Tulsian's

ACCOUNTANCY for CA-IPC (Group-I)

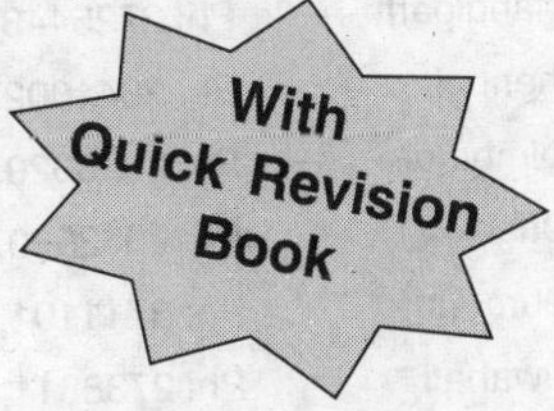

CA (Dr) P C TULSIAN

M.Com., PhD, FCA, PGDFM

Additional Director (Former)
Board of Studies
The Institute of Chartered Accountants of India, New Delhi
Head
Department of Commerce
Ramjas College
University of Delhi
DELHI

*Recipient of an Award for **Exemplary Services Contributed to the Cause of Profession** by The Institute of Chartered Accountants of India, New Delhi*

CA BHARAT TULSIAN

Chartered Accountant

Manager, KPMG
Alumnus of Sri Ram College of Commerce (SRCC)
University of Delhi
DELHI

*Recipient of an Award for the **Best Article on Foreign Exchange** at the all-India level by The Institute of Chartered Accountants of India, New Delhi*

S Chand And Company Limited

(AN ISO 9001 : 2008 COMPANY)

RAM NAGAR, NEW DELHI - 110 055

S Chand And Company Limited
(An ISO 9001 : 2008 Company)
Head Office: 7361, RAM NAGAR, NEW DELHI - 110 055
Phone: 23672080-81-82, 9899107446, 9911310888 Fax: 91-11-23677446
www.**schandpublishing.com**; e-mail: **helpdesk@schandpublishing.com**

Branches

Ahmedabad : Ph: 27541965, 27542369, ahmedabad@schandpublishing.com
Bengaluru : Ph: 22268048, 22354008, bangalore@schandpublishing.com
Bhopal : Ph: 4274723, 4209587, bhopal@schandpublishing.com
Chandigarh : Ph: 2725443, 2725446, chandigarh@schandpublishing.com
Chennai : Ph. 28410027, 28410058, chennai@schandpublishing.com
Coimbatore : Ph: 2323620, 4217136, coimbatore@schandpublishing.com (Marketing Office)
Cuttack : Ph: 2332580, 2332581, cuttack@schandpublishing.com
Dehradun : Ph: 2711101, 2710861, dehradun@schandpublishing.com
Guwahati : Ph: 2738811, 2735640, guwahati@schandpublishing.com
Hyderabad : Ph: 27550194, 27550195, hyderabad@schandpublishing.com
Jaipur : Ph: 2219175, 2219176, jaipur@schandpublishing.com
Jalandhar : Ph: 2401630, 5000630, jalandhar@schandpublishing.com
Kochi : Ph: 2378740, 2378207-08, cochin@schandpublishing.com
Kolkata : Ph: 22367459, 22373914, kolkata@schandpublishing.com
Lucknow : Ph: 4026791, 4065646, lucknow@schandpublishing.com
Mumbai : Ph: 22690881, 22610885, mumbai@schandpublishing.com
Nagpur : Ph: 6451311, 2720523, 2777666, nagpur@schandpublishing.com
Patna : Ph: 2300489, 2302100, patna@schandpublishing.com
Pune : Ph: 64017298, pune@schandpublishing.com
Raipur : Ph: 2443142, raipur@schandpublishing.com (Marketing Office)
Ranchi : Ph: 2361178, ranchi@schandpublishing.com
Siliguri : Ph: 2520750, siliguri@schandpublishing.com (Marketing Office)
Visakhapatnam : Ph: 2782609, visakhapatnam@schandpublishing.com (Marketing Office)

First Edition 2009; Second Edition 2010, Revised Edition 2011 (Twice), 2012, 2013 (Twice), 2014, 2015 Revised Edition 2016, Reprint with updates 2016

Reprint with updates 2018

ISBN: 978-93-525-3135-6 **Code:** 1007I 474

PRINTED IN INDIA

By Vikas Publishing House Pvt. Ltd., Plot 20/4, Site-IV, Industrial Area Sahibabad, Ghaziabad-201010 and published by S Chand And Company Limited, 7361, Ram Nagar, New Delhi -110 055.

PREFACE TO THE ELEVENTH EDITION

We are thankful to readers and teachers for their response and encouragement given to the Tenth Edition. This edition is thoroughly revised and substantially expanded; all chapters have been updated and expanded.

Salient Features

The book adopts a fresh and novel approach to the study of Accountancy for the students of CA Integrated Professional Competence Course (IPC) Group-I. It has been written in teach yourself style strictly following a student-friendly approach, and is essentially meant to serve as a tutor at home.

PEDAGOGICAL FEATURES

Simple Language	The text is presented in the simplest language "meant to serve beginners"
Heading for each Paragraph	Each paragraph has been arranged under a suitable heading for easy retention of concepts
Tabular Form	Wherever possible, the text matter relating to a particular topic/sub-topic has been presented in a tabular form
Eye-catching Screens	All important equations, formulae, figures and practical steps have been presented in screen format to catch the eye
Uniform Format of Chapter	Each chapter has been uniformly organised under suitable headings, viz., text supported by suitable illustrations, solved problems

DISTINCTIVE FEATURES

Exhibits	Over 130 exhibits to acquaint students with various accounting treatment and formats
Illustrations	Over 530 illustrations have been provided for a better understanding of the text
Solved Problems	Over 250 solved problems along with necessary working notes and alternative solution have been provided throughout the text

Tulsian's Quick Revision for Accountancy for CA-IPC (Group-I)

Section 1	**Fully Solved Scanner Chapter-wise (CA Professional Examination Problems with Authentic Solutions)**
Section 2	**Revision One Day Before Examination**
Section 3	**Tulsian's Model Test Papers**
Section 4	**IPC Examination Papers**

ACKNOWLEDGEMENTS

We wish to express our sincere thanks to several individuals who have been a source of inspiration and support personally and professionally including Dr. R P Tulsian, Dr. S C Gupta, Dr. S P Gupta, Dr. Naresh Gupta, Dr. Amit Singhal, Dr. J B Gupta, Dr. Renu Gupta, Dr. Manju Gupta, Dr. C P Gupta, CA M K Aggarwal, CA S K Aggarwal, CA N D Gupta, CA Naveen Gupta, CA Anil Jindal, CA Madhu Sudan Goyal, CA Vinod Aggarwal, CA Sunil Gupta, CA Arun Jain, CA Virender Aggarwal, CA. S K Gupta, CA Ishwar Khemka, CA Prem Bansal, CA Ashish Gupta, CA M K Sharda, CA Rajeev Rastogi, CA Atul Gupta, CA Kuldeep Bhardwaj, CA Neeraj Chabra, CA Kishore Paul, CA Pradeep Narang, CA S K Gupta, CA R Devarajan, CA Tapas Dutta, CA Arnav Chakrabarty, CA Seema Gupta, CA Shilpa Aggarwal, CA Vishal Pandey, CA Vineet Jain, CA Nimish Bhatia, CA Ankit Mohan, CA Antima Jain, CA Prarthana Mittal and CA Aman Mittal.

Special word of thanks is also due to our favourite students **Piyush, Pranav, Antima, Arushi and Aman Mittal** who provided incisive comments and useful feedback.

We must conclude that this book could never have been written without the support, encouragement and prodding of our family members. Many thanks to them.

Any criticisms or suggestions for further improvement of the book will be gratefully acknowledged and appreciated.

CA (Dr) P C Tulsian
pctulsian@gmail.com

CA Bharat Tulsian
bharattulsian88@gmail.com

SYLLABUS

INTEGRATED PROFESSIONAL COMPETENCE COURSE (IPC) SYLLABUS

Paper 1: Accounting

Time: 3 Hours

Level of Knowledge: **Working Knowledge** **Marks-100**

Objectives:

(a) To lay a foundation for the preparation and presentation of financial statements;

(b) To gain working knowledge of the principles and procedures of accounting and their application to different practical situations;

(c) To gain the ability to solve simple problems and cases relating to sole proprietorship, partnership and companies; and

(d) To familiarise students with the fundamentals of computerised system of accounting.

S. No.	*Contents*	*Relevant Chapter of the Book*
1.	A general knowledge of the framing of the accounting standards, national and international accounting authorities, adoption of international financial reporting standards	**Sec. B**
2.	Accounting Standards Working knowledge of: AS 1: Disclosure of Accounting Policies AS 2: Valuation of Inventories AS 3: Cash Flow Statements AS 6: Depreciation Accounting AS 7: Construction Contracts (Revised 2002) AS 9: Revenue Recognition AS 10: Accounting for Fixed Assets AS 13: Accounting for Investments AS 14: Accounting for Amalgamations	**Sec. B**
3.	Company Accounts	
	(a) Preparation of financial statements – Profit and Loss Account, Balance Sheet, Cash Flow Statement and Statement of Changes in Equity and Explanatory Notes	**1, 2, 3**
	(b) Profit (Loss) prior to incorporation	**4**
	(c) Alteration of share capital, Conversion of fully paid shares into stock and stock into shares, Accounting for bonus issue	**5**
	(d) Simple problems on Accounting for business acquisition, Amalgamation and reconstruction (excluding problems of amalgamation on inter-company holding)	**6, 7**
4.	Average Due Date, Account Current, Self-Balancing Ledgers	**8, 9**
5.	Financial Statements of Not-for-Profit Organisations	**10A, 10B**
6.	Accounts from Incomplete Records	**11**

7.	Accounting for Special Transactions (a) Hire purchase and instalment sale transactions (b) Investment accounts (c) Insurance claims for loss of stock and loss of profit	12 13 14
8.	Issues in Partnership Accounts Final accounts of partnership firms – Admission, retirement and death of a partner including treatment of goodwill	15, 16, 17, 18
9.	Accounting in Computerized Environment – An overview of computerized accounting system – Salient features and significance, Concept of grouping of accounts, Codification of accounts, Maintaining the hierarchy of ledger, Accounting packages and consideration for their selection, Generating Accounting Reports	19

Note:
If either old Accounting Standards (ASs), Announcements and Limited Revisions to ASs are withdrawn or new ASs, Announcements and Limited Revisions to ASs are issued by the Institute of Chartered Accountants of India in place of existing ASs, Announcements and Limited Revisions to ASs, the syllabus will accordingly include/exclude such new developments in place of the existing ones with effect from the date to be notified by the Institute.

CONTENTS

PAPER 1: ACCOUNTING (GROUP I)

(One Paper – Three Hours – 100 Marks)

SECTION A–TEXTBOOK

SECTION B–ACCOUNTING STANDARDS

SECTION C–QUESTIONS BASED ON REVISED SCHEDULE III TO THE COMPANIES ACT, 2013

Tulsian's

Quick Revision for

ACCOUNTANCY

for CA-IPC (Group-I)

SECTION 1

FULLY SOLVED SCANNER

CHAPTER-WISE

(CA PROFESSIONAL EXAMINATION PROBLEMS WITH AUTHENTIC SOLUTIONS)

SCANNER FOR CA EXAMINATION PROBLEMS
SHORT ANSWER CARRYING 4-6 MARKS &
LONG ANSWER CARRYING 8-16 MARKS

SCANNER FOR ACCOUNTING STANDARDS CA EXAMINATION PROBLEMS CARRYING 4-6 MARKS

SECTION 2

REVISION ONE DAY BEFORE EXAMINATION

SECTION 3

TULSIAN'S MODEL TEST PAPERS WITH ANSWERS

SECTION 4

IPC EXAMINATION PAPERS

SECTION A

PAPER 1: ACCOUNTING [GROUP-I]

Textbook

1 FINANCIAL STATEMENTS OF A COMPANY

LEARNING OBJECTIVES

After studying this chapter, you should be able to understand:

- ◇ Meaning of Financial Statements
- ◇ Legal Requirements
- ◇ Contents and Forms
- ◇ Form of Preparing a Statement of Profit and Loss of a Company
- ◇ Accounting Treatment of Provision for Tax
- ◇ Dividend
- ◇ Option to Transfer to Reserves
- ◇ Declaration of Dividend out of Reserves
- ◇ Capital Reserve
- ◇ Interim Dividend
- ◇ Final Dividend
- ◇ Payment of Dividend
- ◇ Unpaid/Unclaimed Dividend
- ◇ Right to dividend, rights shares and bonus shares to be held in abeyance pending registration of transfer of shares
- ◇ Punishment for failure to distribute dividends
- ◇ Payment of Dividend on Partly Paidup Shares
- ◇ Dividend on Preference Shares
- ◇ Dividend Distribution Tax (D.D.T)
- ◇ Capitalisation of Profits
- ◇ Accounting Treatment of Dividend, Dividend Distribution Tax, Transfer to Reserves, Bonus, Etc.
- ◇ Form of Preparing a Balance Sheet of a Company
- ◇ Vertical Form of Summarised Balance Sheet of a Company
- ◇ Vertical Form of Detailed Balance Sheet of a Company
- ◇ Distinction Between a Company's Balance Sheet and Firm's Balance Sheet
- ◇ Managerial Remuneration

1.0 MEANING OF FINANCIAL STATEMENTS

GENERAL MEANING

The financial statements are historical documents which show the organised summaries of detailed information about the financial performance of an accounting entity for an accounting period and financial position at the end of an accounting period.

There are two basic financial statements, viz., Income statement and Balance Sheet.

1. **An Income Statement** is a Statement of Revenue from Operations, Other Incomes and Expenses during a given accounting period. It indicates the Financial Performance of an enterprise for an accounting period.
2. **A Balance Sheet** is a Statement of Assets (Current and Non-Current), Liabilities (Current and Non-Current) and Equity (i.e., Shareholders' Funds) indicating the Financial Position of an enterprise at a given date.

LEGAL MEANING

As per Section 2(40) of the Companies Act, 2013, Financial Statements include-

(i) a Balance Sheet as at the end of the financial year;

(ii) a Profit and Loss Account, *or* in the case of a company carrying on any activity not for profit, an Income and Expenditure Account for the financial year;

(iii) Cash Flow Statement for the financial myear;

(iv) a Statement of Changes in Equity, if applicable; and

(v) any explanatory note annexed to, *or* forming part of, any document referred to in sub-clause (i) to (iv):

Provided that the Financial Statements, with respect to One Person Company, small company and dormant company, may not include the Cash Flow Statement.

2.0 LEGAL REQUIREMENTS

1. **Company's Duty to prepare Books of Account, etc., [Sec 128 (1)]**

   Every company must prepare and keep at its registered office books of account and other relevant books and papers and financial statement for every financial year which give a true and fair view of the state of the affairs of the company, including that of its branch office *or* offices, if any, and explain the transactions effected both at the registered office and its branches.

2. **On Accrual Basis:** Such books must be kept on accrual basis and according to the double entry system of accounting [Sec 128(1)].
3. **At Place other than Registered Office:** All *or* any of the books of account aforesaid and other relevant papers may be kept at such other place in India as the Board of Directors may decide and where such a decision is taken, the company must, within 7 days thereof, file with the Registrar a notice in writing giving the full address of that other place [Provisio to Sec 128(1)].
4. **In Electronic Mode:** The company may keep such books of account *or* other relevant papers in electronic mode in such manner as may be prescribed. [Provisio to Sec 128(1)]
5. **In Case of Branch Books of Account:** Where a company has a branch office in India *or* outside India, it shall be deemed to have complied with the provisions of the Act, if proper books of account relating to the transactions effected at the branch office are kept at that office and proper summarized returns periodically are sent by the branch office to the company at its registered office *or* such other place where accounts are kept. [Sec 128 (2)]

6. **Director's Right to Inspect:** The books of account and other books and papers maintained by the company within India shall be open for inspection at the registered office of the company *or* at such other place in India by any director during business hours, and in the case of financial information, if any, maintained outside the country, copies of such financial information shall be maintained and produced for inspection by any director subject to such conditions as may be prescribed.

   However, the inspection in respect of any subsidiary of the company shall be done only by the person authorised in this behalf by a resolution of the Board of Directors. [Sec 128 (3)]

   Employees' Duty to give Assistance: Where an inspection is made by any director, the officers and other employees of the company must give to the person making such inspection all assistance in connection with the inspection which the company may reasonably be expected to give. [Sec 128 (4)]

7. **Preservation of Books etc:** The books of account of every company relating to a period of atleast 8 financial years immediately preceding a financial year, *or* where the company had been in existence for a period *less* than 8 years, in respect of all the preceding years together with the vouchers relevant to any entry in such books of account shall be kept in good order.

   However, where an investigation has been ordered in respect of the company under Chapter XIV, the Central Government may direct that the books of account may be kept for such longer period as it may deem fit [Sec 128 (5)].

8. **Penalty:** In case of contravention of Sec 128, Managing Director, Whole-time Director in charge of finance, Chief Financial Officer *or* any other person charged by the Board with the duty of complying with the provisions of Sec.128, shall be punishable with imprisonment for a term which may extend to 1 year *or* with fine which shall be at least ₹ 50,000 but which may extend to ₹ 5,00,000 *or* with both [Sec 128 (6)].

9. **Compliance with AS and in Forms as per Schedule III:** The Financial Statements must give a true and fair view of the state of affairs of the company *or* companies, comply with the accounting standards notified under Sec 133 and must be in the form *or* forms as may be provided for different class *or* classes of companies in Schedule III [Sec 129 (1)]:

10. **BOD's Responsibility to lay:** At every annual general meeting of a company, the Board of Directors of the company must lay before such meeting Financial Statements for the financial year [Sec 129 (2)].

11. **Consolidated Financial Statements:** Where a company has one *or* more subsidiaries, it must, in addition to financial statements, prepare a consolidated financial statement of the company and of all the subsidiaries in the same form and manner as that of its own which must also be laid before the annual general meeting of the company along with the laying of its Financial Statements.

    Provided that the company must also attach along with its financial statement, a separate statement containing the salient features of the financial statement of its subsidiary *or* subsidiaries in Form AOC-1.

    Provided further that the Central Government may provide for the consolidation of accounts of companies in such manner as may be prescribed.

    Explanation.— For the purposes of this sub-section, the word "subsidiary" shall include Associate Company and Joint Venture [Sec 129 (3)].

    Note: The provisions of this Act applicable to the preparation, adoption and audit of the financial statements of a holding company shall, mutatis mutandis, apply to the consolidated financial statements [Sec 129 (4)].

12. **Reasons for Deviation from AS:** Where the financial statements of a company do not comply with the accounting standards the company must disclose in its financial statements, the deviation from the accounting standards, the reasons for such deviation and the financial effects, if any, arising out of such deviation [Sec 129 (5)].

13. **Penalty:** If a company contravenes the provisions of Sec.129, the Managing Director, the Whole-time Director in charge of finance, the Chief Financial Officer *or* any other person charged by the Board with the duty of complying with the requirements of this section and in the absence of any of the officers mentioned above, all the directors shall be punishable with imprisonment for a term which may extend to 1 year *or* with fine which shall be atleast ₹ 50,000 but which may extend to ₹ 5,00,000, *or* with both. [Sec 129(7)]

    Explanation.—For the purposes of this section, except where the context otherwise requires, any reference to the financial statement must include any notes annexed to *or* forming part of such financial statement, giving information required to be given and allowed to be given in the form of such notes under this Act.

14. **Voluntary Revision of Financial Statements *or* Board's Report:** If it appears to the directors of a company that—

    (a) the financial statement of the company; *or*

    (b) the report of the Board,

    do not comply with the provisions of Sec.129 *or* 134, they may prepare revised financial statement *or* a revised report in respect of any of the 3 preceding financial years after obtaining approval of the Tribunal on an application made by the company in such form and manner as may be prescribed and a copy of the order passed by the Tribunal shall be filed with the Registrar. [Sec 131(1)]

Notes

(i) Tribunal shall give notice to the Central Government and the Income tax authorities and shall take into consideration the representations, if any, made by that Government *or* the authorities before passing any order under this section:

(ii) Such revised Financial Statement *or* Report shall not be prepared *or* filed more than once in a financial year:

(iii) The detailed reasons for revision of such financial statement *or* report shall also be disclosed in the Board's report in the relevant financial year in which such revision is being made.

Scope of Revision: Where copies of the previous financial statement *or* report have been sent out to members *or* delivered to the Registrar *or* laid before the company in general meeting, the revisions must be confined to—

(a) the correction in respect of which the previous Financial Statement *or* Report do not comply with the provisions of section 129 *or* 134; and

(b) the making of any necessary consequential alternation. [Sec 131(2)]

15. **Approval of and Signature on Financial Statement:** The financial statement, including consolidated financial statement, if any, must be approved by the Board of Directors before they are signed on behalf of the Board at least by the chairperson of the company where he is authorised by the Board *or* by two directors out of which one shall be Managing Director and the Chief Executive Officer, if he is a director in the company, the Chief Financial Officer and the Company Secretary of the company, wherever they are appointed, *or* in the case of a One Person Company, only by one director, for submission to the Auditor for his Report thereon [Sec 134 (1)].

16. **Auditor's Report to be Attached:** The Auditors' Report shall be attached to every financial statement [Sec 134 (2)].

17. **BOD's Report to be Attached:** The Board's Report must be attached to statements laid before a company in general meeting.

18. **Contents of BOD's Report:** BOD Report must include—

    (a) the extract of the Annual Return as provided u/s 92 (3);

    (b) Number of Meetings of the Board;

(c) Directors' Responsibility Statement;

(d) a Statement on Declaration given by Independent Directors u/s 149 (6);

(e) in case of a company covered u/s 178 (1), company's policy on directors' appointment and remuneration including criteria for determining qualifications, positive attributes, independence of a director and other matters provided u/s 178 (3);

(f) explanations *or* comments by the Board on every qualification, reservation *or* adverse remark *or* disclaimer made—

(i) by the auditor in his report; and

(ii) by the company secretary in practice in his secretarial audit report;

(g) particulars of loans, guarantees *or* investments under section 186;

(h) particulars of contracts *or* arrangements with related parties referred to in sub-section (1) of section 188 in the prescribed **Form AOC-2;**

(i) the state of the company's affairs;

(j) the amounts, if any, which it proposes to carry to any reserves;

(k) the amount, if any, which it recommends should be paid by way of dividend;

(l) material changes and commitments, if any, affecting the financial position of the company which have occurred between the end of the financial year of the company to which the financial statements relate and the date of the report;

(m) the conservation of energy, technology absorption, foreign exchange earnings and outgo, in such manner as may be prescribed;

(n) a statement indicating development and implementation of a risk management policy for the company including identification therein of elements of risk, if any, which in the opinion of the Board may threaten the existence of the company;

(o) the details about the policy developed and implemented by the company on corporate social responsibility initiatives taken during the year;

(p) in case of a listed company and every other public company having such paid-up share capital as may be prescribed, a statement indicating the manner in which formal annual evaluation has been made by the Board of its own performance and that of its committees and individual directors;

(q) such other matters as may be prescribed under Rule 8 of the Companies (Account) Rules, 2015.

19. Signature on BOD's Report: The Board's Report and any annexures must be signed by its chairperson of the company if he is authorised by the Board and where he is not so authorised, must be signed by at least two directors, one of whom shall be a managing director, *or* by the director where there is one director. [Sec 134 (6)]

20. BOD's Report in case of One Person Company [Sec 134 (4)]: The BOD's Report of in case of a One Person Company, means a report containing explanations *or* comments by the Board on every qualification, reservation *or* adverse remark *or* disclaimer made by the Auditor in his Report.

21. Contents of Directors' Responsibility Statement [Sec 134 (5)]:

The Directors' Responsibility Statement must state that—

(a) **Compliance with AS:** in the preparation of the annual accounts, the applicable accounting standards had been followed along with proper explanation relating to material departures;

(b) **Accounting Policies:** the directors had selected such accounting policies and applied them consistently and made judgments and estimates that are reasonable and prudent so as to give a true and fair view of the state of affairs of the company at the end of the financial year and of the profit and loss of the company for that period;

(c) **Maintenance of Adequate Accounting Records:** the directors had taken proper and sufficient care for the maintenance of adequate accounting records in accordance with the provisions of this Act for safeguarding the assets of the company and for preventing and detecting fraud and other irregularities;

(d) **Accounts on a Going Concern Basis:** the directors had prepared the annual accounts on a going concern basis; and

(e) **Internal Financial Controls:** the directors, in the case of a listed company, had laid down internal financial controls to be followed by the company and that such internal financial controls are adequate and were operating effectively.

Explanation.— For the purposes of this clause, the term "Internal Financial Controls" mean the policies and procedures adopted by the company for ensuring the orderly and efficient conduct of its business, including adherence to company's policies, the safeguarding of its assets, the prevention and detection of frauds and errors, the accuracy and completeness of the accounting records, and the timely preparation of reliable financial information;

(f) **Proper Systems to ensure compliance with Law:** the directors had devised proper systems to ensure compliance with the provisions of all applicable laws and that such systems were adequate and operating effectively.

22. Circulation: A signed copy of every financial statement, including consolidated financial statement, if any, must be issued, circulated *or* published along with a copy each of—

(a) any notes annexed to *or* forming part of such financial statement;

(b) the auditor's report; and

(c) the Board's report [Sec 134 (7)].

23. Penalty: If a company contravenes the provisions of Sec 134, the company shall be punishable with fine which shall be atleast ₹ 50,000 but which may extend to ₹ 25,00,000 and every officer of the company who is in default shall be punishable with imprisonment for a term which may extend to 3 years *or* with fine which shall be atleast ₹ 50,000 but which may extend to ₹ 5,00,000 *or* with both.

24. Corporate Social Responsibility (CSR):

1. Every company having **Net Worth of atleast ₹ 500 hundred crore** *or* **Turnover of atleast ₹ 1,000 crore** *or* **a Net Profit of atleast ₹ 5 crores** during any financial year must constitute a Corporate Social Responsibility Committee of the Board consisting of atleast 3 directors, out of which at least one director shall be an Independent Director [Sec 135 (1)].
2. The Board's Report must disclose the composition of the Corporate Social Responsibility Committee [Sec 135 (2)].
3. **The Corporate Social Responsibility Committee is required,—**

   (a) To Formulate and recommend to the Board, a Corporate Social Responsibility Policy which shall indicate the activities to be undertaken by the company as specified in Schedule VII;

   (b) To Recommend the amount of expenditure to be incurred on the activities referred to in clause (a); and

   (c) To Monitor the Corporate Social Responsibility Policy of the company from time to time. [Sec 135(3)]
4. **The Board of every company is required,—**

   (a) after taking into account the recommendations made by the Corporate Social Responsibility Committee, approve the Corporate Social Responsibility Policy for the company and disclose contents of such Policy in its report and also place it on the company's website, if any, in such manner as may be prescribed; and

(b) ensure that the activities as are included in Corporate Social Responsibility Policy of the company are undertaken by the company. [Sec 135(4)]

5. **Spending of 2% of Average Net Profits on CSR:** The Board of every company must ensure that the company spends, in every financial year, **at least 2 of the Average Net Profits (as per Sec 198)** of the company made **during 3 immediately preceding financial years**, in pursuance of its Corporate Social Responsibility Policy. [Sec 135(5)]

Notes

(i) The company must give preference to the local area and areas around it where it operates, for spending the amount earmarked for Corporate Social Responsibility activities. [Proviso to Sec 135(5)]

(ii) If the company fails to spend such amount, the Board must, in its report made u/s 134, specify the reasons for not spending the amount. [Proviso to Sec 135(5)]

(ii) As per Rule 2(1)(e) of the Companies (CSR Policy) Rules, 2015, "CSR Policy" relates to the activities to be undertaken by the company as specified in Schedule VII to the Act and the expenditure thereon, excluding activities undertaken in pursuance of normal course of business of a company.

(iv) As per Rule 2(1)(f) "Net Profit" means the Net Profit of a company as per its financial statement prepared in accordance with the applicable provisions of the Act, but shall not include the following, namely:—

(a) any profit arising from any overseas branch *or* branches of the company, whether operated as a separate company *or* otherwise; and

(b) any dividend received from other companies in India, which are covered under and complying with the provisions of Sec 135.

(v) As per Rule 4(5), the CSR projects *or* programs *or* activities that benefit only the employees of the company and their families shall not be considered as CSR activities in accordance with Sec 135.

25. **Right of members to copies of Audited Financial Statement [Sec 136]:** Without prejudice to the provisions of Sec 101, a copy of the financial statements, including consolidated financial statements, if any, Auditor's Report and every other document required by law to be annexed *or* attached to the financial statements, which are to be laid before a company in its general meeting, must be sent to every member of the company, to every trustee for the debenture-holder of any debentures issued by the company, and to all persons other than such member *or* trustee, being the person so entitled, atleast 21 days before the date of the meeting. [Sec 136(1)]

However, in the case of a listed company, the provisions of Sec 136(1) shall be deemed to be complied with, if the copies of the documents are made available for inspection at its registered office during working hours for a period of 21 days before the date of the meeting and a statement containing the salient features of such documents in Form AOC-3 *or* copies of the documents, as the company may deem fit, is sent to every member of the company and to every trustee for the holders of any debentures issued by the company atleast 21 days before the date of the meeting unless the shareholders ask for full financial statements. [Provisio to Sec 136(1)]

However, that the Central Government may prescribe the manner of circulation of financial statements of companies having such Net Worth and Turnover as may be Prescribed. [Provisio to Sec 136(1)]

26. **Manner of Circulation of Financial Statements in certain cases (Rule 11 of the Companies (Account) Rules, 2015):** In case of all listed companies and such public companies which have a **Net Worth of more than ₹ 1 crore** and **Turnover of more than ₹ 10 crore**, the financial statements may be sent-

(a) by electronic mode to such members whose shareholding is in dematerialised format and whose email Ids are registered with Depository for communication purposes;

(b) where Shareholding is held otherwise than by dematerialised format, to such members who have positively consented in writing for receiving by electronic mode; and

(c) by despatch of physical copies through any recognised mode of delivery as specified u/s 20 of the Act, in all other cases.

27. Duty to File with Registrar [Sec 137]:

1. Where Financial Statements adopted	at AGM A copy of the financial statements, including consolidated financial statement, if any, along with all the documents which are required to be *or* attached to such financial statements under this Act, duly adopted at the AGM of the company, must be filed with the Registrar **within 30 days of the date of AGM** in such manner, with such fees *or* additional fees as may be prescribed within the time specified u/s 403.
2. Where Financial Statements Not adopted at AGM	Where the financial statements are not adopted at AGM *or* Adjourned AGM, such unadopted financial statements along with the required documents must be filed with the Registrar **within 30 days of the date of AGM** and the Registrar shall take them in his records as provisional till the Financial Statements are filed with him after their adoption in the Adjourned AGM for that purpose:
3. Where Financial Statement adopted at Adjourned AGM	Financial Statements adopted in the Adjourned AGM must be filed with the Registrar **within 30 days of the date of such Adjourned AGM** with such fees *or* such additional fees as may be prescribed within the time specified u/s 403:
4. In case of One Person Company	A One Person Company must file a copy of the financial statements duly adopted by its member, along with all the documents which are required to be attached to such financial statements, **within 180 days from the closure of the financial year**.
5. In case of Subsidiary/ Subsidiaries	A company must, along with its financial statements to be filed with the Registrar, attach the accounts of its subsidiary *or* subsidiaries which have been incorporated outside India and which have not established their place of business in India.
6. Where AGM not held	Where the AGM of a company for any year has not been held, the financial statements along with the documents required to be attached duly signed along **with the Statement of Facts and Reasons for not holding the AGM** must be filed with the Registrar **within 30 days of the last date before which the AGM** should have been held and in such manner, with such fees *or* additional fees as may be prescribed within the time specified, u/s 403.

Penalty for Failure to File: If a company fails to file the copy of the financial statements before the expiry of the specified period the company shall be punishable with fine of ₹ 1,000 *or* every day during which the failure continues but which shall not be more than ₹ 10,00,000, and the Managing Director and the Chief Financial Officer of the company, if any, and, in the absence of the Managing Director and the Chief Financial Officer, any other director who is charged by the Board with the responsibility of complying with the provisions of this section, and, in the absence of any such director, all the directors of the company, shall be punishable with imprisonment for a term which may extend to 6 months *or* with fine which shall be atleast ₹ 1,00,000 but which may extend to ₹ 5,00,000, *or* with both.

28. **Internal Audit [Sec 138]:** Such class *or* classes of companies as may be prescribed shall be required to appoint an internal auditor, who shall either be a Chartered Accountant *or* a Cost Accountant, *or* such other professional as may be decided by the Board to conduct internal audit of the functions and activities of the company.

    Note: The Central Government may, by rules, prescribe the manner and the intervals in which the internal audit shall be conducted and reported to the Board.

3.0 CONTENTS AND FORMS [SECTION 129]

1. The Balance Sheet is required to give a true and fair view of the state of affairs of the company as at the end of the financial year and is to be in the form set out in Part I of Schedule III.
2. The Statement of Profit and Loss is required to give a true and fair view of the profit *or* loss of the company for the financial year and is to be in the form set out in Part II of Schedule III.

4.0 FORM OF PREPARING A STATEMENT OF PROFIT AND LOSS

1. **Vertical form** has been prescribed under The Companies Act, 2013 for Statement of Profit and Loss of a company.
2. A format of Statement of Profit and Loss has been given on next page:

SPECIMEN OF STATEMENT OF PROFIT & LOSS

NAME OF THE COMPANY.........................

STATEMENT OF PROFIT AND LOSS FOR THE YEAR ENDED ....

Particulars	*Note No.*	*Figures for the Current Reporting Period*	*Figures for the Previous Reporting Period*
		₹	₹
I. Revenue from Operations	1	xxx	xxx
II. Other Income	2	xxx	xxx
III. Total Revenue [I + II]		xxx	xxx
IV. Expenses:			
Cost of Materials consumed	3	xxx	xxx
Purchases of Stock-in-Trade		xxx	xxx
Changes in Inventories	4	xxx	xxx
Employee Benefits Expense	5	xxx	xxx
Finance Costs	6	xxx	xxx
Depreciation and Amortization Expense	7	xxx	xxx
Other Expenses	8	xxx	xxx
Total Expenses		xxx	xxx
V. Profit before Tax(III–IV)		xxx	xxx
VI. Exceptional Items		xxx	xxx

VII.	**Profit Before Extraordinary Items and Tax (V – VI)**	xxx	xxx
VIII.	**Extraordinary Items**	xxx	xxx
IX.	**Profit before tax (VII – VIII)**	xxx	xxx
X.	**Tax Expense:**		
	(1) Current Tax	xxx	xxx
	(2) Deferred Tax	xxx	xxx
		xxx	xxx
XI.	**Profit (Loss) for the period**	xxx	xxx
XII.	**Earnings per Equity Share:**		
	(1) Basic	xxx	xxx
	(2) Diluted	xxx	xxx

Notes to Accounts:

NOTE 1: REVENUE FROM OPERATIONS

(a)	From Sale of Products	xxx	xxx
(b)	From Sale of Services	xxx	xxx
(c)	From Other Operating Revenues [Trading Commission]	xxx	xxx
(d)	*Less:* Excise Duty	(xxx)	(xxx)
		xxx	xxx

NOTE 2: OTHER INCOME

(a)	Interest Income (in case of a company other than a finance company)	xxx	xxx
(b)	Dividends From Subsidiary Companies	xxx	xxx
(c)	Dividend Income From Companies other than Subsidiary Companies	xxx	xxx
(d)	Net Gain/Loss on Sale of Investments [Gain – Loss)]	xxx	xxx
(e)	Other Non-Operating Income (Net of Expenses directly attributable to such income) [Income – Expenses)]	xxx	xxx
(f)	Net Gain on Foreign Currency Transaction of Translation (other than considered as Finance Cost)	xxx	xxx
		xxx	xxx

NOTE 3: COST OF MATERIALS CONSUMED

(a)	Opening Stock of Materials	xxx	xxx
(b)	*Add:* Purchases of Materials	xxx	xxx
(c)	*Less:* Closing Stock of Materials	(xxx)	(xxx)
	Cost of Materials consumed	xxx	xxx

NOTE 4: CHANGES IN INVENTORIES

Particulars	Work-in-Progress (₹)	Finished Goods (₹)	Total
Closing Stock	xxx	xxx	xxx
Less: Opening Stock	(xxx)	(xxx)	(xxx)
	xxx	xxx	xxx

NOTE 5: EMPLOYEE BENEFITS EXPENSE

Salaries and Wages	xxx	xxx
Contribution To Provident and Other Funds	xxx	xxx
Expense On Employee Stock Option Scheme (ESOP) and Employee Stock Purchase Plan (ESPP)	xxx	xxx
Staff Welfare Expenses	xxx	xxx
	xxx	xxx

NOTE 6: FINANCE COSTS

(a) Interest Expense	xxx	xxx
(b) Other Borrowing Costs	xxx	xxx
(c) Applicable Net Gain/Loss on Foreign Currency Transactions and Translation	xxx	xxx
	xxx	xxx

NOTE 7: DEPRECIATION AND AMORTIZATION EXPENSE

Buildings	xxx	xxx
Plant and Equipment	xxx	xxx
Vehicles	xxx	xxx
Office Equipment	xxx	xxx
Brands	xxx	xxx
Computer Software	xxx	xxx
	xxx	xxx

NOTE 8: OTHER EXPENSES

(a) Consumption of Stores and Spare Parts	xxx	xxx
(b) Power and Fuel	xxx	xxx
(c) Rent.	xxx	xxx
(d) Repairs to Buildings	xxx	xxx
(e) Repairs to Machinery	xxx	xxx
(f) Insurance	xxx	xxx
(g) Rates and Taxes [Excluding Taxes on Income]	xxx	xxx
(h) Miscellaneous Expenses	xxx	xxx

(i) Provisions for Losses of Subsidiary Companies	xxx	xxx
(j) Net Gain on Foreign Currency Transaction of Translation (other than considered as Finance Cost)	xxx	xxx
(k) Provisions, if material	xxx	xxx
(l) Withdrawl from Provisions, if material	xxx	xxx
(m) Expenditure on Corporate Social Responsibility (CSR)	xxx	xxx
(j) Payments to the Auditor as:		
(a) Auditor	xxx	xxx
(b) For Taxation Matters	xxx	xxx
(c) For Company Law Matters	xxx	xxx
(d) For Management Services	xxx	xxx
(e) For Other Services	xxx	xxx
(f) For Reimbursement of Expenses	xxx	xxx
	xxx	xxx

NOTE 9: SURPLUS I.E. BALANCE IN THE STATEMENT OF P&L TO BE TAKEN TO BALANCE SHEET

Opening Balance	xxx	xxx
Add: Profit for the period	xxx	xxx
Less: Transfer to Reserve	(xxx)	(xxx)
Less: Interim Dividend	(xxx)	(xxx)
Less: Proposed Preference Dividend	(xxx)	(xxx)
Less: Proposed Equity Dividend	(xxx)	(xxx)
Less: Dividend Distribution Tax	(xxx)	(xxx)
Closing Balance	xxx	xxx

Notes

1. Any item of Income *or* Expenditure which exceeds **1% of the Revenue from Operations *or* ₹ 1,00,000, *whichever is higher*** is to be disclosed separately.
2. The Statement of Profit and Loss shall also contain by way of a note the following information, namely:

(a) **Value of imports calculated on C.I.F. basis** by the company during the financial year in respect of—

I. Raw Materials; II. Components and spare parts; III. Capital Goods;

(b) **Expenditure in Foreign Currency** during the financial year on account of royalty, know-how, professional and consultation fees, interest, and other matters;

(c) **Total Value of all imported raw materials, spare parts and components** consumed during the financial year and the total value of all indigenous raw materials, spare parts and components similarly consumed and the percentage of each to the total consumption;

(d) **The amount remitted during the year in Foreign Currencies** on account of dividends with a specific mention of the total number of Non-Resident Shareholders, the total number of shares held by them on which the dividends were due and the year to which the dividends related.

(e) **Earnings in Foreign Exchange** classified under the following heads, namely:—

I. Export of Goods calculated on F.O.B. basis;

II. Royalty, know-how, professional and consultation fees;

III. Interest and Dividend;

IV. Other Income, indicating the nature thereof.

ILLUSTRATION 1

From the following information, prepare Statement of Profit and Loss for the year ended 31st March, 2016:

Particulars	*(₹ in lacs)*
Revenue from Operations	2605
Other Income	40
Cost of Materials consumed	1000
Changes in Inventories	(275)
Employee Benefits Expense	850
Finance Costs	20
Depreciation and Amortization Expense	150
Other Expenses	100
Tax Rate @ 30%	

SOLUTION

TULSIAN LTD.
STATEMENT OF PROFIT AND LOSS FOR THE YEAR ENDED 31ST MARCH, 2016

Particulars	*Note No.*	*(₹ in lacs)*
I. Revenue from Operations		2605
II. Other Income		40
III. Total Revenue [I + II]		2645
IV. Expenses:		
Cost of Materials consumed		1000
Changes in Inventories		(275)
Employee Benefits Expense		850
Finance Costs		20
Depreciation and Amortization Expense		150
Other Expenses		100
Total Expenses		1845
V. Profit before Tax(III – IV)		800
VI. Tax Expense@30%		(240)
VII. Profit for the period		560

ILLUSTRATION 2

From the following information, prepare the relevant Notes to Accounts:

Particulars	*(₹ in lacs)*
Sales of Products	2700
Sales of Services	30
Trading Commission	60
Excise Duty	185
Interest Income	20
Dividends From Companies	10
Net Loss on Sale of Investments	4
Rental Income	15
Rental Collection Expenses	1

SOLUTION

1. REVENUE FROM OPERATIONS

Particulars	*(₹ in lacs)*
(a) From Sale of Products	2700
(b) From Sale of Services	30
(c) From Other Operating Revenues [Trading Commission]	60
(d) *Less:* Excise Duty	(185)
	2605

2. OTHER INCOME

Particulars	*(₹ in lacs)*
(a) Interest Income	20
(b) Dividends From Companies	10
(c) Net Loss on Sale of Investments	(4)
(d) Rental Income (15 lacs – 1lac Collection Expenses)	14
	40

ILLUSTRATION 3

From the following information, prepare the relevant Notes to Accounts:

Particulars	*(₹ in lacs)*
Opening Stock of Materials	84.6
Purchases of Materials	955.2
Closing Stock of Materials	39.8
Opening Stock of WIP	150
Closing Stock of WIP	200

Opening Stock of Finished Goods	175
Closing Stock of Finished Goods	400

SOLUTION

3. COST OF MATERIALS CONSUMED

Particulars	*(₹ in lacs)*
(a) Opening Stock of Materials	84.6
(b) *Add:* Purchases of Materials	955.2
(c) *Less:* Closing Stock of Materials	(39.8)
Cost of Materials consumed	1000

4. CHANGES IN INVENTORIES

Particulars	*Work-in-Progress (₹ in lacs)*	*Finished Goods (₹ in lacs)*	*Total (₹ in lacs)*
Opening Stock	150	175	325
Less: Closing Stock	200	400	600
	(50)	(225)	(275)

ILLUSTRATION 4

From the following information, prepare the relevant Notes to Accounts:

Particulars	*(₹ in lacs)*
Salaries and Wages	600
Contribution To Provident and Other Funds	72
Expense on Employee Stock Option Scheme (ESOP) and Employee Stock Purchase Plan (ESPP)	28
Staff Welfare Expenses	150
Interest Expense	24
Other Borrowing Costs(Brokerage)	4
Gain on Foreign Currency Transactions and Translation	8

SOLUTION

5. EMPLOYEE BENEFITS EXPENSE

Particulars	*(₹ in lacs)*
Salaries and Wages	600
Contribution To Provident and Other Funds	72
Expense on Employee Stock Option Scheme (ESOP) and Employee Stock Purchase Plan (ESPP)	28
Staff Welfare Expenses	150
	850

6. FINANCE COSTS

Particulars	(₹ in lacs)
(a) Interest Expense	24
(b) Other Borrowing Costs(Brokerage)	4
(c) Gain on Foreign Currency Transactions and Translation	(8)
	20

ILLUSTRATION 5

From the following information, prepare the relevant Notes to Accounts:

Particulars	(₹ in lacs)	Particulars	(₹ in lacs)
Buildings	400	Provision for Doubtful Debts	2
Plant and Equipment	200	Consumption of Stores and Spare Parts	14
Vehicles	50	Power and Fuel	16
Furniture and Fixtures	60	Rent	10
Brands	200	Repairs to Buildings	8
Computer Software	90	Repairs to Machinery	6
Insurance	4	Rates and Taxes	2
Sundry Debtors	80	Miscellaneous Expenses	2
Payments to the Auditor	32		

(a) Depreciate Buildings @ 5%, Plant and Equipment @ 20%, Vehicles @ 20%, Furniture and Fixtures @ 10% and Brands@ 10%,Computer Software@60%.

(b) Maintain a Provision for Doubtful Debts @ 10%

SOLUTION

7. DEPRECIATION AND AMORTIZATION EXPENSE

Particulars	(₹ in lacs)
Buildings [5% of ₹ 400 lacs]	20
Plant and Equipment [20% of ₹ 200 lacs]	40
Vehicles [20% of ₹ 50 lacs]	10
Furniture & Fixtures [10% of ₹ 60 lacs]	6
Brands [10 % of ₹ 200 lacs]	20
Computer Software [60% of ₹ 90 lacs]	54
	150

8. OTHER EXPENSES

Particulars	(₹ in lacs)
(a) Consumption of Stores and Spare Parts	14
(b) Power and Fuel	16
(c) Rent.	10

(d) Repairs to Buildings	8
(e) Repairs to Machinery	6
(f) Insurance	4
(g) Rates and Taxes	2
(h) Miscellaneous Expenses	2
(i) Provision for Doubtful Debts [(10% of ₹ 80 lacs) – ₹ 2 lac]	6
(j) Payments to the Auditor	32
	100

ILLUSTRATION 6

From the following information, prepare the relevant Notes to Accounts:

Particulars	*(₹ in lacs)*
Opening Balance of Profit and Loss Statement	452
Profit for the period	560
Transfer to Reserve @ 5%	
Interim Dividend	100
Proposed Preference Dividend	140
Proposed Equity Dividend	200
Corporate Dividend Tax	85
Debenture Redemption Reserve	100

SOLUTION

9. SURPLUS IN THE STATEMENT OF P&L TO BE TAKEN TO BALANCE SHEET

Particulars	*(₹ in lacs)*
Opening Balance	452
Add: Profit for the period	560
Less: Transfer to Reserve @ 5%	(28)
Less: Interim Dividend	(100)
Less: Proposed Preference Dividend	(140)
Less: Proposed Equity Dividend	(200)
Less: Corporate Dividend Tax	(85)
Less: Debenture Redemption Reserve	(100)
Closing Balance	359

ILLUSTRATION 7

The following items appear in the Trial Balance of Bharat Ltd. as at 31st March, 2016:

Particulars	₹
a) Revenue from Operations	48,00,000
b) Other Income	2,00,000
c) Expenses other than Interest	7,60,000

d) 12%, 20,000 Debentures of ₹ 100 each fully paid up

e) Opening Balance of Profit and Loss Statement ₹ 6,56,000.

f) Transfer to Reserve @ 5%

g) Interim Dividend ₹ 1,60,000

h) 14%, 10,000 Preference Shares of ₹ 100 each fully paid up

i) The recommendation of the company's Board of Directors include Proposed Equity Dividend ₹ 80,000. Transfer to Debenture Redemption Reserve @ 25% of Debentures.

j) Corporate Tax 30% and Corporate Dividend Tax 20%.

Required: Show the above items in Statement of Profit and Loss and calculate Surplus i.e. Balance in Statement of Profit & Loss.

SOLUTION

BHARAT LTD.
STATEMENT OF PROFIT AND LOSS FOR THE YEAR ENDED 31ST MARCH, 2016

Particulars	*Note No.*	*(₹ in lacs)*
I. Revenue from Operations		48
II. Other Income		2
III. Total Revenue [I + II]		50
IV. Expenses:		
Finance Costs		2.4
Other Expenses		7.6
Total Expenses		10.0
V. Profit before Tax(III – IV)		40
VI. Tax Expense [30% of ₹ 40 lacs]		(12)
VII. Profit for the period		28

SURPLUS I.E. BALANCE IN STATEMENT OF PROFIT & LOSS

Opening Balance	6.56
Add: Profit for the period	28.00
Less: Transfer to Reserve @ 5%	(1.4)
Less: Interim Dividend	(1.6)
Less: Proposed Preference Dividend	(1.4)
Less: Proposed Equity Dividend	(0.8)
Less: Corporate Dividend Tax[(1.6 + 1.4+ 0.8) x 20/80]	(0.95)
Less: Debenture Redemption Reserve [25% of ₹ 20 lacs]	(5)
	23.41

ILLUSTRATION 8

TULSIAN Ltd. provides the following information for the year ended 31st March, 2016:

Particulars	₹	*Particulars*	₹
Excise Duty paid	92.5	Sale of Products	1350

Net Loss on Sale of Investments	2	Sale of Services	15
Rental Collection Expenses	0.5	Trading Commission received	30
Opening Stock of Materials	42.3	Interest Income	10
Opening Stock of WIP	75	Dividends From Companies	5
Opening Stock of Finished Goods	87.5	Rental Income	7.5
Purchases of Materials	477.6	Gain on Foreign Currency	
Salaries and Wages	300	Transactions and Translation	4
Contribution To Provident and Other Funds	36	50 lacs Equity Shares of ₹ 10 each, ₹ 8 paid up	400
Expense on Employee Stock Option		60 lacs Equity Shares of ₹ 10 each	600
Scheme (ESOP) & Emp. Stock		Profit and Loss Account [01.04.2015]	226
Purchase Plan (ESPP)	14	10%, 70 lacs Pref. Shares of ₹ 10 each	700
Staff Welfare Expenses	75	General Reserve	80
Interest Expense	12	12% Debentures	100
Other Borrowing Costs(Brokerage)	2	Provision for Doubtful Debts	1
Buildings	200	Consum. of Stores and Spare Parts	7
Plant and Equipment	100	Power and Fuel	8
Vehicles	25	Rent	5
Furniture and Fixtures	30	Repairs to Buildings	4
Brands	100	Repairs to Machinery	3
Computer Software	45	Insurance	2
Prepaid Expenses	1	Rates and Taxes	1
Interim Dividend paid	50	Miscellaneous Expenses	1
Sundry Debtors	40		
Payments to the Auditor	16		

Additional Information:

(a) Closing Stocks: Materials ₹ 19.9 lacs, WIP ₹ 100,Finished Goods ₹ 200 lacs

(b) Depreciate Buildings @ 5%, Plant and Equipment @ 20%, Vehicles @ 20%, Furniture and Fixtures @ 10% and Brands@ 10%,Computer Software@60%.

(c) Payments to the Auditor include as Auditor ₹ 5 lacs,For Taxation Matters ₹ 4 lacs, For Company Law Matters ₹ 3 lacs, For Management Services ₹ 2 lacs, For Other Services ₹ 1 lac, For Other Services ₹ 1 lac

(d) Make a Provision for Doubtful Debts @ 10%

(e) The director's recommended:(i)An Equity Dividend of 15% including Interim Dividend.(ii) Transfer to Debenture Redemption Reserve @ 25% of Debentures. (iii) Transfer to General Reserve @ 5%.

(f) Income Tax Rate 30%,Corporate Dividend Tax Rate 20%

Required: Prepare Statement of Profit and Loss for the year ended 31st March, 2016 and a Note showing the computation of Surplus in the Statement of Profit and Loss to be taken to the Balance Sheet (as per Schedule III toThe Companies Act, 2013) as on that date.

SOLUTION

TULSIAN LTD.
STATEMENT OF PROFIT AND LOSS FOR THE YEAR ENDED 31ST MARCH, 2016

Particulars	*Note No.*	*(₹ in lacs)*
I. Revenue from Operations	1	1302.5
II. Other Income	2	20.0
III. Total Revenue [I + II]		1322.5
IV. Expenses:		
Cost of Materials consumed	3	500
Changes in Inventories	4	(137.5)
Employee Benefits Expense	5	425
Finance Costs	6	10
Depreciation and Amortization Expense	7	75
Other Expenses	8	50
Total Expenses		922.5
V. Profit before Tax(III – IV)		400
VI. Tax Expense@30%		(120)
VII. Profit for the period		280
Basic Earnings per Equity Share: = (280 – 70)/100 = ₹ 2.10		

Notes to Accounts: [₹ in lacs]

1. REVENUE FROM OPERATIONS

(a) From Sale of Products	1350
(b) From Sale of Services	15
(c) From Other Operating Revenues [Trading Commission]	30
(d) *Less:*Excise Duty	(92.5)
	1302.5

2. OTHER INCOME

(a) Interest Income	10
(b) Dividends From Companies	5
(c) Net Loss on Sale of Investments	(2)
(d) Rental Income (7. 5 lacs – 0.5 lac Collection Expenses)	7
	20

3. COST OF MATERIALS CONSUMED

(a) Opening Stock of Materials	42.3
(b) *Add:* Purchases of Materials	477.6
(c) *Less:* Closing Stock of Materials	(19.9)
Cost of Materials consumed	500

4. CHANGES IN INVENTORIES

Particulars	*Work-in-Progress (₹ in lacs)*	*Finished Goods (₹ in lacs)*	*Total (₹ in lacs)*
Opening Stock	75	87.5	162.5
Less: Closing Stock	100	200	300
	(25)	(112.5)	(137.5)

5. EMPLOYEE BENEFITS EXPENSE

Salaries and Wages	300
Contribution To Provident and Other Funds	36
Expense on Employee Stock Option Scheme (ESOP) and Employee Stock Purchase Plan (ESPP)	14
Staff Welfare Expenses	75
	425

6. FINANCE COSTS

(a) Interest Expense	12
(b) Other Borrowing Costs(Brokerage)	2
(c) Gain on Foreign Currency Transactions and Translation	(4)
	10

7. DEPRECIATION AND AMORTIZATION EXPENSE

Buildings [5% of ₹ 200 lacs]	10
Plant and Equipment [20% of ₹ 100 lacs]	20
Vehicles [20% of ₹ 25 lacs]	5
Furniture & Fixtures [10% of ₹ 30 lacs]	3
Brands [10 % of ₹ 100 lacs]	10
Computer Software [60% of ₹ 45 lacs]	27
	75

8. OTHER EXPENSES

(a) Consumption of Stores and Spare Parts	7
(b) Power and Fuel	8
(c) Rent.	5
(d) Repairs to Buildings	4
(e) Repairs to Machinery	3
(f) Insurance	2
(g) Rates and Taxes	1
(h) Miscellaneous Expenses	1
(i) Provision for Doubtful Debts [(10% of ₹ 40 lacs) – ₹ 1 lac]	3

(j) Payments to the Auditor as:	
1) Auditor	5
2) For Taxation Matters	4
3) For Company Law Matters	3
4) For Management Services	2
5) For Other Services	1
6) For Other Services	1
	50

9. SURPLUS IN THE STATEMENT OF P&L TO BE TAKEN TO BALANCE SHEET

Opening Balance	226
Add: Profit for the period	280
Less: Transfer to General Reserve @ 5%	(14)
Less: Interim Dividend	(50)
Less: Proposed Preference Dividend [10% of ₹ 700 lacs]	(70)
Less: Proposed Equity Dividend[15% of (600 lacs + 400 lacs) – 50 lacs]	(100)
Less: Corporate Dividend Tax [(50 + 70 + 100) x 20/80]	(55)
Less: Debenture Redemption Reserve [25% of ₹ 100 lacs]	(25)
Closing Balance	192

5.0 ACCOUNTING TREATMENT OF PROVISION FOR TAX

The worth noting points in this regard are as follows:

1. **Provision for tax for Current Year**	It is shown in Statement of Profit and Loss Statement.
2. **Advance Payment of Tax**	It is shown under the head **'Current Assets'** and sub-head **'Short-term Loans and Advances'** in the Balance Sheet.
3. **Tax Deducted at source (T.D.S.) from Incomes received from Others**	It is shown under the head **'Current Assets'** and sub-head **'Short term Loans and Advances'** in the Balance Sheet.
4. **Advance Tax and T.D.S. (Dr. Balance)**	These are usually adjusted against the Income Tax liability at the time of settlement of liability for income tax.

The accounting entries to be passed in this regard are summarised on next page:

JOURNAL ENTRIES

1. On Making Provision for Tax for current year	
Profit & Loss A/c	Dr.
To Provision for Tax A/c	
2. On Converting Provision into Liability on Settlement	
Provision for Tax A/c	Dr.
To Income Tax payable A/c	

3. On Adjustment of Advance tax and T.D.S. (Dr. Balance) Income Tax Payable A/c Dr. [with Actual Settled Liability] Income Tax Refund Due A/c Dr. [with Refund, *if any* Due] To Advance Tax A/c To T.D.S. A/c (Debit Balance)	
4. On Payment of Balance of tax payable (if any) Income Tax Payable A/c Dr. To Bank A/c	
5. On Receipt of Income tax Refund Due (if any) Bank A/c Dr. To Income Tax Refund due A/c	

ILLUSTRATION 9

The following items appear in the Trial Balance of Tulsian Ltd. as at 31st March 2016:

Particulars	*Dr. (₹)*	*Cr. (₹)*
Advance Payment of Tax (2014–2015)	4,50,000	—
Advance Payment of Tax (2015–2016)	6,00,000	
Provision for Tax (2014–2015)		5,00,000
Net Profit subject to Tax @ 35%		20,00,000

Required: Prepare Journal, Statement of Profit & Loss and Balance Sheet if the actual tax liability for 2014–2015 was settled and paid for ₹ 5,00,000 on 31.3.2016 but no accounting effect has yet been given.

SOLUTION

JOURNAL OF TULSIAN LTD.

Date	*Particulars*	*L.F.*	*Dr. (₹)*	*Cr. (₹)*
31.3.2016	Profit & Loss A/c Dr. To Provision for Income Tax A/c (Being the provision for I.T. for current year made)		7,00,000	 7,00,000
31.3.2016	Provision for Income Tax A/c Dr. To Income Tax Payable A/c (Being the tax for previous year finally settled)		5,00,000	 5,00,000
31.3.2016	Income Tax Payable A/c Dr. To Advance Tax A/c To Bank A/c (Being the advance tax for 2013–2015 adjusted against tax payable and Balance paid)		5,00,000	 4,50,000 50,000

AN EXTRACT OF STATEMENT OF PROFIT & LOSS FOR THE YEAR ENDED 31ST MARCH, 2016

Particulars	₹
Net Profit before Tax	20,00,000
Tax Expense	(7,00,000)
Profit for the period	13,00,000

AN EXTRACT OF BALANCE SHEET AS AT 31ST MARCH, 2016

Particulars	₹
Reserves & Surplus (Balance in Statement of Profit & Loss)	13,00,000
Current Liabilities [Short-term Provisions (Provisions for Tax)]	7,00,000
Current Assets [Short-term Loans & Advances (Advance Payment of Tax)]	6,00,000

6.0 DIVIDEND

MEANING OF DIVIDEND

(a) Dividend ordinarily means that portion of divisible profits *or* reserves which is distributed among the shareholders of a company which is a going concern.

(b) In case of a liquidating company, dividend means a division of the realised assets among the creditors and contributories according to their respective rights.

[CIT v. *Girdhar Dass & Co. (P) Ltd.* Supreme Court]

(c) The Institute of Chartered Accountants of India has defined 'dividend' as a "a distribution to shareholders out of profits *or* reserves available for this purpose."

[Guidance Note on terms used in Financial Statements]

(d) As per Sec 2(35), the term 'Dividend' includes Interim Dividend also.

CAN A COMPANY DECLARE AND DISTRIBUTE DIVIDEND IF THE MEMORANDUM AND ARTICLES ARE SILENT?

Yes, a company can declare and distribute dividend even if its Memorandum and Articles are silent because it has an inherent power to declare and distribute dividend. Such power need not expressly be given by the Memorandum *or* Articles though the Articles may regulate the manner in which dividends are to be distributed.

LEGAL PROVISIONS RELATING TO DIVIDEND

1. Sources from which Dividends can be Declared *or* Paid [Section 123(1)]

Section 123(1) of The Companies Act, 2013 specifies the following 4 sources from which dividends can be declared *or* paid:

(i) out of Profits of Current Financial Year;

(ii) out of Undistributed Profits of the Previous Financial Year *or* Years;

(iii) out of both above;

(iv) out of Moneys provided by the Central Government *or* State Government for payment of dividend in pursuance of a guarantee given by that government.

2. Provision for Depreciation [Section 123(2)]

Before declaring any dividend, the company must provide for:

(i) depreciation for current financial year, and

(ii) arrears of depreciation for previous financial year *or* years.

3. Extent of Depreciation [Section 123(2)]

Depreciation must be provided to the extent specified in Schedule II. Further, when the asset is sold, discarded, demolished *or* destroyed in any financial year, the Excess of the Written Down Value over its Sale Proceeds as scrap, if any should be written off in the same financial year.

Note: A company need not provide for depreciation if it does not want to declare dividends. In such a case, the fact that depreciation has not been provided for *or* written off, together with the quantum of arrears of depreciation must be disclosed in the Financial Statements.

4. Provision relation to Past Losses and Arrears of Depreciation [Rule 3(5)]

Before declaring any dividend, the company must provide for Past Losses and Arrears of Depreciation relating to previous year(s).

5. Out of Free Reserves only: No dividend shall be declared *or* paid by company from its reserves other than free reserves.

Note: Meaning of Free Reserves: As per Sec 2(43) of the Companies Act, 2013, "Free Reserves" mean such reserves which, as per the latest audited balance sheet of a company, are available for distribution as dividend.

ILLUSTRATION 10

Particulars	*₹ (in lakh)*		
	2012-2013	*2013-2014*	*2015-2016*
A. Profit (Loss) before charging Depreciation	(5)	6	16
B. Depreciation Chargeable u/s 123 (2)	3	7	6
C. Profit (Loss) after charging depreciation	(8)	(1)	10

Required: Calculate the Divisible Profits for the year 2015-2016

SOLUTION

COMPUTATION OF DIVISIBLE PROFIT FOR THE YEAR 2015-2016

Particulars	*₹ in (lakh)*
A. Profits for the Current Year	16
B. *Less:*	
(a) Depreciation for Current Year	(6)
(b) Past Loss for 2012-2013	(8)
(c) Past Loss for 2013-2014	(1)
C. Divisible Profits for the Current Year	1

7.0 OPTION TO TRANSFER PROFITS TO RESERVES

According to Proviso to Sec 123(1), a company may transfer an appropriate % of Current Profits to Reserve before declaring a dividend.

8.0 DECLARATION OF DIVIDEND OUT OF RESERVES [PROVISO TO SEC 123(1)]

According to The Companies *(Declaration and Payment of Dividend out of Reserves)* Rules, 2015, in the event of inadequacy *or* absence of profit in any financial year, dividend may be declared by a company for that year out of free reserves subject to fulfilment of the following 4 conditions:

1. Maximum Rate of Dividend	The rate of the dividend declared must not exceed the Average Rate of Dividend declared in 3 years immediately preceding that year.
2. Maximum Withdrawal	The total amount so drawn from the reserves must not exceed 10% of the sum of its Paid up Capital and Free Reserves as appearing in latest Audited Financial Statement.
3. First Set-off Losses	The amount so drawn shall first be utilised to set off the losses incurred in the financial year before any dividend in respect of equity shares is declared; and
4. Minimum Balance after Withdrawal	The balance of Reserves after such drawal must be at least 15% of its Paid up share capital as appearing in latest Audited Financial Statement.

ILLUSTRATION 11

Bharat Ltd. provides you the following information:

Year	*Rate of dividend declared*	*Paid up capital*
2010-2011	9%	₹ 1,00,000
2011-2012	8%	₹ 1,00,000
2012-2013	10%	₹ 1,00,000
2013-2014	8%	₹ 1,00,000
2014-2015	6%	₹ 1,00,000

Reserves as on 1.4.2015 ₹ 50,000

Loss after charging depreciation for the year 2015-2016 ₹ 6,000

Depreciation for year 2015-2016 ₹ 6,000

Required: X Ltd. desires to declare dividend @ 8.5% for the loss year 2015-2016. Can it do so? State giving reasons.

SOLUTION

Step 1 Maximum withdrawal of Reserve if condition (i) is satisfied

= 10% of Paid up Capital and free reserves

= 10% of (₹ 1,00,000 + 50,000) = ₹ 15,000

Step 2 Maximum withdrawal of Reserve if condition (ii) is satisfied

A. Opening Balance of Reserves in the beginning of the year	50,000
B. *Less:* Closing Balance of Reserve being 15% of paid up share capital	15,000
C. Reserve available (A – B)	35,000

Step 3 Permissible withdrawal of Reserve if conditions (i) and (ii) are satisfied

= ₹ 15,000 (being lower of limits as per Step 1 and Step 2)

Step 4 Maximum Permissible Divisible Profits

A. Permissible withdrawal of Reserve (as per Step 3)	15,000
B. *Less:* Loss to the extent of depreciation	6,000
C. Maximum Permissible Divisible profit [A – B]	9,000

Step 5 Actual Permissible Rate of Dividend

A. Maximum Permissible Rate of Dividend $\left(\frac{₹\,9000}{₹\,1,00,000} \times 100\right) = 9\%$

B. Average Rate of Dividend based on 3 years [(10% + 8% + 6%)/3] = 8%

C. Actual Permissible Rate of Dividend being lowest of two i.e. 8%

Comment: The management can declare dividend only upto a rate of 8% and not 8.5%.

ILLUSTRATION 12

Tushar Ltd. provides you the following information:

1. Equity shares of ₹ 10 Each on 31.3.2016	₹ 100 lakh
2. Free Reserves as on 31.3.2015	₹ 20 lakh
3. Loss for the year ending 31.3.2016	₹ 1 lakh

4. Rates of equity Dividend for the past eight years immediately preceeding the year 2015-2016:

1	2	3	4	5	6	7	8
6%	5%	4%	8%	7%	9%	10%	11%

The management recommends a dividend of 8% on equity share capital. As an expert comment upon the management's decision.

SOLUTION

As per the Companies Act, 2013 dividend out of reserves may be declared in accordance with the Companies (Declaration and Payment of Dividend out of Reserves) Rules, 2015. These rules provide the following four conditions to be fulfilled:

Step 1 Maximum withdrawal of Reserve if condition (i) is satisfied

= 10% of Paid up Capital and free reserves = 10% of (₹ 100 lakh + 20 lakh) = 12 lakh

Step 2: Maximum withdrawal of Reserve if condition (ii) is satisfied

A. Opening Balance of Reserves in the beginning of the year	20,00,000
B. *Less:* Closing Balance of Reserve being 15% of paid up share capital	15,00,000
C. Reserve available (A – B)	5,00,000

Step 3 Permissible withdrawal of Reserve if conditions (i) and (ii) are satisfied

= ₹ 5,00,000 (being lower of limits as per Step 1 and Step 2)

Step 4 Maximum Permissible Divisible Profits

A. Permissible withdrawal of Reserve (as per Step 3)	5,00,000
B. *Less:* Loss	1,00,000
C. Maximum Permissible Divisible profit [A – B]	4,00,000

Step 5 Actual Permissible Rate of Dividend

A. Maximum Permissible Rate of Dividend $\frac{₹\,4\text{ lakh}}{₹\,100\text{ lakh}} \times 100 = 4\%$

B. Average Rate of Dividend based on 3 years [(11% + 10% + 9%)/3] = 10%

C. Actual Permissible Rate of Dividend being lowest of two i.e. 4%

Comment: The management can declare dividend only upto a rate of 4%. Hence, the management's dividend decision of 8% is not as per Rules.

ILLUSTRATION 13

Due to inadequency of profits during the year ended 31st March, 2016, PQR Ltd. proposes to declare 8.5% dividend out of general reserves. From the following particulars, ascertain the amount that can be utilized from general reserves for this purpose, according to the Companies (Declaration of Dividend out of Reserves) Rules, 2014.

8% Preference shares of ₹ 100 each, fully paid up	₹ 15,00,000
Equity shares of ₹ 10 each, fully paid up	₹ 1,10,00,000
General Reserves as on 1.4.2015	₹ 25,00,000
Capital Reserves as on 1.4.2015	₹ 10,00,000
Revaluation Reserves as on 1.4.2015	₹ 15,00,000
Net Profit for the year ended 31st March, 2016	₹ 4,85,000

Average rate of dividend during the last three years has been 12%.

SOLUTION

As per the Companies Act, 2013 dividend out of reserves may be declared in accordance with the Companies (Declaration and Payment of Dividend out of Reserves) Rules, 2015. These rules provide the following four conditions to be fulfilled:

Step 1 Maximum withdrawal of Reserve if condition (i) is satisfied

= 10% of Paid up Capital and free reserves

= 10% of (₹ 15 lakh + 110 lakh + 25 lakh) = 15 lakh

Step 2 Maximum withdrawal of Reserve if condition (ii) is satisfied

A.	Opening Balance of Reserves in the beginning of the year	25,00,000
B.	*Less:* Closing Balance of Reserve being 15% of paid up share capital	18,75,000
C.	Reserve available (A – B)	6,25,000

Step 3 Permissible withdrawal of Reserve if conditions (i) and (ii) are satisfied

= ₹ 6,25,000 (being lower of limits as per Step 1 and Step 2)

Step 4 Maximum Permissible Divisible Profits

A.	Permissible withdrawal of Reserve (as per Step 3)	6,25,000
B.	*Add:* Profit [₹ 4,85,000 – ₹ 1,20,000 (Preference Dividend)]	3,65,000
C.	Maximum Permissible Divisible profit [A – B]	9,90,000

Step 5 Actual Permissible Rate of Dividend

A. Maximum Permissible Rate of Dividend $\left(\frac{₹\ 9,90,000}{₹\ 110,00,000} \times 100\right) = 9\%$

B. Average Rate of Dividend based on 3 years 12%

C. Actual Permissible Rate of Dividend being lowest of two i.e. 9%

Comment: The management can declare dividend only upto a rate of 9%. To declare dividend @ 8.5% the Company can utilize ₹ 5,70,000 (i.e. ₹ 9,35,000 – ₹ 3,65,000) out of General Reserves.

9.0 CAPITAL RESERVE

MEANING OF CAPITAL RESERVE

Capital Reserve is the reserve which does not include any amount regarded as free for distribution through the Statement of Profit and Loss. Only profits *or* a surplus of a capital nature are credited to such a reserve.

EXAMPLES OF PROFITS OR SURPLUSES WHICH ARE CREDITED TO CAPITAL RESERVE

1. Profit on Re-issue of Forfeited Shares.
2. Profit prior to incorporation.
3. The excess of the value of Net Assets over the price paid for the acquisition of a business.
4. Profit on Redemption/Cancellation of Debentures.
5. The credit balance in the Capital Reduction/Reconstruction Account, where there has been a reduction of capital with the consent of the Tribunal.

ITEMS NOT CREDITED TO CAPITAL RESERVE

1. Securities Premium as per Sec 52
2. Capital Redemption Reserve as per Sec.55 & Sec 69

These accounts are to be kept separately.

10.0 INTERIM DIVIDEND

MEANING OF INTERIM DIVIDEND

Interim dividend is the dividend which is declared between two AGMs. It is declared during the current year for the current year.

NO LIMIT ON NUMBER OF INTERIM DIVIDENDS [REGULATION 83 OF TABLE F]

The Board may from time to time pay to the members such interim dividends as appear to it to be justified by the profits of the company. Thus, there is no limit on the number of interim dividends a company may declare in a year.

LEGAL PROVISIONS AS TO INTERIM DIVIDEND

1. As per Sec 123(3) the Board of Directors of a company may declare interim dividend during any financial year out of the Surplus in the Profit and Loss Account and out of profits of the financial year in which such interim dividend is sought to be declared: However, in case the company has incurred loss during the current financial year up to the end of the quarter immediately preceding the date of declaration of interim dividend, such interim dividend shall not be declared at a rate higher than the average dividends declared by the company during the immediately preceding 3 financial years.

2. The term 'Dividend' includes Interim Dividend also [Section 2(35)].

3. All provisions of the Companies Act which apply to dividends have now become applicable to interim dividends also.

LEADING CASE LAWS AS TO INTERIM DIVIDEND

1. It is declared by the Board of directors. It does not require approval of members at General Meeting. *[Scott v. Scott, (1943)]*

2. Before declaring an interim dividend, the directors must satisfy themselves that the financial position of the company warrants the payment of such dividend out of its distributable profits because

"the declaration of interim dividends depends much more upon estimates and opinions than the declaration of final dividend which is made upon the information contained in a formal balance sheet."

[Lucas v. Fitzgarald (1903)]

11.0 FINAL DIVIDEND

WHO TAKES DIVIDEND DECISION?

The dividend decision is taken by the Board of Directors and is then recommended to the shareholders for their final approval at AGM (i.e., Annual General Meeting) of the company. The shareholders can reduce the amount of dividend even to zero but can not increase the amount of dividend as recommended by the Board of Directors. If the directors decide not to declare and dividend, the shareholders in general meeting cannot themselves declare it. *[Regulation 80 of Table F]*

DECLARATION OF FINAL DIVIDEND AT AGM/EGM [REGULATION 80 OF TABLE F]

1. A company usually declares dividend at its Annual General Meeting. But it may declare dividend at any other general meeting unless the articles provide otherwise.
2. A company cannot declare a further dividend after having declared a final dividend at its annual general meeting.
3. It may also be noted that there can be no declaration of dividend for past years in respect of which the accounts have already been closed at previous annual general meetings.

12.0 LEGAL PROVISIONS AS TO PAYMENT OF DIVIDEND [SEC 123(4) & (5)]

1. The amount of dividend including interim dividend must be deposited in a separate bank account within 5 days of the declaration of such dividend and the same shall be used for payment of dividend.
2. No dividend shall be paid by a company in respect of any share therein except to the registered shareholder of such share *or* to his order *or* to his banker and shall not be payable except in cash.
3. Any dividend payable in cash may be paid by cheque *or* warrant *or* in any electronic mode to the shareholder entitled to the payment of the dividend.

13.0 UNPAID/UNCLAIMED DIVIDEND [SEC 124 & 125]

DUTY OF COMPANY TO TRANSFER TO SPECIAL DIVIDEND ACCOUNT [SEC 124(1)]

The company must transfer the total amount of dividend which remains unpaid/unclaimed within 30 days of its declaration, to a special account 'Unpaid Dividend Account of ... Company limited/ Company (Private) Limited, within 7 days of the expiry of aforesaid 30 days. This account is to be opened in a Scheduled Bank.

DUTY OF COMPANY TO PREPARE A STATEMENT OF SHAREHOLDERS TO WHOM UNPAID DIVIDEND RELATES [SEC 124(2)]

The company must, within a period of 90 days of making any transfer of an amount to the Unpaid Dividend Account, prepare a statement containing the names, their last known addresses and the unpaid dividend to be paid to each person and place it on the website of the company, if any, and also on any other website approved by the Central Government for this purpose, in such form, manner and other particulars as may be prescribed.

PENALTY FOR DEFAULT IN TRANSFER [SEC 124(3)]

If unpaid/unclaimed dividend is not transferred to Unpaid Dividend Account within the stipulated period of 7 days, the company shall be liable to pay interest @ 12% p.a. The interest accruing on such an amount must ensure to the benefit to the members of the company, in proportion to the amount remaining unpaid to them.

PAYMENT OF UNCLAIMED/UNPAID DIVIDEND [SEC 124(4)]

Any person claiming to be entitled to any money transferred to the Unpaid/Unclaimed Dividend Account may make an application to the Company within 7 years from the date of transfer for payment of money claimed.

TRANSFER OF UNCLAIMED/UNPAID DIVIDEND AFTER 7 YEARS[SEC 124(5)]

If any amount transferred to Unpaid Dividend Account remains unclaimed/unpaid for 7 years, it must be transferred by the company to the 'Investor Education and Protection Fund' along with Interest Accrued.

TRANSFER OF SHARES [SEC 124(6)]

All shares in respect of which unpaid *or* unclaimed dividend has been transferred to Investor Education and Protection Fund must also be transferred by the company in the name of Investor Education and Protection Fund along with a statement containing such details as may be prescribed. However, any claimant of shares transferred above shall be entitled to claim the transfer of shares and unclaimed dividend from Investor Education and Protection Fund in accordance with such procedure and on submission of such documents as may be prescribed.

INVESTOR EDUCATION AND PROTECTION FUND [SEC 125]

Objective of the Fund	The Fund shall be used for promotion of investors' awareness and protection of interests of investors in accordance with such rules as may be prescribed.
Amount to be Credited to Fund	The following amounts shall be credited to the fund: (a) Unpaid dividends (b) Matured deposits with companies other than Banking Companies (c) Refund of application money (d) Matured debentures with the companies (e) Interest accrued on the amounts referred to in Clauses (a) to (d) above. (f) Grants and donations given to the fund by the Central Government, State Government, Companies *or* any other institution. (g) The interest *or* other income received out of instruments made from the fund. (h) sale proceeds of fractional shares arising out of issuance of bonus shares, merger and amalgamation for 7 *or* more years; (i) redemption amount of preference shares remaining unpaid *or* unclaimed for 7 *or* more years; and

Utilization of Fund	The Fund shall be utilised for— a) Refund of Unclaimed Dividends, b) Refund of Matured Deposits, c) Refund of Matured Debentures, d) Refund of the Application Money due for refund and Interest thereon; e) Promotion of Investors' Education, Awareness and Protection; f) Reimbursement of Legal Expenses, g) Any other purpose as per Rules
Power of Central Government to Constitute Committee	The Central Government shall by notification in the Official Gazette, constitute a committee to administer the Fund, and maintain separate accounts and other relevant records in relation to the Fund in such form as may be prescribed in consultation with the Comptroller and Auditor General of India (CAG).
Power of Committee to Spend	The committee shall be entitled to spend money out of the fund for carrying out the objectives of the fund.

14.0 RIGHT TO DIVIDEND, RIGHTS SHARES AND BONUS SHARES TO BE HELD IN ABEYANCE PENDING REGISTRATION OF TRANSFER OF SHARES [SEC 126]

Where any instrument of transfer of shares has been delivered to any company for registration and the transfer of such shares has not been registered by the company, it must, irrespective of anything contained in any other provision of this Act,—

(a) transfer the dividend in relation to such shares to the Unpaid Dividend Account unless the company is authorised by the registered holder of such shares in writing to pay such dividend to the transferee specified in such instrument of transfer; and

(b) keep in abeyance in relation to such shares, any offer of rights shares and any issue of fully paid-up bonus shares.

15.0 PUNISHMENT FOR FAILURE TO DISTRIBUTE DIVIDENDS [SEC 127]

Where a dividend has been declared by a company but has not been paid *or* the warrant in respect thereof has not been posted within 30 days from the date of declaration to any shareholder entitled to the payment of the dividend, every director of the company shall, if he is knowingly a party to the default, be punishable with imprisonment which may extend to 2 years and with fine which shall be atleast ₹ 1,000 for every day during which such default continues and the company shall be liable to pay simple interest at the rate of 18% p.a. during the period for which such default continues:

Circumstances under which No Offence (Provisio to Sec 127): No offence under this section shall be deemed to have been committed:—

(a) where the dividend could not be paid by reason of the operation of any law;

(b) where a shareholder has given directions to the company regarding the payment of the dividend and those directions cannot be complied with and the same has been communicated to him;

(c) where there is a dispute regarding the right to receive the dividend;

(d) where the dividend has been lawfully adjusted by the company against any sum due to it from the shareholder; *or*

(e) where, for any other reason, the failure to pay the dividend *or* to post the warrant within the period under this section was not due to any default on the part of the company.

16.0 PAYMENT OF DIVIDEND ON PARTLY PAID-UP SHARES [SEC 51 AND REGULATION 83]

As per Sec 51 a company may, if so authorised by its articles, pay dividends in proportion to the amount paid up on each share where a larger amount is paid up on some shares than on others.

Note: If the articles do not contain any such provision, dividend will have to be paid only in proportion to the nominal value of shares. *[Oak Bank Oil Co. v. Crum, (1882)]*

Note: In the case of fresh issue of capital, the holders thereof, unless precluded by the terms of issue, are entitled to receive dividend pari passu with the shares already issued. *[Regulation 83 of Table F]*

LEGAL POSITION AS TO DIVIDEND ON PARTLY PAID-UP SHARES

Case	*Dividend on Partly paid shares*
1. Where the Articles specify provision in this regard	Dividend is payable on the nominal/called up/ paid up amount of shares as per Articles.
2. Where the Articles are silent In this regard and Table F has not been excluded.	
(a) If some amount has been paid on any of the shares of the company.	Dividend must be declared and paid on the amount paid up (excluding calls-in-advance) on shares.
(b) If nothing has been paid on any of the shares of the company.	Dividend may be declared and paid according to the nominal amounts of the shares.
3. Where the Articles are silent in this regard and Table F has been excluded.	Dividend must be declared and paid on nominal amount of shares.

ILLUSTRATION 14

X Ltd. provides you the following information:

10,000 Equity Shares of ₹ 10 each, ₹ 6 per share called up	₹ 60,000
Less: Calls-in-arrears on 1,000 shares @ ₹ 2 per share	₹ 2,000
	₹ 58,000
Add: Calls-in advance on 500 shares @ ₹ 3 per share	₹ 1,500
The Board of Directors recommend a dividend @ 10%	₹ 59,500

Required: Calculate the amount of Proposed Dividend in each of the following alternative cases:

Case (a) If no other information is given.

Case (b) If the Articles prescribe the payment of dividend on the nominal amount of shares.

Case (c) If the Articles prescribe the payment of dividend on the called up amount of shares.

Case (d) If the Articles prescribe the payment of dividend on the paid up amount of shares.

Case (e) If the Articles are silent and Table F has been excluded.

SOLUTION

Case (a) 10% of ₹ 58,000 = ₹ 5,800 [As per Regulation 83 of Table F]

Case (b) 10% of ₹ 1,00,000 = 10,000 [As per Articles]

Case (c) 10% of ₹ 60,000 = ₹ 6,000 [As per Articles]

Case (d) 10% of ₹ 58,000 = ₹ 5,800 [As per Articles]

Case (e) 10% of ₹ 1,00,000 = ₹ 10,000 [Oak Bank Oil Co. v. Crum, (1882)]

ILLUSTRATION 15

X Ltd. was registered with an authorised capital of ₹ 40,00,000 divided into 10,000 12% Preference Shares of ₹ 100 each and 3,00,000 Equity Shares of ₹ 10 each. On 1st April 2015, all the preference shares and 2,00,000 equity shares had been issued and were fully paid with the exception of 40,000 of equity shares on which only ₹ 5 per share had been called up. On 1st Nov. 2015 the director made the final call of ₹ 5 per share on the partly paid equity shares and the call was dully paid except by a shareholders-holding 2,000 shares. The recommendation of directors include the dividend on equity shares @ 15% p.a.

Required: Calculate the amount of proposed dividend in each of the following alternative cases:

Case (a) If no other information is given;

Case (b) If the shares on which calls were in arrears were duly forfeited before the end of the accounting year.

Case (c) If the shares on which calls were in arrears were duly forfeited and were reissued @ ₹ 9 per share before the end of the accounting year.

SOLUTION

Case (a)

I	On 12% Preference Shares (12% on ₹ 10,00,000)		1,20,000
II	On Equity shares		
	On 1,60,000 Equity Shares (1,60,000 × ₹ 10 × 15/100)	2,40,000	
	On 40,000 Equity Shares (40,000 × ₹ 5 × 15/100)	30,000	
	On 38,000 Equity Shares (38,000 × ₹ 5 × 15/100 × 5/12)	11,875	2,81,875
III	Total Proposed Dividend [I + II]		4,01,875

Case (b)

I	On 12% Preference Shares (12% on ₹ 10,00,000)		1,20,000
II	On Equity shares		
	On 1,60,000 Equity Shares (1,60,000 × ₹ 10 × 15/100)	2,40,000	
	On 38,000 Equity Shares (38,000 × ₹ 5 × 15/100)	28,500	
	On 38,000 Equity Shares (38,000 × ₹ 5 × 15/100 × 5/12)	11,875	2,80,375
III	Total Proposed Dividend [I + II]		4,00,375

Case (c)

I	On 12% Preference Shares (12% on ₹ 10,00,000)		1,20,000
II	On Equity Shares		
	On 1,60,000 Equity Shares (1,60,000 × ₹ 10 × 15/100)	2,40,000	
	On 40,000 Equity Shares (40,000 × ₹ 5 × 15/100)	30,000	
	On 40,000 Equity Shares (40,000 × ₹ 5 × 15/100 × 5/12)	12,500	2,82,500
III	Total Proposed Dividend [I + II]		4,02,500

7.0 DIVIDEND ON PREFERENCE SHARES

RIGHT TO RECEIVE PREFERENCE DIVIDEND

Holders of preference shares are entitled to receive a dividend at a fixed rate before any dividend is declared on equity shares. They can exercise this right only when there are sufficient divisible profits and a dividend is declared as per the provisions of the Act.

ARREARS OF DIVIDEND IN CASE OF CUMULATIVE PREFERENCE SHARES

1. If the company is a going concern	Holders of Cumulative Preference Shares are entitled to receive the arrears of dividend out of the profits of subsequent years before any dividend is paid on equity shares.
2. If the company goes into liquidation (i) ***Where Articles contain an express provision to that effect.*** (ii) ***Where Articles are silent*** (a) *If such dividends have been declared.*	(i) Arrears of dividend are payable alongwith return of preference share capital before return of equity capital. (a) Arrears of dividend are payable alongwith return of preference share capital before return of equity capital.
(b) *If such dividends have not been declared*	(b) Arrears of undeclared dividends are payable out of any surplus if any left after the return of full preference and equity share capital.

Note: In India Unless otherwise stated, all Preference Shares are assumed to be Cumulative.

DIVIDEND IN CASE OF NON-CUMULATIVE PREFERENCE SHARES

Holders of non-cumulative preference shares are not entitled to receive the arrears of dividend out of the profits of subsequent years if no divided is declared in a particular year *or* years. In other words, they are entitled to receive the dividend only for the year in which the dividend is declared.

DIVIDEND IN CASE OF PARTICIPATING PREFERENCE SHARES

Holders of Participants Preference shares are entitled to receive their fixed dividend before any dividend is paid on the equity shares *plus* a fixed percentage of surplus profits remaining after a certain fixed percentage of equity dividend has been paid to equity shareholders.

ILLUSTRATION 16

Tulsian Ltd provides you the following information:

9% Participating Pref. Share Capital	₹ 100 lakhs
10% Preference Share Capital	₹ 200 lakhs
11% Non-Cumulative Preference Share Capital	₹ 300 lakhs
Equity Share Capital	₹ 400 lakhs
Current Year's Net Profit after tex	₹ 231 lakhs

Participating Pref. Shareholders are entitled to participate to the extent of 25% of Surplus Profits as per Articles. Last year no dividend could be paid on any share due to absence of profits. At end of current year, the Board decided to propose dividend on Equity Shares @ 20%. Calculate the amont of Proposed Dividend on all shares.

SOLUTION

On 9% Participating Pref. Share Capital [₹ 9 lakhs (arrears) + ₹ 9 lakhs (current) + ₹ 15 lakhs*]	₹ 33 lakhs
On 10% Preference Share Capital [₹ 20 lakhs (arrears) + ₹ 20 lakhs (current)]	₹ 40 lakhs
On 11% Non-Cumulative Preference Share Capital [₹ 11% of 300 lakhs (current)]	₹ 33 lakhs
On Equity Share Capital [₹ 20% of 400 lakhs (current)]	₹ 80 lakhs
	₹ 180 lakhs

* Surplus Profit = Profits available – Dividend
= ₹ 231 lakhs – [₹ 18 lakhs (on Participating) + ₹ 40 lakhs (on 10% Pref. Shares) + ₹ 33 lakhs (on 11% Pref. Shares) + ₹ 80 lakhs (on Equity)] = ₹ 60 lakhs

25% share of participating pref. shareholders = 25% of ₹ 60 lakhs = ₹ 15 lakhs

Note: In India Unless otherwise stated, all Preference Shares are assumed to be Cumulative.

18.0 DIVIDEND DISTRIBUTION TAX (D.D.T)

Meaning	Dividend Distribution Tax (DDT) is a tax on any amount declared, distributed *or* paid by way of dividends (whether Interim *or* otherwise).		
Recognition	DDT Liability should be recognised in the same financial year in which dividend concerned is recognised since it is directly linked to dividend.		
Disclosure in Notes to Reserves & Surplus	DDT should be disclosed along with Proposed/Interim Dividend in the Notes to Reserves & Surplus as follows:		
	Proposed/Interim Dividend	XXX	
	Dividend Distribution Tax	XXX	XXX
Disclosure in Balance Sheet	DDT should be disclosed separately under the sub head **'Short-term Provisions'** & the head **'Current Liabilities'**.		
Current Rate of C.D.T.	For Financial year 2016–2017, the Current Rate of DDT. is 15% with an additional surcharge of 12% *plus* 3% for education cess. It means the effective rate comes out at 20.358% [i.e.(15/85) +12%] +3%]		
Time Limit for Payment	DDT must be paid within 14 days from the date of declaration, distribution *or* payment of dividend (whichever is earliest)		

19.0 CAPITALISATION OF PROFITS

MEANING OF CAPITALISATION OF PROFITS AND BONUS SHARES

Capitalisation of profits refers to the process of converting profits *or* reserves into paid up capital. A bonus share is a free share issued without any consideration to an existing shareholder in the ratio of number of shares held by that shareholder. Issue of Bonus share, decreases the Reserve & Surplus, increases the Issued Capital but does not bring any change in Cash Flow and Net Worth of the Company.

HOW TO CAPITALISE PROFITS OR RESERVES? [SEC 123(5)]

A company may capitalise its profits *or* reserves—

(a) by paying up amounts unpaid on existing partly paid shares so as to make them fully paid up shares, or

(b) by issuing fully paid bonus shares to the existing members.

THREE SOURCES FOR ISSUE OF FULLY PAID-UP BONUS SHARES [SEC 63(1)]

As per Sec 63(1), a company may issue fully paid-up bonus shares to its members out of—

(i) Its Free Reserves

(ii) The Secutiries Premium Account*; or*

(iii) The Capital Redemption Reserve Account:

Notes

1. **Not out of Revaluation Reserves:** No issue of bonus shares shall be made by capitalising reserves created by the Revaluation of Assets.
2. **Meaning of Free Reserves:** As per Sec 2(43) of the Companies Act, 2013, "Free Reserves" mean such reserves which, as per the latest audited balance sheet of a company, are available for distribution as dividend.
3. **Items not treated as Free Reserves:**

(i) Any amount representing unrealised gaints, notional gains *or* revaluation of assets, whether shown as a reserve *or* otherwise, *or*

(ii) Any change in carrying amount of an asset *or* of a liability recognised in equity, including Surplus in Profit and Loss Account on measurement of the Asset *or* the Liability at Fair Value.

CONDITIONS FOR ISSUE OF FULLY PAID-UP BONUS SHARES [SEC 63(2) & REGULATION 39 OF TABLE F]

1. **Authorised by Articles** — A company can issue bonus shares if its Articles expressly authorise to do so.
2. **Board's Resolution** — A resolution is to be passed by the Board of Directors recommending its decision to issue bonus shares.
3. **Member's Resolution** — A resolution is to be passed by the members in the general meeting to approve the Board's resolution recommending the issue of bonus shares.

   Members' resolution must state—

(a) an intention to capitalize the profits *or* reserves, and

(b) the amount of profits *or* reserves to be capitalized.

4. **No Default in Payment of Interest/Principle:** The company has not defaulted in payment of interest *or* principal in respect of fixed deposits *or* debt securities issued by it.
5. **No Default in Payment of Statutory dues:** The company has not defaulted in respect of payment of statutory dues of the employees such as contribution to provident fund, gratuity and bonus.
6. **No O/s Partly-Paid-up Shares:** The partly-paid shares, if any, outstanding on the date of allotment are made fully paid-up.
7. **Compliance with Prescribed Conditions:** The company must comply with Prescribed Conditions.
8. **Not in lieu of Dividend:** The Bonus Shares shall not be issued in lieu of dividend.

20.0 ACCOUNTING TREATMENT OF DIVIDEND, DIVIDEND DISTRIBUTION TAX TRANSFER TO RESERVES BONUS, ETC.

1. On Transfer of Profits to General Reserve (Board's Option)

Profit & Loss (Appropriation) A/c	Dr.
*To General Reserve	

2.	**For Making Provision for Final Dividend recommended by the Board of Directors and Provision for Dividend Distribution Tax**	
	Profit & Loss (Appropriation) A/c	Dr.
	*To Proposed Preference Dividend A/c	
	*To Proposed Equity Dividend A/c	
	*To Provision for Dividend Distribution Tax A/c	
3.	**On Declaration of Final Dividend for the previous year at Annual General Meeting**	
	Proposed Pref. Dividend A/c	Dr.
	Proposed Equity Dividend A/c	Dr.
	To Pref. Dividend Payable A/c	
	To Equity Dividend Payable A/c	
4.	**On Payment of Dividend Distribution Tax**	
(a)	Provision for Dividend Distribution Tax A/c	Dr.
	To Dividend Distribution Tax Payable A/c	
(b)	Dividend Distribution Tax Payable A/c	Dr.
	To Bank A/c	
5.	**On Transfer of the amount of Dividend Payable to a Separate Bank Account**	
	Dividend Bank A/c	Dr.
	To Bank A/c	
6.	**On Payment of a Dividend Payable out of Dividend Bank**	
	Pref. Dividend Payable A/c	Dr.
	Equity Dividend Payable A/c	Dr.
	To Dividend Bank A/c	
7.	**On giving Bonus by converting partly paid shares into fully paid shares**	
(a)	**On declaration of such Bonus**	
	General Reserve A/c	Dr.
	Profit & Loss A/c	Dr.
	To Bonus to Shareholders A/c	
(b)	**On Making the final call due**	
	Share Final Call A/c	Dr.
	To Share Capital A/c	
(c)	**On Adjustment of final call**	
	Bonus to Shareholders A/c	Dr.
	To Share Final Call A/c	
8.	**On Issue of fully paid Bonus shares**	
(a)	**On Declaration of such Bonus**	
	Capital Redemption Reserve A/c	Dr.
	Securities Premium A/c (Realised in Cash)	Dr.
	Capital Reserve (realised in cash only)	Dr.
	General Reserve A/c	Dr.

Profit & Loss A/c	Dr.
To Bonus to Shareholders A/c	
(b) **On Issue of fully paid Bonus Shares**	
Bonus to Shareholders A/c	Dr.
To Share Capital A/c	

*These Appropriations shall be shown by way of deduction while computing, 'Surplus' in the Statement of Profit & Loss, in the Note as to 'Reserves and Surplus'.

Important Note: For Converting Partly Paid up Shares into Fully Paid up shares, the company can utilise only the Free Reserves and not the Balance of Securities Premium A/c and Capital Redemption Reserve A/c.

ILLUSTRATION 17

An Extract of the Balance Sheet of Tulsian Ltd. as at 31st March, 2015 is as follows:

Share Capital:	
Authorised:	
1,40,000 Equity Shares of ₹ 10 Each	14,00,000
10% 7,000 Preference Shares of ₹ 100 each	7,00,000
Issued & Subscribed:	
10% 7,000 Preference Shares of ₹ 100 each	7,00,000
60,000 Equity Shares of ₹ 10 each fully paid	6,00,000
50,000 Equity Shares of ₹ 10 each ₹ 8 per share paid up	4,00,000
Reserves & Surplus:	
Capital Redemption Reserve	60,000
Revaluation Reserve	60,000
Securities Premium Account	40,000
General Reserve	3,00,000
Profit & Loss Account	1,78,000
Proposed Preference Dividend	70,000
Proposed Equity Dividend	1,50,000
Provision for Dividend Distribution Tax	55,000
Cash at Bank	6,00,000

At the Annual General Meeting held on 30th Sept 2015, it was resolved:

(a) To declare and pay the dividend as proposed by Directors.

(b) To convert the partly paid equity shares into fully paid up equity shares by way of bonus and to issue fully paid bonus shares to the holders of fully paid equity shares in the same ratio.

(c) To give existing shareholders the option to subscribe one ₹ 10 Right share at ₹ 15 for every four shares held after the bonus distribution.

The aforesaid right shares were subscribed by all the shareholders. The bonus shares and right shares were fully allotted on 1st Jan. 2016.

On 31st March 2016, the recommendation of the company's board of directors include equity dividend @ 15% p.a. for the year 2015-2016 and Transfer of Profits to General Reserve @5%. Net profit after tax for the year 2015-2016 amounted to ₹ 4,00,000.

Required: Give the necessary journal entries on 30th Sept., 2015, 1st Jan 2016 and 31st March, 2016. (Assume Dividend Distribution Tax @ 20%)

SOLUTION

JOURNAL OF TULSIAN LTD.

Particulars		*L.F.*	*Dr. (₹)*	*Cr. (₹)*
Proposed Pref. Dividend A/c	Dr.		70,000	
Proposed Equity Dividend A/c	Dr.		1,50,000	
To Pref. Dividend Payable A/c				70,000
To Equity Dividend Payable A/c				1,50,000
(Being final pref. dividend & equity dividend declared at AGM).				
Dividend Bank A/c	Dr.		2,20,000	
To Bank A/c				2,20,000
(Being the amount of dividend payable t/f to separate Bank A/c)				
Pref. Dividend Payable A/c	Dr.		70,000	
Equity Dividend Payable A/c	Dr.		1,50,000	
To Dividend Bank A/c				2,20,000
(Being the payment of dividend)				
Provisions for Dividend Distribution Tax A/c	Dr.		55,000	
To Dividend Distribution Tax Payable A/c				55,000
(Being the DDT payable on declaration of final dividend)				
Dividend Distribution Tax Payable A/c	Dr.		55,000	
To Bank A/c				55,000
(Being Dividend Tax paid)				
General Reserve	Dr.		1,00,000	
To Bonus to Shareholders A/c				1,00,000
(Being the bonus declared for making partly paid shares fully paid as per General Body's resolution dated 30th Sept. 2015)				
Equity Share Final Call A/c	Dr.		1,00,000	
To Equity Share Capital A/c				1,00,000
(Being the final call of ₹ 2 per share due on 50,000 shares as per Board's resolution dated....)				
Bonus to Shareholders A/c	Dr.		1,00,000	
To Equity Share Final Call A/c				1,00,000
(Being amount of bonus dividend utilized towards payment of the final call of ₹ 2 per share on 50,000 shares)				
Capital Redemption Reserve A/c	Dr.		60,000	
Securities Premium A/c	Dr.		40,000	
General Reserve A/c	Dr.		50,000	
To Bonus to Shareholders A/c				1,50,000

(Being the bonus declared for issuing fully paid bonus shares at the rate of 1 share for every 4 shares held as per General Body's resolution dated 30th Sept. 2015)			
Bonus to Shareholders A/c Dr.		1,50,000	
To Equity Share Capital A/c			1,50,000
(Being the issue of 15,000 equity shares of ₹10 each by way of bonus shares in the ratio of 1 for every 4 held)			
Bank A/c Dr.		4,68,750	
To Equity Share Application & Allotment A/c			4,68,750
(Being application money received on 31,250 @ ₹ 15 per share to be issued as right shares in the ratio of 1 : 4)			
Equity Share Application & Allotment A/c Dr.		4,68,750	
To Equity Share Capital A/c			3,12,500
To Securities Premium A/c			1,56,250
(Being application money on 31,250 shares @ ₹ 10 per share transferred to Share Capital Account and ₹ 5 per share to Securities Premium Account)			
Profit & Loss (Appropriation) A/c Dr.		20,000	
To General Reserve			20,000
(Being the t/f of 5% of current Profits ₹ 4,00,000 to reserve)			
Profit & Loss (Appropriation) A/c Dr.		2,41,093.75	
To Proposed Pref. Dividend A/c			70,000
To Proposed Equity Dividend A/c			1,71,093.75
(Being the provision made for pref. and equity dividend)			
Profit & Loss (Appropriation) A/c Dr.		60,273	
To Provision for Dividend Distribution Tax A/c			60,273
(Being DDT provided for[241093.75 x 20/80])			

Working Notes

1. CALCULATION OF EQUITY DIVIDEND @ 15% P.A.

On paid-up capital of ₹ 10,00,000 for 1 year	1,50,000.00
On additional capital (on conversion of partly paid shares into fully paid shares) of ₹ 1,00,000 for 3 months	3,750.00
On additional capital (issued by way of bonus shares) of ₹ 1,50,000 for 3 months	5,625.00
On additional capital (issued by way of Right shares) of ₹ 3,12,500 for 3 months	11,718.75
	1,71,093.75

1. Ratio of bonus dividend in case of partly paid shares @ ₹ 2 for every ₹ 8 paid up capital is 1 for every 4. Hence, the amount of bonus dividend to be declared to the holders of fully paid share = 1/4 × 60,000 × ₹ 10 = ₹ 1,50,000.

ILLUSTRATION 18

The paid up capital of COJHI Ltd. is ₹ 10,00,000 consisting of 60,000 Equity Shares of ₹ 10 each fully paid up and 50,000 Equity Shares of ₹ 10 each, ₹ 8 per share paid up.

It has ₹ 40,000 in Securities Premium Account, ₹ 2,00,000 in Profit and Loss Account (Cr.) ₹ 3,00,00 in General Reserve and ₹ 60,000 in Capital Redemption Reserve Account.

By way of Bonus Dividend the partly paid-up shares are converted into fully paid-up shares and th holders of fully paid up shares are also allotted fully paid-up Bonus shares in the same ratio.

Required: Pass Journal Entries showing separately the two types of Bonus issues stated above. is desired that there should be minimum reduction in free reserves.

SOLUTION

JOURNAL

Particulars		*L.F.*	*Dr. (₹)*	*Cr. (₹)*
General Reserve A/c	Dr.		1,00,000	
To Bonus Shareholders A/c				1,00,00
(Being the Bonus declared for making partly paid shares fully paid as per Shareholders Resolution dated.....):				
Share Final Call A/c	Dr.		1,00,000	
To Equity Share Capital A/c				1,00,00
(Being the Final call of ₹ 2 per share due on 50,000 shares as per Board's Resolution dated....)				
Bonus Shareholders A/c	Dr.		1,00,000	
To Share Final Call A/c				1,00,00
(Being the Utilisation of Bonus towards payment of the final call of ₹ 2 per share on 50,000 shares)				
Securities Premium A/c	Dr		40,000	
Capital Redemption Reserve A/c	Dr.		60,000	
General Reserve A/c	Dr.		50,000	
To Bonus Shareholders A/c				1,50,00
(Being the Bonus declared for issuing fully paid-up shares as per Share-holder's Resolution dated....)				
Bonus Shareholders A/c	Dr.		1,50,000	
To Equity Share Capital A/c				1,50,0
(Being the Issue of 15,000 fully paid shares of ₹ 10 each to be distributed in the ratio of 1 share for every 4 hold, as per Board's Resolution dated....)				

Note 1: *General Reserve has been utilised for making partly paid shares fully paid, because Securi Premium A/c or Capital Redemption Reserve A/c cannot be utilised for the purpose.*

Note 2: *Ratio of Bonus declared is ₹ 2 for every ₹ 8 paid-up capital is 1/4th or 1 for every 4. Her the amount of Bonus to be declared to the holders of fully paid shares is:*

= (60,000 × 1/4) × ₹ 10 = ₹ 1,50,000.

21.0 FORM OF PREPARING A BALANCE SHEET OF A COMPANY

VERTICAL FORM OF BALANCE SHEET

Part I of Schedule III to The Companies Act, 2013 prescribes only vertical form of Balance Shee

GENERAL INSTRUCTIONS FOR PREPARATION OF BALANCE SHEET

1. Current Assets	An asset shall be classified as current when it satisfies **any of the following criteria**: (a) it is expected to be realized in, *or* is intended for sale *or* consumption in, the company's normal operating cycle; (b) it is held primarily for the purpose of being traded; *or* (c) it is expected to be realized within 12 months after the reporting date; *or* (d) it is cash *or* cash equivalent unless it is restricted from being exchanged *or* used to settle a liability for at least 12 months after the reporting date.
2. Non-Current Assets	All other assets shall be classified as non-current.
3. An Operating Cycle	An operating cycle is the time between the acquisition of assets for processing and their realization in cash *or* cash equivalents. Where the normal operating cycle cannot be identified, it is assumed to have a duration of 12 months.
4. Current Liabilities	A liability shall be classified as current when it satisfies **any of the following criteria:** (a) it is expected to be settled in the company's normal operating cycle; (b) it is held primarily for the purpose of being traded; (c) it is due to be settled within 12 months after the reporting date; *or* (d) the company does not have an unconditional right to defer settlement of the liability for at least twelve months after the reporting date. Terms of a liability that could, at the option of the counterparty, result in its settlement by the issue of equity instruments do not affect its classification.
5. Non-Current Liabilities	All other liabilities shall be classified as non-current.
6. Trade Receivable	A receivable shall be classified as a 'Trade Receivable' if it is in respect of the amount due on account of goods sold *or* services rendered in the normal course of business.
7. Trade Payable	A payable shall be classified as a 'Trade Payable' if it is in respect of the amount due on account of goods purchased *or* services received in the normal course of business.
8. Use of Prefix 'At' instead of 'On'	It may be noted that the prescribed form of Balance Sheet prefixes 'At' instead of 'On'. For example, if a Balance Sheet of X Ltd. is prepared on 31st march, then the date of the balance-sheet will be stated as 'At 31st March, 2016' and not as 'On 31st March, 2016. The word 'On' refers to the entire duration (which consists of 24 hours) of the day whereas the word 'At' refers to a specific point of time. Since the balance-sheet is prepared to represent the financial position of the concern at a particular point of time (viz. at the end of the day's business hours), it is **appropriate to use the word 'At' instead of 'On'.**

22.0 VERTICAL FORM OF SUMMARISED BALANCE SHEET [WITH MAJOR HEADINGS ONLY]

...NAME OF THE COMPANY...
BALANCE SHEET AS AT...

(Rupees in...

Particulars	*Note No.*	*Figures for the Current Reporting Period*	*Figures for the Previous Reporting Period*
I. EQUITY AND LIABILITIES			
(1) Shareholders' Funds		xxx	xxx
(2) Share Application Money pending Allotment		xxx	xxx
(3) Non-Current Liabilities		xxx	xxx
(4) Current Liabilities		xxx	xxx
Total		xxx	xxx
II. ASSETS			
(1) Non-Current Assets		xxx	xxx
(2) Current Assets		xxx	xxx
Total		xxx	xxx

23.0 VERTICAL FORM OF DETAILED BALANCE SHEET

...NAME OF THE COMPANY...
BALANCE SHEET AS AT...

(Rupees in...

Particulars	*Note No.*	*Figures for the Current Reporting Period*	*Figures for the Previous Reporting Period*
I. EQUITY AND LIABILITIES			
(1) Shareholders' Funds			
(a) Share Capital	1	....	....
(b) Reserves and Surplus [e.g. Debit Balance of Profit & Loss A/c as negative figure]	2	....	....
(c) Money received against Share Warrants		....	....
(2) Share Application Money pending Allotment		....	....
(3) Non-Current Liabilities			
(a) Long-term Borrowings [e.g. Bonds/ Debentures/Loans repayableafter 12 months]	3	....	....

(b) Deferred Tax Liabilities (Net)		....	....
(c) Other Long term Liabilities [e.g. Trade Payables to be settled after 12 months]		....	....
(d) Long-term Provisions [e.g. Provision for Employee Benefits to be settled after 12 months]		....	....
(4) Current Liabilities			
(a) Short-Term Borrowings [e.g. Loans repayable on demand *or* within 12 months]	4	....	....
(b) Trade Payables [e.g. Trade Creditors,Bills Payables to be settled within 12 months]	5	....	....
(c) Other Current Liabilities [e.g. Bank Overdraft,Unpaid Dividend/ matured Deposits/ matured Debentures, That portion of Long-term Borrowings repayable within 12 months, Interest accrued(whether due *or* not) on borrowings,Calls-in-Advance,Outstanding Expenses, Tax Payable]	6	....	....
(d) Short-Term Provisions [e.g. Provision for Tax, Proposed Dividend, Provision for Employee Benefits to be settled within 12 months]	7	....	....
Total		....	....
II. ASSETS			
(1) Non-Current Assets			
(a) Fixed Assets			
(i) Tangible Assets [e.g. Land, Buildings, Plant & Equipment]	8	....	....
(ii) Intangible Assets [e.g.Goodwill Purchased, Goodwill on Consolidation,Brands/Trademarks]	9	....	....
(iii) Capital Work-in-Progress [e.g. Building under construction]		....	....
(iv) Intangible Assets under Development [e.g. Computer Software under Development]		....	....
(b) Non-Current Investments [e.g. Investment in Property/Partnership Firms]	10	....	....
(c) Deferred Tax Assets (Net)		....	....

(d) Long-Term Loans and Advances [e.g. Capital Advances, Security Deposits, Loans & Advances receivable after 12 months]	11	....	....
(e) Other Non-Current Assets [e.g.Unamortised Expenses like Discount/Loss on issue of Debentures to be amortised after 12 months, Amalgamation Adjustment A/c]	12	....	....
(2) Current Assets			
(a) Current Investments	13	....	....
(b) Inventories [e.g. Raw- Materials, Work-in-Progress, Finished Goods,Loose Tools,Stores & Spares]	14	....	....
(c) Trade Receivables [e.g. Trade Debtors,Bills Receivables to be realized within 12 months, Provision for Doubtful Debts by way of deduction]	15	....	....
(d) Cash and Cash Equivalents [e.g. Cheques/Drafts on hand, Bank Deposits with more than 12 months maturity]	16	....	....
(e) Short-term Loans and Advances [e.g. Loans & Advances receivable within 12 months]	17	....	....
(f) Other Current Assets [e.g.Prepaid Expenses]	18	....	....
Total		....	....

Notes To Accounts:

NOTE 1: SHARE CAPITAL

Particulars	₹	₹
Authorised Capital		
..... Shares of ₹... each	xxx	xxx
Issued Capital		
..... Shares of ₹... each	xxx	xxx
Subscribed Capital and fully paid		
..... Shares of ₹... each ₹... per share paid up	xxx	xxx
*Subscribed Capital but not fully paid		
..... Shares of ₹... each ₹... per share paid up	xxx	xxx
Less: Calls unpaid:		
(a) by Directors & Officers	(xxx)	(xxx)
(b) by Others	(xxx)	(xxx)
Add: Forfeited Shares	xxx	xxx
	xxx	xxx

otes

1. For the period of 5 years immediately preceding the date as at which the Balance Sheet is prepared
   (a) Aggregate Number and Class of **Shares** allotted as fully paid up pursuant to a contract **without payments being received in cash**
   (b) Aggregate Number and Class of **Shares** allotted as fully paid up by way of **Bonus Shares**
   (c) Aggregate Number and Class of Shares bought back
2. Shares in the company held by each shareholder holding more than 5% shares specifying the number of shares
3. Shares Reserved for issue under options and contracts/commitments for the sale of shares/ disinvestment, including the terms and amounts
4. Shares held by Holding Company/Ultimate Holding Company/Subsidiaries/Associates of Holding Company/Ultimate Holding Company.
5. **Reconciliation** of the No of shares outstanding at the beginning and at the end of the reporting period

Particulars	*Figures for the Current Reporting Period*	*Figures for the Previous Reporting Period*
A. Shares at the beginning of the year		
B. *Add:* Shares allotted as fully paid up pursuant to a contract without payments being received in cash		
C. *Add:* Shares issued on RIght/Preferential/Private Placement basis		
D. *Add:* Shares allotted as fully paid up by way of Bonus Shares		
E. *Add:* Shares Issued on exercise of Employee Stock Options		
F. *Add:* Shares Issued on conversion/surrender of Debentures/ Bonds/Term Loan.		
G. *Less:* Shares cancelled on buy back of Shares		
H. *Less:* Shares Foreited but not ressued during the current year		
I. Shares at the end of the year		

Note: *Subscribed and Paid up Share Capital will include Unpaid Amount on Shares subscribed by Subscribers to Memorandum of Association and such Unpaid Amount will be disclosed under the head* **'Current Assets' and sub-head 'Other Current Assets'.**

NOTE 2: RESERVES AND SURPLUS

Particulars	₹	₹
Capital Reserve		
Capital Redemption Reserve		
Securities Premium Reserve		
Debenture Redemption Reserve		
Revaluation Reserve		
Share Options Outstanding Account		

Other Reserves – (specify the nature and purpose of each reserve and the amount in respect thereof)		
General Reserve, Dividend Equalisation Reserve, Reserve for Contingent Liabilities, Reserve for bad debts, Tonnage Tax Reserve created under the Income-tax Act, 1961.		
Surplus i.e. Balance in Statement of Profit & Loss		
Opening Balance		
Add: Profit for the period		
Less: Transfer to Reserve		
Less: Used for Bonus Shares		
Less: Interim Dividend		
Less: Proposed Preference Dividend		
Less: Proposed Equity Dividend		
Less: Dividend Distribution Tax		
Closing Balance		

Notes

1. Debit Balance of Profit & Loss A/c is to be shown as negative figure.
2. Similarly Debit Balance of Reserve & Surplus is shown as negative figure.
3. 'Fund' is to be used if Reserve is earmarked for specific purpose.

NOTE 3: LONG-TERM BORROWINGS

Particulars	₹	₹
Bonds/Debentures		
Term Loans from Banks		
Term Loans from Other Parties		
Deferred Payment Liabilities		
Deposits		
Loans and Advances from Related Parties		
Long term Maturities of Finance Lease Obligations		
Other Loans and Advances (specify nature)		

Notes

1. Aggregate Amount of Secured Borrowings along with Nature of security.
2. Aggregate Amount of Unsecured Borrowings
3. Aggregate Amount of Loans guaranteed by Directors *or* Others under each head
4. Bonds/debentures (along with the Rate of Interest and particulars of redemption *or* conversion, as the case may be) in descending order of maturity *or* conversion, starting from farthest redemption *or* conversion date, as the case may be. Where bonds/debentures are redeemable by installments, the date of maturity for this purpose must be reckoned as the date on which the first installment becomes due.
5. Particulars of any Redeemed Bonds/Debentures which the company has power to reissue shall be disclosed.
6. Terms of Repayment of Term Loans and Other Loans

7. Period and amount of continuing default as on the Balance Sheet Date in repayment of Loans and Interest

NOTE 4: SHORT-TERM BORROWINGS

Particulars	₹	₹
Loans repayable on demand from Banks		
Loans repayable on demand from Other Parties		
Loans and Advances from Related Parties		
Deposits		
Other Loans and Advances (specify nature)		

Notes

1. Aggregate Amount of Secured Borrowings along with Nature of security and Unsecured Borrowings.
2. Aggregate Amount of Unsecured Borrowings
3. Aggregate Amount of Loans guaranteed by Directors *or* Others under each head
4. Period and amount of continuing default as on the Balance Sheet Date in repayment of Loans and Interest

NOTE 5: TRADE PAYABLES

Particulars	₹	₹
Sundry Creditors		
Bills Payables		

NOTE 6: OTHER CURRENT LIABILITIES

Particulars	₹	₹
Current maturities of Long-term Debt		
Current maturities of Finance Lease Obligations		
Interest accrued but not due on Borrowings		
Interest accrued and due on Borrowings		
Income received in advance		
Unpaid Dividends		
Application Money received for allotment of securities and due for refund and interest accrued thereon.		
Unpaid matured Deposits and Interest accrued thereon		
Unpaid matured Debentures and Interest accrued thereon		
Other Payables (specify nature e.g.)		
Bank Overdraft		
Outstanding Expenses		
Calls-in-Advance		

NOTE 7: SHORT-TERM PROVISIONS

Particulars	₹	₹
Provision for Employees' Benefit		
Provision for Income Tax		
Provision for Dividend Distribution Tax		
Proposed Equity Dividend		
Proposed Preference Dividend		

NOTE 8: TANGIBLE ASSETS

Asset	*Original Cost in the beg*	*Additions*	*Disposal*	*Original Cost at the end*	*Total Depreciation in the beg*	*Depreciation for Current year*	*Depreciation on Asset Disposed off*	*Total Depreciation at the end*	*W.D.V at the end*
A	*B*	*C*	*D*	*E = B + C − D*	*F*	*G*	*H*	*I = F + G − H*	*J = E − I*
Land									
Building									
Plant & Equipment									
Furniture and Fixtures									
Vehicles									
Office Equipment									
Others (specify nature)									
Assets under Lease									

Notes

1. Impairment Losses/Reversals
2. Every Balance Sheet subsequent to date of Capital Reduction/Revaluation must show the reduced *or* increased figures and must by way of a note also show the amount of the reduction *or* increase together with the date thereof for the first 5 years subsequent to the date of such reduction *or* increase.

NOTE 9: INTANGIBLE ASSETS

Asset	*Original Cost in the beg*	*Additions*	*Disposal*	*Original Cost at the end*	*Total Depreciation in the beg*	*Depreciation for Current year*	*Depreciation on Asset Disposed off*	*Total Depreciation at the end*	*W.D.V at the end*
A	*B*	*C*	*D*	*E = B + C − D*	*F*	*G*	*H*	*I = F + G − H*	*J = E − I*
Goodwill									
Brands									
Trademarks									
Computer Software									
Mastheads and Publishing Titles.									

Mining Rights.									
Copyrights, and Patents and Other Intellectual Property Rights, Services & Operating Rights.									
Recipes, Formulae, Models, Designs and Prototypes.									
Licenses and Franchise.									
Others (Specify Nature).									

Notes: Same as for Tangible Assets

NOTE 10: NON-CURRENT INVESTMENTS

Particulars	₹	₹
Trade Investments		
Investment in Property		
Investments In Equity Instruments		
Investments In Preference Shares		
Investments In Government *or* Trust Securities		
Investments In Debentures *or* Bonds		
Investments In Mutual Funds		
Investments In Partnership Firms		
Other Non-Current Investments (Specify Nature)		

Notes

1. Basis for Valuation in case of Investments carried at other than at cost
2. Aggregate amount of Quoted Investments and Market Value thereof;
3. Aggregate amount of Unquoted Investments;
4. Aggregate Provision for Diminution in Value of Investments

NOTE 11: LONG-TERM LOANS AND ADVANCES

Particulars	₹	₹
Capital Advances		

Security Deposits		
Loans and Advances to Related Parties		
Other Loans and Advances (specify nature)		

Notes

1. Amount of Secured Loans & Advances considered good
2. Amount of Unsecured Loans & Advances considered good
3. Amount of Loans & Advances considered Doubtful
4. Allowance for Bad and Doubtful on Loans and Advances
5. Loans and advances due by directors *or* other officers of the the company *or* any of them either severally *or* jointly with any other persons *or* amounts due by firms *or* private companies respectively in which any director is a partner *or* a director *or* a member

NOTE 12: OTHER NON-CURRENT ASSETS

Particulars	₹	₹
Long Term Trade Receivables (including trade receivables on deferred credit terms)		
Others (specify nature e.g.)		
Discount/Loss on Issue of Debentures		
Amalgamation Adjustment A/c		

Notes Same as for Long-term Loans and Advances

NOTE 13: CURRENT INVESTMENTS

Particulars	₹	₹
Investments In Equity Instruments		
Investments In Preference Shares		
Investments In Government *or* Trust Securities		
Investments In Debentures *or* Bonds		
Investments In Mutual Funds		
Investments In Partnership Firms		
Other Current Investments (Specify Nature)		

Notes: Same as for Non-Current Investments

NOTE 14: INVENTORIES

Particulars	₹	₹
Raw- Materials		
Work-in-Progress		
Finished Goods		
Stock-in-Trade		
Stores & Spares		
Loose Tools		
Others (specify nature)		

Notes

1. Goods-in-transit
2. Mode of Valuation

NOTE 15: TRADE RECEIVABLES

Particulars	₹	₹
Sundry Debtors		
Less: Provision for Doubtful Debts		
Bills Receivables		

Notes

1. Aggregate amount of Trade Receivables outstanding for a period exceeding six months from the date they are due for payment
2. Other Notes Same as for Long-term Loans and Advances

NOTE 16: CASH AND CASH EQUIVALENTS

Particulars	₹	₹
Bank Balance		
Cheques/Drafts on hand		
Cash Balance		
Others (specify nature)		

Notes

1. Earmarked balances with banks (***For Example*** for unpaid dividend)
2. Balances with banks to the extent held as margin money *or* security against the borrowings, guarantees, other commitments
3. Repatriation restrictions, if any, in respect of cash and bank balances
4. Bank deposits with more than 12 months maturity

NOTE 17: SHORT-TERM LOANS AND ADVANCES

Particulars	₹	₹
Loans and Advances to Related Parties		
Other Loans and Advances (specify nature)		

Notes: Same as for Long-term Loans and Advances

NOTE 18: OTHER CURRENT ASSETS (SPECIFY NATURE E.G.)

Particulars	₹	₹
Prepaid Expenses		
Unpaid Amount on Shares subscribed by Subscribers to Memorandum of Association		

NOTE 19: CONTINGENT LIABILITIES AND COMMITMENTS (TO THE EXTENT NOT PROVIDED FOR)

Particulars	₹	₹
(i) CONTINGENT LIABILITIES		
(a) Claims against the company not acknowledged as debt (e.g., Towards Excise, Customs, VAT, Service Tax, Income Tax, Suppliers, Customers)		
(b) Guarantees (e.g. to Banks on behalf of others)		
(c) Other money for which the company is contingently liable (e.g.Bills Discounted but not yet matured)		
(ii) COMMITMENTS		
(a) Estimated amount of contracts remaining to be executed on Capital Account and not provided for;		
(b) Uncalled Liability on Shares and Other Investments(e.g. Debentures) partly paid		
(c) Other Commitments (e.g. Arrears of Fixed Cumulative Dividends on Preference Shares)		

QUESTION 1

How will you disclose the following items while preparing the Balance Sheet of a company, as per the Schedule III to The Companies Act, 2013?

1. Bank Overdraft
2. Preliminary Expenses
3. Arrears of Fixed Cumulative Dividends on Preference Shares
4. Proposed Dividend

ANSWER:

DISCLOSURE AS PER SCHEDULE III TO THE COMPANIES ACT, 2013

Item	Major Head	Sub- Head
1. Bank Overdraft	Current Liabilities	Other Current Liabilities
2. Preliminary Expenses	NO WHERE AS PER AS 26	
3. Arrears of Fixed Cumulative Dividends on Preference Shares	Notes to Accounts	Contingent Liabilities and Commitments–Commitments
4. Proposed Dividend	Current Liabilities [Note: This treatment is as per ICAI's Guidance Note and AS4] It may be noted that Schedule III requires merely the disclosure in Notes to Accounts.	Short-Term Provisions

QUESTION 2

How will you disclose the following items while preparing the Balance Sheet of a company, as per the Schedule III to The Companies Act, 2013?

1. Debit Balance of Profit & Loss A/c
2. Computer Software under Development
3. Building under construction
4. Uncalled Liability on partly paid Debentures held as Investments

ANSWER:

DISCLOSURE AS PER SCHEDULE III TO THE COMPANIES ACT, 2013

Item	Major Head	Sub- Head	Sub- Sub- Head
1. Debit Balance of Profit & Loss A/c	Shareholders' Funds	Reserves and Surplus (As a negative figure)	
2. Computer Software under Development	Non-Current Assets	Fixed Assets	Intangible Assets under Development
3. Building under construction	Non-Current Assets	Fixed Assets	Capital Work-in-Progress
4. Uncalled Liability on partly paid Debentures held as Investments	Notes to Accounts	Contingent Liabilities and Commitments	Commitments

QUESTION 3

How will you disclose the following items while preparing the Balance Sheet of a company, as per the Schedule III to The Companies Act, 2013?

1. Premium on Redemption of Debentures
2. Employees'earned leave payable on retirement
3. Security Deposit for Telephone
4. Share Application Money pending Allotment

ANSWER:

DISCLOSURE AS PER SCHEDULE III TO THE COMPANIES ACT, 2013

Item	Major Head	Sub- Head
1. Premium on Redemption of Debentures	Non-Current Liabilities	Other Long-term Liabilities
2. Employees'earned leave payable on retirement	Non-Current Liabilities	Long-term Provisions
3. Security Deposit for Telephone	Non-Current Liabilities	Long-term Loans & Advances
4. Share Application Money pending Allotment	Equity and Liabilities	

QUESTION 4

How will you disclose the following items while preparing the Balance Sheet of a company, as per the Schedule III to The Companies Act, 2013?

1. Cheques/Drafts on hand
2. Calls-in-Advance
3. Calls Unpaid
4. Investment in Land & Building

ANSWER:

DISCLOSURE AS PER SCHEDULE III TO THE COMPANIES ACT, 2013

Item	Major Head	Sub- Head
1. Cheques/Drafts on hand	Current Assets	Cash and Cash Equivalents
2. Calls-in-Advance	Current Liabilities	Other Current Liabilities
3. Calls Unpaid	Notes to Accounts	
4. Investment in Land & Building	Non-Current Assets	Non-Current Investments

QUESTION 5

How will you disclose the following items while preparing the Balance Sheet of a company, as per the Schedule III to The Companies Act, 2013?

1. Investment in Bonds of Reliance Ltd. (Redeemable within 1 year)
2. Interest accrued on Bonds of Reliance Ltd.
3. Tonnage Tax Reserve

ANSWER:

DISCLOSURE AS PER SCHEDULE III TO THE COMPANIES ACT, 2013

Item	Major Head	Sub- Head	Sub- Sub- Head
1. Investment in Bonds of Reliance Ltd. (Redee mable within 1 year)	Current Assets	Current Investments	
2. Interest accrued on Bonds of Reliance Ltd.	Current Assets	Other Current Assets	
3. Tonnage Tax Reserve	Shareholders' Funds	Reserves and Surplus	Other Reserves

QUESTION 6

State under which head these accounts should be classified in Balance Sheet, as per Schedule III to The Companies Act 2013:

1. Share application money received in excess of issued share capital.
2. Share option outstanding account.

3. Unpaid matured debenture and interest accrued thereon.
4. Uncalled liability on shares and other partly paid investments.

ANSWER:

DISCLOSURE AS PER SCHEDULE III TO THE COMPANIES ACT, 2013

Item	Accounts	Head
1.	Share application money received in excess of issued share capital	1. Other Current Liabilities
2.	Share option outstanding account	2. Reserves & Surplus
3.	Unpaid matured debentures and interest accrued thereon	3. Other Current Liabilities
4.	Uncalled liability on shares and other partly paid investments	4. Contingent Liabilities and commitments-commitments to the extent not provided for

QUESTION 7

State under which head these accounts should be classified in Balance Sheet, as per Schedule III to The Companies Act 2013:

1. Calls unpaid.
2. Intangible Assets under development.
3. Money received against share warrant.
4. Long term maturity of finance lease obligation.

ANSWER:

DISCLOSURE AS PER SCHEDULE III TO THE COMPANIES ACT, 2013

Item	Accounts	Head
1.	Calls unpaid	1. Share Capital
2.	Intangible Assets under development	2. Fixed Assets
3.	Money received against share warrant	3. Shareholder's Funds
4.	Long term maturity of finance lease obligation	4. Long Term Borrowings

ILLUSTRATION 21 [DISCLOSURE OF SHARE CAPITAL]

Tulsian Ltd. was formed with a capital of ₹ 1,00,000 divided into 10,000 Equity Shares of ₹ 10 each. Out of these 2,000 Equity Shares were issued to the Vendors as fully paid as purchase consideration for a fixed asset acquired. 6,000 Equity Shares were offered to the public and the issue was fully subscribed. The directors called ₹ 6 per share and received the entire amount except a call of ₹ 2 per share on 500 shares out of which 200 shares were forfeited.

Required: How would you show the relevant items in the Balance Sheet of Tulsian Ltd., as per Schedule III to The Companies Act, 2013.

SOLUTION

AN EXTRACT OF BALANCE SHEET OF TULSIAN LTD AS AT ....

Particulars	*Note No*	*Current Year* ₹	*Previous Year* ₹
Equity & Liabilities			
I. Shareholders' Funds			
Share Capital	1	55,000	

Notes To Accounts:

NOTE 1: SHARE CAPITAL

Particulars	₹	₹
Authorised Capital:		
10,000 Equity Shares of ₹ 10 each		1,00,000
Issued Capital:		
8,000 Equity Shares of ₹ 10 each		80,000
Subscribed Capital and fully paid		
2,000 Equity Shares of ₹ 10 each		20,000
(allotted as fully paid up pursuant to a contract without payments being received in cash)		
Subscribed Capital but not fully paid		
5,800 Equity Shares of ₹ 10 each ₹ 6 paid up		34,800
Less: Calls unpaid (300 × ₹ 2)		(600)
Add: Forfeited Shares (200 × ₹ 4)		800
		55,000

ILLUSTRATION 22 [DISCLOSURE OF SHARE CAPITAL]

X Ltd. has authorised capital of ₹ 70,00,000 divided into 7,00,000 equity shares of ₹ 10 each. X Ltd. allotted 10,000 equity shares of ₹ 10 each as fully paid to the signatories to the Memorandum of Association and 5,000 equity shares of ₹ 10 each as fully paid to the vendors against the purchase of building and offered 5,00,000 equity shares of ₹ 10 each (₹ 8 called up). The issue was fully subscribed. All money were duly received with the following exceptions.

Mr. X who holds 4,000 shares has not paid anything after Application Money (₹ 2 per share).

Mr. Y (director of X Ltd.) who holds 600 shares, has paid only ₹ 6 per share.

Mr. Z who holds 400 shares, has paid only ₹ 6 per share. 4,000 shares held by Mr. X were forfeited.

Required: Show how the Share Capital will appear in the Balance Sheet of X Ltd., as per Schedule III to The Companies Act, 2013.

SOLUTION

AN EXTRACT OF BALANCE SHEET OF X LTD AS AT ....

Particulars	Note No	Current Year ₹	Previous Year ₹
Equity & Liabilities			
I. Shareholders' Funds			
Share Capital	1	41,24,000	

Notes To Accounts:

NOTE 1: SHARE CAPITAL

Particulars		₹
Authorised Capital:		
7,00,000 Equity Shares of ₹ 10 each		70,00,000
Issued Capital:		
5,15,000 Equity Shares of ₹ 10 each		51,50,000
Subscribed Capital and Fully paid		
15,000 Equity Shares of ₹ 10 each		1,50,000
(5,000 Shares allotted as fully paid up pursuant to a contract without payments being received in cash)		
Subscribed Capital but not Fully Paid		
4,96,000 Equity Shares of ₹ 10 each, ₹ 8 per share paid up		39,68,000
Less: Calls unpaid		
(a) By Directors (600 × ₹ 2)	(1,200)	
(b) By Others (400 × ₹ 2)	(800)	(2,000)
Add: Forfeited Shares (4,000 × ₹ 2)		8,000
		41,24,000

ILLUSTRATION 23

Prepare Reconciliation of the No of Shares outstanding at the beginning and at the end of the reporting period from the following information:

Shares at the beginning of the year	90,00,000
Shares allotted as fully paid up pursuant to a contract without payments being received in cash	50,00,000
Shares allotted as fully paid up by way of Bonus Shares	45,00,000
Shares Issued on exercise of Employee Stock Options	5,00,000
Shares Issued on conversion/surrender of Debentures, Bonds and Term Loan.	10,00,000
Shares cancelled on buy back of Shares	20,00,000

SOLUTION

RECONCILIATION OF NO SHARES

	Particulars	*2015-2016*	*2013-2015*
A.	Shares at the beginning of the year	90,00,000	
B.	*Add:* Shares allotted as fully paid up pursuant to a contract without payments being received in cash	50,00,000	
C.	*Add:* Shares allotted as fully paid up by way of Bonus Shares	45,00,000	
D.	*Add:* Shares Issued on exercise of Employee Stock Options	5,00,000	
E.	*Add:* Shares Issued on conversion/surrender of Debentures, Bonds &Term Loan.	10,00,000	
F.	*Less:* Shares cancelled on buy back of Shares	(20,00,000)	
G.	Shares at the end of the year	1,80,00,000	

QUESTION 8

How will you disclose the following items while preparing the Balance Sheet of a company?

1. Trade Receivables
2. Trade Payables
3. Current Maturities of Long-term Debt

ANSWER:

1. Trade Receivables are to be classified as Current Assets if Expected Realisation Period is either within the Operating Cycle Period *or* within the 12 Months Period.
2. Trade Payables are to be classified as Current Liabilities if Expected Payment Period is either within the Operating Cycle Period *or* within the 12 Months Period.
3. Current Maturities of Long-term Debt represents that portion of Long-term Borrowings which is due within 12 Months from the date of Balance Sheet *or* with in Operating Cycle Period. It appears under the head 'Current Liabilities' and sub-head 'Other Current Liabilities'. For Example, 12% Debentures of Reliance Ltd. ₹ 100 lacs [20% Redeemable within 1 year]. ₹ 20 lacs will appear as Current Maturities of Long-term Debt under the head 'Current Liabilities' and sub-head 'Other Current Liabilities' and ₹ 80 lacs will appear under the head 'Non-Current Liabilities' and sub head 'Long-term Borrowings'.

QUESTION 9

X Ltd. provides you the following information:

1. Raw material stock holding period: 3 months
2. Work-in-progress holding period: 1 month
3. Finished goods holding period: 4 months
4. Debtors collection period: 6 months

You are required to compute the operating cycle

ANSWER:

As per Schedule III "An operating cycle is the time between the acquisition of assets for processing and their realization in cash *or* cash equivalents".

Operating Cycle = Raw material stock holding period + Work-in-progress holding period + Finished goods holding period + Debtors collection period = 3 + 1 + 4 + 6 = 14 months.

QUESTION 10

State giving reason whether the Trade Receivables are Current Assets *or* Non-Current Assets as per Schedule III in the following cases:

Case	*Operating Cycle Period*	*Expected Realisation Period*
1.	11 Months	10 Months
2.	11 Months	12 Months
3.	11 Months	13 Months
4.	14 Months	13 Months
5.	14 Months	15 Months

ANSWER:

Case	*Current Assets or Non-Current Assets*	*Reason*
1.	Current Assets	Expected Realisation Period — is *less* than the Operating Cycle Period and — is within 12 Months.
2.	Current Assets	Expected Realisation Period is within 12 Months although it is more than the Operating Cycle Period.
3.	Non-Current Assets	Expected Realisation Period is more than the Operating Cycle Period and 12 Months Period.
4.	Current Assets	Expected Realisation Period is *less* than the Operating Cycle Period although it is more than the 12 Months Period.
5.	Non-Current Assets	Expected Realisation Period is more than the Operating Cycle Period and the 12 Months Period.

QUESTION 11

State giving reason whether the Trade Payables are Current Liabilities *or* Non-Current Liabilities as per Schedule III in the following cases:

Case	*Operating Cycle Period*	*Expected Payment Period*
1.	11 Months	10 Months
2.	11 Months	12 Months
3.	11 Months	13 Months
4.	14 Months	13 Months
5.	14 Months	15 Months

ANSWER:

Case	*Current Assets or Non-Current Assets*	*Reason*
1.	Current Assets	Expected Payment Period — is *less* than the Operating Cycle Period and — is within 12 Months.
2.	Current Assets	Expected Payment Period is within 12 Months although it is more than the Operating Cycle Period.
3.	Non-Current Assets	Expected Payment Period is more than the Operating Cycle Period and 12 Months Period.
4.	Current Assets	Expected Payment Period is *less* than the Operating Cycle Period although it is more than the 12 Months Period.
5.	Non-Current Assets	Expected Payment Period is more than the Operating Cycle Period and the 12 Months Period.

QUESTION 12

PCT Ltd. is in the process of finalizing its accounts for year ended 31st March, 2016 and furnishes the following information:

(i) Finished goods normally are held for 1 month before sale.

(ii) Sales realization from Debtors usually takes 2 months from date of credit invoice.

(iii) Raw materials are held in stock to cover 1 month's production requirements.

(iv) Packing materials, being specifically made for the company and having lead time of 3 months is held in stock for 3 months.

(v) The holding period in respect of unfinished goods is 1 month.

(vi) Being a monopoly KAY Ltd. enjoys a credit period of 12.5 months from its suppliers who sometimes at the end of their credit period opt for conversion of their dues into long term debt of KAY Ltd.

You are required to compute the operating cycle of PCT Ltd. as per Schedule III of The Companies Act, 2013. As the suppliers of the company are paid off after a credit period of 12.5 months should this be part of Current Liability? Would your answer be the same if the creditors are settled in 330 days?

ANSWER:

Operating Cycle = 1 + 1 + 3 + 1 + 2 = 8 months

Classification of liability to suppliers: Schedule III provides that:

"A liability shall be classified as current when it satisfies any of the following criteria:

(i) it is expected to be settled in the company's normal operating cycle;

(ii) it is held primarily for the purpose of being traded;

(iii) it is due to be settled within 12 months after the reporting date; *or*

(iv) the company does not have an unconditional right to defer settlement of the liability for at least 12 months after the reporting date. Terms of a liability that could, at the option of the counterparty, result in its settlement by the issue of equity instruments and do not affect its classification."

(a) **When credit period is 12.5 months:** It will be treated as non-current liability since it is not due to be settled within 12 months after the reporting date.

(b) **When credit period is 330 days (i.e. 11 months approx.):** It will be treated as current liability since it is due to be settled within 12 months after the reporting date.

QUESTION 13

The management of X Ltd. contends that the work in process is not valued since it is difficult to ascertain the same in view of the multiple processes involved. They opined that the value of opening and closing work in process would be more or *less* the same. Accordingly, the management had not separately disclosed work in process in its financial statements. Comment in line with Schedule III.

ANSWER:

Schedule III to the Companies Act, 2013 requires the disclosure of opening and closing WIP under broad heads by way of additional information [General Instructions 5 (iii)]. In addition, AS-2 also requires the valuation of WIP. Therefore, the non-disclosure in the financial statements by the company amounts to violation of Schedule III.

QUESTION 14

TULSIAN Ltd is having the following Fixed Deposit Receipts:

Bank	*Date of FDR*	*Maturity Date*	*Amount*
Yes Bank Limited	01–Jan–2016	2–Jan–2016	30,00,000
Bank of Baroda	01–Jan–2016	31–Mar–2016	20,00,000
State Bank of India	28–Feb–2016	30–May–2016	10,00,000
ICICI Bank	1–Jan–2015	1–Apr–2016	40,00,000

Prepare Notes to Accounts showing the above Deposits in accordance with the requirements of Schedule III as at the Balance Sheet date i.e. 31st March, 2016.

ANSWER:

NOTE 'X': CASH & BANK BALANCES AS AT 31ST MARCH, 2016 (BALANCE SHEET DATE)

Particulars	₹
A. Cash in Hand	xxx
B. Balances with Bank	
(i) Less than *or* equal to 12 Months Maturity.	
– Cash Equivalent as per AS–3 (less than 3 Months Maturity) [SBI]	10,00,000
– Other Bank Balances [30,00,000 + 20,00,000]	50,00,000
(ii) More than 12 Months Maturity [ICICI]	40,00,000
	100,00,000

QUESTION 15

Z Ltd. has flexi deposit linked current account with various banks. Cheques are issued from the current amount and as per the requirements of funds, the flexi deposits are encashed and transferred to current accounts. As of 31st March 2016 certain cheques issued to vendors are not presented for payment resulting in the credit balance in the books of the company. The management wants to present the books overdraft under current liabilities and flexi deposits under cash and bank balances. Comment.

ANSWER:

<table>
<tr><td>Schedule III</td><td>Presentation of Bank Overdraft as per Schedule III: The instructions in accordance with which "Cash and Cash Equivalents" should be presented as per Schedule III to the Companies Act, 2013 are as follows:
(i) Cash and Cash Equivalents shall be classified as:
(a) Balances with banks;
(b) Cheques, drafts on hand;
(c) Cash on hand;
(d) Others (specify nature).
(ii) Earmarked balances with banks (For Example, for unpaid dividend) shall be separately stated.
(iii) Balances with banks to the extent held as margin money or security against the borrowings, guarantees, other commitments shall be disclosed separately
(iv) Repatriation restrictions, if any, in respect of cash and bank balances shall be separately stated.
(v) Bank deposits with more than 12 months maturity shall be disclosed separately.</td></tr>
<tr><td>Advice</td><td>It is evident that is substance the position is that the composite bank balance including the balance in flexi deposit accounts are positive, even though physical set-off has not been made as on the balance sheet date. Further the bank has got the right to set off of flexi deposits against the cheques issued and hence it would be more information and useful to the readers of the financial statements to disclosed the book credit balance as a set-off from the flexi deposit accounts. The disclosure of the said book credit balance as book overdraft under the head current liabilities as proposed by the management is not correct.</td></tr>
</table>

QUESTION 16

Is non-disclosure of source from which Bonus shares have been issued, a violation of Schedule III to the Companies Act, 2013?

ANSWER:

No since Schedule III does not require such disclosure. Schedule III merely requires the disclosure of aggregate number and class of shares allotted as fully paid up bonus shares for a period of 5 years immediately preceding the Balance Sheet date in the Notes to Accounts.

QUESTION 17

X Ltd. paid ₹ 25 lakhs as advance to Y Ltd. towards the purchase of printing machinery on 15-01-2016 with delivery instruction to deliver the same in the last week of June, 2016. Further on 15-02-2016 X Ltd. purchased two diesel generator sets from Y Ltd. for ₹ 30 lakhs on 90 days Credit term. In the accounts for 2015-2016, X Ltd. intends to adjust the advance paid against Credit purchase and show the net amount of ₹ 5 lakhs as due from them. As the statutory auditor, how would you deal with this?

ANSWER:

Since X Ltd. has paid advance amount to the supplier of machinery to be used in the project, such advance amount should be grouped under the main heading 'Non-Current Assets' with the sub-head as Fixed Assets with a sub-classification as 'Capital Work-in-Progress.' This is as per requirement of Schedule III to The Companies Act, 2013 and the existing accounting practice.

If the advance is for purchase of other machinery, it should be grouped under a separate head – 'Long Term Loan and Advance' with a sub-classification as 'Capital advance' under the main heading 'Non-current Assets'. In view of the above, the proposal of X Ltd., to show the net balance in the personal account of Y Ltd. is not correct. Such proposal will conceal the two material items in the balance sheet – one, expenditure towards capital asset and the other current liability for purchase of the generator set.

Hence, the auditor should advice X Ltd., to show these tow items separately. If X Ltd. does not accept the advice, the auditor should qualify his report with suitable quantification of amount involved.

asset and the other current liability for purchase of the generator set.

Hence, the auditor should advice X Ltd., to show these tow items separately. If X Ltd. does not accept the advice, the auditor should qualify his report with suitable quantification of amount involved.

QUESTION 18

The Balance Sheet of G Ltd is as under: Comment on the presentation in terms of Schedule III and Accounting Standards issued by NACAS.

BALANCE SHEET AS AT ... *(Rupees in ...)*

Particulars	*Note No.*	*31.03.2016*	*31.03.2015*
I. EQUITY AND LIABILITIES			
Share Capital	1	xxx	xxx
Reserves & Surplus	2	0	0
Employee stock option outstanding	3	xxx	xxx
Share application money	4	xxx	xxx
Non-Current Liabilities			
Deferred tax liability (Arising from Indian Income Tax)	5	xxx	xxx
Current Liabilities			
Trade Payables	6	xxx	xxx
Total		xxx	xxx
II. ASSETS			
Non-Current Assets			
Fixed Assets-Tangible	7	xxx	xxx
CWIP (including capital advances)	8	xxx	xxx
Current Assets			
Trade Receivables	9	xxx	xxx
Deferred Tax Asset (Arising from Indian Income Tax)	10	xxx	xxx
P & L Debit balance			
Total		xxx	xxx

ANSWER:

Following Errors are noticed in presentation as per Schedule III:

(i) Share Capital & Reserve & Surplus are to be reflected under the heading "Shareholders' funds", which is not shown while preparing the balance sheet. Although it is a part of Equity and Liabilities yet it must be shown under head "shareholders' funds". The heading "Shareholders' funds" is missing in the balance sheet given in the question.

(ii) Reserve & Surplus is showing zero balance, which is not correct in the given case. Debit balance of statement of profit & Loss should be shown as a negative figure under the head 'Surplus'. The balance of 'Reserves and Surplus', after adjusting negative balance of surplus shall be shown under the head 'Reserves and Surplus' even if the resulting figure is in the negative.

(iii) Schedule III requires that Employee Stock Option outstanding should be disclosed under the heading "Reserves and Surplus"

(iv) Share application money refundable shall be shown under the sub-heading "Other Current Liabilities". As this is refundable and not pending for allotment, hence it is not a part of equity.

(v) Deferred Tax Liability has been correctly shown under Non-Current Liabilities. But Deferred tax assets and deferred tax liabilities, both, cannot be shown in balance sheet because only the net balance of Deferred Tax Liability *or* Asset is to be shown

(vi) Under the main heading of Non-Current Assets, Fixed Assets are further classified as under:

(i) Tangible assets

(ii) Intangible assets

(iii) Capital work in Progress

(iv) Intangible assets under development.

Keeping in view the above, the CWIP shall be shown under Fixed Assets as Capital Work in Progress. The amount of Capital advances included in CWIP shall be disclosed under the sub-heading "Long term loans and advances" under the heading Non-Current Assets.

(vii) Deferred Tax Asset shall be shown under Non-Current Asset. It should be the net balance of Deferred Tax Asset after adjusting the balance of deferred tax

ILLUSTRATION 24

From the following information extracted from the books of XY Ltd., prepare a Balance Sheet of the company as at 31st March, 2016 as per Schedule III of the Companies Act. 2013:

Particulars	*(₹ in "000)*
Long term borrowings	500
Share Capital	390
Fixed Assets (tangible)	600
Trade Receivables	80
Share Application Money pending Allotment	10
Trade Payables	20
Reserve and Surplus	90
Inventories	20
Cash and Cash Equivalents	120
Non-Current Investments	200
Proposed Dividend	10

SOLUTION

XY LTD.
BALANCE SHEET AS AT 31ST MARCH, 2016

Particulars	*Note No*	*2015-2016 (₹ in "000)*	*2014-2015 (₹ in "000)*
I. EQUITY AND LIABILITIES			
(1) Shareholders' Funds			
(a) Share Capital		390	
(b) Reserves and Surplus		90	
(2) Share Application Money pending Allotment		10	
(3) Non-Current Liabilities			
(a) Long term Borrowings		500	
(4) Current Liabilities			
(a) Trade Payables		20	
(b) Short-term Provisions (Proposed Dividend)		10	
Total		1020	
II. ASSETS			
(1) Non-Current Assets			
(a) Fixed Assets			
(i) Tangible Assets		600	
(b) Non-Current Investments		200	
(2) Current Assets		–	
(a) Inventories		20	
(b) Trade Receivables		80	
(c) Cash and Cash Equivalents		120	
Total		1020	

ILLUSTRATION 25

From the following information, prepare the relevant Notes to Accounts:

Capital Reserve	20
Capital Redemption Reserve	40
Securities Premium	60
General Reserve	160
Opening Balance of Profit and Loss Statement	452
Profit for the period	560
Transfer to General Reserve @ 5%	
Interim Dividend	100
Proposed Preference Dividend	140
Proposed Equity Dividend	200

Dividend Distribution Tax	88
Transfer to Debenture Redemption Reserve	100

SOLUTION

2. RESERVES AND SURPLUS

Capital Reserve		20
Capital Redemption Reserve		40
Securities Premium		60
Debenture Redemption Reserve		100
General Reserve [160 + 28]		188
Profit & Loss Account:		
Opening Balance	452	
Add: Profit for the period	560	
Less: Transfer to General Reserve @ 5%	(28)	
Less: Interim Dividend	(100)	
Less: Proposed Preference Dividend	(140)	
Less: Proposed Equity Dividend	(200)	
Less: Dividend Distribution Tax @20%	(85)	
Less: Debenture Redemption Reserve	(100)	356
		764

ILLUSTRATION 26

From the following information, prepare the relevant Notes to Accounts:

Sundry Creditors	40
Bills Payables	20
Bank Overdraft	10
Unpaid Dividend	2
Outstanding Expenses	4
Calls-in-Advance	2
Interest accrued on Borrowings	24
Current Maturity of 12% Debentures	40
Provision for Tax	240
Proposed Preference Dividend	140
Proposed Equity Dividend	200
Dividend Distribution Tax @20%	85

SOLUTION

3. TRADE PAYABLES

Sundry Creditors	40
Bills Payables	20
	60

4. OTHER CURRENT LIABILITIES

Bank Overdraft	10
Unpaid Dividend	2
Outstanding Expenses	4
Calls-in-Advance	2
Interest accrued on Borrowings [12% of ₹ 100 lacs (12% Debentures)]	24
Current Maturity of 12% Debentures	40
	82

5. SHORT-TERM PROVISIONS

Provision for Tax	240
Proposed Preference Dividend	140
Proposed Equity Dividend	200
Dividend Distribution Tax	85
	665

ILLUSTRATION 27

From the following information, prepare the relevant Notes to Accounts:

Particulars	*Cost*	*Provision for Depreciation/ Amortization*
Buildings	400	20
Plant and Equipment	200	40
Vehicles	50	10
Furniture and Fixtures	60	6
Brands	200	20
Computer Software	90	54

SOLUTION

6. TANGIBLE ASSETS

Particulars	*Cost*	*Provision for Depreciation*	*Closing WDV*
Buildings	400	20	380
Plant and Equipment	200	40	160

Vehicles	50	10	40
Furniture and Fixtures	60	6	54
	710	76	634

7. INTANGIBLE ASSETS

Particulars	*Cost*	*Provision for Amortization*	*Closing WDV*
Brands	200	20	180
Computer Software	90	54	36
	290	74	216

ILLUSTRATION 28

From the following information, prepare the relevant Notes to Accounts:

Trade Investments	
300 lacs Shares of X Ltd of ₹ 10 each,₹ 8 paid up	2400
6 lacs,14% Debentures of ₹ 100 each,₹ 80 paid up	480
Other Investments	26
Discount/Loss on Issue of Debentures	2
Amalgamation Adjustment A/c	4

SOLUTION

8. NON-CURRENT INVESTMENTS

Trade Investments		
300 lacs Shares of X Ltd of ₹ 10 each,₹ 8 paid up	2400	
6 lacs,14% Debentures of ₹ 100 each,₹ 80 paid up	480	2880
Other Investments		26
		2906

9. OTHER NON-CURRENT ASSETS

Discount/Loss on Issue of Debentures	2
Amalgamation Adjustment A/c	4
	6

ILLUSTRATION 29

From the following information, prepare the relevant Notes to Accounts:

Closing Stock of Materials	39.8
Closing Stock of WIP	200.00
Closing Stock of Finished Goods	400.00
Loose Tools	12.00

Stores & Spares	8.00
Sundry Debtors	80
Provision for Doubtful Debts	8
Bills Receivables	20
Cash Balance	4
Bank Balance	16
Cheques/Drafts on hand	4
Prepaid Expenses	2
Interest accrued on Investments	2

SOLUTION

10. INVENTORIES

Closing Stock of Materials	39.80
Closing Stock of WIP	200.00
Closing Stock of Finished Goods	400.00
Loose Tools	12.00
Stores & Spares	8.00
	659.8

11. TRADE RECEIVABLES

Sundry Debtors	80
Less: Provision for Doubtful Debts	(8)
Bills Receivables	20
	92

12. CASH AND CASH EQUIVALENTS

Cash Balance	4
Bank Balance	16
Cheques/Drafts on hand	4
	24

13. OTHER CURRENT ASSETS

Prepaid Expenses	2
Interest accrued on Investments	2
	4

ILLUSTRATION 30

From the following information, prepare the relevant Notes to Accounts:

1. Bills Discounted but not yet matured 2
2. 300 lacs Shares of X Ltd of₹ 10 each,₹ 8 paid up held as Investments
3. 6 lacs,14% Debentures of ₹ 100 each, ₹ 80 paid up held as Investments

SOLUTION

14. CONTINGENT LIABILITIES AND COMMITMENTS (TO THE EXTENT NOT PROVIDED FOR)

(i) Contingent Liabilities	
Bills Discounted but not yet matured	2
(ii) Commitments	
(a) Uncalled Liability on partly paid Shares [300 lacs Shares of X Ltd of ₹ 10 each,₹ 8 paid up]	600
(b) Uncalled Liability on partly paid Debentures held as Investments [6 lacs,14% Debentures of ₹ 100 each, ₹ 80 paid up]	120

ILLUSTRATION 31

From the details given below prepare Balance Sheet of TULSIAN Ltd. as at 31st March, 2016, as per the Schedule III to The Companies Act 2013:

	(₹ in "000)
P & L A/c (Dr.)	200
12% Debentures	200
Proposed Dividend	20
Equity Share Capital (₹ 10 each)	500
Cheques & Drafts on hand	48
15% Pref. Share Capital (₹ 100 each)	400
Prepaid Expenses	50
Bank Overdraft	45
Interest accrued on Debentures of Tata Steels	12
Building under construction	115
2,500,12% Tata Steel Deb. of ₹ 100 each, ₹ 80 paid up	200
Premium on Red. of Debentures	20
Application Money pending allotment	40
Bills Payables	75
Calls-in Advance	5
Employees'earned leave payble on Retirement	45
Stores & Spares	50
Securities Deposit for Telephone	5
Brands	110
Computer Software under development	20
Bills Receivables	120
Plant & Machinery	120
12% Debentures of Reliance Ltd. [20% Redeemable within 1 year]	100
Investment in Land & Building	200

Note: Bills Discounted but not yet matured ₹ 25,000, Dividends on Preference Shares are in arrear for 2 years

SOLUTION

TULSIAN LTD.
BALANCE SHEET AS AT 31ST MARCH, 2016

Particulars	*Note No*	*2015-2016 (₹ in "000)*	*2013-2015 (₹ in "000)*
I. EQUITY AND LIABILITIES			
(1) Shareholders' Funds			
(a) Share Capital	1	900	
(b) Reserves and Surplus [P & L A/c (Dr.)]		(200)	
(2) Share Application Money pending Allotment		40	
(3) Non - Current Liabilities			
(a) Long term Borrowings [12% Debentures]		200	
(b) Other Long term Liabilities			
(Premium on Red. of Debentures)		20	
(c) Long term Provisions (Earned Leave)		45	
(4) Current Liabilities			
(a) Trade Payables (B/P)		75	
(b) Other Current Liabilities	2	50	
(c) Short term Provisions (Proposed Dividend)		20	
Total		1150	
II. ASSETS			
(1) Non-Current Assets			
(a) Fixed Assets			
(i) Tangible Assets (Plant & Machinery)		120	
(ii) Intangible Assets (Brands)		110	
(iii) Capital Work in progress (Building)		115	
(iv) Intangible Assets under development		20	
(b) Non-Current Investments	3	480	
(c) Long-term Loans & Advances (Security)		5	
(2) Current Assets			
(a) Current Investments (Deb. of Reliance Ltd.)		20	
(b) Inventories (Stores & Spares)		50	
(c) Trade Receivables (B/R)		120	
(d) Cash and Cash Equivalents (Ch. & DD)		48	
(e) Other Current Assets	4	62	
Total		1150	

Notes to Accounts:

NOTE 1: SHARE CAPITAL

Particulars	*2015-2016 (₹ in "000)*	*2013-2015 (₹ in "000)*
50,000 Equity Shares of ₹10 each	500	
4,000, 15% Pref. Shares of ₹100 each	400	
	900	

NOTE 2: OTHER CURRENT LIABILITIES

Particulars	*2015-2016 (₹ in "000)*	*2013-2015 (₹ in "000)*
Bank Overdraft	45	
Calls-in-advance	5	
	50	

NOTE 3: NON-CURRENT INVESTMENTS

Particulars	*2015-2016 (₹ in "000)*	*2013-2015 (₹ in "000)*
2,500,12% Tata Steel Deb. of ₹100 each, ₹80 paid up	200	
12% Debentures of Reliance Ltd. [100 – 20]	80	
Investment in Land & Building	200	
	480	

NOTE 4: OTHER CURRENT ASSETS

Particulars	*2015-2016 (₹ in "000)*	*2013-2015 (₹ in "000)*
Prepaid Expenses	50	
Interest accrued on Debentures of Tata Steels	12	
	62	

NOTE 5: CONTINGENT LIABILITIES & COMMITMENTS

Particulars	*2015-2016 (₹ in "000)*	*2013-2015 (₹ in "000)*
i. Contingent Liabilities		
Bills Discounted but not yet matured	25	
ii. Commitments		
(a) Uncalled Liability on partly paid Debentures held as Investments [2,500,12% Tata Steel Debentures of ₹ 100 each, ₹ 80 paid up] [2,500 × ₹ 20]	50	
(b) Arrears of Fixed Cumulative Dividends on Preference Shares [₹ 4,00,000 × 15/100 × 2]	120	

ILLUSTRATION 32

The following items appear in the Trial Balance of Bharat Ltd. as at 31st March, 2016:

Particulars	₹
1. Revenue from Operations	24,00,000
2. Other Income	1,00,000
3. Expenses other than Interest	3,80,000
4. General Reserve (as on 1st April, 2015)	1,30,000

5. Profit and Loss Account (as on 1.4.2015) ₹ 3,28,000. The recommendation of the company's Board of Directors include equity dividend of 15% (Including Interim Dividend of ₹ 80,000). Transfer to Debenture Redemption Reserve @ 50% of Debentures and Transfer to General Reserve @ 5%. (Assume Corporate Tax 30% and Dividend Distribution Tax @ 20%).
6. 12%, 10,000 Debentures of ₹ 100 each fully paid up
7. 16%, 5,000 Preference Shares of ₹ 100 each fully paid up
8. 6,000 Equity Shares of ₹ 100 each
9. 8,000 Equity Shares ₹ 100 each, ₹ 25 paid up

Required: Show the above items in Statement of Profit and Loss and Balance Sheet.

SOLUTION

BHARAT LTD.
STATEMENT OF PROFIT AND LOSS FOR THE YEAR ENDED 31ST MARCH, 2016

Particulars	*Note No.*	*(₹ in lacs)*
I. Revenue from Operations		24
II. Other Income		1
III. Total Revenue [I + II]		25
IV. Expenses:		
Finance Costs		1.2
Other Expenses		3.8
Total Expenses		5.0
V. Profit before Tax(III – IV)		20
VI. Tax Expense [30% of ₹ 20 lacs]		(6)
VII. Profit for the period		14
Basic Earnings per Equity Share:		
= [Profit for the period – Pref. Dividend] /No.of Equity Shares		
= (14 – 0.70)/8000 = ₹ 166.25		

AN EXTRACT OF BALANCE SHEET OF BHARAT LTD. AS AT 31ST MARCH, 2016

Particulars	*Note No.*	*(₹ in lacs)*
I. EQUITY AND LIABILITIES		
(1) Shareholders' Funds		
(a) Share Capital	1	13.00
(b) Reserves and Surplus	2	16.08

(2) Non-Current Liabilities		
(a) Long-term Borrowings [10% Debentures]		10.00
(3) Current Liabilities		
(a) Other Current Liabilities [Interest accrued on Debentures]	4	1.20
(b) Short-Term Provisions	5	7.70
Total		47.98

Notes To Accounts:

1. SHARE CAPITAL

Authorised Capital	?
Issued Capital	
14,000 Equity Shares of ₹ 100 each	14.00
5,000, 14% Pref. Shares of ₹ 100 each	5.00
	19.00
Subscribed Capital and fully paid	
6,000,Equity Shares of ₹ 100 each	6
14%,5,000 Pref. Shares of ₹ 100 each	5
Subscribed Capital but not fully paid	
8,000, Equity Shares of ₹ 100 each,₹ 25 paid up	2
	13

2. RESERVES AND SURPLUS

Debenture Redemption Reserve		5.00
General Reserve [1.30 + 0.70]		2.00
Surplus i.e. Balance in Statement of Profit & Loss:		
Opening Balance	3.28	
*Add:*Profit for the period	14.00	
Less: Transfer to General Reserve @ 5%	(0.70)	
Less: Interim Dividend	(0.8)	
Less: Proposed Preference Dividend	(0.8)	
Less: Proposed Equity Dividend[15% of(6 lacs + 2 lacs) – 0.80 lacs]	(0.4)	
Less: Dividend Distribution Tax [(0.8 + 0.8 + 0.4) 20/80]	(0.50)	
*Less:*Debenture Redemption Reserve [50% of ₹ 10 lacs]	(5)	9.08
		16.08

3. SHORT-TERM PROVISIONS

Provision for Tax	6.00
Proposed Preference Dividend	0.80
Proposed Equity Dividend	0.40
Corporate Dividend Tax	0.50
	7.70

ILLUSTRATION 33

Fine Products Ltd. was registered with a nominal capital of ₹ 5,00,000 divided into shares of ₹ 100 each. The following Trial Balance is extracted from the books on 31st March, 2016:

Dr. *Cr.*

Particulars	₹	*Particulars*		₹
Buildings	2,90,000	Sales		5,20,000
Machinery	1,00,000	Outstanding Expenses		2,000
Closing Stock	90,000	Provision for Doubtful Debt (1-4-2015)		3,000
Purchases (adjusted)	2,10,000	Equity Share Capital		2,00,000
Salaries	60,000	General Reserve		40,000
Directors Fees	10,000	Profit and Loss A/c (1-4-2015)		25,000
Rent	26,000	Creditors		92,000
Depreciation	20,000	Provision for depreciation:		
Bad Debts	6,000	on Building	50,000	
Interest accrued on Investment	2,000	on Machinery	55,000	1,05,000
12,000 shares of X Ltd. of		14% Debentures		2,00,000
₹ 10 each ₹ 8 paid up	1,20,000	Interest on Debentures		
Debenture Interest	28,000	accrued but not due		14,000
Loose Tools	23,000	Interest on Investments		12,000
Advance Tax	60,000	Unclaimed dividend		5,000
Sundry expenses	18,000	(Bills Discounted but not yet		
Debtors	1,25,000	matured ₹ 10,000)		
bank	30,000			
	12,18,000			12,18,000

You are required to prepare Statement of Profit and Loss for the year ending 31st March, 2016 and Balance Sheet as at that date after taking into consideration the following information:

(a) Closing stock is more than opening stock by ₹ 80,000; (b) Provide for doubtful debts @ 4% on Debtors: (c) Make a provision for income tax @ 30%; (d) Depreciation expense includes depreciation of ₹ 8,000 on Buildings and that of ₹ 12,000 on Machinery; (e) The directors recommend a dividend @ 25% and Transfer to General Reserve @ 10%. (Assume Dividend Distribution Tax @ 20%)

SOLUTION

FINE PRODUCTS
PROFIT AND LOSS STATEMENT FOR THE YEAR ENDED 31ST MARCH, 2016

Particulars	*Note No.*	*(₹ in lacs)*
I. Revenue from Operations		5,20,000
II. Other Income		12,000
III. Total Revenue [I + II]		5,32,000
IV. Expenses:		

Cost of Purchases [2,10,000 + 80,000]		2,90,000
Changes in Inventories [10,000 – 90,000]		(80,000)
Employee Benefits Expense		60,000
Finance Costs		28,000
Depreciation and Amortization Expense		20,000
Other Expenses	1	62,000
Total Expenses		3,80,000
V. Profit before Tax(III – IV)		1,52,000
VI. Tax Expense@30%		(45,600)
VII. Profit for the period		1,06,400
Basic Earnings per Equity Share: = 1,06,400/20,000 = ₹ 5.32		

Notes to Accounts:

1. Other Expenses	
Rent.	26,000
Miscellaneous Expenses	18,000
Directors' Fees	10,000
Bad Debts	6,000
Provision for Doubtful Debts[(4% of ₹ 1,25,000) – ₹ 3,000]	2,000
	62,000

BALANCE SHEET OF FINE PRODUCTS LTD. AS AT 31ST MARCH, 2016

Particulars	*Note No.*	*(₹ in lacs)*
I. EQUITY AND LIABILITIES		
(1) Shareholders' Funds		
(a) Share Capital	1	2,00,000
(b) Reserves and Surplus	2	1,08,900
(2) Non-Current Liabilities		
(a) Long-term Borrowings [Debentures]		2,00,000
(3) Current Liabilities		
(a) Trade Payables [Sundry Creditors]		92,000
(b) Other Current Liabilities	3	21,000
(c) Short-Term Provisions	4	1,08,100
Total		7,30,000
II. ASSETS		
(1) Non-Current Assets		
(a) Fixed Assets		
(i) Tangible Assets	5	2,85,000
(b) Non-Current Investments [12,000 Shares of X Ltd of ₹ 10 each, ₹ 8 paid up]		1,20,000

(2) Current Assets		
(a) Inventories	6	1,13,000
(b) Trade Receivables	7	1,20,000
(c) Cash and Cash Equivalents		30,000
(d) Short-term Loans and Advances [Advance Payment of Tax]		60,000
(f) Other Current Assets Interest accrued on Investments		2,000
Total		7,30,000

Notes To Accounts:

1. SHARE CAPITAL

Authorised Capital	
5,000 Equity Shares of ₹ 100 each	5,00,000
Issued Capital	
2,000 Equity Shares of ₹ 100 each	2,00,000
Subscribed Capital and fully paid	
2,000 Equity Shares of ₹ 100 each	2,00,000
	2,00,000

2. RESERVES AND SURPLUS

General Reserve [40,000 + 10,640]		50,640
Balance of Statement of Profit & Loss Account:		
Opening Balance	25,000	
Add: Profit for the period [(412 – 12) × (1 – 0.30)]	1,06,400	
Less: Transfer to General Reserve @ 10%	(10,640)	
Less: Proposed Equity Dividend [25% of 2,00,000]	(50,000)	
Less: Dividend Distribution Tax [50,000 x 20/80]	(12,500)	58,260
		1,08,900

3. OTHER CURRENT LIABILITIES

Unclaimed Dividend	5,000
Outstanding Expenses	2,000
Interest accrued on Borrowings	14,000
	21,000

4. SHORT-TERM PROVISIONS

Provision for Tax	45,600
Proposed Equity Dividend	50,000
Corporate Dividend Tax	12,500
	1,08,100

5. TANGIBLE ASSETS

Particulars	*Cost*	*Provision for Depreciation*	*Closing WDV*
Buildings	2,90,000	50,000	2,40,000
Plant and Equipment	1,00,000	55,000	45,000
	3,90,000	1,05,000	2,85,000

6. INVENTORIES

Closing Stock of Finished Goods	90,000
Loose Tools	23,000
	1,13,000

7. TRADE RECEIVABLES

Sundry Debtors	1,25,000
Less: Provision for Doubtful Debts	(5,000)
	1,20,000

8. CONTINGENT LIABILITIES AND COMMITMENTS (TO THE EXTENT NOT PROVIDED FOR)

i.	**Contingent Liabilities**	
	Bills Discounted but not yet matured	10,000
ii.	**Commitments**	
	(a) Uncalled Liability on partly paid Shares [12,000 Shares of X Ltd of ₹ 10 each, ₹ 8 paid up]	24,000

ILLUSTRATION 43

CSDIJ Ltd. have authorised capital of ₹ 50 lakhs divided into 5,00,000 equity shares of ₹ 10 each. Their books show the following balances as on 31st March, 2016:

	₹
Opening Stock	6,65,000
Discounts & Rebates	30,000
Carriage Inwards	57,500
Patterns	3,75,000
Rates, Taxes and Insurance	55,000
Furniture & Fixtures	1,50,000
Purchases	12,32,500
Wages	13,68,000
Freehold Land	12,50,000
Plant & Machinery	7,50,000
Engineering Tools	1,50,000
Goodwill	3,75,000

Sundry Debtors	2,66,000
Bills Receivables	1,34,500
Advertisement	15,000
Commission & Brokerage	67,500
Business Expenses	56,000
Bank Current Account	20,000
Cash in hand	8,000
Debenture Interest Paid	10,000
Interest on Bank overdraft	91,000
Preliminary Expenses	10,000
Calls in Arrear @ ₹ 2 per share	10,000
Equity Share Capital (2,00,000 shares of ₹ 10 each)	20,00,000
4% Debentures (repayable after 10 years)	5,00,000
Bank Overdraft	7,57,000
Sundry Creditors (for goods)	2,40,500
Sales	36,17,000
Rent (Cr.)	30,000
Transfer Fees received	6,500
Profit & Loss A/c (Cr.)	67,000
Repairs to Building	46,500
Bad debts	25,500

The stock (valued at cost *or* market value, which is lower) as on 31st March. 2016 was ₹ 7,08,000. Outstanding liabilities for wages ₹ 25,000 and business expenses ₹ 36,000. Dividend declared @ 12% on paid-up capital.

Change depreciation: Plant and Machinery @ 5%, Engineering Tools @ 20%; Patterns @ 10%; and Furniture & Fixtures @ 10%. Provide 10% on debtors as doubtful debts after writing off ₹ 16,000 as bad debts. Write off preliminary expenses fully. Create Debenture Redemption Reserve @10% of Debentures. Transfer to General Reserve @ 2.5%. Provide for Income Tax @ 30%. Dividend Distribution Tax Rate @ 20%.

Required: Prepare Statement of Profit & Loss for the year ended 31st March 2016 and (ii) Balance Sheet as on that date.

SOLUTION

CSDIJ LTD.
PROFIT AND LOSS STATEMENT FOR THE YEAR ENDED 31ST MARCH, 2016

Particulars	*Note No.*	*(₹ in lacs)*
I. Revenue from Operations		36,17,000
II. Other Income	1	36,500
III. Total Revenue [I + II]		36,53,500
IV. Expenses:		
Cost of Purchases		12,32,500

Changes in Inventories [6,65,000 – 7,08,000]		(43,000)
Employee Benefits Expense[13,68,000 + 25,000]		13,93,000
Finance Costs [20,000 + 91,000]		1,11,000
Depreciation and Amortization Expense		1,20,000
Other Expenses	2	4,40,000
Total Expenses		32,53,500
V. Profit before Tax (III – IV)		4,00,000
VI. Tax Expense@30%:		(1,20,000)
VII. Profit for the period		2,80,000
Basic Earnings per Equity Share: = 2,80,000/2,00,000 = ₹ 1.40		

Notes to Accounts:

1. OTHER INCOME

Miscellaneous Income (Transfer fees)	6,500
Rental Income	30,000
	36,500

2. OTHER EXPENSES

Carriage Inward	57,500
Discount & Rebates	30,000
Advertisement	15,000
Rent.	55,000
Repairs to Buildings	46,500
Preliminary Expenses	10,000
Commission & Brokerage	67,500
Miscellaneous Expenses [56,000 + 36,000]	92,000
Bad Debts [25,500 + 16,000]	41,500
Provision for Doubtful Debts [10% of (2,66,000 – 16,000)]	25,000
	4,40,000

CSDIJ LTD.
BALANCE SHEET AS AT 31ST MARCH, 2016

Particulars	*Note No.*	*(₹ in lacs)*
I. EQUITY AND LIABILITIES		
(1) Shareholders' Funds		
(a) Share Capital	1	19,90,000
(b) Reserves and Surplus	2	48,500
(2) Non-Current Liabilities		
(a) Long-term Borrowings [Debentures]		5,00,000
(3) Current Liabilities		
(a) Trade Payables [Sundry Creditors]		2,40,500

(b) Other Current Liabilities	3	8,28,000
(c) Short-Term Provisions	4	4,18,500
Total		40,25,500
II. ASSETS		
(1) Non-Current Assets		
(a) Fixed Assets		
(i) Tangible Assets	5	25,55,000
(ii) Intangible Assets (Goodwill)		3,75,000
(2) Current Assets		
(a) Inventories		7,08,000
(b) Trade Receivables	6	3,59,500
(c) Cash and Cash Equivalents	7	28,000
Total		40,25,500

Notes To Accounts:

1. SHARE CAPITAL

Authorised Capital	
5,00,000 Equity Shares of ₹ 10 each	50,00,000
Issued Capital	
2,00,000 Equity Shares of ₹ 10 each	20,00,000
Subscribed Capital and fully paid	
1,95,000 Equity Shares of ₹ 10 each	19,50,000
Subscribed Capital but not fully paid	
5,000 Equity Shares of ₹ 10 each ₹ 8 paid	40,000
Note: Call unpaid ₹ 10,000	19,90,000

2. RESERVES AND SURPLUS

Debenture Redemption Reserve		50,000
General Reserve		7,000
Surplus i.e. Balance in Statement of Profit & Loss:		
Opening Balance	67,000	
Add: Profit for the period	2,80,000	
Less: Transfer to General Reserve @ 2.5%	(7,000)	
Less: Proposed Equity Dividend [12% of(20,00,000 – 10,000)]	(2,38,800)	
Less: Dividend Distribution Tax [2,38,800 x 20/80]	(59,700)	
Less: Debenture Redemption Reserve [10% of ₹ 5,00,000]	(50,000)	8,500
		48,500

3. OTHER CURRENT LIABILITIES

Bank Overdraft	7,57,000
Outstanding Expenses [25,000 + 36,000]	61,000
Interest accrued on Borrowings [20,000 – 10,000]	10,000
	8,28,000

4. SHORT-TERM PROVISIONS

Provision for Tax	1,20,000
Proposed Equity Dividend	2,38,800
Corporate Dividend Tax	59,700
	4,18,500

5. TANGIBLE ASSETS

Particulars	*Value given* ₹	*Depreciation charged* ₹	*Written down Value at the end* ₹
Land	12,50,000	—	12,50,000
Plant & Machinery	7,50,000	37,500	7,12,500
Furniture & Fixtures	1,50,000	15,000	1,35,000
Patterns	3,75,000	37,500	3,37,500
Engineering Tools	1,50,000	30,000	1,20,000
	26,75,000	1,20,000	25,75,000

6. TRADE RECEIVABLES

Sundry Debtors[2,66,000 – 16,000]	2,50,000
Less: Provision for Doubtful Debts	(25,000
Bills Receivables	1,34,500
	3,59,500

7. CASH AND CASH EQUIVALENTS

Cash Balance	8,000
Bank Balance	20,000
	28,000

ILLUSTRATION 35

TULSIAN Ltd. provides the following information for the year ended 31st March, 2016:

Particulars	₹
Buildings	20
Plant and Equipment	10
Vehicles	2

Furniture and Fixtures	30
Brands	100
Computer Software	45
Buildings under construction	100
Computer Software under Development	40
Trade Investments	
150 lacs Shares of X Ltd of ₹ 10 each, ₹ 8 paid up	1200
3 lacs,14% Debentures of ₹ 100 each, ₹ 80 paid up	240
Other Investments	13
Long-Term Loans and Advances (Dr)	17.6
Discount/Loss on Issue of Debentures	1
Amalgamation Adjustment A/c	2
Current Investments	100
Closing Stock of Materials	19.9
Closing Stock of WIP	100
Closing Stock of Finished Goods	200
Loose Tools	6
Stores & Spares	4
Sundry Debtors	40
Bills Receivables	10
Cash Balance	2
Bank Balance	8
Cheques/Drafts on hand	2
Advance Payment of Tax	50
Prepaid Expenses	1
Interest accrued on Investments	1
Interim Dividend	50
60 lacs Equity Shares of ₹ 10 each	600
50 lacs Equity Shares of ₹ 10 each, ₹ 8 paid up	400
10%, 70 lacs Pref. Shares of ₹ 10 each	700
Profit and Loss Statement (Opening Balance)	226
Profit before Interest & tax for the year 2015-15	412
General Reserve	80
Capital Reserve	10
Capital Redemption Reserve	20
Securities Premium	30
12% Debentures (20% Redeemable within 1 year)	100
Long term Loans and Advances (Cr)	3
Provision for Gratuity & Provident Fund	7.5
Short-Term Borrowings	1

Sundry Creditors	20
Bills Payables	10
Bank Overdraft	5
Unpaid Dividend	1
Outstanding Expenses	2
Calls-in-Advance	1
Provision for Doubtful Debts	4
Provision for Depreciation:	
Buildings	10
Plant and Equipment	20
Vehicles	5
Furniture and Fixtures	3
Provision for Amortization:	
Brands	10
Computer Software	27

Additional Information:

(a) The directors recommended: (a) An Equity Dividend of 15% including Interim Dividend. (b) Transfer to Debenture Redemption Reserve @50% of Debentures (c) Transfer to General Reserve @ 5%.

(b) Income Tax Rate 30%, Dividend Distribution Tax Rate 20%.

(c) Bills Discounted but not yet matured ₹ 1 lac

Required: Prepare the Balance Sheet (as per Schedule III to The Companies Act, 2013) as at 31st March, 2016.

SOLUTION

TULSIAN LTD.
BALANCE SHEET AS AT 31ST MARCH, 2016

Particulars	*Note No.*	*(₹ in lacs)*
I. EQUITY AND LIABILITIES		
(1) Shareholders' Funds		
(a) Share Capital	1	1,700.00
(b) Reserves and Surplus	2	371.00
(2) Non-Current Liabilities		
(a) Long-term Borrowings [Debentures]		80.00
(b) Deferred Tax Liabilities (Net)		
(c) Other Long term Liabilities (Long-term Loans & Adv.)		3.00
(d) Long-term Provisions [Provision for Gratuity & Provident Fund]		7.50
(3) Current Liabilities		
(a) Short-Term Borrowings		1.00
(b) Trade Payables	3	30.00

(c) Other Current Liabilities	4	41.00
(d) Short-Term Provisions	5	345.00
Total		2,578.50
II. ASSETS		
(1) Non-Current Assets		
(a) Fixed Assets		
(i) Tangible Assets	6	317.00
(ii) Intangible Assets	7	108.00
(iii) Capital Work-in-Progress [Buildings under construction]		100.00
(iv) Intangible Assets under Development		40.00
(b) Non-Current Investments	8	1,453.00
(c) Deferred Tax Assets (Net)		
(d) Long-Term Loans and Advances		17.60
(e) Other Non-Current Assets	9	3.00
(2) Current Assets		
(a) Current Investments		100.00
(b) Inventories	10	329.90
(c) Trade Receivables	11	46.00
(d) Cash and Cash Equivalents	12	12.00
(e) Short-term Loans and Advances [Advance Payment of Tax]		50.00
(f) Other Current Assets	13	2.00
Total		2,578.50

Notes To Accounts:

1. SHARE CAPITAL

Authorised Capital	
250 lacs shares of ₹ 10 each	2,500
Issued Capital	
110 lacs Equity Shares of ₹ 10 each	1,100
70 lacs, 10% Pref. Shares of ₹ 10 each	700
	1,800
Subscribed Capital and Fully paid up	
60 lacs Equity Shares of ₹ 10 each	600
70 lacs 10%, Pref. Shares of ₹ 10 each	700
Subscribed Capital but not fully paid up	
50 lacs Equity Shares of ₹ 10 each,₹ 8 paid up	400
	1,700

2. RESERVES AND SURPLUS

Capital Reserve		10
Capital Redemption Reserve		20
Securities Premium		30
Debenture Redemption Reserve		50
General Reserve [80 + 14]		94
Profit & Loss Statement:		
Opening Balance	226	
Add: Profit for the period [(412 – 12) × (1 – 0.30)]	280	
Less: Transfer to Reserve @ 5% [since Rate of Equity Dividend is 15%]	(14)	
Less: Interim Dividend	(50)	
Less: Proposed Preference Dividend	(70)	
Less: Proposed Equity Dividend [15% of(600 lacs + 400 lacs) – 50 lacs]	(100)	
Less: Corporate Dividend Tax[(50 + 70 + 100) 20/80]	(55)	
Less: Debenture Redemption Reserve [50% of ₹ 100 lacs]	(50)	167
		371

3. TRADE PAYABLES

Sundry Creditors	20
Bills Payables	10
	30

4. OTHER CURRENT LIABILITIES

Bank Overdraft	5
Unpaid Dividend	1
Outstanding Expenses	2
Calls-in-Advance	1
Interest accrued on Borrowings [12% of ₹ 100 lacs (12% Debentures)]	12
Current Maturity of 12% Debentures	20
	41

5. SHORT-TERM PROVISIONS

Provision for Tax [(412 – 12) × (0.30)]	120
Proposed Preference Dividend	70
Proposed Equity Dividend [15% of (600 lacs + 400 lacs) – 50 lacs]	100
Corporate Dividend Tax [(50 + 70 + 100)x 20/80]	55
	345

6. TANGIBLE ASSETS

Particulars	*Cost*	*Provision for Depreciation*	*Closing WDV*
Buildings	200	10	190
Plant and Equipment	100	20	80
Vehicles	25	5	20
Furniture and Fixtures	30	3	27
	355	38	317

7. INTANGIBLE ASSETS

Particulars	*Cost*	*Provision for Amortization*	*Closing WDV*
Brands	100	10	90
Computer Software	45	27	18
	145	37	108

8. NON-CURRENT INVESTMENTS

Trade Investments		
150 lacs Shares of X Ltd of ₹ 10 each,₹ 8 paid up	1,200	
3 lacs,14% Debentures of ₹ 100 each,₹ 80 paid up	240	1440
Other Investments		13
		1453

9. OTHER NON-CURRENT ASSETS

Discount/Loss on Issue of Debentures	1
Amalgamation Adjustment A/c	2
	3

10. INVENTORIES

Closing Stock of Materials	19.90
Closing Stock of WIP	100.00
Closing Stock of Finished Goods	200.00
Loose Tools	6.00
Stores & Spares	4.00
	329.90

11. TRADE RECEIVABLES

Sundry Debtors	40
Less: Provision for Doubtful Debts	(4)
Bills Receivables	10
	46

12. CASH AND CASH EQUIVALENTS

Cash Balance	2
Bank Balance	8
Cheques/Drafts on hand	2
	12

13. OTHER CURRENT ASSETS

Prepaid Expenses	1
Interest accrued on Investments	1
	2

14. CONTINGENT LIABILITIES AND COMMITMENTS (TO THE EXTENT NOT PROVIDED FOR)

i. Contingent Liabilities	
Bills Discounted but not yet matured	1
ii. Commitments	
(a) Uncalled Liability on partly paid Shares [150 lacs Shares of X Ltd of ₹ 10 each,₹ 8 paid up]	300
(b) Uncalled Liability on partly paid Debentures held as Investments [3 lacs,14% Debentures of ₹ 100 each, ₹ 80 paid up]	60

ILLUSTRATION 36

An Extract of the Balance Sheet of a CAMHC Limited as at 31st March 2016 is as follows:

Particulars	₹
Share Capital:	
Authorised:	
30,000 Equity Shares of ₹ 10 each	3,00,000
Issued and Subscribed:	
20,000 Equity Shares of ₹ 10 each fully paid	2,00,000
Profit and Loss Account	1,16,000
12% Debentures	1,20,000
Creditors	1,15,000
Proposed Dividends	20,000
Provision for Dividend Distribution Tax	4,000
Tangible Assets [Freehold Property]	1,15,000
Inventories	1,35,000
Trade Receivables	75,000
Cash at Bank	2,51,000

At the Annual General Meeting it was resolved: (a) To increase the authorised capital to ₹ 4,00,000. (b) To pay the proposed dividend of 10 per cent in cash. (c) To issue one bonus share for every four shares held. (d) To give existing shareholders the option to purchase one ₹ 10 share, at ₹ 15 for every four shares held prior to the bonus distribution, this option being taken up by all the shareholders. (e) To repay the debentures at a premium of 3 per cent.

Required: Pass the necessary Journal Entires and the Company's Balance Sheet after these transactions are completed. (Assume Dividend Distribution Tax @ 20%)

SOLUTION

JOURNAL

Date	*Particulars*		*L.F.*	*Dr. (₹)*	*Cr. (₹)*
1	Proposed Dividend A/c	Dr.		20,000	
	Provision for Dividend Distribution Tax A/c	Dr.		5,000	
	To Dividend Payable A/c				20,000
	To Dividend Distribution Tax Payable A/c				5,000
	(Being dividend declared DDT thereon)				
2	Dividend Bank A/c	Dr.		25,000	
	To Bank A/c				25,000
	(Being the t/f of Balance to Dividend Bank A/c)				
3	Dividend Payable A/c	Dr.		20,000	
	Dividend Distribution Tax Payable A/c	Dr.		5,000	
	To Dividend Bank A/c				25,000
	(Being payment of dividend & DDT)				
4	Bank A/c	Dr.		75,000	
	To Equity Share Application & Allotment A/c				75,000
	(Being the Application money received on 5,000 shares @ ₹ 15 per share to be issued as rights shares in the ratio of 1 : 4)				
5	Equity Share Application & Allotment A/c	Dr.		75,000	
	To Equity Share Capital A/c				50,000
	To Securities Premium A/c				25,000
	(Share application money on 5,000 shares @ ₹ 10 per share transferred to Share Capital Account and ₹ 5 per share to Securities Premium Account, vide Board's Resolution dated....)				
6	Securities Premium A/c	Dr.		25,000	
	Profit & Loss A/c	Dr.		37,500	
	To Bonus to Shareholders A/c				62,500
	(Amount transferred for issue of bonus shares to existing shareholders in the ratio of 1 : 4 vide General Body's Resolution dated....)				
7	Bonus to Shareholders A/c	Dr.		62,500	
	To Equity Share Capital A/c				62,500
	(Issue of bonus shares in the ratio of 1 for 4)				
8	Profit & Loss A/c	Dr.		30,000	
	To Debentures Redemption Reserve A/c				30,000

	(Being the t/f of Profit equal to 25% of Nominal Value to DRR)			
9	12% Debentures A/c	Dr.	1,20,000	
	Premium Payable on Redemption A/c	Dr.	3,600	
	To Debenture holders A/c			1,23,600
	(Amount due to Debentures on redemption, at a premium of 3%, transferred to Debentures A/c)			
10	Debentures A/c	Dr.	1,23,600	
	To Bank A/c			1,23,600
	(Amount paid to debentures holders)			
11	Profit & Loss A/c	Dr.	3,600	
	To Premium Payable on Redemption A/c			3,600
	(Premium payable on redemption charged to P&L A/c)			
12	Debenture Redemption Reserve A/c	Dr.	30,000	
	To General Reserve A/c			30,000
	(Being the Transfer of DRR to General Reserves)			

BALANCE SHEET OF CAMHC LTD AS AT 31.3.2016

Particulars	*Note No.*	*₹ (in lacs)*
I. EQUITY AND LIABILITIES		
(1) Shareholders' Funds		
(a) Share Capital	1	3,12,500
(b) Reserves and Surplus	2	74,900
(2) Non-Current Liabilities		—
(3) Current Liabilities		
Trade Payables		1,15,000
Total		5,02,400
II. ASSETS		
(1) Non-Current Assets		
(a) Fixed Assets		
(b) Tangible Assets [Freehold Property]		1,15,000
(2) Current Assets		
(a) Inventories		1,35,000
(b) Trade Receivables		75,000
(c) Cash and Cash Equivalents		1,77,400
Total		5,02,400

Note to Accounts:

NOTE 1: SHARE CAPITAL

31,250 Equity Shares of ₹ 10 each	3,12,500
(Of the above 6,250 Shares were issued as Bonus Shares)	

NOTE 2: RESERVES AND SURPLUS

General Reserve	30,000
Profit & Loss Account	44,900
	74,900

ILLUSTRATION 37

The following is the Balance Sheet of Bumbum Limited as at 31st March, 2016:

Particulars	
Sources of Funds:	
Authorized capital:	
50,000 Equity Shares of ₹ 10 each	5,00,000
10,000 Preference Shares of ₹ 100 each	10,00,000
	15,00,000
Issued subscribed and paid up	
30,000 Equity shares of ₹ 10 each	3,00,000
5,000 Redeemable 8% Preference shares of ₹ 100 each	5,00,000
Reserves & Surplus	
Securities Premium	6,00,000
General Reserve	6,50,000
Profit & Loss A/c	1,80,000
2500, 9% Debentures of ₹ 100 each	2,50,000
Sundry Creditors	1,70,000
	26,50,000
Application of Funds:	
Fixed Assets (net)	7,80,000
Investments (Market Value ₹ 6,80,000)	4,90,000
Deferred Tax Assets	3,40,000
Sundry Debtors	6,20,000
Cash & Bank balance	2,80,000
Preliminary expenses	1,40,000
	26,50,000

In Annual General Meeting held on 20th June the company passed the following resolutions:

a) To split equity share ₹ 10 each into 5 equity shares of ₹ 2 each from 1st July.

b) To redeem 8% Preference Shares at a premium of 5%.

c) To redeem 9% Debentures by making offer to debenture holders to convert their holdings into equity shares at ₹ 10 per share *or* accept cash on redemption.

d) To issue fully paid bonus shares in the ratio of one equity share for every 3 shares held on record date.

On 10th July investments were sold for ₹ 5,55,000 and preference shares were redeemed. 40% of Debentureholder exercised their option to accept cash & their claims were settled on 1st Aug.

The company fixed 5th September as record date and bonus issue was concluded by 12th September. You are requested to journalize the above transactions including cash transactions and prepare Balance Sheet as at 30th September.

SOLUTION

JOURNAL OF BUMBUM LIMITED

Date	Particulars	L.F.	Dr. (₹)	Cr. (₹)
July 01	Equity Share Capital A/c (10 each) Dr.		3,00,000	
	To Equity share Capital A/c (2 each)			3,00,000
	(Being equity shares of ₹ 10 each splitted into 5 equity shares of ₹ 2 each)			
July 10	Cash & Bank A/c Dr.		5,55,000	
	To Investment A/c			4,90,000
	To Profits Loss A/c			65,000
	(Being investment sold out and profit on sale credited to Profit & Loss A/c)			
July 10	8% Redeemable Preference Share Capital A/c Dr.		5,00,000	
	Premium on redemption of Preference Share A/c Dr.		25,000	
	To Preference shareholders A/c			5,25,000
	(Being amount payable to preference share holders on redemption)			
July 10	Preference Shareholders A/c Dr.		5,25,000	
	To Cash & bank A/c			5,25,000
	(Being amount paid to preference shareholders)			
July 10	General Reserve A/c Dr.		5,00,000	
	To Capital Redemption Reserve A/c			5,00,000
	(Being amount equal to nominal value of preference shares transferred to Capital Redemption Reserve A/c on its redemption as per the law)			
Aug 1	9% Debentures A/c Dr.		2,50,000	
	Interest on debentures A/c Dr.		7,500	
	To Debentureholders A/c			2,57,500
	(Being amount payable to debentureholders along with interest payable)			
Aug. 1	Debentureholders A/c Dr.		2,57,500	
	To Cash & Bank A/c (1,00,000 + 7,500)			1,07,500
	To Equity share capital A/c			30,000
	To Securities premium A/c			1,20,000
	(Being claims of debenture holders satisfied)			
Sept. 5	Capital Redemption Reserve A/c Dr.		1,10,000	
	To Bonus to shareholders A/c			1,10,000
	(Being CRR capitalized to issue bonus shares)			

Sept. 12	Bonus to Shareholders A/c	Dr.	1,10,000	
	To Equity Share Capital A/c			1,10,000
	(Being 55,000 fully paid equity shares of ₹ 2 each issued as bonus in ratio of 1 share for every 3 shares held)			
Sept. 30	Securities Premium A/c	Dr.	25,000	
	To Premium on redemption of Preference Shares A/c			25,000
	(Being premium on preference shares adjusted from securities premium account)			
Sept. 30	Profit & Loss A/c	Dr.	7,500	
	To Interest on Debentures A/c			7,500
	(Being interest on debentures transferred to Profit and Loss Account)			
Sept. 30	Profit & Loss A/c	Dr.		1,40,000
	To Preliminary expenses A/c			1,40,000
	(Being the Preliminary Exp w/o the per para 56 of AS 26)			

Note: For capitalisation of Bonus shares and transfer to Capital Redemption Reserve Account any other free reserves given in the Balance Sheet may also be used.

BALANCE SHEET AT 30TH SEPTEMBER, 2016

Particulars	*Note*	₹
I. Equity & Liabilities		
1. Share Capital	1	4,40,000
2. Reserves & Surplus	2	13,32,500
3. Current Liabilities [Sundry Creditors]		1,70,000
Total		19,42,500
II. Assets		
1. Non-Current Assets		
Fixed Assets (Net)		7,80,000
Deferred Tax Assets		3,40,000
2. Current Assets		
Trade Receivables [Sundry Debtors]		6,20,000
Cash & Cash Equivalents		2,02,500
Total		19,42,500

Notes to Accounts:

1. Share Capital	₹
Authorized Share capital	
2,50,000 Equity Shares of 2 each	5,00,000
10,000 Preference Shares of 100 each	10,00,000
	15,00,000
Issued, Share Capital	
2,20,000 Equity Shares of ₹ 2 each	4,40,000

Subscribed and fully paid up	
2,20,000 Equity Shares of 2 each	4,40,000
2. Reserves & Surplus	
Securities Premium	6,95,000
Capital Redemption Reserve	3,90,000
General Reserve	1,50,000
Profit & Loss A/c (1,80,000 + 65,000 – 7,500 – 1,40,000)	97,500
	13,32,500

Notes:

1. Amount payable to Preference Shareholders = ₹ 5,00,000 + 5% = ₹ 5, 25,000
2. Equity shares issued on conversion = (2,50,000 – 1,00,000)/10 = 15,000 shares
3. Bonus shares to be issued = (150000 + 15000)/3 = 55,000 shares

4. SECURITIES PREMIUM A/C

Balance as per Balance Sheet	6,00,000
Add: Premium on equity shares issued on conversion of debentures (15,000 × 8)	1,20,000
Less: Adjustment for premium on preference shares	25,000
Balance	6,95,000

5. CASH AND BANK BALANCE

Balance as per balance sheet	2,80,000
Add: Realization on sale of investment	5,55,000
Less: Paid to preference share holders	5,25,000
Paid to Debenture holders (7,500 + 1,00,000)	1,07,500
Balance	2,02,500

6. Interest of ₹ 7,500 paid to debenture holders have been debited to Profit & Loss Account.

24.0 MANAGERIAL REMUNERATION

MEANING OF REMUNERATION [SEC 2(78)]

As per Sec. 2(78) the term 'Remuneration' means any money *or* its equivalent given *or* passed to any person for services rendered by him and includes perquisities as defined under the Income-tax Act, 1961.

OVERALL LIMIT OF MANAGERIAL REMUNERATION [SEC 197]

As per Sec197, the total managerial remuneration payable by a public company to its directors (including Managing Director and Whole Time Director) and Manager in respect of any financial year must not exceed 11 per cent of the Net Profits of that company for that financial year. In computing the aforesaid ceiling of 11 per cent fees payable to directors for attending Board meetings shall not be included.

CAN A COMPANY PAY REMUNERATION EXCEEDING 11% OF NET PROFITS?

The company in general meeting may, with the approval of the Central Government, authorise the payment of remuneration exceeding 11% of the Net Profits of the company, subject to the provisions of Schedule V [Provisio to Sec 197(1)].

Note: The remuneration of the directors shall not be deducted from the gross profits.

MAXIMUM LIMIT OF REMUNERATION PAYABLE TO DIRECTORS AND MANAGER [PROVISO TO SEC 197]

Maximum limit of remuneration payable to directors and Manager is given below:

Case	*Max. limit as % of Net Profits*
1. For Whole Time Director or Managing Director or Manager	
(a) If there is one such director	5% to any such person.
(b) If there is more than one such director	10% for all of them together.
2. For directors other than whole time director or managing director	
(a) If there is a managing director or whole time director or manager	1% for all of them together.
(b) In any other case	3% for all of them together.

Note: The company in general meeting may authorise the payment of remuneration exceeding the aforesaid limits subject to the overall limit of 11% of the Net Profits of the company.

CALCULATION OF NET PROFITS [SEC 198]

Sec 198 lays down the manner in which net profits for the purposes of calculation of managerial remuneration shall be calculated.

The various items which are required to be included *or* excluded *or* deducted *or* not to be deducted as per Sec. 198 are given on next page:

ITEMS TO BE INCLUDED IN/EXCLUDED FROM PROFITS FOR COMPUTING MANAGERIAL REMUNERATION

Items to be included in profits	Items to be excluded from profits
1. Bounties and subsidies received from any Government *or* any public authority constituted *or* authorised in this behalf by any government.	1. Premium on shares *or* debentures. 2. Profit on sale of forfeited shares. 3. Profits of capital nature including those from the sale of the undertaking of the company. 4. Profits of capital nature from the sale of any immovable property *or* fixed assets. 5. Any change in carrying amount of an asset *or* of a liability recognised in equity reserves including surplus P & L A/c on measurement of the asset *or* the liability at fair value.

ITEMS TO BE / NOT TO BE DEDUCTED FROM PROFIT FOR COMPUTING MANAGERIAL REMUNERATION

Item to be deducted from profits	Item not to be deducted from profits
1. All the usual working charges; 2. Directors' remuneration; 3. Bonus *or* Commission paid *or* payable to any person employed *or* engaged by the company; 4. Excess Profit Tax and Business Tax; 5. Interest on Debentures, Mortgages, Loans and Advances.	1. Income-tax and super tax paid by the company *or* any other tax on the income of the company not falling under Clause (d) above. 2. Capital Losses 3. Any Compensation, Damages *or* Payments made **voluntarily** and not paid due to any legal liability.
6. Expenses of Repairs not of Capital Nature 7. Contribution to Charitable and other funds, not directly related to the business of the company **not exceeding 5% of the average net profit** during the **three financial years** immediately preceding,. However, these limits can be exceeded with the prior permission of the company in general meeting; 8. Depreciation to the extent specified in Sec. 123; 9. Past losses arising after the commencement of this Act to the extent not already deducted in any subsequent year; 10. Any compensation *or* damages to be paid due to any legal liability including the one arising from a breach of contract; 11. Any sum paid by way of insurance to cover any liability discussed in above clause. 12. Bad debts written off *or* adjusted during the accounting year.	4. Any change in carrying amount of an asset *or* of a liability recognised in equity reserves including surplus P & L A/c on measurement of the asset *or* the liability at fair value.

MODE OF PAYMENT OF REMUNERATION

A director *or* a Manager may be paid remuneration—

(a) by way of a monthly payment, or

(b) at a specified percentage of the net profits of the company, or

(c) partly by one way and partly by the other.

REMUNERATION PAYABLE BY COMPANIES HAVING NO PROFIT OR INADEQUATE PROFIT WITHOUT CENTRAL GOVERNMENT APPROVAL [SEC 197 (3) & SCHEDULE V (PART II, SEC II)]

In accordance with the Provisions of Schedule V a company having no profit *or* inadequate profit may, without Central Government approval, pay remuneration to the managerial person not exceeding the higher of the limits under (A) and (B) given below:

LIMITS (A)

Effective Capital	Max. Yearly Remuneration
1. Negative (i.e. *less* than 0) or *less* than 5 crores	₹ 30 lakhs
2. 5 crores and above but *less* than 100 crores	₹ 42 lakhs
3. 100 crores and above but *less* than 250 crores	₹ 60 lakhs
4. 250 crores and above	₹ 60 lakhs *plus* 0.01% of the effective capital in excess of ₹ 250 crores.

Notes

1. *The above limits shall be doubled if special resolution is passed by the shareholders.*
2. *The above limits shall be prorated (i.e. on Proportionate basis) for a period less than 1 year.*

LIMITS (B)

In the case of a managerial person not holding securities of the company of nominal value of atleast ₹ 5,00,000 *or* an Employee *or* a Director of the company *or* not related to any director *or* promoter at any time during the 2 years prior to his appointment as a managerial person: 2.5% of the Current Relevant Profit.

Note: *The above limits shall be doubled if special resolution is passed by the shareholders.*

HOW TO CALCULATE EFFECTIVE CAPITAL?

1. Effective Capital is *to be calculated as on the last date of the financial year preceding the financial year in which appointment is made.*
2. Application Money pending allotment and Advance against Shares are not included while Computing Effective Capital.
3. Effective Capital is calculated as under:

Paid-up Equity Share Capital	XXX
Paid-up Preference Share Capital	XXX
Reserves & Surplus [including Securities Premium but excluding Revaluation Reserves]	XXX
Long term Loans	XXX
Deposits Payable after 1year	XXX
Less:	
Accumulated Losses not yet written off	(XXX)
Preliminary Expenses not written off	(XXX)
Investments (Not held by Investment co)	(XXX)
Effective Capital	XXX

HOW TO CALCULATE CURRENT RELEVANT PROFIT?

Current Relevant Profit means the profit as calculated u/s 198 but without deducting the losses of past years during which the managerial person was not an employeee, director *or* shareholder of the company *or* its holding *or* subsidiary companies.

ILLUSTRATION 38

The following is the Profit & Loss Account of Tulsian Ltd. for the year ended 31st March 2016.

Particulars	₹	*Particulars*	₹
To Salaries & wages	1,92,000	By Gross Profit	10,15,200
To Bonus for 2014-2015	5,000	By Premium on Issue of shares &	
To Interest an Debentures	12,000	Debentures	50,000
To Interest an unsecured Loan	6,000	By Profit on sale of forfeited shares	5,000
To Repairs to		By Profit on sale of Building	
To Moveable Property	1,000	(Cost-₹ 2 lakhs WDV ₹ 1.30 lakh)	90,000
To Immovable Property	2,000	By Bounties & Subsidies	
To Contributions	25,000	Received from Govt.	60,000
To Depreciation	82,000		
To Compensation for breach			
To of contract	1,000		
To Insurance Premium against			
the risk *or* meeting Liability on A/c			
of compensation for breach			
of contract	5,000		
To Loss on Sale of Investments	5,000		
To Loss on sale of Machinery			
(Cost ₹ 2,00,000 Sale Proceeds			
₹ 1,10,000 W.D.V. ₹ 1,30,000)	20,000		
To Expenditure on Scientific			
Research & cost of an operation	20,000		
To Provision for Income Tax	1,60,000		
To Provision for Doubtful Debts	7,500		
To Directors' fees	5,000		
To Ex-gratia, payments to			
employees	2,200		
To Balance c/d	6,69,500		
	12,20,200		12,20,200
To Proposed Dividend	1,60,000	By Profit for the year	6,69,500
To Corporate Dividend Tax	16,000		
To Balance c/d	4,93,500		
	6,69,500		6,69,500

Notes.

1. *Estimated liability on account of Bonus in respect of 2015-2016 in accordance with the Payment of Bonus Act 1965 is ₹ 10,000.*
2. *Depreciation admissible as per Schedule II amounts to ₹ 67,000.*

Required: Calculate the Maximum managerial remuneration payable in each of the following alternative cases:

(a) Overall managerial remuneration u/s 197
(b) If the Company has one managing director.
(c) If the company has one managing director & one whole time director.
(d) If the company has only three part time directors.
(e) If the company has three part-time directors & one managing director.
(f) If the company has three part time directors & two whole time directors.
(g) If the company has three part-time directors & one whole time director.
(h) If the company has three whole time directors & two part time directors. The remuneration payable to the whole time directors is to be calculated on net profits remaining after charging remuneration to part-time directors & the remuneration to part-time directors is to be calculated on net profits remaining after charging remuneration to whole time directors.

SOLUTION

STATEMENT SHOWING THE COMPUTATION OF NET PROFIT FOR THE PURPOSE OF CALCULATING MANAGERIAL REMUNERATION

Particulars		₹
A. Net Profit As Per Profit & Loss Account		6,69,500
B. *Add:* Items not to be deducted		
(a) Bonus for 2014-2015	5,000	
(b) Depreciation (to be taken separately)	82,000	
(c) Loss on Sale of Investments (Being Loss of Capital nature)	5,000	
(d) Expenditure on Scientific Research	20,000	
(e) Provision for I. Tax	1,60,000	
(f) Provision for Doubtful Debts	7,500	
(g) Ex-gratia payment to employees	2,200	
		2,81,700
C. *Less:* Items not to be credited		
(a) Premium on issue of shares & Deb.	50,000	
(b) Profit on sale of forfeited share	5,000	
(c) Profit on sale of Building (Being of capital nature) (i.e. Sales proceeds-Original Cost) (1,30,000 + 90,000 – 2,00,000)	20,000	75,000
D. *Less:* Items yet to be deducted		
(a) Depreciation Admissible	67,000	
(b) Bonus for 2013-2015	10,000	77,000
E. Net Profit for the purpose of calculating managerial remuneration (A + B – C – D)		7,99,200

(a) Max. Overall Managerial Remuneration = 11% of ₹ 7,99,200 = ₹ 87,912
(b) One Managing Director's Remuneration = 5% ₹ 7,99,200 = ₹ 39,960
(c) One Managing Director & one Whole Time Director's Remuneration
= 10% of ₹ 7,99,200 = ₹ 79,920
(d) Three part time Directors' Remuneration = 3% of ₹ 7,99,200 = ₹ 23,976.

	Managerial Personnel	*Rate*	*Amount* ₹
(e)	Three Part-Time Directors	1% of ₹ 7,99,200	7,992
	One Managing director	5% of ₹ 7,99,200	39,960
	Total		47,952
(f)	Three Part Time Directors	1% ₹ 7,99,200	7,992
	Two Whole Time directors	10% ₹ 7,99,200	79,920
	Total		87,912
(g)	Three Part Time directors	1% of ₹ 7,99,200	7,992
	One Whole Time Director	5% of ₹, 7,99,200	39,960
	Total		47,952

(h) Rummuneration payable to whole time Directors = 10% of Net Profit after charging commission to Part Time Directors. Max. Remuneration payable to Part Time Directors = 1% of net profit after charging commission to Whole Time Directors. Let the remuneration to Whole Time Directors be x & the remuneration to Part-time directors be 'y'

$x = 10\%$ of (₹ 7,99,200 – y)

$= 1/10$ (₹ 7,99,200 – y)

$10x + y =$ ₹ 7,99,200 I

Again $y = 1\%$ of (₹ 7,99,200 – x)

$= 1/100$ (₹ 7,99,200 – x)

$100y =$ ₹ 7,99,200 – x

$x + 100y =$ ₹ 7,99,200 II

Multiplying Equation II by 10

$10x + 1000y =$ ₹ 79,92,000 III

Substracting Equation I from equation III

$999y = 71,92,800$

$y =$ ₹ 7,200

Now, putting the value of y in equation I, we get

$10x + 7200 = 7,99,200$

$10x = 7,99,200 - 7,200$

$x = 7,92,000/10 = 79,200$

Therefore, Remuneration to

a)	Whole Time Director—	₹ 79,200
b)	Part Time Directors—	₹ 7,200
		₹ 86,400

Max. Limit for Whole Time Directors = ₹ 7,99,200 × 10% = ₹ 79,920

Max. Limit for Part Time Directors = ₹ 7,99,200 × 1% = ₹ 7,992

Hence the actual remuneration is within the limits.

ILLUSTRATION 39

The following Profit & Loss Account is presented by X Ltd. for the year ended March 2016:

Dr. **PROFIT & LOSS ACCOUNT** *Cr.*

Particulars	₹	*Particulars*		₹
To Salaries & Wages	4,00,000	By Gross Profit b/d		12,00,000
To Sundry Expenses	63,000	By Subsidy from the State Govt.		1,50,000
To Directors' Remuneration	77,000	By Profit on Sale of Plant &		
To Depreciation	1,30,000	Machinery:		
To Expenditure on Scientific		Cost	2,90,000	
Research		WDV	2,40,000	
(cost of New laboratory set up)	25,000	Sale Proceeds	3,20,000	80,000
To Provision for Income Tax	1,39,000			
To Provision for Doubtful Debts	3,000			
To Provision for Repairs	2,000			
To Ex-Gratia Payment on employee	3,000			
To Proposed Dividend	1,00,000			
To Manager's Salary	48,000			
To Commission to Manager (on A/c)	10,000			
To Net Profit	4,30,000			
	14,30,000			14,30,000

Note:

(i) Depreciation As per Schedule II amount to ₹ 90,000

(ii) Directors' Remuneration represent the remuneration payable to one whole Time Director.

Required: Calculate the remuneration payable to the Manager who is entitled to a salary of ₹ 4,000 per month *plus* 2% commission on the net profits of the company after such salary & commission & Comment about the remuneration paid/payable by the company in light of the legal requirements.

SOLUTION

	Particulars	₹	₹
A	Net Profit as per Profit & Loss Account		4,30,000
B	*Add:* Items not to be deducted		
	(a) Depreciation (to be taken separately	1,30,000	
	(b) Expenditure on Scientific Research (being Capital Expenditure)	25,000	
	(c) Provision for I. Tax	1,39,000	
	(d) Provision for Doubtful Debts	3,000	
	(e) Provision for Repairs	2,000	
	(f) Ex-Gratia Payments	3,000	
	(g) Proposed Dividend	1,00,000	
	(h) Manager's Salary	48,000	
	(i) Manager's Commission	10,000	4,60,000

C	*Less:* Items not to be credited capital Profit on sale of Pant & Machinery (i.e. Excess of sale process over original cost)		30,000
D	*Less:* Items yet to be debited: Depreciation as per Schedule II		90,000
E	Net Profit as Per Sec. 198 [A + B – C – D]		7,70,000
F	Net Profit Before salary & commission		7,70,000
G	*Less:* Salary		48,000
H	Net Profit After salary but before commission [F – G]		7,22,000
I	Commission Due [₹ 7,22,000 × 2/102]		14,157
J	Commission already paid		10,000
K	Commission Still Payable [H – I]		4,157

Comment About Manager's Remuneration:

Net Profit for the purpose of computing managerial remuneration (Before the debit of Directors' Remuneration) = ₹ 7,70,000 + ₹ 77,000 = ₹ 8,47,000

Max. Remuneration of a Manager = × 8,47,000 = ₹ 42,350

Since the actual amount (paid & payable) (i.e. ₹ 62,157) exceeds the Max. Remuneration payable to the manager, it has been assumed that the approval of Central Govt. has already been obtained for the amount already paid & payable to the manager.

Comment About Whole Time Director' Remuneration:

Max. Remuneration of One Whole Time Director = 5% of [₹ 8,47,000 – ₹ 62,157 (Manager's Rem.)] = ₹ 39,242.

Since the actual payment exceeds the maximum limit prescribed, hence approval of Central Govt. is required.

ILLUSTRATION 40

TULSIAN Ltd. provides the following information:

Particulars	*31.03.2015 ₹ [in lacs]*	*31.03.2016 ₹ [in lacs]*
Paid-up Equity Share Capital	60	420
Paid-up Preference Share Capital	10	62
Reserves [including Revaluation Reserves ₹ 5 lacs]	75	75
Securities Premium	20	20
Long term Loans	350	350
Deposits Payable after 1year	10	10
Application Money pending allotment	360	0
Accumulated Losses not written off	8	10
Preliminary Expenses not written off	2	2
Investments	90	90

Required: Calculate the Remuneration that can be paid to one Whole-time Director appointed during the year 2015-2016 if TULSIAN Ltd is (a) Non- Investment company (b) an Investment company

SOLUTION

CALCULATION OF EFFECTIVE CAPITAL & MAXIMUM LIMIT OF MONTHLY REMUNERATION

Particulars	*If Non-Investment company ₹ [in lacs]*	*If Investment company ₹ [in lacs]*
Paid-up Equity Share Capital	60	60
Paid-up Preference Share Capital	10	10
Reserves [other than Revaluation Reserves][75-5]	70	70
Securities Premium	20	20
Long term Loans	350	350
Deposits Payable after 1 year	10	10
Less:		
Accumulated Losses not written off	(8)	(8)
Preliminary Expenses not written off	(2)	(2)
Investments	(90)	
Effective Capital	420	510
Yearly Remuneration shall not exceed	**₹ 30**	**₹ 42**
[Under Option I if No Special Resolution is passed]		
Yearly Remuneration shall not exceed	**₹ 60**	**₹ 84**
[Under Option II if Special Resolution is passed but no Prior Approval of Central Government is obtained]		

Notes

1. The effective capital is to be calculated as on the last date of the financial year preceding the financial year in which appointment is made.
2. Revaluation Reserves, Application Money pending allotment and Investments **(Not held by Investment co)** are not included while computing Effective Capital.

SOLVED PROBLEMS

PROBLEM 1

The following is the Profit & Loss A/c of CAS Ltd., the year ended 31st March, 2016:

Particulars	₹	*Particulars*		₹
To Adm. & Selling Expenses	8,00,000	By Balance b/d		5,72,000
To Donation to charitable funds	25,000	By Balance from Trading A/c		40,25,000
To Directors fees	66,000	By Subsidies received from Govt.		2,32,000
To Interest on Debentures	31,000	By Interest on Investments		16,000
To Compensation for breach of contract	42,000	By Transfer fees		1,000
		By Profit on sales of Machinery:		
To Managerial remuneration	2,85,000	Amount realised	55,000	

To Depreciation on fixed assets	5,22,000	Written down value	30,000	25,000
To Provision for Taxation	12,42,000			
To General Reserve	4,00,000			
To Investment Revaluation Reserve	12,000			
To Balance c/d	14,46,600			
	48,71,000			48,71,000

Additional Information:

(1) Original Cost of the machinery sold was ₹ 40,000.

(2) Depreciation on fixed assets as per Schedule II of the Companies Act, 2013 was ₹ 6,00,000.

Your are required to comment on the managerial remuneration in the following situations:

(a) there is only one whole time director;

(b) there are two whole time directors;

(c) there are two whole time directors and one part time director.

SOLUTION

CALCULATION OF NET PROFIT U/S 198 OF THE COMPANIES ACT, 2013

Particulars	₹	₹
Balance from Trading A/c		40,25,000
Add: Subsidies received from Government	2,32,000	
Interest on investment	16,000	
Transfer fees	1,000	
Profit on sale of machinery (40,000 – 30,000)	10,000	2,59,000
Less: Adm. & Selling Expenses	8,00,000	
Donation to charitable funds	25,000	
Direction's Fees	66,000	
Interest on debentures	31,000	
Compensation for breach of contract	42,000	
Depreciation on fixed assets as per Schedule II	6,00,000	(15,64,000)
Net Profit as per 198		27,20,000

SITUATION

(a) When there is only one whole time director: Managerial remuneration [5% of ₹ 27,20,000]	₹ 1,36,000
(b) When there are two whole time directors: Managerial remuneration [10% of ₹ 27,20,000]	₹ 2,72,000
(c) When there are two whole time directors and one part time director: Managerial remuneration [11% of ₹ 27,20,000]	₹ 2,99,200

Comment: In situations (a) and (b) since managerial remuneration as per Statement of Profit and Loss ₹ 2,85,000 exceeds the maximum amount payable, the company is required to obtain permission for such excess payment.

PROBLEM 2

The following are extracts of Balance Sheet of CAS Ltd.:

AN EXTRACT OF BALANCE SHEET AS AT 31ST MARCH 2016

Particulars	₹
Authorised Capital:	
20,000, 14% preference shares of ₹ 100	40,00,000
2,00,000 Equity shares of ₹ 100 each	4,00,00,000
	4,40,00,000
Issued and Subscribed Capital:	
15,000, 14% Preference Shares of ₹ 100 each fully paid	30,00,000
1,20,000 Equity Shares of ₹ 100 each, ₹ 80 paid-up	192,00,000
Share Suspense Account	40,00,000
Capital reserves (60% is revaluation reserve)	5,00,000
Securities Premium	1,00,000
15% Debentures	3,30,00,000
Public deposits	7,40,000
Cash credit loan from IDBI	9,30,000
Sundry Creditors	6,90,000
Investment in Shares, Debentures, etc.	150,00,000
Profit and Loss Account	30,50,000
Preliminary expenses not written off	1,10,000

Share Suspense Account represents application money received on shares, the allotment of which is not yet made.

CAS Ltd. has been sustaining loss for the last few years. CAS Ltd. has only one whole-time director.

Required: Find out how much remuneration CAS Ltd. can pay to its managerial person as per the provisions of Part II of Schedule V. Would your answer differ if CAS Ltd. is an investment company?

SOLUTION

CALCULATION OF EFFECTIVE CAPITAL AND MAXIMUM LIMIT OF REMUNERATION

Particulars	*Where CAS Ltd. is a Non-investment Company* ₹	*Where CAS Ltd. is an investment Company* ₹
Paid-up Share Capital		
15,000, 14% Preference Shares	30,00,000	30,00,000
1,20,000 Equity Shares	192,00,000	192,00,000
Capital Reserves	2,00,000	2,00,000
Securities Premium	1,00,000	1,00,000
15% Debentures	3,30,00,000	3,30,00,000

Public Deposits	7,40,000	7,40,000
Total (A)	562,40,000	562,40,000
Investments in Shares, Debentures etc.	150,00,000	
Profit and Loss Account (Dr. balance)	30,50,000	30,50,000
Preliminary Expenses not written off	1,10,000	1,10,000
Total (B)	181,60,000	31,60,000
Effective Capital [A – B]	**3,80,80,000**	**5,30,80,000**
Yearly Remuneration shall not exceed	**30,00,000**	**42,00,000**
[Under Option I if no Special Resolution is passed]		
Yearly Remuneration shall not exceed	**60,00,000**	**84,00,000**
[Under Option II if Special Resolution is passed but No Prior Approval of Central Government is obtained]		

PROBLEM 3

On 31st March, 2016 Bose and Sen Ltd. provides to you the following ledger balances after preparing its Profit and Loss Account for the year ended 31st March, 2016:

Credit Balances:

Particulars	₹
Equity Share Capital, fully paid shares of ₹ 10 each	70,00,000
General Reserve	15,49,100
Loan from State Finance Corporation	10,50,000
Secured by hypothecation of Plant & Machinery	
(Repayable within one year ₹ 2,00,000)	
Loans: Unsecured (Long term)	8,47,000
Sundry Creditors for goods & expenses	14,00,000
(Payable within 6 months)	
Profit & Loss Account	7,00,000
Provision for Taxation	3,25,500
Proposed Dividend	4,20,000
Provision for Dividend Distribution Tax	71,400
	1,33,63,000

Debit Balances:

Particulars	₹
Calls in arrear	7,000
Land	14,00,000
Buildings	20,50,000
Plant and Machinery	36,75,000
Furniture & Fixture	3,50,000
Stocks: Finished goods	14,00,000

Raw Materials	3,50,000
Sundry Debtors	14,00,000
Advances: Short-term	2,98,900
Cash in hand	2,10,000
Balances with banks	17,29,000
Preliminary Expenses	93,100
Patents & Trade marks	4,00,000
	1,33,63,000

The following additional information is also provided:

(i) 4,20,000 fully paid equity shares were allotted as consideration for land & buildings.

(ii) Cost of Building ₹ 28,00,000

Cost of Plant & Machinery ₹ 49,00,000

Cost of Furniture & Fixture ₹ 4,37,500

(iii) Sundry Debtors for ₹ 3,80,000 are due for more than 6 months.

(iv) The amount of Balances with Bank includes ₹ 18,000 with a bank which is not a scheduled Bank and the deposits of ₹ 5 lakhs are for a period of 9 months.

(v) Unsecured loan includes ₹ 2,00,000 from a Bank and ₹ 1,00,000 from related parties.

Required: Prepare the Balance Sheet of the Company as at 31st March, 2016 as required under Schedule III to the Companies Act, 2013.

SOLUTION

BALANCE SHEET OF BOSE AND SON LTD.
AS AT 31ST MARCH, 2016

Particulars	*Notes*	*Figures at the end of current reporting period* ₹
Equity and Liabilities		
1. Shareholders' funds		
(a) Share capital	1	69,93,000
(b) Reserves and Surplus	2	21,56,000
2. Non-current liabilities		
(a) Long-term borrowings	3	16,97,000
3. Current liabilities		
(a) Trade Payables		14,00,000
(b) Other current liabilities	4	2,00,000
(c) Short-term provisions	5	8,16,900
Total		1,32,62,900
Assets		
1. Non-current assets		
(a) Fixed assets		
Tangible assets	6	74,75,000

Intangible assets (Patents & Trade Marks)		4,00,000
2. Current assets		
(a) Inventories	7	17,50,000
(b) Trade receivables	8	14,00,000
(c) Cash and cash equivalents	9	19,39,000
(d) Short-term loans and advances		2,98,900
Total		1,32,62,900

Notes to Accounts:

Particulars		
1. Share Capital		
Equity share capital		
Issued, subscribed and called up		
7,00,000 Equity Shares of ₹ 10 each fully paid		
(Out of the above 4,20,000 shares have been issued for consideration other than cash)	70,00,000	
Less: Calls unpaid	(7,000)	69,93,000
Total		69,93,000
2. Reserves and Surplus		
General Reserve		15,49,100
Surplus (Profit & Loss A/c)		7,00,000
Less: Preliminary expenses	(93,100)	6,06,900
Total		21,56,000
3. Long-term borrowings		
Secured		
Term Loans		
Loan from State Finance Cor. (₹10,50,000 – ₹ 2,00,000)		8,50,000
(Secured by hypothecation of Plant and Machinery)		
Unsecured		
Bank Loan		2,00,000
Loan from related parties		1,00,000
Others	5,47,000	8,47,000
Total		16,97,000
4. Other current liabilities		
Loan Instalment repayable within one year		2,00,000
5. Short-term provisions		
Provision for taxation		3,25,500
Proposed Dividend		4,20,000
Provision for Dividend Distribution Tax		71,400
Total		8,16,900

6.	**Tangible assets**		
	Land		14,00,000
	Buildings		28,00,000
	Less: Depreciation	7,50,000	20,50,000
	Plant & Machinery		49,00,000
	Less: Depreciation	12,25,000	36,75,000
	Furniture & Fittings		4,37,500
	Less: Depreciation	87,500	3,50,000
	Total		74,75,000
7.	**Inventories**		
	Raw Material		3,50,000
	Finished goods		14,00,000
8.	**Trade receivables**		
	Debts outstanding for a period exceeding six months		3,80,000
	Other Debts		10,20,000
	Total		14,00,000
9.	**Cash and Cash Equivalents**		
	Cash at bank with Scheduled Banks including Bank	17,11,000	
	deposits for period of 9 months amounting ₹ 5,00,000 with others	18,000	17,29,000
	Cash in hand		2,10,000
	Total		19,39,000

2 CASH FLOW STATEMENT

LEARNING OBJECTIVES

After studying this chapter, you should be able to understand:

- ◇ Meaning of Cash Flow Statement
- ◇ Objectives of Cash Flow Statement
- ◇ Uses/Advantages of Cash Flow Statement
- ◇ Limitations of Cash Flow Statement
- ◇ What is meant by the term 'Cash Flows'?
- ◇ Cash and Cash Equivalents
- ◇ Operating Activities
- ◇ Investing Activities
- ◇ Financial Activities
- ◇ Practical Steps involved in the Preparation of Cash Flow Statement

1.0 MEANING OF CASH FLOW STATEMENT

The Cash Flow Statement means the Statement of Changes in Cash and Cash equivalents during a particular accounting period. It shows—

1. Net Cash flows from Operating Activities;
2. Net Cash flows from Investing Activities;
3. Net Cash flows from Financing Activities;
4. Net Change in Cash and Cash Equivalents.

Notes

1. *Cash Flow Statement is* ***not a substitute for Income Statement*** *because it does not disclose the calculation of Profit or Loss.*
2. *Cash Flow Statement is* ***not a substitute for Position Statement (Balance Sheet)*** *because it does not disclose the Total Financial Position [i.e. Total Equity,Non-Current Liabilities, Current Liabilities, Non-Current Assets and Current Assets].*
3. *Cash Flow Statement is historical in nature because it is prepared on the basis of Historical Financial Statements.*

2.0 OBJECTIVES OF CASH FLOW STATEMENT

The objectives of Cash Flow Statement are as follows:

1. **To ascertain Net Cash Flows from Operating, Investing and Financing Activities of an enterprise**

2. **To ascertain the Net Change in Cash & Cash Equivalents** indicating the aggregate of Net Cash Flows from Operating, Investing and Financing Activities of an enterprise between the dates of two consecutive Balance Sheets.

3.0 USES/ADVANTAGES OF CASH FLOW STATEMENT

The various uses of Cash Flow Statement are as follows:

1. **Facilitates to ascertain Net Cash flows:** Cash Flow Statement facilitates to ascertain Net Cash Flows from Operating, Investing and Financing Activities and Net Change in Cash and Cash Equivalents.
2. **Facilitates to evaluate Cash Financial Performance:** It facilitates to evaluate Cash Financial Performance by providing information on Net Cash flows from Operating Activities.
3. **Facilitates to evaluate Cash Financial Position:** It facilitates to evaluate Cash Financial Position by providing information on Net Cash flows from investing Activities and Financing Activities.
4. **Facilitates Efficient Cash Management.:** The management can know the situation of shortage *or* surplus cash and can plan for the effective use of surplus cash *or* can make the necessary arrangement in case of an shortage of cash.
5. **Facilitates Comparision:** It facilitates the comparative study of the operating performance of different enterprises because it eliminates the effects of using different accounting treatments for the same transactions and events.
6. **Facilitates Capital Budgeting Decisions:** It facilitates Capital Budgeting Decisions by providing information on Net Cash flows from Investing Activities .
7. **Facilitates Capital Structure Decisions:** It facilitates Capital Structure Decisions by providing information on Net Cash flows from Financing Activities.
8. **Facilitates Planning:** The Projected Cash Flow Statement enables the management to plan its future investments, operating and financial activities such as the repayment of long-term loans and interest thereon, modernisation *or* expansion of plant, payment of cash dividend etc.
9. **Answers some of the important financial questions:** As a tool of historical analysis, it provides an answer to some of the important financial questions such as:
   (i) How was it possible to distribute dividend in excess of current earnings *or* in the presence of a net loss for the period?
   (ii) Why has the cash decreased although the net income for the period has gone up?
   (iii) Why has the cash increased even though there has been a net loss for the period?
   (iv) What happened to the proceeds of the sale of land and equipments?
   (v) Why did the firm resort to long-term borrowings inspite of large profits?
   (vi) Why did the firm issue new equity *or* preference shares?
   (vii) How was the retirement of long-term debts *or* redemption of redeemable preference shares accomplished?

4.0 LIMITATIONS OF CASH FLOW STATEMENT

The major limitations of Cash Flow Statement are as follows:

1. Ignores Non-Cash Transactions	It ignores the non-cash transactions. In other words, it does not take into consideration those transactions which do not affect the cash ***For Example***, Issue of Shares against the purchase of Fixed Assets *or* Stock-in-trade, Conversion of Debentures into Shares.

2. Secondary Data Based Statement	It is a secondary data based statement. It merely rearranges the primary data already appearing in other statements viz., Income Statement and Balance Sheet.
3. Historical Statement	It is basically historical in nature because it is prepared on the basis of Historical Financial Statements.
4. Ignores Accural Concept	It ignores the Fundamental Assumption of Accural.

5.0 WHAT IS MEANT BY THE TERM 'CASH FLOWS'?

MEANING OF CASH FLOWS

Cash Flows are inflows and outflows of Cash and Cash equivalents.

MEANING OF CASH INFLOWS

Cash Inflow arises when the net effect of transaction is increase in the amount of **Cash *or* Cash Equivalents.**

MEANING OF CASH OUTFLOWS

Cash Outflow arises when the net effect of transaction is to decrease in the amount of **Cash *or* Cash Equivalents.**

EXAMPLES OF CASH FLOWS

Cash Inflows	***Cash Outflows***
1. Cash Sales of Goods	1. Cash Purchases of Goods
2. Cash received from Trade Debtors	2. Cash paid to Trade Creditors
3. Cash received from commission & Royalty	3. Operating Expenses paid (e.g. Salaries & Wages, Administration Exp. Selling Exp.)
4. Sale of Fixed Assets for Cash	4. Income Tax paid
5. Sale of Investments (whether Current *or* Non-Current) for Cash	5. Cash Purchase of Fixed Assets
6. Loans & Advances repayment received (whether Short term *or* Long term)	6. Cash Purchase of Investments (whether Short term *or* Long term)
7. Income received on Investments (whether Current *or* Non-Current)	7. Loans & Advances granted (whether Short term *or* Long term)
8. Issue of Equity Shares for Cash	8. Buy-back of Equity Shares for Cash
9. Issue of Preference Shares for Cash	9. Redemption of Preference Shares for Cash
10. Issue of Debentures for Cash	10. Redemption of Debentures for Cash
11. Loans taken (whether Short term *or* Long term)	11. Loans repaid (whether Short term *or* Long term)
	12. Interest on Debentures & Loans paid. (whether Short term *or* Long term)
	13. Final Dividend on Equity Shares paid.
	14. Dividend on Preference Shares paid.
	15. Interim Dividend on Equity Shares paid.

6.0 CASH AND CASH EQUIVALENTS

THE TERM 'CASH'

Meaning	Cash comprises Cash on hand and Demand Deposits with banks.
Examples	Cash in hand, Cash at Bank

THE TERM 'CASH EQUIVALENTS'

Meaning	Cash Equivalents are short term, highly liquid investments that are readily convertible into known amounts of cash and which are subject to an insignificant risk of changes in value.
Purpose	Cash Equivalents are held for the purpose of meeting short-term cash commitments rather than for Investment *or* other purposes.
Two Conditions for an Investment to qualify as a Cash Equivalent	1. It must be readily convertible to a known amount of cash. 2. It must be subject to an insignificant risk of changes in value. Therefore, an investment normally qualifies as a cash equivalent only when it has a **short maturity of, say, 3 months *or* less from the date of acquisition.**
Examples	Treasury Bills, Commercial Papers, Commercial Bills, Call Money, Certificate of Deposit

7.0 TRANSACTIONS NOT CONSIDERED AS CASH FLOWS

Meaning	Transactions which represent movements between items of Cash *or* Cash Equivalents are not considered as Cash Flows.
Reason	These components are part of the cash management of an enterprise rather than part of its Operating, Investing and Financing Activities.
Examples	1. Cash deposited into Bank; 2. Cash withdrawn from Bank; 3. Purchase/Sale of Short-term Marketable Securities (neither held as Current Investments nor held as Non-current Investments).

8.0 NON-CASH TRANSACTIONS

Meaning	Non-Cash transactions are those transactions which do not involve Cash.
Examples [Verification by Journal Entry]	**1. Issue of Equity Shares *or* Debentures against the purchase of an Asset** **JOURNAL ENTRY** Asset A/c Dr To Equity Share Capital A/c/Debentures A/c **2. Issue of Equity Shares on conversion of Convertible** Debentures **JOURNAL ENTRY** Convertible Debentures A/c Dr To Equity Share Capital A/c

	3. Charging of Depreciation on a Fixed Tangible Asset **JOURNAL ENTRY** Depreciation A/c Dr To Fixed Tangible Asset A/c **4. Amortization of a Fixed Intangible Asset** **JOURNAL ENTRY** Profit & Loss A/c Dr To Intangible Asset A/c **5. Written off of an old Fixed Tangible Asset** **JOURNAL ENTRY** Profit & Loss A/c Dr To Fixed Tangible Asset A/c **6. Declaration of Final Dividend on Shares** **JOURNAL ENTRY:** Proposed Dividend A/c Dr To Dividend Payable A/c
Why ignored in CFS?	Non-Cash transactions are ignored while preparing Cash Flow Statement because these do not involve Cash.

9.0 OPERATING ACTIVITIES

MEANING OF OPERATING ACTIVITIES

Operating Activities are the principal revenue-producing activities of the enterprise and other activities that are not investing *or* financing activities.

EXAMPLES OF CASH FLOWS FROM OPERATING ACTIVITIES

Cash Inflows	***Cash Outflows***
1. Cash Sales of Goods	1. Cash Purchases of Goods
2. Cash received from Trade.Debtors	2. Cash paid to Trade Creditors
3. Cash received from Trading Commission & Royalty	3. Operating Expenses paid (e.g. Salaries & Wages, Administration Exp. Selling Exp.)
	4. Income Tax (related to Operating Activities only) paid.

TUTORIAL NOTE

In case of Financial Enterprises the following activities are classified as Operating Activities since they relate to the main revenue-producing activity of that enterprise:

1. *Purchases and Sales of Shares & Debentures of other companies for Cash*
2. *Dividend received on Shares of other companies*
3. *Interest received on Debentures of other companies*
4. *Loans & Advances granted*
5. *Interest received on Loans & Advances granted*

DISTINCTION BETWEEN NET PROFIT AND CASH FROM OPERATING ACTIVITIES

Basis of Distinction	*Net Profit*	*Cash from Operating Activities*
1. **Meaning**	It indicates the net result of Operating & non-operating activities carried out during an accounting year.	It indicates the Cash Flow as a result of operating activities.
2. **Non-Cash Operating Item (Depreciation)**	It is calculated **after taking into account the effect of non-cash operating items.**	It is calculated **excluding the effect of non-cash operating items** since these items merely represent the book entries.
3. **Non-Operating Items**	It is calculated **after taking into account the effect of non-operating items.**	It is calculated **excluding the effect of non-operating items** since these items do not relate to operating activities.

10.0 INVESTING ACTIVITIES

MEANING OF INVESTING ACTIVITIES

Investing Activities are the acquisition and disposal of Long-term Assets and other Investments not included in Cash Equivalents.

EXAMPLES OF INVESTING ACTIVITIES

Cash Inflows	*Cash Outflows*
1. Cash Sale of Fixed Assets	1. Cash Purchase of Fixed Assets
2. Cash Sale of Investments (whether Current *or* Non-Current)	2. Cash Purchase of Investments (whether Short term *or* Long term)
3. Loans & Advances repayment received (whether Short term *or* Long term)	3. Loans & Advances granted (whether Short term *or* Long term)
4. Income received on Investments (whether Current *or* Non-Current)	4. Brokerage paid on Purchase of Investments (whether Short term *or* Long term)

11.0 FINANCING ACTIVITIES

MEANING OF FINANCING ACTIVITIES

Financing Activities are activities that result in changes in the size and composition of the Owners' Capital (including Preference Share Capital in the case of a company) and Borrowings (whether Short term *or* Long term) of the enterprise.

EXAMPLES OF FINANCING ACTIVITIES

Cash Inflows	*Cash Outflows*
1. Issue of Equity Shares for Cash	1. Buy-back of Equity Shares for Cash.
2. Issue of Preference Shares for Cash	2. Redemption of Preference Shares for Cash.
3. Issue of Debentures for Cash	3. Redemption of Debentures for Cash
4. Loans taken (whether for short-term *or* long-term)	4. Loans repaid (whether Short term *or* Long term)

5. Interest received on Calls-in-arrears. (whether Short term *or* Long term).	5. Interest on Debentures & Loans paid 6. Final Dividend on Equity Shares paid 7. Dividend on Preference Shares paid 8. Interim Dividend on Equity Shares paid 9. Brokerage & Underwriting commission paid on Issue of Shares & Debentures.

ILLUSTRATION 1

Classify the following activities as (i) Operating Activities; (ii) Investing Activities; (iii) Financing Activities:

(i) Purchase of Machinery
(ii) Sale of Land
(iii) Payment of Income Tax
(iv) Refund of Income Tax
(v) Payment of Dividend
(vi) Receipt of Dividend
(vii) Payment of Interest on Debenture
(viii) Receipt of Interest on Debenture
(ix) Issue of Debentures
(x) Buy-back of Equity Shares

SOLUTION

(i) Investing Activity
(ii) Investing Activity
(iii) Operating Activity
(iv) Operating Activity
(v) Financing Activity
(vi) Investing Activity
(vii) Financing Activity
(viii) Investing Activity
(ix) Financial Activity
(x) Financing Activity

ILLUSTRATION 2

Classify the following activities as (a) Operating Activities, (b) Investing Activities, (c) Financing Activities, (d) Cash *or* Cash Equivalents.

1. Purchase of Machinery	21. Dividend received on Shares
2. Issue of Equity Share Capital	22. Rent received on property
3. Cash Sales	23. Selling & Distribution Exp paid
4. Interest on Short-term Borrowings	24. Income Tax paid
5. Sale of Machinery	25. Dividend paid on Pref. Shares
6. Cash receipts from Debtors	26. Underwriting Commission paid
7. Commission and Royalty received	27. Rent paid
8. Purchase of Current Investments	28. Brokerage paid on issue of shares
9. Redemption of Preference shares	29. Brokerage paid on purchase of Investments
10. Cash Purchases of Goods	30. Bank Overdraft
11. Sale of Investments	31. Cash Credit
12. Purchase of Goodwill	32. Short-term Deposits having maturity of 3 months
13. Cash paid to suppliers of Goods.	
14. Interim Dividend paid on Equity Shares	33. Marketable Securities having maturity of 3 months
15. Wages & Salaries paid	

16. Sale of Patents	34. Refund of Income Tax received
17. Interest received on Debentures held as Investments	35. Discount allowed to customers
	36. Discount received from Suppliers
18. Interest paid on borrowings	37. Purchase of Marketable Securities having maturity of 6 months
19. Office & Adm. Expenses paid	
20. Manufacturing Overheads paid	

SOLUTION

CLASSIFICATION OF ACTIVITIES

(a) Operating Activities	3, 6, 7, 10, 13, 15, 19, 20, 23, 24, 27, 34, 35, 36
(b) Investing Activities	1, 5, 8, 11, 12, 16, 17, 21, 22, 29, 37
(c) Financing Activities	2, 4, 9, 14, 18, 25, 26, 28, 30, 31
(d) Cash *or* Cash Equivalents	32, 33

ILLUSTRATION 3

Classify the following activities as (i) Operating Activities; (ii) Investing Activities; (iii) Financing Activities in case of (a) a Manufacturing Enterprise; (b) a Financial Enterprise.

1. Purchase of Investments.
2. Proceeds from Sale of Investments.
3. Brokerage paid on purchase & sale of Investments.
4. Interest received on Debentures held as Investments.
5. Dividend received on shares held as Investments.
6. Loans & Advances made to third parties.
7. Receipts from the repayments of loans & advances made to third parties.
8. Receipt of Interest on loans & advances made to third parties.

SOLUTION

(a) In case of a **Manufacturing Enterprise**, all the given activities are **Investing Activities** since they relate to acquisition and disposal of long-term assets.

(b) In case of a **Financial Enterprise**, all the given activities are **Operating Activities** since they relate to the main revenue-producing activity of the enterprise.

ILLUSTRATION 4

Classify the following activities as (i) Operating Activities; (ii) Investing Activities; (iii) Financing Activities in case of (a) Manufacturing Enterprise; (b) a Real Estate Enterprise.

1. Purchase of Land.
2. Purchase of Building.
3. Sale of Land.
4. Sale of Building.
5. Brokerage paid on purchase and sale of Land & Building.
6. Rent received from a Building.
7. Payment of Construction Cost of a Building.

SOLUTION

(a) In case of a **Manufacturing Enterprise**, all the given activities are **Investing Activities** since they relate to acquisition and disposal of long-term assets.

(b) In case of a **Real Estate Enterprise**, all the given activities are **Operating Activities** since they relate to the main revenue-producing activity of the enterprise.

ILLUSTRATION 5

When is Dividend received considered as Operating Activity?

SOLUTION

Dividend received by a Financial Enterprise is considered as Operating Activity.

ILLUSTRATION 6

Classify the following into Operating, Investing and Financing Activities:

(a) Refund of Income Tax
(b) Sale of Shares & Debentures of other companies by a Finance Co
(c) Dividend on Shares and Interest on Debentures paid by a Mutual Fund Company
(d) Dividend on Shares and Interest on Debentures received by a Bank.
(e) Payment of Brokerage on Purchase of Shares of a Finance Company.

SOLUTION

(a) Operating Activity (b) Operating Activity (c) Financing Activity
(d) Investing Activity (e) Investing Activity

ILLUSTRATION 7

If you want neither Inflow nor Outflow of Cash, which of the following transactions will you select?

(a) A Long-term Loan from Bank
(b) Goodwill written off
(c) Issue of Equity Shares *or* Debentures against the purchase of a Fixed Asset
(d) Issue of Equity shares on conversion of Debentures
(e) Cash deposited into Bank
(f) Cash withdrawn from Bank
(g) Charging Depreciation on Furniture
(h) Declaration of Final Dividend
(i) Purchase of Stock-in-trade on credit

SOLUTION

(b) (i)

ILLUSTRATION 8

Mention the net amount of 'Source' *or* 'Use' of Cash in the following cases:

1. When Fixed asset (having book value of ₹ 15,000) is sold at a loss of ₹ 5,000.

2. When Goods costing ₹ 10,000 are sold for ₹ 15,000.
3. When ₹ 19,000 received from a debtor and allowed ₹ 1,000 as discount.
4. When Discount of ₹ 1,000 is received on making payment to a creditor of ₹ 10,000.
5. When Issue of shares for ₹ 7,00,000 against purchase of business comprising of fixed assets ₹ 6,00,000; current assets ₹ 2,00,000 and took over current liabilities ₹ 1,00,000.
6. When Old Furniture (Book value ₹ 1,000) written off.
7. When Deferred Revenue Expenditure (₹ 1,000) charged to Profit.

SOLUTION

1. Source ₹10,000,
2. Source ₹ 15,000,
3. Source ₹19,000,
4. Use ₹ 9,000,
5. Nil because this transaction does not involve Cash.
6. Nil because this transaction does not involve Cash.
7. Nil because this transaction does not involve Cash.

12.0 HOW TO COMPUTE CASH FROM OPERATING ACTIVITIES

The amount of cash from operating activities may be computed by following either the Direct Method *or* the Indirect Method.

HOW TO COMPUTE NET CASH FLOW FROM OPERATING ACTIVITIES (UNDER DIRECT METHOD)

Particulars	₹	₹
A. *Operating Receipts in Cash (e.g.)*		
Cash Sales	xxx	
Cash receipts from Debtors	xxx	
Trading Commission received	xxx	xxx
B. *Operating Payments in Cash (e.g.)*		
Cash Purchases	xxx	
Cash paid to Suppliers	xxx	
Wages & Salaries paid	xxx	
Office and Administration Expenses paid	xxx	
Manufacturing Overheads paid	xxx	
Selling and Distribution Expenses paid	xxx	xxx
C. Cash generated from Operations before taxes (A – B)		xxx
D. Income Tax paid (Net of Refund of Tax)		xxx
E. Cash flow before extraordinary item (C – D)		xxx
F. Extraordinary item		xxx
G. Net Cash from (used in) Operating Activities		xxx

ILLUSTRATION 9

From the following particulars, Calculate Cash Flows from Operating Activities:

Particulars	₹	*Particulars*	₹
Cash Sales	2,00,000	Manufacturing Overheads paid	30,000
Cash Purchases	50,000	Office & Administration Exp. paid	20,000
Cash receipts from customers	4,00,000	Selling & Distribution Expenses paid	10,000
Cash paid to suppliers	1,00,000	Income Taxes paid	1,18,000
Trading Commission received	1,00,000	Insurance proceeds from earthquake disaster settlement	1,00,000
Trading Commission Paid	25,000		
Wages & Salaries paid	40,000	Income Tax Refund received	3,000
Rent paid	10,000		

SOLUTION **CASH FLOW FROM OPERATING ACTIVITIES**

Particulars	₹
A. Operating Receipts in Cash:	
Cash Sales	2,00,000
Cash receipts from customers	4,00,000
Trading Commission received	1,00,000
	7,00,000
B. Operating Payments in Cash:	
Cash Purchases	50,000
Cash paid to suppliers	1,00,000
Trading Commission paid	25,000
Wages & Salaries paid	40,000
Rent paid	10,000
Manufacturing Overheads paid	30,000
Office & Administrative Expenses paid	20,000
Selling & Distribution Expenses paid	10,000
	2,85,000
C. Cash generated from Operations before taxes [A – B]	4,15,000
D. Income Tax paid (Net of refund) [₹ 1,18,000 – ₹ 3,000]	1,15,000
E. Cash flow before extraordinary items	3,00,000
F. Insurance proceeds from earthquake disaster settlement	1,00,000
G. Net Cash from Operating Activities	4,00,000

HOW TO COMPUTE NET CASH FLOW FROM OPERATING ACTIVITIES (UNDER INDIRECT METHOD)

Particulars	₹	₹
Step 1: ***Calculate Net Profit before Taxation and Extraordinary Item as follows:***		
A. Closing Balance of P & L A/c		xxx

Less: Opening Balance of P&L A/c [or *Add:* Opening Bal. of P & L A/c (Dr.)]		xxx
Add: Proposed Dividend for the current year		xxx
Add: Interim Dividend paid during the current year		xxx
Add: Transfer to Reserve [or *Less:* Transfer from Reserve]		xxx
Add: Provision for Tax made during the Current Year		xxx
Less: Refund of Tax credited to P&L A/c		(xxx)
Less: Extraordinary item, if any, credited to P&L A/c (e.g., Insurance proceeds from earthquake disaster settlement)		(xxx)
Add: Extraordinary Debit Items (e.g., Loss due to earthquake)		xxx
B. Net Profit before Taxation and Extraordinary Item		xxx
Step 2: *Calculate Operating Profit before Working Capital Changes as follows:*		
A. Net Profit before Taxation and Extraordinary Item		xxx
B. Adjustments for Non-Cash and Non-Operating Items : (***For Example***)		
Depreciation	xxx	
Interest on Debentures & Loans (whether Short term *or* Long term)	xxx	
Preliminary Expenses/Underwriting Commission/Discount on	xxx	
Issue of Debentures/Shares written off	xxx	
Goodwill/Patents/Trade Marks/Copyright amortised	xxx	
Loss on Sale of Investments (whether Current *or* Non-Current).	xxx	
Premium payable on redemption of Preference shares/Debentures	xxx	
Interest Income from Investments (whether Current *or* Non-Current)	(xxx)	
Dividend Income	(xxx)	
Rental Income	(xxx)	
Profit on Sale of Investments (whether Current *or* Non-Current)	(xxx)	xxx
C. Operating Profit before Working Capital Changes		xxx
Step 3: *Calculate Cash from Operations before Tax & Extraordinary Item as follows:*		
A. Operating Profit before Working Capital Changes		xxx
B. Add : Changes in Current Assets (Excluding Cash and Cash Equivalents) &		
Current Liabilities (Excluding Bank Overdraft & Cash Credit):		
Decrease in Inventories, Trade Receivables etc.	xxx	
Increase in Trade Payables, O/s Exp. etc.	xxx	
Increase in Inventories, Trade Receivables etc.	(xxx)	
Decrease in Trade Payables, O/s Exp. etc.	(xxx)	xxx
C. Cash generated from Operations		xxx
Step 4: Calculate Cash generated from Operations after Tax but before Extraordinary Item as follows:		
A. Cash generated from Operations		xxx
B. *Less:* Income taxes paid (Including Advance Tax but Excluding Refund of Tax)		(xxx)
[**Note:** Income Tax should be related to Operating Activities only]		
C. Cash Flow before Extraordinary Item		xxx

Step 5: ***Calculate Net Cash from (used in) Operating Activities as follows:***	
A. Cash Flow before Extraordinary Items	xxx
B. *Add:* Extraordinary Credit Items (e.g., Insurance proceeds from earthquake disaster settlement, Govt. Grant)	xxx
C. *Less:* Extraordinary Debit Items (e.g., Loss due to earthquake)	(xxx)
D. Net Cash Flow from (used in) Operating Activities	xxx

Note: *Negative items which are to be deducted have been shown in brackets.*

ILLUSTRATION 10

From the following information, calculate Net Profit before Taxation and Extraordinary Item:

Particulars	*Closing* ₹	*Opening* ₹
Profit & Loss Account	3,36,000	1,00,000
Reserve	1,50,000	50,000
Proposed Dividend	72,000	60,000

Interim Dividend paid during the year	90,000
Provision for Tax made during the current year	1,50,000
Refund of Tax	3,000
Loss due to Earthquake	2,00,000
Insurance Proceeds from earthquake disaster settlement	1,00,000

SOLUTION

CALCULATION OF NET PROFIT BEFORE TAXATION AND EXTRAORDINARY ITEM

Particulars	₹
A. Net Profit as per Profit & Loss A/c [₹ 3,36,000 – ₹ 1,00,000]	2,36,000
Add: Proposed Dividend for the current year	72,000
Add: Interim Dividend paid during the year	90,000
Add: Transfer to Reserve	1,00,000
Add: Provision for Tax made during the Current Year	1,50,000
Less: Refund of Tax	(3,000)
Add: Extraordinary Item (Loss due to Earthquake)	2,00,000
Less: Extraordinary items (i.e., Insurance proceeds from earthquake disaster settlement)	(1,00,000)
B. Net Profit before Taxation and Extraordinary Item	7,45,000

ILLUSTRATION 11

From the following information, calculate Net Cash Flow from Operating Activities:

Particulars	₹
Net Profit before Taxation and Extraordinary Item	7,45,000

Depreciation	1,40,000
Loss on Sale of Machinery	30,000
Interest on Debentures	24,850
Interest on Bank Loan	6,650
Goodwill amortised	9,000
Preliminary Expenses written off	2,000
Premium on Redemption of Preference Shares	10,000
Interest Income on Non-Current Investments	6,000
Interest Income on Current Investments	2,000
Profit on Sale of Current Investments	5,000
Loss on Sale of Non-Current Investments	10,000
Tax paid during the Current Year	1,18,000
Refund of Tax	3,000
Loss due to Earthquake	2,00,000
Insurance Proceeds from earthquake disaster settlement	1,00,000

POSITION OF CURRENT ASSETS & CURRENT LIABILITIES

Particulars	*Closing (₹)*	*Opening (₹)*
Inventories	1,06,000	1,00,000
Trade Receivables	10,000	6,70,000
Trade Payables	25,000	1,80,000
Outstanding Expenses	14,000	10,000
Cash & Cash Equivalents	30,000	49,000

SOLUTION

CALCULATION OF OPERATING PROFIT BEFORE WORKING CAPITAL CHANGES

Particulars		₹
A. Net Profit before Taxation and Extraordinary Item		7,45,000
B. *Adjustments for Non-Cash and Non-Operating Items:*		
Depreciation	1,40,000	
Loss on Sale of Machinery	30,000	
Interest on Debentures	24,850	
Interest on Bank Loan	6,650	
Goodwill amortised	9,000	
Preliminary Expenses written off	2,000	
Premium on Redemption of Preference Shares	10,000	
Interest Income on Non-Current Investments	(6,000)	
Interest Income on Current Investments	(2,000)	
Profit on Sale of Current Investments	(5,000)	
Loss on Sale of Non-Current Investments	10,000	2,19,500

C. Operating Profit before Working Capital Changes		9,64,500
D. Changes in Current Assets & Current Liabilities:		
Decrease in Inventories	6,000	
Increase in Trade Payables	1,55,000	
Increase in Trade Receivables	(6,60,000)	
Decrease in Outstanding Expenses	(4,000)	(5,03,000)
E. Cash generated from operations before Taxes		4,61,500
F. *Less:* Income taxes paid (Net of Refund) [₹ 1,18,000 – ₹ 3,000]		(1,15,000)
G. Cash Flow before Extraordinary Items		3,46,500
Add: Extraordinary items (i.e., Insurance proceeds from earthquake disaster settlement)		1,00,000
Less: Extraordinary items (i.e., Loss due to earthquake)		(2,00,000)
H. Net Cash Inflow from Operating Activities		2,46,500

ILLUSTRATION 12

From the following particulars, calculate the Net Cash Flow from Operating Activities:

(i) Profit made during the year was ₹ 1,00,000 after considering the following items:

Particulars	₹
(a) Depreciation on fixed assets	4,000
(b) Amortization of goodwill	2,000
(c) Transfer to Reserve	2,800
(d) Profit on Sale of Land	1,700
(e) Loss on Sale of Furniture	500
(f) Provision for Taxation	80,000

(ii) The following is the position of Current Assets and Current Liabilities

Particulars	*Closing (₹)*	*Opening (₹)*
Trade Receivables	6,000	4,800
Trade Payables	4,000	6,000
Inventories	3,200	4,000
Outstanding Expenses	2,400	1,600
Provision for Taxation	80,000	70,000

SOLUTION

CALCULATION OF NET CASH FLOW FROM OPERATING ACTIVITIES

Particulars		₹
Net Profit before Tax		1,82,800
Adjustments for Non-Cash and Non-Operating Items:		
Depreciation	4,000	
Goodwill amortized	2,000	
Loss on sale of Furniture	500	

Profit on sale of Land	(1,700)	4,800
Operating Profit before Working Capital Changes		1,87,600
Changes in Current Assets & Current Liabilities:		
Decrease in Inventories	800	
Increase in Outstanding Expenses	800	
Increase in Trade Receivables	(1,200)	
Decrease in Trade Payables	(2,000)	(1,600)
Cash generated from operations		1,86,000
Less: Income taxes paid (Net of Refund)		(70,000)
Net Cash Inflow from Operating Activities		1,16,000

Working Note:

CALCULATION OF NET PROFIT BEFORE TAX

Net Profit as per Profit & Loss A/c	1,00,000
Add: Transfer to Reserve	2,800
Add: Provision for Tax	80,000
Net Profit before Tax	1,82,800

TREATMENT OF SPECIAL ITEMS WHILE CALCULATING NET PROFIT BEFORE TAX

Item	*Treatment and Reason*	*Remarks*
Increase in General Reserve	**Add back** to Balance of P & L A/c to find out **Net Profit Before Tax** **Reason:** It represents an appropriation out of Current year's profits.	
Decrease in General Reserve	**Subtract** from Balance of P&L A/c to find out **Net Profit Before Tax** **Reason:** It represents utilization of past reserves and not of Current year's profits.	
Provision for Tax for Current Year	**Add back Tax provided** to Balance of P & L A/c to find out **Net Profit Before Tax** **Reason:** It is merely a book entry and does not involve any Cash outflow.	1. If only Opening & Closing amounts of Provision for Tax are given,Take Provision for Tax for Current Year as Tax provided during the current year. 2. **If Tax Paid is also given,** Prepare Provision for Tax Account to ascertain the amount of Tax provided during the current year.
Provision for Tax for Previous Year	**Subtract Tax paid** from Cash from Operating Activities before tax **Reason:** It involves Cash outflow.	1. If only Opening & Closing amounts of Provision for Tax are given, Take Provision for Tax for previous year as Tax paid during the current year. 2. **If Tax provided is also given,** Prepare Provision for Tax Account to ascertain the amount of Tax paid during the current year.

Proposed Dividend for Current Year [It represents the amount of dividend proposed by the Board of Directors for the current year.]	**Add back** to Balance of P & L A/c to find out **Net Profit Before Tax** **Reason:** It is merely a book entry and does not involve any Cash outflow.	
Interim Dividend Board of [An Interim Dividend is that dividend which is declared by the Directors for the current year during the current year.]	**Add back** to Balance of P & L A/c to find out **Net Profit Before Tax** **Reason:** It represents an appropriation out of Current Year's Profits.	
Dividend on Pref. Shares	**Add back** to Balance of P & L A/c to find out **Net Profit Before Tax** **Reason:** It represents an appropriation out of Current year's profits.	If the date of Fresh issue / Redemption of Pref. Shares is not given, Calculate Dividend on opening balance of Pref. Shares.

TREATMENT OF SPECIAL ITEMS WHILE CALCULATING CASH FROM OPERATING ACTIVITIES

Item	***Treatment and Reason***	***Remarks***
Depreciation for the Current year	**Add back** to Current year's profits in order to find out Cash from Operating Activities. **Reason:** It does not involve any Cash outflow.	In case of Missing Figure,Prepare Fixed Asset A/c (on WDV Basis) OR Provision for Depreciation A/c to ascertain the amount of Depreciation.
Loss on Sale of Fixed Asset / Investments	**Add back** to Current year's profits in order to find out Cash from Operating Activities. **Reason:** It does not represent an operating cost.	In case of Missing Figure, Prepare Fixed Asset A/c / Investments A/c to ascertain the amount of Loss on Sale.
1. Profit on Sale of Fixed Assets/ Investments **2. Income from Investments (whether Current *or* Non-Current)**	**Subtract** from Current year's profits in order to find out Cash from Operating Activities. **Reason:** It does not represent an operating income.	In case of Missing Figure, Prepare Fixed Asset A/c´Investments A/c to ascertain the amount of Profit on Sale.
Goodwill/Patents Amortized	**Add back** to Current year's profits in order to find out Cash from Operating Activities. **Reason:** It merely represents a book entry and does not involve any Cash flow.	
Preliminary Expenses/ Discount on issue of Debentures written off	**Add back** to Current year's profits in order to find out Cash from Operating Activities. **Reason:** It merely represents a book entry and does not involve any Cash flow.	

Interest on Debentures/ Loans (whether disclosed as Current *or* Non-Current)	**Add back** to Current year's profits in order to find out Cash from Operating Activities. **Reason:** It does not represent an operating cost.	If the date of Fresh issue/ Redemption of Debentures is not given, Calculate Interest on opening balance of Debentures.
Premium on Redemption of Debentures/ Pref. Shares	**Add back** to Current year's profits in order to find out Cash from Operating Activities. **Reason:** It does not represent an operating cost.	
Increase in Provision for Doubtful Debts	**Add like** an Increase in Current Liability	
Decrease in Provision for Doubtful Debts	**Subtract like** a Decrease in Current Liability	
Increase in Inventories, Trade Receivables/ Payables against issue of Shares/Debentures	Exclude from Respective Closing Balances **Reason:** These do not involve any cash flow.	

ILLUSTRATION 13

From the following particulars, Calculate the Net Cash Flow from Operating Activities:

Particulars	*Closing* ₹	*Opening* ₹
Profit and Loss A/c	7,000	1,000
General Reserve	15,000	10,000
Proposed Dividend	25,000	21,000
Provision for Taxation	25,000	15,000
10% Debentures	25,000	21,000
Trade Payables	1,17,500	8,500
Machinery	44,000	50,000
Goodwill	8,000	10,000
Discount on issue of Debentures	—	200
Current Investments	8,000	3,000
Inventories	24,500	6,000
Trade Receivables	1,12,300	7,300
Cash & Cash Equivalents	17,700	0

Income tax paid during the year ₹ 20,000

SOLUTION

CALCULATION OF NET CASH FLOW FROM OPERATING ACTIVITIES

Particulars	₹	₹
Net Profit before Tax		66,000

Adjustments for Non-Cash and Non-Operating Items :		
Depreciation	6,000	
Discount on issue of Debentures	200	
Goodwill Amortised	2,000	
Interest on Debentures [₹ 21,000 × 10/110]	2,100	10,300
Operating Profit before Working Capital Changes		76,300
Changes in Current Assets & Current Liabilities:		
Increase in Trade Payables	1,09,000	
Increase in Inventories	(18,500)	
Increase in Trade Receivables	(1,05,000)	(14,500)
Cash generated from operations		61,800
Less: Income taxes paid		(20,000)
Net Cash Inflow from Operating Activities		41,800

Working Notes:

1. CALCULATION OF NET PROFIT BEFORE TAX

A. Closing balance as per Profit & Loss A/c:	7,000
Less: Opening Balance as per Profit & Loss A/c	1,000
Add: Proposed Dividend for current year	25,000
Add: Transfer to Reserve	5,000
Add: Provision for Tax for current year	30,000
B. Net Profit before Tax	66,000

2. *It has been assumed that new Debentures have been issued at the end of current accounting year*

Dr. **3. PROVISION FOR TAX ACCOUNT** *Cr.*

Particulars	₹	*Particulars*	₹
To Bank A/c	20,000	By Balance b/d	15,000
To Balance c/d	25,000	By P & L A/c (balancing figure)	30,000
	45,000		45,000

ILLUSTRATION 14

From the following particulars, Calculate the Net Cash Flow from Operating Activities:

Particulars	*Closing* ₹	*Opening* ₹
Profit & Loss A/c	7,000	1,000 (Dr)
General Reserve	10,000	15,000
Proposed Dividend	25,000	21,000
Provision for Taxation	25,000	15,000
15% Debentures	34,000	22,000

Trade Payables	22,000	24,000
Fixed Assets (Gross)	74,000	74,000
Accumulated Depreciation	30,000	24,000
10% Current Investments	20,000	10,000
Trade Receivables (Gross)	48,400	15,000
Provision for Doubtful Debts	10,000	5,000
Inventories	15,000	25,000
Cash & Cash Equivalents	5,600	1,000

Income tax provided during the year ₹ 30,000

SOLUTION

CALCULATION OF NET CASH FLOW FROM OPERATING ACTIVITIES

Particulars	₹	₹
Net Profit before Tax		58,000
Adjustments for Non-Cash and Non-Operating Items :		
Depreciation [₹ 30,000 – ₹ 24,000]		6,000
Interest on Debentures [₹ 22,000 × 15/100]		3,300
Interest Income on Current Investments		(1,000)
Operating Profit before Working Capital Changes		53,800
Changes in Current Assets & in Current Liabilities:		
Decrease in Inventories	10,000	
Increase in Trade Receivables (Gross)	(33,400)	
Increase in Provision for Doubtful Debts	5,000	
Decrease in Trade Payables	(2,000)	(20,400)
Cash generated from operations before tax		33,400
Less: Income taxes paid		(20,000)
Net Cash Inflow from Operating Activities		13,400

Working Notes:

1. CALCULATION OF NET PROFIT BEFORE TAX

Particulars	₹
A. Closing Balance as per Profit & Loss A/c	7,000
Add: Opening Balance as per Profit & Loss A/c(Dr)	1,000
Add: Proposed dividend	25,000
Less: Transfer to Reserve	(5,000)
Add: Provision for Tax	30,000
B. Net Profit before Tax	58,000

Dr. **2. PROVISION FOR TAX ACCOUNT** *Cr.*

Particulars	₹	*Particulars*	₹
To Bank A/c (balancing figure)	20,000	By Balance b/d	15,000
To Balance c/d	25,000	By P & L A/c	30,000
	45,000		45,000

3. *It has been assumed that new Debentures have been issued at the end of current accounting year.*
4. *It has been assumed that new Current Investments have been acquired at the end of current accounting year.*

ILLUSTRATION 15

From the following information, calculate the Net Cash Flow from Operating Activities:

Particulars	*Closing* ₹	*Opening* ₹
Equity Share Capital	4,00,000	3,00,000
15% Preference Share Capital	1,00,000	1,50,000
General Reserve	70,000	40,000
Profit and Loss A/c	48,000	30,000
Proposed Dividend	50,000	42,000
Provision for Tax	50,000	40,000
Trade Payables	1,22,000	88,000
Tangible Fixed Assets	3,70,000	2,80,000
Intangible Assets [Goodwill]	90,000	1,15,000
Trade Receivables & Inventories	3,39,000	2,57,000

During the year a machine costing ₹ 50,000 (depreciation provided thereon ₹ 30,000) was sold for ₹ 10,000. A machine was purchased for ₹ 1,30,000. Interim Dividend paid, ₹ 20,000, Income-tax, ₹ 35,000 paid.

SOLUTION

CALCULATION OF NET CASH FLOW FROM OPERATING ACTIVITIES

Particulars	₹	₹
I. Cash Flow from Operating Activities		
A. Net Profit before tax		1,63,000
B. *Adjustments for Non-Cash and Non-Operating Items :*		
Depreciation	20,000	
Loss on Sale of Machinery	10,000	
Goodwill amortised	25,000	55,000
C. Operating Profit before Working Capital Changes		2,18,000
D. Changes in Current Assets & Current Liabilities:		
Increase in Trade Payables	34,000	

	Increase in Trade Receivables & Inventories	(82,000)	(48,000)
E.	Net Cash Flow from Operating Activities before Tax		1,70,000
F.	*Less:* Tax paid		(35,000)
G.	**Net Cash Inflow from Operating Activities after Tax**		1,35,000

Working Notes:

1. CALCULATION OF NET PROFIT BEFORE TAX

Particulars	₹
Closing Balance of P&L A/c	48,000
Less: Opening Balance of P&L A/c	(30,000)
Add: Transfer to Reserve	30,000
Add: Proposed Dividend	50,000
Add: Interim Dividend on Equity Shares	20,000
Add: Tax	45,000
Net Profit before Tax	1,63,000

Dr. **2. FIXED ASSETS ACCOUNT** *Cr.*

Particulars	₹	*Particulars*	₹
To Balance b/d	2,80,000	By Depreciation A/c (b.f.)	20,000
To Bank A/c (Purchases)	1,30,000	By Bank A/c (Sale)	10,000
		By P&L A/c (Loss) [₹20,000 - ₹10,000]	10,000
		By Balance c/d	3,70,000
	4,10,000		4,10,000

Dr. **3. PROVISION FOR TAX ACCOUNT** *Cr.*

Particulars	₹	*Particulars*	₹
To Bank A/c	35,000	By Balance b/d	40,000
To Balance c/d	50,000	By P & L A/c (balancing figure)	45,000
	85,000		85,000

ILLUSTRATION 16

From the following information, calculate the Net Cash Flow from Operating Activities:

Particulars	*Closing* ₹	*Opening* ₹
Equity Share Capital	5,50,000	4,50,000
5% Preference Share Capital	2,00,000	3,00,000
General Reserve	1,50,000	1,20,000
Profit and Loss A/c	1,50,000	(1,40,000)
Securities Premium	10,000	—

Provision for Tax	50,000	40,000
Non-Current Liabilities [8% Debentures]	2,60,000	1,50,000
Short-term Borrowings (8% Bank Loan)	40,000	50,000
Trade Payables	1,05,000	1,00,000
Tangible Fixed Assets	8,60,000	6,20,000
Intangible Assets [Goodwill]	15,000	20,000
Trade Receivables & Inventories	3,95,000	3,00,000
Other Non-Current Assets [Preliminary Exp.]	—	20,000

During the year a machinery costing ₹ 60,000 on which depreciation charged was ₹ 20,000 was sold for ₹ 20,000. Depreciation provided on Fixed Assets ₹ 60,000. Additional Debentures were issued at par on 1st October and Bank Loan was repaid on the same date. Dividend on equity shares @ 8% was paid on opening balance.Income Tax ₹ 45,000 has been provided during the year. Preference Shares were redeemed at a premium of 5% at the end of the year.

SOLUTION

CALCULATION OF NET CASH FLOW FROM OPERATING ACTIVITIES

Particulars	₹	₹
Net Profit before tax		4,16,000
Adjustment for Non-Cash and Non-Operating Items :		
Depreciation on Fixed Assets	60,000	
Loss on Sale of Machinery	20,000	
Interest on Debentures [(₹ 1,50,000 × 8/100) + (₹ 1,10,000 × 8/100 × 6/12)]	16,400	
Interest on Bank Loan [(₹ 50,000 × 8/100 × 6/12) + (₹ 40,000 × 8/100 × 6/12)	3,600	
Goodwill Amortised	5,000	
Preliminary Expenses Written off	20,000	
Premium on Redemption of Preference Shares	5,000	1,30,000
Operating Profit before Working Capital Changes		5,46,000
Changes in Current Assets & Current Liabilities:		
Increase in Trade Receivables & Inventories	(95,000)	
Increase in Trade Payables	5,000	(90,000)
Net Cash Flow from Operating Activities before Tax		4,56,000
Less: **Tax paid**		(35,000)
Net Cash Inflow from Operating Activities after Tax		4,21,000

Working Notes:

1. CALCULATION OF NET PROFIT BEFORE TAX

Particulars	₹
Closing Balance of P&L A/c	1,50,000
Add: Opening Balance of P&L A/c (Debit)	1,40,000
Add: Provision for tax	45,000

Add: Transfer to Reserve	30,000
Add: Dividend on Equity Shares	36,000
Add: Dividend on Preference Shares	15,000
Net Profit before Tax	4,16,000

Dr. **2. FIXED ASSETS ACCOUNT** Cr

Particulars	₹	*Particulars*	₹
To Balance b/d	6,20,000	By Depreciation A/c	60,000
To Bank A/c (Purchases) (b.f.)	3,40,000	By Bank A/c (Sale)	20,000
		By P&L A/c (Loss)	20,000
		By Balance c/d	8,60,000
	9,60,000		9,60,000

Dr. **3. PROVISION FOR TAX ACCOUNT** Cr

Particulars	₹	*Particulars*	₹
To Bank A/c (balancing figure)	35,000	By Balance b/d	40,000
To Balance c/d	50,000	By P & L A/c	45,000
	85,000		85,000

ILLUSTRATION 17

From the following information calculate Cash Flow from Operating Activities:

Particulars	*Closing* ₹	*Opening* ₹
Trade Payables	1,65,000	40,000
Intangible Assets [Goodwill]	21,000	10,000
Inventories	1,69,000	54,000
Trade Receivables	3,76,000	4,06,000

During the year, the business of Y Ltd. was purchased for ₹60,000 payable in fully paid equity shares of ₹10 each at 20% premium. The assets included Inventories ₹15,000. Trade Receivables ₹10,000 and machine ₹30,000. Trade Payables of ₹15,000 were also taken over. Net Profit before tax for the year was ₹ 7,98,000. Tax paid during the year ₹ 10,000.

SOLUTION

CALCULATION OF CASH FLOW FROM OPERATING ACTIVITIES

Particulars		₹
A. Net Profit before tax		7,98,000
B. *Add:* Goodwill amortised		9,000
C. Operating Profit before Working Capital Changes		8,07,000
D. Changes in Current Assets & Current Liabilities:		
Increase in Inventories [(1,69,000 – 15,000) – 54,000]	(1,00,000)	
Decrease in Trade Receivables [(3,76,000 – 10,000) – 4,06,000]	40,000	

	Increase in Trade Payables [(1,65,000 – 15,000) – 40,000]	1,10,000	50,000
E.	Net Cash Flow from Operating Activities before Tax		8,57,000
F.	*Less:* Tax paid		(10,000)
G.	Net Cash Inflow From Operating Activities After Tax		8,47,000

Note: Goodwill Amortised

= Goodwill Purchased + Opening Goodwill – Closing Goodwill

= [₹ 60,000 – (₹ 15,000 + ₹ 10,000 + ₹ 30,000 – ₹ 15,000] + ₹ 10,000 – ₹ 21,000 = ₹ 9,000

13.0 HOW TO COMPUTE CASH FLOW FROM INVESTING ACTIVITIES

TREATMENT OF SPECIAL ITEMS WHILE COMPUTING CASH FLOW FROM INVESTING ACTIVITIES

Item	Treatment	Reason
1. Sale of Fixed Assets *or* Investments*	CashInflow from Investing Activities.	It involves Cash Inflow.
2. Purchase of Fixed Assets *or* Investments*	Cash Outlow in Investing Activities.	It involves Cash Outflow.
3. Interest *or* Dividend on Investments* *or* Rent from Property	Cash Inflow from Investing Activities.	It represents the receipt of Non-Operating Income. **Note:** If the date of Fresh Purchase /Sale of Investments is not given, Calculate Interest on Opening Bal. of Investments.
4. Increase in Accrued Interest on Investments*	**Subtract** from the Total Interest on Investments to ascertain the Net Amount of interest received.	It represents the amount of Interest not yet received.

**whether Current or Non-Current*

CALCULATION OF CASH FLOW FROM INVESTING ACTIVITIES

Particulars	₹
A. Cash Inflow from Investing Activities:	
Sale of Tangible Fixed Assets (e.g. Machinery) for cash	xxx
Sale of Intangible Assets (e.g. Goodwill/Patents/Trademark/Copyright) for cash	xxx
Sale of Investments(whether Current *or* Non-Current) for cash	xxx
Loans & Advances repayments received (whether Short term *or* Long term)	xxx
Incomes from Investments (whether Current *or* Non-Current)(***For Example***)	xxx
Dividend received on Shares held as Investments	xxx
Interest received on Debentures held as Investments	xxx
Rent received from Immovable Property held as Investments	xxx
	xxx
B. Cash used in Investing Activities:	
Purchase of Tangible Fixed Assets (e.g. Machinery) for cash	(xxx)

	Purchase of Intangible Assets (e.g. Goodwill/Patents/Trademark/Copyright) for cash	(xxx)
	Purchase of Investments(whether Current *or* Non-Current) for cash	(xxx)
	Loans & Advances granted (whether Short term *or* Long term)	(xxx)
		(xxx)
C.	**Net Cash Inflow from Investing Activities [if A > B]**	xxx
	or	***or***
	Net Cash used in Investing Activities [If A < B]	(xxx)

ILLUSTRATION 18

From the following particulars, Calculate Net Cash Flow from Investing Activities:

Particulars	*Closing* ₹	*Opening* ₹
Goodwill	90,000	1,10,000
Patents	1,15,000	90,000
Land	90,000	1,00,000
Plant & Machinery (Net)	1,60,000	1,80,000
Furniture (Gross)	4,25,000	2,00,000
Provision for Depreciation on Furniture	42,500	20,000
10% Non-Current Investments	1,10,000	1,50,000
10% Current Investments	60,000	50,000

SOLUTION

CALCULATION OF NET CASH FLOW FROM INVESTING ACTIVITIES

Particulars	₹
Purchase of Patents [₹ 1,15,000 – ₹ 90,000]	(25,000)
Sale of Land [₹ 1,00,000 – ₹ 90,000]	10,000
Purchase of Furniture [₹ 4,25,000 – ₹ 2,00,000]	(2,25,000)
Sale of Non-Current Investments [₹ 1,50,000 – ₹ 1,10,000]	40,000
Purchase of Current Investments [₹ 60,000 – ₹ 50,000]	(10,000)
Interest on 10% Non-Current Investments [₹ 1,50,000 × 10/100]	15,000
Interest on 10% Current Investments [₹ 50,000 × 10/100]	5,000
Net Cash used in Investing Activities	(1,90,000)

Notes

1. *It has been assumed that Investments have been sold & purchased at the end of current accounting year.*
2. *Decrease in Goodwill represents Goodwill Amortised.*
3. *Decrease in Plant & Machinery (Net) represents Depreciation.*

HOW TO ASCERTAIN MISSING FIGURES (E.G. SALES, PURCHASES AND PROFIT/LOSS ON SALE) RELATED TO INVESTMENTS

To ascertain Missing Figures (e.g. Sales, Purchases and Profit/Loss on Sale) related to Investments, prepare Investments Account as follows:

Dr. **INVESTMENTS ACCOUNT** *Cr.*

Particulars	₹	*Particulars*	₹
To Balance b/d	....	By Bank A/c (Sale Proceeds)	....
To Bank A/c (Purchases)	....	By P&L A/c (Loss on Sale)	....
To P&L (Profit)	....	By Balance c/d	....
	....		....

ILLUSTRATION 19

Particulars	*Closing* ₹	*Opening* ₹
10% Non-Current Investments	1,60,000	60,000
10% Current Investments	60,000	20,000

At the end of the year Some Non-Current Investments costing ₹ 40,000 were sold at a loss of 1/3rd on sale and Some Current Investments costing ₹ 20,000 were sold at a profit of 25%. Net Profit before Tax ₹ 1,00,000. How will you disclose these items while preparing Cash Flow Statement as per AS–3 issued by ICAI?

SOLUTION

Dr. **1. NON-CURRENT INVESTMENTS ACCOUNT** *Cr.*

Particulars	₹	*Particulars*	₹
To Balance b/d	60,000	By Bank A/c [₹ 40,000 – ₹ 10,000]	30,000
To Bank A/c (Purchases) (b.f.)	1,40,000	By P&L A/c (Loss)	10,000
		By Balance c/d	1,60,000
	2,00,000		2,00,000

Dr. **2. CURRENT INVESTMENTS ACCOUNT** *Cr.*

Particulars	₹	*Particulars*	₹
To Balance b/d	20,000,	By Bank A/c	25,000
To Bank A/c (Purchase)	60,000	By Balance c/d	60,000
To P&L A/c (Profit) [25% of ₹ 20,000]	5,000		
	85,000		85,000

CASH FLOW STATEMENT FOR THE YEAR ENDED ...

A	**Cash Flow from Operating Activities**	₹
	Net Profit before Tax	1,00,000

	Add: Loss on Sale of Non-Current Investments	10,000
	Less: Profit on Sale of Current Investments	5,000
	Less: Interest Income on Non-Current Investments	6,000
	Less: Interest Income on Current Investments	2,000
	Operating Profit before Working Capital changes	87,000
B	**Cash Flow from Investing Activities**	
	Purchase of Non-Current Investments	(1,40,000)
	Purchase of Current Investments	(60,000)
	Interest Income on Non-Current Investments	6,000
	Interest Income on Current Investments	2,000
	Sale of Non-Current Investments	30,000
	Sale of Current Investments	25,000
	Cash used in Investing Activities	(1,37,000

ILLUSTRATION 20

Particulars	*Closing* ₹	*Opening* ₹
10% Non-Current Investments	1,60,000	60,000
10% Current Investments	60,000	20,000

At the end of the year Some Non-Current Investments costing ₹ 40,000 were sold at a loss of 1/3rd on sale and Some Current Investments costing ₹ 20,000 were sold at a profit of 25%. Profit / Loss on Investments was adjusted against the Capital Reserve. Net Profit before Tax ₹ 1,00,000. How will you disclose these items while preparing Cash Flow Statement as per AS–3 issued by ICAI?

SOLUTION

Dr. **1. NON-CURRENT INVESTMENTS ACCOUNT** *Cr.*

Particulars	₹	*Particulars*	₹
To Balance b/d	60,000	By Bank A/c [₹ 40,000 – ₹ 10,000]	30,000
To Bank A/c (Purchases) (b.f.)	1,40,000	By Capital Reserve A/c (Loss)	10,000
		By Balance c/d	1,60,000
	2,00,000		2,00,000

Dr. **2. CURRENT INVESTMENTS ACCOUNT** *Cr.*

Particulars	₹	*Particulars*	₹
To Balance b/d	20,000,	By Bank A/c	25,000
To Bank A/c (Purchase)	60,000	By Balance c/d	60,000
To Capital Reserve A/c (Profit) [25% of ₹ 20,000]	5,000		
	85,000		85,000

CASH FLOW STATEMENT OF TULSIAN LTD FOR THE YEAR ENDED .....

A	**Cash Flow from Operating Activities**	₹
	Net Profit before Tax	1,00,000
	Less: Interest Income on Non-Current Investments	6,000
	Less: Interest Income on Current Investments	2,000
	Operating Profit before Working Capital changes	92,000
B	**Cash Flow from Investing Activities**	
	Purchase of Non-Current Investments	(1,40,000)
	Purchase of Current Investments	(60,000)
	Interest Income on Non-Current Investments	6,000
	Interest Income on Current Investments	2,000
	Sale of Non-Current Investments	30,000
	Sale of Current Investments	25,000
	Cash used in Investing Activities	(1,37,000)

HOW TO ASCERTAIN MISSING FIGURES (E.G. SALES, PURCHASES AND PROFIT/LOSS ON SALE) RELATED TO DEPRECIABLE FIXED ASSETS

To ascertain Missing Figures (e.g. Sales, Purchases and Profit/Loss on Sale) related to Depreciable Fixed Assets, prepare Fixed Assets Account as follows:

Dr. **FIXED ASSETS ACCOUNT** *Cr.*

Particulars	₹	*Particulars*	₹
To Balance b/d	....	By Depreciation A/c	....
To Bank A/c (Purchases)	....	By Bank A/c (Sale)	....
To Profit & Loss A/c (Profit)	....	By P&L A/c (loss)	....
To Equity Share Capital A/c (Purch.)	....	By Balance c/d	....
	....		....

ILLUSTRATION 21

Tangible Fixed Assets (Net): Closing ₹ 8,60,000, Opening ₹ 6,20,000. During the year a machine costing ₹ 60,000 (depreciation provided thereon ₹ 20,000) was sold at a loss of ₹ 10,000. Depreciation charged was ₹ 60,000. Net Profit before Tax ₹ 1,00,000. How will you disclose these items while preparing Cash Flow Statement as per AS–3 issued by ICAI?

SOLUTION

Dr. **FIXED ASSETS ACCOUNT** Cr.

Particulars	₹	*Particulars*	₹
To Balance b/d	6,20,000	By Depreciation A/c	60,000
To Bank A/c (Purchases) (b.f.)	3,40,000	By Bank A/c (Sale)	30,000
		By P&L A/c (Loss)	10,000
		By Balance c/d	8,60,000
	9,60,000		9,60,000

CASH FLOW STATEMENT FOR THE YEAR ENDED ...

		₹
A	**Cash Flow from Operating Activities**	
	Net Profit before Tax	1,00,000
	Add: Depreciation	60,000
	Add: Loss on Sale	10,000
	Operating Profit before Working Capital changes	1,70,000
B	**Cash Flow from Investing Activities**	
	Purchase of Machinery	(3,40,000)
	Sale of Machinery	30,000
	Cash used in Investing Activities	(3,10,000

ILLUSTRATION 22

Tangible Fixed Assets (Net): Closing ₹ 12,70,000, Opening ₹ 10,20,000. During the year a machine costing ₹ 1,40,000 (depreciation provided thereon ₹ 60,000) was sold for ₹ 50,000. Depreciation charged was ₹ 1,40,000. A machine costing ₹ 30,000 was purchased by issue of Equity Shares of ₹ 10 each at a premium of 20%.Net Profit before Tax ₹ 1,00,000. How will you disclose these items while preparing Cash Flow Statement as per AS–3 issued by ICAI?

SOLUTION

Dr. **FIXED ASSETS ACCOUNT** Cr.

Particulars	₹	*Particulars*	₹
To Balance b/d	10,20,000	By Bank A/c (Sale)	50,000
To Bank A/c (Purchases) (b.f.)	4,40,000	By P&L A/c (Loss on Sale)	30,000
To Equity Share Capital A/c	25,000	By Depreciation A/c	1,40,000
To Securities Premium	5,000	By Balance c/d	12,70,000
	14,90,000		14,90,000

CASH FLOW STATEMENT FOR THE YEAR ENDED ...

		₹
A	**Cash Flow from Operating Activities**	
	Net Profit before Tax	1,00,000
	Add: Depreciation	1,40,000
	Add: Loss on Sale	30,000
	Operating Profit before Working Capital changes	2,70,000
B	**Cash Flow from Investing Activities**	
	Purchase of Machinery	(4,40,000)
	Sale of Machinery	50,000
	Cash used in Investing Activities	(3,90,000

HOW TO ASCERTAIN MISSING FIGURES (E.G. SALES, PURCHASES AND PROFIT/LOSS ON SALE) RELATED TO DEPRECIABLE FIXED ASSETS WHEN PROVISION FOR DEPRECIATION ACCOUNT IS MAINTAINED.

To ascertain Missing Figures (e.g. Sales, Purchases and Profit/Loss on Sale) related to Depreciable Fixed Assets when Provision for Depreciation Account is maintained, prepare the following three accounts as follows:

Dr. **1. FIXED ASSETS ACCOUNT (AT COST)** *Cr.*

Particulars	₹	*Particulars*	₹
To Balance b/d	....	By Machinery Disposal A/c	....
To Bank A/c (Purchases)	....	[T/f of Cost of Machine sold]	
To Equity Share Capital A/c (Purch.)	....	By Balance c/d	....
	....		....

Dr. **2. PROVISION FOR DEPRECIATION ACCOUNT** *Cr.*

Particulars	₹	*Particulars*	₹
To Machinery Disposal A/c	....	By Balance b/d	....
[T/f of Acc. Dep. on Machine sold]		By P&L A/c	
		(Dep. Provided during the	
To Balance c/d	....	current year)	....
	....		....

Dr. **3. MACHINERY DISPOSAL ACCOUNT** *Cr.*

Particulars	₹	*Particulars*	₹
To Plant & Machinery A/c (Cost)	....	By Provision for Depreciation A/c	....
To Profit & Loss A/c (Profit)	....	By Bank A/c (Sale proceeds)	....
		By Profit & Loss A/c (Loss on sale)	....
	....		....

ILLUSTRATION 23

Particulars	Closing (₹)	Opening (₹)
Tangible Fixed Assets	16,20,000	13,20,000
Accumulated Depreciation	3,80,000	3,00,000

During the year a machine having book value of ₹ 80,000 (depreciation provided thereon ₹ 60,000) was sold at a loss of ₹ 30,000. Net Profit before Tax ₹ 1,00,000. How will you disclose these items while preparing Cash Flow Statement as per AS–3 issued by ICAI?

SOLUTION

Dr. **1. FIXED ASSETS ACCOUNT (AT COST)** *Cr.*

Particulars	₹	*Particulars*	₹
To Balance b/d	13,20,000	By Machinery Disposal A/c	1,40,000
To Bank A/c (Purchases)	4,40,000	By Balance c/d	16,20,000
	17,60,000		17,60,000

Dr. **2. PROVISION FOR DEPRECIATION ACCOUNT** Cr.

Particulars	₹	Particulars	₹
To Machinery Disposal A/c	60,000	By Balance b/d	3,00,000
To Bank c/d	3,80,000	By P&L A/c (Depreciation for current year) (Balancing figure)	1,40,000
	4,40,000		4,40,000

Dr. **3. MACHINERY DISPOSAL ACCOUNT** Cr.

Particulars	₹	Particulars	₹
To Fixed Assets A/c	1,40,000	By Provision for Depreciation A/c	60,000
		By Bank A/c (b.f.)	50,000
		By Profit and Loss A/c (Loss)	30,000
	1,40,000		1,40,000

CASH FLOW STATEMENT FOR THE YEAR ENDED ...

		₹
A	**Cash Flow from Operating Activities**	
	Net Profit before Tax	1,00,000
	Add: Depreciation	1,40,000
	Add: Loss on Sale	30,000
	Operating Profit before Working Capital changes	2,70,000
B	**Cash Flow from Investing Activities**	
	Purchase of Machinery	(4,40,000)
	Sale of Machinery	50,000
	Cash used in Investing Activities	(3,90,000

ILLUSTRATION 24

Particulars	*Closing* ₹	*Opening* ₹
Tangible Fixed Assets	16,50,000	13,20,000
Accumulated Depreciation	3,80,000	3,00,000

During the year a machine having book value of ₹ 80,000 (depreciation provided thereon ₹ 60,000) was sold at a loss of 37.5%. A machine costing ₹ 30,000 was purchased by issue of Equity Shares of ₹ 10 each at a premium of 20%. Net Profit before Tax ₹ 1,00,000. How will you disclose these items while preparing Cash Flow Statement as per AS–3 issued by ICAI?

SOLUTION

Dr. **1. FIXED ASSETS ACCOUNT (AT COST)** Cr.

Particulars	₹	Particulars	₹
To Balance b/d	13,20,000	By Machinery Disposal A/c	1,40,000
To Bank A/c (Purchases)	4,40,000	By Balance c/d	16,50,000

	₹		₹
To Equity Share Capital A/c	25,000		
To Securities Premium	5,000		
	17,90,000		17,90,000

Dr. **2. PROVISION FOR DEPRECIATION ACCOUNT** Cr.

Particulars	₹	*Particulars*	₹
To Machinery Disposal A/c	60,000	By Balance b/d	3,00,000
To Bank c/d	3,80,000	By P&L A/c (Depreciation for current year) (Balancing figure)	1,40,000
	4,40,000		4,40,000

Dr. **3. MACHINERY DISPOSAL ACCOUNT** Cr.

Particulars	₹	*Particulars*	₹
To Fixed Assets A/c	1,40,000	By Provision for Depreciation A/c	60,000
		By Bank A/c (b.f.)	50,000
		By Profit and Loss A/c (Loss)	30,000
	1,40,000		1,40,000

CASH FLOW STATEMENT FOR THE YEAR ENDED ...

		₹
A	**Cash Flow from Operating Activities**	
	Net Profit before Tax	1,00,000
	Add: Depreciation	1,40,000
	Add: Loss on Sale	30,000
	Operating Profit before Working Capital changes	2,70,000
B	**Cash Flow from Investing Activities**	
	Purchase of Machinery	(4,40,000)
	Sale of Machinery	50,000
	Cash used in Investing Activities	(3,90,000

ILLUSTRATION 25

Particulars	Closing ₹	Opening ₹
Tangible Fixed Assets	16,50,000	13,20,000
Accumulated Depreciation	3,80,000	3,00,000

During the year a machine costing ₹ 1,40,000 was sold at a loss of 37.5%. Depreciation of ₹ 1,40,000 was provided during the current year. A machine costing ₹ 30,000 was purchased by issue of Equity Shares of ₹ 10 each at a premium of 20%. Net Profit before Tax ₹ 1,00,000. How will you disclose these items while preparing Cash Flow Statement as per AS–3 issued by ICAI?

SOLUTION

Same as in case of Previous ILLUSTRATION.

ILLUSTRATION 26

From the following information, Calculate Net Cash Flow from Operating Activities and Investing Activities:

Particulars	Closing ₹	Opening ₹
Profit and Loss A/c	3,92,000	(1,08,000)
General Reserve	1,40,000	3,20,000
Proposed Dividend	1,50,000	1,20,000
Provision for Tax	40,000	20,000
Trade Payables	2,00,000	1,00,000
Tangible Fixed Assets (Net)	12,40,000	10,20,000
Intangible Assets [Goodwill]	1,000	10,000
10% Non-Current Investments	1,60,000	60,000
10% Current Investments	60,000	20,000
Trade Receivables & Inventories	5,20,000	4,60,000

During the year a machine costing ₹ 1,40,000 (depreciation provided thereon ₹ 60,000) was sold fo ₹ 50,000. Depreciation charged was ₹ 1,40,000. Tax paid was ₹ 10,000. At the end of the year some Non-Current Investments costing ₹ 40,000 were sold at a profit of 25%,

SOLUTION

CALCULATION OF NET CASH FLOW FROM OPERATING ACTIVITIES AND INVESTING ACTIVITIES

Particulars	₹	₹
I. Cash Flow from Operating Activities:		
A. Net Profit before tax		5,00,000
B. Adjustments for Non-Cash and Non-Operating Items :		
Depreciation	1,40,000	
Loss on Sale of Machinery	30,000	
Goodwill amortised	9,000	
Profit on Sale of Non-Current Investments	(10,000)	
Interest Income on Non-Current Investments	(6,000)	
Interest Income on Current Investments	(2,000)	1,61,000
C. Operating Profit before Working Capital Changes		6,61,000
D. Changes in Current Assets & Current Liabilities:		
Increase in Trade Payables	1,00,000	
Increase in Trade Receivables & Inventories	(60,000)	40,000
E. Net Cash Flow from Operating Activities before Tax		7,01,000
F. *Less:* Tax paid		(10,000)
G. Net Cash Inflow from Operating Activities after Tax		6,91,000
II. Cash Flow from Investing Activities:		
Sale of Machinery		50,000

Purchases of Fixed Assets		(4,40,000)
Purchases of Non-Current Investments		(1,40,000)
Purchases of Current Investments		(40,000)
Sale of Non-Current Investments		50,000
Interest received on Non-Current Investments		6,000
Interest received on Current Investments		2,000
Net Cash used in Investing Activities		(5,12,000)

Working Notes:

1. CALCULATION OF NET PROFIT BEFORE TAX

Particulars	₹
Closing Balance of P&L A/c	3,92,000
Add: Opening Balance of P&L A/c (Debit)	1,08,000
Less: Transfer from Reserve	(1,80,000)
Add: Proposed Dividend	1,50,000
Add: Tax	30,000
Net Profit before Tax	5,00,000

2. FIXED ASSETS ACCOUNT

Dr. Cr.

Particulars	₹	*Particulars*	₹
To Balance b/d	10,20,000	By Bank A/c (Sale)	50,000
To Bank A/c (Purchases) (b.f.)	4,40,000	By P&L A/c (Loss)	30,000
		By Depreciation A/c	1,40,000
		By Balance c/d	12,40,000
	14,60,000		14,60,000

3. NON-CURRENT INVESTMENTS ACCOUNT

Dr. Cr.

Particulars	₹	*Particulars*	₹
To Balance b/d	60,000	By Bank A/c [₹ 40,000 + ₹ 10,000]	50,000
To Bank A/c (Purchases) (b.f.)	1,40,000	By Balance c/d	1,60,000
To Profit and Loss A/c (Profit) [₹ 40,000 × 25/100]	10,000		
	2,10,000		2,10,000

4. PROVISION FOR TAX ACCOUNT

Dr. Cr.

Particulars	₹	*Particulars*	₹
To Bank A/c [Tax paid]	10,000	By Balance b/d	20,000
To Balance c/d	40,000	By Profit and Loss A/c (b.f.) [Provision made]	30,000
	50,000		50,000

14.0 HOW TO COMPUTE CASH FLOW FROM FINANCING ACTIVITIES

TREATMENT OF SPECIAL ITEMS WHILE CALCULATING CASH FROM FINANCING ACTIVITIES

Item	Treatment	Reason
1. Increase in Equity Share Capital/Pref. Share Capital/Debentures/ Loans*	Cash Inflow from Financing Activities.	It represents the issue of New Shares/Debentures.
2. Decrease in Equity Share Capital/ Pref. Share Capital/ Debentures/Loans*	Cash Outlow in Financing Activities.	It represents the buy-back of Equity Shares *or* Redemption of Pref. Share Capital/Debentures.
3. Increase in Securities Premium	Cash Inflow from Financing Activities.	It represents the issue of New Shares/Debentures at premium.
4. Increase in Discount on Issue of Debentures/ Shares	**Subtract** from the increase in amount of Share Capital/ Debentures to ascertain the Net amount of issue.	It represents the issue of New shares/Debentures at discount.
5. Increase in Underwriting Commission	Cash Outlow in Financing Activities.	It represents the payment of underwriting commission in raising Share Capital/ Debentures.
6. Interest on Debentures/ Loans*	Cash Outlow in Financing Activities.	It represents the payment of interest on Debentures. **Note:** *If the date of Fresh issue /Redemption of Debentures is not given, Calculate Interest on Opening Balance of Debentures.*
7. Increase in Unpaid Interest on Debentures/ Loans*	Subtract from the Total Interest on Debentures to ascertain the Net amount of Interest paid.	It represents the amount of Interest not yet paid.
8. Proposed Dividend for Previous Year [It represents the amount of dividend proposed by the Board of Directors for the Previous year.]	Cash Outlow in Financing Activities.	It represents the payment of Dividend.
9. Increase in Unclaimed Dividend	Subtract from the amount of Proposed Dividend for the previous year to ascertain the Net amount of dividend paid.	It represents the amount of Dividend not yet paid.
10. Interim Dividend [An Interim Dividend is that dividend which is declared by the Board of Directors for the current year during the current year.]	Cash Outlow in Financing Activities.	It represents the payment of Dividend.

11. Dividend on Pref. Shares	Cash Outlow in Financing Activities.	It represents the payment of Pref. Dividend. **Note:** *If the date of Fresh issue/ Redemption of Pref. Shares is not given, Calculate Dividend on Opening Balance of Pref. Share.*

**whether Short-term or Long-term*

CALCULATION OF NET CASH FLOW FROM FINANCING ACTIVITIES

Particulars	₹
A. Cash Inflows from Financing Activities:	
Issue of Equity Share Capital for cash [including Premium but excl. Discount]	xxx
Issue of Pref. Share Capital for cash [including Premium but excl. Discount]	xxx
Issue of Debentures for cash [including Premium but excl. Discount]	xxx
Loans raised (whether Short term *or* Long term)	xxx
	xxx
B. Cash used in Financing Activities:	
Buy back of Equity Shares [including Premium]	(xxx)
Redemption of Preference Shares for cash [including Premium]	(xxx)
Redemption of Debentures for cash [including Premium]	(xxx)
Repayment of Loans (whether Short term *or* Long term)	(xxx)
Interim Dividend paid on Equity Shares	(xxx)
Final Dividend paid on Equity Shares	(xxx)
Final Dividend paid on Preference Shares	(xxx)
Interest paid on Debentures & Loans (whether Short term *or* Long term)	(xxx)
	(xxx)
C. Net Cash Inflow from Financing Activities [If A > B]	xxx
or	***or***
Net Cash Flow used in Financing Activities [If A < B]	(xxx)

ILLUSTRATION 27

From the following particulars, Calculate Net Cash Flow from Financing Activities:

Particulars	*Closing* ₹	*Opening* ₹
Equity Share Capital	4,00,000	3,00,000
Pref. Share Capital	1,00,000	1,50,000
Securities Premium	15,000	5,000
Proposed Dividend on Equity. Shares	35,000	30,000
Proposed Dividend on Pref. Shares	15,000	15,000
10% Debentures	4,00,000	3,00,000

SOLUTION

CALCULATION OF NET CASH FLOW FROM FINANCING ACTIVITIES

Particulars	₹
Proceeds from Issue of Equity Share Capital [(₹ 4,00,000 – ₹ 3,00,000) + ₹ 10,000 Premium]	1,10,000
Proceeds from Issue of Debentures [₹ 4,00,000 – ₹ 3,00,000]	1,00,000
Redemption of Preference Shares [₹ 1,50,000 – ₹ 1,00,000]	(50,000)
Interest on Debentures paid [₹ 3,00,000 × 10/100]	(30,000)
Dividend on Equity. Shares	(30,000)
Dividend on Pref. Shares	(15,000)
Net Cash Inflow from Financing Activities	85,000

Notes

1. *It has been assumed that the new Debentures have been issued at par at the end of current accounting year.*
2. *It has been assumed that Preference Shares have been redeemed at the end of current accounting year.*

ILLUSTRATION 28

From the following particulars of BT Ltd., calculate Net Cash Flow from Financing Activities:

Particulars	*Closing* ₹	*Opening* ₹
Equity Share Capital	9,00,000	6,00,000
18% Pref. Share Capital	1,00,000	4,00,000
Securities Premium	1,30,000	1,00,000
14% Debentures	3,00,000	2,00,000

Additional Information: During the year Preference Dividend on preference shares and an Interim Dividend on equity shares @ 15% were paid on 30th Sept. New Shares and Debentures were issued on 1st Oct. Preference shares were redeemed at the end of the year at a premium of 5%. Such premium has been provided out of profits.

SOLUTION

CALCULATION OF NET CASH FLOW FROM FINANCING ACTIVITIES

Particulars	₹
Issue of Equity Share Capital [₹ 9,00,000 – ₹ 6,00,000 + ₹ 30,000 (Premium)]	3,30,000
Issue of Debentures [₹ 3,00,000 – ₹ 2,00,000]	1,00,000
Redemption of Preference Shares [₹ 3,00,000 + ₹ 15,000]	(3,15,000)
Interest paid on Debentures [(₹ 2,00,000 × 14/100) + ₹ 1,00,000 × 14/100 × 6/12)]	(35,000)
Interim Dividend paid on Equity Shares [₹ 6,00,000 × 15/100]	(90,000)
Dividend paid on Pref. Shares [₹ 4,00,000 × 18/100]	(72,000)
Net Cash used in Financing Activities	(82,000)

ILLUSTRATION 29

Particulars	*31.03.2016* ₹	*31.03.2015* ₹
14% Debentures	2,60,000	1,50,000
14% Short-term Bank Loan	40,000	50,000

New Debentures were issued on 01.01.2016 and Bank Loan was repaid on the same date. Unpaid Interest on Debentures on 31.03.2016 ₹ 10,000. Net Profit before Tax ₹ 1,00,000 How will you disclose these items while preparing Cash Flow Statement as per AS–3 issued by ICAI?

SOLUTION

CASH FLOW STATEMENT FOR THE YEAR ENDED 31ST MARCH, 2016

A	**Cash Flow from Operating Activities**	₹
	Net Profit before Tax	1,00,000
	Add: Interest on Debentures [(1,50,000 x 14%)+(1,10,000 x 14% x3/12]	24,850
	Add: Interest on Bank Loan [(50,000 x 14% x 9/12)+(40,000 x 14% x 3/12]	6,650
	Operating Profit before Working Capital changes	1,31,500
B	**Cash Flow from Financing activities**	
	Issue of Debentures	1,10,000
	Bank Loan repaid	(10,000)
	Interest on Debentures [24,850 – 10,000]	14,850
	Interest on Bank Loan	6,650
	Cash Flow from Financing activities	78,500

ILLUSTRATION 30

From the following information, Calculate Net Cash Flow from Operating Activities & Financing Activities:

Particulars	*31.03.2016* ₹	*31.03.2015* ₹
Equity Share Capital	5,50,000	4,50,000
5% Preference Share Capital	2,00,000	3,00,000
General Reserve	1,50,000	1,20,000
Profit and Loss A/c	1,50,000	(1,40,000)
Securities Premium	10,000	—
Provision for Tax	50,000	40,000
Non-Current Liabilities [8% Debentures]	2,60,000	1,50,000
Short-term Borrowings (8% Bank Loan)	40,000	50,000
Increase in Trade Payables	2,00,000	1,00,000
Increase in Trade Receivables & Inventories	5,20,000	4,60,000

Additional Information: During the year Additional Debentures were issued at par on 1st October, and Bank Loan was repaid on the same date. Dividend on equity shares @ 8% was paid on opening balance. Income Tax ₹ 45,000 has been provided during the year. Preference Shares were redeemed at a premium of 5% at the end of the year.

SOLUTION

CALCULATION OF CASH FLOW FROM OPERATING ACTIVITIES AND FINANCING ACTIVITIES

Particulars	₹	₹
I. Cash Flow from Operating Activities:		
Net Profit before tax		4,16,000
Adjustment for Non-Cash and Non-Operating Items :		
Interest on Debentures [(₹ 1,50,000 × 8/100) + (₹ 1,10,000 × 8/100 × 6/12)]		16,400
Interest on Bank Loan [(₹ 50,000 × 8/100 × 6/12) + (₹ 40,000 × 8/100 × 6/12)		3,600
Premium on Redemption of Preference Shares		5,000
Operating Profit before Working Capital Changes		4,41,000
Changes in Current Assets & Current Liabilities:		0
Increase in Trade Payables	1,00,000	
Increase in Trade Receivables & Inventories	(60,000)	40,000
Net Cash Flow from Operating Activities before Tax		4,81,000
Less: **Tax paid**		(35,000)
Net Cash Inflow from Operating Activities after Tax		4,46,000
II. Cash Flow from Financing Activities:		
Issue of Share Capital [₹ 1,00,000 + ₹ 10,000 (Premium)]		1,10,000
Issue of Debentures		1,10,000
Interest on Debentures		(16,400)
Interest on Bank Loan		(3,600)
Dividend on Equity Shares [₹4,50,000 × 8/100]		(36,000)
Dividend on Preference Shares [₹3,00,000 × 5/100]		(15,000)
Redemption of Preference Shares[₹ 1,00,000 + ₹ 5,000]		(1,05,000)
Bank Loan Repaid [₹ 50,000 + ₹ 40,000]		(10,000)
Net Cash from in Financing Activities		34,000

Working Notes:

1. CALCULATION OF NET PROFIT BEFORE TAX

Particulars	₹
Closing Balance of P&L A/c	1,50,000
Add: Opening Balance of P&L A/c (Debit)	1,40,000
Add: Provision for tax	45,000
Add: Transfer to Reserve	30,000
Add: Dividend on Equity Shares	36,000
Add: Dividend on Preference Shares	15,000
Net Profit before Tax	4,16,000

Dr. **2. PROVISION FOR TAX ACCOUNT** Cr.

Particulars	₹	Particulars	₹
To Bank A/c (balancing figure)	35,000	By Balance b/d	40,000
To Balance c/d	50,000	By P & L A/c	45,000
	85,000		85,000

15.0 PRACTICAL STEPS INVOLVED IN THE PREPARATION OF CASH FLOW STATEMENT

The various steps involved in the preparation of Cash Flow Statement are given below:

PRACTICAL STEPS INVOLVED IN THE PREPARATION OF CASH FLOW STATEMENT

Step 1: ***Calculate the Cash from Operating Activities.***

Step 2: ***Calculate the Cash Flow from Investing Activities.***

Step 3: ***Calculate the Cash Flow from Financing Activities.***

Step 4: ***Calculate the Net Increase (Decrease) in Cash and Cash Equivalents***

Step 4 = Step 1 + Step 2 + Step 3

Step 5: ***Calculate the Cash and Cash Equivalents at the Beginning of Period***

Step 6: ***Calculate the Cash and Cash Equivalents at the End of Period***

Step 6 = Step 4 + Step 5

IMPORTANT INSTRUCTIONS FOR WORKING NOTES

1. Net Profit before Tax	Calculate Net Profit before Tax *[Refer to Working Note No. 1 under Para 16.0].*
2. Fixed Assets Account	Prepare Fixed Assets Account to ascertain Missing Figures (e.g. Sales, Purchases and Profit/Loss on Sale) related to Depreciable Fixed Assets *[Refer to Working Note No. 2 under Para 16.0].*
3. Investments Account	Prepare Investments Account to ascertain Missing Figures (e.g. Sales, Purchases and Profit/Loss on Sale) related to Investments *[Refer to Working Note No. 3 under Para 16.0].*
4. Provision for Tax Account	Prepare Provision for Tax Account to ascertain Missing Figure (e.g. Tax provided *or* Tax paid) *[Refer to Working Note No. 4 under Para 16.0].*
5. Interest on Debentures/ Loans (whether Current *or* Non-Current)	Calculate Interest on Opening Balance of Debentures/Loan if the date of Fresh issue/Redemption of Debentures/Loan is not given.
6. Dividend on Pref.Shares	Calculate Dividend on Opening Balance of Pref. Shares if the date of Fresh issue /Redemption of Pref. Shares is not given.
7. Premium on Redemption of Pref. Share Capital/ Debentures	Calculate Premium on Redemption of Pref. Share Capital/ Debentures on Pref. Share Capital/Debentures redeemed during the year.
8. Interest on Investments (whether Current *or* Non-Current)	Calculate Interest at given % on Opening Balance of Investments if the date of Fresh Purchase/Sale of Investments is not given.

9. Proposed Dividend for Previous Year	Unless otherwise stated it is presumed that the 'Proposed Dividend for Previous Year' has been declared subsequently at the Annual General Meeting and has been paid during the current accounting period.
10. Provision for Tax for Previous Year	Unless otherwise stated, it presumed that the' Provision for Tax for Previous Year' has been paid subsequently during the current year.
11. Transactions which do not appear in CFS	1. Issue of Shares/Debentures on conversion of Debentures and 2. Purchase of an Asset against the issue of Shares/ Debentures **Reason:** These transactions do not involve any inflow/ outflow of cash.

PRECAUTIONS WHILE PREPARING CASH FLOW STATEMENT

1. *Check whether Current Year's Figures are given first or Previous Year's Figures are given first*
2. *Check whether Balance of Profit & Loss Account is Debit or Credit. If Balance of Profit & Loss Account is Debit, Add or Less very carefully.*
3. *Check whether Balance of General Reserve during current year has increased or decreased. If Balance of General Reserve during current year has decreased, Subtract Transfer from General Reserve from Closing Balance of Profit & Loss Account.*
4. *Check whether Interest % on Investments is given or not. If Interest % on Investments is given, Do not forget to make adjustment for Interest on Investments (whether Current or Non-Current) while computing Cash from Operating Activities and Investing Activities.*
5. *Do not forget to make adjustment for Interest on Borrowings (whether Short term or Long term) while computing Cash from Operating Activities and Financing Activities.*
6. *Exclude Increase in Inventories, Trade Receivables/ Payables against issue of Shares / Debentures from Respective Closing Balances. Reason: These do not involve any cash flow.*

16.0 FORMAT OF CASH FLOW STATEMENT

A Format of Cash Flow Statement is given below:

CASH FLOW STATEMENT OF M/S ....

for the year ended 31st March, ...

Particulars	₹	₹
I. Cash Flow from Operating Activities:		
A. *Net Profit before taxation, and extraordinary item*		xxx
B. *Adjustment for Non-Cash and Non-Operating Items:* ***(For Example)***		
Depreciation	xxx	
Interest on Debentures & Loans (whether Short term *or* Long term)	xxx	
Preliminary Expenses/Underwriting Commission/Discount on	xxx	
Issue of Debentures/Shares written of	xxx	
Goodwill/Patents/Trade Marks/Copyright amortised	xxx	

	Loss on Sale of Investments (whether Current *or* Non-Current)	xxx	
	Premium payable on redemption of Preference shares/Debentures		
	Profit on Sale of Investments (whether Current *or* Non-Current)	(xxx)	
	Income from Investments (whether Current *or* Non-Current)	(xxx)	xxx
C.	*Operating Profit before Working Capital Changes*		xxx
D.	*Changes in Current Assets (Excluding Cash and Cash Equivalents) & Current Liabilities: (Excluding Bank over Draft & Cash Credit) other than due to issue of Shares /Debentures*		
	Decrease in Inventories	xxx	
	Decrease in Trade Receivables	xxx	
	Decrease in Prepaid expenses	xxx	
	Decrease in Accrued Commission	xxx	
	Increase in Trade Payables	xxx	
	Increase in Outstanding expenses	xxx	
	Increase in Commission received in advance	xxx	
	Increase in Provision for Doubtful Debts *or* Discount on Debtors	xxx	
	Increase in Inventories	(xxx)	
	Increase in Trade Receivables	(xxx)	
	Increase in Prepaid Expenses	(xxx)	
	Increase in Accrued Commission	(xxx)	
	Decrease in Trade Payables	(xxx)	
	Decrease in Outstanding expenses	(xxx)	
	Decrease in Commission received in advance	(xxx)	
	Decrease in Provision for Doubtful Debts/Discount on Debtors	(xxx)	xxx
E.	*Net Cash Flow from Operating Activities before Tax*	xxx	
F.	*Less: Income taxes paid (Net of Refund)*	(xxx)	
G.	*Net Cash Flow from Operating Activities before extraordinary item*	xxx	
H.	*Extraordinary items*		xxx
I.	*Net Cash Flow from (used in) Operating Activities*		xxx
II.	**Cash Flow from Investing Activities:**		
	Sale of Machinery/Land & Building for cash		xxx
	Sale of Investments (whether Current *or* Non-Current) for cash		xxx
	Sale of Patents/Trademarks/Copyrights for cash		xxx
	Income received from Investments (whether Current *or* Non-Current)	xxx	
	Purchase of Machinery/Land & Building for cash		(xxx)
	Purchase of Investments (whether Current *or* Non-Current) for cash		(xxx)
	Purchase of Patents/Trademarks/Copyrights/Goodwill for cash		(xxx)
	Net Cash Flow from (used in) Investing Activities		xxx
III.	**Cash Flow from Financing Activities:**		

Issue of Share Capital for cash		xxx
Issue of Debentures for cash		xxx
Loans raised (whether Short term *or* Long term)		xxx
Redemption of Preference Shares/Buy - back of Equity shares		(xxx)
Redemption of Debentures for cash		(xxx)
Loans repaid (whether Short term *or* Long term)		(xxx)
Interest paid on Debentures/Loans(whether Short term *or* Long term)	(xxx)	
Interim Dividend paid (Excluding Unpaid/Unclaimed)		(xxx)
Final Dividend paid (Excluding Unpaid/Unclaimed)		(xxx)
Net Cash Flow from (used in) Financing Activities		xxx
IV. Net Increase (Decrease) in Cash and Cash Equivalents [I + II + III]	xxx	
V. Cash and Cash Equivalents at the Beginning of Period		
Cash in hand	xxx	
Cash at bank	xxx	
Cash Equivalents (Investments having maturity of 3 months *or* less)	xxx	xxx
VI. Cash and Cash Equivalents at End of Period [IV + V]		
Cash in hand	xxx	
Cash at bank	xxx	
Cash Equivalents (Investments having maturity of 3 months *or* less)	xxx	xxx

Working Notes:

1. CALCULATION OF NET PROFIT BEFORE TAX

Particulars	₹
Closing Balance of P&L A/c	xxx
Less: Opening Balance of P&L A/c(Cr.)[*Add:* Opening Balance of P&L A/c(Dr.)]	xxx
Add: Proposed Dividend for the current year.	xxx
Add: Interim Dividend paid during the Current year	xxx
Add: Transfer to Reserve [*Less:* Transfer from Reserve]	xxx
Add: Provision for Tax made during the Current Year	xxx
Less: Refund of Tax credited to P&L A/c	xxx
Net Profit before Tax	xxx

Dr. **2. FIXED ASSETS ACCOUNT** *Cr.*

Particulars	₹	*Particulars*	₹
To Balance b/d	....	By Bank A/c (Sale)	....
To Bank A/c (Purchases)	....	By P&L A/c (Loss)	....
To P & L A/c (Profit)		By Depreciation A/c	....
To Equity Share Capital A/c (Purch.)	....	By Balance c/d	....
	....		....

Dr. **3. INVESTMENTS ACCOUNT** Cr.

Particulars	₹	Particulars	₹
To Balance b/d	....	By Bank A/c (Sale Proceeds)	....
To Bank A/c (Purchases)	....	By P&L A/c (Loss on Sale)	....
To P&L (Profit)	....	By Balance c/d	....
	....		....

Dr. **4. PROVISION FOR TAX ACCOUNT** Cr.

Particulars	₹	Particulars	₹
To Bank A/c	....	By Balance b/d	....
To Balance c/d	....	By P & L A/c	....
	....		....

ILLUSTRATION 31

From the following information, prepare a Cash Flow Statement:

BALANCE SHEETS AS AT ...

Particulars	Note	31.03.2016 ₹	31.03.2015 ₹
I. EQUITY AND LIABILITIES			
(1) Shareholders' Funds			
(a) Share Capital	1	5,00,000	4,50,000
(b) Reserves and Surplus	2	1,28,000	70,000
(2) Non-Current Liabilities		–	–
(3) Current Liabilities			
Trade Payables		99,000	75,000
Other Current Liabilities (Bank Overdraft)		23,000	13,000
Short-term Provisions	3	1,00,000	82,000
Total		8,50,000	6,90,000
II. ASSETS			
(1) Non-Current Assets			
Tangible Fixed Assets		3,70,000	2,80,000
Intangible Assets [Goodwill]		90,000	1,15,000
(2) Current Assets			
Current Investments		10,000	15,000
Cash & Cash Equivalents		41,000	23,000
Other Current Assets		3,39,000	2,57,000
Total		8,50,000	6,90,000

Notes to Accounts:

Particulars	*31.03.2016* ₹	*31.03.2015* ₹
1. Share Capital		
Equity Share Capital	4,00,000	3,00,000
15% Preference Share Capital	1,00,000	1,50,000
	5,00,000	4,50,000
2. Reserves and Surplus		
General Reserve	70,000	40,000
Profit and Loss A/c	48,000	30,000
Securities Premium	10,000	–
	1,28,000	70,000
3. Short-Term Provisions		
Proposed Dividend	50,000	42,000
Provision for Tax	50,000	40,000
	1,00,000	82,000

Additional Informtion: A machine costing ₹ 50,000 (depreciation provided thereon ₹ 30,000) was sold for ₹ 10,000. Depreciation charged during the year was ₹ 20,000. Interim Dividend paid, ₹ 20,000 paid, Income-tax, ₹ 35,000 paid.

SOLUTION

CASH FLOW STATEMENT
for the year ended 31st March, 2016

Particulars	₹	₹
I. Cash Flow from Operating Activities		
A. Net Profit before tax		1,63,000
B. Adjustments for Non-Cash and Non-Operating Items :		
Depreciation	20,000	
Loss on Sale of Machinery	10,000	
Goodwill amortised	25,000	55,000
C. Operating Profit before Working Capital Changes		2,18,000
D. Changes in Current Assets & Current Liabilities:		
Increase in Trade Payables	24,000	
Increase in Other Current Assets	(82,000)	(58,000)
E. Net Cash Flow from Operating Activities before Tax		1,60,000
F. *Less:* Tax paid		(35,000)
G. Net Cash Inflow from Operating Activities after Tax		1,25,000
II. Cash Flow from Investing Activities:		
Sale of Machinery		10,000
Purchases of Fixed Assets		(1,30,000)

	Sale of Current Investments		5,000
	Net Cash used in Investing Activities		(1,15,000)
III.	**Cash Flow from Financing Activities:**		
	Issue of Share Capital [₹ 1,00,000 + ₹ 10,000]		1,10,000
	Interim Dividend paid on Equity Shares		(20,000)
	Final Dividend paid		(42,000)
	Redemption of Preference Shares		(50,000)
	Net Cash used in Financing Activities		(2,000)
IV.	**Net Increase in Cash and Cash Equivalents [I + II + III]**		8,000
V.	**Opening Cash and Cash Equivalents** [₹ 23,000 – ₹ 13,000]		10,000
VI.	**Closing Cash and Cash Equivalents** [₹ 41,000 – ₹ 23,000]		18,000

Working Notes:

1. CALCULATION OF NET PROFIT BEFORE TAX

Particulars	₹
Closing Balance of P&L A/c	48,000
Less: Opening Balance of P&L A/c	(30,000)
Add: Transfer to Reserve	30,000
Add: Proposed Dividend	50,000
Add: Interim Dividend on Equity Shares	20,000
Add: Tax	45,000
Net Profit before Tax	1,63,000

Dr. **2. FIXED ASSETS ACCOUNT** *Cr.*

Particulars	₹	*Particulars*	₹
To Balance b/d	2,80,000	By Depreciation A/c	20,000
To Bank A/c (Purchases) (b.f.)	**1,30,000**	By Bank A/c (Sale)	10,000
		By P&L A/c (Loss)	10,000
		By Balance c/d	3,70,000
	4,10,000		4,10,000

Dr. **3. PROVISION FOR TAX ACCOUNT** *Cr.*

Particulars	₹	*Particulars*	₹
To Bank A/c	35,000	By Balance b/d	40,000
To Balance c/d	50,000	By P & L A/c (balancing figure)	**45,000**
	85,000		85,000

ILLUSTRATION 32

From the following information, prepare a Cash Flow Statement:

BALANCE SHEETS AS AT ...

Particulars	*Note*	*31.03.2016* ₹	*31.03.2015* ₹
I. EQUITY AND LIABILITIES			
(1) Shareholders' Funds			
(a) Share Capital	1	7,50,000	7,50,000
(b) Reserves and Surplus	2	3,10,000	(20,000)
(2) Non-Current Liabilities [8% Debentures]		2,60,000	1,50,000
(3) Current Liabilities			
Short-term Borrowings (8% Bank Loan)		40,000	50,000
Trade Payables		1,05,000	1,00,000
Other Current Liabilities (Bank Overdraft)		15,000	10,000
Short term Provisions (Provision for tax)		50,000	40,000
Total		15,30,000	10,80,000
II. ASSETS			
(1) Non-Current Assets			
Tangible Fixed Assets		8,60,000	6,20,000
Intangible Assets [Goodwill]		15,000	20,000
Non-Current Investments		1,25,000	80,000
Other Non-Current Assets [Preliminary Exp.]		—	20,000
(2) Current Assets			
Current Investments		5,000	15,000
Cash & Cash Equivalents		1,30,000	25,000
Other Current Assets		3,95,000	3,00,000
Total		15,30,000	10,80,000

Notes to Accounts:

Particulars	*31.03.2016* ₹	*31.03.2015* ₹
1. Share Capital		
Equity Share Capital	5,50,000	4,50,000
5% Preference Share Capital	2,00,000	3,00,000
	7,50,000	7,50,000
2. Reserves and Surplus		
General Reserve	1,50,000	1,20,000
Profit and Loss A/c	1,50,000	(1,40,000)
Securities Premium	10,000	—
	3,10,000	(20,000)

Additional Information: A piece of machinery costing ₹ 60,000 on which depreciation charged was ₹ 20,000 was sold for ₹ 20,000. Depreciation provided on Fixed Assets ₹ 60,000. Preference Shares were redeemed at a premium of 5% at the end of the year. Additional Debentures were issued at par on 1st October, 2015 and Bank Loan was repaid on the same date. Dividend on equity shares @ 8% was paid on opening balance.Income Tax ₹ 45,000 has been provided during the year.

SOLUTION

CASH FLOW STATEMENT

for the year ended 31st March, 2016

Particulars	₹	₹
I. Cash Flow from Operating Activities:		
Net Profit before tax		4,16,000
Adjustment for Non-Cash and Non-Operating Items :		
Depreciation on Fixed Assets	60,000	
Loss on Sale of Machinery	20,000	
Interest on Debentures [(₹ 1,50,000 × 8/100) + (₹ 1,10,000 × 8/100 × 6/12)]	16,400	
Interest on Bank Loan [(₹ 50,000 × 8/100 × 6/12) + (₹ 40,000 × 8/100 × 6/12)	3,600	
Goodwill Amortised	5,000	
Preliminary Expenses Written off	20,000	
Premium on Redemption of Preference Shares	5,000	1,30,000
Operating Profit before Working Capital Changes		5,46,000
Changes in Current Assets & Current Liabilities:		
Increase in Other Current Assets	(95,000)	
Increase in Trade Payables	5,000	(90,000)
Net Cash Flow from Operating Activities before Tax		4,56,000
***Less:* Tax paid**		(35,000)
Net Cash Inflow from Operating Activities after Tax		4,21,000
II. Cash Flow from Investing Activities:		
Sale of Machinery		20,000
Purchase of Fixed Assets		(3,40,000)
Purchase of Non-Current Investments		(45,000)
Sale of Current Investments		10,000
Net Cash used in Investing Activities		(3,55,000)
III. Cash Flow from Financing Activities:		
Issue of Share Capital [₹ 1,00,000 + ₹ 10,000 (Premium)]		1,10,000
Issue of Debentures		1,10,000
Interest on Debentures		(16,400)
Interest on Bank Loan		(3,600)
Dividend on Equity Shares		(36,000)
Dividend on Preference Shares		(15,000)

Redemption of Preference Shares[₹ 1,00,000 + ₹ 5,000]		(1,05,000)
Bank Loan Repaid		(10,000)
Net Cash from in Financing Activities		34,000
IV. Net Increase Cash and Cash Equivalents [I + II + III]		1,00,000
V. Opening Cash and Cash Equivalents [₹ 25,000 – ₹ 10,000]		15,000
VI. Closing Cash and Cash Equivalents [₹ 1,30,000 – ₹ 15,000]		1,15,000

Working Notes:

1. CALCULATION OF NET PROFIT BEFORE TAX

Particulars	₹
Closing Balance of P&L A/c	1,50,000
Add: Opening Balance of P&L A/c (Debit)	1,40,000
Add: Provision for tax	45,000
Add: Transfer to Reserve	30,000
Add: Dividend on Equity Shares	36,000
Add: Dividend on Preference Shares	15,000
Net Profit before Tax	4,16,000

Dr. **2. FIXED ASSETS ACCOUNT** *Cr.*

Particulars	₹	*Particulars*	₹
To Balance b/d	6,20,000	By Depreciation A/c	60,000
To Bank A/c (Purchases) (b.f.)	3,40,000	By Bank A/c (Sale)	20,000
		By P&L A/c (Loss)	20,000
		By Balance c/d	8,60,000
	9,60,000		9,60,000

Dr. **3. PROVISION FOR TAX ACCOUNT** *Cr.*

Particulars	₹	*Particulars*	₹
To Bank A/c (balancing figure)	35,000	By Balance b/d	40,000
To Balance c/d	50,000	By P & L A/c	**45,000**
	85,000		85,000

ILLUSTRATION 33

From the following information, prepare a Cash Flow Statement:

BALANCE SHEETS AS AT ...

Particulars	*Note*	*31.03.2016* ₹	*31.03.2015* ₹
I. EQUITY AND LIABILITIES			
(1) Shareholders' Funds			
(a) Share Capital		12,50,000	10,00,000

(b) Reserves and Surplus	1	4,90,000	4,00,000
(2) Non-Current Liabilities [Loan]		4,00,000	5,00,000
(3) Current Liabilities			
Trade Payables		4,00,000	5,00,000
Short-term Provisions	2	1,85,000	1,50,000
Total		27,25,000	25,50,000
II. ASSETS			
(1) Non-Current Assets			
Tangible Fixed Assets	3	14,00,000	12,50,000
Non-Current Investments		50,000	1,00,000
(2) Current Assets			
Inventories		2,80,000	3,00,000
Trade Receivables		4,20,000	4,00,000
Cash & Cash Equivalents		5,75,000	5,00,000
Total		27,25,000	25,50,000

Notes to Accounts:

Particulars	*31.03.2016* ₹	*31.03.2015* ₹
1. Reserves and Surplus		
General Reserve	3,00,000	2,50,000
Profit and Loss A/c	1,80,000	1,50,000
Capital Reserve	10,000	—
	4,90,000	4,00,000
2. Short-Term Provisions		
Proposed Dividend	1,25,000	1,00,000
Provision for Tax	60,000	50,000
	1,85,000	1,50,000
3. Tangible Fixed Assets		
Land & Building	4,80,000	5,00,000
Machinery	9,20,000	7,50,000
	14,00,000	12,50,000

During the year the company purchased a machinery for ₹ 2,25,000. They paid ₹ 1,25,000 in cash and issued 10,000 equity shares of ₹ 10 each at par. The company sold some investments at a profit of ₹ 10,000, which was credited to Capital Reserve. Income-tax provided during the year ₹ 55,000.

SOLUTION

CASH FLOW STATEMENT FOR THE YEAR ENDING 31ST MARCH, 2016

Particulars	₹
I. Cash Flows from Operating Activities	
Net Profit made during the year	2,60,000

	Adjustment for depreciation on Machinery	55,000
	Adjustment for depreciation Land and Building	20,000
	Operating profits before change in Working Capital	3,35,000
	Decrease in Inventories	20,000
	Increase in Trade Receivables	(20,000)
	Decrease in Trade Payables	(1,00,000)
	Income Tax paid	(45,000)
	Net Cash from operating activities	1,90,000
II.	**Cash flows from Investing Activities**	
	Purchase on Machinery	(1,25,000)
	Sale of Investments	60,000
	Cash flows from Investing Activities	(65,000)
III.	**Cash flows from Financing Activities**	
	Issue of Equity Shares (2,50,000 – 1,00,000)	1,50,000
	Repayment of Long term Loan	(1,00,000)
	Dividend Paid	(1,00,000)
	Cash flows from Financing Activities	(50,000)
	Net Increase in cash and cash equivalent	75,000
	Cash and cash equivalents at the beginning of the period	5,00,000
	Cash and cash equivalents at the end of the period	5,75,000

Working Notes:

1. NET PROFIT BEFORE TAX

Particulars	₹
Increase in P & L A/c (Cr.) Balance	30,000
Add: Transfer to general reserve	50,000
Add: Provision for taxation made during the year	55,000
Add: Proposed Dividend during the year	1,25,000
	2,60,000

Dr. **2. MACHINERY ACCOUNT** *Cr.*

Particulars	₹	*Particulars*	₹
To Balance b/d	7,50,000	By Depreciation A/c (Bal. Fig.)	55,000
To Bank A/c	1,25,000	By Balance c/d	9,20,000
To Equity Share Capital A/c	1,00,000		
	9,75,000		9,75,000

Dr. **3. PROVISION FOR TAXATION ACCOUNT** *Cr.*

Particulars	₹	*Particulars*	₹
To Cash A/c (Bal. Fig.)	45,000	By Balance b/d	50,000

To Balance c/d	60,000	By P & L A/c	55,000
	1,05,000		1,05,000

Dr. **4. PROPOSED DIVIDEND ACCOUNT** Cr.

Particulars	₹	*Particulars*	₹
To Dividend Payable A/c	1,00,000	By Balance b/d	1,00,000
To Balance c/d	1,25,000	By P & L A/c (bal. fig.)	1,25,000
	2,25,000		2,25,000

Dr. **5. INVESTMENTS ACCOUNT** Cr.

Particulars	₹	*Particulars*	₹
To Balance b/d	1,00,000	By Bank A/c	60,000
To Capital Reserve A/c	10,000	(Bal. figure for investment sold)	
(Profit on sale of investment)		By Balance c/d	50,000
	1,10,000		1,10,000

ILLUSTRATION 34

From the following information, prepare a Cash Flow Statement of SRCC Ltd.:

BALANCE SHEETS AS AT ...

Particulars	*Note*	*31.03.2016 (₹)*	*31.03.2015 (₹)*
I. EQUITY AND LIABILITIES			
(1) Shareholders' Funds			
(a) Share Capital	1	10,00,000	10,00,000
(b) Reserves and Surplus	2	5,62,000	2,32,000
(2) Non-Current Liabilities [14% Debentures]		2,60,000	1,50,000
(3) Current Liabilities			
Short-term Borrowings (14% Bank Loan)		40,000	50,000
Trade Payables		1,50,000	40,000
Other Current Liabilities	3	80,000	60,000
Short-term Provisions	4	1,90,000	1,40,000
Total		22,82,000	16,72,000
II. ASSETS			
(1) Non-Current Assets			
Tangible Fixed Assets (Net)		12,40,000	10,20,000
Intangible Assets [Goodwill]		1,000	10,000
10% Non-Current Investments		1,60,000	60,000
Other Non-Current Assets	5	1,000	2,000
(2) Current Assets			
10% Current Investments		60,000	20,000
Cash & Cash Equivalents		3,00,000	1,00,000

Other Current Assets		5,20,000	4,60,000
Total		22,82,000	16,72,000

Notes to Accounts:

Particulars	*31.03.2016 (₹)*	*31.03.2015 (₹)*
1. Share Capital		
Equity Share Capital	8,00,000	6,00,000
18% Preference Share Capital	2,00,000	4,00,000
	10,00,000	10,00,000
2. Reserves and Surplus		
General Reserve	1,40,000	3,20,000
Profit and Loss A/c	3,92,000	(1,08,000)
Securities Premium	30,000	20,000
	5,62,000	2,32,000
3. Other Current Liabilities		
Bank Overdraft	50,000	60,000
Unpaid Dividend	20,000	–
Unpaid Interest on Debentures	10,000	–
	80,000	60,000
4. Short-Term Provisions		
Proposed Dividend	1,50,000	1,20,000
Provision for Tax	40,000	20,000
	1,90,000	1,40,000
5. Other Non-Current Assets		
Underwriting Commission	1,000	—
Preliminary Expenses	—	2,000
	1,000	2,000

Additional Information:

(a) During the year a machine costing ₹ 1,40,000 (depreciation provided thereon ₹ 60,000) wa sold for ₹ 50,000. Depreciation charged was ₹ 1,40,000. Tax paid was ₹ 10,000.

(b) At the end of the year some Non-Current Investments costing ₹ 40,000 were sold at a profit c 25%, New Shares and debentures were issued and Preference Shares were redeemed at premium of 5%.

(c) An Interim Dividend @ 15% was paid on equity shares.

SOLUTION

***CASH FLOW STATEMENT* FOR THE YEAR ENDED 31ST MARCH, 2016**

Particulars	₹	₹
I. Cash Flow from Operating Activities:		
A. Net Profit before tax		5,90,000

B. Adjustments for Non-Cash and Non-Operating Items :		
Depreciation	1,40,000	
Loss on Sale of Machinery	30,000	
Interest on Debentures	21,000	
Interest on Bank Loan	7,000	
Goodwill amortised	9,000	
Preliminary Expenses written off	2,000	
Premium on Redemption of Preference Shares	10,000	
Profit on Sale of Non-Current Investments	(10,000)	
Interest Income on Non-Current Investments	(6,000)	
Interest Income on Current Investments	(2,000)	2,01,000
C. Operating Profit before Working Capital Changes		7,91,000
D. Changes in Current Assets & Current Liabilities:		
Increase in Other Current Assets	(60,000)	
Increase in Trade Payables	1,10,000	50,000
E. Net Cash Flow from Operating Activities before Tax		8,41,000
F. *Less:* Tax paid		(10,000)
G. Net Cash Inflow from Operating Activities after Tax		8,31,000
II. Cash Flow from Investing Activities:		
Sale of Machinery		50,000
Purchases of Fixed Assets		(4,40,000)
Purchases of Non-Current Investments		(1,40,000)
Purchases of Current Investments		(40,000)
Sale of Non-Current Investments		50,000
Interest received on Non-Current Investments		6,000
Interest received on Current Investments		2,000
Net Cash used in Investing Activities		(5,12,000)
III. Cash Flow from Financing Activities:		
Issue of Share Capital [₹ 2,00,000 + ₹ 10,000]		2,10,000
Issue of Debentures		1,10,000
Interest paid on Debentures [₹ 21,000 – ₹ 10,000]		(11,000)
Interest paid on Bank Loan		(7,000)
Interim Dividend paid on Equity Shares		(90,000)
Final Dividend paid [₹ 1,20,000 – ₹ 20,000]		(1,00,000)
Redemption of Preference Shares [₹ 2,00,000 + 5%]		(2,10,000)
Under writing commission paid		(1,000)
Bank Loan repaid		(10,000)
Net Cash used in Financing Activities		(1,09,000)
IV. Net Increase in Cash and Cash Equivalents [I + II + III]		2,10,000

V. Opening Cash and Cash Equivalents [₹ 1,00,000 – ₹ 60,000]		40,000
VI. Closing Cash and Cash Equivalents [₹ 3,00,000 – ₹ 50,000]		2,50,000

Working Notes:

1. CALCULATION OF NET PROFIT BEFORE TAX

Particulars	₹
Closing Balance of P&L A/c	3,92,000
Add: Opening Balance of P&L A/c (Debit)	1,08,000
Less: Transfer from Reserve	(1,80,000)
Add: Proposed Dividend	1,50,000
Add: Interim Dividend on Equity Shares	90,000
Add: Tax	30,000
Net Profit before Tax	5,90,000

Dr. **2. FIXED ASSETS ACCOUNT** *Cr.*

Particulars	₹	*Particulars*	₹
To Balance b/d	10,20,000	By Bank A/c (Sale)	50,000
To Bank A/c (Purchases) (b.f.)	4,40,000	By P&L A/c (Loss)	30,000
		By Depreciation A/c	1,40,000
		By Balance c/d	12,40,000
	14,60,000		14,60,000

Dr. **3. NON-CURRENT INVESTMENTS ACCOUNT** *Cr.*

Particulars	₹	*Particulars*	₹
To Balance b/d	60,000	By Bank A/c [₹ 40,000 + ₹ 10,000]	50,000
To Bank A/c (Purchases) (b.f.)	1,40,000	By Balance c/d	1,60,000
To Profit and Loss A/c (Profit) [₹ 40,000 × 25/100]	10,000		
	2,10,000		2,10,000

Dr. **4. PROVISION FOR TAX ACCOUNT** *Cr.*

Particulars	₹	*Particulars*	₹
To Bank A/c [Tax paid]	10,000	By Balance b/d	20,000
To Balance c/d	40,000	By Profit and Loss A/c (b.f.) [Provision made]	30,000
	50,000		50,000

ILLUSTRATION 35

From the following information, prepare a Cash Flow Statement:

BALANCE SHEETS AS AT ...

Particulars	*Note*	*31.03.2016* ₹	*31.03.2015* ₹
I. EQUITY AND LIABILITIES			
(1) Shareholders' Funds			
(a) Share Capital		7,87,500	6,75,000
(b) Reserves and Surplus	1	5,06,250	3,20,625
(2) Non-Current Liabilities [15% Debentures]		2,25,000	3,37,500
(3) Current Liabilities			
Trade Payables		2,81,250	1,80,000
Other Current Liabilities		13,500	11,250
Short-term Provisions	2	1,23,750	1,12,500
Total		19,37,250	16,36,875
II. ASSETS			
(1) Non-Current Assets			
Tangible Fixed Assets		13,50,000	11,25,000
Accumulated Depreciation		(2,81,250)	(2,25,000)
Non-Current Investments		2,02,500	2,02,500
(2) Current Assets			
Inventories		3,03,750	2,25,000
Trade Receivables		4,05,000	3,43,125
Provision for Doubtful debts		(56,250)	(45,000)
Other Current Assets (Prepaid Expenses)		13,500	11,250
Total		19,37,250	16,36,875

Notes to Accounts:

Particulars	*31.03.2016* ₹	*31.03.2015* ₹
1. Reserves and Surplus		
General Reserve	2,81,250	2,25,000
Profit and Loss A/c	2,13,750	95,625
Capital Reserve	11,250	—
	5,06,250	3,20,625
2. Short-Term Provisions		
Proposed Dividend	38,250	33,750
Provision for Tax	85,500	78,750
	1,23,750	1,12,500

Additional Information:

(i) During the year Fixed assets with a net book value of ₹ 11,250 (accumulated depreciation, ₹ 33,750) were sold for ₹ 9,000.

(ii) During the year Investments costing ₹ 90,000 were sold, and also Investments costing ₹ 90,000 were purchased. Profit on Sale was credited to Capital Reserve.

(iii) Debentures were retired at a Premium of 10%

(iv) Tax of ₹ 61,875 was paid during the year

(v) During the year, bad debts of ₹ 15,750 were written off against the provision for Doubtful Debt account

SOLUTION

CASH FLOW STATEMENT FOR THE YEAR ENDED 31ST MARCH, 2016

Particulars	₹	₹
I. Cash Flows from Operating Activities:		
A. Balance as per Profit and Loss Account		2,13,750
Less: Opening Balance as per Profit and Loss Account		(95,625)
Add: Proposed dividend for the current year		38,250
Add: Transfer to reserve		56,250
Add: Provision for Tax during the current year		68,625
B. Net Profit before Taxation, and Extraordinary item		2,81,250
C. *Add:* Items to be added		
Depreciation	90,000	
Intrest on Debentures	50,625	
Loss on sale of Fixed Assets	2,250	
Premium payable on redemption of Debentures	11,250	1,54,125
D. Operating Profit before Working Capital Changes		4,35,375
E. *Add:* Decrease in Current Assets and Increase in Current Liabilities		
Increase in Trade Payables	1,01,250	
Increase in other current liabities	2,250	
F. *Less:* Increase in Current Assets&Decrease in Current Libilities		
Increase in Inventories	78,750	
Increase in Trade Receivables	50,625	
Increase in Prepaid Expenses	2,250	(28125)
G. Cash generated from operations		4,07,250
H. *Less:* Income taxes paid		(61,875)
I. Net Cash from Operating Activties		3,45,375
II. Cash Flows from financing Activities:		
Proceeds from sale Assets		9,000
Proceeds from sale of Investments [₹ 90,000 + ₹ 11,250]		1,01,250
Purchase of Fixed Assets		(2,70,000)

	Purchase of Investments		(90,000)
	Net Cash used in Investing Activities		(2,49,750)
III.	**Cash Flow from Financing Activities:**		
	Proceeds from issuance of share capital		1,12,500
	Repayment of Debentures		(1,23,750)
	Interest paid on Debentures		(50,625)
	Final Dividend paid		(33,750)
	Net cash from Financing Activities		(95,625)
IV.	**Net Increase in cash and cash Equivalents [I + II + III]**		0
V.	**Cash and cash Equivalents at beginning of period**		0
VI.	**Cash and cash Equivalents at End of period [IV + V]**		0

Working Notes:

Dr. **1. FIXED ASSETS ACCOUNT** *Cr.*

Particulars	₹	*Particulars*	₹
To Balance b/d	11,25,000	By Fixed Assets Disposal A/c	45,000
To Bank (purchases) (Bal fig.)	2,70,000	By Balance c/d	13,50,000
	13,95,000		13,95,000

Dr. **2. ACCUMULATED DEPRECIATION ACCOUNT** *Cr.*

Particulars	₹	*Particulars*	₹
To Fixed Assets A/c	33,750	By Balance b/d	2,25,000
To Balance c/d	2,81,250	By Profit and Loss A/c (Provision for dep.) (Bal.fig.)	90,000
	3,15,000		3,15,000

Dr. **3. FIXED ASSETS DISPOSAL ACCOUNT** *Cr.*

Particulars	₹	*Particulars*	₹
To Fixed Assets A/c	45,000	By Accumulated Dep,A/c	33,750
		By Bank A/c	9,000
		By Profit&Loss A/c (Loss)	2,250
	45,000		45,000

Dr. **4. PROVISION FOR TAX ACCOUNT** *Cr.*

Particulars	₹	*Particulars*	₹
To Bank A/c (Tax paid)	61,875	By Balance b/d	78,750
To Balance c/d	85,500	By P&L A/c (Prov.) (Bal.fig.)	68,625
	1,47,375		1,47,375

ILLUSTRATION 36

From the following information, prepare a Cash Flow Statement:

BALANCE SHEETS AS AT ...

Particulars	Note	31.03.2016 ₹	31.03.2015 ₹
I. EQUITY AND LIABILITIES			
(1) Shareholders' Funds			
(a) Share Capital		4,00,000	3,00,000
(b) Reserves and Surplus	1	1,45,000	1,02,000
(2) Non-Current Liabilities [10% Debentures]		1,00,000	1,50,000
(3) Current Liabilities			
Trade Payables		70,000	90,000
Other Current Liabilities (Dividend Payable)		4,000	—
Short-term Provisions	2	80,000	80,000
Total		7,99,000	7,22,000
II. ASSETS			
(1) Non-Current Assets			
Tangible Fixed Assets		4,29,250	2,98,000
Intangible Assets [Goodwill]		90,000	1,00,000
Non-Current Investments		60,000	1,00,000
(2) Current Assets			
Inventories		80,000	50,000
Trade Receivables		1,10,000	1,60,000
Cash & Cash Equivalents		24,000	10,000
Other Current Assets (Prepaid Expenses)		5,750	4,000
Total		7,99,000	7,22,000

Notes to Accounts:

Particulars	31.03.2016 ₹	31.03.2015 ₹
1. Reserves and Surplus		
General Reserve	1,00,000	80,000
Profit and Loss A/c	45,000	22,000
	1,45,000	1,02,000
2. Short-Term Provisions		
Proposed Dividend	40,000	30,000
Provision for Tax	40,000	50,000
	80,000	80,000

Additional Inofrmation:

1. 15% depreciation has been charged in the accounts on plant and machinery.

2. Old machines costing ₹.50,000 (WDV. ₹.20,000) have been sold for ₹.35,000.
3. A machine costing ₹.10,000 (WDV. ₹.3,000) has been discarded.
4. ₹.10,000 profit has been earned by sale of investments.
5. Debentures have been redeemed at 5% premium at the end.
6. ₹ 45,000 income tax has been paid and adjusted against Income Tax Provision Account.

SOLUTION

CASH FLOW STATEMENT FOR THE YEAR ENDING 31.03.2016

	Particulars	₹	₹
I.	**Cash Flows from Operating Activities**		
A.	Closing balance as per Profit and Loss Account		45,000
	Less: Opening Balance as per Profit and Loss Account		(22,000)
	Add: Proposed dividend during the year		40,000
	Add: Transfer to Reserve		20,000
	Add: Provision for Tax		35,000
	Add: Premium on Redemption of Debentures		2,500
B.	Net Profit before taxation and extraordinary item		1,20,500
C.	*Add:* Items to be added		
	Depreciation	75,750	
	Interest on Debentures	15,000	
	Goodwill written off	10,000	
	Loss on Machinery	3,000	1,03,750
D.	*Less:* Items to be deducted		
	Profit on sale of Machinery	(15,000)	
	Profit on sale of Investments	(10,000)	(25,000)
E.	Operating Profit before working capital changes [B + C – D]		1,99,250
F.	Decrease in Trade Receivables		50,000
G.	*Less:* Increase in Current Assets & Decrease in Current Liabilities		
	Increase in Inventories	(30,000)	
	Increase in Prepaid Expenses	(1,750)	
	Decrease in Trade Payables	(20,000)	(51,750)
H.	Cash generated from operations [E + F – G]		1,97,500
I.	*Less:* Income taxes paid (Net of Refund)		(45,000)
J.	Net Cash from Operating Activities		1,52,500
II.	**Cash Flows from Investing Activities**		
	Purchase of Machinery		(2,30,000)
	Proceeds for sale of Machinery		35,000
	Proceeds from sale of Investments		50,000
	Net Cash used in investing activities		(1,45,000)

III. Cash Flows from Financing Activities	
Proceeds from issuance of share capital	1,00,000
Redemption of Debentures	(52,500)
Interest on Debentures	(15,000)
Final dividend paid [₹.30,000 – ₹.4,000]	(26,000)
Net Cash from financing activities	6,500
IV. Net Increase in Cash and Cash Equivalents [I + II + III]	14,000
V. Cash and Cash Equivalents at beginning of Period	10,000
VI. Cash and Cash Equivalents at end of Period [IV + V]	24,000

Working Notes:

Dr. **1. PLANT AND MACHINERY ACCOUNT** *Cr.*

Particulars	₹	*Particulars*	₹
To Balance b/d	2,98,000	By Bank A/c (Sale)	35,000
To Bank A/c (Balancing figure)	2,30,000	By Profit and Loss A/c (written off)	3,000
To Profit and Loss A/c (Profit)	15,000	By Depreciation A/c	
		(4,29,250 × 15/85)	75,750
		By Balance c/d	4,29,250
	5,43,000		5,43,000

Dr. **2. PROVISION FOR TAX ACCOUNT** *Cr.*

Particulars	₹	*Particulars*	₹
To Bank A/c	45,000	By Balance b/d	50,000
To Balance c/d	40,000	By P&L A/c(b.f.)	35,000
	85,000		85,000

ILLUSTRATION 37

From the following information, prepare a Cash Flow Statement of IPCC (1) Ltd.:

BALANCE SHEETS AS AT ...

Particulars	*Note*	*31.03.2016* ₹	*31.03.2015* ₹
I. EQUITY AND LIABILITIES			
(1) Shareholders' Funds			
(a) Share Capital	1	10,25,000	10,00,000
(b) Reserves and Surplus	2	5,67,000	2,32,000
(2) Non-Current Liabilities [14% Debentures]		2,60,000	1,50,000
(3) Current Liabilities			
Short-term Borrowings (14% Bank Loan)		40,000	50,000
Trade Payables		1,50,000	40,000
Other Current Liabilities	3	80,000	60,000

Short-term Provisions	4	1,90,000	1,40,000
Total		23,12,000	16,72,000
II. ASSETS			
(1) Non-Current Assets			
Tangible Fixed Assets (Net)		12,70,000	10,20,000
Intangible Assets [Goodwill]		1,000	10,000
10% Non-Current Investments		1,60,000	60,000
Other Non-Current Assets	5	1,000	2,000
(2) Current Assets			
10% Current Investments		60,000	20,000
Cash & Cash Equivalents		3,00,000	1,00,000
Other Current Assets		5,20,000	4,60,000
Total		23,12,000	16,72,000

Notes to Accounts:

Particulars	*31.03.2016* ₹	*31.03.2015* ₹
1. Share Capital		
Equity Share Capital of ₹ 10 each	8,25,000	6,00,000
5% Preference Share Capital of ₹ 100 each	2,00,000	4,00,000
	10,25,000	10,00,000
2. Reserves and Surplus		
General Reserve	1,40,000	3,20,000
Profit and Loss A/c	3,92,000	(1,13,000)
Securities Premium	35,000	20,000
Capital Reserve	—	5,000
	5,67,000	2,32,000
3. Other Current Liabilities		
Bank Overdraft	50,000	60,000
Unpaid Dividend	20,000	–
Unpaid Interest on Debentures	10,000	–
	80,000	60,000
4. Short-Term Provisions		
Proposed Dividend	1,50,000	1,20,000
Provision for Tax	40,000	20,000
	1,90,000	1,40,000
5. Other Non-Current Assets		
Underwriting Commission	1,000	—
Preliminary Expenses	—	2,000
	1,000	2,000

Additional Information:

(a) During the year a machine costing ₹ 1,40,000 (depreciation provided thereon ₹ 60,000) was sold for ₹ 50,000. Depreciation charged was ₹ 1,40,000. A machine costing ₹ 30,000 was purchased by issue of Equity Shares of ₹ 10 each at a premium of 20%.

(b) At the end of the year Some Non-Current Investments costing ₹ 40,000 were sold at a loss of 25% and Some Current Investments costing ₹ 20,000 were sold at a profit of 25%. Profit / Loss on Investments was adjusted against the Capital Reserve.

(c) An Interim Dividend @ 15% was paid on equity shares on 31.12.2015. New Shares and Debentures were issued on 01.01.2016 and Bank Loan was repaid on the same date.

(d) Tax paid during the year was ₹ 10,000.

(e) Preference Shares were redeemed at the end of the year at a premium of 5%.

SOLUTION

CASH FLOW STATEMENT FOR THE YEAR ENDED 31ST MARCH, 2016

Particulars	₹	₹
I. Cash Flow from Operating Activities:		
A. Net Profit before tax		5,95,000
B. Adjustments for Non-Cash and Non-Operating Items :		
Depreciation	1,40,000	
Loss on Sale of Machinery	30,000	
Interest on Debentures	24,850	
Interest on Bank Loan	6,650	
Goodwill amortised	9,000	
Preliminary Expenses written off	2,000	
Premium on Redemption of Preference Shares	10,000	
Interest Income on Non-Current Investments	(6,000)	
Interest Income on Current Investments	(2,000)	2,14,500
C. Operating Profit before Working Capital Changes		8,09,500
D. Changes in Current Assets & Current Liabilities:		
Increase in Other Current Assets	(60,000)	
Increase in Trade Payables	1,10,000	50,000
E. Net Cash Flow from Operating Activities before Tax		8,59,500
F. *Less:* Tax paid		(10,000)
G. Net Cash Inflow from Operating Activities after Tax		8,49,500
II. Cash Flow from Investing Activities:		
Sale of Machinery		50,000
Purchases of Fixed Assets		(4,40,000)
Purchases of Non-Current Investments		(1,40,000)
Purchases of Current Investments		(60,000)
Sale of Non-Current Investments		30,000

	Sale of Current Investments		25,000
	Interest received on Non-Current Investments		6,000
	Interest received on Current Investments		2,000
	Net Cash used in Investing Activities		(5,27,000)
III.	**Cash Flow from Financing Activities:**		
	Issue of Share Capital [₹ 2,00,000 + ₹ 10,000 (Premium in cash)]	2,10,000	
	Issue of Debentures		1,10,000
	Interest paid on Debentures [₹ 24,850 – ₹ 10,000]		(14,850)
	Interest paid on Bank Loan		(6,650)
	Interim Dividend paid on Equity Shares		(90,000)
	Final Dividend paid [₹ 1,20,000 – ₹ 20,000]		(1,00,000)
	Redemption of Preference Shares [₹ 2,00,000 + 5%]		(2,10,000)
	Under writing commission paid		(1,000)
	Bank Loan repaid		(10,000)
	Net Cash used in Financing Activities		(1,12,500)
IV.	**Net Increase in Cash and Cash Equivalents [I + II + III]**		2,10,000
V.	**Opening Cash and Cash Equivalents** [₹ 1,00,000 – ₹ 60,000]		40,000
VI.	**Closing Cash and Cash Equivalents** [₹ 3,00,000 – ₹ 50,000]		2,50,000

Working Notes:

1. CALCULATION OF NET PROFIT BEFORE TAX

Particulars	₹
Closing Balance of P&L A/c	3,92,000
Add: Opening Balance of P&L A/c (Debit)	1,13,000
*Less:*Transfer from Reserve	(1,80,000)
Add: Proposed Dividend	1,50,000
Add: Interim Dividend on Equity Shares	90,000
Add: Tax	30,000
Net Profit before Tax	5,95,000

Dr. **2. FIXED ASSETS ACCOUNT** *Cr.*

Particulars	₹	*Particulars*	₹
To Balance b/d	10,20,000	By Bank A/c (Sale)	50,000
To Bank A/c (Purchases) (b.f.)	4,40,000	By P&L A/c (Loss)	30,000
To Equity Share Capital A/c	25,000	By Depreciation A/c	1,40,000
To Securities Premium	5,000	By Balance c/d	12,70,000
	14,90,000		14,90,000

Dr. **3. NON-CURRENT INVESTMENTS ACCOUNT** *Cr.*

Particulars	₹	*Particulars*	₹
To Balance b/d	60,000	By Bank A/c [₹ 40,000 – ₹ 10,000]	30,000

To Bank A/c (Purchases) (b.f.)	1,40,000	By Capital Reserve A/c (Loss)	10,000
		By Balance c/d	1,60,000
	2,00,000		2,00,000

Dr. **4. CURRENT INVESTMENTS ACCOUNT** *Cr.*

Particulars	₹	*Particulars*	₹
To Balance b/d	20,000	By Bank A/c	25,000
To Bank A/c (Purchase)	60,000	By Balance c/d	60,000
To Capital Reserve A/c (Profit) [25% of ₹ 20,000]	5,000		
	85,000		85,000

Dr. **5. PROVISION FOR TAX ACCOUNT** *Cr.*

Particulars	₹	*Particulars*	₹
To Bank A/c [Tax paid]	10,000	By Balance b/d	20,000
To Balance c/d	40,000	By Profit and Loss A/c (b.f.) [Provision made]	30,000
	50,000		50,000

ILLUSTRATIVE PROBLEM 38

From the following information, prepare a Cash Flow Statement of IPCC (2) Ltd.:

BALANCE SHEETS AS AT ...

Particulars	*Note*	*31.03.2016* ₹	*31.03.2015* ₹
I. EQUITY AND LIABILITIES			
(1) Shareholders' Funds			
(a) Share Capital	1	10,50,000	10,00,000
(b) Reserves and Surplus	2	5,72,000	2,32,000
(2) Non-Current Liabilities [14% Debentures]		2,60,000	1,50,000
(3) Current Liabilities			
Short-term Borrowings (14% Bank Loan)		40,000	50,000
Trade Payables		1,65,000	40,000
Other Current Liabilities	3	80,000	60,000
Short-term Provisions	4	1,90,000	1,40,000
Total		23,57,000	16,72,000
II. ASSETS			
(1) Non-Current Assets			
Tangible Fixed Assets		16,50,000	13,20,000
Accumulated Depreciation		(3,80,000)	(3,00,000)
Intangible Assets [Goodwill]		21,000	10,000

10% Non-Current Investments		1,60,000	60,000
Other Non-Current Assets	5	1,000	2,000
(2) Current Assets			
10% Current Investments		60,000	20,000
Cash & Cash Equivalents		3,00,000	1,00,000
Inventories		1,69,000	54,000
Trade Receivables		3,76,000	4,06,000
Total		23,57,000	16,72,000

Notes to Accounts:

Particulars	*31.03.2016* ₹	*31.03.2015* ₹
1. Share Capital		
Equity Share Capital of ₹ 10 each	8,50,000	6,00,000
5% Preference Share Capital of ₹ 100 each	2,00,000	4,00,000
	10,50,000	10,00,000
2. Reserves and Surplus		
General Reserve	1,40,000	3,20,000
Profit and Loss A/c	3,92,000	(1,13,000)
Securities Premium	40,000	20,000
Capital Reserve	—	5,000
	5,72,000	2,32,000
3. Other Current Liabilities		
Bank Overdraft	50,000	60,000
Unpaid Dividend	20,000	–
Unpaid Interest on Debentures	10,000	–
	80,000	60,000
4. Short-Term Provisions		
Proposed Dividend	1,50,000	1,20,000
Provision for Tax	40,000	20,000
	1,90,000	1,40,000
5. Other Non-Current Assets		
Underwriting Commission	1,000	—
Preliminary Expenses	—	2,000
	1,000	2,000

Additional Information:

(a) During the year a machine having book value of ₹ 80,000 (depreciation provided thereon ₹ 60,000) was sold at a loss of 37.5%.

(b) On 01.01.2016, Some Non-Current Investments costing ₹ 1,40,000 were purchased and Some Non-Current Investments were sold at a loss of 1/3rd on sale. At the end of the year Some Current Investments costing ₹ 20,000 were sold at a profit of 25%. Profit / Loss on Investments was adjusted against the Capital Reserve.

(c) An Interim Dividend @ 15% was paid on equity shares on 31.12.2015. New Shares and Debentures were issued on 01.01.2016 and Bank Loan was repaid on the same date.

(d) Tax provided during the year was ₹ 30,000. Preference Shares were redeemed at the end of the year at a premium of 5%.

(e) On 01.01.2016, the Business of Y Ltd. was purchased for ₹ 60,000 payable in fully paid equity shares of ₹ 10 each at 20% premium. The assets included Stock ₹ 15,000. Debtors ₹ 10,000 and Machine ₹ 30,000. Creditors of ₹ 15,000 were also taken over.

SOLUTION

CASH FLOW STATEMENT FOR THE YEAR ENDED 31ST MARCH, 2016

Particulars	₹	₹
I. Cash Flow from Operating Activities:		
A. Net Profit before tax		5,95,000
B. Adjustments for Non-Cash and Non-Operating Items :		
Depreciation	1,40,000	
Loss on Sale of Machinery	30,000	
Interest on Debentures	24,850	
Interest on Bank Loan	6,650	
Goodwill amortised	9,000	
Preliminary Expenses written off	2,000	
Premium on Redemption of Preference Shares	10,000	
Interest Income on Non-Current Investments	(8,500)	
Interest Income on Current Investments	(2,000)	2,12,000
C. Operating Profit before Working Capital Changes		8,07,000
D. Changes in Current Assets & Current Liabilities:		
Increase in Inventories [(1,69,000 – 15,000) – 54,000]	(1,00,000)	
Decrease in Trade Receivables [(3,76,000 – 10,000) – 4,06,000]	40,000	
Increase in Trade Payables [(1,65,000 – 15,000) – 40,000]	1,10,000	50,000
E. Net Cash Flow from Operating Activities before Tax		8,57,000
F. *Less:* Tax paid		(10,000)
G. Net Cash Inflow from Operating Activities after Tax		8,47,000
II. Cash Flow from Investing Activities:		
Sale of Machinery		50,000
Purchases of Fixed Assets		(4,40,000)
Purchases of Non-Current Investments		(1,40,000)
Purchases of Current Investments		(60,000)
Sale of Non-Current Investments		30,000
Sale of Current Investments		25,000
Interest received on Non-Current Investments		8,500
Interest received on Current Investments		2,000

Net Cash used in Investing Activities		(5,24,500)
III. Cash Flow from Financing Activities:		
Issue of Share Capital [₹ 2,00,000 + ₹ 10,000 (Premimum in cash)]		2,10,000
Issue of Debentures		1,10,000
Interest paid on Debentures [₹ 24,850 – ₹ 10,000]		(14,850)
Interest paid on Bank Loan		(6,650)
Interim Dividend paid on Equity Shares		(90,000)
Final Dividend paid [₹ 1,20,000 – ₹ 20,000]		(1,00,000)
Redemption of Preference Shares [₹ 2,00,000 + 5%]		(2,10,000)
Under writing commission paid		(1,000)
Bank Loan repaid		(10,000)
Net Cash used in Financing Activities		(1,12,500)
IV. Net Increase in Cash and Cash Equivalents [I + II + III]		2,10,000
V. Opening Cash and Cash Equivalents [₹ 1,00,000 – ₹ 60,000]		40,000
VI. Closing Cash and Cash Equivalents [₹ 3,00,000 – ₹ 50,000]		2,50,000

Working Notes:

1. CALCULATION OF NET PROFIT BEFORE TAX

Particulars	₹
Closing Balance of P&L A/c	3,92,000
Add: Opening Balance of P&L A/c (Debit)	1,13,000
Less: Transfer from Reserve	(1,80,000)
Add: Proposed Dividend	1,50,000
Add: Interim Dividend on Equity Shares	90,000
Add: Tax	30,000
Net Profit before Tax	5,95,000

Dr. **2. FIXED ASSETS ACCOUNT (AT COST)** *Cr.*

Particulars	₹	*Particulars*	₹
To Balance b/d	13,20,000	By Asset Sold A/c	1,40,000
To Bank A/c (Purchases)	4,40,000	By Balance c/d	16,50,000
To Business Purchase A/c	30,000		
	17,90,000		17,90,000

Dr. **3. PROVISION FOR DEPRECIATION ACCOUNT** *Cr.*

Particulars	₹	*Particulars*	₹
To Assets Sold A/c	60,000	By Balance b/d	3,00,000
To Bank c/d	3,80,000	By P&L A/c (Depreciation for current year) (Balancing figure)	1,40,000
	4,40,000		4,40,000

Dr. **4. ASSET SOLD ACCOUNT** *Cr.*

Particulars	₹	*Particulars*	₹
To Fixed Assets A/c	1,40,000	By Provision for Depreciation A/c	60,000
		By Bank A/c (b.f.)	50,000
		By Profit and Loss A/c (Loss)	30,000
	1,40,000		1,40,000

Dr. **5. NON-CURRENT INVESTMENTS ACCOUNT** *Cr.*

Particulars	₹	*Particulars*	₹
To Balance b/d	60,000	By Bank A/c [₹ 40,000 – ₹ 10,000]	30,000
To Bank A/c (Purchases) (b.f.)	1,40,000	By Capital Reserve A/c (Loss)	10,000
		By Balance c/d	1,60,000
	2,00,000		2,00,000

Dr. **6. CURRENT INVESTMENTS ACCOUNT** *Cr.*

Particulars	₹	*Particulars*	₹
To Balance b/d	20,000	By Bank A/c	25,000
To Bank A/c (Purchase)	60,000	By Balance c/d	60,000
To Capital Reserve A/c (Profit) [25% of ₹ 20,000]	5,000		
	85,000		85,000

Dr. **7. PROVISION FOR TAX ACCOUNT** *Cr.*

Particulars	₹	*Particulars*	₹
To Bank A/c [Tax paid] (b.f.)	10,000	By Balance b/d	20,000
To Balance c/d	40,000	By Profit and Loss A/c [Provision made]	30,000
	50,000		50,000

8. Goodwill Amortised = Goodwill Purchased + Opening Goodwill – Closing Goodwill
   = [₹ 60,000 – (₹ 15,000+ ₹ 10,000 + ₹ 30,000 – ₹ 15,000] + ₹ 10,000 – ₹ 21,000
   = ₹ 9,000
9. Following Items will not appear in the Cash Flow Statement since these are non- cash transactions:

   (i) Issue of Equity Shares for ₹ 50,000,(ii) Securities Premium of ₹ 10,000,(iii) Increase in Stock (₹ 15,000), Debtors (₹ 10,000), Creditors (₹ 15,000) and Machine(₹ 30,000) due to purchase of business.

ILLUSTRATION 39

10% Investments: Opening ₹ 1,00,000, Closing ₹ 80,000, Accrued Interest on Investments: Opening ₹ 2,000, Closing ₹ 3,000. How will you disclose these items while preparing Cash Flow Statement as per AS–3 issued by ICAI?

SOLUTION

A.	Cash Flow from Operating Activities	₹
	Net Profit as per Profit & Loss A/c	
	Less: Interest on 10% Investments	(10,000)
B.	Cash Flow from Investing Activities	
	Sale of 10% Investments [1,00,000 – 80,000]	20,000
	Interest on Investments [10,000 – (3,000 – 2,000)]	9,000

ILLUSTRATION 40

10% Debentures: Opening ₹ 2,00,000, Closing ₹ 1,40,000, Unpaid interest on Debentures: Opening ₹ 500, Closing ₹ 2,000. Debentures were redeemed at 5% premium at the end of the year. How will you disclose these items while preparing Cash Flow Statement as per AS–3 issued by ICAI?

SOLUTION

A.	Cash Flow from Operating Activities	
	Net Profit as per Profit & Loss A/c	
	Add: Premium on Redemption of Debentures *Less:* Interest on 10% Debentures	3,000 (20,000)
B.	Cash Flow from Financing activities	
	Interest on Debentures paid [20,000 – (2,000 – 500)]	(18,500)
	Redemption of Debentures [(2,00,000 – 1,40,000) + 5% premium]	(63,000)

ILLUSTRATION 41

Investment in Shares: Opening ₹ 10,000,Closing ₹ 35,000, Dividend received amounted to ₹ 2,100 which included pre acquisition dividend of ₹ 600. How will you disclose these items while preparing Cash Flow Statement as per AS–3 issued by ICAI?

SOLUTION

A.	Cash Flow from Operating Activities	₹
	Net Profit as per Profit & Loss A/c	
	Less: Dividend (₹ 2,100 – ₹ 600)	(1,500)
B.	Cash Flow from Investing Activities	
	Purchase of investment in shares [(35,000 + 600) – 10,000]	(25,600)
	Dividend Income	2,100

ILLUSTRATION 42

Compensation received in a suit filed by the company ₹ 90,000 .How will you disclose this item while preparing Cash Flow Statement as per AS–3 issued by ICAI?

SOLUTION

A.	Cash Flow from Operating Activities	₹
	Net Profit as per Profit & Loss A/c	

	Less: Compensation received	(90,000)
B.	**Operating Profit before extraordinary items**	
	Add: Compensation received	90,000

ILLUSTRATION 43

Capital Grant: Opening ₹ Nil, Closing ₹ 8,00,000. Grant of ₹ 10,00,000 amortised in P&L A/c. How will you disclose these items while preparing Cash Flow Statement as per AS–3 issued by ICAI?

SOLUTION

A.	**Cash Flow from Operating Activities**	₹
	Net Profit as per Profit & Loss A/c	
	*Less:*Capital Grant amortised	(10,00,000)
B.	**Cash Flow from Financing activities**	
	Grant Received	18,00,000

ILLUSTRATION 44

Voluntary Separation Payments : Opening ₹ 65,000, Closing ₹ 1,25,000. Voluntary Separation Payments ₹ 50,000 adjusted against General Reserve. How will you disclose these items while preparing Cash Flow Statement as per AS–3 issued by ICAI?

SOLUTION

A.	**Cash Flow from Operating Activities**	₹
	Operating Profit before extraordinary items	
	Less: Voluntary Separation Payments [(125,000+50,000) – 65,000]	(1,10,000)

ILLUSTRATION 45

Debtors of ₹ 2,30,000 were written off against the Provision for Doubtful Debts A/c during the year. Short-term Investments (held for 2 months) costing ₹ 10,000 were sold for ₹ 12,000. How will you disclose these items while preparing Cash Flow Statement as per AS–3 issued by ICAI?

SOLUTION

Profit on sale of short term investments and debtors written off against provision for doubtful debts do not require any further adjustment in **Cash Flow Statement.**

ILLUSTRATION 46

Following are the Extracts of Balance Sheets of Tulsian Ltd.:

Paticulars	*31.3.2016 (₹)*	*31.3.2015 (₹)*
Equity Share Capital	9,10,000	5,00,000
General Reserve	2,10,000	2,50,000
Profit & Loss A/c	9,50,000	(40,000)

Securities Premium	50,000	—
Capital Redemption Reserve	—	1,00,000
Capital Grant	8,00,000	Nil
Convertible Debentures (into equity shares at 25% premium)	—	2,00,000
Trade Payables	1,00,000	1,05,000
Goodwill	15,000	—
Plant & Machinery	7,65,000	5,00,000
Inventories	95,640	54,000
Trade Receivables	7,50,000	6,25,000
Less: Provision for Doubtful Debts	(1,90,000)	(1,50,000)
Voluntary Separation Payments	1,25,000	65,000

Additional Information:

(a) Depreciation on Plant & Machinery written off @ 15%.

(b) It was decided to value Inventories at cost whereas previously the practice was to value Inventories at cost less 10%. However the closing stock on 31.03.2016 was correctly valued at cost.

(c) On 31st March 2016, the business of Y Ltd. was purchased for ₹ 60,000 payable in fully paid equity shares of ₹ 10 each at a premium of 20%. The assets included Inventories ₹ 26,640, Trade Receivables ₹ 10,000, and Machine ₹ 18,360. In addition Trade Payables of ₹ 15,000 were taken over.

(d) Debtors of ₹ 2,30,000 were written off against the Provision for Doubtful Debts A/c during the year. Grant of ₹ 10,00,000 amortised in P&L A/c. Compensation received in a suit filed by the company ₹ 90,000. Voluntary Separation Payments ₹ 50,000 adjusted against General Reserve.

Required: How will you disclose these items while preparing Cash Flow Statement as per AS–3 issued by ICAI.

SOLUTION

CASH FLOW STATEMENT OF TULSIAN LTD FOR THE YEAR ENDED 31ST MARCH, 2016

A	**Cash Flow from Operating Activities**		₹
	Net Profit [9,50,000 – (40,000) + 10,000 (t/f to Reserve)]		10,00,000
	Add: Depreciation [(7,65,000 x 15/85)]		1,35,000
	Add: Goodwill amortised		5,000
	[60,000 – (26,640 + 10,000 + 18,360 – 15,000)]–15,000		
	Less: Under valuation of Opening stock (54,000 × 10/90)		(6,000)
	Less: Compensation received		(90,000)
	*Less:*Capital Grant amortised		(10,00,000)
	Operating Profit before Working Capital changes		44,000
	Add: Increase in Provision for doubtful debts	40,000	
	Less: Increase in Inventories [(95,640 – 26,640) – (54,000 + 6,000)]	(9,000)	
	Increase in Trade Receivables [(7,50,000 – 10,000) – 6,25,000]	(1,15,000)	

	Decrease in Trade Payables [(1,05,000 – 15,000) – 1,00,000]	(10,000)	(94,000)
	Operating Profit before extraordinary items		(50,000)
	Add: Compensation received		90,000
	Less: Voluntary Separation Payments [(125,000+50,000) – 65,000]		(1,10,000)
	Cash used in Operating Activities		(70,000)
B	**Cash Flow from Investing Activities**		
	Purchase of Machinery		(3,81,640)
	[(7,65,000+1,35,000) – 5,00,000 – 18,360]		
C	**Cash Flow from Financing Activities**		
	Issue of Equity Share Capital [(9,10,000 – 50,000 – 1,00,000 –1,60,000) – 5,00,000]		1,00,000
	Grant Received		18,00,000

Note: Debtors written off against provision for doubtful debts do not require any further adjustment in **Cash Flow Statement.**

SOLVED PROBLEMS

PROBLEM 1

CAMJI Limited provides you the following information for the preparation of Cash Flow Statement:

Particulars	*(₹. in lakhs)*
Net Profit	25,000
Dividend (including dividend tax) paid	8,535
Provision for Income Tax	5,000
Income tax paid during the year	4,248
Loss on sale of assets (net)	40
Book value of the assets sold	185
Depreciation charged to Profit and Loss Account	20,000
Amortisation of Capital grant	6
Profit on sale of Investments	100
Carrying amount of Investment sold	27,765
Interest income on investments	2,506
Interest expenses	10,000
Interest paid during the year	10,520
Increase in Working Capital (excluding Cash and Bank balance)	56,075
Purchase of fixed assets	14,560
Investment in joint venture	3,850
Expenditure on construction work in progress	34,740
Proceeds from calls in arrears	2
Receipt of grant for capital projects	12

Proceeds from long-term borrowings	25,980
Proceeds from short-term borrowings	20,575
Opening Cash and Bank balance	5,003
Closing Cash and Bank balance	6,988

SOLUTION

CASH FLOW STATEMENT FOR THE YEAR ENDED 31ST MARCH......

Particulars	*(₹. in lakhs)*
Cash flows from Operating Activities:	
Net Profit before taxation (₹. 25,000 + ₹. 5,000)	30,000
Adjustment for:	
Depreciation	20,000
Loss on sale of assets (Net)	40
Amortisation of capital grant	(6)
Profit on sale of investments	(100)
Interest income on investments	(2,506)
Interest expenses	10,000
Operating profit before working capital changes	57,428
Changes in working capital (excluding cash and bank balance)	(56,075)
Cash generated from operations	1,353
Income taxes paid	(4,248)
Net cash used in operating activities	(2,895)
Cash flows from Investing Activities:	
Sale of assets (185 – 40)	145
Sale of investments (27,765 + 100)	27,865
Interest income on investments	2,506
Purchase of fixed assets	(14,560)
Investment in joint venture	(3,850)
Expenditure on construction work-in-progress	(34,740)
Net cash used in investing activities	(22,634)
Cash flows from Financing Activities:	
Proceeds from calls in arrears	2
Receipts of grant for capital projects	12
Proceeds from long-term borrowings	25,980
Proceeds from short-term borrowings	20,575
Interest paid	(10,520)
Dividend (including dividend tax) paid	(8,535)
	27,514

Net increase in cash and cash equivalents	1,985
Cash and cash equivalents at the beginning of the period	5,003
Cash and cash equivalents at the end of the period	6,988

PROBLEM 2

J. Ltd. presents you the following information for the year ended 31st March, 2016:

	Particulars	*(₹ in lacs)*
(i)	Net profit before tax provision	36,000
(ii)	Dividend paid	10,202
(iii)	Income-tax paid	5,100
(iv)	Book value of assets sold	222
	Loss on sale of asset	48
(v)	Depreciation debited in P&L Account	24,000
(vi)	Capital grant received - amortized in P&L A/c	10
(vii)	Book value of investment sold	33,318
	Profit on sale of investment	120
(viii)	Interest income from investment credited in P&L A/c	3,000
(ix)	Interest expenditure debited in P&L A/c	12,000
(x)	Interest actually paid (Financing activity)	13,042
(xi)	Increase in working capital [Excluding cash and bank balance]	67,290
(xii)	Purchase of fixed assets	22,092
(xiii)	Expenditure on construction work	41,688
(xiv)	Grant received for capital projects	18
(xv)	Long term borrowings from banks	55,866
(xvi)	Provision for Income-tax debited in P&L A/c	6,000
	Cash and bank balance at the beginning	6,000
	Cash and bank balance at the end	8,000

You are required to prepare a Cash Flow Statement as per AS 3 (Revised)

SOLUTION

CASH FLOW STATEMENT FOR THE YEAR ENDED 31ST MARCH, 2016

Particulars	*(₹ in lacs)*
A. Cash Flows from Operating Activities:	
Net profit before tax provision	36,000
Add: Non-cash expenditures	
Depreciation	24,000
Loss on sale of assets	48
Interest expenditure	12,000
	72,048

	Less: Non-cash income	
	Amortisation of capital grant received	(10)
	Profit on sale of investments	(120)
	Interest income from investment	(3,000)
	Operating Profit before Working Capital Changed	68,918
	Less: Increase in working capital	(67,290)
	Cash from operations	1,628
	Less: Income tax paid	(5,100)
	Net cash used in operating activities	(3,472)
B.	**Cash flows from investing activities**	
	Sale of assets (222 – 48)	174
	Sale of investments (33,318 + 120)	33,438
	Interest income from investments	3,000
	Purchase of fixed assets	(22,092)
	Expenditure on construction work	(41,688)
	Net cash used in investing activities	(27,168)
C.	**Cash flows from financing activities**	
	Grants for capital projects	18
	Long term borrowings	55,866
	Interest paid	(13,042)
	Dividend paid	(10,202)
	Net cash from financing activities	32,640
D.	Net increase in Cash & Cash Equivalents	2,000
E.	Cash & Cash Equivalents at the beginning of the year	6,000
F.	Cash & Cash Equivalents at the end of the year	8,000

Note: No effect for 'provision for income tax debited in P&L A/c' has been given since the figure of 'net profit before tax provision' has been considered for calculation.

PROBLEM 3

Raj Ltd. gives you the following information for the year ended 31st March, 2016:

(i) Sales for the year ₹ 48,00,000. The Company sold goods for cash only.

(ii) Cost of goods sold was 75% of sales.

(iii) Closing inventory was higher than opening inventory by ₹ 50,000.

(iv) Closing Trade Payables exceed the Opening Trade Payables by ₹ 1,00,000

(v) Tax paid during the year amounts to ₹ 1,50,000.

(vi) Amounts paid to Trade Payables during the year ₹ 35,50,000.

(vii) Administrative and Selling expenses paid ₹ 3,60,000.

(viii) One new machinery was acquired during the year for ₹ 6,00,000.

(ix) Dividend paid during the year ₹ 1,20,000.

(x) Cash in hand and of Bank at the end ₹ 70,000.

(xi) Cash in hand and at Bank at the begining ₹ 50,000.

Required: Prepare Cash Flow Statement as per Accounting Standard 3.

SOLUTION

CASH FLOW STATEMENT FOR THE YEAR ENDED 31ST MARCH 2016

Particulars	₹
Cash flow from operating activities:	
Cash receipt from customers (sales)	48,00,000
Cash paid to suppliers and expenses (₹ 35,50,000 + ₹ 3,60,000)	(39,10,000)
Cash flow from operations	8,90,000
Less: Tax paid	(1,50,000)
Net cash from operating activities	7,40,000
Cash flow from investing activities:	
Purchase of fixed assets	(6,00,000)
Net cash used in investing activities	(6,00,000)
Cash flow from financing activities:	
Dividend Paid	(1,20,000)
Net cash from financing activities	(1,20,000)
Net Increase in Cash & Cash Equivalents	20,000
Cash & Cash Equivalents at the beginning of the year	50,000
Cash & Cash Equivalents at the end of the year	70,000

PROBLEM 4

The following figures have been extracted from the Books of X Ltd. for the year ended on 31.3.2016. You are required to prepare a cash flow statement.

(i) Net profit before taking into account Income Tax and Income from law suits but after taking into Account the following items was ₹ 20 lakhs:
   (a) Depreciation on Fixed Assets ₹ 5 lakhs.
   (b) Discount on issue of Debentures written off ₹ 30,000.
   (c) Interest on Debentures paid ₹ 3,50,000.
   (d) Books value of investments ₹ 3 lakhs (Sale of Investments for ₹ 3,20,000).
   (e) Interest received on investments ₹ 60,000.

(ii) Compensation received ₹ 90,000 by the company in a suit filed.

(iii) Income tax paid during the year ₹ 10,50,000.

(iv) 15,000, 10% preference shares of ₹ 100 each were redeemed at the end at a premium of 5%. Further the company issued 50,000 equity shares of ₹ 10 each at a premium of 20%. Dividend on preference shares were paid at the time of redemption.

(v) Final Dividends paid ₹ 5 lakhs and Interim dividend paid ₹ 3 lakhs.

(vi) Land was purchased for ₹ 2,40,000 for which the company issued 20,000 equity shares of ₹ 10 each at a premium of 20% to the land owner as consideration.

(vii) Current assets and Current liabilities in the beginning and at the end of the years were as detailed below:

Particulars	*Opening* ₹	*Closing* ₹
Inventories	12,00,000	13,18,000
Trade Receivables	2,58,000	2,53,100
Cash in hand	1,96,300	35,300
Trade Payables	2,11,000	2,11,300
Outstanding expenses	75,000	81,800

SOLUTION

CASH FLOW STATEMENT FOR THE YEAR ENDED 31ST MARCH, 2016

Particulars	₹
Net Profit before income tax and extraordinary items:	20,00,000
Adjustments for:	
Depreciation on Fixed Assets	5,00,000
Discount on issue of Debentures	30,000
Interest on Debentures paid	3,50,000
Interest on Investments received	(60,000)
Profit on Sale of Investments	(20,000)
Operating profit before working capital changes	28,00,000
Adjustments for:	
Increase in Inventories	(1,18,000)
Decrease in Trade Receivables	4,900
Increase in Trade Payables	300
Increase in outstanding expenses	6,800
Cash flow from operation	26,94,000
Income Tax paid	(10,50,000)
	16,44,000
Cash flow from extraordinary items:	
Compensation received in a suit filed	90,000
Net Cash flow from operating activities	17,34,000
Cash flow from investing activities:	
Sale proceeds of investments	3,20,000
Interest received on investment	60,000
Net cash flow from investing activities	3,80,000
Cash flow from financing activities:	
Proceeds by issue of equity shares at a premium	6,00,000
Redemption of preference shares at a premium	(15,75,000)
Preference Dividend paid	(1,50,000)
Interest on debentures paid	(3,50,000)

Dividend paid (5,00,000 + 3,00,000)	(8,00,000)
	(22,75,000)
Net Decrease in Cash and Cash Equivalents	(1,61,000)
Cash & Cash Equivalents at the beginning of the year	1,96,300
Cash & Cash Equivalents at the end of the year	35,300

PROBLEM 5

From the following information, prepare a Cash Flow Statement:

BALANCE SHEETS AS AT ...

Particulars	*Note*	*31.03.2016* ₹	*31.03.2015* ₹
I. EQUITY AND LIABILITIES			
(1) Shareholders' Funds			
(a) Share Capital	1	18,80,000	16,00,000
(b) Reserves and Surplus	2	11,00,000	8,40,000
(2) Non-Current Liabilities [9% Debentures]		2,80,000	4,00,000
(3) Current Liabilities			
Trade Payables		5,20,000	4,80,000
Other Current Liabilities (Unpaid Dividend)		16,000	—
Short-term Provisions	3	4,84,000	4,80,000
Total		42,80,000	38,00,000
II. ASSETS			
(1) Non-Current Assets			
Tangible Fixed Assets		38,00,000	32,00,000
Accumulated Depreciation		(11,60,000)	(9,20,000)
Non-Current Investments		3,20,000	4,00,000
(2) Current Assets			
Cash & Cash Equivalents		10,000	10,000
Other Current Assets		13,10,000	11,10,000
Total		42,80,000	38,00,000

Notes to Accounts:

Particulars	*31.03.2016* ₹	*31.03.2015* ₹
1. Share Capital		
Equity Share Capital	16,00,000	12,00,000
10% Preference Share Capital	2,80,000	4,00,000
	18,80,000	16,00,000
2. Reserves and Surplus		
General Reserve	8,00,000	6,80,000

Profit and Loss A/c	2,60,000	1,60,000
Capital Reserve	40,000	—
	11,00,000	8,40,000
3. Short-Term Provisions		
Proposed Dividend	1,44,000	1,20,000
Provision for Tax	3,40,000	3,60,000
	4,84,000	4,80,000

Additional Information:

(i) The company sold one fixed asset for ₹ 1,00,000, the cost of which was ₹ 2,00,000 and the depreciation provided on it was ₹ 80,000. The company also decided to write off another fixed asset costing ₹ 56,000 on which depreciation amounting to ₹ 40,000 has been provided. Depreciation on fixed assets provided ₹ 3,60,000.

(ii) Sold some investment at a profit of ₹ 40,000, which was credited to capital reserve.

(iii) Debentures and preference share capital redeemed at 5% premium.

(iv) Company decided to value Inventories at cost, whereas previously the practice was to value Inventories at cost *less* 10%. The opening Inventories was ₹ 2,16,000. The Closing Inventories was correctly valued at ₹ 3,00,000.

SOLUTION

CASH FLOW STATEMENT FOR THE YEAR ENDED 31ST MARCH, 2016

Particulars	₹	₹
I. Cash Flow from operating activities		
Profit after appropriation		
Increase in Profit and Loss Account after inventory adjustment [₹ 2,60,000 – (₹ 1,60,000 + ₹ 24,000)]	76,000	
Transfer to general reserve	1,20,000	
Proposed dividend	1,44,000	
Provision for tax	3,40,000	
Net profit before taxation and extraordinary item	6,80,000	
Adjustments for:		
Depreciation	3,60,000	
Loss on sale of fixed assets	20,000	
Interest on Debentures	36,000	
Decrease in value of fixed assets	16,000	
Premium on redemption of preference share' capital	6,000	
Premium on redemption of debentures	6,000	
Operating profit before working capital changes	11,24,000	
Increase in Trade Payables (₹ 5,20,000 – ₹ 4,80,000)	40,000	
Increase in other current assets [₹ 13,10,000 – (₹ 11,10,000 + ₹ 24,000))	(1,76,000)	
Cash generated from operations	9,88,000	

	Income taxes paid	(3,60,000)	
	Net Cash from operating activities		6,28,000
II.	**Cash Flow from investing activities**		
	Purchase of fixed assets	(8,56,000)	
	Proceeds from sale of fixed assets	1,00,000	
	Proceeds from sale of investments	1,20,000	
	Net Cash from investing activities		(6,36,000)
III.	**Cash Flow from financing activities**		
	Proceeds from issuance of Share Capital		4,00,000
	Redemption of Preference Share Capital (₹ 1,20,000 + ₹ 6,000)		(1,26,000)
	Redemption of Debentures (₹ 1,20,000 + ₹ 6,000)		(1,26,000)
	Dividend paid (₹ 1,20,000 – ₹ 16,000)		(1,04,000)
	Interest on Debentures		(36,000)
	Net Cash from financing activities		8,000
	Net increase/decrease in cash and cash equivalent during the year		Nil
	Cash and Cash equivalent at the beginning of the year		10,000
	Cash and Cash equivalent at the end of the year		10,000

Working Notes:

1. Revaluation of Inventories will increase opening Inventories by ₹ 24,000 (i.e. 2,16,000 × 10/90)

   Opening of other current assets ₹ 11,10,000 + ₹ 24,000 = ₹ 11,34,000

   Due to under valuation of Inventories, the opening balance of Profit and Loss Account be increase by ₹ 24,000.

   The opening balance Profit and Loss Account after revaluation of Inventories will be

   ₹ 1,60,000 + ₹ 24,000 = ₹ 1,84,000

Dr. **2. INVESTMENTS ACCOUNT** *Cr.*

Particulars	₹	*Particulars*	₹
To Balance bld	4,00,000	By Bank A/c (Balancing figure being investment sold)	1,20,000
To Capital Reserve Account (Profit on sale of investment)	40,000	Balance c/d	3,20,000
	4,40,000		4,40,000

Dr. **3. FIXED ASSETS ACCOUNT** *Cr.*

Particulars	₹	*Particulars*	₹
To Balance bld	32,00,000	By Bank A/c (sale of Assets)	1,00,000
To Bank A/c (Bal. figure being assets purchased)	8,56,000	By Accumulated depreciation A/c	80,000
		By Profit and Loss A/c (Loss on sale of assets)	20,000
		By Accumulated Depreciation A/c	40,000
		By Profit and Loss A/c	16,000

		(Assets written off)	
		By Balance c/d	38,00,000
	40,56,000		40,56,000

Dr. **4. ACCUMULATED DEPRECIATION ACCOUNT** Cr.

Particulars	₹	*Particulars*	₹
To Fixed Assets A/c	80,000	By Balance b/d	9,20,000
To Fixed Assets A/c	40,000	By Profit and Loss A/c	3,60,000
To Balance c/d	11,60,000	(Depreciation for the period)	
	12,80,000		12,80,000

PROBLEM 6

From the following information, prepare a Cash Flow Statement:

BALANCE SHEETS AS AT ...

Particulars	*Note*	*31.03.2016* ₹	*31.03.2015* ₹
I. EQUITY AND LIABILITIES			
(1) Shareholders' Funds			
(a) Share Capital	1	6,00,000	7,00,000
(b) Reserves and Surplus	2	3,60,000	2,75,000
(2) Non-Current Liabilities [9% Debentures]		2,00,000	—
(3) Current Liabilities			
Trade Payables		1,15,000	1,10,000
Other Current Liabilities		30,000	20,000
Short-term Provisions	3	1,85,000	1,20,000
Total		14,90,000	12,25,000
II. ASSETS			
(1) Non-Current Assets			
Tangible Fixed Assets	4	9,15,000	7,00,000
Non-Current Investments		50,000	80,000
Other Non-Current Assets	5	1,25,000	65,000
(2) Current Assets			
Inventories		95,000	90,000
Trade Receivables		2,40,000	2,00,000
Cash & Cash Equivalents		65,000	90,000
Total		14,90,000	12,25,000

Notes to Accounts:

Particulars	*31.03.2016* ₹	*31.03.2015* ₹
1. Share Capital		
Equity Share Capital	6,00,000	5,00,000
10% Preference Share Capital	—	2,00,000
	6,00,000	7,00,000
2. Reserves and Surplus		
General Reserve	1,00,000	2,50,000
Profit and Loss A/c	60,000	25,000
Capital Reserve	1,00,000	—
Capital Redemption Reserve	1,00,000	—
	3,60,000	2,75,000
3. Short-Term Provisions		
Proposed Dividend	90,000	60,000
Provision for Tax	95,000	60,000
	1,85,000	1,20,000
4. Tangible Fixed Assets		
Land & Building	1,50,000	2,00,000
Machinery	7,65,000	5,00,000
	9,15,000	7,00,000
5. Other Non-Current Assets		
Voluntary Separation Payments	1,25,000	65,000

Additional Information:

(i) A piece of land has been sold out for ₹ 1,50,000 (Cost: ₹ 1,20,000) and the balance land was revalued. Capital Reserve consisted of profit on sale and profit on revaluation.

(ii) During the year on 1st April, 2015 a plant was sold for ₹ 90,000 (Original Cost: ₹ 70,000 and W.D.V.: ₹ 50,000) and Debentures worth ₹ 1 lakhs was issued at par as part consideration for plant of ₹ 4.5 lakhs acquired. Depreciation @ 15% has been written off from Plant account but no depreciation has been charged on Land and Building.

(iii) Part of the investments (Cost ₹ 50,000) was sold for ₹ 70,000.

(iv) Income tax liability for the current year was estimated at ₹ 1,35,000.

(v) Pre-acquisition dividend received ₹ 5,000 was adjusted against cost of investment.

(vi) Voluntary separation cost of ₹ 50,000 was adjusted against General Reserve.

SOLUTION

CASH FLOW STATEMENT FOR THE YEAR ENDED 31ST MARCH, 2016

Particulars	₹
Net Profit before taxation	2,60,000

Adjustment for:	
Depreciation	1,35,000
Profit on sale of plant	(40,000)
Profit on sale of investments	(20,000)
Interest on debentures	18,000
Operating profit before working capital changes	3,53,000
Increase in Inventories	(5,000)
Increase in Trade Receivables	(40,000)
Increase in Trade Payables	5,000
Increase in other current liabilities	10,000
Cash generated from operations	3,23,000
Income taxes paid	(1,00,000)
	2,23,000
Voluntary separation payments	(1,10,000)
Net Cash from operating activities	1,13,000
Cash Flow from investing activities	
Proceeds from sale of land	1,50,000
Proceeds from sale of plant	90,000
Proceeds from sale of investments	70,000
Purchase of plant	(3,50,000)
Purchase of investments	(25,000)
Pre-acquisition dividend received	5,000
Net cash used in investing activities	(60,000)
Cash Flow from financing activities	
Proceeds from issue of equity shares	1,00,000
Proceeds from issue of debentures	1,00,000
Redemption of preference shares	(2,00,000)
Dividends paid	(60,000)
Interest paid on debentures	(18,000)
Net cash used in financing activities	(78,000)
Net decrease in cash and cash equivalents	(25,000)
Cash and cash equivalents at the beginning of the year	90,000
Cash and Cash equivalents at the end of the year	65,000

Working Notes:

1. NET PROFIT BEFORE TAXATION

Particulars	₹
Retained profit	60,000
Less: Opening Balance	(25,000)
Proposed dividend	90,000

Provision for taxation	1,35,000
	2,60,000

Dr. **2. LAND AND BUILDING ACCOUNT** Cr.

Particulars	₹	Particulars	₹
To Balance b/d	2,00,000	By Cash (Sale)	1,50,000
To Capital Reserve (Profit on sale)	30,000	By Balance c/d	1,50,000
To Capital Reserve (Revalua. Profit)	70,000		
	3,00,000		3,00,000

Dr. **3. PLANT AND MACHINERY ACCOUNT** Cr.

Particulars	₹	Particulars	₹
To Balance b/d	5,00,000	By Cash (Sale)	90,000
To Profit and Loss A/c	40,000	By Depreciation A/c (b.f.)	1,35,000
To Debentures	1,00,000	By Balance c/d	7,65,000
To Bank A/c	3,50,000		
	9,90,000		9,90,000

Dr. **4. INVESTMENTS ACCOUNT** Cr.

Particulars	₹	Particulars	₹
To Balance b/d	80,000	By Cash (Sale)	70,000
To Profit and Loss Account	20,000	By Dividend (Pre-acquisition)	5,000
To Bank A/c (Balancing figure)	25,000	By Balance c/d	50,000
	1,25,000		1,25,000

Dr. **5. PROVISION FOR TAXATION ACCOUNT** Cr.

Particulars	₹	Particulars	₹
To Bank (Balancing figure)	1,00,000	By Balance b/d	60,000
To Balance c/d	95,000	By Profit and Loss Account	1,35,000
	1,95,000		1,95,000

Dr. **6. CAPITAL RESERVE ACCOUNT** Cr.

Particulars	₹	Particulars	₹
To Balance c/d	1,00,000	By Profit on Sale of Land	30,000
		By Profit on Reval. of Land	70,000
	1,00,000		1,00,000

Dr. **7. GENERAL RESERVE ACCOUNT** Cr

Particulars	₹	Particulars	₹
To Voluntary separation cost	50,000	By Balance b/d	2,50,000
To Capital redemption reserve	1,00,000		

To Balance c/d	1,00,000		
	2,50,000		2,50,000

Dr. **8. VOLUNTARY SEPARATION PAYMENTS ACCOUNT** *Cr.*

Particulars	₹	*Particulars*	₹
To balance b/d	65,000	By General Reserve	50,000
To Bank (Balancing figure)	1,10,000	By Balance c/d	1,25,000
	1,75,000		1,75,000

PROBLEM 7

From the following information, prepare a Cash Flow Statement:

BALANCE SHEETS AS AT ...

Particulars	*Note*	*31.03.2016* ₹	*31.03.2015* ₹
I. EQUITY AND LIABILITIES			
(1) Shareholders' Funds			
(a) Share Capital	1	3,50,000	3,00,000
(b) Reserves and Surplus	2	82,000	38,000
(2) Non-Current Liabilities			
(3) Current Liabilities			
Trade Payables		65,000	44,000
Other Current Liabilities (Dividend Payable)		4,000	—
Short-term Provisions	3	65,000	55,000
Total		5,66,000	4,37,000
II. ASSETS			
(1) Non-Current Assets			
Tangible Fixed Assets	4	2,66,000	1,90,000
Intangible Assets [Goodwill]		47,000	60,000
Non-Current Investments		35,000	10,000
(2) Current Assets			
Inventories		78,000	85,000
Trade Receivables		1,08,000	75,000
Cash & Cash Equivalents		32,000	17,000
Total		5,66,000	4,37,000

Particulars	*31.03.2016* ₹	*31.03.2015* ₹
1. Share Capital		
Equity Share Capital	2,50,000	1,50,000
8% Preference Share Capital	1,00,000	1,50,000

	3,50,000	3,00,000
2. Reserves and Surplus		
General Reserve	30,000	20,000
Profit and Loss A/c	27,000	18,000
Capital Reserve	25,000	—
	82,000	38,000
3. Short-Term Provisions		
Proposed Dividend	33,000	27,000
Provision for Tax	32,000	28,000
	65,000	55,000
4. Tangible Fixed Assets		
Land & Building	75,000	1,00,000
Machinery	1,91,000	90,000
	2,66,000	1,90,000

Addition Information:

(i) ₹ 18,000 depreciation has been written off Plant and Machinery and no depreciation has been charged on Land and Building.

(ii) A piece of land has been sold out and the balance has been revalued, profit on such sale and revaluation being transferred to Capital Reserve. There is no other entry in Capital Reserve Account.

(iii) A plant was sold for ₹ 12,000 (WDV being ₹ 15,000).

(iv) Dividend received amounted to ₹ 2,100 which included pre acquisition dividend of ₹ 600.

(v) An interim dividend of ₹ 10,000 has been paid.

SOLUTION

CASH FLOW STATEMENT FOR THE YEAR ENDING 31ST MARCH, 2016

Particulars	₹	₹
I. Cash Flows from Operating Activities		
A. Closing balance as per Profit and Loss Account		27,000
Less: Opening balance as per Profit and Loss Account		(18,000)
Add: Proposed dividend during the year		33,000
Add: Interim dividend paid during the year		10,000
Add: Transfer to reserve		10,000
Add: Provision for Tax		32,000
B. Net profit before taxation, and extra ordinary item		94,000
C. *Add:* Items to be added		
Depreciation	18,000	
Loss on sale of Plant	3,000	
Goodwill w/o	13,000	34,000
D. *Less:* Dividend Income		(1,500)

E. Operating profit before working capital changes [B + C – D]		1,26,500
F. *Add:* Decrease in Current Assets and Increase in current Liabilities		
Decrease in Inventories	7,000	
Increase in Trade Payables	21,000	28,000
G. *Less:* Increase in Trade Receivables (Gross)		(33,000)
H. Cash generated from operations [E + F – G]		1,21,500
I. *Less:* Income taxes paid		(28,000)
J. Net Cash from (used in) operating activities		93,500
II. Cash Flows from Investing Activities:		
Purchase of Plant		(1,34,000)
Sale of Land		50,000
Sale of Plant		12,000
Purchase of Investments		(25,600)
Dividend Received		2,100
Net Cash used in investing activities		(95,500)
III. Cash Flows from Financing Activities:		
Proceeds from issuance of share capital		1,00,000
Redemption of preference shares		(50,000)
Interim Dividend paid		(10,000)
Final Dividend paid [₹.27,000 – ₹.4,000]		(23,000)
Net Cash from Financing Activities		17,000
IV. Net Increase in Cash and Cash Equivalents [I + II + III]		15,000
V. Cash and Cash Equivalents at beginning of Period		17,000
VI. Cash and Cash Equivalents at end of Period [IV + V]		32,000

Working Notes:

Dr. **1. LAND AND BUILDING ACCOUNT** *Cr.*

Particulars	₹	*Particulars*	₹
To Balance b/d	1,00,000	By Bank A/c (sale)	50,000
To Capital Reserve A/c (Profit on sale and revaluation)	25,000	By Balance c/d	75,000
	1,25,000		1,25,000

Cr. **2. PLANT AND MACHINERY ACCOUNT** *Dr.*

Particulars	₹	*Particulars*	₹
To Balance b/d	90,000	By Depreciation A/c	18,000
To Bank A/c (Purchase)	1,34,000	By Bank A/c (Sale)	12,000
		By Profit and Loss A/c	
		By (Loss on sale)	3,000
		By Balance c/d	1,91,000
	2,24,000		2,24,000

Dr. **3. INVESTMENTS ACCOUNT** *Cr.*

Particulars	₹	*Particulars*	₹
To Balance b/d	10,000	By Bank A/c (Div. received)	600
To Bank A/c (Purchases)	25,600	By Balance c/d	35,000
	35,600		35,600

4. It has been assumed that proposed dividend includes preference dividend also.

PROBLEM 8

From the following information, prepare a Cash Flow Statement:

BALANCE SHEETS AS AT ...

Particulars	*Note*	*31.03.2016 ₹ '000*	*31.03.2015 ₹ '000*
I. EQUITY AND LIABILITIES			
(1) Shareholders' Funds			
(a) Share Capital		1500	1250
(b) Reserves and Surplus		3410	1380
(2) Non-Current Liabilities [Long Term Debt]		1110	1040
(3) Current Liabilities			
Trade Payables		150	1890
Other Current Liabilities	1	630	1100
Total		6800	6660
II. ASSETS			
(1) Non-Current Assets			
Tangible Fixed Assets		2180	1910
Accumulated Depreciation		(1450)	(1060)
Non-Current Investments		2500	2500
(2) Current Assets			
Inventories		900	1950
Trade Receivables		1700	1200
Cash & Cash Equivalents		870	160
Other Current Assets (Interest Receivable)		100	—
Total		6800	6660

Notes to Accounts:

Particulars	*31.03.2016 ₹*	*31.03.2015 ₹*
1. Other Current Liabilities		
Interest Payable	230	100

Income Tax Payable	400	1000
	630	1100

STATEMENT OF PROFIT OR LOSS FOR THE YEAR ENDED 31ST MARCH, 2016

Particulars	*₹ '000*
Sales	30,650
Cost of sales	(26,000)
Gross profit	4,650
Depreciation	(450)
Administrative and selling expenses	(910)
Interest expenses	(400)
Interest income	300
Dividend income	200
Net profit before taxation and extraordinary items	3,390
Extraordinary items:	
Insurance proceeds from earthquake disaster settlement	140
Net Profit after extraordinary items	3,530
Income tax	(300)
	3,230

Additional Information:

(i) An amount of ₹ 250 was raised from the issue of share capital and a further ₹250 was raised from long-term borrowings.

(ii) Interest expense was ₹ 400 of which ₹ 170 was paid during the period ₹ 100 relating to interest expense of the prior period was also paid during the period.

(iii) Dividends paid were ₹ 1,200.

(iv) Tax deducted at source on dividends received (including in the tax expense of ₹ 300 for the year) amounted to ₹ 40.

(v) During the period the enterprise acquired fixed assets for ₹ 350. The payment was made in cash.

(vi) Plant with original cost of ₹ 80 and accumulated depreciation of ₹ 60 was sold for ₹ 20.

(vii) Trade Receivables and Trade Payables include amounts relating to credit sales and credit purchase only.

SOLUTION

CASH FLOW STATEMENT (DIRECT METHOD)

Particulars	*(₹)*
Cash flows from Operating Activities	
Cash receipts from customers (30,650 + 1,200 – 1,700)	30,150
Cash paid to suppliers (24,950 + 1,890 – 150)	(26,690)
Cash paid to employees and for expenses	(910)
Cash generated from operations	2,550

Income tax paid (300 + 1000 – 400 – 40)	(860)
Cash flow before extraordinary item:	1,690
Proceeds from earthquake disaster settlement	140
Net cash from operating activities	1,830
Cash flows from Investing Activities	
Purchase of fixed assets	(350)
Proceeds from sale of equipment	20
Interest received (300 – 100)	200
Dividends received (200 – 40)	160
Net cash from investing activities	30
Cash flows from Financing Activities	
Proceeds from issuance of share capital	250
Proceeds from long term borrowings	250
Repayment of long term borrowings (1,040 + 250 – 1,110)	(180)
Interest paid (400 + 100 – 230)	(270)
Dividends paid	(1,200)
Net Cash used in financial activities	1,150
Net increase in cash and cash equivalents	710
Cash and Cash Equivalents at beginning of the period	160
Cash and Cash Equivalents at end of the period	870

Working Note:

CASH PAID TO SUPPLIERS, EMPLOYEES AND FOR EXPENSES

Particulars	₹
Cost of sales	26,000
Add: Closing Inventories	900
Less: Opening Inventories	(1,950)
Credit Purchases	24,950

PROBLEM 9

The following particulars relate to Bee Ltd., for the year ended 31st March, 2016:

(i) Furniture of Book Value of ₹ 15,500 was disposed off for ₹ 12,000.

(ii) Machinery costing ₹ 3,10,000 was purchased and ₹ 20,000 were spent on its erection.

(iii) Fully paid 8% preference shares of the face value of ₹ 10,00,000 were redeemed at a premium of 3%. In this connection 60,000 equity shares of ₹ 10 each were issued at a premium of ₹ 2 per share. The entire money being received with applications.

(iv) Dividend was paid as follows:

On 8% Preference Shares	₹ 40,000
On equity shares	₹ 1,10,000

(v) Total sales were ₹ 32,00,000 out of which cash sales were ₹ 11,50,000.

(vi) Total purchases were ₹ 8,00,000 including cash purchases of ₹ 60,000.

(vii) Total expenses were ₹ 12,40,000 charged to Profit and Loss A/c.

(viii) Taxes paid including dividend distribution tax of ₹ 22,500 were ₹ 3,30,000.

(ix) Closing Cash and cash equivalents were ₹ 1,25,000.

Prepare Cash Flow Statement as per AS 3 after taking into consideration the following also:

Particulars	*Opening (₹)*	*Closing (₹)*
Trade Receivables	1,50,000	1,47,000
Trade Payables	78,000	83,000
Unpaid Expenses	63,000	55,000

SOLUTION

CASH FLOW STATEMENT FOR THE YEAR ENDED 31ST MARCH, 2016

	Particulars	₹
I.	**Cash Flow from Operating Activities**	
	Cash receipts from customers	32,03,000
	Less: Cash paid to suppliers	(7,95,000)
	Less: Cash paid for expenses	(12,48,000)
	Casn generated from operations	11,60,000
	Income tax paid (₹ 3,30,000 – ₹ 22,500)	(3,07,500)
	Net Cash from Operating Activities	8,52,500
II.	**Cash Flows from Investing Activities**	
	Sale of Furniture	12,000
	Purchase of Machinery	(3,30,000)
	Net Cash used in Investing Activities	(3,18,000)
III.	**Cash Flow from Financing Activities**	
	Proceeds from issue of equity shares	7,20,000
	Redemption of 8% preference shares	(10,30,000)
	Dividend paid (₹ 40,000 + ₹ 1,10,000)	(1,50,000)
	Dividend distribution tax paid	(22,500)
	Net Cash used in Financing Activities	(4,82,500)
	Net Increase in Cash and Cash equivalents	52,000
	Add: Cash and Cash Equivalents at the beginning (Bal. fig)	73,000
	Cash and Cash Equivalents at the end	1,25,000

Working Notes:

1. Credit sales = ₹32, 00,000 – ₹ 11,50,000 = ₹ 20,50,000

Dr. **2. TOTAL TRADE RECEIVABLES ACCOUNT** *Cr.*

Particulars	₹	*Particulars*	₹
To Balance b/d	1,50,000	By Cash/Bank A/c (Bal. fig.)	20,53,000
To Credit Sales	20,50,000	By Balance c/d	1,47,000
	22,00.000		22,00,000

3. Total Sale Receipts = ₹ 20,53,000 + ₹ 11,50,000 = ₹ 32,03,000
4. Credit Purchases = ₹ 8,00,000 – ₹ 60,0000 = ₹ 7,40,000

Dr. **5. TOTAL TRADE PAYABLES ACCOUNT** *Cr.*

Particulars	₹	*Particulars*	₹
To Cash/Bank A/c (Bal. fig.)	7,35,000	By Balance b/d	78,000
To Balance c/d	83,000	By Credit Purchases	7,40,000
	8,18,000		8,18,000

6. Total Payments to suppliers = ₹ 7,35,000 + ₹ 60,000 = ₹ 7,95,000
7. Payment for Expenses = ₹ 12,40,000 + ₹ 63,000 – ₹ 55,000 = ₹ 12,48,000

COMPERHENSIVE REVISIONAL PROBLEMS

PROBLEM 10

From the following information, prepare a Cash Flow Statement:

BALANCE SHEETS AS AT ...

Particulars	*Note*	*31.03.2016* ₹	*31.03.2015* ₹
I. EQUITY AND LIABILITIES			
(1) Shareholders' Funds			
(a) Share Capital	1	6,60,000	7,00,000
(b) Reserves and Surplus	2	10,18,300	3,06,000
(2) Non-Current Liabilities [10% Debentures]		1,40,000	2,00,000
(3) Current Liabilities			
Trade Payables		1,05,000	1,00,000
Other Current Liabilities	3	1,06,000	91,500
Short-term Provisions	4	44,100	36,000
Total		20,73,400	14,33,500
II. ASSETS			
(1) Non-Current Assets			
Tangible Fixed Assets		7,65,000	5,00,000
Intangible Assets [Goodwill]		15,000	—
Non-Current Investments	5	1,15,000	1,10,000
Other Non-Current Assets (Voluntary Separation Payments)		1,25,000	65,000
(2) Current Assets			
Current Investments		21,500	31,500
Inventories		95,640	54,000
Trade Receivables		7,50,000	6,25,000
Provision for Doubtful debts		(1,90,000)	(1,50,000)

Cash & Cash Equivalents		3,73,260	1,96,000
Other Current Assets (Accrued Interest on Invst.)		3,000	2,000
Total		20,73,400	14,33,500

Notes to Accounts:

Particulars	*31.03.2016* ₹	*31.03.2015* ₹
1. Share Capital		
Equity Share Capital	6,60,000	5,00,000
Preference Share Capital	—	2,00,000
	6,60,000	7,00,000
2. Reserves and Surplus		
General Reserve	1,00,000	2,50,000
Profit and Loss A/c	18,300	48,000
Securities Premium	—	8,000
Capital Grant	8,00,000	—
Capital Redemption Reserve	1,00,000	—
	10,18,300	3,06,000
3. Other Current Liabilities		
Bank Overdraft	1,00,000	90,000
Unpaid Dividend	4,000	1,000
Unpaid Interest on Debentures	2,000	500
	1,06,000	91,500
4. Short-Term Provisions		
Proposed Dividend	36,000	30,000
Provision for Tax	8,100	6,0000
	44,100	36,000
6. Non-Current Investments		
10% Investments	80,000	1,00,000
Investments in Shares	35,000	10,000
	1,15,000	1,10,000

Additional Information:

(a) Depreciation on Plant & Machinery written off @ 15%.

(b) Dividend received amounted to ₹ 2,100 which included pre acquisition dividend of ₹ 600

(c) Debentures and Preference Shares were redeemed at 5% premium at the end.

(d) Compensation received in a suit filed by the company ₹ 90,000.

(e) Grant of ₹ 10,00,000 amortised in P&L A/c.

(f) It was decided to value Inventories at cost whereas previously the practice was to value Inventories at cost *less* 10%. However the closing Inventories were correctly valued at cost.

(g) Trade Receivables of ₹ 2,30,000 were written off against the Provision for Doubtful Debts A/c during the year.

(h) Current Investments costing ₹ 10,000 were sold for ₹ 12,000.

(i) Voluntary Separation payment ₹ 50000 adjusted against General Reserve.

(j) At the end of the year the business of Y Ltd. was purchased for ₹ 60,000 payable in fully paid equity shares. The assets included Inventories ₹ 26,640, Trade Receivables ₹ 10,000, and Machine ₹ 18,360. In addition Trade Payables of ₹ 15,000 were taken over.

SOLUTION

CASH FLOW STATEMENT OF TULSIAN LTD FOR THE YEAR ENDED 31ST MARCH, 2016

	Particulars	₹	₹
A	Cash Flow from Operating Activities		
	Difference between Closing and Opening balance of P & L A/c		(29,700)
	Add: Proposed dividend for the current year	36,000	
	Provision for tax:	7,100	
	Depreciation	1,35,000	
	Premium on redemption of debentures	3,000	
	Premium on redemption of Preference		
	Shares (₹ 10,000 – ₹ 8,000)	2,000	
	Interest on Debentures	20,000	
	Goodwill amortised	5,000	2,08,100
	Less: Capital Grant amortised	10,00,000	
	Under valuation of Opening Inventories (54,000 × 10/90)	6,000	
	Compensation received	90,000	
	Interest on 10% Investment	10,000	
	Dividend (₹ 2,100 – ₹ 600)	1,500	
	Profit on Sale of Current Investments	2,000	(11,09,500)
	Operating profit before working capital changes		(9,31,100)
	Add: Increase in Provision for doubtful debts		40,000
	Less: Increase in Inventories [(95,640 – 26,640) – (54,000 + 6,000)]	9,000	
	Increase in Trade Receivables [(7,50,000–10,000)–6,25,000]	1,15,000	
	Decrease in Trade Payables [(1,05,000 – 15,000) – 1,00,000]	10,000	(1,34,000)
	Operating Profit before extraordinary items		(10,25,100)
	Add: Compensation received		90,000
	Less: Voluntary Separation Payment		(1,10,000)
	Operating Profit before Income tax		(10,45,100)
	Less: Income Tax paid		(5,000)
	Net Cash Flow from Operating activities		(10,50,100)
B	**Cash Flow from Investing Activities**		
	Purchase of machinery		(3,81,640)
	Sale of 10% investment		20,000

	Interest on investments[10,000 - (3,000 - 2,000)]		9,000
	Purchase of investment in shares		(25,600)
	Dividend income		2,100
	Sale of Current Investments		12,000
	Net Cash Flow from Investing activities		(3,64,140)
C	**Cash flow from Financing activities**		
	Grant Received		18,00,000
	Dividend paid [30,000 – (4,000 – 1,000)]		(27,000)
	Interest on debentures paid [20,000 – (2,000 – 500)]		(18,500)
	Issue of Equity Share Capital [(6,60,000 – 60,000) – 5,00,000]		1,00,000
	Redemption of Red. Preference Shares [2,00,000 + 5% premium]		(2,10,000)
	Redemption of Debentures [60,000 + 5% premium]		(63,000)
	Net Cash Flow from Financing Activities		15,81,500
D	**Net Decrease in Cash & cash equivalents [A + B + C]**		1,67,260
E	**Opening Balance of Cash & Cash Equivalents (1,96,000 – 90,000)**		1,06,000
F	**Closing Balance of Cash & Cash Equivalents (3,73,260 – 1,00,000)**		2,73,260

Working Notes:

Dr. **1. PROVISION FOR TAX ACCOUNT** *Cr.*

Particulars	₹	*Particulars*	₹
To Bank A/c (bal. fig.)	5,000	By Balance b/d	6,000
To Balance c/d	8,100	By P & L A/c (Current year Provision)	7,100
	13,100		13,100

Dr. **2. PLANT & MACHINERY ACCOUNT** *Cr.*

Particulars	₹	*Particulars*	₹
To Balance b/d	5,00,000	By P & L - Dep. (7,65,000 × 15/85)	1,35,000
To Business Purchase A/c	18,360	By Balance c/d	7,65,000
To Bank A/c (bal. fig.)	3,81,640		
	9,00,000		9,00,000

Dr. **3. GOODWILL ACCOUNT** *Cr.*

Particulars	₹	*Particulars*	₹
To Balance b/d	-	By P & L A/c (Amortised)	5,000
To Business Purchase [60,000 – (26,640 + 10,000 + 18,360 – 15,000)]	20,000	By Balance c/d	15,000
	20,000		20,000

Dr. **4. VOLUNTARY SEPARATION PAYMENTS ACCOUNT** Cr.

Particulars	₹	Particulars	₹
To Balance b/d	65,000	By General Reserve	50,000
To Bank A/c (bal. fig.)	1,10,000	By Balance c/d	1,25,000
	1,75,000		1,75,000

Dr. **5. 10% INVESTMENTS ACCOUNT** Cr.

Particulars	₹	Particulars	₹
To Balance b/d	1,00,000	By Bank A/c (Sale) (b.f)	20,000
		By Balance c/d	80,000
	1,00,000		100,000

Dr. **6. INVESTMENT IN SHARES ACCOUNT** Cr.

Particulars	₹	Particulars	₹
To Balance b/d	10,000	By Bank A/c [Pre-acquisition Div.]	600
To Bank A/c (bal. fig.)	25,600	By Balance c/d	35,000
	35,600		35,600

Dr. **7. GENERAL RESERVE ACCOUNT** Cr.

Particulars	₹	Particulars	₹
To Voluntary Seperation A/c	50,000	By Balance b/d	2,50,000
To Capital Redemption Reserve	1,00,000		
To Balance c/d	1,00,000		
	2,50,000		2,50,000

8. Trade Receivables written off against provision for doubtful debts do not require any further adjustment.

PROBLEM 11

From the following information, prepare a Cash Flow Statement of Bharat Tushar Ltd.:

BALANCE SHEETS AS AT ...

Particulars	Note	31.03.2016 ₹	31.03.2015 ₹
I. EQUITY AND LIABILITIES			
(1) Shareholders' Funds			
(a) Share Capital		6,63,000	3,00,000
(b) Reserves and Surplus	1	2,72,500	2,15,000
(2) Non-Current Liabilities [10% Debentures]		1,40,000	2,00,000
(3) Current Liabilities			
Trade Payables		1,05,000	1,00,000
Other Current Liabilities	2	29,000	20,000

Short-term Provisions	3	1,21,000	1,20,000
Total		13,30,500	9,55,000
II. ASSETS			
(1) Non-Current Assets			
Tangible Fixed Assets	4	7,28,360	5,75,000
Intangible Assets	5	21,000	10,000
Non-Current Investments		80,000	1,00,000
(2) Current Assets			
Inventories		95,640	54,000
Trade Receivables (All Good)		2,50,000	1,25,000
Provision for Doubtful debts		(20,000)	(10,000)
Cash & Cash Equivalents		95,500	71,000
Short Term Loans and Advances (Advance Tax)		80,000	30,000
Total		13,30,500	9,55,000

Notes to Accounts:

Particulars	*31.03.2016* ₹	*31.03.2015* ₹
1. Reserves and Surplus		
General Reserve	1,09,550	1,70,000
Profit and Loss A/c	14,300	40,000
Securities Premium	88,650	—
Capital Reserve	60,000	5,000
	2,72,500	2,15,000
2. Other Current Liabilities		
Bank Overdraft	23,000	20,000
Unpaid Dividend	4,000	—
Unpaid Interest on Debentures	2,000	—
	29,000	20,000
3. Short-Term Provisions		
Proposed Dividend	36,000	30,000
Provision for Tax	85,000	90,000
	1,21,000	1,20,000
4. Tangible Fixed Assets		
Land (at Cost)	50,000	5,000
Machinery	9,68,360	8,00,000
Less: Depreciation on Machinery	(2,90,000)	(2,30,000)
	7,28,360	5,75,000
5. Intangible Fixed Assets		
Goodwill	15,000	—

Patents	6,000	10,000
	21,000	10,000

Additional Information:

1. One machine having a book value of ₹ 29,000 (Depreciation provided thereon ₹ 21,000) was sold for ₹ 25,000.
2. One machine costing ₹ 14,000 (fully depreciation) was discarded and written off.
3. An interim Dividend of ₹ 10,000 has also been paid on 30th June, 2013.
4. An Income Tax liability upto previous year has been settled and paid for ₹ 75,000.
5. 30% of the Debentures are to be redeemed converting into fully paid Equity Shares at a premium of 3% on 30.09.2012.
6. Marketable securities (having maturity of 2 months) costing ₹ 30,000 were disposed off at a profit of 20%.
7. At the end of the year, the Business of Y Ltd. was purchased for ₹ 60,000 payable in fully paid equity shares. The assets included Inventories ₹ 26,640. Trade Receivables ₹ 10,000 and Machine ₹ 18,360. Trade Payables of ₹ 15,000 were also taken over.
8. Land was revalued by 900% and the surplus was credited to Capital Reserve Account.
9. There is no entry (other than on account of profit on sale of investment @ 25% on cost and on revaluation of land) in Capital Reserve Account.
10. Dividend received amounted to ₹ 2,100 which includes pre-acquisition dividend of ₹ 600.
11. It was decided to value Inventories at cost whereas previously the practice was to value Inventories at cost *less* 10%. However, the Closing Inventories were correctly valued at cost.
12. On 01.07.2013, Tulsian Ltd. issued Bonus Shares to the equity shareholders.
13. On 01.10.2013, Tulsian Ltd. announced one share for every 3 shares held as right at 20% *less* than the market price during the last 6 months. Average market price was ₹ 20. The right issue was fully subscribed and allotted accordingly.
14. Trade Receivables of ₹ 2,30,000 were written off against the provision for doubtful debts account during the year.

SOLUTION

CASH FLOW STATEMENT FOR THE YEAR ENDING 31ST MARCH, 2016

Particulars	₹	₹
I. Cash Flows from Operating Activities:		
A. Closing Balance as per Profit and Loss Account		14,300
Less: Opening Balance as per Profit and Loss Account [₹40,000+₹6,000]		(46,000)
Add: Proposed dividend during the year		36,000
Add: Interim dividend paid during the year		10,000
Add: Transfer to Reserve		30,000
Add: Provision for Tax Current Year		85,000
Less: Excise Provision for Tax for previous year		(15,000)
Add: Increase in provision for doubtful debts (since all Trade Receivables are good)		10,000

B. Net Profit before Taxation, and Extraordinary item		1,24,300
C. *Add:* Items to be added Depreciation	95,000	
Add: Interest on Debentures [₹10,000 + ₹7,000]	17,000	
Add: Patents amortised	4,000	
Add: Loss on sale of Machinery	4,000	
Add: Goodwill amortised	5,000	1,25,000
D. *Less:* Items to be deducted		
Less: Dividend Income		(1,500)
E. Operating Profit before Working Capital Changes [B + C – D]		2,47,800
F. *Less:* Decrease in Trade Payables [₹1,05,000 – ₹15,000– ₹1,00,000]	(10,000)	
Less: Increase in Inventories [₹95,640–₹26,640–(₹54,000 + ₹6,000)	(9,000)	
Less: Increase in Trade Receivables [₹2,50,000 – ₹10,000 – ₹1,25,000]	(1,15,000)	(1,34,000)
G. Cash Generated from Operations [E + F - G]		1,13,800
H. *Less:* Income taxs paid: for previous year		(45,000)
for current year		(80,000)
I. Net Cash used in Operating Activities		(11,200)
II. Cash Flows from Investing Activities:		
Purchase of Machinery		(2,14,000)
Proceeds from sale of Machinery		25,000
Purchase of Investments		(20,600)
Proceeds from sale of Investments		50,000
Dividend Received		2,100
Net Cash used in Investing Activities		(1,57,500)
III. Cash Flows from Financing Activities:		
Proceeds from issuance of share capital (including Premium)		2,41,200
Interest paid on Debentures [₹ 17,000 – ₹ 2,000]		(15,000)
Interim Dividend paid		(10,000)
Final Dividend paid [₹ 30,000 – ₹ 4,000]		(26,000)
Net Cash from Financing Activities		1,90,200
IV. Net Increase in Cash and Cash Equivalents [I + II + III]		21,500
V. Cash and Cash Equivalents at beg. of Period (71,000 – 20,000)		51,000
VI. Cash and Cash Equivalents at End of Period (95,500 – 23,000)		72,500

Working Notes:

Dr. **1. CAPITAL RESERVE ACCOUNT** *Cr.*

Particulars	₹	*Particulars*	₹
To Balance c/d	60,000	By Balance b/d	5,000
		By Land A/c (900% of ₹5,000)	45,000

		By Investments A/c (Profit on Sale)	10,000
		By (Balancing figure)	
	60,000		60,000

2. Cost of Investments sold = ₹ 10,000/0.25 = ₹ 40,000

   Sale Proceeds = ₹ 40,000 + ₹ 10,000 = ₹ 50,000

Dr. **3. INVESTMENTS ACCOUNT** *Cr.*

Particulars	₹	*Particulars*	₹
To Balance b/d	1,00,000	By Bank A/c (Sale Proceeds)	50,000
To Capital Reserve A/c (Profit)	10,000	By Bank A/c (Dividend out of	600
To Bank A/c (Purchases)	20,600	By Pre-acquisition profits)	
		By Balance c/d	80,000
	1,30,600		1,30,600

Dr. **4. PLANT AND MACHINERY ACCOUNT (AT COST)** *Cr.*

Particulars	₹	*Particulars*	₹
To Balance b/d	8,00,000	By Machine Disposal A/c (Sold)	50,000
To Business Purchase A/c	18,360	By Machinery Disposal A/c	14,000
To Bank A/c (Purchases) (b/f)	2,14,000	(Discarded)	
		By Balance c/d	9,68,360
	10,32,360		10,32,360

Dr. **5. ACCUMULATED DEPRECIATION ACCOUNT** *Cr.*

Particulars	₹	*Particulars*	₹
To Machinery Disposal A/c	21,000	By Balance b/d	2,30,000
To Machinery Disposal A/c	14,000	By Profit and Loss A/c (b/f)	95,000
To Balance c/d	2,90,000		
	3,25,000		3,25,000

Dr. **6. MACHINERY DISPOSAL AND DISCARDED ACCOUNT** *Cr.*

Particulars	₹	*Particulars*	₹
To Plant and Machinery A/c (Cost)	50,000	By Accumulated Depreciation A/c	21,000
To Plant and Machinery A/c (Cost)	14,000	By Accumulated Depreciation A/c	14,000
		By Bank A/c	25,000
		By Profit and Loss A/c (Loss)	4,000
	64,000		64,000

Dr. **7. PROVISION FOR TAX ACCOUNT** *Cr.*

Particulars	₹	*Particulars*	₹
To Advance Tax A/c	30,000	By Balance b/d	90,000
To Bank A/c (Paid)	45,000	By P & L A/c (Provision)	85,000

To P&L A/c (Excess Provision)	15,000		
To Balance c/d	85,000		
	1,75,000		1,75,000

Dr. **8. ADVANCED TAX ACCOUNT** Cr.

Particulars	₹	Particulars	₹
To Balance b/d	30,000	By Provision for Tax A/c	30,000
To Bank A/c	80,000	By Balance c/d	80,000
	1,10,000		1,10,000

9. As per SEBI Guidelines, no Company can issue bonus shares to its shareholders without extending similar benefit to holders of convertible debentures through reservation of bonus shares in proportion to such convertible part of debentures.

Thus, Redeemable amount of convertible debentures are as follows:

Particulars	₹
Face value of Convertible Debentures	60,000
Add: Premium on Redemption @ 3%	1,800
Total Redeemable Amount	61,800
Number of Equity Shares to be issued	618

10. CALCULATION OF BONUS SHARES AND RIGHT SHARE CAPITAL

A. Total Capital eligible for Bonus [₹3,00,000 + ₹61,800]	3,61,800
B. *Add:* Bonus (assuming X)	X
C. Total Capital eligible for Right [A + B]	3,61,800 + X
D. *Add:* Right Share Capital [1:3]	1/3[3,61,800 + X]
E. Total Capital after right issue	4,82,400 + 4/3X
F. *Add:* Shares issued for consideration other than cash to Y Ltd.	60,000
G. Closing Balance of Share Capital [E + F]	5,42,400 + 4/3X

Thus 5,42,400 + (3/4)X = ₹ 6,63,000

X = (₹6,63,000 – ₹ 5,42,400) × 3/4 = ₹ 90,450

Thus 1 Bonus share is to be issued for 4 shares held

Right Share Capital = 1/3(₹ 3,61,800 + ₹ 90,450) = ₹ 1,50,750

Dr. **11. EQUITY SHARE CAPITAL ACCOUNT** Cr.

Particulars	₹	Particulars	₹
To Balance c/d	6,63,000	By Balance b/d	3,00,000
		By General Reserve [Bonus]	90,450
		By Debenture holders A/c	61,800
		By Bank A/c (Rights)	1,50,750
		By Y Ltd.	60,000
	6,63,000		6,63,000

Dr. **12. GENERAL RESERVE** Cr.

Particulars	₹	*Particulars*	₹
To Equity Share Capital A/c	90,450	By Balance b/d	1,70,000
To Balance c/d	1,09,550	By Profit and Loss A/c	30,000
	2,00,000		2,00,000

Dr. **13. SECURITIES PREMIUM ACCOUNT** Cr.

Particulars	₹	*Particulars*	₹
To Premium on Red of Deben. A/c	1,800	By Bank A/c [15,075 × ₹ 6]	90,450
To balance c/d	88,650	Issue Price = ₹ 20 – 20% = ₹ 16	
		Premium = ₹ 16 – ₹ 10 = 6	
	90,450		90,450

14. Goodwill Amortised = Goodwill Purchased – Closing Balance of Goodwill A/c
= [₹ 60,000 – (₹ 26,640 + ₹ 10,000 + ₹ 18,360 – ₹ 15,000] – ₹ 15,000
= ₹ 5,000

PROBLEM 12

CAMHI Limited gives you its Balance Sheet as on 31st March, 2016 and its Projected Profit and Loss Account for the year ended 31st March, 2016:

BALANCE SHEETS AS AT ...

Particulars	*Note*	*31.03.2016* ₹
I. EQUITY AND LIABILITIES		
(1) Shareholders' Funds		
(a) Share Capital	1	7,00,000
(b) Reserves and Surplus	2	2,30,000
(2) Non-Current Liabilities [12% Debentures]		2,00,000
(3) Current Liabilities		
Trade Payables		2,85,000
Short-term Provisions	3	2,15,000
Total		16,30,000
II. ASSETS		
(1) Non-Current Assets		
Tangible Fixed Assets		6,10,000
Other Non-Current Assets (Preliminary Expenses)		20,000
(2) Current Assets		
Inventories		5,60,000
Trade Receivables		2,20,000
Cash & Cash Equivalents		1,20,000

Short term loans & Adcances (Advance Tax)		1,00,000
Total		16,30,000

Notes to Accounts:

Particulars	*31.03.2014* ₹
1. Share Capital	
Equity Share Capital of ₹ 100 each	5,00,000
10% Preference Share Capital of ₹ 100 each	2,00,000
	7,00,000
2. Reserves and Surplus	
General Reserve	1,30,000
Profit and Loss A/c	80,000
Securities Premium	20,000
	2,30,000
3. Short-Term Provisions	
Proposed Dividend (Equity)	75,000
Provision for Tax	1,40,000
	2,15,000
4. Tangible Fixed Assets	
Motor car	80,000
Less: Depreciation	(30,000)
Machinery	7,00,000
Less: Depreciation	(1,40,000)
	6,10,000

PROJECTED PROFIT & LOSS ACCOUNT FOR THE YEAR ENDED 31ST MARCH, 2016

Particulars	*Note No.*	*(₹)*
I. Revenue from Operations	1	21,70,000
II. Other Income	2	10,000
III. Total Revenue [I + II]		21,80,000
IV. Expenses:		
Cost of Purchases	3	14,40,000
Changes in Inventories	4	1,40,000
Employee Benefits Expense	5	80,000
Finance Costs	6	24,000
Depreciation and Amortization Expense	7	70,000
Other Expenses	8	1,40,000
Total Expenses		18,94,000
V. Profit before Tax(III – IV)		2,86,000
VI. Tax Expense		1,36,000

VII. Profit for the period		1,50,000

Notes to Accounts: [₹ in lacs]

1. REVENUE FROM OPERATIONS

(a) Cash Sale of Products	3,70,000
(b) Credit Sale of Products	18,00,000
	21,70,000

2. OTHER INCOME

(a) Profit on sale of machinery	10,000

3. COST OF MATERIALS CONSUMED

Purchases	14,40,000

4. CHANGES IN INVENTORIES

Particulars	*Finished Goods (₹)*
Opening Inventories	5,60,000
Less: Closing Inventories	4,20,000
	1,40,000

5. EMPLOYEE BENEFITS EXPENSE

Salaries and Wages	80,000

6. FINANCE COSTS

(a) Interest on Debentures Expense	24,000

7. DEPRECIATION AND AMORTIZATION EXPENSE

Machinery	56,000
Car	14,000
	70,000

8. OTHER EXPENSES

(h) Manufacturing Expenses	40,000
(h) Office & Adm. Expenses	50,000
(h) Selling and distibution Expenses	30,000
(h) Preliminary Expenses w/o	20,000
	1,40,000

9. SURPLUS IN THE STATEMENT OF PROFIT & LOSS TO BE TAKEN TO BALANCE SHEET

Opening Balance	80,000
Add: Profit for the period	1,50,000

Less: Proposed Preference Dividend	20,000
Less: Proposed Equity Dividend	80,000
Add: Excess tax provision of previous year	20,000
Closing Balance	1,50,000

(a) Preference shares will be redeemed at the end of the year. The company proposes to issue equity shares with a nominal value of ₹.3,00,000 at a premium of 10%. Machineries will be acquired for ₹.1,00,000.

(b) The cost of machinery to be sold in the year ended 31st March, 2016 is ₹.80,000 with a depreciation provision of ₹.45,000.

It is expected that:

(i) Tax liabilities upto previous year will be settled for ₹.1,20,000 during the year.

(ii) Advance Incorne-tax amounting to ₹.1,30,000 is proposed to be paid in current year.

(iii) Trade Receivables will be 20% more than that warranted by the credit period of one month.

(iv) Trade Payables will continue to extend one month's credit and manufacturing expenses outstanding at the end of the year will be ₹.5,000.

You are required to:

(i) Draft the company's projected Balance Sheet as at 31st March, 2016.

(ii) Draft Cash Flow Statement for the year ended 31st March, 2016.

SOLUTION

PROJECTED BALANCE SHEET AS AT 31ST MARCH, 2016

Particulars	Note	*31.03.2016* ₹
I. EQUITY AND LIABILITIES		
(1) Shareholders' Funds		
(a) Share Capital	1	8,00,000
(b) Reserves and Surplus	2	3,30,000
(2) Non-Current Liabilities [12% Debentures]		2,00,000
(3) Current Liabilities		
Trade Payables		1,20,000
Short-term Provisions	3	2,16,000
Other Current liabities (Outstanding exp.)		5,000
Total		16,71,000
II. ASSETS		
(1) Non-Current Assets		
Tangible Fixed Assets		6,05,000
(2) Current Assets		
Inventories		4,20,000
Trade Receivables		1,80,000
Cash & Cash Equivalents		3,36,000
Short term loans & Advances (Advance Tax)		1,30,000

Total		16,71,000

Notes to Accounts:

Particulars	*31.03.2015* ₹
1. Share Capital	
Equity Share Capital of ₹ 100 each	8,00,000
10% Preference Share Capital of ₹ 100 each (2,00,000 – 2,00,000)	—
	8,00,000
2. Reserves and Surplus	
General Reserve	1,30,000
Profit and Loss A/c	1,50,000
Securities Premium	50,000
	3,30,000
3. Short-Term Provisions	
Proposed Dividend (Equity)	80,000
Provision for Tax	1,36,000
	2,16,000
4. Tangible Fixed Assets	
Motor car	80,000
Less: Depreciation	(44,000)
Machinery	7,20,000
Less: Depreciation	(1,51,000)
	6,05,000

SOLUTION

CASH FLOW STATEMENT FOR THE YEAR ENDING 31ST MARCH, 2016

Particulars	₹
I. Cash Flows from Operating Activities	
A. Closing balance as per Profit and Loss Account	1,50,000
Less: Opening Balance as per Profit and Loss Account	(80,000)
Add: Proposed dividend during the year	80,000
Add: Preference dividend paid during the year	20,000
Add: Provision for Tax (Net of Excess Provision)	1,16,000
B. Net profit before taxation, and extraordinary item	2,86,000
C. *Add:* Items to be added	
Depreciation	70,000
Interest on Debentures	24,000
Preliminary Exp. written off	20,000
D. *Less:* Profit on sale of Machinery	(10,000)

E. Operating profit before working capital changes [B + C - D]	3,90,000
F. *Add:* Decrease in Current Assets and Increase in Current Liabilities	
Decrease in Inventories	1,40,000
Decrease in Trade Receivables	40,000
Increase in Outstanding Expenses	5,000
G. *Less:* Increase in Current Assets and Decrease in Current Liabilities	
Decrease in Trade Payables for goods	(1,65,000)
H. Cash generated from operations [E + F - G]	4,10,000
I. *Less:* Income taxes paid (including Advance Tax)	(1,50,000)
J. Net Cash from (used in) operating activities	2,60,000
II. Cash Flows from Investing Activities	
Purchase of Machinery	(1,00,000)
Proceeds from sale of Machinery	45,000
Net Cash used in investing Activities	(55,000)
III. Cash Flows from Financing Activities	
Proceeds from issuance of share capital	3,30,000
Redemption of Preference shares	(2,00,000)
Interest on Debentures	(24,000)
Final Dividend paid	(75,000)
Pref. Dividend paid	(20,000)
Net Cash from financing activities	11,000
IV. Net Increase in Cash and Cash Equivalents [I + II + III]	2,16,000
V. Cash and Cash Equivalents at Beginning of Period	1,20,000
VI. Cash and Cash Equivalents at end of Period	3,36,000

Working Notes:

1. Closing Trade Receivables = (₹ 18,00,000/12) + 20% = ₹ 1,80,000
2. Closing Trade Payables = (₹ 14,40,000/12) = ₹ 1,20,000.

Dr. **3. PLANT AND MACHINERY ACCOUNT** *Cr.*

Particulars	₹	*Particulars*	₹
To Balance (b/d)	7,00,000	By Bank A/c	45,000
To Profit & Loss A/c (Profit on Sale)	10,000	By Provision for Depreciation A/c	45,000
To Bank A/c	1,00,000	By Balance c/d	7,20,000
	8,10,000		8,10,000

Dr. **4. PROVISION FOR DEPRECIATION ACCOUNT** *Cr.*

Particulars	₹	*Particulars*	₹
To Machinery A/c	45,000	By Balance b/d	1,40,000
To Balance c/d	1,51,000	By Profit and Loss A/c	56,000
	1,96,000		1,96,000

Dr. **5. CASH/BANK ACCOUNT** *Cr*

Particulars	₹	*Particulars*		₹
To Balance b/d	1,20,000	By Pref. Share Capital (Redemption)		2,00,000
To Equity Share Capital	3,00,000	By Machinery (Purchase)		1,00,000
To Securities Premium	30,000	By Trade Payables		16,05,000
To Sale of Machinery	45,000	By Wages		80,000
To Trade Receivables	18,40,000	By Manufacturing Expenses		35,000
To Sales (cash)	3,70,000	By Office etc. Expenses		50,000
		By Selling etc. Expenses		30,000
		By Interest		24,000
		By Taxes paid (p/y)		20,000
		By Advance Tax paid		1,30,000
		By Dividend paid		
		(2012 - 2013))	75,000	
		(2013 - 2014)	20,000	95,000
		By Balance c/d		3,36,000
	27,05,000			27,05,000

Dr. **6. TRADE RECEIVABLES ACCOUNT** *Cr*

Particulars	₹	*Particulars*	₹
To Balance b/d	2,20,000	By Bank A/c (Balancing figure)	18,40,000
To Credit Sales	18,00,000	By Balance c/d	
		[(18,00,000/12) + 20%]	1,80,000
	20,20,000		20,20,000

Dr. **7. TRADE PAYABLES ACCOUNT** *Cr*

Particulars	₹	*Particulars*	₹
To Bank A/c (Balancing figure)	16,05,000	By Balance b/d	2,85,000
To Balance c/d [14,40,000/12]	1,20,000	By Purchase A/c	14,40,000
	17,25,000		17,25,000

Dr. **8. PROVISION FOR TAX ACCOUNT** *Cr*

Particulars	₹	*Particulars*	₹
To Advance Tax A/c	1,00,000	By Balance b/d	1,40,000
To Bank A/c	20,000	By Profit & Loss A/c	1,36,000
To Profit and Loss A/c (Excess)	20,000	By (Net Provision)	
To Balance c/d	1,36,000		
	2,76,000		2,76,000

PROBLEM 13

From the following information, calculate Cash Flow from Operating Activities:

Cash Sales one forth of Net Credit Sales

Net Credit purchases are four times the Cash Purchases

Discount allowed to customers..	₹ 6,000
Discount received from Suppliers..	₹ 3,000
Returns Inward..	₹ 10,000
Returns Outward..	₹ 5,000
Office & Selling Expenses	₹ 51,000
Depreciation..	₹ 19,000
Provision for Tax..	₹ 40,000
Trading Commission earned	₹ 1,02,000
Total Sales (Net of Returns)	₹ 2,00,000
Total Purchases (Net of Returns)	₹ 1,00,000
Bad Debts	₹ 4,000

Particulars	*Opening*	*Closing*
Trade Receivables	₹ 1,00,000	₹ 2,00,000
Trade Payables	₹ 1,00,000	₹ 50,000
Outstanding Office & Selling Expenses	₹ 500	₹ 1,000
Prepaid Office & Selling Expenses	₹ 1,000	₹ 500
Accrued Trading Commission	₹ 1,000	₹ 2,000
Advance Trading Commission	₹ 2,000	₹ 1,000
Provision for Tax	₹ 50,000	₹ 60,000

SOLUTION

STATEMENT SHOWING THE COMPUTATION OF CASH FLOW FROM OPERATING ACTIVITIES

Particulars	₹
A. Operating Receipts in Cash:	
(a) Cash Sales	40,000
(b) Collection from Trade Receivables	50,000
(c) Trading Commission received	1,00,000
	1,90,000
B. Operating Payments in Cash:	
(a) Cash Purchases	20,000
(b) Payments made to Trade Payables	1,27,000
(c) Office & Selling Expenses paid	50,000
	1,97,000
C. Cash used in Operations before taxes	7,000

D. Income Tax paid	30,000
E. Net Cash used in Operating Activities	37,000

Working Notes:

1. *Calculation of Cash Sales, Net Credit Sales and Gross Credit Sales*

   Total Sales = Net Credit Sales + Cash Sales

   Let Net Credit Sales be X

   ₹ 2,00,000 = X + ¼X

   Multiplying the above equation by 4

   ₹ 8,00,000 = 4 X + X

   X = ₹ 8,00,000/5 = ₹ 1,60,000

   Cash Sales = ¼ × ₹ 1,60,000 = ₹ 40,000

   Gross Credit Sales = Net Credit Sales + Returns Inwara = ₹ 1,60,000 + ₹ 10,000 = ₹ 1,70,000

2. *Calculation of Cash Purchases, Net Credit Purchases and Gross Credit Purchases*

   Total Purchases = Net Credit Purchases + CasJrPurchases

   Let Cash Purchases be X

   ₹ 1,00,000 = 4X + X

   X = ₹ 1,00,000/5 = ₹ 20,000

   Net Credit Purchases = 4 × ₹ 20,000 = ₹ 80,000

   Gross Credit Purchases = Net Credit Purchases + Returns Outward

   = ₹ 80,000 + ₹ 5,000 = ₹ 85,000

Dr. **3. TOTAL TRADE RECEIVABLES ACCOUNT** Cr.

Particulars	₹	*Particulars*	₹
To Balance b/d	1,00,000	By Sales Returns	10,000
To Credit Sales	1,70,000	By Discount Allowed	6,000
		By Bad Debts	4,000
		By Cash Received (b.f.)	50,000
		By Balance c/d	2,00,000
	2,70,000		2,70,000

Dr. **4. TOTAL TRADE PAYABLES ACCOUNT** Cr.

Particulars	₹	*Particulars*	₹
To Purchases Returns	5,000	By Balance b/d	1,00,000
To Discount Received	3,000	By Credit Purchases	85,000
To Cash paid [Balancing Figure]	1,27,000		
To Balance c/d	50,000		
	1,85,000		1,85,000

Dr. **5. OFFICE & SELLING EXPENSES ACCOUNT** *Cr.*

Particulars	₹	*Particulars*	₹
To Prepaid Expenses A/c (in the beginning)	1,000	By Outstanding Expenses A/c (in the beginning)	500
To Bank A/c (Balancing figure)	50,000	By P & L A/c	51,000
To Outstanding Expenses A/c (af the end)	1,000	By Prepaid Expenses A/c (at the end)	500
	52,000		52,000

Dr. **6. TRADING COMMISSION ACCOUNT** *Cr.*

Particulars	₹	*Particulars*	₹
To Accrued Commission A/c (in the beginning)	1,000	By Advance Commission A/c	2,000
To P&L A/c	1,02,000	By Cash/Bank A/c (Balancing figure)	1,00,000
To Advance Commission A/c (at the end)	1,000	By Accrued Commission A/c (at the end)	2,000
	1,04,000		1,04,000

Dr. **7. PROVISION FOR TAX ACCOUNT** *Cr.*

Particulars	₹	*Particulars*	₹
To Bank A/c (Tax Paid) (Balancing figure)	30,000	By Balance b/d	50,000
		By P&L A/c (Provision made)	40,000
To Balance c/d	60,000		
	90,000		90,000

3 STATEMENT OF CHANGES IN EQUITY

LEARNING OBJECTIVES

After studying this chapter, you should be able to understand:

- ◇ Meaning of Equity
- ◇ Meaning of Statement of Changes in Equity
- ◇ Format of Statement of Changes in Equity

1.0 MEANING OF EQUITY

Equity represents owners' stake in the entity which is the residual interest in the Assets of the entity after deducting all of its external liabilities.

2.0 MEANING OF STATEMENT OF CHANGES IN EQUITY

A Statement of Changes in Shareholders' Equity is a Financial Statement which reconciles the opening balances of Equity Accounts with their closing balances by showing a summary of the changes in Shareholders' Equity Accounts over the reporting period.

The Change in Shareholders' Equity over the reporting period usually occurs due to the following:

1. **Corrections of Prior Period errors and Changes in Accounting Policy**
2. **Changes in Net Income for the period,**
3. **Effect of Revaluation of Non-Current Fixed Assets, Changes on re- measuring of Financial Assets held as Available for Sale, Effect of Foreign Exchange Translation (if not included in Net Income Determination), Effective Portion of Change in Fair Value of Hedging Instruments in Cash Flow Hedges and Actuarial Gains & Losses on Defined Benefit Plans**
4. **Transactions with Shareholders such as Issue/ Buy back of Shares, Payment of Dividends, Issue of Bonus Shares etc.**
5. **Changes in Ownership Interests in Subsidiaries that do not result in a loss of control**

Note: The Consolidated Statement of Changes in Equity (of a group that includes one *or* more partly-owned subsidiaries) also provides information about the share of equity attributable to the owners of the parent and that attributable to the non-controlling interests and information about changes in such interests.

3.0 FORMAT OF STATEMENT OF CHANGES IN EQUITY

STATEMENT OF CHANGES IN EQUITY

For the period ended 31st March, 20...

Particulars	*Share Capital*	*Reserves & Surplus*					*Total Equity*
		Retained Earnings	*Securities Premium*	*Capital Reserve*	*Capital Red. Reserve*	*Revaluation Reserve*	
A. Balance in the beg.	XXX	XXX	XXX	XXX	XXX	XXX	XXX
B. Corrections of Prior Period errors		XXX					XXX
C. Changes in Accounting Policy		XXX					XXX
D. Re–stated Balance in the beg. (A + B + C)	XXX	XXX	XXX	XXX	XXX	XXX	XXX
E. Net Income for the period		XXX					XXX
F. Effect of Revaluation							
(i) Revaluation of Non-Current Fixed Assets						XXX	XXX
(ii) Change on re measuring of Financial Assets held as Available for Sale						XXX	XXX
(iii) Effective Portion of Change in Fair Value of Hedging Instruments in Cash Flow Hedges						XXX	XXX
(iv) Effect of Foreign Exchange Translation (if not included in net income determination)					XXX	XXX	
(v) Actuarial Gains and Losses on Defined Benefit Plans						XXX	XXX
TOTAL (F)	-	-	-	-	-	XXX	XXX
G. Transactions with Shareholders							
(i) Dividends		(XXX)					(XXX)
(ii) Issue of New Shares	XXX		XXX				XXX
(iii) Buy back of Shares	(XXX)	(XXX)	(XXX)		XXX		(XXX)
(iv) Issue of Bonus Shares	XXX		(XXX)		(XXX)		
TOTAL (G)	XXX	(XXX)	XXX		XXX	-	XXX
H. Balance at the end [D + E + F + G]	XXX	XXX	XXX	XXX	xxx	XXX	XXX

ILLUSTRATION 1

From the following Information, Prepare Statement of Changes in Equity of TULSIAN IPC LTD For the period ended 31st March, 2016:

Share Capital in the beg.	₹ 50 crores
Retained Earnings in the beg.	₹ 100 crores
Securities Premium in the beg.	₹ 50 crores
Capital Redemption Reserve in the beg.	₹ 50 crores
Revaluation Reserve in the beg.	₹ 50 crores

Corrections of Prior Period errors resulting in increase in Profits	₹ 5 crores
Changes in Accounting Policy resulting in increase in Profits	₹ 10 crores
Net Income for the period (incl. ₹ 4 crores	
Net Gains on Foreign ExchangeTranslation)	₹ 20 crores
Revaluation Gain on Non-Current Fixed Assets	₹ 30 crores
Dividends	₹ 5 crores
Issue of 50 lacs New Shares of ₹ 10 each at ₹ 100 each	
Buy back of 20 lacs Shares of of ₹ 10 each at ₹ 50 each out of Securities Premium Issue of Bonus Shares out of Capital Redemption Reserve	₹ 45 crores

SOLUTION

STATEMENT OF CHANGES IN EQUITY OF TULSIAN IPC LTD

For the period ended 31st March, 2016

Particulars	*Share Capital*	*Reserves & Surplus*				*Total Equity*
		Retained Earnings	*Securities Premium*	*Capital Red. Reserve*	*Revaluation Reserve*	
A. Balance in the beg.	50	100	50	50	50	300
B. Corrections of Prior Period errors		5				5
C. Changes in Accounting Policy		10				10
D. Re–stated Balance in the beg. (A + B + C)	50	115	50	50	50	315
E. Net Income for the period		20				20
F. Effect of Revaluation of Non-Current Fixed Assets			10	10		
G. Transactions with Shareholders						
(i) Dividends		(5)				(5)
(ii) Issue of New Shares	5		45			50
(iii) Buy back of Shares	(2)	(2)	(8)	2		(10)
(iv) Issue of Bonus Shares	45			(45)		0
TOTAL (G)	**48**	**(7)**	**37**	**(43)**	**0**	**35**
H. Balance at the end [D + E + F + G]	**98**	**128**	**87**	**7**	**60**	**380**

ILLUSTRATION 2

From the following Information, Prepare Statement of Changes in Equity of TULSIAN FINAL LTD For the period ended 31st March, 2016:

Share Capital in the beg.	₹ 100 crores
Retained Earning in the beg.	₹ 200 crores
Securities Premium in the beg.	₹ 100 crores
Capital Redemption Reserve in the beg.	₹ 100 crores

Revaluation Reserve in the beg.	₹ 100 crores
Corrections of Prior Period errors resulting in increase in Profits	₹ 10 crores
Changes in Accounting Policy resulting in increase in Profits	₹ 20 crores
Net Income for the period (incl. ₹ 4 crores Net Gains on Foreign ExchangeTranslation)	₹ 40 crores
Revaluation Gain on Non-Current Fixed Assets	₹ 20 crores
Profit on re-measuring of Financial Assets held as Available for Sale	₹ 40 crores
Effective Portion of Upward Change in Fair Value of Hedging Instruments in Cash Flow Hedges	₹ 10 crores
Actuarial Gain on Defined Benefit Plans	₹ 10 crores
Dividends	₹ 10 crores
Issue of 1 crore New Shares of ₹ 10 each at ₹ 100 each	
Buy back of 40 lacs Shares of of ₹ 10 each at ₹ 50 each out of Securities Premium	
Issue of Bonus Shares out of Capital Red. Reserve	₹ 90 crores

SOLUTION

STATEMENT OF CHANGES IN EQUITY OF TULSIAN FINAL LTD

For the period ended 31st March, 2016

Particulars	*Share Capital*	*Reserves & Surplus*				*Total Equity*
		Retained Earnings	*Securities Premium*	*Capital Red. Reserve*	*Revaluation Reserve*	
A. Balance in the beg.	100	200	100	100	100	600
B. Corrections of Prior Period errors		10				10
C. Changes in Accounting Policy		20				20
D. Re–stated Balance in the beg. (A + B + C)	100	230	100	100	100	630
E. Net Income for the period		40				40
F. Effect of Revaluation						
(i) Revaluation of Non-Current Fixed Assets				20	20	
(ii) Change on re measuring of Financial Assets held as Available for Sale					40	40
(iii) Effective Portion of Change in Fair Value of Hedging Instruments in Cash Flow Hedges				10	10	
(iv) Actuarial Gains and Losses on Defined Benefit Plans					10	10
TOTAL (F)	**0**	**0**	**0**	**0**	**80**	**80**
G. Transactions with Shareholders						
(i) Dividends		(10)				(10)
(ii) Issue of New Shares	10		90			100

(iii) Buy back of Shares	(4)	(4)	(16)	4		(20)
(iv) Issue of Bonus Shares	90			(90)		0
TOTAL (G)	**96**	**(14)**	**74**	**(86)**	**0**	**70**
H. Balance at the end [D + E + F + G]	**196**	**256**	**174**	**14**	**180**	**820**

ILLUSTRATION 3

CEO of XYZ Ltd. has asked you to prepare a statement of changes in equity for the year ended 31st March 2016.

The components of the company's shareholders equity as at 1 April 2015 was as follows:

Particulars	*₹ (in crores)*
Authorized Share Capital 40 crores, Issued 10 crores shares of ₹ 10 each	100
Securities Premium	240
Capital Reserve	60
Retained earnings	180
Revaluation Reserve	30

Additional Information:

(a) On 31 July 2015, the company declared and issued 10% bonus shares. Market Price per share at the date was ₹ 40.

(b) On 30 June 2015, the company issued 2 crore new shares for total consideration of ₹ 90 crores.

(c) Profit for the financial year ended 31 March 2016 amounted to ₹100 crores and the company paid dividends totaling ₹ 32 crores.

(d) The company set aside 10% of net income for the period for transfer to capital reserve.

(e) 1 crore shares were bought back on 30 December 2015 at ₹ 40 per share.

(f) The company reversed upward revaluation of an asset by ₹ 10 crores. The revaluation surplus already includes ₹ 14 crores of such initial upward revaluation.

SOLUTION

STATEMENT OF CHANGES IN EQUITY OF XYZ LTD
For the period ended 31st March, 2016

Particulars	*Share Capital*	*Reserves & Surplus*					*Total Equity*
		Retained Earnings	*Securities Premium*	*Capital Reserve*	*Capital Red. Reserve*	*Revaluation Reserve*	
A. Balance in the beg.	100	180	240	60	0	30	610
B. Corrections of Prior Period errors						0	
C. Changes in Accounting Policy						0	
D. Re-stated Balance in the beg. (A + B + C)	100	180	240	60	0	30	610
E. Net Income for the period		100					100
F. Revaluation of Non-Current Fixed Assets						(10)	(10)

G.	**Transactions with Shareholders**							
(i)	Issue of Bonus Shares	10		(10)				0
(ii)	Issue of New Shares	20		70				90
(iii)	Dividend		(32)					(32)
(iii)	Transfer to Capital Reserve		(10)		10			0
(iv)	Buy back of Shares	(10)	(10)	(30)		10		(40)
TOTAL (G)		**20**	**(52)**	**30**	**10**	**10**	**0**	**18**
H.	**Balance at the end [D + E + F + G]**	**120**	**228**	**270**	**70**	**10**	**20**	**718**

ILLUSTRATION 4

From the following information, prepare Statement of Equity of IPC (1) Ltd.:

BALANCE SHEETS AS AT. ..

Particulars	*Note*	*31.03.2016* ₹	*31.03.2015* ₹
I. EQUITY AND LIABILITIES			
(1) Shareholders' Funds			
(a) Share Capital	1	10,25,000	10,00,000
(b) Reserves and Surplus	2	5,67,000	2,32,000
(2) Non-Current Liabilities [14% Debentures]		2,60,000	1,50,000
(3) Current Liabilities			
Short-term Borrowings (14% Bank Loan)		40,000	50,000
Trade Payables		1,50,000	40,000
Other Current Liabilities		80,000	60,000
Short-term Provisions	3	1,90,000	1,40,000
Total		**23,12,000**	**16,72,000**
II. ASSETS			
(1) Non-Current Assets			
Tangible Fixed Assets (Net)		12,70,000	10,20,000
Intangible Assets [Goodwill]		1,000	10,000
10% Non-Current Investments		1,60,000	60,000
(2) Current Assets			
10% Current Investments		60,000	20,000
Cash & Cash Equivalents		3,00,000	1,00,000
Other Current Assets		5,21,000	4,62,000
Total		**23,12,000**	**16,72,000**

Notes to Account:

Particulars	*31.03.2016* ₹	*31.03.2015* ₹
1. Share Capital		
Equity Share Capital of ₹ 10 each	8,25,000	6,00,000
5% Preference Share Capital of ₹ 100 each	2,00,000	4,00,000
	10,25,000	10,00,000
2: Reserves And Surplus		
Retained Earnings	5,32,000	1,92,000
Securities Premium	35,000	20,000
Capital Remption Reserve	—	5,000
Revaluation Reserve	—	15,000
	5,67,000	2,32,000
3: Short-Term Provisions		
Proposed Dividend	1,50,000	1,20,000
Provision for Tax	40,000	20,000
	1,90,000	1,40,000

SOLUTION

STATEMENT OF CHANGES IN EQUITY OF XYZ LTD

For the period ended 31st March, 2016

Particulars	*Share Capital*	*Reserves & Surplus*				*Total Equity*
		Retained Earnings	*Securities Premium*	*Capital Red. Reserve*	*Revaluation Reserve*	
A. Balance in the beg.	10,00,000	3,12,000	20,000	5000	15,000	13,52,000
E. Net Income for the period	4,90,000					4,90,000
F. Revaluation of Non-Current Fixed Assets				(15,000)	(15,000)	
G. Transactions with Shareholders						
(i) Dividend		(1,20,000)				(1,20,000)
(ii) Issue of New Shares	2,20,000		15000			2,35,000
(iii) Redemption of Pref.Shares	(2,00,000)					(2,00,000)
(iv) Issue of Bonus Shares	5,000			(5,000)		0
TOTAL (G)	25,000	(1,20,000)	15000	(5,000)		(85,000)
H. Balance at the end [D + E + F + G]	10,25,000	6,82,000	35000	0	0	17,42,000

Notes:

1. Opening & Closing Balances of Retained Earnings include the Opening & Closing Balances of Proposed Dividend respectively.
2. Net Profit for the year = Balance of Retained Earnings at 31 March 2015 + Proposed Dividend for the year 2014 - 2015 – (Balance of Retained Earnings at 31 March 2014) = ₹ 5,32,000 + ₹ 1,50,000 – ₹ 1,92,000 = ₹ 4,90,000
3. Issue of Bonus Share is equal to ₹ 5000 since Balance of Capital Redemption Reserve in beginning was ₹ 5,000 and it can only be utilized to issue fully paid bonus shares.

ILLUSTRATION 5

From the following information, prepare Statement of Equity of IPC (2) Ltd.:

BALANCE SHEETS AS AT. ..

Particulars	*Note*	*31.03.2016* ₹	*31.03.2015* ₹
I. EQUITY AND LIABILITIES			
(1) Shareholders' Funds			
(a) Share Capital	1	10,25,000	10,00,000
(b) Reserves and Surplus	2	5,67,000	2,32,000
(2) Non-Current Liabilities [14% Debentures]		2,60,000	1,50,000
(3) Current Liabilities			
Short-term Borrowings (14% Bank Loan)		40,000	50,000
Trade Payables		1,50,000	40,000
Other Current Liabilities		80,000	60,000
Short-term Provisions	3	1,90,000	1,40,000
Total		**23,12,000**	**16,72,000**
II. ASSETS			
(1) Non-Current Assets			
Tangible Fixed Assets (Net)		12,70,000	10,20,000
Intangible Assets [Goodwill]		1,000	10,000
10% Non-Current Investments		1,60,000	60,000
(2) Current Assets			
10% Current Investments			
Cash & Cash Equivalents		60,000	20,000
Other Current Assets		5,21,000	4,62,000
Total		**23,12,000**	**16,72,000**

Notes to Accounts:

Particulars	*31.03.2016* ₹	*31.03.2015* ₹
1. Share Capital		
Equity Share Capital of ₹ 10 each	8,25,000	6,00,000
5% Preference Share Capital of ₹ 100 each	2,00,000	4,00,000
	10,25,000	10,00,000
2. Reserves And Surplus		
Retained Earnings	5,32,000	1,92,000
Securities Premium	35,000	20,000
Capital Remption Reserve	—	5,000
Revaluation Reserve	—	15,000
	5,67,000	2,32,000

3. Short-Term Provisions		
Proposed Dividend	1,50,000	1,20,000
Provision for Tax	40,000	20,000
	1,90,000	1,40,000

Additional Information:

(a) During the year a machine costing ₹ 1,40,000 (depreciation provided thereon ₹ 60,000) was sold for ₹ 50,000. Depreciation charged was ₹ 1,40,000. A machine was purchased by issue of Equity Shares of ₹ 10 each at a premium of 25%. Some Machines were purchased during the year by a cheque of ₹ 4,61,000. Some Machines were revalued at year end.

(b) An Interim Dividend @ 15% was paid on equity shares on 31.12.2015.

(c) ₹ 10,000 New Shares of ₹ 10 each were issued on 01.01.2016 and Bank Loan was repaid on the same date.

(d) Preference Shares were redeemed at the end of the year at a premium of 5% and Premium was provided out of Securities Premium.

(e) Bonus shares were issued out of Capital Redemption Reserve on 31/03/2016

SOLUTION

STATEMENT OF CHANGES IN EQUITY OF XYZ LTD

For the period ended 31st March, 2016

Particulars	*Share Capital*	*Reserves & Surplus*				*Total Equity*
		Retained Earnings	*Securities Premium*	*Capital Red. Reserve*	*Revaluation Reserve*	
A. Balance in the beg.	10,00,000	3,12,000	20,000	5000	15,000	13,52,000
E. Net Income for the period	6,80,000					6,80,000
F. Revaluation of Non-Current Fixed Asts				(15,000)	(15,000)	
G. Transactions with Shareholders						
(i) Dividend [₹ 1,20,000 + ₹ 90,000]		(2,10,000)				(2,10,000)
(ii) Issue of New Shares	1,20,000		25,000			1,45,000
(iii) Redemption of Pref.Shares	(2,00,000)	(1,00,000)	(10,000)	1,00,000		(2,10,000)
(iv) Issue of Bonus Shares	1,05,000			(1,05,000)		0
TOTAL (G)	25,000	(3,10,000)	15,000	(5,000)		(2,75,000)
H. Balance at the end [D + E + F + G]	10,25,000	6,82,000	35,000	0	0	17,42,000

Working Notes:

1. Opening & Closing Balances of Retained Earnings include the Opening & Closing Balances of Proposed Dividend respectively.
2. Redemption of Preference Shares of ₹ 2,00,000 has been made out of Issue of new shares to the extent of ₹ 1,00,000 and the balance of ₹ 1,00,000 out of Retained earnings by transfer to Capital Redemption Reserve.
3. Net Income for the period = Balance of Retained Earnings at 31 March 2016 +Transfer to Capital Redemption Reserve+ Interim Dividend+ Proposed Dividend for the year 2015 - 2016 – (Balance of Retained Earnings at 31 March 2014) = ₹ 5,32,000 + ₹ 1,00,000 + ₹ 90,000 + ₹ 1,50,000 – ₹ 192,000 = ₹ 6,80,000.

Dr. **4. CAPITAL REDEMPTION RESERVE ACCOUNT** Cr.

Particulars	₹	Particulars	₹
To Bonus to Shareholders A/c [b.f.]	1,05,000	By Balance b/d	5,000
		By Profit and Loss A/c	1,00,000
	1,05,000		1,05,000

Dr. **5. EQUITY SHARE CAPITAL ACCOUNT** Cr.

Particulars	₹	Particulars	₹
To Balance c/d	8,25,000	By Balance b/d	6,00,000
		By Vendor of Fixed Assets A/c (b.f.)	20,000
		By Bank A/c (new shares)	1,00,000
		By Bonus to Shareholders A/c	1,05,000
	8,25,000		8,25,000

Dr. **6. SECURITIES PREMIUM ACCOUNT** Cr.

Particulars	₹	Particulars	₹
To Pref. Shareholders A/c	10,000	By Balance b/d	20,000
To Balance c/d	35,000	By Vendor of Fixed Assets A/c	5,000
		By Bank A/c (new shares) (b.f.)	20,000
	45,000		45,000

Dr. **7. FIXED ASSETS ACCOUNT** Cr.

Particulars	₹	Particulars	₹
To Balance b/d	10,20,000	By Bank A/c (Sale)	50,000
To Bank A/c (Purchases) (b.f.)	4,61,000	By P&L A/c (Loss)	30,000
To Vendor of Fixed Assets A/c	25,000	By Depreciation A/c	1,40,000
		By Revalution Reserve A/c (b.f.)	15,000
		By P & L A/c (b.f.)	1,000
		By Balance c/d	12,70,000
	15,06,000		15,06,000

Note: Total Revaluation loss amounts to ₹ 16,000. Revaluation loss is first provided from Revaluation Reserve to the extent available i.e. ₹ 15,000 and the remaining balance of ₹ 1,000 is provided from Profit & Loss A/c.

4 PROFIT PRIOR TO INCORPORATION AND ACCOUNTING FOR BUSINESS ACQUISITION

LEARNING OBJECTIVES

After studying this chapter, you should be able to understand:

- Acquisition of Existing Business
- Meaning of Purchase Consideration
- Methods of Calculating Purchase Consideration
- Treatment of Difference Between Purchase Consideration and Net Assets taken Over
- Accounting Entries in the books of Purchasing Company
- Distributioin of Shares (Received from the Purchasing Company) Among the Partners
- Profit or Loss Prior to Incorporation
- Statutory Report (Section 165)

1.0 ACQUISITION OF EXISTING BUSINESS

When a company is formed to acquire an existing business, it may take over:

(a) the entire business [i.e., all assets (excluding fictitious assets) and all outsiders liabilities;

(b) only the assets (i.e., both fixed and current assets) with *or* without trade liabilities (i.e., trade creditors, Bills payable);

(c) only the fixed assets with *or* without all liabilities/trade liabilities;

(d) only the floating assets (i.e., Current Assets like Trade Debtors, Inventory. Cash and Bank, Bills Receivable) with *or* without all liabilities/trade liabilities.

2.0 MEANING OF PURCHASE CONSIDERATION

SIMPLY SPEAKING PURCHASE CONSIDERATION MEANS THE AMOUNT PAYABLE BY THE PURCHASING COMPANY TO THE VENDOR OF AN EXISTING BUSINESS.

PRACTICALLY SPEAKING, PURCHASE CONSIDERATION MEANS THE AGGREGATE OF THE SHARES AND OTHER SECURITIES ISSUED AND THE PAYMENT MADE IN THE FORM OF CASH OR OTHER ASSETS BY THE PURCHASING COMPANY TO THE VENDOR OF AN EXISTING BUSINESS.

3.0 METHODS OF CALCULATING PURCHASE CONSIDERATION

Depending upon the availability of information, the purchase consideration may be calculated on Net Assets basis *or* Net Payment basis.

The following criteria may be adopted to select the basis of purchase consideration.

Case	*Basis of Purchase Consideration*
I. If All the Modes of Discharging Purchase Consideration alongwith their individual figures are specifically given	Net Payment basis must be used and accordingly, Purchase Consideration = Cash + Issue Price of Securities
II. In Other Cases	Net Assets basis must be used and accordingly, Purchase Consideration = Agreed value of Assets taken over – Agreed Amount of Liabilities taken over

4.0 TREATMENT OF DIFFERENCE BETWEEN PURCHASE CONSIDERATION AND NET ASSETS TAKEN OVER

If the amount of the purchase consideration is greater than the value of the net assets acquired (i.e., the difference between the agreed value of assets taken over and the agreed amount of liabilities taken over), the difference should be treated as an amount paid for goodwill and hence should be debited to Goodwill Account.

If the amount of the purchase consideration is lower than the value of the net assets acquired, the difference should be treated as capital profit and hence should be credited to Capital Reserve Account.

5.0 ACCOUNTING ENTRIES IN THE BOOKS OF PURCHASING COMPANY

Step 1: Record the Acquision of business from the Vendor.

JOURNAL ENTRY

Business Purchase A/c	Dr. (with Purchase Consideration)
To Vendor/Liquidator of Vendor Co. (in case Vendor is a company)	

Step 2: Record the Assets and Liabilities taken over at their respective agreed values (i.e., not their book values) and debit the Goodwill Account with the excess of purchase consideration over the net assets taken over (if any) or credit the Capital Reserve Account with the excess of net assets over the purchase consideration (if any).

JOURNAL ENTRY

Assets (Individually)	Dr.	(with the respective agreed values of the assets taken over)
Goodwill A/c	Dr.	(with the excess of Purchase Consideration over the Net Assets)
To Liabilities (Individually)		(with the respective agreed amount of the liabilities taken over)
To Business Purchase A/c		(with the Purchase Consideration)
To Capital Reserve A/c		(with the excess of Net Assets over the Purchase Consideration)

Step 3: Make Payment to Vendor

Vendor/Liquidator *or* Vendor Co. A/c	Dr.	(with the Purchase Consideration)
Discount on Issue of Shares A/c	Dr.	(with the Discount allowed on shares)
To Equity Share Capital A/c		(with the Paid up value of Equity Shares issued)
To Preference Share Capital A/c		(with the Paid up value of Pref. Shares issued)
To Securities Premium A/c		(with the Securities Premium)
To Cash A/c/Bank A/c		(with the Cash Payment)

Tutorial Note: *The shares issued by way of purchase consideration must be recorded at their paid up values (i.,e., not at their issue prices) after giving due credit to Securities Premium Account (in case the shares have been issued at premium) or after giving due debit to 'Discount on issue of Shares A/c' (In case the shares have been issued at discount).*

Step 4:* *Where the purchasing company merely agrees to act as an agent of the Vendor for collection of Vendor's Debtors and payment of Vendor's Creditors, for an agreed commission, record the following entries:

(a) On taking over the Vendor's Debtors

Vendor's Debtors A/c	Dr.	
To Vendor's Suspense A/c		

(b) On taking over Vendor's Creditors

Vendor's Suspense A/c	Dr.	
To Vendor's Creditors A/c		

(c) On Collection of Vendor's Debtors

Cash/Bank A/c	Dr.	[with Actual Amount received]
Vendor's Suspense A/c	Dr.	[with loss on collection]
To Vendor's Debtors A/c		[with total]

(d) On Recovery of Vendor's Bad Debts already written off

Cash/Bank A/c	Dr.	
To Vendor's Suspense A/c		

(e) On Payment of Vendor's creditors

Vendor's Creditors A/c	Dr.	[with total]
To Vendor's Suspense A/c		[with Profit on Payment]
To Cash/Bank A/c		[with Actual Amount paid]

(f) On Discharge of Vendor's Contingent Liability

Vendor's Suspense A/c	Dr.	
To Cash/Bank A/c		

(g) On Making the Commission due from Vendor

Vendor's Suspense A/c	Dr.	
To Commission A/c		

(h) On Making Final Payment to Vendor

Vendor's Suspense A/c	Dr.	
To Cash/Bank A/c		

Step 5:* *Record the Interest on Delayed Payment (if any). due to Vendor

Interest to Vendor A/c	Dr.	
To Vendor's A/c		

Step 6:* *Record the Payment to Vendor

Vendor's A/c	Dr.	
To Cash/Bank A/c		

Step 7: Record the payment of Preliminary Expenses

Preliminary Expenses A/c	Dr.
To Cash/Bank A/c	

Note: *Usually the Vendor makes use of P&L Adjustment A/c in place of Nominal Accounts in his books of accounts.*

ILLUSTRATION 1 [TREATMENT OF VENDOR'S DEBTORS & CREDITORS]

X Ltd acquired the business of Mr X taking over all the assets with the exception of Debtors and all liabilities with the exception of creditors. The company under took to collect the Vendor's debtors and to pay the Vendor's creditors out the proceeds collected for an agreed commission of 3% on amount collected and 1% on amounts paid. At the date of transfer the Vendor's debtors and Vendor's creditors amounted to ₹ 2,00,000 and ₹1,10,000 respectively. The company could collect only the good book debts which amounted to 90% after allowing them 10% discount. In addition, the company collected 60% from Z who owed ₹10,000 and whose account was written off as bad by the Vendor. The company paid all the creditors after receiving a discount of 10% on net payment made. In addition, the company discharged a contingent liability of ₹10,000 by paying ₹ 9,000 in full & final settlement.

Required: Pass the necessary journal entries in the books of X and X Ltd. assuming that X Ltd. remitted the final balance.

SOLUTION

JOURNAL OF X LTD.

Date	*Particulars*		*L.F.*	*Dr. (₹)*	*Cr. (₹)*
	X's Debtors A/c	Dr.		2,00,000	
	To X's Suspense A/c				2,00,000
	(Being Debtors Accounts taken over for collection)				
	X's Suspense A/c	Dr.		1,10,000	
	To X's Creditors A/c				1,10,000
	(Being creditors Accounts taken over for payment)				
	Cash A/c [90% of ₹2,00,000 – 10% of ₹1,80,000]	Dr.		1,62,000	
	X's Suspense A/c [₹20,000 + ₹ 18,000]	Dr.		38,000	
	To X's Debtors A/c				2,00,000
	(Being 90% of X's Debtors collected after allowing a discount of 10%, Balance debtors 10% become bad)				
	Cash A/c	Dr.		6,000	
	To X's Suspense A/c				6,000
	(Being Bad Debts recovered from X's debtors)				
	X's Suspense A/c	Dr.		5,040	
	To Commission A/c				5,040
	(Being commission due from X @3% on Total Collection of on ₹ 1,68,000 i.e. ₹1,62,000 + ₹ 6,000)				
	X's Creditors	Dr.		1,10,000	
	To X's Suspense A/c [₹1,10,000 × 10/110]				10,000

	To Cash A/c (Being all creditors of X discharged after receiving a discount of 10% on net payment)			1,00,000
	X's Suspense A/c Dr. To Cash A/c (Being a Contingent liability of X discharged)		9,000	9,000
	X's Suspense A/c Dr. To Commission A/c (Being commission due from X @1% on ₹1,09,000 being paid, i.e. ₹1,00,000 + ₹ 9,000)		1,090	1,090
	X's Suspense A/c Dr. To Cash A/c (Being the final payment made to X ₹ 1,62,000 + ₹ 6,000 – ₹1,00,000 – ₹ 9,000 – ₹ 6,130]		52,870	52,870

JOURNAL OF X

Particulars	*L.F.*	*Dr. (₹)*	*Cr. (₹)*
X Ltd. Suspense A/c Dr. To Debtors A/c (Being Debtors Account transferred for collection)		2,00,000	2,00,000
Creditors A/c Dr. To X Ltd. Suspense A/c (Being Creditors Accounts transferred for payment)		1,10,000	1,10,000
Profit & Loss Adjustment A/c Dr. To X Ltd. Suspense A/c (Being discount allowed to debtors (₹18,000 & Debtors of ₹ 20,000 became bad)		38,000	38,000
X Ltd. Suspense A/c Dr. To Profit & Loss Adjustment A/c (Being Bad Debts recovered by X Ltd.)		6,000	6,000
Profit & Loss Adjustment A/c Dr. To X Ltd. Suspense A/c (Being Commission due to X Ltd. @ 3% on total collection of ₹ 1,68,000 i.e. ₹1,62,000 + 6,000)		5,040	5,040
X Ltd. Suspense A/c Dr. To Profit & Loss Adjustment A/c (Being discount received from creditors)		10,000	10,000
Profit & Loss Adjustment A/c Dr. To X Ltd. Suspense A/c (Being a Contingent liability discharged)		9,000	9,000

Profit & Loss Adjustment A/c Dr. To X Ltd. Suspense A/c (Being Commission due to X Ltd. @ 1% on ₹1,09,000 i.e. ₹1,00,000 + 9,000)			1,090	1,090
Cash A/c Dr. To X Ltd. Suspense A/c (Being final payment received from X Ltd. (₹1,62,000 + ₹6,000 – ₹ 1,00,000 – ₹ 9,000 – ₹ 6,130)			52,870	52,870
Capital A/c Dr. To Profit & Loss Adjustment A/c (Being the Profit & Loss Adjustment A/c closed by transferring to the X 's Capital A/c) [i.e. ₹38,000 + 9,000 + 5,040 + 1,090 – 10,000 – 6,000]			37,130	37,130
Capital A/c [₹ 2,00,000 – ₹ 1,10,000 – ₹ 37,130] Dr. To Bank A/c (Being the payment made to X)			52,870	52,870

ILLUSTRATION 2

CAS Ltd. a public company purchased on July 1st, 2013 goodwill and assets (except the cash balance in the bank) of X Ltd. the summarized balance sheet of which is given below:

Particulars		₹
20,000 Equity Shares of ₹ 10 each		4,00,000
Revenue Reserve		1,60,000
Current Liabilities		57,000
Fixed Assets:		
Plants & Machinery	3,60,000	
Less: Depreciation	80,000	2,80,000
Investment:		
4% Bombay State		
Loan at par		1,30,000
Current Assets:		
Stock-in-trade	1,10,000	
Debtors	40,000	
Balance at Bank	57,000	2,07,000

The assets would be taken over at their book values except that (i) the value of stock-in-trade would be reduced by ₹ 10,000; (ii) goodwill be valued at ₹ 2,00,000 and (iii) a provision of 5% would be made against book debts.

The purchase price would be discharged by CAS Ltd. by allotting equity shares of ₹ 100 each in their capital at ₹ 150 per share only in multiples of 100 shares and the balance would be paid in cash.

X Ltd. would discharge its own liabilities. The cost of transfer would be wholly payable by CAS Ltd. Costs amounted to ₹ 17,000 out of which an amount of ₹ 1,000 was in respect of shares issued.

Required: Prepare Journal of CAS Ltd.

OLUTION

JOURNAL OF CAS LTD.

Date	*Particulars*		*L.F.*	*Dr. (₹)*	*Cr. (₹)*
2013	Business Purchase A/c	Dr.		7,48,000	
July 01	To X Ltd.				7,48,000
	(Being the assets of X Ltd. purchased as per agreement dated....)				
	Plant & Machinery A/c	Dr.		2,80,000	
	4% Bombay State Loan A/c	Dr.		1,30,000	
	Stock-in-trade A/c	Dr.		1,00,000	
	Debtors	Dr.		40,000	
	Goodwill A/c	Dr.		2,00,000	
	To Business Purchase A/c				7,48,000
	To Provision against Doubtful Debts				2,000
	(Being assets purchased recorded)				
	X Ltd.	Dr.		7,48,000	
	To Equity Share Capital A/c				4,90,000
	To Securities Premium A/c				2,45,000
	To Cash A/c				13,000
	(Being the purchase consideration discharged in the form of cash and 4,900 shares of ₹ 100 each at ₹ 150, as per agreement)				
	Goodwill A/c	Dr.		16,000	
	Cost of Issue of Shares A/c	Dr.		1,000	
	To Cash A/c				17,000
	(Being Payment of costs of transfer of assets & Issued Shares)				
	Securities Premium A/c	Dr.		1,000	
	To Cost of Issue of Shares A/c				1,000
	(Being the cost of issue of Shares w/o against Securities Premium)				

LUSTRATION 3

ul and Behari, who have been carrying on a partnership business, agree on conversion of the firm to a private limited company with effect from April 1, 2013. The agreement among other things, cludes the following terms:-

(a) Since the bank desires that the term loan should be liquidated, the partners bring in the required amount in proportion to their capitals.

(b) Goodwill of the firm is to be valued at ₹ 1,20,000.

(c) Tangible Fixed assets are to be revalued at ₹ 4,53,000;

The partners further agree that the revaluation be carried out before dissolution and the surplus be adjusted in their current accounts.

(d) The new company to be called CAMHE (P) Ltd. shall issue shares of ₹10 each to the partners in consideration of take-over of the business.

(e) The new company shall not assume the debtors and creditors but shall assist the vender-firm in realisation and settlement.

The Balance Sheet of Atul and Behari on 31st March, 2013 immediately before putting the agreement into effect reads as below:

Particulars	₹
Sundry creditors	1,60,000
Cash credit from bank	1,52,000
Term loan from bank	1,60,000
Partner's capitals:	
Atul	1,60,000
Behari	80,000
Cash and bank	50,000
Sundry debtors	60,000
Stock and stores	2,00,000
Tangible Fixed Assets	3,62,000
Partner's Current A/cs:	
Atul	15,000
Behari	25,000

Required:

(a) To calculate the number of shares to be allotted by the new company by way of purchase consideration and suggest the equitable distribution thereof between the partners; and

(b) To prepare the Balance Sheet of the new company assuming the agreement is implemented

SOLUTION

STATEMENT SHOWING THE CALCULATION OF PURCHASE CONSIDERATION AND DISTRIBUTION THEREOF

	Particulars	₹
	Goodwill	1,20,000
	Tangible Fixed Assets	4,53,000
	Stocks and Stores	2,00,000
A	Total Assets taken over	7,73,000
B	*Less:* Cash Credit taken over	1,52,000
C	Net Assets taken over *or* Purchase consideration payable	6,21,000
D	Number of shares to be allocated [₹ 6,21,000/₹ 10]	62,100
E	2/3 Share of Atul	41,400
F	1/3 Share of Behari	20,700

The most equitable proportion of distributing the shares between the partners would be the ratio of capitals prior to dissolution. Any balance due from/to any partner could be settled in cash. Alternatively subject to agreement between the partners, such shares can be allotted in profit sharing ratio as well

BALANCE SHEET OF CAMHE LTD AS AT 1ST APRIL,2013

Particulars	Note No.	₹
I. EQUITY AND LIABILITIES		
(1) Shareholders' Funds		
(a) Share Capital	1	6,21,000
(b) Reserves and Surplus		
(2) Non-Current Liabilities		
(3) Current Liabilities		
Short-Term Provisions Borrowings [Cash Credit]		1,52,000
Trade Payables [Trade Creditors (1,60,000) – Vender's Suspense (1,60,000)]		—
Total		7,73,000
II. ASSETS		
(1) Non-Current Assets		
(a) Fixed Assets		
(i) Tangible Assets		4,53,000
(ii) Intangible Assets [Goodwill]		1,20,000
(2) Current Assets		
Inventories		2,00,000
Trade Receivables [Sundry Debtors (60,000) – Vender's Suspense (60,000)]		—
Total		7,73,000

Notes to Accounts:

NOTE 1: SHARE CAPITAL

62,100 Equity Shares of ₹ 10 each (Of the above all Shares were issued for consideration otherwise than cash)	6,21,000

ILLUSTRATION 4

ACS Ltd. was incorporated for taking over the business of B from 1st April, 2013. The following is the Balance Sheet of B as on 31st March, 2013:

Particulars	₹
Capital	1,00,800
Loans	1,20,000
Creditors	71,200
Tangible Fixed Assets	2,08,000
Sundry Debtors	84,000

The company takes over the business with fixed assets and loans on the following terms:

(i) The fixed assets should be depreciated at 10%.

(ii) The value of goodwill is estimated at ₹ 80,000.

The company realised ₹ 80,000 from sundry debtors as the agent of the Vendor in full settlement and discharged all the trade creditors by paying ₹ 68,000 for a commission of 3% on the amount collected and 2% on the amount paid.

The creditors accepted 10% preference shares of ₹ 100 each in discharge of the loans.

After realisation of the debts and discharge of the liabilities, the total amount due to the Vendor was settled by payment of ₹ 5,440 in cash and the balance in the share of fully paid equity shares of ₹ 10 each.

Required: Show purchase consideration and pass journal entries in the books of the company. Also give the Balance Sheet of the company after taking over the business of B.

SOLUTION

COMPUTATION OF PURCHASE CONSIDERATION

Particulars	₹
Assets taken over:	
Land and Building	1,60,000
Plant and Machinery	28,000
Furniture	20,000
	2,08,000
Less: Depreciation @10%	20,800
	1,87,200
Add: Goodwill	80,000
	2,67,200
Less: Loans	1,20,000
Purchase consideration	1,47,200

JOURNAL OF ACS LTD.

Date	*Particulars*		*L.F.*	*Dr. (₹)*	*Cr. (₹)*
01.04.12	Business Purchase A/c	Dr.		1,47,200	
	To B				1,47,200
	(Being purchase consideration due for taking over the business)				
	Tangible Fixed Assets	Dr.		1,87,200	
	Goodwill	Dr.		80,000	
	To Loans				1,20,000
	To Business Purchase A/c				1,47,200
	(Being assets and liabilities taken over)				
	Vendor's Debtors	Dr.		84,000	
	To Vendor's Suspense A/c				84,000
	(Being Vendor's Creditors to be paid off)				
	Vendor's Suspense A/c	Dr.		71,200	
	To Vendor's Creditors				71200
	(Being Vendor's creditors to be paid off)				

	Bank A/c Dr. Vendor's Suspense A/c Dr. To Vendor's Debtors A/c (Being Vendor's Debtors collected at loss)		80,000 4,000	 84,000
	Vendor's Creditors Dr. To Bank A/c To Vendor's Suspense A/c (Being Profit on payment to Vendor's Creditors)		71,200	 68,000 3,200
	Vendor's Suspense A/c Dr. To Commission (Being the commission @3% on Vendor's Debtors collected & @2% on payment of Vendor's Creditors)		3,760	 3,760
	Vendor's Suspense A/c Dr. To B (Being transfer of the balance left net after realisation of debtors and payment to creditors)		8,240	 8,240
	B Dr. To Equity Share Capital A/c To Bank A/c (Being allotment of 15,000 Equity Shares of ₹ 10 each as fully paid up to Vendor's and payment of cash as per agreement dated....)		1,55,440	 1,50,000 5,440
	Loans Dr. To 10% Preference Share Capital A/c (Being issue of 1,200 10% preference share capital for discharge of loans)		1,20,000	 1,20,000

BALANCE SHEET OF ACS LTD AS AT 1ST APRIL,2013

Particulars	*Note No.*	₹
I. EQUITY AND LIABILITIES		
(1) Shareholders' Funds		
(a) Share Capital	1	2,70,000
(b) Reserves and Surplus [Capital Reserve (commission)]		3,760
(2) Non-Current Liabilities		
(3) Current Liabilities		
Total		2,73,760
II. ASSETS		
(1) Non-Current Assets		
(a) Fixed Assets		
(i) Tangible Assets		1,87,200
(ii) Intangible Assets [Goodwill]		80,000

(2) Current Assets		
Cash and Cash Equivalents		6,560
Total		2,73,760

Notes to Accounts:

NOTE 1: SHARE CAPITAL

15,000 Equity Shares of ₹ 10 each	1,50,000
1,200, 10% Pref. Shares of ₹ 100 each	1,20,000
(Of the above15,000, Equity Shares were issued for consideration otherwise than cash)	
	2,70,000

Note: The commission received on collection of Vendor's debtors and payment of Vendor's Creditors has been treated as a pre-incorporation profit and hence transferred to capital reserve. This amount may be used to write off goodwill to extent. In such a case the net amount of goodwill (i.e., ₹ 80,000 – ₹ 3,760 = ₹ 76,240) may be shown in the Balance Sheet.

ILLUSTRATION 5

M/s X, Y, & Z, the Balance Sheet of whose business is given below transferred their business to a limited company with the same name on January 1, 2013. It was agreed that the company would take over the assets except cash and book debts at their book values, would pay ₹ 40,000 for the goodwill of business and would collect the book debts at commission of 5% out of the collection from the debtors, the liabilities to sundry creditors would be first discharged as and when the amount is available, and the balance, if any, would be paid to vendors after six months. The partners undertook to pay off bank overdraft. You are required to show the computation of the purchase consideration and the Vendors Collection Account, assuming that only ₹ 1,30,000 collected out of debtor's balance and the remaining debtors were taken over by the vendors at the end of six months. Collection from debtors were : January, ₹ 60,000; February, ₹30,000; March ₹ 20,000; April ₹ 10,000; May ₹ 10,000; June nil.

BALANCE SHEET OF M/S X, Y, Z AS ON 31ST DECEMBER, 2012

Particulars	₹
Capital Accounts of Partners:	
X	1,50,000
Y	1,20,000
Z	80,000
General Reserve	1,60,000
Sundry Creditors	1,12,000
Bank Overdraft	8,000
Land & Building	50,000
Machinery	3,00,000
Stock	1,20,000
Book Debts	1,50,000
Cash	10,000

SOLUTION

PURCHASE CONSIDERATION PAYABLE

Particulars		₹
Total of Assets		6,30,000
Add: amount of Goodwill		40,000
		6,70,000
Less: Assets not taken over:		
Cash Balance	10,000	
Book Debts	1,50,000	1,60,000
		5,10,000

Dr. **VENDOR'S DEBTORS' ACCOUNT 2013** *Cr.*

Date	*Particulars*	₹	*Date*	*Particulars*	₹
2013			2013		
Jan. 01	To Balance of Debtors		Jan. 31	By Cash A/c	60,000
	takeover for collection	1,50,000	Feb. 28	By Cash A/c	30,000
			Mar. 31	By Cash A/c	20,000
			Apr. 30	By Cash A/c	10,000
			May 30	By Cash A/c	10,000
			June 30	By Balance transferred	
				to Debtor's Suspense A/c	20,000
		1,50,000			1,50,000

Dr. **DEBTOR'S SUSPENSE ACCOUNT** *Cr.*

Date	*Particulars*	₹	*Date*	*Particulars*	₹
2013			2013		
Jan. 31	To Amt. transferred		Jan. 31	By Balance of Vendor's	
	to Vendor's			debtors taken over for	
	Collection A/c	57,000		collection	1,50,000
	To Commission A/c	3,000			
Feb. 28	To Amt. transferred to				
	Vendor's Colletion A/c	28,500			
	To Commission A/c	1,500			
Mar. 31	To Amt. transferred to				
	Vendors' Collection A/c	19,000			
	To Commission A/c	1000			
April 29	To Amt. transferred to				
	Vendor's Collection A/c	9,500			
	To Commission A/c	500			

May 31	To Amt. transferred to Vendor's Collection A/c	9,500			
	To Commission A/c	500			
June 30	To Amt. transferred from Vendor's Debtors A/c	20,000			
		1,50,000			1,50,000

Dr. **CREDITOR'S SUSPENSE ACCOUNT** Cr.

Date	Particulars	₹	Date	Particulars	₹
2013			2013		
Jan. 01	To Amount recoverable from vendors in respect of liabilities taken over	1,12,000	Jan, 31	By Vendor's Collec. A/c	57,000
			Feb. 28	-do-	28,500
			Mar. 31	-do-	19,000
			April 30	-do-	7,500
		1,12,000			1,12,000

Dr. **VENDOR'S CREDITOR'S ACCOUNT** Cr.

Date	Particulars	₹	Date	Particulars	₹
2013			2013		
Jan. 31	To Cash A/c	57,000	Jan. 01	By Amount payable on behalf of vendors	1,12,000
Feb. 28	To Cash A/c	28,500			
Mar. 31	To Cash A/c	19,000			
Apr. 30	To Cash A/c	7,500			
		1,12,000			1,12,000

Dr. **VENDOR'S COLLECTION ACCOUNT** Cr.

Date	Particulars	₹	Date	Particulars	₹
2013			2013		
Jan. 31	To Creditor's Suspense A/c	57,000	Jan. 31	By Debtors Suspense A/c	57,000
Feb. 28	To Creditor's Suspense A/c	28,500	Feb. 28	"	28,500
Mar. 31	To Creditor's Suspense A/c	19,000	Mar. 31	"	19,000
April 30	To Creditor's Suspense A/c	7,500	Apr. 29	"	9,500
June 30	To Cash A/c (amt. paid to vendors)	11,500	May 31	"	9,500
		1,23,500			1,23,500

6.0 DISTRIBUTION OF SHARES (RECEIVED FROM THE PURCHASING COMPANY) AMONG THE PARTNERS

In the absence of an agreement as to the division of shares (received from the Purchasing Company) among the partners, such shares should be distributed among the partners in the ratio of their final claims (i.e., in the ratio of capitals standing after making all adjustments like transfer of profit/loss on realisation, accumulated profits/ reserves/losses) in accordance with the provisions of Section 48(b) (ii) of the Indian Partnership Act 1932.

Notes:

(i) For the purpose of payment to partners, the shares should be treated as cash equivalents and should be distributed like cash in an ordinary case of dissolution.

(ii) A share being an indivisible unit, should be given in nearest whole number and not in fraction. The necessary adjustment should be made in cash.

In case of conversion of a firm into a company if it is specifically given that the partners agree to preserve the same rights as regards the interest on capital and the sharing of profits and losses as they had in the partnership, the question of equity shares and the preference shares to be issued to partners may be dealt with in any one of the following two ways:

Method	*Manner*
I. ***If it is desired to receive the same amount on Interest on Fixed Capital***	I. (a) Issue Preference Shares in the ratio of Fixed Capitals. (b) Issue Equity Shares for the balance in the profits sharing ratio.
II. ***If it is desired to compensate those partners who contribute Capital in excess of what is required as per profit sharing ratio.***	II. (a) Issue Equity Shares in the ratio of Proportionate Capitals (taking the capital of a partner who contributed the least, as base) (b) Issue Preference Shares for the Surplus Capitals

Note: In the opinion of Author, II Method seems to be more appropriate.

ILLUSTRATION 6

P, Q and R were carrying on business in partnership, sharing profits and losses in the ratio of 5 : 4 : 3 respectively. The trial balance of the firm as on 31st March, 2013 was the following:

Particulars		*Debit (₹)*	*Credit (₹)*
Plant and Machinery		85,000	—
Stock		64,200	—
Sundry Debtors		66,500	—
Sundry Creditors		—	84,700
Capital Accounts:	P	—	63,000
	Q	—	42,000
	R	—	21,000
Drawings Accounts:	P	20,000	—
	Q	20,000	—
	R	15,000	—
Depreciation on Plant and Machinery		—	25,000

Trading profit for the year	—	1,23,300
cash at Bank	88,300	—
	3,59,000	3,59,000

Interest on Capital accounts @ 5% p.a. on the amount standing to the credit of partner's Capital Account at the beginning of the year was not provided before preparing the above Trial Balance. On 31st March, they formed a Private Limited Co. with an authorised share capital of ₹ 2,00,000 in shares of ₹ 10 each to be divided in different classes to take over the business of partnership.

You are informed as under:

(a) Plant and Machinery is to be transferred at ₹ 66,000.

(b) Shares in the company are to be issued to the partners, in such numbers and such classes as will give the partners, by reason of their share holdings alone, the same rights as regards interest on capitals and the sharing of profit and losses as they had in the partnership.

(c) Before transferring the business, the partners wish to draw from the partnership their profit to such an extent that the Bank balance is reduced to ₹ 50,000. For this purpose, sufficient profits of the year are to be retained in profit sharing ratio.

(d) All assets and liabilities except plant and machinery and the bank balance are to be transferred at their values in the books of the partnership as on 31st March.

You are required to prepare:

(i) Profit and Loss Account for the year ending on 31.3.2013.

(ii) Capital Accounts showing all the adjustments required to dissolve the partnership.

(iii) A statement showing the number of shares of each class to be issued by the company to each of the partners and details of rights attaching to those shares.

(iv) The Balance Sheet of the company immediately after acquiring the partnership and issuing of shares.

SOLUTION

(I) PROFIT AND LOSS ACCOUNT

for the year ending on 31st March, 2013

Dr. *Cr.*

Particulars		₹	*Particulars*	₹
To Interest on Capitals:			By Trading Profit	123,300
P	3,150			
Q	2,100			
R	1,050	6,300		
To Profit transferred to Capital A/cs:				
P	48,750			
Q	39,000			
R	29,250	1,17,000		
		1,23,300		1,23,300

(II) CAPITAL ACCOUNTS OF PARTNERS

Dr. *Cr.*

Particulars	*P* ₹	*Q* ₹	*R* ₹	*Particulars*	*P* ₹	*Q* ₹	*R* ₹
To Drawings	20,000	20,000	15,000	By Balance b/d	63,000	42,000	21,000

To Bank (drawings)	19,400	11,100	7,800	By Interest on Capital	3,150	2,100	1,050
To 5% Preference Shares	28,000	14,000	—	By P & L A/c	48,750	39,000	29,250
To Equity Shares	50,000	40,000	30,000	By Plant & Machinery (Profit on transfer)	2,500	2,000	1,500
	1,17,400	85,100	52,800		1,17,400	85,100	52,800

The question of preference and equity shares to be issued to P, Q and R can be dealt with in the following manner:

	Particulars	*P* ₹	*Q* ₹	*R* ₹
A	Total amount due as capital	78,000	54,000	30,000
B	Proportionate Capitals taking R's Capital as the Base Capital (for which Equity Shares should be issued)	50,000	40,000	30,000
C	Surplus Capital (for which 5% Non-cumulative Pref. Shares should be issued) (A – B)	28,000	14,000	Nil

The above is based on the principle that the function of interest in case of partnership is to compensate those partners who contribute capital more than proportionate capital as per profit sharing ratio.

BALANCE SHEET OF ... PVT. LTD. AS AT 1ST APRIL,2013

	Particulars	*Note No.*	₹
I.	**EQUITY AND LIABILITIES**		
	(1) Shareholders' Funds		
	(a) Share Capital	1	1,62,000
	(2) Non-Current Liabilities		
	(3) Current Liabilities [Trade Payables]		84,700
	Total		2,46,700
II.	**ASSETS**		
	(1) Non-Current Assets		
	(a) Fixed Assets		
	(i) Tangible Assets (Plant & Machinery)		66,000
	(2) Current Assets		
	Inventories		64,200
	Trade Receivables		66,500
	Cash and Cash Equivalents		50,000
	Total		2,46,700

Notes to Accounts:

NOTE 1: SHARE CAPITAL

Authorised Capital	
20,000 Shares of ₹ 10 each	2,00,000
Issued & Subscribed Capital	
12,000 Equity Shares of ₹ 10 each	1,20,000

4,200, 5% Pref. Shares of ₹ 10 each (Of the above all Shares were issued for consideration otherwise than cash)	42,000
	1,62,000

Working Notes:

(i) Calculation of Additional Drawings

Drawings (already made: ₹ 55,000, *plus* those to be made ₹ 38,300, (i.e. ₹ 88,300 – 50,000), are ₹ 93,300. Of these, ₹ 6,300 is for interest. The remaining ₹ 87,000 is to be drawn by the partners in the ratio of 5 : 4 : 3.

STATEMENT SHOWING THE CALCULATION OF ADDITIONAL DRAWINGS

	Particulars	*P* ₹	*Q* ₹	*R* ₹
A	Total Drawings (excluding interest) (Ratio 5 : 4 : 3)	36,250	29,000	21,750
B	*Add:* Interest on Capital	3,150	2,100	1,050
		39,400	31,100	22,800
C	*Less:* Amount already drawn	20,000	20,000	15,000
D	Additional Drawings to be made (A + B – C)	19,400	11,100	7,800

(ii) Purchase Consideration = Agreed Value of Assets taken over – Agreed amount of Liabilities taken over

= ₹ 66,000 + ₹ 64,200 + ₹ 66,500 + ₹ 50,000 – ₹ 84,700

= ₹ 1,62,000.

ILLUSTRATION 7

A and B carried on business as partners sharing profits and losses equally. The business was being carried on in two departments, called R and W. The following is the Balance Sheet as on 31st March, 2013:

Particulars		₹
Creditors:		
R. Department	3,38,800	
W. Department	57,200	3,96,000
Loans		26,400
Bank Overdraft		1,96,900
Capital Accounts:		
A	5,78,600	
B	3,56,400	9,35,000
Land and Building (at cost)		4,21,300
Debtors:		
R. Department	1,40,800	
W. Department	2,37,600	3,78,400
Stock in Trade:		
R. Department	5,06,000	

W. Department	2,47,500	7,53,500
Cash in hand		1,100

Additional Information:

(a) As from 1st April, 2013, it was decided that the business should be taken over by two Limited Companies, A and Co. to take over R Department, and B and Co. Ltd. to take over W, Department.

(b) The lenders agreed to accept 7% Preference Shares of the Companies as follows:

A and Co. Ltd. ₹ 15,840; B & Co. Ltd.: ₹ 10,560.

(c) A and Co. Ltd. took over the Land and Building, Cash and Liabilities to bank at book values, partners were to be paid goodwill for R Department, amount to ₹ 1,10,000 and for W Departments, ₹ 88,000.

(d) The whole of the purchase price was satisfied by allotment of fully paid equity shares as under:

A received shares of ₹ 5,22,500 in A and Co. Ltd. and balance in the form of shares of B and Co. Ltd.

B received shares of ₹ 3,50,240 in B and Co. Ltd. and balance in the form of shares of A and co. Ltd.

(e) The formation expenses payable by respective companies were as under:

A and Co. Ltd.: ₹ 14,300; B and Co. LTD.: ₹ 8,800.

(f) Bank overdraft, was settled at book value by A and Co. Ltd. out of the proceeds of a loan of ₹ 2,20,000 raised on mortgage of land and building.

(g) Both companies issued further equity shares for cash as under:

A and Co. Ltd.: ₹ 22,000; B and Co. Ltd.: ₹ 33,000

Required: Prepare the Balance Sheet of A and Co. Ltd. after taking into consideration the above transactions and to state the amount of shares allotted to A and B in both the companies.

SOLUTION

BALANCE SHEET OF A AND CO. LTD AS AT 1ST APRIL,2013

Particulars	*Note No.*	₹
I. EQUITY AND LIABILITIES		
(1) Shareholders' Funds		
(a) Share Capital	1	6,65,500
(b) Reserves and Surplus	2	(14,300)
(2) Non-Current Liabilities		
Long-term Borrowings [Mortgage on Land & Building]		2,20,000
(3) Current Liabilities		
Trade Payables		3,38,800
Total		12,10,000
II. ASSETS		
(1) Non-Current Assets		
(a) Fixed Assets		
(i) Tangible Assets		4,21,300

(ii) Intangible Assets [Goodwill]		1,10,000
(2) Current Assets		
Inventories		5,06,000
Trade Receivables		1,40,800
Cash and Cash Equivalents		31,900
Total		12,10,000

Notes to Accounts:

NOTE 1: SHARE CAPITAL

Equity Shares of ₹ 10 each	6,49,660
7% Pref. Shares of ₹ 10 each	15,840
(Of the above all Shares were issued for consideration otherwise than cash)	
	6,65,500

Note: *Profit on Realisation is equal to the amount paid for goodwill as other assets have been taken over at book value.*

NOTE 2: RESERVES AND SURPLUS

Profit & Loss Account [0 – 14,300 (*Preliminary Expenses as per AS 26)]	(14,300)

STATEMENT SHOWING THE ALLOTMENT OF EQUITY SHARES

Particulars	*A & Co. Ltd. (₹)*	*B & Co. Ltd. (₹)*	*Total (₹)*
A. Shares allotted to A	5,22,500	1,55,100	6,77,600
B. Shares allotted to B	1,05,160	3,50,240	4,55,400
	6,27,660	5,05,340	11,33,000
C. Shares allotted for cash	22,000	33,000	55,000
	6,49,660	5,38,340	11,88,000

Working Notes:

Dr. **(I) CAPITAL ACCOUNS OF PARTNERS** *Cr.*

Particulars	*A(₹)*	*B(₹)*	*Particulars*	*A(₹)*	*B(₹)*
To Shares in A & Co. Ltd.	5,22,500	1,05,160	By Balance b/d	5,78,600	3,56,400
To Shares in B & Co. Ltd.	1,55,100	3,50,240	By Realisation A/c	99,000	99,000
	6,77,600	4,55,400		6,77,600	4,55,400

(II) STATEMENT SHOWING THE COMPUTATION OF PURCHASE CONSIDERATION

Particulars	*A & Co. Ltd.* ₹	*B & Co. Ltd.* ₹
A. Total Assets taken over:		
Debtors	1,40,800	2,37,600
Stock in trade	5,06,000	2,47,500
Land and Buildings	4,10,300	

	Fixtures	11,000	
	Cash	1,100	
	Goodwill	1,10,000	88,000
		11,79,200	5,73,100
B.	Total Liabilities taken over:		
	Creditors	3,38,800	57,200
	Loan	15,840	10,560
	Overdraft	1,96,900	
		5,51,540	67,760
C.	Net Assets taken over (A – B)	6,27,660	5,05,340

Dr. **(III) A & CO. LTD.'S CASH ACCOUNT** *Cr.*

Particulars	₹	*Particulars*	₹
To Balance taken over	1,100	By Bank Overdraft	1,96,900
To Equity Share Capital;	22,000	By Formation Expenses	14,300
To Mortgage Loan	2,20,000	By Balance c/d	31,900
	2,43,100		2,43,100

ILLUSTRATION 8

Ram, Rahim and Rogers carry business in partnership under the style of M/s. R & Co, sharing profit and losses in the ratio of 5:3:2. They have floated CANHB(P) Ltd. for the purpose of takeover of their business. The following is the Balance Sheet of the firm as on 30 September, 2013.

Particulars		₹
Creditors		50,000
Capitals:		
Ram		1,01,000
Rahim		1,51,000
Rogers		1,33,000
Cash		6,000
Bank		14,000
Debtors	60,000	
Less: Provision	2,000	58,000
Stock		42,000
Fixed assets (WDV)		3,00,000
Expenditure in relation to CANHB (P). Ltd: Formation expenses	12,000	
Bank A/c in the name		
of CANHB (P). Ltd: Deposit of par value of 300 equity share of ₹ 10 each subscribed equally by Ram, Rahim and Rogers as subscribers to the memorandum and articles of association	3,000	15,000

On that day CANHB (P) Ltd. took over the business for a total consideration of ₹ 5,00,000. The purchase consideration was to be discharged by the allotment of equity shares of ₹10 each at par in the profit sharing ratio and 15% Debentures of ₹100 each at par for surplus capital. The directors of CANHB (P). Ltd. revalued the fixed assets of R & Co at ₹ 4,00,000.

Required:

(a) State the number of equity shares and debentures allotted by CANHB (P). Ltd. to Ram, Rahim and Rogers.

(b) Show journal entries in connection with the above transactions in the books of CANHB (P) Ltd.

SOLUTION

(A) DISTRIBUTION OF PURCHASE CONSIDERATION AMONGST PARTNERS

	Particulars	*Ram* ₹	*Rahim* ₹	*Rogers* ₹
A	Balance of Capital Accounts (Given)	1,01,000	1,51,000	1,33,000
B	*Add:* Profit on Sale of business	59,000	35,400	23,600
C	Actual Capitals	1,60,000	1,86,400	1,56,600
D	Profit Sharing Ratio	5	3	2
E	Capital/Profit sharing ratio [C/D]	32,000	62,133	78,300
F	Proportionate Capitals taking Ram's Capital as basis	1,60,000	96,000	64,000
G	Total Equity shares to be issued including initial allotment of ₹ 3,000	1,60,000	96,000	64,000
H	Initial allotment	1,000	1,000	1,000
I	Further allotment [G – H]	1,59,000	95,000	63,000
J	Allotment of Debentures for the balance [C – G]	—	90,400	92,600
K	No. of Equity Shares Issued [G/₹ 10]	16,000	9,600	6,400
L	No. of Debentures Issued [J/₹ 100]	—	904	926

JOURNAL

Particulars		*L.F.*	*Dr. (₹)*	*Cr. (₹)*
Bank A/c	Dr		3,000	
To Equity Share Capital A/c				3,000
(For Allotment of 300 Equity shares of ₹ 10 each for Ram, Rahim and Rogers as subscribed to Memorandum)				
Business Purchase A/c	Dr.		5,00,000	
To R & Co.				5,00,000
(For purchase of firms business by CANHB (P) Ltd. for ₹ 5,00,000 vide agreement dated...)				
Goodwill A/c	Dr.		18,000	
Fixed Assets A/c	Dr.		4,00,000	
Stock A/c	Dr.		42,000	
Debtors A/c	Dr.		60,000	
Bank A/c	Dr.		14,000	
Cash A/c	Dr.		6,000	
Prelminary Expenses A/c	Dr.		12,000	

To Sundry Creditor			50,000
To Provision for Doubtful Debts			2,000
To Business Purchase A/c			5,00,000
(For various assets and liabilities taken over from vendors as per agreement dated...; difference debited to Goodwill Account)			
R & Co. Dr.		5,00,000	
To Equity Share Capital A/c			3,17,000
To Debentures A/c			1,83,000
(Allotment of 31,700 Shares and 1,830 Debentures to venders in settlement of purchase consideration vide agreement dated...)			

Working Notes: CANHB(P) Ltd. has allotted ₹ 3,000 shares to subscribers of Memorandum ₹ 1,000 each to Ram, Rahim and Rogers. After this allotment total balance of capital A/cs will be ₹ 3,82,000 representing net assets of the business. This has been taken over for ₹ 5,00,000 giving a profit of ₹ 1,18,000

Alternative Solution: In case one assumes that after allotment of ₹ 3,000 shares, the amount payable to the firm will be ₹ 4,97,000 only, the profit on sale of business will be ₹ 1,15,000 with consequential changes in allotment of shares and debentures to the partners.

7.0 PROFIT *or* LOSS PRIOR TO INCORPORATION

MEANING OF PROFIT OR LOSS PRIOR TO INCORPORATION

When a running business is taken over by the promoters of a company as at a date prior to the date of incorporation of company, the profit *or* loss of such a business for the period from the date of purchase of the business to the date of incorporation of the company, is called 'Profit *or* Loss prior to incorporation'.

NATURE OF PROFIT OR LOSS PRIOR TO INCORPORATION

The profit *or* loss prior to incorporation is regarded as of capital nature because a company can not do any business before its incorporation.

ACCOUNTING TREATMENT OF PROFIT OR LOSS PRIOR TO INCORPORATION

The accounting treatment of profit *or* loss prior to incorporation is summarised as follows:

Profit or Loss	*Accounting Treatment*
(a) ***Profit Prior to Incorporation***	It is credited to Capital Reserve A/c and the balance of Capital Reserve A/c is shown under the head 'Reserves and Surplus'. ***or*** It is credited to Goodwill A/c (if Good will has been debited as an asset at the time of acquisition of business)
(b) ***Loss Prior to Incorporation***	It is debited to Goodwill A/c. ***or*** It is debited to Capital Reserve A/c (if Capital Reserve has been credited at the time of acquisition of business)

METHODS OF COMPUTING PROFIT OR LOSS PRIOR TO INCORPORATION

The profit *or* loss prior to incorporation can be ascertained in any of the following two methods:

1. Separate Final Accounts Method	Under this method, the books of the business taken over are balanced off and a trial balance is prepared as on the date of incorporation of the company. Then a Profit and Loss Statement is prepared for the period from the date of acquisition of business to the date of incorporation of the company to ascertain Profit *or* Loss prior to incorporation.
2. Single Final Accounts Method	Under this method, a trial balance is prepared only at the end of the accounting period and a Profit and Loss Statement is prepared for the whole period covering the pre-incorporation period and the post-incorporation period. Then the profit *or* Loss for the whole period is apportioned between pre-incorporation period and post-incorporation period on some appropriate basis.

BASIS OF APPORTIONMENT

The following guiding principles may be followed in this regard:

Item	*Basis of Apportionment*
(a) **Gross Profit or Gross Loss**	On the basis of Turnover in the respective periods ***or*** On the basis of Cost of Goods Sold in the respective periods in the absence of any information regarding turnover ***or*** On the basis of Time in the respective periods in the absence of any information regarding turnover and cost of goods sold.
(b) **Expenses related to Turnover** [e.g. Carriage/ Cartage Outward. Selling and Distribution Expenses, Commission to selling agents/ travelling agents, Advertisement expenses, Bad debts (if actual bad debts for the two periods are not given), Brokerage, Travelling Expenses relating to Sales Promotion.]	On the basis of Turnover in the respective periods.
(c) **Expenses related to TIme** [e.g. Salaries, Office and Administration Expenses, Rent, Rates and Taxes, Printing and Stationery, Telephone, Telegram and Postage, Depreciation, Miscellaneous Expenses]	On the basis of Time in the respective periods
(d) **Expenses exclusively relating to pre-incorporation period** [e.g. Vendor's salary, Interest on Vendor's Capital]	Charge to Pre-incorporation period
(e) **Expenses exclusively relating to post-incorporation period** [e.g. Interest on Debentures, Director' fees, Directors' remuneration, Preliminary Expenses, Share issue Expenses, Underwriting Commission, Discount on issue of Shares/Debentures, formation Expenses]	Charge to Post-incorporation period

(f) Interest on purchase consideration to Vendor	
(i) For the period from the date of acquisition of business to date of incorporation	Charge to Pre-incorporation period
(ii) For the period from the date of incorporation to the date of payment	Charge to Post-incorporation period
(g) Audit Fees	
(i) For Company's Audit under section 227 of the Companies Act 1956	Charge to Post-incorporation period
(ii) For Tax Audit under section 44AB of the Income Tax Act 1961	On the basis of Turnover in the respective periods

RELEVANT DATE FOR THE APPORTIONMENT OF PROFIT IN CASE OF A PUBLIC LIMITED COMPANY

Some accountants contends that in case of public limited company any profit made before the date of certificate of commencement of business should be taken as capital profit because a public company can commence business only after obtaining the certificate of commencement of business. However, it has now been widely accepted that when a company receives the certificate of commencement of business, the company's right to carry on the business relates back to the date of incorporation. Hence, the Date of incorporation should be taken as the relevant date for the apportionment of profits between pre and post incorporation periods even in case of a public limited company.

ILLUSTRATION 9 [CALCULATION OF SALES RATIO]

Accounting Period	—	*Calender year*
Date of taking over of Business	—	1.1.2013
Date of Incorporation	—	1.5 2013
Date Commencement of Business	—	1.7.2013
Total Sales during 2013	—	₹ 9,60,000

Required: Calculate the Sales Ratio in each of the following alternative cases:—

Case (a) Sales were uniform throughout the period.

Case (b) 80% Sales upto 1.9.2013 and the balance for the remaining period

Case (c) Sales were as under:-

(i) For January—twice the average sale

(ii) For February—Equal to average Sale

(iii) From May to August—one fourth of the average Sale in each month.

(iv) For October & November—Three times the average Sale in each month

Case (d) The monthly average of turnover during the first four months of 2013 was half the corresponding figure for remaining period.

Case (e) The monthly average of turnover during the first eight months of 2013 was twice the corresponding figure for the remaining period.

Case (f) The monthly sales in Jan, Nov and Dec. are double the monthly sales for the remaining months of the year.

Case (g) The turnover was evenly upto the date of the certificate of commencement, where after the same spurted to record an increase of two-thirds during the rest of the year.

SOLUTION

Case (a) Time Ratio = Pre-in Corporation Period: Post Incorporation Period = 4 : 8 = 1 : 2

Sales Ratio = Time Ratio = 1 : 2

Case (b) 80% of Sales = ₹ 9,60,00,000 × 80/100 = ₹ 7,68,000

Sales from Jan to Aug. = ₹ 7,68,000

Average Sales during these 8 months = ₹ 7,68,000/8 = ₹ 96,000

Sales from Jan. to April = ₹ 96,000 × 4 = ₹ 3,84,000

Sales from May to Dec. = ₹ 9,60,000 – ₹ 3,84,000 = ₹ 5,76,000

Thus, Sales Ratio = ₹ 3,84,000: ₹ 5,76,000 = 2:3

Case (c) (i) Average Sales = ₹ 9,60,000/12 = ₹ 80,000

(ii) For
Jan = ₹ 80,000 × 2 = ₹ 1,60,000
Feb = ₹ 80,000 × 1 = ₹ 80,000
May = ₹ 80,000 × 1/4 = ₹ 20,000
Jun = ₹ 80,000 × 1/4 = ₹ 20,000
Jul = ₹ 80,000 × 1/4 = ₹ 20,000
Aug= ₹ 80,000 × 1/4 = ₹ 20,000
Oct = ₹ 80,000 × 3 = ₹ 2,40,000
Nov = ₹ 80,000 × 3 = ₹ 2,40,000

Sales for 8 Months. = ₹ 8,00,000

(iii) Sales for March, Apr. Sept., & Dec = ₹ 9,60,000 – ₹ 8,00,000 = ₹ 1,60,000

(iv) Average Sales for these 4 months = ₹ 1,60,000/4 = ₹ 40,000

(v) Sales for Pre-in Corporation Period

Jan. = ₹ 1,60,000.
Feb. = ₹ 80,000.
Mar. = ₹ 40,000.
April = ₹ 40,000.
₹ 3,20,000.

(vi) Sales for Post Incorporation Period ₹ 9,60,000 – ₹ 3,20,000 = ₹ 6,40,000

(vii) Sales Ratio ₹ 3,20,000 : ₹ 6,40,000 = 1:2

Case (d) Time Ratio = 4 : 8, Average Ratio = 1 : 2

Sales Ratio = 4 × 1: 8 × 2 = 4 : 16 = 1 : 4

Case (e)

Time Ratio	8 : 4,
Average Ratio	2 : 1
Actual Sales Ratio (8 × 2 : 4 × 1 = 16:4)	4 : 1
Sales for first Eight Months from Jan to Aug (₹ 96,000 × 4)	₹ 3,84,000
Average Sales for First Eight Months (₹ 7,68,000/8)	₹ 96,000
Sales from Jan to Apr. (₹ 96,000 × 4)	₹ 3,84,000
Sales from May to Dec. (₹ 9,60,000 – ₹ 3,84,000)	₹ 5,76,000

Case (f)

SALES FOR JAN, NOV & DEC: SALES FOR FEB TO OCT.

Time Ratio	3 : 9
Average Ratio	2 : 1
Actual Sales Ratio (3 × 2 : 9 × 1)	6 : 9
Sales for Jan, Nov & Dec (₹ 9,60,000 × 6/15)	₹ 3,84,000
Monthly Average for Jan, Nov. & Dec. (₹ 3,84,000/3)	₹ 1,28,000
Sales for Feb to Oct (₹ 9,60,000 – ₹ 3,84,00)	₹ 5,76,000
Monthly Average for Feb to Oct (₹ 5,76,000/9)	₹ 64,000
Sales from Jan to April (₹ 1,28,000 + ₹ 64,000 + ₹ 64,000 + ₹ 64,000)	₹ 3,20,000
Sales from May to Dec. (₹ 9,60,000 – ₹ 3,20,000)	₹ 6,40,000

Case (g)

SALES UPTO 30TH JUNE : SALES FROM 1ST JULY TO 31ST DEC.

Sales upto 30th June: Sales from 1st July to 31 Dec. = 1 : 5/3, *or* 3 : 5

Sales upto 30th June (₹ 9,60,000 × 3/8)	₹ 3,60,000
Average (₹ 3,60,000/6)	₹ 60,000
Pre-Incorporation Sales (₹ 60,000 × 4)	₹ 2,40,000
Post-Incorporation Sales (₹ 9,60,000 – ₹ 2,40,000)	₹ 7,20,000

ILLUSTRATION 10 [CALCULATION OF WAGES RATIO]

Date of Taking over Business	–1.1.2013
Date of Incorporation	–1.5.2013
Date of Commencement of Business	–1.7.2013
Accounting Period	–Calender year
Total wages incurred during 2013	–₹ 72,000

Required: Calculate the wage ratio in each of the following alternative cases:-

Case (a) Wages were paid uniformly during the period

Case (b) 50% of wages pertain to the first 8 months and the balance for the remaining period.

Case (c) No. of workers employed during the First 4 months – 4

No. of workers employed during remaining period – 8

Case (d) Rate of wages during first 4 month was half of the corresponding figure for the remaining period

Case (e) No. of workers during first four month was twice the corresponding figure for the remaining period & the rate of wages during the first four months was half the corresponding figure for the remaining period.

Case (f) No. of workers & rate of wages during first six months was half the corresponding figure for the remaining period.

Case (g) The rates of wages tripled from 1st April 2013.

SOLUTION

Case (a) Time Ratio Pre-incorporation Period: Post incorporation Period

= 4 Months : 8 Months = 1 : 2

Wages Ratio = Time Ratio = 1 : 2

Case (b) Wages for first 8 months = ₹ 72,000 × 1/2 = ₹ 36,000

Average wages = ₹ 36,000/8 = ₹ 4,500

Wages for pre-incorporation period = ₹ 4,500 × 4 = ₹ 18,000

Wages for post incorporation period = ₹ 72,000 – ₹ 18,000 = ₹ 54,000

Wages Ratio = ₹ 18,000 : ₹ 54,000 = 1 : 3

Case (c) Time Ratio = 1 : 2, No. of workers Ratio = 4 : 8

Weighted wages Ratio = 1 × 4 : 2 × 8 = 4 : 16 = 1 : 4

Case (d) Time Ratio = 1 : 2, Rate of wages Ratio = 1 : 2

Weighted wages Ratio = 1 × 1 : 2 × 2 = 1 : 4

Case (e)

Time Ratio	1:2
No. of workers Ratio	2:1
Rate of wages Ratio	1:2
Weighted wages Ratio (1 × 2 × 1 : 2 × 1 × 2 = 2 : 4)	1:2
Pre-Incorporation Wages (₹ 72,000 × 2/6)	₹ 24,000
Post-Incorporation Wages (₹ 72,000 – ₹ 24,000)	₹ 48,000

Case (f)

Time Ratio	1:1
No. of workers Ratio	1: 2
Rate of wages Ratio	1:2
Weighted wages Ratio (1 × 1 × 1 : 1 × 2 × 2)	1: 4
Wages for first 6 months (₹ 72,000 × 1/5)	₹ 14,400
Average wages (₹ 14,400/6)	₹ 2,400
Pre-Incorporation wages (₹ 2,400 × 4)	₹ 9,600
Post-Incorporation wages (₹ 72,000 – ₹ 9,600)	₹ 62,400

Case (g)

Time Ratio	1:3
Rate of Wages Ratio	1:3
Weighted Wages Ratio (1 × 1:3 × 3)	1 : 9
Wages for last 9 months (₹72,000 × 9/10)	₹64,800
Average wages for 9 months (₹64,800/9)	₹7,200
Pre-Incorporation wages (₹ 72,000 × 1/10 + ₹7,200)	₹ 14,400
Post-In corporation wages (₹ 72,000 – ₹ 14,400)	₹ 57,600

ILLUSTRATION 11 [CALCULATION OF COST OF GOODS SOLD RATIO]

Date of acquisition of business 1st April 2012, Date of incorporation of Public Ltd. Company 1st Aug. 2012, Date of Certificate to Commence business 1st Oct. 2012, Sales from 1st April to 31st July ₹ 2,40,000 and sales from 1st Aug. to 31st March ₹ 7,20,000. The company deals in one type of product. The unit cost of sales was reduced by 10% since 1st Aug as compared to pre-incorporation period. The cost of goods sold from 1st April to 31st March 2013 amounted to ₹ 7,77,000. Calculate the Gross Profit for pre-incorporation and post-incorporation period.

SOLUTION

Let Cost of goods sold in the pre-incoperation period be ₹ 100. Then, Cost of goods sold in the post-incorporation period = ₹ 90

Sales Ratio = 2,40,000 : 7,20,000 = 1 : 3

Thus, Cost of goods sold Ratio = 100 × 1 : 90 × 3 = 100 : 270 = 10 : 27

Particulars	*Pre incorporation*	*Post incorporation*
A. Sales	₹ 2,40,000	₹ 7,20,000
B. *Less:* Cost of Goods sold (10 : 27)	₹ 2,10,000	₹ 5,67,000
C. Gross Profit (A – B)	₹ 30,000	₹ 1,53,000

ILLUSTRATION 12 [COMPREHENSIVE]

Tulsian Ltd. was formed to take over a running business of Mr. Tulsian with effect from 1st April 2012. The company was incorporated in 1st Aug. 2012 and the certificate of Commencement of business was received on 1st Oct. 2012. No entries relating to the transfer of the business were entered in the books which were continued until 31st March 2013. The following Trial Balance was extracted from the books as on 31st March 2013:

JOURNAL

Particulars	*Dr. (₹)*	*Cr. (₹)*
Sales		9,60,000
Cost of Goods Sold	7,77,000	
Rent	40,000	
Salaries	21,000	
Travelling Expenses	8,400	
Depreciation	4,800	
Carriage outward	400	
Printing & Stationary	2,400	
Advertisement	8,000	
Miscellaneous Expenses	12,600	
Directors' fees	600	
Managing Director's Remuneration	4,100	
Bad Debts	1,600	
Commission & Brokerage to Selling Agents	8,000	
Audit Fees	3,000	

Interest on Debentures	1,500	
Interest paid to Vendors	2,100	
Selling & Distribution Expenses	12,000	
Preliminary Expenses	1,500	
Underwriting Commission	900	
Fixed Assets	3,65,000	
Current Assets	43,800	
TULSIAN's capital as on 1.4.2012		2,78,000
Current Liabilities		30,700
Debentures		50,000
	13,18,700	13,18,700

Additional Information:

(a) Total sales for the year arose evenly upto the date of the certificate of Commencement whereafter they spurted to record an increase of two-thirds during the rest of the year

(b) The Company deals in one type of product. The unit cost of goods sold was reduced by 10% since 1st Aug. 2012 as compared to the pre-incorporation period.

(c) Rent of old office building was increased by 20% since 1st Nov. 2012. It had to occupy additional space from 1st July 2012 for which rent was ₹ 3000 p.m.

(d) The salaries were Tripled from 1st July 2012

(e) Travelling Expenses include ₹ 2,400 towards sales promotion.

(f) Depreciation includes ₹ 300 for new assets acquired in Aug 2012.

(g) Purchase consideration was discharged by the company on 30th Sept. 2012 by issuing 30,000 Equity shares of ₹ 10 each.

Required: Prepare the Profit & Loss Statement in a Columnary form, showing the allocation of profits between pre-incorporation and post-incorporation periods indicating the basis of apportionment.

SOLUTION

PROFIT & LOSS STATEMENT OF TULSIAN LTD.

for the year ended 31st March 2013

Particulars	*Ratio*	*Pre-Incorporation* ₹	*Post-Incorporation* ₹
I. Revenue from Operations	1 : 3	2,40,000	7,20,000
II. Expenses:			
Cost of Goods sold	10 : 27	2,10,000	5,67,000
Employee Benefits Expense	Note	4,200	20,900
Finance Costs	Note	1,400	2,200
Depreciation and Amortization Expense	W.N. (vi)	1,500	3,300
Other Expenses	Note	22,100	77,300
Total Expenses		2,39,200	6,70,700
III. Profit for the period		800	49,300

Note: *Profit for the Pre-Incorporation period will be treated as of capital nature and hence will be credited to Capital Reserve Account but Profit for the Post-Incorporation period will be treated as of revenue nature hence will remain in the Profit & Loss Account.*

NOTE AS TO APPORIONMENT OF EXPENSES

Particulars	*Basis of Apportionment*	*Pre-Incorporation*	*Post-Incorporation*
Employee Benefits Expense			
Salaries	W.N. (iv)	4,200	16,800
MD Remmuneration		—	4,100
		4,200	**20,900**
Finance Costs			
Interest on Debentures		—	1,500
Interest to Vendors	4 : 2	1,400	700
		1,400	**2,200**
Other Expenses			
Rent for old office	W.Note (iii)	4,000	9,000
Rent for new office	1 : 8	3,000	24,000
Travelling Exp.	W. Note(v)	2,600	5,800
Carriage outwards	Sales Ratio		
	To 1 : 3	100	300
Printing & stationery	Time Ratio	800	1,600
		4 : 8	
Advertisements	Sales Ratio	2,000	6,000
Misc. Trade Exp.	Time Ratio	4,200	8,400
Director's fees	—	—	600
Bad Debt.	Sales Ratio	400	1,200
Commission	Sales Ratio	2,000	6,000
Audit fees	—	—	3,000
Selling & Dist. Exp.	Sales Ratio	3,000	9,000
*Preliminary Expenses	—	—	1,500
*Underwriting Comm.	—	—	900
		22,100	**77,300**

**As per Para 56 of AS 26, 'Intangible Assets', Preliminary Expenses & underwriting commission are to be recognized as expenses as and when they are incurred. Hence, these Expenses are not to appear in the Balance Sheet.*

BALANCE SHEET OF TULSIAN LTD AS AT 1ST APRIL,2013

Particulars	*Note No.*	₹
I. EQUITY AND LIABILITIES		
(1) Shareholders' Funds		
(a) Share Capital	1	3,00,000

(b) Reserves and Surplus	2	49,300
(2) Non-Current Liabilities		
Long-term Borrowings [Debentures]		50,000
(3) Current Liabilities		30,700
Total		4,30,000
II. ASSETS		
(1) Non-Current Assets		
(a) Fixed Assets		
(i) Tangible Assets		3,65,000
(ii) Intangible Assets [Goodwill] [22,000 – 800 (Capital Reserve)]		21,200
(2) Current Assets		43,800
Total		4,30,000

Notes to Accounts:

NOTE 1: SHARE CAPITAL

30,000, Equity Shares of ₹ 10 each	3,00,000
(Of the above all Shares were issued for consideration otherwise than cash)	

NOTE 2: RESERVES AND SURPLUS

Profit & Loss Account	49,300

Working Notes:

(i) Calculation of Sales Ratio

If sale upto 30th Sept. (for 6 month) is X, it will be 5/3 X for remaining 6 months.

X + 5/3X = ₹ 9,60,000

X = ₹ 9,60,000 × 3/8 = 3,60,000

Thus, sales upto 31st July (for 4 months) = ₹ 3,60,000 × 4/6 = ₹ 2,40,000

Sales from 1st Aug to 31st March = ₹ 9,60,000 – ₹ 2,40,000 = ₹ 7,20,000

Thus, the Sales Ratio = 1 : 3

(ii) Calculation of Cost of Goods Sold

Let cost of goods sold in the pre-incorporation period be ₹100

Then cost of goods sold in the post-incorporation period is ₹ 90.

Sales Ratio (as calculated above) = 1 : 3

Then, cost of Goods sold Ratio = (100 × 1) : (90 × 3) = 100 : 270 = 10 : 27

(iii) Calculation of Rent

A Additional Rent for new office premises = ₹ 3,000 × 9 = ₹ 27,000

B Rent for old office premises = Total Rent – Additional Rent

= ₹ 40,000 – ₹ 27,000 = ₹ 13,000

If monthly average upto oct (7 months) is X then the monthly average from Nov to Dec. (5 months) will be 1.2 X

Thus, Rent for 7 months = 7 × X = 7X and Rent for 5 months = 5 × 1.2X = 6X.

Thus, the ratio for division is 7 : 6

Rent for 7 months upto Oct. = ₹ 13,000 × 7/13 = ₹ 7,000

Rent for 4 months upto July = ₹ 7,000 × 4/7 = ₹ 4,000

Rent for 8 months from Aug. to Dec. = ₹ 13,000 – ₹ 4,000 = ₹ 9,000

(iv) Calculation of Salaries

If monthly average upto June (3 months) is X, then monthly average from July to March (9 months) will be 3X

Thus, Salaries for 3 months = 3X and Salaries for 9 months = 27 X

Thus, the ratio for division is 3 : 27 *or* 1 : 9

Thus, Salaries from Apr-June = 21,000 × 1/10 = 2,100

Salaries for July–March = ₹ 21,000 × 9/10 = 18,900

Salaries for July = ₹ 18,900/9 = ₹ 2,100

Thus, Salaries from Apr to July = ₹ 2,100 + ₹ 2,100 = 4,200

Salaries from Aug. to March = ₹ 18,900 – ₹ 2,100 = ₹ 16,800

(V) CALCULATION OF TRAVELLING EXPENSES

Particulars	*Pre incorporation*	*Post incorporation*
Towards Sales Promotion	2,400 × 1/4 = 600	2,400 × 3/4 = 1,800
other (8,400 – 2,400)	6,000 × 4/12 = 2,000	6,000 × 8/12 = 4,000
	2,600	5,800

(VI) CALCULATION OF DEPRECIATION

Particulars	*Pre incorporation*	*Post incorporation*
On Addition in Aug.	—	₹ 300
On Others (₹ 4,800 – ₹ 300)	₹ 4500 × 4/12 = 1,500	₹ 4,500 × 8/12 = ₹ 3,000
	₹ 1,500	₹ 3,300

(vii) Goodwill = Purchase Consideration – Capital = ₹3,00,000 – ₹ 2,78,000 = ₹ 22,000

PROBLEM 3.14

XYZ (P) Limited was incorporated on 01.08.2012 to take over the business of Mis Rank & Co. from 01.04.2012.The Profit & Loss Account as given by XYZ (P) Limited for the year ending 31.03.2013 is as under:

Dr. **PROFIT & LOSS ACCOUNT FOR THE YEAR ENDING 31. 03.2013** *Cr.*

Particulars	₹	*Particulars*	₹
To Advertisement	99,000	By Gross Profit b/d	9,45,000
To Audit fee	15,000	By Interest on Investments	16,000
To Bad debts (related to sales)	27,000		
To Depreciation	21,000		
To Discount	9,000		
To Interest on debentures	80,000		
To Preliminary expenses	12,000		
To Rent	1,40,000		

To Salaries	4,48,000		
To Underwriting commission	20,000		
To Net Profit	90,000		
	9,61,000		9,61,000

Prepare Profit & Loss Statement showing allocation of pre-incorporation and post-incorporation profits after considering the following information:

(1) Gross profit ratio was constant throughout the year.

(2) Sales for August 2012 to November 2012 were 1½ times the average monthly sales while for December, 2012 to March, 2013 were 2 times the average sales.

(3) Company had to occupy additional space from 01st December, 2012 for which rent was ₹ 5,000 per month.

(4) Bad debts are shown after adjusting a recovery of ₹ 9,000 of bad debts for a sale made in July, 2012.

(5) Salary of one manager was increased by ₹ 2,000 p.m. from August, 2012. Salary of other employees remains unchanged.

(6) All investments were sold in May, 2012 at a profit of ₹ 27,000. Profit on sale of investment inadvertently included to sales and ultimately to gross profit.

SOLUTION

PROFIT & LOSS STATEMENT FOR THE YEAR ENDED 31ST MARCH, 2013

Particulars	*Ratio*	*Pre-Incorporation* ₹	*Post-Incorporation* ₹
I. **Gross Profit** [9,45,000 – 27,000]	4 : 14	2,04,000	7,14,000
II. **Other Income** [9,000 + 27,000 + 16,000]		52,000	—
III. **Total Revenue [1 + II]**		2,56,000	7,14,000
II. **Expenses:**			
Employee Benefits Exp. [Refer to working Note]		1,44,000	3,04,000
Finance Costs [Interest on Co's Debentures]		—	80,000
Depreciation and Amortization Expense	1 : 2	7,000	14,000
*Other Expenses		77,000	2,54,000
Total Expenses		2,28,000	6,52,000
III. **Profit for the period**		28,000	62,000

Note: *Profit for the Pre-Incorporation period will be treated as of capital nature and hence will be credited to Capital Reserve Account but Profit for the Post-Incorporation period will be treated as of revenue nature hence will remain in the Profit & Loss Statement.*

NOTE AS TO APPORIONMENT OF OTHER EXPENSES

Particulars	*Ratio*	*Pre-Incorporation* ₹	*Post-Incorporation* ₹
Advertisement	4 : 14	22,000	77,000
Audit Fee	1 : 2	5,000	10,000

Bad debts	4 : 14	8,000	28,000
Discount	4 : 14	2,000	7,000
Preliminary expenses	Post	—	12,000
Rent	W.N. (v)	40,000	1,00,000
Underwriting commission	Post	—	20,000
		77,000	2,54,000

Working Notes:

(i) Calculation of Sales Ratio

Let us assume average monthly sales be X

Average sales during pre- in corporation period:

April – July = 4 × X = 4X

Average sales during post-incorporation period:

August – November = 4 × 1.5X = 6X

December – March = 4 × 2X = 8X

Total average sales during post-incorporation period = 14X

Ratio of sales between pre incorporation and post incorporation period is 4X : 14X i.e. 4: 14.

(ii) Calculation of time ratio

4 months : 8 months = 1:2

(III) GROSS PROFIT RELATED TO TRADING ACTIVITY

Particulars	₹
Gross profit as per Profit & Loss A/c	9,45,000
Less: Profit on sale of investment	(27,000)
Gross profit related to trading activity	9,18,000

Gross profit apportioned in the ratio of sale 4:14 between pre incorporation and post incorporation period i.e. ₹ 2,04,000 and ₹ 7,14,000 respectively.

(IV) APPORTIONMENT OF BAD DEBTS

Particulars	₹
Bad debts as per Profit and Loss A/c	27,000
Add: Bad debts recovered considered separately	9,000
	36,000

Bad debts apportioned in the ratio of sales 4:14 between pre incorporation and post incorporation period i.e. ₹ 8,000 and ₹ 28,000 respectively

(V) APPORTIONMENT OF RENT

Particulars	₹
Total rent	1,40,000
Less: Additional rent on new premises for 4 months (December to March)	(20,000)
Rent for old premises for 12 months	1,20,000

Particulars	Pre Inc ₹	Post Inc ₹
Rent for old premise in time ratio 1:2	40,000	80,000
Rent for new premise	—	20,000
Apportioned rent	40,000	1,00,000

(VI) APPORTIONMENT OF SALARY

Particulars	₹
Total salary	4,48,000
Less: Increased salary of manager for 8 months @ ₹ 2,000 p.m.	(16,000)
Normal salary for 12 months	4,32,000

Particulars	Pre Inc ₹	Post Inc ₹
Normal salary in time ratio 1: 2	1,44,000	2,88,000
Increased salary of manager for post incorporation period only	—	16,000
Apportioned salary	1,44,000	3,04,000

(vii) Interest on debentures, underwriting commission and preliminary expenses are related to post incorporation period.

PROBLEM 3.15

A firm M/s. Alag, which was carrying on business from 1st July, 2012 gets itself incorporated as a company on Ist November, 2012. The first accounts are drawn upto March 31, 2013. The gross profit for the period is ₹ 56,000. The general expenses are ₹ 14,220; Director's fees ₹ 12,000 p.a.; incorporation expenses ₹ 1,500. Rent upto 31st December was ₹ 1,200 p.a., after which it is increased to ₹ 3,000 p.a. Salary of the manager, who upon incorporation of the company was made a director, is ₹ 6,000 p.a. His remuneration thereafter is included in the above figure of fees to the directors. Give Profit and Loss Statement showing pre and post incorporation profit. The net sales are ₹ 8,20,000, the monthly average of which for the first four months is one-half of that of the remaining period. The company earned a uniform profit. Interest and tax may be ignored.

SOLUTION

PROFIT & LOSS STATEMENT FOR 9 MONTHS ENDED ON 31ST MARCH, 2013

Particulars	Ratio	Pre-Incorporation ₹	Post-Incorporation ₹
I. **Gross Profit**	2 : 5	16,000	40,000
II. **Expenses:**			
Employee Benefits Expense		2,000	—
*Other Expenses		6,720	15,350
Total Expenses		8,720	15,350
III. **Profit for the period**		7,280	24,650

Note: *Profit for the Pre-Incorporation period will be treated as of capital nature and hence will be credited to Capital Reserve Account but Profit for the Post-Incorporation period will be treated as of revenue nature hence will remain in the Profit & Loss Statement.*

***APPORIONMENT OF EXPENSES**

Particulars	*Ratio*	*Pre-Incorporation* ₹	*Post-Incorporation* ₹
General Expenses	4 : 5	6,320	7,900
Directors' Fees	—	—	5,000
Formation Expenses	—	—	1,500
Rent	W.N.(ii)	400	950
		6,720	15,350

Working Notes:

(i) Calculation of Sales Ratio

Let the Average Monthly Sales of first four months = 100 and next five months = 200

Total Sales of first four months = 100 × 4 = 400 and total sales of next five months = 200 × 5 = 1,000

The Ratio of Sales = 400 : 1,000 = 2 : 5

(ii) Rent

Till 31st December, 2010, Rent was ₹1,200 p.a. i.e. ₹ 100 p.m.

So, Pre-incorporation Rent = ₹ 100 × 4 months = ₹ 400

Post-incorporation Rent = (₹ 100 × 2 months) + (₹ 250 × 3 months) = ₹ 950

8.0 STATUTORY REPORT (SECTION 165)

WHICH COMPANIES ARE REQUIRED TO HOLD STATUTORY MEETING?

Every Public limited company having share capital is required to hold such meeting. However, if a private company converts itself into a Public company within period of 6 months from date of its incorporation, it shall be required to hold such meeting.

WHEN IS STATUTORY MEETING TO BE HELD?

Statutory meeting is to be held within a period of not *less* than 1 month and not more than 6 months from the date on which the company is entitled to commence business.

OBJECT OF THE STATUTORY MEETING

The object of this meeting is to provide an opportunity to the members of the company to discuss all matters relating to the formation of the company.

STATUTORY REPORT

A report containing prescribed information relating to formation of the company is sent by the directors to the members. Such a report is called as Statutory Report.

DIRECTOR'S DUTY TO FORWARD THE STATUTORY REPORT TO THE MEMBERS [SEC. 165 (2)]

The Directors must forward at least 21 days before the statutory meeting is held, a statutory report to every member of the company. However such report can be sent at shorter notice provided it is condoned unanimously by members entitled to attend and vote at the meeting.

CONTENTS OF STATUTORY REPORT [SEC. 165 (3)]

(a) The **total number of shares allotted**, distinguishing shares allotted as fully paid *or* partly paid, otherwise than in cash, and in case of partly paid up share stating the extent to which they are so paid up, and in both cases the consideration for which they have been allotted.

(b) The total amount of cash received in respect of shares allotted for cash.

(c) **An abstract of the Receipts and Payment A/c** up to date within 7 days of the report, showing under the different headings the receipts of the company from shares, debentures and other sources, payments made, balance in hand, and an account *or* estimate of the preliminary expenses of the company, showing separately any commission *or* discount paid, *or* to be paid on the issue *or* sale of shares *or* debentures.

(d) The **names, addresses and occupations of the director, auditor, manager and secretary and the change** if any which have occurred in such names, addresses and occupations since the date of its incorporation.

(e) The **particulars of any contract** which, *or* the modification *or* the proposed modification of which, is to be submitted to the meeting for its approval together in the latter case with the particulars of the modification *or* the proposed modification.

(f) The extent, if any, to which each **underwriting contract** has not been carried out and the reasons thereof.

(g) The **call-in-arrears from director and manager** of the company.

(h) The **particulars of any commission or brokerage** paid *or* payable in connection with the issue *or* sale of shares and debentures to any director *or* manager.

CERTIFICATION OF STATUTORY REPORT

Statutory Report is to be certified by at least 2 directors of the company one of them must be managing director if any. [Section 165(4)].

AUDITOR CERTIFICATION OF STATUTORY REPORT

Auditors are required to certify the statutory report after the certification by directors on the matters which relates to the shares allotted by the company and the receipts and payments of the company.

DELIVER OF THE REPORT TO REGISTER [SECTION 165 (5)]

After the copies of the report have been sent to the members of the company then the company must send a certified copy of the report to the Registrar of the company for registration.

CONSEQUENCES OF DEFAULT

The court may order for the compulsory winding up of the company if default is made in delivering the statutory report to the registrar *or* in holding the statutory meeting. [Section 433(b)] *or* the court, instead of winding up order, may direct the company to deliver statutory report *or* hold statutory meeting. [Section 443 (3)]

PRESCRIBED FORM

The statutory report must be prepared in form No. 22 of the general forms. A performa of Statutory Report is given below:

FORM NO. 22

Name of Company .... **Nominal Capital ₹ ....**

THE COMPANIES ACT, 1956
Statutory Report
(Pursuant to Section 165)

Name of Company ....

Statutory Report of the .... Limited Certified and filed pursuant to Section 165 (5)

Date of notice of holding statutory meeting ....

Date of meeting ....

Place where the meeting is to be held ....

Presented by ....

....

The Board of Directors submits this statutory reports to the members in pursuance of Section 165.

1. SHARES ALLOTED AND CASH RECEIVED UP TO ....

Particulars	*No. of shares*	*Nominal value of each*	*Cash received share up to ....*
(a) Alloted subject to payment thereof in cash.	------	------	------
(i) Equity	------	------	------
(ii) Redeemable Preference Shares	------	------	------
(iii) Preference Shares other than Redeemable Preference Shares	------	------	------

(b) Alloted as fully paid-up otherwise than in cash and the consideration for which they have been allotted.

(i) Equity

(ii) Redeemable Preference Shares

(iii) Preference Shares other than Redeemable Preference Shares.

(c) Allotted as partly paid-up to the extent of ₹ .... per share, and the consideration for which they have been so allotted.

(i) Equity

(ii) Redeemable Preference Shares

(iii) Preference Shares other than Redeemable preference Shares.

2. ABSTRACT OF RECEIPTS AND PAYMENTS UP TO ....

Receipts	₹	*Payments*	₹
Shares:		Preliminary Expenses	...
Equity	...	Commission on issue *or* sale of shares	...
Redeemable Preference Shares	...	Discount on issue *or* sale of shares ...	
Preference Shares other than Redeemable Preference Shares	...	**Capital Expenditure:**	
		Land	...

Advance payment for shares	...	Buildings	...
Debentures	...	Plant	...
Loans	...	Machinery	...
Deposits	...	**Other items to be specified:**	...
Other sources (to be specified)	...	Balances:	
		In Hand	...
		At Bank	...
		At Post Office Savings Bank	...
Total	...	Total	...

3. PRELIMINARY EXPENSES AS ESTIMATED IN THE PROSPECTUS OR STATEMENT IN LIEU OF PROSPECTUS

Particulars	*Preliminary expenses actually incurred up to aforesaid date (₹)*	*Preliminary expenses estimated to be incurred after the aforesaid date (₹)*
Law Charges Other charges in connection with the preparation of the Memorandum and Aricles of Association Printing expenses Registration charges Advertisement charges Commission on issue *or* sale of shares Discount on issue *or* sale of shares Other initial expenses (to be specified as far as possible)		
Total ₹		

4. NAMES, ADDRESSES AND OCCUPATIONS OF THE COMPANY'S DIRECTOR'S, AUDITORS, MANAGER AND SECRETARY.

Name(s)	*Address(es)*	*Occupation(s)*	*Particulars of change(s) date of changes, if any, in entries in columns (1), (2) and (3) since the date of incorporation*
A. Directors B. Auditors C. Manager D. Secretary			

These particulars must include dates of changes.

(If any modification *or* propsed modification of a contract is to be submitted for such approval brief particulars of contract and particulars of modification *or* proposed modification should be given).

5. Particulars of any contract which is to be submitted to the statutory meeting for approval.

6. Underwriting contracts.
   Brief description of each contract.
   If contract not carried out fully, extent to which it has not been carried out and reasons therefore.

7. THE ARREARS IF ANY, DUE ON CALLS FROM DIRECTORS AND MANAGER

	Names of Directors	*Amount due*
1.		...
2.		...

8. Particulars of any commission *or* brokerage paid *or* to be paid in connection with the issue *or* sale of shares to any director *or* manager.

Name of Directors	*Commission or brokerage paid or to be paid*	
	On Shares	*On Debentures*
________	________	________
________	________	________

Dated this .... day of .... 19 ....

We hereby certify that the above report is correctSignatures of two *or* more Directors

We hereby certify as correct so much of the report as relates to the shares allotted by the company and to the cash received in respect of such shares and to the receipts and payments.

Date this .... day of .... 19 ....

Auditors

ILLUSTRATION 13

From the particulars given below prepare a Receipts and Payments Account to be included in the Statutory Report of CAS Ltd. made upto March 31, 2013.

Total number of shares subscribed was 15000 shares of ₹ 10 each of which 5,000 shares were issued as fully paid up to vendors. Of the remaining shares 50% of their nominal value was called up and had been received except that allotment money of ₹ 2.50 per share on 1,000 shares remained unpaid by Mr. X a director, The company sold off all the assets acquired from the vendors for ₹ 70,000 and advanced a sum of ₹ 60,000 to a contractor for the construction of a building and further entered into an agreement to purchase machinery valued at ₹ 2,00,000 against which it only paid a deposit of ₹ 20,000. The preliminary expenses amounted to ₹ 28,845 (Advertisement charges ₹ 15,000; Stamping of Documents and Registration Fee ₹ 1845 Solicitors' fee ₹ 11,000; and printing of Memorandum ₹ 1,000 out of which ₹ 4,000 was still payable to solicitors and printers in respect of their bills on March 31, 2013. The preliminary expenses were estimated at ₹ 15,000 in the Statement in lieu of Prospectus.

SOLUTION

RECEIPTS AND PAYMENTS ACCOUNT OF CAS LTD.

Dr. *for the period ending 31st March, 2013* *Cr.*

Receipts	₹	*Payments*	₹
Amount received on application and allotment of 10,000 shares	47,500	Preliminary Expenses	24,845
		Advance paid for the construction of building	60,000

Amount received on sale of assets	70,000	Deposit against purchase of machinery	20,000
		Cash and balance in hand	12,655
	1,17,500		1,17,500

The following is an estimate of the preliminary expenses incurred by the company and that of its expenditure on the acquisition of machinery:

(1) Preliminary expenses including fees, etc.,	₹	₹
Advertisement charges	15,000	
Stamping of documents and Registration fees	1,845	
Solicitors' fees	11,000	
Printing memorandum	1,000	28,845

(Preliminary expenses were estimated only at ₹ 15,000 in the Statement in lieu of Prospectus)

(2) The cost of machinery order is ₹ 2,00,000 against which a sum of ₹ 20,000 only was paid till 31.03.2013.

(3) 5,000 fully paid-up shares of ₹ 10 each were allotted to the vendors for purchase of their assets.

(4) Shri X, a director of the company had not paid the allotment money of ₹ 2.50 on 1000 shares allotted to him.

ILLUSTRATION 14

Megabyte Ltd. was incorporated on 1st April, 2013 to take over the running business of Mr. X. The purchase consideration was satisfied by allotment of:

(i) 20,000 equity shares of ₹ 10 each at par.

(ii) 10,000 10% Redeemable Preference shares of ₹ 10 each at par, redeemable on 31.3.2016.

(iii) ₹ 50,000 paid in cash.

The company issued a prospectus for raising capital by issue of 30,000 equity shares of ₹ 10 each, at par and 15,000 10% Redeemable Preference shares of ₹ 10 each, at par. The entire amount in respect of the issue was received by 30th June, 2013 except final call of ₹ 2.50 per share on 1,000 shares issued to Mr. Y, a director. Underwriting commission @ 2% on equity shares and @ 3% on preference shares were paid to a merchant banker.

The preliminary expenses were estimated at ₹ 50,000 in the prospectus but the actual expenses incurred were as under:

Particulars		₹
Solicitor's fee	—	10,000
Printing of memorandum	—	15,000 (of which ₹ 5,000 remained unpaid)
Stamping and registration	—	20,000
Advertisement expenses	—	30,000

The company purchased a plot of land for ₹ 75,000. Further, it advanced ₹ 1,00,000 for construction of office building and ₹ 1,50,000 to a supplier, being 40% of contract price for supply of machinery. A part of the investments taken over from Mr. X was sold for ₹ 50,000 (₹ 5,000 in excess of their book value).

Required: Prepare a Receipts and Payments Account and other relevant financial information to be included in the Statutory Report pursuant to Section 165 of the Companies Act, 1956 in respect of Megabyte Ltd. made upto 30th June, 2013.

SOLUTION

MEGABYTE LTD

(I) ABSTRACTS OF RECEIPTS AND PAYMENTS A/C OF MEGABYTE LTD

for the Period ending 30 June 2013

Receipts	₹	*Payments*		₹
Amt. received on issue of shares:		Preliminary Expenses		70,000
Equity shares	2,97,500	Underwriting commission		
10% Red. Pref. shares	1,50,000	2% on ₹ 3,00,000	6,000	
Amt. received on sale of investment	50,000	3% on ₹ 1,50,000	4,500	10,500
		Purchase of land		75,000
		Paid to vendors in statisfaction of purchase consideration		50,000
		Advance for building		1,00,000
		Advance for machinery		1,50,000
		Cash & bank balance		42,000
	4,97,500			4,97,500

(ii) Relevant financial information for inclusion in Statutory Report

1. Shares alloted

(A) ALLOTED SUBJECT TO PAYMENT IN CASH

Particulars	*No. of shares* ₹	*Nominal Value* ₹	*Amount received* ₹
Equity shares	30,000	10	2,97,500
10% Redeemable Pref shares	15,000	10	1,50,000

(B) ALLOTED FOR CONSIDERATION OTHER THAN CASH

Particulars	No.	₹	₹
Equity shares	20,000	10	2,00,000
10% Redeemable Pref shares	10,000	10	1,00,000

2. Mr. Y, a director of the company had not paid the call money of ₹ 2.50 on 1,000 equity shares alloted to him.

3. ESTIMATE OF PRELIMINARY EXPENSES INCURRED BY THE COMPANY:

Particulars	₹
Solicitor's fee	10,000
Printing of Memorandum	15,000
Stamping & registration	20,000
Advertisement expenses	30,000
	75,000

Preliminary expenses estimated in the Prospectus—₹ 50,000

4. Particulars of contracts
   (a) The cost of machinery on order is ₹ 3,75,000 against which a sum of ₹ 1,50,000 was paid till 30th June 2013.
   (b) Advance for building made for ₹ 1,00,000

5 ACCOUNTING FOR BONUS ISSUE

LEARNING OBJECTIVES

After studying this chapter, you should be able to understand:

- ◇ Meaning of Capitalisation of Profits and Bonus Shares
- ◇ How to Capitalise Profits or Reserves?
- ◇ Three Sources for Fully Paid-up Bonus Shares [Sec 63(1)]
- ◇ Distinction between Bonus Shares and Right Shares
- ◇ Conditions for Issue of Bonus Shares
- ◇ SEBI Guidelines on Bonus Issues
- ◇ Accounting Treatment of Bonus Issue

1.0 MEANING OF CAPITALISATION OF PROFITS AND BONUS SHARES

Capitalisation of profits refers to the process of converting profits *or* reserves into paid up capital. A bonus share is a free share issued without any consideration to an existing shareholder in the ratio of number of shares held by that shareholder. Issue of Bonus share, decreases the Reserve & Surplus, increases the issued capital but does not bring any change in cash flow and Net worth of the company.

2.0 HOW TO CAPITALIZE PROFITS *or* RESERVES?

A company may capitalise its profits *or* reserves—

(a) by paying up amounts unpaid on existing partly paid shares so as to make them fully paid up shares, or

(b) by issuing fully paid bonus shares to the existing members.

3.0 THREE SOURCES FOR FULLY PAID-UP BONUS SHARES [SEC 63]

As per Sec 63(1), a company may issue fully paid-up bonus shares to its members out of—

(i) Its Free Reserves

(ii) The Secutiries Premium Account; or

(iii) The Capital Redemption Reserve Account:

Notes:

1. **Not out of Revaluation Reserves:** No issue of bonus shares shall be made by capitalising reserves created by the Revaluation of Assets.
2. **Meaning of Free Reserves:** As per Sec 2(43) of the Companies Act, 2015, "Free Reserves" mean such reserves which, as per the latest audited balance sheet of a company, are available for distribution as dividend.

3. **Items not treated as Free Reserves:**

(i) Any amount representing unrealised gaints, notional gains *or* revaluation of assets, where shown as a reserve *or* otherwise, *or*

(ii) Any change in carrying amount of an asset *or* of a liability recognised in equity, including surplus in Profit and Loss Account on measurement of the Asset *or* the Liability at Fair Value

4.0 DISTINCTION BETWEEN BONUS SHARES AND RIGHT SHARES

Basis of Distinction	Bonus Shares	Right Shares
1. Manner of Issue	These are issued by Capitalizing the accumulated profits *or* reserves.	These are issued by issuing new share capital. In case of further issue of shares, further shares must be offered to the existing shareholders in proportion to their existing shareholdings at that date.
		Such shares are called 'Rights Shares.' Such right is available when it is proposed to increase the subscribed capital of the company by allotment of further shares at any time after the expiry of 2 years from the formation of a company *or* after the expiry of 1 year from the first allotment of shares, whichever is earlier.
2. Consideration	These are issued without any consideration.	These are issued for cash.
3. T/f of Right to Receive	Right to receive bonus shares can not be transferred to another person.	Right to subscribe for right shares can be transferred to another person.
4. Apply	Shareholders are not required to apply for bonus shares.	Shareholders are required to apply to subscribe for right shares.
5. Option	Shareholders have no option to receive bonus shares *less* than/ more than those offered.	Shareholders have an option to apply for right shares *less* than/more than those offered.
6. Cash Inflow	There is no cash inflow.	There is cash inflow.

5.0 CONDITIONS FOR ISSUE OF FULLY PAID-UP BONUS SHARES [SEC 63(2)]

1. **Authorised by Articles** — A company can issue bonus shares if its Articles expressly authorise to do so.

2. **Board's Resolution** — A resolution is to be passed by the Board of Directors recommending its decision to issue bonus shares.

3. **Member's Resolution** — A resolution is to be passed by the members in the general meeting to approve the Board's resolution recommending the issue of bonus shares.

   Members' resolution must state—

(a) an intention to capitalize the profits *or* reserves, and

(b) the amount of profits *or* reserves to be capitalized.

4. **No Default in Payment of Interest/Principle:** The company has not defaulted in payment of interest *or* principal in respect of fixed deposits *or* debt securities issued by it.
5. **No Default in Payment of Statutory dues:** The company has not defaulted in respect of payment of statutory dues of the employees such as contribution to provident fund, gratuity and bonus.
6. **No O/s Partly-Paid-up Shares:** The partly-paid shares, if any, outstanding on the date of allotment are made fully paid-up.
7. **Compliance with Prescribed Conditions:** A Company must comply with Prescribed Conditions.
8. **Not in lieu of Dividend:** The bonus shares shall not be issued in lieu of dividend.

6.0 SEBI GUIDELINES ON BONUS ISSUES

A listed company proposing to issue bonus shares shall comply with the following:

1.(a) The articles of association of the company must contain a provision for capitalisation of reserves, etc.

(b) If there is no such provision in the articles the company must pass a resolution at its general body meeting making provision in the articles of association for capitalisation.

2. The company has not defaulted in payment of interest *or* principal in respect of fixed deposits and interest on existing debentures *or* principal on redemption
3. The company has not defaulted in respect of payment of statutory dues of the employees such as contribution to provident fund, gratuity, bonus etc.
4. The partly-paid shares, if any, outstanding on the date of allotment are made fully paid-up.

5.(a) No company shall, pending conversion of FCDs/PCDs, issue any by way of bonus unless similar benefit is extended to the holders of such FCDs/though reservation of shares in proportion to such convertible part of FCDs *or* PCDs.

(b) The shares so reserved may be issued at the time of conversion(s) of such debentures on the same terms on which the bonus issues were made.

6. The bonus issue shall be made out of free reserves built out of the genuine profits *or* securities premium collected in cash only.
7. Reserves created by revaluation of fixed assets shall not be capitalised.
8. The declaration of bonus issue, in lieu of dividend, shall not be made.
9. A company which announces its bonus issue after the approval of the Board of directors must implement the proposal within a period of 15 days from the date of such approval (if Shareholders' approval is not required) *or* 2 months (if Shareholders' approval is required).
10. Once the decision to make a bonus issue is announced, the same can not be withdrawn.

7.0 ACCOUNTING TREATMENT OF BONUS ISSUE

The various accounting entries relating to bonus issue are given below:

(a). On giving Bonus by converting partly paid shares into fully paid shares

1. On declaration of such Bonus

Capital Reserve A/c (realised in cash only)	Dr.
General Reserve A/c	Dr.
Profit & Loss A/c	Dr.
To Bonus to Shareholders A/c	

2. On Making the final call due	
Share Final Call A/c	Dr.
To Share Capital A/c	
3. On Adjustment of final call	
Bonus to Shareholders A/c	Dr.
To Share Final Call A/c	
(b) On issue of fully paid Bonus shares	
1. On Declaration of such bonus	
Capital Redemption Reserve A/c	Dr.
Securities Premium A/c	Dr.
Capital Reserve (realised in cash only)	Dr.
General Reserve A/c	Dr.
Profit & Loss A/c	Dr.
To Bonus to Shareholders A/c	
2. On issue of fully paid Bonus shares	
Bonus to Shareholders A/c	Dr.
To Share Capital A/c	

ILLUSTRATION 1 [Bonus by converting partly paid shares into fully paid shares]

Following items appear in the Trial Balance of Tulsian Ltd. as at 31st March 2015:

1. 40,000 Equity Shares of ₹ 10 each, ₹ 7.50 paid up	₹ 3,00,000
2. Capital Redemption Reserve	₹ 30,000
3. Plant Revaluation Reserve	₹ 10,000
4. Securities Premium Account	₹ 35,000
5. General Reserve	₹ 1,00,000
6. Profit & Loss Account	₹ 50,000
7. Capital Reserve (including ₹ 25,000 being Profit on Sale of Machinery)	₹ 75,000

The company decided to convert the partly paid equity shares into fully paid shares by way of bonus.

Required: Pass the necessary journal entries. It is desired that there should be minimum reduction in free reserves.

SOLUTION

JOURNAL

Date	*Particulars*		*L.F.*	*Dr. (₹)*	*Cr. (₹)*
(i)	Equity Share Final Call A/c	Dr.		1,00,000	
	To Equity Share Capital A/c				1,00,000
	(Being the final call of ₹ 2.50 each on 40,000 equity shares to make them fully paid up)				
(ii)	Capital Reserve A/c	Dr.		25,000	
	General Reserve A/c	Dr.		75,000	

	To Bonus to Shareholders A/c			1,00,000
	(Being the t/f of ₹ 25,000 from Capital Reserve & ₹ 75,000 from General Reserve to make the partly paid up shares fully paid up)			
(iii)	Bonus to Shareholders A/c Dr.		1,00,000	
	To Equity Share Final Call A/c			1,00,000
	(Being the amount due on final call adjusted against transfer from General Reserves to Bonus to Shareholders A/c)			

Notes: (i) Capital Redemption Reserve, Plant Revaluation Reserve and Securities Premium can not be capitalized for converting partly paid shares into fully paid shares.

(ii) Capital Reserve realised in cash can be utilized for bonus issue.

ILLUSTRATION 2 [Bonus by Issue of Fully Paid Shares]

Following items appear in the Trial Balance of Tulsian Ltd. as at 31st March, 2015:

1.	40,000 Equity Shares of ₹ 10 each	₹ 4,00,000
2.	Capital Redemption Reserve	₹ 30,000
3.	Plant Revaluation Reserve	₹ 10,000
4.	Securities Premium Account	₹ 35,000
5.	General Reserve	₹ 1,00,000
6.	Profit & Loss Account	₹ 50,000
7.	Capital Reserve (including ₹ 25,000 being Profit on Sale of Machinery)	₹ 75,000

The company decided to issue bonus shares to its shareholders at the rate of one share for every four shares held.

Required: Pass the necessary journal entries. It is desired that there should be minimum reduction in free reserves.

SOLUTION

JOURNAL

Date	*Particulars*	*L.F.*	*Dr. (₹)*	*Cr. (₹)*
(i)	Capital Reserve A/c Dr.		25,000	
	Capital Redemption Reserve A/c Dr.		30,000	
	Securities Premium A/c Dr.		35,000	
	General Reserve A/c Dr.		10,000	
	To Bonus to Shareholders A/c			1,00,000
	(Being the bonus declared by issuing 1 bonus share for every 4 shares held as per general body's resolution dated...)			
(ii)	Bonus to Shareholders A/c Dr.		1,00,000	
	To Equity Share Capital A/c			1,00,000
	(Being the issue of 10,000 shares of ₹ 10 each by way of bonus)			

Notes: (i) Plant Revaluation Reserve can not be utilized to issue bonus shares.

(ii) Capital Reserve realised in cash can be utilized for bonus issue.

ILLUSTRATION 3

Following items appear in the Trial Balance of Tulsian Ltd. as at 31st March 2015:

1.	40,000 Equity Shares of ₹ 10 each, ₹ 7.50 paid up	₹ 3,00,000
2.	60,000 Equity Shares of ₹ 10 each	₹ 6,00,000
3.	Capital Redemption Reserve	₹ 1,30,000
4.	Plant Revaluation Reserve	₹ 10,000
5.	Securities Premium Account	₹ 60,000
6.	General Reserve	₹ 1,00,000
7.	Profit & Loss Account	₹ 50,000
8.	Capital Reserve (including ₹ 25,000 being Profit on Sale of Machinery)	₹ 75,000

The company decided to convert the partly paid equity shares into fully paid shares by way of bonus and to issue fully paid-up Bonus Shares to the holders of fully paid up shares in the same ratio.

Required: Pass the necessary journal entries. It is desired that there should be minimum reduction in free reserves.

SOLUTION

JOURNAL

Date	*Particulars*		*L.F.*	*Dr. (₹)*	*Cr. (₹)*
(i)	Equity Share Final Call A/c	Dr.		1,00,000	
	To Equity Share Capital A/c				1,00,000
	(Being the final call of ₹ 2.50 each on 40,000 equity shares to make them fully paid up)				
(ii)	Capital Reserve A/c	Dr.		25,000	
	General Reserve A/c	Dr.		75,000	
	To Bonus to Shareholders A/c				1,00,000
	(Being the transfer of ₹ 25,000 from Capital Reserve & ₹ 75,000 from General Reserve to make the partly paid up shares fully paid up)				
(iii)	Bonus to Shareholders A/c	Dr.		1,00,000	
	To Equity Share Final Call A/c				1,00,000
	(Being the amount due on final 1call adjusted against transfer from Capital Reserve & General Reseives to Bonus to Shareholders A/c)				
(iv)	Capital Redemption Reserve A/c	Dr.		1,30,000	
	Securities Premium A/c	Dr.		60,000	
	General Reserve A/c	Dr.		10,000	
	To Bonus to Shareholders A/c				2,00,000
	(Being the bonus declared by issuing 1 bonus share for every 3 shares held as per general body's resolution dated...)				

(v)	Bonus to Shareholders A/c Dr. To Equity Share Capital A/c (Being the issue of 20,000 shares of ₹ 10 each by way of bonus)		2,00,000	2,00,000

Notes:

(i) Capital Redemption Reserve and Securities Premium can be utilized to issue fully paid-up Bonus Shares and not for converting partly paid shares into fully paid shares.

(ii) Capital Reserve realised in cash can be utilized for bonus issue.

(iii) Plant Revaluation Reserve can not be utilized to issue bonus shares.

(iv) Ratio of Bonus declared is ₹ 2.50 for every ₹ 7.50 paid-up capital i.e. 1/3rd *or* 1 for every 3. Hence, the amount of Bonus = (60,000 × 1/3) × ₹ 10 = ₹ 2,00,000.

SOLVED PROBLEMS

PROBLEM 1

The paid up capital of COJHI Ltd. is ₹ 10,00,000 consisting of 60,000 Equity Shares of ₹ 10 each fully paid up and 50,000 Equity Shares of ₹ 10 each, ₹ 8 per share paid up. It has ₹ 40,000 in Securities Premium Account, ₹ 2,00,000 in Profit and Loss Account (Cr.), ₹ 3,00,000 in General Reserve and ₹ 60,000 in Capital Redemption Reserve Account. By way of Bonus Dividend the partly paid-up shares are converted into fully paid-up shares and the holders of fully paid up shares are also allotted fully paid-up Bonus shares in the same ratio.

Required: Pass Journal Entries showing separately the two types of Bonus issues stated above.

SOLUTION

JOURNAL

Date	*Particulars*	*L.F.*	*Dr. (₹)*	*Cr. (₹)*
	General Reserve A/c Dr. To Bonus to Shareholders A/c (Being the bonus to Shareholders declared for making partly paid shares fully paid as per Shareholders Resolution dated.....):		1,00,000	1,00,000
	Share Final Call A/c Dr. To Equity Share Capital A/c (Being the final call of ₹ 2 per share due on 50,000 shares as per Board's Resolution dated....)		1,00,000	1,00,000
	Bonus to Shareholders A/c Dr. To Share Final Call A/c (Being the utilisation of Bonus to Shareholders towards payment of the final call of ₹ 2 per share on 50,000 shares)		1,00,000	1,00,000
	Securities Premium A/c Dr Capital Redemption Reserve A/c Dr. General Reserve A/c Dr. To Bonus to Shareholders A/c		40,000 60,000 50,000	1,50,000

	(Being the bonus to Shareholders declared for issuing fully paid-up shares as per Share-holder's Resolution dated....)		
	Bonus to Shareholders A/c Dr.	1,50,000	
	To Equity Share Capital A/c		1,50,000
	(Being the utilisation of Bonus to Shareholders towards issue of 15,000 fully paid shares of ₹ 10 each to be distributed in the ratio of one share for every four held, as per Board's Resolution dated....)		

Notes:

(a) General Reserve has been utilised for making partly paid shares fully paid, because Securities Premium A/c *or* Capital Redemption Reserve A/c cannot be utilised for the purpose.

(b) Ratio of Bonus declared is ₹ 2 for every ₹ 8 paid-up capital i.e. 1/4th *or* 1 for every 4. Hence, the amount of Bonus = (60,000 × 1/4) × ₹ 10 = ₹ 1,50,000.

PROBLEM 2

Following is the extract of the Balance Sheet of CAS Ltd. as at 31st March, 2015:

Particulars	₹
Authorised Capital	
10,000 12% Preference shares of ₹ 10 each	1,00,000
1,00,000 Equity shares of ₹ 10 each	10,00,000
	11,00,000
Issued and Subscribed Capital:	
8,000 12% Preference shares of ₹ 10 each fully paid	80,000
90,000 Equity shares of ₹ 10 each, ₹ 8 paid up	7,20,000
Reserves and Surplus:	
Capital Redemption Reserve	20,000
General Reserve	1,20,000
Capital Reserve	75,000
Securities Premium	25,000
Profit and Loss Account	1,80,000
Secured Loans:	
12% Partly Convertible Debentures @ ₹ 100 each	5,00,000

On 1st April, 2015 the Company has made final call @ 2 each on 90,000 equity shares. The call money was received by 20th April, 2015. Thereafter the company decided to capitalise its reserves by way of bonus at the rate of one share for every four shares held. Securities premium of ₹ 25,000 includes a premium of ₹ 5,000 for shares issued to vendors pursuant to a scheme of amalgamation. Capital reserves include ₹ 40,0000, being profit on sales of plant and machinery. 20% of 12% Debentures are convertible into equity shares of ₹ 10 each fully paid on 1st June 2015.

Required: Show necessary entries in the books of the company and prepare the extract of the Balance Sheet immediately after bonus issue but before conversion of debentures. Are the convertible debenture holders entitled to bonus shares?

SOLUTION

JOURNAL OF CAS LTD.

Date	Particulars		L.F.	Dr. (₹)	Cr. (₹)
April 1	Equity Share Final Call A/c	Dr.		1,80,000	
	To Equity Share Capital A/c				1,80,000
	(Being the Final call of ₹ 2 per share on 90,000 equity shares due as per Board's Resolution dated...)				
April 20	Bank A/c	Dr.		1,80,000	
	To Equity Share Final Call A/c				1,80,000
	(Being the Final Call money on 90,000 equity shares received)				
	Capital Redemption Reserve A/c	Dr.		20,000	
	Capital Reserve A/c [Realized in cash]	Dr.		40,000	
	Securities Premium A/c [25,000 – 5,000]	Dr.		20,000	
	General Reserve A/c	Dr.		1,20,000	
	Profit and Loss A/c	Dr.		25,000	
	To Bonus to Shareholders A/c				2,25,000
	(Being the Bonus issue @ one share for every four shares held by utilising various reserves as per Board's Resolution dated...)				
April 20	Bonus to Shareholders A/c	Dr.		2,25,000	
	To Equity Share Capital A/c				2,25,000
	(Being the Capitalisation of profits)				

AN EXTRACT OF BALANCE SHEET AS AT 30TH APRIL, 2015 (AFTER BONUS ISSUE)

Particulars	Note No.	₹
I. EQUITY AND LIABILITIES		
(1) Shareholders' Funds		
(a) Share Capital	1	12,05,000
(b) Reserves and Surplus	2	1,95,000
(2) Non-Current Liabilities		
(a) Long-term borrowings	3	5,00,000
Total		19,00,000

Notes to Accounts:

Particulars	₹
1. Share Capital	
Authorised Share Capital	
1,25,000 Equity Shares of ₹ 10 each	12,50,000
10,000, 12% Preference Shares of ₹ 10 each	1,00,000
	13,50,000

	Issued, Subscribed and fully paid Share Capital	
	1,12,500 Equity Shares of ₹ 10 each, fully paid (Out of above, 22,500 equity shares @ ₹ 10 each were issued by way of bonus)	11,25,000
	8,000 12% Preference Shares of ₹ 10 each	80,000
	Total	12,05,000
2.	**Reserves and Surplus**	
	Capital Reserves [75,000 – 40,000]	35,000
	Securities Premium Reserves [25,000 – 20,000]	5,000
	Surplus (Profit & Loss Account) [1,80,000 – 25,000]	1,55,000
	Total	1,95,000
3.	**Long-term borrowings**	
	Secured	
	Secured 12% Convertible Debentures @ ₹ 100 each (out of above 1,00,000 Debentures @ ₹ 100 each to be converted into 10,000 Equity shares @ ₹ 10 each on 1st July, 2015)	5,00,000
	Total	5,00,000

Working Notes:

(i) Capital Reserve realised in cash can be utilised for issue of fully paid bonus shares.

(ii) As per SEBI guidelines, securities premium collected in cash can only be utilised for bonus issue.

(iii) As per pare (ii) of SEBI guidelines, no-company can issue bonus shares to its shareholders without extending similar benefit to convertible debentures holders. Pending such conversion, necessary number of shares should be earmarked for convertible debentures holders. Therefore, convertible debenture holders are also entitled to the bonus shares in the same ratio as the equity shareholders.

(iv) It is assumed that the company will pass necessary resolution at its general body meeting for increasing the authorised capital by ₹ 2,50,000.

Issue of Bonus Shares to equity shareholders [22,500 × ₹ 10]	2,25,000
Issue of Bonus Shares to be issued to Debenture holders after conversion	25,000
[(20% of 5,00,000)/₹ 10] × 1/4 × ₹ 10]	
	2,50,000

PROBLEM 3

Following is the Balance Sheet of Happy Limited as on March 31, 2015:

BALANCE SHEET AS ON 31-3-2015

Particulars	₹
Authorised Share Capital:	
2,00,000 Equity shares of ₹ 10 each	20,00,000
Issued and Subscribed Share Capital:	
2,00,000 Equity shares of ₹ 10 each, ₹ 7 paid up	14,00,000
Reserves and Surplus:	

Capital reserve (Profit on sale of Fixed Assets)	1,30,000
Securities Premium (Includes ₹ 20,000 received otherwise than in cash)	90,000
General reserve	2,40,000
Profit & Loss A/c	5,20,000
Secured loans:	
12% Fully convertible debentures @ ₹ 100 each	4,00,000
Current Liabilities	2,20,000
Fixed assets	20,00,000
Investments	4,40,000
Current Assets	5,60,000

On April 01, 2015, company has made final call @ ₹ 3 on 2,00,000 equity shares and received complete call money by April 30, 2015.

The company wants to issue bonus shares to its shareholders @ one share for every four shares held.

12% Debentures are convertible into equity shares of ₹ 10 each fully paid on June 01, 2015. Necessary resolutions were passed and requisite legal requirements were complied with. For issue of bonus shares it was decided that reserves and surplus, other than Profit and Loss Account, should be first capitalized.

Required: Prepare Balance Sheet as on May 15, 2015, date on which all the formalities related to the issue of bonus shares completed.For the purpose of preparation of Balance Sheet, assume that, Balance Sheet items as on March 31, 2015, which are not effected by issue of bonus shares as above, remains unchanged as on May 15, 2015. Also pass necessary Journal Entries in the books of the company related to issue of bonus shares, for the period from April 01, 2015 to May 15, 2015.

SOLUTION

BALANCE SHEET OF HAPPY LTD. AS AT 15.5.2015

	Particulars	*Note No*	*₹ (lacs)*
I.	**Equity and Liabilities**		
	(1) Shareholders' Funds		
	(a) Share Capital (10 each)	1	25,00,000
	(b) Reserves and Surplus	2	4,80,000
	(2) Non-Current Liabilities [12% Debentures]		4,00,000
	(3) Current Liabilities		2,20,000
	Total		36,00,000
II.	**Assets**		
	(1) Non-Current Assets		
	(a) Fixed Assets		
	Tangible Assets		20,00,000
	(b) Non-Current Investments		4,40,000
	(2) Current Assets [5,60,000 + 6,00,000]		11,60,000
	Total		36,00,000

Notes To Accounts:

	Particulars	₹ *(lacs)*
1.	**Share Capital**	
	2,50,000 Equity Shares of ₹ 10 each (Of the above 50,000 Shares were issued by way of bonus for consideration otherwise than cash)	25,00,000
2.	**Reserves and Surplus**	
	Debentures Redemption Reserve	
	Profit & Loss Account [5,20,000 – 60,000]	4,60,000
	Securities Premium	20,000
	Total	4,80,000

JOURNAL

Date	*Particulars*		*Dr. (₹)*	*Cr. (₹)*
01.04.2015	Equity Share Final Call A/c	Dr.	6,00,000	
	To Equity Share Capital A/c			6,00,000
	(Being final call of ₹ 3 per share on 2,00,000 equity shares made)			
30.04.2015	Bank A/c	Dr.	6,00,000	
	To Equity Share Final Call A/c			6,00,000
	(Being final call money on 2,00,000 equity shares received)			
15.05.2015	Capital Reserve A/c	Dr.	1,30,000	
	Securities Premium A/c (90,000 – 20, 000)	Dr.	70,000	
	General Reserve A/c	Dr.	2,40,000	
	Profit & Loss A/c	Dr.	60,000	
	To Bonus to Shareholders A/c			5,00,000
	(Being bonus issue @ one share for every four shares held, by utilizing various reserves)			
15.05.2015	Bonus to Shareholders A/c	Dr.	5,00,000	
	To Equity Share Capital A/c			5,00,000
	(Being capitalization of reserves and profits)			

Working Notes:

(I) AUTHORISED SHARE CAPITAL

Particulars	*Number of shares*
Existing number of authorised share capital	2,00,000
Add: Issue of bonus shares to existing equity shareholders	50,000
Add: Shares required for conversion of debentures	40,000
Add: Bonus shares to be issued to debentureholders after conversion	10,000
Total authorised share capital as on May 15, 2015 should be	3,00,000

(ii) As per SEBI guidelines, no company can issue bonus shares to its shareholders without extending similar benefit to convertible debentureholders. Pending such conversion, necessary number of shares should be earmarked for convertible debenture holders. Therefore, convertible debentureholders are also entitled to the bonus shares in the same ratio as the equity shareholders on conversion.

(iii) As per SEBI guidelines, securities premium collected in cash can only be utilised for bonus issue.

6 AMALGAMATION OF COMPANIES

LEARNING OBJECTIVES

After studying this chapter, you should be able to understand:

- ◇ General Meaning
- ◇ Legal Meaning of Amalgamation
- ◇ Provisions of Accounting Standard (AS) 14 Issued By ICAI
- ◇ Amalgamation in the Nature of Merger
- ◇ Amalgamation in the Nature of Purchase
- ◇ Distinction between Amalgamation in the Nature of Purchase and Amalgamation in the Nature of Merger
- ◇ Purchase Consideration
- ◇ Accounting Treatment in the Books of Transferor Company or VSendor Company
- ◇ Treatment of Difference between the Purchase Consideration and the Net Assets of the Transferor Company arising on Amalgamation in the Nature of Purchase
- ◇ Accounting Treatment in the Books of Transferee Company or Purchasing Company in case of Purchase
- ◇ Treatment of Reserves arising on Amalgamation in the Nature of Merger
- ◇ Accounting Treatment in the Books of Transferee Company or Purchasing Company In case of Merger

1.0 GENERAL MEANING

Amalgamation	Usually, the term 'Amalgamation' is used when two *or* more existing companies go into liquidation and a new company is formed to take over their business. ***For Example**, if a new company XY Ltd. is formed to take over the businesses of two existing companies, X Ltd. and Y Ltd., it is a case of Amalgamation.*
Absorption	The term 'Absorption' is used when one *or* more existing company(s) goes into liquidation and some existing company takes over its business. ***For Example**, if the business of an existing company X Ltd. is taken over by another existing company Y Ltd., it is a case of absorption.*
External Reconstruction	The term 'External Reconstruction' is used when one existing company goes into liquidation and a new company is formed to take-over its business. ***For Example**, if a new company X (New) Ltd. is formed to take over the business of an existing company X Ltd., it is a case of 'External Reconstruction'.*

2.0 PROVISIONS OF ACCOUNTING STANDARD (AS) 14 ISSUED BY ICAI

Effective date	Accounting Standard (AS) 14 on 'Accounting for Amalgamations' came into effect in respect of accounting periods commencing on *or* after 1.4.1995.
Mandatory	AS 14 is mandatory in nature.
Meaning of Amalgamation	Amalgamation means an amalgamation pursuant to the provisions of the Companies Act, 1956 *or* any other statute which may be applicable to companies.
Types of Amalgamations	An amalgamation may be either (a) an amalgamation in the nature of merger *or* (b) and amalgamation in the nature of purchase.

3.0 AMALGAMATION IN THE NATURE OF MERGER

MEANING OF AMALGAMATION IN THE NATURE OF MERGER

Amalgamation in the nature of merger is an amalgamation which satisfies all the following **five** conditions:

1. Transfer of All Assets & Liabilities	All the assets and liabilities of the transferor company (i.e., the company which is amalgamated into another company) become, after amalgamation, the assets and liabilities of the transferee company (i.e., the company into which a transferor company is amalgamated).
2. Same Equity Shareholders Holding 90%	Shareholders holding at least 90% of the face value of the equity shares of the transferor company (other than the equity shares already held therein, immediately before the amalgamation, by the transferee company *or* its subsidiaries *or* their nominees) become equity shareholders of the transferee company by virtue of the amalgamation.
3. Purchase Consideration in Equity Shares	The consideration for the amalgamation receivable by those equity shareholders of the transferor company who agree to become equity shareholders of the transferee company is discharged by the transferee company wholly by the issue of equity shares in the transferee company, except that cash may be paid in respect of any fractional shares.
4. Same Business	The business of the transferor company is intended to be carried on, after the amalgamation, by the transferee company.
5. Recording of Assets & Liabilities at Book Values	No adjustment is intended to be made to the book values of the assets and liabilities of the transferor company when they are incorporated in the financial statements of the transferee company expect to ensure uniformity of accounting policies.

METHOD OF ACCOUNTING FOR AMALGAMATION IN THE NATURE OF MERGER

The **'Pooling of Interests Method'** should be used in accounting for amalgamation in the nature of merger. The salient features of this method are as follows:

Recording of Assets and Liabilities	In preparing the transferee company's financial statements, the assets and liabilities of the transferor company should be recorded at their existing carrying amounts and in the same form as at the date of amalgamation.

Recording of Reserves (whether capital or revenue or arising on revaluation)	The reserves should be recorded at their existing carrying amounts and in the same form as at the date of the amalgamation.
Recording of Balance of Profit and Loss A/c	The balance of the Profit and Loss Account of the transferor company should be aggregated with the corresponding balance of the transferee company *or* transferred to the General Reserve, if any.
Difference between the purchase consideration and the amount of share capital of the transferor company	The difference between the amount recorded as share capital issued *plus* any additional consideration in the form of cash *or* other assets and the amount of share capital of the transferor company should be adjusted in reserves.
Uniform Set of Accounting Policies	If, at the time of the amalgamation, the transferor and the transferee companies have conflicting accountant policies, a uniform set of accounting policies should be adopted following the amalgamation. The effects on the financial statements of any changes in a accounting policies should be reported in accordance with Accounting Standard (AS) 5, 'Prior Period and Extraordinary items and changes in Accounting Policies'.

4.0 AMALGAMATION IN THE NATURE OF PURCHASE

MEANING OF AMALGAMATION IN THE NATURE OF PURCHASE

Amalgamation in the nature of purchase is an amalgamation which does not satisfy anyone *or* more of the conditions specified for Amalgamation in the nature of merger.

METHOD OF ACCOUNTING FOR AMALGAMATION IN THE NATURE OF PURCHASE

The **'Purchase Method'** should be used in accounting for amalgamation in the nature of purchase. The salient features of this method are as follows:

Recording of Assets and Liabilities	In preparing the transferee company's financial statements, the assets and liabilities of the transferor company should be incorporated **at their existing carrying amounts or, alternatively,** the consideration should be allocated to individual identifiable assets and liabilities on the basis of their **fair values** at the date of amalgamation.
Recording of Statutory Reserves	Where the requirements of the relevant statute for recording the statutory reserves in the books of the transferee company are complied with, statutory reserves of the transferor company should be recorded in the financial statements of the transferee company. The corresponding debit should be given to a suitable account head (e.g., 'Amalgamation Adjustment Account') which should be disclosed as a part of "Miscellaneous Expenditure" *or* other similar category in the Balance Sheet. When the identity of the statutory reserves is no longer required to be maintained, both the reserves and the aforesaid account should be reversed.
Recording of Reserves other than Statutory Reserves	The reserves (whether capital *or* revenue *or* arising on revaluation) of the transferor company, other than the statutory reserves, should *not be included* in the financial statements of the transferee company.

Balance of Profit and Loss A/c	The balance of the Profit and Loss Account of the transferor company whether debit *or* credit *loses its identity.*
Difference between the Purchase Consideration and the Net Assets of the transferor company	Any **excess of** the amount of the **consideration over the value of the net assets** of the transferor company acquired by the transferee company should be recognised in the transferee company's financial statements **as goodwill** arising on amalgamation. If the amount of the consideration is lower than the value of the net assets acquired, the difference should be treated as **Capital Reserve**. The goodwill arising on amalgamation should be amortised to income on a systematic basis over its useful life. The amortisation period should not exceed 5 years unless a somewhat longer period can be justified.

5.0 DISTINCTION BETWEEN AMALGAMATION IN THE NATURE OF PURCHASE AND AMALGAMATION IN THE NATURE OF MERGER

Basis of Distinction	*Amalgamation in nature of Merger*	*Amalgamation in nature of Purchase*
1. **Method of Accounting**	Pooling of Interest Method	Purchase Method
2. **T/f of Assets & Liabilities**	There is transfer of all assets & liabilities.	There need not be transfer of all assets & liabilities.
3. **Equity Shareholders holding 90%**	Equity shareholders holding 90% equity shares in transferer company **become shareholders of transferee company.**	Equity shareholders, need **not become shareholders of transferee company.**
4. **Purchase Consideration**	Purchase consideration is discharged **wholly by issue of equity shares** (except cash for fractional shares)	Purchase consideration **need not** be discharged wholly by issue of equity shares.
5. **Same Business**	The **same business** of the transferor company is intended to be carried on by the transferee company.	The business of the transferor company **need not** be intended to be carried on by the transferee company.
6. **Recording of Assets & Liabilities**	The assets & liabilities taken over are recorded **at their existing carrying amounts** except where adjustment is required to ensure uniformity of accounting policies.	The assets & liabilities taken over are recorded at their existing carrying amounts *or* the basis of their **fair values.**
7. **Recording of Reserves of Transferor Co.**	**All reserves** are recorded at their **existing carrying amounts** and in the same form.	(a) **only statutory reserves** are recorded at their existing carrying amounts as follows: Amalagamation Adjustment A/c Dr. To Statutory Reserve A/c (b) Other reserves are not recorded at all.

8. Reording of Balance of Profit & Loss A/c of Transferor Co.	The balance of P&L A/c should be **aggregated** with the corresponding balance of the transferee co. *or* transferred to the General Reserve.	The balance of P&L A/c losses its identify and is **not recorded** at all.
9. Difference between the Purchase Consideration and Share Capital/Net Assets of transfer co.	The excess of the purchase consideration over the share capital of transferor company is **debited to Reserves** and the excess of share capital over purchase consideration is **creditted to reserves.**	The excess of purchase consideration over the net assets is treated as **Goodwill** and the excess of net assets over purchase consideration is treated as **Capital Reserve.**

6.0 PURCHASE CONSIDERATION

MEANING OF PURCHASE CONSIDERATION

Consideration for the amalgamation means the aggregate of the shares and other securities issued and the payment made in the form of cash *or* other assets by the transferee company to the shareholders of the transferor company.

The analysis of the aforesaid definition of 'Purchase Consideration' makes it clear that the payments made by the transferee company to discharge the debentureholders and other outside liabilities and the cost of winding up of transferor company shall not be considered as part of purchase consideration.

METHODS OF CALCULATING PURCHASE CONSIDERATION

(a) Depending upon the availability of information, the purchase consideration may be calculated on 'Net Assets taken over basis', *or* 'Net Payments to shareholders basis'.

(b) The following criteria may be adopted to select the basis of purchase consideration:

Case	*Basis of Purchase Consideration*
I. If all the modes of discharging the Purchase Consideration (e.g. Pref. Shares, Equity Shares or Cash payable to shareholders of transferor company) are given alongwith their individual amount	'Net Payment to Shareholders basis' should be used.
II. In other cases	'Net Assets taken over basis' should be used.

COMPUTATION OF PURCHASE CONSIDERATION (NET ASSETS BASIS)

Particulars	₹
A. Total Assets taken over at their agreed values	xxx
B. *Less:* Total Liabilities taken over at their agreed amounts	xxx
C. Net Assets taken over at their agreed values *or* Total Purchase Consideration [A – B]	xxx

$$\text{No. of Shares to be issued by Purchasing Co.} = \frac{\text{Amount to be discharged by issue of shares}}{\text{Issue Price of a share}}$$

COMPUTATION OF PURCHASE CONSIDERATION (ON NET PAYMENT BASIS)

Mode of Discharging Purchase Consideration	*No. of Shares*	*Issue Price*	₹
A. Preference Shares	xxx	xxx	xxx
B. Cash for Preference Shareholders	—	—	xxx
C. Equity Shares	xxx	xxx	xxx
D. Cash for Equity Shareholders	—	—	xxx
E. Total Purchase Consideration (A + B + C + D)			xxx

Notes

1. *The payment made by the transferee Company to discharge the debentureholders and other outside liabilities and the cost of winding up of transferor company* ***shall not be considered as part of purchase consideration.***
2. *The shares shall be issued in whole number and not in fraction.* ***For Example,*** *if no. of shares to be issued comes to 28454.55, only 28454 shares will be issued.*
3. *The fraction share shall be valued at market value and shall be paid in cash.* ***For Example****, if the market price of a share is ₹ 100 and the fractional share is 0.55, ₹ 55 (i.e., 0.55 × ₹ 100) will be paid in cash.*
4. *When it is decided to make entries relating to issue of shares at par value only, the number of shares to be issued by the purchasing company are calculated in the usual manner but thereafter are multiplied by par value only for the purposes of computing the purchase consideration.*

ILLUSTRATION 1

Given below are the extracts from the Balance Sheet of V Ltd. as at 31st March, 2016:

Particulars	₹
Equity Share Capital of ₹ 10 each	2,00,000
8% Pref. Share Capital of ₹ 100 each	50,000
Reserves & Surplus	41,100
10% Debentures	50,000
Current Liabilities	1,40,000
Tangible Fixed Assets	1,50,000
Current Assets	3,31,100

The business of V Ltd. is taken over by P Ltd. as on that date on the following terms:

(a) The issue of such an amount of fully paid 14% Debentures in P Ltd at 96 per cent as is sufficient to discharge 10% Debentures in V Ltd. at a premium of 20 per cent.

(b) The issue of such an amount of fully paid 10% Pref. Shares in P Ltd. at 125% as is sufficient to discharge 9% Pref. Shares in V Ltd. at a premium of 20%.

(c) One Equity Share of ₹ 10 each, ₹ 8 paid up valued at ₹ 15 per share and Cash ₹ 1.86 for every two Equity Shares held in V Ltd. The market value of an equity share of P Ltd. at present is ₹ 100.

(d) Expenses of liquidation of V Ltd. are to be reimbursed by P Ltd. to the extent of ₹ 10,000. Actual Expenses amounted to ₹ 12,000.

Show the calculation and discharge of Purchase Consideration.

SOLUTION

CALCULATION AND DISCHARGE OF PURCHASE CONSIDERATION

A. 10,000, Equity Shares to be issued [(20,000 × 1/2) × ₹ 15]	1,50,000
B. 480, 9% Pref. Shares to be issued [(50,000 × 120%)/125] × 125	60,000
C. Cash to Equity Shareholders [(20,000 × 1/2) × ₹ 1.86]	18,600
D. Total Purchase Consideration (A + B + C)	2,28,600

Note: *According to AS-14, the amount paid by purchasing Company to discharge the debentures holders and the liquidation expenses of Vendor Company are not considered as part of purchase consideration.*

ILLUSTRATION 2

Given below are the extracts from the Balance Sheets of B Ltd. as at 31.03.2016:

Particulars	*(₹ in lacs)*
Equity Share Capital of ₹ 100 each	75
12% Pref. Share Capital of ₹ 100 each	20
Reserves & Surplus	33
10% Debentures of ₹ 100 each	3
Current Liabilities	19
Tangible Fixed Assets	70
Current Assets	80

A Ltd. absorbs B Ltd.as on that date on the following terms:

(a) 10% Debentures of the transferor company are to be discharged by transferee company by issuing such number of its 15% Debentures of ₹ 100 each so as to maintain the same amount of interest.

(b) 12% Preference Shares of the transferor company are to be discharged by transferee company by issuing equivalent numbers of 15% preference Shares of ₹ 100 each at ₹ 150 each.

(c) The transferee company shall issue 4 equity shares of ₹ 10 each at ₹ 30 each for each equity share in the transferor company.

(d) The transferee company shall pay the cost of absorption which amounts to ₹ 1,00,000

Show the calculation and discharge of Purchase Consideration.

SOLUTION

CALCULATION OF PURCHASE CONSIDERATION

20,000,12% Preference Shares [(20,00,000/100) × ₹ 150]	30,00,000
3,00,000 Equity Shares [{(75,00,000/100) × 4} × ₹ 30]	90,00,000
	120,00,000

Note: *According to AS-14, the amount paid by purchasing Company to discharge the debentures holders and the liquidation expenses of Vendor Company are not considered as part of purchase consideration.*

ILLUSTRATION 3

Given below are the extracts from the Balance Sheets of Y Ltd. as at 31st March 2016:

Particulars	*(₹ in lacs)*
Equity Share Capital of ₹ 10 each	10.00
8% Pref. Share Capital of ₹ 100 each	2.00
Reserves & Surplus	3.00
12% Debentures of ₹ 100 each	1.00
Current Liabilities	2.20
Non-Current Assets	12.80
Current Assets	5.40

X Ltd. absorbs Y Ltd.as on that date on the following terms:

(a) 12% Debentures of Y Ltd. are to be discharged by X Ltd. by issuing such number of its 15% Debentures of ₹ 100 each so as to maintain the same amount of interest.

(b) The issue of such an amount of fully paid 9% Pref. Shares in X Ltd. at 125% as is sufficient to discharge 8% Pref. Shares in Y Ltd. at a premium of 20%.

(c) The Equity Shareholders of Y Ltd. will receive the requisite number of Equity Shares of X Ltd. The Equity Shares of X Ltd are to be of a nominal value of ₹ 10 each credited as ₹ 8 paid up and valued at ₹ 15 per share.

(d) The transferee company shall pay the cost of absorption which amounts to ₹ 1,00,000

Show the calculation and discharge of Purchase Consideration.

SOLUTION

CALCULATION OF PURCHASE CONSIDERATION

1920,9% Pref. Shares [(2,00,000 + 20%)/125) × ₹ 125]	2,40,000
1,00,000 Equity Shares [1,00,000 × 15]	15,00,000
	17,40,000

Note: *According to AS-14, the amount paid by purchasing Company to discharge the debentures holders and the liquidation expenses of Vendor Company are not considered as part of purchase consideration.*

ILLUSTRATION 4

Given below are the extracts from the Balance Sheet of V Ltd. as at 31st March, 2016:

Particulars	₹
Equity Share Capital of ₹ 10 each	2,00,000
8% Pref. Share Capital of ₹ 100 each	50,000
General Reserve	20,000
Profit & Loss A/c	16,100
Statutory Reserves	5,000
10% Debentures	50,000
Trade Payables	1,40,000
Tangible Assets	1,50,000

Goodwill	1,19,500
Inventories	55,000
Trade Receivables	65,000
Cash at Bank	91,600

The business of V Ltd. is taken over by P Ltd. as on that date on the following terms:

(a) 50% of Tangible Fixed Assets are taken over at 100% more than the book value and the remaining Tangible Fixed Assets are taken over at $16\frac{2}{3}\%$ less than the book value.

(c) Goodwill of V Ltd. is to be valued at ₹ 50,000.

(d) Inventories are taken over at book value less 10% and Trade Receivables are taken over at book value subject to an allowance of 10% to cover doubtful debts.

(e) Trade Payables are to be taken over subject to a discount of 5% and Unrecorded Loan Liability of ₹ 38,500 to be discharged by P Ltd. at book value.

(f) The purchase consideration payable by P Ltd. was agreed as follows:

(i) The issue of such an amount of fully paid 14% Debentures in P Ltd at 96 per cent as is sufficient to discharge 10% Debentures in V Ltd. at a premium of 20 per cent.

(ii) The issue of such an amount of fully paid 10% Pref. Shares in P Ltd. at 125% as is sufficient to discharge 9% Pref. Shares in V Ltd. at a premium of 20%.

(iii) One Equity Share of ₹ 10 each, ₹ 8 paid up valued at ₹ 15 per share for every two Equity Shares held in V Ltd. and the balance in cash. The market value of an equity share of P Ltd. at present is ₹ 100.

(iv) Expenses of liquidation of V Ltd. are to be reimbursed by P Ltd. to the extent of ₹ 10,000. Actual Expenses amounted to ₹ 12,000.

Show the calculation and discharge of Purchase Consideration.

SOLUTION

1. CALCULATION OF PURCHASE CONSIDERATION

	Particulars	₹
A	Assets taken over at agreed values	
	Tangible Fixed Assets [(₹ 1,50,000 × 50%) + 100%]	1,50,000
	Tangible Fixed Assets [(₹ 1,50,000 × 50%) – $16\frac{2}{3}\%$]	62,500
	Inventories [₹ 55,000 – ₹ 5,500]	49,500
	Trade Receivables [₹ 65,000 – ₹ 6,500]	58,500
	Cash at Bank [91,600 – 2,000 (Expenses)]	89,600
	Goodwill	50,000
		4,60,100
B	*Less:* Liabilities taken over:	
	Trade Payables [₹ 1,40,000 – 5%]	1,33,000
	10% Debentures [₹ 50,000 + 20%]	60,000
	Unrecorded Loan	38,500
		2,31,500
C	Net Assets taken over (A – B)	2,28,600

2. DISCHARGE OF PURCHASE CONSIDERATION

A. 10,000, Equity Shares to be issued [(20,000 × 1/2) × ₹ 15]	1,50,000
B. 480, 9% Pref. Shares to be issued [(500 × 120%)]	60,000
C. Cash to Equity Shareholders [Balancing figure]	**18,600**
D. Total Purchase Consideration (A + B + C)	2,28,600

Note: *According to AS-14, the amount paid by purchasing Company to discharge the debentures holders and the liquidation expenses of Vendor Company are not considered as part of purchase consideration.*

ILLUSTRATION 5

Given below are the extracts from the Balance Sheet of V Ltd. as at 31st March, 2016:

Particulars	₹
Equity Share Capital of ₹ 10 each	2,00,000
8% Pref. Share Capital of ₹ 100 each	50,000
General Reserve	20,000
Profit & Loss A/c	16,100
Statutory Reserves	5,000
10% Debentures	50,000
Trade Payables	1,40,000
Tangible Assets	1,50,000
Goodwill	1,19,500
Inventories	55,000
Trade Receivables	65,000
Cash at Bank	91,600

The business of V Ltd. is taken over by P Ltd. as on that date on the following terms:

(a) 50% of Tangible Fixed Assets are taken over at 100% more than the book value and the remaining Tangible Fixed Assets are taken over at $16\frac{2}{3}\%$ less than the book value.

(c) Goodwill of V Ltd. is to be valued at ₹ 50,000.

(d) Inventories are taken over at book value less 10% and Trade Receivables are taken over at book value subject to an allowance of 10% to cover doubtful debts.

(e) Trade Payables are to be taken over subject to a discount of 5% and Unrecorded Loan Liability of ₹ 38,500 to be discharged by P Ltd. at book value.

(f) The purchase consideration payable by P Ltd. was agreed as follows:

(i) The purchase consideration is to be discharged to the extent of 20% in cash.

(ii) The issue of such an amount of fully paid 14% Debentures in P Ltd at 96 per cent as is sufficient to discharge 10% Debentures in V Ltd. at a premium of 20 per cent.

(iii) The issue of such an amount of fully paid 10% Pref. Shares in P Ltd. at 125% as is sufficient to discharge 9% Pref. Shares in V Ltd. at a premium of 20%.

(iv) The balance in the form of equity shares of ₹ 10 each, ₹ 8 paid up at a premium of ₹ 7 per share. The market value of an equity share of P Ltd. at present is ₹ 100.

(v) Expenses of liquidation of V Ltd. are to be reimbursed by P Ltd. to the extent of ₹ 10,000. Actual Expenses amounted to ₹ 12,000.

Show the calculation and discharge of Purchase Consideration.

SOLUTION

1. CALCULATION OF PURCHASE CONSIDERATION

	Particulars	₹
A	Assets taken over at agreed values	
	Tangible Fixed Assets [(₹ 1,50,000 × 50%) + 100%]	1,50,000
	Tangible Fixed Assets [(₹ 1,50,000 × 50%) − $16\frac{2}{3}$%]	62,500
	Inventories [₹ 55,000 – ₹ 5,500]	49,500
	Trade Receivables [₹ 65,000 – ₹ 6,500]	58,500
	Cash at Bank [91,600 – 2,000(Expenses)]	89,600
	Goodwill	50,000
		4,60,100
B	*Less:* Liabilities taken over:	
	Trade Payables [₹ 1,40,000 – 5%]	1,33,000
	10% Debentures [₹ 50,000 + 20%]	60,000
	Unrecorded Loan	38,500
		2,31,500
C	Net Assets taken over (A – B)	2,28,600

2. DISCHARGE OF PURCHASE CONSIDERATION

A. Cash to Equity Shareholders [2,28,600 × 20%]	45,720
B. 480, 9% Pref. Shares to be issued [(500 × 120%)]	60,000
C. 8,192, Equity Shares to be issued [(2,28,600 – 45,720 – 60,000)/ ₹ 15] × ₹ 15	**1,22,880**
D. Total Purchase Consideration (A + B + C)	2,28,600

Note: *According to AS-14, the amount paid by purchasing Company to discharge the debentures holders and the liquidation expenses of Vendor Company are not considered as part of purchase consideration.*

ILLUSTRATION 6

Given below are the extracts from the Balance Sheet of V Ltd. as at 31st March, 2016:

Particulars	₹
Equity Share Capital of ₹ 10 each	2,00,000
8% Pref. Share Capital of ₹ 100 each	50,000
General Reserve	20,000
Profit & Loss A/c	16,100
Statutory Reserves	5,000
10% Debentures	50,000
Trade Payables	1,40,000
Tangible Assets	1,50,000
Goodwill	1,19,500

Inventories	55,000
Trade Receivables	65,000
Cash at Bank	91,600

Prior to absorption, V Ltd. decides to declare and pay equity dividend @ 5%.(Ignore Dividenc Distribution Tax). The business of V Ltd. is taken over by P Ltd. as on that date on the following terms

(a) 50% of Tangible Fixed Assets are taken over at 100% more than the book value and the remaining Tangible Fixed Assets are taken over at $16\frac{2}{3}\%$ less than the book value.

(c) Goodwill of V Ltd. is to be valued at ₹ 50,000.

(d) Inventories are taken over at book value less 10% and Trade Receivables are taken over a book value subject to an allowance of 10% to cover doubtful debts.

(e) Trade Payables are to be taken over subject to a discount of 5% and Unrecorded Loan Liabilit of ₹ 38,500 to be discharged by P Ltd. at book value.

(f) The purchase consideration payable by P Ltd. was agreed as follows:

(i) The issue of such an amount of fully paid 14% Debentures in P Ltd at 96 per cent as i sufficient to discharge 10% Debentures in V Ltd. at a premium of 20 per cent.

(ii) The issue of such an amount of fully paid 10% Pref. Shares in P Ltd. at 125% as i sufficient to discharge 9% Pref. Shares in V Ltd. at a premium of 20%.

(iii) One Equity Share of ₹ 10 each, ₹ 8 paid up valued at ₹ 15 per share for every two Equit Shares held in V Ltd. and the balance in cash. The market value of an equity share of P Ltd. at present is ₹ 100.

(iv) Expenses of liquidation of V Ltd. are to be reimbursed by P Ltd. to the extent of ₹ 10,000 Actual Expenses amounted to ₹ 14,100.

Show the calculation and discharge of Purchase Consideration.

SOLUTION

1. CALCULATION OF PURCHASE CONSIDERATION

	Particulars	₹
A	Assets taken over at agreed values	
	Tangible Fixed Assets [(₹ 1,50,000 × 50%) + 100%]	1,50,000
	Tangible Fixed Assets [(₹ 1,50,000 × 50%) – $16\frac{2}{3}\%$]	62,500
	Inventories [₹ 55,000 – ₹ 5,500]	49,500
	Trade Receivables [₹ 65,000 – ₹ 6,500]	58,500
	Cash at Bank [91,600 – 10,000(ED) – 4,000(PD) – 4,100(Exp.)]	73,500
	Goodwill	50,000
		4,44,000
B	*Less:* Liabilities taken over:	
	Trade Payables [₹ 1,40,000 – 5%]	1,33,000
	10% Debentures [₹ 50,000 + 20%]	60,000
	Unrecorded Loan	38,500
		2,31,500
C	Net Assets taken over (A – B)	2,12,500

2. DISCHARGE OF PURCHASE CONSIDERATION

A. 10,000, Equity Shares to be issued [(20,000 × 1/2) × ₹ 15]	1,50,000
B. 480, 9% Pref. Shares to be issued [(500 × 120%)]	60,000
C. Cash to Equity Shareholders [Balancing figure]	**2,500**
D. Total Purchase Consideration (A + B + C)	2,12,500

Note: *According to AS-14, the amount paid by purchasing Company to discharge the debentures holders and the liquidation expenses of Vendor Company are not considered as part of purchase consideration.*

ILLUSTRATION 7

X Ltd. takes over Y Ltd. Given below are the extracts from the Balance Sheets of these companies at 31.03.2016:

Particulars	*X Ltd. (₹)*	*Y Ltd. (₹)*
Equity Share Capital of ₹ 10 each	30,00,000	12,00,000
Reserves & Surplus		10,00,000
15% Debentures	—	8,00,000
Current Liabilities	3,00,000	1,00,000
Tangible Block	24,00,000	18,00,000
Goodwill	—	1,50,000
Non-Current Investments (₹ 1,00,000, 6% tax free G.P. Notes)	1,00,000	—
Inventories	1,90,000	2,20,000
Other Current Assets	6,10,000	9,30,000

Additional Information:

	X Ltd.	*Y Ltd.*
Tangible Block	Valued at 25% more than the book value	Valued at $16\frac{2}{3}\%$ less than the book value
Goodwill	₹ 17,90,000	₹ 70,000
Inventories	Undervalued by ₹10,000	Overvalued by ₹ 20,000

X Ltd. to issue shares to share-holders of Y Ltd., on the basis of the intrinsic value of shares on the date of take-over. Calculate Purchase Consideration and show the discharge thereof.

SOLUTION

CALCULATION OF PURCHASE CONSIDERATION

Particulars	*X Ltd.* ₹	*Y Ltd.* ₹
Tangible Block	24,00,000	18,00,000
Add: Undervaluation (24,00,000 × 25%)	6,00,000	
Less: Overvaluation (18,00,000 × $16\frac{2}{3}\%$]		(3,00,000)
Net Tangible Block at Revalued figure	30,00,000	15,00,000

Goodwill	17,90,000	70,000
Non-Current Investments (₹ 1,00,000, 6% tax free G.P. Notes)	1,00,000	—
Inventories	1,90,000	2,20,000
Add: Undervaluation of Cl. Inventory	10,000	
Less: Overvaluation of Cl. Inventory		(20,000)
Other Current Assets	6,10,000	9,30,000
	57,00,000	27,00,000
Less: 15% Debentures	—	(8,00,000)
Less: Current Liabilities	(3,00,000)	(1,00,000)
Net Assets	54,00,000	18,00,000
No. of Shares	3,00,000	1,20,000
Intrinsic Value	18	15
No. of Equity Shares to be issued (1,20,000 × 15/18)		1,00,000
Share Capital [1,00,000 × ₹ 10]		10,00,000
Securities Premium [1,00,000 × ₹ 8]		8,00,000
Purchase Consideration		18,00,000

ILLUSTRATION 8

X Ltd. takes over Y Ltd. Given below are the extracts from the Balance Sheets of these companies at 31.03.2016:

Particulars	*X Ltd. (₹)*	*Y Ltd. (₹)*
Equity Share Capital of ₹ 10 each	30,00,000	12,00,000
Reserves & Surplus		10,00,000
15% Debentures	—	8,00,000
Current Liabilities	3,00,000	1,00,000
Tangible Block	24,00,000	18,00,000
Goodwill	—	1,50,000
Non-Current Investments (₹ 1,00,000, 6% tax free G.P. Notes)	1,00,000	—
Inventories	1,90,000	2,20,000
Other Current Assets	6,10,000	9,30,000

Additional Information:

	X Ltd.	*Y Ltd.*
Tangible Block	Understated by 20%	Overstated by 20%
Goodwill	17,90,000	70,000
Inventories	Understated by 5%	Overstated by 10%

X Ltd. to issue shares to share-holders of Y Ltd.at a price of ₹1 above the intrinsic value of its shares on the date of take-over.The market value of an equity share of X Ltd. at present is ₹ 100. The scheme of amalgamation was not supported by 100 shareholders of Y Ltd., and had to be paid ₹ 10 per share above their intrinsic value as consideration. The amount of the dissenting shareholders was borne by X Ltd.,Calculate Purchase Consideration and show the discharge thereof.

SOLUTION

CALCULATION OF PURCHASE CONSIDERATION

Particulars	*X Ltd.* ₹	*Y Ltd.* ₹
Tangible Block	24,00,000	18,00,000
Add: Undervaluation (24,00,000 × 20/80)	6,00,000	
Less: Overvaluation (18,00,000 × 20/120)		(3,00,000)
Net Tangible Block at Revalued figure	30,00,000	15,00,000
Goodwill	17,90,000	70,000
Non-Current Investments (₹ 1,00,000, 6% tax free G.P. Notes)	1,00,000	—
Inventories	1,90,000	2,20,000
Add: Undervaluation of Cl. Inventory (1,90,000 × 5/95)	10,000	
Less: Overvaluation of Cl. Inventory (2,20,000 × 10/110)		(20,000)
Other Current Assets	6,10,000	9,30,000
	57,00,000	27,00,000
Less: 15% Debentures	—	(8,00,000)
Less: Current Liabilities	(3,00,000)	(1,00,000)
Net Assets	54,00,000	18,00,000
No. of Shares	3,00,000	1,20,000
Intrinsic Value	18	15
Issue Price [₹18 + ₹1]	19	
No. of Equity Shares to be issued [(1,20,000 – 100) × 15/19]		94,657.89
Share Capital [94,657 × ₹ 10]		9,46,570
Securities Premium [94,657 × ₹ 9]		8,51,913
Cash for fraction [0.89 × ₹ 100]		89
Payment to dissenting shareholders[100 × (₹15 + ₹ 10)]		2,500
Purchase Consideration		18,01,072

ILLUSTRATION 8A

IN THE PREVIOUS ILLUSTRATION Calculate Purchase Consideration and show the discharge thereof if it is also decided to make the entries relating to the issue of shares at par value only.

SOLUTION

No. of Equity Shares to be issued [(1,20,000 – 100) × 15/19]	94,657.89
Share Capital [94,657 × ₹ 10]	9,46,570
Cash for fraction [0.89 × ₹ 100]	89
Payment to dissenting shareholders [100 × (₹15 + ₹ 10)]	2,500
Purchase Consideration	9,49,159

ILLUSTRATION 9

Given below are the extracts from the Balance Sheets of A Ltd. and B Ltd. on at 31st March 2016:

Particulars	₹
80,000 Equity shares of ₹ 10 each fully paid up	8,00,000
Reserves & Surplus	1,00,000
Current Liabilities	1,00,000
Non-Current Assets	7,00,000
Current Assets	3,00,000

The consideration was agreed to be paid as follows:

(a) A payment in cash of ₹ 5 per share in B Ltd., and

(b) The issue of shares of ₹ 10 each in A Ltd. on the basis of 2 equity shares (valued at ₹ 15) and one 10% Cumulative Preference shares (valued at ₹ 10) for every five shares held in B Ltd.

The whole of the share capital consists of shareholdings in exact multiple of five except the followings holdings:

A	116
B	76
C	72
D	28
Other individual	8 (each member holding one share each)
	300

It was agreed that A Ltd. will pay in cash for fractional shares equivalent at agreed value of shares in B Ltd.

Required: Prepare a Statement showing the purchase consideration receivable in shares and cash.

SOLUTION

STATEMENT SHOWING THE COMPUTATION OF PURCHASE CONSIDERATION

Particulars	₹
31,994 Equity Shares @ ₹ 15 each	4,79,910
15,997 Preference Shares @ ₹ 10 each	1,59,970
Cash [(80,000 – 15) × ₹ 5]	3,99,925
	10,39,805
Add: Cash for fractional shares [15 × ₹ 13]	195
	10,40,000

Working Notes:

(I) SCHEDULE SHOWING FRACTIONAL SHARES

Share holder	*Holding of Shares*	*Exchangeable in multiple of five*	*Non Exchangeable Shares*
A	116	115	1
B	76	75	1

C	72	70	2
D	28	25	3
Others	8	–	8
	300	285	15

(ii) Equity Shares to be issued by A Ltd. = [(80,000 – 15) × 2/5] = 31,994

(iii) Preference Shares to be issued by A Ltd. = [(80,000 – 15) × 1/5] = 15,997

(IV) VALUATION OF FRACTIONAL SHARES

Cash for 5 equity shares [5 × ₹5]	₹ 25
2 equity shares for 5 equity shares [2 × ₹15]	₹ 30
1 Pref. share for 5 equity shares [1 × ₹ 10]	₹ 10
Total	₹ 65
Value for 1 equity share [₹65/5]	₹13
No. of fractional shares	15
Cash for fractional shares [15 × ₹ 13]	195

7.0 ACCOUNTING TREATMENT IN THE BOOKS OF TRANSFER OR COMPANY OR VENDOR COMPANY

Step 1: Open a Realisation Account and transfer all the recorded assets [including intangible assets like goodwill at their respective book values (i.e., the values at which they are appearing in the books of vendor company) irrespective of the fact whether the purchasing company has taken over *or* not. However, Cash and Bank Balances are transferred to Realisation Account only to the extent it is taken over by the purchasing company.

JOURNAL ENTRY

Realisation A/c	Dr.	*(with the total)*
To Sundry Assets (individually)		*(with their individual book values)*

Notes

(i) An asset against which a provision or reserve has been created should be transferred at its gross figure and not at its net figure e.g., debtors.

(ii) Provision/Reserve against a liability is a separate account and thus, it should be transferred to Realisation Account separately like other assets e.g., reserve for discount on creditors.

(iii) The cash and bank balances should not be transferred to Realisation account if these are not taken over by the purchasing company.

Step 2: Transfer all third parties liabilities which are taken over by the purchasing company, at their respective book figures.

JOURNAL ENTRY

Sundry Assets (individually)	Dr.	*(with their individual book values)*
To Realisation A/c		*(with the total)*

Notes

(i) A liability against which a provision or reserve has been created should be transferred at its gross figure and not at its net figure, e.g., creditors.

(ii) *Items in the nature of 'Provisions' (e.g., Provision for taxation, Employees Provident Fund, Pension Fund, Provision for Doubtful Debt, Provision for Depreciation) should be transferred to Realisation Account.*

(iii) *Items in the nature of "Reserve" (e.g., credit balance of Profit and Loss Account, General Reserve, Dividend Equalisation Fund, Workmen Compensation Fund) should not be transferred to Realisation Account but that portion of any reserve/fund which represents a liability expected to arise in future should be transferred to Realisation Account (e.g., Estimated Workmen Compensation Claim out of Workmen Compensation Reserve).*

Step 3: Make due the Purchase Consideration from the Purchasing Company.

JOURNAL ENTRY

Purchasing Company's A/c	Dr.	*(with the Purchase Consideration Due)*
To Realisation A/c		

Step 4: Receive the Purchase Consideration from the Purchasing Company.

Cash/Bank A/c	Dr.	*(with Cash Received)*
Preference Shares in Purchasing Company	Dr.	*(with Issue Price of Pref. Shares)*
Equity Shares in Purchasing Company	Dr.	*(with Issue Price of Equity Shares)*
To Purchasing Company		*(With the total)*

Step 5: Do the Treatment of Liquidation/Realisation expenses.

Case	**JOURNAL ENTRY**
(a) If these expenses are to be borne and paid by the Vendor Company	Realisation A/c To Bank A/c
(b) If these expenses are to be reimbursed by the purchasing company	
(i) *On Payment by Vendor Company*	Purchasing Company Dr. *(with agreed amount)* Realisation A/c Dr. *(with excess)* To Bank A/c (with the total)
(ii) *On reimbursement*	Bank A/c To Purchasing Company

Step 6: Realise those assets which have not been taken over by the purchasing company.

JOURNAL ENTRY

Bank A/c	Dr.	*(with the amount realised)*
To Realisation A/c		

Step 7: Discharge the Claims of Preference Shareholders and transfer the difference between the amount actually payable and the book figure to the Realisation Account.

(A) JOURNAL ENTRY ON MAKING DUE

Preference Share Capital A/c	Dr.	*(with book figure)*
Realisation A/c	Dr.	*(with the loss)*

To Preference Shareholders' A/c's	*(with the amount actually payable)*
To Realisation A/c	*(with the profit)*

(B) JOURNAL ENTRY ON MAKING PAYMENT

Preference Shareholders' A/cs	Dr.
To Bank A/c	
To Preference Shares in purchasing Co.	

Step 8: Ascertain the Profit *or* Loss on Realisation and transfer the same to the Equity Shareholders' A/c.

(a) In case of Profit on Realisation	Realisation A/c	Dr.
	To Equity Shareholders' A/c	
(b) In case of Loss on Realisation	Equity Shareholders' A/c	Dr.
	To Realisation A/c	

Step 9: Transfer the Equity Share Capital A/c, Accumulated Profits, Reserve and losses to the Equity Shareholders' A/cs.

(a) For Transfer of Equity Share Capital, Accumulated Profits and Reserves [after making adjustment for Dividend, Dividend Tax etc.]	Equity Share Capital A/c	Dr.
	Profit and Loss A/c	Dr.
	General Reserve A/c	Dr.
	Dividend Equalisation Reserve	Dr.
	Workmen Compensation reserve	Dr.
	Capital Reserve A/c	Dr.
	Securities Premium A/c	Dr.
	Debenture redemption Reserve	Dr.
	Capital Redemption Reserve	Dr.
	Statutory Reserves	Dr.
	To Equity Shareholders' A/c	
(b) For Transfer of Accumulated Losses	Equity Shareholders' A/c	Dr.
	To Profit and Loss A/c (Dr. Balance)	
	To Preliminary Expenses	
	To Underwriting Commission	
	To Discount on Issue of Shares/Debentures	
	To Deferred Advertisement Expenditure	

Step 10: Make Final Payment to Equity Shareholders:

Equity Shareholders' A/c	Dr. *(with the total)*
To Equity Shares in Purchasing Co.	
To Cash/Bank A/c	

Note: *The net amount payable to the equity shareholders must be equal to the amount of shares in Purchasing Co. and Cash and Bank Balance left after the discharge of all outsiders' liabilities and claims of Preference Shareholders.*

8.0 TREATMENT OF DIFFERENCE BETWEEN THE PURCHASE CONSIDERATION AND THE NET ASSETS OF THE TRANSFEROR COMPANY ARISING ON AMALGAMATION IN THE NATURE OF PURCHASE

Case	Accounting Treatment
If Purchase Consideration > Net Assets	The excess of Purchase Consideration over the value of Net Assets acquired should be Treated as **Goodwill arising on amalgamation.** Such goodwill should be amortised on a systematic basis over a period not exceeding 5 years unless longer period can be justified.
If Net Assets > Purchase Consideration	The excess of net assets acquired over the Purchase Consideration should be treated as **Capital Reserve arising on Amalgamation.**

ILLUSTRATION 10 [Treatment of Reserves arising on Amalgamation in the nature of Purchase]

(₹ in lacs)

Particulars	*Case I* ₹	*Case II* ₹	*Case III* ₹
Share Capital issued by Transferee Co.	9.50	9.50	9.50
Cash for fractional Share paid by Transferee Co.	.50	.50	.50
Assets acquired by Transferee Co.	11.20	11.00	10.80
Liabilities undertaken by Transferee Co.	1.00	1.00	1.00

SOLUTION

CALCUALTION OF CAPITAL RESERVE/GOODWILL

Particulars	*Case I* ₹	*Case II* ₹	*Case III* ₹
A. Purchase Consideration (9.50 + 0.50)	10.00	10.00	10.00
B. Net Assets acquired (Assets – Liabilities)	10.20	10.00	9.80
C. Goodwill	—	—	.20
or			
Capital Reserve	0.20	—	—

9.0 ACCOUNTING TREATMENT IN THE BOOKS OF TRANSFEREE COMPANY OR PURCHASING COMPANY IN CASE OF PURCHASE

Step 1: Record the Acquisition of business from the Vendor Company.

JOURNAL ENTRY

Business Purchase A/c	Dr.	*(with purchase consideration)*
To Liquidator of the Vendor Co.		

Step 2A: In case of Amalgamation in the nature of Purchase.

"Record the Assets and Liabilities taken over at their respective agreed values (i.e., not their book values) and debit the Goodwill Account with the excess of Purchase Consideration over the Net Assets taken over (if any) *or* credit the Capital Reserve Account with the excess of Net Assets over the Purchase Consideration (if any)".

JOURNAL ENTRY

Assets (Individually)	Dr.	*(with their respective agreed values of the assets taken over)*
Goodwill A/c	Dr.	*(with excess of Purchase Consideration over the Net Assets)*
To Liabilities (Individually)		*(with the respective agreed amount of the liabilities taken over)*
To Business Purchase A/c		*(with the Purchase consideration)*
To Capital Reserve A/c		*(with excess of Net Assets over the Purchase Consideration)*

Step 2B: In case of Amalgamation in the nature of Purchase.

"Record the Statutory Reserves of the Transferor Company"

JOURNAL ENTRY

Amalgamation Adjustment A/c	Dr.	*(with the total)*
To Statutory Reserves A/c (Individually)		*(with their respective book balances)*

Note: *Amalgamation Adjustment should be disclosed under the head 'Other Non-current Assets' on the Assets side of the Balance Sheet.*

Step 3: Make Payment to Vendor Company.

JOURNAL ENTRY

Liquidator of Vendor Co.'s A/c	Dr.	*(with the total)*
Discount on Issue of Shares A/c	Dr.	*(with the Discount allowed on shares)*
To Equity Share Capital A/c		*(with the paid up value of Equity Shares issued)*
To Preference Share Capital A/c		*(with the paid up value of Pref. Shares issued)*
To Securities Premium A/c		*(with the Securities Premium)*
To Cash A/c/Bank A/c		*(with the Cash Payment)*

Note: *The Shares issued by way of purchase consideration must be recorded at their paid up values (i.e., not at their issued prices) after giving due credit to Securities Premium Account (in case the shares have been issued at premium) or after giving due debit to "Discount on issue of Shares A/c' (in case the shares have been issued at discount).*

Step 4: Record the Issue of Debentures (if any) to discharge the existing Debentureholders of vendor company.

JOURNAL ENTRY

Debentures in Vendor Company	Dr.	*(with the amount of debentures)*
Discount on Issue of Debentures in Purchasing Company	Dr.	*(with the Debentures Discount)*
To Debentures in Purchasing Company		*(with the Nominal Value)*
To Securities Premium A/c		*(with the Debenture Premium)*

Step 5: Record the Reimbursement of the Liquidation Expenses of the Vendor Company.

JOURNAL ENTRY

Goodwill A/c (in case of Purchase)	Dr.
To Bank A/c	

Step 6: Eliminate the unrealised profit included in the unsold stock.

(a) Where the Unsold Inventories of the purchasing company includes the goods purchased from the vendor company

Goodwill A/c (in case of Purchase)	Dr.
To Inventories A/c	

(b) Where the Unsold Inventories of the vendor company includes goods purchased from the purchasing company, only the amount of stock is reduced to its cost while passing the entries on acquisition. (i.e., Entry in Step 2).

Note: *In case of sale of goods at loss, no adjustment is required*

Step 7: Eliminate the Inter Company Owings

(a) To eliminate the Debts owed by Vendor Company	Trade Payables of Vendor Co To Trade Receivables	Dr.
(b) To eliminate the Debts owed by Purchasing Company	Trade Payables To Trade Receivables of Vendor Co.	Dr.
(c) To eliminate the Bills drawn and retained by Vendor Co. upon Purchasing Company	Bills Payable A/c To Bills Receivable of Vendor Co.	Dr.
(d) To eliminate the Bills drawn and retained by Purchasing Company upon Vendor Co.	Bills Payable of Vendor Co. To Bills Receivable A/c	Dr.
(e) To eliminate the Debentures held by Vendor Co. in Purchasing Co.	Debentures A/c Goodwill A/c To Investment in Debentures A/c (Vendor Co.) To Capital Reserve A/c	Dr. [Face value] Dr. [If FV < BV] [Book Value] [If FV > BV]
(f) To eliminate the Debentures held by Purchasing Co. in Vendor Co.	Debentures in Vendor Co. Goodwill A/c To Investment in Debentures A/c To Capital Reserve A/c	Dr. [Face Value] Dr. [If FV < BV] Dr. [Book value] [If FV > BV]

Notes

(i) *Bills drawn by one company upon the other company and discounted with the bank should not be eliminated because these bills represent owing between the bank and the company and not the inter-company owings.*

(ii) *Where the debtors of a company include a sum due from another company but the creditors of another company include a lesser sum due to the former company. The difference should be treated as Cash-in-transit.*

(iii) *The entry (f) in Step 7 should be merged with entry in Step 4 so that the new debentures will be issued to discharge those debentures of vendor company which are held by outsiders (i.e., holders other than the purchasing company).*

(iv) *In case of entries (e) and (f), the loss should be debited to Goodwill A/c (in case of purchase) and the profit should be credited to Capital Reserve A/c.*

Step 8: Set off Goodwill against Capital Reserve

JOURNAL ENTRY

Capital Reserve A/c	Dr.
To Goodwill A/c	

Note: *The objective of passing the aforesaid journal entry is to disclose only one item (i.e., out of Capital Reserve and Goodwill) which is net of other item.*

ILLUSTRATION 11

Given below are the extracts from the Balance Sheet of V Ltd. as at 31st March, 2016:

Particulars	₹
Equity Share Capital of ₹ 10 each	2,00,000
8% Pref. Share Capital of ₹ 100 each	50,000
General Reserve	20,000
Profit & Loss A/c	16,100
Statutory Reserves	5,000
10% Debentures	50,000
Trade Payables	1,40,000
Tangible Assets	1,50,000
Goodwill	1,19,500
Inventories	55,000
Trade Receivables	65,000
Cash at Bank	91,600

The business of V Ltd. is taken over by P Ltd. as on that date on the following terms:

(a) 50% of Tangible Fixed Assets are taken over at 100% more than the book value and the remaining Tangible Fixed Assets are taken over at $16\frac{2}{3}\%$ less than the book value.

(c) Goodwill of V Ltd. is to be valued at ₹ 50,000.

(d) Inventories are taken over at book value less 10% and Trade Receivables are taken over at book value subject to an allowance of 10% to cover doubtful debts.

(e) Trade Payables are to be taken over subject to a discount of 5% and Unrecorded Loan Liability of ₹ 38,500 to be discharged by P Ltd. at book value.

(f) The purchase consideration payable by P Ltd. was agreed as follows:

(i) The issue of such an amount of fully paid 14% Debentures in P Ltd at 96 per cent as is sufficient to discharge 10% Debentures in V Ltd. at a premium of 20 per cent.

(ii) The issue of such an amount of fully paid 10% Pref. Shares in P Ltd. at 125% as is sufficient to discharge 9% Pref. Shares in V Ltd. at a premium of 20%.

(iii) One Equity Share of ₹ 10 each, ₹ 8 paid up valued at ₹ 15 per share for every two Equity Shares held in V Ltd. and the balance in cash. The market value of an equity share of P Ltd. at present is ₹ 100.

(iv) Expenses of liquidation of V Ltd. are to be reimbursed by P Ltd. to the extent of ₹ 10,000. Actual Expenses amounted to ₹ 12,000.

(g) Statutory Reserves are to be maintained for 2 more years.

Required: *Pass Journal Entries in the books of V Ltd and P Ltd.*

SOLUTION

JOURNAL OF V LTD.

Date	Particulars		L.F.	Dr. (₹)	Cr. (₹)
1	Realisation A/c	Dr.		4,79,100	
	To Goodwill				1,19,500
	To Tangible Fixed Assets				1,50,000
	To Inventories				55,000
	To Trade Receivables				65,000
	To Cash at Bank [91,600 – 2,000 Exp.]				89,600
	(Being the transfer of various assets to Realisation A/c)				
2	10% Debentures	Dr.		50,000	
	Trade Payables	Dr.		1,40,000	
	To Realisation A/c				1,90,000
	(Being the transfer of various liabilities to Realisation A/c)				
3	P Ltd	Dr.		2,28,600	
	To Realisation A/c				2,28,600
	(Being the purchase consideration due)				
4	Equity Shares in P Ltd.	Dr.		1,50,000	
	9% Pref. Shares in P Ltd.	Dr.		60,000	
	Cash at Bank	Dr.		18,600	
	To P Ltd.				2,28,600
	(Being the receipt of purchase consideration)				
5	P Ltd.	Dr.		10,000	
	Realiasation A/c	Dr.		2,000	
	To Bank A/c				12,000
	(Being liquidation expenses paid out of which ₹ 10,000 are to be reimbursed by purchasing company)				
6	Bank A/c	Dr.		10,000	
	To P Ltd.				10,000
	(Being liquidation expenses reimbursed by purchasing company)				
7	8% Pref. Share Capital A/c	Dr.		50,000	
	Realiasation A/c	Dr.		10,000	
	To Pref. Shareholders' A/c				60,000
	(Being the transfer of Pref. Share Capital to Pref. shareholders' A/c & loss on discharge to Realiasation A/c)				
8	Pref. Shareholders' A/c	Dr.		60,000	
	To 9% Pref. Shares in P Ltd.				60,000
	(Being the claims of Pref. share holders discharged)				

9	Equity Shareholders' A/c Dr.		72,500	
	To Realisation A/c			72,500
	(Being the transfer of loss on Realisation)			
10	Equity Share Capital A/c Dr.		2,00,000	
	General Reserve Dr.		20,000	
	Profit & Loss A/c Dr.		16,100	
	Statutory Reserves A/c Dr.		5,000	
	To Equity Shareholders' A/c			2,41,100
	(Being the transfer of Share Capital & balance of P&L A/c & Reserves to Equity Shareholders' Account)			
11	Equity Shareholders' A/c Dr.		1,68,600	
	To Equity Shares in P Ltd.			1,50,000
	To Bank A/c			18,600
	(Being the claims of Equity Shareholders discharged)			

JOURNAL OF P LTD.

Date	*Particulars*	*L.F.*	*Dr. (₹)*	*Cr. (₹)*
1	Business Purchase A/c Dr.		2,28,600	
	To Liquidators of V Ltd.			2,28,600
	(Being the purchase of the business)			
2	Goodwill Dr.		50,000	
	Tangible Fixed Assets[₹ 1,50,000 + ₹ 62,500] Dr.		2,12,500	
	Inventories Dr.		49,500	
	Trade Receivables Dr.		65,000	
	Bank Dr.		89,600	
	Reserve for Discount on Trade Payables [5% of ₹ 1,40 000] Dr.		7,000	
	To Provision for Doubtful Debts [10% of ₹ 65,000]			6,500
	To Trade Payables			1,40,000
	To 10% Debentures [₹ 50,000 + 20%]			60,000
	To Unrecorded Loan			38,500
	To Business Purchase A/c			2,28,600
	(Being the Assets and Liabilities taken over)			
3	Liquidators of V Ltd. Dr.		2,28,600	
	To Equity Share Capital A/c [10,000 × ₹ 8]			80,000
	To 9% Pref. Share Capital A/c [480 × ₹ 100]			48,000
	To Securities Premium A/c [(10,000 × ₹ 7) + (480 × ₹ 25)]			82,000
	To Bank A/c			18,600
	(Being the purchase consideration discharged)			

4	Goodwill A/c	Dr.	10,000	
	To Bank A/c			10,000
	(Being the payment of Liquidation Expenses of Vendor co.)			
5	10% Debentures of V Ltd.	Dr.	60,000	
	Discount on Issue of 14% Debentures A/c	Dr.	2,500	
	To 14% Debentures A/c			62,500
	(Being 10% Debentures of Vendor co. redeemed by issue of 625, 14% Debentures of ₹ 100 each at a discount of 4%) [Face Value of Debentures = ₹ 60,000/96% = ₹ 62,500]			
6	Unrecorded Loan A/c	Dr.	38,500	
	To Bank A/c			38,500
	(Being the liabilities of Vendor co. discharged)			
7	Amalgamation Adjustment A/c	Dr.	5,000	
	To Statutory Reserves			5,000
	(Being the identity of Statutory Reserves retained)			

Working Notes:

1. CALCULATION OF PURCHASE CONSIDERATION

	Particulars	₹
A	Assets taken over at agreed values	
	Tangible Fixed Assets [(₹ 1,50,000 × 50%) + 100%]	1,50,000
	Tangible Fixed Assets [(₹ 1,50,000 × 50%) – $16\frac{2}{3}$%]	62,500
	Inventories [₹ 55,000 – ₹ 5,500]	49,500
	Trade Receivables [₹ 65,000 – ₹ 6,500]	58,500
	Cash at Bank [91,600 – 2,000 (Expenses)]	89,600
	Goodwill	50,000
		4,60,100
B	*Less:* Liabilities taken over:	
	Trade Payables [₹ 1,40,000 – 5%]	1,33,000
	10% Debentures [₹ 50,000 + 20%]	60,000
	Unrecorded Loan	38,500
		2,31,500
C	Net Assets taken over (A – B)	2,28,600

2. DISCHARGE OF PURCHASE CONSIDERATION

A. 10,000, Equity Shares to be issued [(20,000 × 1/2) × ₹ 15]	1,50,000
B. 480, 9% Pref. Shares to be issued [(500 × 120%)]	60,000
C. Cash to Equity Shareholders [Balancing figure]	18,600
D. Total Purchase Consideration (A + B + C)	2,28,600

Note: *According to AS-14, the amount paid by purchasing Company to discharge the debentures holders and the liquidation expenses of Vendor Company are not considered as part of purchase consideration.*

ILLUSTRATION 12

What shall be the change in the solution of Previous Illustration 11 if the following information is also provided:

"V Ltd. owed P Ltd. ₹ 60,000 for the purchases of stock from P Ltd. which made a profit of 20% on cost. Four fifth of such stock were sold till 31.3.2016."

SOLUTION

1. There will be no change in the Journal Entries of V Ltd.

JOURNAL OF P LTD.

Date	*Particulars*		*L.F.*	*Dr. (₹)*	*Cr. (₹)*
1	Business Purchase A/c	Dr.		2,28,600	
	To Liquidators of V Ltd.				2,28,600
	(Being the purchase of the business)				
2	**Goodwill (Balancing figure)**	**Dr.**		**53,000**	
	Tangible Fixed Assets	Dr.		2,12,500	
	Inventories	Dr.		49,500	
	Trade Receivables	Dr.		65,000	
	Bank	Dr.		89,600	
	Reserve for Discount on Trade Payables [5% of ₹(1,40 000 – 60,000)]	**Dr.**		**4,000**	
	To Provision for Doubtful Debts [10% of ₹ 65,000]				6,500
	To Trade Payables				1,40,000
	To 10% Debentures [₹ 50,000 + 20%]				60,000
	To Unrecorded Loan				38,500
	To Business Purchase A/c				2,28,600
	(Being the Assets and Liabilities taken over)				
3	Liquidators of V Ltd.	Dr.		2,28,600	
	To Equity Share Capital A/c [10,000 × ₹ 8]				80,000
	To 9% Pref. Share Capital A/c [480 × ₹ 100]				48,000
	To Securities Premium A/c [(10,000 × ₹ 7) + (480 × ₹ 25)]				82,000
	To Bank A/c				18,600
	(Being the purchase consideration discharged)				
4	Goodwill A/c	Dr.		10,000	
	To Bank A/c				10,000
	(Being the payment of Liquidation Expenses of Vendor co.)				

5	10% Debentures of V Ltd. Dr. Discount on Issue of 14% Debentures A/c Dr. To 14% Debentures A/c (Being 10% Debentures of Vendor co. redeemed by issue of 625, 14% Debentures of ₹ 100 each at a discount of 4%) [Face Value of Debentures = ₹ 60,000/96% = ₹ 62,500]		60,000 2,500	 62,500
6	Unrecorded Loan A/c Dr. To Bank A/c (Being the liabilities of Vendor co. discharged)		38,500	 38,500
7	Amalgamation Adjustment A/c Dr. To Statutory Reserves (Being the identity of statutory Reserves retained)		5,000	 5,000
8	**Goodwill A/c Dr.** **To Inventories** **(Being the elimination of unrealized profit included in goods purchased by V Ltd.)[(20% of ₹ 60,000 × 1/6) – (10% of ₹ 12,000)]**		**800**	 **800**
9	**Trade Payables (V Ltd.) A/c Dr.** **To Trade Receivables A/c** **(Being the cancellation of Inter Co. Owing)**		**60,000**	 **60,000**

ILLUSTRATION 13

What shall be the change in the solution of Illustration 11 if the following information is also provided: "Prior to 31st March 2016 V Ltd. sold goods costing ₹ 30,000 to P Ltd. for ₹ 40,000. ₹ 25,000 worth of goods were still in stock of P Ltd.Trade Receivables include ₹ 20,000 still due from P Ltd."

SOLUTION

1. There will be no change in the Journal Entries of V Ltd.

JOURNAL OF P LTD.

Date	*Particulars*	*L.F.*	*Dr. (₹)*	*Cr. (₹)*
1	Business Purchase A/c Dr. To Liquidators of V Ltd. (Being the purchase of the business)		2,28,600	 2,28,600
2	**Goodwill (balancing figure) Dr.** Tangible Fixed Assets Dr. Inventories Dr. Trade Receivables Dr. Bank Dr. Reserve for Discount on Trade Payables [5% of ₹ 1,40 000] Dr. **To Pro. for Doubtful Debts [10% of ₹ (65,000 – 20,000)]**		**48,000** 2,12,500 49,500 65,000 89,600 7,000	 **4,500**

	To Trade Payables			1,40,000
	To 10% Debentures [₹ 50,000 + 20%]			60,000
	To Unrecorded Loan			38,500
	To Business Purchase A/c			2,28,600
	(Being the Assets and Liabilities taken over)			
3	Liquidators of V Ltd.	Dr.	2,28,600	
	To Equity Share Capital A/c [10,000 × ₹ 8]			80,000
	To 9% Pref. Share Capital A/c [480 × ₹ 100]			48,000
	To Securities Premium A/c [(10,000 × ₹ 7) + (480 × ₹ 25)]			82,000
	To Bank A/c			18,600
	(Being the purchase consideration discharged)			
4	Goodwill A/c	Dr.	10,000	
	To Bank A/c			10,000
	(Being the payment of Liquidation Expenses of Vendor co.)			
5	10% Debentures of V Ltd.	Dr.	60,000	
	Discount on Issue of 14% Debentures A/c	Dr.	2,500	
	To 14% Debentures A/c			62,500
	(Being 10% Debentures of Vendor co. redeemed by issue of 625, 14% Debentures of ₹ 100 each at a discount of 4%)			
	[Face Value of Debentures = ₹ 60,000/96% = ₹ 62,500]			
6	Unrecorded Loan A/c	Dr.	38,500	
	To Bank A/c			38,500
	(Being the liabilities of Vendor co. discharged)			
7	Amalgamation Adjustment A/c	Dr.	5,000	
	To Statutory Reserves			5,000
	(Being the identity of statutory Reserves retained)			
8	**Goodwill**	**Dr.**	**6,250**	
	To Inventories A/c			**6,250**
	(Being the Elimination of unrealized profit on unsold goods worth ₹ 25,000 bought from V Ltd. still unsold (25,000 × 10,000/40,000)			
9	**Trade Payables A/c**	**Dr.**	**20,000**	
	To Trade Receivables (V Ltd.) A/c			**20,000**
	(Being Elimination of the amount owed by us to V Ltd.)			

ILLUSTRATION 14

Given below are the extracts from the Balance Sheet of **PRARTHANA** Ltd. as at 31st March, 2016:

Particulars	₹
Share Capital [Equity Shares of ₹ 10 fully paid]	6,00,000
Statutory Reserves	1,70,000

General Reserve	10,000
Profit & Loss A/c	1,00,000
12% Debentures	1,00,000
Trade Payables	20,000
Tangible Assets	6,00,000
Intangible Assets [Goodwill]	1,00,000
Inventories	2,08,000
Trade Receivables	36,000
Cash at Bank	56,000

PIYUSH Ltd. agreed to absorb the business of PRARTHANA Ltd. with effect from 1st Apr. 2016. The purchase consideration payable by Piyush Ltd. was agreed as follows:

(a) A cash payment equivalent to ₹ 2.50 for every ₹ 10 share in PRARTHANA Ltd.

(b) The issue of 90,000 Equity Shares of ₹ 10 each fully paid in PIYUSH Ltd. having an agreed value of ₹ 15 per share.

(c) The issue of such an amount of fully paid 14% Debentures in PIYUSH Ltd. at 96 per cent as is sufficient to discharge 12% Debentures in PRARTHANA Ltd. at a premium of 20 per cent.

While computing purchase consideration, PIYUSH Ltd. valued Tangible Fixed Assets at 100% more than the book value, Inventories at ₹ 1,42,000 and Trade Receivables at their face value subject to a provision of 5 per cent for doubtful debts. The actual cost of liquidation of PRARTHANA Ltd. was ₹ 15,000. Liquidation cost of PRARTHANA Ltd. is to be reimbursed by PIYUSH Ltd. to the extent of ₹ 10,000. Statutory Reserves are to be maintained for 2 more years.

Required: (i) Close the books of PRARTHANA Ltd. by preparing Realisation Account, Piyush Ltd Account, Shareholders' Account and Debentures Account; and

(ii) Pass Journal Entries in the books of PIYUSH Ltd. regarding acquisition of business.

SOLUTION

BOOKS OF PRARTHANA LTD.

REALISATION ACCOUNT

Dr. Cr.

Particulars	₹	Particulars	₹
To Goodwill	1,00,000	By Trade Payables	20,000
To Tangible Fixed Assets	6,00,000	By PIYUSH Ltd.	15,00,000
To Inventories	2,08,000	By 12% Debentures	1,00,000
To Trade Receivables	36,000		
To Cash & Bank [₹ 56,000 – ₹ 5,000]	51,000		
To Cash & Bank (Expenses)	5,000		
To Profit on Realisation	6,20,000		
	16,20,000		16,20,000

PIYUSH LTD. ACCOUNT

Dr. Cr.

Particulars	₹	Particulars	₹
To Realisation A/c	15,00,000	By Bank A/c	1,50,000
To Bank A/c	10,000	By Equity Shares in PIYUSH Ltd.	13,50,000

		By Bank A/c	10,000
	15,10,000		15,10,000

Dr. **EQUITY SHAREHOLDERS' ACCOUNT** Cr.

Particulars	₹	Particulars	₹
To Cash A/c	1,50,000	By Share Capital	6,00,000
To Equity Shares in PIYUSH Ltd.	13,50,000	By Statutory Reserves	1,70,000
		By General Reserve	10,000
		By Profit & Loss A/c	1,00,000
		By Realisation A/c	6,20,000
	15,00,000		15,00,000

Dr. **12% DEBENTURES ACCOUNT** Cr.

Particulars	₹	Particulars	₹
To Realisation A/c	1,00,000	By Balance b/d	1,00,000

Dr. **CASH & BANK ACCOUNT** Cr.

Particulars	₹	Particulars	₹
To Balance b/d	56,000	By Realisation A/c (transfer)	51,000
To PIYUSH Ltd.	1,50,000	By Realisation A/c (Expenses)	5,000
To PIYUSH Ltd.	10,000	By PIYUSH Ltd.	10,000
		By Equity Shareholders' A/c	1,50,000
	2,16,000		2,16,000

JOURNAL OF PIYUSH LTD.

Particulars		L.F.	Dr. (₹)	Cr. (₹)
Business Purchase A/c	Dr.		15,00,000	
To Liquidators of PRARTHANA Ltd.				15,00,000
(Being the Purchase of the business of PRARTHANA Ltd. as per agreement dated ...)				
Goodwill A/c (Balancing Figure)	Dr.		2,12,800	
Tangible Fixed Assets	Dr.		12,00,000	
Inventories	Dr.		1,42,000	
Trade Receivables	Dr.		36,000	
Cash & Bank	Dr.		51,000	
To Trade Payables				20,000
To 12% Debentures in PRARTHANA Ltd.				1,20,000
To Provision for Doubtful Debts A/c				1,800
To Business Purchase A/c				15,00,000
(Being the assets & liabilities taken over recorded, Goodwill being the balancing figure)				

Liquidators of PRARTHANA Ltd.	Dr.		15,00,000	
To Equity Share Capital A/c				9,00,000
To Securities Premium A/c				4,50,000
To Bank A/c				1,50,000
(Being the purchase consideration discharged)				
12% Debentures in PRARTHANA Ltd. A/c	Dr.		1,20,000	
Discount on Issue of Debentures A/c	Dr.		5,000	
To 14% Debentures A/c				1,25,000
(Being the Issue of 14% Debentures to 12% Debenture holders of PRARTHANA Ltd. at a discount of 4%) [Face Value of Debentures ₹ 1,20,000/. 96 = ₹ 1,25,000]				
Amalgamation Adjustment A/c	Dr.		1,70,000	
To Statutory Reserves A/c				1,70,000
(Being the identity of Statutory Reserves retained)				
Goodwill A/c	Dr.		10,000	
To Bank A/c				10,000
(Being the payment of Liquidation Exp. of Vendor Co.)				

Working Notes:

(I) CALCULATION OF PURCHASE CONSIDERATION

Particulars	₹
Cash [₹ 2.50 × 60,000]	1,50,000
Equity Shares [90,000 × 15]	13,50,000
	15,00,000

(ii) It is assumed that PRARTHANA Ltd. will retain the required cash for expenses.

ILLUSTRATION 15

Ajanta Limited agreed to acquire the business of Elora Limited as on 31st March 2016. Given below are the extracts from the Balance Sheet of Elora Ltd. as at 31st March, 2016:

Particulars	₹
20,000 Equity Shares of ₹ 10 each	2,00,000
10,000, 12% Pref. Shares of ₹ 10 each	1,00,000
Statutory Reserves	13,000
General Reserve	2,000
Profit & Loss A/c	30,000
12% Debentures	1,00,000
Trade Payables	1,50,000
Tangible Assets	2,50,000
Inventories	2,50,000
Trade Receivables	50,000
Cash at Bank	45,000

The consideration payable by Ajanta Limited was agreed as under:

(a) The Preference Shareholders of Elora Limited were to be allotted 8% Preference Shares of ₹ 1,10,000.

(b) Equity Shareholders to be allotted six Equity Shares of ₹ 10 each issued at a premium of 10% and ₹ 3 cash against every five shares held.

(c) 12% Debenture holders of Elora Limited to be paid @ 8% premium by issue of 14% Debentures at 10% discount.

While arriving at the agreed consideration, the directors of Ajanta Limited valued Tangible Fixed Assets at 40% more than the book value. Inventories at 12% less than book value, and Trade Receivables at their book value subject to an allowance of 5% to cover doubtful debts. Trade Receivables of Elora Limited included ₹ 10,000 due from Ajanta Limited. It was agreed that before acquisition, Elora Limited will pay dividend at 10% on Equity Shares. Actual Liquidation expenses are ₹ 15,000. Liquidation Expenses are to be reimbursed by Ajanta Ltd. to the extent of ₹ 10,000. Ignore Corporate Dividend Tax.

Required: Pass Journal entries necessary to close the books of Elora Limited and to record acquisition in the books of Ajanta Limited.

SOLUTION

JOURNAL OF ELORA LTD.

Particulars		*L.F.*	*Dr. (₹)*	*Cr. (₹)*
Profit & Loss A/c	Dr.		30,000	
Reserve A/c	Dr.		2,000	
To Dividend Payable A/c				32,000
(Being the Dividend @ 10% on equity shares & @ 12% as Pref. shares declared)				
Dividend Payable A/c	Dr.		32,000	
To Bank A/c				32,000
(Being the payment of Divided)				
Realisation A/c	Dr.		5,58,000	
To Tangible Fixed Assets				2,50,000
To Inventories				2,50,000
To Trade Receivables				50,000
To Cash At Bank [₹ 45,000 – ₹ 32,000 (Div)– ₹ 5,000(Exp)]				8,000
(Being the transfer of Sundry assets to realisation account)				
12% Debentures A/c	Dr.		1,00,000	
Trade Payables A/c	Dr.		1,50,000	
To Realisation A/c				2,50,000
(Being the transfer of various liabilities taken over)				
Ajanta Limited A/c	Dr.		3,86,000	
To Realisation A/c				3,86,000
(Being the purchase consideration due from purchasing company)				
8% Preference Shares in Ajanta Ltd. A/c	Dr.		1,10,000	
Equity Shares in Ajanta Limited A/c	Dr.		2,64,000	

Particulars		L.F.	Dr. (₹)	Cr. (₹)
Bank A/c	Dr.		12,000	
To Ajanta Limited				3,86,000
(Being the receipt of purchase consideration)				
Realisation A/c	Dr.		5,000	
Ajanta Ltd.	Dr.		10,000	
To Bank A/c				15,000
(Being the payment of realisation expenses)				
Bank A/c	Dr.		10,000	
To Ajanta Ltd.				10,000
(Being the receipt of reimbursement of Exp.)				
12% Preference Share Capital A/c	Dr.		1,00,000	
Realisation A/c	Dr.		10,000	
To Preference Shareholders' A/c				1,10,000
(Being the transfer of Pref. share capital to Pref. shareholders' A/c and provision made for redemption of shareholders)				
Realisation A/c	Dr.		63,000	
To Equity Shareholders' A/c				63,000
(Being the transfer of Profit on realisation)				
Preference Shareholders' A/c	Dr.		1,10,000	
To 8% Preference Shares in Ajanta Ltd.				1,10,000
(Being the payment made to pref. shareholders)				
Equity Share Capital A/c	Dr.		2,00,000	
Statutory Reserves A/c	Dr.		13,000	
To Equity Shareholders' A/c				2,13,000
(Being the transfer of equity share capital and Reserve)				
Equity Shareholders' A/c	Dr.		2,76,000	
To Equity Shares in Ajanta Ltd.				2,64,000
To Bank A/c				12,000
(Being the final Payment made to equity shareholders)				

JOURNAL OF AJANTA LIMITED

Particulars		*L.F.*	*Dr. (₹)*	*Cr. (₹)*
Business Purchase A/c	Dr.		3,86,000	
To Liquidators of Elora Limited				3,86,000
(Being the purchase of business as per agreement dated...)				
Goodwill A/c (Balancing figure)	Dr.		18,000	
Tangible Fixed Assets	Dr.		3,50,000	
Inventories A/c	Dr.		2,20,000	
Trade Receivables A/c	Dr.		50,000	
Cash at Bank A/c	Dr.		8,000	

To Trade Payables A/c			1,50,000
To 12% Debentures in Elora Ltd.			1,08,000
To Provision for Doubtful Debts A/c [5% of ₹ (50,000 – 10,000)]			2,000
To Business Purchase A/c			3,86,000
(Being the assets & liabilities taken over recorded)			
Liquidators of Elora Ltd.	Dr.	3,86,000	
To 8% Preference Share Capital A/c			1,10,000
To Equity Share Capital A/c			2,40,000
To Securities Premium A/c			24,000
To Bank A/c			12,000
(Being the purchase consideration discharged)			
12% Debentures in Elora Ltd. A/c	Dr.	1,08,000	
Discount on Issue of Debentures A/c	Dr.	12,000	
To 14% Debentures A/c			1,20,000
(Being the Issue of 14% Debentures of Debentureholders of Elora Ltd.) [face value of Debentures = ₹ 1,08,000 / .90 = ₹ 1,20,000]			
Ajanta Ltd.'s Trade Payables A/c	Dr.	10,000	
To Elora Ltd.'s Trade Receivables A/c			10,000
(Being the inter-company's debt's cancelled)			
Amalgamation Adjustment A/c	Dr.	13,000	
To Statutory Reserves A/c			13,000
(Being the identity of Statutory Reserves retained)			
Goodwill A/c	Dr.	10,000	
To Bank A/c			10,000
(Being the liquidation expenses reimbursed)			

Working Notes:

(I) CALCULATION OF PURCHASE CONSIDERATION

Particulars	₹	₹
8% Preference Shares		1,10,000
Equity Shares (20,000 × × ₹ 10)	2,40,000	
Securities Premium	24,000	2,64,000
Cash (3/5 × 20,000)		12,000
		3,86,000

(ii) It has been assured that Elora Ltd. will retain the adequate cash for liquidation expenses.

ILLUSTRATION 16

Given below are the extracts from the Balance Sheets of P Ltd. and V Ltd. as at 31st March, 2016:

Particulars	*P Ltd. (₹)*	*V Ltd. (₹)*
Equity Share Capital of ₹ 10 each	6,00,000	2,00,000

General Reserve	1,50,000	20,000
Profit & Loss A/c	1,77,000	10,000
Statutory Reserves	—	5,000
10% Debentures of ₹ 100 each	—	50,000
Trade Payables	37,500	1,40,000
Goodwill	—	1,19,500
Tangible Assets	4,75,000	1,50,000
Non-Current Investments (including 100 Debentures of V Ltd. purchased @ of ₹ 90)	1,09,000	—
Inventories	95,000	55,000
Trade Receivables	1,40,000	65,000
Cash at Bank	1,45,500	35,500

The business of V Ltd. is taken over by P Ltd. as on that date on the following terms:

(a) Prior to absorption, V Ltd and P Ltd decide to declare and pay equity dividend @ 5%.(Ignore Dividend Distribution Tax)

(b) 50% of Tangible Fixed Assets are taken over at 100% more than the book value and the remaining Tangible Fixed Assets are taken over at $16\frac{2}{3}\%$ less than the book value.

(c) Goodwill of V Ltd. is to be valued at ₹ 50,000.

(d) Inventories are taken over at book value less 10% and Trade Receivables are taken over at book value subject to an allowance of 10% to cover doubtful debts.

(e) Trade Payables are to be taken over subject to a discount of 5% and Unrecorded Loan Liability of ₹ 38,500 to be discharged by P Ltd. at book value.

(f) The purchase consideration is to be discharged to the extent of 20% in cash and the balance in the form of equity shares of ₹ 10 each, ₹ 8 paid up at a premium of ₹ 7 per share, The market value of an equity share of P Ltd. at present is ₹ 100.

(g) The issue of such an amount of fully paid 14% Debentures in P Ltd at 96 per cent as is sufficient to discharge 10% Debentures in V Ltd. at a premium of 20 per cent.

(h) Expenses of liquidation of V Ltd. are to be reimbursed by P Ltd. to the extent of ₹ 10,000. Actual Expenses amounted to ₹ 12,000.

(i) Statutory Reserves are to be maintained for 2 more years.

Prior to 31st March 2016 V Ltd. sold goods costing ₹ 30,000 to P Ltd. for ₹ 40,000. ₹ 25,000 worth of goods were still in stock of P Ltd.Trade Receivables include ₹ 20,000 still due from P Ltd. On the date of absorption, V Ltd. owed P Ltd. ₹ 60,000 for the purchases of stock from P Ltd. which made a profit of 20% on cost. Four fifth of such stock were sold till 31.3.2016. Investments of P Ltd. include ₹ 9,000 representing the cost of 10% Debentures of V Ltd.

Required: *(a) Prepare Realisation Account, Bank Account, Equity Shareholders Account and Shares in P Ltd. Account in the books of V Ltd. (b) Pass Journal Entries in the books of P Ltd. and prepare Balance Sheet.*

SOLUTION

IN THE BOOKS OF V LTD.

Dr. **REALISATION ACCOUNT** *Cr.*

Particulars	₹	*Particulars*	₹
To Goodwill	1,19,500	By 10% Debentures	50,000

To Tangible Fixed Assets	1,50,000	By Trade Payables	1,40,000
To Inventories	55,000	By P Ltd. (Purchase Consideration)	1,62,557
To Trade Receivables	65,000	By Equity Shareholders' A/c (Loss)	62,443
To Bank [35,500 – 10,000 (Div.) – 2,000 (Exp.)]	23,500		
To Bank A/c (Expenses)	2,000		
	4,15,000		4,15,000

Dr. **BANK ACCOUNT** Cr.

Particulars	₹	*Particulars*	₹
To Balance b/d	35,500	By Dividend Payable A/c	10,000
To P Ltd. (Expenses)	10,000	By Realisation A/c (Takeover)	23,500
To P Ltd. (Consideration)	32,567	By Realisation A/c (Expenses)	2,000
		By P Ltd. (Expenses)	10,000
		By Equity Shareholders A/c	32,567
	78,067		78,067

Dr. **EQUITY SHAREHOLDERS' ACCOUNT** Cr.

Particulars	₹	*Particulars*	₹
To Realisation A/c (Loss)	62,443	By Share Capital	2,00,000
To Bank A/c	32,567	By General Reserve	20,000
To Shares in P Ltd.	1,29,990	By Statutory Reserves	5,000
	2,25,000		2,25,000

Dr. **SHARES IN P LTD. ACCOUNT** Cr.

Particulars	₹	*Particulars*	₹
To P Ltd.	1,29,990	By Sundry Shareholders (transfer)	1,29,990

JOURNAL OF P LTD.

Particulars		*L.F.*	*Dr. (₹)*	*Cr. (₹)*
Profit & Loss A/c	Dr.		30,000	
To Dividend Payable a/c				30,000
(Being the Dividend declared @ 5%)				
Dividend Payable A/c	Dr.		30,000	
To Bank A/c				30,000
(Being the Dividend paid)				
Business Purchase A/c	Dr.		1,62,557	
To Liquidators of V Ltd.				1,62,557
(Being the purchase price agreed to be paid for the business of V Ltd.)				

Particulars			Dr. (₹)	Cr. (₹)
Goodwill (Balancing figure)	Dr.		51,057	
Tangible Fixed Assets	Dr.		2,12,500	
Inventories	Dr.		49,500	
Trade Receivables	Dr.		65,000	
Bank	Dr.		23,500	
Reserve for Discount on Trade Payables [5% of ₹(1,40 000 – 60,000)]	Dr.		4,000	
To Provision for Doubtful Debts [10% of ₹ (65,000 – 20,000)]				4,500
To Trade Payables				1,40,000
To 10% Debentures [₹ 50,000 + 20%]				60,000
To Unrecorded Loan				38,500
To Business Purchase A/c				1,62,557
(Being the assets and liabilities taken over from V Ltd.)				
Liquidators of V Ltd.	Dr.		1,62,557	
To Bank A/c				32,567
To Equity Share Capital A/c				69,328
To Securities Premium A/c				60,662
(Being the issue of Shares and payment in cash in satisfaction of purchase consideration)				
Goodwill A/c	Dr.		10,000	
To Bank A/c				10,000
(Being the payment of Realization Expenses of V Ltd.)				
Goodwill	Dr.		6,250	
To Inventories A/c				6,250
(Being the Elimination of unrealized profit on unsold goods worth ₹ 25,000 bought from V Ltd. still unsold (25,000 × 10,000/40,000)				
Trade Payables A/c	Dr.		20,000	
To Trade Receivables (V Ltd.) A/c				20,000
(Being Elimination of the amount owed by us to V Ltd.)				
Goodwill A/c	Dr.		800	
To Inventories				800
(Being the elimination of unrealized profit included in goods purchased by V Ltd.)[(20% of ₹ 60,000 x1/6) –(10% of ₹ 12,000)]				
Trade Payables (V Ltd.) A/c	Dr.		60,000	
To Trade Receivables A/c				60,000
(Being the cancellation of Inter Co. Owing)				
10% Debentures of V Ltd.	Dr.		60,000	
Discount on Issue of 14% Debentures A/c	Dr.		2,000	
To Investments in 10% Debentures of V Ltd.				9,000
To 14% Debentures A/c				50,000
To Capital Reserve A/c				3,000

(Being the Investment in 10% Debentures of V Ltd. cancelled and the remaining debentures redeemed by issue of 500, 14% Debentures of ₹ 100 each at a discount of 4%) [Face Value of Debentures = ₹ 48,000/96% = ₹ 50,000]			
Unrecorded Loan A/c	Dr.	38,500	
To Bank A/c			38,500
(Being the liabilities of V Ltd. discharged)			
Amalgamation Adjustment A/c	Dr.	5,000	
To Statutory Reserves			5,000
(Being the identity of statutory Reserves retained)			
Capital Reserve A/c	Dr.	3,000	
To Goodwill A/c			3,000
(Being the goodwill adjusted against Capital Reserve)			

BALANCE SHEET OF P LTD. AS AT 31.03.2016

Particulars	*Note No*	X Ltd. (₹)
I. Equity and Liabilities		
(1) Shareholders'Funds		
(a) Share Capital	1	6,69,328
(b) Reserves and Surplus	2	3,60,662
(2) Non–Current Liabilities		
(a) Long–term Borrowings (14% Debentures)		50,000
(3) Current Liabilities		
(a) Trade Payables [(37,500 – 20,000) + (1,40,000 – 4,000 – 60,000)]		93,500
Total		11,73,490
II. Assets		
(1) Non–Current Assets		
(a) Fixed Assets		
Tangible Assets [4,75,000 + 2,12,500]		6,87,500
Intangible Assets [Goodwill] [51,057 + 10,000 + 6,250 + 800 – 3,000]		65,107
(b) Non–Current Investments[1,09,000 –9,000]		1,00,000
(c) Other Non–Current Assets[Amalgamation Adjustment A/c]		5,000
(2) Current Assets		
(a) Inventories [(95,000 – 6,250)+(49,500 – 800)]		1,37,450
(b) Trade Receivables [(1,40,000 – 60,000)+(65,000 – 4,500 – 20,000)]		1,20,500
(c) Cash and Cash Equivalents [Cash at Bank] [(1,45,500 –30,000 – 10,000 – 32,567 – 38,500) + (23,500)]		57,933
Total		11,73,490

Notes To Accounts:

	Particulars	X Ltd. (₹)
1.	**Share Capital**	
	Equity Shares of ₹ 10 each	6,00,000
	Equity Shares of ₹ 10 each,₹ 8 paid up	69,328
		6,69,328
2.	**Reserves and Surplus**	
	General Reserve	1,50,000
	Profit & Loss A/c[1,77,000 – 30,000]	1,47,000
	Statutory Reserves	5,000
	Securities Premium	60,662
	Less: Discount on Issue of 14% Debentures A/c	(2,000)
		3,60,662

Working Notes:

1. CALCULATION OF PURCHASE CONSIDERATION

	Particulars		₹
A	Assets taken over at agreed values		
	Tangible Fixed Assets [(₹ 1,50,000 × 50%) + 100%]		1,50,000
	Tangible Fixed Assets [(₹ 1,50,000 × 50%) – $16\frac{2}{3}\%$]		62,500
	Inventories [₹ 55,000 – ₹ 5,500]		49,500
	Trade Receivables [₹ 65,000 – ₹ 6,500]		58,500
	Cash at Bank [35,500 – 10,000 – 2,000]		23,500
	Goodwill		50,000
			3,94,000
B	*Less:* Liabilities taken over:		
	Trade Payables	1,40,000	
	Less: Reserve for Discount @ 5%	7,000	1,33,000
	10% Debentures[₹ 50,000 + 20%]		60,000
	Unrecorded Loan		38,500
			2,31,500
C	Net Assets taken over (A – B)		1,62,500

2. DISCHARGE OF PURCHASE CONSIDERATION

Particulars	₹
Payable in Cash(20% of ₹ 1,62,500)	32,500
In shares—[(80% of ₹ 1,62,500)/₹15]	
8,666 shares of ₹ 10 each, ₹ 8 paid up valued at ₹ 15 per share	1,29,990

Cash for Fractional Share(.67 × ₹ 100)	67
	1,62,557

ILLUSTRATION 17

Given below are the extracts from the Balance Sheet of V Ltd. as at 31st March, 2016:

Particulars	*P Ltd* ₹	*V Ltd* ₹
Equity Share Capital of ₹ 10 each	6,00,000	2,00,000
12% Pref. Share Capital of ₹ 100 each	1,00,000	50,000
General Reserve	1,50,000	20,000
Profit & Loss A/c	1,75,200	14,000
Statutory Reserves	—	5,000
10% Debentures	—	50,000
Trade Payables	37,500	1,40,000
Tangible Assets	4,75,000	1,50,000
Goodwill	—	1,19,500
Non-Current Investments (including 100 Debentures of V Ltd. purchased @ of ₹ 90)	1,09,000	—
Inventories	95,000	55,000
Trade Receivables	1,40,000	65,000
Cash at Bank	2,43,700	89,500

Prior to absorption, both the companies decide to declare and pay equity dividend @ 5%.(Ignore Dividend Distribution Tax). The business of V Ltd. is taken over by P Ltd. as on that date on the following terms:

(a) 50% of Tangible Fixed Assets are taken over at 100% more than the book value and the remaining Tangible Fixed Assets are taken over at $16\frac{2}{3}\%$ less than the book value.

(b) Goodwill of V Ltd. is to be valued at ₹ 50,000.

(c) Inventories are taken over at book value less 10% and Trade Receivables are taken over at book value subject to an allowance of 10% to cover doubtful debts.

(d) Trade Payables are to be taken over subject to a discount of 5% and Unrecorded Loan Liability of ₹ 38,500 to be discharged by P Ltd. at book value.

(e) The purchase consideration payable by P Ltd. was agreed as follows:

  (i) The purchase consideration is to be discharged to the extent of 20% in cash.

  (ii) The issue of such an amount of fully paid 14% Debentures in P Ltd at 96 per cent as is sufficient to discharge 10% Debentures in V Ltd. at a premium of 20 per cent.

  (iii) The issue of such an amount of fully paid 10% Pref. Shares in P Ltd. at 125% as is sufficient to discharge 9% Pref. Shares in V Ltd. at a premium of 20%.

  (iv) The balance in the form of equity shares of ₹ 10 each, ₹ 8 paid up at a premium of ₹ 7 per share. The market value of an equity share of P Ltd. at present is ₹ 100.

  (v) Expenses of liquidation of V Ltd. are to be reimbursed by P Ltd. to the extent of ₹ 10,000. Actual Expenses amounted to ₹ 12,000.

Show the calculation & discharge of Purchase Consideration & prepare the Balance Sheet of P Ltd.

SOLUTION

1. CALCULATION OF PURCHASE CONSIDERATION

	Particulars	₹
A	Assets taken over at agreed values	
	Tangible Fixed Assets [(₹ 1,50,000 × 50%) + 100%]	1,50,000
	Tangible Fixed Assets [(₹ 1,50,000 × 50%) – $16\frac{2}{3}\%$]	62,500
	Inventories [₹ 55,000 – ₹ 5,500]	49,500
	Trade Receivables [₹ 65,000 – ₹ 6,500]	58,500
	Cash at Bank [89,500 – 10,000(ED) – 4,000(PD) – 2,000(Exp.)]	73,500
	Goodwill	50,000
		4,44,000
B	*Less:* Liabilities taken over:	
	Trade Payables [₹ 1,40,000 – 5%]	1,33,000
	10% Debentures [₹ 50,000 + 20%]	60,000
	Unrecorded Loan	38,500
		2,31,500
C	Net Assets taken over (A – B)	2,12,500

2. DISCHARGE OF PURCHASE CONSIDERATION

Particulars	₹
A. Cash to Equity Shareholders [2,12,500 × 20%]	42,500
B. 480, 9% Pref. Shares to be issued [(500 × 120%)]	60,000
C. 7,333, Equity Shares to be issued [(2,12,500 – 42,500 – 60,000)/ ₹ 15]	1,09,995
D. Cash for Fractional Share(.33 × ₹ 100)	33
E. Total Purchase Consideration (A + B + C + D)	2,12,528

Note: *According to AS-14, the amount paid by purchasing Company to discharge the debentures holders and the liquidation expenses of Vendor Company are not considered as part of purchase consideration.*

BALANCE SHEET OF P LTD. AS AT 31.03.2016

Particulars	Note No	X Ltd. (₹)
I. Equity and Liabilities		
(1) Shareholders' Funds		
(a) Share Capital	1	8,06,664
(b) Reserves and Surplus	2	3,49,531
(2) Non–Current Liabilities		
(a) Long–term Borrowings (14% Debentures)		50,000
(3) Current Liabilities		
(a) Trade Payables [(37,500 – 20,000) + (1,40,000 – 4,000 – 60,000)]		93,500
Total		12,99,695

II. Assets		
(1) Non–Current Assets		
(a) Fixed Assets		
Tangible Assets [4,75,000 + 2,12,500]		6,87,500
Intangible Assets [Goodwill] [51,028 + 10,000 + 6,250 + 800 – 3,000]		65,078
(b) Non–Current Investments[1,09,000 – 9,000]		1,00,000
(c) Other Non–Current Assets [Amalgamation Adjustment A/c]		5,000
(2) Current Assets		
(a) Inventories [(95,000 – 6,250) + (49,500 – 800)]		1,37,450
(b) Trade Receivables [(1,40,000 – 60,000) + (65,000 – 4,500 – 20,000)]		1,20,500
(c) Cash and Cash Equivalents [Cash at Bank] [(2,43,700 – 30,000 – 12,000 – 10,000 – 42,533 – 38,500) + (73,500)]		1,84,167
Total		12,99,695

Notes To Accounts:

Particulars	₹
1. Share Capital	
60,000, Equity Shares of ₹ 10 each	6,00,000
7,333, Equity Shares of ₹ 10 each,₹ 8 paid up	58,664
1,000, 8% Pref. Shares of ₹ 100 each	1,00,000
480, 9% Pref. Shares of ₹ 100 each	48,000
	8,06,664
2. Reserves and Surplus	
General Reserve	1,50,000
Profit & Loss A/c [1,75,200 – 30,000 – 12,000]	1,33,200
Statutory Reserves	5,000
Securities Premium [51,331 + 12,000]	63,331
Less: Discount on Issue of 14% Debentures A/c	(2,000)
	3,49,531

ILLUSTRATION 18 [Take-over on a date other than Balance Sheet Date]

Given below are the extracts from the Balance Sheets of CANHA Ltd. and Krishna Ltd., as at 31st March, 2016:

Particulars	*CAHANA Ltd.* ₹	*Krishna Ltd.* ₹
Equity Share Capital of ₹ 10 each	6,00,000	4,00,000
General Reserve	1,40,000	42,500
Statutory Reserves	—	60,000

Profit & Loss A/c	69,000	56,000
Trade Payables	37,500	30,000
Tangible Fixed Assets	5,00,000	3,50,000
Inventories	95,000	82,500
Trade Receivables	1,40,000	1,00,000
Cash at Bank	1,11,500	56,000

CANHA Ltd., took over and absorbed Krishna Ltd., as on 1st Oct. 2016. No Balance Sheet of Krishna Ltd. was prepared on the date of take-over. But the following information is made available to you:

(a) For the six months ended 30th Sept. 2016, CANHA Ltd and Krishna Ltd., made net profits of ₹ 1,51,000 and ₹ 64,000 after providing for depreciation at 10% per annum on fixed assets;

(b) Both the companies had distributed dividends @ 10% on 1st July 2016.

(c) Goodwill of Krishna Ltd. on the date of take-over was estimated at ₹ 25,000 and it was agreed that the Inventories of Krishna Ltd., subject to an abnormal item of ₹ 7,500 to be fully written off, would be appreciated by 20% for the purpose of take-over:

(d) CANHA Ltd. to issue shares to share-holders of Krishna Ltd., on the basis of the intrinsic value of shares on the date of take-over.

Required: Draft the Balance Sheet of CANHA Ltd., after absorption. (Ignore Corporate Dividend Tax Rate).

SOLUTION

BALANCE SHEET OF CANHA LTD. AS AT 1.10.2016

Particulars	*Note No*	*₹ (lacs)*
I. Equity and Liabilities		
(1) Shareholders' Funds		
(a) Share Capital	1	10.100
(b) Reserves and Surplus	2	5.650
(2) Non-Current Liabilities		
(3) Current Liabilities Trade Payables [0.375 + 0.30]		0.675
Total		16.425
II. Assets		
(1) Non-Current Assets		
(a) Fixed Assets		
Tangible Assets [5 + 3.325 – 0.25]		8.075
Intangible Assets		0.250
(b) Other Non-Current Assets	3	0.600
(2) Current Assets		
(a) Inventories [0.95 + (82,500 – 7,500) + 20%]		1.850
(b) Trade Receivables [1.40 + 1.00]		2.400
(c) Cash and Cash Equivalents	1	3.250
Total		16.425

Notes To Accounts:

	Particulars	₹ *(lacs)*
1.	**Share Capital**	
	101,000 Equity Shares of ₹ 10 each	10.10
	(Of the above 41,000 Shares were issued for consideration otherwise than cash)	
2.	**Reserves and Surplus**	
	Securities Premium [41,000 x ₹ 5]	2.05
	General Reserve	1.40
	Statutory Reserves	0.60
	Profit & Loss Account [0.69 + 1.51 – 0.60]*	1.60
		5.65
3.	**Other Non-Current Assets** [Amalgamation Adjustment A/c]	0.60

Working Notes:

(I) CALCULATION OF CLOSING CASH & BANK BALANCE

	Particulars	*CAHANA Ltd.* ₹	*Krishna Ltd.* ₹
A	Opening Balance	1,11,500	56,000
B	Add Net Profit	1,51,000	64,000
C	*Add:* Depreciation	25,000	17,500
		2,87,500	1,37,500
D	*Less:* Dividend	60,000	40,000
E	Closing Cash & Bank Balance (A + B + C – D)	2,27,500	97,500

(II) CALCULATION OF INTRINSIC VALUE OF SHARES

	Particulars	*CAHANA Ltd.* ₹	*Krishna Ltd.* ₹
A	Total Assets at current values		
	Goodwill	—	25,000
	Fixed Assets	4,75,000	3,32,500
	Trade Receivables	1,40,000	1,00,000
	Inventories *[(82,500 -7,500) + 20%]	95,000	90,000*
	Cash & Bank [Refer to Working Note (i)]	2,27,500	97,500
		9,37,500	6,45,000
B	*Less:* Liabilities	(37,500)	(30,000)
C	Net Assets at current values [A – B]	9,00,000	6,15,000
D	No. of shares	60,000	40,000
E	Intrinsic value per share {C/D}	15	15.375

(III) CALCULATION OF NO. OF SHARES TO BE ISSUED BY PURCHASING COMPANY

A	Net assets of vendor company take over	6,15,000
B	Intrinsic value of an equity share of Purchasing company	15
C	No of shares to be issued by Purchasing company (A/B)	41,000

Note: *In the absence of information about changes in other assets, it is assumed that the profit has resulted in cash only.*

10.0 TREATMENT OF RESERVES ARISING ON AMALGAMATION IN THE NATURE OF MERGER

1. **Provision as per AS-14 [Paragraph 35]**

   The difference betwen the amount recorded as share capital issued (*plus any additional consideration in the form of cash and other assets*) and the amount of the share capital of the transferor company should be adjusted in reserves.

2. **Opinon of the Expert Advisory Committee of ICAI [Published in 22nd Volume]**

   (a) The difference between the share capital of the transferor companies and share capital issued by company on amalgamation should be treated as **Capital Reserve** for the purpose of paragraph 35 of AS-14.

   (b) Reserve created on amalgamation is not available for the purpose of distribution to shareholders as dividend and/or bonus shares.

3. **Author's Opinion**

   (a) The excess of share capital of the transferor company over the purchase consideration should be treated as **Capital Reserve** which shall not be available for distribution as dividend *or* bonus.

   (b) The excess of purchase consideration over the share capital of the transferor company should be treated as Capital loss and should be adjusted:

   (i) first against the Capital Reserves

   (ii) then against the Revenue Reserves (if capital reserves are insufficient)

Note: *If Revenue Reserves are also insuficient, the necessary required amount should be transferred to Revenue Reserves by debting Profit & Loss Account. After such transfer if Profit & Loss Account shows debit balance it will be shown as a negative item under Reserves and Surplus.*

ILLUSTRATION 19 [Treatment of Reserves arising on Amalgamation in the nature of Merger]

X Ltd. took over all the assets & liabilities of Y Ltd. and discharged the consideration by issue of equity shares and cash for fractional shares. Calculate the balances of Reserves and Profit & Loss Account which are to appear in the Balance Sheet of X Ltd. in each of the following cases:

(*₹ in lacs*)

Particulars	*Case I* ₹	*Case II* ₹	*Case III* ₹	*Case IV* ₹	*Case V* ₹
Share Capital issued by X Ltd.	9.50	9.50	9.50	9.50	9.50
Cash for Fractional Shares paid by X Ltd.	.50	.50	.50	.50	.50
Share Capital of Y Ltd.	9.65	9.45	9.15	9.00	8.80
Capital Reserves of Y Ltd.	.40	.40	.40	.40	.40
Revenue Reserves of Y Ltd.	.30	.30	.30	.30	.30
Statutory Reserves of Y Ltd.	.20	.20	.20	.20	.20
Profit & Loss A/c of Y Ltd.	.10	.10	.10	.10	.10
Capital Reserve of X Ltd.	.10	.10	.10	.10	.10

Revenue Reserve of X Ltd.	.20	.20	.20	.20	.20
Profit & Loss Account of X Ltd.	.05	.05	.05	.05	.05

SOLUTION

CALCULATION OF BALANCES OF RESERVES AND PROFIT & LOSS ACCOUNT *[₹ in lacs]*

Particulars	₹	₹	₹	₹	₹
A. Purchase Consideration					
Share Capital Issued:	9.50	9.50	9.50	9.50	9.50
Cash for Fractional Shares paid	.50	.50	.50	.50	.50
	10.00	10.00	10.00	10.00	10.00
B. *Less:* Share Capital of Transferor Co.	9.65	9.45	9.15	9.00	8.80
C. Difference to be adjusted (A–B)	0.35	0.55	0.85	1.00	1.20
D. Debited to:					
Capital Reserves (of Both Co.)	0.35	.50	.50	.50	.50
Revenue Reserves (of Both Co.)	—	.05	.35	.50	.50
Profit & Loss A/c (of Both Co.)	—	—	—	—	.20
	.35	.55	.85	1.00	1.20
Balances of Reserves & P&L A/c:					
Capital Reserves	.15	—	—	—	—
Revenue Reserves	.50	.45	.15	—	—
Statutory Reserves	.20	.20	.20	.20	.20
Profit & Loss A/c (Credit)	.15	.15	.15	.15	—
Profit & Loss A/c (Debit)	—	—	—	—	0.05

11.0 ACCOUNTING TREATMENT IN THE BOOKS OF TRANSFEREE COMPANY *or* PURCHASING COMPANY IN CASE OF MERGER

Step 1: Record the Acquisition of business from the vendor company.

JOURNAL ENTRY

Business Merger A/c	Dr.	*(with Purchase Consideration)*
To Liquidator of the Vendor Co.		

Step 2: In case of Amalgamation in the nature of Merger

"Record the Assets, Liabilities and Reserves (whether Statutory Reserves *or* not) at their respective book values".

JOURNAL ENTRY

Assets (Individually)	Dr.	*[with their respective book values]*
To Liabilities (Individually)		*[with their respective book values]*
To Provision for Doubtful Debts		*[with the book balance]*
To Provision for Depreciation etc.		*[with the book balance]*

To Reserves (other than Revenue Reserves)	*[with their respective book balances]*
To General Reserve	*[Balancing figure]*
To Business Merger A/c	*[with Purchase Consideration]*

Step 3: Make Payment to Vendor Company.

JOURNAL ENTRY

Liquidator of Vendor Co.'s A/c	Dr.	*(with the total)*
Discount on Issue of Shares A/c	Dr.	*(with the Discount allowed on shares)*
To Equity Share Capital A/c		*(with the paid up value of Equity Shares issued)*
To Preference Share Capital A/c		*(with the paid up value of Pref. Shares issued)*
To Securities Premium A/c		*(with the Securities Premium)*
To Cash A/c Bank A/c		*(with the Cash Payment)*

Note: *The Shares issued by way of purchase consideration must be recorded at their paid up values (i.e., not at their issued prices) after giving due credit to Securities Premium Account (in case the shares have been issued at premium) or after giving due debit to "Discount on issue of Shares A/c' (in case the shares have been issued at discount).*

Step 4: Record the Issue of Debentures (if any) to discharge the existing debentureholders of Vendor Company.

JOURNAL ENTRY

Debentures in Vendor Company	Dr.	*(with the amount of debentures)*
Discount on Issue of Debentures in Purchasing Company	Dr.	*(with the debentures discount)*
To Debentures in Purchasing Company		*(with the nominal value)*
To Securities Premium A/c		*(with the debenture premium)*

Step 5: Record the Reimbursement of the Liquidation Expenses of the vendor company.

JOURNAL ENTRY

Profit & Loss A/c (in case of Merger)	Dr.
To Bank A/c	

Step 6: Eliminate the Unrealised Profit included in the Unsold Inventories.

(a) ***Where the Unsold Inventories of the purchasing company includes the goods purchased from the vendor company***

P&L A/c (in Case of Merger)	Dr.
To Inventories A/c	

(b) ***Where the Unsold Inventories of the vendor company includes goods purchased from the purchasing company, only the amount of stock is reduced to its cost while passing the entries on acquisition. (i.e., Entry in Step 2).***

Note: *In case of sale of goods at loss, no adjustment is required.*

Step 7: Eliminate the Inter Company Owings

(a) To eliminate the Debts owed by Vendor Company	Trade Payables of Vendor Co	Dr.
	To Trade Receivables	

(b) To eliminate the Debts owed by Purchasing Company	Trade Payables Dr. To Trade Receivables of Vendor Co.
(c) To eliminate the Bills drawn and retained by Vendor Co. upon Purchasing Company	Bills Payable A/c Dr. To Bills Receivable of Vendor Co.
(d) To eliminate the Bills drawn and retained by Purchasing Company upon Vendor Co.	Bills Payable of Vendor Co. Dr. To Bills Receivable A/c
(e) To eliminate the Debentures held by Vendor Co. in Purchasing Co.	Debentures A/c Dr. [Face value] Profit & Loss A/c Dr. [If FV < BV] To Investment in Debentures A/c (*Vendor Co.*) [Book Value] To Capital Reserve A/c [If FV > BV]
(f) To eliminate the Debentures held by Purchasing Co. in Vendor Co.	Debentures in Vendor Co. Dr. [Face Value] Profit & Loss A/c Dr. [If FV < BV] To Investment in Debentures A/c Dr. [Book value] To Capital Reserve A/c [If FV > BV]

Notes

(i) *Bills drawn by one company upon the other company and discounted with the bank should not be eliminated because these bills represent owing between the bank and the company and not the inter-company owings.*

(ii) *Where the debtors of a company include a sum due from another company but the creditors of another company include a lesser sum due to the former company. The difference should be treated as cash-in-transit.*

(iii) *The entry (f) in* ***Step 7*** *should be merged with entry in* ***Step 4*** *so that the new debentures will be issued to discharge those debentures of vendor company which are held by outsiders (i.e., holders other than the purchasing company).*

(iv) *In case of entries (e) and (f), the loss should be debited to P & L A/c (in case of merger) and the profit should be credited to Capital Reserve A/c.*

ILLUSTRATION 20

V Ltd has Equity Share Capital of ₹ 95,00,000, Tangible Fixed Assets of ₹ 65,00,000 and Current Assets of ₹ 85,00,000 , Statutory Reserves of ₹ 5,00,000 and General Reserve of ₹ 28,00,000 , Current Liabilities of ₹ 19,00,000, Non-Current Liabilities of ₹ 3,00,000 as at 31.3.2016. Statutory Reserves are to be maintained for 2 more years. The business of V Ltd. is taken over by P Ltd. by issue of 1,00,000 equity shares of ₹ 100 each at 20% premium. Journalise in the books of P Ltd.

SOLUTION

JOURNAL OF P LTD.

Date	Particulars	L.F.	Dr. (₹)	Cr. (₹)
	Business Merger A/c. Dr. To Liquidator of V Ltd. A/c. (Being the Business taken over)		120,00,000	120,00,000

	Tangible Fixed Assets	Dr.	65,00,000	
	Current Assets	Dr.	85,00,000	
	To Non-Current Liabilities			3,00,000
	To Current Liabilities			19,00,000
	To Business Merger A/c			120,00,000
	To General Reserve *(balancing figure)*			**3,00,000**
	To Statutory Reserves			5,00,000
	(Being the assets, liabilities and reserves taken over recorded)			
	Liquidator of V Ltd.	Dr.	120,00,000	
	To Equity Share Capital A/c.			100,00,000
	To Securities Premium A/c.			20,00,000
	(Being the purchase consideration discharged)			

Note: Closing Balance of General Reserve = Given Balance of General Reserve – Difference between purchase consideration and the amount of Share capital of the transferor company

= ₹28,00,000 – (₹120,00,000 – ₹ 95,00,000)

= ₹ 3,00,000

ILLUSTRATION 21

Given below are the extracts from the Balance Sheets of A Ltd. and B Ltd. as at 31.03.2016:

Particulars	*A Ltd. (₹ in lacs)*	*B Ltd. (₹ in lacs)*
Equity Share Capital of ₹ 100 each	80	75
12% Pref. Share Capital of ₹ 100 each	30	20
Capital Reserve	1	1
Capital Redemption Reserve	3	3
Statutory Reserves	5	5
General Reserve	31	22
Profit & Loss A/c	2	2
10% Debentures of ₹ 100 each	6	3
Current Liabilities	42	19
Tangible Fixed Assets	90	65
Non-Current Investments	15	5
Current Assets	95	80

Additional Information:

(a) 10% Debentures of the transferor company are to be discharged by transferee company by issuing such number of its 15% Debentures of ₹ 100 each so as to maintain the same amount of interest.

(b) 12% Preference shares of the transferor company are to be discharged by transferee company by issuing equivalent numbers of 15% preference Shares of ₹ 100 each at ₹ 150 each.

(c) The transferee company shall issue 4 equity shares of ₹ 10 each at ₹ 30 each for each equity share in the transferor company.

(d) The Statutory Reserves are to be maintained for 2 more years.

(e) The transferee company shall pay the cost of absorption which amount to ₹ 1,00,000

Required: (a) Prepare Journal of transferor company (b) Prepare the Journal and Balance Sheet of Transferee Company in each of the following alternative cases:

Case I If A Ltd. absorbs B Ltd. and the amalgamation is in the nature of a purchase.

Case II If A Ltd. absorbs B Ltd., and the amalgamation is in the nature of a merger.

SOLUTION

JOURNAL OF B LTD. *(₹ in lacs)*

Particulars		*L.F.*	*Dr. (₹)*	*Cr. (₹)*
Realisation A/c	Dr.		150	
To Tangible Fixed Assets				65
To Investments				5
To Current Assets				80
(Being the transfer of various assets)				
10% Debentures A/c	Dr.		3	
Current Liabilities	Dr.		19	
To Realisation A/c				22
(Being the t/f of various liabilities taken over by the Purchasing Co.)				
A Ltd.	Dr.		120	
To Realisation A/c				120
(Being the purchase Consideration due from A Ltd.)				
15% Pref. Shares in A Ltd.	Dr.		30	
Equity Shares in A Ltd.	Dr.		90	
To A Ltd.				120
(Being the receipt of purchase consideration)				
12% Preference Share Capital A/c	Dr.		20	
Realisation A/c	Dr.		10	
To 12% Preference Shareholders' A/c				30
(Being the amount due to 12% Pref. shareholders)				
12% Preference Shareholders' A/c	Dr.		30	
To 15% Pref. Shares in A Ltd.				30
(Being the payment made to pref. shareholders)				
Equity Shareholders' A/c	Dr.		18	
To Realisation A/c				18
(Being the transfer of loss on realisation)				
Equity Share Capital A/c	Dr.		75	
Capital Reserve	Dr.		1	

Capital Redemption Reserve	Dr.		3	
Statutory Reserves	Dr.		5	
General Reserve	Dr.		22	
Profit & Loss A/c	Dr.		2	
To Equity Shareholders' A/cs				108
(Being the transfer of Equity Share capital, Reserves and accumulated profits)				
Equity Shareholders' A/cs	Dr.		90	
To Equity Shares in A Ltd.				90
(Being the final payment made to Equity shareholders)				

CASE I: IF THE AMALGAMATION IN THE NATURE OF PURCHASE

JOURNAL OF A LTD.

[₹ in lacs]

Particulars		L.F.	Dr. (₹)	Cr. (₹)
Business Purchase A/c	Dr.		120	
To Liquidator of B Ltd.				120
(Being the purchase of business as per agreement dated...)				
Tangible Fixed Assets	Dr.		65	
Investments	Dr.		5	
Current Assets	Dr.		80	
To 10% Debentures A/c				2
To Current Liabilities				19
To Business Purchase A/c				120
To Capital Reserve A/c				9
(Being the assets & liabilities taken over recorded)				
Amalgamation Adjustment A/c	Dr.		5	
To Statutory Reserves A/c				5
(Being the identity of statutory Reserves retained)				
Liquidator of B Ltd.	Dr.		120	
To Equity Share Capital A/c				30
To 15% Pref. Share Capital A/c				20
To Securities Premium A/c [60 + 10]				70
(Being the purchase consideration discharged)				
Goodwill A/c	Dr.		1	
To Bank A/c				1
(Being the cost of absorption of B Ltd. paid)				
10% Debentures A/c	Dr.		2	
To 15% Debentures A/c				2
(Being the issue of 15% Debentures to 10% Debentureholders of B Ltd.) [No. of 15% Debentures = ₹ 30,000/15 = 2,000]				

Capital Reserve A/c Dr.		1	
To Goodwill A/c			1
(Being the goodwill adjusted against Capital Reserve)			

BALANCE SHEET OF A LTD. AS AT 31.3.2016

Particulars	*Note No*	*₹ (lacs)*
I. Equity and Liabilities		
(1) Shareholders' Funds		
(a) Share Capital	1	160
(b) Reserves and Surplus	2	125
(2) Non-Current Liabilities		
(a) Long-term Borrowings	3	8
(3) Current Liabilities [42 + 19]		61
Total		354
II. Assets		
(1) Non-Current Assets		
(a) Fixed Assets		
Tangible Assets [90 + 65]		155
(b) Non-Current Investments [15 + 5]		20
(c) Other Non-Current Assets [Amalgamation Adjustment A/c]		5
(2) Current Assets [95 + 80 – 1]		174
Total		354

Notes To Accounts:

Particulars	*₹ (lacs)*
1. Share Capital	
80,000 Equity Shares of ₹ 100 each	80
3,00,000 Equity Shares of ₹ 10 each	30
30,000 Pref. Shares of ₹ 100 each	30
20,000, 15% Pref. Shares of ₹ 100 each	20
(Of the above 3 lacs equity Shares were issued for consideration otherwise than cash)	
	160
2. Reserves and Surplus	
Securities Premium [60 + 10]	70
General Reserve	31
Profit & Loss Account	2
Capital Reserve	1
Capital Reserve on Amalgamation	8
Capital Redemption Reserve	3
Statutory Reserves	10
	125

3. **Long-term Borrowings**	
10% Debentures of ₹ 100 each	6
15% Debentures of ₹ 100 each	2
	8

Working Notes:

(I) CALCULATION OF PURCHASE CONSIDERATION

for preference Shareholders [(20,00,000/100) × ₹ 150]	30,00,000
for Equity Shareholders [{(75,00,000/100) × 4} × ₹ 150]	90,00,000
	120,00,000

(II) CALCULATION OF NET ASSETS TAKEN OVER AT THEIR AGREED VALUES

A	Total Assets taken over at their agreed values	
	Fixed Assets	65,00,000
	Investments	5,00,000
	Current Assets	80,00,000
		150,00,000
B	*Less:* Liabilities taken over at their agreed amounts	
	10% Debentures	2,00,000
	Current Liabilities	19,00,000
		21,00,000
C	Net Assets taken over (A – B)	129,00,000

(iii) *Calculation of Capital Reserve on amalgamation*

Capital Reserve = Net Assets taken over at their agreed values – Purchase consideration

= ₹ 129,00,000 – ₹ 120,00,000 = ₹ 9,00,000

CASE II: IF AMALGAMATION IS IN THE NATURE OF MERGER
JOURNAL OF A LTD.

(₹ in lacs)

Particulars		*L.F.*	*Dr. (₹)*	*Cr. (₹)*
Business Merger A/c	Dr.		120	
To Liquidator of B Ltd.				120
(Being the purchase of business as per agreement dated....)				
Tangible Fixed Assets	Dr.		65	
Investments	Dr.		5	
Current Assets	Dr.		80	
To 10% Debentures A/c				3
To Current Liabilities				19
To Business Merger A/c				120
To Capital Redemption Reserve				3
To Statutory Reserves				5
(Being the assets, liabilities and reserves taken over recorded)				

Liquidator of B Ltd.	Dr.	120	
To Equity Share Capital A/c			30
To 15% Preference Share Capital A/c			20
To Securities Premium A/c (60 + 10)			70
(Being the purchase consideration discharged)			
Profit & Loss A/c	Dr.	1	
To Bank A/c			1
(Being the cost of absorption of B Ltd. paid)			
10% Debentures A/c	Dr.	3	
To 15% Debentures, A/c			2
To Capital Reserve A/c			1
(Being the issue of 15% Debentures to 10% Debentureholders of B Ltd.) No. of 15% Debenturers = ₹ 30,000/.15 = 20,000]			

BALANCE SHEET OF A LTD. AS AT 31.3.2016

Particulars	Note No	₹ *(lacs)*
I. Equity and Liabilities		
(1) Shareholders'Funds		
(a) Share Capital	1	160
(b) Reserves and Surplus	2	120
(2) Non-Current Liabilities [Long-term Borrowings]	3	8
(3) Current Liabilities [42 + 19]		61
Total		349
II. Assets		
(1) Non-Current Assets		
(a) Fixed Assets		
Tangible Assets [90 + 65]		155
(b) Non-Current Investments [15 + 5]		20
(2) Current Assets [95 + 80 – 1]		174
Total		349

Notes To Accounts:

Particulars	₹ *(lacs)*
1. Share Capital	
80,000 Equity share of ₹ 100 each	80
3,00,000 Equity Shares of ₹ 10 each	30
30,000 Pref. Shares of ₹ 100 each	30
20,000, 15% Pref. Sahres of ₹ 100 each	20
(Of the above 3 lacs equity Shares were issued for consideration otherwise than cash)	
	160

2.	**Reserves and Surplus**	
	Securities Premium [60 + 10]	70
	General Reserve[Refer to WN]	31
	Profit & Loss Account [2 + 2 – 1]	3
	Capital Redemption Reserve	6
	Statutory Reserves	10
		120
3.	**Long-term Borrowings**	
	10% Debentures of ₹ 100 each	6
	15% Debenture of ₹ 100 each	2
		8

Working Notes:

(I) CALCULATION OF PURCHASE CONSIDERATION

Particulars	*No. of Shares*	*Issue Price*	*Total*
For Preference Shareholders	20,000	₹ 150	30,00,000
For Equity Shareholders (75000 × 4)	3,00,000	₹ 30	90,00,000
			120,00,000

(ii) *Calculation of the difference between purchase consideration and the amount of share capital of the transferor company*

Difference = ₹ 120,00,000 – ₹ 95,00,000 (Equity + Pref.) = ₹ 25,00,000

(iii) *Calculation of the difference between the amount of Debentures of transferor company taken over and the amount of Debentures of the transferee company issued in exchange*

Difference = ₹ 3,00,000 – ₹ 2,00,000 = ₹, 1,00,000 (Profit)

(IV) ADJUSTMENT OF DIFFERENCE AGAINST THE RESERVES AND ACCUMULATED PROFITS OF TRANSFEREOR CO.

A	Difference between Purchase Consideration & Share Capital	25.00
B	*Less:* Capital Reserves of both Co. (1+1 + 1)	(3.00)
C	Balance to be adjusted against Revenue Reserve	22.00
D	General Reserves of both Co. (31 + 22)	53.00
E	Closing Balance of General Reserves [D–C]	31.00

AMALGAMATION OF TWO OR MORE COMPANIES IN THE NATURE OF PURCHASE WHEN A NEW COMPANY IS FORMED

ILLUSTRATION 22

Sun Ltd. and Moon Ltd. were amalgamated on and from 1st April, 2016. A new company Star Ltd. was formed to take over the business of the existing companies. Given below are the extracts from the Balance Sheets of Sun Ltd. and Moon Ltd. as at 31st March, 2016 :

(₹ in lakhs)

Particulars	*Sun Ltd.*	*Moon Ltd.*
Equity Shares of ₹ 100 each	400	375
12% Preference Shares of ₹100 each	150	100
Reserves & Surplus	210	165
10% Debentures (₹100 each)	30	15
Current Liabilities	210	95
Tangible Fixed Assets	450	275
Non-Current Investments	75	25
Current Assets	575	450

Additional Information:

(a) Star Ltd. will issue 5 equity shares for each equity share of Sun Ltd. and 4 equity shares for each equity share of Moon Ltd. The shares are to be issued @ ₹ 30 each, having a face value of ₹ 10 per share.

(b) Preference shareholders of the two companies are issued equivalent number of 15% preference shares of Star Ltd. at a price of ₹ 150 per share (face value ₹ 100).

(c) 10% Debentureholders of Sun Ltd. and Moon Ltd. are discharged by Star Ltd., issuing such number of its 15% Debentures of ₹100 each so as to maintain the same amount of interest.

(d) Investment allowance reserve is to be maintained for 4 more years.

(e) Liquidation expenses are: Sun Ltd. ₹ 2,00,000 Moon Ltd. ₹ 1,00,000. It was decided that these expenses would be borne by Star Ltd.

(f) All the assets and liabilities of Sun Ltd. and Moon Ltd. are taken over at book value.

Required: Calculate Purchase Consideration and show the discharge thereof.

SOLUTION

CALCULATION OF PURCHASE CONSIDERATION

Particulars	*X Ltd.*	*Y Ltd.*	*Total*
A. No of Equity Shares	4,00,000	3,75,000	
B. Exchange Ratio	5:1	4:1	
C. No of Equity Shares to be issued by [A × B]	20,00,000	15,00,000	35,00,000
Equity Share Capital @ ₹ 20	400,00,000	300,00,000	700,00,000
Securities Premium@ ₹ 10	200,00,000	150,00,000	350,00,000
D. No of 15% Pref.Shares to be issued	1,50,000	1,00,000	2,50,000
15% Pref. Share Capital @ ₹ 100	150,00,000	100,00,000	250,00,000

Securities Premium@ ₹ 50	75,00,000	50,00,000	125,00,000
Total Purchase Consideration	825,00,000	600,00,000	1425,00,000

Note: *According to AS-14, the amount paid by purchasing Company to discharge the debentures holders and the liquidation expenses of Vendor Company are not considered as part of purchase consideration.*

ILLUSTRATION 23

Given below are the extracts from the Balance Sheets of X Ltd and Y Ltd. as at 31st March 2016:

Particulars	*X Ltd. (₹ in lacs)*	*Y Ltd. (₹ in lacs)*
Equity Share Capital of ₹ 10 each	5.00	10.00
8% Pref. Share Capital of ₹ 100 each	1.00	2.00
Reserves & Surplus	21.71	3.00
12% Debentures of ₹ 100 each	2.00	1.00
Current Liabilities	1.00	2.20
Net Tangible Assets	19.00	7.60
Non-Current Investments	3.45	5.20
Current Assets	8.26	5.40

The two companies agree to amalgamate as on Ist April, 2016 and form a new company XY Ltd.

Additional Information:

(a) Goodwill of X Ltd. and Y Ltd. on the date of take-over was valued at ₹ 48,000 and ₹ 38,000 respectively and Net Tangible Blocks of X Ltd. and Y Ltd were valued at 10% above their book values on the date of take-over.Investments of X Ltd. and Y Ltd. are considered worth ₹ 4,16,000 and ₹ 6,26,000 respectively.

(b) 12% Debentures of X Ltd. and Y Ltd. are discharged by XY Ltd. by issuing such number of its 15% Debentures of ₹ 100 each so as to maintain the same amount of interest.

(c) The issue of such an amount of fully paid 10% Pref. Shares in X Y Ltd. at 125% as is sufficient to discharge 9% Pref. Shares in X Ltd. & Y Ltd. at a premium of 20%.

(d) The Equity Shares of XY Ltd are to be of a nominal value of ₹ 10 each credited as ₹ 8 paid up and valued at ₹ 15 per share.

(e) Liquidation expenses are: X Ltd. ₹ 2,000 ,Y Ltd. ₹ 1,000. It was decided that these expenses would be borne by XY Ltd.Expenses on incorporation of XY Ltd. were ₹ 1,000.

Required: Calculate Purchase Consideration and show the discharge thereof.

SOLUTION

(I) COMPUTATION OF VALUE OF NET ASSETS FOR EQUITY SHAREHOLDERS ₹ (LAKHS)

Particulars	*X Ltd.*	*Y Ltd.*
A. Total Assets at their Current Values:		
Goodwill	0.48	0.38
Net Tangible Block	20.90	8.36
Non-Current Investments	4.16	6.26
Current Assets	8.26	5.40

	33.80	**20.40**
B. *Less:* Liabilities at their Current Amounts:		
12% Debentures [Interest/15%]	1.60	0.80
Current Liabilities	1.00	2.20
8% Pref. Share Capital	1.20	2.40
	3.80	**5.40**
C. Net Assets for Equity Shareholders [A – B]	**30.00**	**15.00**

(II) CALCULATION OF NO. OF EQUITY SHARES TO BE ISSUED BY PURCHASING COMPANY

Particulars	*X Ltd.*	*Y Ltd.*	*Total*
A. Total Value (as calculated above)	30,00,000	15,00,000	45,00,000
B. Issue Price of an Equity Share	15	15	15
C. No of Equity Shares to be issued by [A/B]	2,00,000	1,00,000	3,00,000
Equity Share Capital @ ₹ 8	16,00,000	8,00,000	24,00,000
Securities Premium@ ₹ 7	14,00,000	7,00,000	21,00,000

(III) CALCULATION OF PURCHASING CONSIDERATION

Particulars	*X Ltd.*	*Y Ltd.*	*Total*
Equity Shares @ ₹ 15	30,00,000	15,00,000	45,00,000
9% Pref. Shares @ ₹ 125	1,20,000	2,40,000	3,60,000
Total	31,20,000	17,40,000	48,60,000

Note: *According to AS-14, the amount paid by purchasing Company to discharge the debentures holders and the liquidation expenses of Vendor Company are not considered as part of purchase consideration.*

ILLUSTRATION 24

P Ltd. and Q Ltd. were carrying on the business of manufacturing of auto components. both the companies decided to amalgamare and a new company PQ Ltd. is to be formed with an Authorized Capital of ₹ 10,00,000 divided into 1,00,000 equity shares of ₹ 10 each. The Balance Sheet of the companies as on 31.03.2016 were as under:

Particulars	*P (₹)*	*Q (₹)*
I. Equity and Liabilities		
1. Shareholder's Fund		
(a) Share Capital	1,40,000	2,50,000
(b) Reserves & Surplus (Profit & Loss A/c)	30,000	1,55,000
2. Non Current Liabilities (8 % Secured Debentures)	1,10,000	—
3. Current Liabilities (Trade Payables)	54,000	1,40,000
Total	3,34,000	5,45,000
II. Assets		
1. Non-current Assets		
(a) Tangible Fixed Assets	1,25,000	2,95,000

2. Current Assets		
(a) Inventories	1,35,000	50,000
(b) Trade Receivables	44,000	1,42,000
(c) Cash at bank	30,000	58,000
Total	3,34,000	5,45,000

The assets and liabilities of the existing companies are to be transferred at book value with the exception of some items detailed below:

(i) Goodwill of P Ltd. was worth ₹ 50,000 and of Q Ltd. was worth ₹ 1,50,000,.

(ii) Tangible Fixed Assets of Q Ltd. was valued at ₹ 3,05,000.

(iii) The Trade Receivables of P Ltd. are realized fully and bank balance of P Ltd. are to be retained by the liquidator and the Trade Payables are to be paid of the proceeds thereof.

(iv) The debentures of P Ltd. are to be dischareged by issue of 8% debentures of PQ Ltd. at a premium of 10%.

You are required to:

(i) Compute the basis on which shares in PQ Ltd. will be issued at par to the shareholders of the existing companies.

(ii) Draw up a Balance Sheet of PQ Ltd. as at 1st April, 2016, the date of completiion of amalgamatiion.

(iii) Write up Journal entires including bank entries for closing the books of P Ltd.

SOLUTION

CALCULATION OF PURCHASE CONSIDERATION

Particulars	*P Ltd. (₹)*	*Q Ltd. (₹)*
Assets taken over:		
Goodwill	50,000	1,50,000
Tangible Fixed Assets	1,20,000	3,05,000
Inventories	1,35,000	50,000
Trade Receivables	–	1,42,000
Cash at Bank	–	58,000
	3,10,000	7,05,000
Less: Liabilities taken over:		
8% Debentures	(1,21,000)	–
Trade Payables	–	(1,40,000)
Net Assets taken over	1,89,000	5,65,000
To be satisfied by issue of shares of PQ Ltd. of ₹ 10 each at par	18,900	56,500

BALANCE SHEET OF PQ LIMITED AS AT 1ST APRIL, 2016

Particulars	*Note No.*	*(₹)*
I. Equity and Liabilities		
(1) Shareholder's Funds		
(a) Share Capital	1	7,54,000
(b) Reserve & Surplus [Securities Premium]		11,000

(2) Non-Current Liabilities	
(a) Long term borrowings [8% Debentures]	1,10,000
(3) Current Liabilities	
(a) Trade Payables	1,40,000
Total	10,15,000
II. Assets	
(1) Non-Current assets	
(a) Fixed Assets	
Tangible [₹ 1,25,000 + ₹ 3,05,000]	4,30,000
Intangible [₹ 50,000 + ₹ 1,50,000]	2,00,000
(2) Current Assets	
(a) Inventories	1,85,000
(b) Trade Receivables	1,42,000
(c) Cash at Bank	58,000
Total	10,15,000

Notes to Accounts:

Particulars	₹
1. Share Capital	
Authorized	
1,00,000 shares of ₹ 10 eac	10,00,000
Issued, Subscribed and Paid up	
75,400 shares of ₹ 10 each (All the above shares are allotted as fully paid up pursuant to scheme of amalgamation withut payments being received in cash)	7,54,000

JOURNAL OF P LTD.

Date	*Particulars*		*L.F.*	*Dr. (₹)*	*Cr. (₹)*
1	Realization A/c	Dr.		3,04,000	
	To Tangible Fixed Assets				1,25,000
	To Inventories				1,35,000
	To Trade Receivables				44,000
	(Being all assets except cash t/f to Realization A/c)				
2	8% Debentures A/c	Dr.		1,10,000	
	Trade Payables	Dr.		54,000	
	To Realization A/c				1,64,000
	(Being all liabilities transferred to Realization Account)				
3	Equity Share Capital A/c	Dr.		1,40,000	
	Profit & Loss A/c	Dr.		30,000	
	To Equity Shareholder's A/c				1,70,000
	(Being Equity transferred to Equity Shareholder's A/c)				

4	PQ Ltd.	Dr.	1,89,000	
	To Realization A/c			1,89,000
	(Being Purchase consideration due)			
5	Bank A/c	Dr.	44,000	
	To Realization A/c			44,000
	(Being cash received from trade receivables in full)			
6	Realization A/c	Dr.	54,000	
	To Bank A/c			54,000
	(Being payment made to Trade Payables)			
7	Share in PQ Ltd.	Dr.	1,89,000	
	To PQ Ltd.			1,89,000
	(Being purchase consideration received in the form of Equity Shares of PQ Ltd.)			
8	Realization A/c (balancing figure)	Dr.	39,000	
	To Equity Shareholder's A/c			39,000
	(Being profit on realization transferred to Equity Shareholder's A/c)			
9	Equity Shareholder's A/c	Dr.	2,09,000	
	To Shares in PQ Ltd.			1,89,000
	To Bank A/c			20,000
	(Being final payment made to shareholders)			

ILLUSTRATION 25

Given below are the extracts of Balance Sheets of M Ltd. and N Ltd. as at 31st March, 2016:

(₹ in lakhs)

Particulars	*M Ltd.*	*N Ltd.*
Equity Shares of ₹10 each	3,600	900
10% Preference Shares of ₹ 10 each	1,200	–
Capital Reserve	600	–
General Reserve	2,100	–
Profit and Loss Account	780	(39)
8% Redeemable Debentures of ₹ 1,000 each	–	300
Trade Payables	3,291	462
Tangible Fixed Assets	6,615	702
Inventories	2,370	444
Trade Receivables	1,044	237
Cash at Bank	1,542	240

A new Company MN Ltd. was incorporated with an authorised capital of ₹ 15,000 lakhs divided into shares of ₹ 10 each. For the purpose of amalgamation in the nature of merger, M Ltd. and N Ltd. were merged into MN Ltd. on the following terms:

(i) Purchase consideration for M Ltd.'s business is to be discharged by issue of 120 lakhs fully paid 11% preference shares and 720 lakhs fully paid equity shares of MN Ltd. to the preference and equity shareholders of M Ltd. in full satisfaction of their claims.

(ii) To discharge purchase consideration for N Ltd. 's business, MN Ltd. to allot 90 lakhs fully paid up equity shares to shareholders of N Ltd. in full satisfaction of their claims.

(iii) Expenses on the liquidation of M Ltd. and N Ltd. amounting to ₹ 6 lakhs are to be borne by MN Ltd.

(iv) 8% Redeemable Debentures of N Ltd. to be converted into 8.5% redeemable debentures of MN Ltd.

(v) Expenses on incorporation of MN Ltd. were ₹15 lakhs.

You are required to:

(a) Pass necessary Journal Entries in the books of MN Ltd. to record above transactions, and

(b) Prepare Balance Sheet of MN Ltd. after merger.

SOLUTION

JOURNAL OF MN LTD. *(₹ in lakhs)*

Date	*Particulars*		*L.F.*	*Dr. (₹)*	*Cr. (₹)*
	Business Purchase A/c	Dr.		9,300	
	To Liquidator of M Ltd.				8,400
	To Liquidator of N Ltd.				900
	(Being consideration payable to liquidators of the two companies taken over)				
	Tangible Fixed Assets (6,615 + 702)	Dr.		7,317	
	Inventories A/c (2,370 + 444)	Dr.		2,814	
	Trade Receivables A/c (1,044 + 237)	Dr.		1,281	
	Cash at Bank A/c (1,542 + 240)	Dr.		1,782	
	Profit and Loss A/c (Refer W.N.)	Dr.		120	
	To 8% Redeemable Debentures of N Ltd. A/c				300
	To Trade Payables A/c (3,291 + 462)				3,753
	To Business Purchase A/c				9,300
	(Being incorporation of all the assets and liabilities and the excess of consideration over the share capital being adjusted against reserves and surplus)				
	Liquidator of M Ltd, A/c	Dr.		8,400	
	Liquidator of N Ltd. A/c	Dr.		900	
	To Equity Share Capital A/c (7,200 + 900)				8,100
	To 11% Preference Share Capital A/c				1,200
	(Being allotment of fully paid shares in discharge of purchase consideration)				
	Profit and Loss A/c	Dr.		6	
	To Bank A/c				6
	(Being payment of liquidation expenses of M Ltd, and N Ltd.)				

	Preliminary Expenses A/c Dr. To Bank A/c (Being expenses on incorporation of MN Ltd.)		15	15
	8% Redeemable Debentures of N Ltd. A/c Dr. To 8.5% Redeemable Debentures A/c (Being conversion of 8% Debentures of N Ltd. into 8.5% Debentures)		300	300
	Profit & Loss A/c Dr. To Preliminary Expenses A/c (Being the Preliminary Exp. and Discount w/o as per Para 56 of AS 26)		15	15

BALANCE SHEET OF MN LTD AS AT 1ST APRIL, 2016

Particulars	*Note No.*	*₹ (in lacs)*
I. EQUITY AND LIABILITIES		
(1) Shareholders' Funds		
(a) Share Capital	1	9,300
(b) Reserves and Surplus [120 + 6 + 48 + 6]		(180)
(2) Non-Current Liabilities		
Long-term Borrowings [Debentures]		300
(3) Current Liabilities		
Trade Payables [₹ 3,291 + ₹ 462]		3,753
Total		13,173
II. ASSETS		
(1) Non-Current Assets		
(a) Fixed Assets		
(i) Tangible Assets [₹ 6,615 + ₹ 702]		7,317
(2) Current Assets		
Inventories [₹ 2,370 + ₹ 444]		2,814
Trade Receivables [₹ 1,044 + ₹ 237]		1,281
Cash and Cash Equivalents [₹ 1,542 + ₹ 240 – 21]		1,761
Total		13,173

Notes To Accounts:

Particulars	₹
1. Share Capital	
810 lakhs Equity Shares of ₹ 10 each	8,100
120 lakhs Pref. Shares of ₹ 10 each	1,200
(Of the above all Shares were issued for consideration otherwise than cash)	9,300

Working Note:

BALANCE OF PROFIT LOSS ACCOUNT (₹ in lakhs)

Total Consideration = ₹ (8,400 + 900) lakhs		9,300
Less: Share Capital of Companies taken over [₹(3,600 + 1,200 + 900) lacs]		5,700
		3,600
Amount to be adjusted:		
Capital Reserve	600	
General Reserve	2,100	
Profit & Loss A/c	780	3,480
Debit balance of Profit & Loss Account		120

ILLUSTRATION 26

Sun Ltd. and Moon Ltd. were amalgamated on and from 1st April, 2016. A new company Star Ltd. was formed to take over the business of the existing companies. The Balance Sheets of Sun Ltd. and Moon Ltd. as at 31st March, 2016 are given below:

(₹ in lakhs)

Particulars	*Sun Ltd.*	*Moon Ltd.*
Equity Shares of ₹ 100 each	400	375
12% Preference Shares of ₹100 each	150	100
Revaluation Reserve	75	50
General Reserve	85	75
Investment Allowance Reserve	25	25
Profit and Loss Account	25	15
10% Debentures (₹100 each)	30	15
Trade Payables	210	95
Tangible Fixed Assets	450	275
Investments	75	25
Inventories	175	125
Trade Receivables	150	175
Cash and Bank balances	250	150

Additional Information:

(a) Star Ltd. will issue 5 equity shares for each equity share of Sun Ltd. and 4 equity shares for each equity share of Moon Ltd. The shares are to be issued @ ₹ 30 each, having a face value of ₹ 10 per share.

(b) Preference shareholders of the two companies are issued equivalent number of 15% preference shares of Star Ltd. at a price of ₹ 150 per share (face value ₹ 100).

(c) 10% Debentureholders of Sun Ltd. and Moon Ltd. are discharged by Star Ltd., issuing such number of its 15% Debentures of ₹100 each so as to maintain the same amount of interest.

(d) Investment allowance reserve is to be maintained for 4 more years.

(e) Liquidation expenses are: Sun Ltd. ₹2,00,000 Moon Ltd. ₹ 1,00,000. It was decided that these expenses would be borne by Star Ltd.

(f) All the assets and liabilities of Sun Ltd. and Moon Ltd. are taken over at book value.

(g) Authorised equity share capital of Star Ltd. is ₹ 5,00,00,000, divided into equity shares of ₹ 10 each. After issuing required number of shares to the Liquidators of Sun Ltd. and Moon Ltd., Star Ltd. issued balance shares to Public. The issue was fully subscribed.

Required: Prepare the Balance Sheet of Star Ltd. as at 1st April, 2016 after amalgamation has been carried out on the basis of Amalgamation in the nature of purchase.

SOLUTION

BALANCE SHEET OF STAR LTD AS AT 1ST APRIL, 2016

Particulars	*Note No.*	*₹ (in lacs)*
I. EQUITY AND LIABILITIES		
(1) Shareholders' Funds		
(a) Share Capital	1	750
(b) Reserves and Surplus	2	875
(2) Non-Current Liabilities		
Long-term Borrowings [Debentures] [20 + 10]		30
(3) Current Liabilities		
Trade Payables (210 + 95)		305
Total		1,960
II. ASSETS		
(1) Non-Current Assets		
(a) Fixed Assets		
(i) Tangible Assets [450 + 325]		775
(ii) Intangible Assets [Goodwill] [10 + 2 + 1]		13
(b) Non-Current Investments [75 + 25]		100
(c) Other Non-Current Assets [Amalgamation Adjustment A/c]		50
(2) Current Assets		
Inventories [175 + 125]		300
Trade Receivables [150 + 175]		325
Cash and Cash Equivalents [250 + 150 – 3]		397
Total		1,960

Notes To Accounts:

Particulars	₹
1. Share Capital	
50 lakhs Equity Shares of ₹ 10 each	500
2.5 lakhs Pref. Shares of ₹ 10 each	250
(Of the above all Shares were issued for consideration otherwise than cash)	750
2. Reserves and Surplus	
Securities Premium [75 + 50 + 400 + 300]	825
Investment Allowance Reserve [25 + 25]	50
	875

Working Notes:

1. CALCULATION OF PURCHASE CONSIDERATION

Particulars	X Ltd.	Y Ltd.	Total
A. No of Equity Shares	4,00,000	3,75,000	
B. Exchange Ratio	5:1	4:1	
C. No of Equity Shares to be issued by [A × B]	20,00,000	15,00,000	35,00,000
Equity Share Capital @ ₹ 20	400,00,000	300,00,000	700,00,000
Securities Premium@ ₹ 10	200,00,000	150,00,000	350,00,000
D. No of 15% Pref.Shares to be issued	1,50,000	1,00,000	2,50,000
15% Pref. Share Capital @ ₹ 100	150,00,000	100,00,000	250,00,000
Securities Premium@ ₹ 50	75,00,000	50,00,000	125,00,000
Total Purchase Consideration	825,00,000	600,00,000	1425,00,000

2. CALCULATION OF NUMBER OF DEBENTURES ISSUED

(₹ in lakhs)

Particulars	Sun Ltd.	Moon Ltd.
10% Debentures of ₹100 each	30	15
15% Debentures to be issued to maintain same amount of interest:		
Interest = ₹30,00,000 × 10% = ₹3,00,000		
Number of 15% Debentures = (₹ 3,00,000/15) × 100	20	
Interest = ₹15,00,000 × 10%		
Number of 15% Debentures = (₹ 1,15,000/15) × 100		10

3. NET ASSETS TAKEN OVER

(₹ in lakhs)

Particulars	Sun Ltd.	Moon Ltd.
A. Assets taken over		
Tangible Fixed Assets	450	325
Investments	75	25
Inventories	175	125
Trade Receivable	150	175
Cash and bank	150	100
	1,000	750
B. Less: Liabilities taken over		
Debentures	20	10
Trade Payable	210	95
	230	105
C. Net assets taken over	770	645
D. Purchase consideration	825	600
E. (Goodwill)/Capital Reserve	(55)	45
F. Net Goodwill		(10)

4. Liquidation expenses of Sun Ltd. and Moon Ltd., ₹ 2 lakhs and ₹ 1 lakhs respectively will be debited to Goodwill account in the books of Star Ltd.

ILLUSTRATION 27

Given below are the extracts from the Balance Sheets of X Ltd and Y Ltd. as at 31st March 2016:

Particulars	*X Ltd. (₹ in lacs)*	*Y Ltd. (₹ in lacs)*
Equity Share Capital of ₹ 10 each	5.00	10.00
8% Pref. Share Capital of ₹ 100 each	1.00	2.00
Reserve	15.46	0.70
Statutory Reserve	2.00	1.00
Profit & Loss A/c	4.25	1.30
12% Debentures of ₹ 100 each	2.00	1.00
Current Liabilities	1.00	2.20
Net Tangible Assets	19.00	7.60
Non-Current Investments	3.45	5.20
Current Assets	8.26	5.40

The two companies agree to amalgamate as on Ist April, 2016 and form a new company XY Ltd.

Additional Information:

(a) Goodwill of X Ltd. and Y Ltd. on the date of take-over was valued at ₹ 48,000 and ₹ 38,000 respectively and Net Tangible Blocks of X Ltd. and Y Ltd were valued at 10% above their book values on the date of take-over.Investments of X Ltd. and Y Ltd. are considered worth ₹ 4,16,000 and ₹ 6,26,000 respectively.

(b) 12% Debentures of X Ltd. and Y Ltd. are discharged by XY Ltd. by issuing such number of its 15% Debentures of ₹ 100 each so as to maintain the same amount of interest.

(c) The issue of such an amount of fully paid 10% Pref. Shares in X Y Ltd. at 125% as is sufficient to discharge 9% Pref. Shares in X Ltd. & Y Ltd. at a premium of 20%.

(d) The Equity Shares of XY Ltd are to be of a nominal value of ₹ 10 each credited as ₹ 8 paid up and valued at ₹ 15 per share.

(e) Statutory Reserve is to be maintained for 3 years more for Income Tax purposes.

(f) Liquidation expenses are: X Ltd. ₹ 2,000 ,Y Ltd. ₹ 1,000. It was decided that these expenses would be borne by XY Ltd.Expenses on incorporation of XY Ltd. were ₹ 1,000.

Required: Draft the Balance Sheet of XY Ltd. after amalgamation.

SOLUTION

BALANCE SHEET OF XY LTD. AS AT 31.3.2016

Particulars	*Note No*	*₹ (lacs)*
I. Equity and Liabilities		
(1) Shareholders' Funds		
(a) Share Capital	1	26.88
(b) Reserves and Surplus	2	24.72
(2) Non-Current Liabilities[Long-term Borrowings]	3	2.40

(3) Current Liabilities		3.20
Total		57.20
II. Assets		
(1) Non-Current Assets		
(a) Fixed Assets		
Tangible Assets (20.90 + 8.36)		29.26
Intangible Assets (Goodwill) (0.48 + 0.38 + 0.02+.01+.01)		0.90
(b) Non-Current Investments		10.42
(c) Other Non-Current Assets [Amalgamation Adjustment A/c]		3.00
(2) Current Assets [8.26+5.40-.02-.01-.01]		**13.62**
Total		57.20

Notes To Accounts:

	Particulars	*₹ (lacs)*
1.	**Share Capital**	
	3,00,000 Equity Shares of ₹ 10 each, ₹ 8 paid up	24.00
	2,880, 9% Pref. Shares of ₹ 100 each	2.88
	(Of the above all Shares were issued for consideration otherwise than cash)	
		26.88
2.	**Reserves and Surplus**	
	Securities Premium [(3,00,000 × ₹ 7) + (2,880 × ₹ 25)]	21.72
	Statutory Reserve	3.00
		24.72
3.	**Long-term Borrowings**	
	15% Debentures (1.60 + 0.80]	2.40

Working Notes:

(I) COMPUTATION OF VALUE OF NET ASSETS FOR EQUITY SHAREHOLDERS ₹ (LAKHS)

	Particulars	*X Ltd.*	*Y Ltd.*
A.	Total Assets at their Current Values:		
	Goodwill	0.48	0.38
	Net Tangible Block	20.90	8.36
	Non-Current Investments	4.16	6.26
	Current Assets	8.26	5.40
		33.80	**20.40**
B.	*Less:* Liabilities at their Current Amounts:		
	12% Debentures [Interest/15%]	1.60	0.80
	Current Liabilities	1.00	2.20
	8% Pref. Share Capital	1.20	2.40
		3.80	**5.40**
C.	Net Assets for Equity Shareholders [A – B]	**30.00**	**15.00**

(II) CALCULATION OF NO. OF EQUITY SHARES TO BE ISSUED BY PURCHASING COMPANY

Particulars	X Ltd.	Y Ltd.	Total
A. Total Value (as calculated above)	30,00,000	15,00,000	45,00,000
B. Issue Price of an Equity Share	15	15	15
C. No of Equity Shares to be issued by [A/B]	2,00,000	1,00,000	3,00,000
Equity Share Capital @ ₹ 8	16,00,000	8,00,000	24,00,000
Securities Premium@ ₹ 7	14,00,000	7,00,000	21,00,000

(III) CALCULATION OF PURCHASE CONSIDERATION

Particulars	X Ltd.	Y Ltd.	Total
Equity Shares @ ₹ 15	30,00,000	15,00,000	45,00,000
9% Pref. Shares @ ₹ 125	1,20,000	2,40,000	3,60,000
Total	31,20,000	17,40,000	48,60,000

7 INTERNAL RECONSTRUCTION

LEARNING OBJECTIVES

After studying this chapter, you should be able to understand:

- ◇ Meaning of Internal Reconstruction
- ◇ Alteration of Share capital
- ◇ Reduction of Share Capital
- ◇ Variation of Shareholders' Rights
- ◇ Scheme of Compromise and Arrangement
- ◇ How to deal with Surrender of Shares?
- ◇ Accounting Entries

1.0 MEANING OF INTERNAL RECONSTRUCTION

In case of internal reconstruction, the company's existing financial structure is reorganised without dissolving the existing Company and without forming a new Company. Taking a wider meaning of the term 'Internal Reconstruction'. It includes:

1. Alteration of Share Capital u/s 61.
2. Reduction of Share Capital u/s 66.
3. Variation of Shareholders' Rights u/s 48.
4. Scheme of Compromise/Arrangement u/s 230 and 231.

2.0 DISTINCTION BETWEEN INTERNAL RECONSTRUCTION AND EXTERNAL RECONSTRUCTION

Basis of Distinction	Internal Reconstruction	External Reconstruction
1. Liquidation of Existing Company	Existing company does not go into liquidation.	Existing company goes into liquidation.
2. Formation of New Company	No new company is formed.	A new company is formed to take over the business of the existing company.
3. Reduction of Share Capital	It involves the reduction of share capital.	It may *or* may not involve reduction of share capital.

.0 ALTERATION OF SHARE CAPITAL [SECTIONS 61]

LEGAL REQUIREMENTS

he main legal requirements in connection with the alteration of Share Capital are summarized as nder:

Authorized by Articles	A Company may alter the Capital Clause of its memorandum only if it is authorised by its articles of association to do so.
Manner	A Company may alter the Capital Clause in the following manner: (i) by increasing its share capital by issue of new shares; [e.g. from 1 crore to 5 crores]. (ii) by consolidating the existing shares into shares of larger amount than its existing shares: [e.g. Conversion of Shares of ₹ 10 each into shares of ₹ 100 each]. (iii) by sub-diving the existing shares into shares of smaller amount than its existing shares; [e.g. Conversion of shares of ₹ 100 each into each into shares of ₹ 10 each]. (iv) by converting fully paid shares into stock *or* vice-versa. (v) by cancelling its unissued shares.
Ordinary Resolution	An ordinary resolution must be passed at a general meeting.
Notice	A notice specifying alteration made must be given to the Registrar within 30 days of alteration.

JOURNAL ENTRIES

The accounting entries in each case of alteration of share capital will be as under:

Particulars	Dr. (₹)	Cr. (₹)
(a) **For increase in Share Capital:**		
Example *X Ltd. issued 10,000 Equity Shares of ₹ 10 each at par.*		
(i) Bank A/c Dr.	1,00,000	
To Equity Share Application and Allotment A/c		1,00,000
(Being the application money received)		
(ii) Equity Share Application and Allotment A/c Dr.	1,00,000	
To Equity Share Capital A/c		1,00,000
(Being 10,000 Equity shares of ₹ 10 each allotted at par)		
(b) **For Consolidation of Shares:**		
Example *X Ltd. having 10,000 Equity Shares of ₹ 10 each decides to convert the Share Capital into Equity Shares of ₹ 100 each.*		
Equity Share Capital (₹ 10) A/c Dr.	1,00,000	
To Equity Share Capital (₹ 100) A/c		1,00,000
(Being 10,000 Equity Shares of ₹ 10 each converted into 1,000 shares of ₹ 100 each)		
(c) **For Sub-division of Shares:**		
Example *X Ltd. having 1,000 Equity Shares of ₹ 100 each decides to convert the Share Capital into Equity Shares of ₹ 10 each.*		
Equity Share Capital (₹ 100) A/c Dr.	1,00,000	
To Equity Share Capital (₹ 10) A/c		1,00,000
(Being 1,000 Equity Shares of ₹ 100 each converted into 10,000 Shares of ₹ 10 each)		

(d) **For Conversion of Shares into Stock:** **Example** *X Ltd. having 10,000 Equity Shares of ₹ 10 each decides to convert the Share Capital into Equity Stock* Equity Share Capital (₹ 10) A/c Dr. To Equity Stock A/c (Being 1,000 Equity Shares of ₹ 10 each converted into equity stock)	1,00,000	1,00,000
(e) **For Conversion of Stock into Shares:** **Example** *X Ltd. having Equity Stock of ₹ 1,00,000 decides to convert the Equity Stock into Equity Share Capital of ₹ 10 each* Equity Stock A/c Dr. To Equity Share Capital (₹ 10) A/c (Being Equity Stock of ₹ 1,00,000 converted into 10,000 Equity Shares of ₹ 10 each)	1,00,000	1,00,000
(f) **For Cancelling Unissued Shares:** No accounting entry is required to be passed. The Authorised Share Capital gets reduced by the amount of unissued shares now cancelled.		

4.0 REDUCTION OF SHARE CAPITAL [SECTION 66]

LEGAL REQUIREMENTS

The main legal requirements for reduction of Share Capital are summarised as follows:

Authorised by Articles	A company limited by shares *or* a company limited by guarantee having a Share Capital may reduce its Share Capital only if it is authorised by its articles of association to do so.
Ways	A company may reduce its Share Capital in any of the following ways: (i) by extinguishing/reducing the liability on any of its shares in respect of uncalled amount on shares; (ii) by cancelling the paid up Share Capital which is lost *or* is not represented by available assets; (iii) by paying off any paid up Share Capital which is in excess of the requirements of the Company.
Special Resolution	A Special Resolution must be passed at a general meeting.
Auditor's Certificate	Auditor's Certificate to the affect that the proposed accounting treatment is as per prescribed Accounting Standard, must be filed with the Tribunal.
Tribunal's Order	A Tribunal's order confirming the reduction must be obtained.
Filing with ROC	A certified copy of Tribunal's order and Minutes approved by the Tribunal must be filed with the Registrar.
Notice	A Company must publish notice of registration in such manner as the Tribunal may direct.
Effective Date	A resolution for reducing Capital as confirmed by the order of the Tribunal shall take effect on its registration by the Registrar.

JOURNAL ENTRIES

The Accounting entries in each case of reduction of share capital will be as follows:

Particulars	Dr. (₹)	Cr. (₹)
(a) **For Reducing the liability in respect of Uncalled Amount**		
Example *X Ltd. having 1,000 Equity Shares of ₹ 100 each ₹ 60 paid up, decides to cancel the liability of member to the extent of ₹ 20 per share and make shares as of ₹ 80 each. ₹ 60 paid up.*		
Equity. Share Capital (₹ 100) A/c Dr.	60,000	
To Equity Share Capital (₹ 80)		60,000
(Being Shares of ₹ 100 each converted into shares of ₹ 80 each)		
Note: *The Paid up Share Capital of the company will remain unchanged.*		
(b) **For Paying off the surplus paid up Capital**		
Example *A Ltd. having 1,000 Equity Shares of ₹ 100 each fully paid decides to repay to its members ₹ 20 per share and make shares as of ₹ 80 each fully paid up.*		
(i) Equity Share Capital (₹ 100) A/c Dr.	1,00,000	
To Equity Share Capital (₹ 80) A/c		80,000
To Sundry Members A/c		20,000
(Being shares of ₹ 100 each converted into shares of ₹ 80 each and make ₹ 20 per share due to members)		
(ii) Sundry Members A/c Dr.	20,000	
To Bank A/c		20,000
(Being the payment made to members)		
(c) **For Writing off the lost paid up Capital**		
Example *Look at the following Balance Sheet of Bad Luck Ltd.:*		

Liabilities	₹	*Assets*	₹
1,000 Shares of ₹ 100 each	*1,00,000*	*Intangible Assets*	*25,000*
Sundry Creditors.	*1,00,000*	*Other Fixed Assets*	*1,00,000*
		Current Assets	*25,000*
		P&L A/c	*50,000*
	2,00,000		*2,00,000*

Assets	*Present Worth (₹)*
Intangible	*Nil*
Other Fixed Assets	*1,05,000*
Current Assets	*15,000*
Thus, the Company has lost ₹ 80,000 if its paid up Capital as under:	
Intangible Assets	*₹ 25,000*
Current Assets	*₹ 10,000*
P&L A/c	*₹ 50,000*

	₹ 85,000
Less: Appreciation in Fixed Assets	5,000
	₹ 80,000

This reduction can be effected in any of the following two ways:

JOURNAL

Particulars		*Dr. (₹)*	*Cr. (₹)*
(i) By reducing the paid-up value (not Nominal Value) of existing shares			
Share Capital (₹ 100) A/c	Dr.	80,000	
To Capital Reduction A/c			80,000
(Being the paid-up value of a share reduced from ₹ 100 to ₹ 20)			
(ii) By reducing both the Nominal values and paid up values of Shares			
Share Capital (₹ 100) A/c	Dr.	1,00,000	
To Share. Capital (₹ 20) A/c			20,000
To Capital Reduction A/c			80,000
(Being the shares reduced to ₹ 20 per share)			

Note: The Shareholders will not ordinarily be willing for the first alternative since it puts additional burden on them.

5.0 VARIATION OF SHAREHOLDERS' RIGHTS [SECTION 48]

LEGAL REQUIREMENTS

The main legal requirements for variation of shareholders' rights are summarised as under:

Separate Meeting	If the rights attached to the shares of any particulars class of shareholders are to be varied, a separate meeting of that particular class of shareholders must be held.
Consent of atleast 3/4th	The consent of the holder of at least 3/4th of the shares of the class concerned (or a higher proportion if so required by the articles/yemorandum) must be obtained.
Right to Apply to the Tribunal	The holders of at least 10% of the issued shares of the class concerned whose rights are being varied, may apply to the Tribunal to have the variation cancelled within 21 days after the consent is obtained *or* the resolution is passed.
Tribunal's Confirmation	If such appeal is made, the variation will not have effect unless it is confirmed by the Tribunal whose decision is final.
Notice	Notice of the variation must be filed with the Registrar within 30 days of the Tribunal's order.

EXAMPLE 1

X Ltd. has 1,000, 10% Cum Pref. shares of ₹ 100 each. At a class meeting of Cum Pref. Shareholders, it was decided that the rate of dividend be reduced to 9%. In such a case following Journal Entry will be passed.

Particulars		*Dr. (₹)*	*Cr. (₹)*
10% Cum Pref. Share Capital A/c	Dr.	1,00,000	
To 9% Cum Pref. Share Capital A/c			1,00,000

EXAMPLE 2

Y Ltd. has 1,000, 10% Cumulative Pref. Shares of ₹ 100 each. At a meeting of Cum Pref. Shareholders, it was decided that the existing Cumulative-Pref-Shares be converted into Non-Cumulative-Pref. Shares.

Particulars		*Dr. (₹)*	*Cr. (₹)*
10% Cum Pref. Share Capital A/c	Dr.	1,00,000	
To 9% Cum Pref. Share Capital A/c			1,00,000

6.0 SCHEME OF COMPROMISE AND ARRANGEMENT [SECTIONS 230 TO 2310]

MEANING OF COMPROMISE

Compromise refers to an amicable settlement of differences by mutual concessions by parties to dispute. It may be noted that the compromise presupposes the existence of some dispute because there can be no compromise unless there is some dispute. The need for compromise may arise for the settlement of some dispute between the company and its creditors/members.

MEANING OF ARRANGEMENT

The term 'Arrangement' carries a wider sense than the term 'Compromise'. It implies re-arrangement of rights and/or liabilities of a member/a class of them/a creditor/a class of them without the existence of any dispute. According to Explanation to Section 230(1), of the Companies Act, 2013 the term 'Arrangement' includes re-organisation of the share capital of the company by the consolidation of shares of different classes *or* by the division of the shares into shares of different classes *or* by both these methods. An arrangement may involve anyone *or* more of the following:

(a) Debenture-holders foregoing their claims in whole *or* in part;

(b) Debentures exchanging their debentures for new debentures/shares;

(c) Creditors foregoing their claims in whole *or* in part;

(d) Creditor agreeing to receive shares/debentures in whole/in part payment of the claims;

(e) Preference shareholders forgoing their claims for arrears of dividend;

(f) Preference shareholders agreeing to accept a reduced rate of dividend in future;

(g) Fresh issue of shares to raise additional working capital;

(h) Writing off lost Paid-up Capital.

Example In the Balance Sheet 10% Debentures 14,70,000, Sundry Creditors 4,50,000

The debenture holders agree to reduce their claims to ₹ 5,00,000 in consideration of their getting 50,000 Equity Shares of ₹ 10 each. Sundry Creditors agree to reduce their claims to 20% and half the balance to be satisfied by the issue of Equity Shares of ₹ 10 each. The following Journal Entries shall be passed to record the aforesaid arrangement:

Particulars		Dr. (₹)	Cr. (₹)
(i) 10% Debentureholders' A/c	Dr.	9,70,000	
To Equity Shares Capital A/c (₹ 10)			5,00,000
To Reconstruction A/c			4,70,000
(ii) Sundry Creditors A/c	Dr.	4,05,000	
To Equity Share Capital A/c (₹ 10)			45,000
To Reconstruction A/c			3,60,000

7.0 HOW TO DEAL WITH SURRENDER OF SHARES?

Under a scheme of reconstruction, the shareholders may be required to surrender a part of their share-holdings. Such surrendered shares may be re-issued to other parties, in whole/in part satisfaction of their claims *or* cancelled. The following Journal Entries may be required to be passed in such connection:

(a) On Surrender of Shares	Share Capital A/c	Dr.
	To Shares Surrendered A/c	
(b) On Re-issue of Surrendered Shares	Shares Surrendered A/c	Dr.
	To Share Capital A/c	
(c) On Cancellation of Surrendered Shares	Shares Surrendered A/c	Dr.
	To Reconstruction A/c	

8.0 ACCOUNTING ENTRIES UNDER INTERNAL RECONSTRUCTION

Date	Particulars		Dr. (₹)	Cr. (₹)
1.	**To Reduce Both the Nominal Value and Paid up Value of Shares**			
	Share Capital A/c (₹ 100 each)	Dr.	100	
	To Share Capital A/c (₹ 80 each)			80
	To Reconstruction A/c/Capital Reduction A/c			20
2.	**To Reduce only the Paid up Value of Shares**			
	Share Capital A/c	Dr.	20	
	To Reconstruction A/c/Capital Reduction A/c			20
3.	**(a) To Pay the Arrears of Preference Dividend**			
	Reconstruction A/c	Dr.		
	To Bank A/c/Share Capital A/c			
	(b) To Cancel the Arrears of Preference Dividend			
	No Journal Entry is required to cancel a Contingent Liability.			
4.	**To Reduce the Claims of Debentureholders**			
	Debentures A/c	Dr.		
	Interest on Debentures A/c	Dr.		
	To New Debentures A/c/Share Capital A/c/Bank A/c			
	To Reconstruction A/c			

5.	**To Reduce the claims of Trade Creditors** Trade Creditors A/c Dr. To Share Capital A/c/Bank A/c To Reconstruction A/c		
6.	**To Settle the Tax Liability** Provision for Tax A/c Dr. To Bank A/c To Reconstruction A/c		
7.	**To Pay Reconstruction Expenses** Reconstruction A/c Dr. To Bank A/c		
8.	**To Pay for Cancellation of Capital Commitments etc.** Reconstruction A/c Dr. To Bank A/c		
9.	**To Record the Bad Debts and Doubtful Debts** Reconstruction A/c Dr. [With total] To Debtors A/c [With Bad Debts] To Provision for Doubtful Debts A/c [With Doubtful Debts]		
10.	**To Record the Appreciation in Value of Assets** Investments A/c/Land and Building A/c Dr. To Reconstruction A/c		
11.	**To Transfer Capital Reserve for Reconstruction Purpose** Capital Reserve A/c Dr. To Reconstruction A/c		
12.	**To write off the Accumulated Losses, Fictitious Assets and the over valuation of Over Valued Assets** Capital Reduction A/c/Reconstruction A/c Dr. To Profit and Loss A/c To Preliminary Expenses A/c To Underwriting Commission A/c To Discount on Issue of Shares/Debentures A/c To Goodwill A/c (To the extent of over valuation) To Patents A/c (To the extent of over valuation) To Trade Marks A/c (To the extent of over valuation) To Copy Right A/c (To the extent of over valuation) To Other Overvalued Assets (individually)		
13.	**To Transfer the Credit Balance of Reconstruction A/c/** Capital Reduction A/c Capital Reduction A/c/Reconstruction A/c Dr. To Capital Reserve A/c		

Tutorial Notes:

(i) *The author recommends the use of 'Reconstruction Account' particularly when the scheme of compromise/arrangement is carried out under the provisions of Sections 391 to 393. The use of 'Capital Reduction Account' is purely justified when the capital reduction scheme is carried out without invoking the provisions of Sections 230 to 231.*

(ii) *Even if the question is silent as to writing off, the debit balance of Profit & Loss Account and Unamortized Expense Items (like Preliminary Expenses, Underwriting Comm., Discount on Issue of Shares/Debentures) should be written off to the extent of credit balance available in Reconstruction/Capital Reduction Account.*

(iii) *So far as Fixed Assets are concerned, the amount written off under a scheme of reconstruction must be shown in each Balance Sheet for five years.*

ILLUSTRATION 1

Pass journal entries for the following transactions:

(i) Conversion of 2 lakh fully paid equity shares of ₹ 10 each into stock of ₹ 1,00,000 and balance has 12% fully convertible Debenture.

(ii) Consolidation of 40 lakh fully paid equity shares of ₹2.50 each into 10 lakh fully paid equity share of ₹10 each.

(iii) Sub-division of 10 lakh fully paid 11% preference shares of ₹ 50 each into 50 lakh fully paid 11% preference shares of ₹ 10 each.

(iv) Conversion of 12% preference shares of ₹ 5,00,000 into 14% preference shares ₹ 3,00,000 and remaining balance as 12% Non-cumulative preference shares.

SOLUTION

JOURNAL

Date	*Particulars*		*Dr. (₹)*	*Cr. (₹)*
(i)	Equity share Capital A/c Dr.		20,00,000	
	To Equity Stock			1,00,000
	To 12% Fully Convertible Debentures			19,00,000
	(Being conversion of 2 lakh equity shares of ₹ 10 each into stock of ₹ 1,00,000 and balance as fully convertible debentures as per resolution)			
(ii)	Equity Share Capital A/c (₹ 2.50) Dr.		100,00,000	
	To Equity Share Capital A/c (₹ 10)			100,00,000
	(Being consolidation of 40 lakh shares of ₹ 2.50 each into 10 lakh shares of ₹ 10 each as per resolution)			
(iii)	11% Preference Shares Capital A/c (₹ 50) Dr.		500,00,000	
	To 11% Preference Share Capital A/c (₹10)			500,00,000
	(Being subdivision of 10 lakh preference shares of ₹ 50 each into 50 lakh shares of ₹ 10 each as per resolution)			
(iv)	12% Preference Share Capital A/c Dr.		5,00,000	
	To 14% Preference Share Capital			3,00,000

	To 12% Non-cumulative Pref. Share Capital (Being conversion of preference shares as per resolution)			2,00,000

ILLUSTRATION 2

V Ltd has Equity Share Capital (of ₹ 10 each) of ₹ 500 lacs. All the equity shares be converted into the same number of equity shares of ₹ 5 each, ₹ 2.50 paid up. Journalise

SOLUTION

JOURNAL

[₹ in Lacs]

Date	*Particulars*	*L.F.*	*Dr. (₹)*	*Cr. (₹)*
	Equity Share Capital (₹ 10 each) A/c Dr.		500	
	To Equity Share Capital (₹ 5 each) A/c			125
	To Reconstruction A/c			375
	(Being the conversion of all the equity shares into the same number of equity shares of ₹ 5 each, ₹ 2.50 paid up as per scheme of reconstruction)			

ILLUSTRATION 3

V Ltd has 6%Cum-Pref.Shares (of ₹ 100 each) of ₹ 100 lacs. The preference shares are converted from 6% to 15% but revalued in a manner in which the total return on them remains unaffected. Journalise

SOLUTION

JOURNAL

[₹ in Lacs]

Date	*Particulars*	*L.F.*	*Dr. (₹)*	*Cr. (₹)*
	6% Cum-Preference Share Capital (₹ 100) A/c Dr.		100	
	To 15% Cum-Pref. Share Capital (₹ 100) A/c			40
	To Reconstruction A/c			60
	(Being 40000 15% cum Pref. share of ₹ 100 each issued so as to maintain the same amount of dividend (i.e. ₹ 6 lacs) vide scheme of reconstruction dated.....)			

ILLUSTRATION 4

V Ltd has 6%Cum-Pref.Shares (of ₹100 each) of ₹ 100 lacs. Dividend on Preference Shares are in arrears for three years. Four equity shares of ₹ 5 each, ₹ 2.50 paid up to be issued for each ₹100 of arrears of preference dividend.Journalise

SOLUTION

JOURNAL

[₹ in Lacs]

Date	*Particulars*	*L.F.*	*Dr. (₹)*	*Cr. (₹)*
	Reconstruction A/c Dr.		1.8	
	To Equity Share Capital (₹ 5 each, ₹ 2.50 paid up) A/c			1.8
	(Being 72000 equity shares of ₹ 5 each, ₹ 2.50 paid up issued to Pref. Shareholders for dividend arrears vide scheme of Reconstruction dated.....)			

ILLUSTRATION 5

V Ltd has 10% first debentures for ₹ 60 lacs, 10% second debentures for ₹ 100 lacs and Interest on Debentures Outstanding ₹ 16 lacs. Mr. A holds 10% first debentures for ₹ 40 lacs and 10% second debentures for ₹ 60 lacs. He is also a creditor for ₹ 10 lacs. Mr. 'A' is to cancel ₹ 60 lacs of his total debt and to pay ₹ 10 lacs to the company and to receive new 12% Debentures for the balance amount.Journalise

SOLUTION

JOURNAL

[₹ in Lacs]

Date	*Particulars*	*L.F.*	*Dr. (₹)*	*Cr. (₹)*
	10% First Debentures A/c Dr.		40	
	10% Second Debentures A/c Dr.		60	
	Trade Creditors A/c Dr.		10	
	Interest on Debentures Outstanding A/c Dr. [16 x 100/160]		10	
	To Mr. A			120
	(Being the total amount due to A t/f to his A/c)			
	Bank A/c Dr.		10	
	To Mr. A			10
	(Being the amount received from Mr. A under the Reconstruc- tion Scheme)			
	Mr. A A/c Dr.		130	
	To 12% New Debentures A/c			70
	To Reconstruction A/c			60
	(Being ₹ 60 lacs due to A (Including creditors) cancelled and 12% new debentures allotted for balance amount as per scheme of reconstruction)			

ILLUSTRATION 6

V Ltd has 10% first debentures for ₹ 60 lacs, 10% second debentures for ₹ 100 lacs and Interest on Debentures Outstanding ₹ 16 lacs. Mr. B holds 10% first debentures for ₹ 20 lacs and 10% second debentures for ₹ 40 lacs and is also a creditor for ₹ 5 lacs. Mr. 'B' is to cancel ₹ 30 lacs of his total debt and to accept new 12% Debentures for the balance amount.Journalise

SOLUTION

JOURNAL

[₹ in Lacs]

Date	Particulars	L.F.	Dr. (₹)	Cr. (₹)
	10% First Debentures A/c Dr.		20	
	10% Second Debentures A/c Dr.		40	
	Trade Creditors A/c Dr.		5	
	Interest on Debentures Outstanding A/c Dr.		6	
	To Mr. B			71
	(Being the total amount due to Mr. B t/f to his A/c)			
	Mr. B		71	
	To 12% New Debentures A/c			41
	To Reconstruction A/c			30
	(Being ₹ 30 lacs due to B (including creditors) cancelled and 12% new debentures allotted for balance amount as per scheme of reconstruction)			

ILLUSTRATION 7

V Ltd has Trade Creditors for ₹ 165 lacs. Mr. A and Mr. B are creditors for ₹ 10 lacs and ₹ 5 lacs respectively. Trade Creditors (other than A and B) are given the option of either to accept equity shares of ₹ 5, ₹ 2.50 paid up each, for the amount due to them *or* to accept 80% of the amount due in cash. 40% Creditors accepted equity shares whereas the balance accepted cash in full settlement. Journalise

SOLUTION

JOURNAL

[₹ in Lacs]

Date	Particulars	L.F.	Dr. (₹)	Cr. (₹)
	Trade Creditors A/c Dr.		150	
	To Equity Share Capital (₹ 5 each, ₹ 2.50 paid up) A/c			60
	To Bank A/c			72
	To Reconstruction a/c			18
	(Being the Trade creditors for ₹ 60 lakhs accepted 24 lakhs shares of ₹ 5 each, ₹ 2.50 paid up for full amount and those for ₹.90 lakhs accepted cash equal to 80% of claim in full settlement)			

ILLUSTRATION 8

There were capital commitments totalling ₹ 300 lacs. These contracts are to be cancelled on payment of 5% of the contract price as a penalty.The Directors refund ₹ 11 lacs of the fees previously received by them. A dissentient shareholder transferred his 100 shares to a director. Journalise

SOLUTION

JOURNAL

[₹ in Lacs]

Date	*Particulars*	*L.F.*	*Dr. (₹)*	*Cr. (₹)*
	Reconstruction A/c Dr.		15	
	To Bank A/c			15
	(Being payment made for cancellation of capital commitments)			
	Bank A/c Dr.		11	
	To Reconstruction A/c			11
	(Being refund of fees by directors credited to Reconstruction A/c)			

Note: *The transfer of 100 Shares by a dissentient shareholder to the director concerned need not be accounted for.*

ILLUSTRATION 9

V Ltd has Provision for Tax for ₹10 lacs. The taxation liability of the company is settled at ₹ 8.88 lacs and the same is paid immediately.Journalise.

SOLUTION

JOURNAL

[₹ in Lacs]

Date	*Particulars*	*L.F.*	*Dr. (₹)*	*Cr. (₹)*
	Provision for Tax A/c Dr.		10	
	To Bank A/c			8.88
	To Reconstruction A/c			1.12
	(Being payment of tax liability in full settlement)			

ILLUSTRATION 10

Following items appear in the Balance Sheet of V Ltd:

Workmen's Compensation Fund:	Pune	₹1 lac
	Bombay	₹ 2 lacs
10% Government Loan Earmarked Against Workmen's Compensation Fund		₹ 3 lacs
Workmen's Compensation Fund (Bombay) disclosed the fact that actually there was a liability of ₹ 20,000 only. As a result the relevant fund amount balance was to be brought down to the required amount. Investments were realised at 10% above the book value. Journalise.		

SOLUTION

JOURNAL

[₹ in Lacs]

Date	Particulars	L.F.	Dr. (₹)	Cr. (₹)
	Bank A/c Dr.		0.88	
	To Investment in 10% Government Loan A/c			0.80
	To Workmen's Compensation Fund (Bombay) A/c			0.08
	(Being the Sale of Investments for Workmen's Compensation Fund (Bombay) and the profit on the sale of same transferred to Workmen Compensation Fund (Bombay) Account)			
	Workmen's Compensation Fund (Bombay) A/c Dr.		0.88	
	To Reconstruction A/c			0.88
	(Being the Surplus in Workmen Compensation Fund at Bombay transferred to Reconstruction Account)			

ILLUSTRATION 11

V Ltd has Investments in Shares in Q Ltd. ₹ 32.4 lacs V Ltd. holds 21,600 shares in Q Ltd. This represents 15% of the share capital of that company. Q Ltd. is not a quoted company. The average net profit (after tax) of the company is ₹ 25 lacs. The shares would be valued based on 12% capitalization rate. Journalise.

SOLUTION

JOURNAL

[₹ in Lacs]

Date	Particulars	L.F.	Dr. (₹)	Cr. (₹)
	Reconstruction A/c Dr.		1.15	
	To Investments in Shares in Q Ltd. A/c			1.15
	(Being reduction in the value of Investments)			

Working Notes:

(i) Valuation of Investments in Shares of Q Ltd.= (₹ 25 lacs/.12) × 15% = ₹ 31.25 lacs

(ii) Reduction in the Value of Investment in Shares of Q Ltd. = ₹ 32.40 lacs – ₹.31.25 = ₹.1.15 lacs

ILLUSTRATION 12

Following items appear in the Balance Sheet of V Ltd:

Capital Reserve	₹ 6 lacs
Profit and Loss Account	(₹ 15 lacs)
Goodwill	₹ 10 lacs
Patents & Copy Rights	₹ 5 lacs

Plant & Machinery	₹ 719.6 lacs
Land & Building	₹ 60 lacs
Debtors	₹ 10 lacs
Cash at Bank	₹ 104 lacs
Discount on issue of Debentures	₹ 1 lac

Goodwill is considered worthless. Land & Building is to be valued at 114% of book value. 80% of Debtors are considered as Bad and 20% of the balance Debtors are considered as Doubtful. Any surplus after writing off the various losses should be utilized in writing down the value of plant & machinery. The credit Balance available in Reconstruction A/c is ₹ 538.05 lacs. Journalise.

SOLUTION

JOURNAL

[₹ in Lacs]

Date	*Particulars*		*L.F.*	*Dr. (₹)*	*Cr. (₹)*
	Capital Reserve A/c	Dr.		6	
	To Reconstruction A/c				6
	(Being the transfer of Capital Reserve for purpose of reconstruction)				
	Land & Building A/c	Dr.		8.40	
	To Reconstruction A/c				8.40
	(Being the Land & Building revalued)				
	Reconstruction A/c	Dr.		8.40	
	To Debtors				8.00
	To Provision for Doubtful Debts.				0.40
	(Being the Debtors revalued)				
	Reconstruction A/c	Dr.		544.05	
	To Goodwill A/c				10
	To Profit and Loss A/c				15
	To Discount on issue of Debentures A/c				1
	To Plant & Machinery (balancing figure)				**518.05**
	(Being writing off of losses and reduction in the value of assets as per scheme of reconstruction)				

ILLUSTRATION 13

The ledger balances of X Ltd. as on 31st March, 2015 are:

Fixed Assets ₹ 7,00,000, Investments ₹ 10,000, Stock ₹ 3,90,000 Debtors ₹ 4,60,000, Preliminary Expenses ₹ 20,000, Equity Share Capital (60% paid) ₹ 6,00,000, 10% First Debentures ₹ 2,00,000, 12% Second Debentures ₹ 5,00,000, Bank overdraft ₹ 50,000, Trade Creditors (including Y for ₹ 8,50,000) ₹ 11,50,000, Outstanding interest for one year on both types of debentures.

Due to heavy losses, the following scheme of re-construction is agreed:

(a) To make the existing ₹ 100 equity shares fully paid up and then to reduce them to ₹ 20 each.

(b) To settle the claims of first debenture-holders by issuing 2,000, 13.5% debentures of ₹ 100 each,

(c) To discharge the claims of the second debenture-holders by issuing 15% 4,000 debentures of ₹ 100 each,

(d) To pay ₹ 3,00,000 to Mr. Y in full settlement of his account,

(e) To allot 15,000 fresh equity shares of ₹ 20 each to discharge the remaining trade creditors,

(f) Market value of investments is ₹ 20,000, and

(g) To write off the fictitious assets and to reduce the fixed assets.

Required: Pass journal Entries and prepare the post-reconstruction Balance-Sheet.

STEP 1: BALANCE SHEET OF X LTD. (BEFORE RECONSTRUCTION) AS AT 31 MARCH, 2015

Liabilities	₹	*Assets*	₹
Equity Share Capital (60% Paid-up)	6,00,000	Fixed Assets	7,00,000
10% First Debentures	2,00,000	Trade Debtors	4,60,000
12% Second Debentures	5,00,000	Stock	3,90,000
Outstanding Interest on Debentures for one year	80,000	Investments (Market value ₹ 20,000)	10,000
Bank Overdraft	50,000	Preliminary Expenses	20,000
Trade Creditors (including Y for ₹ 8,50,000)	11,50,000	Profit and Loss Account (Balancing figure)	10,00,000
	25,80,000		25,80,000

JOURNAL

Particulars		*L.F.*	*Dr. (₹)*	*Cr. (₹)*
Share Final Call A/c	Dr.		4,00,000	
To Equity Share Capital A/c				4,00,000
(Final call made for the balance on equity share)				
Bank A/c	Dr.		4,00,000	
To Equity Share Final Call A/c				4,00,000
(Receipt of Final Call money)				
Equity Share Capital (₹ 100 Shares) A/c	Dr.		10,00,000	
To Equity Shares (₹ 20 Shares) A/c				2,00,000
To Reconstruction A/c				8,00,000
(Reduction of ₹ 100 share capital to ₹ 20 each)				
10% First Debentures A/c	Dr.		2,00,000	
Debenture Interest (outstanding) A/c	Dr.		20,000	
To 13.5% Debentures A/c				2,00,000
To Reconstruction A/c				20,000
(Redemption of First Debentures)				
12% Second Debentures A/c	Dr.		5,00,000	
Debenture Interest (outstanding) A/c	Dr.		60,000	

To 15% Debentures A/c			4,00,000
To Reconstruction A/c			60,000
(Redemption of Second Debentures)			
Sundry Creditors A/c Dr.		11,50,000	
To Bank A/c			3,00,000
To Equity Share Capital A/c			3,00,000
To Reconstruction A/c			5,50,000
(Settlement of creditors' account)			
Reconstruction A/c Dr.		15,30,000	
To Profit and Loss A/c			10,00,000
To Preliminary Expenses A/c			20,000
To Fixed Assets A/c			5,10,000
(Utilisation of reconstruction account for writing of past losses and fixed assets)			

BALANCE SHEET OF CONTINENTAL CONSTRUCTION LTD. (AND REDUCED) AS AT 31.3.2015

	Particulars	Note No	₹
I.	**Equity and Liabilities**		
	(1) Shareholders' Funds		
	(a) Share Capital (₹ 20 each)		5,00,000
	(2) Non-Current Liabilities		
	(a) Long-term Borrowings	1	6,00,000
	(3) Current Liabilities		
	Total		11,00,000
II.	**Assets**		
	(1) Non-Current Assets		
	(a) Fixed Assets		
	Tangible Assets [7,00,000 – 5,10,000 (Amt. w/o)]		1,90,000
	(b) Non-Current Investments [Market Value ₹ 20,000]		10,000
	(2) Current Assets		
	(a) Inventories		3,90,000
	(b) Trade Receivables [Debtors]		4,60,000
	(c) Cash and Cash Equivalents		50,000
	Total		11,00,000

Notes To Accounts:

1. Long-term Borrowings		
13.5% Debentures	2,00,000	
15% Debentures	4,00,000	6,00,000

ILLUSTRATION 14

Given below are the extracts from the Balance Sheet of Road Block Ltd. as at March 31, 2014:

Particulars		*(₹ in lakhs)*
Equity Shares of ₹ 10 each		500
6%Cum-Pref.Shares of ₹ 100 each		100
Capital Reserve		6
Workmen's Compensation Fund:		
Pune	2	
Bombay	1	3
10% First Debentures		60
10% Second Debentures		100
Debentures Interest outstanding		16
Trade Creditors		165
Provision for Tax		10
Goodwill		10
Patents & Copy Rights		5
Plant & Machinery		719.6
10% Government Loan Earmarked Against Workmen's Compensation Fund		3
Investments in Shares in Q Ltd.		32.4
Stock		60
Debtors		10
Cash at Bank		104
Discount on issue of Debentures		1
Profit and Loss Account		15

Note: *Dividend on Preference Shares are in arrears for three years.*

The following scheme of internal reconstruction was approved by the Court and implemented:

(a) All the equity shares be converted into the same number of equity shares of ₹ 5 each, ₹ 2.50 paid up.

(b) The preference shares are converted from 6% to 15% but revalued in a manner in which the total return on them remains unaffected. Four equity shares of ₹ 5 each, ₹ 2.50 paid up to be issued for each ₹ 100 of arrears of preference dividend.

(c) Mr. A holds 10% first debentures for ₹ 40 lacs and 10% second debentures for ₹ 60 lacs. He is also a creditor for ₹ 10 lacs. Mr. 'A' is to cancel ₹ 60 lacs of his total debt and to pay ₹ 10 lacs to the company and to receive new 12% Debentures for the balance amount.

(d) Mr. B holds 10% first debentures for ₹ 20 lacs and 10% second debentures for ₹ 40 lacs and is also a creditor for ₹ 5 lacs. Mr. 'B' is to cancel ₹ 30 lacs of his total debt and to accept new 12% Debentures for the balance amount

(e) Trade Creditors (other than A and B) are given the option of either to accept equity shares of ₹ 5, ₹ 2.50 paid up each, for the amount due to them *or* to accept 80% of the amount due in cash. 40% Creditors accepted equity shares whereas the balance accepted cash in full settlement.

(f) There were capital commitments totalling ₹ 300 lacs. These contracts are to be cancelled on payment of 5% of the contract price as a penalty.

(g) The Directors refund ₹ 11 lacs of the fees previously received by them.

(h) Workmen's Compensation Fund (Bombay) disclosed the fact that actually there was a liability of ₹ 20,000 only. As a result the relevant fund amount balance was to be brought down to the required amount. Investments were realised at 10% above the book value.

(i) The taxation liability of the company is settled at ₹ 8.88 lacs and the same is paid immediately.

(j) Road Block Ltd. holds 21,600 shares in Q Ltd. This represents 15% of the share capital of that company. Q Ltd. is not a quoted company. The average net profit (after tax) of the company is ₹ 25 lacs. The shares would be valued based on 12% capitalization rate.

(k) A dissentient shareholder transferred his 100 shares to a director.

(l) Stock is to be valued at 114% of book value. 80% of Debtors are considered as Bad and 20% of the balance Debtors are considered as Doubtful. Any surplus after writing off the various losses should be utilized in writing down the value of plant & machinery.

(m) All equity shareholders paid the balance to make the shares fully paid up and then all equity shares were consolidated into the shares of ₹ 10 each.

Required: Pass the Journal Entries and prepare the Reconstruction Account, Bank Account and Balance Sheet after Reconstructon assuming that the Authorised Capital was incresed to 500 lacs by compling with the necessary formalaties.

SOLUTION

JOURNAL *[₹ in Lacs]*

Date	*Particulars*		*L.F.*	*Dr. (₹)*	*Cr. (₹)*
(a)	Equity Share Capital (₹ 10 each) A/c	Dr.		500	
	To Equity Share Capital (₹ 5 each) A/c				125
	To Reconstruction A/c				375
	(Being the conversion of all the equity shares into the same number of equity shares of ₹ 5 each, ₹ 2.50 paid up as per scheme of reconstruction)				
(b)(i)	6% Cum-Preference Share Capital (₹ 100) A/c	Dr.		100	
	To 15% Cum-Pref. Share Capital (₹ 100) A/c				40
	To Reconstruction A/c				60
	(Being 40000 15% cum Pref. share of ₹ 100 each issued so as to maintain the same amount of dividend (i.e. ₹ 6 lacs) vide scheme of reconstruction dated.....)				
(b)(ii)	Reconstruction A/c	Dr.		1.8	
	To Equity Share Capital (₹ 5 each, ₹ 2.50 paid up) A/c				1.8
	(Being 72000 equity shares of ₹ 5 each, ₹ 2.50 paid up issued to pref. Shareholders for dividend arrears vide scheme of Reconstruction dated.....)				
(c)(i)	10% First Debentures A/c	Dr.		40	
	10% Second Debentures A/c	Dr.		60	
	Trade Creditors A/c	Dr.		10	
	Interest on Debentures Outstanding A/c	Dr.		10	
	To Mr. A				120
	(Being the total amount due to A t/f to his A/c)				

(c)(ii)	Bank A/c	Dr.	10	
	To Mr. A			10
	(Being the amount received from Mr. A under the Reconstruction Scheme)			
(c)(iii)	Mr. A A/c	Dr.	130	
	To 12% New Debentures A/c			70
	To Reconstruction A/c			60
	(Being ₹ 60 lacs due to A (Including creditors) cancelled and 12% new debentures allotted for balance amount as per scheme of reconstruction)			
(d)(i)	10% First Debentures A/c	Dr.	20	
	10% Second Debentures A/c	Dr.	40	
	Trade Creditors A/c	Dr.	5	
	Interest on Debentures Outstanding A/c	Dr.	6	
	To Mr. B			71
	(Being the total amount due to Mr. B t/f to his A/c)			
d(ii)	Mr. B		71	
	To 12% New Debentures A/c			41
	To Reconstruction A/c			30
	(Being ₹ 30 lacs due to B (including creditors) cancelled and 12% new debentures allotted for balance amount as per scheme of reconstruction)			
(e)	Trade Creditors A/c	Dr.	150	
	To Equity Share Capital (₹ 5 each, ₹ 2.50 paid up) A/c			60
	To Bank A/c			72
	To Reconstruction a/c			18
	(Being the Trade creditors for ₹ 60 lakhs accepted 24 lakhs shares of ₹ 5 each, ₹ 2.50 paid up for full amount and those for ₹.90 lakhs accepted cash equal to 80% of claim in full settlement)			
(f)	Reconstruction A/c	Dr.	15	
	To Bank A/c			15
	(Being payment made for cancellation of capital commts.)			
(g)	Bank A/c	Dr.	11	
	To Reconstruction A/c			11
	(Being refund of fees by directors credited to Reconstruction A/c)			
(h)(i)	Bank A/c	Dr.	0.88	
	To Investment in 10% Government Loan A/c			0.80
	To Workmen's Compensation Fund (Bombay) A/c			0.08
	(Being the Sale of Investments for Workmen's Compensation Fund (Bombay) and the profit on the sale of same transferred to Workmen Compensation Fund (Bombay) Account)			

(h)(ii)	Workmen's Compensation Fund (Bombay) A/c Dr. To Reconstruction A/c (Being the Surplus in Workmen Compensation Fund at Bombay transferred to Reconstruction Account)		0.88	 0.88
(i)	Provision for Tax A/c Dr. To Bank A/c To Reconstruction A/c (Being payment of tax liability in full settlement)		10	 8.88 1.12
(j)	Reconstruction A/c Dr. To Investments in Shares in Q Ltd. A/c (Being reduction in the value of Investments)		1.15	 1.15
(k)	No Journal Equity is to be passed			
(l)(i)	Capital Reserve A/c Dr. To Reconstruction A/c (Being the transfer of Capital Reserve for purpose of reconstruction)		6	 6
(l)(ii)	Stock A/c Dr. To Reconstruction A/c (Being the Stock revalued)		8.40	 8.40
(l)(iii)	Reconstruction A/c Dr. To Debtors To Provision for Doubtful Debts. (Being the Debtors revalued)		8.40	 8.00 0.40
(l)(iv)	Reconstruction A/c Dr. To Goodwill A/c To Profit and Loss A/c To Discount on issue of Debentures A/c To Plant & Machinery (balancing figure) (Being writing off of losses and reduction in the value of assets as per scheme of reconstruction)		544.05	 10 15 1 518.05
(m)(i)	Equity Share First & Final Call A/c Dr. To Equity Share Capital A/c (Being the first & final call due on 74.72 lakhs Share @ ₹ 2.50)		186.80	 186.80
(m)(ii)	Bank A/c Dr. To Equity Share First & Final Call A/c (Being the First & Final Call received)		186.80	 186.80
(m)(iii)	Equity Share Capital (₹ 5 each) A/c Dr. To Equity Share Capital (₹ 10 each) A/c (Being the consolidation of 74.72 lakhs equity shares of ₹ 5 each into 37.36 lakhs equity shares of ₹ 10 each)		373.60	 373.60

Working Notes:

(i) Valuation of Investments in Shares of Q Ltd.= (₹ 25 lacs/.12) × 15% = ₹ 31.25 lacs

(ii) Reduction in the Value of Investment in Shares of Q Ltd.

= ₹ 32.40 lacs – ₹.31.25 = ₹.1.15 lacs

(iii) *The transfer of 100 Shares by a dissentient shareholder to the director concerned and waiver of the right to arrears of pref., dividend need not be accounted for.*

Dr. **RECONSTRUCTION ACCOUNT** *Cr.*

Particulars	*₹ (lacs)*	*Particulars*	*₹ (lacs)*
To Equity Share Capital A/c (₹ 5 each)	1.80	By Equity Share Capital (₹ 10 each)	375.00
To Bank A/c	15.00	By 6% Cum. Pref. Share Capital	60.00
To Investment in Shares in Q Ltd.	1.15	By Mr. A (Sundries)	60.00
To Debtors	8.00	By Mr. B (Sundries)	30.00
To Provision for Doubtful Debts	0.40	By Trade Creditors	18.00
To Goodwill A/c	10.00	By Bank A/c	11.00
To Profit & Loss A/c	15.00	By Workmen's Compensation	
To Discount on Issue of		Fund (Bombay) A/c	0.88
Debentures A/c	1.00	By Provision for Tax A/c	1.12
To Plant & Machinery A/c	518.05	By Capital Reserve A/c	6.00
		By Stock A/c	8.40
	570.40		570.40

Dr. **BANK ACCOUNT** *Cr.*

Particulars	*₹ (lacs)*	*Particulars*	*₹ (lacs)*
To Balance b/d	104.00	By Trade Creditors	72.00
To Mr. A	10.00	By Reconstruction A/c	15.00
To Reconstruction A/c	11.00	By Provision for Tax	8.88
To Investment in Govt. Loan A/c	0.88	By Balance c/d	216.80
To Equity Share Capital A/c (₹ 5 each)	186.80		
	312.68		312.68

BALANCE SHEET OF ROAD BLOCK LTD. (AND REDUCED) AS AT 31.3.2014

Particulars	*Note No*	*₹ (lacs)*
I. Equity and Liabilities		
(1) Shareholders'Funds		
(a) Share Capital	1	413.60
(b) Reserves and Surplus [Workmen's Compensation Fund] [2.00 + 0.20]		2.20
(2) Non-Current Liabilities [12% Debentures]		111.00
(3) Current Liabilities		
Total		526.80

II. Assets		
(1) Non-Current Assets		
(a) Fixed Assets		
Tangible Assets [719.60 – 518.05 (Amt. w/o)]		201.55
Intangible Assets [Patents & Copy Rights]		5.00
(b) Non-Current Investments	2	33.45
(2) Current Assets		
(a) Inventories		68.40
(b) Trade Receivables [Debtors][2.00 – 0.40]		1.60
(c) Cash and Cash Equivalents		216.80
Total		526.80

Notes To Accounts:

Particulars	₹ *(lacs)*
1. Share Capital	
37.36 lacs Equity Shares of ₹ 10 each	373.60
40,000,15% Pref. Shares of ₹ 100 each	40.00
	413.60
2. Non-Current Investments	
10% Govt. Loan earmarked against Workmen's Compensation Fund	2.20
Investments in Shares of Q Ltd.	31.25
	33.45

ILLUSTRATION 15

Given below are the extracts from the Balance Sheet of Unfortunate Bad Luck Ltd. as at 31.3.2014:

Particulars	₹
6% Cum-Pref. Shares of ₹ 100 each	1,00,000
Equity Shares of ₹ 100 each	8,00,000
Securities Premium	70,000
Capital Reserve	10,000
10% Debentures	14,00,000
Accrued Interest on Debentures	70,000
Sundry Creditors	4,50,000
Provision for Tax	10,000
Goodwill	1,00,000
Plant & Machinery	10,00,000
Other Fixed Assets	4,30,000
Investments	15,000
Stock	1,00,000
Sundry Debtors	40,000

Cash at Bank	25,000
Other Current Assets	80,000
P & L A/c	10,60,000
Preliminary Expenses	30,000
Underwriting Commission	20,000
Discount on Issue of Shares & Debentures	10,000

Notes:(i) *Dividend on Preference shares are in arrears for three years.*

(ii) *There is a Bill receivable for ₹ 10,000 under discount. The bill was received from Z.*

The following scheme of reconstruction is sanctioned:

(a) Equity Shares to be sub-divided into shares of ₹ 10 each.

(b) Equity Shareholders to surrender 90% of their holdings.

(c) The preference shares are converted from 6% to 15% but revalued in a manner in which the total return on them remains unaffected.

(d) Five equity shares out of those surrendered to be issued for each ₹ 100 of arrears of preference dividend.

(e) The debentureholders agree to reduce their total claims to ₹ 5,00,000 in consideration of their getting equity shares of ₹ 5,00,000 out of the surrendered equity shares.

(f) Sundry Creditors agree to reduce their claims to 20% and 80% of the balance shall be satisfied by issue of equity shares out of those surrendered.

(g) the taxation liability was settled (but not discharged) at ₹ 15,000.

(h) Expenses of re-organization amounted to ₹ 10,000

(i) Z proved insolvent and a dividend of 10% was received from his estate.

(j) Shares surrendered and not re-issued to be cancelled.

(k) The balance in Securities Premium a/c and Capital Reserve A/c to be utilized.

(l) Goodwill is considered worthless.

(m) The company expected to earn profit @ ₹ 45,000 p.a. from the current year which would be utilized entirely for reducing the debit balance of profit & loss account for the next three consecutive years. The remaining balance of the said account would be written off at the time of Capital Reduction process.

(n) Plant & Machinery to be written down by 40%.

(o) Other fixed assets to be written down to ₹ 4,10,000.

(p) Stock to the extent of rs. 10,000 considered to be obsolete.

(q) Debtors to the extent of ₹ 11,000 considered irrecoverable.

(r) Other current assets to be revalued at 75,000.

(s) Any surplus after writing off the various losses & reducing the value of over-valued assets, should be utilized in writing down value of plant & machinery further.

(t) A dissentient shareholder transferred his 100 shares to a director.

Required: Pass the necessary journal entries and prepare the Balance-Sheet reconstruction.

SOLUTION

JOURNAL OF UNFORTUNATE BAD LUCK LTD.

Date	*Particulars*	*Dr. (₹)*	*Cr. (₹)*
(a)	Equity Share Capital (₹ 100) A/c Dr.	8,00,000	
	To Equity Share Capital (₹ 10) A/c		8,00,000
	(Being equity of ₹ 100 each converted into equity shares of ₹ 10 each vide scheme of reconstruction dated......)		
(b)	Equity Share Capital (₹ 10) A/c Dr.	7,20,000	
	To Shares Surrendered A/c		7,20,000
	(Being 90% of equity shares surrendered vide scheme of reconstruction dated.....)		
(c)	6% Cum-preference Shares Capital (₹ 100) A/c Dr.	1,00,000	
	To 15% Cum-Pref. Share capital (₹ 100) A/c		40,000
	To Reconstruction A/c		60,000
	(Being 400 15% cum Pref. share of ₹ 100 each issued so as to maintain the same amount of dividend (i.e. ₹ 6,000) vide scheme of reconstruction dated.....)		
(d)	Shares Surrendered A/c Dr.	9,000	
	To Equity Share Capital (₹ 10) A/c		9,000
	(Being 900 equity shares out of those surrendered issued to pref. Shareholders on their surrendering a claim for arrears vide scheme of Reconstruction dated.....)		
(e)(i)	10% Debentures A/c Dr.	9,00,000	
	Accrued Interest on Debentures A/c Dr.	70,000	
	To Reconstruction A/c		9,70,000
	(Being the amount sacrificed by debentureholders as per reconstruction scheme dated......)		
(e)(ii)	Shares surrendered A/c Dr.	5,00,000	
	To Equity shares capital (₹ 10) A/c		5,00,000
	(Being 50,000 equity shares out of those surrendered issued to debentureholders on their surrendering a claim of 9,70,000)		
(f)(i)	Shares Surrendered A/c Dr.	72,000	
	To Equity Share Capital (₹ 10) A/c		72,000
	(Being 7,200 Equity shares out of those surrendered issued to creditors in part satisfaction of their balance claim)		
(f)(ii)	Sundry Creditors A/c Dr.	4,32,000	
	To Reconstruction A/c		4,32,000
	(Being total reduction in the claim of sundry creditors from 4,50,000 to ₹ 18,000)		
(g)(i)	Reconstruction A/c Dr.	5,000	
	To Provision for Tax A/c		5,000
	(Being the writing up the provision for tax as per Reconstruction scheme dated.......)		

(g)(ii)	Provision for Tax A/c	Dr.	15,000	
	To Tax Payable A/c			15,000
	(Being the conversion of provision into settled liability)			
(h)	Reconstruction A/c	Dr.	10,000	
	To Bank A/c			10,000
	(Being the reconstruction expenses paid)			
(i)(i)	Z	Dr.	10,000	
	To Bank A/c			10,000
	(Being the discounted B/R dishonourd)			
(i)(ii)	Bank A/c	Dr.	1,000	
	Reconstruction A/c	Dr.	9,000	
	To Z A/c			10,000
	(Being the ₹ 1,000 received from Z in respect of Discounted B/R met)			
(j)	Shares Surrendered A/c	Dr.	1,39,000	
	To Reconstruction A/c			1,39,000
	(Being shares surrendered but not re-issued cancelled)			
(k)	Capital Reserve A/c	Dr.	10,000	
	Securities Premium A/c	Dr.	70,000	
	To Reconstruction A/c			80,000
	(Being the transfer of balances of Capital Reserve A/c and Share Premium A/c vide Scheme of reconstruction dated......)			
(l to s)	Reconstruction A/c	Dr.	16,57,000	
	To Goodwill A/c			1,00,000
	To P & L A/c			9,25,000
	To Preliminary Expenses A/c			30,000
	To Underwriting Commission A/c			20,000
	To Discount on Issue of Shares/Deb. A/c			10,000
	To Other fixed assets			20,000
	To Stock			10,000
	To Debtors			11,000
	To Other Current Assets			5,000
	To Plant & Machinery			5,26,000
	(Being the balance of Reconstruction A/c utilized to written off various losses & to reduce the value of various overvalued assets vide Reconstruction scheme dated.....)			

BALANCE SHEET OF UNFOTUNATE BAD LUCK LTD. (AND REDUCED) AS AT 31.3.2014

Particulars	*Note No*	₹
I. Equity and Liabilities		
(1) Shareholders' Funds		
(a) Share Capital	1	7,01,000

(b) Reserves and Surplus [Profit & Loss A/c (Dr.)]		(1,35,000)
(2) Non-Current Liabilities [10%Debentures]		5,00,000
(3) Current Liabilities		
(a) Trade Payables[Creditors]		18,000
(b) Short-term Provisions [Provision for Tax]		15,000
Total		10,99,000
II. Assets		
(1) Non-Current Assets		
(a) Fixed Assets		
Tangible Assets	2	8,84,000
Intangible Assets [Goodwill] [1,00,000 -1,00,000(Amt. w/o)]		0
(b) Non-Current Investments		15,000
(2) Current Assets		
(a) Inventories		90,000
(b) Trade Receivables [Debtors]		29,000
(c) Cash and Cash Equivalents		6,000
(d) Other Current Assets		75,000
Total		10,99,000

Notes To Accounts:

Particulars		₹
1. Share Capital		
66100 Equity Shares of ₹ 10 each,₹ paid		6,61,000
400,15% Pref. Shares of ₹ 100 each, ₹ paid		40,000
		7,01,000
2. Tangible Assets		
Plant & Machinery	10,00,000	
Less: Amt. w/o under Reconstruction Scheme	5,26,000	4,74,000
Other Fixed Assets	4,30,000	
Less: Amt. w/o under Reconstruction Scheme	20,000	4,10,000
Total		8,84,000

Note: *The transfer of 100 Shares by a dissentient shareholder to the director concerned and waiver of the right to arrears of pref., dividend need not be accounted for.*

Working Notes:

(i) *Calculation of the amount of Shares Surrendered to be transferred to Reconstruction Account.*

Dr. **SHARES SURRENDERED ACCOUNT** *Cr.*

Particulars	₹	*Particulars*	₹
To Equity Shares Capital A/c (Issued to Debentureholders)	5,00,000	By Equity Share Capital A/c (₹ 10)	7,20,000
To Equity Shares Capital A/c (Issued to sundry Creditors)	72,000		

To Equity Share Capital A/c (Issued to Pref. Shareholders)	9,000		
To Reconstruction A/c (b.f.)	1,39,000		
	7,20,000		7,20,000

(ii) *Calculation of Debit Balance of P & L A/c to be written off now*

= ₹ 10,60,000 – (₹ 45,000 × 3) = ₹ 9,25,000.

(iii) *Calculation of the amount by which the value of Plant & Machinery is to be written down*

Dr. **RECONSTRUCTION ACCOUNT** *Cr.*

Particulars	₹	*Particulars*	₹
To To Provision for tax	5,000	By 6% Cum Pref. Share Capital A/c	60,000
To Bank A/c (Expenses)	10,000	By 10% Debentures A/c	9,00,000
To Bank A/c (Discounted B/R)	9,000	By Accrued Interest	70,000
To Goodwill A/c	1,00,000	By Sundry Creditors	4,32,000
To P & L A/c	9,25,000	By Share Surrendered A/c	1,39,000
To Preliminary Expenses	30,000	By Capital Reserve A/c	10,000
To Underwriting Commission	20,000	By Securities Premium A/c	70,000
To Discount on Issue of Shares/ Deb. A/c	10,000		
To Other Fixed Assets	20,000		
To Stock	10,000		
To Debtors	11,000		
To Other Current Assets	5,000		
To Plant & Machinery (b.f.)	5,26,000		
	16,81,000		16,81,000

SOLVED PROBLEMS

PROBLEM 1

The following is the balance sheet of CSJHB Ltd. as at 31st March, 2014:

Particulars	₹
Share Capital:	
Authorised:	
30,000 Equity Shares of ₹ 10 each	3,00,000
30,000, 13% Pref. Shares of ₹ 10 each	3,00,000
	6,00,000
Subscribed, Issued and Paid-up:	
20,000 Equity Shares of ₹ 10 each fully paid	2,00,000
18,000 13% Pref. Shares of ₹ 10 fully paid	1,80,000

Reserves & Surplus:		
Workmen's compensation fund:		
Pune	20,000	
Bombay	10,000	30,000
Secured loans:		
12% 'A' Debentures secured on Pune Property	30,000	
12% 'B' Debentures secured on Bombay Property	35,000	65,000
Current Liabilities & Provisions:		
(A) Current Liabilities:		
Sundry Creditors		25,000
(B) Provisions:		
Fixed Assets:		
Pune Property		1,60,000
Bombay Property		1,20,000
Plant and Machinery		1,50,000
Investments:		
10% Government loan earmarked against Workmen's compensation Fund		30,000
Miscellaneous expenditure and losses:		
Profit and Loss Account		40,000

The following scheme of reconstruction was duly approved:

(a) Equity shares were to be reduced to ₹ 1 each.

(b) Preference shares were to be reduced by ₹ 2 per share.

(c) Debentureholders were to forgo their unpaid interest ₹ 5,200 which is included in sundry creditors.

(d) 'B' Debentureholders agreed to take over the Bombay property at ₹ 50,000 and paid the balance amount due from them in cash.

(e) Workmen's compensation fund (Bombay) disclosed the fact that actually there was a liability of ₹ 2,000 only. As a result the relevant fund amount balance was to be brought down to the required amount. Investments were realised at 10% above the book value.

(f) The Plant and machinery were to be written down by ₹ 90,000.

(g) Any balance remaining was to be applied as to 75% in writing down Pune property and 25% transferred to capital reserve.

Required: Pass the necessary journal entries and prepare the Balance Sheet after reconstruction.

SOLUTION

JOURNAL

Particulars		*L.F.*	*Dr. (₹)*	*Cr. (₹)*
Equity Share Capital (Old) A/c	Dr.		2,00,000	
Preference Share Capital A/c	Dr.		36,000	
To Equity Share Capital (New) A/c				20,000
To Reconstruction A/c				2,16,000

(Being the reduction of 20,000 equity shares of ₹ 10 each to ₹ 1 and 18,000 13% preference shares by ₹ 2 per share vide special Resolution No..... dated .... confirmed by court vide order dated......)			
Sundry Creditors A/c	Dr.	5,200	
To Reconstruction A/c			5,200
(Being the Cancellation of debenture interest)			
12% 'B' Debentures A/c	Dr.	35,000	
To 'B' Debentureholders A/c			35,000
(Being Transfer of 'B' Debentures to debentureholders)			
₹B' Debentureholders A/c	Dr.	35,000	
Bank A/c	Dr.	15,000	
To Bombay Property			50,000
(Being the Payment to 'B' debentureholders by transfer of Bombay Property, the balance received from them in cash)			
Bank A/c	Dr.	8,800	
To Investment in 10% Government Loan A/c			8,000
To Workmen's Compensation Fund (Bombay) A/c			800
[Being the Sale of investments for workmen's compensation fund (Bombay) and the profit on the sale of same transferred to workmen compensation fund (Bombay) account]			
Workmen's Compensation Fund (Bombay) A/c	Dr.	8,800	
To Reconstruction A/c			8,800
(Being the Surplus in workmen compensation fund at Bombay transferred to reconstruction account)			
Reconstruction A/c	Dr.	2,30,000	
To Profit and Loss A/c			40,000
To Plant and Machinery A/c			90,000
To Bombay Property			70,000
To Pune Property			22,500
To Capital Reserve A/c			7,500
(Being the utilisation of the amount available in the reconstruction account to write off the debit balance in the profit and loss account and to write down the value of various assets as per scheme of reconstruction)			

BALANCE SHEET OF CSJHB LTD. (AND REDUCED) AS AT 31.03.2014

Particulars	*Note No*	₹
I. **Equity and Liabilities**		
(1) Shareholders'Funds		
(a) Share Capital (₹ 10 each)	1	1,64,000
(b) Reserves and Surplus	2	29,500
(2) Non-Current Liabilities [10%Debentures]		30,000

	(3) Current Liabilities		
	(a) Trade Payables[Creditors]		19,800
	Total		2,43,300
II.	**Assets**		
	(1) Non-Current Assets		
	(a) Fixed Assets		
	Tangible Assets	3	1,97,500
	(b) Non-Current Investments[10% Govt. Loan]		22,000
	(2) Current Assets		
	(a) Cash and Cash Equivalents		23,800
	Total		2,43,300

Notes To Accounts:

	Particulars		₹
1.	**Share Capital**		
	20000 Equity Shares of ₹ 1 each		20,000
	18000,15% Pref. Shares of ₹ 10 each, ₹ 8 paid		1,44,000
			1,64,000
2.	**Reserves and Surplus**		
	Capital Reserve		7,500
	[Workmen's Compensation Fund] [20,000 + 2,000]		22,000
	Total		29,500
3.	**Tangible Assets**		
	Pune Property	1,60,000	
	Less: Amt. w/o under Reconstruction Scheme	22,500	1,37,500
	Plant & Machinery	1,50,000	
	Less: Amt. w/o under Reconstruction Scheme	90,000	60,000
	Total		1,97,500

PROBLEM 2

Green Limited had decided to reconstruct the Balance Sheet since it has accumulated huge losses. The following is the Balance Sheet of the Company on 31.3.2014 before reconstruction:

BALANCE SHEET OF GREEN LIMITED AS AT 31.3.2014

Particulars	₹
Share Capital:	
Authorised:	
1,50,000 Equity Shares of ₹ 50 each	75,00,000
Subscribed 50,000 Equity Shares of ₹ 50 each	25,00,000
1,00,000 Equity Shares of ₹ 50 each, ₹ 40 per share paid up	40,00,000
Secured Loans:	

12% First Debentures	5,00,000
12% Second Debentures	10,00,000
Current Liabilities:	
Sundry Creditors	5,00,000
Fixed Assets:	
Goodwill	20,00,000
Building	10,00,000
Plant	10,00,000
Computers	25,00,000
Investments	Nil
Current Assets	Nil
Profit and Loss A/c (Loss)	20,00,000

The Following is the interest of Mr. X and Mr. Y in Green Limited:

Particulars	*Mr. X* ₹	*Mr. Y* ₹
12% First Debentures	3,00,000	2,00,000
12% Second Debentures	7,00,000	3,00,000
Sundry Creditors	2,00,000	1,00,000
	12,00,000	6,00,000
Fully paid up ₹ 50 shares	3,00,000	2,00,000
Parly paid shares (₹ 40 paid up)	5,00,000	5,00,000

The following Scheme of Reconstruction is approved by all parties interested and also by the Court:

(a) Uncalled capital is to be called up in full and such shares and the other fully paid up shares be converted into equity shares of ₹ 20 each.

(b) Mr. X is to cancel ₹ 7,00,000 of his total debt (other than share amount) and to pay ₹ 2 lakhs to the company and to receive new 14% First Debentures for the balance amount.

(c) Mr. Y is to cancel ₹ 3,00,000 of his total debt (other than equity shares) and to accept new 14% First Debentures for the balance.

(d) The amount thus rendered available by the scheme shall be utilised in writing off of Goodwill, Profit and Loss A/c Loss and the balance to write off the value of computers.

Required: Pass the Journal Entires and prepare the Balance Sheet of the reconstructed company.

SOLUTION

JOURNAL

Particulars		*L.F.*	*Dr. (₹)*	*Cr. (₹)*
Bank A/c	Dr.		10,00,000	
To Equity Share Capital A/c				10,00,000
(Being the balance of ₹ 10 per share on 1,00,000 equity shares called up as per reconstruction scheme)				
Equity Share Capital A/c (₹ 50)	Dr.		75,00,000	
To Equity Share Capital A/c (₹ 20)				30,00,000

Particulars		Dr. (₹)	Cr. (₹)
To Capital Reduction A/c			45,00,000
(Being the reduction of equity shares of ₹ 50 each to shares of ₹ 20 each as per reconstruction scheme)			
12% First Debentures A/c	Dr.	3,00,000	
12% Second Debentures A/c	Dr.	7,00,000	
Sundry Creditors A/c	Dr.	2,00,000	
To X			12,00,000
(Being the total amount due to X, transferred to his account)			
Bank A/c	Dr.	2,00,000	
To X			2,00,000
(Being the amount paid by X under the reconstruction scheme)			
12% First Debentures A/c	Dr.	2,00,000	
12% Second Debentures A/c	Dr.	3,00,000	
Sundry Creditors A/c	Dr.	1,00,000	
To Y			6,00,000
(Being the total amount due to Y, transferred to his account)			
X	Dr.	14,00,000	
To 14% First Debentures A/c			7,00,000
To Capital Reduction A/c			7,00,000
(Being the cancellation of ₹ 7,00,000 out of total debt of Mr. X and issue of 14% first debentures for the balance amount as per reconstruction scheme)			
Y	Dr.	6,00,000	
To 14% First Debentures A/c			3,00,000
To Capital Reduction A/c			3,00,000
(Being the cancellation of ₹ 3,00,000 out of total debt of Mr. Y and issue of 14% first debentures for the balance amount as per reconstruction scheme)			
Capital Reduction A/c	Dr.	55,00,000	
To Goodwill A/c			20,00,000
To Profit and Loss A/c			20,00,000
To Computers A/c (balancing figure)			15,00,000
(Being the balance amount of capital reduction account utilised in writing off goodwill, profit and loss account, and computers)			

BALANCE SHEET OF GREEN LTD. (AND REDUCED) AS AT 31.03.2014

Particulars	*Note No*	₹
I. Equity and Liabilities		
(1) Shareholders' Funds		
(a) Share Capital (₹ 10 each)		30,00,000
(2) Non-Current Liabilities[14% Debentures]		10,00,000

(3) Current Liabilities		
(a) Trade Payables[Creditors]		2,00,000
Total		42,00,000
II. Assets		
(1) Non-Current Assets		
(a) Fixed Assets		
Tangible Assets	3	30,00,000
(2) Current Assets		
(a) Cash and Cash Equivalents		12,00,000
Total		42,00,000

Notes To Accounts:

1. Tangible Assets	
Land & Building	10,00,000
Plant & Machinery	10,00,000
Computers	10,00,000
Total	30,00,000

Working Note:

Dr. **CAPITAL REDUCTION ACCOUNT** *Cr.*

Particulars	₹	*Particulars*	₹
To Goodwill A/c	20,00,000	By Equity Share Capital A/c	45,00,000
To P & L A/c	20,00,000	By X	7,00,000
To Computers (Bal. Fig.)	15,00,000	By Y	3,00,000
	55,00,000		55,00,000

PROBLEM 3

The following is the Balance Sheet of Rocky Ltd. as at March 31, 2014:

Particulars	*₹ in lacs*
Fully paid Equity Shares of ₹ 10 each	500
Capital Reserve	6
12% Debentures	400
Debenture Interest Outstanding	48
Trade Creditors	165
Director's Remuneration Outstanding	10
Other Outstanding Expenses	11
Provisions	33
Goodwill	15
Land and Building	184
Plant and Machinery	286

Furniture and Fixtures	41
Stock	142
Debtors	80
Cash at Bank	27
Discount on Issue of Debentures	8
Profits and Loss Account	390

The following scheme of internal reconstruction was framed, approved by the Court, all the concerned parties and implemented:

(i) All the equity shares be converted into the same number of fully-paid equity shares of ₹ 2.50 each.

(ii) Directors agree to forego their outstanding remuneration.

(iii) The debentureholders also agree to forego outstanding interest in return of their 12% debentures being converted into 13% debentures.

(iv) The existing shareholders agree to subscribe for cash, fully paid equity shares of ₹ 2.50 each for ₹ 125 lacs.

(v) Trade creditors are given the option of either to accept fully-paid equity shares of ₹ 2.50 each for the amount due to them *or* to accept 80% of the amount due in cash. Creditors for ₹ 65 lacs accept equity shares whereas those for ₹ 100 lacs accept ₹ 80 lacs in cash in full settlement.

(vi) The Assets are revalued as under:

Particulars	*₹ in lacs*
Land and building	230
Plant and Machinery	220
Stock	120
Debtors	76

Required: Pass Journal Entries and prepare Balance Sheet after reconstruction.

SOLUTION

JOURNAL

[₹ in lacs]

Particulars		*L.F.*	*Dr. (₹)*	*Cr. (₹)*
Equity Share Capital (₹ 10 each) A/c	Dr.		500	
To Equity Share Capital (₹ 2.50 each) A/c				125
To Reconstruction A/c				375
(Being the conversion of all the equity shares into the same number of fully paid equity shares of ₹ 2.50 each as per scheme of reconstruction)				
Director's Remuneration Outstanding A/c	Dr.		10	
To Reconstruction A/c				10
(Being the outstanding remuneration foregone by the directors as per scheme of reconstruction)				
12% Debentures A/c	Dr.		400	
Debenture Interest Outstanding A/c	Dr.		48	

To 13% Debentures A/c			400
To Reconstruction A/c			48
(Being the conversion of 12% debentures into 13% debentures, Debentureholders forgoing outstanding debenture interest)			
Bank Dr.		125	
To Equity Share Application and Allotment A/c			125
(Being the application money received for equity shares)			
Equity Share Application and Allotment A/c Dr.		125	
To Equity Share Capital (₹ 2.50 each) A/c			125
(Being the application money transferred to share capital)			
Trade Creditors A/c Dr.		165	
To Equity Share Capital (₹ 2.50 each) A/c			65
To Bank A/c			80
To Reconstruction A/c			20
(Being the Trade creditors for ₹ 65 lakhs accepting shares for full amount and those for ₹ 100 lakhs accepting cash equal to 80% of claim in full settlement)			
Capital Reserve A/c Dr.		6	
To Reconstruction A/c			6
(Being the Capital Reserve being used for purpose of reconstruction)			
Land and Building Dr.		46	
To Reconstruction A/c			46
(Being the appreciation made in the value of land and building as per scheme of reconstruction)			
Reconstruction A/c Dr.		505	
To Goodwill			15
To Plant and Machinery			66
To Stock			22
To Debtors			4
To Discount on issue of Debentures			8
To Profit and Loss A/c			390
(Being the writing off losses and reduction in the values of assets as per scheme of reconstruction)			

BALANCE SHEET OF ROCKY LTD. (AND REDUCED) AS AT 31.03.2014

Particulars	*Note No*	₹
I. Equity and Liabilities		
(1) Shareholders' Funds		
(a) Share Capital (₹ 10 each)		315
(b) Reserves and Surplus		
(2) Non-Current Liabilities [13% Debentures]		400

	(3) Current Liabilities		
	(a) Trade Payables[Creditors]		
	(b) Short-term Provisions		33
	(c) Other Current Liabilities[O/S Expenses]		11
	Total		759
II.	**Assets**		
	(1) Non-Current Assets		
	(a) Fixed Assets		
	Tangible Assets	2	491
	Intangible Assets [Goodwill] [15 – 15]		0
	(2) Current Assets		
	(a) Inventories		120
	(b) Trade Receivables [Debtors – Prov] [80 – 4]		76
	(c) Cash and Cash Equivalents		72
	Total		759

Notes To Accounts:

	Particulars		₹
1.	**Share Capital**		
	126000 Equity Shares of ₹ 2.50 each		315
	(Of the above 26000 Shares were issued for consideration otherwise than cash)		
2.	**Tangible Assets**		
	Land & Building	184	
	Add: Amt. increased under Reconstruction Scheme	46	230
	Plant & Machinery	286	
	Less: Amt. w/o under Reconstruction Scheme	66	220
	Furniture& Fixtures		41
	Total		491

Working Notes:

Dr. **(I) REDUCTION ACCOUNT** *(₹ in lacs) Cr.*

Particulars	₹	*Particulars*	₹
To Goodwill	15	By Equity Share Capital A/c	375
To Plant and Machinery	66	By Director's Remuneration	
To Stock	22	By Outstanding A/c	10
To Debtors	4	By Deben. Interest Outstanding A/c	48
To Discount on issue of Debentures	8	By Trade Creditors	20
To Profit and Loss A/c	390	By Capital Reserve	6
		By Land and Building	46
	505		505

	₹
(ii) Equity share capital (after reconstruction)	₹
Equity Share Capital (₹ 2.50 each)	125
Add: Fresh issue	125
Add: Equity share issued to creditors	65
	315
(iii) Cash at bank (after reconstruction)	
Cash at bank (before reconstruction)	27
Add: Proceeds from issue of equity shares	125
	152
Less: Payment made to creditors	80
	72

PROBLEM 4

Following are the extracts of Balance Sheets as at March 31, 2013:

(₹ '000)

Particulars	*K Ltd.*	*W Ltd.*
Share capital:		
Equity Shares of ₹ 100 each	2,000	1,500
9% Preference Shares of ₹ 100 each	700	400
General Reserve	240	170
Profit & Loss A/c	—	15
12% Debentures of ₹ 100 each	600	200
Sundry Creditors	560	315
Goodwill	20	—
Other Fixed Assets	2,400	1,150
Debtors	625	615
Stock	412	680
Cash at bank	38	155
Own debentures [Nominal value ₹ 2,00,000]	192	—
Discount on issue of debentures	2	—
Profit & Loss A/c	411	—

On 1.4.2013, K Ltd. adopted the following scheme of reconstruction:

(a) Each equity share shall be sub-divided into 10 equity shares of ₹ 10 each fully paid up. 50% of the equity share capital would be surrendered to the company.

(b) Preference dividends are in arrear for 3 years. Preference shareholders agreed to waive 80% of the dividend claim and accept payment for the balance.

(c) Own debentures of ₹ 80,000 were sold at ₹ 98 own-interest and remaining own debentures were cancelled.

(d) Debentureholders of ₹ 3,00,000 agreed to accept one machinery of book value of ₹ 3,20,000 in full settlement.

(e) Creditors, Debtors and Stocks were valued at ₹ 5,00,000, ₹ 6,00,000 and ₹ 4,00,000 respectively. The goodwill, discount on issue of Debentures & Profit and Loss (Dr.) are to be written off.

(f) The Company paid ₹ 20,000 as penalty to avoid capital commitments of ₹ 4,00,000.

On 2.4.2013 a scheme of absorption was adopted. K Ltd. would take over W Ltd. The purchase consideration was fixed as below:

(i) Equity shareholders of W Ltd. will be given 50 equity shares of ₹ 10 each fully paid up, in exchange for every 5 shares held in W Ltd.

(ii) Issue of 10% Preference Shares of ₹ 100 each in the ratio of 4 Preference Shares of K Ltd. for every 5 Preference Shares held in W Ltd.

(iii) Issue of one 12% Debentures of ₹ 100 each of K Ltd. for every 12% Debentures in W Ltd.

Required: Give journal entries in the books of K Ltd. and draw the resultant Balance Sheet as at 2nd April, 2013.

SOLUTION

JOURNAL

Date	*Particulars*		*L.F.*	*Dr. (₹)*	*Cr. (₹)*
01.04.13	Equity Share Capital A/c	Dr.		20,00,000	
	To Equity Share Capital A/c				20,00,000
	(Being the sub-division of one share of ₹ 100 each into 10 shares of ₹ 10 each)				
	Equity Share Capital A/c	Dr.		10,00,000	
	To Reconstruction A/c				10,00,000
	(Being the reduction of capital by 50%)				
	Reconstruction A/c	Dr.		42,000	
	To Bank A/c				42,000
	(Being the payment in cash for 20% of arrears of preference dividend)				
	Bank A/c	Dr.		78,400	
	To Own Debentures A/c [(1,92,000/2,00,000) × 80,000]			76,800	
	To Reconstruction A/c				1,600
	(Being the T/f of profit on sale of own Debentures)				
	12% Debentures A/c	Dr.		1,20,000	
	To Own debentures A/c [(1,92,000/2,00,000) × 1,20,000]			1,15,200	
	To Reconstruction A/c				4,800
	(Being the T/f of profit on cancellation of own Debentures)				
	12.% Debentures A/c	Dr.		3,00,000	
	Reconstruction A/c	Dr.		20,000	
	To Machinery A/c				3,20,000
	(Being the machinery taken up by debentureholders)				

	Reconstruction A/c Dr. To Debtors A/c To Stock A/c (Being the Assets revalued)	Dr.	37,000	 25,000 12,000
	Creditors A/c To Reconstruction A/c (Being the liabilities revalued)	Dr.	60,000	 60,000
	Reconstruction A/c To Goodwill A/c To Discount on debentures A/c To Profit and Loss A/c (Being the losses w/o)	Dr.	4,33,000	 20,000 2,000 4,11,000
	Reconstruction A/c To Bank A/c (Being the penalty paid for avoidance of capital commitments)	Dr.	20,000	 20,000
	Reconstruction A/c To Capital Reserve A/c (Being the transfer of Balance to Capital Reserve)	Dr.	5,14,400	 5,14,400
02.04.13	Business Purchase A/c To Liquidators of W Ltd. (Being the purchase of business)	Dr.	18,20,000	 18,20,000
	Fixed assets A/c Stock A/c Debtors A/c Cash at bank A/c To Sundry Ceditors A/c To 12% Debentures A/c of W Ltd. To Profit and loss A/c To General Reserve A/c ₹ (1,70,000 + 80,000*) To Business Purchase A/c (Being the recording over of all assets and liabilities taken over)	Dr. Dr. Dr. Dr.	11,50,000 6,80,000 6,15,000 1,55,000	 3,15,000 2,00,000 15,000 2,50,000 18,20,000
	Liquidators of W Ltd. A/c To Equity share capital A/c To 10% Preference share capital A/c (Being the purchase consideration discharged)	Dr.	18,20,000	 15,00,000 3,20,000
	12% Debentures of W Ltd. A/c To 12% Debentures A/c (Being the issue of 12% Debentures against Debentures of W Ltd.)	Dr.	2,00,000	 2,00,000

**₹ 80,000 is the balancing figure adjusted to General Reserve Account as per AS 14 "Accounting for Amalgamation".

BALANCE SHEET OF K LTD. AS AT 02.04.2013

	Particulars	*Note No*	₹
I.	**Equity and Liabilities**		
	(1) Shareholders' Funds		
	(a) Share Capital	1	35,20,000
	(b) Reserves and Surplus	2	10,19,400
	(2) Non-Current Liabilities [12%Debentures]	3	3,80,000
	(3) Current Liabilities		
	(a) Trade Payables [Creditors]	4	8,15,000
	Total		57,34,400
II.	**Assets**		
	(1) Non-Current Assets		
	(a) Fixed Assets		
	Tangible Assets	5	32,30,000
	(2) Current Assets		
	(a) Inventories	6	10,80,000
	(b) Trade Receivables [Debtors]	7	12,15,000
	(c) Cash and Cash Equivalents	8	2,09,400
	Total		57,34,400

Notes To Accounts:

	Particulars	₹
1.	**Share Capital**	
	2,50,000 Equity Shares of ₹ 10 each	25,00,000
	10,200,9% Pref. Shares of ₹ 100 each	10,20,000
	(Of the above 1,50,000 Equity Shares & 3200,9% Pref. Shares were issued for consideration otherwise than cash)	
	Total	35,20,000
2.	**Reserves and Surplus**	
	General Reserve (2,40,000 + 2,50,000)	4,90,000
	Profit & Loss Account	15,000
	Capital Reserve	5,14,400
	Total	10,19,400
3.	**Long-term Borrowings**	
	12% Debentures	6,00,000
	Less: Settled in consideration of machinery	(3,00,000)
	Less: Cancelled debentures	(1,20,000)
	Add: 12% Debentures issue to W Ltd.	2,00,000
	Total	3,80,000

4.	**Trade Payables**	
	of K Ltd.	5,60,000
	Less: Reduction due to revaluation	(60,000)
	Add: Trade Payables of W Ltd.	3,15,000
	Total	8,15,000
5.	**Tangible assets**	
	Balance of Other Fixed Assets	24,00,000
	Less: Machinery taken up by debenture holders	(3,20,000)
	Add: Other Fixed Assets of W Ltd.	11,50,000
	Total	32,30,000
6.	**Inventories**	
	of K Ltd.	4,12,000
	Less: Reduction due to revaluation	(12,000)
	Add: Inventories of W Ltd.	6,80,000
	Total	10,80,000
7.	**Trade Receivables**	
	of K Ltd.	6,25,000
	Less: Reduction due to revaluation	(25,000)
	Add: Trade Receivables of W Ltd.	6,15,000
	Total	12,15,000
8.	**Cash and Cash Equivalents**	
	of K Ltd.	38,000
	Less: Payment of Arrear of Preference dividend	(42,000)
	Add: Profit on Sale of own Debentures	78,400
	Less: Penalty Paid	(20,000)
	Add: Cash and Cash Equivalents of W Ltd.	1,55,000
	Total	2,09,400

Working Notes:

(i)	Purchase Consideration:	₹
	Equity share capital [(15,000 × 50/5) × ₹ 10]	15,00,000
	9% Preference share capital [(4,000 × 4/5) × ₹ 100]	3,20,000
		18,20,000
(ii)	General Reserve:	₹
	Share capital of W Ltd. (Equity + Preference)	19,00,000
	Less: Share capital issued by K Ltd.	18,20,000
	General reserve (resulted due to absorption)	80,000

PROBLEM 5

The summarized Balance Sheet of Bad Luck Ltd. as on 31st March, 2013 was as follows:

Particulars	*Note No*	*₹ (lacs)*
I. Equity and Liabilities		
(1) Shareholders' Funds		
(a) Share Capital	1	7.50
(b) Reserves and Surplus	2	(10.00)
(2) Non-Current Liabilities (Long-term Borrowings)	3	5.00
(3) Current Liabilities		
(a) Short-term Borrowings	4	5.00
(b) Trade Payables [Creditors]		2.50
Total		10.00
II. Assets		
(1) Non-Current Assets		
(a) Fixed Assets		
Tangible Assets	5	5.50
Intangible Assets [Goodwill]	6	1.50
(2) Current Assets		
(a) Inventories		1.50
(b) Trade Receivables		1.25
(c) Deferred revenue expenditure		0.25
Total		10.00

Notes To Accounts:

Particulars	*₹ (lacs)*
1. Share Capital	
5000 Equity Shares of ₹ 100 each	5.00
2500, 8% Pref. Shares of ₹ 100 each	2.50
	7.50
2. Reserves and Surplus (Profit and Loss A/c)	(10.00)
3. Long-term Borrowings (8% Debentures)	5.00
4. Short-term Borrowings	
Loan from Directors	3.00
Bank Overdraft	2.00
	5.00
5. Tangible Assets	
Freehold Property	4.00
Plant & Machinery	1.50
Total	5.50

6.	**Intangible Assets**	
	Goodwill	1.00
	Trademark	0.50
		1.50

The followig scheme of internal reconstruction was framed, approved by the Court, all the concerned parties and implemented:

(i) The preference shares to be written down to ₹ 25 each and the equity shares to ₹ 20 each. Each class of shares then to be conveted into shares of ₹ 100 each.

(ii) The debenture holders to take over freehold property (book value ₹ 2,00,000) at a valuation of ₹ 2,50,000 in part repayment of their holdings. Remaining freehold property to be revalued at ₹ 6,00,000.

(iii) Loan from directors to be waived off in full.

(iv) Stock of ₹ 50,000 to be written off, ₹ 12,500 to be provided for bad debts.

(v) Profit and Loss account balance, Trademark, Goodwill and Deferred Revenue Expenditure to be written off.

Pass Journal Entries for all the above mentioned transactions. Also, Prepare Capital Reducation account and company's Balance Sheet immediately after reconstruction.

SOLUTION

JOURNAL OF BAD LUCK LTD.

Date	*Particulars*		*Dr. (₹)*	*Cr. (₹)*
(i)	8% Preference Share Capital A/c (₹ 100)	Dr.	2,50,000	
	To 8% Preference Share Capital A/c (₹ 25)			62,500
	To Capital Reduction A/c			1,87,500
	(Being preference shares of ₹100 each reduced to ₹ 25 each as per the scheme)			
(ii)	Equity Share Capital A/c (₹ 100)	Dr.	5,00,000	
	To Equity Share Capital A/c (₹ 20)			1,00,000
	To Capital Reduction A/c			4,00,000
	(Being equity shares of ₹ 100 each reduced to ₹ 20 each as per the scheme)			
(iii)	8% Preference Share Capital A/c (₹ 25)	Dr.	62,500	
	To 8% Preference Share Capital A/c (₹ 100)			62,500
	(Being the conversion of 2,500 shares of ₹ 25 each into 625 shares of ₹ 100 each as per the scheme)			
(iv)	Equity Share Capital A/c (₹ 20)	Dr.	1,00,000	
	To Equity Share Capital A/c (₹ 100)			1,00,000
	(Being the conversion of 5,000 shares of ₹ 20 each in to 1,000 shares of ₹ 100 each as per the scheme)			
(v)	Freehold Property A/c	Dr.	50,000	
	To Capital Reduction A/c			50,000
	(Being appreciation in the value of property)			

(vi)	8% Debentures A/c	Dr.	2,50,000	
	To Freehold Property A/c			2,50,000
	(Being claim of debentureholders settled in part by transfer of freehold property as per the scheme)			
(vii)	Freehold Property A/c	Dr.	4,00,000	
	To Capital Reduction A/c			4,00,000
	(Being appreciation in the value of remaining property)			
(viii)	Director's Loan A/c	Dr.	3,00,000	
	To Capital Reduction A/c			3,00,000
	(Being Director's loan waived in full)			
(ix)	Capital Reduction A/c	Dr.	13,37,500	
	To Profit and Loss A/c			10,00,000
	To Deferred Revenue Expenditure A/c			25,000
	To Inventories A/c			50,000
	To Provision for Doubtful Debts A/c			12,500
	To Goodwill A/c			1,00,000
	To Trademark			50,000
	To Capital Reserve A/c			1,00,000
	(Being the various assets written off as per the scheme)			

Dr. **CAPITAL REDUCTION ACCOUNT** *Cr.*

Particulars	₹	*Particulars*	₹
To Provision for Doubtful Debts A/c	12,500	By Preference Share Capital A/c	1,87,500
To Inventories A/c	50,000	By Freehold Property A/c	4,50,000
To Trademark A/c	50,000	By Equity Share Capital A/c	4,00,000
To Deferred Revenue Exp. A/c	60,000	By Director's loan A/c	3,00,000
To Goodwill A/c	1,00,000		
To Profit and loss A/c	10,00,000		
To Capital reserve A/c	1,00,000		
	13,37,500		13,37,500

BALANCE SHEET OF BAD LUCK LTD. (AND REDUCED) AS AT 31.03.2013

Particulars	*Note No*	₹
I. Equity and Liabilities		
(1) Shareholders' Funds		
(a) Share Capital	1	1,62,500
(b) Reserves and Surplus[Capital Reserve]		1,00,000
(2) Non-Current Liabilities		
Long-term Borrowings [8% Debentures]		2,50,000
(3) Current Liabilities		
(a) Short-term Borrowings [Bank Overdraft]		2,00,000

(b) Trade Payables [Creditors]		2,50,000
Total		9,62,500
II. Assets		
(1) Non-Current Assets		
(a) Fixed Assets		
Tangible Assets	2	7,50,000
(2) Current Assets		
(a) Inventories		1,00,000
(b) Trade Receivables [1,50,000 – 12,500]		1,12,500
Total		9,62,500

Notes To Accounts:

Particulars	₹
1. Share Capital	
1,000 Equity Shares of ₹ 100 each	1,00,000
625,8% Pref. Shares of ₹ 100 each	62,500
	1,62,500
2. Tangible Assets	
Frehold Property	6,00,000
Plant & Machinery	1,50,000
Total	7,50,000

PROBLEM 6

Given below are the extracts from the Balance Sheet of CANIC Limited as at 31st March, 2015:

Particulars	₹
2,00,000 Equity Shares of ₹ 10 each, ₹ 5 paid	10,00,000
6,000 8% Preference Shares of ₹ 100 each	6,00,000
Profit & Loss Account (Dr.)	(4,08,000)
9% Debentures	6,00,000
Interest accrued on debentures	1,08,000
Bank overdraft	1,50,000
Interest accrued on Bank overdraft	15,000
Creditors	69,000
Fixed Assets	11,40,000
Patents and Copyrights	80,000
Investments at cost (Market value ₹ 55,000)	65,000
Inventories	4,00,000
Debtors	4,39,000
Bank	10,000

Preference dividend is in arrear for one year:

(a) Preference shareholders to give up their claims, inclusive of dividends, to the extent of 30% and desire to be paid off, (b) Debenture-holders agree to give up their claims to interest in consideration of their interest being enhanced to 12%, (c) Bank agrees to give up 50% of its interest outstanding in consideration of its being paid off at once, (d) Creditors would like to grant a discount of 5% if they are paid immediately, (e) Balance of Profit & Loss Account, Patents and Copyright and Debtors of ₹ 30,000 to be written off, (f) Fixed Assets to be written down by ₹ 34,000, (g) Investments are to reflect their market value, (h) To the extent not specifically stated, equity shareholders suffer on reduction of their rights. Cost of reconstruction is ₹ 3,350.

Required: Pass journal entries assuming that the scheme has been put through fully with the equity shareholders bringing in necessary cash to pay off the parties and to leave a Balance of ₹ 30,000 and prepare the Balance Sheet after reconstruction.

SOLUTION

JOURNAL

Particulars		*L.F.*	*Dr. (₹)*	*Cr. (₹)*
8% Preference Share Capital A/c	Dr.		6,00,000	
To Preference Shareholders' A/c				4,20,000
To Reconstruction A/c				1,80,000
(Being 30% of claim given up by preference shareholders as per reconstruction scheme dated....)				
Reconstruction A/c	Dr.		33,600	
To Preference Shareholders A/c				33,600
(Being 70% of arrears preference dividend payable to preference shareholders as per reconstruction scheme)				
9% Debentures A/c	Dr.		6,00,000	
Interest accrued on debentures A/c	Dr.		1,08,000	
To 12% Debentures A/c				6,00,000
To Reconstruction A/c				1,08,000
(Being 9% debentures converted into equivalent number of 12% debentures and the accrued debenture interest sacrificed as per Reconstruction scheme)				
Equity Share Capital A/c	Dr.		3,00,000	
To Reconstruction A/c				3,00,000
(Being equity shareholders rights reduced to a share of ₹ 3.50 vide Board's Resolution No....dated....., the amount of sacrifice credited to Reconstruction Account) (Working Notes i)				
Bank A/c	Dr.		7,00,000	
To Equity Share Capital A/c				7,00,000
(Being the amount received on 2,00,000 equity shares @₹ 3.50 per share as per reconstruction scheme) (Working Notes ii)				
Bank of India A/c	Dr.		1,50,000	
Interest Accrued on Bank overdraft A/c	Dr.		15,000	
To Bank A/c				1,57,500

To Reconstruction A/c (Being the Bank overdraft paid off including 50% of accrued interest as per reconstruction scheme, the interest sacrificed credited to Reconstruction A/c)			7,500
Creditors A/c Dr. To Bank A/c To Reconstruction A/c (Being the Creditors claim discharged to the extent of 95% as per reconstruction scheme, the balance of the claim sacrificed)		69,000	 65,550 3,450
Reconstruction A/c Dr. To Bank A/c (Being the Reconstruction expenses paid)		3,350	 3,350
Preference shareholders' A/c Dr. To Bank A/c (Being the Amount due to preference shareholders discharged)		4,53,600	 4,53,600
Reconstruction A/c Dr. To Profit and Loss A/c To Patents & copyright A/c To Debtors A/c To Investment A/c To Fixed Assets A/c (Being the debit balance of profit and loss account, patents & copy rights writing off and the value of debtors, investments and fixed assets written down as per reconstruction scheme)		5,62,000	 4,08,000 80,000 30,000 10,000 34,000

BALANCE SHEET OF CANIC LTD. (AND REDUCED) AS AT 31.03.2014

Particulars	Note No	₹
I. Equity and Liabilities		
(1) Shareholders' Funds		
(a) Share Capital (₹ 10 each, ₹ 7 paidup)		14,00,000
(b) Reserves and Surplus		
(2) Non-Current Liabilities [12%Debentures]		6,00,000
(3) Current Liabilities		
Total		20,00,000
II. Assets		
(1) Non-Current Assets		
(a) Fixed Assets		
Tangible Assets [11,40,000 – 34,000 (Amt. w/o)]		11,06,000
(b) Non-Current Investments [65,000 – 10,000 (Amt. w/o)]		55,000
(2) Current Assets		
(a) Inventories		4,00,000

(b) Trade Receivables [Debtors – Prov][80 – 4]		4,09,000
(c) Cash and Cash Equivalents		30,000
Total		20,00,000

Working Notes:

(I) STATEMENT SHOWING LIABILITIES AND EQUITY SACRIFICED AND THEIR USES AS PER SCHEME

Liabilities & Equity Sacrified	₹	*Uses*	₹
Preference shareholders:		Writing off:	
30% of ₹ 6,00,000	1,80,000	Reconstruction expenses	3,350
Debenture holders:		Profit and Loss account balance	4,08,000
Interest on Debentures	1,08,000	Patents and copyrights	80,000
Bank of India: Interest on bank overdraft (50%)	7,500	Pref. dividend Arrears (70% of ₹ 48,000)	33,600
Creditors:		Writing down:	
5% of ₹ 69,000	3,450	Debtors	30,000
Equity Shareholders:		Investment	10,000
Sacrifice @ ₹ 1.50 per share (Balancing figure)	3,00,000	Fixed Assets	34,000
	5,98,950		5,98,950

(II) CASH TO BE BROUGHT IN BY EQUITY SHAREHOLDERS:

Payments to: Preference shareholders (including arrears of preference dividend)	₹
70% of ₹ 6,48,000	4,53,600
Bank of India (including interest on bank overdraft) ₹ [1,50,000 + ₹ 7,500]	1,57,500
Creditors 95% of ₹ 69,000	65,550
Reconstruction expenses	3,350
Additional cash for working capital [₹ 30,000 – ₹ 10,000]	20,000
	7,00,000

Therefore, Contribution per Equity Share = ₹ 7,00,000/2,00,000 = ₹ 3.50

PROBLEM 7

Given below are the extracts from the Balance Sheet of Sickness Ltd. as at 31st March, 2015:

Particulars	₹
Share Capital:	
8,000 equity shares of ₹ 100 each, ₹ 50 per share paid up	4,00,000
4,000 11% Cumulative Preference shares of ₹ 100 each, fully paid up	4,00,000
Securities Premium A/c	40,000
General Reserve	60,000
Current Liabilities	3,10,000

Contingent liability not provided:	
Preference dividends are in arrears for three years including the year ended 31st March, 2014	—
Fixed Assets	
Tangible Fixed Assets	8,50,000
Less: Depreciation	(2,70,000)
Goodwill at cost	40,000
Investments	25,000
Inventories	2,10,000
Trade Debtors	2,55,000
Cash and Bank Balances	1,00,000

The funds of the Company are sufficient to discharge its liabilities including Preference Dividends in arrears. However, the company does not want to deplete its resources. It would also like to reflect the values of some of its assets in a realistic manner. The Board of Directors of the Company decided and proposed the following scheme of rehabilitation/reconstruction to be effective from 1st April, 2015.

(a) The cumulative preference shareholders are to be issued, in exchange of their holdings, 13% Debentures of the face value of ₹ 100 each at a premium of 10% Fractional holdings are to be paid off in cash.

(b) Arrears in preference dividends to be converted into equity shares of ₹ 100, ₹ 50 per share paid up.

(c) After the issue of the equity shares mentioned in (ii) above, the paid up value of all the equity shares is to be reduced to ₹ 25 each.

(d) The face value of all the equity shares to be reduced to ₹ 50 each and the balance of the unpaid portion is to be called up fully.

(e) Goodwill has lost its value and has to be written off. Market value of Tangible Fixed Assets is determined, as at 31st March, 2015 at ₹ 5,00,000.

(f) Investments have no market value and have to be written off.

(g) Inventories is to be valued at 110% of its book value and Trade Debtors are to be discounted by 5%.

The scheme, as approved by the Directors, is duly accepted by all authorities and put into effect.

During the working for the half year ended 30th September, 2015, it is noticed that the trading for the period has resulted in an increase of bank balances by ₹ 55,100, Sundry Debtors by ₹ 40,000, Trade Creditors by ₹ 26,000 and a decrease in stock by ₹ 8,000. Depreciation for the half year on fixed assets at 10% per annum is to be provided. The increase in the bank balances was prior to the company paying the half yearly interest on the debentures and redeeming one half of the debentures on 30th September, 2014.

Required: Prepare Journal, and the Balance Sheet of Sickness Ltd. as at 30th September, 2015.

SOLUTION

JOURNAL

Particulars		*L.F.*	*Dr. (₹)*	*Cr. (₹)*
11% Cumulative Preference Share Capital A/c	Dr.		4,00,000	
To 13% Debentures A/c				3,63,600
To Securities Premium A/c				36,360

Particulars		Dr. (₹)	Cr. (₹)
To Cash and Bank A/c (Being the issue of 3,636 13% debentures of ₹ 100 each at a premium of ₹ 10 to cancel 4,000 11% cumulative preference shares of ₹ 100 each, fraction ₹ 40 was paid in cash)			40
Capital Reduction A/c To Equity Share Capital A/c (Being the Issue of 2,640 equity shares of ₹ 100 each ₹ 50 paid-up for arrears preference dividend)	Dr.	1,32,000	1,32,000
Equity Share Capital A/c To Capital Reduction A/c (Being the Reduction of paid up value of 10,640 equity shares of ₹ 100 each, ₹ 50 paid up to shares of ₹ 50 each, ₹ 25 paid up)	Dr.	2,66,000	2,66,000
Equity Share Capital (₹ 100 each) A/c To Equity Share Capital (₹ 50 each) A/c (Being the face value of ₹ 100 reduced to ₹ 50 each as per scheme of reconstruction)	Dr.	2,66,000	2,66,000
Cash and Bank A/c To Equity Share Capital A/c (Being the Call money on 10,640 equity shares @ ₹ 25 to make the equity shares fully paid up)	Dr.	2,66,000	2,66,000
Capital Reduction A/c To Goodwill A/c To Investment A/c To Fixed Assets A/c (₹ 8,50,000 – ₹ 2,70,000) – ₹ 5,00,000 To Sundry Debtors A/c (Being the Value of Sundry assets written down)	Dr.	1,57,750	 40,000 25,000 80,000 12,750
Stock A/c To Capital Reduction A/c (Beig the Value of Stock written up	Dr.	21,000	21,000
General Reserve A/c To Capital Reduction A/c (Being the Transfer from General Reserve)	Dr.	2,750	2,750

BALANCE SHEET OF SICKNESS LTD. (AND REDUCED) AS AT 30.09.2015

Particulars	*Note No*	₹
I. Equity and Liabilities		
(1) Shareholders'Funds		
(a) Share Capital [₹ 50 each]		5,32,000
(b) Reserves and Surplus	1	1,46,076
(2) Non-Current Liabilities [13%Debentures]		1,81,800
(3) Current Liabilities		3,36,000
Total		11,95,876

II.	**Assets**		
	(1) Non-Current Assets		
	(a) Fixed Assets		
	Tangible Assets [5,80,000 – 80,000 (Amt. w/o) – 25,000]		4,75,000
	Intangible Assets [Goodwill] [40,000 – 40,000(Amt. w/o)]		0
	(b) Non-Current Investments[25,000 – 25,000(Amt. w/o)]		0
	(2) Current Assets		
	(a) Inventories		2,23,000
	(b) Trade Receivables [Debtors]		2,82,250
	(c) Cash and Cash Equivalents		2,15,626
	Total		11,95,876

Notes To Accounts:

1.	**Reserves and Surplus**	
	General Reserve	57,250
	Profit & Loss Account	12,466
	Securities Premium	76,360
	Total	1,46,076

Working Notes:

Dr. **(I) CAPITAL REDUCTION ACCOUNT** *Cr.*

Particulars	₹	*Particulars*	₹
To Equity Share Capital A/c	1,32,000	By Equity Share Capital A/c	2,66,000
To Sundries	1,57,750	By Stock	21,000
		By General Reserve	2,750
	2,89,750		2,89,750

Dr. **(II) CASH AND BANK ACCOUNT** *Cr.*

Particulars	₹	*Particulars*	₹
To Balance b/d	1,00,000	By 11% Cumulative Preference	
To Equity Share Capital A/c	2,66,000	Shares A/c	40
		By Balance c/d	3,65,960
	3,66,000		3,66,000

(III) BALANCE SHEET (AFTER INTERNAL RECONSTRUCTION)

Liabilities	₹	*Assets*		₹
Share Capital:		Fixed Assets:		
10,640 Equity Shares of ₹ 50 each fully paid	5,32,000	Goodwill	40,000	
Reserves and Surplus:		*Less:* Amt w/o under Reconstruction		—
Securities Premium A/c	76,360	Scheme	40,000	
General Reserve	57,250	Other Fixed Assets	5,80,000	

Secured Loans:		*Less:* Amt w/o under Reconstruction		5,00,000
13% Debentures	3,63,600	Scheme	80,000	
Current Liabilities:	3,10,000	Investments	25,000	
		Less: Amt w/o under		
		Reconstruction Scheme	25,000	—
		Current Assets:		
		Stock in Trade		2,31,000
		Sundry Debtors		2,42,250
		Cash and Bank		3,65,960
	13,39,210			13,39,210

Working Notes:

(I) CALCULATION OF HALF-YEARLY PROFIT

Particulars	₹	₹
Increase in bank balances	55,100	
Increase in sundry debtors	40,000	95,100
Less: Decrease in stock	8,000	
Less: Increase in trade creditors	26,000	34,000
Trading Profit before interest and depreciation		61,100
Less: Interest for 1/2 year @13% on ₹ 3,63,600	23,634	
Less: Depr. for 1/2 year on ₹ 5,00,000 @ 10% p.a	25,000	48,634
Net Profit		12,466

(II) CALCULATION OF CASH AND BANK BALANCE AS ON 30.9.2015

Particulars	₹	₹
Balance as on 31.3.2015		3,65,960
Add: Increase		55,100
Less: Interest	23,634	
Less: Redemption of 1/2 of 13% debentures	1,81,800	2,05,434
		2,15,626

PROBLEM 8

Given below are the extracts from the Balance Sheet of Munna Ltd. on 31st March, 2015:

Particulars	₹
20,000, Equity shares of ₹ 100 each	20,00,000
10,000, 7% preference shares of ₹ 100 each	10,00,000
Profit & Loss Account (Dr.)	(7,00,000)
Sundry Creditors	7,00,000
Bank overdraft	3,00,000
Goodwill	2,00,000

Plant and Machinery	18,00,000
Stock	3,00,000
Debtors	7,50,000
Cash	1,50,000
Preliminary Expenses	1,00,000

Two years' preference dividend are in arrears. The company had been bad time during the last two years and hopes for better business in future, earning profit and paying dividend provided the capital base is reduced.

An internal reconstruction scheme as follows was agreed to by all concerned:

(i) Creditors agreed to forego 50% of the claim.

(ii) Preference shareholders withdrew arrears dividend claim. They also agreed to lower their capital claim by 20% by reducing nominal value in consideration of 9% dividend effective after reorganisation in case equity shareholders' loss exceeded 50% on the application of the scheme.

(iii) Bank agreed to convert overdraft into term loan to the extent required for making current ratio equal to 2 : 1.

(iv) Revalued figure for plant and machinery was accepted as ₹ 15,00,000.

(v) Debtors to the extent of ₹ 4,00,000 were considered good.

(vi) Equity shares shall be exchanged for the same number of equity shares at a revised denomination as required after the reorganisation.

Required:

(a) Total loss to be borne by the equity and preference shareholders for the reorganisation;

(b) Shares of loss to the individual classes of shareholders;

(c) New structure of share capital after reorganisation;

(d) Working capital of the reorganised Co.; and

(e) A proforma balance sheet after reorganisation.

SOLUTION

(A) LOSS TO BE BORNE BY EQUITY AND PREFERENCE SHAREHOLDERS

Particulars	₹
Profit and Loss A/c (debit balance)	7,00,000
Preliminary Expenses	1,00,000
Goodwill	2,00,000
Plant and Machinery (₹ 18,00,000 – ₹ 15,00,000)	3,00,000
Debtors	3,50,000
Amount to be written off	16,50,000
Less: 50% of Sundry Creditors	3,50,000
Loss to be borne by equity and preference shareholders	13,00,000

Note: *Since preference dividend for 2 years which is in arrears is sacrificed by preference shareholders, the same may be ignored in the above calculation or alternatively may be included in the amount to be written off and then reduced therefrom as preference shareholders' sacrifice.*

(B) SHARES OF LOSS TO PREFERENCE SHAREHOLDERS AND EQUITY SHAREHOLDERS

Total loss being more than 50% of equity share capital:	
Preference shareholders' share of loss = 20% of ₹ 10,00,000	₹ 2,00,000
Equity shareholders' share of loss (₹ 13,00,000 – ₹ 2,00,000)	₹ 11,00,000
Total	₹ 13,00,000

(C) NEW STRUCTURE OF CAPITAL

Equity Shares	₹
20,000 shares of ₹ 45 each fully paid	9,00,000
Preference Shares	
10,000, 9% shares of ₹ 80 each fully paid	8,00,000
	17,00,000

(D) WORKING CAPITAL OF THE REORGANISED COMPANY

Current Assets	₹	₹
Stock		3,00,000
Debtors		4,00,000
Cash		1,50,000
		8,50,000
Less: Current Liabilities		
Creditors	3,50,000	
Bank overdraft (see Note)	75,000	4,25,000
Working Capital		4,25,000

Note: *Current ratio shall be 2: 1, i.e., total current liabilities shall be 50% of ₹ 8,50,000 = ₹ 4,25,000. Therefore, Bank overdraft = ₹ 4,25,000 – ₹ 3,50,000 = ₹ 75,000.*

BALANCE SHEET OF MUNNA LTD. (AND REDUCED) AS AT 31.3.2015

Particulars	*Note No*	₹
I. Equity and Liabilities		
(1) Shareholders' Funds		
(a) Share Capital	1	17,00,000
(b) Reserves and Surplus		
(2) Non-Current Liabilities [Term Loan with Bank]		2,25,000
(3) Current Liabilities		
(a) Trade Payables [Creditors]		3,50,000
(b) Other Current Liabilities [Bank overdraft]		75,000
Total		23,50,000
II. Assets		
(1) Non-Current Assets		
(a) Fixed Assets		
Tangible Assets [18,00,000 – 3,00,000(Amt. w/o)]		15,00,000

Intangible Assets [Goodwill] [2,00,000 – 2,00,000(Amt. w/o)]		0
(2) Current Assets		
(a) Inventories		3,00,000
(b) Trade Receivables [Debtors]		4,00,000
(c) Cash and Cash Equivalents		1,50,000
Total		23,50,000

Notes To Accounts:

Particulars	₹
1. Share Capital	
20000 Equity Shares of ₹ 45 each	9,00,000
10000,9% Pref. Shares of ₹ 80 each	8,00,000
	17,00,000

PROBLEM 9

Given below are the extracts from the Balance Sheet of X Ltd. as at March 31st, 2015.

Particulars	*(₹ in lakhs)*
Equity Shares of ₹ 100 each	600
14% Preference Shares of ₹ 100 each	200
Profit and Loss Account (Dr.)	(525)
13% Debentures	200
Debenture Interest accrued	26
Loan from bank	74
Trade creditors	340
Land and Building	200
Plant and Machinery	300
Furniture and Fixtures	50
Inventory	150
Sundry Debtors	70
Cash at bank	130
Preliminary expenses	10
Cost of issue of debentures	5

The company did not perform well and has suffered sizable losses during the last few years. However, it is that the company could be nursed back to health by proper financial restructuring. Consequently the following scheme of reconstruction has been drawn up.

(a) Equity shares are to be reduced to ₹ 25 per share, fully paid up;

(b) Preference shares are to be reduced (with coupon rate of 10%) to equal number of shares of ₹ 50 each, fully paid up

(c) Debenture holders have agreed to forgo the accrued interest due to them. In the future, the rate of interest on debentures is to be reduced to 9 percent.

(d) Trade creditors will forego 25% of the amount due to them.

(d) The company issued 6 lakh of equity shares at ₹ 25 each and the entire sum was to be paid on application. The entire amount was fully subscribed by promoters.

(f) Land and Building was to be revalued at ₹ 450 lakhs, Plant and Machinery was to be written down by ₹ 120 lakhs and a provision of ₹ 15 lakhs had to be made for doubtful debts.

Required:

(i) Show the impact of financial restructuring on the company's activities.

(ii) Prepare the fresh balance sheet after the reconstructions is completed on the basis of the above proposals.

SOLUTION

(A) IMPACT OF FINANCIAL RESTRUCTURING

(i) Benefits of X Ltd.	
A. Reduction of Liabilities payable	₹ in lakhs
Reduction in equity share capital (6 lakh shares × ₹ 75 per share)	450
Reduction in preference share capital (2 lakh shares × ₹ 50 per share)	100
Waiver of outstanding debenture Interest	26
Waiver from trade creditors (₹ 340 lakhs × 0.25)	85
	661
B. Revaluation of Assets	
Appreciation of Land and Building (₹ 450 lakhs – ₹ 200 lakhs)	250
	911
(ii) Amount of ₹ 911 lakhs utilized to write off losses, fictitious assets and over-valued assets.	
Writing of Profit and Loss Account	525
Cost of Issue of Debentures	5
Preliminary Expenses	10
Provision for Doubtful Debts	15
Revaluation of Plant and Machinery (₹ 300 lakhs – ₹ 104 lakhs)	120
	675
C. Capital Reserve [A – B]	236

(III) BALANCE SHEET OF X LTD. (AFTER RECONSTRUCTION) AS AT 31.3.2015

Particulars	*Note No*	*₹ (lacs)*
I. Equity and Liabilities		
(1) Shareholders' Funds		
(a) Share Capital	1	400
(b) Reserves and Surplus (Capital Reserve)		236
(2) Non-Current Liabilities [9% Debentures + Loan from Bank [200 + 74]		274
(3) Current Liabilities		
(a) Trade Payables [Creditors]		255

Total		1,165
II. Assets		
(1) Non-Current Assets		
(a) Fixed Assets		
Tangible Assets	2	680
(2) Current Assets		
(a) Inventories		150
(b) Trade Receivables [Debtors – Prov] [70 – 15]		55
(c) Cash and Cash Equivalents [balancing figure]		280
Total		1,165

Notes To Accounts:

Particulars		*₹ (lacs)*
1. Share Capital		
12 lacs Equity Shares of ₹ 25 each		300
2 lacs, 10% Pref. Shares of ₹ 50		100
		400
2. Tangible Assets		
Land & Building	200	
Add: Amt. increased under Reconstruction scheme	250	450
Plant & Machinery	300	
Less: Amt. w/o under Reconstruction scheme	(120)	180
Furniture & Fixtures		50
Total		680

PROBLEM 10

The Shareholders of Sunrise Ltd decided on a corporate restructuring exercise necessitated due to economic recession and a slump in business. From the audited prepare:

(i) Balance Sheet after the completion of the restructuring exercise,

(ii) The Capital Reduction Amount,

(iii) The Cash Account of the entity.

BALANCE SHEET OF SUNRISE LTD AS ON 31-03-2015

Particulars	₹
Share Capital	
30,000 Equity Shares (₹ 10 each)	3,00,000
40,000 8% Cumulative Preference Shares (₹ 10 each)	4,00,000
Reserves and Surplus	
Securities Premium Account	10,000
Profit & Loss Account	(1,38,400)
Non-Current Liabilities (Debentures)	1,25,400

Current Liabilities		
Creditors		1,20,000
Deferred Vat Payable		50,000
Temporary Bank Overdraft		2,23,100
Fixed Assets		
Trade Marks and Patents		1,10,000
Goodwill at cost		36,100
Freehold Land		1,20,000
Freehold Premises		2,44,000
Plant and Equipment		3,20,000
Investment (Market to Market)		64,000
Current Assets		
Inventories:		
Raw materials and packing		
Materials	60,000	
Finished goods	16,000	76,000
Trade receivable		1,20,000

Note: Preference Dividends are in arrears for 4 years.

The scheme of reconstruction that received the permission of the Court was on the following lines:

(1) The Authorized capital of the Company to be re-fixed at ₹ 10 Lakhs (Preference Capital ₹ 3 Lakhs and Equity Capital ₹ 7 Lakhs both ₹ 10/- shared each).

(2) The Preference shares are to be reduced to ₹ 5 each and equity share reduced by ₹ 3 per share. Post reduction, both classes of shares to be e-consolidated into ₹ 10 shares.

(3) Trade Investments are to be liquidation in open market

(4) One fresh equity share of ₹ 10 to issued for every ₹ 40 of preference dividends in arrears (ignore taxation).

(5) The Securities premium is to be fully utilized to meet the reconstruction programme.

(6) The debenture holder took over freehold land at ₹ 2,10,000 and settled the balance after adjusting their dues.

(7) Unprovided contingent Liabilities were settled at ₹ 54,000 and a pending insurance claim receivable settled at ₹ 12,500 on condition that claim will be immediately settled.

(8) The Intangible assets were all the written off along with ₹ 10,000 worth obsolete packing material and 10% of the Receivables.

(9) Reconstruction expenses amounted to ₹ 10,000.

(10) Remaining cash available as a result of the above transactions is to be utilised to pay off the bank overdraft to that extent.

(11) The equity shareholder agree that they who bring in cash to liquidate the balance outstanding on the overdraft account and also agree the sufficient funds will be brought in to bring up the net working capital, after completing the re-structuring exercise, to ₹ 2 lakhs. The Equity Shares will be issued at par for this purpose.

SOLUTION

(I) BALANCE SHEET OF SUNRISE LTD. (AND REDUCED) AS AT 31.03.2015

Particulars	Note No	₹
I. Equity and Liabilities		
(1) Shareholders' Funds		
(a) Share Capital	1	7,64,000
(b) Reserves and Surplus		—
(2) Non-Current Liabilities		
(3) Current Liabilities		
(a) Trade Payables [Creditors]		1,20,000
(b) Other Current Liabilities [Deferred VAT Payable]		50,000
Total		9,34,000
II. Assets		
(1) Non-Current Assets		
(a) Fixed Assets		
Tangible Assets	2	5,64,000
(2) Current Assets		
(a) Inventories [50,000 + 16,000]		66,000
(b) Trade Receivables [Debtors]		1,08,000
(c) Cash and Equivalents		1,96,000
Total		9,34,000

Notes to Accounts:

Particulars	₹
1. Share Capital	
56,400 Equity Shares of ₹ 10 each	5,64,000
20,000, 8% Pref. Shares of ₹ 10 each, ₹ 10 paid	2,00,000
(of the above 3,200 Equity Shares were issued for consideration otherwise than case)	
	7,64,000
2. Tangible Assets	
Free hold Premises	2,44,000
	3,20,000
	5,64,000

Dr. **(II) CAPITAL REDUCTION ACCOUNT** *Cr.*

Particulars	₹	Particulars	₹
To Equity Share Capital A/c [(4,00,000 × 8% × 4)/₹ 40] × ₹ 10	32,000	By 8% Cumulative Preference Share Capital A/c [40,000 × ₹ 5]	2,00,000
To Trademarks & Patents w/o	1,10,000	By Equity Share Capital [30,000 × ₹ 3]	90,000
To Goodwill w/o	36,100		

To Bank A/c (Contingent Liability)	54,000	By Securities Premium A/c	10,000
To Bank A/c (Expenses paid)	10,000	By Bank A/c (Insurance Claim)	12,500
To Trade Receivables (1,20,000 × 10%)	12,000	By Freehold Land (Profit on Transfer) [2,10,000 – 1,20,000]	90,000
To P&L A/c (Debit Bal. w/o)	1,38,400		
	4,02,500		4,02,500

Dr. **(III) CASH ACCOUNT** *Cr.*

Particulars	₹	*Particulars*	₹
To Investments A/c	64,000	By Capital Reduction A/c (Expenses)	10,000
To Capital Reduction (Insurance Claim)	12,500	By Capital Reduction A/c (Unrecorded Liability)	54,000
To Debentures Holders A/c [2,10,000 – 1,25,400]	84,600	By Bank Overdraft A/c (Settlement) (Balancing Figure)	97,100
	1,61,100		1,61,100

Working Notes:

(i) **Shortage of Working Capital** = ₹ 2,00,000 – Existing Working Capital

= ₹ 2,00,000 – [(60,000 – 10,000) + 16,000 + 1,08,000 – (1,20,000 + 50,000)]

= ₹ 1,96,000 (to be maintained by Bank Balance)

(ii) **Additional Equity Share Capital to be issued to have desired Bank Balance of ₹ 1,96,000**

Dr. **BANK ACCOUNT** *Cr.*

Particulars	₹	*Particulars*	₹
To Cash A/c	97,100	By Balance b/d (given)	2,23,100
To Equity Share Capital (b/f)	3,22,000	By Balance c/d (Desired Balance)	1,96,000
	4,19,100		4,19,100

(III) NO. OF SHARES AFTER RECONSTRUCTION

A.	No. of Equity Shares After Consolidation into Shares of ₹ 10 Each = [2,10,000/10]	21,000
B.	*Add:* Issued for Arrears of Dividend	3,200
C.	*Add:* Issued for Cash Consideration [3,22,000/10]	32,200
D.	No. of Shares After Reconstruction	56,400

8 AVERAGE DUE DATE AND ACCOUNT CURRENT

LEARNING OBJECTIVES

After studying this chapter, you should be able to understand:

- ◇ Meaning of Average Due Date
- ◇ Practical Steps to Calculate Average Due Date
- ◇ Short-cut Method in Case of Equal Instalments
- ◇ Account Current

1.0 MEANING OF AVERAGE DUE DATE

Average due date is a break-even date at which neither the party making the payment nor the receiving the payment suffers if the payment is made on that date. The person who has make the payment is able to make the payment in one instalment in lieu of several payments due on different dates. The person who has to receive the payment is able to calculate the interest on the total amount due for the days from the average due date to the settlement date. Thus, average due date facilitates the calculation of interest on total amount due for the period from the average due date to the actual date of settlement.

2.0 PRACTICAL STEPS TO CALCULATE AVERAGE DUE DATE

The practical steps to calculate the Average Due Date are given below:

Step 1	Take any date as base date (**Note:** Usually the due date of the first transaction is taken as the base date)	
Step 2	Calculate the due date of each transaction as under:	
	(a) **When the invoice/bill is made payable on a specific date**	(a) That specific date will be the due date.
	(b) **When the invoice/bill is made payable at a stated number of month(s) after date**	(b) That date on which the term of the invoice/bill shall expire will be the due date. **Note:** *The term shall expire on that day of the month which corresponds with the day on which the invoice bill is dated. If the month in which the period terminates has no corresponding day, The period shall be deemed* to expire on the last day of such a month.
	(c) **When the invoice/bill is made payable at a stated no. of days after date**	(c) That date which comes after adding stated number of days to the date of invoice/bill, shall be the due date **Note:** *The date of invoice/bill is excluded.*

(d) **When the due date is a public holiday**	(d) The preceeding business day will be the due date.
(e) **When the due date is an emergency/unforeseen holiday.**	(e) The next following day will be the due date.

Notes:

(i) In case of time or tenor bills, three days (called days to grace) are added to the due date to arrive at the date of maturity.

(ii) The term of a Bill after sight commences from the date of acceptance of the bill where as the term of a Bill after date commences from the date of drawing a bill.

(iii) Public Holidays include all Sundays, 26th Jan. (Republic Day), 15th Aug. (independence Day) 30th Sept., (bank holiday) and 1st April, (bank holiday)

Step 3	Calculate the number of days from the base date to the due date.
Step 4	Find out the product by multiplying the amount of transaction by corresponding number of days so calculated
Step 5	Find out the total of the product column.
Step 6	Find out the total of the amount column
Step 7	Divide the total of the product column by the total of the amount column to know the number of days to be adjusted to the base date.
Step 8	Calculate the Average Due Date by adding the aforesaid days to the base date (if quotient calculated as per Step 7 is positive) *or* by subtracting the aforesaid days from the base date (if quotient calculated as per Step 7 is negative).

ILLUSTRATION 1

Find out the due date of the following invoices:

Date of Invoice (year 2015)	*Credit Period Allowed*
31st Jan.	1 month
29th Jan.	30 days
2nd Mar.	30 days
16th July	30 days
30th June	3 months
26th Dec.	1 month

SOLUTION

Date of Invoice	*Due Date*	
31st Jan.	28.02.2015	
29th Jan.	28.02.2015	
2nd Mar.	31.03.2015	Since 1st April (being a bank holiday) is a public holiday.
16th July	14.08.2015	Since 15th Aug. (being Independence Day) is a public holiday.
30th June	29.09.2015	Since 30th Sept. (being a bank holiday) is a public holiday.
26th Dec.	25.01.2016	Since 26th Jan. (being Republic Day) is a public holiday.

ILLUSTRATION 2

Find out the date of maturity of the following Bills Receivable:

Bill No.	*Date of Drawing*	*Date of Acceptance*	*Payable*
A-1	31.01.2015	02.02.2015	1 month after date
A-2	29.01.2015	03.02.2015	30 days after date
A-3	29.01.2015	02.02.2015	2 months after date
A-4	12.07.2015	14.07.2015	1 month after date
A-5	27.06.2015	28.06.2015	3 months after date
A-6	28.09.2015	01.10.2015	2 months after sight
A-7	23.12.2015	24.12.2015	1 month
A-8	02.01.2016	03.01.2016	On demand
A-9	05.01.2016	06.01.2016	At sight
A-10	10.01.2016	11.01.2016	On presentment

Drawer demanded the amount of last three bills on 24th Jan., 2016.

SOLUTION

Bill No.	*Date of Drawing*	*Date of Maturity*	
A - 1	31.01.2015	03.03.2015	
A - 2	29.01.2015	03.03.2015	
A - 3	29.01.2015	31.03.2015	Since 1st April (being a bank holiday) is a public holiday.
A - 4	12.07.2015	14.08.2015	Since 15th Aug., (being Independence Day) is a public holiday.
A - 5	27.06.2015	29.09.2015	Since 30th Sept, (being a bank holiday) is a public holiday.
A - 6	28.09.2015	04.12.2015	
A - 7	23.12.2015	25.01.2016	Since 26th Jan. (being Republic Day) is a public holiday.
A - 8	02.01.2016	24.01.2016	
A - 9	05.01.2016	24.01.2016	
A - 10	10.01.2016	24.01.2016	

Notes:

(i) *Three days of grace have been considered in case of Bills after date and Bills after sight, to ascertain the date of maturity.*

(ii) *The term of a 'Bill after sight' commences from the date of acceptance.*

ILLUSTRATION 3

Calculate No. of days from the base date (i.e. 16th Aug.) X owes Y ₹ 2,000 on 16th Aug.

Date of Bill	*Term*	*Amount*
20th Oct.	2 months	5,000
20th Oct.	60 days	6,000

SOLUTION

Due Date of Bill (including 3 grace days)	*No. of Days from Base Date*	*Amount*
16th Aug.	0	2,000
23rd Dec.	15 + 30 + 31 + 30 + 23 = 129	5,000
22nd Dec.	15 + 30 + 31 + 30 + 22 = 128	6,000

ILLUSTRATION 4

Calculate Average Due Date from the following:

Base Date	1st April
Sum of Products	₹ 7,02,000
Sum of Amount	₹ 20,000

SOLUTION

Average Due Date = 1st April + Sums of Products/Sum of Amount

= 1st April + 7,02,000/20,000 = 1st April + 35.1 days = 6th May

ILLUSTRATION 5

From the following, calculate the amount of interest if X desires to pay the whole amount including interest @ 15% p.a. on 30th June: Average Due Date 6th May, Amount Due ₹ 20,000

SOLUTION

Period from 6th May to 30th June = 26 + 29 = 55 days

Interest = ₹ 20,000 × 55/365 × 15/100 = ₹ 452

ILLUSTRATION 6

X purchased the following goods from Y:

Date of Invoice	*Amount (₹)*	*Credit Period Allowed*
30.01.2015	1,000	30 days
31.01.2015	2,000	1 month
13.07.2015	1,000	30 days
28.09.2015	1,000	3 months

Y agreed to draw a bill for the total amount due on the average due date. Ascertain that date taking (i) the due date on 1st transaction as base date; (ii) 1st Jan., 2015 as base (iii) 1st April 2015 as base date. (iv) the due date of last transaction as base date.

SOLUTION

(I) CALCULATION OF AVERAGE DUE DATE (BASE DATE: 29.02.2015)

A *Due Date*	*B* *Amount*	*C* *No. of days from Base Date to Due Date*	*D = B × C* *Products*
29.02,2015	1,000	0	0
29.02.2015	2,000	0	0

12.08.2015	1,000	31 + 30 + 31 + 30 + 31 + 12 = 165	1,65,000
28.12.2015	1,000	31 + 30 + 31 + 30 + 31 + 31 + 30 + 31 + 30 + 28 = 303	3,03,000
	5,000		4,68,000

Average Due Date $= \text{Base Date} + \dfrac{\text{Total of Products}}{\text{Total Amount}} = \text{29th Feb.} + \dfrac{4,68,000}{5,000}\text{days}$

= 29th Feb. + 93.6 days = 2nd June, 2015

(II) CALCULATION OF AVERAGE DUE DATE (BASE DATE: 01.01.2015)

A *Due Date*	*B* *Amount*	*C* *No. of days from Base Date to Due Date*	*D = B × C* *Products*
29.02.2015	1,000	30 + 29 = 59	59,000
29.02.2015	2,000	30 + 29 = 59	1,18,000
12.08.2015	1,000	30 + 29 + 31 + 30 + 31 + 30 + 31 + 12 = 224	2,24,000
28.12.2015	1,000	366 – 4 = 362	3,62,000
	5,000		7,63,000

Average Due Date $= \text{Base Date} + \dfrac{\text{Total of Products}}{\text{Total Amount}} = \text{1st Jan.} + \dfrac{7,63,000}{5,000}\text{days}$

= 1st Jan. + 152.6 days = 2nd June, 2015

(III) CALCULATION OF AVERAGE DUE DATE (BASE DATE: 01.04.2015)

A *Due Date*	*B* *Amount*	*C* *No. of days from Base Date to Due Date*	*D = B × C* *Products*
29.02.2015	1,000	31 + 1 = (32)	(32,000)
29.02.2015	2,000	31 + 1 = (32)	(64,000)
12.08.2015	1,000	29 + 31 + 30 + 31 + 12 = 133	1,33,000
28.12.2015	1,000	29 + 31 + 30 + 31 + 31 + 30 + 31 + 30 + 28 = 271	2,71,000
	5,000		3,08,000

Average Due Date $= \text{Base Date} + \dfrac{\text{Total of Products}}{\text{Total Amount}} = \text{1st Apr.} + \dfrac{3,08,000}{5,000}\text{days}$

= 1st April + 61.6 days = 2nd June 2015

(IV) CALCULATION OF AVERAGE DUE DATE (BASE DATE: 28.12.2015)

A *Due Date*	*B* *Amount*	*C* *No. of days from Base Date to Due Date*	*D = B × C* *Products*
29.02.2015	1,000	28 + 30 + 31 + 30 + 31 + 31 + 30 + 31 + 30 + 31 = (303)	(3,03,000)
29.02.2015	2,000	= (303)	(6,06,000)
12.08.2015	1,000	28 + 30 + 31 + 30 + 19 = (138)	(1,38,000)
28.12.2015	1,000	0	0
	5,000		(10,47,000)

Average Due Date $= \text{Base Date} + \dfrac{\text{Total of Products}}{\text{Total Amount}} = \text{28th Dec.} + \dfrac{(10,47,000)}{5,000}\text{days}$

= 28th Dec – 209.4 Days = 2nd June, 2015

ILLUSTRATION 7

X has accepted the following bills payable on different dates. He wants to accept only one bill on average due date and requests you to find out that date.

Serial No.	*Date of Drawing*	*Amount (₹)*	*Payable After*
101	31.01.2015	1,000	30 days
102	31.01.2015	2,000	1 month
103	12.07.2015	1,000	1 month
104	27.08.2015	1,000	1 month

Note: *On 1st July, 2015 the day was Friday.*

SOLUTION

CALCULATION OF AVERAGE DUE DATE: (BASE DATE: 3RD MARCH, 2015)

A *Serial*	*B* *Date of Maturity*	*C* *Amount*	*D* *No. of days from Base Date to Date of Maturity*	*E = C × D* *Product*
101	03.03.2015	1,000	0	0
102	03.03.2015	2,000	0	0
103	13.08.2015	1,000	28 + 30 + 31 + 30 + 31 + 13 = 163	1,63,000
104	29.09.2015	1,000	28 + 30 + 31 + 30 + 31 + 31 + 29 = 210	2,10,000
		5,000	3,73,000	

Average Due Date $= \text{Base Date} + \dfrac{\text{Total of Products}}{\text{Total Amount}} = \text{3rd Mar.} + \dfrac{3,73,000}{5,000}\text{days}$

= 3rd March + 74.6 days = 17th May, 2015

Notes:

(i) *Three days of grace have been considered in each case to ascertain the date of maturity.*

(ii) *In case of Bill No. 103, due date has been taken as 13th August instead of 15th Aug. since 15th Aug. being Independence Day and 14th Aug. being Sunday are public holidays.*

(iii) *In case of Bill No. 104, due date has been taken as 29th Sept instead of 30th Sept since 30th Sept being a Bank Holiday is a public holiday.*

ILLUSTRATION 8

X and Y had the following mutual dealings and desire to settle their account on the average due date:

01.01.2016	Balance owing by Mr X ₹ 5,000
30.01.2016	Goods sold to Y (credit period 30 days) ₹ 1,000
31.01.2016	Goods purchased by X (credit period 1 month) ₹ 2,000
13.07.2016	Goods sold to Y (credit period 30 days) ₹ 1,000
28.09.2016	Goods purchased by X (credit period 3 months) ₹ 1,000

Required: Ascertain the average due date.

SOLUTION

Let the Base Date be 01.01.2016

FOR OWINGS BY MR X

A *Due Date*	*B* *Amount*	*C* *No. of days from Base Date to Date*	*D = B × C* *Product*
01.01.2016*	5,000	1	5,000
29.02.2016	2,000	30 + 29 = 59	1,18,000
28.12.2016	1,000	366 – 4 = 362	3,62,000
	8,000		4,85,000

*It is the date of brought down balance and not the date of transaction.

FOR OWINGS TO MR X

A *Due Date*	*B* *Amount*	*C* *No. of days from Base Date to Date*	*D = B × C* *Product*
29.02.2016	1,000	30 + 29 = 59	59,000
12.08.2016	1,000	30 + 29 + 31 + 30 + 31 + 30 + 31 + 12 = 224	2,24,000
	2,000		2,83,000

Average Due Date $= \text{Base Date} + \frac{\text{Total of Products}}{\text{Total Amount}}\text{days}$

$= 01.01.2015 + \frac{₹4,85,000 - ₹2,83,000}{₹8,000 - ₹2,000}\text{ Days}$

$= 01.01.2015 + 33.67\text{ Days} = 04.02.2016$

ILLUSTRATION 9

X owes Y ₹ 5,000. The average due date of mutual transactions is 2nd June 2015. Calculate the amount to be paid by X to Y if X wants to pay off (a) on 2.6.2015 (b) on 14.8.2015 (c) On 21.3.2015. Interest is charged @ 18% P.a.

SOLUTION

A *Case*	*B* *Principal*	*C* *Interest from Average Date to Actual Date of Payment*	*D = B ± C* *Total Amount to be paid*
(a)	5,000	₹ 5,000 × 18/100 × 0/365 = 0	₹ 5,000
(b)	5,000	₹ 5,000 × 18/100 × 73/365 = ₹ 180 **Note:** *Interest has been charged for deferred period of 73 days from 2.6.2015 to 14.8.2015.*	₹ 5,180
(c)	5,000	₹ 5,000 × 18/100 × (73)/365 = (₹ 180) **Note:** *Rebate has been allowed for unexpired credit period of 73 days from 21.3.2015 to 2.6.2015.*	₹ 4,820

ILLUSTRATION 10

X owes Y ₹ 10,000. The average due date of mutual transactions is 2nd June. Calculate the date on which X has to make the payment if X wants to pay (a) ₹ 10,000 only (b) ₹ 10,360 (c) ₹ 9,640. Interest is charged @ 18% p.a.

SOLUTION

Let the period from average due date to actual date of payment be x

Interest $= \text{Principal} \times \frac{\text{Rate}}{100} \times \frac{\text{Period in Days}}{365 \text{ Days}}$

(a) Interest = Actual Payment – Principal Amount ₹ 10,000 – ₹ 10,000 = 0

$= ₹10,0000 \times \frac{18}{100} \times \frac{x}{365} = 0$

Thus, x = 0

Actual Date of Payment

= Average Due Date + Period from average due date to actual date of payment

= 2nd June + 0 = 2nd June

(b) Interest = ₹ 10,360 – ₹ 10,000 = ₹ 360

$= ₹10,0000 \times \frac{18}{100} \times \frac{x}{365} = ₹360$

$x = 360 \times 365 \times \frac{100}{18} \times \frac{1}{10,000} = 73 \text{ Days}$

Actual Date of Payment

= Average Due Date + Period from average due date to actual date of payment

= 2nd June + 73 Days = 14th Aug.

(c) Interest = ₹ 9,640 – ₹ 10,000 = – ₹ 360

$= ₹10,0000 \times \frac{18}{100} \times \frac{x}{365} = -₹360$

$x = -360 \times 365 \times \frac{100}{18} \times \frac{1}{10,000} = -73 \text{ Days}$

Actual Date of Payment

= Average Due Date – Period from average date to actual date of payment.

= 2nd June – 73 Days = 21st March

3.0 SHORT CUT METHOD IN CASE OF EQUAL INSTALMENTS

In case of equal instalments, the Short Cut method may be used instead of Product method as explained above. Under the short cut method, the time units (e.g. years, months *or* days) are added up and are divided by the number of instalments and its quotient (which shall be expressed in the same unit in which the time has been expressed) is then added to the lending date to arrive at the average due date. In the form of an equation, it may be expressed as follows:

$$\text{Average Due Date} = \text{Date of Lending} + \frac{\text{Sum of the periods' Digits from the date of loan to the date of repayment of each instalment}}{\text{Number of Periodic Intalments}}$$

Note: *The periods may be expressed in terms of years, quarters, months, weeks or days.*

ILLUSTRATION 11

Mr X lends ₹ 25,000 to Mr Y on 1st Jan., 2015. Calculate the average due date and interest if interest @ 18% p.a. to be charged by X in each of the following alternative cases:

(a) If the amount is repayable in 5 equal annual instalments commencing from 1st January, 2016.

(b) If the amount is repayable in 5 half yearly equal installments commencing from 1st Jan. 2016.

(c) If the amount is repayable in three equal instalments at an interval of two years commencing from 30th June, 2015.

(d) If the amount is repayable in 5 equal instalments; as under:— I (01.01.2016); II (1.7.2016); III (1.7.2017); IV (01.01.2018): V (01.01.2019)

SOLUTION

Case (a)

$$\text{Average Due Date} = \text{Date of Lending} + \frac{\text{Sum of Years' Digits}}{\text{Number of Intalments}}$$

= 01.01. 2015 + (1 + 2 + 3 + 4 + 5) / 5 = 01.01.2015 + 3 years = 1st Jan, 2016

Interest = ₹ 25,000 × 3 ×18/100 = ₹ 13,500

Case (b)

$$\text{Average Due Date} = \text{Date of Lending} + \frac{\text{Sum of Years' Digits}}{\text{Number of Intalments}}$$

= 01.01.2015 + (12 + 18 + 24 + 30 + 36) / 5 = 01.01.2015 + 120/5 months

= 01.01.2015 + 24 Months = 1st Jan., 2015

Interest = ₹ 25,000 × 24/12 ×18/100 = ₹ 9,000

Case (c)

$$\text{Average Due Date} = \text{Date of Lending} + \frac{\text{Sum of Years' Digits}}{\text{Number of Intalments}}$$

= 01.01.2015 + (2.5 + 4.5 + 6.5) / 3 = 01.01.2015 + 4.5 years

= 1st July, 2017

Interest = ₹ 25,000 × 4.5 × 18/100 = ₹ 20,250

Case (d)

$$\text{Average Due Date} = \text{Date of Lending} + \frac{\text{Sum of Years' Digits}}{\text{Number of Intalments}}$$

= 01.01.2015 + (12 + 18 + 30+ 36 + 48) / 5 = 01.01.2015 + 28.8 months

= 25th May, 2015

Interest = ₹ 25,000 × 27.8/12 × 18/100 = ₹ 10,800

4.0 ACCOUNT CURRENT

MEANING OF ACCOUNT CURRENT

Account Current is a running statement in the form of a ledger account showing the transactions between two parties for a given period of time together with the interest due *or* payable. The heading of this statement is written as under:

"—(Name of Receiving Party)—In Account Current with—(Name of Sending Party)—" to—(date)

For example, if X sends the Account Current to Y, it will be headed as "Y in Account Current with X'. If Y sends the Account Current to X, it will be headed as — X in Account Current with Y'.

Account Current is usually sent by (a) a banker to its customer (b) a lender to its borrower (c) a supplier to its customer (d) an agent to its principal (e) a co-venturer to another co-venturer.

METHODS OF PREPARING ACCOUNT CURRENT

There are three methods of preparing Account Current viz. Interest on Individual Transaction Method, Product of Individual Transaction Method, Product of Balances Method.

INTEREST ON INDIVIDUAL TRANSACTION METHOD

Under this method three additional columns on each of the sides of a ledger account are provided— One column to record the Due Date, Second to record the number of days counted from the due date of each transaction to the date of closing the account and third column to record the interest due on individual transaction. The format of Account Current according to this method is given on next page. The practical steps involved in the preparation of Account Current are given below:

PRACTICAL STEPS INVOLVED IN THE PREPARATION OF ACCOUNT CURRENT

Step 1	*Provide three additional columns on each of the sides of a ledger account— one for Due Date, second for Days and third for 'Interest'.*
Step 2	*Calculate the due date of each transaction and enter in due date column.*
Step 3	*Calculate the number of days from the due date of each transaction to the date of closing the account and enter the number of days in 'Days' column.*
Step 4	*Calculate the interest at the given rate of interest on the amount of individual transaction for the number of days entered against that item in 'Days' Column and enter the interest in 'Interest Column'.*
Step 5	*Calculate the balance of the 'interest' columns, enter such balance on the appropriate side in the 'Interest' column and total up the 'Interest' columns.*
Step 6	*Enter the net interest on the appropriate side in the 'Amount' column. This entry is made on the side other than that on which the balance of interest appears.*

FORMAT OF ACCOUNT CURRENT (ACCORDING TO INTEREST ON INDIVIDUAL TRANSACTION METHOD)

Dr. **— (NAME OF RECEIVING PARTY)—IN ACCOUNT CURRENT WITH—(NAME OF SENDING PARTY)—AS AT—(DATE)—** Cr.

Date	Particulars	L.F.	Due Date	Amt. ₹	Days	Interest ₹ P	Date	Particulars	L.F.	Due Date	Amt. ₹	Days	Interest ₹ P

Solution to Illustration 12

Dr. **MR Y IN ACCOUNT CURRENT WITH MR X (INTEREST TO 31ST DEC., 2015 @ 18% P.A.)** Cr.

Date	Particulars	L.F.	Due Date	Amt. ₹	Days	Interest ₹ P	Date	Particulars	L.F.	Due Date	Amt. ₹	Days	Interest ₹ P
01.07.2015	To Balance b/d			600	184	54.44	01.08.2015	By Purchase A/c		Sep. 1	200	121	11.93
30.07.2015	To Sales A/c		Aug 30	300	123	18.20	01.09.2015	By Cash A/c		Sep. 1	100	121	5.97
31.12.2015	To Interest A/c			54			01.09.2015	By B/R A/c		Dec. 4	100	27	1.33
							01.10.2015	By B/R A/c		4.1.14	300	(4)	(0.59)
							31.12.2015	By Balance of Interest					54.00
							31.12.2015	By Balance c/d			254		
				954		72.64					954		72.64

ILLUSTRATION 12

From the following particulars, make up an Account Current to be rendered by Mr X to Mr Y on 31st December, 2015 taking interest into account at the rate of 18% p.a.

01.07.2015	Balance owing by Mr Y	₹ 600
30.07.2015	Goods sold to Mr Y (Credit Period allowed 1 Month)	₹ 300
01.08.2015	Goods purchased from Mr Y (Credit Period received 1 Month)	₹ 200
01.09.2015	Cash received from Mr Y	₹ 100
01.09.2015	Mr Y accepted Mr X's Draft at 3 Months date	₹ 100
01.10.2015	Mr Y accepted Mr X's Draft at 3 Months date	₹ 300

Required: Prepare the Account Current according to Interest on Individual Transaction Method.

SOLUTION

See previous page for solution.

PRODUCT OF INDIVIDUAL TRANSACTION METHOD

Under this method, **three additional columns** on each of the sides of a ledger account are provided—one column to record the **due date**, second column to record **number of days** counted from the due date of each transaction to the date of closing the account and third column to record the **product** (i.e. the amount multiplied by the number of days for which it has been outstanding). The format of Account Current according to this method is given on next page. The practical steps involved in the preparation of the Account Current are given below:

PRACTICAL STEP INVOLVED IN THE PREPARATION OF ACCOUNT CURRENT

Step 1 *Provide three additional columns on each of the sides of a ledger account-one for Due Date, Second for 'Days' and third for 'Product'.*

Step 2 *Calculate the due date of transaction and enter in Due Date Column.*

Step 3 *Calculate the number of days from the due date of each transaction to the date of closing the account and enter the number of days in 'Days' column.*

Step 4 *Calculate the product by multiplying the amount of transaction by corresponding number of days and enter the product in 'Product' column.*

Note: *In case of transactions the due date of which falls after the date of closing the account, the product must be written either as negative product on the same side or as positive product on the opposite side (i.e. the side other than that on which the transaction appears). Traditionally, such product was used to be written in 'Red Ink' and interest on such 'Red Ink Product' was used to be called as "Red Ink Interest".*

Step 5 *Calculate the balance of the 'Product' columns, enter such balance on the appropriate side in the 'Product' column and total up the 'Product' columns.*

Step 6 *Calculate the interest at the given rate of interest on the bal. of the products for a single day.*

Step 7 *Enter the interest on the appropriate side in the 'Amount' Column. This entry is made on the side other than that on which the balance of product appears if the number of days are calculated from the due date of transaction to the date of closing the account.*

FORMAT OF ACCOUNT CURRENT (ACCORDING TO PRODUCT OF INDIVIDUAL TRANSACTION METHOD

Dr. **— (NAME OF RECEIVING PARTY)—IN ACCOUNT CURRENT WITH—(NAME OF SENDING PARTY)—AS AT—(DATE)—** *Cr.*

Date	*Particulars*	*L.F.*	*Due Date*	*Amt.* ₹	*Days*	*Product* ₹ *P*	*Date*	*Particulars*	*L.F.*	*Due Date*	*Amt.* ₹	*Days*	*Product* ₹ *P*

METHODS OF COMPUTING THE NUMBERS OF DAYS

Usually any of the following two methods is used for calculating the number of days:

1. **Forward Method** — Under this Method the number of days are calculated from the due date of the transaction to the date of closing the account.
2. **Backward (or Epoque Method)** — Under this method, the number of days are calculated from the opening date of statement to the due date of transaction.

Notes:

(i) *In the case of brought down balance, the date of the balance is to be counted, For example, if the opening balance is on 1st July and the date of closing the account is 31st December, the number of days will be counted as under:*

31 (July) + 31 (Aug.) + 30 (Sept.) + 31 (Oct.) + 30 (Nov.) + 31 (Dec,) = 184 days,

(ii) *In the case of transaction, the date of transaction is to be excluded, For example, if the cash is received on 1st July and the date of closing the account is 31st December the number of days will be counted as under:*

30 (July) + 31 (Aug.) + 30 (Sept.) + 31 (Oct.) + 30 (Nov.) + 31 (Dec.) = 183 days.

(iii) *In the case of sale or purchase transactions, if any credit period is allowed then only the due date should be considered as an effective date of transaction. For example, if goods are sold (on one month credit) on 1st July and the date of closing the account is 31st Dec., the number of days will be counted as under.,*

30 (Aug.) + 30 (Sept.) + 31 (Oct.) + 30 (Nov,) + 31 (Dec.) = 152 days

(iv) *In the case of Time Bills Receivable/Bills Payable, the due date (including days of grace) will be the effective date. For example, if a Bill Receivable for 3 months is received on 1st July, and the date of closing the account is 31st Dec. the number of days will be counted as under*

27 (Oct) + 30 (Nov.) + 31 (Dec.) = 88 days

(v) *In case the effective due date of any transaction falls after the date of closing the account, the interest is calculated for the number of days by which the due date falls after closing date and charged to party's account. For example, if a Bill Receivable for 3 months is received on 1st Oct, 2015 and the date of closing the account is 31st Dec., 2015 the interest for 4 days from 1st Jan., 20X2 to 4th Jan., 20X2 will have to be charged.*

ILLUSTRATION 13

Taking the same information as given in Illustration 12 prepare the Account Current according to Product of Individual Transaction Method.

SOLUTION

For the purposes of computing products, the number of days may be calculated either from the due date of transaction to the closing date of account (Forward method) *or* from the opening date of account to the due date of transaction (Epoque Method). Here, Account Current has been shown according to both these methods.

(a) Product of Individual Transaction Method (Forward Method) (see next page)

(b) Product of Individual Transaction Method (Epoque Method) (see next page)

PRODUCT OF BALANCES METHOD

This method, also known as 'Periodic Balance Method', is usually adopted by enterprises dealing it, finance (e.g. banks) where the balance of account is taken out after every transaction. The format of Account Current according to this method is given on next page.

The practical steps involved in the preparation of Account Current are given on next page:

Solution to Illustration 13

(a) Product of Individual Transaction Method (Forward Method)

Dr. **MR Y IN ACCOUNT CURRENT WITH MR X (INTEREST TO 31ST DEC., 2015 @ 18% P.A.)** *Cr.*

Date	Particulars	L.F.	Due Date	Amt. ₹	Days	Product ₹ P	Date	Particulars	L.F.	Due Date	Amt. ₹	Days	Product ₹ P
01.07.2015	To Balance b/d			600	184	1,10,400	01.08.2015	By Purchases A/c		Sep. 1	200	121	24,200
30.07.2015	To Sales A/c		Aug 30	300	123	36,900	01.09.2015	By Cash A/c		Sep. 1	100	121	12,100
31.12.2015	To Interest on Balance			54			01.09.2015	By B/R A/c		Dec. 4	100	27	2,700
	for 1 day @ 18%						01.10.2015	By B/R A/c		4.1.14	300	(4)	(1,200)
	$\left[\frac{1,09,500 \times 18 \times 1}{100 \times 365}\right]$						31.12.2015	By Bal. of Products					1,09,500
							31.12.2015	By Balance c/d			254		
				954		1,47,300					954		1,47,300

(b) Product of Individual Transaction Method (Epoque Method)

Dr. **MR Y IN ACCOUNT CURRENT WITH MR X (INTEREST TO 31ST DEC., 2015 @ 18% P.A.)** *Cr.*

Date	Particulars	L.F.	Due Date	Amt. ₹	Days	Product ₹ P	Date	Particulars	L.F.	Due Date	Amt. ₹	Days	Product ₹ P
01.07.2015	To Balance b/d			600	—	—	01.08.2015	By Purchases A/c		Sep. 1	200	63	12,600
30.07.2015	To Sales A/c		Aug 30	300	61	18,300	01.09.2015	By Cash A/c		Sep. 1	100	63	6,300
31.12.2015	To Balance of Product					1,09,500	01.09.2015	By B/R A/c		Dec. 4	100	157	15,700
31.12.2015	To Interest on Balance			54			01.10.2015	By B/R A/c		4.1.14	300	188	56,400
	for 1 day @ 18%						31.12.2015	By Bal. of Products				184	36,800
	$\left[\frac{1,09,500 \times 18 \times 1}{100 \times 365}\right]$							[200 × 184]					
							31.12.2015	By Balance c/d			254		
				954	—	1,27,800					954		1,27,800

ORMAT OF ACCOUNT CURRENT (ACCORDING TO PRODUCT OF BALANCES METHOD)

Dr. **(NAME OF CUSTOMER) ...... IN ACCOUNT CURRENT WITH .... (NAME OF BANKERS) .... AS AT ...... (DATE) .....** *Cr.*

Date	Particulars	Dr. ₹ P	Cr. ₹ P	Dr. or Cr.	Balance ₹ P	Days	Dr Product ₹	Cr Product ₹

Solution to Illustration 14

MR Y IN ACCOUNT CURRENT WITH THE CANARA BANK AS AT 31ST MARCH, 2015

Date	Particulars	Dr. ₹ P	Cr. ₹ P	Dr. or Cr.	Balance ₹ P	Days	Dr Product ₹	Cr Product ₹
2015								
Jan. 1	By Balance b/d	—	—	Cr.	10,000	11	—	1,10,000
Jan. 12	To Self	11,000	—	Dr.	1,000	34	34,000	—
Feb. 15	By Deposit	—	10,000	Cr.	9,000	23	—	2,07,000
Mar. 10	To Self	10,000	—	Dr.	1,000	6	6,000	—
Mar. 16	By Cleaning	—	10,000	Cr.	9,000	16	—	1,44,000
Mar. 31	By Interest upto 31st Mar.	—	6	Cr.	9006	—	—	—
							40,000	4,61,000

PRACTICAL STEPS INVOLVED IN THE PREPARATION OF ACCOUNT CURRENT

Step 1 *Provide three additional columns in the ledger account—One for Days, one for 'Dr. Product' and one for 'Cr. Product'.*

Step 2 *Calculate the number of days from the date of one transaction to the date of next transaction and enter the number of days in 'Days' column.*

Step 3 *Calculate the product by multiplying the balance by corresponding number of days and enter the product of debit balance in 'Dr. Product' column and the credit balance in 'Cr. Product' column.*

Step 4 *Calculate the total of 'Dr. Product' column and Cr. Product' columns.*

Step 5 *Calculate the interest on 'Total Dr Product' and 'Total Cr. Product' at the given rates of Interest.*

Step 6 *Calculate the net interest (i.e. the difference between the interest on 'Total Dr. Product' and Interest on 'Total Cr. product.')*

Step 7 *Enter the net interest payable to the customer as 'By Interest A/c' and the net interest receivable from the customer as 'To Interest—A/c'.*

DAILY BALANCE METHOD OF COMPUTING THE NUMBER OF DAYS

Under this method, the number of days are calculated from the effective date of last transaction to the effective date of next transaction. It is to be noted that if a cheque *or* draft is deposited in a Bank, the effective date will be the date when credit for cheque/draft is given and not the date of deposit of cheque/draft. This method is usually—adopted by financial institutions.

ILLUSTRATION 14

Mr X, a customer of Canara Bank has the following transactions during the quarter ending 31st March, 2015:

Jan. 1	Credit Balance	₹ 10,000
Jan. 12	Withdrew	₹ 11,000
Feb. 15	Deposited	₹ 10,000
Mar. 10	Withdrew	₹ 10,000
Mar. 12	Deposited an outstation cheque (Cleared on March 16)	₹ 10,000

Required: Show Mr Y's Account as at 31st March in the bank's books assuming that the bank allows interest @ 2% p.a. and charges interest @ 18% p.a.

SOLUTION *(See previous page)*

Working Notes:

A. Interest charged on ₹ 40,000 for 1 Day @ 18% p.a.

$$= \frac{40{,}000 \times 18 \times 1}{365 \times 100} = ₹\ 19.73$$

B. Interest allowed on ₹ 4,61,000 for 1 day @ 2% p.a.

$$= \frac{4{,}61{,}000 \times 2 \times 1}{365 \times 100} = ₹\ 25.26$$

C. Net Interest allowed (B – A) = ₹ 5.53. rounded off to ₹ 6.

SOLVED PROBLEMS

PROBLEM 1

From the following calculate the average due date and interest @ 10% p.a. if Mr X lent ₹ 25,000 to Mr Y on 1st Jan. 2015 which is repayable in 5 half yearly instalments commencing from 1st Jan. 2016.

SOLUTION

$$\text{A.D.D.} = \text{Date of Lending} + \frac{\text{Sum of months from 1.1.2000 to date of each instalment}}{\text{Number of Intalments}}$$

= 1.1.2015 + (12 + 18 + 24 + 30 + 36) / 5 months

= 1.1.2015 + 24 months = 1.1.2015

$$\text{Interest} = ₹25{,}000 \times \frac{10}{100} \times 2 \text{ years} = ₹5{,}000$$

PROBLEM 2

Rames drew upon Vinod several bills of exchange due for payment on different dates as under:

Date of the Bill	*Amount ₹*	*Tenure of the Bill*
1st June	1,200	3 Months
19th June	1,600	2 Months
10th July	2,000	3 Months
27th July	1,500	3 Months
7th Aug.	1,800	1 Month
15th Aug.	2,400	2 Months

Find out average due date in which payment may be made in one single amount.

SOLUTION

CALCULATION OF AVERAGE DUE DATE [BASE DATE: 22ND AUG.]

A *Date of Maturity*	*B* *Amount*	*C* *No. of days from base date*	*D = B × C* *Product*
4th Sept.	1,200	13	15,600
22nd Aug.	1,600	0	0
13th Oct.	2,000	52	1,04,000
30th Oct.	1,500	69	1,03,500
10th Sept.	1,800	19	34,200
18th Oct.	2,400	57	1,36,800
	10,500		3,94,100

Average Due Date $= \text{22nd Aug.} + \frac{\text{Total of Products}}{\text{Total Amount}} \text{ days}$

$= \text{22nd Aug.} + \frac{3{,}94{,}100}{10{,}500} \text{ days}$

= 22nd Aug. + 38 Days = 29th Sep.

PROBLEM 3

R owes S the following sums of money due from him on the dates stated:

₹ 300 due on March 9, ₹ 1,000 due on April 2, ₹ 4,000 due on April 30, ₹ 100 due on June 1,

He wants to make the complete payment on 30th June. Calculate interest @ 5% p.a. with the help of average due date method.

SOLUTION

CALCULATION OF AVERAGE DUE DATE [BASE DATE 9TH MARCH]

A *Date of Maturity*	*B* *Amount*	*C* *No. of days from base date*	$D = B \times C$ *Product*
9th March	300	0	
2nd April	1,000	24	24,000
30th April	4,000	52	2,08,000
1st June	100	84	8,400
	5,400		2,40,400

Average Due Date $= \text{Base Date} + \frac{\text{Total of Products}}{\text{Total Amount}} \text{days} = \text{9th Mar.} + \frac{2,40,400}{5,400} \text{days}$

= 9th March + 44.52 days = 23rd April

Interest for 68 days from A.D.D. to date of payment = ₹ 5,400 × 5/100 × 68/365 = ₹ 50.30

PROBLEM 4

A partner has withdrawn the following sum during the half year ending 30th June:

Particulars	₹
January 15	500
February 10	400
March 12	700
April 5	800
May 20	1,000
June 18	900

Interest is to be charged at 10 per annum. Find out the average due date and calculate the interest on drawings.

SOLUTION

CALCULATION AVERAGE DUE DATE (BASE DATE 15TH JAN.]

A *Date of Maturity*	*B* *Amount*	*C* *No. of days from base date*	$D = B \times C$ *Product*
January 15	500	0	0
February 10	400	26	10,400
March 12	700	56	39,200
April 5	800	80	64,000

May 20	1,000	125	1,25,000
June 18	900	154	1,38,600
	4,300		3,77,200

Average Due Date $= \text{Base Date} + \dfrac{\text{Total of Products}}{\text{Total Amount}}\text{days}$

= 15th Jan. + (3,77,200/4,300) = 87.72 (or) 88 days.

Average Due Date = 13th April, Interest from 13th April to 30th June @ ₹ 10%

= ₹ 4300 × (78/365) × (10/100) = ₹ 91.89

PROBLEM 5

Shankar owed to Ramesh the following sums of money on the due dates given below:

Due Date	*Amount Due*
10th Aug.	500
25th Aug.	300
5th Sep.	1,000
10th Sep.	800
15th Sep.	400

Calculation the average due date on which Shankar may pay the total sum due.

SOLUTION

CALCULATION OF AVERAGE DUE DATE [BASE DATE: 10TH AUG.]

A *Date of Maturity*	*B* *Amount*	*C* *No. of days from base date*	*D = B × C* *Product*
10th Aug.	500	0	0
25th Aug.	300	15	4,500
5th Sept.	1,000	26	26,000
10th Sept.	800	31	24,800
15th Sept.	400	36	14,400
	3,000		69,700

Average Due Date $= \text{Base Date} + \dfrac{\text{Total of Products}}{\text{Total Amount}}\text{days}$

= 10th Aug. + (69,700/3,000) days

Average Due Date = 10th Aug. + 23.23 days = 2nd September

PROBLEM 6

Find the Average Due Date for the following bills:

Date of drawing of the bill	*Amount (₹)*	*Period*
January 15	250	3 months
March 4	400	5 months

April 10		500	1 month
April 22		200	2 months

SOLUTION

CALCULATION OF AVERAGE DUE DATE [BASE DATE: 18 APRIL]

A *Date of Maturity*	*B* *Amount*	*C* *No. of days from base date*	*D = B × C* *Product*
18th April	250	0	0
7th Aug.	400	111	44,400
13th May	500	25	12,500
25th June	200	68	13,600
	1,350		70,500

Average Due Date $= \text{Base Date} + \dfrac{\text{Total of Products}}{\text{Total Amount}}\text{days}$

$= \text{18th Apr.} + \dfrac{70{,}500}{1{,}350}\text{days}$

= 18th April + 52.22 days = 9th June

PROBLEM 7

Mr Arvind purchases goods on credit. His due dates for payments were as under:

	₹		
March 5	300	due date	April 8
April 15	200	due date	May 18
May 10	275	due date	June 13
June 5	400	due date	July 8

Calculate his average due date.

SOLUTION

CALCULATION OF AVERAGE DUE DATE [BASE DATE: 8TH APRIL]

A *Date of Maturity*	*B* *Amount*	*C* *No. of days from base date*	*D = B × C* *Product*
8th April	300	0	0
18th May	200	40	8,000
13th June	275	66	18,150
8th July	400	91	36,400
	1175		62,550

Average Due Date $= \text{Base Date} + \dfrac{\text{Total of Products}}{\text{Total Amount}}\text{days} = \text{8th Apr.} + \dfrac{62{,}550}{1{,}175}\text{days}$

= 8th April + 53.23 days = 31st May

PROBELM 8

From the following particulars, you are required to ascertain the Average Due Date:

Due Date	*Amount of the Bill (₹)*
18th May	1,100
24th June	625
30th July	1,800
18th Aug.	1,750
20th Oct.	1,000
24th Nov.	500

SOLUTION

CALCULATION OF AVERAGE DUE DATE [BASE DATE: 18TH MAY]

A *Date of Maturity*	*B* *Amount*	*C* *No. of days from Base Date*	*D = B × C* *Products*
18th May	1,100	0	0
24th June	625	13 + 24 = 37	23,125
30th July	1,800	13 + 30 + 30 = 73	1,31,400
18th Aug	1,750	13 + 30 + 31 + 18 = 92	1,61,000
20th Oct.	1,000	13 + 30 + 31 + 31 + 30 + 20 = 155	1,55,000
24th Nov.	500	13 + 30 + 31 + 31 + 30 + 31 + 24 = 190	95,000
	6,775		5,65,525

Average Due Date $= \text{Base Date} + \dfrac{\text{Total of Products}}{\text{Total Amount}} \text{ days}$

$= \text{18th May} + \dfrac{5,65,525}{6,775} = 83.47$ Days or 83 Days

= 18th May + 83 days = 9th August,

PROBLEM 9

From the following transactions in the books of Anand, prepare an account current to be sent by Anand to Basu for the quarter ending 31st March, 2015 charging and following interest at 12% per annum.

Particulars	₹
January 1, Balance in Basu's account	3,000
January 14, sold goods to Basu	5,000
February 11, cash received from Basu	4,000
February 17, sold goods to Basu	3,000
February 19, received a bill of exchange from B one month after date	5,000

SOLUTION

BASU IN ACCOUNT CURRENT WITH ANAND
for the year ending on 31st March 2O13

Date	Particulars	₹	Days	Product	Date	Particulars	₹	Days	Product
2015					2015				
Jan. 1	To Balance	3,000	90	2,70,000	Feb. 11	By Cash	4,000	48	1,92,000
Jan. 14	To Sales	5,000	76	3,80,000	Feb. 19	By Bills Receivable			
Feb. 17	To Sales	3,000	42	1,26,000		(Due date 22nd Mar.)	5,000	9	45,000
Mar. 31	To Interest	177			Mar. 31	By Balance c/d	2,177		5,39,000
		11,177		7,76,000			11,11,7		7,76,000
2015									
April	To Balance b/d	2,177		5,39,000					

$$\text{Interest} = 5,39,000 \times \frac{12}{100} \times \frac{1}{365} = 177$$

PROBLEM 10

From the following, prepare an account current as sent by Arun to Bhola on 30th June, 2015, charging interest on debits @ 6% p.a. and on credits @ 4% p.a.:

2015	*Particulars*	₹
Jan. 1	Balance due from Bhola	600
Jan. 10	Sold goods to Bhola,	520
Jan. 17	Bhola returned goods	125
Feb. 10	Bhola paid by cheque	400
Feb. 14	Bhola accepted Arun's draft for one month	300
Apr. 29	Goods sold to Bhola	615
May 15	Received cash from Bhola	700
June 5	Bhola accepted Arun's bill for 3 months	500

SOLUTION

BHOLA IN ACCOUNT CURRENT WITH ARUN
for the year ending on 30th June 2015

Date	Particulars	₹	Days	Product	Date	Particulars	₹	Days	Product
2015					2015				
Jan 1	To Balance b/d	600	181	1,08,600	Jan 17	By Sale Return	125	164	20,500
Jan 10	To Sales A/c	520	171	88,920	Feb 10	By Bank A/c	400	140	56,000
Apr 29	To Sales A/c	615	62	38,130	Feb 14	By B/R A/c (Due			
Jun 30	To Interest A/c	27.21	—	—		date: Mar. 17)	300	105	31,500
	To Balance c/d	262.79	—	—	May 15	By Cash A/c	700	46	32,200
				—	June 5	By B/R (Due			
						date: 8th Sept.	500	(70)	–35,000
		2,025	—	2,35,650			2,025	–	1,05,200

Interest on Debit side Product Total [2,35,650 × 6/100 × 1/365]	38.74
Interest on Credit side Product Total [1,05,200 × 4/100 × 1/365]	11.53
Net	27.21

PROBLEM 11

Mehra owed ₹ 3,000 on 1st Jan, 2015 to Somesh. The following are the transactions that took place between them during 2015. It is agreed between the parties that interest @ 6% p.a. is to be calculated on all transactions.

2015	*Particulars*	₹
January 16	Somesh sold goods to Mehra	2,000
January 29	Somesh purchase goods from Mehra	1,500
February 10	Somesh pays cash	1,500
March 7	Mehra accepts bill drawn by Somesh for one month	2,000

They desire to settle their accounts by one single, payment on 15th March 2015. Ascertain the amount to be paid to the earnest rupee. Ignore days of grace.

SOLUTION

MR MEHRA ACCOUNT CURRENT WITH MR SORNESH

for the period ended 15th March 2015

Date	*Particulars*	₹	*Days*	*Product*	*Date*	*Particulars*	₹	*Days*	*Product*
2015					2015				
Jan 1	To Balance b/d	3,000	74	2,22,000	Jan. 29	By Purchases	1,500	45	67,500
Jan 16	To Sales	2,000	58	1,16,000	Mar. 7	By B/R (Due date: Apr. 7)	2,000	–23	–46,000
Feb. 10	To Cash	1,500	33	49,500					
Mar 15	To Interest	60			15 Mar.	By Bal. of Product	—		3,66,000
						By Balance c/d	3,060	—	—
		6,560	—	3,87,500			6,560	—	3,87,500

Interest = $3,66,000 \times \frac{6}{100} \times \frac{1}{365}$ = 60.16 (or) ₹ 60.

Single Payment on 15-3-2015 = ₹ 3,060

PROBLEM 12

From the following transactions, draw up an account current by means of product up to 31st December, 2015 to be rendered by X to Y and give the amount of interest charging @ 8% per annum.

Date	*Particulars*	*Amounts (₹ thousands)*
2015		
July 01	Balance owing by Y	600
July 15	Goods sold to Y	900
Aug. 21	Goods bought from Y	700
Aug. 23	Cash received from Y	450
Oct. 23	Y accepted X's bill at 3 months	300

Nov. 01	Goods bought from Y	950
Dec.03	Accepted a bill drawn by Y at 3 months (due date of bill is on Sunday)	400

On 31st December, 2015, X and Y settled their account after considering the interest factor. Show the cash amount received *or* paid by X on that date.

SOLUTION

Y IN ACCOUNT CURRENT WITH X FOR THE PERIOD FROM

Dr. *1st July, 2015 to 31st December, 2015* *Cr.*

Date	*Due Date*	*Particulars*	*Days upto 31st Dec.*	*Amt. (₹ in 000s)*	*Product*	*Date*	*Due Date*	*Particulars*	*Days upto 31st Dec.*	*Amt. (₹ in 000s)*	*Product*
2015 July 01	July 01	To Bal. b/d	184	600	1,10,400	2015	Aug. 21 Aug. 21	By Purch. A/c	132	700	92,400
July 15	July 15	To Sales	169	900	1,52,100	Aug. 23	Aug. 23	By Cash A/c	130	450	58,500
Dec. 03	Mar. 05	To Bills Payable	(64)	400	(25,600)	Oct. 23	Jan.25	By Bills Receivable	(25)	300	(7,500)
						Nov. 01	Nov.01	By Purchases A/c	60	950	57,000
Dec. 31	Dec.31	To Interest [36,500 × 8%/365]		8			Dec. 31	By Bal. of Product			36,500
Dec. 31	Dec.31	To Cash A/c		492							
				2,400	2,36,900					2,400	2,36,900

PROBLEM 13

On 1st January 2015, X's Account in Y's Ledger showed a debit balance of ₹ 5,000. The following transactions took place between Y and X during the quarter ended 31st March 2015:

2015	*Particulars*	₹
Jan. 11	Y sold goods to X	6,000
Jan. 24	Y received a Promissory Note from X, 3 months date	5,000
Feb. 01	X sold goods to Y	10,000
Feb. 04	Y sold goods to X	8,200
Feb. 07	X returned goods to Y	1,000
March 01	X sold goods to Y	5,600
March 18	Y sold goods to X	9,200
March 23	X sold goods to Y	4,000

Accounts were settled on 31st March 2015, by means of a cheque. Prepare an Account Current to be submitted by Y to X as on 31st March 2015, taking interest into account at 10% per annum. Calculate Interest to the nearest multiple of a rupee.

SOLUTION

IN THE BOOKS OF Y (LEDGER FROM 1ST JAN 2015 TO 31ST MAR 2015)

Dr. **X IN ACCOUNT CURRENT WITH Y (INTEREST UPTO 31ST MARCH 2015 AT 10% P.A.)** *Cr.*

Date	*Particulars*	₹	*Days*	*Product*	*Date*	*Particulars*	₹	*Days*	*Product*
Jan 1	To Bal. b/d	5,000	90	4,50,000	Jan 24	By B/R	5,000	(27)	(1,35,000)
Jan 11	To Sales	6,000	79	4,74,00	Feb 1	By Purchases	10,000	58	5,80,00
Feb 4	To Sales	8,200	55	4,51,000	Feb 7	By Sales Returns	1,000	52	52,000
Mar 18	To Sales	9,200	13	1,19,600	Mar 1	By Purchases	5,600	30	1,68,000
Mar 31	To Interest	219			Mar 23	By Purchases	4,000	8	32,0000
					Mar 31	By Bal. of Products			7,97,600
						By bal. c/d	3,019		
		28,619		14,94,600			28,619		14,94,600

9 SELF BALANCING AND SECTIONAL BALANCING SYSTEM

LEARNING OBJECTIVES

After studying this chapter, you should be able to understand:

◇ Which Company can Issue Redeemable Preference Shares?

◇ Division of Ledger

◇ Sectional Balancing System

◇ Transfer from one Ledger to another (Under SectionaL Balancing System)

◇ Self Balancing System

◇ Self Balancing Entries in Relation to Debtors' Ledger

◇ Self Balancing Entries in Relation to Creditors' Ledger

◇ Transfer from One Ledger to another (Under Self Balancing System)

1.0 DIVISION OF LEDGER

Normally, the firms maintain one ledger for all the accounts involved. So long as the volume of transactions is small and the number of accounts is limited, this works fairly well. But, as the business expands and the number of accounts increases, especially those of the debtors and creditors, maintaining all accounts in a single ledger becomes impractical. The ledger becomes too bulky and location of errors involves more time. Hence many firms decide to introduce multiple ledger system whereby the ledger is usually divided into three parts as follows:

(a) General Ledger	It contains all the real and nominal accounts as well as the personal accounts other than trade debtors and trade creditors. Thus, accounts like Building Plant & machinery, Goodwill, Interest, Rent, Capital, Loan, Rent outstanding etc. are maintained in this ledger.
(b) Debtors Ledger	It is also known as 'Sales Ledger' *or* 'Sold Ledger'. It contains the accounts of trade debtors only i.e., the customers to whom goods are sold on credit. The accounts of persons/firms who are not the buyers of goods from the business, are maintained in the General Ledger.
(c) Creditors Ledger	It is also known as 'Purchase Ledger' *or* 'Bought Ledger'. It contains the accounts of trade creditors only i.e., persons *or* firms who have supplied goods on credit to the business. The accounts of persons/ firms who are not suppliers of goods *or* raw-materials are maintained in the General Ledger.

In case the number of trade debtors and trade creditors is fairly large, Debtors Ledger and Creditors Ledger can be further subdivided. For this, any suitable criteria may be adopted. Normally, the firms sub-divide them on alphabetical basis, say, A to F, G to K, L to P, and Q to Z *or* on geographical basis, say district-wise *or* nation-wise. Look at following figures for sub-division of ledger.

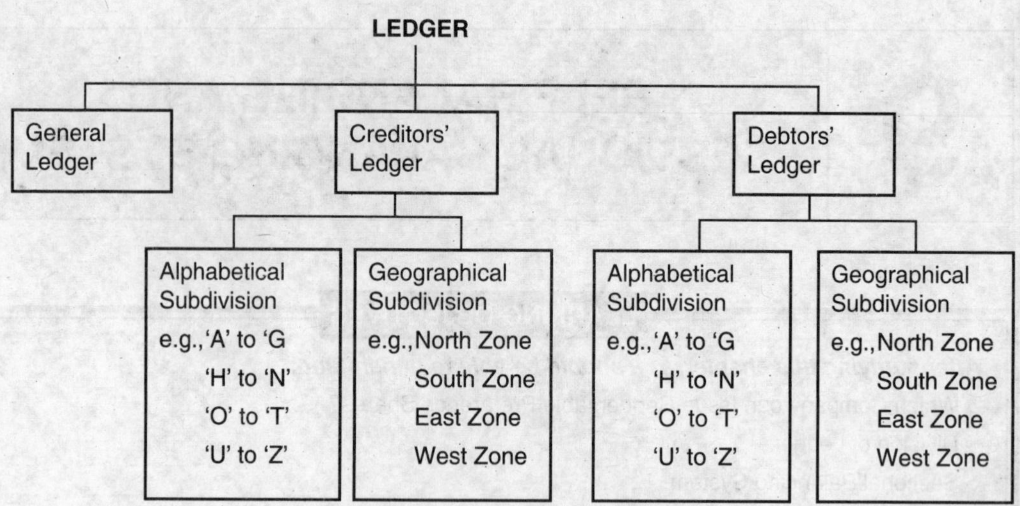

Fig. Sub-division of a Ledger

2.0 SECTIONAL BALANCING SYSTEM

Meaning	Under this system, only the total account for each of the subsidiary ledgers is opened in the General Ledger and no Control Account/Adjustment Account/Self Balancing Account is opened in the subsidiary ledger. Since in the subsidiary ledger, a double entry is not completed, a separate trial balance cannot be taken out from these ledgers.
Features	(a) Accounts of individual customers are maintained in the Debtors' Ledger and no Control Account is set up in the Debtors' Ledger. Individual items are posted to these accounts without completing the double entry in this ledger. (b) Accounts of individual suppliers are maintained in the Creditors' Ledger and no Control Account is set up in the Creditors' Ledger. Individual items are posted to these accounts without completing the double entry in this ledger. (c) Total Debtors' Account and Total Creditors' Account are maintained in the General Ledger. (d) The accuracy of individual customers' accounts may be checked by comparing the total of their balances with the balance in the Total Debtors' Account. (e) The accuracy of individual suppliers' accounts may be checked by comparing the total of their balances with the balance in the Total Creditors' Account. (f) A trial balance can be prepared only of General Ledger and not of Debtors' Ledger *or* Creditors' Ledger since the double entry is completed in respect of General Ledger and not in respect of Debtors' Ledger and Creditors' Ledger.

3.0 TRANSFER FROM ONE LEDGER TO ANOTHER (UNDER SECTIONAL BALANCING SYSTEM)

The transfer of an amount in an account in one ledger to the same account in another ledger requires one usual transfer entry and one self balancing entry. For example. Goods sold to A ₹ 1,000 and Goods purchased from A, ₹ 700.

Date	*Particulars*	*Dr. (₹)*	*Cr. (₹)*
(a)	Transfer Entry		
	A's A/c (in the Creditors' Ledger) Dr.	700	
	To A's A/c (in the Debtors' Ledger)		700
(b)	Self Balancing Entry		
	Total Creditors' Account Dr.	700	
	To Total Debtors' Account		700

ILLUSTRATION 1

From the following information, prepare Total Debtors Account for the year ending on 31st March, 2016:

Particulars	₹
Trade Debtors as on 1.4.2015	1,00,000
Credit Sales	6,10,000
Return Inwards	10,000
Discount Allowed	5,000
Cheque Dishonoured	1,00,000
Bad Debts Received	10,000
Cash received from Debtors	1,00,000
Cheques received from Debtors	2,00,000
Bills Receivable drawn	3,00,000
Bad Debts	5,000
B/R Dishonoured	1,00,000

SOLUTION

Dr. **TOTAL DEBTORS ACCOUNT** *Cr.*

Date	*Particulars*	₹	*Date*	*Particulars*	₹
01.04.2015	To Balance b/d	1,00,000	2015-2016	By Return Inwards	10,000
2015-2016	To Credit Sales	6,10,000		By Discount Allowed	5,000
	To B/R A/c	1,00,000		By Cash A/c	1,00,000
	To Bank A/c	1,00,000		By Bank A/c	3,00,000
				By Bills Receivable A/c	4,00,000
				By Bad Debts	5,000
				By Balance c/d	90,000
		9,10,000			9,10,000

ILLUSTRATION 2

From the following information, prepare Total Debtors Account for the year ending on 31st March, 2016:

(a) Trade Debtors as on 1.4.2015 ₹ 2,00,000

(b) Gross Sales (including Cash Sales of ₹ 4,00,000) ₹ 16,20,000

(c) Return Inwards ₹ 20,000

(d) Discount Allowed ₹ 11,000 (of which later on ₹ 1,000 disallowed)

(e) Cash received from Debtors ₹ 2,20,000 (including ₹ 20,000 from a person to whom an old fixed asset was sold)

(f) Cheques received from Debtors ₹ 4,40,000 of which cheques amounting to ₹ 40,000 were dishonoured. Out of these dishonoured cheques a cheque for ₹ 10,000 was dishonoured for non-payment as the customer became insolvent and his estate realised nothing.

(g) Bills Receivables drawn during the year totalled ₹ 6,60,000 of which bills amounting to ₹ 60,000 were endorsed in favour of suppliers. Bills dishonoured ₹ 30,000 (including Bills of ₹ 10,000 endorsed to suppliers).

(h) Interest on Overdue Accounts ₹ 45,000

(i) Bad Debts written off in earlier years recovered ₹ 20,000

(j) Provision for Doubtful Debts on Debtors ₹ 25,000.

(k) Transfer to Bought Ledger ₹ 15,000.

SOLUTION

Dr. **TOTAL DEBTORS ACCOUNT** *Cr.*

Date	*Particulars*	₹	*Date*	*Particulars*	₹
01.04.2015	To Balance b/d	2,00,000	31.03.2016	By Returns Inward	20,000
31.03.2016	To Credit Sales	12,20,000		By Discount Allowed	11,000
	To Disc. disallowed	1,000		By Cash A/c	2,00,000
	To Bank A/c (Ch. dish.)	40,000		By Bank A/c	4,40,000
	To Bills Rece. A/c			By Bad Debts	10,000
	(B/R Dish.)	20,000		By Bills Receivable	6,60,000
	To Total Creditors A/c			By Total Creditors A/c	15,000
	(Endor. B/R Disc.)	10,000		By Balance c/d	1,80,000
	To Interest	45,000			
		15,36,000			15,36,000

Note: *Cash Sales, Bad Debts Recovered and Provision for Doubtful Debts do not appear in the Total Debtors Account.*

ILLUSTRATION 3

From the following information, prepare Total Creditors Account for the year ending on 31st March 2016:

Particulars	₹
Creditors as on 1.4.2015	2,00,000
Credit Purchases	12,20,000
Returns Outward	20,000
Discount Received	10,000
Cash paid to creditors	2,00,000

Cheque issued to Creditors [Cheque ₹ 1,00,000 dishonoured]	5,00,000
Bills Payables accepted [B/P ₹ 1,00,000 cancelled]	7,00,000

SOLUTION

Dr. **TOTAL CREDITORS ACCOUNT** *Cr.*

Date	*Particulars*	₹	*Date*	*Particulars*	₹
31.03.2016	To Returns Outward	20,000	01.04.2015	By Balance b/d	2,00,000
	To Discount Received	10,000	31.03.2016	By Credit Purchases	12,20,000
	To Cash A/c	2,00,000		By Bank A/c	1,00,000
	To Bank A/c	5,00,000		By B/P	1,00,000
	To Bills Payable A/c	7,00,000			
	To Balance c/d	1,90,000			
		16,20,000			16,20,000

ILLUSTRATION 4

From the following information, prepare Total Creditors' Account for the year ending on 31st March, 2016:

(a) Trade Creditors as on 1.4.2015 ₹ 4,00,000.

(b) Gross Purchases (including Cash Purchases of ₹ 8,00,000) ₹ 32,40,000.

(c) Returns Outward ₹ 40,000.

(d) Discount Received ₹ 22,000 (of which later on ₹ 2,000 returned)

(e) Cash paid to Creditors ₹ 4,40,000 (including ₹ 40,000 to a supplier of a fixed asset)

(f) Cheques issued to Creditors ₹ 8,80,000 of which cheque amounting to ₹ 80,000 were dishonoured due to technical reasons.

(g) Bills Payable accepted (including renewals) during the year totalled ₹ 13,20,000. Bills payable withdrawn upon renewals amounted to ₹ 20,000.

(h) Bills amounting to ₹ 1,20,000 were endorsed in favour of suppliers. Out of these endorsed B/R, B/R for ₹ 20,000 was dishonoured.

(i) Interest on Overdue Accounts ₹ 90,000.

(j) Transfer from Sales Ledger ₹ 30,000.

(k) Reserve for Discount on Creditors ₹ 50,000.

SOLUTION

Dr. **TOTAL CREDITORS ACCOUNT** *Cr.*

Date	*Particulars*	₹	*Date*	*Particulars*	₹
31.03.2016	To Return Outward	40,000	01.04.2015	By Balance b/d	4,00,000
	To Discount Received	22,000	31.03.2016	By Credit Purchases	24,40,000
	To Cash A/c	4,00,000		By Discount Returned	2,000
	To Bank A/c	8,80,000		By Bank A/c (Ch. dish)	80,000
	To Bills Payable A/c	13,20,000		By Bills Payable A/c	20,000
	To Bills Receivable A/c	1,20,000		(Cancelled upon	

	To Transfer from Sales Ledger	30,000		renewal)	
				By Interest A/c	90,000
	To Balance c/d	2,40,000		By Total Debtors A/c (Endorsed B/R Dish.)	20,000
		30,52,000			30,52,000

Note: *Cash Purchases and Reserve for Discount on Creditors do not appear in the Total Creditors' Account.*

4.0 SELF BALANCING SYSTEM

MEANING OF SELF BALANCING SYSTEM

A self balancing ledger system implies a system of ledger keeping under which—

(a) Separate ledger (e.g. Debtors ledger, Creditors ledger) are maintained for different nature of transactions.

(b) A General Ledger Adjustment Account is opened in each subsidiary ledger in order to make each such ledger self-balancing. General Ledger Adjustment Account in the Debtors Ledger gives a summary of all transactions of the Debtors Ledger in a reverse manner and similarly, General Ledger Adjustment Account in the Creditors Ledger gives a summary of all transactions of the Creditors Ledger in a reverse manner.

(c) A Control Account/Adjustment Account is opened for each subsidiary ledger in the General Ledger in order to complete the double entry. For example, Debtors Ledger Adjustment Account for Debtors Ledger and Creditors Ledger Adjustment Account for Creditors Ledger are opened in the General Ledger.

(d) The accuracy of individual balances in each ledger is checked by comparing the total of their balances with the balance of the Control Account.

(e) Usually the following accounts are maintained:

Ledger	*Accounts Opened in the Ledger*
(i) Debtors' Ledger	(a) Personal accounts of all Trade Debtors, (b) General Ledger Adjustment Account.
(ii) Creditors' Ledger	(a) Personal accounts of all Trade Creditors, (b) General Ledger Adjustment Account.
(iii) General Ledger	(a) Personal accounts (other than those of Trade Debtors & Creditors), (b) All Real Accounts, (c) All Nominal Accounts, (d) Debtors' Ledger Adjustment Account, (e) Creditors' Ledger Adjustment Account.

Example

In case of Banking Companies, separate ledgers are maintained each for Saving Bank Account Holders, Current Account Holders, Borrowers, Fixed Depositors.

OBJECT

The object of the self balancing ledger system is to locate the errors quickly with minimum effort.

ADVANTAGES OF SELF BALANCING SYSTEM

(i) It identifies errors and facilitates in the quick detection of errors with the minimum efforts.

(ii) It fixes the responsibility of ledger keeper, as to the balancing of the ledger under his/her charge and the person responsible for the mistake can be called upon to work overtime to locate it. Errors are localized.

(iii) It facilitates the preparation of interim accounts without personal ledgers having to be balanced.

(iv) It facilitates the ascertainment of the figures of total debtors and creditors readily.

WORKING OF SELF BALANCING SYSTEM

(a) Debtors' Ledger (also known as Sold Ledger/Sale Ledger) is kept in which the following accounts are opened:

   (i) Personal Accounts of Trade Debtors (i.e., those to whom the goods, in which the firm deals in are sold on credit basis) to which individual items are posted.

   (ii) General Ledger Adjustment Account which is debited when the debtors' accounts are credited and is credited when the debtor's accounts are debited. This account helps in completing the double entry in this ledger and making it self-balancing.

   This account is just reverse of the Debtors' Ledger Adjustment Account in the General Ledger.

(b) Creditors' Ledger (also known as Purchase Ledger/Bought Ledger) is kept in which the following accounts are opened:

   (i) Personal Accounts of Trade Creditors (i.e. those from whom the goods, in which the firm deals in, are purchased on credit basis) to which individual items are posted.

   (ii) General Ledger Adjustment Account which is debited when the creditors' accounts are credited and is credited when the creditors' accounts are debited. This account helps in completing the double entry in this ledger and making it self-balancing. This account is just reverse of the Creditors' Ledger Adjustment Account in the General Ledger.

(c) General Ledger (also known as Main Ledger) is kept in which the following accounts are opened:

   (i) Personal Accounts other than those of customers and suppliers which have already been opened in a separate ledgers of Debtors and Creditors.

   (ii) Real Accounts

   (iii) Nominal Accounts

   (iv) Debtors' Ledger Adjustment Account which is debited when Trade debtors' accounts are debited and is credited when trade debtors accounts are credited. This account helps in completing the double entry in this ledger and making it self-balancing. This account is just reverse of the General Ledger Adjustment Account in Debtors' Ledger.

   (v) Creditors Ledger Adjustment Account which is debited when creditors' accounts are debited and is credited when trade creditors' accounts are debited. This account helps in completing the double entry in this ledger and making it self- balancing. This account is just the reverse of the General Ledger Adjustment account in Creditors' Ledger.

5.0 SELF BALANCING ENTRIES IN RELATION TO DEBTORS' LEDGER

The self balancing entries in relation to Debtors' Ledger are made with help of two accounts, viz. Debtors' Ledger Adjustment Account and General Ledger Adjustment Account with the object of making the Debtors' Ledger, self balanced. For this purpose, we take only the total of such items for the period as a whole and pass the necessary self-balancing journal entries. Some of the examples are as follows:

Case	Self-Balancing Journal Entry
(a) For Goods sold on credit or, For B/R or Cheque dishonoured	(a) Debtors' Ledger Adjustment A/c (In G.L.) Dr. To General Ledger Adjustment A/c (In D.L.)
(b) For Sales returns, or For Cash received, or cheque received or B/R drawn Discount/Rebate/Allowances allowed or Bad Debts	(b) General Ledger Adjustment A/c (In D.L.) Dr. To Debtors' Ledger Adjustment A/c (In G.L.)

The format of Debtors' Ledger Adjustment Account as it appears in General Ledger is given below:

FORMAT OF DEBTORS' LEDGER ADJUSTMENT ACCOUNT

Dr. **DEBTORS' LEDGER ADJUSTMENT ACCOUNT IN GENERAL LEDGER** *Cr.*

Particulars	₹	*Particulars*	₹
To Balance b/d		By Balance b/d	
(Dues from Customers in the beg.)	xxx	(Advs. from Customers in the beg.)	xxx
To General Ledger Adjustment A/c:		**By General Ledger Adjustment A/c:**	
Credit Sales	xxx	Cash (Received)	xxx
B/R (Dishonoured)	xxx	Bank (Cheque Received)	xxx
Bank (Cheque dishonoured)	xxx	B/R (Drawn)	xxx
Interest & Cartage charged	xxx	Returns inwards	xxx
B/R (Cancelled upon Renewal)	xxx	Discount allowed	xxx
Discount (Disallowed)	xxx	Rebate & allowances	xxx
Creditors (Endorsed B/R Dish)	xxx	Bad Debt w/o	xxx
To Balance c/d (Advances from	xxx	Transfer to Creditors	xxx
Customers at the end)		By Balance c/d	xxx
		(Dues from Customers at the end)	
	xxx		xxx

Note: *Provision for Doubtful Debts, Provision for Discount on Debtors, Bad Debts recovered, Trade Discount allowed, B/R Discounted do not affect the aforesaid account.*

FORMAT OF GENERAL LEDGER ADJUSTMENT ACCOUNT

Dr. **GENERAL LEDGER ADJUSTMENT ACCOUNT IN DEBTORS' LEDGER** *Cr.*

Particulars	₹	*Particulars*	₹
To Balance b/d (Advances from		By Balance b/d (Dues from	
Customers in the beginning)	xxx	Customers in the Beginning)	xxx
To Debtors' Ledger Adjustment A/c:		**By Debtors' Ledger Adjustment A/c:**	
Cash (received)	xxx	Credit Sales	xxx
Bank (Cheque received)	xxx	B/R (Dishonoured)	xxx
B/R (Drawn)	xxx	Bank (Cheque dishonoured)	xxx
Returns inwards	xxx	Interest & Cartage charged	xxx
Discount allowed	xxx	B/R cancelled upon renewal	xxx
Rebate & allowances	xxx	Discount (Disallowed)	xxx
Transfer to Creditors	xxx	Creditors (Endorsed B/R Dish)	xxx

To Balance c/d (Dues from Customers at the end)	xxx	By Balance c/d (Advances from customers at the end)	
	xxx		xxx

Note: *Provision for Doubtful Debts, Provision for Discount on Debtors, Bad Debts recovered, B/R Discounted and Trade discount allowed do not affect the aforesaid account.*

ILLUSTRATION 5

Taking the same information is given in Illustration 1, prepare Debtors' Ledger Adjustment Account in General Ledger and General Ledger Adjustment Account in Debtors' Ledger.

SOLUTION

Dr. **DEBTORS' LEDGER ADJUSTMENT ACCOUNT** Cr.

Date	*Particulars*	₹	*Date*	*Particulars*	₹
01.04.2015	To Balance b/d	1,00,000	31.03.2016	By General Ledger	
31.03.2016	To General Ledger			Adjustment A/c:	
	Adjustment A/c:			Cash (Received)	1,00,000
	Credit Sales	6,10,000		Bank (Cheque Rec.)	2,00,000
				B/R (Drawn)	3,00,000
				Returns inwards	10,000
				Discount allowed	5,000
				Bad Debt w/o	5,000
				By Balance c/d	90,000
		7,10,000			7,10,000

Dr. **GENERAL LEDGER ADJUSTMENT ACCOUNT IN DEBTORS LEDGER** Cr.

Date	*Particulars*	₹	*Date*	*Particulars*	₹
31.03.2016	To Debtors Ledger		01.04.2015	By Balance b/d	1,00,000
	Adjustment A/c:		31.03.2016	By Debtors Ledger	
	Cash (Received)	1,00,000		Adjustment A/c:	
	Bank (Cheque Rec.)	2,00,000		Credit Sales	6,10,000
	B/R (Drawn)	3,00,000			
	Returns inwards	10,000			
	Discount allowed	5,000			
	Bad Debt w/o	5,000			
	By Balance c/d	90,000			
		7,10,000			7,10,000

ILLUSTRATION 6

Taking the same information as given in Illustration 2, prepare Debtors' Ledger Adjustment Account in General Ledger and General Ledger Adjustment Account in Debtors' Ledger.

SOLUTION

Dr. **DEBTORS' LEDGER ADJUSTMENT ACCOUNT** *Cr.*

Date	*Particulars*	₹	*Date*	*Particulars*	₹
01.04.2015	To Balance b/d	2,00,000	31.03.2016	By General Ledger	
31.03.2016	To General Ledger			Adjustment A/c:	
	Adjustment A/c:			Cash (Received)	2,00,000
	Credit Sales	12,20,000		Bank	
	B/R (Dishonoured)	20,000		(Cheque Received)	4,40,000
	Bank (Cheque			B/R (Drawn)	6,60,000
	dishonoured)	40,000		Returns inward	20,000
	Interest charged	45,000		Discount allowed	11,000
	Total Creditors			Transfer to Bought	
	(Endorsed)	10,000		Ledger	15,000
	Discount (Disall.)	1,000		Bad Debt w/o	10,000
				By Balance c/d	1,80,000
		15,36,000			15,36,000

Dr. **GENERAL LEDGER ADJUSTMENT ACCOUNT IN DEBTORS' LEDGER** *Cr.*

Date	*Particulars*	₹	*Date*	*Particulars*	₹
31.03.2016	To Debtors Ledger		01.04.2015	By Balance b/d	2,00,000
	Adjustment A/c:		31.03.2016	By Debtors Ledger	
	Cash (Received)	2,00,000		Adjustment A/c:	
	Bank			Credit Sales	12,20,000
	(Cheque Received)	4,40,000		B/R (Dishonoured)	20,000
	B/R (Drawn)	6,60,000		Bank (Cheque	
	Returns inwards	20,000		dishonoured)	40,000
	Discount allowed	11,000		Interest charged	45,000
	Transfer to Bought			Total Creditors	
	Ledger	15,000		(Endor. B/R Dish.)	10,000
	Bad Debt w/o	10,000		Discount (Disall.)	1,000
	By Balance c/d	1,80,000			
		15,36,000			15,36,000

Note: *Cash Sales, Bad Debts Recovered and Provision for Doubtful Debts do not appear in the Debtors' Ledger Adjustment Account/General Ledger Adjustment Account.*

6.0 SELF BALANCING ENTRIES IN RELATION TO CREDITORS' LEDGER

The self balancing entries in relation to Creditor's Ledger are made with the help of two accounts, viz. Creditors' Ledger Adjustment Account and General Ledger Adjustment Account with the object of making the Creditors' Ledger self balanced. For this purpose we take only the total of such items for the period as a whole and pass that necessary self-balancing journal entries. Some of the examples are as under:

Case	Self Balancing Journal Entry
(a) For Goods purchased or For B/P renewed	General Ledger Adjustment A/c (In C.L.) Dr. To Creditors' Ledger Adjustment A/c (In G.L.)
(b) For Purchase returns or For Cash paid or Cheques Issued or For Discount/Rebate/ Allowance Received or For Bills accepted	Creditors' Ledger Adjustment A/c (In G.L.) Dr. To General Ledger Adjustment A/c (In C.L)

The format of Creditors' Ledger Adjustment Account as it appears in General Ledger is given below:

FORMAT OF CREDITORS' LEDGER ADJUSTMENT ACCOUNT

Dr. **CREDITORS' LEDGER ADJUSTMENT ACCOUNT IN GENERAL LEDGER** *Cr.*

Particulars	₹	*Particulars*	₹
To Balance b/d	xxx	By Balance b/d	xxx
(Advances to Suppliers in the Beg.)		(Due to Suppliers in the Beginning)	
To General Ledger Adjustment A/c:		**By General Ledger Adjustment A/c:**	
Cash (paid)	xxx	Credit Purchases	xxx
Bank (Cheque Issued)	xxx	Cheque dishonoured	xxx
B/P (Accepted)	xxx	Endorsed B/R (dishonoured)	xxx
B/R (Endorsed)	xxx	Interest & Cartage	
Returns Outwards	xxx	(Charged by Suppliers)	xxx
Discount Received	xxx	B/P (Withdrawn)	xxx
Rebate & Allowances	xxx	Discount Returned	xxx
T/F from Debtors Ledger	xxx	By Balance c/d (Advances to	
To Balance c/d	xxx	Suppliers at the end)	xxx
(Due to Suppliers at the end)	xxx		
	xxx		xxx

Note: *Reserve for Discount on Creditors does not affect the aforesaid account since this item directly relates to Profit & Loss Account.*

The format of General Ledger Adjustment Account as it appears in Creditors' Ledger is given below:

FORMAT OF GENERAL LEDGER ADJUSTMENT ACCOUNT

Dr. **GENERAL LEDGER ADJUSTMENT ACCOUNT IN CREDITORS' LEDGER** *Cr.*

Particulars	₹	*Particulars*	₹
To Balance b/d	xxx	By Balance b/d (Advances to	xxx
(Due to Suppliers in the Beginning)		Suppliers in the Beginning)	
To Creditors' Ledger Adjustment A/c:		By Creditors' Ledger Adjustment A/c:	
Credit Purchases	xxx	Cash (Paid)	xxx
Cheque Dishonoured	xxx	Bank (Cheque Issued)	xxx
Endorsed B/R (dishonoured)	xxx	B/P (Accepted)	xxx
Interest & Cartage (charged by		B/R (Endorsed)	xxx
Suppliers)	xxx	Returns Outwards	xxx
B/P (Withdrawn)	xxx	Discount Received	xxx
Discount Returned	xxx	Rebate & Allowances	xxx

To Balance c/d (Advances to Suppliers at the end)	xxx	T/F to Debtors Ledger	xxx
		By Balance c/d (Due to Suppliers at the end)	xxx
	xxx		xxx

Note: *Reserve for Discount on Creditors does not affect the aforesaid account since this item directly relates to Profit & Loss Account.*

ILLUSTRATION 7

Taking the same information as given in Illustration 3, prepare Creditors' Ledger Adjustment Account in General Ledger and General Ledger Adjustment Account in Creditors' Ledger.

SOLUTION

Dr. **CREDITORS' LEDGER ADJUSTMENT ACCOUNT IN GENERAL LEDGER** *Cr.*

Date	*Particulars*	₹	*Date*	*Particulars*	₹
31.03.2016	To General Ledger		01.04.2015	By Balance b/d	2,00,000
	Adjustment A/c:		31.03.2016	By General Ledger	
	Cash (Paid)	2,00,000		Adjustment A/c:	
	Bank (Cheque Issued)	4,00,000		Credit Purchases	12,20,000
	B/P Accepted	6,00,000			
	Returns outwards	20,000			
	Discount Received	10,000			
	By Balance c/d	1,90,000			
		14,20,000			14,20,000

Dr. **GENERAL LEDGER ADJUSTMENT ACCOUNT IN CREDITORS' LEDGER** *Cr.*

Date	*Particulars*	₹	*Date*	*Particulars*	₹
01.04.2015	To Balance b/d	2,00,000	31.03.2016	By Creditors' Ledger	
31.03.2016	To Creditors Ledger			Adjustment A/c:	
	Adjustment A/c:			Cash (Paid)	2,00,000
	Credit Purchases	12,20,000		Bank (Cheque Issued)	4,00,000
				B/P Accepted	6,00,000
				Returns outwards	20,000
				Discount Received	10,000
				By Balance c/d	1,90,000
		14,20,000			14,20,000

ILLUSTRATION 8

Taking the same information as given in Illustration 4, prepare Creditors' Ledger Adjustment Account in General Ledger and General Ledger Adjustment Account in Creditors' Ledger.

SOLUTION

Dr. **CREDITORS' LEDGER ADJUSTMENT ACCOUNT IN GENERAL LEDGER** Cr.

Date	*Particulars*	₹	*Date*	*Particulars*	₹
31.03.2016	To General Ledger		01.04.2015	By Balance b/d	4,00,000
	Adjustment A/c:		31.03.2016	By General Ledger	
	Cash (Paid)	4,00,000		Adjustment A/c:	
	Bank			Credit Purchases	24,40,000
	(Cheque Issued)	8,80,000		Endorsed B/R	
	B/P Accepted	13,20,000		(Dishonoured)	20,000
	B/R (Endorsed)	1,20,000		Bank (Cheque	
	Returns outwards	40,000		dishonoured)	80,000
	Discount received	22,000		Interest charged	90,000
	Transfer from			B/P (Cancelled	
	Sales Ledger	30,000		upon renewal)	20,000
	By Balance c/d	240,000		Discount (Returned)	2,000
		30,52,000			30,52,000

Dr. **GENERAL LEDGER ADJUSTMENT ACCOUNT IN CREDITORS' LEDGER** Cr.

Date	*Particulars*	₹	*Date*	*Particulars*	₹
01.04.2015	By Balance b/d	4,00,000	31.03.2016	To Creditors Ledger	
31.03.2016	By Creditors Ledger			Adjustment A/c:	
	Adjustment A/c:			Cash (Paid)	4,00,000
	Credit Purchases	24,40,000		Bank	
	Endorsed B/R			(Cheque Issued)	8,80,000
	(Dishonoured)	20,000		B/P Accepted	13,20,000
	Bank (Cheque			B/R (Endorsed)	1,20,000
	dishonoured)	80,000		Returns outwards	40,000
	Interest charged	90,000		Discount received	22,000
	B/P (Cancelled)	20,000		Transfer from	
	Discount (Returned)	2,000		Sales Ledger	30,000
				By Balance c/d	2,40,000
		30,52,000			30,52,000

Note: Reserve for Discount on creditors does not affect the aforesaid accounts since this item directly relates to Profit & Loss Account.

7.0 TRANSFER FROM ONE LEDGER TO ANOTHER (UNDER SELF BALANCING SYSTEM)

The transfer of an amount in an account in one ledger to the same account in another requires one usual transfer entry and two self balancing entries. For example: Goods sold to A for ₹ 1,000, and purchased goods from A for ₹ 700.

JOURNAL

Date	Particulars		L.F.	Dr. (₹)	Cr.(₹)
(a)	Transfer Entry				
	A's A/c (In Creditors' Ledger)	Dr.		700	
	To A's A/c (In Debtors' Ledger)				700
(b)	Self Balancing Entries				
(i)	Creditors' Ledger Adjustment A/c (in G.L.)	Dr.		700	
	To General Ledger Adjustment A/c (in C.L.)				700
(ii)	General Ledger Adjustment A/c (in D.L.)	Dr.		700	
	To Debtors' Ledger Adjustment A/c (in G.L.)				700

ILLUSTRATION 9

X Ltd. maintains three Debtors Ledgers viz. (A-J) Debtors Ledger, (K-P) Debtors Ledger and (Q-Z) Debtors Ledger. Debtors list include ₹ 5,000 owed by Miss Kansal who became Mrs. Bansal after marriage. Give the necessary journal entries for transfer assuming Self Balancing System.

SOLUTION

JOURNAL

Particulars		L.F.	Dr. (₹)	Cr.(₹)
Mrs. Bansal (In A-J Debtors' Ledger)	Dr.		5,000	
To Miss Kansal (In K-P Debtors' Ledger)				5,000
(Being transfer of A/c of Miss Kansal to A-J Debtors' Ledger)				
General Ledger Adjustment A/c (In K-P Debtors' Ledger)	Dr.		5,000	
To (K-P) Debtors' Ledger Adjustment A/c (In G.L.)				5,000
(Being reduction in total K-P Debtors)				
(A-J) Debtors' Ledger Adjustment A/c (In G.L.)	Dr.		5,000	
To General Ledger Adjustment A/c (In A-J Debtors' Ledger)				5,000
(Being increase in (A-J) Debtors)				

ILLUSTRATION 10

Debtors List of ₹ 1,00,000 includes ₹ 1,000 owed by X and ₹ 500 by Y. Similarly, Creditors List of ₹ 2,00,000 covers ₹ 3,000 owed to X and ₹ 300 to Y. Give the necessary Journal Entries for the transfer under (i) Self Balancing System and (ii) under Sectional Balancing System.

SOLUTION

JOURNAL

Date	Particulars		L.F.	Dr. (₹)	Cr.(₹)
(i)	Under Self Balancing System				
(a)	X (In Creditors' Ledger)	Dr.		1,000	
	To X (In Debtors' Ledger)				1,000

	(Being T/f of X's A/c from Debtors' Ledger to Creditors' Ledger)			
(b)	Y (In Creditors' Ledger) Dr.		300	
	To Y (In Debtors' Ledger)			300
	(Being t/f of Y's A/c from Creditors' Ledger to Debtors' Ledger)			
(c)	General Ledger Adjustment A/c (In Debtors' Ledger) Dr.		1,300	
	To Debtors Ledger Adjustment A/c (In General Ledger)			1,300
	(Being reduction in Total Debtors)			
(d)	Creditors' Ledger Adjustment A/c (In General Ledger) Dr.		1,300	
	To General Ledger Adjustment A/c (In Creditors' Ledger)			1,300
	(Being reduction in Total Creditors)			
(ii)	Under Sectional Balancing System			
(a)	X (In Creditor Ledger) Dr.		1,000	
	To X (In Debtors' Ledger)			1,000
	(Being T/f of X's A/c from Debtors to Creditor Ledger)			
(b)	Y (In Creditors' Ledger) Dr.		300	
	To Y (In Debtors' Ledger)			300
	(Being T/f of Y's A/c from Creditors Ledger to Debtors Ledger)			
(c)	Total Creditors A/c Dr.		1,300	
	To Total Debtors A/c			1,300
	(Being reduction in Total Creditors and Total Debtors)			

ILLUSTRATION 11

M. Shyam keeps self balancing ledgers. Record the following transactions in the General Ledger Adjustment Account in the Sales Ledger.

Date	*Particulars*
01.04.2016	Received ₹ 475 from Mr X in full settlement. He was allowed a discount of ₹ 25.
02.04.2016	Received ₹ 2,000 from Mr Y towards his dues in full.
03.04.2016	Goods supplied to Mr T ₹ 700 and received ₹ 300 after adjustment of an advance of ₹ 400.
04.04.2016	Bad debts recovered from Mr Q ₹ 1,000
05.04.2016	Goods sold to the following: Mr A ₹ 1,000, Mr B ₹ 1,500, Mr C ₹ 2,000.
15.04.2016	Mr P paid ₹ 750 towards dues. Balances thereafter due was ₹ 250.
25.04.2016	Amounts received from Mr A ₹ 750, Mr B ₹ 1,000, Mr C ₹ 2,000.
30.04.2016	Advance received from Mr R for supply ₹ 2,000

SOLUTION

Dr. **GENERAL LEDGER ADJUSTMENT ACCOUNT (IN SALES LEDGER)** *Cr.*

Date	Particulars	₹	Date	Particulars	₹
2016			2016		
Apr. 01	To Balance b/d [See Note (ii)]	400	Apr. 01	By Balance b/d [See Note (i)]	3,500
Apr. 01	To Sales Ledger Adjustment A/c (X)	475	Apr. 03	By Sales Ledger Adjustment A/c (Sales)	700
Apr. 01	To Sales Ledger Adju stment A/c (Disc.)	25	Apr. 05	By Sales Ledger Adjustment A/c (Sales) [₹ 1,000 + ₹ 1,500 + ₹ 2,000]	4,500
Apr. 02	To Sales Ledger Adjustment A/c (Y)	2,000			
Apr. 02	To Sales Ledger Adjustment A/c (T)	300	Apr. 30	By Balance c/d [See Note (iii)]	2,000
Apr. 15	To Sales Ledger Adjustment A/c (P)	750			
Apr. 25	To Sales Ledger Adjustment A/c (A,B,C)	3,750			
Apr. 30	To Sales Ledger Adjustment A/c (R)	2,000			
Apr. 30	To Balance c/d (A,B & P) [See Note (iv)]	1,000			
		10,700			10,700
May 01	To Balance b/d	2,000	May 01	By Balance b/d	1,000

Working Notes:

(i) Opening credit balance = ₹ 500 (X) + ₹ 2,000 (Y) + ₹ 1,000 (P) = ₹ 3,500

(ii) Opening debit balance ₹ 400, is advance from T.

(iii) Closing debit balance represents advance from R, ₹ 2,000.

(iv) Closing credit balance = ₹ 250 (A) + ₹ 500 (B) + ₹ 250 (P) = ₹ 1,000.

ILLUSTRATION 12

From the following particulars, prepare the relevant adjustment account as should appear in the General Ledger of Mr Vasu for the month of March 2016.

Date	Particulars
March 01	Purchased from Mr X ₹ 2,000.
02	Paid ₹ 1,600 after adjusting the initial advance in full to Mr X.
13	Paid ₹ 1,000 to Mr R towards the purchases made in February, in full.
13	Paid Advance to Mr Y ₹ 3,000
14	Purchased goods from Mr A ₹ 4,000.

25	Returned Goods worth ₹ 500 to Mr A.
26	Settled the balance due to A at discount of 10 per cent.
27	Goods purchased from Mr Y ₹ 2,500 against the advance paid on 13th March.
28	Received back the advance from Mr P (Paid on 28th February, 2013, ₹ 2,000).
30	Purchased from B ₹ 2,000.
31	Goods returned to Q ₹ 750. The goods were originally purchased for cash in February.

SOLUTION

Dr. **CREDITORS' LEDGER ADJUSTMENT ACCOUNT (IN GENERAL LEDGER)** *Cr.*

Date	*Particulars*	₹	*Date*	*Particulars*	₹
2016			2016		
Mar. 1	To Balance b/d (X, P)		Mar. 1	By Balance (R) b/d	1,000
	[₹ 400 + ₹ 2,000]	2,400	Mar. 31	By General Ledger	
Mar. 31	To General Ledger			Adjustment A/c:	
	Adjustment A/c:			(In Bought Ledger):	
	(In Bought Ledger):			Purchases	
	Bank (X,R,Y & A)			[See Note (i)]	10,500
	[See Note (ii)]	8,750		Bank (refund) (From P)	2,000
	Returns (A,Q)				
	[₹ 500 + ₹ 750]	1,250			
	Discount	350			
Mar. 31	To Balance c/d (B)	2,000	Mar. 31	By Balance c/d (Y,Q)	1,250
		14,750			14,750
April 1	To Balance b/d (Y,Q)	1,250	April 1	By Balance b/d (B)	2,000

Working Notes:

(i) Purchases = ₹ 2,000 + ₹ 4,000 + ₹ 2,500 + ₹ 2,000 = ₹ 10,500

(ii) Payments = ₹ 1,600 + ₹ 1,000 + ₹ 3,000 + (₹ 3,500 – 10% of ₹ 3,500) = ₹ 8,750

ILLUSTRATION 13

On 1st June, the Debtors' Balance in a Trader's Ledger were as follows:

A. Bose ₹ 1,700. B. Kumar ₹ 1,800, C. Dutta ₹ 1,650,G. Emery ₹ 2,100, F. Francis ₹ 1,300, G. Ghose ₹ 1,900.

The following transactions occurred during the month:

Date	*Particulars*	₹
June 2	Sold goods to A. Bose	1,850
8	Received from G. Ghose on account	900
9	A. Bose accepted the Trader's Draft (Discount ₹ 50)	950
11	F. Francis returned goods	300
12	Sold goods to H. Hamid	2,000

14	Received from F. Francis (Discount ₹ 10)	990
19	Sold goods to B. Kumar	1,500
21	Received from G Emery (Discount ₹ 100)	2,000
22	Sold goods to G Emery	1,600
25	H. Hamid returned goods	230
27	Received from B. Kumar (Discount ₹ 60)	1,740
28	Sold goods to F. Francis	2,200
28	Received from H. Hamid (Discount ₹ 70)	1,700
29	G. Ghose accepted the Trader's Draft (Discount ₹ 40)	960
30	Sold goods to G. Ghose	1,600
30	Received from A. Bose on accounts	700

Prepare the necessary accounts in the Sales Ledger under Self Balancing System.

SOLUTION

Dr. **A. BOSE** *Cr.*

Date	*Particulars*	₹	*Date*	*Particulars*	₹
June 1	To Balance b/d	1,700	June 9	By B/R	950
2	To Sales	1,850	9	By Discount	50
			30	By Cash	700
			30	By Balance c/d	1,850
		3,550			3,550
July 1	To Balance b/d	1,850			

Dr. **B. KUMAR** *Cr.*

Date	*Particulars*	₹	*Date*	*Particulars*	₹
June 1	To Balance b/d	1,800	June 27	By Cash	1,740
19	To Sales	1,500	27	By Discount	60
			30	By Balance c/d	1,500
		3,300			3,300
July 1	To Balance b/d	1,500			

Dr. **C. DUTTA** *Cr.*

Date	*Particulars*	₹	*Date*	*Particulars*	₹
June 1	To Balance b/d	1,650	June 30	By Balance c/d	1,650
July 1	To Balance b/d	1,650			

Dr. **G. EMERY** *Cr.*

Date	*Particulars*	₹	*Date*	*Particulars*	₹
June 1	To Balance b/d	2,100	June 21	By Cash	2,000
June 22	To Sales	1,600	June 21	By Discount	100

			June 30	By Balance c/d	1,600
		3,700			3,700
July 1	To Balance b/d	1,600			

Dr. **F. FRANCIS** Cr.

Date	Particulars	₹	Date	Particulars	₹
June 1	To Balance b/d	1,300	June 11	By Sales Returns	300
June 28	To Sales	2,200	June 14	By Cash	990
			June 14	By Discount	10
			June 30	By Balance c/d	2,200
		3,500			3,500
July 1	To Balance b/d	2,200			

Dr. **G. GHOSE** Cr.

Date	Particulars	₹	Date	Particulars	₹
June 1	To Balance b/d	1,900	June 8	By Cash	900
June 30	To Sales	1,600	June 29	By B/R	960
			June 29	By Discount	40
			June 30	By Balance c/d	1,600
		3,500			3,500
July 1	To Balance b/d	1,600			

Dr. **H. HAMID** Cr.

Date	Particulars	₹	Date	Particulars	₹
June 12	To Sales	2,000	June 25	By Sales Returns	230
			June 28	By Cash	1,700
			June 28	By Discount	70
		2,000			2,000

Dr. **GENERAL LEDGER ADJUSTMENT ACCOUNT (IN SALES LEDGER)** Cr.

Date	Particulars	₹	Date	Particulars	₹
June 30	To Sales Ledger		June 1	By Balance b/d	10,450
	Adjustment A/c:		June 30	By Sales Ledger	
	Cash Received	8,030		Adjustment A/c:	
	Discount allowed	330		Sales	10,750
	Returns	530			
	B/R	1,910			
June 30	To Balance c/d	10,400			
		21,200			21,.200
			July 1	By Balance b/d	10,400

ILLUSTRATION 14

Samaresh keeps his ledger on Self Balancing System. From the following particulars, you are required to write up the individual Debtor's Account and the General Ledger Adjustment Account (in Sales Ledger) during the month of January.

(i) Individual Debtors Balances on 1st January, 2013: A - ₹ 1,530, B - ₹ 1,620, C - ₹ 1,890 and D - ₹ 1,170.

(II) TRANSACTIONS DURING THE MONTH

January 2	Sold goods to A ₹ 1,710.
January 9	Received from B on account ₹ 300
January 11	Received from A ₹ 1,500 full settlement of his balance on 1st January.
January 12	Sold goods to B ₹ 600.
January 14	B returned goods which were damaged in transit amounting to ₹ 180.
January 18	Received from C ₹ 1,800 and allowed him discount ₹ 90.
January 19	Received from A a Bill of Exchange for ₹ 1,200 accepted by X payable on 25th January.
January 22	Received from B ₹ 900.
January 25	A's Bill returned dishonoured.
January 28	D became insolvent and 30 paise in the rupee was received from his estate in full and final settlement.
January 31	Sold goods to C ₹ 1,020.

SOLUTION

Dr. **GENERAL LEDGER ADJUSTMENT ACCOUNT (IN SALES LEDGER)** *Cr.*

Date	*Particulars*	₹	*Date*	*Particulars*	₹
	To Sales Ledger		Jan. 01	By Balance b/d	6,210
	Adjustment A/c:		Jan. 31	By Sales Ledger	
	Cash	4,851		Adjustment A/c:	
	Discount Allowed	120		Sales	3,330
	Bills Receivable	1,200		Bills Receivable	1,200
	Returns Inwards	180			
	Bad Debts	819			
Jan. 31	To Balance c/d	3,570			
		10,740			10,740
			Feb. 01	By Balance b/d	3,570

Dr. **A'S ACCOUNT** *Cr.*

Date	*Particulars*	₹	*Date*	*Particulars*	₹
Jan. 01	To Balance b/d	1,530	Jan. 11	By Cash	1,500
Jan. 02	To Sales	1,710	Jan. 11	By Discount Allowed	30
Jan. 25	To B/R (Dishonoured)	1,200	Jan. 19	By B/R	1,200

			Jan. 31	By Balance c/d	1,710
		4,440			4,440
Feb. 01	To Balance b/d	1,710			

Dr. **B 'S ACCOUNT** *Cr.*

Date	*Particulars*	₹	*Date*	*Particulars*	₹
Jan. 01	To Balance b/d	1,620	Jan. 09	By Cash	300
Jan. 12	To Sales	600	Jan. 14	By Return Inwards	180
			Jan. 22	By Cash	900
			Jan. 31	By Balance c/d	840
		2,220			2,220
Feb. 01	To Balance b/d	840			

Dr. **C 'S ACCOUNT** *Cr.*

Date	*Particulars*	₹	*Date*	*Particulars*	₹
Jan. 01	To Balance b/d	1,890	Jan. 18	By Cash	1,800
Jan. 31	To Sales	1,020	Jan. 18	By Discount Allowed	90
			Jan. 31	By Balance c/d	1,020
		2,910			2,910
Feb. 01	To Balance b/d	1,020			

Dr. **D 'S ACCOUNT** *Cr.*

Date	*Particulars*	₹	*Date*	*Particulars*	₹
Jan. 01	To Balance b/d	1,170	Jan. 28	By Cash	351
			Jan. 28	By Bad Debts	819
		1,170			1,170

Working Notes:

(i) Total Debtors Balance as on 1st Jan. = ₹ 1,530 + ₹ 1,620 + ₹ 1,890 + ₹ 1,170 = ₹ 6,210

(ii) Total Sales = ₹ 1,710 + 600 + ₹ 1,020 = ₹ 3,330

(iii) Total Cash received = ₹ 300 + ₹ 1,500 + ₹ 1,800 + ₹ 900 + ₹ 351 = ₹ 4,851

(iii) Total Discount allowed = ₹ 30 + ₹ 90 = ₹ 120

(v) Returns Inward (B) = ₹ 180

(vi) B/R Received (A) = ₹ 1,200

(vii) Bad Debt (D) = ₹ 819

(viii) B/R dishonoured (A) = ₹ 1,200

(ix) Total Debtors balance as on 31st Jan. = ₹ 1,710 + ₹ 840 + ₹ 1,020 = ₹ 3,570

ILLUSTRATION 15

CANIG Ltd. maintains accounts on self-balancing system for customers and suppliers. You are required to pass journal entries for "Control Account" purpose in respect of the following transactions for September:

(a) Bills of exchange for ₹ 3,00,000 drawn on customers against credit sales;

(b) Bills of exchange for ₹ 2,50,000 accepted by customers earlier now endorsed to suppliers;

(c) An endorsed bill of exchange for ₹ 13,000 dishonoured; noting charges ₹ 150 incurred by holder in due course; endorsement was not "sans recourse";

(d) An acceptor of a bill of exchange of ₹ 12,000 retires the bill by paying ₹ 11,800, this bill was already endorsed to the supplier. The business contacts and pays the supplier by cheque on the due date.

SOLUTION

JOURNAL

Date	*Particulars*	*L.F.*	*Dr. (₹)*	*Cr. (₹)*
	General ledger Control A/c (in customers ledger) Dr.		3,00,000	
	To Customers' Ledger Control A/c (in general ledger)			3,00,000
	(Being the Self-balancing entry for bills of exchange drawn on and accepted by customers)			
	Suppliers' Ledger Control A/c (in general ledger) Dr.		2,50,000	
	To General Ledger Control A/c (in suppliers' ledger)			2,50,000
	(Being the Self-balancing entry for bills of exchange accepted by customers now endorsed to suppliers)			
	Customers Ledger Control A/c (in general ledger) Dr.		13,150	
	General Ledger Control A/c (in suppliers' ledger) Dr.		13,150	
	To General Ledger Control A/c (in customers' ledger)			13,150
	To Suppliers Ledger Control A/c (in general ledger)			13,150
	(Being the entry to record dishonour of an endorsed bill of exchange, along with nothing charges of ₹ 150)			
(i)	General Ledger Control A/c (in customers ledger) Dr.		12,000	
	To Customer's Ledger Control A/c (in general ledger)			12,000
	(Being the retirement by a customer of an endorsed bill of exchange)			
(ii)	Supplier's Ledger Control A/c (in general ledger) Dr.		12,000	
	To General Ledger Control A/c (in suppliers' ledger)			12,000
	(Being the payment made to supplier on due date).			
(iii)	Customers' Ledger Control A/c (in general ledger) Dr.		12,000	
	General Ledger Control A/c (in supplier's ledger) Dr.		12,000	
	To General Ledger Control A/c (in customers' ledger)			12,000
	To Supplier's Ledger Control A/c (in general ledger)			12,000
	(Being the transfer of balance from customers' account to suppliers' account)			

ILLUSTRATION 16

How will you show the following items in General Ledger Adjustment Account in Debtors Ledger and General Ledger Adjustment Account in Creditors Ledger:

Particulars	₹
(a) Transfer from Debtors' Ledger to Creditors' Ledger	1,100
(b) Transfer from Creditors' Ledger to Debtors' Ledger	1,900
(c) B/R endorsed to Creditors	4,000
(d) Endorsed Bills dishonoured	1,000
(e) Bad Debts written off (after deducting bad debts recovered ₹ 300)	2,200
(f) Provision for Doubtful Debts	550
(g) Provision for Discount on Debtors	1,000
(h) Reserve for Discount on Creditors	2,000
(i) Cash Sales	3,000
(j) Cash Purchases	4,000
(k) Bill Receivable Collected on maturity	5,000
(l) Bills Receivable discounted	6,000
(m) Bills Payable matured	7,000
(n) Discount allowed	1,500
(o) Discount received	600
(p) Allowances from Creditors	3,200
(q) Discount allowed to debtors ₹ 500 was recorded as discount received from creditors.	
(r) Closing Debtors Balance (As per General Ledger Adjustment Account)	60,000 (Cr)
(s) Closing Creditors Balance (As per General Ledger Adjustment Account)	30,000 (Dr)

SOLUTION

Dr. **GENERAL LEDGER ADJUSTMENT ACCOUNT (IN DEBTOR LEDGER)** *Cr.*

Particulars	₹	*Particulars*	₹
To Debtors Ledger Adjustment A/c:		By Debtors Ledger Adjustment A/c:	
Discount Allowed (₹ 1,500 + ₹ 500)	2,000	Endorsed B/R dish.	1,000
Bad Debts (2,200+300)	2,500		
T/f from Drs Ledger to Crs. Ledger	1,100		
T/f from Cr. Ledger to Drs. Ledger	1,900		
To Balance c/d (60,000 – 500)	59,500		

Dr. **GENERAL LEDGER ADJUSTMENT ACCOUNT (IN CREDITORS LEDGER)** *Cr.*

Particulars	₹	*Particulars*	₹
To Creditors Ledger Adjustment A/c:		By Creditors Ledger Adjustment A/c:	
Endorsed B/R Dish.		T/f from Drs. Ledger to Crs. Ledger	1,100
	1,000	T/f from Crs. Ledger to Drs. Ledger	1,900

		B/R Endorsed to Crs.	4,000
		Discount received (₹ 600–₹ 500)	100
		Allowances	3,200
		By Balance c/d (30,000 + 500)	30,500

Notes:

(i) *The following items do not appear in GLA Account.*

1. Cash Sales
2. Provision for Doubtful Debts
3. Provision for Discount on Debtors
4. Bad Debts Recovered
5. Bills Receivable matured/collected on maturity
6. Bills Receivable discounted
7. Bills Receivable endorsed

(ii) *The following items do not appear in GLA Account.*

1. Cash Purchases
2. Reserve for Discount on Creditors
3. Bills Payable matured / discharged

8.0 RECTIFICATION OF ERRORS

The following points are worth noting while rectifying the errors:

(a) In case of Sectional Balancing System, any error in the Debtors' Ledger and Creditors Ledger can be rectified as follows:

Case	*Manner of Rectification*
(a) Before opening the Suspense Account	(a) By correcting the Concerned Personal A/c
(b) After opening the Suspense Account	(b) With the help of Concerned Personal A/c and Suspense A/c

In case, the error affects the total accounts also, an additional rectifying entry will have to be passed:

(b) In case of Self balancing system, in addition to be usual rectifying entry, one more entry will be required for rectifying the error in the Adjustment Account also.

ILLUSTRATION 17

Pass the necessary journal entries using a Suspense Account presuming (i) when the system of self-balancing is not in use and (ii) when the system of self-balancing is in use.

(a) Goods of the value of ₹ 500 returned by Mr Sharma were entered in the Sales Day Book and posted therefrom to the credit of his account.

(b) An amount of ₹ 300, entered in the Sales Returns Book, has been posted to the debit of Mr Philip, who returned the goods.

(c) A sale of ₹ 100 made to Mr Ghanshyam was correctly entered in the Sales Day Book but wrongly posted to the debit of Mr Radhesham as ₹ 10.

(d) Bad Debts aggregating ₹ 150 were written off during the year in the Sales Ledger but were not adjusted in General Ledger.

(e) The total of "Discount Allowed" column in the Cash Book for the month of Jan, amounting to ₹ 1,000 was not posted.

SOLUTION

(i) When the System of Self Balance is not in use

JOURNAL

Date	*Particulars*	*L.F.*	*Dr. (₹)*	*Cr. (₹)*
(a)	Sales A/c Dr.		500	
	Sales Returns A/c Dr.		500	
	To Suspense A/c			1,000
	(The value of goods returned by Mr Sharma wrongly posted to Sales and omission of debit to Sales Returns A/c, now rectified)			
(b)	Suspense A/c Dr.		600	
	To Mr Philip			600
	(Wrong debit to Mr Philip for goods, returned by him, now rectified)			
(c)	Mr Ghanshyam Dr.		100	
	To MR Radhesham			10
	To Suspense A/c			90
	(Omission of debit to Mr Ghanshyam and wrong credit to Mr Radhesham for sale of ₹ 100, now rectified)			
(d)	Bad Debts A/c Dr.		150	
	To Suspense A/c			150
	(The amount of Bad Debts written off not adjusted in General Ledger, now rectified)			
(e)	Discount A/c Dr.		1,000	
	To Suspense A/c			1,000
	(The total of Discounts allowed during Jan, not posted from the Cash Book, error now rectified)			

(ii) When the System of Self Balancing is in use

JOURNAL

Date	*Particulars*	*L.F.*	*Dr. (₹)*	*Cr. (₹)*
(a)(i)	Sales A/c Dr.		500	
	Sales Returns A/c Dr.		500	
	To Suspense A/c (in Sales Ledger)			1,000
(ii)	General Ledger Adjustment A/c (In Sales Ledger) Dr.		1,000	
	To Sales Ledger Adjustment A/c (In General Ledger)			1,000
(b)	Suspense A/c Dr.		600	
	To Mr Philips (In Sales Ledger)			600

(c)	Mr Ghanshyam Dr.		100	
	To Mr Radhesham			10
	To Suspense A/c (In Sales Ledger)			90
(d)	Bad Debts A/c Dr.		150	
	To Suspense (In Sales Ledger)			150
(e)	Discount A/c Dr.		1,000	
	To Suspense A/c (In Sales Ledger)			1,000

ILLUSTRATION 18

X Ltd. provides you the following informations:

(a) The Sales Book was found undercast by ₹ 5,000

(b) Discount allowed to Ram ₹ 500, correctly recorded in the Cash Book was not posted to his account.

(c) Credit balance of ₹ 1,500 in Mahesh's Account in the Purchase Ledger was to be transferred to his account in Sales Ledger.

Give journal entries both under the Self Balancing System and the Sectional Balancing System.

SOLUTION

Self Balancing System

JOURNAL OF X LTD.

Date	*Particulars*	*L.F.*	*Dr. (₹)*	*Cr. (₹)*
(a)	Sales Ledger Adjustment A/c (In General Ledger) Dr.		5,000	
	To General Ledger Adjustment A/c (In Sales Ledger)			5,000
	(Being the error, of undercasting Sales Book, rectified)			
	Suspense A/c (In General Ledger) Dr.		5,000	
	To Sales A/c			5,000
	(Being rectification of the error resulting from undercasting of the Sales Book)			
(b)	Suspense A/c (In Sales Ledger) Dr.		500	
	To Ram (In Sales Ledger)			500
	(Being rectification of the error by which Ram was not credited, accounts in the general ledger are not affected)			
(c)	Mahesh (In Purchase Ledger) Dr.		1,500	
	To General Ledger Adjustment A/c (In Bought Ledger)			1,500
	(Being transfer of Mahesh's credit Balance in the Purchase Ledger to his account in the Sales Ledger)			
	Bought Ledger Adjustment A/c (In General Ledger) Dr.		1,500	
	To General Ledger Adjustment A/c (In Bought Ledger)			1,500
	(Being correction of the adjustment relating to the Bought Ledger because of the transfer of Mahesh's A/c, in the Purchase Ledger)			

	General Ledger Adjustment A/c (In Sales Ledger) Dr.		1,500	
	To Sales Ledger Adjustment A/c (In General Ledger)			1,500
	(Being correction of the Adjustment A/c relating to the Sales Ledger because of transfer of Mahesh's A/c)			

Note: *It is assumed that if a ledger has not balanced, a Suspense Account has been opened.*

Sectional Balancing System:

JOURNAL OF X LTD.

Date	*Particulars*	*L.F.*	*Dr. (₹)*	*Cr. (₹)*
(a)	Total Debtors' A/c Dr.		5,000	
	To Sales A/c			5,000
	(Being rectification of the consequences of the undercasting the Sales Book)			
(b)	Credit Ram with ₹ 500 (in the Sales Ledger)			
(c)	Mahesh's A/c (in Purchase Ledger) Dr.		1,500	
	To Mahesh's A/c (In Sales Ledger)			1,500
	(Being transfer of Mahesh's credit balance, ₹ 1,000 in the purchase Ledger to his account in the sales ledger)			
	Total Creditor's A/c Dr.		1,500	
	To Total Debtor's A/c			1,500
	(Being adjustment of total accounts because of the transfer of Mahesh's A/c in the Purchase Ledger to the Sales Ledger)			

ILLUSTRATION 19

How would you rectify the following errors made during the year ending on 31st March by the staff of Kumar & Co., who keep their Sales Ledger (A-M and N-Z) on the self Balancing System.

(a) Goods returned ₹ 200 by Rajiv were not entered in the books.

(b) A cheque for ₹ 1,000 received from Uttam was wrongly posted to the account of Bihari.

(c) The N-Z Sales Book for Feb., 2013 was overcast by ₹ 300.

SOLUTION

JOURNAL

Date	*Particulars*	*L.F.*	*Dr. (₹)*	*Cr. (₹)*
(a)(i)	Return Inward A/c Dr.		200	
	To Rajiv			200
	(For goods returned by Rajiv previously omitted from books)			
(ii)	General Ledger Adjustment A/c (In N-Z Sales Ledger) Dr.		200	
	To N-Z Sales Ledger Adjustment A/c (In General Ledger)			200
	(For entry in adjustment accounts necessitated by entry for sales returns			

(b)(i)	Bihari Dr. To Uttam (For correction of wrong credit to Bihari for cheque received from Uttam)		1,000	1,000
(ii)	A-M Sales Ledger Adjustment A/c (In General Ledger) Dr. To General Ledger Adjustment A/c (In A-M Sales Ledger) (For entry in adjustment accounts necessitated by correction in personal accounts of debtors)		1,000 1,000	
(b)(ii)	General Ledger Adjustment A/c (In N-Z General Ledger) Dr. To N-Z Sales Ledger Adjustment A/c (In General Ledger) (For correction in adjustment accounts necessitated by changes in debtors individual accounts)		1,000	1,000
(c)(i)	Sales Account in General Ledger will have to be debited by ₹ 300			
(c)(ii)	General Ledger Adjustment A/c (In N-Z Sales Ledger) Dr. To N-Z Sales Ledger Adjustment A/c (For adjustment arising out of correction of N-Z Sales Book)		300	300

10A FINANCIAL STATEMENTS OF NOT-FOR-PROFIT ORGANISATIONS

LEARNING OBJECTIVES

After studying this chapter, you should be able to understand:

◇ Meaning and Examples of Not-for-Profit Organisations
◇ Distinction between Profit Seeking and Not-for-Profit Organisations
◇ Fund Based Accounting
◇ Accounting for Not-for-Profit Organisations
◇ Receipts and Payments Account – Meaning, Features and Format
◇ Income and Expenditure Account – Meaning, Features and Format
◇ Meaning and Accounting Treatment of Some Peculiar Items
◇ Distinction between Receipts and Payments Account and Income and Expenditure Account
◇ Distinction between Income and Expenditure Account and Profit & Loss Account
◇ Preparation of an Income and Expenditure Account from a Receipts and Payments Account
◇ Preparation of Balance Sheet of A Not-for-Profit Organisation
◇ Practical steps Involved in the Preparation of a Receipts & Payments Account from an Income and Expenditure Accounts
◇ Practical steps Involved in the Preparation of a Balance Sheet from Receipts and Payments Account and Income and Expenditure Account
◇ Accounts of a Professional Firm

1.0 MEANING OF NOT-FOR-PROFIT ORGANISATIONS

Not-for-Profit organisations refer to those organisations which:

(a) are formed for the purpose of promoting commerce, art, science, religion, charity *or* any other useful object,
(b) intend to spend their income in promoting their objectives, and
(c) prohibit the payment of any dividend to their members.

EXAMPLES OF NOT-FOR-PROFIT ORGANISATIONS

The examples of such organisations include Sports Clubs, Social Clubs, Libraries, Charitable Hospitals, Charitable Educational Institutions, Temples, Churches, Gurudwaras, Masjids and Professional Bodies (e.g. The Institute of Chartered Accountants of India, The Institute of Cost Accountants of India, The Institute of Company Secretaries of India).

RESTRICTION ON APPLICATION OF INCOME AND NOT ON EARNING OF INCOME

Not-for-Profit Organisations may *or* may not have trading activities. If trading activities are carried on by such entities, then the profit arising therefrom is used for the purposes of promoting the objectives for which such entities were formed. ***For Example***, if a Sports Club also runs a Restaurant, the profit of such a Restaurant is used to promote the service objectives.

It may be noted that the restriction is on the Application of Income and not on the Earning of Income by not-for-profit organisations.

2.0 DISTINCTION BETWEEN A PROFIT SEEKING ORGANISATION AND A NOT-FOR-PROFIT ORGANISATION

A Profit seeking Organisation may be distinguished from a Not-for-Profit Organisation as under:

Basis of Distinction	Profit seeking organisation	Not-for-profit organization.
1. Primary Motive	The primary motive of such an entity is to earn profit.	The primary motive of such an entity is to provide services.
2. Owner's Fund Vs. Capital Fund	Interest of owners is known as Owner's Fund which represents the owner's investments *plus* accumulated reserves and surplus.	Interest of members is known as Capital Fund which represents the accumulated surplus of subscriptions, donations and net Income from activities carried on by such an entity.
3. Net Result of activities	The net result of the activities of such an entity is known as the profit/loss.	The net result of the activities of such an entity is known as the surplus/deficit.
4. Accounting Statements	The accounting statements of such type of entity include: (a) a Manufacturing A/c (b) a Trading A/c; (c) a Profit and Loss A/c; (d) a Balance Sheet.	The accounting statements of such an entity includes: (a) a Receipts and Payments A/c; (b) an Income and Expenditure A/c (c) a Trading A/c; (d) a Balance Sheet.

3.0 FUND BASED ACCOUNTING

MEANING OF FUND BASED ACCOUNTING

(a) Fund theory calls for fund based accounting rather than entity based accounting (which is done in case of profit seeking organizations).

(b) Fund based accounting essentially involves preparation of financial statements fundwise and consolidation of those statements to represent the financial results/position of the organisation as a whole.

(c) According to Governmental Accounting Standards Board, USA Codification of Governmental Accounting and Financial Reporting Standards, A fund may be defined as an accounting entity "with a self balancing set of accounts regarding cash and/or other resources together with all related liabilities and residual equities *or* balances, and changes therein, which is segregated for the purpose of carrying specific activities *or* attaining certain objectives in accordance with special regulations, restrictions *or* limitations." Thus, every fund is aimed at fulfilling some purpose and the services embodied in the assets are the primary means to achieve that purpose.

(d) The accounting for these not-for-profit entities is primarily based on the fund theory. The fund theory is based on the following equation:

Assets = Restrictions on Assets

(e) Assets represent prospective services to the fund and liabilities represent restrictions against the assets of the fund. ***For Example***, in case of a university, the most commonly used specific funds are endowment funds, development funds etc.

(f) Each of these funds has its specific assets restricted for particular purposes. Under the fund theory, the balance sheet is considered an 'inventory statement' of assets and those restrictions applicable to the assets.

(g) In fund-based accounting, the following statements are to be prepared to get a consolidated picture of the organization as a whole:

1. Income and Expenditure Account for each of the Revenue Funds. [Whether restricted *or* Unrestricted] *or* Statement of Activity
2. Statement showing changes in Balances of each Fund [Whether Revenue Fund *or* Specific Fund]
3. Balance Sheet of each of the Funds [Whether Revenue Fund *or* Specific Fund]
4. General Balance Sheet of the organization as a whole.

(h) Some academicians argue that the income and expenditure account should better be called 'Statement of activity' A not-for-profit organization may have no income other than grants and gifts received from government and well wishers. In that situation, it is proper to name the statement showing the normal revenue operations of the organization as the statement of Activity. But in case of educational institutions like Schools, Colleges *or* Universities, fees from students form a significant portion of revenue receipts. Therefore, we can continue to call the Statement of Activity as Income and Expenditure Account.

CLASSIFICATION OF FUNDS

Funds may be classified as follows:

1. **Revenue Funds**
   - Restricted Revenue Fund
   - Unrestricted Revenue Fund
2. **Specific Funds** e.g. Endowment Fund, Loan Funds, Life Income Funds

REVENUE FUNDS

Revenue Funds essentially record normal revenue transactions. In other words, revenue funds are received to meet operating expenses. The accrual basis of accounting is used to recognize revenue and expense in the revenue fund (or Operating Funds). However, the use of Revenue Fund may be restricted *or* unrestricted.

(a) Restricted Funds Account for resources whose use is restricted by the donor. Restrictions may be externally imposed by the grantors of gifts *or* endowments. In addition, the governing body of the organisation may designate monies for specific purpose. In case of restricted funds revenue is recognised to the extent of resources expended.

(b) The Unrestricted Fund Account for the resources that may be expended to carry out the primary purposes of the institution (e.g. instructions, research, maintenance etc.) and that are not restricted to specific purposes. The accounting basis of the unrestricted fund is the accrual method as used for commercial entities. The primary sources of income for this fund are membership fees, unrestricted government grants, gifts from individuals, income from investments. Another important source of revenue in the unrestricted fund is from auxiliary enterprises/operations. Such enterprises include students canteen, book stores, hostel accommodation etc. There may be transfers out of revenue funds to specific funds and vice-versa. Some transfers are mandatory and some are non-mandatory. There may be a provision for life membership fees wherein a willing member is required to make a life time contribution. The lump sum lifetime contribution is determined in such a manner that the income from such contribution is more *or less* equal to the annual membership fees. Such lifetime contribution is directly credited to life membership fund. That fund is simultaneously invested in outside securities. Income from such investment is credited to unrestricted operating fund. When a life member expires *or* his membership terminated for some reasons, the proportionate fund balance is transferred from life membership fund to unrestricted operating fund. The corresponding investment may *or* may not be sold.

(c) **Mandatory and non-mandatory transfers:** Inter fund transfers are permissible for any type of not-for-profit entities. However, the terms mandatory and non-mandatory transfers are unique to college and universities accounting and reporting. Mandatory transfers are transfers out of the revenue funds to other funds resulting from binding legal agreements *or* grant agreements. Non-mandatory transfers are discretionary transfers specified by the governing board for a variety of purposes such as new additions to building, repairs & replacement of plant etc. Non-mandatory transfers may also be made from specific funds to the revenue funds. Both mandatory and non-mandatory transfers are reported separately in the financial statements of the revenue funds. Also the governing board may designate unrestricted revenue fund resources for specific purposes in future periods. These board – designated funds are internal designations similar to appropriations of retained earnings for a commercial entry.

SPECIAL FUNDS

Special Funds essentially record transactions of capital nature. There funds account for those resources which may not be currently expended.

For Example — Endowment Fund. Development Fund, Membership Fund, Loan Fund. The main features of Special Funds are:

(i) These funds record the transaction of capital nature,

(ii) Contributions and transfers are directly credited to the respective fund accounts.

(iii) A statement showing changes in balances of each of specific funds is prepared.

(iv) Balance Sheet of each of specific funds is prepared.

(v) No Income & Expenditure Account (or Statement of Activity) is prepared for such funds.

4.0 ACCOUNTING FOR NOT-FOR-PROFIT ORGANISATIONS

1. The following books are generally kept by every not-for-profit organisation:
   (a) Cash book with *or* without Analysis Column
   (b) Members' Register
   (c) Register of Assets
2. In case of large not-for-profit organisations, almost the same accounting system is followed as in the case of profit seeking organisations.
3. In case of small not-for-profit organisations, usually the Cash Book is prepared and with the help of such a cash book, a Receipts & Payments Account is prepared and with the help of such account and additional information, an Income & Expenditure Account and a Balance Sheet are prepared.

5.0 RECEIPTS AND PAYMENTS ACCOUNT

MEANING OF RECEIPTS & PAYMENTS ACCOUNT

The 'Receipts & Payment Account' is an Asset Account (or Real Account) which shows the classified summary of transactions of a Cash Book along with the Cash & Bank balances in the beginning and at the end of an accounting period.

In other words, it is an Asset Account which shows all Receipts and Payments (whether Capital *or* Revenue *or* whether relating to previous, current *or* following accounting year) alongwith Cash and Bank Balance in the beginning and at the end of an accounting period.

FEATURES OF RECEIPTS & PAYMENTS ACCOUNT

1. It starts with the Opening Balance of Cash in hand and Cash at Bank.
2. It is debited with all sums received.
3. It is credited with all sums paid out.
4. It records all receipts and payments whether they are of revenue nature *or* capital nature.
5. It records all receipts and payments whether they relate to the previous, current *or* following accounting year.
6. It does not record non-cash items (e.g. Depreciation).
7. It ends with Closing Balance of Cash in hand and Cash at bank.

FORMAT OF RECEIPTS & PAYMENTS ACCOUNT

RECEIPTS AND PAYMENTS ACCOUNT

Dr. *for the period ending on ...* *Cr.*

Receipts		₹	*Payments*		₹
To Balance b/f:			By Balance b/d (Bank overdraft)		xxx
Cash	xxx		By Annual Sports Expenses		xxx
Bank	xxx	xxx	By Salaries & Wages		xxx
To Subscription:			By Rent, Rates & Taxes		xxx
for previous year	xxx		By Insurance		xxx
for current year	xxx		By Furniture		xxx
for next year	xxx	xxx	By Sports Equipments		xxx
To Entrance Fees		xxx	By Books & Periodicals		xxx
To Donation for Building		xxx	By Audit Fees		xxx
To General Donations		xxx	By Printing & Stationery		xxx
To Life Membership Fees		xxx	By Honorarium		xxx
To Legacy		xxx	By Bank Charges		xxx
To Grant from Govt.		xxx	By Postage & Telegrams		xxx
To Contribution for Annual Dinner		xxx	By Water & Electricity		xxx
To Dividend		xxx	By Conveyance & Travelling		xxx
To Interest		xxx	By Repairs & Maintenance		xxx
To Rent		xxx	By Sundry Expenses		xxx
To Receipt on Annual Sports		xxx	By Annual Dinner Expenses		xxx
To Sale of Old Sports Materials		xxx	By 12% Investments		xxx
To Sale of Old Magazines		xxx	By Balance c/f:		xxx
To Sundry Receipts		xxx	Cash	xxx	
To Balance c/d (Bank overdraft)		xxx	Bank	xxx	xxx
		xxx			xxx

ILLUSTRATION 1

From the information given below, prepare Receipts & Payments Account of Tulsian Club, Delhi for the year ending on March 31, 2016.

Particulars	₹	Particulars	₹
Cash as at 1.4.2015	1,025	Sale of old Bats etc.	50
Subscription received (including ₹ 40 for 2015-2016 & ₹ 60 for 2016-2017)	2,150	12% General Investments (made on 1.11.2015)	500
Upkeep of fields	220	12% Tournament Fund Investments (made on 1.11.2015)	1,500
Admission Fees	40	Tournament Expenses	1,200
Salaries	600	Sale of old furniture (cost ₹ 100)	60
Drama Expenses	450	Bats and Balls purchased	700
Life Membership Subscription	100	Proceeds of drama tickets	950
Newspapers purchased	150	Interest on 12% General Invest. Recei.	12.50
Books purchased	100	Printing & Stationery	100
Subscription for Tournament received (on 1.11.2015)	1,500	Interest on 12% Tournament Fund & Investment received	37.50
Donations received (on 1.11.2015)	500	Furniture	250
Municipal Taxes	40		
Charity given	350	Subscription received for Governor's Party	3,450
Sale of old newspapers	45		

SOLUTION

RECEIPTS AND PAYMENTS ACCOUNT OF TULSIAN CLUB, DELHI

Dr. *for the year ending on 31st March, 2016* *Cr.*

Receipts		₹	Payments	₹
To Balance b/f (Cash)		1,025	By Upkeep of fields	220
To Subscription			By Salaries	600
2014-2015	40		By Drama Expenses	450
2015-2016	2,050		By Newspapers	150
2016-2017	60	2,150	By Books	100
To Admission Fees		40	By Municipal Taxes	40
To Life Membership Subscription		100	By Charity	350
To Donations (on 1.11.2015)		500	By Tournament Expenses	1,200
To Subscription for Tournament (on 1.11.2015)		1,500	By 12% General Investments (on 1.11.2015)	500
To Sale of old furniture (costing ₹ 100)		60	By 12% Tournament Fund Investments (on 1.11.2015)	1,500
To Sale of old bats etc.		50	By Bats, Balls etc.	700
To Proceeds of drama tickets		950	By Printing & Stationery	100
To Sales of old newspapers		45	By Furniture	250
To Interest on 12% General Investments		12.50	By Balance c/f (Cash)	3,760

To Interest on 12% Tournament Fund Investments	37.50		
To Subscription for Governor's Party	3,450		
	9,920		9,920

6.0 INCOME AND EXPENDITURE ACCOUNT

MEANING OF INCOME & EXPENDITURE ACCOUNT

An Income and Expenditure Account is a final account like Profit & Loss Account, which shows the classified summary of Revenue Incomes, Revenue Expenses and Losses for Current Accounting Period along with Surplus (i.e., the Excess of Income over Expenditure) *or* Deficit (i.e., Excess of Expenditure over Income) which is transferred to the Capital Fund.

FEATURES OF INCOME & EXPENDITURE ACCOUNT

1. It is debited with the Expenses and Losses.
2. It is credited with the Incomes.
3. It records only those Incomes, Expenses and Losses which are of **Revenue Nature.**
4. It records only those Incomes, Expenses and Losses which **relates to Current Accounting Year.**
5. It records Non-Cash Items also (e.g. depreciation).
6. Its balance at the end which represents either the Net Surplus (if credit side exceeds debit side) *or* Net Deficit (if debit side exceeds credit side) is transferred to the Capital Fund in the Balance Sheet.

FORMAT OF INCOME & EXPENDITURE ACCOUNT

INCOME AND EXPENDITURE ACCOUNT

Dr. *for the year ending on ......* Cr.

Expenditure		₹	*Income*		₹
To Salaries and Wages paid	xxx		By Subscription Received	xxx	
Add: Outstanding at the end	xxx		*Add:* Outstanding at the end	xxx	
Less: Prepaid at the end	xxx		*Less:* Advance at the end	xxx	
Add: Prepaid in the beginning	xxx		*Add:* Advance in the beginning	xxx	
Less: Outstanding in the beg.	xxx	xxx	*Less:* Outstanding in the beginning	xxx	xxx
To Rent, Rates and Taxes		xxx	By Entrance Fees (only that portion which is to be treated as revenue)		xxx
To Insurance Premium		xxx	By General Donations		xxx
To Depreciation on Furniture and		xxx	By Life membership Fees (only that portion which is to be treated as revenue)		xxx
Sports equipments		xxx			
To Books and Periodicals		xxx	By Profit from Annual Dinner		
To Audit fees		xxx	Contribution	xxx	
To Printing & Stationery		xxx			
To Honorarium		xxx			
To Bank Charges		xxx			

To Postage & Telegram	xxx	*Less:* Expenses	xxx	xxx
To Electricity & Water	xxx	By Profit on Annual sports		
To Conveyance & Travelling	xxx	(Receipts – expenses)		xxx
To Sundry Expenses	xxx	By Profit on sale of provisions		
To* Surplus i.e., excess of income		(Sale + Closing Stock –		
over expenditure	xxx	Purchases – Opening Stock)		xxx
		By Rent of Club Hall		xxx
		By Dividend & Interest		xxx
		By Sundry Receipts		xxx
		By* Deficit i.e. Excess of		
		expenditure over income		xxx
	xxx			xxx

**Either Surplus or Deficit shall appear.*

7.0 MEANING AND ACCOUNTING TREATMENT OF SUBSCRIPTION

MEANING OF SUBSCRIPTION

Subscription is the major source of revenue income of a not-for-profit entity. Subscriptions are the amounts paid by the members of such entity to maintain their membership. Subscriptions may be paid periodically (usually on yearly basis) *or* as a lump sum for lifetime membership.

ACCOUNTING TREATMENT OF SUBSCRIPTION

(a) Periodical Subscriptions	These are treated as **Revenue Receipts** and hence **credited to Income & Expenditure Account.**
(b) Life Membership Subscriptions	These subscriptions are treated as a **Capital Receipt** and hence are **added to the Capital Fund.**

HOW TO CALCULATE INCOME FROM SUBSCRIPTIONS

Where the accrual basis of accounting is used, only that amount of subscriptions which relates to current accounting period, should be treated as revenue income of that period. In order to calculate this amount, the amount of subscriptions received during the current accounting period should be adjusted in the light of outstanding and advance subscriptions in the beginning and at the end of the current accounting period. The subscription income for current accounting period may be computed in any of the following three ways:

(a) In Statement Form,

(b) In Account Form, and

(c) In Equation Form.

(a) In Statement Form:

COMPUTATION OF INCOME FROM SUBSCRIPTIONS FOR THE CURRENT YEAR

Particulars		₹
A. Subscriptions received during the current year		xxx
B. *Add:* (i) Outstanding Subscriptions at the end of current year	xxx	

	(ii) Advance Subscriptions in the beginning of current year	xxx	xxx
C.	*Less:* (i) Outstanding Subscriptions in the beginning of current year	xxx	
	(ii) Advance Subscriptions at the end of current year	xxx	xxx
D.	Subscription Income to be credited to Income & Expenditure Account (A + B – C)		xxx

(b) In Account Form:

Dr. **SUBSCRIPTION ACCOUNT** *Cr.*

Particulars	₹	*Particulars*	₹
To Outstanding Subscription A/c (Outstanding Subscription in the beginning)	xxx	By Advance Subscription A/c (Advance Subscription in the beginning)	xxx
To Income & Expenditure A/c (balancing figure)	xxx	By Bank A/c (Total Subscription received during the current year)	xxx
To Advance Subscription A/c (Advance Subscription at the end)	xxx	By Outstanding Subscription A/c (Outstanding subscription at the end)	xxx
	xxx		xxx

(c) In Equation Form: The entire process of computation of subscription income for the current year may be described through the following equation:

$$S_1 = SR + OS_2 + AS_1 - OS_1 - AS_2$$

Where, S_1 = Subscription Income for the current accounting period

SR = Subscription received during the current accounting period

OS_2 = Outstanding Subscription at the end of the current year

AS_1 = Advance Subscription in the beginning of the current year

OS_1 = Outstanding Subscription in the beginning of the current year

AS_2 = Advance Subscription at the end of the current year

ILLUSTRATION 2 [Income From Subscription]

(a) Subscription received during the year 2015-2016 ₹ 60,000. Compute the Income from Subscription for the year 2015-2016.

(b) Subscription received during the year 2015-2016 ₹ 60,000. Subscription ₹ 30,000 is still outstanding. Compute the Income from Subscription for the year 2015-2016.

(c) Subscription received during the year 2015-2016 ₹ 60,000. Subscription ₹ 20,000 received in advance for the year 2016-2017. Compute the Income from Subscription for the year 2015-2016.

(d) Subscription received during the year 2015-2016 ₹ 60,000. Subscription ₹ 40,000 was outstanding at the end of the previous year. Compute the Income from Subscription for the year 2015-2016.

(e) Subscription received during the year 2015-2016 ₹ 60,000. Subscription ₹ 90,000 was received in advance at the end of the previous year. Compute the Income from Subscription for the year 2015-2016.

SOLUTION

COMPUTATION OF INCOME FROM SUBSCRIPTION

Particulars	*(a)*	*(b)*	*(c)*	*(d)*	*(e)*
Subscription Received	60,000	60,000	60,000	60,000	60,000
Add: O/s at the end	–	30,000	–	–	–
Less: Advance at the end	–	–	(20,000)	–	–
Add: Advance in the beg.	–	–	–	–	90,000
Less: O/s in the beg.	–	–	–	(40,000)	–
	60,000	**90,000**	**40,000**	**20,000**	**1,50,000**

ILLUSTRATION 3

Compute the Income from Subscription for the year 2015-2016 from the following particulars relating to a club:

Particulars	*1.4.2015*	*31.3.2016*
Outstanding Subscription	₹ 9,500	₹ 7,000
Advance Subscription	₹ 2,800	₹ 5,200

Subscription received during 2015-2016, ₹ 1,48,900, Subscriptions of ₹ 1,000 are still in arrears for the year 2014-2015.

SOLUTION

(a) In Statement Form:

COMPUTATION OF INCOME FROM SUBSCRIPTION

Particulars			₹	₹
A.	Subscription received			1,48,900
B.	*Add:*	(a) Outstanding Subscription at the end	7,000	
		(b) Advance Subscription at the beginning	2,800	9,800
C.	*Less:*	(a) Outstanding Subscription at the beginning	9,500	
		(b) Advance Subscription at the end	5,200	14,700
D.	Subscription Income for the year (A + B – C)			1,44,000

(b) In Account Form:

Dr. **SUBSCRIPTION ACCOUNT** *Cr.*

Particulars	₹	*Particulars*	₹
To Outstanding Subscription A/c (in the beginning)	9,500	By Advance Subscription A/c (in the beginning)	2,800
To Income & Expenditure A/c (balancing figure)	1,44,000	By Outstanding Subscription A/c (at the end)	7,000
To Advance Subscription A/c	5,200	By Bank A/c	1,48,900
	1,58,700		1,58,700

(c) In Equation Form:

$$S_1 = SR + OS_2 + AS_1 - OS_1 - AS_2$$
$$= ₹\ 1,48,900 + ₹\ 7,000 + ₹\ 2,800 - ₹\ 9,500 - ₹\ 5,200 = ₹\ 1,44,000$$

Where, S_1 = Subscription Income, SR = Subscription Received,
OS_2 = Outstanding Subscription at the end,
AS_1 = Advance Subscription in the beginning,
OS_1 = Outstanding Subscription in the beginning,
AS_2 = Advance Subscription at the end.

ILLUSTRATION 4

From the following information,Compute the Outstanding Subscription as on 31.3.2016:

(a) A Club has 75 members, each paying annual subscription of	₹ 1,000
(b) Subscription received during 2015-2016	₹ 80,000
(c) Subscription received in advance as at 31.3.2015	₹ 15,000
(d) Subscription received in advance as at 31.3.2016	₹ 10,000
(e) Subscription outstanding as at 31.3.2015	₹ 26,000
(f) Subscription of ₹ 12,000 are still in arrears for the year 2014-2015	

SOLUTION

Dr. **SUBSCRIPTION ACCOUNT** *Cr.*

Particulars	₹	*Particulars*	₹
To Outstanding Subscription A/c (in the beginning)	26,000	By Advance Subscription A/c (in the beginning)	15,000
To Income & Expenditure A/c (75 × ₹ 1,000)	75,000	By Outstanding Subscription A/c (at the end) (B.f.)	16,000
To Advance Subscription A/c	10,000	By Bank A/c	80,000
	1,11,000		1,11,000

ILLUSTRATION 5

From the following information, Compute the Outstanding Subscription for the year 2015-2016:

(a) A Club has 70 members, each paying annual subscription of	₹ 1,000
(b) Subscription received during 2015-2016	₹ 70,000
(c) Subscription received in advance as at 31.3.2015	₹ 12,000
(d) Subscription received in advance as at 31.3.2016	₹ 11,000
(e) Subscription outstanding as at 31.3.2015	₹ 16,000
(f) Subscription of ₹ 8,000 are still in arrears for the year 2014-2015	

SOLUTION

Dr. **SUBSCRIPTION ACCOUNT** *Cr.*

Particulars	₹	*Particulars*	₹
To Outstanding Subscription A/c (in the beginning)	16,000	By Advance Subscription A/c (in the beginning)	12,000
To Income & Expenditure A/c (70 × ₹ 1,000)	70,000	By Outstanding Subscription A/c (at the end) (B.f.)	70,000
To Advance Subscription A/c	11,000	By Bank A/c	15,000
	97,000		97,000

Outstanding Subscription for the year 2015-2016 = ₹ 15,000 – ₹ 8,000 = ₹ 7,000

ILLUSTRATION 6

From the following information, Compute the Advance Subscription for the year 2015-2016:

(a) A Club has 39 members, each paying annual subscription of	₹ 1,000
(b) Subscription received during 2015-2016	₹ 50,000
(c) Subscription received in Advance as at 31.3.2015	₹ 10,000
(d) Subscription outstanding as at 31.3.2016	₹ 9,000
(d) Subscription outstanding as at 31.3.2015	₹ 18,000
(e) Subscription of ₹ 7,000 are still in arrears for the year 2014-2015	

SOLUTION

Dr. **SUBSCRIPTION ACCOUNT** *Cr.*

Particulars	₹	*Particulars*	₹
To Outstanding Subscription A/c (in the beginning)	18,000	By Advance Subscription A/c (in the beginning)	10,000
To Income & Expenditure A/c (39 × ₹ 1,000)	39,000	By Outstanding Subscription A/c (at the end) (B.f.)	50,000
To Advance Subscription A/c	12,000	By Bank A/c	9,000
	69,000		69,000

ILLUSTRATION 7

How will you deal with the following items while preparing the Income & Expenditure Account for the year ended March 31, 2016 and the Balance Sheet as on that date?

Dr. **AN EXTRACT OF RECEIPTS AND PAYMENTS ACCOUNT** *Cr.*

Receipts		₹	*Payments*	₹
To Subscription				
2014-2015	250			
2015-2016	1,000			
2016-2017	200	1,450		

Information:

The club has 50 members, each paying annual subscription of ₹ 25. Subscriptions outstanding on March 31, 2016 were ₹ 300.

SOLUTION

AN EXTRACT OF INCOME AND EXPENDITURE ACCOUNT

Dr. *for the year ended 31st March, 2016* *Cr.*

Expenditure	₹	*Income*	₹
		By Subscription (50 × ₹ 25)	1,250

AN EXTRACT OF BALANCE SHEET AS AT 31ST MARCH, 2016

Liabilities	₹	*Assets*		₹
Subscription received in advance	200	Subscription Outstanding		
		for 2014-2015	50	
		for 2015-2016	250	300

ILLUSTRATION 8

From the following extracts of Receipts & Payments Account and the additional information, you are required to calculate the Income from Subscriptions for the year ending March 31, 2016 and show them in the Income & Expenditure Account, and the Balance Sheet of a Club.

AN EXTRACT OF RECEIPTS & PAYMENTS ACCOUNT

Dr. *for the year ended 31st March, 2016* *Cr.*

Receipts		₹	*Payments*	₹
To Subscription				
2014-2015	5,000			
2015-2016	30,000			
2016-2017	6,000	41,000		

Information:

(a) Subscription outstanding on 31.3.2015	₹ 6,000
(b) Subscription outstanding on 31.3.2016	₹ 5,000
(c) Subscription received-in-advance on 31.3.2015	₹ 6,000

SOLUTION

AN EXTRACT OF INCOME AND EXPENDITURE ACCOUNT

Dr. *for the year ended 31st March, 2016* *Cr.*

Expenditure	₹	*Income*	₹
		By Subscription	40,000

AN EXTRACT OF BALANCE SHEET

for the year ended 31st March, 2016

Liabilities	₹	*Assets*	₹
Subscription in advance	6,000	Subscription Outstanding	
		for 2014-2015 (6000 – 5000) 1,000	
		for 2015-2016 (5000 – 1000) 4,000	5,000

Working Note:

CALCULATION OF SUBSCRIPTION INCOME FOR 2015-2016

A. Subscription received during 2015-2016 for 2015-2016	₹ 30,000
B. Subscription received during 2014-2015 for 2015-2016	₹ 6,000
C. Subscription outstanding for 2015-2016 as at 31.3.2016	₹ 4,000
	₹ 40,000

ILLUSTRATION 9

How will you deal with the following case while preparing the final accounts for the year 2015-2016:

(a) Subscription received during 2015-2016: for 2014-2015 ₹ 5,000, for 2015-2016 ₹ 30,000, for 2016-2017 ₹ 6,000

(b) Subscription received in advance as at 31.3.2015 — ₹ 6,000

(c) Subscription Outstanding as at 31.3.2015 — ₹ 6,000

(d) Subscription Outstanding for the year 2015-2016 — ₹ 4,000

SOLUTION

AN EXTRACT OF INCOME & EXPENDITURE ACCOUNT

for the year ended 31st March, 2016

Dr. *Cr.*

Expenditure	₹	*Income*	₹
		By Subscription	40,000

AN EXTRACT OF BALANCE SHEET AS AT 31ST MARCH, 2016

for the year ended 31st March, 2016

Liabilities	₹	*Assets*	₹
Subscription received in advance	6,000	Subscription Outstanding	
		for 2014-2015 (6,000 – 5,000) 1,000	
		for 2015-2016 4,000	5,000

ILLUSTRATION 10

Prepare the Subscription Account from the following items for the year ending on March 31, 2016:

(a) Subscription in arrears on 31.3.2015 — ₹ 500

(b) Subscription received in advance on 31.3.2015 — ₹ 1,100

(c) Total Subscription received during 2015 – 2016 (including ₹ 400 for 2014 – 2015, ₹ 900 for 2016 – 2017 and ₹ 300 for 2017 – 2018), — ₹ 35,400.

(d) Subscription outstanding for 2015 – 2016 — ₹ 400

SOLUTION

Dr. **SUBSCRIPTION ACCOUNT** *Cr.*

Particulars		₹	*Particulars*		₹
To Outstanding Subscription A/c		500	By Advance Subscription A/c		1,100
To Income & Expenditure A/c		35,300	By Bank A/c		35,400
To Advance Subscription A/c			By Outstanding Subscription A/c		
for 2016 – 2017	900		for 2014 – 2015	100	
for 2017 – 2018	300	1,200	for 2015 – 2016	400	500
		37,000			37,000

ILLUSTRATION 11

From the following extracts of the Receipts and Payments Account and the additional information, you are required to compute the income from subscription for the year ending on March 31, 2016 and show the subscription items in the Income and Expenditure Account and the Balance Sheet as on 31.3.2016.

AN EXTRACT OF RECEIPTS AND PAYMENTS ACCOUNT

Dr. *for the year ending on 31st March, 2016* *Cr.*

Receipts	₹	*Payments*	₹
To Subscription			
2014-2015	9,000		
2015-2016	1,34,400		
2016-2017	5,200		

Information: Subscription outstanding as on 31.3.2015 ₹ 9,200. Subscription received in advance as on 31.3.2015 ₹ 2,800 (including ₹ 800 for 2015-2016). There are 1,440 members each paying an annual subscription of ₹ 100.

SOLUTION

AN EXTRACT OF INCOME AND EXPENDITURE ACCOUNT

Dr. *for the year ending on 31st March, 2016* *Cr.*

Expenditure	₹	*Income*	₹
		By Subscription Income	1,44,000

AN EXTRACT OF BALANCE SHEET AS AT 31ST MARCH, 2016

Liabilities	₹	*Assets*		₹
Subscription received in advance	7,200	Subscription outstanding for 2011 (₹ 9,200 – ₹ 9,000)	200	
		for 2012 (₹ 9,000 – ₹ 200)	8,800	9,000

Working Note: *Calculation of Subscription outstanding for 2015-2016*

Dr. **SUBSCRIPTION ACCOUNT** *Cr.*

Particulars	₹	*Particulars*	₹
To O/s Account (Beg.)	9,200	By Advance Subsc. A/c (Beg.)	2,800
To Income & Expenditure A/c	1,44,000	By Bank A/c	1,48,600
To Advance Subscription A/c	7,200	By Outstanding Subscription A/c (Balancing figure)	9,000
	1,60,400		1,60,400

ILLUSTRATION 12

How will you deal with the following items while preparing the Income and Expenditure Account for the year ending on 31st March, 2016 and the Balance Sheet as on that date'?

Subscription outstanding as on 31.3.2015: ₹ 9,500 (including ₹ 500 for 2013-2014) Subscription received in advance as on 31.3.2015: ₹ 3,000 (including ₹ 200 for 2016-2017)

Subscription received during 2015-2016: for 2013-2014 ₹ 400, for 2014-2015 ₹ 8,900, for 2015-2016 ₹ 1,34,400, for 2016-2017 ₹ 4,000, for 2017-2018 ₹ 1,200.

Subscription outstanding as on 31.3.2016: ₹ 7,000.

Subscription of 2013-2014 written off during 2015-2016 ₹ 50.

SOLUTION

AN EXTRACT OF INCOME AND EXPENDITURE ACCOUNT

Dr. *for the year ended 31st March, 2016* *Cr.*

Expenditure	₹	*Income*	₹
To Supscriptions w/o	50	By Subscriptions (See working note)	1,44,000

AN EXTRACT OF BALANCE SHEET AS AT 31ST MARCH, 2016

Liabilities	₹	*Assets*	₹
Subscription received in advance		Subscription Outstanding	
for 2016-2017 (₹ 200 + ₹ 4,000) 4,200		for 2013-2014 (₹ 500 – ₹ 400 – ₹ 50) 50	
for 2017-2018 1,200	5,400	for 2014-2015 (₹ 9,000 – ₹ 8,900) 100	
		for 2015-2016 (₹ 7,000 – ₹ 100 – ₹ 100) 6,800	6,950

Working Note:

CALCULATION OF SUBSCRIPTION INCOME FOR THE YEAR 2015-2016

Dr. **SUBSCRIPTION ACCOUNT** *Cr.*

Particulars	₹	*Particulars*	₹
To O/s A/c (Beg.)	9,500	By Advance Subscription A/c (Beg.)	3,000
To Income & Exp. A/c (b.f.)	1,44,000	By Bank A/c	1,48,900
To Advance Subscription (end)	5,400	By Income & Exp. A/c (w/o)	50

		By Outstanding Subscription A/c	6,950
	1,58,900		1,58,900

8.0 TREATMENT OF ENTRANCE FEE/ADMISSION FEE

MEANING OF ENTRANCE FEE/ADMISSION FEE

Entrance Fee (or Admission Fee) is an initial amount payable at the time of seeking admission by a person who intends to become a member of a club, association, *or* society.

ACCOUNTING TREATMENT OF ENTRANCE FEE/ADMISSION FEE

The entrance fees may be accounted for in any of the following three ways:

1. It may be treated exclusively as a Revenue Receipt and thus, be credited to Income & Expenditure Account.
2. It may be treated exclusively as a Capital Receipt and thus, be added to the Capital Fund on the liabilities side of the Balance Sheet.
3. Some portion of Entrance Fee (say 40%) may be treated as a Revenue receipt and thus, be credited to Income & Expenditure Account and remaining portion (say 60%) may be treated as a Capital receipt and thus, be, added to the Capital Fund on the liabilities side of the Balance Sheet as per the Accounting Policy of the organisation.

ILLUSTRATION 13

How will you deal with the Entrance fees while preparing the final accounts for the year ending on 31st March 2016 in each of the following alternative cases:

Case (a) During the year 2015–2016, Entrance Fees received ₹ 1,00,000

Case (b) During the year 2015–2016 Entrance Fees received ₹ 1,00,000. The accounting policy of the club is to treat the entrance fees as of revenue nature.

Case (c) During the year 2015–2016 Entrance Fees received ₹ 1,00,000. The accounting policy of the club is to treat the entrance fees as of capital nature.

Case (d) During the year 2015–2016 Entrance Fees received ₹ 1,00,000. According to accounting policy of the club, 40% of the entrance fees is to be capitalised. There was no pending membership as on 31st March 2016.

SOLUTION

Case (a) Entrance Fees ₹ 1,00,000 may either be credited to Income & Expenditure Account (if entrance fees is treated as of revenue nature), *or* be added to the Capital Fund (if entrance fee is to be treated as of capital nature) by giving a specific note to that effect.

Case (b) Entrance Fees ₹ 1,00,000 must be credited to Income & Expenditure Account

Case (c) Entrance Fees ₹ 1,00,000 must be added to the Capital Fund.

Case (d) Entrance Fees ₹ 60,000 (i.e., 60% of ₹ 1,00,000) must be credited to Income & Expenditure Account and ₹ 40,000 (i.e., 40% of ₹ 1,00,000) must be added to Capital Fund.

9.0 TREATMENT OF DONATIONS AND LEGACIES

MEANING OF DONATIONS AND LEGACIES

Donations represent the amount donated by any person (whether member *or* outsider) to the organisation for a general *or* specific purpose. Legacies represent the donations which are given under a will on the death of a donor.

ACCOUNTING OF TREATMENT OF DONATIONS AND LEGACIES

The accounting treatment is summarised below:

Types of Donations and Legacies	Accounting Treatment
(a) General Donations and Legacies	These donations & legacies are treated as **Revenue Receipts** and thus, are credited to **Income & Expenditure Account.**
(b) Specific Donations and Legacies	1. These donations & legacies are treated as **Capital Receipts** and thus, are transferred to a **'Special Fund Account' (e.g., Building Fund)** maintained for the purpose. 2. Any **Income** relating to such 'Special Fund Account' is **added to the Respective Fund.** 3. Any **Revenue Expenditure** relating to 'Special Fund Account' is **deducted from the Respective Fund.** 4. However,any **expenditure of capital nature** on account of this Special Fund (e.g., Expenditure on the construction of building out of Building Fund) should be shown **on the Assets side** of the Balance Sheet and an equal amount should be **transferred from that Special Fund to the Capital Fund.**

ILLUSTRATION 14

Show how will you deal with the Prizes awarded ₹ 2,000 while preparing the final accounts of a Club for the year ending on March 31, 2016.

SOLUTION

AN EXTRACT OF INCOME AND EXPENDITURE ACCOUNT

Dr. *for the year ended 31st March, 2016* *Cr.*

Expenditure	₹	*Income*	₹
To Prizes awarded	2,000		

Reason: There does not exist any Prize Fund.

ILLUSTRATION 15

Show how will you deal with the following items while preparing the final accounts of a Club for the year ending on March 31, 2016:

Prizes awarded ₹ 2,000, Prize Fund as at 31.3.2015 ₹ 12,000.

SOLUTION

AN EXTRACT OF BALANCE SHEET AS AT 31ST MARCH, 2016

Liabilities		₹	*Assets*	₹
Prize Fund:				
Opening Balance	12,000			
Less: Prizes awarded	2,000	10,000		

ILLUSTRATION 16

Show how will you deal with the following items while preparing the final accounts of a Club for the year ending on March 31, 2016:

Prizes awarded ₹ 2,000, Prize Fund as at 31.3.2015 ₹ 12,000,Donations for Prizes received during the year 2015–2016 ₹ 2,800.

SOLUTION

AN EXTRACT OF BALANCE SHEET AS AT 31ST MARCH, 2016

Liabilities		₹	*Assets*	₹
Prize Fund:				
Opening Balance	12,000			
Add: Donations	2,800			
Less: Prizes awarded	2,000	12,800		

ILLUSTRATION 17

Show how will you deal with the following items while preparing the final accounts of a Club for the year ending on March 31, 2016:

Prizes awarded ₹ 2,000,

Prize Fund as at 31.3.2015 ₹ 12,000,

Donations for Prizes received during the year 2015–2016 ₹ 2,800,

10% Prize Fund Investments as at 31.3.2015 ₹ 12,000.

Interest on Prize Fund Investments ₹ 1,200.

SOLUTION

AN EXTRACT OF BALANCE SHEET AS AT 31ST MARCH, 2016

Liabilities		₹	*Assets*	₹
Prize Fund:			10% Prize Fund Investments	12,000
Opening Balance	12,000			
Add: Donations	2,800			
Add: Interest on Prize fund Investments	1,200			
Less: Prizes awarded	2,000	14,000		

ILLUSTRATION 18

Show how will you deal with the following items while preparing the final accounts of a Club for the year ending on March 31, 2016:

Prizes awarded ₹ 17,000, Prize Fund as at 31.3.2015 ₹ 12,000, Donations for Prizes received during the year 2015–2016 ₹ 2,800, 10% Prize Fund Investments as at 31.3.2015 ₹ 12,000.Interest on Prize Fund Investments ₹ 1,200.

SOLUTION

AN EXTRACT OF INCOME AND EXPENDITURE ACCOUNT

Dr. *for the year ended 31st March, 2016* *Cr.*

Expenditure	₹	*Income*	₹
To Prizes awarded	1,000		

AN EXTRACT OF BALANCE SHEET AS AT 31ST MARCH, 2016

Liabilities		₹	*Assets*	₹
Prize Fund:				
Opening Balance	12,000			
Add: Donations	2,800			
Add: Interest on Prize Fund Investments	1,200			
Less: Prizes awarded	17,000			
T/F to I & E Exp. A/c	**(1,000)**			

ILLUSTRATION 19

Show how will you deal with the following items while preparing the final accounts for the year ending on 31st March 2016:

Expenditure on Construction of Building ₹ 3,00,000. The construction work is in progress and has not yet completed. Opening Capital Fund ₹ 9,00,000.

SOLUTION

AN EXTRACT OF BALANCE SHEET AS AT 31ST MARCH, 2016

Liabilities	₹	*Assets*	₹
Capital Fund:		Building-in-progress	3,00,000
Opening Balance	9,00,000		

ILLUSTRATION 20

Show how will you deal with the following items while preparing the final accounts for the year ending on 31st March 2016:

Expenditure on construction of Building ₹ 3,00,000. The construction work is in progress and has not yet completed. Opening Building Fund ₹ 4,00,000, Opening Capital Fund ₹ 9,00,000

SOLUTION

AN EXTRACT OF BALANCE SHEET AS AT 31ST MARCH, 2016

Liabilities		₹	*Assets*	₹
Capital Fund:			Building-in-progress	3,00,000
Opening Balance	9,00,000			
Add: T/f from Building Fund	3,00,000	12,00,000		

Building Fund:					
Opening Balance	4,00,000				
Less: T/f to Capital Fund	3,00,000	1,00,000			

ILLUSTRATION 21

Show how will you deal with the following items while preparing the final accounts for the year ending on 31st March 2016:

Opening Building Fund	₹ 4,00,000
Donation for Building received	₹ 5,00,000
Opening Capital Fund	₹ 9,00,000
Expenditure on construction of Building . The construction work is in progress and has not yet completed.	₹ 3,00,000.

SOLUTION

AN EXTRACT OF BALANCE SHEET AS AT 31ST MARCH, 2016

Liabilities		₹	*Assets*	₹
Capital Fund:			Building in progress	3,00,000
Opening Balance	9,00,000			
Add: T/f from Building fund	3,00,000	12,00,000		
Building Fund:				
Opening Balance	4,00,000			
Add: Donations	5,00,000			
Less: T/f to Capital Fund	3,00,000	6,00,000		

ILLUSTRATION 22

Show how will you deal with the following items while preparing the final accounts for the year ending on 31st March 2016:

Opening Building Fund	₹ 4,00,000
Opening 10% Building Fund Investments	₹ 4,00,000
Donation for Building received	₹ 5,00,000
Interest received on Building Fund Investments	₹ 40,000
Opening Capital Fund	₹ 9,00,000.
Expenditure on construction of Building The construction work is in progress and has not yet completed.	₹ 3,00,000.

SOLUTION

AN EXTRACT OF BALANCE SHEET AS AT 31ST MARCH, 2016

Liabilities		₹	*Assets*	₹
Capital Fund:			Building in progress	3,00,000
Opening Balance	9,00,000		10% Building Fund Investments	4,00,000

Add: T/f from Building Fund	3,00,000	12,00,000		
Building Fund:				
Opening Balance	4,00,000			
Add: Donations	5,00,000			
Add: Interest on B.F. Investments	40,000			
Less: T/f to Capital Fund	3,00,000	6,40,000		

ILLUSTRATION 23

How will you deal with the following items while preparing for the Tulsian Cricket Club's Income and Expenditure Account for the year ending on March 31, 2016 and its Balance Sheet as on March 31, 2016.

Particulars	₹
(i) Building Fund as on 1.04.2015	2,00,000
Donations received for the Building	5,54,000
Expenditure on Building construction	5,92,000
The construction work is continuing,	
(ii) Tournament Fund: as on April 1, 2015	3,760
Donation received for Tournament	18,400
Tournament Expenses	30,200
Proceeds from Sale of Tournament Tickets	10,000
(iii) Life Membership fees received during the year	16,000
(iv) Subscription for Governor's Party received	20,000
Outstanding Subscription for Governor's Party	5,000
(v) Capital Fund as on 1.04.2015.	10,00,000

SOLUTION

All the receipts mention in the above Illustration are of capital nature. Hence these are capitalised and are shown in Balance Sheet as under:

AN EXTRACT OF BALANCE SHEET OF TULSIAN CRICKET CLUB

as at 31st March, 2016

Liabilities		₹	*Assets*	₹
Capital Fund:			Building in progress	5,92,000
Add: Transferred from Building Fund	5,92,000		Outstanding Subscription for Governor's Party	5,000
Opening Balance	10,00,000			
Add: Life Membership fees	16,000	6,08,000		
Building Fund:				
Opening Balance	2,00,000			
Add: Donations received	5,54,000			
Less: T/F to Capital Fund	5,92,000	1,62,000		

Tournament Fund:				
Opening Balance	3,760			
Add: Donations Received	18,400			
Add: Sale Proceeds	10,000			
	32,160			
Less: Expenses	30,200	1,960		
Subscription for Governor's Party (₹ 20,000 + ₹ 5,000)		25,000		

10.0 TREATMENT OF SALE OF OLD NEWSPAPERS AND PERIODICALS

The sale proceeds of old newspapers and periodicals are treated as **Revenue Receipts** and thus, are **credited to the Income & Expenditure Account.**

11.0 TREATMENT OF SALE OF OLD FIXED ASSETS

The sale proceeds of old fixed assets are treated as **Capital Receipts** and thus, are **credited to the Respective Fixed Asset Account.** However, the **Profit *or* Loss on Sale** of fixed assets is **shown in the Income & Expenditure Account.**

ILLUSTRATION 24

Furniture as on 31.3.2015 ₹ 1,10,000, Furniture (having a book value as on 1.4.2015 of ₹ 10,000) sold at a profit of 20% on 31.12.2015, Furniture purchased on 1.10.2015 ₹ 50,000. Furniture is to be depreciated @ 10% p.a. Prepare the Furniture account for the year ending on March 31, 2016

SOLUTION

Dr. **FURNITURE ACCOUNT** *Cr.*

Particulars	₹	*Particulars*	₹
To Balance b/d	1,10,000	By Depreciation A/c	750
To Bank A/c (Purchases)	1,850	$\left[₹10,000 \times \frac{10}{100} \times \frac{9}{12}\right]$	
To Income & Expenditure A/c [Profit @ 20% on ₹ 9,250]	50,000	By Bank A/c (Sale proceeds) [(10,000 – 750) + 20% of 9,250]	11,100
		By Depreciation A/c:	
		on 1,00,000 for 1 year 10,000	
		on 50,000 for 1/2 year 2,500	12,500
		By Balance c/d	1,37,500
	1,61,850		1,61,850

ILLUSTRATION 25

Furniture as on 31.3.2015 ₹ 2,20,000. Furniture (having a book value as on 1.4.2015 of ₹ 20,000) sold at a loss of 20% on 31.12.2015, Furniture is to be depreciated @ 10% p.a. Furniture costing ₹ 1,50,000 was also purchased on 1.10.2015. Prepare the Furniture Account for the year ending on March 31, 2016.

SOLUTION

Dr. **FURNITURE ACCOUNT** *Cr.*

Particulars	₹	*Particulars*		₹
To Balance b/d	1,10,000	By Depreciation A/c		750
To Balance b/d	2,20,000	By Depreciation A/c $\left[₹20,000 \times \frac{10}{100} \times \frac{9}{12}\right]$		1,500
To Bank A/c (Purchases)	1,50,000	By Bank A/c (Sale Proceeds) [(₹ 20,000 – ₹ 1,500) – 20% of ₹ 18,500]		14,800
		By Income & Expenditure A/c [20% of ₹ 18,500]		3,700
		By Depreciation A/c		
		on ₹ 2,00,000 for 1 year,	20,000	
		on ₹ 1,50,000 for 1/2 year	7,500	27,500
		By Balance c/d		3,22,500
	3,70,000			3,70,000

12.0 TREATMENT OF AID FROM GOVERNMENT AND OTHER INSTITUTIONS

Aids from the government and other institutions are accounted for as follows:

Type of Aid	Accounting treatment
(a) General Aids	(a) These aids are treated as **Revenue Receipts** and thus, are **credited to the Income & Expenditure Account.**
(b) Special Aids	(b) These aids are treated as **Capital Receipts** and thus, are **added to the Capital Fund.**

13.0 TREATMENT OF CONSUMABLE ITEMS CONSUMED DURING THE YEAR

1. Sometimes Not-for-profit organisations consume some consumable item e.g. Stationery, Sports Materials, Medicines.
2. In such a case Total Creditors Account should be prepared to ascertain Credit Purchases *(if missing).*
3. A separate Stock Account for each of the consumable items is prepared to ascertain the amount of consumable item consumed during the year.
4. Such amount consumed is debited to Income & Expenditure Account.

ILLUSTRATION 26

How will you deal with the following items while preparing the Income and Expenditure Account for the year ending on March 31, 2016 and a Balance Sheet as on that date?

Particulars	*As at 1.4.2015* ₹	*As at 31.3.2016* ₹
Creditors for Sports Materials	2,000	1,200
Stock of Sports Materials	2,100	500

During 2015–2016, the payment made to these creditors was ₹ 10,800. Cash Purchases 10% of Credit purchases.

SOLUTION

AN EXTRACT OF INCOME AND EXPENDITURE ACCOUNT

Dr. *for the year ending on 31st March, 2016* Cr.

Expenditure	₹	*Income*	₹
To Sports Materials consumed	12,600		

AN EXTRACT OF BALANCE SHEET AS AT 31ST MARCH, 2016

Liabilities	₹	*Assets*	₹
Creditors for Sports Materials	1,200	Stock of Sports Materials	500

Working Notes:

Dr. **(I) CREDITORS FOR SPORTS MATERIALS ACCOUNT** Cr.

Particulars	₹	*Particulars*	₹
To Bank A/c	10,800	By Balance b/d	2,000
To Balance c/d	1,200	By Stock of Sports Materials A/c (Credit purchases) (b. f.)	10,000
	12,000		12,000

Dr. **(II) STOCK OF SPORTS MATERIALS ACCOUNT** Cr.

Particulars	₹	*Particulars*	₹
To Balance b/d	2,100	By Income and Expenditure A/c	
To Creditors for Sports Materials		*(Sports Materials consumed)*	
(transfer)	10,000	*(Balancing figure)*	12,600
To Bank A/c (cash purchases)	1,000	By Balance c/d	500
	13,100		13,100

ILLUSTRATION 27

How will you deal with the following items while preparing the Income and Expenditure Account for the year ending on March 31, 2016 and a Balance Sheet as on that date?

Particulars	*As at 1.4.2015* ₹	*As at 31.3.2016* ₹
Amount due to suppliers of Sports Materials	15,000	9,750
Advances to suppliers of Sports Materials	5,000	3,750
Stock of Sports Materials	10,500	2,500

During 2015–2016, the payment made to the suppliers of Sports Materials was ₹ 54,000. Cash Purchases 10% of Credit purchases.

SOLUTION

AN EXTRACT OF INCOME AND EXPENDITURE ACCOUNT

Dr. *for the year ending on 31st March, 2016* *Cr.*

Expenditure	₹	*Income*	₹
To Sports Materials consumed	63,000		

AN EXTRACT OF BALANCE SHEET AS AT 31ST MARCH, 2016

Liabilities	₹	*Assets*	₹
Creditors for Sports Materials	9,750	Advance for Sports Materials	3,750
		Stock of Sports Materials	2,500

Working Notes:

Dr. **(I) CREDITORS FOR SPORTS MATERIALS ACCOUNT** *Cr.*

Particulars	₹	*Particulars*	₹
To Balance b/d	5,000	By Balance b/d	15,000
To Bank A/c	54,000	By Stock of Sports Materials A/c	
To Balance c/d	9,750	(Credit purchases)	
		(Balancing figure)	50,000
		By Balance c/d	3,750
	68,750		68,750

Dr. **(II) STOCK OF SPORTS MATERIALS ACCOUNT** *Cr.*

Particulars	₹	*Particulars*	₹
To Balance b/d	10,500	By Income and Expenditure A/c	
To Creditor for Sports Materials		*(Sports Materials consumed)*	
(transfer)	50,000	*(Balancing figure)*	63,000
To Bank A/c (cash purchases)	5,000	By Balance c/d	2,500
	65,500		65,500

14.0 TREATMENT OF PROFIT/LOSS FROM TRADING ACTIVITIES

1. Sometimes Not-for-profit organisations carry on trading activities e.g. A Restaurant/Bar run by a club, Chemist shop by a hospital, Book-Shop by a library.
2. In such a case, a separate Trading Account for each of the trading activities is prepared to ascertain the Profit/Loss from each of such trading activities.
3. Such Profit/Loss is transferred to Income & Expenditure Account.
4. Trading Account is prepared in the same manner as in case of commercial organisations.
5. Sometimes the figures of Credit Purchases and Credit Sales are missing in the questions, in such case Total Creditors' Account and Total Debtors' Account should be prepared to ascertain credit purchases and credit sales respectively.

ILLUSTRATION 28

Bharat Club provides you the following information:

Stock in Restaurant on 31.3.2015 ₹ 3,900, and on 31.3.2016 ₹ 4,500, Restaurant Takings ₹ 3,61,600, Restaurant Purchases ₹ 2,04,800, Wages (including ₹ 50,000 for Restaurant) ₹ 92,300, Fuel ₹ 17,700, China Glass Cutlery on 31.3.2015 ₹ 2,500, Depreciation @ 20% is to be provided on China Glass Cutlery.

Required: Show how will you deal with the above items while preparing Restaurant Trading Account, Income & Expenditure Account and Balance Sheet.

SOLUTION

RESTAURANT TRADING ACCOUNT

for the year ended 31st March, 2016

Dr. *Cr.*

Particulars	₹	*Particulars*	₹
To Opening Stock	3,900	By Restaurant Takings	3,61,600
To Purchases	2,04,800	By Closing Stock	4,500
To Wages	50,000		
To Fuel	17,700		
To Depreciation on China Glass Cutlery	500		
To Surplus transferred to Income & Expenditure A/c	89,200		
	3,66,100		3,66,100

AN EXTRACT OF INCOME & EXPENDITURE ACCOUNT

for the year ended 31st March, 2016

Dr. *Cr.*

Expenditure	₹	*Income*	₹
To Wages	42,300	By Profit from Restaurant	89,200

AN EXTRACT OF BALANCE SHEET AS AT 31ST MARCH, 2016

Liabilities	₹	*Assets*		₹
		Restaurant Stock		4,500
		China Glass Cutlery	2,500	
		Less: Depreciation @ 20%	500	2,000

15.0 DISTINCTION BETWEEN RECEIPTS AND PAYMENTS ACCOUNT AND INCOME AND EXPENDITURE ACCOUNT

A 'Receipt & Payment Account' and 'Income & Expenditure Account' can be distinguished as follows:

Basis of Distinction	Receipts & Payments A/c	Income & Expenditure A/c
1. Nature of Account	It is a **real** account.	It is a **nominal** account.

2. Period to which items relate	It records the receipts and payments whether they relate to **previous**, **current** or **following** accounting periods.	It records only those incomes, expenses and losses which relate to **current** accounting period.
3. Nature of items recorded—Revenue Vs. Capital.	It records all the receipts and payments **whether of capital *or* revenue nature.**	It records the incomes, expenditures and losses of **revenue nature**.
4. Non-cash Items	Non-cash items are **not shown** in this account.	Non-cash items such as depreciation, bad debts, etc., are **shown**.
5. Items of Debit side	It is debited with all the **sums received**.	It is debited with the **expenses and losses**.
6. Items of Credit side	It is credited with all the **sums paid out**.	It is credited with the **incomes**.
7. Closing balance	Closing balance represents **cash *or* bank balance (or bank overdraft) at the end** of the accounting period.	Its closing balance represents either **net surplus *or* net deficit**.
8. Treatment of closing balance	Its closing balance is **carried forward** in the same account of the **next period**.	Its closing balance is transferred to the **Capital Fund** in the Balance Sheet.
9. Opening balance	Opening balance represents **cash *or* bank balances (or Bank Overdraft) in the beginning** of the accounting period.	It has **no** opening balance.
10. Basic Structure	It is **basically a summarised Cash Book**.	It is **like a Profit & Loss Account**.
11. Object	It is prepared to present a summary of cash transactions during an accounting period.	It is prepared to ascertain the net results of all the transactions during an accounting period.

16.0 DISTINCTION BETWEEN INCOME AND EXPENDITURE ACCOUNT AND PROFIT AND LOSS ACCOUNT

Income & Expenditure Account differs from Profit & Loss Account in the following respects:

Basis of Distinction	Income & Expenditure A/c	Profit & Loss A/c
1. Object	The main object of Income and Expenditure Account is **to ascertain excess of income over expenditure *or* excess of expenditure over income.**	The main object of Profit and Loss Account is **to ascertain Net Profit *or* Net Loss.**
2. Who prepares?	This account is prepared by **Non-Profit Organisations.**	This account is prepared by **Trading Institutions.**
3. Basis of Preparation	This account is prepared on the basis of **Receipts and Payments Account and other information.**	This account is prepared on the basis of **Trial Balance.**
4. Balance	The balance of this account represents **Surplus *or* Deficit**	The balance of this account represents **Net Profit *or* Net Loss.**

17.0 HOW TO PREPARE AN INCOME AND EXPENDITURE ACCOUNT FROM A RECEIPTS AND PAYMENTS ACCOUNT

The practical steps involved in the preparation of an Income & Expenditure Account from the Receipts & Payments Account are given as follows:

PRACTICAL STEPS INVOLVED IN THE PREPARATION OF AN INCOME & EXPENDITURE ACCOUNT FROM THE RECEIPTS & PAYMENTS ACCOUNT

			₹
Step 1:	Ascertain the Revenue Income (e.g. Subscriptions) for the current accounting period as under and show on the credit side of Income & Expenditure Account:		
	A. Revenue Receipts during the current year		xxx
	B. *Add:* (a) Outstanding income at the end of current year	xxx	
	(b) Advance income in the beginning of current year	xxx	xxx
	C. *Less:* (a) Outstanding income in the beginning of current year	xxx	
	(b) Advance income at the end of current year	xxx	xxx
	D. Revenue Income for the current year (A + B – C)		xxx
Step 2:	Ascertain 'Revenue Expense' (e.g. Salaries) for the current accounting period as under and show on the debit side of Income & Expenditure Account;		₹
	A. Revenue Payments during the current year		xxx
	B. *Add:* (a) Outstanding expenses at the end of current year	xxx	
	(b) Prepaid expenses in the beginning of current year	xxx	xxx
	C. *Less:* (a) Outstanding expenses in the beginning of current year	xxx	
	(b) Prepaid expenses at the end of current year	xxx	xxx
	D. Revenue Expenses for the current year (A + B – C)		xxx
Step 3:	Ascertain the Non-Cash Expenses (e.g. depreciation on fixed assets) from the additional information and show such charges on the debit side of Income & Expenditure Account.		
Step 4:	Calculate the amount of Profit *or* Loss on Trading Activities and show the amount of profit on the credit side of Income & Expenditure Account *or* the amount of Loss on the debit side of Income & Expenditure Account separately.		
Step 5:	Calculate the difference between the total of debit side and the total of credit side. If the total of credit side exceeds the total of debit side, show the **Surplus** (i.e. excess of Income over Expenditure) on the debit side. If the total of debit side exceeds the total of credit side, show the **Deficit** (i.e. excess of Expenditure over Income) on the credit side of Income & Expenditure Account.		

TUTORIAL NOTE

The following items appearing in the Receipts & Payments Account are not shown in the Income & Expenditure Account:

1. *Opening Cash and Bank Balances*
2. *Closing Cash and Bank Balances*
3. *Capital Receipts (e.g. Special Donations, Sale Proceeds of Fixed Assets), Entrance Fees & Life Membership Fees to the extent Capitalised)*
4. *Capital Payments (e.g. Purchase of Fixed Assets)*

5. *Expenses paid for the previous year(s) or following year(s)*
6. *Incomes received for the previous year(s) or following year(s).*

ILLUSTRATION 29

(a) Salaries paid during the year 2015-2016 ₹ 60,000. Compute the Salaries for the year 2015-2016.

(b) Salaries paid during the year 2015-2016 ₹ 60,000. Salaries ₹ 30,000 is still outstanding. Compute the Salaries for the year 2015-2016.

(c) Salaries paid during the year 2015-2016 ₹ 60,000. Salaries ₹ 20,000 paid in advance for the year 2016-2017. Compute the Salaries for the year 2015-2016.

(d) Salaries paid during the year 2015-2016 ₹ 60,000. Salaries ₹ 40,000 was outstanding at the end of the previous year. Compute the Salaries for the year 2015-2016.

(e) Salaries paid during the year 2015-2016 ₹ 60,000. Salaries ₹ 90,000 was paid in advance at the end of the previous year. Compute the Salaries for the year 2015-2016.

SOLUTION

COMPUTATION OF SALARIES FOR THE CURRENT YEAR

Particulars	*(a)*	*(b)*	*(c)*	*(d)*	*(e)*
Salaries paid	60,000	60,000	60,000	60,000	60,000
Add: O/s at the end	—	30,000	—	—	—
Less: Advance at the end	—	—	(20,000)	—	—
Add: Advance in the beg.	—	—	—	—	90,000
Less: O/s in the beg.	—	—	—	(40,000)	—
Salaries for the Current Year	**60,000**	**90,000**	**40,000**	**20,000**	**1,50,000**

ILLUSTRATION 30

Compute the Salaries for the year 2015-2016 from the following information:

Particulars	*1.4.2015*	*31.3.2016*
Outstanding Salaries	₹ 9,500	₹ 7,000
Prepaid Salaries	₹ 2,800	₹ 5,200
Salaries paid during 2015-2016 ₹ 1,48,900		

SOLUTION

Dr. **SALARIES ACCOUNT** *Cr.*

Particulars	₹	*Particulars*	₹
To Prepaid Salaries A/c (in the beginning)	2,800	By Outstanding Salaries A/c (in the beginning)	9,500
To Bank A/c	1,48,900	By Income & Expenditure A/c	1,44,000
To Outstanding Salaries A/c	7,000	(balancing figure)	
(at the end)		By Prepaid Salaries A/c (at the end)	5,200
	1,58,700		1,58,700

ACCOUNTING TREATMENT OF SPECIAL ITEMS

Item	Accounting Treatment
1. Subscriptions	These are treated as **Revenue Receipts** and hence are **credited to Income & Expenditure Account.**
2. Life Membership Subscriptions	These are treated as **Capital Receipts** and hence are **added to the Capital Fund** in the Balance Sheet.
3.Entrance Fees	1. **If** treated as a **Revenue Receipt** and is **credited to Income & Expenditure Account.** 2. **If** treated as a **Capital Receipt** and is **added to the Capital Fund** in the Balance Sheet.
4. Amount of Consumable Item (e.g. Stationery, Sports Material, Medicines) consumed during the year	Such Amount is **debited to Income & Expenditure Account.**
5(a). Profit on Sale of Asset [Sale Proceeds – Book Value]	It is **credited to Income & Expenditure Account.**
5(b). Loss on Sale of Asset [Book Value – Sale Proceeds]	It is **debited to Income & Expenditure Account.**
6. Sale of Old Sports Materials already w/o	It is **credited to Income & Expenditure Account.**
7. Sale of Old Newspapers & Periodicals	It is **credited to Income & Expenditure Account.**
8. Depreciation	It is **debited to Income & Expenditure Account.**
9. General Donations and Legacies	These donations & legacies are treated as **Revenue Receipts** and hence, are **Credited to Income & Expenditure Account.**
10. Specific Donations and Legacies	1. These donations & legacies are treated as **Capital Receipts** and hence, are **credited to a 'Special Fund Account'** (e.g., Prize Fund,Tournament Fund,Building Fund) maintained for the purpose. 2. Any **Income** relating to such 'Special Fund Account' is **added to** the respective Fund. (e.g., Interest on Prize Fund Investments is added to Prize Fund) 3. Any **Revenue Expenditure** out of 'Special Fund Account' is **deducted** from the respective Fund. (e.g., Prize Expenses are deducted from Prize Fund) 4. However, any **Capital Expenditure** out of Special Fund should be shown on the **Assets side** of the Balance Sheet **and** an equal amount should be **transferred from that Special Fund to the Capital Fund.** (e.g., Expenditure on the construction of building out of Building Fund should be shown on the assets side of the Balance Sheet and an equal amount should be transferred from Building Fund to the Capital Fund.)
11. General Aids	General aids are treated as **Revenue Receipts** and hence, are **Credited to Income & Expenditure Account.**

12. Special Aids	Special aids are treated as **Capital Receipts** and hence, are **Added to the Capital Fund.**
13. Interest on General Fund Investments	It is treated as **Revenue Receipt** and hence is **credited to Income & Expenditure Account.**
14. Interest on Specific Fund Investments	It is **added to the Respective Fund.** (e.g., Interest on Prize Fund Investments is added to Prize Fund)

ILLUSTRATION 31

Given below in the Receipts and Payments Accounts of Tulsian Sports Club for the year ended 31.3.2016:

RECEIPTS AND PAYMENTS ACCOUNT OF TULSIAN SPORTS CLUB

Dr. *for the year ended 31st March, 2016* *Cr.*

Receipts		₹	*Payments*		₹
Balance b/f:			Salary (inclu. ₹ 1,000 for 2014-2015)		11,000
Cash	400		Billiards table		8,000
Bank	3,600	4,000	Office Expenses		
Subscriptions		11,000	(including ₹ 1,000 for 2016-2017)		4,400
Lift membership fee		8,000	Stationary		700
Tournament fund		15,000	Tournament expenses		16,000
Donation for Building		40,000	Furniture purchased		5,000
Locker rent		2,000	Sports equipments purchased		6,000
Sale of Old Sports Material			Fixed deposit on 1.4.2015		5,900
(Costing ₹ 5,000)		3,000	@ 12% p.a.		
Sale of Old Newspapers		2,000	Balance c/f:		
Legacy		10,000	Cash	200	
Entrance fee		5,000	Bank	53,154	53,354
Interest on Fixed Deposit		354			
Interest on Building Fund		10,000			
		1,10,354			1,10,354

Additional Information:

(a) On 1.4.2015 subscriptons outstanding were ₹ 800 and on 31.3.2016 ₹ 900.

(b) On 1.4.2015 the Club had Building ₹ 50,000; Furntirue ₹ 20,000 and Sports Equipment ₹ 14,000. Charge depreciation @ 10% on these items (including purchases).

(c) Stock of Stationery at the begining and at the end of year was ₹ 3,000 and ₹ 1,000.

(d) Donation for Building includes ₹ 4,000 General Donation.

Prepare Income and Expenditure Account of the Club for the year ended 31.3.2016.

SOLUTION

INCOME AND EXPENDITURE ACCOUNT

Dr. *for the year ended 31st March., 2016* *Cr.*

Expenditure	₹	*Income*		₹
To Salary [₹ 11,000 – ₹ 1,000]	10,000	By Subscriptions	11,000	
To Office Expenses		*Less:* O/s in the Beg.	800	
[₹ 4,400 – ₹ 1000]	3,400	*Add:* O/s at end	900	11,100
To Stationery	2,700	By Locker Rent		2,000
[₹ 3,000 + ₹ 700 – ₹ 1,000]		By Sale of Old Newspapers		2,000
To Loss on Sale of Sports material	2,000	By Entrance Fee		5,000
To Depreciation on		By General Denations		4,000
Building	5,000	By Interest on Fixed Deposit		
Furniture		Received	354	
10/100 [20,000 + 5,000]	2,500	Accrued	354	708
Sports Equipment		By Deficit		4,592
10/100 [14,000 + 6,000 + 800]	2,800			
To Tournament Expenses	1,000			
[₹ 16,000 – ₹ 15,000]				
	29,400			29,400

Notes:

1. Billiards Table has been treated as part of Sports Equipments.
2. Entrance Fees have been treated as of Revenue nature.
3. Excess Tournament Expenses have been charged to Income & Exp. A/c.

ILLUSTRATION 32

From the following Receipts & Payments Account, prepare the Income & Expenditure Account for the year 31st March, 2016:

Receipts	₹	*Payments*	₹
To Balance b/f	10,000	By Rent	
		(including ₹ 1,500 for 2014-2015)	6,000
To Entrance Fees:		By Insurance Premium	
2014-2015	1,000	(including ₹ 1,500 for 2016-2017)	6,000
2015-2016	5,000	By Sports Materials	5,000
To Subscriptions:		By Sports Equipment	6,000
2014-2015	1,000	(Purchased on 31.3.2016)	
2015-2016	9,000	By 8% Fixed Deposits	12,000
2016-2017	500	(made on 1.10.2015)	
To Life Membership Subscription	2,000	By Tournament Expenses	1,000
To Donations	12,000	By Purchase of Books	2,000
To Donation for Tournament	5,000	By Postage Stamps	500
To Subsc. for Governor's Party	1,500	By Printing & Stationery	1,500
To Interest on 8% Fixed Deposit	240	By Newspapers & Periodicals	2,000
To Sale of Old Sports Materials	30	By Balance c/f	6,000

To Sale of Old Sports Equipment (Book Value ₹ 120)	50		
To Locker Rents (including ₹ 60 for 2014-2015)	500		
To Sale of Old Newspapers & Periodicals	180		
	48,000		48,000

SOLUTION

INCOME & EXPENDITURE ACCOUNT

Dr. *for the year ended 31st March, 2016* Cr.

Expenditure		₹	*Income*		₹
To Loss on Sale of Sports Equip. (₹ 120 – 50)		70	By Entrance Fees		5,000
To Rent			By Subscription		9,000
Paid	6,000		By Donations		12,000
Less: O/s in the beginning	1,500	4,500	By Interest on Deposits		
To Insurance Premium:			Received	240	
Paid	6,000		*Add:* Accrued	240	480
Less: Prepaid at the end	1,500	4,500	By Sale of Sports Materials		30
To Sports Materials		5,000	By Locker Rent		440
To Postage Stamps		500	By Sale of Old Newspapers & Periodicals		180
To Printing & Stationery		1,500			
To Newspapers & Periodicals		2,000			
To Surplus t/f to Capital Fund		9,060			
		27,130			27,130

Notes:

1. Sports Equipments, 8% Fixed Deposits and Books represent assets which will appear in the closing Balance Sheet.
2. In the absence of any information regarding the rate of depreciation on Sports Equipments & Books, no depreciation has been provided.
3. Tournament Expenses will be deducted from Tournament Fund.
4. Donation for Tournament & Subscription for Governor's party will appears on liabilities side of Balance Sheet.
5. Entrance Fees have been treated as of revenue nature.
6. Life Membership Subscription has been treated as of Capital nature and hence, not shown on the credit side of Income & Expenditure Account.
7. It has been assumed that there is no Stock of Sports Materials in hand.

18.0 PREPARATION OF BALANCE SHEET OF A NOT-FOR-PROFIT ORGANISATION

MEANING OF A BALANCE SHEET

1. A Balance Sheet is the Statement of Assets and Liabilities of an accounting unit at a given date.
2. It is prepared at the end of an accounting period after the Income & Expenditure Account has been prepared.
3. It is called a Balance Sheet because it is a sheet of balances of ledger accounts which are open even after the preparation of Income & Expenditure Account.
4. In Not-for-Profit organisations, the excess of Total Assets over Total Outside Liabilities is known as Capital Fund. While preparing the Balance Sheet, the excess of income over expenditure is added to the opening Capital Fund and the excess of expenditure over the income is deducted from the opening Capital Fund.

FORMAT OF BALANCE SHEET

A general format of a Balance Sheet of a Not-for-Profit Organisation is given below:

BALANCE SHEET OF... AS AT...

Liabilities		₹	*Assets*		₹
Capital Fund:			**Fixed Assets:**		
Opening Balance	xxx		Building		
Add: Surplus	xxx		Opening Balance	xxx	
(or *Less:* Deficit)	xxx		*Add:* Additions	xxx	
Add: Entrance Fees	xxx		*Less:* Depreciation	xxx	xxx
(to the extent capitalised)			Furniture		
Add: Life Membership			Opening Balance	xxx	
Subscriptions	xxx		*Add:* Additions	xxx	
(to the extent capitalised)			*Less:* Book Value of asset sold	xxx	
Add: Amt. of Capital Expenditure			*Less:* Depreciation	xxx	xxx
transferred from A Special			Sports Equipment	xxx	
Fund (e.g. Building Fund)	xxx	xxx	*Less:* Depreciation	xxx	xxx
Prize Fund:			**Investments:**		
Opening Balance	xxx		Prize Fund Investments		xxx
Add: Donation for prizes	xxx		Building Fund Investments		xxx
Add: Income from			10% Govt. Securities		xxx
Prize Fund Investments	xxx		Fixed Deposits		xxx
Less: Expenses	xxx	xxx	**Current Assets:**		
Building Fund:			Sports Materials		xxx
Add: Donation for Building	xxx		Outstanding Subscriptions		xxx
Add: Income from			Accrued Interest		xxx
Building Fund Investments	xxx		Accrued Rent		xxx
Less: Transfer to Capital Fund	xxx	xxx	Cash in hand		xxx
Current Liabilities:			Cash at bank		xxx
Subscription received in Advan.	xxx				
Outstanding Expenses		xxx			

Bank Overdraft	xxx		
Creditors	xxx		
	xxx		xxx

ILLUSTRATION 33

From the following information, prepare Opening and Closing Balance Sheets:

Particulars	*31st March 2015* ₹	*31st March 2016* ₹
Building (subject to 10% depreciation)	30,000	?
Furniture (subject to 10% depreciation)	–	10,000
Stock of Sports Materials	2,500	1,000
Prepaid Insurance	1,500	3,000
Outstanding Subscription	6,000	4,000
Advance Subscription	3,000	2,000
Outstanding Locker Rent	—	3,000
Advance Locker Rent received	—	1,000
Outstanding Rent for Godown	3,000	1,500
12% General Fund Investments	1,00,000	?
Accrued Interest on above	—	2,000
Cash Balance	500	32,000
Bank Balance	1,000	—
Bank Overdraft	—	1,000

Note: Entrance Fees received ₹ 10,000, Life Membership Fees received ₹ 10,000, Surplus from Income & Expenditure Account ₹ 30,000. It is the policy of the club to treat 60% of Entrance Fees and 40% of Life Membership Fees as of revenue nature.

SOLUTION

BALANCE SHEET AS AT 31ST MARCH 2015

Liabilities	₹	*Assets*	₹
Outstanding Rent	3,000	Building	30,000
Advance Subscription	3,000	Stock of Sports Materials	2,500
Capital Fund **(Balancing Figure)**	1,35,500	Prepaid Insurance	1,500
		Outstanding Subscription	6,000
		12% General Fund Investments	1,00,000
		Cash Balance	500
		Bank Balance	1,000
	1,41,500		1,41,500

BALANCE SHEET AS AT 31ST MARCH 2016

Liabilities		₹	*Assets*		₹
Outstanding Rent		1,500	Building		
Advance Subscription		2,000	Book Value	30,000	
Advance Locker Rent		1,000	*Less:* Depreciation	3,000	27,000
Bank Overdraft		1,000	Furniture Cost	10,000	
Capital Fund:			*Less:* Depreciation	1,000	9,000
Opening Balance	1,35,500		Stock of Sports Materials		1,000
Add: Entrance Fees			Prepaid Insurance		3,000
[10,000 × 40%]	4,000		Outstanding Subscription		4,000
Add: Life Membership Fees			Outstanding Locker Rent		3,000
[₹ 10,000 × 60%]	6,000		12% General Fund Investments		1,00,000
Add: Surplus	30,000	1,75,500	Accrued Interest on 12% General		
			Fund Investments		2,000
			Cash Balance		32,000
		1,81,000			1,81,000

PREPARATION OF AN INCOME & EXPENDITURE A/C AND THE BALANCE SHEET

ILLUSTRATION 34

From the following Receipts and Payments A/c of Mumbai Club, prepare Income and Expenditure A/c for the year ended 31.3.2016 and its Balance Sheet as on that date:

Receipts	₹	*Payments*	₹
Cash in Hand	4,000	Salary	2,000
Cash at Bank	10,000	Repair Expenses	500
Donations	5,000	Purchase of Furniture	6,000
Subscriptions	12,000	Misc. Expenses	500
Entrance Fees	1,000	Purchase of Investments	6,000
Interest on Investments	100	Insurance Premium	200
Interest Received from Bank	400	Billiard Table	8,000
Sale of Old Newspaper	150	Paper, Ink, etc.	150
Sale of Drama Tickets	1,050	Drama Expenses	500
		Cash in Hand (Closing)	2,650
		Cash at bank (Closing)	7,200
	33,700		33,700

Information:

(a) Subscriptions in arrears for 2015-2016 ₹ 900 and Subscription in advance for 2016-2017 ₹ 350,

(b) Insurance premium Outstanding ₹ 40, Misc. Expenses Prepaid ₹ 90,

(c) 50% of donation is to be capitalised, Entrance Fees are to be treated as revenue income,

(d) 8% Interest has accrued on Investment for five months,

(e) Billiard Table costing ₹ 30,000 was purchased during the last year and ₹ 22,000 were paid for it.

SOLUTION

INCOME AND EXPENDITURE ACCOUNT

Dr. *for the year ended 31st March, 2016* Cr.

Expenditure		₹	*Income*		₹
To Salary		2,000	By Subscriptions	12,000	
To Repair Expenses		500	*Add:* Outstanding in beg.	900	
To Misc. Expenses	500			12,900	
Less: Prepaid	90	410	*Less:* Advance at end	350	12,550
To Insurance Premium	200		By Entrance Fees		1,000
Add: Outstanding	40	240	By Interest on Investment		
			(100 + 200)		300
To Paper, ink, etc.		150	By Sale of Drama Tickets		1,050
To Drama expenses		500	By Interest received from Bank		400
To Surplus — Excess of Income			By Sale of Newspaper		150
over Expenditure		14,150	By Donation	5,000	
			Less: Capitalised (50%)	2,500	2,500
		17,950			17,950

BALANCE SHEET OF MUMBAI CLUB AS AT 31ST MARCH, 2016

Liabilities		₹	*Assets*	₹
Outstanding Expenses		40	Billiards table	30,000
Subscription in advance		350	Furniture	6,000
Capital Fund	36,000		Prepaid Expenses (Misc.)	90
Add: Surplus	14,150		Subscription receivable	900
Add: Donations	2,500	52,650	Investments	6,000
			Interest accrued	200
			Bank balance	7,200
			Cash on hand	2,650
		53,040		53,040

Working Note: *Calculation of Opening Capital Fund*

BALANCE SHEET OF MUMBAI CLUB AS AT 31ST MARCH, 2015

Liabilities	₹	*Assets*	₹
Creditors for Billiards Table	8,000	Billiards table	30,000
Capital Fund (Balancing figure)	**36,000**	Bank Balance	10,000
		Cash on Hand	4,000
	44,000		44,000

ILLUSTRATION 35

Excellent Library Society showed the following position on 31st March 2015:

Liabilities	₹	*Assets*	₹
Capital Fund	7,93,000	Electrical Fittings	1,50,000
Expenses Due	7,000	Furniture	50,000
		Books	4,00,000
		Investments in Securities	1,50,000
		Cash at Bank	25,000
		Cash on Hand	25,000
	8,00,000		8,00,000

The Receipts and Payments Account for the year ending on 31st March 2016 is given below:

Receipts	₹	*Payments*	₹
To Balance b/f		By Electric charges	7,200
Cash at Bank	25,000	By Postage & Stationery	5,000
Cash on Hand25,000	50,000	By Telephone charges	5,000
To Entrance Fees	30,000	By Books purchased (on 1.4.2015)	60,000
To Membership Subscription	2,00,000	By Outstanding Expenses Paid	70,00
To Sale Proceeds of old Papers	1,500	By Rent Account	88,000
To Hire of Lecture Hall	20,000	By Investment in Securities	40,000
To Interest on Securities	8,000	By Salaries	66,000
		By Balance c/f:	
		Cash at Bank	20,000
		Cash on Hand	11,300
	3,09,500		3,09,500

You are required to prepare an Income and Expenditure Account for the year ending 31.03.2016 and a Balance Sheet as on that date after making the following adjustments:

(a) Membership subscriptions included ₹ 10,000 received in advance.

(b) Provide for Outstanding Rent ₹ 4,000 and Salaries ₹ 3,000.

(c) Books to be depreciated @ 10% including additions. Electrical Fittings and Furniture are also to be depreciated at the same rate.

(d) 75% of the Entrance fees is to be capitalised.

(e) Interest on Securities is to be calculated @ 5% p.a. including purchases of investments made on 1.7.2015 for ₹ 40,000.

SOLUTION

INCOME AND EXPENDITURE ACCOUNT

for the year ended on 31st March, 2016

Dr. *Cr.*

Expenditure	₹	*Income*	₹
To Electric changes	7,200	By Entrance Fees	7,500
To Postage & Stationary	5,000	By Membership Subscription	

To Telephone Charges		5,000	Received	2,00,000	
To Rent	88,000		*Less:* Advance at the end	10,000	1,90,000
Add: Due	4,000	92,000	By Sale proceeds of old papers		1,500
To Salaries	66,000		By Interest on Securities	8,000	
Add: Due	3,000	69,000	*Add:* Due	500	8,500
To Depreciation:			By Hire of Lecture Hall		20,000
Electrical Fittings	15,000		By Deficit i.e., Excess of		
Furniture	5,000		expenditure over income		16,700
Books	46,000	66,000			
		2,44,200			2,44,200

Working Note:

CALCULATION OF INTEREST ON INVESTMENTS

@ 5% on ₹ 1,50,000 for one year	₹ 7,500
@ 5% on ₹ 40,000 for 6 months	₹ 1,000
Less: Received	₹ 8,500
Due	₹ 8,000
	₹ 500

BALANCE SHEET AS AT 31ST MARCH, 2016

Liabilities		₹	*Assets*		₹
Capital Fund:			Electrical Fittings	1,50,000	
Opening Balance	7,93,000		*Less:* Depreciation	15,000	1,35,000
Add: Entrance Fees	22,500		Furniture	50,000	
	8,15,500		*Less:* Depreciation	5,000	45,000
Less: Deficit	16,700	7,98,800	Books	4,00,000	
Expenses Due:			Additions	60,000	
Rent	4,000			4,60,000	
Salaries	3,000	7,000	*Less:* Depreciation	46,000	4,14,000
Subscription received in advance		10,000	Investments	1,50,000	
			Additions	40,000	1,90,000
			Accrued interest on Securities		500
			Cash at bank		20,000
			Cash on hand		11,300
		8,15,800			8,15,800

ILLUSTRATION 36

Prepare the Income & Expenditure Account and the Balance Sheet from the following information:

RECEIPTS AND PAYMENTS ACCOUNT OF TULSIAN CLUB, DELHI

Dr. *for the year ending on 31st March, 2016* *Cr.*

Receipts			₹	*Payments*	₹
To Balance b/f (cash)			1,025	By Upkeep of fields	220
To Subscriptions:				By Salaries	600
2014-2015	40			By Drama Expenses	450
2015-2016	2,050			By Newspapers	150
2016-2017	60		2,150	By Books	100
To Admission Fees		40		By Municipal Taxes	40
To Life Membership subscription		100		By Charity	350
To Donations (on 1.11.2015)		500		By 12% General Investments	
To Subscription for Tournament				(on 1.11.2015)	500
(on 1.11.2015)			1,500	By 12% Tournament Fund	
To Sales of old newspapers		45		Investments (on 1.11.2015)	1,500
To Sale of old bats etc.		50		By Tournament Expenses	1,200
To Proceeds of drama tickets		950		By Bats, Balls etc.	700
To Sale of old furniture		60		By Printing & Stationery	100
(costing ₹ 100)				By Furniture	250
To Interest on 12% General			12.50	By Prizes	1,115
Investments				By Balance c/f (Cash)	3,725
To Interest on 12% Tournament					
Fund Investments			37.50		
To Subscription for Governor's Party			3,450		
To Prize Fund			1,080		
			11,000		11,000

Additional Information:

(a) There are 500 members each paying an annual subscription of ₹ 5. ₹ 50 are still in arrear, for the year 2014-2015.

(b) Municipal taxes amounting to ₹ 40 per year have been paid upto June 30, 2016 and ₹ 50 are outstanding for salaries.

(c) On 1.4.2015 the club owned building valued at ₹ 5,000, Stock of Bats and Balls ₹ 1,500, Printing and Stationery ₹ 200, Cash at Bank ₹ 3,000, Books ₹ 500 and Furniture ₹ 600.

(d) Write 50% off Bats and Balls (without considering sale), 25% off printing and stationery.

(e) Special subscription for governor's party outstanding ₹ 550.

(f) Admission fees to be treated as of revenue nature but Life Membership is to be treated as of Capital nature.

SOLUTION

INCOME & EXPENDITURE ACCOUNT OF TULSIAN CLUB

Dr. *for the year ending on 31st March, 2016* Cr.

Expenditure		₹	*Income*		₹
To Upkeep of fields		220	By Subscription (500 × ₹ 5)		2,500
To Salaries paid	600		By Admission Fees		40
Add: Outstanding at end	50	650	By Donations		500
To Drama Expenses		450	By Sale of old newspapers		45
To Newspapers		150	By Sale of old bats etc.		50
To Municipal Taxes Paid	40		By Proceeds of drama tickets		950
Add: Pre. in the beginning	10		By Interest on General Invest..		
Less: Prepaid at end	10	40	(500 × 12/100 × 5/12)		
To Charity		350	Received	₹ 12.5	
To Loss on sale of furniture		40	Accrued	₹ 12.5	25
To Printing & Stationery		75			
To Bats & balls consumed		1,100			
To Prize Exp. (1,115 – 1,080)		35			
To Surplus		1,000			
		4,110			4,110

BALANCE SHEET OF TULSIAN CLUB AS AT 31ST MARCH, 2016

Liabilities		₹	*Assets*		₹
Capital Fund:			Cash in hand		3,725
Opening Balance	11,925		Cash at bank		3,000
Add: Surplus	1,000		Outstanding Subscription:		
Add: Life Membership			for 2014-2015	50	
subscription	100	13,025	for 2015-2016	450	500
Tournament Fund:			Printing & Stationery:		
Opening Balance	Nil		Opening Balance	200	
Add: Subscription	1,500		*Add:* Purchases	100	
Add: Interest on				300	
Tournament Fund			*Less:* Charged	75	225
Invest. [1500 × 12% × 5/12]	75		Stock of Bats & Ball:		
Less: Tournament expenses	1,200	375	Opening Balance	1,500	
Subscription for Governor's			*Add:* Purchases	700	
Party Received	3,450			2,200	
Add: Outstanding	550	4,000	*Less:* Charged	1,100	1,100
Outstanding Salaries		50	Books:		
Advance Subscription		60	Opening Balance	500	
			Add: Additions	100	600
			12% Investments		2,000

		Furniture:	
		Opening Balance 600	
		Add: Additions 250	
		Less: Sale 100	750
		Building	5,000
		Accrued Interest:	
		on General Investments 12.5	
		on Tournament Fund	
		Investments 37.5	50
		Outstanding subscription for	
		Governor's Party	550
		Prepaid Municipal Taxes	10
	17,510		17,510

Working Note:

BALANCE SHEET OF TULSIAN CLUB AS AT 31ST MARCH, 2015

Liabilities	₹	*Assets*	₹
Capital Fund (balancing figure)	11,925	Cash in hand	1,025
		Cash at bank	3,000
		O/s subscription (50 + 40)	90
		Printing & Stationery	200
		Stock of Bats & Balls	1,500
		Books	500
		Furniture	600
		Building	5,000
		Prepaid Municipal Taxes	10
	11,925		11,925

Notes:

1. Since yearly municipal charges are ₹ 40, ₹ 10 must have been paid during the previous year for current year.
2. Excess Prize Expenses have been charged to Income & Expenditure Account.

ILLUSTRATION 37

Following is the Trial Balance of the Tulsian Public School on 31st March 2016:

Debit Balances	₹	*Credit Balances*	₹
Land	50,000	Capital Fund	15,60,000
School Building	15,00,000	Tuition Fees Received	25,10,000
Furniture	3,00,000	Salaries Payable	1,75,000
Salaries:		Prize Fund	2,00,000
Teaching Staff	12,00,000	Tournament Fund	3,00,000
Adm. Staff	2,60,000	General Reserve Fund	2,00,000
Investments	7,00,000	Interest received on	
Stationery, Postage	1,73,000	Fund Investments	77,000

Lighting	36,000	Donation for School Hall	1,50,000
General Expenses	65,000		
Prizes awarded	20,000		
Tournament Expenses	30,000		
Library Books	3,75,000		
Bank Balance	4,63,000		
	51,72,000		51,72,000

Depreciation is to be provided as follows: Building 2%, Furniture 10% and Library Books 20%. The investments were made against the various funds commonly. Prepare the Income and Expenditure Account for 2015–2016 and the Balance Sheet as at March 31, 2016.

SOLUTION

INCOME AND EXPENDITURE ACCOUNT

Dr. *for the year ending on 31st March, 2016* Cr.

Expenditure		₹	*Income*	₹
To Salaries:			By Interest on Investments	22,000
Teaching Staff	12,00,000		[₹ 77,000 × ₹ 2,00,000/₹ 7,00,000]	
Adm. Staff	2,60,000	14,60,000	By Tuition Fees	25,10,000
To Stationery, Postage		1,73,000		
To Lighting		36,000		
To General Expenses		65,000		
To Depreciation:				
Buildings	30,000			
Furniture	30,000			
Library Books	75,000	1,35,000		
To Surplus		6,63,000		
		25,32,000		25,32,000

BALANCE SHEET AS AT 31ST MARCH, 2016

Liabilities		₹	*Assets*		₹
Capital Fund:	15,60,000		**Fixed Assets:**		
Add: Surplus	6,63,000	22,23,000	Land		50,000
General Reserve Fund		2,00,000	School Building	15,00,000	
Tournament Fund:			*Less:* Depreciation	30,000	14,70,000
Opening Balance	3,00,000		Furniture	3,00,000	
Add: Interest on TFI	33,000		*Less:* Depreciation	30,000	2,70,000
[₹ 77,000 × ₹ 3,00,000/ ₹ 7,00,000]			Library Books	3,75,000	
Less: Tournament Ext.	30,000	3,03,000	*Less:* Depreciation	75,000	3,00,000
Prize Fund:			**Investments:**		
Opening Balance	2,00,000		Tournament Fund		

Add: Interest on PFI 22,000		Investments	3,00,000	
[₹ 77,000 × ₹ 2,00,000/ ₹ 7,00,000]		Prize Fund Investments	2,00,000	
Less: Cost of Prize awarded 20,000	2,02,000	General Reserve Fund		
School Hall Fund	1,50,000	Investment	2,00,000	7,00,000
Current Liabilities:		**Current Assets:**		
Salaries Payable	1,75,000	Bank Balance		4,63,000
	32,53,000			32,53,000

ILLUSTRATION 38

The following is the Receipts and Payments Account of the Social Club in respect of the year ended 31st March, 2016:

Receipts		₹	*Payments*	₹
To Balance b/d		10,250	By Salaries	20,800
To Subscriptions:			By Stationery	4,000
2014-2015	450		By Rates	6,000
2015-2016	21,100		By Telephone	1,000
2016-2017	750	22,300	By Investment	12,500
To Profit on sports meet		15,500	By Sundry expenses	9,250
To Income from investments		10,000	By Balance c/d	4,500
		58,050		58,050

The following additional information is provided to you:

(i) There are 450 members each paying an annual subscription of ₹ 50; ₹ 500 were in arrears for 2014-2015 as on 1st April, 2015.

(ii) On 31st March, 2016, the rates were prepaid to 30th June, 2016; the charge paid every year being ₹ 6,000.

(iii) There was an outstanding telephone bill for ₹ 350 on 31st March, 2016.

(iv) Outstanding sundry expenses as on 31st March, 2015 totalled ₹ 700.

(v) Stock of stationery on 31st March, 2015 was ₹ 500; on 31st March, 2016 it was ₹ 900.

(vi) On 31st March, 2015, building stood in the books at ₹ 1,00,000 and it was subject to depreciation at 5% per annum.

(vii) Investments on 31st March, 2015 stood at ₹ 2,00,000.

(viii) On 31st March, 2016 income accrued on investments purchased during the year amounted ₹ 375.

Required: Prepare an Income and Expenditure Account for the year ended 31st March, 2016 and the Balance Sheet as at that date.

SOLUTION

INCOME AND EXPENDITURE ACCOUNT
for the year ending on 31st March, 2016

Dr. Cr.

Expenditure	₹	*Income*	₹
To Salaries	20,800	By Subscriptions	22,500

To Stationery-Stock	500		By Profit on sports meet		15,500
Add: Purchases	4,000	4500	By Income on investments	10,000	
Less: Closing stock	900	3,600	*Add:* Income accrued	375	10,375
To Rates	6,000				
Less: Prepaid at the end	1,500	4,500			
Add: Prepaid in the beg.	1,500	6,000			
To Telephone	1,000				
Add: Outstanding at the end	350	1,350			
To Sundry Expenses	9,250				
Less: Outstanding in the beg.	700	8,550			
To Depreciation on Building		5,000			
To Surplus		3,075			
		48,375			48,375

BALANCE SHEET AS AT 31ST MARCH, 2016

Liabilities		₹	*Assets*		₹
Capital Fund	3,12,050		Outstanding Subscriptions		1,450
Add: Surplus	3,075	3,15,125	Investments (2,00,000 + 12,500)		2,12,500
Advance Subscription in		750	Building	1,00,000	
Outstanding telephone bill		350	*Less:* Depreciation	5,000	95,000
			Prepaid rates		1,500
			Stock of stationery		900
			Cash		4,500
			Income on investments accrued		375
		3,16,225			3,16,225

Working Notes:

Dr. **(I) SUBSCRIPTION ACCOUNT** Cr

Particulars	₹	*Particulars*	₹
To Outstanding Subscription A/c Beg.	500	By Cash A/c	22,300
To Income and Expenditure A/c (₹ 50 × 450)	22,500	By Outstanding Subscription A/c End. *(balancing figure)*	1,450
To Advance Subscription A/c	750		
	23,750		23,750

(II) BALANCE SHEET AS AT 31ST MARCH, 2015

Liabilities	₹	*Assets*	₹
Outstanding sundry expenses	700	Building	1,00,000
Capital Fund (Balancing figure)	3,12,050	Investments	2,00,000
		Stock of stationery	500

		Cash	10,250
		Prepaid rates	1,500
		Outstanding Subscriptions	500
	3,12,750		3,12,750

ILLUSTRATION 39*

From the following Receipts and Payments Account of Excellent Recreation Club for the year ended 31.3.2016 and additional information given, prepare an Income and Expenditure Account for the year ended 31.3.2016 and Balance Sheet as on 31.3.2016:

Receipts	₹	*Payments*	₹
Opening Balance:		Secretary's Salary	12,000
Cash in hand and at bank	3,180	Salaries to Staff	25,000
Subscription	18,000	Charities	1,000
Sale of Old Newspapers	2,500	Printing and Stationery	600
Legacies	4,000	Postage Expenses	120
Interest on Investments	2,000	Rates and Taxes	1,500
Endowment Fund Receipts	20,000	Upkeep of the Land	2,000
Proceeds of Sport and Concerts	4,020	Purchase of Sports Materials	10,000
Advertisement in the Year Book	5,000	Telephone Expenses	3,480
		Closing Balance:	
		Cash in hand and at bank	3,000
	58,700		58,700

Assets and Liabilities were as follows:

Particulars	*Opening* ₹	*Closing* ₹
Subscription in arrears	2,000	1,000
Subscription received in advance	500	400
Furniture	2,000	1,800
Land	10,000	10,000

Depreciation shall be charged at 10% p.a. under the diminishing value method. Legacies received shall be capitalised. Investments were made in Securities, the rate of interest being 12% p.a., the date of investment was 1.6.2014 and the amount of investments was ₹ 20,000. Due date of interest 31st March every year. Stock of sports materials on 31.3.2016 were useless and valued at NIL price

SOLUTION

INCOME AND EXPENDITURE ACCOUNT

Dr. *for the year ending on 31st March, 2016* *Cr.*

Expenditure	₹	*Income*		₹
To Secretary's salary	12,000	By Subscription		17,100
To Salaries to staff	25,000	By Sale of old newspapers		2,500
To Charities	1,000	By Interest on securities	2,000	

To Printing and stationary	600	*Add:* Amount due 400	2,400
To Postage expenses	120	By Proceeds of sport and concerts	4,020
To Rates & Taxes	1,500	By Advertisement in the Year Book	5,000
To Upkeep of Land	2,000	By Deficit, Excess of	
To Sports materials written off	10,000	Expenditure over Income	24,880
To Telephone expenses	3,480		
To Depreciation on furniture	200		
	55,900		55,900

BALANCE SHEET OF EXCELLENT RECREATION CLUB AS AT 31ST MARCH, 2016

Liabilities	₹	₹	*Assets*	₹	₹
Capital Fund:			Land		10,000
Opening balance	36,680		Furniture	2,000	
Less: Deficit.	24,880		*Less:* Depreciation	200	1,800
Add: Legacies	4,000	15,800	Sports Materials	10,000	
Endowment Fund		20,000	*Less:* Written off	10,000	—
Advance Subscription		400	Investment in Securities		20,000
			Outstanding Subscriptions		1,000
			Interest Due		400
			Cash in hand and at Bank		3,000
		36,200			36,200

Working Notes:

(I) BALANCE SHEET OF EXCELLENT RECREATION CLUB AS AT 31ST MARCH, 2015

Liabilities	₹	*Assets*	₹
Capital (*Balancing Figure*)	36,680	Land	10,000
Advance Subscription	500	Furniture	2,000
		Investments in Securities	20,000
		Outstanding Subscription	2,000
		Cash in hand and at Bank	3,180
	37,180		37,180

Dr. **(II) SUBSCRIPTION ACCOUNT** *Cr.*

Particulars	₹	*Particulars*	₹
To Outstanding Subscription A/c	2,000	By Advance Subscription A/c	500
To Income & Expenditure A/c (b/f)	17,100	By Bank A/c	18,000
To Advance Subscription A/c	400	By Outstanding Subscription A/c	1,000
	19,500		19,500

ILLUSTRATION 40

The Accountant of Diana Club furnishes you the following Receipts and Payments account for the year ending 31st March, 2016:

Receipts	₹	*Payments*	₹
Opening Balance:		Honoraria to Secretary	9,600
Cash and Bank	16,760	Misc. Expenses	3,060
Subscriptions	21,420	Rates and Taxes	2,520
Sale of Old Newspapers	4,800	Groundman's Wages	1,680
Entertainment Fees	8,540	Printing and Stationery	940
Bank Interest	460	Telephone Expenses	4,780
Bar Receipts	14,900	Payment for Bar Purchases	11,540
		Repairs	640
		New car (Less-sale Proceeds of Old Car ₹ 6,000)	25,200
		Closing Balance:	
		Cash and Bank	6,920
	66,880		66,880

Additional Informations:

Particulars	*Opening* ₹	*Closing* ₹
(i) Subscription due (not received)	2,400	1,960
(ii) Cheques issued, but not presented for payment of printing	180	60
(iii) Club premises at cost	58,000	—
(iv) Depreciation on club premises provided so far	37,600	—
(v) Car at cost	24,380	—
(vi) Depreciation on car	20,580	—
(vii) Value of Bar stock	1,420	1,740
(viii) Amount unpaid for bar purchases	1,180	860

(ix) Depreciation is to be provided @ 5% p.a. on the written down value of the club premises and @ 15% p.a. on car for the whole year.

Required: Prepare an Income and Expenditure account of Diana Club for the year ending 31st March, 2016 and Balance Sheet as on that date.

SOLUTION

INCOME AND EXPENDITURE ACCOUNT

for the year ended 31st March, 2016

Dr. Cr.

Expenditure	₹	*Income*	₹
To Honoraria to Secretary	9,600	By Subscriptions	20,980
To Misc. Expenses	3,060	By Sale of Old Newspapers	4,800
To Rates and Taxes	2,520	By Entertainment Fees	8,540
To Groundman's Wages	1,680	By Bank Interest	460
To Printing and Stationary	940	By Bar Receipts	14,900

To Telephone Expenses		4,780	By Profit on Sale of Car	2,200
To Bar Expenses Opening Bar Stock	1,420			
Add: Purchases	11,220			
Less: Closing Bar Stock	1,740	10,900		
To Repairs		640		
To Depreciation:				
Club Premises	1,020			
Car	4,680	5,700		
To Surplus t/f to Capital Fund		12,060		
		51,880		51,880

BALANCE SHEET AS AT 31ST MARCH, 2016

Liabilities		₹	*Assets*	₹
Capital Fund			Club Premises	19,380
Opening Balance	43,600		Car	26,520
Add: Excess of Income			Bar Stock	1,740
over Expenditure	12,060	55,660	Outstanding Subscription	1,960
Outstanding Liabilities for			Cash and Bank	6,920
Bar Purchases		860		
		56,520		56,520

Working Note:

(I) BALANCE SHEET OF DIANA CLUB

as at 31st March, 2015

Liabilities	₹	*Assets*		₹
Amount Due for Bar Purchases	1,180	Club Premises	58,000	
Capital Fund on 1.10.2002	43,600	*Less:* Depreciation	37,600	20,400
(Balancing Figure)		Car	24,380	
		Less: Depreciation	20,580	3,800
		Bar Stock		1,420
		Outstanding Subscription		2,400
		Cash and Bank		16,760
	44,780			44,780

(II) CALCULATION OF BAR PURCHASES FOR THE YEAR

Particulars	₹
A. Bar payments as per receipts and payments account	11,540
B. *Add:* Amount due at the end	860
C. *Less:* Amount due in the beginning	(1,180)
	11,220

(III) CALCULATION OF SUBSCRIPTIONS ACCRUED DURING THE YEAR

	Particulars	₹
A.	Subscriptions received	21,420
B.	*Add:* Outstanding at the end	1,960
C.	*Less:* Outstanding at the beginning	(2,400)
		20,980

(IV) DEPRECIATION ON CLUB PREMISES AND W.D.V

	Particulars	₹
A.	Written down value on 1st April (58,000 – 37,600)	20,400
B.	*Less:* Depreciation for the year @ 5% p.a.	(1,020)
		19,380

(V) CALCULATION OF PROFIT ON SALE OF CAR

	Particulars		₹
A.	Sale Proceeds of old car		6,000
B.	*Less:* Written down value of old car:		
	Cost of car	24,380	
	Less: Depreciation	20,580	3,800
			2,200

(VI) DEPRECIATION ON CAR AND WRITTEN DOWN VALUE

	Particulars	₹
A.	Cost of new car purchased (25,200 + 6,000)	31,200
B.	*Less:* Depreciation for the year @ 15% p.a.	4,680
C.	Written down value	26,520

Note: The opening and closing balance of cash and bank shown in the Receipts and Payments Account (given in the question), include the bank balance as per cash book. Therefore, no adjustment has been made in the above solution on account of cheques issued, but not presented for payment of printing.

19.0 PRACTICAL STEPS INVOLVED IN THE PREPARATION OF A RECEIPTS AND PAYMENTS ACCOUNT FROM AN INCOME AND EXPENDITURE ACCOUNT

The practical steps involved in the preparation of a Receipts & Payments Account from an Income & Expenditure Account are given below:

Step 1: *Ascertain the opening Cash and Bank balances (or Bank Overdraft) from the additional information or from the opening Balances Sheet (if available) and show the Cash and Bank Balance on the debit side and Bank Overdraft on the credit side of Receipts & Payments account.*

Step 2: *Ascertain 'Revenue Receipts' (e.g. Subscription) received during the current accounting period as under and show on the debit side of Receipts & Payments Account:*

Particulars			₹
A. Revenue Income for the current year			xxx
B. *Add:*	(a) Outstanding income in the beginning of current year	xxx	
	(b) Advance income at the end of current year	xxx	xxx
C. *Less:*	(a) Outstanding income at the end of current year	xxx	
	(b) Advance income in the beginning of current year	xxx	xxx
D. Revenue Receipts during the current year (A + B – C)			xxx

Step 3: *Ascertain revenue Payments' (e.g. rent) made during the current accounting period as under and show on the credit side of Receipts & Payments Account.*

Particulars			₹
A. Revenue Expenses for the current year			xxx
B. *Add:*	(a) Outstanding expenses in the beginning of current year	xxx	
	(b) Prepaid expenses at the end of current year	xxx	
C. *Less:*	(a) Outstanding expenses at the end of current year	xxx	
	(b) Prepaid expenses in the beginning of current year	xxx	xxx
D. Revenue payments during the current year (A + B – C)			xxx

Step 4: *Ascertain all capital receipts (e.g. Life Membership Fees/Entrance Fees) and capital payments (e.g. purchase of fixed assets) from the additional information or Balance Sheets (if available) or by preparing the Accounts of Capital Items such as fixed assets, special funds and show the capital receipts on the debit side and the capital payments on the credit side of the Receipts & Payments account.*

Step 5: *Calculate the difference between the total of debit side and the total of credit side. If the total of debit side exceeds the total of credit side, show the Cash balance (if the Bank Balance is given) or the Bank Balance (if the Cash Balance is given) on the credit side of the Receipts & Payments Account. If the total of credit side exceeds the total of debit side, show the Bank Overdraft on the debit side of Receipts & Payments Account.*

Tutorial Note: *The following items appearing in the Income & Expenditure Account are not shown in the Receipts & Payments Account:*

(a) Non-Cash items (e.g. Depreciation, Loss on sale of a fixed asset) (b) Outstanding or Prepaid Expenses (c) Accrued or Unaccrued Incomes (d) Surplus or Deficit.

ILLUSTRATION 41 [SUBSCRIPTION RECEIVED]

(a) Income from Subscription for the year 2015-2016 ₹ 60,000. Compute the Subscription received during the year 2015-2016.

(b) Income from Subscription for the year 2015-2016 ₹ 90,000. Subscription ₹ 30,000 is still outstanding. Compute the Subscription received during the year 2015-2016.

(c) Income from Subscription for the year 2015-2016 ₹ 40,000. Subscription ₹ 20,000 received in advance for the year 2015-2016. Compute the Subscription received during the year 2015-2016.

(d) Income from Subscription for the year 2015-2016 ₹ 20,000. Subscription ₹ 40,000 was outstanding at the end of the previous year. Compute the Subscription received during the year 2015-2016.

(e) Income from Subscription for the year 2015-2016 ₹ 1,50,000. Subscription ₹ 90,000 was received in advance at the end of the previous year. Compute the Subscription received during the year 2015-2016

SOLUTION

COMPUTATION OF SUBSCRIPTION RECEIVED

Particulars	*(a)*	*(b)*	*(c)*	*(d)*	*(e)*
Subscription Income	60,000	90,000	40,000	20,000	1,50,000
Less: O/s at the end	–	(30,000)	–	–	–
Add: Advance at the end	–	–	20,000	–	–
Less: Advance in the beg.	–	–	–	–	(90,000)
Add: O/s in the beg.	–	–	–	40,000	–
Subscription Received	**60,000**	**60,000**	**60,000**	**60,000**	**60,000**

ILLUSTRATION 42

Compute the Subscription received during the year 2015-2016 from the following particulars relating to a club:

Particulars	*1.4.2015*	*31.3.2016*
Outstanding Subscription	₹ 9,500	₹ 7,000
Advance Subscription	₹ 2,800	₹ 5,200

Subscription income for the year 2015-2016, ₹ 1,44,000, Subscriptions of ₹ 1,000 are still in arrears for the year 2015-2016.

SOLUTION

(a) In Statement Form:

COMPUTATION OF SUBSCRIPTION RECEIVED

Particulars	₹	₹
A. Subscription Income for the year		1,44,000
B. *Less:* (a) Outstanding Subscription at the end	7,000	
(b) Advance Subscription at the beginning	2,800	(9,800)
C. *Add:* (a) Outstanding Subscription at the beginning	9,500	
(b) Advance Subscription at the end	5,200	14,700
D. Subscription received (A + B – C)		1,48,900

(b) In Account Form:

Dr. **SUBSCRIPTION ACCOUNT** *Cr.*

Particulars	₹	*Particulars*	₹
To Outstanding Subscription A/c (in the beginning)	9,500	By Advance Subscription A/c (in the beginning)	2,800
To Income & Expenditure A/c	1,44,000	By Bank A/c (balancing figure)	1,48,900
To Advance Subscription A/c	5,200	By Outstanding Subscription A/c (at the end)	7,000
	1,58,700		1,58,700

(c) In Equation Form:

$$SR = S_1 - OS_2 - AS_1 + OS_1 + AS_2$$
$$= ₹\ 1,44,000 - ₹\ 7,000 - ₹\ 2,800 + ₹\ 9,500 + ₹\ 5,200 = ₹\ 1,48,900$$

Where, S_1 = Subscription Income, SR = Subscription Received,
OS_2 = Outstanding Subscription at the end,
AS_1 = Advance Subscription in the beginning,
OS_1 = Outstanding Subscription in the beginning,
AS_2 = Advance Subscription at the end.

ILLUSTRATION 43

(a) Salaries for the year 2015-2016 ₹ 60,000. Compute Salaries paid during the year 2015-2016.

(b) Salaries for the year 2015-2016 ₹ 90,000. Salaries ₹ 30,000 is still outstanding. Compute Salaries paid during the year 2015-2016.

(c) Salaries for the year 2015-2016 ₹ 40,000. Salaries ₹ 20,000 paid in advance for the year 2015-2016. Compute Salaries paid during the year 2015-2016.

(d) Salaries for the year 2015-2016 ₹ 20,000. Salaries ₹ 40,000 was outstanding at the end of the previous year. Compute Salaries paid during the year 2015-2016.

(e) Salaries for the year 2015-2016 ₹ 1,50,000. Salaries ₹ 90,000 was paid in advance at the end of the previous year. Compute Salaries paid during the year 2015-2016.

SOLUTION

COMPUTATION OF SALARIES PAID DURING THE CURRENT YEAR

Particulars	*(a)*	*(b)*	*(c)*	*(d)*	*(e)*
Salaries for the year	60,000	90,000	40,000	20,000	1,50,000
Less: O/s at the end	–	(30,000)	–	–	–
Add: Advance at the end	–	–	20,000	–	–
Less: Advance in the beg.	–	–	–	–	(90,000)
Add: O/s in the beg.	–	–	–	40,000	–
Salaries Paid	**60,000**	**60,000**	**60,000**	**60,000**	**60,000**

ILLUSTRATION 44

Compute the Salaries paid during the year 2015-2016 from the following information:

Particulars	*1.4.2015*	*31.3.2016*
Outstanding Salaries	₹ 9,500	₹ 7,000
Prepaid Salaries	₹ 2,800	₹ 5,200
Salaries for the year 2015-2016 ₹ 1,44,000		

SOLUTION

Dr. **SALARIES ACCOUNT** Cr.

Particulars	₹	Particulars	₹
To Prepaid Salaries A/c (in the beginning)	2,800	By Outstanding Salaries A/c (in the beginning)	9,500
To Bank A/c (balancing figure)	1,48,900	By Income & Expenditure A/c	1,44,000
To Outstanding Salaries A/c (at the end)	7,000	By Prepaid Salaries A/c (at the end)	5,200
	1,58,700		1,58,700

ILLUSTRATION 45

From the following Income & Expenditure Account, prepare the Receipts & Payments Account for the year 2015-2016:

Dr. **INCOME & EXPENDITURE ACCOUNT** Cr.

Expenditure		₹	Income		₹
To Loss on Sale of Sports Material			By Subscription:		
[Book value ₹ 500]		300	Received	10,000	
To Rent:			*Add:* O/s at the end	4,000	
Paid	6,000		*Add:* Advance in the beg.	3,000	
Add: O/s at the end	1,500		*Less:* O/s in the beg.	6,000	
Less: O/s in the beg.	3,000	4,500	*Less:* Advance at the end	2,000	9,000
To Insurance Premium:			By Entrance Fees		6,000
Paid	6,000		(40% capitalised)		
Add: Prepaid in the beginning	1,500		By Life Membership Fees		
Less: Prepaid at the end	3,000	4,500	(60% capitalised)		4,000
To Sports Materials	4,000		By General Donations		10,000
Add: Opening Stock	2,000		By Locker Rent:		
Less: Closing Stock	1,000	5,000	Received	4,000	
To Newspapers & Periodicals		1,200	*Add:* Outstanding at the end	3,000	
To Dep. @ 10% on old Building		3,000	*Less:* Advance at the end	1,000	6,000
To Depreciation @ 10% on			By Interest on 12%		
New Furniture			General Fund Investments:		
(Purchased on 1.4.2015)		1,000	Received	10,000	
To Salaries		4,500	*Add:* Accrued	2,000	12,000
To Surplus		30,000	By Sale of Newspapers		100
			By Income from Charity Show:		
			Charity Show Proceeds	10,900	
			Less: Show Expenses	4,000	6,900
		54,000			54,000

Note: Cash Balance as on 1.4.2015 and on 31.3.2016 ₹ 500 and ₹ 32,000 respectively. Bank Balance as on 1.4.2015 ₹ 1,000.

SOLUTION

RECEIPTS & PAYMENTS ACCOUNT
Dr. *for the year ending 31st March, 2016* Cr.

Receipts	₹	Payments	₹
To Balance b/d		By Rent	6,000
Cash	500	By Insurance Premium	6,000
Bank	1,000	By Sports Materials Purchased	4,000
To Subscription	10,000	By Newspapers & Periodicals	1,200
To Entrance Fees [₹ 6,000/.60]	10,000	By Furniture [₹ 1,000/.10]	10,000
To Life Materialship Fees [₹ 4,000/.40]	10,000	By Salaries	4,500
To General Donations	10,000	By Charity Show Expenses	4,000
To Locker Rent	4,000	By Balance c/d:	
To Interest on 10% General Fund		Cash	32,000
Investment	10,000		
To Sale of Newspapers	100		
To Proceeds of Charity Show	10,900		
To Sale of Sports Materials			
[₹ 500 – ₹ 300]	200		
To Balance c/d:			
[Bank overdraft] (Balancing Figure)	1,000		
	67,700		67,700

ILLUSTRATION 46

Jalan Cricket Club provides you the following formation:

INCOME & EXPENDITURE ACCOUNT
Dr. *for the year ended 31st March, 2016* Cr.

Expenditure	₹	Income		₹
To Remuneration to coach	18,000	By Donation and Subscription		1,00,000
To Salaries and Wages	24,000	By Bar Room:		
To Rent	23,000	Receipts	24,000	
To Miscellaneous expenses	7,000	*Less:* Expenses	20,000	4,000
To Honorarium to Secretary	18,000	By Bank Interest		2,000
To Depreciation on Equipment	5,000	By Hire-Club-Hall		14,000
To Surplus	25,000			
	1,20,000			1,20,000

BALANCE SHEETS

Particulars	31.3.2015 ₹	31.3.2016 ₹
Capital Fund	48,000	48,000
Add: Entrance Fees		10,000
Add: Surplus		25,000
Subscription in advance	4,000	3,000
Miscellaneous expenses	5,500	5,000
Salaries & Wages	—	1,000
Honorarium to Secretary	1,000	
Equipment	25,000	20,000
Outstanding subscription	6,000	6,000
Cash in hand	4,000	2,000
Cash at bank	2,500	10,000
Fixed Deposit	20,000	50,000
Accrued Hire charges of Club Hall	—	2,000
Prepaid Rent	1,000	2,000

Required: Prepare the Receipts & Payments Account of the Club for the year ended March 31, 2016

SOLUTION

RECEIPTS & PAYMENTS ACCOUNT OF JALAN CRICKET CLUB

Dr. *for the year ending on 31st March, 2016* Cr.

Receipts	₹	Payments	₹
To Balance b/d:		By remuneration to Cash	18,000
Cash in hand	4,000	By Rent	24,000
Cash at bank	2,500	By Miscellaneous Expenses	7,500
To Donations & Subscriptions	99,000	By Salaries & wages	23,000
To Entrance Fees	10,000	By Honorarium to Secretary	19,000
To Bar Receipts	24,000	By Fixed deposits	30,000
To Bank Interest	2,000	By Bar expenses	20,000
To Hire of Club Hall	12,000	By balance c/d	
		Cash in hand	2,000
		Cash at bank	10,000
	1,53,500		1,53,500

Working Notes:

Dr. **(I) DONATIONS AND SUBSCRIPTIONS ACCOUNT** Cr.

Particulars	₹	Particulars	₹
To Balance b/d	6,000	By Balance b/d	4,000
To Income & Expenditure A/c	1,00,000	By Bank A/c (balancing figure)	99,000
To Balance c/d	3,000	By Balance c/d	6,000
	1,09,000		1,09,000

Dr. **(II) MISCELLANEOUS EXPENSES ACCOUNT** Cr.

Particulars	₹	Particulars	₹
To Bank A/c (balancing figure)	7,500	By balance b/d	5,500
To Balance c/d	5,000	By Income & Expenditure a/c	7,000
	12,500		12,500

Dr. **(III) SALARIES AND WAGES ACCOUNT** Cr.

Particulars	₹	Particulars	₹
To Bank A/c (balancing figure)	23,000	By Income & Expenditure A/c	24,000
To Balance c/d	1,000		
	24,000		24,000

Dr. **(IV) HONORARIUM TO SECRETARY ACCOUNT** Cr.

Particulars	₹	Particulars	₹
To Bank A/c (balancing figure)	19,000	By Balance b/d	1,000
		By Income & Expenditure A/c	18,000
	19,000		19,000

Dr. **(V) RENT ACCOUNT** Cr.

Particulars	₹	Particulars	₹
To Balance b/d	1,000	By Income & Expenditure A/c	23,000
To Bank A/c (balancing figure)	24,000	By Balance c/d	2,000
	25,000		25,000

Dr. **(VI) CLUB HALL HIRE CHARGES ACCOUNT** Cr.

Particulars	₹	Particulars	₹
To Income & Expenditure A/c	14,000	By Bank A/c (balancing figure)	12,000
		By Balance c/d	2,000
	14,000		14,000

ILLUSTRATION 47

The Lok Kalyan Dispensary had the following:

INCOME AND EXPENDITURE ACCOUNT
for the year ending on 31st March, 2016

Expenditure	₹	Income	₹
Salaries	23,500	Subscriptions	25,000
Surgery & Dispensary	3,000	Interest	9,000
Rent and Taxes	500	Donations	4,000
Insurance	200	Miscellaneous Receipts	300
Office expenses	800		

Depreciation:				
Building	3,750			
Furniture	120			
Instruments	100	3,970		
Surplus		6,330		
		38,300		38,300

Information:

Particulars	*31.03.2015*	*31.03.2016*
Cash in hand and at bank	?	18,700
4.5% Tax free Government securities (Face value ₹ 2,00,000)	1,80,000	1,80,000
Subscription outstanding	7,000	10,000
Subscription received in advance	200	600
Salaries unpaid	1,000	1,500
Furniture	2,000	1,980
Land & Buildings	1,00,000	96,250
Instruments	3,500	3,900
Surgery expenses due	200	300
Stock of medicines	300	100

Prepare Receipts and Payments Account for 2015-2016 and also the Balance Sheet.

SOLUTION

RECEIPTS AND PAYMENTS ACCOUNT
for the year ending on 31st March, 2016

Dr. Cr.

Receipts	₹	*Payments*	₹
To Balance b/d		By Salaries	23,000
Cash in hand and at bank		By Surgery and Dispensary:	2,700
(balancing figure)	10,800	By Rent & taxes	500
To Subscriptions:	22,400	By Insurance	200
To Interest	9,000	By Office expenses	800
To Donation	4,000	By Instruments bought	500
To Miscellaneous receipts	300	By Furniture bought	100
		Cash in hand and at bank	18,700
	46,500		46,500

BALANCE SHEET AS AT 31ST MARCH, 2016

Liabilities		₹	*Assets*		₹
Capital Fund:			Land and Building	1,00,000	
Opening Balance	3,02,200		*Less:* Depreciation	3,750	96,250
Add: Surplus	6,330	3,08,530	Instruments		3,900

Subscriptions received in advance	600	Furniture	1,980
Salaries outstanding	1,500	Govt. Securities	1,80,000
Surgery expenses due	300	Stock of medicines	100
		Subscriptions outstanding	10,000
		Cash in hand and at bank	18,700
	3,10,930		3,10,930

Working Notes

(I) BALANCE SHEET AS AT 31ST MARCH, 2015

Liabilities	₹	*Assets*	₹
Subscriptions received in advance	200	Cash in hand and at bank	10,800
Salaries unpaid	1,000	Govt. Securities	1,80,000
Surgery expenses due	200	Subscriptions outstanding	7,000
Capital Fund (balancing figure)	3,02,200	Furniture	2,000
		Land and Buildings	1,00,000
		Instruments	3,500
		Stock of medicines	300
	3,03,600		3,03,600

Dr. **(II) SUBSCRIPTION ACCOUNT** *Cr.*

Particulars	₹	*Particulars*	₹
To Balance b/d (O/s in the beg.)	7,000	By Balance b/d	
To Income and Expenditure A/c	25,000	(O/s Advance in the beg.)	200
To Balance c/d (Advance at the end)	600	By Bank A/c (b.f.)	22,400
		By Balance c/d (O/s at the end)	10,000
	32,600		32,600

Dr. **(III) SALARIES ACCOUNT** *Cr.*

Particulars	₹	*Particulars*	₹
To Bank A/c (b.f.)	23,000	By Salaries Outstanding A/c (beg.)	1,000
To Salaries outstanding A/c (end)	1,500	By Income and Expenditure A/c	23,500
	24,500		24,500

Dr. **(IV) STOCK OF MEDICINES ACCOUNT** *Cr.*

Particulars	₹	*Particulars*	₹
To Balance b/d	300	By Income & Expenditure A/c	3,000
To Creditors for medicine etc.		By Balance c/d	100
(Purchases)	2,800		
	3,100		3,100

Dr. **(V) CREDITORS FOR MEDICINES ETC. ACCOUNT** Cr.

Particulars	₹	*Particulars*	₹
To Bank A/c (b.f)	2,700	By Balance b/d	200
To Balance c/d	300	By Stock of Medicine A/c	
		(Cr. Purchases)	2,800
	3,000		3,000

Dr. **(VI) INSTRUMENTS ACCOUNT** Cr.

Particulars	₹	*Particulars*	₹
To Balance b/d	3,500	By Depreciation A/c	100
To Bank A/c (Purchases) (b.f.)	500	By Balance c/d	3,900
	4,000		4,000

Dr. **(VII) FURNITURE ACCOUNT** Cr.

Particulars	₹	*Particulars*	₹
To Balance b/d	2,000	By Depreciation A/c	120
To Bank A/c (b.f.)	100	By Balance c/d	1,980
	2,100		2,100

ILLUSTRATION 48

Following is the Income and Expenditure Account of Victoria Club for the year ending 31st March, 2016:

Expenditure		₹	*Income*		₹
To Salaries & Wages		19,000	By Subscription		30,000
To Misc. Expenses			By Entrance Fees received		1,000
(including Insurance)		2,000	By Annual Sports Income		
To Audit fees		1,000	Receipts	6,000	
To Chief Executives' Honorarium		4,000	*Less:* Expenses	3,000	3,000
To Printing & Stationery		1,800			
To Annual day					
Celebration Exp.	6,000				
Less: Donation	4,000	2,000			
To Interest on Bank loan		600			
To Dep. on Sports Equipment		1,200			
To Excess of Income over Expen.		2,400			
		34,000			34,000

Additional Information:

Particulars	*Opening* ₹	*Closing* ₹
(i) Subscription outstanding	2,400	3,000
(ii) Subscription received in advance	1,800	1,080
(iii) Salaries outstanding	1,600	1,800
(iv) Sports equipment (after deducting depreciation)	10,400	10,800
(v) Prepaid Insurance	—	240
(vi) Cash in Hand	?	6,400

(vi) The Club owned a Sports' ground of ₹ 40,000

(vii) The Club took a loan of ₹ 8,000 from a bank during the year 2014-2015, which was not paid in 2015-2016.

(viii) Audit fee of 2015-2016 was outstanding, but Audit fees of ₹ 800 for 2014-2015 was paid in 2015-2016.

Prepare Receipts and Payments Account for the year ending 31st March, 2016 and a Balance Sheet on that date.

SOLUTION

VICTORIA CLUB
RECEIPT AND PAYMENT ACCOUNT
for the year ended 31st March, 2016

Dr. *Cr.*

Receipts		₹	*Payments*		₹
To Balance b/d		5,560	By Salaries & wages		
To Donation for Annual Day		4,000	for current year	19,000	
To Subscription			+ O/s into beg.	1,600	
for current year	30,000		– O/s at the end	1,800	18,800
+ O/s in the beg.	2,400		By Misc. expenses		
– O/s at the end	3,000		for current year	2,000	
+ Advance at the end	1,080		+ Prepaid at the end	240	2,240
– Advance in the beg.	1,800	28,680	By Audit fees for current year	1,000	
To Entrance fees		1,000	+ O/s in the beg.	800	
To Annual sports receipts		6,000	– O/s at the end	1,000	800
			By Chief Executive's Honorarium		4,000
			By Printing & Stationery		1,800
			By Annual Day Expenses		6,000
			By Interest on Bank Loan		600
			By Annual Sport Expenses		3,000
			By Sports Equipment		1,600
			By Balance c/d		6,400
		45,240			45,240

BALANCE SHEET AS AT 31ST MARCH, 2016

Liabilities		₹	*Assets*		₹
Capital fund:			Sports Ground		40,000
Opening Balance	46,160		Sports equipment		
Add: Surplus	2,400	48,560	Opening balance	10,400	
Loan from Bank		8,000	*Add:* Addition	1,600	
Subscription received in advance		1,080	*Less:* Depreciation	1,200	10,800
Salaries outstanding		1,800	Subscription Outstanding		3,000
Audit fees outstanding		1,000	Prepaid Insurance		240
			Cash		6,400
		60,440			60,440

Working Notes:

Dr. **(I) SPORTS EQUIPMENT ACCOUNT** *Cr.*

Particulars	₹	*Particulars*	₹
To Balance b/d	10,400	By Depreciation A/c	1,200
To Cash A/c (b/f)	1,600	By Balance b/d	10,800
	12,000		12,000

(II) OPENING BALANCE SHEET AS AT 31.3.2015

Liabilities	₹	*Assets*	₹
Loan from Bank	8,000	Sports ground	40,000
Subscription received in advance	1,800	Sports equipment	10,400
Salaries outstanding	1,600	Subscription outstanding	2,400
Audit fees o/s	800	Cash	5,560
Capital fund (b/f)	46,160		
	58,360		58,360

ILLUSTRATION 49

The Income and Expenditure Account of City Sports Club for the year ended 31st March, 2016 was as follows:

Expenditure	₹	*Income*	₹
To Salaries	1,20,000	By Subscriptions	1,60,000
To Printing and Stationery	6,000	By Entrance Fees	10,000
To Rent	12,000	By Contribution for Annual dinner	20,000
To Repairs	10,000	By Profit on Annual Sports meet	20,000
To Sundry Expenses	8,000		
To Annual Dinner Expenses	30,000		
To Interest to Bank	6,000		
To Depreciation of Sports equipment	6,000		
To Surplurs	12,000		
	2,10,000		**2,10,000**

The above account had been prepared after the following adjustments:

Particulars	₹
Subscriptions outstanding in the beg.	12,000
Subscriptions received in advance in the beg.	9,000
Subscriptions received in advance at the end.	5,400
Subscriptions outstanding at the end.	15,000

Salaries outstanding at the beginning and at the end of the financial year were ₹ 8,000 and ₹ 10,000 respectively. Sundry expenses included prepaid insurance expenses of ₹ 1,200.

The Club owned a freehold ground valued ₹ 2,00,000. The Club has sports equipment on 01.04.2008 valued at ₹ 52,000. At the end of the year, after depreciation, the sports equipment amounted to ₹ 54,000. The Club raised a loan of ₹ 40,000 from a bank on 01.01.2015, which was unpaid till 31.03.2016. On 31.03.2016, cash in hand was ₹ 32,000.

Required: Prepare Receipts and Payments account of the Club for the year ended 31st March, 2016 and Balance Sheet as on that date.

SOLUTION

Dr. **RECEIPT AND PAYMENTS ACCOUNT FOR THE YEAR ENDED 31ST MARCH, 2016** *Cr.*

Receipts	*(₹)*	*Payments*	*(₹)*
To Balance b/d (Bal. Fig.)	27,800	By Salaries:	
To Subscription:		for 2014-2015	8,000
for 2014-2015	12,000	for 2015-2016	1,10,000
for 2015-2016	1,36,000	By Printing & Stationery	6,000
for 2016-2017	5,400	By Rend	12,000
To Entrance Fees	10,000	By Repairs	10,000
To Contribution for Annual Dinner	20,000	By Sundry Expenses (8,000 + 1,200)	9,200
To Profit on Annual Sports Meet	20,000*	By Annual Dinner Expenses	30,000
		By Interest to Bank	6,000
		By Sports Equipment	8,000
		By Balance c/d	32,000
	2,31,200		**2,31,200**

BALANCE SHEET AS AT 31ST MARCH, 2016

Liabilities	*(₹)*	*(₹)*	*Assets*	*(₹)*	*(₹)*
Capital Fund	2,34,800		Freehold Ground		2,00,000
Add: Surplus	12,000	2,46,800	Sports Equipment	52,000	
Bank Loan		40,000	*Add:* Additions	8,000	
Outstanding Salaries		10,000		**60,000**	
Subscription in Advance		5,400	*Less:* Depreciation	(6,000)	54,000
			Subscription in Arrear		15,000
			Prepaid Insurance		1,200
			Cash in Hand		32,000
		3,02,200			**3,02,200**

Working Notes:

(I) BALANCE SHEET AS AT 31ST MARCH, 2015

Liabilities	₹	*Assets*	₹
Capital Fund (Bal. Fig.)	2,34,800	Freehold Ground	2,00,000
Bank Loan	40,000	Sports Equipment	52,000
Outstanding Salaries	8,000	Subscription in Arrear	12,000
Subscription in Advance	9,000	Cash in hand	27,800
	2,91,800		2,91,800

Dr. **(II) SPORTS EQUIPMENT ACCOUNT** Cr.

Particulars	₹	*Particulars*	₹
To Balance b/d	52,000	By Depreciation A/c	6,000
To Bank A/c	8,000	By Balance c/d	54,000
	60,000		60,000

Dr. **(III) SUBSCRIPTION ACCOUNT** Cr.

Particulars	₹	*Particulars*	₹
To Income & Exp. A/c	1,60,000	By Advance Subscription A/c	9,000
		By Bank A/c	1,36,000
		By O/s Subscription A/c	15,000
	1,60,000		1,60,000

20.0 PRACTICAL STEPS INVOLVED IN THE PREPARATION OF A BALANCE SHEET FROM RECEIPTS AND PAYMENTS ACCOUNT AND INCOME AND EXPENDITURE ACCOUNT

The practical steps involved in the preparation of a Balance sheet are shown below:

Step 1: *Open only one account for each of the various items given in Receipts & Payments Account, Income & Expenditure Account and additional information avoiding duplication (i.e. no account should be opened twice).*

Step 2: *Post the following items in various ledger accounts as under:*

(a) Receipts shown on the debit side of Receipts & Payments Account	*Show on the credit side of respective account*
(b) Payments shown on the credit side of Receipts & Payments Account	*Show on the debit side of respective account*
(c) Revenue Expenses and losses shown on the debit side of Income	*Show on the credit side of respective account*
(d) Revenue Incomes shown on the credit side of Income & expenditure Account account	*Show on the debit side of respective account*

Step 3: *Calculate the difference between the total of debit side and the total of credit side of each account. Show the difference as Opening Balance (if the credit side exceeds the debit side) or as Closing Balance (if the debit side exceeds the credit side).*

Step 4: *Prepare Opening Balance Sheet on the basis of opening Balances (including opening cash and Bank Balances) and Closing Balance Sheet on the basis of Closing Balances (including Closing Cash and Bank Balances).*

Tutorial Note: *Expenses paid for the current year and Income received for the current year will not appear in the Balance Sheet.*

ILLUSTRATION 50

Taking the same information as given in Illustration 45, prepare Opening and Closing Balance Sheets:

SOLUTION

BALANCE SHEET AS AT 31ST MARCH, 2015

Liabilities	₹	*Assets*	₹
Outstanding Rent	3,000	Building [₹ 3,000/.10]	30,000
Advance Subscription	3,000	Stock of Sports Materials	
Capital Fund (Balancing Figure)	1,35,500	[₹ 500 + ₹ 2,000]	2,500
		Prepaid Insurance	1,500
		Outstanding Subscription	6,000
		12% General Fund Investments	1,00,000
		[₹ 12,000/.12]	
		Cash Balance	500
		Bank Balance	1,000
	1,41,500		1,41,500

BALANCE SHEET AS AT 31ST MARCH, 2016

Liabilities		₹	*Assets*		₹
Outstanding Rent		1,500	Building		
Advance Subscription		2,000	Book Value	30,000	
Advance Locker Rent		1,000	*Less:* Depreciation	3,000	27,000
Bank Overdraft		1,000	Furniture [Cost [₹ 1,000/.10]	10,000	
Capital Fund:			*Less:* Depreciation	1,000	9,000
Opening Balance	1,35,500		Stock of Sports Materials		1,000
Add: Entrance Fees			Prepaid Insurance		3,000
[6,000 × 4/.6]	4,000		Outstanding Subscription		4,000
Add: Life Membership Fees			Outstanding Locker Rent		3,000
[₹ 4,000 × 6/.4]	6,000		12% General Fund Investments		1,00,000
Add: Surplus	30,000	1,75,500	Accrued Interest on 12% General		
			Fund Investments		2,000
			Cash Balance		32,000
		1,81,000			1,81,000

ILLUSTRATION 51

The following particulars relate to a sports club's Income & Expenditure Account for the year ended 31st March, 2016:

Dr. **INCOME & EXPENDITURE ACCOUNT** *Cr.*

Expenditure	₹	*Income*	₹
To Salaries	1,500	By Entrance Fees	10,100
To Printing and Stationery	2,200	By Subscriptions	15,600
To Advertising	1,600	By Rent	4,000
To Audit Fees	100		
To Fire Insurance	1,000		
To Dep. on Sports Equipments	9,000		
To Excess of Income over Expen.	14,300		
	29,700		29,700

RECEIPTS & PAYMENTS ACCOUNT
for the year ended 31st March, 2016

Dr. *Cr.*

Receipts	₹	*Payments*	₹
To Balance b/d	4,200	By Salaries	1,000
To Entrance Fee	10,100	By Printing & Stationery	2,600
To Subscriptions		By Advertising	1,600
2012	600	By Fire Insurance	1,200
2013	15,000	By Investments	20,000
2014	400	By Balance c/d	7,400
To Rent Received	3,500		
	33,800		33,800

The assets on 1st April, 2015 included club grounds and pavilion ₹ 44,000, sports equipments ₹ 25,000 and furniture and fixture ₹ 4,000. Subscription in arrears on that date was ₹ 800. Prepare Opening and Closing Balance Sheets.

SOLUTION

BALANCE SHEET AS AT 31.3.2015

Liabilities	₹	*Assets*	₹
Capital Fund (Balancing figure)	78,000	Cash	4,200
		Sports Equipments	25,000
		Club Ground & Pavilion	44,000
		Furniture & Fixture	4,000
		Subscription in arrear	800
	78,000		78,000

BALANCE SHEET AS AT 31.3.2016

Liabilities		₹	*Assets*		₹
Salaries outstanding		500	Cash in hand		7,400
Audit Fees outstanding		100	Sports Equipments	25,000	
Subscription received in advance		400	*Less:* Depreciation	9,000	16,000
Capital Fund	78,000		Club Ground & Pavilion		44,000
Add: Surplus	14,300	92,300	Furniture & Fixtures		4,000
			Investments		20,000
			Prepaid Printing & Stationery		400
			Prepaid Insurance		200
			Rent Receivable		500
			Subscriptions Due: 2012	200	
			2013	600	800
		93,300			93,300

ILLUSTRATION 52

The following particulars relate to Hanuman Sports Club:

INCOME & EXPENDITURE ACCOUNT
for the year ending on 31st March, 2016

Dr. *Cr.*

Expenditure	₹	*Income*	₹
To Secretary's Salary	1,500	By Entrance Fees	10,500
To Printing & Stationery	2,200	By Subscriptions	15,600
To Advertising	1,600	By rent	2,800
To Audit Fees	500	By Interest on Investments	1,200
To Fire Insurance	1,000		
To Depreciation:			
—Sports Equipments	9,000		
—Furniture	500		
To Surplus	13,800		
	30,100		30,100

RECEIPTS & PAYMENTS ACCOUNT
for the year ending on 31st March, 2016

Dr. *Cr.*

Receipts		₹	*Payments*	₹
To Balance b/d		4,200	By Secretary's Salary	1,000
To Entrance Fee	2014-2015	1,000	By Printing & stationery	2,600
-do-	2015-2016	10,000	By Advertising	1,600
To Subscriptions	2014-2015	600	By Fire Insurance	1,200
To Subscription	2015-2016	15,000	By 12% Investments	

-do- 2016-2017	400	(purchased on 1.7.2013)	20,000
To Rent received	2,400	By Furniture	2,000
To Interest received	600	By Balance c/d	5,800
	34,200		34,200

The assets on 1st April, 2015 included Club Grounds & Pavilion ₹ 44,000, Sports Equipments ₹ 25,000 and Furniture and Fixtures ₹ 4,000. Subscriptions in arrear on that date were ₹ 800. Subscriptions received in advance on that date were ₹ 200. Creditors for Printing & Stationery on that date were ₹ 500.

Requirements: Prepare opening and closing Balance Sheets.

SOLUTION

BALANCE SHEET OF HANUMAN SPORTS CLUB
as at 31st March, 2015

Liabilities	₹	*Assets*	₹
Funds:		Fixed Assets:	
Capital Fund (b.f)	78,300	Club Grounds & Pavilion	44,000
Current Liabilities:		Furniture & Fixture	4,000
Subscription received in advance	200	Sports Equipments	25,000
Creditors for Printing & Stationery	500	Current Assets:	
		Entrance Fees Outstanding	1,000
		Subscription Outstanding	800
		Cash at Bank	4,200
	79,000		79,000

BALANCE SHEET OF HANUMAN SPORTS CLUB
as at 31st March, 2016

Liabilities		₹	*Assets*		₹
Funds:			Fixed Assets:		
Capital fund:			Club Grounds & Pavilion		44,000
Opening Balance	78,300		Furniture & Fixtures	4,000	
Add: surplus	13,800	92,100	*Add:* Additions	2,000	
Current Liabilities:				6,000	
Outstanding Salary		500	*Less:* Depreciation	500	5,500
Outstanding Audit Fees		500	Sports Equipments	25,000	
Creditors for Printing & Stationery		100	*Less:* Depreciation	9,000	16,000
Subscription received in advance		400	Investments:		
			Investments (at cost)		20,000
			Current Assets:		
			Accrued rent		400
			Subscription outstanding		
			for 2014-2015	200	

		for 2015-2016 400	600
		Entrance Fees Outstanding	500
		Cash at Bank	5,800
		Prepaid Insurance	200
		Accrued Interest [₹ 1,200 – ₹ 600]	600
	93,600		93,600

CORRECTION OF WRONG STATEMENTS

ILLUSTRATION 53

Modern (India) Citizens Club was registered in a city and the accountant prepared the following Receipts and Payments Account for the year ended on March 31, 2016 and showed a deficit of ₹ 14,520:

Receipts	₹	*Payments*	₹
Subscriptions	62,130	Premises	30,000
Fair Receipts	7,200	Honorarium to Secretary	12,000
Variety Show Receipts (Net)	12,810	Rent	2,400
Interest	690	Rates and Taxes	3,780
Bar Collections	22,350	Printing and Stationery	1,410
Cash Spent More	1,000	Wages	2,520
Deficit	14,520	Sundry Expenses	5,350
		Fair Expenses	7,170
		Bar Purchases Payments	17,310
		Repairs	960
		New Car (Less proceeds of old Car ₹ 9,000)	37,800
	1,20,700		1,20,700

Information:

Particulars	*1.4.2015* ₹	*31.3.2016* ₹
Cash in hand	450	—
Bank Balance as per Pass Book	24,690	10,440
Cheque issued not presented for sundry expenses	270	90
Subscriptions Due	3,600	2,940
Premises at Cost	87,000	1,17,000
Accumulated Depreciation on Premises	56,400	?
Car at Cost	36,570	46,800
Accumulated Depreciation—Car	30,870	?
Bar Stock	2,130	2,610
Creditors for Bar Purchases	1,770	1,290

(a) Cash overspent represents honorarium to Secretary not withdrawn due to cash deficit. His annual honorarium is ₹ 12,000.

(b) Depreciation on Premises and Car is to be provided at 5% and 20% on written down value.

Required: Prepare the Correct Receipts and Payments Accounts, Income and Expenditure Account for the year 2015-2016 and Balance Sheet as on 31st March 2016.

SOLUTION

RECEIPTS AND PAYMENTS ACCOUNT

Dr. *for the year ending on 31st March, 2016* *Cr.*

Receipts	₹	*Payments*	₹
Opening Balances		Premises	30,000
Cash Balance as per Cash Book	450	Honorarium to secretary	11,000
Bank Balance as per Pass Book	24,690	Rent	2,400
Subscriptions	62,130	Rates and Taxes	3,780
Fair Receipts	7,200	Printing and Stationery	1,410
Variety Show Receipts	12,810	Sundry Expenses (5,350 + 270 – 90)	5,530
Interest	690	Wages	2,520
Bar Collections	22,350	Fair Expenses	7,170
		Bar Purchases	17,310
		Repairs	960
		New Car (less proceeds of old car)	37,800
		Bank Balance as per Pass Book	10,440
	1,30,320		1,30,320

INCOME AND EXPENDITURE ACCOUNT

Dr. *for the year ending on 31st March, 2016* *Cr.*

Expenditure	₹	*Income*	₹
To Honorarium to Secretary	12,000	By Subscriptions	61,470
To Rent	2,400	By Fair Receipts	7,200
To Rates and Taxes	3,780	By Variety Show Receipts	12,810
To Printing and Stationery	1,410	By Interest	690
To Sundry Expenses		By bar Collections	22,350
(5,530 – 270 + 90)	5,350	By Profit on Sale of old car	3,300
To Wages	2,520		
To Fair Expenses	7,170		
To Bar Stock Consumed	16,350		
To Repairs	960		
To Depreciation on:			
Premises (5% on 60,600)	3,030		
Car (20% on 46,800)	9,360		
To Surplus t/f to Capital Fund	43,490		

	1,07,820		1,07,820

BALANCE SHEET AS AT 31ST MARCH, 2016

Liabilities		₹	*Assets*	₹
Creditors for Bar Purchases		1,290	Premises	57,570
Secretary—honorarium outstanding		1,000	Car	37,440
Capital Fund			Subscriptions Due	2,940
Opening Balance	65,130		Bar Stock	2,610
Add: Surplus	43,490		Cash at Bank as per Cash Book	
		1,08,620	(10,440 – 90)	10,350
		1,10,910		1,10,910

Working Notes:

BALANCE SHEET AS AT 31ST MARCH, 2015

Liabilities	₹	*Assets*		₹
Creditors for Bar Purchases	1,770	Cash in Hand		450
Capital Fund (Balancing figure)	65,130	Bank Balance as per Cash Book		
		(24,690 – 270)		24,420
		Subscriptions Due		3,600
		Premises (at cost)	87,000	
		Less: Depreciation	56,400	30,600
		Car (at cost)	36,570	
		Less: Depreciation	30,870	5,700
		Bar Stock		2,130
	66,900			66,900

Dr. **(II) SUBSCRIPTION ACCOUNT** *Cr.*

Particulars	₹	*Particulars*	₹
To Balance b/d	3,600	By Bank A/c	62,130
To Income & Expenditure (b.f.)	61,470	By Balance c/d	2,940
	65,070		65,070

Dr. **(III) CREDITORS FOR BAR ACCOUNT** *Cr.*

Particulars	₹	*Particulars*	₹
To Bank A/c	17,310	By balance b/d	1,770
To Balance c/d	1,290	By Bar Stock A/c (Purchases) (b.f.)	16,830
	18,600		18,600

Dr. **(IV) BAR STOCK ACCOUNT** *Cr.*

Particulars	₹	*Particulars*	₹
To Balance b/d	2,130	By Income & Expenditure A/c (b.f.)	16,350

To Creditors for Bar Stock (Purchas.)	16,830	By Balance c/d	2,610
	18,960		18,960

(v) Premises	
Original Cost (as on 1.4.2015)	87,000
Less: Accumulated Depreciation on 1.4.2015	56,400
Add: Purchases during the year	30,000
	60,600
Less: Depreciation @ 5%	3,030
	57,570
(vi) Profit on sale of car	
Original cost (as on 1.4.2015)	36,570
Less: Accumulated Depreciation as on 1.4.2015	30,870
	5,700
Sale Price (given)	9,000
Profit on sale	3,300
(vii) New Car	
Purchase price (₹ 37,800 + ₹ 9,000)	46,800
Less: Depreciation @ 20%	9,360
	37,440

ILLUSTRATION 54

The Receipts and Payments account of Trustwell Club prepared on 31st March, 2016 is as follows:

RECEIPTS AND PAYMENTS ACCOUNT

Receipts		₹	*Payments*	₹
To Balance b/d		450	By Expenses (including	
To Annual Income from Subscription			Payment for sports material ₹ 2,700)	6,300
Add: Outstanding of	4,590		By Loss on Sale of Furniture	
last year received this year	180		(cost price ₹ 450)	180
	4,770		By Balance c/d	90,450
Less: Prepaid of last year	90	4,680		
To Other fees		1,800		
To Donation for Building		90,000		
		96,930		96,930

Additional Information:

Trustwell club had balances as on 1.4.2015:

Furniture ₹ 1,800; Investment at 5% ₹ 27,000; Sports material ₹ 6,660; Balance as on 31.3.2016: Subscription Receivable ₹ 270; Subscription received in advance ₹ 90; Stock of sports material ₹ 1,800.

Do you agree with above Receipts and Payments account? If not, prepare correct Receipts and

Payments account and Income and Expenditure account for the year ended 31st March, 2016 and Balance Sheet on that date.

SOLUTION

CORRECTED RECEIPTS AND PAYMENTS ACCOUNT OF TRUSTWELL CLUB

Dr. *for the year ended 31st March, 2016* *Cr.*

Receipts		₹	*Payments*	₹
To Balance b/d		450	By Expenses (₹ 6,300 – ₹ 2,700)	3,600
To Subscription			By Sports Material	2,700
Annual Income	4,590		By Balance c/d	90,720
Less: Receivable at end	270		(Cash in Hand and at Bank)	
Add: Advance at end	90			
Add: Receivable at the end	180			
Less: Advance received at end	90	4,500		
To Other fees		1,800		
To Donation for Building		90,000		
To Sale of Furniture		270		
		97,020		97,020

INCOME AND EXPENDITURE ACCOUNT OF TRUSTWELL CLUB

Dr. *for the year ended 31st March, 2016* *Cr.*

Expenditure		₹	*Income*	₹
To Sundry Expenses		3,600	By Subscription	4,590
To Sports Material			By Other fees	1,800
Balance as on 1.4.2016	6,660		By Interest on investment	1,350
Add: Purchases	2,700		(5% on ₹ 27,000)	
Less: Balance as on			By Deficit: Excess of	
31.3.2016	(1,800)	7,560	Expenditure over Income	3,600
To Loss on Sale of Furniture		180		
		11,340		11,340

BALANCE SHEET OF TRUSTWELL CLUB

as on 31st March, 2016

Liabilities		₹	*Assets*		₹
Capital Fund	36,000		Furniture	1,800	
Less: Excess of Expenditure			*Less:* Sold	(450)	1,350
over Income	(3,600)	32,400	5% Investment		27,000
Building Fund		90,000	Interest Accrued on Investment		1,350
Subscription Received in Advance		90	Sports Material		1,800
			Subscription Receivable		270
			Cash in Hand and at Bank		90,720
		1,22,490			1,22,490

Working Note:

BALANCE SHEET OF TRUSTWELL CLUB AS ON 1ST APRIL, 2015

Liabilities	₹	*Assets*	₹
Subscription Received in Advance	90	Furniture	1,800
Capital Fund (Balancing Figure)	36,000	Investment	27,000
		Sports Material	6,660
		Subscription Receivable	180
		Cash in Hand and at Bank	450
	36,090		36,090

SOLVED PROBLEMS

PROBLEM 1

How will you deal with the following items while preparing the Income and Expenditure Account of Tulsian Club for the year ending on March 31, 2016 and a Balance Sheet as on that date?

Particulars	*As at 1.4.2015* ₹	*As at 31.3.2016* ₹
Outstanding Subscription	9,500	7,000
Advance Subscription	2,800	5,200
Outstanding Salaries	15,000	9,000
Prepaid Salaries	5,000	3,000
Amount due to Suppliers of Sports Materials	15,000	9,000
Advances to Suppliers of Sports Materials	5,000	3,000
Stock of Sports Materials	15,000	7,000

During 2015–2016, the payment made to the suppliers of Sports Materials was ₹ 54,000 and Cash Purchases amounted to 10% of Credit Purchases. Subscription received ₹ 1,48,900, Salaries paid ₹ 54,000.

SOLUTION

AN EXTRACT OF INCOME AND EXPENDITURE ACCOUNT

Dr. *for the year ended 31st March, 2016* Cr.

Expenditure	₹	*Income*	₹
To Sports Materials consumed	63,000	By Subscription	1,44,000
To Salaries	50,000		

AN EXTRACT OF BALANCE SHEET AS AT 31ST MARCH, 2016

Liabilities	₹	*Assets*	₹
Advance Subscription	5,200	Outstanding Subscription	7,000

Creditors for Sports Materials	9,000	Advance for Sports Materials	3,000
		Stock of Sports Materials	7,000

Working Notes:

Dr. **1. SUBSCRIPTION ACCOUNT** *Cr.*

Particulars	₹	*Particulars*	₹
To Outstanding Subscription A/c (in the beginning)	9,500	By Advance Subscription A/c (in the beginning)	2,800
To Income & Expenditure A/c (balancing figure)	**1,44,000**	By Bank A/c	1,48,900
To Advance Subscription A/c	5,200	By Outstanding Subscription A/c (at the end)	7,000
	1,58,700		1,58,700

Dr. **2. SALARIES ACCOUNT** *Cr.*

Particulars	₹	*Particulars*	₹
To Prepaid Salaries A/c (in the beginning)	5,000	By Outstanding Salaries A/c (in the beginning)	15,000
To Bank A/c	54,000	By Income & Expenditure A/c (balancing figure)	50,000
To Outstanding Salaries A/c (at the end)	9,000	By Prepaid Salaries A/c (at the end)	3,000
	68,000		68,000

Dr. **3. CREDITORS FOR SPORTS MATERIALS ACCOUNT** *Cr.*

Particulars	₹	*Particulars*	₹
To Balance b/d	5,000	By Balance b/d	15,000
To Bank A/c	54,000	By Stock of Sports Materials A/c (Credit purchases) (Balancing figure)	50,000
To Balance c/d	9,000	By Balance c/d	3,000
	68,000		68,000

Dr. **4. STOCK OF SPORTS MATERIALS ACCOUNT** *Cr.*

Particulars	₹	*Particulars*	₹
To Balance b/d	15,000	By Income and Expenditure A/c (Sports Materials consumed) (Balancing figure)	63,000
To Creditor for Sports Materials (transfer)	50,000		
To Cash Purchases [₹ 50,000 × 10/100]	5,000	By Balance c/d	7,000
	70,000		70,000

PROBLEM 2

Show how will you deal with the following items while preparing the final accounts of Tulsian Club for the year ending on March 31, 2016:

AN EXTRACT OF RECEIPTS AND PAYMENTS ACCOUNT OF TULSIAN CLUB, DELHI

Dr. *for the year ended 31st March, 2016* Cr.

Receipts	₹	*Payments*	₹
Admission Fees	5,000	Prizes awarded	2,000
Life Membership Subscription	50,000	Tournament Expenses	1,00,000
Donations	1,00,000	Construction of Building	3,00,000
Tournament Fund	50,000	12% Fixed Deposit on 1.7.2015	1,00,000
Proceeds of Tournament tickets	40,000		
Donations for Prizes	2,800		
Donation for Building	5,00,000		
Interest on 12% Fixed Deposit	6,000		
Subscription for Governor's Party	3,450		
Interest on Prize Fund Inves.	1,200		
Interest on Building Fund Inves.	40,000		

Additional Information:

Particulars	*As at 1.4.2015* ₹	*As at 31.3.2016* ₹
Tournament Fund	5,000	?
Prize Fund	12,000	?
10% Prize Fund Investments	12,000	?
Building Fund	4,00,000	?
10% Building Fund Investments	4,00,000	?
Capital Fund	9,00,000	?
Subscription for Governor's party outstanding	—	550

SOLUTION

AN EXTRACT OF INCOME AND EXPENDITURE ACCOUNT

Dr. *for the year ended 31st March, 2016* Cr.

Expenditure	₹	*Income*		₹
To Tournament Expenses	5,000	By Interest on 12% Fixed Deposit		
		Received	6,000	
		Accrued	3,000	9,000
		By Admission Fees		5,000
		By Donations		1,00,000

AN EXTRACT OF BALANCE SHEET AS AT 31ST MARCH, 2016

Liabilities		₹	*Assets*	₹
Capital Fund:			Building in progress	3,00,000
Opening Balance	9,00,000		10% Building Fund Investments	4,00,000
Add: T/F from			10% Prize Fund Investments	12,000
Building Fund	3,00,000		12% Fixed Deposit	1,00,000
Add: Life Membership			Interest Accru. on Fixed Deposit	3,000
Subscription	50,000	12,50,000	Subscription for Governor's	
Building Fund:			party outstanding	550
Opening Balance	4,00,000			
Add: Donations	5,00,000			
Add: Interest	40,000			
Less: T/F to Capital Fund	3,00,000	6,40,000		
Prize Fund:				
Opening Balance	12,000			
Add: Donations	2,800			
Add: Interest on Prize fund				
Investments	1,200			
Less: Prizes awarded	2,000	14,000		
Tournament Fund:				
Opening Balance	5,000			
Add: Donations	50,000			
Add: Proc. of tickets	40,000			
Less: Expenses	1,00,000			
T/F to I & E Exp. A/c	**(5,000)**	Nil		
Subscription for				
Governor's Party	3,450			
Add: Outstanding	550	4,000		

PROBLEM 3

The following is the Receipts and Payments Account of the Calcutta Club for the year ending 31.3.2016

Receipts	₹	*Payments*	₹
Opening Balances:		Salaries	6,000
Cash	1,025	Sports Expenses	6,900
Stamps	50	Electricity	1,000
Bank F.D.	10,000	Telephone	1,200
S.B. Account	4,200	Postage Expenses	200
Current Account	2,100	General Body Expenses	700

10% Govt. Securities	1,80,000	Printing and Stationery	850
Subscriptions:		Building Purchase Account	12,000
2014-2015	1,010	Repairs	400
2015-2016	18,900	Closing Balances:	
2016-2017	900	Cash	1,740
Donations	7,000	Stamps	25
Bank Interest Received	1,340	Bank F.D.	11,000
Receipts from Sports	2,600	S.B. Account	22,310
Telephone Recoveries	900	Current Account	3,700
Interest on Govt Securities	18,000	10% Govt. Securities	1,80,000
(After T.D.S. 10%)			
	2,48,025		2,48,025

A building costing one lac of rupees was purchased during the last year and ₹ 88,000 was paid for it.

Subscription outstanding for 2015-2016	₹ 1,100
Salaries outstanding	₹ 200
Interest accrued on Bank deposits but not received	₹ 200

The Government Securities of the face value of ₹ 2,00,000 (cost ₹ 1,80,000) present investment of the Endowment Fund.

Required: From the above, prepare Income and Expenditure Account for the year 2015-2016 and also the Balance Sheet as on 31.3.2016 of the Calcutta Club.

SOLUTION

INCOME AND EXPENDITURE ACCOUNT

Dr. *for the year ending on 31st March, 2016* *Cr.*

Expenditure		₹	*Income*		₹
To Salaries	6,000		By Subscriptions	18,900	
Add: Outstanding	200	6,200	*Add:* Outstanding	1,100	20,000
To Sports Expenses		6,900	By Donations		7,000
To Electricity		1,000	By Bank Interest	1,340	
To Telephone		1,200	*Add:* Accrued	200	1,540
To Postage Expenses:			By Receipts from Sports		2,600
Cash	175		By Telephone Recoveries		900
Stamps	25	200			
To General Body Expenses		700			
To Printing and Stationery		850			
To Repairs		400			
To Surplus (Excess of Income over Expenditure)		14,590			
		32,040			32,040

BALANCE SHEET AS AT 31ST MARCH 2016

Liabilities		₹	*Assets*	₹
Subscription Received in Advance		900	Building	1,00,000
Outstanding Salary		200	Govt. Securities	1,80,000
Endowment Fund:			Fixed Deposit	11,000
Opening Balance	1,80,000		T.D.S. on Interest (18,000 × 10/90)	2,000
Add: Interest	20,000	2,00,000	Saving Bank Account	22,310
(10% of ₹ 2,00,000)			Current Account	3,700
Capital Fund:			Stamps	25
Opening Balance	1,06,385		Cash	1,740
Add: Surplus	14,590	1,20,975	Subscriptions Receivable	1,100
			Accrued Bank Interest	200
		3,22,075		3,22,075

Working Note:

BALANCE SHEET AS AT 31ST MARCH 2015

Liabilities	₹	*Assets*	₹
Loan (For Building)	12,000	Building	1,00,000
Capital Fund (Balancing Figure)	1,06,385	10% Govt Securities	1,80,000
Endowment Fund	1,80,000	Fixed Deposit	10,000
		Saving Bank Account	4,200
		Current Account	2,100
		Stamps	50
		Cash	1,025
		Subscription Receivable	1,010
	2,98,385		2,98,385

PROBLEM 4

Prepare Income and Expenditure Account and Balance Sheet of Tulsian Sports Club, Delhi from the following information:

RECEIPTS AND PAYMENTS ACCOUNT OF TULSIAN SPORTS CLUB, DELHI

Dr. *for the year ending on 31st March, 2016* *Cr.*

Receipts			₹ *'000*	*Payments*	₹ *'000*
To Balance b/d:	Cash	150		By Balance b/d (Bank Overdraft)	3,000
	Stamps	50	200	By Insurance (paid up to 30.6.2016)	300
To Subscriptions			7,000	By Miscellaneous Expenses	3,875
To Entrance fees			200	By Postage Expenses	200
To Life Membership Subscription			500	By Refreshment Room Expenditure	2,100
To General Donations			2,000	By Furniture (Purchased on	600

To Cricket Fees	250	1.10.2015)		
To Refreshment Room Receipts	3,100	By Honorarium to Cricket coach		600
To Sale of Old periodicals	72	By Sports Equipments		2,200
To Interest on Govt. Securities	144	(on 1.10.2015)		
(T.D.S. @ 20%)		By 10% RBI Tax Free Bonds		
To Donation for Club Pavilion		(on 1.1.2016) (Pavilion)		10,000
(on 1.1.2016)	10,000	By Balance c/d:		
		Cash in hand	52	
		Cash at bank	514	
		Stamps	25	591
	23,466			23,466

Information:

Particulars	*1.4.2015* *₹ '000*	*31.3.2016* *₹ '000*
Club Pavilion Fund	5,000	?
Sports Equipments	4,500	?
Furniture	3,200	?
Stock of Foodstuff	120	80
6% Government Securities (Face Value ₹ 30,00,000)	2,580	?
Subscription Outstanding	600	250
Subscription in Advance	—	300
Outstanding Miscellaneous Expenses	200	250

Accounting policies followed by Tulsian Sports Club, Delhi are, provide as under:

(a) The sports equipments and furniture are to be depreciated @ 25% and 19% p.a. respectively.

(b) One half of the entrance fees and life membership fee are to be treated as income.

SOLUTION

INCOME AND EXPENDITURE ACCOUNT

Dr. *for the year ending on 31st March, 2016* *Cr.*

Expenditure		*₹ '000*	*Income*		*₹ '000*
To Insurance		225	By Subscription		6,350
To Honorarium to Cricket Coach		600	By General Donations		2,000
To Miscellaneous Expenses		3,925	By Entrance Fees		100
To Postage			By Life Membership subscription		250
Cash	175		By Cricket Fees		250
Stamps	25	200	By Sale of old periodicals		72
To Depreciation on			By Interest on Secur. (144 × 100/80)		180
— Sports equipment	1,675		By Profit on sale of foodstuff		
— Furniture	665	2,340	Sales	3,100	
To Surplus transferred to			*Add:* Closing Stock	80	

Capital Fund	2,872	*Less:* Opening Stock 120	
		Less: Purchases 2,100	960
	10,162		10,162

BALANCE SHEET AS AT 31ST MARCH, 2016

Liabilities		₹ *'000*	*Assets*		₹ *'000*
Capital Fund:			**Fixed Assets:**		
Opening Balance	3,000		Furniture		
Add: 50% of Entrance Fees	100		Opening balance	3,200	
Add: 50% of Life			*Add:* Additions	600	
Membership fees	250			3,800	
Add: Surplus	2,872	6,222	*Less:* Depreciation	665	3,135
Club Pavilion Fund:			Sports Equipments		
Opening Balance	5,000		Opening Balance	4,500	
Add: Donations	10,000		*Add:* Additions	2,200	
Add: Interest on Club Pavilion				6,700	
Fund Investments	250	15,250	*Less:* Depreciation	1,675	5,025
Current Liabilities:			**Investments:**		
Subscription received in advance		300	6% Government Securities		2,580
Outstanding Miscellaneous Exp.		250	10% Club Pavilion Fund Investments		10,000
			Current Assets:		
			Stock of foodstuff		80
			Subscription in arrears		250
			Cash in hand		52
			Cash at bank		514
			Stamps		25
			T.D.S. on interest on: Government		
			Securities (144 × 20/80)		36
			Accrued Interest on Club		
			Pavilion Fund		
			Investments (RBI Bonds)		250
			Prepaid Insurance		75
		22,022			22,022

Working Notes:

(I) BALANCE SHEET AS AT 1ST APRIL, 2015

Liabilities	₹ *'000*	*Assets*	₹ *'000*
Capital Fund (balancing figure)	3,000	Sports Equipments	4,500
Club Pavilion Fund	5,000	Furniture	3,200
Bank Overdraft	3,000	Stock of Foodstuff	120

Outstanding Miscellaneous Exp.	200	Government Securities	2,580
		Subscription in arrears	600
		Cash in hand	150
		Stamps	50
	11,200		11,200

Dr. **(II) SUBSCRIPTION ACCOUNT** *Cr.*

Particulars	*₹ '000*	*Particulars*	*₹ '000*
To Outstanding Subscription A/c	600	By Cash A/c	7,000
(in the beginning)		By Outstanding Subscription A/c	
To Income and Expenditure A/c (b.f.)	6,350	(at the end)	250
To Advance Subscription A/c			
(at the end)	300		
	7,250		7,250

Dr. **(III) MISCELLANEOUS EXPENSES ACCOUNT** *Cr.*

Particulars	*₹ '000*	*Particulars*	*₹ '000*
To Cash A/c	3,875	By Outstanding Expenses A/c	
To Outstanding Expenses A/c		(in the beginning)	200
(at the end)	250	By Income and Expenditure A/c	
		(Balancing figure)	3,925
	4,125		4,125

(iv) Interest on Fixed Deposits has accrued for 3 months @ 10% p.a. and has been credited to Pavilion Fund, since Fixed Deposit has been made out of the donation for Pavilion Fund.

(v) Blanket Rate of Depreciation (without p.a.) has been given on sports equipment.

PROBLEM 5

Prepare Income and Expenditure Account and Balance Sheet of Bhagat Singh College Sports Club, Delhi from the following information:

RECEIPTS AND PAYMENTS ACCOUNT OF BHAGAT SINGH COLLEGE SPORTS CLUB, DELHI

Dr. *for the year ended on 31st March, 2016* *Cr.*

Receipts		*₹ '000*	*Payments*	*₹ '000*
To Balance b/d: Cash		500	By Rent	9,750
Bank		4,000	By Miscellaneous Expenses	28,800
Stamps		300	By Postage Expenses	1,200
To Subscription			By Furniture	8,000
2015-2016	4,650		By Creditors for Sports Material	12,200
2016-20X3	67,200		By Cost of prizes (to be awarded)	4,150
20X3-2015	2,600	74,450	By Cash purchase of Sports Materials	2,000
To Entrance Fees		8,000	By Match Expenses	7,030

To General Donations	4,050	By Balance c/d:		
To Donations for Prize Fund	2,800	Cash	545	
To Sale of old Sports Materials	5,200	Bank	26,000	
To Interest on Prize Fund Investments	300	Stamps	150	26,695
To Miscellaneous Receipts	225			
	99,825			99,825

Information:

Particulars	*1.4.2015* ₹	*31.3.2016* ₹
Sports Materials	4,000	5,000
Furniture	40,000	?
5% Prize Fund Investments (Face Value ₹ 12,000)	11,700	?
Creditors for Sports Materials	1,400	2,950
Subscription in arrears	4,750	?
Subscription in advance	1,400	?
Prize Fund	12,000	?
Rent paid in advance	—	750
Outstanding Rent	750	—
Outstanding Miscellaneous Expenses	2,280	4,020
Miscellaneous Expenses paid in advance	750	850

Book Value of Sports Materials sold was ₹ 4,000. Depreciation on furniture is to be provided @ 10%. Half of entrance fees to be capitalised. There are 720 members, each paying an annual subscription of ₹ 100.

SOLUTION

BHAGAT SINGH COLLEGE SPORTS CLUB, DELHI
INCOME AND EXPENDITURE ACCOUNT
for the year ending on 31st March, 2016

Dr. *Cr.*

Expenditure		₹ *'000*	*Income*	₹ *'000*
To Rent		8,250	By Subscriptions	72,000
To Miscellaneous Expenses		30,440	By General Donations	4,050
To Postage Expenses:			By Entrance Fees	4,000
Cash	1,050		By Profit on sale of old sports materials	1,200
Stamps	150	1,200	By Miscellaneous Receipts	225
To Sports Materials consumed		10,750		
To Depreciation on Furniture		4,800		
To Match Expenses		7,030		
To Surplus trans. to Capital Fund		19,005		
		81,475		81,475

BHAGAT SINGH COLLEGE SPORTS CLUB, DELHI
BALANCE SHEET AS AT 31ST MARCH, 2016

Liabilities		*₹ '000*	*Assets*		*₹ '000*
Capital Fund:			**Fixed Assets:**		
Opening Balance	48,170		Furniture		43,200
Add: Surplus	19,005		Investments:		
Add: Entrance Fees	4,000	71,175	5% Prize Fund Investments		11,700
Prize Fund:			**Current Assets:**		
Opening Balance	12,000		Sports Materials		5,000
Add: Donations	2,800		Subscription in arrears		
Add: Income @ 5% on ₹ 12,000	600		for 2015-2016	₹ 100	
	15,400		for 2016-20X3	₹ 3,400	3,500
Less: Expenses	4,150	11,250	Prepaid Miscellaneous Expenses		850
Current Liabilities:			Cash Balance		545
Creditors for sports materiels		2,950	Bank Balance		26,000
Subscription in advance		2,600	Stamps		150
Outstanding Miscellaneous			Prepaid Rent		750
Expenses		4,020	Accrued Interest on Prize		
			Fund Investments (₹ 600 – ₹ 300)		300
		91,995			91,995

Working Notes:

(I) BALANCE SHEET AS AT 31ST MARCH, 2016

Liabilities	₹	*Assets*	₹
Capital Fund (Balancing figure)	48,170	Fixed Assets:	
Prize Fund	12,000	Furniture	40,000
Current Liabilities:		Investments:	11,700
Creditors for Sports Materials	1,400	5% Prize Funds Investments	
Subscription in advance	1,400	Current Assets:	
Outstanding Miscellaneous Exp.	2,280	Subscription in arrears	4,750
Rent Outstanding	750	Sports materials	4,000
		Miscellaneous Exp. paid in advance	750
		Cash Balance	500
		Bank Balance	4,000
		Stamps	300
	66,000		66,000

Dr. **(II) SUBSCRIPTION ACCOUNT** *Cr.*

Particulars	*₹ '000*	*Particulars*	*₹ '000*
To Outstanding Subscription A/c	4,750	By Advance Subscriptions A/c	1,400

(In the beginning)		(in the beginning)	
To Income and Expenditure A/c		By Bank A/c	74,450
(720 × ₹ 100)	72,000	By Outstanding Subscription A/c	
To Advance Subscription A/c		(at the end)	3,500
(at the end)	2,600		
	79,350		79,350

Dr. **(III) MISCELLANEOUS EXPENSES ACCOUNT** Cr.

Particulars	₹	*Particulars*	₹
To Prepaid Expenses A/c	750	By Outstanding Expenses A/c	2,280
(in the beginning)		(in the beginning)	
To Bank A/c	28,800	By Income and Expenditure A/c	
To Outstanding Expenses A/c		(Balancing figure)	30,440
(at the end)	4,020	By Prepaid Expenses A/c	
		(at the end)	850
	33,570		33,570

Dr. **(IV) RENT ACCOUNT** Cr.

Particulars	₹	*Particulars*	₹
To Bank A/c	9,750	By Outstanding Rent A/c	750
		By Income and Expenditure A/c	
		(Balancing figure)	8,250
		By Prepaid Rent A/c (at the end)	750
	9,750		9,750

Dr. **(V) CREDITORS FOR SPORTS MATERIALS ACCOUNT** Cr.

Particulars	₹	*Particulars*	₹
To Bank A/c	12,200	By Balance b/d	1,400
To Balance c/d	2,950	By Stock of Sports Materials	
		(Credit purchases)	
		(Balancing figure)	13,750
	15,150		15,150

Dr. **(VI) STOCK OF SPORTS MATERIALS ACCOUNT** Cr.

Particulars	₹	*Particulars*	₹
To Balance b/d	4,000	By Income and Expenditure A/c (b/f)	10,750
To Creditors for Sports Materials	13,750	By Bank A/c	5,200
(Credit purchases)		By Balance c/d	5,000
To Bank A/c (Cash purchases)	2,000		
To Income and Expenditure A/c			

(Profit on sale)	1,200		
	20,950		20,950

Dr. **(VII) FURNITURE ACCOUNT** Cr.

Particulars	₹	*Particulars*	₹
To Balance b/d	40,000	By Depreciation A/c	4,800
To Bank A/c	8,000	By Balance c/d	43,200
	48,000		48,000

PROBLEM 6

The following balances have been extracted from the books of XYZ Club for the year ended on 31st March, 2016.

Furniture as on 31st March, 2016: ₹ 8,400, Additions to Furniture during the year ₹ 5,400, Billiard Table and other accessories as on 31st March, 2016: ₹ 8,900, China Glass Cutlery and Linex as on 31st March, 2016: ₹ 2,500, Restaurant receipts during the year: ₹ 3,61,600, Restaurant stock as on 31st March, 2016: ₹ 3,900, Receipts from Billard room during the year: ₹ 25,600, Subscriptions received during the year: ₹ 31,500, Interest on deposit received during the year: ₹ 1,500, Secretary's honorarium; ₹ 30,000, Purchases for restaurant: ₹ 2,07,800, Rent and Rates: ₹ 34,900, Wages (restaurant ₹ 50,000) ₹ 92,300, Repairs and Renewals: ₹ 17,900, Fuel: ₹ 17,700, Lighting: ₹ 2,200, Sundry Expenses: ₹ 13,400, Cash in Hand as on 31st March, 2016: ₹ 1,350, Bank Balances as on 31st March, 2016: ₹ 9,150, Bank Deposit at 10% as on 31st March, 2016: ₹ 30,000.

The Payment for purchases includes ₹ 3,000 for the year ending on 31st March, 2016. Restaurant stock on 31st March, 2016: ₹ 4,500. Included in the subscriptions received were ₹ 4,800 for the previous year and ₹ 1,200 for the year ending on 31st March, 2015. Subscriptions outstanding on 31st March, 2016 were ₹ 5,000. Depreciation should be provided as follows:

China glass and cutlery at 20%. Furniture 10% and Billiard Table and Accessories 15%. The cost of the boarding expenses of the staff is estimated at ₹ 27,500 of which ₹ 20,000 is to be charged to the restaurant. Cash in hand on March 31, 2016: ₹ 2,600.

Required: Prepare the Receipts and Payments Account, Income and Expenditure Account and the Balance Sheet showing the working of the restaurant separately.

SOLUTION

RECEIPTS AND PAYMENTS ACCOUNTS

Dr. *for the year ending on 31st March, 2016* Cr.

Receipts	₹	*Payments*	₹
To Balance b/d		By Furniture	5,400
Cash in hand	1,350	By Purchases for Restaurant	2,07,800
Cash at bank	9,150	By Rent and Rates	34,900
Bank Deposit	30,000	By Wages	92,300
To Restaurant Receipts	3,61,600	By Repairs and Renewals	17,900
To Billiard Receipts	25,600	By Fuel	17,700
To Subscriptions	31,500	By Lighting	2,200
To Interest on Deposit	1,500	By Sundry Expenses	13,400
		By Secretary's Honorarium	30,000

		By Balance c/d	
		Cash in hand	2,600
		Cash at bank (Balancing figure)	6,500
		Bank Deposit	30,000
	4,60,700		4,60,700

RESTAURANT TRADING ACCOUNT

Dr. *for the year ending on 31st March, 2016* Cr.

Particulars		₹	*Particulars*	₹
To Opening Stock		3,900	By Restaurant's receipts	3,61,600
To Purchases	2,07,800		By Cost of boarding of staff	27,500
Less: Outstanding in the beg.	3,000	2,04,800	By Closing stock	4,500
To Wages		50,000		
To Board Exp. of Restaurant staff		20,000		
To Fuel		17,700		
To Dep. of China glass, cutlery		500		
To Surplus transferred to Income & Expenditure Account		96,700		
		3,93,600		3,93,600

INCOME AND EXPENDITURE ACCOUNT

Dr. *for the year ending on 31st March, 2016* Cr.

Expenditure		₹	*Income*		₹
To Repairs and Renewals		17,900	By Subscription	31,500	
To Wages (₹ 92,300 – ₹ 50,000)		42,300	*Less:* for 2015-2016	4,800	
To Secretary's Honorarium		30,000	20X3-2015	1,200	
To Rent and Rates		34,900	*Add:* Outstanding	25,500	
To Lighting		2,200	for 2016-20X3	5,000	30,500
To Boarding Expenses		7,500	By Billiards receipts		25,600
To Sundry Expenses		13,400	By Interest received	1,500	
To Depreciation on:			*Add:* Outstanding	1,500	3,000
Furniture	1,380		By Profit from Restaurant		96,700
Billiard Tables	1,335	2,715			
To Excess of Income over Expenditure transferred to Capital Fund		4,885			
		1,55,800			1,55,800

BALANCE SHEET OF XYZ CLUB AS AT 31ST MARCH, 2016

Liabilities	₹	*Assets*	₹
Capital Fund		Cash in hand	2,600

Opening Balance	66,000		Cash at bank		6,500
Add: Surplus	4,885	70,885	Bank Deposit		30,000
Subscription received in advance		1,200	Accrued Interest		1,500
			Subscription receivable		5,000
			Restaurant stock		4,500
			Furniture:		
			Opening balance	8,400	
			Addition	5,400	
				13,800	
			Less: Depreciation	1,380	12,420
			Billiard table	8,900	
			Less: Depreciation	1,335	7,565
			China glass etc.	2,500	
			Less: Depreciation	500	2,000
		72,085			72,085

Note: *It has been assumed that depreciation on furniture is to be charged to Income & Expenditure Account.*

PROBLEM 7

From the following Trial Balance and the necessary information given below for a public school, prepare Income and Expenditure Account for the year 2016, and a Balance Sheet as at March 31, 2016.

Debit Balances	₹	*Credit Balances*	₹
Buildings	2,50,000	Admission fees	5,000
Furnitures and Fittings	40,000	Tuition and other fees received	2,00,000
Library books	60,000	Creditors for supplies	6,000
9% Investments	2,00,000	Rent for the Hall	4,000
Salaries	2,00,000	Miscellaneous Receipts	12,000
Stationery	15,000	Govt. Grant	1,40,000
General expenses	8,000	General Fund	4,00,000
Annual Sports—Expenses	6,000	Donation received for purchase	
Cash at bank	20,000	of library books	25,000
Cash in hand	1,000	Sale of Old Furniture	8,000
	8,00,000		8,00,000

Fees yet to be received for the year ₹ 10,000. Salaries yet to be paid amount to ₹ 12,000. Furniture costing ₹ 15,000 was purchased on 1.10.2015. The book value of the Furniture sold (on 30.9.2015) was ₹ 20,000 on 1.4.2015. Depreciation is to be charged @ 10% per annum on Furniture and Fittings; 15% on Library Books and 5% on Buildings.

SOLUTION

INCOME AND EXPENDITURE ACCOUNT

Dr. *for the year ending on 31st March, 2016* Cr.

Expenditure		₹	*Income*		₹
To Salaries	2,00,000		By Admission fees		5,000
Add: Outstanding	12,000	2,12,000	By Tuition fees	2,00,000	
To Stationery		15,000	Add Accrued	10,000	2,10,000
To General Expenses		8,000	By Hall Rent		4,000
To Annual Sports Expenses		6,000	By Miscellaneous Receipts		12,000
To Depreciation on furniture		2,250	By Govt Grants		1,40,000
To Loss on Sale of Furniture		11,000	By Accrued Interest on Investment		18,000
To Depreciation on Library Books		9,000			
To Depreciation on Buildings		12,500			
To Surplus t/f to Capital fund		1,13,250			
		3,89,000			3,89,000

BALANCE SHEET AS AT 31ST MARCH, 2016

Liabilities		₹	*Assets*		₹
Creditors for suppliers		6,000	Buildings	2,50,000	
Library funds		25,000	*Less:* Depreciation	12,500	2,37,500
Salaries due		12,000	Furniture and Fittings	20,000	
General fund	4,00,000		*Less:* Depreciation	1,250	18,750
Add: Surplus	1,13,250	5,13,250	Library Books	60,000	
			Less: Depreciation	9,000	51,000
			9% Investments		2,00,000
			Interest Accrued on Inve. @ 9% p.a.		18,000
			Bank		20,000
			Cash		1,000
			Tution Fees Due		10,000
		5,56,250			5,56,250

Working Note:

Since Sale of old furniture for ₹ 8,000 appears in the Trial Balance, it means, no accounting effect has yet been given in respect of Furniture Account. After passing the rectifying entry the Furniture Account will appear as under:

Opening Balance of furniture as at 1.4.2015 = ₹ 40,000 – ₹ 15,000 = ₹ 25,000

Book Value of Unsold Old Furniture = ₹ 25,000 – ₹ 20,000 = ₹ 5,000

Dr. **FURNITURE ACCOUNT** Cr.

Particulars	₹	*Particulars*	₹
To Balance (Unadjusted given)	40,000	By Depreciation on old furniture	
		(20,000 × 10/100 × 612)	1,000
		By Sale of Furniture A/c	8,000
		By Income & Expenditure A/c (Loss)	11,000

		By Depreciation A/c:	
		On Old furniture of ₹ 5,000	500
		On New furniture of ₹ 15,000	750
		By Balance c/d	18,750
	40,000		40,000

PROBLEM 8

The following is the Income and Expenditure Account of the Red Roses Club for the year ended on March, 31 2016.

Expenditure	₹	*Income*	₹
To Salaries	24,000	By Subscriptions	72,000
To Rent	10,800	By Entrance fees	8,000
To Rates and Taxes	600	By Surplus on Publication of brochure	4,500
To Postage and Telephones	720	By Profit on sale of old sports as sets	1,200
To Affiliation fees to the All-India Lawn Tennis Association	1,200	By Interest on 4% investments	600
		By Miscellaneous Income	225
To Sports Materials	15,750		
To Electricity Charges	1,200		
To Repairs and Maintenance to tennis court	9,600		
To Depreciation on assets at 10% of gross book value at end of year	4,800		
To Surplus carried to Capital Fund	17,855		
	86,525		86,525

The following further information is made available:

Particulars	*Balances on 31.3.2015* ₹	*Balances as at 31.3.2016* ₹
(a) Sundry assets	44,000	?
Bank Balance	4,800	?
Subscriptions in arrear	4,750	3,500
Subscription received in advance	1,400	2,600
4% Investments [Face value ₹ 15,000]	12,000	12,000
(b) Expenses Outstanding:		
Salaries	600	1,200
Rent	900	1,800
Rates & Taxes	Nil	600
Tennis court maintenance	780	320
(c) Outstanding for purchase of sports materials	1,400	2,950
(d) Prize Fund	4,600	3,250

(e) The book value, as on 1.4.2015 of sports goods sold in the year was ₹ 4,000.

(f) Prize Fund is separately maintained. All receipts are credited to it separately and expenditure is met out of the fund directly. During the year, credits to the account amounted to ₹ 2,800.

(g) Interest received this year was only for two quarters.

(h) The club was admitted as a member of the All India Lawn Tennis Federation on 1.10.2015 when it paid subscription till 30.9.2016.

(i) Advertisement charges on brochure—yet to be collected—₹ 450.

(j) A fixed deposit of ₹ 25,000 was made on 31st March, 2016.

Prepare the Receipts and Payments Account for the year ended on March 31, 2016 and the Balance-Sheet as on that date of the Red Roses Club.

SOLUTION

RECEIPTS AND PAYMENT ACCOUNTS OF RED ROSES CLUB

Dr. *for the year ending on 31st March, 2016* *Cr.*

Receipts	₹	*Payments*	₹
To Balance b/d	4,800	By Electricity Charges	1,200
To Subscription	74,450	By Salaries	23,400
To Entrance fee	8,000	By Rent	9,900
To Brochure receipts, Surplus	4,050	By Postage and Telephone	720
To Old Sports material	5,200	By A.I. and T.F. Affiliation fee	2,400
To Interest on Investments	300	By Purchase of Sports Material	14,200
To Miscellaneous receipts	225	By Repairs and Maintenance to	
To Prize Fund receipts	2,800	tennis court	10,060
		By Sundry assets	8,000
		By Prize Fund	4,150
		By Fixed deposit	25,000
		By Balance c/d	795
	99,825		99,825

BALANCE SHEET OF RED ROSES CLUB AS AT 31ST MARCH, 2016

Liabilities		₹	*Assets*		₹
General Fund	55,870		Sundry Assets	48,000	
Add: Surplus for the year	17,855	73,725	*Less:* Depreciation	4,800	43,200
Prize Fund		3,250	4% Investments [FV ₹ 15,000]		12,000
Liability for purchases and expenses		6,870	Fixed Deposit		25,000
Subscription received in advance		2,600	Subscriptions receivable		3,500
			Advance affiliation fee paid		1,200
			Advt. charges receivable		450
			Interest due to Investments		300
			Cash at Bank		795
		86,445			86,445

Working Notes:

(I) BALANCE SHEET AS AT 31ST MARCH, 2015

Liabilities	₹	*Assets*	₹
Subscriptions received in advance	1,400	5% Investments	12,000
Expenses Outstanding	2,280	Sports Materials	4,000
Sundry suppliers (sports materials)	1,400	Sundry Assets	40,000
Prize Fund	4,600	Bank Balance	4,800
Capital Fund (Balancing figure)	55,870	Subscriptions receivable	4,750
	65,550		65,550

Dr. **(II) SUBSCRIPTION ACCOUNT** *Cr.*

Particulars	₹	*Particulars*	₹
To Outstanding Subscription A/c		By Advance Subscription A/c (Beg.)	1,400
(Opening)	4,750	By Bank (Balancing figure)	74,450
To Income and Expenditure Account	72,000	By Outstanding Subscription A/c	
To Advance Subscription A/c (end)	2,600	(Closing)	3,500
	79,350		79,350

Dr. **(III) SUNDRY ASSETS ACCOUNT** *Cr.*

Particulars	₹	*Particulars*	₹
To Balance b/d (₹ 44,000 – ₹ 4,000)	40,000	By Depreciation A/c	4,800
To Bank A/c (Balancing figure)	8,000	By Balance c/d	43,200
		[₹ 4,800 (Dep.) × 100/10) – ₹ 4,800]	
	48,000		48,000

Dr. **(IV) STOCK OF SPORTS MATERIALS ACCOUNT** *Cr.*

Particulars	₹	*Particulars*	₹
To Balance b/d	4,000	By Bank A/c	5,200
To Income & Expenditure A/c (Profit)	1,200	By Income & Expenditure A/c	
To Creditors for Sports Materials A/c	15,750	(Materials Consumed)	15,750
	20,950		20,950

Dr. **(V) CREDITORS FOR SPORTS MATERIALS ACCOUNT** *Cr.*

Particulars	₹	*Particulars*	₹
To Bank A/c (b.f.)	14,200	By Balance b/d	1,400
To Balance c/d	2,950	By Credit Purchases	15,750
	17,150		17,150

Dr. **(VI) PRIZE FUND ACCOUNT** *Cr.*

Particulars	₹	*Particulars*	₹
To Bank (Prize Awarded) (b.f.)	4,150	By Balance b/d	4,600
To Balance c/d	3,250	By Bank A/c	2,800
	7,400		7,400

(vii) Total interest due @ 4% on ₹ 15,000 i.e. ₹ 600; half of it is received and the other half is still due.

(viii) AILTF Affiliation fee paid is ₹ 1,200 (October-March) i.e. for the current year and advance payment is also ₹ 1,200 (April-September).

PROBLEM 9

Tulsian Sports Club which is also running a Restaurant provides you the following information:

1. OPENING AND CLOSING BALANCES

Particulars	*As on 1.4.2015* ₹	*As on 31.3.2016* ₹
Furniture	2,20,000	?
Sports Equipment	2,20,000	?
China Glass, Cutlery etc.,	25,000	?
6% Govt. Securities [Face value ₹ 3,00,000]	2,50,000	?
Stock of Sports Materials	3,000	500
Advances to Suppliers of Sports Materials	1,000	500
Due to Suppliers of Sports Materials	3,000	1,800
Stock of Stationery	2,000	?
Unpresented cheques being payment for stationery	900	300
Subscription Outstanding	4,750	3,500
Subscription Received-in-Advance	1,400	2,600
Outstanding Miscellaneous Expenses	4,750	3,500
Miscellaneous Expenses paid in advance	1,400	2,600
Outstanding Wages	5,000	4,000
Cash Balance	10,000	30,000
Bank Balance as per Pass Book	5,00,000	?
Stock of Provisions	30,000	3,80,000
Debtors for Provisions	30,000	40,000
Creditors for Provisions	1,00,000	50,000

2. PAYMENTS

Particulars	₹
Suppliers of Sports Materials	10,800
Miscellaneous Expenses	74,450
Wages	51,000
Stationery	1,600
Furniture (Purchased on 1.10.2015)	1,50,000

Sports Equipment (purchased on 1.10.2015)	1,50,000
8% R.B.I Tax Free Bonds (Purchased on 1.1.2016)	79,200
[Face Value ₹ 1,00,000]	
Creditors for Provisions	10,50,000
Cash Purchases of Provisions – 1/11th of Total Purchases	

3. RECEIPTS

Particulars	₹
Subscription	74,450
Interest on 6% Govt. Securities (After T.D.S. @ 10%)	8,100
Collection from Debtors for Provisions	8,90,000
Cash Sales of Provisions –10% of Total Sales	

4. **Depreciation Rates:**
   (a) On China Glass & Cutlery — 20%
   (b) On Furniture — 10% p.a.
   (c) On Sports Equipment — 10%
5. The cost of the boarding expenses—Restaurant staff ₹ 20,000—other staff ₹ 7,500.
6. Furniture (having a book value of ₹ 20,000) as on 1.4.2015 was sold at a loss of 20% on 31.12.2015.
7. Write 25% off Stationery.

Required: Prepare Restaurant Trading Account, Income & Expenditure Account and the Closing Balance Sheet.

SOLUTION

RESTAURANT TRADING ACCOUNT

Dr. *for the year ended 31st March, 2016* Cr.

Particulars		₹	*Particulars*		₹
To Opening Stock		30,000	By Sales of Provisions		
To Purchases Of Provisions			Cash Sales	1,00,000	
Cash Purchases	1,00,000		Credit Sales	9,00,000	10,00,000
Credit Purchases	10,00,000	11,00,000	By Boarding Expenses		
To Restaurant & Other Staff Expenses		20,000	of Restaurant Staff		27,500
To Wages		50,000	By Stock of Provisions		3,80,000
To Depreciation on Cutlery		5,000			
To Profit t/f to Income & Expenditure A/c		2,02,500			
		14,07,500			14,07,500

INCOME & EXPENDITURE ACCOUNT

Dr. *for year ended 31st March 2016* Cr.

Particulars	₹	*Particulars*	₹
To Depreciation on Furniture	29,000	By Profit from Restaurant	2,02,500

To Depreciation on Sport Equipment	37000	By Subscription A/c	72,000
To Sports Materials Consumed	12,600	By Interest on Govt. Securities	
To Stationery w/o	750	Received 8,100	
To Miscellaneous Expenses A/c	72,000	T.D.S 900	
To Loss on Sale	3,700	*Add:* Accrued Interest 9,000	18,000
To Boarding Expenses of other Staff	7500	By Accrued Interest on	
To Surplus	1,31,950	8% RBI Tax free Bonds	2,000
	2,94,500		2,94,500

BALANCE SHEET AS AT 31 MARCH, 2016

Liabilities		₹	*Assets*		₹
Capital Fund:			Furniture		3,22,500
Opening Balance	11,82,100		Sport Equipment		
Add: Surplus	1,31,950	13,14,050	Opening Balance	2,20,000	
Subscription received in advance		2,600	*Add:* Purchases	1,50,000	
Outstanding Misc. Expenses		3,500	*Less:* Depreciation	(37,000)	3,33,000
Outstanding Wages		4,000	China, Glass Cutlery		20,000
Due to Suppliers of Sports Materials		1,800	Govt. Securities		
Creditors for Provisions		50,000	(Face Value ₹ 3,00,000)		2,50,000
Bank overdraft as per Cash Book		1,00,000	8% RBI Tax free Bonds		
			(Face Value ₹ 1,00,000)		79,200
			Stock of Provisions		3,80,000
			Stock of Sports Material		500
			Stock of Stationery		2,250
			Debtors for Provisions		40,000
			Ad. to Suppliers of Sports Materials		500
			Subscription Outstanding		3,500
			Prepaid Misc. Expenses		2,600
			Accrued Interest on Govt. Securities		9,000
			Accrued Interest on		
			8% RBI Tax free Bonds		2,000
			T.D.S		900
			Cash		30,000
		14,75,950			14,75,950

Working Notes:

Dr. **(I) SUBSCRIPTION ACCOUNT** *Cr.*

Particulars	₹	*Particulars*	₹
To Subscription Outstanding A/c (beginning)	4,750	By Subscription received in advance A/c (beg)	1,400

To Income & Expenditure A/c	72,000	By Bank A/c	74,450
To Subscription received in advance A/c (end)	2,600	By Subscription Outstanding A/c (end)	3,500
	79,350		79,350

Dr. **(II) MISCELLANEOUS EXPENSES ACCOUNT** *Cr.*

Particulars	₹	*Particulars*	₹
To Expenses Prepaid A/c (beginning)	1,400	By Expenses Outstanding A/c (beg.)	4,750
To Expenses Outstanding A/c (end)	3,500	By Expenses Prepaid A/c (end)	2,600
To Bank A/c	74,450	By Income & Expenditure A/c	72,000
	79,350		79,350

Dr. **(III) SUPPLIERS OF SPORTS MATERIALS ACCOUNT** *Cr.*

Particulars	₹	*Particulars*	₹
To Balance b/d (advance)	1,000	By Balance b/d (outstanding)	3,000
To Bank A/c	10,800	By Stock of Sports Material A/c	10,100
To Balance c/d (outstanding)	1,800	By Balance c/d (advance)	500
	13,600		13,600

Dr. **(IV) STOCK OF SPORTS MATERIALS ACCOUNT** *Cr.*

Particulars	₹	*Particulars*	₹
To Balance b/d	3,000	By Income & Expenditure A/c	
To Supplier's A/c	10,100	(consumed)	12,600
		By Balance c/d	500
	13,100		13,100

(v) Purchases of stationery = Payment as per Pass Book + Unpresented cheques at the end – Unpresented cheques at the beginning 1600 + 300 – 900 = 1,000

Dr. **(VI) STOCK OF STATIONERY ACCOUNT** *Cr.*

Particulars	₹	*Particulars*	₹
To Balance b/d	2,000	By Income & Expenditure A/c	
To Purchases A/c	1,000	(consumed)	750
		By Balance c/d	2,250
	3,000		3,000

Dr. **(VII) DEBTORS FOR PROVISIONS ACCOUNT** *Cr.*

Particulars	₹	*Particulars*	₹
To Balance b/d	30,000	By Bank A/c	8,90,000
To Credit Sales	9,00,000	By Balance c/d	40,000
	9,30,000		9,30,000

Dr. **(VIII) CREDITORS FOR PROVISIONS ACCOUNT** Cr.

Particulars	₹	Particulars	₹
To Bank A/c	10,50,000	By Balance b/d	1,00,000
To Balance c/d	50,000	By Credit purchases	10,00,000
	11,00,000		11,00,000

Dr. **(IX) FURNITURE ACCOUNT** Cr.

Particulars	₹	Particulars	₹
To Balance b/d	2,20,000	By Depreciation A/c	
To Bank A/c	1,50,000	Sold (20,000 × 10% × 9/12)	1,500
		By Bank A/c (sales)	14,800
		By Income & Expenditure A/c (Loss)	3,700
		By Dep. A/c (Old (2,00,000 × 10%)	20,000
		New (1,50,000 × 10% × 6/12)	7,500
		By Balance c/d	3,22,500
	3,70,000		3,70,000

Dr. **(X) CASH & BANK ACCOUNT** Cr.

Particulars	₹	Particulars	₹
To Balance b/d: Cash	10,000	By Creditors for Provisions A/c	10,50,000
Bank Balance as per Pass Book	5,00,000	By Wages A/c	51,000
To Debtors for Provisions A/c	8,90,000	By Suppliers of Sports Materials A/c	10,800
To Interest on Govt. Securities	8,100	By Furniture A/c	1,50,000
To Subscription	74,450	By Miscellaneous Expenses A/c	74,450
To Cash Sales of Provisions	1,00,000	By Sport Equipment	1,50,000
To Furniture	14,800	By Stationery A/c	1,600
To Balance c/d:		By Cash Purchases of Provisions	1,00,000
Bank Overdraft as per Pass Book	99,700	By 8% RBI Tax free Bonds	79,200
		By Balance c/d (cash)	30,000
	16,97,050		16,97,050

(XI) BANK RECONCILIATION STATEMENT

Particulars	31.3.2015 (₹)	31.3.2016 (₹)
A. Bank Balance (overdraft) as per Pass Book	5,00,000	(99,700)
B. *Less:* Unpresented cheques for stationery	(900)	(300)
C. Bank Balance (overdraft) as per Cash Book	4,99,100	(1,00,000)

(XII) BALANCE SHEET AS AT 31 MARCH, 2015

Liabilities	₹	*Assets*	₹
Capital Fund	11,82,100	Furniture	2,20,000
Creditors for Provisions	1,00,000	Sport Equipment	2,20,000
Due to Suppliers of Sports Materials	3,000	China, Glass Cutlery	25,000
Subscription received in advance	1,400	Govt. Securities	
Outstanding Misc. Expenses	4,750	(Face Value ₹ 3,00,000)	2,50,000
Outstanding Wages	5,000	Stock of Provisions	30,000
		Stock of Sports Material	3,000
		Stock of Stationery	2,000
		Debtors for Provisions	30,000
		Advance to Supp. of Sports Materials	1,000
		Subscription Outstanding	4,750
		Prepaid Misc. Expenses	1,400
		Cash	10,000
		Bank Balance As per Cash Book	4,99,100
	12,96,250		12,96,250

PROBLEM 10

The accountant of City Club gave the following information about the receipts and payments of the Club for the year ended on 31st March, 2016:

Receipts: Subscriptions: ₹ 62,130; Fair Receipts: ₹ 7,200; Variety Show Receipts (net): ₹ 12,810; Interest: ₹ 690; Bar Collections: ₹ 22,350.

Payments: Premises: ₹ 30,000; Rent: ₹ 2,400; Rates and Taxes: ₹ 3,780; Printing and Stationery: ₹ 1,410; Sundry Expenses: ₹ 5,350; Wages: ₹ 2,520; Bar Purchases (Payments): ₹ 17,310; Repairs: ₹ 960; New Car (less proceeds of old car ₹ 9,000): ₹ 37,800, Fair Expenses ₹ 7,170, Honorarirum to Secretary ₹ 11,000.

Information:

Particulars	*Opening* ₹	*Closing* ₹
Cash in Hand	450	Nil
Bank Balance as per Cash-book	24,420	10,350
Cheque issued for Sundry Expenses not presented to the bank (entry has been duly made in the cash-book)	270	90
Subscriptions Due	3,600	2,940
Premises (at cost)	87,000	1,17,000
Provision for Depreciation on Premises	56,400	
Car (at cost)	36,570	46,800
Accumulated Depreciation on Car	30,870	
Bar Stock	2,130	2,610
Creditors for Bar Purchases	1,770	1,290

Annual Honorarium to Secretary is ₹ 12,000. Depreciation on Premises is to be provided at 5% on written down value. Depreciation on new Car is to be provided at 20%.

You are required to prepare the Receipts and Payments Account and Income and Expenditure Account for the year ended on 31.3.2016.

SOLUTION

RECEIPTS AND PAYMENTS ACCOUNT

for the year ending on 31st March, 2016

Dr. *Cr.*

Receipts	₹	*Payments*	₹
To Opening Balances:		By Premises	30,000
Cash in Hand	450	By Rent	2,400
Bank Balance	24,420	By Rates and Taxes	3,780
To Subscriptions	62,130	By Printing and Stationery	1,410
To Fair Receipts	7,200	By Sundry Expenses	5,350
To Variety Show Receipts (Net)	12,810	By Wages	2,520
To Interest	690	By Fair Expenses	7,170
To Bar Collections	22,350	By Honorarium to Secretary	11,000
To Sale Proceeds of old car	9,000	By Bar Purchases (Payments)	17,310
		By Repairs	960
		By New Car	46,800
		By Closing Balances:	
		Cash on hand	Nil
		Bank balance	10,350
	1,39,050		1,39,050

INCOME AND EXPENDITURE ACCOUNT

for the year ending on 31st March, 2016

Dr. *Cr.*

Expenditure		₹	*Income*		₹
To Rent		2,400	By Subscriptions	62,130	
To Rent and Taxes		3,780	*Add:* O/s at the end	2,940	
To Printing and Stationery		1,410	*Less:* O/s in the beg.	3,600	61,470
To Wages		2,520	By Surplus from Fair:		
To Honorarium to Secretary		12,000	Fair receipts	7,200	
To Sundry Expenses		5,350	*Less:* Fair expenses	7,170	30
To Repairs		960	By Surplus from variety show		12,810
To Depreciation on:			By Interest		690
Premises @ 5%	3,030		By Profit from Bar		6,000
Car @ 20%	9,360	12,390	By Profit on sale of car		3,300
To Excess of Income over Expenditure transferred to Capital Fund		43,490			
		84,300			84,300

Working Notes:

(I) BAR CREDITORS ACCOUNT

Dr. Cr.

Particulars	₹	Particulars	₹
To Bank A/c	17,310	By Balance b/d	1,770
To Balance c/d	1,290	By Bar Purchases (Balancing figure)	16,830
	18,600		18,600

(ii) Profit on sale of car = Sale Proceeds – WDV = ₹ 9,000 – ₹ 5,700 = ₹ 3,300

(iii) Bar Stock Consumed = Opening Stock + Purchases – Closing Stock
= ₹ 2,130 + ₹ 16,830 – ₹ 2,610 = ₹ 16,350

(iv) Profit from Bar = Bar Collection – Bar Stock Consumed = ₹ 22,350 – ₹ 16,350 = ₹ 6,000

PROBLEM 11

The following informations were obtained from the books of Delhi Club as on 31.3.2016 at the end of the first year of the Club. You are required to prepare Receipts and Payments Account, Income and Expenditure Account for the year ended 31.3.2016 and a Balance Sheet as at 31.3.2016 on mercantile basis:

(i) Donations received for Building and Library Room ₹ 2,00,000

(ii) Other revenue income and actual receipts:

Particulars	Revenue Income ₹	Actual Receipts ₹
Entrance Fees	17,000	17,000
Subscription	20,000	19,000
Locker Rents	600	600
Sundry Income	1,600	1,060
Refreshment Account	—	16,000

(iii) Other revenue expenditure and actual payments:

Particulars	Revenue Income ₹	Actual Payments ₹
Land (cost ₹ 10,000)	—	10,000
Furniture (cost ₹ 1,46,000)	—	1,30,000
Salaries	5,000	4,800
Maintenance of Playgrounds	2,000	1,000
Rent	8,000	8,000
Refreshment Account	—	8,000

Donations to the extent of ₹ 25,000 were utilised for the purchase of Library Books, balance was still unutilised. In order to keep it safe, 9% Govt. Bonds of ₹ 1,60,000 were purchased on 31.3.2016. Remaining amount was put in the Bank on 31.3.2016 under the term deposit. Depreciation at 10% p.a. was to be provided for the whole year on Furniture and Library Books.

SOLUTION

RECEIPTS AND PAYMENTS ACCOUNT

for the year ending on 31st March, 2016

Dr. Cr.

Receipts	₹	*Payments*	₹
To Donation for Building & Library Room	2,00,000	By Purchase of Land	10,000
To Entrance Fees	17,000	By Purchase of Furniture	1,30,000
To Subscription	19,000	By Salaries	4,800
To Locker Rents	600	By Maintenance of Play grounds	1,000
To Sundry Income	1,060	By Rent	8,000
To Refreshment Receipts	16,000	By Refreshment Payments	8,000
To Balance c/d [Bank overdraft]	1,08,140	By Library Books	25,000
		By 9% Govt Bonds	1,60,000
		By Term Deposit with Bank	15,000
	3,61,800		3,61,800

INCOME & EXPENDITURE ACCOUNT

for the year ended 31st March, 2016

Dr. Cr.

Expenditure	₹	*Income*		₹
To Salaries [₹ 4,800 + ₹ 200]	5,000	By Entrance Fees		17,000
To Maintenance of playgrounds	2,000	By Subscription [₹ 19,000 + ₹ 1,000]		20,000
To Rent	8,000	By Locker Rents		600
To Depreciation on Furniture	14,600	By Sundry Income [₹ 1,060 + ₹ 540]		1,600
To Depreciation on Library Books	2,500	By Profit on Refreshment A/c		
To Surplus t/f to Capital fund	15,100	Receipts	16,000	
		Less: Expenses	8,000	8,000
	47,200			47,200

BALANCE SHEET AS AT 31ST MARCH, 2016

Liabilities		₹	*Assets*		₹
Capital Fund:			Fixed Assets:		
Surplus	15,100		Land		10,000
Add: Trans. from Library F.	25,000	40,100	Furniture Cost	1,46,000	
Building & Library Fund:			*Less:* Depreciation	14,600	1,31,400
Donation Received	2,00,000		Library books cost	25,000	
Less: utilized and t/f Capital Fund	25,000	1,75,000	*Less:* Depreciation	2,500	22,500
Supplier of Furniture		16,000	Investments:		
Outstanding Salary		200	9% Govt. Bonds (Face Value ₹ 1,60,000)		1,60,000
Outstanding Maintenance of Playgrounds		1,000	Term Deposit with bank		15,000
			Current Assets:		

Bank Overdraft	1,08,140	Outstanding Subscription	1,000
		Accused Sundry Income	540
	3,40,440		3,40,440

PROBLEM 12

Summary of Receipts and Payments of Bombay Medical Aid Society for the year ended 31st March, 2016 are as follows:

Opening Cash balance in hand ₹ 8,000, Subscription ₹ 50,000, donation ₹ 15,000. Interest on Investments @ 9% p.a. ₹ 9,000, Payments for medicine supply ₹ 30,000, Honorarium to Doctors ₹ 10,000, Salaries ₹ 28,000 sundry Expenses ₹ 1,000, Equipment purchase ₹ 15,000, Charity show expenses ₹ 1,500, Charity show collections. ₹ 12,500.

Additional informations:

Particulars	*Opening*	*Closing*
Subscription due	1,500	2,200
Subscription received in advance	1,200	700
Stock of medicine	10,000	15,000
Amount due for medicine supply	9,000	13,000
Value of equipment	21,000	30,000
Value of building	50,000	48,000

Required: Prepare Receipts and Payments Account and Income and Expenditure Account for the year ended 31st March, 2016 and Balance Sheet as on 31st March, 2016.

SOLUTION

RECEIPTS AND PAYMENTS ACCOUNT
for the year ended 31st March, 2016

Dr. *Cr.*

Receipts	₹	*Payments*	₹
To Cash in hand (Opening)	8,000	By Medicine supply	30,000
To Subscription	50,000	By Honorarium to doctors	10,000
To Donation	15,000	By Salaries	28,000
To Interest on investments	9,000	By Sundry expenses	1,000
To Charity show collections	12,500	By Purchase of Equipment	15,000
		By Charity show expenses	1,500
		By Cash in hand (closing)	9,000
	94,500		94,500

INCOME AND EXPENDITURE ACCOUNT
for the year ended 31st March, 2016

Dr. *Cr.*

Expenditure	₹	*Income*	₹
To Medicine consumed	29,000	By Subscription	51,200
To Honorarium to doctors	10,000	By Donation	15,000
To Salaries	28,000	By Interest on investments	9,000

To Sundry expenses		1,000	By Profit on charity show:		
To Depreciation on:			Show collections	12,500	
Equipment	6,000		Show expenses	1,500	11,000
Building	2,000	8,000			
To Surplus-Excess of Income Over Expenditure		10,200			
		86,200			86,200

BALANCE SHEET

as on 31st March, 2016

Liabilities		₹	*Assets*		₹
Capital Fund:			Building	50,000	
Opening Balance	1,80,300		*Less:* Depreciation	2,000	48,000
Add: surplus	10,200	1,90,500	Equipment	21,000	
Subscription received in advance		700	*Add:* Purchase	15,000	
Amount due for medicine supply		13,000		36,000	
			Less: Depreciation	6,000	30,000
			Stock of medicine		15,000
			Investments		1,00,000
			Subscription receivable		2,200
			Cash in hand		9,000
		2,04,200			2,04,200

Working Notes:

Dr. **(I) SUBSCRIPTION ACCOUNT** *Cr.*

Particulars	₹	*Particulars*	₹
To Outstanding Subscription A/c (beg.)	1,500	By Advance Subscription A/c (beg.)	1,200
To Income & Expenditure A/c	51,200	By Bank A/c	50,000
To Advance Subscription A/c	700	By Outstanding Subscription A/c (end)	2,200
	53,400		53,400

Dr. **(II) CREDITORS FOR MEDICINES ACCOUNT** *Cr.*

Particulars	₹	*Particulars*	₹
To Bank A/c	30,000	By Balance b/d	9,000
To Balance c/d	13,000	By Credit Purchases	34,000
	43,000		43,000

Dr. **(III) STOCK OF MEDICINES ACCOUNT** Cr.

Particulars	₹	Particulars	₹
To Balance b/d	10,000	By Income & Expenditure A/c	29,000
To Purchases	34,000	By Balance c/d	15,000
	44,000		44,000

Dr. **(IV) EQUIPMENT ACCOUNT** Cr.

Particulars	₹	Particulars	₹
To Balance b/d	21,000	By Depreciation A/c	6,000
To Bank A/c (Purchases)	15,000	By Balance c/d	30,000
	36,000		36,000

(V) BALANCE SHEET OF MEDICAL AID SOCIETY

as on 31st March, 2015

Liabilities	₹	Assets	₹
Capital fund (balancing figure)	1,80,300	Building	50,000
Subscription received in advance	1,200	Equipment	21,000
Amount due for medicine supply	9,000	Stock of medicine	10,000
		Investments	1,00,000
		Subscription receivable	1,500
		Cash in hand	8,000
	1,90,500		1,90,500

Note: *Donation has been credited directly to the income and expenditure account assuming that donation is of revenue nature. Alternatively, donation may be treated as of capital nature and thus, be credited to capital fund.*

21.0 ACCOUNTS OF A PROFESSIONAL FIRM

Professionals (like solicitors, doctors, chartered accountants, architects etc.) *or* Professionals firms generally prefer to prepare Income and Expenditure Account to find out surplus generated from professional activities during a particular accounting period, Receipts and Expenditure Account for allocation of such surplus and Balance Sheet to show financial position at the end of a particular period.

MEANING OF RECEIPTS AND EXPENDITURE ACCOUNT

1. Receipts and Expenditure Account is an income statement which is prepared by professionals (like Chartered Accountants) *or* professional firms to ascertain the final results of their professional activities during an accounting period.
2. In Receipts and Expenditure Account, all **expenses** are recognised **on accrual basis** and all **incomes** are recognised on cash basis. In other words, all outstanding expenses are considered but all outstanding fees and charges *or* work-in-progress are not considered.

REASON FOR NON-RECOGNITION OF OUTSTANDING FEES

The reason for non-recognition of outstanding fees is that professionals consider it imprudent and risky to recognize the outstanding fees.

REASON FOR DIFFERENCE BETWEEN THE PROFIT AS SHOWN BY THE INCOME & EXPENDITURE ACCOUNT AND RECEIPTS AND EXPENDITURE ACCOUNT.

Such difference arises because of non-recognition of outstanding fees and charges and work-in-progress in Receipts & Expenditure Account.

PRACTICAL GUIDELINES FOR PREPARING FINAL ACCOUNTS OF A PROFESSIONAL FIRM

1. Prepare the Income and Expenditure Account in the usual manner after taking into account the following:
   (i) Fees and Charges for Completed Work in respect of which bills have been submitted,
   (ii) Value of the Incomplete Work in the beginning, and
   (iii) Value of the Incomplete Work at the end.
2. Transfer the Surplus from the Income and Expenditure Account to the credit of Receipts and Expenditure Account
3. Make 'Provision for Outstanding fees and charges (for Completed Work) and for the Value of Incomplete Work' at the end by debiting the Receipts and Expenditure Account.
4. Take credit of 'Provision for Outstanding fees and charges (for Completed Work) and for the value of Incomplete Work' existing at the beginning by crediting the Receipts and Expenditure Account.
5. Give credit to partners for the share in direct business at an agreed rate (if any).
6. Allocate the balance of surplus among the partners in an agreed profit sharing ratio.

FORMAT OF INCOME AND EXPENDITURE ACCOUNT OF A PROFESSIONAL FIRM

INCOME AND EXPENDITURE ACCOUNT OF A PROFESSIONAL FIRM

for the year ending on...

Dr. *Cr.*

Expenditure		₹	*Income*		₹
To Incomplete Work (in the beg.):			By Bills of Cost Rendered (Fees Bills):		
A's Clients	xxx		A's Clients	xxx	
B's Client	xxx	xxx	B's Clients	xxx	xxx
To Salaries & Wages		xxx	By Incomplete Work (at the end):		
To Stipend to Trainees		xxx	A's Clients	xxx	
To Printing & Stationary		xxx	B's Clients	xxx	xxx
To Conveyance Charges		xxx			
To Travelling Expenses		xxx			
To Postage, Telephone, Telegram Expenses		xxx			
To General Office Expenses		xxx			
To Depreciation		xxx			
To Surplus transferred to Receipts and Expenditure A/c		xxx			
		xxx			xxx

FORMAT OF RECEIPTS AND EXPENDITURE ACCOUNT OF A PROFESSIONAL FIRM

RECEIPTS AND EXPENDITURE ACCOUNT OF A PROFESSIONAL FIRM

for the year ending on.....

Dr. Cr.

Expenditure		₹	*Receipts*		₹
To Provision for Outstanding Fees & value of Incomplete Work (at the end):			By Surplus transferred from Income & Expenditure A/c		xxx
A's Clients	xxx		By Provision for Outstanding Fees & value of Incomplete Work (in the beginning):		
B's Clients	xxx	xxx	A's Clients	xxx	
To Partner's Capital Accounts (Share in direct business)			B's Client	xxx	xxx
A	xxx				
B	xxx	xxx			
To Partner's Capital Accounts (Balance of Surplus)					
A	xxx				
B	xxx	xxx			
		xxx			xxx

ILLUSTRATION 55

Dr Arun Gupta's Receipts and Payments for the year ending on 31st March 2016 was as follows:

Receipts	₹	*Payments*	₹
To Balance b/d	66,100	By Rent (for 18 months to 30.6.2016)	45,000
To Fees	2,14,200	By Telephone Charges	4,500
To Miscellaneous Receipts	200	By Salaries to assistants	33,000
To Sale of old Equipment	4,000	By Journals etc.	1,000
		By Library Books (Purchased on 1.7.2015)	5,000
		By Medical Equipments	8,000
		By Furniture (Purchased on 1.10.2015)	7,000
		By Purchases of Medicines	43,000
		By Conveyance Expenses	50,000
		By Drawings	60,000
		By Misc. Expenses	1,000
		By Balance c/d	27,000
	2,84,500		2,84,500

Information:

(a) Fees outstanding: on 31.3.2015 ₹ 2,000, on 31.3.2016 ₹ 5,000

(b) Stock of Medicines: on 31.3.2015 ₹ 10,000, on 31.3.2016 ₹ 18,600

(c) Creditors for Medicines: on 31.3.2015 ₹ 100, on 31.3.2016 ₹ 300

(d) Medical Equipment on 31.3.2015 ₹ 50,000. Medical Equipment was sold as well as purchased on 1st Jan. 2016. The book value of the equipment sold being ₹ 6,000 as on 1.4.2015. Equipment is subject to depreciation @ 20% p.a.

(e) Furniture on 31.3.2015 ₹ 5,000, Library Books on 31.3.2015 ₹ 1,000 Depreciate furniture by 10% and Library Books by 20%.

(f) Salary to assistant still payable is ₹ 3,000.

(g) 40% of conveyance is for domestic purposes.

Required: Prepare the Receipts and Expenditure Account of Dr. Arun for the year 2015-2016 and the Balance Sheet as at 31.3.2016.

SOLUTION

RECEIPTS AND EXPENDITURE ACCOUNT OF DR. ARUN

Dr. *for the year ending on 31st March, 2016* *Cr.*

Expenditure		₹	*Receipts*	₹
To Medicine Consumed		34,600	By Fees	2,14,200
To Rent [₹ 45,000 × 12/18]		30,000	By Misc. Receipts	200
To Telephone charges		4,500		
To Salaries to assistants paid	33,000			
Add: O/s at the end	3,000	36,000		
To Journals etc.		1,000		
To Misc. Expenses		1,000		
To Depreciation Medical Equipment		10,100		
To Depreciation on Library Books		1,200		
To Depreciation on furniture		1,200		
To Loss on sale of Equipment		1,100		
To Conveyance [60% of ₹ 50,000]		30,000		
To Surplus t/f to Capital Fund		63,700		
		2,14,400		2,14,400

BALANCE SHEET AS AT 31ST MARCH, 2016

Liabilities			₹	*Assets*		₹
Creditors for Medicines			300	Cash in hand		27,000
Salary outstanding			3,000	Medical Equipments		42,800
Capital				Furniture		10,800
Opening Balance		1,24,500		Library Books		4,800
Add: Surplus		63,700		Stock of Medicines		18,600
		1,88,200		Fees Outstanding	5,000	
Less: Drawings				*Less:* Provision against		
Cash	60,000			Outstanding Fees	5,000	—

Conveyance 20,000 (40% of ₹ 50,000)	80,000	1,08,200	Prepaid Rent [₹ 45,000 × 3/18]	7,500
		1,11,500		1,11,500

Working Notes:

(I) BALANCE SHEET AS AT 31ST MARCH, 2015

Liabilities	₹	*Assets*		₹
Creditors for Medicines	100	Cash in hand		66,100
Rent Outstanding [₹ 45,000 × 3/18]	7,500	Medical Equipment		50,000
Capital (Balancing figure)	1,24,500	Furniture		5,000
		Library Books		1,000
		Stock of Medicines		10,000
		Fees Outstanding	2,000	
		Less: Provision	2,000	—
	1,32,100			1,32,100

Dr. **(II) CREDITORS FOR MEDICINES ACCOUNT** *Cr.*

Particulars	₹	*Particulars*	₹
To Cash A/c	43,000	By Balance b/d	100
To Balance c/d	300	By Stock of Medicines A/c (Purchases)	43,200
	43,300		43,300

(III) STOCK OF MEDICINES ACCOUNT

Particulars	₹	*Particulars*	₹
To Balance b/d	10,000	By Income & Expenditure A/c (b.f.)	34,600
To Creditors for Medicines A/c	43,200	By Balance c/d	18,600
	53,200		53,200

Dr. **(IV) MEDICAL EQUIPMENT ACCOUNT** *Cr.*

Particulars	₹	*Particulars*	₹
To Balance b/d	50,000	By Depreciation A/c	900
To Cash A/c (Purchases)	8,000	By Cash A/c (Sale Proceeds)	4,000
		By Income & Expenditure A/c (Loss) [(₹ 6,000 – ₹ 900) – ₹ 4,000]	1,100
		By Depreciation A/c	
		on ₹ 44,000 for 1 year	8,800
		on ₹ 8,000 for 1/4 year	400
		By Balance c/d	42,800
	58,000		58,000

Dr. **(V) FURNITURE ACCOUNT** Cr.

Particulars	₹	Particulars	₹
To Balance b/d	5,000	By Depreciation A/c	1,200
To Cash A/c (Purchases)	7,000	By Balance c/d	10,800
	12,000		12,000

Dr. **(VI) LIBRARY BOOKS ACCOUNT** Cr.

Particulars	₹	Particulars	₹
To Balance b/d	1,000	By Depreciation A/c	1,200
To Bank A/c (Purchases)	5,000	By Balance c/d	4,800
	6,000		6,000

Dr. **(VII) PROVISION AGAINST OUTSTANDING FEES ACCOUNT** Cr.

Particulars	₹	Particulars	₹
To Fees A/c		By Balance b/d	2,000
[Ope. Reserve no longer required]	2,000	By Fees A/c	5,000
To Balance c/d	5,000		
	7,000		7,000

Dr. **(VIII) FEES ACCOUNT** Cr.

Particulars	₹	Particulars	₹
To Balance b/d	2,000	By Provision against outstanding	
To Provision against outstanding		fees A/c	2,000
fees A/c	5,000	By Cash A/c	2,14,200
To Income & Expenditure A/c (t/f)	2,14,200	By Balance c/d	5,000
	2,21,200		2,21,200

ILLUSTRATION 56

M/s Sagar and Boond are a firm of solicitors whose partners Anand and Ashok share profits in equal shares, after charging a management fee of 5% thereof to Anand. For the year ended on 31st March 2016, the books maintained by the firm reveal the following particulars:

Particulars	₹	Particulars	₹
Capitals:	33,000	Office Rent	12,000
Drawings: Anand	20,000	Office Expenses	3,600
Ashok	18,000	Furniture and Library books	24,600
Life Insurance Premium paid: Anand	6,000	Client's disbursements	2,600
Ashok	12,000	Amount owing by clients for	
Salaries to staff and juniors	46,000	bills of cost rendered	17,200
Amounts received from clients on		Profit costs	1,42,000
accounts of pending matters	32,000	Fixed deposits with Bank	15,000

Salary debts owing by the firm	3,400	Bank accounts: Clients	31,800
Reserve against bills of costs not		Office	6,600
collected and work-in-progress		Work-in-progress on 31.3.2016	8,200
as on 1.4.2015	5,000		

The following additional information is also available:

(a) Capital accounts of partners, at the beginning of the year, were of equal amounts.

(b) Included in the bills of costs sent to clients are sundry disbursements like postage, telephone charges, etc. debited in the books to office expenses account. At the end of the year, items on the debit side of Clients' Disbursements Account, amounting to ₹ 3,200, had not been charged to clients in bills of costs. Of these, ₹ 200 was received and credited to their accounts in the year.

Required: Prepare the Receipts and Expenditure Account for the year ended on 31st March 2016, and a Balance Sheet of the firm as on that date.

SOLUTION

RECEIPTS AND EXPENDITURE ACCOUNT

Dr. *for the year ending on 31st March, 2016* *Cr.*

Expenditure		₹	*Receipts*	₹
To Salaries for staff		46,000	By Reserve against Bills of	
To Office Rent		12,000	Cost not collected and W.I.P.	5,000
To Office Expenses			By Profit Costs	1,42,000
[(₹ 3,600) – (₹ 3,200 – ₹ 2,600)]		3,000	By Work-in-progress	8,200
To Reserve against Bills of cost not				
collected and work-in-progress		25,400		
(₹ 17,200 + ₹ 8,200)				
To Management fee to Anand				
(5% of ₹ 68,800)		3,440		
(Contd)				
To Net Profit transferred to				
Partners' Capital A/cs:				
Anand	32,680			
Ashok	32,680	65,360		
		1,55,200		1,55,200

BALANCE SHEET OF M/S SAGAR AND BOOND AS AT 31ST MARCH, 2016

Liabilities		₹	*Assets*	₹
Capital Accounts:			Furniture and Library	24,600
Anand:			Fixed Deposits with Bank	15,000
Opening balance	16,500		Debtors for Bills of cost rendered	17,200
Add: Management fee	3,440		Work-in-progress	8,200
Net Profit	32,680		Debtors for Disbursements	

Less: Drawings and Insurance			(₹ 3,200 – ₹ 200)		3,000
Premium	26,000	26,620	Cash at Bank:		
Ashok:			Office	6,600	
Opening Balance	16,500		Clients	31,800	38,400
Add: Net Profit	32,680				
Less: Drawings and					
Insurance premium	30,000	19,180			
Reserve against Debtors not collected & WIP [₹ 17,200 + ₹ 8,200]		25,400			
Sundry Creditors		3,400			
Clients Deposit (₹ 32,000 – ₹ 200)		31,800			
		1,06,400			1,06,400

ILLUSTRATION 57

A doctor, after retiring from Government Service, started private practice on 1st April, 2011 with ₹ 20,000 of his own and ₹ 30,000 borrowed at an interest of 15% per annum on the security of his life policies. His accounts for the year were kept on a cash basis and the following is his summarized Cash Account:

Dr. *Cr.*

Receipts	₹	*Payments*	₹
Own Capital	20,000	Medicines purchased	24,500
Loan	30,000	Surgical Equipments	25,000
Prescription Fees	52,500	Motor Car	32,000
Gifts from Patients	13,500	Motor Car Expenses	12,000
Visiting Fees	25,000	Wages and Salaries	10,500
Fees from Lectures	2,400	Rent of Clinic	6,000
Pension received	30,000	General Charges	4,900
		Household Expenses	18,000
		Household Furniture	2,500
		Expenses on daughter's Marriage	21,500
		Interest on loan	4,500
		Balance at Bank	11,000
		Cash in Hand	1,000
	1,73,400		1,73,400

You are required to prepare his Capital Account and Income and Expenditure Account for the year ended 31st March, 2016 and a Balance Sheet as on that date. One-third of the motor car expenses may be treated as applicable to the private use of car and ₹ 3,000 of the wages and salaries are in respect of domestic servants.

The stock of medicines in hand on 31st March, 2016 was valued at ₹ 9,500.

SOLUTION

CAPITAL ACCOUNT

Dr. *For the year ended 31st March, 2016* Cr.

Particulars	₹	*Particulars*	₹
To Drawings		By Cash/bank	20,000
Motor Car expenses (one-third of ₹ 12,000)	4,000	By cash/bank (Pension)	30,000
Household expenses	18,000	By Net income from Practice (derived from Income and Expenditure A/c)	47,500
Daughter's marriage exp.	21,500		
Wages of domestic servants	3,000		
Household furniture	2,500		
To Balance c/d	48,500		
	97,500		97,500

INCOME AND EXPENDITURE ACCOUNT
FOR THE YEAR ENDED 31ST MARCH, 2016

Dr. Cr.

Particulars		₹	*Particulars*	₹
To Medicines consumed			By Prescription fees	52,500
Purchases	24,500		By Gifts from patients	13,500
Less: Cl.Stock	9,500	15,000	By Visiting fees	25,000
To Motor car expenses		8,000	By Fees from lectures	2,400
To Wages and Salaries (₹ 10,500 – ₹ 3000)		7,500		
To Rent of clinic		6,000		
To General charges		4,900		
To Interest on loan		4,500		
To Net Income		47,500		
		93,400		93,400

BALANCE SHEET
as on 31st March, 2016

Liabilities	₹	*Assets*	₹
Capital	48,500	Motor Car	32,000
Loan	30,000	Surgical Equipments	25,000
		Stock of medicines	9,500
		Cash at bank	11,000
		Cash in hand	1,000
	78,500		78,500

ILLUSTRATION 58

Old and New are in partnership, practising as Chartered Accountants under the name and style Oldnew & Co., sharing profits in the manner stated below. They close their accounts on 31st March. The following was their Balance Sheet as on 31st March, 2015.

Liabilities		₹	*Assets*		₹
Partners' Capitals:			Motor Car		20,000
Old	26,000		Office Machinery		3,000
New	18,000	44,000	Furniture		8,000
Audit Fees Collected in		1,000	Outstanding Audit Fees:		
Advance (old clients)			Old's clients	4,000	
Client Accounts		2,000	New's clients	5,000	9,000
Liabilities for Establishment exp.		500	Cash at bank		12,500
Provision against Outstanding			Cash in hand		1,500
Audit Fees		9,000	Library Books		2,500
		56,500			56,500

The following is the summary of their Cash Transactions for the year ended on 31st March 2016.

Receipts		₹	*Disbursements*		₹
Opening Cash and Bank Balance		14,000	Establishment charges		24,000
Audit Fees:			Motor car expenses		10,000
Old clients	90,000		Printing and Stationery		700
New clients	50,000	1,40,000	Postage and Telegrams		300
Fees for other service:			Subscription for journals		600
Old's Account	40,000		Library Books		1,500
New's Account	20,000	60,000	Calculating Machine		7,500
Miscellaneous Income		500	Travelling and Conveyance		2,500
			Member Fees	400	
			Drawings:		
			Old	50,000	
			New	40,000	90,000
			Disbursement on Clients		1,500
			Cash in hand		2,500
			Cash in bank		73,000
		2,14,500			2,14,500

The following particulars are further available:

(a) Depreciation to be provided on: Books @ 10%, Motor Cars @ 20% p.a., Furniture @ 10% p.a., Office Machine @ 15%.

(b) Audit Fees Receivable: New's clients: ₹ 2,000, Old's clients: ₹ 6,000.

(c) Outstanding liability for establishment expenses at the end: ₹ 1,000.

(d) It has been agreed that 40% of Audit Fees and 20% of Fees for other services should be transferred to Income and Expenditure Account in respect of each partner's account, the balance being credited directly to the Capital Accounts, Profits and Losses are to be divided between the partners in the ratio at 2:1.

Required: Prepare the Income and Expenditure Account for the year 2015-2016 and a Balance Sheet as on 31st March, 2016.

SOLUTION

INCOME AND EXPENDITURE ACCOUNT

Dr. *for the year ended on 31st March, 2016* Cr.

Expenditure		₹	*Income*	₹
To Establishment		24,500	By Audit Fees (₹ 36,400 + ₹ 20,000)	56,400
To Motor Car expenses		10,000	By Fee for other Services	12,000
To Printing and Stationery		700	By Miscellaneous Receipts	500
To Postage and Telegrams		300		
To Subscription for Journals		600		
To Travelling and Conveyance		2,500		
To Membership Fees		400		
To Depreciation		6,775		
To Profit:				
Old's Share	15,417			
New's Share	7,708	23,125		
		68,900		68,900

BALANCE SHEET AS AT 31ST MARCH, 2016

Liabilities		₹	*Assets*		₹
Capital Accounts:			Library Books (₹ 4,000 – ₹ 400)		3,600
Old	78,017		Motor Car (₹ 20,000 – ₹ 4,000)		16,000
New	31,708	1,09,725	Furniture (₹ 8,000 – ₹ 800)		7,200
Liabilities for establishment			Office Machinery		
expenses		1,000	(₹ 10,500 – ₹ 1,575)		8,925
Clients Accounts		500	Outstanding Audit Fees:		
Provision against Audit Fees			Old's clients	6,000	
Receivable		8,000	New's clients	2,000	8,000
			Cash in hand		2,500
			Cash in bank		73,000
		1,19,225			1,19,225

Working Notes:

(I) AUDIT FEES ACCOUNT

Dr. Cr.

Particulars	*Old* ₹	*New* ₹	*Particulars*	*Old* ₹	*New* ₹
To Balance b/d (Beg.)	4,000	5,000	By Provision against		
To Capital A/c (60%)	54,600	30,000	outstanding Fees A/c	4,000	5,000

To Income and Expenditure A/c (40%)	36,400	20,000	By Advance Fees A/c (in the beginning)	1,000	
To Provision against Outstanding Fees A/c			By Cash A/c	90,000	50,000
(at the end)	6,000	2,000	By Balance c/d (at the end)	6,000	2,000
	1,01,000	57,000		1,01,000	57,000

Dr. **(II) PROVISION AGAINST OUTSTANDING AUDIT FEE ACCOUNT** *Cr.*

Particulars	*Old* ₹	*New* ₹	*Particulars*	*Old* ₹	*New* ₹
To Audit Fees A/c	4,000	5,000	By Balance b/d	4,000	5,000
To Balance c/d	6,000	2,000	By Audit fees A/c	6,000	2,000
	10,000	7,000		10,000	7,000

Dr. **(III) FEES FOR OTHER SERVICE ACCOUNT** *Cr.*

Particulars	*Old* ₹	*New* ₹	*Particulars*	*Old* ₹	*New* ₹
To Capital A/c (80%)	32,000	16,000	By Cash A/c	40,000	20,000
To Income & Expenditure A/c (20%)	8,000	4,000			
	40,000	20,000		40,000	20,000

Dr. **(IV) CAPITAL ACCOUNTS OF PARTNERS** *Cr.*

Particulars	*Old* ₹	*New* ₹	*Particulars*	*Old* ₹	*New* ₹
To Drawings	50,000	40,000	By Balance b/d	26,000	18,000
To Balance c/d	78,017	31,708	By Audit fees (60%)	54,600	30,000
			By Other Services 80%	32,000	16,000
			By Share of Profit	15,417	7,708
	1,28,017	71,708		1,28,017	71,708

10B ACCOUNTING FOR EDUCATIONAL INSTITUTIONS

LEARNING OBJECTIVES

After studying this chapter, you should be able to understand:

- ◇ Organisational Pattern & Salient Features of an Educational Institution
- ◇ Sources of Finance for Running the Educational Institution
- ◇ Technique of Maintaining Fund Accounts

1.0 ORGANISATIONAL PATTERN & SALIENT FEATURES OF AN EDUCATIONAL INSTITUTION

1.1 Registration — The educational institutions in India are registered as Societies under the Indian Societies Registration Act, 1860, and/or are registered under the Public Trust Act. ***For Example***, in the State of Maharastra, all the Educational Societies have simultaneously been registered under the Bombay Public Trust Act, 1950.

1.2 Governing Body — The Governing Body consists of office bearers viz. President, Secretary, Treasurer and Executive Committee Members. The General Body consists of all the Members of the Society. The function of the Governing Body is to manage and supervise the affairs of the individual school *or* college. The Principal of the School/College is an Ex-officio Secretary of the said Governing Body.

2.0 SOURCES OF FINANCE FOR RUNNING THE EDUCATIONAL INSTITUTION

The sources of finance for running the Aided Educational Institutions and Self-financing Educational Institutions are as follows:

(a) Sources of Finance for Aided Educational Institutions.

(i) Grants received from the Government and/or Local Authorities.

(ii) Donations from Public;

(iii) Fees in the from of annual tuition fees, term fees, admission fees, laboratory fee etc., and

(b) Sources of Finance for Self-Financing Educational Institutions.

(i) Capitation Fee/Admission Fee

(ii) Contributions towards Development Fund, Building Fund etc.

(iii) Fees in the from of annual tuition fees, term fees, admission fees, laboratory fee etc., and

The Government grants are of four kinds namely Maintenance Grant, Equipment grant, Building Grant and such other grants as may be sanctioned by the Government from time to time.

2.1 Donation from Public — These are received either for recurring *or* non-recurring purposes, Donations are received either in cash *or* in kind. The 'in kind' donations are in the form of land and building, shares and securities, furnitures and fixtures.

2.2 Capitation Fee *or* Admission Fees — Capitation Fees *or* Admission Fees are collected by the Parent Body from parents/guardians of the students who seek admission in the educational institution.

2.3 Laboratory and Library Deposit — These are generally collected by schools and colleges and they remain with the institution till the student finally leaves it.

2.4 Use of Term Fee — A separate account of receipts and expenditures shall be maintained and surplus carried over to the next year. The following are main items on which term fee can be used:

(i) Examination expenses i.e. printing, including cyclo-styling of question papers and supply of answer books if there is sufficient balance.

(ii) Sports and Games-major and minor.

(iii) Contribution to athletic and cultural associations, connected with school activities.

(iv) Inter-class and Inter-school tournaments.

(v) School Magazine manuscript and/or printing.

(vi) School Functions and festivals.

(vii) Medical Inspection.

(viii) School Band.

(ix) School competitions.

(x) Newspapers and magazines.

(xi) Scouting and Guiding.

(xii) Vocational Guidance in general.

2.5 Recurring Grants — Recurring grants in the form of Maintenance Grants are received in instalments spread out throughout the year.

2.6 Use of Grant-in-Aid — The School Code provides a detailed list of items of expenditure which are admissible for grant-in-aid:

(i) Staff salaries and allowances

(ii) Leave Allowance

(iii) Bad Climate Allowance

(iv) Water Allowance

(v) Leave Salary

(vi) Expenditure on Training of Teachers

(vii) Pension and Gratuity as may be applicable.

(viii) Expenditure on the appointment of Librarian.

(ix) Rent, Taxes and Insurance.

(x) Other Contingencies — Under this head is covered expenditure of printing and stationery, conveyance expenditure, expenditure on purchase of books and furniture equipment (for which no special grant has been claimed provided it is upto the limit of 12 percent of the total admissible expenditure in Maharashtra.

(xi) Current repairs to the extent of 5 percent of the amount of grant of total expenditure of the School *or* 1-1/2 percent of the cost of the calculated as directed under Government Resolution No. 2321 dated 1.9.1923 as modified from time to time.

(xii) Miscellaneous Expenses: School Garden, Physical Education.

(xiii) Prizes.

(xiv) Expenditure on co-operative stores.

(xv) Registration fee paid to the board for recognition.

(xvi) Maintenance of Tiffin Rooms.

(xvii) Bonus to Teachers.

(xviii) Electrical Charges.

(xix) Telephone Charges.

(xx) Expenditure in connection with Conferences.

(xxi) Subscription to educational Association etc.

(xxii) Medical Charges.

(xxiii) Audit fees of the auditors in accordance with prescribed scale. The minimum being ₹ 75 upto admissible expenditure ₹ 50,000 and minimum ₹ 300 for expenditure over ₹ 50,000.

(xxiv) Sales-tax and General tax on purchase of the school requirements.

(xxv) Payments for merit scholarships.

ILLUSTRATION 1

From the following Trial Balance of Education Society as on 31st March, 2016; prepare an Income & Expenditure Account and a Balance Sheet.

Particulars	*Dr. (₹)*	*Cr. (₹)*
Furniture & Fittings	12,500	
Additions to Furniture (during the year)	3,200	
Library Books	17,500	
Addition to Library (during the year)	4,300	
Building	2,75,000	
General Investment	1,50,000	
Investment Reserve Fund		15,000
Sundry Debtors and Creditors	5,000	14,500
Entrance Fee	15,200	
Examination Fee		2,400
Subscription Received		20,000
Certificate Fee		500
Hire of Society's Hall		6,500
Interest on Investment		5,500
Sundry receipts		600
Staff Salaries	10,200	
Printing, Stationery & Advertising	1,000	
Taxes & Insurance	800	
Examination Expenses	600	
Subscription of Periodicals	1,200	
Prize Trust Fund		16,000
Prize Trust Investment	15,800	
Prize Trust Income		650
Prize Awarded	450	
Prize Fund Bank	275	

Donations received (to be capitalised)		18,000
General Expenses	375	
Capital Fund		3,89,150
Cash at Bank	5,500	
Cash in hand	300	
	5,04,000	5,04,000

The following further information is supplied to enable you to make the necessary adjustments:

Particulars	₹
Subscriptions receivable	4,500
Subscription received in advance	500
Interest on General Investment accrued	450
Staff salaries outstanding	1,800
Taxes & Insurance Paid in Advance	500
Provide depreciation at the following rates (including the additions):	
Library Books	15% p.a.
Furniture & Fittings	5% p.a.
Building	5% p.a.

The market value of General Investments was ₹ 1,30,000. You are not required to make any provision for this fall in value.

SOLUTION

BHARAT EDUCATION SOCIETY INCOME AND EXPENDITURE ACCOUNT

Dr. *for the year ended at 31st March, 2016* Cr.

Particulars		₹	*Particulars*		₹
To Staff salaries	10,200		By Subscription	20,000	
To *Add:* Outstanding	1,800	12,000	*Add:* Outstanding	4,500	
To Printing, Stationery & Advertising		1,000		24,500	
To Taxes & Insurance	800		*Less:* Received in advance	500	24,000
Less: Prepaid	500	300	By Entrance Fee		15,200
To Examination Expenses		600	By Examination Fee		2,400
To Subscription to Periodicals		1,200	By Certificate Fee		500
To General Expenses		375	By Hire of Society's Hall		6,500
To Depreciation:			By Interest on Investment		
Library Books	3,270		Received	5,500	
Furniture & Fittings	785		*Add:* Accrued	450	5,950
Building	13,750	17,805	By Sundry Receipts		600
To Excess of Income over Expen.		21,870			
		55,150			55,150

BALANCE SHEET OF BHARAT EDUCATION SOCIETY AS ON 31ST MARCH, 2016

Liabilities		₹	*Assets*		₹
Capital Fund	3,89,150		Building cost	2,75,000	
Add: Surplus	21,870	4,11,020	*Less:* Depreciation	13,750	2,61,250
Investment Res. Fund		15,000	Furniture & Fittings	12,500	
Prize Trust Fund	16,000		*Add:* Additions	3,200	
Income *less* Prizes	200	16,200		15,700	
Capital Reserve		18,000	*Less:* Depreciation	785	14,915
Subscription received in advance		500	Library Books	17,500	
Salaries Outstanding		1,800	*Add:* Additions	4,300	
Sundry Creditors		14,500		21,800	
			Less: Depreciation	3,270	18,530
			General Investment (M.V. ₹ 1,30,000)		1,50,000
			Interest Accrued		450
			Sundry Debtors		5,000
			Prize Trust Investments		15,800
			Prize Fund cash at Bank		275
			Cash at Bank		5,500
			Cash in Hand		300
			Subscription due		4,500
			Taxes & Insurance prepaid		500
		4,77,020			4,77,020

ILLUSTRATION 2

From the following balances and particulars of Republic College prepare Income & Expenditure Account for the year ended March, 2016 and a Balance Sheet as on the date:

Particulars	*Dr.* (₹)	*Cr.* (₹)
Seminars & Conference Receipts		4,80,000
Consultancy Receipts		1,28,000
Security Deposit Students		1,50,000
Capital Fund		16,06,000
Reseach Fund		8,00,000
Building Fund		25,00,000
Provident Fund		5,10,000
Tuition Fee received		8,00,000
Government Grants		5,00,000
Donations		50,000
Interest & Dividends on Investments		1,85,000

Hostel Room Rent		1,75,000
Mess Receipts (Net)		2,00,000
College Stores – Sales		7,50,000
Outstanding expenses		2,25,000
Stock of stores and Supplies	3,00,000	
Purchases – Stores & Supplies	8,00,000	
Salaries – Teaching	8,50,000	
Research	1,20,000	
Scholarships	80,000	
Students Welfare expenses	38,000	
Repairs & Maintenance	1,12,000	
Games & Sports Expenses	50,000	
Misc. Expenses	65,000	
Research Fund Investments	8,00,000	
Other Investments	18,50,000	
Provident Fund Investment	5,10,000	
Seminar & Conference Expenses	4,50,000	
Consultancy Expenses	28,000	
Land	1,00,000	
Building	16,00,000	
Plant and Machinery	8,50,000	
Furniture and Fittings	6,00,000	
Motor Vehicle	1,80,000	
Provision for Depreciation:		
Building		4,80,000
Plant & Equipment		5,10,000
Furniture & Fittings		3,36,000
Cash at Bank	6,42,000	—
Library	3,60,000	—
	1,03,85,000	1,03,85,000

Adjustments:

	₹
(1) Materials & Supplies consumed:	
Teaching	50,000
Research	1,50,000
Students Welfare	75,000
Games *or* Sports	25,000
(2) Tuition fee receivable from Government for backward class Scholars	80,000
(3) Stores selling prices are fixed to give a net profit of 10% on selling price	
(4) Depreciation is provided on straight line basis at the following rates:	

(i) Building	5%
(ii) Plant & Equipment	10%
(iii) Furniture & Fixtures	10%
(iv) Motor Vehicle	20%

SOLUTION

REPUBLIC COLLEGE INCOME AND EXPENDITURE ACCOUNT

for the year ending 31st March, 2016

Dr. Cr.

Expenditure		₹	*Income*		₹
To Salaries: Teaching		8,50,000	By Tuitions & Other Fee		8,80,000
Research		1,20,000	By Govt. Grants		5,00,000
To Material & Supplies Consumed:			By Income from Investments		1,85,000
— Teaching		50,000	By Hostel room Rent		1,75,000
— Research		1,50,000	By Mess Receipts		2,00,000
To Repairs & Maintenance		1,12,000	By Profit-stores Sales		75,000
To Sports & Games Expenses:			By Seminar and Conferences		
Cash	50,000		Income	4,80,000	
Materials	25,000	75,000	*Less:* Expenses	4,50,000	30,000
To Students Welfare Exp.:			By Consultancy charges:		
Cash	38,000		Income	1,28,000	
Materials	75,000	1,13,000	*Less:* Expenses	28,000	1,00,000
To Misc. Expenses		65,000	By Donations		50,000
To Scholarships		80,000			
To Depreciation:					
— Building		80,000			
— Plant & Equipment		85,000			
— Furniture		60,000			
— Motor Vehicle		36,000			
To Excess of Income over Expen.		3,19,000			
		21,95,000			21,95,000

BALANCE SHEET OF REPUBLIC COLLEGE AS ON 31ST MARCH, 2016

Liabilities		₹	*Assets*		₹
Capital Fund:			**Fixed Assets:**		
Opening Balance	16,06,000		Land		1,00,000
Add: Surplus	3,19,000	19,25,000	Building: Cost	16,00,000	
Other Funds:			*Less:* Dep.	5,60,000	10,40,000
Research Fund		8,00,000	**Equipment:**		
Building Fund		25,00,000	Cost	8,50,000	
Current Liabilities:			*Less:* Dep.	5,95,000	2,55,000

Outstanding Expenses	2,25,000	**Furniture & Fittings:**		
Provident Fund	5,10,000	Cost	6,00,000	
Security Deposit	1,50,000	*Less:* Dep.	3,96,000	2,04,000
		Motor Vehicles:		
		Cost	1,80,000	
		Less: Dep.	36,000	1,44,000
		Library		3,60,000
		Investments:		
		Capital Fund Investments		18,50,000
		Research Fund Investment		8,00,000
		P.F. Investment		5,10,000
		Current Assets:		
		Stock of Material & Supplies		1,25,000
		Grants receivable		80,000
		Cash in hand & at Bank		6,42,000
	61,10,000			61,10,000

Working Notes:

Dr. **(I) MATERIAL & SUPPLIES STOCK ACCOUNT** *Cr.*

Particulars	₹	*Particulars*	₹
To Balance b/d	3,00,000	By Income & Expenditure	3,00,000
To Purchases	8,00,000	By Sales	6,75,000
		By Balance c/d (b.f.)	1,25,000
	11,00,000		11,00,000

(II) PROVISIONS FOR DEPRECIATION

Particulars	*Building* ₹	*Plant & Equipment* ₹	*Furniture & Fitting* ₹
Opening Balance	4,80,000	5,10,000	3,36,000
Addition	80,000	85,000	60,000
Closing Balance	5,60,000	5,95,000	3,96,000

3.0 TECHNIQUE OF MAINTAINING FUND ACCOUNTS

3.1 Meaning of Fund Based Accounting — Fund based accounting essentially involves preparation of financial statements fund-wise. Separate ledgers are maintained for each fund. Fund ledgers are self-balancing in nature. A fund may be created for purchase, *or* construction of fixed assets *or* for any specific activities of the organisations *or* for both. ***For Example***, a building fund may be created with a view to purchase, *or* construct buildings. All receipts in connection with the purchase *or* construction of buildings are to be credited to the Building Fund. Any capital expenditure incurred for the purpose of construction *or* acquisition of building is debited to Building Fund.

When building is ultimately acquired *or* constructed, the asset is recognised in the general balance sheet and consequently that portion of the building fund which has been utilised for the acquisition *or* construction of the building is transferred to General Fund. Depreciation on assets can be charged only after its completion *or* acquisition.

In the same way, separate funds may be created for equipments, major repairs to fixed assets and for other developmental activities.

3.2 Journal Entries in Relation to Specific Fund

(a)	**On Receipt of Donation/Legacy/Grant for Specific Purpose (say Building, Prize, Sports)** Cash A/c / Bank A/c Dr. To Respective Fund A/c (Being the receipt of donations/Legacy/Grant for ....)
(b)	**On Investment of Amount of Specific Fund** Respective Fund Investment A/c Dr. To Cash A/c / Bank A/c (Being the purchase of ... Fund Investments)
(c)	**On Receipt *or* Accrual of Interest on Specific Fund Investments** Cash A/c / Bank A/c Dr. Accrued Interest A/c Dr. To Interest on Respective Fund Investment A/c (Being the receipt & accrual of Interest on ... Fund Investments)
(d)	**On Transfer of Interest on Respective Fund Investment to Respective Fund Account** Interest on Respective Fund Investment A/c Dr. To Respective Fund A/c (Being the transfer of interest on ... Fund Investments to ... Fund Account)
(e)	**On making due the Capital Expenditure Out of Fund** Capital Work-in-progress A/c Dr. To Contractor's A/c (Being the amount due to contractor in respect of part of work completed and certified)
(f)	**On making payment to contractor** Contractor's A/c Dr. To Cash A/c / Bank A/c (Being the payment made to contractor)
(g)	**On Transfer of Capital Work-in-progress to Respective Asset Account on Completion of Work** Respective Asset A/c Dr. To Capital Work-in-progress A/c (Being the transfer of Capital WIP to Respective Asset A/c)
(h)	**On Transfer of Corresponding Specific Fund to General Fund on Completion of Work** Respective Fund A/c Dr. To General Fund A/c (Being the transfer of corresponding specific fund to General Fund)

ILLUSTRATION 3

Tulsian Public School which maintains a Building Fund provides you the following information:

1.	Building Fund as at 1.4.2015	₹ 1,50,000
2.	12% Building Fund Investments as at 1.4.2015	₹ 1,00,000
3.	Building Fund Bank Balance as at 1.4.2015	₹ 50,000
4.	On 30.9.08 Received Interest on 12% Building Fund Investments	₹ 6,000
5.	Donations received for Building on 30.9.2015	₹ 8,50,000
6.	10% Building Fund Investments purchased on 1.10.2015	₹ 5,00,000
7.	Expenditure on construction of Building as per contractor's bill dated 31.12.2015 was ₹ 3,00,000 of which only 75% was certified and paid.	
8.	On 1.2.2016 contractor finished the remaining work and was paid.	

Required: Pass the necessary journal entries, prepare the Trial Balance of Building Fund Ledger and show the disclosure of related items in the Balance Sheet.

SOLUTION

JOURNAL

Date	*Particulars*	*L.F.*	*Dr. (₹)*	*Cr. (₹)*
30.9.2015	Bank A/c Dr.		6,000	
	To Interest on Building Fund Investment A/c			6,000
	(Being the receipt of interest as Building Fund Investment)			
30.9.2015	Bank A/c Dr.		8,50,000	
	To Building Fund A/c			8,50,000
	(Being the receipt of donations for Building)			
1.10.2015	10% Building Fund Investments A/c Dr.		5,00,000	
	To Bank A/c			5,00,000
	(Being the purchase of 10% Building Fund Investments)			
31.12.2015	Capital Work-in-Progress A/c Dr.		2,25,000	
	To Contractor's A/c			2,25,000
	(Being the amount due to contractor)			
31.12.2015	Contractor's A/c Dr.		2,25,000	
	To Bank A/c			2,25,000
	(Being the payment made to contractors)			
01.02.2016	Capital Work-in-Progress A/c Dr.		75,000	
	To Contractor's A/c			75,000
	(Being the amount due to contractor)			
01.02.2016	Contractor's A/c Dr.		75,000	
	To Bank A/c			75,000
	(Being the payment made to contractors)			

01.02.2016	Building A/c Dr.		3,00,000	
	To Capital Work-in-progress A/c			3,00,000
	(Being the transfer of completed Building to Asset A/c)			
01.02.2016	Building Fund A/c Dr.		3,00,000	
	To General Fund A/c			3,00,000
	(Being the transfer of Building Fund to General Fund to the extent of expenditure booked on Building)			
31.03.2016	Accrued Interest on 12% B F Investments A/c Dr.		6,000	
	Accrued Interest on 10% B F Investments A/c Dr.		25,000	
	To Interest on 12% BF Investments A/c Dr.			6,000
	To Interest on 10% BF Investments A/c Dr.			25,000
	(Being the interest accrued)			
31.03.2016	Interest on 12% B F Investments A/c Dr.		12,000	
	Interest on 10% B F Investments A/c Dr.		25,000	
	To Building Fund A/c Dr.			37,000
	(Being the transfer of interest to Building Fund A/c)			

TRIAL BALANCE OF BUILDING FUND AS AT 31.3.2016

Particulars	*Dr. (₹)*	*Cr. (₹)*
Building Fund		7,37,000
12% Building Fund Investments A/c	1,00,000	
10% Building Fund Investments A/c	5,00,000	
Building Fund Bank A/c	1,06,000	
Accrued Interest on 12% Building Fund Investments	6,000	
Accrued Interest on 10% Building Fund Investments	25,000	
	7,37,000	7,37,000

AN EXTRACT OF BALANCE SHEET AS AT 31.03.2016

Liabilities		₹	*Assets*	₹
General Fund:			Building	3,00,000
Opening Balance	?		12% Building Fund Investments	1,00,000
Add: Surplus	?		10% Building Fund Investments	5,00,000
Less: Deficit	?		Building Fund Bank	1,06,000
Add: T/f from Building Fund	3,00,000		Accrued Interest on 12% Building	
Building Fund:			Fund Investments	6,000
Opening Balance	1,50,000		Accrued Interest on 10% Building	
Add: Donations	8,50,000		Fund Investments	25,000
Add: Interest	37,000			
Less: T/f to General Fund	3,00,000	7,37,000		

ILLUSTRATION 4

Delhi School maintains separate building fund. As on 31.3.2015, balance of building fund was ₹ 20,00,000 and it was represented by 15% fixed deposit of ₹ 12,00,000 and current account balance of ₹ 8,00,000. During the year 2015-2016, the school collected as donations towards the building fund ₹ 11,20,000 and transferred 40% of developmental fees collected ₹ 45,13,000 to Building Fund. Capital work progress as on 31st March, 2015 was ₹ 16,50,000 for which contractors' bill upto 75% was paid on 30.09.2015. The extension of building was finished on 31.12.2015 costing ₹ 14,50,000 for which contractors' bill was fully met. It was decided to transfer the cost of completed building (₹ 31,00,000) to the corresponding asset account.

Required: Pass journal entries to incorporate the above transactions in the books of Delhi School for the year 2015-2016 and show the trial balance of Building Fund Ledger.

SOLUTION

JOURNAL ENTRIES FOR BUILDING FUND LEDGER

Date	*Particulars*		*L.F.*	*Dr. (₹)*	*Cr. (₹)*
(i)	Bank A/c	Dr.		11,20,000	
	To Building Fund A/c				11,20,000
	(Being the receipt of donations)				
(ii)	Bank A/c	Dr.		18,05,200	
	To Building Fund A/c				18,05,200
	(Being the transfer of 40% of the development fees directly)				
(iii)	Fixed Deposit A/c	Dr.		1,80,000	
	To Interest A/c				1,80,000
	(Being the accrual of interest on F.D.)				
(iv)	Interest A/c	Dr.		1,80,000	
	To Building Fund				1,80,000
	(Being the transfer of interest accrued on fixed deposit)				
(v)	Capital work in progress A/c	Dr.		14,50,000	
	To Contractors' A/c				14,50,000
	(Being the work completed and certified during the year)				
(vi)	Contractors' A/c	Dr.		26,87,500	
	To Bank A/c				26,87,500
	(Being the payments made to contractors)				
(vii)	Building A/c	Dr.		31,00,000	
	To Capital work-in-progress				31,00,000
	(Being the transfer of completed buildings to Asset A/c)				
(viii)	Building Fund A/c	Dr.		31,00,000	
	To General Fund A/c				31,00,000
	(Being the transfer of corresponding Building Fund to General Fund)				

TRIAL BALANCE OF BUILDING FUND AS ON 31ST MARCH, 2016

Particulars	*Dr. (₹)*	*Cr. (₹)*
Building Fund		20,05,200
Contractors' A/c		4,12,500
12% Fixed Deposit A/c	13,80,000	
Current A/c	10,37,700	
	24,17,700	24,17,700

SOLVED PROBLEMS

PROBLEM 1

Yougman Association is running a hostel for college students. There are 150 single bedrooms and 250 double bedrooms. Monthly room rent, payable for full year by each occupant is ₹ 90 p.m. for double bedrooms and ₹ 150 p.m. for single bedroom. Occupancy rate of double bedrooms is 90% and of single bedroom is 100%. From the following balances and additional information, prepare on Income and Expenditure Account for the year ending on 31st March, 2016 and a Balance Sheet as on that date.

Particulars	*₹ (Lakhs)*	*Particulars*	*₹ (Lakhs)*
Land	10.00	Income from Investments	96
Building	80.00	Room Rent	7.56
Furniture and Fixtures	2.00	Security Deposit @ ₹ 100 each	.60
Room Coolers,	2.00	Rent from Room Coolers, Heaters etc.	46
Heaters	.30	Electricity and Water charges @	
Telephones	6.00	₹ 10 p.m. for 10 months	.60
Investment—Govt. Securities	8.00	Mess fee for 10 months @ ₹200 p.m.	13.00
Opening Stock: Food (10 days)	.30	Mess Charges extra—Guests	.60
Fuel	.03	Room Services charges	15
Drinks	.055	Rent for Bankers/General Stores	.18
Sundries	.045	Annual Day Collection	.12
Purchases:		Grants—Youth Welfare Deptt.	1.50
Food	9.00	Rent of Hall	.54
Fuel	.81	Capital Fund	100.00
Drinks	1.20	General Fund	2.15
Sundries	.14	Annual Day Expenses	.15
Wages: Mess	4.32	Medical and First Aid expenses	.12
Others	.68	Repairs and Maintenance	.16
Electricity and Water Charges	.35	Indoor Games Material	.18
Common Room Expenses	.125	Cash at Bank	2.46

Additional Information: Closing stock of food, fuel drinks and sundries were valued at ₹ 35,000, ₹ 3,500, ₹ 6,000 and ₹ 5,400 respectively. Provide depreciation on Building @ 5% on Furniture and fittings, @ 10% p.a., on room coolers, heaters and telephone apparatus @ 20% p.a.

SOLUTION

INCOME AND EXPENDITURE ACCOUNT OF YOUNGMAN ASSOCIATION

Dr. *for the year ending on 31st March 2016* *Cr.*

Expenditure	₹	*Income*	₹
To Mess Expenses:		By Room Rent	7,56,000
Consumption of Materials		By Rent of Coolers etc.	46,000
Food (₹ 9,30,000 – ₹ 35,000)	8,95,000	By Electricity and Water charges	60,000
Fuel (₹ 84,000 – ₹ 3,500)	80,500	By Mess Receipts:	
Drinks (₹ 1,25,500 – ₹ 6,000)	1,19,500	Students	13,00,000
Sundries (₹ 18,500 – ₹ 5,400)	13,100	Guests	60,000
Wages: Mess	4,32,000	Charges	15,000
Wages: Others	68,000	Rent of Shop Apartment	18,000
To Electricity and Water Charges	35,000	By Annual Day Collection	12,000
(600 × ₹ 10 × 10)		By Grants	1,50,000
To Common Room Expenditure	12,500	By Rent of Hall	54,000
To Annual Day Expenditure	15,000	By Income from Investments	96,000
To Medical and First Aid	12,000		
To Repairs and Maintenance	16,000		
To Indoor Games Materials	18,000		
To Depreciation on:			
Building	4,00,000		
Furniture	20,000		
Room Coolers etc.	46,000		
Telephone Apparants	1,20,000		
To Surplus	38,400		
	23,41,000		23,41,000

BALANCE SHEET OF YOUNGMAN ASSOCIATION AS ON 31ST MARCH, 2016

Liabilities		₹	*Assets*		₹
Capital Fund		1,00,00,000	Land		10,00,000
General Fund:			Building	80,00,000	
Opening Balance	2,15,500		*Less:* Depreciation	4,00,000	76,00,000
Add: Surplus	38,400	2,53,900	Furniture	2,00,000	
Security Deposit (600 × ₹ 100)		60,000	*Less:* Depreciation	20,000	1,80,000
			Room Coolers etc.	2,30,000	
			Less: Depreciation	46,000	1,84,000
			Telephones	6,00,000	
			Less: Depreciation	1,20,000	4,80,000
			Investments		8,00,000
			Cash at Bank		20,000

		Stock of Consumables:		
		Food	35,000	
		Fuel	3,500	
		Drinks	6,000	
		Sundries	5,400	49,900
	1,03,13,900			1,03,13,900

Working Notes:

(i) No. of Students = (250 × 2 × 90%) + 150 = 600

(ii) Room Rent = (150 × ₹ 150 × 12) + (450 × ₹ 90 × 12) = ₹ 7,56,000.

11 ACCOUNTS FROM INCOMPLETE RECORDS [OR SINGLE ENTRY SYSTEM]

LEARNING OBJECTIVES

After studying this chapter, you should be able to understand:

- ◇ Meaning of Incomplete Records
- ◇ Reasons of Incomplete Records
- ◇ Limitations of Incomplete Records
- ◇ Distinction between Double Entry System and Incomplete Records (Popularly known as Single Entry System)
- ◇ Preparation of Accounts From Incomplete Records
- ◇ Statement of Affairs Method
- ◇ Final Accounts Method

1.0 MEANING OF INCOMPLETE RECORDS

1. Incomplete Accounting Records are those accounting records which, **at present**, are not complete according to Double Entry Accounting Principles.

   Example: Mr Smart Master Mind, a trader, maintains his books of accounts according to Double Entry Accounting Principles. On 31st March, a fire took place and some of the accounting records destroyed. In this case, his records are Incomplete Accounting Records at present even though these were maintained according to Double Entry Accounting Principles.

2. Many authors describe it as the Single Entry System but according to the majority of accountants, it is appropriate to describe it as Incomplete Records because incomplete records contain:

   1. Both the aspects of some of the transactions; *e.g., Cash received from Debtors.*
   2. Only one aspect of some of the transactions; *e.g., Cash Sales, Cash Purchases.*
   3. No aspect of some of the transactions. *e.g., Depreciation, Provision for Doubtful Debts.*

2.0 REASONS OF INCOMPLETE RECORDS

Accounting records may be incomplete due to any one *or* more of the following reasons:

1. The businessman may be ignorant of the separate legal entity assumption:
2. The businessman may be ignorant of the double entry accounting principles;
3. The businessman may not intentionally maintain proper accounts to evade taxation;
4. Destruction of the books of accounts due to fire, flood etc.

3.0 LIMITATIONS OF INCOMPLETE RECORDS

Maintenance of incomplete records suffers from the following limitations:

1. **No checking of Arithmetical Accuracy**—Arithmetical accuracy of the accounts can not be checked because no agreed trial balance can be prepared.
2. **No True Financial Performance**—True financial performance can not be ascertained because Trading and Profit & Loss Account cannot be prepared.
3. **No True Financial Position**—True financial position cannot be ascertained because balance sheet cannot be prepared.
4. **No Recognition under Laws**—Such records are not recognised by the Courts, Sales Tax and Income Tax authorities.
5. It is difficult to conduct the audit of such records.
6. It is difficult to operate internal control system.
7. It is difficult to operate internal check system.
8. It is difficult to exercise control over assets.
9. It is difficult to detect fraud.

4.0 DISTINCTION BETWEEN DOUBLE ENTRY SYSTEM AND INCOMPLETE RECORDS (POPULARLY KNOWN AS SINGLE ENTRY SYSTEM)

Basis of Distinction	*Double Entry System*	*Incomplete Records System*
1. Assumptions and principles	It is **based** on certain assumptions and principles.	It is **not based** on certain assumptions and principles.
2. Both aspects of all transactions	Both the aspects of all transactions are **recorded.**	Both the aspects of all transactions are **not recorded.**
3. Nature of accounts maintained	**All** types of accounts—Personal, Real & Nominal, are maintained.	**Usually, cash and Personal** accounts are maintained.
4. Trial Balance	Arithmetical accuracy of the records can be checked by **preparing a Trial Balance.**	Arithmetical accuracy of the records cannot be checked since Trial Balance **cannot be prepared.**
5. Determination of True Profit or Loss	**True profits *or* losses** can be determined by preparing Trading and Profit & Loss Account.	**Only estimated profit *or* losses** can be determined since Trading & Profit and Loss Account cannot be prepared.
6. Financial position	**True** financial position can be known by preparing a Balance Sheet.	**Only estimated** financial position can be known on the basis of Statement of Affairs.
7. Adjustments	**All types** of adjustments are made while preparing final accounts.	**No special attention** is given to adjustments.
8. Utility	It is used by **all types of traders.**	It is used only by **small traders.**
9. Recognition	Records maintained according to this system are **recognized by the government.**	Records maintained according to this system are **not recognized by the government.**

5.0 METHOD OF PREPARATION OF ACCOUNTS FROM INCOMPLETE RECORDS

To ascertain the financial performance and the financial position of the business, the information available from the incomplete records can be used in the following methods:

1. Statement of Affairs Method 2. Final Accounts Method

6.0 STATEMENT OF AFFAIRS METHOD

PRACTICAL STEPS INVOLVED IN THE ASCERTAINMENT OF THE PROFIT/LOSS ACCORDING TO THE STATEMENT OF AFFAIRS METHOD

Step 1: ***Ascertain closing capital*** *by preparing a Statement of Affairs at the end of the accounting period.*

Step 2: ***Add:*** *the amount of* ***drawings*** *(whether in cash or in kind) to the Closing Capital, (calculated as per Step 1).*

Step 3: ***Deduct*** *the amount of* ***additional capital*** *introduced from the Closing Capital (calculated as per Step 1).*

Step 4: ***Ascertain Opening Capital*** *by preparing a Statement of Affairs at the beginning of the accounting period.*

Step 5: ***Ascertain Profits or Losses*** *by deducting Opening capital from the Adjusted Closing Capital.*

Note: *Adjusted Closing Capital = Closing Capital + Drawings – Additional Capital*

Step 6: ***Make Adjustment*** *for items not yet adjusted while calculating closing capital e.g. interest on capital and salary of the proprietor or partner(s).*

FORMAT OF STATEMENT OF AFFAIRS

STATEMENT OF AFFAIRS OF... AS AT...

Liabilities	₹	*Assets*	₹
Sundry Creditors	xxx	Cash in Hand	xxx
Bills Payable	xxx	Cash at Bank	xxx
Outstanding Expenses	xxx	Sundry debtors	xxx
Bank Overdraft	xxx	Bills Receivable	xxx
Capital (Balancing figure)	xxx	Stock in trade	xxx
		Prepaid Expenses	xxx
		Fixed Assets	xxx
	xxx		xxx

FORMAT OF STATEMENT SHOWING PROFIT *or* LOSS

STATEMENT SHOWING PROFIT *or* LOSS FOR THE PERIOD ENDING...

	Particulars	₹
A.	Capital at the end of accounting period	xxx
B.	*Add:* Drawings (whether in cash *or* in kind) during the accounting period	xxx
C.	*Less:* additional Capital introduced (whether in cash *or* in kind) during the accounting period	xxx
D.	Adjusted Capital at the end of accounting period (A + B – C)	xxx
E.	Capital at the beginning of accounting period	xxx
F.	Profit (if Adjusted Capital is *more* than the Opening Capital) *or* Loss (if Adjusted Capital is *less* than the Opening Capital)	xxx

DISTINCTION BETWEEN STATEMENT OF AFFAIRS AND BALANCE SHEET

Basis of Distinction	*Statement of Affairs*	*Balance Sheet*
1. Basis of preparation	It is prepared on the basis of **some ledger accounts and estimates.**	It is prepared on the basis of **ledger accounts.**
2. Balance of Capital Account	Balance of Capital Account is arrived at as a **balancing figure.**	Balance of Capital Account is **taken from the ledger**
3. Omission ofAssets/ Liabilities	Omission of an asset *or* liability **cannot be easily traced.**	Omission of an asset *or* liability **can be easily traced** because of non-agreement of both the sides of Balance Sheet.
4. Estimated Vs True Financial Position	It shows only the **estimated** financial position.	It shows the **true** financial position.

ILLUSTRATION 1

Mr X could not keep complete records. He furnishes you the following information for the year 2012–2013:

(A) PARTICULARS OF ASSETS AND LIABILITIES

Particulars	*1st April* ₹	*31st March* ₹
Stock-in-trade	37,400	46,800
Sundry Debtors	24,000	28,000
Sundry Creditors	18,000	3,000
Bills Receivable	8,000	10,000
Bills Payable	2,000	400
Furniture & Fixtures	1,200	1,200
Buildings	24,000	24,000
Bank Balance	8,700	1,660(Cr.)

(b) Additional Information: He sold his private investments of ₹ 4,000 at 25% premium and brought this money into his business. His drawings were ₹ 1,000 p.m.; Stock costing ₹ 3,000 was taken by Mr X for his personal use. A provision @ 10% is required for doubtful debts and depreciation @ 5% p.a. is to be written-off for furniture and fixtures and buildings, Prepaid Insurance amounted to ₹ 400, Outstanding Expenses are ₹ 9,800.

Required: From the above particulars, find out by Statement of Affairs method, the Profit *or* Loss made by Mr X during 2012–2013. Also prepare his Balance Sheet as at 31 March 2013.

SOLUTION

Step 1: Calculation of Opening Capital and Closing Capital

STATEMENT OF AFFAIRS OF MR X AS AT 31.3.2012 AND 31.3.2013

Liabilities	*31.3.2012* ₹	*31.3.2013* ₹	*Assets*	*31.3.2012* ₹	*31.3.2013* ₹
Sundry Creditors	18,000	3,000	Cash at Bank	8,700	—
Bills Payable	2,000	400	Stock-in-trade	37,400	46,800

Bank Overdraft	–	1,660	Sundry Debtors	24,000	28,000
Capital (b.f.)	83,300	1,04,940	Bills Receivable	8,000	10,000
			Furniture & Fixtures	1,200	1,200
			Buildings	24,000	24,000
	1,03,300	1,10,000		1,03,300	1,10,000

Step 2: Calculation of Profit *or* Loss

STATEMENT OF PROFIT *or* LOSS FOR THE YEAR ENDING ON 31.3.2013

Particulars		₹
A. Capital at the end		1,04,940
B. Add.: Drawings during the year [Cash (₹ 1,000 × 12) + Stock of ₹ 3,000]		15,000
C. *Less:* Additional capital introduced during the year [₹ 4,000 + 25% of ₹ 4,000]		(5,000)
D. Adjusted Capital at the end (A + B – C)		1,14,940
E. *Less:* Capital in the beginning		(83,300)
F. Profit subject to adjustments (D – E)		31,640
G. *Less:* Adjustments		
Provision for Doubtful Debts	2,800	
Depreciation on furniture	60	
Depreciation on Building	1,200	
Outstanding Expenses	9,800	
Prepaid Insurance	(400)	(13,460)
H. Net Profit for the year [F – G]		18,180

Step 3: Preparation of Closing Balance Sheet

BALANCE SHEET OF MR X AS AT 31ST MARCH, 2013

Liabilities		₹	*Assets*		₹
Sundry Creditors		3,000	Stock in trade		46,800
Bills Payable		400	Sundry Debtors	28,000	
Bank Overdraft		1,660	*Less:* Provision	2,800	25,200
Outstanding expenses:		9,800	Bills Receivable		10,000
Capital:			Prepaid Expenses		400
Opening Balance	83,300		Furniture & Fixtures	1,200	
Add: Profit	18,180		*Less:* Depreciation	60	1,140
Add: Additional Capital	5,000		Buildings	24,000	
	1,06,480		*Less:* Depreciation	1,200	22,800
Less: Drawings	(15,000)	91,480			
		1,06,340			1,06,340

ILLUSTRATION 2

On 1.7.2012, Nikita Mittal commenced her business with ₹5,00,000. On 1st Oct. she sold her private investments (Cost ₹50,000, Face value ₹40,000) at 125% of face value and brought the proceeds into her bussiness. Her drawings were ₹1,000 p.m. Goods costing ₹11,000 were taken by her for personal use. On 31.3.2013, Capital before adjustments ₹7,00,000, Outstanding Expenses ₹21,000 and Prepaid Expenses ₹4,000.Provide Interest on Capital @ 12% p.a and for group incentive to staff @5% on Net Profit after charging such incentive and interest on capital. Calculate the Profit/Loss for the year ended 31st March, 2013.

SOLUTION

STATEMENT OF PROFIT *or* LOSS FOR THE YEAR ENDING ON 31.3.2013

	Particulars		₹
A.	Capital at the end		7,00,000
B.	*Add:* Drawings during the year [Cash (₹ 1,000 × 9) + Goods of ₹ 11,000]		20,000
C.	*Less:* Additional capital introduced during the year [₹ 40,000 + 25% of ₹ 40,000]		50,000
D.	Adjusted Capital at the end (A + B – C)		6,70,000
E.	*Less:* Capital in the beginning		5,00,000
F.	Profit subject to adjustments (D – E)		1,70,000
G.	*Less:* Adjustments		
	Outstanding Expenses	(21,000)	
	Prepaid Expenses	4,000	
	Interest on Capital		
	(12% x 5,00,000 x 9/12) 45,000		
	(12% x 50,000 x 6/12) 3,000	(48,000)	65,000
H.	Net Profit before Group Commission for the year [F – G]		1,05,000
I.	*Less:* Group Commission [₹ 1,05,000 × 5/105]		5,000
J.	Net Profit [H – I]		1,00,000

ILLUSTRATION 3

Mr. X could not keep complete records. He furnishes you the following information for the year 2012-2013:

(A) PARTICULARS OF ASSETS AND LIABILITIES

Particulars	*Opening* ₹	*Closing* ₹
Stock-in-trade	37,400	46,800
Sundry Debtors	24,000	28,000
Sundry Creditors	18,000	3,000
Bills Receivable	8,000	10,000
Bills Payable	2,000	400
Fixed Assets	25,200	25,200
Bank Balance	8,700	1,690(Cr.)

Information: On 1.10.2012 he sold his private investments of ₹ 4,000 at 25% premium and brought this money into his business. His drawings were ₹ 1,000 p.m.; Goods costing ₹ 3,000 were taken away by Mr X for his personal case. A provision @ 10% is required for doubtful debts and depreciation @ 5% p.a. is to be written-off on fixed assets, ₹ 6,000 is outstanding for wages and ₹ 3,800 for salaries, prepaid insurance amounted to ₹ 400. Provide Interest on Capital @ 5% p.a. and for group incentive to staff @ 5% on net profit after charging such incentive and interest on capital.

Required: From the above particulars, (i) find out profit *or* loss by Statement of Affairs method, and (ii) prepare the Balance Sheet as at 31 March 2013.

SOLUTION

Step 1: Calculation of Opening Capital and Closing Capital

STATEMENT OF AFFAIRS OF MR. X AS AT 31.3.2012 AND 31.3.2013

Liabilities	*31.3.2012* ₹	*31.3.2013* ₹	*Assets*	*31.3.2012* ₹	*31.3.2013* ₹
Sundry Creditors	18,000	3,000	Cash at Bank	8,700	—
Bills Payable	2,000	400	Stock-in-trade	37,400	46,800
Bank Overdraft	—	1,690	Sundry debtors	24,000	28,000
Capital (b.f.)	83,300	1,04,910	Bills Receivable	8,000	10,000
			Fixed Assets	25,200	25,200
	1,03,300	1,10,000		1,03,300	1,10,000

Step 2: Calculation of Profit *or* Loss

STATEMENT OF PROFIT *or* LOSS FOR THE YEAR ENDING ON 31.3.2013

	Particulars			₹
A.	Capital at the end			1,04,910
B.	*Add:* Drawings during the year [Cash (₹ 1,000 × 12) + Goods of ₹ 3,000]			15,000
C.	*Less:* Additional capital introduced during the year [₹ 4,000 + 25% of ₹ 4,000]			5,000
D.	Adjusted Capital at the end (A + B – C)			1,14,910
E.	*Less:* Capital in the beginning			83,300
F.	Profit subject to adjustments (D – E)			31,610
G.	*Less:* Adjustments			
	Provision for Doubtful Debts		2,800	
	Depreciation on Fixed Assets		1,260	
	Outstanding Wages		6,000	
	Outstanding Salaries		3,800	
	Interest on Capital			
	5% on 83,300	4,165		
	5% on 5,000 (1/2 year)	125	4,290	
	Prepaid Insurance		(400)	17,750
H.	Net Profit before Group Commission for the year [F – G]			13,860
I.	*Less:* Group Commission [₹ 13,860 × 5/105]			660
J.	Net profit [H – I]			13,200

Step 3: Preparation of Closing Balance Sheet

BALANCE SHEET OF MR. X AS AT 31ST MARCH, 2013

Liabilities		₹	*Assets*		₹
Sundry Creditors		3,000	Stock in trade		46,800
Bills Payable		400	Sundry Debtors	28,000	
Bank Overdraft		1,690	*Less:* Provision	2,800	25,200
Outstanding expenses:			Bills Receivable		10,000
Wages	6,000		Prepaid Expenses		400
Salaries	3,800		Fixed Assets	25,200	
Group Commission	660	10,460	*Less:* Depreciation	1,260	23,940
Capital:					
Opening Balance	83,300				
Add: Additional capital	5,000				
Add: Int. on Capital	4,290				
Less: Drawings	15,000				
Add: Profit	13,200	90,790			
		1,06,340			1,06,340

7.0 FINAL ACCOUNTS METHOD

Practical steps involved in the preparation of the Final Accounts from incomplete records:

PRACTICAL STEPS INVOLVED IN THE PREPARATION OF FINAL ACCOUNTS FROM INCOMPLETE RECORDS

Step 1: Prepare Cash and Bank Summary (if not available in proper form with both sides tallied) to ascertain the missing information (such as opening and closing balance, cash sales/cash purchases, drawings).

Step 2: Prepare Total Debtors Account to ascertain the missing information (such as opening/closing balance, credit sales, collection, B/R drawn).

Step 3: Prepare Bills receivable Account to ascertain the missing information (such as opening/closing balance, B/R drawn, B/R collected, B/R endorsed).

Step 4: Prepare Total Creditors Account to ascertain the missing information (such as opening/closing balance, credit purchases, payment made, B/P accepted, B/R endorsed).

Step 5: Prepare Bills Payable Account to ascertain the missing information (such as opening/closing balance, B/P accepted, B/P discharged).

Step 6: Prepare Stock Account to ascertain the missing information (such as opening stock/closing stock, total purchases, cost of goods sold, shortage).

Step 7: Prepare Revenue Expense Account to ascertain the missing information (such as opening/closing balance of outstanding/prepaid expenses, expenses paid, current year's expenses).

Step 8: Prepare Revenue Income Account to ascertain the missing information (such as opening/closing balance of accrued/unaccrued income, income received, current year's income).

Step 9: Prepare Fixed Asset Account to ascertain the missing information (such as opening/closing balance, purchases/sale, depreciation provided, profit/loss on sale).

Step 10: Ascertain Opening capital by preparing Statement of Affairs at the beginning of the accounting period.

Step 11: Prepare Trial balance to check the arithmetical accuracy.

Step 12: Prepare Trading and Profit and Loss Account and the Balance Sheet.

Let us Discuss each of the aforesaid steps in detail as follows:

STEP 1: PREPARE CASH AND BANK SUMMARY (IF NOT AVAILABLE IN PROPER FORM WITH BOTH SIDES TALLIED).

(a) If both the sides of a cash Book are not tallied, then the difference in both the sides may be treated as one of the following items:

If credit side exceeds debit side	***If debit side exceeds credit side***
1. Opening cash *or* Bank Balance *or* Closing Bank overdraft	1. Closing Cash *or* Bank Balance *or* Opening Bank overdraft
2. Cash Sales	2. Cash Purchases
3. Collection from debtors	3. Payment to creditors
4. Bills Receivable collected	4. Bills Payables discharged
5. Additional Capital	5. Drawings
6. Sale of a fixed Asset	6. Purchase of a fixed Asset
7. Sundry Incomes	7. Sundry Expenses
	8. Cash Embezzlement by Cashier

(b) Format of Cash Book—A format of Cash Book is given below:

Dr. **CASH BOOK** *Cr.*

Receipts	*Cash (₹)*	*Bank (₹)*	*Payments*	*Cash (₹)*	*Bank (₹)*
To Balance b/d	xxx	xxx	By Balance b/d (overdraft)	—	xxx
To Cash Sales	xxx		By Cash Purchases	xxx	
To Collection from Debtors	xxx	xxx	By Payment to creditors	xxx	xxx
To Bills Receivable collected	xxx	xxx	By Bills Payable discharged	xxx	xxx
To Additional Capital	xxx	xxx	By Drawings	xxx	xxx
To Sale of a Fixed Asset	xxx	xxx	By Purchase of a fixed asset	xxx	xxx
To Sundry Incomes	xxx	xxx	By Sundry Expenses	xxx	xxx
To Balance c/d (overdraft)	—	xxx	By Balance c/d	xxx	xxx
	xxx	xxx		xxx	xxx

ILLUSTRATION 4

Ascertain the appropriate missing figure by preparing the Cash Book, from the following information: (Note: all transactions are made through cheque).

Collection from debtors ₹ 75,800, Payment to Creditors ₹ 52,200, Bills receivable Collected ₹ 24,000, Bills Payables discharged ₹ 18,600, Cash Sales deposited ₹ 17,200, cash purchases ₹ 1,000 (by cheque), Capital introduced on ₹ 5,000, drawings ₹ 15,000, commission received ₹ 3,000, wages paid ₹ 24,000, Salaries paid ₹ 13,000, Rent paid ₹ 8,800, Insurance Premium paid ₹ 1,600, carriage inwards paid ₹ 500, Advertising paid ₹ 660. Opening Bank Balance ₹ 8,700.

SOLUTION

Dr. **CASH BOOK (BANK COLUMN)** Cr.

Receipts	₹	Payments	₹
To Balance b/d	8,700	By Cash Purchases	1,000
To Sundry Debtors	75,800	By Drawings	15,000
To Bills Receivable	24,000	By Trade Creditors	52,200
To Commission	3,000	By Bills Payable	18,600
To Cash Sales	17,200	By Salaries	13,000
To Capital Introduced	5,000	By Wages	24,000
To Balance c/d (b.f.)	1,660	By Rent & Taxes	8,800
		By Insurance	1,600
		By Carriage Inwards	500
		By Advertising	660
	1,35,360		1,35,360

Step 2: Prepare total Debtors Account

(a) If both the sides of this account are not tallied, then the difference of both the sides may be treated as one of the following items:

If credit side exceeds debit side	*If debit side exceeds credit side*
1. Opening Debtors	1. Closing debtors
2. Credit Sales	2. Collection from debtors
3. Bills receivable dishonoured	3. Bills receivable drawn
	4. Sales returns
	5. Discount allowed
	6. Bad debts

(b) Format of Total Debtors Account—A format of total debtors Account is given below:

Dr. **TOTAL DEBTORS ACCOUNT** Cr

Particulars	₹	Particulars	₹
To Balance b/d	xxx	By Sales Returns	xxx
To Bills Receivable A/c	xxx	By Cash A/c (Cash received)	xxx
(B/R dishonoured)		By Bank A/c (Cheques received)	xxx
To Bank A/c		By Bills Receivable A/c (B/R drawn)	xxx
(Discounted B/R Dishonoured)	xxx	By Discount Allowed	xxx
To Bank A/c		By Bad Debts	xxx
(Cheque dishonoured)	xxx	By Balance c/d	xxx
To Total Creditors A/c	xxx		
[Endorsed B/R dishonoured]			
To Credit Sales	xxx		
	xxx		xxx

Tutorial Note: Provision for Doubtful Debts, Provision for Discount on Debtors, Bad Debts recovered, Trade Discount allowed, B/R Discounted do not effect the Total Debtors Account.

ILLUSTRATION 5

Ascertain the appropriate missing figure by preparing the Total Debtors Account from the following information:

Closing Debtors ₹ 28,000, Opening debtors ₹ 24,000, Sales returns ₹ 1,000, Cash received from debtors ₹ 74,800, Bills Receivable drawn ₹ 26,000, discount allowed ₹ 1,000, Bad Debts ₹ 1,000, Cheques received from Debtors ₹ 10,000, Bills Receivable dishonoured ₹ 4,000, Cheques dishonoured ₹ 6,000.

SOLUTION

Dr. **TOTAL DEBTORS ACCOUNT** *Cr.*

Particulars	₹	*Particulars*	₹
To Balance b/d	24,000	By Sales Returns	1,000
To Bills Receivable A/c (B/R dish)	4,000	By Cash A/c	74,800
To Bank A/c (Ch. dish.)	6,000	By Bank A/c	10,000
To Credit Sales (b.f.)	1,07,800	By Bills Receivable A/c (B/R drawn)	26,000
		By Discount allowed	1,000
		By Bad Debts	1,000
		By Balance b/d	28,000
	1,41,800		1,41,800

Step 3: Prepare Bills Receivable Account.

(a) If both the sides of this account are not tallied, then the difference in both the sides may be treated as one of the following items:

If credit side exceeds debit side	***If debit side exceeds credit side***
1. Opening B/R	1. Closing B/R
2. B/R drawn	2. B/R collected
	3. B/R dishonoured
	4. B/R discounted
	5. Banker's discount charges
	6. B/R endorsed

(b) Format of Bills Receivable Account—A format of Bills Receivable Account is given below:

Dr. **BILLS RECEIVABLE ACCOUNT** *Cr.*

Particulars	₹	*Particulars*	₹
To Balance b/d	xxx	By Cash A/c (B/R collected)	xxx
To Total Debtors A/c	xxx	By Bank A/c (B/R discounted)	xxx
(Bills Receivable received)		By Banker's Discount A/c	xxx
		(Discounting charges)	
		By Total Creditors A/c (B/R endorsed)	xxx

		By Total Debtors A/c (B/R dishonoured)	xxx
		By Balance c/d	xxx
	xxx		xxx

Tutorial Note: Provision for Doubtful Bills does not affect the Bills Receivable Account

ILLUSTRATION 6

Ascertain the appropriate missing figure from the following information:

Closing Bills receivables ₹ 10,000, Opening Bills receivables ₹ 8,000, Bills collected ₹ 10,500. Bills Receivable of ₹ 50,000 discounted with a Bank at a discount of ₹ 2,000, Bills Receivable of ₹ 25,000 endorsed in favour of creditors. Bills Receivable (which were retained) dishonoured ₹ 12,500.

SOLUTION

Dr. **BILLS RECEIVABLE ACCOUNT** *Cr.*

Particulars	₹	*Particulars*	₹
To Balance b/d	8,000	By Cash A/c (B/R collected)	10,500
To Total Debtors A/c (B/R drawn) (b.f.)	1,00,000	By Bank A/c (B/R discounted)	48,000
		By Discount A/c	2,000
		By Total Creditors' A/c	25,000
		By Total Debtors' A/c	12,500
		By Balance c/d	10,000
	1,08,000		1,08,000

Step 4: Prepare Total Creditors Account.

(a) If both the sides of this account are not tallied, then the difference in both the sides may be treated as one of the following items:

If credit side exceeds debit side	***If debit side exceeds credit side***
1. Closing Creditors	1. Opening Creditors
2. Payment to Creditors	2. Credit Purchases
3. Bills Payables accepted	3. Bills Payable cancelled
4. B/R endorsed to creditors	4. Endorsed B/R Dishonoured
5. Purchases returns	
6. Discount Received	

(b) Format of Total Creditor Account—A format of total Creditors Account is given below:

Dr. **TOTAL CREDITORS ACCOUNT** *C*

Particulars	₹	*Particulars*	₹
To Purchases Returns	xxx	By Balance b/d	xxx
To Cash A/c (Cash paid)	xxx	By Bills Payable A/c (B/R dishonoured/cancelled)	xxx
To Bank A/c (Cheque issued)	xxx	By Bank A/c	
To Bills Payable A/c			

(B/P accepted)	xxx	(cheque dishonoured)	xxx
To Bills Receivable A/c		By Total Debtors A/c	
(B/R endorsed)	xxx	(Endorsed B/R dishonoured)	xxx
To Discount Received	xxx	By Credit Purchases	xxx
To Purchases Returns	xxx		
To Balance c/d	xxx		
	xxx		xxx

Tutorial Note: Reserve for Discount on Creditors does not effect the Total Creditors Account

ILLUSTRATION 7

Ascertain the appropriate missing figures by preparing Total Creditors Account from the following information:

Closing Creditors ₹ 3,000, Opening creditors ₹ 18,000, Cash paid to creditors ₹ 52,200, Discount allowed by creditors ₹ 1,000, Purchases returns ₹ 1,000, Bills Payables accepted ₹ 17,000. Cheques issued to creditors ₹ 10,000, Bills Receivables endorsed in favour of creditors ₹ 20,000 out of which 25% bills were dishonoured.

SOLUTION

Dr. **TOTAL CREDITORS ACCOUNT** *Cr.*

Particulars	₹	*Particulars*	₹
To Purchase Returns	1,000	By Balance b/d	18,000
To Cash A/c	52,200	By Total Debtors' A/c	
To Bank A/c	10,000	(25% of ₹ 20,000)	5,000
To Bills Payable A/c	17,000	By Credit Purchases (b.f)	81,200
To Bills Receivable A/c	20,000		
To Discount	1,000		
To Balance c/d	3,000		
	1,04,200		1,04,200

Step 5: Prepare Bills Payable Account.

(a) If both the sides of this account are not tallied, then the difference in both sides may be treated as one of the following items:

If credit side exceeds debit side	***If debit side exceeds credit side***
1. Closing B/P	1. Opening B/P
2. B/P discharged/cancelled	2. B/P accepted

(b) Format of Bills Payable Account—A format of Bills Payable Account is given below:

Dr. **BILLS PAYABLE ACCOUNT** *Cr.*

Particulars	₹	*Particulars*	₹
To Cash/Bank/A/c	xxx	By Balance b/d	xxx
(Bills Payable discharged)		By Total Creditors A/c	
To Creditors A/c	xxx	(Bills Payable accepted)	xxx

(Bills Payable dishonoured/cancelled)			
To Balance c/d	xxx		
	xxx		xxx

ILLUSTRATION 8

Ascertain the appropriate missing figure by preparing Bills Payable Account from the following information:

Opening Bills Payable ₹ 2,000, Bills discharged ₹ 18,600, Closing Bills Payable ₹ 400.

SOLUTION

Dr. **BILLS PAYABLE ACCOUNT** *Cr.*

Particulars	₹	*Particulars*	₹
To Cash A/c (B/P discharged)	18,600	By Balance b/d	2,000
To Balance c/d	400	By Total Creditors A/c (Bills accepted)	17,000
	19,000		19,000

Step 6: Prepare Revenue Expenses Account.

(a) If both the sides are not tallied, then the difference in both the sides may be treated as one of the following items.

If credit side exceeds debit side	***If debit side exceeds credit side***
1. Prepaid Expenses in the beginning	1. Outstanding Expenses in the beginning
2. Expenses paid	2. Expenses chargeable for current year
3. Outstanding Expenses at the end	3. Prepaid at the end

(b) Format of Revenue Expense Account—A format of Revenue Expenses Account is given below:

Dr. **REVENUE EXPENSES ACCOUNT (SAY SALARIES ACCOUNT)** *Cr.*

Particulars	₹	*Particulars*	₹
To Balance b/d (Prepaid in the beginning)	xxx	By Balance b/d (Outstanding in the beginning)	xxx
To Cash/Bank A/c (Expenses paid during the current accounting period)	xxx	By Trading and Profit & Loss A/c (Expenses chargeable for the current accounting period)	xxx
To Balance c/d (Outstanding at the end)	xxx	By Balance c/d (Prepaid at the end)	xxx
	xxx		xxx

ILLUSTRATION 9

Ascertain the appropriate missing figure from the following information:

Particulars	*Opening*	*Closing*
Outstanding Salary	₹ 10,000	₹ 15,000
Prepaid Salary	₹ 20,000	₹ 30,000

Salary paid during the year 2012-2013 ₹ 1,00,000.

SOLUTION

Dr. **SALARIES ACCOUNT** *Cr.*

Particulars	₹	*Particulars*	₹
To Balance b/d (Prepaid in the beg.)	20,000	By Balance b/d (O/s in the beg.)	10,000
To Cash A/c	1,00,000	By Profit & Loss A/c (b.f.)	95,000
To Balance c/d (O/s at the end)	15,000	By Balance c/d (Prepaid at the end)	30,000
	1,35,000		1,35,000

Step 7: Prepare Revenue Income Account.

(a) If both the sides are not tallied, then the difference in both the sides may be treated as one of the following items:

If credit side exceeds debit side	***If debit side exceeds credit side***
1. Accrued income in the beginning	1. Unaccrued income at the beginning
2. Income earned during current year	2. Income received during current year
3. Unaccrued income at the end	3. Accrued Income at the end

(b) Format of Revenue Income Account—A format of Revenue Income Account is given below:

Dr. **REVENUE INCOME ACCOUNT (SAY INTEREST ACCOUNT)** *Cr.*

Particulars	₹	*Particulars*	₹
To Balance b/d (Accrued in the beginning)	xxx	By Balance b/d (Unaccrued in the beginning)	xxx
To Profit & Loss A/c (Income earned during the current accounting period)	xxx	By Cash/Bank A/c (Income received during the current accounting period)	xxx
To Balance c/d (Unaccrued at the end)	xxx	By Balance c/d (Accrued at the end)	xxx
	xxx		xxx

ILLUSTRATION 10

Ascertain the appropriate missing figure from the following information:

Particulars	*Opening*	*Closing*
Accrued Interest	₹ 10,000	₹ 15,000
Interest received in advance	₹ 20,000	₹ 30,000

Interest received during the year ₹ 1,00,000.

SOLUTION

Dr. **INTEREST ACCOUNT** Cr.

Particulars	₹	*Particulars*	₹
To Balance b/d	10,000	By Balance b/d	20,000
To P & L A/c (b.f.)	95,000	By Cash A/c	1,00,000
To Balance c/d	30,000	By Balance c/d	15,000
	1,35,000		1,35,000

Step 8: Prepare the Trial Balance

After ascertaining all the missing figures, a trial balance should be prepared to check the mathematical accuracy.

Step 9: Prepare statement of affairs at the beginning of accounting period to ascertain the opening capital.

Format of Statement of Affairs—A format of Statement of Affairs is given below:

STATEMENT OF AFFAIRS OF...AS AT...

Liabilities	₹	*Assets*	₹
Sundry Creditors	xxx	Cash in Hand	xxx
Bills Payable	xxx	Cash at Bank	xxx
Outstanding Expenses	xxx	Sundry Debtors	xxx
Bank Overdraft	xxx	Bills receivable	xxx
Capital (Balancing figure)	xxx	Stock in trade	xxx
		Prepaid Expenses	xxx
		Fixed Assets	xxx
	xxx		xxx

Step 10: Prepare Trading and Profit & Loss Account and the Balance Sheet.

8.0 HINTS FOR TRACING MISSING INFORMATION

The various hints for tracing the various missing information are given below:

HINTS FOR TRACING MISSING INFORMATION

Missing Information	*Hints for Tracing*
(a) *Cash Sales*	I Cash & Bank Account Summary II Total Sales – Net Credit Sales
(b) *Net Credit Sales*	I Prepare Total Debtors Account II Total Sales – Cash Sales – Sales Returns III Closing Debtors × [12/credit period allowed (in months)]
(c) *Net Sales*	I Cash Sales + Credit Sales – Sales Returns II Cost of goods sold + Gross Profit III Gross profit × 100/Rate of Gross Profit on sale

(d) Cost of Goods Sold	I	Opening Stock + Purchases + Direct Expenses (e.g. Carriage/Cartage/Freight inward) – Closing Stock
	II	Net Sales – Gross Profit
	III	Stock Account
(e) Gross Profit	I	Net Sales × Rate of Gross Profit/100
	II	Net Sales – Cost of Goods sold
(f) Cash Purchases	I	Prepare Cash & Bank Account summary
	II	Total Purchases – Net Credit purchases
(g) Net Credit Purchases	I	Prepare Total Creditors Account
	II	Total Purchases – Cash Purchases – Purchases Returns
	III	Closing Creditors × [(12/credit period received (in months)]
(h) Net Purchases	I	Cash Purchases + Credit Purchases – Purchases Returns
	II	Cost of Goods sold + Closing Stock – Opening Stock — Direct Expenses
	III	Stock Account
(i) Collection from Debtors	I	Total Debtors Account
	II	Cash & Bank Account Summary
(j) Payments to Creditors	I	Total Creditors Account
	II	Cash & Bank Account Summary
(k) B/R drawn	I	Bills Receivable Account
	II	Total Debtors Account
(l) B/P accepted	I	Bills Payable Account
	II	Total Creditors Account
(m) B/R collected	I	Bills Receivable Account
	II	Cash & Bank Account Summary
(n) B/P discharged	I	Bills Payable Account
	II	Cash & Bank Account Summary
(o) B/R dishonoured	I	Bills Receivable Account
	II	Total Debtors Account
(p) B/R endorsed dishonoured	I	Total Debtors Account
	II	Total Creditors Account
(q) Drawings/Operating Expenses paid/Loan Repayment/Additional Capital introduced/Loans raised/Income received	I	Cash and Bank Account Summary
(r) Cash and Bank Balance/ Cash stolen by Cashier	I	Cash and Bank Account Summary
(s) Opening Capital	I	Opening Balance Sheet

(t) *Current year's Sales*	I	Previous year's Sales ± change due to change in Sales Price and/or Sales Volume
(u) *Current year's Revenue Expense*	I	Prepare Revenue Expense Account
	II	Expenses paid + Outstanding at the end + Prepaid in the beginning – Outstanding in the beginning – Prepaid at the end.
(v) *Current year's Revenue Income*	I	Prepare Revenue Income Account
	II	Income received + Accrued at the end + Unaccrued in the beginning – Accrued in the beginning – Unaccrued at the end.
(w) *Opening and Closing Balance of any other item*	I	Prepare the Account of Respective Item

ILLUSTRATION 11

From the following information, calculate the amount of Net Sales, Net Purchases and Closing Stock:

Particulars	*Opening* ₹	*Closing* ₹
Debtors	31,800	26,500
Creditors	24,000	16,000
Bills Payable	21,000	29,000
Stock-in-trade	10,000	?
Bills Receivable	8,800	7,000

Transactions during the year—Discount allowed to Customers ₹ 1,000; Discount allowed by Suppliers ₹ 800; Bills Payable discharged ₹ 35,600; Bills Receivable collected ₹ 20,900; Returns inwards ₹ 8,700; Returns outwards ₹ 4,800; Bad debts ₹ 2,800; Bills Receivable dishonoured ₹ 1,800; Cash Paid to creditors ₹ 1,20,000; Cash received from debtors ₹ 69,000; Cash Sales ₹ 40,900; Cash purchases ₹ 1,03,200; Uniform sale price of goods being cost *plus* 25%.

SOLUTION

Dr. **(I) BILLS RECEIVABLE ACCOUNT** *Cr*

Particulars	₹	*Particulars*	₹
To Balance b/d	8,800	By Cash/Bank A/c	20,900
To Total Debtors A/c		By Total Debtors A/c (B/R dish.)	1,800
(B/R drawn) (b.f.)	20,900	By Balance c/d	7,000
	29,700		29,700

Dr. **(II) TOTAL DEBTORS ACCOUNT** *Cr*

Particulars	₹	*Particulars*	₹
To Balance b/d	31,800	By Cash/Bank A/c	69,000
To Bill Receivable A/c (B/R dish.)	1,800	By Discount allowed	1,000
To Credit Sales (b.f.)	95,300	By Bad Debts	2,800
		By Returns inwards	8,700

		By Bills Receivable (transfer)	20,900
		By Balance c/d	26,500
	1,28,900		1,28,900

(III) STATEMENT OF NET SALES

Particulars	₹
A. Credit Sales (as per Total Debtors Account)	95,300
B. Cash Sales (as per Cash Book)	40,900
C. Gross Total Sales (A + B)	1,36,200
D. *Less:* Returns Inward	8,700
E. Net Sales (C – D)	1,27,500

Dr. **(IV) BILLS PAYABLE ACCOUNT** *Cr.*

Particulars	₹	Particulars	₹
To Cash/Bank A/c	35,600	By Balance b/d	21,000
To Balance c/d	29,000	By Total Creditors A/c	
		(B/P accepted) (b.f.)	43,600
	64,600		64,600

Dr. **(V) TOTAL CREDITORS ACCOUNT** *Cr.*

Particulars	₹	Particulars	₹
To Discount received	800	By Balance b/d	24,000
To Bills Payable (transfer)	43,600	By Credit Purchases (b.f)	1,61,200
To Returns outward	4,800		
To Cash A/c	1,20,000		
To Balance c/d	16,000		
	1,85,200		1,85,200

(VI) STATEMENT OF NET PURCHASES

Particulars	₹
A. Credit Purchases (as per Total Creditors Account)	1,61,200
B. Cash Purchases (as per Cash Book)	1,03,200
C. Gross Total Purchases (A + B)	2,64,400
D. *Less:* Return outwards	4,800
E. Net Purchases	2,59,600

Dr. **(VII) STOCK ACCOUNT** *Cr.*

Particulars	₹	Particulars	₹
To Opening Stock	10,000	By Cost of Goods Bold (80% of ₹ 1,27,500)	1,02,000
To Net Purchases	2,59,600	By Closing Stock (balance figure)	1,67,600
	2,69,600		2,69,600

ILLUSTRATION 12

From the following find out net sales and net purchases:

Particulars	₹	Particulars	₹
Opening Debtors	15,000	Bad debts recovered	300
Opening Creditors	14,000	Bills Receivable endorsed to	
Closing Debtors	14,000	creditors	4,000
Closing Creditors	16,000	Bills Receivable dishonoured	
Bills Receivable received	10,000	by customers	1,000
Closing Bills Receivable	8,000	Endorsed bills receivable dish.	500
Cash received from customers	30,000	Bills Receivable discounted	
Cash returned to customers	500	(Discount 20)	2,000
Cash paid to suppliers	20,230	Discounted bills receivable dish.	700
Discount allowed by suppliers	270	Sales returns	250
Discount allowed to customers	500	Purchases returns	670
Bills Payable discharged	1,000	Bills Receivable collected	5,000
Opening Bills Payable	1,000	Opening Bills Receivable	10,000
Closing Bills Payable	8,000		
Bad debts written off	1,200		

Cash Sales 20% Net Sales and Cash Purchases 20% of Net Purchases.

SOLUTION

Dr. **1. BILLS RECEIVABLE ACCOUNT** *Cr.*

Particulars	₹	Particulars	₹
To Balance b/d	10,000	By Cash A/c (B/R collected)	5,000
To Total Debtors A/c	10,000	To Bank A/c (B/R discounted)	1,980
(Bills Receivable received)		By Banker's Discount A/c	20
		(Discounting charges)	
		By Total Debtors A/c (B/R dish.)	1,000
		By Total Creditors A/c	
		(B/R endorsed)	4,000
		By Balance c/d	8,000
	20,000		20,000

Dr. **2. TOTAL DEBTORS ACCOUNT** *Cr.*

Particulars	₹	Particulars	₹
To Balance b/d	15,000	By Bills Receivable A/c	10,000
To Cash A/c (returned)	500	By Cash A/c	30,000
To B/R (dishonoured)	1,000	By Discount Allowed	500
To Total Creditors' A/c	500	By Bad debts	1,200

To Bank A/c (Discounted B/R Dish)	700	By Sales returns	250
		By Balance c/d	14,000
To Credit sales (Balancing figure)	38,250		
	55,950		55,950

Dr. **3. BILLS PAYABLE ACCOUNT** Cr.

Particulars	₹	*Particulars*	₹
To Cash/Bank/A/c (Bills Payable discharged)	1,000	By Balance b/d	1,000
To Balance c/d	8,000	By Total Creditors A/c (b.f.) (Bills Payable accepted)	8,000
	9,000		9,000

Dr. **4. TOTAL CREDITORS ACCOUNT** Cr.

Particulars	₹	*Particulars*	₹
To Bills Payable A/c	8,000	By Balance b/d	14,000
To Cash A/c	20,230	By Total Debtors A/c (bills endorsed and dishonoured)	500
To Discount	270		
To Bills Receivable A/c (endorsed)	4,000	By Purchases (Balancing figure)	34,670
To Purchases returns	670		
To Balance c/d	16,000		
	49,170		49,170

5. STATEMENT OF NET SALES

Particulars	₹
A. Credit Sales (as per Total Debtors Account)	38,250
B. *Less:* Returns Inward	250
C. Net Credit Sales	38,000
D. Cash Sales [20% of Net Sales *or* 25% of Net Credit Sales] [₹ 38,000 × 25/100]	9,500
E. Net Sales	47,500

6. STATEMENT OF NET PURCHASES

Particulars	₹
A. Credit Purchases (as per Total Creditors Account)	34,670
B. *Less:* Return outwards	670
C. Net Purchases	34,000
D. Cash Purchases (20% of Net Purchases *or* 25% of Net Cr. Purchases) [₹ 34,000 × 25/100]	8,500
E. Net Purchases	42,500

Note: *Bad debts recovered, Bills Receivable discounted and Bills Receivable endorsed to creditors do not affect Total Debtors Account.*

ILLUSTRATION 13

Mr. X could not keep complete records. He furnishes you the following information.

(A) PARTICULARS OF ASSETS AND LIABILITIES:

Particulars	*Opening* ₹	*Closing* ₹
Stock	37,400	46,800
Sundry Debtors	24,000	28,000
Sundry Creditors	18,000	3,000
Bills Receivable	8,000	10,000
Bills Payable	2,000	400
Fixed Assets	25,200	?
Bank Balance	8,700	?

(b) *Bank Transactions*—Collection from debtors ₹ 74,800, payment to creditors ₹ 52,200, Bills Receivable collected ₹ 24,000, Bills Payable discharged ₹ 18,600, Cash Sales deposited ₹ 17,200, Cash Purchases (by cheque) rs 4,000, Additional Capital (on 1st Oct.) ₹ 5,000, Wages paid ₹ 24,000, commission received ₹ 3,000, Salaries paid ₹ 13,000, Carriage outward ₹ 8,490, Insurance premium paid ₹ 1,600, Carriage inward ₹ 500, Drawings were ₹1,000 p.m. Goods costing ₹3,000 were taken away by Mr. X for his personal use.

(c) *Information*: A provision @ 10% is required for doubtful debts and depreciation@ 5% p.a. is to be written-off on Fixed Assets. Provide Interest on Capital @ 5% p.a. and for group incentive to staff @ 5% on net profit after charging such incentive and interest on capital. ₹ 6,000 is outstanding for wages and ₹ 3,800 for salaries, Prepaid Insurance ₹ 400, Discount allowed ₹ 1,000, Discount earned ₹ 1,000, Returns Inwards ₹ 1,000, Returns outwards ₹ 1,000, Bad Debts ₹ 1,000.

Required: Prepare Trading and Profit & Loss Account and the Balance Sheet.

SOLUTION

TRADING AND PROFIT & LOSS ACCOUNT

Dr. *for the year ending on 31st March ...* Cr.

Particulars		₹	*Particulars*		₹
To Opening Stock		37,400	By Sales: Cash	17,200	
To Purchases:			Credit	1,07,800	
Cash	4,000		*Less:* Returns	1,000	1,24,000
Credit	56,200		By Closing Stock		46,800
Less: Returns	1,000				
Less: Drawings	3,000	56,200			
To Wages Paid	24,000				
Add: Outstanding	6,000	30,000			
To Carriage Inward		500			
To Gross Profit c/d		46,700			
		1,70,800			1,70,800
To Salaries: Paid	13,000		By Gross Profit b/d		46,700

		₹		₹
Add: Outstanding	3,800	16,800	By Commission Received	3,000
To Carriage outward		8,490	By Discount earned	1,000
To Bad Debt		1,000		
To Discount allowed		1,000		
To Insurance: Paid	1,600			
Less: Prepaid	400	1,200		
To Provision for doubtful debts		2,800		
To Depreciation on Fixed Assets		1,260		
To Interest on Capital				
5% on ₹ 83,300	4,165			
5% on ₹ 5,000 (1/2 year)	125	4,290		
To Group Commission to Staff (13,860 × 5/105)		660		
To Net Profit t/f to Capital Account		13,200		
		50,700		50,700

BALANCE SHEET OF MR. X AS AT 31ST MARCH ...

Liabilities		₹	*Assets*		₹
Sundry Creditors		3,000	Stock-in-trade		46,800
Bills Payable		400	Sundry debtors	28,000	
Outstanding wages		6,000	*Less:* Provision	2,800	25,200
Outstanding salaries		3,800	Bills receivable		10,000
Outstanding Group Commission		660	Prepaid insurance		400
Bank Overdraft		1,690	Fixed Assets	25,200	
Capital:			*Less:* Depreciation	1,260	23,940
Opening Balance	83,300				
Add: Additional Capital	5,000				
Add: Interest on Capital	4,290				
Less: Drawings (₹12,000 + ₹3,000)	(15,000)				
Add: Net Profit	13,200	90,790			
		1,06,340			1,06,340

Working Notes:

Dr. **(I) CASH BOOK** *Cr.*

Receipts	₹	*Payments*	₹
To Balance b/d	8,700	By Wages	24,000
To Debtors	74,800	By Trade Creditors	52,200
To Bills Receivable	24,000	By Bills Payable	18,600
To Cash Sales	17,200	By Cash Purchases	4,000

To Add. Capital	5,000	By Drawings	12,000
To Commission	3,000	By Salaries	13,000
To Balance c/d (Balancing figure)	1,690	By Carriage outward	8,490
		By Insurance	1,600
		By Carriage Inwards	500
	1,34,390		1,34,390

Dr. **(II) BILLS RECEIVABLE ACCOUNT** Cr.

Particulars	₹	*Particulars*	₹
To Balance b/d	8,000	By Cash A/c	24,000
To Total Debtors A/c [Bills received (b.f)]	26,000	By Balance c/d	10,000
	34,000		34,000

Dr. **(III) TOTAL DEBTORS ACCOUNT** Cr.

Particulars	₹	*Particulars*	₹
To Balance b/d	24,000	By Cash A/c	74,800
To Credit Sales (b.f)	1,07,800	By Bills Receivable A/c	26,000
		By Discount Allowed	1,000
		By Return Inwards	1,000
		By Bad debt	1,000
		By Balance c/d	28,000
	1,31,800		1,31,800

Dr. **(IV) BILLS PAYABLE ACCOUNT** Cr.

Particulars	₹	*Particulars*	₹
To Cash A/c	18,600	By Balance b/d	2,000
To Balance c/d	400	By Total Creditors A/c (Bills Issued) (b.f)	17,000
	19,000		19,000

Dr. **(V) TOTAL CREDITORS ACCOUNT** Cr.

Particulars	₹	*Particulars*	₹
To Cash A/c	52,200	By Balance b/d	18,000
To Discount Received	1,000	By Credit Purchases (b.f.)	56,200
To Bills Payable A/c	17,000		
To Returns Outwards	1,000		
To Balance c/d	3,000		
	74,200		74,200

(VI) STATEMENT OF AFFAIRS OF MR. X AS AT 1ST APRIL ...

Liabilities	₹	*Assets*	₹
Sundry Creditors	18,000	Cash at bank	8,700
Bills Payable	2,000	Stock-in-trade	37,400
Capital (b.f)	83,300	Sundry Debtors	24,000
		Bills Receivable	8,000
		Fixed Assets	25,200
	1,03,300		1,03,300

ILLUSTRATION 14

From the following information prepare the Trading and Profit & Loss Account for the year ended 31st March 2014 and the Balance Sheet of Shri Ganesh:

1. Mr X commenced business with ₹ 20,00,000 (Fixed Assets ₹ 8,00,000 & balance cash)
2. He opened a Current Account and deposited ₹ 2,00,000.
3. Goods purchased for cash ₹ 10,00,000, Goods purchased for ₹ 50,00,000 on credit, Goods returned – 20% of goods purchased on credit, Goods costing ₹8,00,000 were sold for Cash ₹ 10,00,000, Goods Costing ₹32,00,000 were sold for ₹ 50,00,000 on credit, Goods returned - 20% of goods sold on credit. Market value of stock-in-hand at the end of accounting period is ₹16,00,000.
4. Cheques received from customers ₹ 20,00,000 of which cheques amounting to ₹ 10,00,000 were endorsed (i.e. transferred) in favour of suppliers.

   Out of these endorsed cheques, Cheques for ₹ 5,00,000 were dishonoured. Out of these dishonoured cheques, drawees of cheques of ₹ 2,50,000 became insolvent and paid 50% only by means of a bank draft.
5. (a) Bills Receivable drawn upon the customers ₹ 10,00,000 of which bills amounting to ₹ 5,00,000 were endorsed in favour of suppliers. Out of these endorsed bills, bills for ₹ 2,50,000 were dishonoured, (b) Bills amounting to ₹ 2,50,000 were discounted at a discount of 10% of which bills amounting to ₹ 1,25,000 were dishonoured, (c) Out of these dishonoured bills, drawees of bills of ₹ 1,87,500 became insolvent and paid 50% only by means of a bank draft, (d) Bills amounting to ₹ 1,25,000 were discharged by drawees before maturity at a discount of 10% by means of a bank draft (e) Bills amounting to ₹ 62,500 were collected at maturity by means of a bank draft.
6. Bills Payables accepted for ₹ 12,50,000 of which bills amounting to ₹ 6,25,000 were discharged before maturity at a discount of 10% by means of a pay order and Bills amounting to ₹ 3,12,500 were also duly discharged at maturity by means of a pay order.
7. Cash received from customers ₹ 4,50,000 after a discount of 10%.
8. Cash paid to suppliers ₹ 5,62,500 after a discount of 10%.
9. Personal Drawings amounted to ₹ 2,00,000 of which ₹ 1,20,000 was in cash.
10. Business Expenses amounted to ₹ 1,60,000 of which ₹ 40,000 were outstanding at the end and ₹ 48,000 was paid by cheque.
11. Depreciate fixed assets by 10%, Make Provision @ 10% for doubtful debts and Bills.
12. The Cashier has absconded with the available cash.

SOLUTION

Dr. **TRADING & PROFIT/LOSS ACCOUNT FOR THE YEAR ENDED 31ST MARCH 2014** *Cr.*

Particulars		₹	*Particulars*		₹
To Purchases			By Sales		
Cash Purchases	10,00,000		Cash Sales	10,00,000	
Credit Purchases	50,00,000		Credit Sales	50,00,000	
Purchase Returns	(10,00,000)	50,00,000	*Less:* Sales Returns	(10,00,000)	50,00,000
To Gross Profit c/d		16,00,000	By Closing Stock		16,00,000
			(Being Cost *or* NRV w.e.l)		
		66,00,000			66,00,000
To Business Expenses		1,60,000	By Gross Profit b/d		16,00,000
To Discount Allowed		50,000	By Discount Received		62,500
To Discounting Charges A/c		25,000	By Rebate on Bill Payable A/c		62,500
To Rebate on Bills Receivable A/c		12,500			
To Bad Debts A/c		2,18,750			
To Loss By Emzellement		6,95,500			
To Provision for Doubtful Debts		93,750			
To Provision for Doubtful B/R		6,250			
To Depreciation		80,000			
To Net Profit t/f to capital A/c		3,83,250			
		17,25,000			17,25,000

BALANCE SHEET OF SHRI GANESH AS AT 31ST MARCH, 2014

Liabilities		₹	*Assets*		₹
Creditors		13,75,000	Cash		0
Bills Payable		3,12,500	Bank		6,90,750
Outstanding Business Expenses		40,000	Debtors	9,37,500	
Capital Account:			*Less:* Provision	(93,750)	8,43,750
Fixed Assets	8,00,000		Bills Receivable	62,500	
Cash	12,00,000		*Less:* Provision	(6,250)	56,250
	20,00,000		Closing Stock		16,00,000
Add: Net Profit	3,83,250		Fixed Assets	8,00,000	
Less: Drawings	(2,00,000)	21,83,250	*Less:* Depreciation	(80,000)	7,20,000
		39,10,750			39,10,750

Working Notes:

Dr. **(I) CASH ACCOUNT** *Cr.*

Particulars	*Cash* ₹	*Bank* ₹	*Particulars*	*Cash* ₹	*Bank* ₹
To X's Capital A/c	12,00,000		By Bank A/c	2,00,000	—

To Cash A/c	—	2,00,000	By Purchases A/c	10,00,000	—
To Sales A/c	10,00,000	—	By Creditors A/c	10,00,000	—
To Debtors A/c	—	10,00,000	By Debtors A/c	—	1,25,000
To Debtors A/c	10,00,000	—	By Bills Payable A/c	—	3,12,500
To Debtors A/c	—	1,25,000	By Bills Payable A/c	—	5,62,500
To B/R A/c	—	2,25,000	By Creditors A/c	5,62,500	—
To Debtors A/c	—	93,750	By Drawings A/c	1,20,000	80,000
To Bills Receivable A/c	—	1,12,500	By Business Exp.	72,000	48,000
To Bills Receivable A/c	—	62,500	By Profit & Loss A/c	6,95,500	—
To Debtors A/c	4,50,000		By Balance c/d	—	6,90,750
	36,50,000	18,18,750		36,50,000	18,18,750

Dr. **(II) DEBTORS ACCOUNT** Cr.

Particulars	₹	*Particulars*	₹
To Bank A/c	1,25,000	By Bank A/c	10,00,000
To Creditors A/c	5,00,000	By Cash A/c	10,00,000
To Creditors A/c	2,50,000	By Bank A/c	1,25,000
To Sales A/c	50,00,000	By Bank A/c	93,750
		By Cash A/c	4,50,000
		By Sales Returns A/c	10,00,000
		By Bad Debts A/c	1,25,000
		By Bad Debts A/c	93,750
		By Bills Receivable A/c	10,00,000
		By Discount Allowed A/c	50,000
		By Balance c/d	9,37,500
	58,75,000		58,75,000

Dr. **(III) BILLS RECEIVABLE ACCOUNT** Cr.

Particulars	₹	*Particulars*	₹
To Debtors A/c	10,00,000	By Bank A/c	2,25,000
		By Bank A/c	1,12,500
		By Bank A/c	62,500
		By Creditors A/c	5,00,000
		By Rebate A/c	12,500
		By Discounting Charges A/c	25,000
		By Balance c/d	62,500
	10,00,000		10,00,000

Dr. **(IV) CREDITORS ACCOUNT** *Cr.*

Particulars	₹	*Particulars*	₹
To Purchase Returns A/c	10,00,000	By Purchases A/c	50,00,000
To Cash A/c	10,00,000	By Debtors A/c	5,00,000
To Cash A/c	5,62,500	By Debtors A/c	2,50,000
To Bills Receivable A/c	5,00,000		
To Bills Payable A/c	12,50,000		
To Discount Received A/c	62,500		
To Balance c/d	13,75,000		
	57,50,000		57,50,000

Dr. **(V) BILLS PAYABLE ACCOUNT** *Cr.*

Particulars	₹	*Particulars*	₹
To Bank A/c	3,12,500	By Creditors A/c	12,50,000
To Bank A/c	5,62,500		
To Rebate A/c	62,500		
To Balance c/d	3,12,500		
	12,50,000		12,50,000

Dr. **(VI) BUSINESS EXPENSES ACCOUNT** *Cr.*

Particulars	₹	*Particulars*	₹
To Cash A/c (Balancing Figure)	72,000	By Profit & Loss A/c	1,60,000
To Bank A/c	48,000		
To Outstanding Business Exp. A/c	40,000		
	1,60,000		1,60,000

(VII) CALCULATION OF CLOSING STOCK

		₹
A. Opening Stock		
B. Net Purchases		
Cash Purchases	10,00,000	
Credit Purchases	50,00,000	
Less: Purchase Returns	(10,00,000)	50,00,000
C. Cost of Goods available for sale		50,00,000
D. *Less:* **Cost of Goods Sold**		
Cost of Goods sold for cash		8,00,000
Cost of Goods Sold on credit (₹32,00,000 – 20% of ₹32,00,000)		25,60,000
Cost of Goods Sold		33,60,000
E. Closing Stock		16,40,000
F. Market Value of Closing Stock at end (as given in question)		16,00,000

ILLUSTRATION 15

The following is the balance sheet of CANJA on 31st March, 2012:

Liabilities	₹	*Assets*	₹
Capital	10,00,000	Fixed Assets	4,00,000
Creditors (Trade)	1,40,000	Stock	3,00,000
Profit & Loss A/c	60,000	Debtors	1,50,000
		Cash & Bank	3,50,000
	12,00,000		12,00,000

The management estimates the purchases and sales for the year ended 31st March, 2013 as under.

Particulars	*upto 28.2.2013*	*31.3.2013*
Purchases	₹ 14,10,000	1,10,000
Sales	19,20,000	2,00,000

It was decided to invest ₹ 1,00,000 in purchases of fixed assets, which are depreciated @ 10% on cost.

The time lag for payment to Trade Creditors for purchase and receipt from Sales is one month. The business earns a gross profit of 30% on turnover. The expenses against gross profit amount to 10% of the turnover. The amount of depreciation is not included in these expenses.

Required: Draft a balance sheet as at 31st March, 2013 assuming that creditors are all Trade Creditors for purchases and debtors for sales and there is no other item of current assets and liabilities apart from stock and cash and bank balances.

SOLUTION

DRAFT BALANCE SHEET AS AT 31ST MARCH 2013

Liabilities		₹	*Assets*		₹
Capital		10,00,000	Fixed Assets	4,00,000	
Profit & Loss Account			Additions	1,00,000	
as on 1-4-2000	60,000			5,00,000	
Add: Net Profit for			*Less:* Depreciation	50,000	4,50,000
the year	3,74,000	4,34,000	Stock in Trade		3,36,000
Creditors (Trade)		1,10,000	Sundry Debtors		2,00,000
			Cash & Balances		5,58,000
		15,44,000			15,44,000

Working Notes:

(I)PROJECTED TRADING & PROFIT & LOSS ACCOUNT

Dr. *for the year ending 31st March, 2013* *Cr.*

Particulars	₹	*Particulars*	₹
To Opening stock	3,00,000	By Sales	21,20,000
To Purchases	15,20,000	By Closing Stock (b.f.)	3,36,000
To Gross Profit (30% on Sales)	6,36,000		
	24,56,000		24,56,000

To Sundry Expenses (10% of the Sales)	2,12,000	By Gross Profit b/d	6,36,000
To Depreciation	50,000		
To Net Profit	3,74,000		
	6,36,000		6,36,000

Dr. **(II) CASH AND BANK ACCOUNT** Cr.

Particulars	₹	*Particulars*	₹
To Balance b/d	3,50,000	By Sundry Creditors	15,50,000
To Sundry Debtors	20,70,000	(₹ 1,40,000 + 14,10,000)	
(₹ 1,50,000 + 19,20,000)		By Expenses	2,12,000
		By Fixed Assets	1,00,000
		By Balance c/d	5,58,000
	24,20,000		24,20,000

(iii) It has been assumed that entire sales and purchases are on credit basis.

ILLUSTRATION 16

The following is the Balance Sheet of the retail business of Sri CAMII as at 31st March 2012

Liabilities	₹	*Assets*	₹
Sri Srinivas's capital	1,00,000	Furniture	10,000
Liabilities for goods	20,500	Stock	70,000
Rent	1,000	Debtors	25,000
		Cash at bank	14,500
		Cash in hand	2,000
	1,21,500		1,21,500

You are furnished with the following information:

(i) Sri CAMII sells his goods at a profit of 20% on sales.

(ii) Goods are sold for cash and credit. Credit customers pay by cheques only.

(iii) Payments for purchases are always made by cheques.

(iv) It is the practice of Sri CAMII to send to the bank every weekend the collections of the week after paying every week, salary of ₹ 300 to the clerk, Sundry expenses of ₹ 50 and personal expenses ₹ 100.

Analysis of the Bank Pass-book for the 13 week period ending on 30 th June, 2013 disclosed the following:

Particulars	₹
Payments to creditors	75,000
Payments of rent upto 30th June 2013	4,000
Amounts deposited into the bank	1,25,000
(include ₹ 30,000 received from debtors by cheques)	

The following are the balances on 30th June 2013:

Particulars	₹
Stock	40,000
Debtors	30,000
Creditors for goods	36,500

On the evening of 30th June 2013 the Cashier absconded with the available cash in the cash box. There was no cash deposit in the week ended on that date.

Required: Prepare a Account showing the amount of cash defalcated by the Cashier and also a Trading & Profit and Loss Account for the period ended 30th June, 2013 and a Balance Sheet as on that date.

SOLUTION

ACCOUNT SHOWING DEFALCATION OF CASH

Dr. *as at 30th June, 2013* Cr.

Receipts	₹	*Payments*	₹
To Balance b/d	2,000	By Salary to Clerk (₹ 300 × 13)	3,900
To Cash Sales	1,16,250	By Sundry Expenses (₹ 50 × 13)	650
		By Drawing (₹ 100 × 13)	1,300
		By Bank (₹ 1,25,000 – ₹ 30,000)	95,000
		By Defalcation (balancing figure)	17,400
	1,18,250		1,18,250

TRADING AND PROFIT & LOSS ACCOUNT

Dr. *for the Period ended 30th June 2013* Cr.

Particulars		₹	*Particulars*	₹
To Opening Stock		70,000	By Sales (116250 + 35000)	1,51,250
To Purchases		91,000	By Closing Stock	40,000
To Gross Profit c/d		30,250	By Drawing (₹ 100 × 13)	1,300
		1,91,250		1,91,250
To Salary to Clerk		3,900	By Gross Profit b/d	30,250
To Sundry Expenses		650		1,18,250
To Rent	4,000			
Less: Outstanding at beg.	1,000	3,000		
To Defalcation		17,400		
To Net Profit t/f to Capital A/c		5,300		
		30,250		30,250

BALANCE SHEET OF SHRI CAMMI AT 30TH JUNE, 2013

Liabilities		₹	*Assets*	₹
Capital	1,00,000		Furniture	10,000
Add: Net Profit	5,300		Stock	40,000

	1,05,300		Debtors	30,000
Less: drawing	1,300	1,04,000	Cash at bank	60,500
Creditors		36,500		
		1,40,500		1,40,500

Working Notes:

(i) Purchases = Payment to Creditors + Closing balance of Creditors – Opening balance of Creditors

Purchases = ₹ 75,000 + ₹ 36,500 – ₹ 20,500 = ₹ 91,000

(ii) Cost of Good Sold = Purchases + Opening Stock – Closing Stock

= ₹ 91,000 + ₹ 70,000 – ₹ 40,000 = ₹ 1,21,000

(iii) Sales = Cost of Goods sold + Gross Profit

= 1,21,000 + 25% on cost = ₹ 1,51,250

(iv) Credit Sales = Cash Received from debtors + Closing balance – Opening balance

= ₹ 30,000 + ₹ 30,000 – ₹ 25,000 = ₹ 35,000

(v) Cash Sales = Total Sales – Credit Sales = ₹ 1,51,250 – ₹ 35,000 = ₹ 1,16,250

Dr. **(VI) BANK ACCOUNT** *Cr.*

Particulars	₹	*Particulars*	₹
To Balance b/d	14,500	By Creditors A/c	75,000
To Debtors A/c	30,000	By Rent A/c	4,000
To Cash A/c	95,000	By Balance c/d (balancing fig.)	60,500
	1,39,500		1,39,500

ILLUSTRATION 17

Shri Rashid furnishes you with the following information relating to his business:

(A) ASSETS AND LIABILITIES

Particulars	*As on 01.04.2012* ₹	*As on 31.03.2013* ₹
Furniture (w.d.v.)	6,000	6,350
Stock at cost	8,000	7,000
Sundry debtors	16,000	?
Sundry creditors	11,000	15,000
Prepaid expenses	600	700
Unpaid expenses	2,000	1,800
Cash in hand and at bank	1,200	625

(b) Receipts and payments during the year:

Collections from debtors, after allowing discount of ₹ 1,500 amounted to ₹ 58,500.

Collections on discounting of bills of exchange, after deduction of discount of ₹ 125 by the bank, totalled to ₹ 6,125.

Creditors of ₹ 40,000 were paid ₹ 39,200 in full settlement of their dues.

Payment for freight inwards ₹ 3,000

Amounts withdrawn for personal use ₹ 7,000.

Payment for office furniture ₹ 1,000.

Investment carrying annual interest of 4% were purchased at ₹ 96 on 1st Oct. and payment made therefor.

Expenses including salaries paid ₹ 14,500.

Miscellaneous receipts ₹ 500.

(c) Bills of exchange drawn on and accepted by customers during the year amounted to ₹ 10,000. Of these, bills of exchange of ₹ 2,000 were endorsed in favour of creditors. An endorsed bill of exchange of ₹ 400 was dishonoured.

(d) Goods costing ₹ 900 were used as advertising materials.

(e) Goods are invariably sold to show a gross profit of 33.1/3% on sales.

(f) Difference in cash book, if any, is to be treated as further drawing *or* introduction by Shri Rashid.

(g) Provide at 2.5% for doubtful debts on closing debtors.

Required: prepare trading and profit and loss Account for the year ended 31st March 2013 and the balance sheet as on that date.

SOLUTION

TRADING AND PROFIT AND LOSS ACCOUNT OF SHRI RASHID

for the year ended 31st March, 2013

Dr. *Cr.*

Particulars		₹	*Particulars*	₹
To Opening Stock		8,000	By Sales	73,050
To Purchases	45,600		By Closing Stock	7,000
Less: For advertising	900	44,700		
To Freight inwards		3,000		
To Gross profit c/d		24,350		
		80,050		80,050
To Sundry expenses:		14,200	By Gross profit b/d	24,350
To Advertisement		900	By Interest on investments	2
To Discount allowed			$\left[₹100 \times \frac{4}{100} \times \frac{1}{2}\right]$	
Debtors	1,500			
Bills receivable	125	1,625	By Discount received	800
To Depreciation on furniture		650	By Miscellaneous income	500
To Provision for doubtful debts		486		
To Net Profit		7,791		
		25,652		25,652

BALANCE SHEET AS AT 31ST MARCH 2013

Liabilities		₹	*Assets*		₹
Capital:			Furniture (w.d.v.)	6,000	
Opening Balance	18,800		Additions during the year	1,000	

Less: Drawings	7,904		*Less:* Depreciation	650	6,350
Add: Net Profit	7,791	18,687	Investment		96
Sundry creditors		15,000	Interest accrued		2
Outstanding expenses		1,800	Closing stock		7,000
			Sundry debtors	19,450	
			Less: Provision for doubtful debts	486	18,964
			Bills receivable		1,750
			Cash in hand and at bank		625
			Prepaid expenses		700
		35,487			35,487

Working Notes:

(I) CALCULATION OF OPENING CAPITAL BALANCE SHEET AS AT 1ST APRIL 2012

Liabilities	₹	*Assets*	₹
Capital *(Balancing figure)*	18,800	Furniture (w.d.v.)	6,000
Creditors	11,000	Stock at cost	8,000
Outstanding expenses	2,000	Sundry debtors	16,000
		Cash in hand and at bank	1,200
		Prepaid expenses	600
	31,800		31,800

(II) CALCULATION OF PURCHASES MADE DURING THE YEAR SUNDRY CREDITORS ACCOUNT

Dr. *Cr.*

Particulars	₹	*Particulars*	₹
To Cash and bank A/c	39,200	By Balance b/d	11,000
To Discount received A/c	800	By Sundry debtors A/c	400
To Bills receivable A/c	2,000	By Purchases A/c *(Balancing figure)*	45,600
To Balance c/d	15,000		
	57,000		57,000

(III) CALCULATION OF SALES MADE DURING THE YEAR

Particulars		₹
Opening Stock		8,000
Purchases	45,600	
Less: For advertising	900	44,700
Freight inwards		3,000
		55,700
Less: Closing Stock		7,000
Cost of goods sold		48,700

Add: Gross profit (@ 50% on cost)	24,350
Sales	73,050

(IV) CALCULATION OF CLOSING DEBTORS
SUNDRY DEBTORS ACCOUNT

Dr. *Cr.*

Particulars	₹	*Particulars*	₹
To Balance b/d	16,000	By Cash and bank A/c	58,500
To Sales A/c	73,050	By Discount allowed A/c	1,500
To Sundry creditors A/c (Bill dish.)		By Bills receivable A/c	10,000
	400	By Balance c/d *(Balancing figure)*	19,450
	89,450		89,450

(V) CASH AND BANK ACCOUNT

Dr. *Cr.*

Particulars	₹	*Particulars*	₹
To Balance b/d	1,200	By Freight inwards A/c	3,000
To Sundry debtors A/c	58,500	By Furniture A/c	1,000
To Bills receivable A/c	6,125	By Investment A/c	96
To Miscellaneous income A/c	500	By Expenses A/c	14,500
		By Creditors A/c	39,200
		By Drawings A/c	7,904
		[₹ 7,000 + ₹ 904 (Add. drawings)]	
		By Balance c/d	625
	66,325		66,325

(VI) EXPENSES ACCOUNT

Dr. *Cr.*

Particulars	₹	*Particulars*	₹
To Prepaid expenses A/c (beg.)	600	By Outstanding expenses A/c (beg.)	2,000
To Bank A/c	14,500	By Profit and loss A/c (b.f.)	14,200
To Outstanding expenses A/c (end)	1,800	By Prepaid expenses A/c (end)	700
	16,900		16,900

(VII) BILLS RECEIVABLE ACCOUNT

Dr. *Cr.*

Particulars	₹	*Particulars*	₹
To Debtors A/c	10,000	By Creditors A/c	2,000
		By Bank A/c	6,125
		By Discount on bills receivable A/c	125
		By Balance c/d (Balancing figure)	1,750
	10,000		10,000

***Note:** As regards investment, it has been assumed that investment purchased for ₹ 96 was of the face value ₹ 100.*

ILLUSTRATION 18

From the following information in respect of a Trader, prepare Trading and Profit and Loss Account for the year ended 31st March 2013, and a Balance Sheet as at that date:

Assets and Liabilities as on	*Opening (₹)*	*Closing (₹)*
Stock-in-Trade	1,60,000	1,40,000
Debtors for Sales	3,20,000	?
Bills Receivable	–	?
Creditors for Purchases	2,20,000	3,00,000
Furniture at Written Down Value	1,20,000	1,27,000
Expenses Outstanding	40,000	36,000
Prepaid Expenses	12,000	14,000
Cash on Hand	4,000	3,000
Bank Balance	20,000	9,500

Receipts and Payments during the year:

Particulars	₹
Collections from Debtors (after allowing 21/2% discount)	11,70,000
Payment to Creditors (after receiving 2% discount)	7,74,000
Proceeds of Bills Receivable discounted at 2%	1,22,500
Proprietor's Drawings	1,40,000
Purchase of Furniture midway through the year	20,000
4% Government Securities purchased at 96% on 1st Oct.	1,92,000
Expenses	3,50,000
Miscellaneous Income	10,000

Other information:

1. Sales are effected so as to realize a Gross Profit of 33-1/3 % on the Sale Proceeds.
2. Goods, costing ₹ 18,000, were issued as Advertisement Articles.
3. During the year, Bills Receivable of ₹ 2,00,000 were drawn on Debtors. Of these, Bills amounting to ₹ 40,000 were endorsed in favour of Creditors. Out of this latter amount, a Bill for ₹ 8,000 was dishonoured by the Debtor.
4. Capital introduced during the year by the Proprietor by cheques was omitted to be recorded in the Cash Book, though the Closing Bank Balance was ₹ 9,500, (as shown above) is after taking the same into account.
5. Purchases and Sales are made only on credit.

SOLUTION

Dr. **TRADING AND PROFIT AND LOSS ACCOUNT FOR THE YEAR ENDED 31.03.2013** *Cr.*

Particulars	₹	*Particulars*	₹
To Opening Stock	1,60,000	By Sales	13,71,000
To Purchases (9,12,000 – 18,000]	8,94,000	By Closing Stock	1,40,000
To Gross Profit (l/3rd on Sales)	4,57,000		
	15,11,000		15,11,000

To Expenses for the year		3,44,000	By Gross Profit b/d	4,57,000
To Discount Allowed:			By Miscellaneous Income	10,000
Debtors	30,000		By Discount Received	16,000
Bills Receivable	2,500	32,500	By Interest on 4% Government	4,000
To Advertisement Expenses		18,000	Securities [2,00,000 × 4% × 6/12]	
To Depreciation on Furniture		13,000		
To Net Profit		79,500		
		4,87,000		4,87,000

BALANCE SHEET AS AT 31.03.2013

Liabilities	₹	*Assets*	₹
Capital	4,87,500	Furhiture	1,27,000
Sundry Creditors	3,00,000	4% Govt. Securities at Cost	1,92,000
Outstanding Expenses	36,000	(NV ₹ 2,00,000)	
		Accused Interest on Govt. Securities	4,000
		Stock in Trade	1,40,000
		Sundry Debtors	2,99,000
		Bills Receivable	35,000
		Cash on Hand	3,000
		Bank Balance	9,500
		Prepaid Expenses	14,000
	8,23,500		**8,23,500**

Working Notes:

(I) BALANCE SHEET AS AT 31.03.2012

Liabilities	₹	*Assets*	₹
Capital (balancing figure)	**3,76,000**	Furniture	1,20,000
Creditors	2,20,000	Stock	1,60,000
Outstanding Expenses	40,000	Debtors	3,20,000
		Cash on Hand	4,000
		Bank Balance	20,000
		Prepaid Expenses	12,000
	6,36,000		6,36,000

Dr. **(II) CREDITORS ACCOUNT** *Cr.*

Particulars	₹	*Particulars*	₹
To Bills Receivable (endorsed)	40,000	By Balance B/d	2,20,000
To Bank (payment)	7,84,000	By Debtors (endorsed bills dish.)	8,000
To Discount Received		By Purchases (balancing figure)	**9,12,000**
[7,84,000 × 2%/98%)	16,000		

To Balance c/d	3,00,000		
	11,40,000		11,40,000

(III) COMPUTATION OF SALES

A. Cost of Goods Sold = 1,60,000 + 8,94,000 – 1,40,000 = ₹ 9,14,000

B. P = l/3rd on Sales = 1/2 on COGS = 1/2 × ₹ 9,14,000 = ₹ 4,57,000

C. Sales = COGS + GP = [A + B] = ₹ 13,71,000

Dr. **(IV) DEBTORS ACCOUNT** *Cr.*

Particulars	₹	*Particulars*	₹
To Balance b/d	3,20,000	By Bills Receivable	2,00,000
To Sales	13,71,000	By Bank (Collections)	11,70,000
To Creditors (endorsed bills dish.)	8,000	By Discount Allowed	
		(11,70,000 × 2.5%/97.5%)	30,000
		By Balance c/d (balancing figure)	**2,99,000**
	16,99,000		16,99,000

Dr. **(V) BILLS RECEIVABLE ACCOUNT** *Cr.*

Particulars	₹	*Particulars*	₹
To Sundry Debtors [B/R received]	2,00,000	By Creditors [B/R endorsed]	40,000
		By Bank [B/R discounted]	1,22,500
		By Discount on Bills Receivable	
		[1,22,500 × 2%/98%]	2,500
		By Balance c/d (balancing figure)	**35,000**
	2,00,000		2,00,000

Dr. **(VI) EXPENSES ACCOUNT** *Cr.*

Particulars	₹	*Particulars*	₹
To Balance b/d	12,000	By Balance b/d	40,000
To Bank A/c	3,50,000	By P&L (b/f)	**3,44,000**
To Balance c/d	36,000	By Balance c/d	14,000
	3,98,000		3,98,000

Dr. **(VII) FURNITURE ACCOUNT** *Cr.*

Particulars	₹	*Particulars*	₹
To Balance b/d	1,20,000	By Depreciation (balancing figure)	**13,000**
To Bank A/c (Purchases)	20,000	By Balance c/d	1,27,000
	1,40,000		1,40,000

Dr. **(VIII) CASH AND BANK ACCOUNT** Cr.

Particulars	Cash	Bank	Particulars	Cash	Bank
To balance b/d	4,000	20,000	By Creditors		7,84,000
To Debtors		11,70,000	By Drawings		1,40,000
To Bills Discounted		1,22,500	By Expenses		3,50,000
To Misc. Income (assumed cash)	10,000		By 4% Govt. Securities		1,92,000
			By Fixed Asset (Purchase)		20,000
To Cash (Contra)		11,000	By Bank (Contra) (bal. fig.)	**11,000**	
To Capital A/c (Additional Cap. (balancing figure)		**1,72,000**	By Balance c/d	3,000	9,500
	14,000	**14,95,500**		**14,000**	**14,95,500**

Dr. **(XI) CAPITAL ACCOUNT** Cr.

Particulars	₹	Particulars	₹
To Drawings	1,40,000	By Balance b/d	3,76,000
To Balance c/d (balancing figure)	**4,87,500**	By Bank A/c (Additional Capital	1,72,000
		By Net Profit for the year (from P&L)	79,500
	6,27,500		**6,27,500**

ILLUSTRATION 19

The following is the Balance Sheet of Bharat, a small trader as a 31.03.2012.

Liabilities	₹	Assets	₹
Capital	1,80,000	Fixed Assets	60,000
Creditors for Goods	25,000	Stock	60,000
Creditors for Business Expenses	55,000	Debtors	50,000
		Cash	5,000
		Bank	65,000
		Prepaid Business Expenses	20,000
	2,60,000		2,60,000

Riots occurred and fire broke out on the evening of 31st March 2013, destroying the books of accounts and factory shed (book value of ₹20,000). The cashier had absconded with the available cash. The following information was available:

1. Uniform Rate of Gross Profit – 20%.
2. **Gross Profit for the year ended 31.03.2012 – ₹80,000.**
3. Cash Sales 33-1/3% of Net Credit Sales, Sales Returns – 1/7th of Gross Credit Sales.
4. Cash Purchases – 20% of Net Credit Purchases Purchase Returns 1/7th of Gross Credit Purchases.
5. His sales for the year ended 21st March, 2013 were 20% higher than the previous year's.
6. On 1st April, 2012 the stock level was raised by ₹48,000 and stock was maintained at this new level all throughout the year.
7. Collections from Debtors (after 5% discount) amounted to ₹3,32,500 of which 80% were in Cash.

8. Payments to Creditors (after 5% discount) amounted to ₹3,37,250 of which 80% were by cheques.
9. Indirect Business Expenses for the year ended 31st March, 2013 amounted to ₹14,250. Of the business expenses ₹10,000 were outstanding and ₹2,750 were prepaid on 31st March, 2013. 80% of Business Expenses were paid by cheque.
10. Fixed Assets purchased (on 30.09.2012) and paid by cheques ₹60,000, Rate of Depreciation on Fixed Assets – 10%.
11. Personal Drawings amounted to ₹1,00,000 of which 80% were in Cash.
12. 4% Govt. Securities purchased by cheque (at 96% on 01.10.2012) for ₹9,600.
13. Cash deposited into the Bank ₹1,40,000.
14. The amount defalcated by the cashier may be written off to Profit and Loss Account.

Required: Prepare Trading & Profit & Loss Account for the year ended 31st March 2013 and the Balance Sheet as at 31st March, 2013.

SOLUTION

TRADING & PROFIT/LOSS ACCOUNT

for the year ended 31st March 2013

Dr. Cr.

Particulars		₹	Particulars		₹
To Opening Stock		60,000	By Sales		
To Purchases			Cash Sales	1,20,000	
Cash Purchases	72,000		Credit Sales	4,20,000	
Credit Purchases	4,20,000		*Less:* Sales Returns	(60,000)	4,80,000
Less: Purchase Returns	(60,000)	4,32,000	By Closing Stock		1,08,000
To Gross Profit c/d		96,000			
		5,88,000			5,88,000
To Business Expenses		14,250	By Gross Profit b/d		96,000
To Discount Allowed		17,500	By Discount Received		17,750
To Loss by fire		20,000	By Interest		200
To Depreciation		10,000			
To Loss by Embezellment		23,150			
To Net Profit t/f to Capital A/c		29,050			
		1,13,950			1,13,950

BALANCE SHEET OF BHARAT

As at 31.03.2013

Liabilities		₹	Assets		₹
X's Capital Account:			**Fixed Assets:**		
Opening Balance	1,80,000		Opening Balance	60,000	
Add: Net Profit	29,050		*Add:* Addition	60,000	
Less: Drawings	(1,00,000)	1,09,050	*Less:*Loss by fire	(20,000)	
Creditors		30,000	*Less:* Depreciation	(10,000)	90,000
Outstanding Business Expenses A/c		10,000	Closing Stock		1,08,000

Bank overdraft	1,21,500	Debtors	60,000
		Prepaid Expenses	2,750
		Govt. Securities	9,600
		Interest Accrued	200
	2,70,550		2,70,550

Working Notes:

(I) CALCULATION OF CASH SALES AND CREDIT SALES DURING THE CURRENT YEAR

Particulars	₹
A. Previous year's Total Sales (Gross Profit/GP Ratio) (₹80,000/.20)	4,00,000
B. *Add:* Increase in Sales during current year @ 20%	80,000
C. Current year's Total Sales (A + B)	4,80,000
D. *Less:* Cash Sales @ 25% of Net Sales (₹4,80,000 × 25%)	1,20,000
E. Net Credit Sales (C – D)	3,60,000
F. *Add:* Sales Returns (₹3,60,000 × 1/6)	60,000
G. Gross Credit Sales (E + F)	4,20,000

(II) CALCULATION OF CASH AND CREDIT PURCHASES DURING THE CURRENT YEAR

Particulars	₹
A. Current year's Total Sales	4,80,000
B. *Less:* Gross Profit @ 20%	96,000
C. Cost of Goods Sold (A – B)	3,84,000
D. *Add:* Closing Stock	1,08,000
E. *Less:* Opening Stock	60,000
F. Total Purchases (C + D – E)	4,32,000
G. *Less:* Cash Purchases (₹4,32,000 × 1/6)	72,000
H. Net Credit Purchases	3,60,000
I. *Add:* Purchase Returns (₹3,60,000 × 1/6)	60,000
J. Gross Credit Purchases	4,20,000

(III) CALCULATION OF BUSINESS EXPENSES
BUSINESS EXPENSES ACCOUNT

Dr. *Cr.*

Particulars	₹	*Particulars*	₹
To Balance b/d	20,000	By Balance b/d	55,000
To Bank A/c (80% of ₹42,000) (b.f.)	33,600	By Profit & Loss A/c	14,250
To Cash A/c (20% of ₹42,000) (b.f.)	8,400	By Balance c/d	2,750
To Balance c/d	10,000		
	72,000		72,000

Dr. **(IV) DEBTORS ACCOUNT** Cr.

Particulars	₹	Particulars	₹
To Balance b/d	50,000	By Sales Returns A/c	60,000
To Sales A/c	4,20,000	By Bank A/c	66,500
		By Cash A/c	2,66,000
		By Discount Allowed A/c [₹3,32,500 × 5/95]	17,500
		By Balance c/d (b.f.)	60,000
	4,70,000		4,70,000

Dr. **(V) CREDITORS ACCOUNT** Cr.

Particulars	₹	Particulars	₹
To Purchase Returns A/c	60,000	By Balance b/d	25,000
To Bank A/c	2,69,800	By Purchases A/c	4,20,000
To Cash A/c	67,450		
To Discount Received A/c [₹3,37,250 × 5/95]	17,750		
To Balance c/d (b.f.)	30,000		
	445,000		4,45,000

Dr. **(VI) FIXED ASSETS ACCOUNT** Cr.

Particulars	₹	Particulars	₹
To Balance b/d	60,000	By Loss by fire	20,000
To Bank A/c	60,000	By Depreciation A/c [10% of (₹ 60,000 + ₹60,000 – ₹20,000]	10,000
		By Balance c/d	90,000
	1,20,000		1,20,000

Dr. **(VII) CASH BOOK** Cr.

Particulars	Cash	Bank	Particulars	Cash	Bank
To Balance b/d	5,000	65,000	By Cash Purchases A/c	72,000	
To Sales A/c	1,20,000		By Creditors A/c	67,450	2,69,800
To Debtors A/c	2,66,000	66,500	By Fixed Assets A/c		60,000
To Cash A/c(C)		1,40,000	By Business Exp.	8,400	33,600
To Balance c/d		1,21,500	By Drawings A/c	80,000	20,000
			By Bank A/c (C)	1,40,000	
			By Profit & Loss A/c (Cash defalcated)	23,150	
			By Govt. Securities		9,600

			By Balance c/d		–
	3,91,000	3,93,000		3,91,000	3,93,000

ILLUSTRATION 20

The following is the Balance Sheet of Bharat, a small trader as a 31.03.2012.

Liabilities	₹	*Assets*	₹
Capital	1,80,000	Fixed Assets	60,000
Creditors for Goods	25,000	Stock	60,000
Creditors for Business Expenses	55,000	Debtors	50,000
		Cash	5,000
		Bank	65,000
		Prepaid Business Expenses	20,000
	2,60,000		2,60,000

Riots occurred and fire broke out on the evening of 31st March 2013, destroying the books of accounts and factory shed (book value of ₹20,000). The cashier had absconded with the available cash. The following information was available:

1. Uniform Rate of Gross Profit – 20%.
2. **Terms of Credit: Debtors – 2 months.**
3. Cash Sales 33-1/3% of Net Credit Sales, Sales Returns – 1/7th of Gross Credit Sales.
4. Cash Purchases – 20% of Net Credit Purchases, Purchase Returns 1/7th of Gross Credit Purchases.
5. His sales for the year ended 21st March, 2013 were 20% higher than the previous year's.
6. On 1st April, 2012 the stock level was raised by ₹48,000 and stock was maintained at this new level all throughout the year.
7. Collections from Debtors (after 5% discount) were 80% in Cash.
8. Payments to Creditors (after 5% discount) amounted to ₹3,37,250 of which 80% were by cheques.
9. Indirect Business Expenses for the year ended 31st March, 2013 amounted to ₹14,250. Of the business expenses ₹10,000 were outstanding and ₹2,750 were prepaid on 31st March, 2013. 80% of Business Expenses were paid by cheque.
10. Fixed Assets purchased (on 30.09.2012) and paid by cheques ₹60,000, Rate of Depreciation on Fixed Assets – 10%.
11. Personal Drawings amounted to ₹1,00,000 of which 80% were in Cash.
12. 4% Govt. Securities purchased by cheque (at 96% on 01.10.2012) for ₹9,600.
13. Cash deposited into the Bank ₹1,40,000.
14. The amount defalcated by the cashier may be written off to Profit and Loss Account.

Required: Prepare Trading & Profit & Loss Account for the year ended 31st March 2013 and the Balance Sheet as at 31st March, 2013.

SOLUTION

STEP 1: CALCULATION OF CASH SALES, CREDIT SALES AND CLOSING DEBTORS DURING THE CURRENT YEAR

	Particulars	₹
A.	Previous year's credit sales (Closing debtors × 12/2) (₹50,000 × 12/2)	3,00,000
B.	*Add:* Previous year's Cash Sales (₹3,00,000 × 1/3)	1,00,000
C.	Previous year's Total Sales [A + B]	4,00,000
D.	*Add:* Increase in sales during current year @ 20%	80,000
E.	Current year's total sales [C + D]	4,80,000
F.	*Less:* Cash Sales @ 25% [₹4,80,000 × 25%]	1,20,000
G.	Net Credit Sales [E – F]	3,60,000
H.	*Add:* Sales Returns [₹3,60,000 × 1/6]	60,000
I.	Gross Credit Sales [G + H]	4,20,000
J.	Closing Debtors [Net Credit Sales × 2/12] (₹3,60,000 × 2/12)	60,000

All other working notes and solutions are same as in Illustration 18.

ILLUSTRATION 21

The following is the Balance Sheet of Bharat, a small trader as a 31.03.2012.

Liabilities	₹	*Assets*	₹
Capital	1,80,000	Fixed Assets	60,000
Creditors for Goods	25,000	Stock	60,000
Creditors for Business Expenses	55,000	Debtors	50,000
		Cash	5,000
		Bank	65,000
		Prepaid Business Expenses	20,000
	2,60,000		2,60,000

Roits occurred and fire broke out on the evening of 31st March 2013, destroying the books of accounts and factory shed (book value of ₹20,000). The cashier had absconded with the available cash. The following information was available:

1. Uniform Rate of Gross Profit – 20%.
2. **Terms of Credit: Creditors – 1 month.**
3. Cash Sales 33-1/3% of Net Credit Sales, Sales Returns – 1/7th of Gross Credit Sales.
4. Cash Purchases – 20% of Net Credit Purchases, Purchase Returns 1/7th of Gross Credit Purchases.
5. His sales for the year ended 21st March, 2013 were 20% higher than the previous year's.
6. On 1st April, 2012 the stock level was raised by ₹48,000 and stock was maintained at this new level all throughout the year.
7. Collections from Debtors (after 5% discount) amounted to ₹3,32,500 of which 80% was by Cash.
8. Payments to Creditors (after 5% discount) were 80% by cheques.
9. Indirect Business Expenses for the year ended 31st March, 2013 amounted to ₹14,250. Of the business expenses ₹10,000 were outstanding and ₹2,750 were prepaid on 31st March, 2013.

80% of Business Expenses were paid by cheque.

10. Fixed Assets purchased (on 30.09.2012) and paid by cheques ₹60,000, Rate of Depreciation on Fixed Assets – 10%.
11. Personal Drawings amounted to ₹1,00,000 of which 80% were in Cash.
12. 4% Govt. Securities purchased by cheque (at 96% on 01.10.2012) for ₹9,600.
13. Cash deposited into the Bank ₹1,40,000.
14. The amount defalcated by the cashier may be written off to Profit & Loss Account.

Required: Prepare Trading & Profit & Loss Account for the year ended 31st March 2013 and the Balance Sheet as at 31st March, 2013.

SOLUTION

STEP 1: CALCULATION OF CASH PURCHASES, CREDIT PURCHASES AND CLOSING CREDITORS DURING THE CURRENT YEAR

Particulars	₹
A. Previous year's credit purchases (Closing Creditors × 12/1) (₹25,000 × 12/1)	3,00,000
B. *Add:* Previous year's Cash Purchases (₹3,00,000 × 20%)	60,000
C. Previous year's Total Purchases [A + B]	3,60,000
D. *Add:* Increase in Sales Volumes @ 20%	72,000
E. Current year's Total Purchases	4,32,000
F. *Less:* Cash Purchases [₹4,32,000 × 1/6]	72,000
G. Net Credit Purchases [E – F]	3,60,000
H. *Add:* Purchase Returns [₹3,60,000 × 1/6]	60,000
I. Gross Credit Purchases [G + H]	4,20,000
J. Closing Creditors [Net Credit Purchases × 1/12] (₹3,60,000 × 1/12)	30,000

STEP 2: CALCULATION OF CASH SALES, CREDIT SALES AND CLOSING DEBTORS DURING THE CURRENT YEAR

Particulars	₹
A. Current year's Total Purchases	4,32,000
B. *Add:* Opening Stock	60,000
C. *Less:* Closing Stock	1,08,000
D. Cost of Goods Sold [A + B – C]	3,84,000
E. *Add:* Gross Profit [₹3,84,000 × 25%]	96,000
F. Total Sales [D + E]	4,80,000
G. *Less:* Cash Sales [₹4,80,000 × 25%]	1,20,000
H. Net Credit Sales [E – G]	3,60,000
I. *Add:* Sales Returns [₹3,60,000 × 1/6]	60,000
J. Gross Credit Sales [H + I]	4,20,000
K. Closing Debtors [Net Credit Sales × 2/12] (₹3,60,000 × 2/12)	60,000

All other working notes and solutions are same as in Illustration 18.

ILLUSTRATION 22

The following is the Balance Sheet of Bharat, a small trader as a 31.03.2012.

Liabilities	₹	*Assets*	₹
Capital	1,80,000	Fixed Assets	60,000
Creditors for Goods	25,000	Stock	60,000
Creditors for Business Expenses	55,000	Debtors	50,000
		Cash	5,000
		Bank	65,000
		Prepaid Business Expenses	20,000
	2,60,000		2,60,000

Riots occurred and fire broke out on the evening of 31st March 2013, destroying the books of accounts and factory shed (book value of ₹20,000). The cashier had absconded with the available cash. The following information was available:

1. Stock as on 1st April 20X6 was ₹20,000.
2. **Rate of Gross Profit – No Change.**
3. **Terms of Credit: Debtors – 2 months, Creditors – 1 month.**
4. Cash Sales 33-1/3% of Net Credit Sales, Sales Returns – 1/7th of Gross Credit Sales.
5. Cash Purchases – 20% of Net Credit Purchases, Purchases Returns 1/7th of Gross Credit Purchases.
6. His sales for the year ended 21st March, 2013 were 20% higher than the previous year's.
7. On 1st April, 2012 the stock level was raised by ₹48,000 and stock was maintained at this new level all throughout the year.
8. Collection from Debtors (after 5% discount) were 80% in Cash.
9. Payment to Creditors (after 5% discount) were 80% by cheques.
10. Indirect Business Expenses for the year ended 31st March, 2013 amounted to ₹14,250. Of the business expenses ₹10,000 were outstanding and ₹2,750 were prepaid on 31st March, 2013. 80% of Business Expenses were paid by cheque.
11. Fixed Assets purchased (on 30.09.2012) and paid by cheques ₹60,000, Rate of Depreciation on Fixed Assets – 10%.
12. Personal Drawings amounted to ₹1,00,000 of which 80% were in Cash.
13. 4% Govt. Securities purchased by cheque (at 96% on 01.10.2012) for ₹9,600.
14. Cash deposited into the Bank ₹1,40,000.
15. The amount defalcated by the cashier may be written off to Profit & Loss Account.

Required: Prepare Trading & Profit & Loss Account for the year ended 31st March 2013 and the Balance Sheet as at 31st March, 2013.

SOLUTION

Same Solution as in Illustration 49

Working Notes:

(I) CALCULATION OF GROSS PROFIT RATIO DURING PREVIOUS YEAR

Particulars	₹
A. Credit Sales[₹50,000 × 12/2]	3,00,000
B. Cash Sales[₹3,00,000 × 1/3]	1,00,000
C. Total Sales [A + B]	4,00,000
D. Credit Purchases[₹25,000 × 12/1]	3,00,000
E. Cash Purchases [₹ 3,00,000 × 20%]	60,000
F. Total Purchases [D + E]	3,60,000
G. *Add:* Opening Stock	20,000
H. *Less:* Closing Stock	(60,000)
I. Cost of Goods sold [F + G – H]	3,20,000
J. Gross Profit [C – I]	80,000
K. Gross Profit Ratio [(Gross Profit/Sales) × 100]	20%

(II) CALCULATION OF CASH & CREDIT SALES AND CLOSING DEBTORS DURING CURRENT YEAR

Particulars	₹
A. Total Sales during Previous Year	4,00,000
B. *Add:* Increase in volume @20%	80,000
C. Total Sales during Current Year	4,80,000
D. Cash Sales[₹4,80,000 × 25%]	1,20,000
E. Credit Sales [c – d]	3,60,000
F. Closing Debtors [₹3,60,000 × 12/2]	60,000

(III) CALCULATION OF CASH & CREDIT PURCHASES AND CLOSING CREDITORS DURING CURRENT YEAR

Particulars	₹
A. Total Sales during Current Year	4,80,000
B. *Less:* Gross Profit	96,000
C. Cost of Goods sold during Current Year	3,84,000
D. *Less:* Opening Stock	(60,000)
E. *Add:* Closing Stock	1,08,000
F. Total Purchases during Current Year	4,32,000
G. *Less:* Cash Purchases[₹ 4,32,000/6]	(72,000)
H. Credit Purchases	3,60,000
I. Closing Creditors [₹ 3,60,000 × 12/1]	30,000

All other working and solution are same as in Illustration 18. The only difference is that in Illustration 18, collection from debtors is the balancing figure since closing debtors are ascertained as per working note (ii) and payments to creditors is the balancing figure since closing creditors are ascertained as per working note (iii).

ILLUSTRATION 23

Riots occurred and fire broke out on the evening of 31st March, 2013, destroying the books of accounts and factory shed (book value ₹20,000) of Bharat, a small trader. The cashier had absconded with the available cash. The following information was available:

1. ASSETS AND LIABILITIES

Particulars	*31.03.2012* ₹	*31.03.2013* ₹
Fixed Assets (after depreciation)	60,000	1,08,000
Stock	60,000	?
Trade Debtors	50,000	60,000
Bills Receivable	–	5,000
Cash	5,000	?
Bank	65,000	?
Prepaid Business Expenses	20,000	4,000
Outstanding Business Expenses	55,000	11,000
Trade Creditors for Goods	25,000	30,000
Bills Payable	–	25,000
Capital	?	1,01,000

2. Uniform Rate of Gross Profit – 20%.
3. Gross Profit for the year ended 31.03.2012 – ₹80,000.
4. Cash Sales 66-2/3% *less* than the net credit sales. Sales Returns – 1/7th of Gross Credit Sales.
5. Cash Purchases – 20% of Net Credit Purchases, Purchases Returns 1/7th of Gross Credit Purchases.
6. His sales for the year ended 21st March, 2013 were 20% higher than the previous year's.
7. On 1st April, 2012 the stock level was raised by ₹42,000 and stock was maintained at this new level all throughout the year.
8. Freight inwards ₹4,000 in cash.
9. Goods costing ₹9,000 were used as advertising materials.
10. Collections from Debtors (after 6% discount) were 80% in cash.
11. Payments to creditors (after 5% discount) amounted to ₹2,18,500 of which 80% were by cheques.
12. 80% of indirect Business Expenses were paid by cheques.
13. On 31.9.2012 Fixed Assets are purchased and paid by cheques. Depreciate Fixed Assets by 10%.
14. (a) Goods costing ₹ 1,000 were used by the proprietor for personal use.
    (b) Personal Drawings amounting to ₹1,00,000 of which 80% were in Cash.
15. 4% Govt. securities purchased by cheque (at 96% on 01.10.2012) for ₹9,600.
16. Cash deposited into the Bank ₹1,00,000.
17. During the year, acceptances amounting to ₹50,000 were discharged before maturity at a discount of 2% by means of a pay order and promissory notes amounting to ₹25,000 were also duly discharged at maturity by means of a pay order.
18. During the year, of the Bills drawn.

(a) Some bills were endorsed in favour of creditors. Out of these endorsed bills, bills for ₹25,000 were dishonoured.

(b) Bills amounting to ₹25,000 were discounted at a discount of 2% of which a bill for ₹12,500 was dishonoured.

(c) Out of these dishonoured bills, drawees of bills of ₹18,750 became insolvent and paid 50% only by means of a bank draft.

(d) Bills amounting to ₹10,000 were discharged by drawees before maturity at a rebate of 2% by means of a bank draft.

(e) Bills amounting to ₹10,000 were collected at maturity by means of bank draft.

19. The amount defalcated by the cashier may be treated as recoverable from him.

Required: Prepare Trading & Profit & Loss Account for the year ended 31st March 2013 and the Balance Sheet as at 31st March, 2013.

SOLUTION

TRADING & PROFIT/LOSS ACCOUNT

Dr. *for the year ended 31st March, 2013* *Cr.*

Particulars		₹	*Particulars*		₹
To Opening Stock		60,000	By Sales		
To Purchases			Cash Sales	1,20,000	
Cash Purchases	72,000		Credit Sales	4,20,000	
Credit Purchases	4,20,000		*Less:* Sales Returns	(60,000)	4,80,000
Less: Purchase Returns	(60,000)		By Closing Stock		1,02,000
Less: Advertisement	(9,000)				
Less: Drawings	(1,000)	4,22,000			
To Freight Inward		4,000			
To Gross Profit		96,000			
		5,82,000			5,82,000
To Advertising		9,000	By Gross Profit B/d		96,000
To Bad Debts		9,375	By Discount Received		11,500
To Rebate Allowed		200	By Rebate Received		1,000
To Discount Allowed		16,125	By Accrued Interest on Govt. Securities		200
To Discount on bill		500			
To Loss by fire		20,000			
To Depreciation		12,000			
To Expenses (Balancing figure)		19,500			
To Net Profit		22,000			
		1,08,700			1,08,700

BALANCE SHEET OF BHARAT AS AT 31.03.2013

Liabilities		₹	*Assets*		₹
X's Capital Account			**Fixed Assets**		
Opening Balance	1,80,000		Opening Balance	60,000	

Add: Net Profit	22,000		*Less:* Loss Due to fire	(20,000)	
Less: Drawings	(1,01,000)	1,01,000	*Add:* Addition	80,000	
Creditors		30,000	*Less:* Depreciation	(12,000)	1,08,000
Outstanding Business Exp. A/c		11,000	**Closing Stock**		1,02,000
Bank overdraft		1,39,700	**Debtors**		60,000
B/P		25,000	**B/R**		5,000
			Prepaid Business Expenses		4,000
			4% Govt.Securities		9,600
			Interest Accrued		200
			Due From Cashier		17,900
		3,06,700			3,06,700

Working Notes:

(I) CALCULATION OF CASH AND CREDIT SALES DURING THE CURRENT YEAR:

	Particulars	₹
A.	Previous year's Total Sales (Gross Profit/GP Ratio) (₹80,000/.20)	4,00,000
B.	*Add:* Increase in Sales during current year @ 20%	80,000
C.	Current year's Total Sales (A + B)	4,80,000
D.	*Less:* Cash Sales @ 25% of Net Sales (₹4,80,000 × 25%)	1,20,000
E.	Net Credit Sales (C – D)	3,60,000
F.	*Add:* Sales Returns (₹3,60,000 × 1/6)	60,000
G.	Gross Credit Sales (E + F)	4,20,000

(II) CALCULATION OF CASH AND CREDIT PURCHASES DURING THE CURRENT YEAR

	Particulars	₹
A.	Current year's Total Sales	4,80,000
B.	*Less:* Gross Profit @ 20%	96,000
C.	Cost of Goods Sold (A – B)	3,84,000
D.	*Add:* Closing Stock (₹60,000 + ₹42,000)	1,02,000
E.	*Add:* Material used in advertising	9,000
F.	*Add:* Goods used as drawings	1,000
G.	*Less:* Opening Stock	60,000
H.	*Less:* Freight inward	4,000
I.	Total Purchases	4,32,000
J.	*Less:* Cash Purchases (₹4,32,000 × 1/6)	72,000
K.	Net Credit Purchases	3,60,000
L.	*Add:* Purchase Returns (₹3,60,000 × 1/6)	60,000
M.	Gross Credit Purchases	4,20,000

Dr. **(III) DEBTORS ACCOUNT** *Cr.*

Particulars	₹	*Particulars*	₹
To Balance b/d	50,000	By Sales Returns A/c	60,000
To Sales A/c	4,20,000	By Bank A/c	9,375
To Creditors (Dish. of Endorsed B/R)	25,000	By Bad Debts A/c	9,375
To Bank A/c (Dish. of Discounted B/R)	12,500	By Discount Allowed A/c [₹2,68,750 × 6%]	16,125
		By Bank A/c [₹2,52,625 × 20%]	50,525
		By Cash A/c	2,02,100
		By B/R A/c	1,00,000
		By Balance c/d	60,000
	5,07,500		5,07,500

Dr. **(IV) CREDITORS ACCOUNT** *Cr.*

Particulars	₹	*Particulars*	₹
To Purchase Returns A/c	60,000	By Balance b/d	25,000
To Bank A/c	1,74,800	By Purchases A/c	4,20,000
To Cash A/c	43,700	By Debtors A/c (Dish. of Endorsed B/R)	25,000
To Discount Received A/c [₹2,18,500 × 5/95]	11,500		
To B/P	1,00,000		
To B/R [Endorsed B/R) (b.f.)	50,000		
To Balance c/d	30,000		
	4,70,000		4,70,000

Dr. **(V) BILLS RECEIVABLE ACCOUNT** *Cr.*

Particulars	₹	*Particulars*	₹
To Debtors A/c (B/R Drawn) *(Balancing Figure)*	1,00,000	By Creditors A/c (Endorsed B/R)	50,000
		By Bank A/c	24,500
		By Discounting Charges A/c	500
		By Bank A/c	9,800
		By Rebate Allowed	200
		By Bank A/c	10,000
		By Balance c/d	5,000
	1,00,000		1,00,000

Dr. **(VI) BILLS PAYABLE ACCOUNT** *Cr.*

Particulars	₹	*Particulars*	₹
To Bank A/c	25,000	By Creditors A/c (B/P Accepted) *(Balancing Figure)*	1,00,000
To Bank A/c	49,000		

To Rebate Received	1,000		
To Balance c/d	25,000		
	1,00,000		1,00,000

Dr. **(VII) FIXED ASSETS ACCOUNT** Cr.

Particulars	₹	*Particulars*	₹
To Balance b/d	60,000	By Loss by fire	20,000
To Bank A/c (Purchases)	80,000	By Depreciation A/c	12,000
(Balancing Figure)		(₹1,08,000 × 10/90)	
		By Balance c/d	1,08,000
	1,40,000		1,40,000

(VIII) CALCULATION OF OPENING CAPITAL
BALANCE SHEET AS AT 31.03.2012

Liabilities	₹	*Assets*	₹
Outstanding Business Expenses	55,000	Fixed Assets	60,000
Trade Creditors for Goods	25,000	Stock	60,000
Capital (Balancing Figure)	1,80,000	Trade Debtors	50,000
		Cash	5,000
		Bank	65,000
		Prepaid Business Expenses	20,000
	2,60,000		2,60,000

(ix) Net Profit for current year = Closing Capital + Drawings – Opening Capital
= ₹1,01,000 + ₹1,01,000 – ₹1,80,000 = ₹22,000.

Dr. **(X) BUSINESS EXPENSES ACCOUNT** Cr.

Particulars	₹	*Particulars*	₹
To Prepaid Expenses A/c (Beg.)	20,000	By Outstanding Exp A/c (Beg.)	55,000
To Bank A/c (80% of ₹ 47,500)	38,000	By Profit & Loss A/c	19,500
To Cash A/c (20% of ₹ 47,500)	9,500	By Prepaid Expenses A/c (End)	4,000
To Outstanding Exp A/c (End)	11,000		
	78,500		78,500

Dr. **(XI) CASH BOOK** Cr.

Particulars	*Cash* ₹	*Bank* ₹	*Particulars*	*Cash* ₹	*Bank* ₹
To Balance b/d	5,000	65,000	By Cash Purchases A/c	72,000	
To Cash Sales A/c	1,20,000		By Creditors A/c	43,700	1,74,800
To Debtors A/c	2,02,100	50,525	By Freight	4,000	
To Cash A/c(C)		1,00,000	By Fixed Assets A/c		80,000
To B/R A/c		24,500	By Business Exp.	9,500	38,000

To Debtors A/c		9,375	By Drawings A/c	80,000	20,000
To B/R A/c		9,800	By Bank A/c (C)	1,00,000	
To B/R A/c		10,000	By Debtor A/c (Dish of B/R)		12,500
To Balance c/d		1,39,700	By B/P		49,000
			By B/P		25,000
			By Govt. Securities		9,600
			By Balance c/d (Defalcated by cashier)	17,900	
	3,27,100	4,08,900		3,27,100	4,08,900

ILLUSTRATION 24

Tulsian Sons is running a Restaurant where sports facilities are also provided in waiting hall and provides you the following information:

1. OPENING AND CLOSING BALANCES

Particulars	*As on 1.4.2012* ₹	*As on 31.3.2013* ₹
Furniture	2,20,000	?
Sports Equipment	2,20,000	?
China Glass, Cutlery etc.,	25,000	?
6% Govt. Securities [Face value ₹ 3,00,000]	2,50,000	?
Stock of Sports Materials	3,000	500
Advances to Suppliers of Sports Materials	1,000	500
Due to Suppliers of Sports Materials	3,000	1,800
Stock of Stationery	2,000	?
Unpresented cheques being payment for stationery	900	300
Interest on loan Outstanding	4,750	3,500
Interest on loan Received-in-Advance	1,400	2,600
Outstanding Miscellaneous Expenses	4,750	3,500
Miscellaneous Expenses paid in advance	1,400	2,600
Outstanding Wages	5,000	4,000
Cash Balance	10,000	30,000
Bank Balance as per Pass Book	5,00,000	?
Stock of Provisions	30,000	3,80,000
Debtors for Provisions	30,000	40,000
Creditors for Provisions	1,00,000	50,000
Loans given	7,20,000	?

2. PAYMENT AS PER PASS BOOK

Particulars	₹
Suppliers of Sports Materials	10,800
Miscellaneous Expenses	74,450
Wages	51,000
Stationery	1,600
Furniture (Purchased on 1.10.2012)	1,50,000
Sports Equipment (purchased on 1.10.2012)	1,50,000
8% R.B.I Tax Free Bonds (Purchased on 1.1.2013) [Face Value ₹ 1,00,000]	79,200
Creditors for Provisions	10,50,000

3. RECEIPTS AS PER PASS BOOK

Particulars	₹
Interest on Loans	74,450
Interest on 6% Govt. Securities (After T.D.S. @ 10%)	8,100
Collection from Debtors for Provisions	8,90,000
Loan Repayments	2,00,000

4.(a) Cash Purchases of Provisions - 1/11th of Total Purchases

4.(b) Cash Sales of Provisions –10% of Total Sales

5. Depreciation Rates:
   (a) On China Glass & Cutlery — 20%
   (b) On Furniture — 10% p.a.
   (c) On Sports Equipment — 10%
6. The cost of the boarding expenses—Restaurant staff ₹ 20,000—other staff ₹ 7,500.
7. Furniture (having a book value of ₹ 20,000 as on 1.4.2012) was sold at a loss of 20% on 31.12.2012 and a cheque was duly received and credited.
8. Write 25% off Stationery.

Required: Prepare Restaurant Trading Account, Profit and Loss Account and the Closing Balance Sheet.

SOLUTION

RESTAURANT TRADING ACCOUNT

Dr. *for the year ended 31st March, 2013* *Cr.*

Particulars		₹	*Particulars*		₹
To Opening Stock		30,000	By Sales of Provisions		
To Purchases of Provisions			Cash Sales	1,00,000	
Cash Purchases	1,00,000		Credit Sales	9,00,000	10,00,000
Credit Purchases	10,00,000	11,00,000	By Boarding Expenses		
To Boarding Expenses of			of Restaurant & other Staff		27,500
Restaurant staff		20,000	By Stock of Provisions		3,80,000

To Wages	50,000		
To Gross Profit t/f to Income & Exp. A/c	2,07,500		
	14,07,500		14,07,500

PROFIT & LOSS ACCOUNT

Dr. *for year ended 31st March 2013* Cr.

Particulars	₹	*Particulars*		₹
To Depreciation on Cutlery	5,000	By Gross Profit from Restaurant		2,07,500
To Depreciation on Furniture	29,000	By Interest on Loan A/c		72,000
To Depreciation on Sport Equipment	37000	By Interest on Govt. Securities		
To Sports Materials Consumed	12,600	Received	8,100	
To Stationery w/o	750	T.D.S	900	
To Miscellaneous Expenses A/c	72,000	*Add:* Accrued Interest	9,000	18,000
To Loss on Sale of Furniture	3,700	By Accrued Interest on		
To Boarding Expenses of other Staff	7500	8% RBI Tax free Bonds		2,000
To Net Profit t/f to Capital A/c	1,31,950			
	2,99,500			2,99,500

BALANCE SHEET AS AT 31 MARCH, 2013

Liabilities		₹	*Assets*		₹
Capital Fund:			Furniture		3,22,500
Opening Balance	19,02,100		Sport Equipment		
Add: Net Profit	1,31,950	20,34,050	Opening Balance	2,20,000	
Interest on Loan received in adva.		2,600	*Add:* Purchases	1,50,000	
Outstanding Misc. Expenses		3,500	*Less:* Depreciation	(37,000)	3,33,000
Outstanding Wages		4,000	China, Glass Cutlery		20,000
Due to Suppliers of Sports Materials		1,800	Govt. Securities		
Creditors for Provisions		50,000	(Face Value ₹ 3,00,000)		2,50,000
			8% RBI Tax free Bonds		
			(Face Value ₹ 1,00,000)		79,200
			Stock of Provisions		3,80,000
			Stock of Sports Material		500
			Stock of Stationery		2,250
			Debtors for Provisions		40,000
			Advance to Suppliers of Sports Materials		500
			Interest on Loan Outstanding		3,500
			Prepaid Misc. Expenses		2,600
			Accrued Interest on Govt. Securities		9,000

		Accrued Interest on 8% RBI Tax free Bonds	2,000
		T.D.S	900
		Cash	30,000
		Bank	1,00,000
		Loan Given	5,20,000
	20,95,950		20,95,950

Working Notes:

Dr. **(I) INTEREST ON LOAN ACCOUNT** *Cr.*

Particulars	₹	*Particulars*	₹
To Interest on Loan Outstanding A/c (beginning)	4,750	By Interest on Loan received in advance A/c (beg)	1,400
To Profit & Loss A/c (b.f.)	72,000	By Bank A/c	74,450
To Interest on Loan received in advance A/c (end)	2,600	By Interest on Loan Outstanding A/c (end)	3,500
	79,350		79,350

Dr. **(II) MISCELLANEOUS EXPENSES ACCOUNT** *Cr.*

Particulars	₹	*Particulars*	₹
To Expenses Prepaid A/c (beginning)	1,400	By Exp. Outstanding A/c (beg.)	4,750
To Bank A/c	74,450	By Profit & Loss A/c (b.f.)	72,000
To Expenses Outstanding A/c (end)	3,500	By Expenses Prepaid A/c (end)	2,600
	79,350		79,350

Dr. **(III) SUPPLIERS OF SPORTS MATERIALS ACCOUNT** *Cr.*

Particulars	₹	*Particulars*	₹
To Balance b/d (advance)	1,000	By Balance b/d (outstanding)	3,000
To Bank A/c	10,800	By Stock of Sports Material A/c (b.f.)	10,100
To Balance c/d (outstanding)	1,800	By Balance c/d (advance)	500
	13,600		13,600

Dr. **(IV) STOCK OF SPORTS MATERIALS ACCOUNT** *Cr.*

Particulars	₹	*Particulars*	₹
To Balance b/d	3,000	By P & L A/c (consumed) (b.f.)	12,600
To Supplier's A/c	10,100	By Balance c/d	500
	13,100		13,100

(v) Purchases of Stationery as per Cash Book = Payment as per Pass Book + Unpresented cheques at the end – Unpresented cheques at the beginning

= ₹ 1,600 + ₹ 300 – ₹ 900 = ₹ 1,000

Dr. **(VI) STOCK OF STATIONERY ACCOUNT** Cr.

Particulars	₹	Particulars	₹
To Balance b/d	2,000	By Profit & Loss A/c (consumed)	750
To Purchases A/c	1,000	By Balance c/d	2,250
	3,000		3,000

Dr. **(VII) DEBTORS FOR PROVISIONS ACCOUNT** Cr.

Particulars	₹	Particulars	₹
To Balance b/d	30,000	By Bank A/c	8,90,000
To Credit Sales	9,00,000	By Balance c/d	40,000
	9,30,000		9,30,000

Dr. **(VIII) CREDITORS FOR PROVISIONS ACCOUNT** Cr.

Particulars	₹	Particulars	₹
To Bank A/c	10,50,000	By Balance b/d	1,00,000
To Balance c/d	50,000	By Credit purchases	10,00,000
	11,00,000		11,00,000

Dr. **(IX) FURNITURE ACCOUNT** Cr.

Particulars	₹	Particulars	₹
To Balance b/d	2,20,000	By Depreciation A/c	
To Bank A/c	1,50,000	Sold (20,000 × 10% × 9/12)	1,500
		By Bank A/c (sales)	14,800
		By Profit & Loss A/c (Loss)	3,700
		By Depreciation A/c	
		Old (2,00,000 × 10%)	20,000
		New (1,50,000 × 10% × 6/12)	7,500
		By Balance c/d	3,22,500
	3,70,000		3,70,000

Dr. **(X) CASH & BANK ACCOUNT** Cr.

Particulars	₹	Particulars	₹
To Balance b/d: Cash	10,000	By Creditors for Provisions A/c	10,50,000
Bank Balance as per Pass Book	5,00,000	By Wages A/c	51,000
To Debtors for Provisions A/c	8,90,000	By Suppliers of Sports Materials A/c	10,800
To Interest on Govt. Securities	8,100	By Furniture A/c	1,50,000
To Interest on Loan	74,450	By Miscellaneous Expenses A/c	74,450
To Cash Sales of Provisions	1,00,000	By Sport Equipment	1,50,000
To Furniture	14,800	By Stationery A/c	1,600
To Loan Repayment	2,00,000	By Cash Purchases of Provisions	1,00,000

		By 8% RBI Tax free Bonds	79,200
		By Balance c/d (cash)	30,000
		Bank	1,00,300
	17,97,350		17,97,350

(XI) BANK RECONCILIATION STATEMENT

Particulars	31.3.2012 ₹	31.3.2013 ₹
A. Bank Balance (overdraft) as per Pass Book	5,00,000	1,00,300
B. *Less:* Unpresented cheques for stationery	(900)	(300)
C. Bank Balance (overdraft) as per Cash Book	4,99,100	1,00,000

(XII) BALANCE SHEET AS AT 31 MARCH, 2012

Liabilities	₹	*Assets*	₹
Capital Account	19,02,100	Furniture	2,20,000
Creditors for Provisions	1,00,000	Sport Equipment	2,20,000
Due to Suppliers of Sports Materials	3,000	China, Glass Cutlery	25,000
Interest on Loan received in ad.	1,400	Govt. Securities	
Outstanding Misc. Expenses	4,750	(Face Value ₹ 3,00,000)	2,50,000
Outstanding Wages	5,000	Stock of Provisions	30,000
		Stock of Sports Material	3,000
		Stock of Stationery	2,000
		Debtors for Provisions	30,000
		Advance to Supp. of Sports Materials	1,000
		Interest on Loan Outstanding	4,750
		Prepaid Misc. Expenses	1,400
		Cash	10,000
		Bank Balance As per Cash Book	4,99,100
		Loan given	7,20,000
	20,16,250		20,16,250

SOLVED PROBLEMS - I

PROBLEM 1

From the following information in respect of BHARAT a trader, prepare a Trading, Profit and Loss Account for the year ended 31st March, 2013 and a Balance Sheet as on that date.

(A) LIABILITIES AND ASSETS

Particulars	Opening ₹	Closing ₹
Stock-in-trade	80,000	70,000

Debtors for Sales	1,60,000	1,49,500
Bills Receivable	—	17,500
Creditors for purchases	1,10,000	1,50,000
Fixed Assets (at written down value)	60,000	63,500
Expenses outstanding	20,000	18,000
Prepaid expenses	6,000	7,000
Cash in hand	2,000	1,500
Bank Balance	10,000	4,750

(B) RECEIPTS AND PAYMENTS DURING THE YEAR

Particulars	₹
Collections from Debtors (after allowing 2.5% discount)	?
Payments to Creditors (after receiving 2% discount)	3,92,000
Proceeds of Bills Receivable, discounted at 2%	61,250
Proprietor's drawings	70,000
Purchases of Fixed Assets midway through the year	10,000
4% Government Securities purchased (at 96% on 1st Oct.)	96,000
Expenses	1,75,000
Miscellaneous income	5,000

(c) Sales are effected so as to realise a gross profit of 33-1/3% on the sale proceeds.

(d) Goods costing ₹ 9,000, were issued as advertisement articles.

(e) During the year, Bills Receivable were drawn on debtors. Of these, Bills amounting to ₹ 20,000 were endorsed in favour of creditors. Of this later amount, a bill for ₹ 4,000 was dishonored by the debtor.

(f) Capital introduced during the year by the proprietor by cheques was omitted to be recorded in Cash Book, though the Bank balance of ₹ 4,750 on 31st March, 2013 (as shown above), takes the same into account.

SOLUTION

TRADING AND PROFIT AND LOSS ACCOUNT OF...

Dr. *for the year ending on 31st March, 2013* *Cr.*

Particulars		₹	*Particulars*	₹
To Opening Stock		80,000	By Sales, (net)	6,85,500
To Purchases	4,56,000		By Closing Stock	70,000
Less: Used for Adv.	(9,000)	4,47,000		
To Gross Profit c/d		2,28,500		
		7,55,500		7,55,500
To Sundry Expenses			By Gross Profit b/d	2,28,500
[₹ 1,75,000 – (2,000 + 1,000]		1,72,000	By Interest on Govt. Securities	2,000
To Depreciation		6,500	By Discount received	8,000
To Discount Allowed		16,250	By Misc. Income	5,000

To Advertisement	9,000		
To Net Profit to transferred Capital Account	39,750		
	2,43,500		2,43,500

BALANCE SHEET AS AT 31ST MARCH, 2013

Liabilities		₹	*Assets*		₹
Capital: Opening Balance	1,88,000		Furniture: Opening Balance	60,000	
Add: Additional Capital	86,000		*Add:* Additions	10,000	
Add: Profit	39,750		*Less:* Depreciation	6,500	63,500
Less: Drawings	70,000	2,43,750	Investment Govt. Securities		96,000
Sundry Creditors		1,50,000	Interest Accrued		2,000
Expenses Outstanding		18,000	Stock in trade		70,000
			Sundry Debtors		1,49,500
			Bills Receivable		17,500
			Cash in hand		1,500
			Cash at Bank		4,750
			Prepaid Expenses		7,000
		4,11,750			4,11,750

Working Notes:

Dr. **(I) TOTAL CREDITORS ACCOUNT** *Cr.*

Particulars	₹	*Particulars*	₹
To Bank A/c	3,92,000	By Balance b/d	1,10,000
To Discount (₹ 3,92,000 × 2/98)	8,000	By Total Debtors A/c- (endorsed bill dishonoured	4,000
To Bills Receivable (Endorsed)	20,000		
To Balance c/d	1,50,000	By Credit Purchases (b.f.)	4,56,000
	5,70,000		5,70,000

Dr. **(II) STOCK ACCOUNT** *Cr.*

Particulars	₹	*Particulars*	₹
To Balance b/d	80,000	By Advertisement A/c	9,000
To Purchases	4,56,000	By Cost of Sales (b.f.)	4,57,000
		By Closing Stock	70,000
	5,36,000		5,36,000

(iii) Sales = Cost of Sales + Gross Profit = ₹ 4,57,000 + 50% of ₹ 4,57,000 = ₹ 6,85,500

Dr. **(IV) BILLS RECEIVABLE ACCOUNT** *Cr.*

Particulars	₹	*Particulars*	₹
To Sundry Debtors	1,00,000	By Bank A/c	61,250
		By Discount (₹ 61,250 × 2/98)	1,250

		By Sundry Creditors (B/R endorsed)	20,000
		By Balance c/d	17,500
	1,00,000		1,00,000

Dr. **(V) TOTAL DEBTORS ACCOUNT** Cr.

Particulars	₹	*Particulars*	₹
To Balance b/d	1,60,000	By Bank (₹ 6,00,000 × 97.5%)	5,85,000
To Sundry Creditors		By Discount (₹ 6,00,000 × 2.5%)	15,000
(Bill endorsed dishonoured)	4,000	By Bills Receivable A/c	1,00,000
To Credit Sales	6,85,500	By Balance c/d	1,49,500
	8,49,500		8,49,500

Dr. **(VI) CASH BOOK** Cr.

Particulars	₹	*Particulars*	₹
To Balance b/d		By Sundry Creditors A/c	3,92,000
(Both Cash & at Bank)	12,000	By Drawings	70,000
To Sundry Debtors A/c	5,85,000	By Furniture	10,000
To Bills Receivable A/c	61,250	By 4% Govt. Securities	96,000
To Misc. Income	5,000	By Expenses	1,75,000
To Capital Introduced (B/f)	86,000	By Balance c/d	6,250
	7,49,250		7,49,250

(VII) BALANCE SHEET AS AT 31ST MARCH, 2012

Liabilities	₹	*Assets*	₹
Sundry Creditors	1,10,000	Furnitures	60,000
Outstanding Expenses	20,000	Stock-in-trade	80,000
Capital (b/f)	1,88,000	Sundry debtors	1,60,000
		Cash in hand	2,000
		Cash in Bank	10,000
		Prepaid Expenses	6,000
	3,18,000		3,18,000

PROBLEM 2

The following is the Balance Sheet of Sri CAMHG as on 31st March, 2012:

Liabilities	₹	*Assets*	₹
Capital Account	96,000	Building	65,000
Loan	30,000	Furniture	10,000
Creditors	62,000	Motor Car	18,000
		Stock	40,000
		Debtors	34,000

		Cash in hand	4,000
		Cash at bank	17,000
	1,88,000		1,88,000

A riot occurred on the night of 31st March, 2013 in which all books and records were lost. The cashier had absconded with the available cash. He gives you the following information.

(a) His sales for the year ended 31st March, 2013 were 20% higher than the previous year's. He always sells his goods at cost *plus* 25%; 20% of the total sales for the year ended 31st March, 2013 were for cash. There were no cash purchases.

(b) On 1st April, 2012, the stock level was raised to ₹ 60,000 and stock was maintained at this new level all throughout the year.

(c) Collection from debtors amounted to ₹ 2,80,000 of which ₹ 70,000 was received in cash. Business expenses amounted to ₹ 40,000 of which ₹ 10,000 was outstanding on 31st March, 2013 and ₹ 12,000 was paid by cheques.

(d) Analysis of the Pass Book revealed the Payment to Creditors ₹ 2,75,000, Personal Drawings ₹ 15,000, Cash deposited in Bank ₹ 1,43,000, Cash withdrawn from Bank ₹ 24,000.

(e) Gross profit as per last year's audited accounts was ₹ 60,000.

(f) Provide depreciation on Building and Furniture at 5% and Motor Car at 20%.

(g) The amount defaulcated by the cashier may be treated as recoverable from him.

Required: Prepare the Trading and Profit and Loss Account for the year ended 31st March, 2013 and the Balance Sheet as on that date.

SOLUTION

TRADING AND PROFIT AND LOSS ACCOUNT

for the year ending on 31st March, 2013

Dr. *Cr.*

Particulars		₹	*Particulars*	₹
To Opening Stock		40,000	By Sales	3,60,000
To Purchases (b.f.)		3,08,000	By Closing Stock	60,000
To Gross Profit c/d (@ 20% on sales)		72,000		
		4,20,000		4,20,000
To Sundry Expenses		40,000	By Gross Profit b/d	72,000
To Depreciation on:				
Building	3,250			
Furniture	500			
Motor	3,600	7,350		
To Net Profit transferred to Capital A/c		24,650		
		72,000		72,000

BALANCE SHEET AS AT 31ST MARCH, 2013

Liabilities		₹	*Assets*		₹
Capital Account:			Building	65,000	
Opening Balance	96,000		*Less:* Depreciation	3,250	61,750

Add: Net Profit	24,650		Furniture	10,000	
	1,20,650		*Less:* Depreciation	500	9,500
Less: Drawings	15,000	1,05,650	Motor Car	18,000	
Loan		30,000	*Less:* Depreciation	3,600	14,400
Sundry Creditors		95,000	Stock in trade		60,000
Outstanding Expenses		10,000	Sundry Debtors		42,000
			Cash at Bank		44,000
			Sundry Advances		9,000
			(Amount recoverable from Cashier)		
		2,40,650			2,40,650

Working Notes:

Dr. **(I) TOTAL DEBTORS ACCOUNT** *Cr.*

Particulars	₹	*Particulars*	₹
To Balance b/d	34,000	By Bank (₹ 2,80,000 – ₹ 70,000)	2,10,000
To Sales (80% of ₹ 3,60,000)	2,88,000	By Cash A/c	70,000
		By Balance c/d	42,000
	3,22,000		3,22,000

Dr. **(II) TOTAL CREDITORS ACCOUNT** *Cr.*

Particulars	₹	*Particulars*	₹
To Bank	2,75,000	By Balance b/d	62,000
To Balance c/d	95,000	By Purchases	3,08,000
	3,70,000		3,70,000

Dr. **(III) CASH BOOK** *Cr.*

Particulars	*Cash* ₹	*Bank* ₹	*Particulars*	*Cash* ₹	*Bank* ₹
To Balance b/d	4,000	17,000	By Sundry Expenses	18,000	12,000
To Sales	72,000	—	By Drawings	—	15,000
To Sundry Debtors	70,000	2,10,000	By Sundry Creditors	—	2,75,000
To Cash (Contra)	—	1,43,000	By Bank (Contra)	1,43,000	—
To Bank (Contra)	24,000	—	By Cash (Contra)	—	24,000
			By Defaulcation (b.f.)	9,000	—
			By Balance c/d (b.f.)	—	44,000
	1,70,000	3,70,000		1,70,000	3,70,000

(iv) Last year's Total Sales = ₹ 60,000 × 100/20 = ₹ 3,00,000.

(v) Current year's Total Sales = ₹ 3,00,00 + 20% of ₹ 3,00,000 = ₹ 3,60,000.

(vi) Current year's Credit Sales = ₹ 3,60,000 × 80% = ₹ 2,88,000.

(vii) Cost of Goods Sold = Sales – G.P. = ₹ 3,60,000 – ₹ 72,000 = ₹ 2,88,000.

(viii) Purchases = Cost of Goods Sold + Closing Stock – Opening Stock

= ₹ 2,88,000 + ₹ 60,000 – ₹ 40,000 = ₹ 3,08,000.

PROBLEM 3

From the following particulars, prepare Trading and Profit & Loss Account for the year ending on 31st March 2013 and the balance Sheet as on that date:

BALANCE SHEET AS AT 31ST MARCH, 2012

Liabilities	₹	*Assets*	₹
Capital	1,72,500	Machinery	70,000
Creditors for goods	62,500	Furniture	15,000
Expenses outstanding	5,000	Stock	35,000
		Debtors	1,00,000
		Cash	5,000
		Bank	15,000
	2,40,000		2,40,000

Information: Debtors' Velocity 2 months, Creditors' Velocity 1.5 month, Stock level uniform, Gross Profit Ratio 33-1/3%, Sales are 20% in cash and 80% on Credit. Sales for the current year is 20% more than the previous year. Receipt from debtors cash ₹ 50,000, balance cheques, Depreciation rate 10%, Payments out of Bank: Machinery ₹ 40,000; Furniture ₹ 5,000, Investments ₹ 40,000, Drawings ₹ 17,500, Business Expenditure ₹ 60,000, Cash Payments: Business Expenditure ₹ 90,000, Cash deposited into Bank 1,00,000.

SOLUTION

TRADING AND PROFIT AND LOSS ACCOUNT

for the year ending on 31st March, 2013

Dr. | *Cr.*

Particulars		₹	*Particulars*	₹
To Opening Stock		35,000	By Sales	9,00,000
To Purchases		6,00,000	By Closing Stock	35,000
To Gross Profit c/d		3,00,000		
		9,35,000		9,35,000
To Business Expenses			By Gross Profit b/d	3,00,000
(₹ 1,50,000 – ₹ 5,000)		1,45,000		
To Depreciation on:				
Machinery	11,000			
Furniture	2,000	13,000		
To Net Profit transferred to				
Capital A/c		1,42,000		
		3,00,000		3,00,000

BALANCE SHEET AS AT 31ST MARCH, 2013

Liabilities		₹	*Assets*		₹
Capital:			Machinery	70,000	
Opening Balance	1,72,500		*Add:* Additions	40,000	
Add: Net Profit	1,42,000		*Less:* Depreciation	11,000	99,000
Less: Drawings	17,500	2,97,000	Furniture	15,000	
Creditors for goods		75,000	*Add:* Addition	5,000	
			Less: Depreciation	2,000	18,000
			Investments		40,000
			Stock		35,000
			Debtors		1,20,000
			Cash at Bank		15,000
			Cash in hand		45,000
		3,72,000			3,72,000

Working Notes:

(I) CALCULATION OF CASH SALES, CREDIT SALES AND COST OF GOODS SOLD

	Particulars	₹
A	Opening Sundry Debtors	1,00,000
B	Debtors' Velocity 2 months	
C	Credit Sales during previous year (₹ 1,00,000 × 12/2)	6,00,000
D	Cash Sales during previous year (₹ 6,00,000 × 25%)	1,50,000
E	Total Sales during previous year (C + D)	7,50,000
F	Total Sales during current year (₹ 7,50,000 + 20% of ₹ 7,50,000)	9,00,000
G	Cash Sales @ 20% = ₹ 1,80,000, Credit Sales @ 80% = ₹ 7,20,000	
H	Closing Sundry Debtors (1/6 of Credit Sales being ₹ 7,20,000)	1,20,000
I	Gross Profit @ 33-1/3% on Total Sales	3,00,000
J	Cost of goods sold (F – I)	6,00,000
K	Purchases = Cost of Goods Sold + Closing Stock – Opening Stock = ₹ 6,00,000 + ₹ 35,000 – ₹ 35,000 = ₹ 6,00,000	

Dr. **(II) TOTAL DEBTORS ACCOUNT** *Cr.*

Particulars	₹	*Particulars*	₹
To Balance b/d	1,00,000	By Cash	50,000
To Sales	7,20,000	By Bank (b.f.)	6,50,000
		By Balance c/d	1,20,000
	8,20,000		8,20,000

Dr. **(III) TOTAL CREDITORS ACCOUNT** Cr.

Particulars	₹	Particulars	₹
To Bank (b.f.)	5,87,500	By Balance b/d	62,500
To Balance c/d	75,000	By Purchases	6,00,000
(₹ 6,00,000 × 1.5/12)			
	6,62,500		6,62,500

Dr. **(IV) CASH BOOK** Cr.

Particulars	Cash ₹	Bank ₹	Particulars	Cash ₹	Bank ₹
To Balance b/d	5,000	15,000	By Machinery	—	40,000
To Sundry Debtors	50,000	6,50,000	By Furniture	—	5,000
To Cash (C)	—	1,00,000	By Investments	—	40,000
To Cash Sales	1,80,000	—	By Drawings	—	17,500
			By Business Expenses	90,000	60,000
			By Bank (C)	1,00,000	—
			By Sundry Creditors	—	5,87,500
			By Balance c/d	45,000	15,000
	2,35,000	7,65,000		2,35,000	7,65,000

Note: *The above solution could also be prepared starting with the figure of creditors (₹ 62,500) instead of Debtors. In that case last year's purchases will amount to ₹ 5,00,000 (62,500 × 12/1.5) creditors velocity being 1.5 month. Current year's purchases will be ₹ 6,00,000.*

PROBLEM 4

The following is the Balance Sheet of A and B as on 1st April 2012:

Liabilities	₹	Assets	₹
Capitals:		Building	65,000
A	1,00,000	Machinery	50,000
B	50,000	Stock	30,000
Creditors for goods	20,000	Debtors	40,000
Creditors for expenses	30,000	Bank	15,000
	2,00,000		2,00,000

Information: Creditors' Velocity 1 month, Debtors' Velocity 1-1/2 months, Stock level uniform in value, Trade Expenses ₹ 75,000, Depreciation on machinery 10%, Depreciation on building 5%. In the current year, cost price will go up by 10%. Sales in the current year will increase by 20% in volume. Rate of gross profit—no change, Drawings—B ₹ 5,000,

Required: prepare Projected Trading, Profit and Loss Account and Balances Sheet.

SOLUTION

PROJECTED TRADING AND PROFIT AND LOSS ACCOUNT

Dr. *for the year ending on 31st March, 2013* Cr.

Particulars		₹	*Particulars*	₹
To Opening Stock		30,000	By Sales	4,22,400
To Purchases		3,16,800	By *Closing Stock (LIFO Basis)	30,000
To Gross Profit (@25% on sales) c/d		1,05,600		
		4,52,400		4,52,400
To Trade Expenses		75,000	By Gross Profit b/d	1,05,600
To Depreciation on:				
Machinery	5,000			
Building	3,250	8,250		
To Net Profit transferred to Capital A/c		22,350		
		1,05,600		1,05,600

*If the closing stock is valued at FIFO basis, gross profit will increase by ₹ 3,000 and purchases will be reduced by ₹ 3,000 with consequential changes in the figure of net profit, creditors and cash at bank.

PROJECTED BALANCE SHEET OF M/S. A & B AS AT 31ST MARCH, 2013

Liabilities		₹	*Assets*		₹
A's Capital	1,00,000		Fixed Assets:		
Add: Profit	11,175	1,11,175	Building	65,000	
B 's Capital	50,000		*Less:* Depreciation	3,250	61,750
Add: Profit	11,175		Machinery	50,000	
Less: Drawings	5,000	56,175	*Less:* Depreciation	5,000	45,000
Sundry Creditors for Goods		26,400	Current Assets:		
			Stock-in-trade		30,000
			Sundry Debtors		52,800
			Cash at Bank		4,200
		1,93,750			1,93,750

Working Notes:

(I) CALCULATION OF RATE OF GROSS PROFIT EARNED DURING PREVIOUS YEAR

	Particulars	₹
A	Sales during previous year (₹ 40,000 × 12/1.5)	3,20,000
B	Purchases (₹ 20,000 × 12/1)	2,40,000
C	Cost of Goods Sold (₹ 30,000 + ₹ 2,40,000 – ₹ 30,000)	2,40,000
D	Gross Profit (A – C)	80,000
E	Rate of Gross Profit	25%

(II) CALCULATION OF SALES AND PURCHASES DURING CURRENT YEAR

	Particulars	₹
A	Cost of goods sold during previous year	2,40,000
B	*Add:* Increases in volume @ 20%	48,000
		2,88,000
C	*Add:* Increase in cost @ 10%	28,800
D	Cost of Goods Sold during Current Year	3,16,800
E	*Add:* Gross Profit @ 33% on cost	1,05,600
F	Sales for current year [D + E]	4,22,400

Dr. **(III) BANK ACCOUNT** *Cr.*

Particulars	₹	*Particulars*	₹
To Balance b/d	15,000	By Sundry Creditors	3,10,400
To Sundry Debtors	4,09,600	By Trade Expenses	75,000
		By Drawings - B	5,000
		By Creditors for Expenses	30,000
		By Balance c/d	4,200
	4,24,600		4,24,600

Dr. **(IV) TOTAL TRADE DEBTORS ACCOUNT** *Cr.*

Particulars	₹	*Particulars*	₹
To Balance b/d	40,000	By Bank A/c (b.f.)	4,09,600
To Sales	4,22,400	By Balance c/d (1/8 of 422,400)	52,800
	4,62,400		4,62,400

Dr. **(V) TOTAL TRADE CREDITORS ACCOUNT** *Cr.*

Particulars	₹	*Particulars*	₹
To Bank (Balancing figure)	3,10,400	By Balancing b/d	20,000
To Balance c/d (1/12 of ₹ 3,16,800)	26,400	By Purchases	3,16,800
	3,36,800		3,36,800

PROBLEM 5

A and B started a business on April 1, 2012 with ₹ 50,000 as capital, contributed equally but the profit sharing ratio was 3:2. Their drawings were ₹ 300 and 200 per month respectively. They had kept no accounts but given you the following information:

Particulars	*31.03.2013*	*31.03.2014*
	₹	₹
Machinery at cost	20,000	25,000
Stock in trade	30,000	30,000
Debtors	50,000	60,000

Cash	2,000	500
Creditors	30,000	20,000
Outstanding Expenses	4,000	3,000
Bank Balance (as per Pass Book)	6,000	8,000

Provision is to be made for depreciation at 10 per cent on the cost of machinery as at the end of each year. Debtors on 31.03.2013 include ₹ 5,000 for goods sent out on consignment at 25 per cent above cost, and the goods were sold only in 2014. A cheque for ₹ 1,000 had been deposited on 31.03.2013 but was credited on 2.4.2013. A cheque for ₹ 2,000 issued on 26.03.2014 was presented on 3.4.2014. A cheque for ₹ 1,000 was directly deposited by a customer on 27.03.2014 but no entry is made either in Pass book *or* in Cash Book. A cheque for ₹ 500 deposited in March, 2014 was dishonoured but no adjustment for this was made.

Required: Determine the profit for 2013-2014 and draw up a Balance Sheet as at 31st March, 2014.

SOLUTION

STATEMENT OF PROFIT EARNED DURING 2012-2013 AND 2013-2014

Particulars	*2012-2013* ₹	*2013-2014* ₹
Closing Capital	72,000	94,500
Add: Drawings	6,000	6,000
	78,000	1,00,500
Less: Opening Capital	50,000	72,000
Profit	28,000	28,500
Share of A (3/5)	16,800	17,100
Share of B (2/5)	11,200	11,400
	28,000	28,500

BALANCE SHEET AS AT 31ST MARCH, 2014

Liabilities		₹	*Assets*		₹
Capital Accounts:			Machinery:		
A:			Cost	25,000	
Opening Balance	25,000		*Less:* Depreciation	4,500	20,500
Add: Profits	33,900		Stock		30,000
	58,900		Debtors		59,500
Less: Drawings	7,200	51,700	Bank balance		7,000
B:			Cash		500
Opening Balance	25,000				
Add: Profits	22,600				
Less: Drawings	4,800	42,800			
Creditors		20,000			
Outstanding Expenses		3,000			
		1,17,500			1,17,500

Working Notes:

(I) BANK BALANCE AS PER CASH BOOK AFTER BANK RECONCILIATION

Particulars	₹
Balance as per Pass Book on 31.03.2013	6,000
Add: Cheque deposited on 31.03.2013	1,000
Balance as per Cash Book on 31.03.2013	7,000
Credit has been given to debtor's account before depositing the cheque to bank.	
Bank Balance as per Pass Book on 31.03.2014	8,000
Less: Cheque issued but not presented	2,000
Add: Direct deposit by customer	1,000
Balance as per Adjusted Cash Book on 31.03.2014	7,000

Dr. **(II) TOTAL DEBTORS ACCOUNT** *Cr.*

Particulars	*31.03.2013* ₹	*31.03.2014* ₹	*Particulars*	*31.03.2013* ₹	*31.03.2014* ₹
To Balance b/d	50,000	60,000	By Stock (adjustment for	5,000	—
To Bank A/c	—	500	goods on consignment)		
(dishonoured cheque)			By Bank (Direct deposit)	—	1,000
			By Balance c/d	45,000	59,500
	50,000	60,500		50,000	60,500

Dr. **(III) STOCK ACCOUNT** *Cr.*

Particulars	₹	*Particulars*	₹
To Balance b/d	30,000	By Stock Reserve A/c	
To Debtors A/c		(₹ 5,000 × 25/125)	1,000
(Adjustment for Goods sent on		By Balance c/d	34,000
consignment)	5,000		
	35,000		35,000

(IV) STATEMENT OF AFFAIRS AS AT 31.03.2013 AND 31.03.2014

Liabilities	*31.03.2013* ₹	*31.03.2014* ₹	*Assets*	*31.03.2013* ₹	*31.03.2014* ₹
Creditors	30,000	20,000	Machinery at cost less		
Outstanding Expenses	4,000	3,000	Depreciation	18,000	20,500
Capital (b.f.)	72,000	94,500	Stock in trade less		
			Stock Reserve	34,000	30,000
			Debtors	45,000	59,500
			Cash	2,000	500
			Bank Balance	7,000	7,000
	1,06,000	1,17,500		1,06,000	1,17,500

PROBLEM 6

From the following information, Calculate Discount Allowed to Debtors of Bharat Tushar & Sons.

Particulars	*Opening*	*Closing*
1. Opening & Closing Balances		
Cash Balance	₹ 5,000	₹ 1,17,900
Debtors	₹ 50,000	₹ 1,95,000

2. Cash Purchases ₹ 72,000, Payment to Creditors ₹ 43,700. Drawings ₹ 80,000. Direct Expenses ₹ 4,000. Indirect Expenses ₹ 9,500.
3. Cash Sales *less* than the Net Credit Sales, Sales Return of Gross Credit Sales.
4. Collection from Debtors received after 6% Discount.

SOLUTION

Dr. **CASH BOOK** *Cr.*

Particulars	₹	*Particulars*	₹
To Balance b/d	5,000	By Cash Purchases	72,000
To Cash Sales	X	By Creditors	43,700
To Collection form Debtors	3,22,100–X	By Drawings	80,000
		By Direct Expensers	4,000
		By Indirect Expensers	9,500
		By Balance c/d	1,17,900
	3,27,100		3,27,100

Dr. **DEBTORS ACCOUNT** *Cr.*

Particulars	₹	*Particulars*	₹
To Balance b/d	50,000	By Discount Allowed	6% (3X – 1,45,000)
To Credit Sales	3X	By Cash A/c	94% (3X – 1,45,000)
		By Balance c/d	1,95,000
	3X + 50,000		3X + 50,000

Equating Collection from Debtors from Cash Book and Debtors Account

3,22,100 – X = 94% (3X – 1,45,000)

3,22,100 – X = 2.82X – 1,36,300

3.82X = 3,22,100 + 1,36,300

3.82X = 4,58,400

X = 4,58,400/3.82 = 1,20,000

Cash Sales = ₹ 1,20,000

Net Credit Sales = ₹ 1,20,000 × 3 = ₹ 3,60,000

Sales Returns = ₹ 3,60,000 × 1/6 = ₹ 60,000

Gross Credit Sales = ₹ 3,60,000 + ₹ 60,000 = ₹ 4,20,000

Collection from Debtors = 94% (1,20,000 × 3 – ₹ 1,45,000) = ₹ 2,02,100

Discount Allowed = 6% (₹ 1,20,000 × 3 – ₹ 1,45,000) = ₹ 12,900

12 ACCOUNTING FOR HIRE PURCHASE AND INSTALMENT PURCHASE

LEARNING OBJECTIVES

After studying this chapter, you should be able to understand:

- ◇ Meaning of Hire Purchase Agreement
- ◇ Contents of Hire Purchase Agreement
- ◇ Terms Used in Hire Purchase Agreement
- ◇ Calculation of Interest When Both the Cash Price and the Rate of Interest are given
- ◇ Calculation of Interest When Cash Price is Given But Rate of Interest is Not Given
- ◇ Calculation of Interest When Both the Cash Price and The Rate of Interest are Not Given
- ◇ Calculation of Cash Price
- ◇ Accounting for Hire Purchase Transactions
- ◇ Meaning of Instalment Purchase Agreement
- ◇ Distinction between Hire Purchase Agreement and Instalment Purchase Agreement
- ◇ Accounting For Instalment Purchase

1.0 MEANING OF HIRE PURCHASE AGREEMENT

Hire Purchase agreement means an agreement under which goods are let on hire and under which the hirer has an option to purchase them in accordance with the terms of the agreement and includes the agreement under which:

1. Possession of goods is delivered by the owner thereof to a person on condition that such person pays the agreed amount, in periodical instalments;
2. The property in the goods (i.e. ownership of goods) is to pass to such a person on the payment of the last instalment; and
3. Such a person has a right to terminate the agreement at any time before the property so passes.

2.0 CONTENTS OF HIRE PURCHASE AGREEMENT

According to Section 4 of the Hire Purchase Act 1972, every hire purchase agreement must state:

1. The hire purchase price of the goods to which the agreement relates.
2. The cash price of the goods, that is to say, the price at which the goods may be purchased by the hirer for cash.
3. The date on which the agreement shall be deemed to have commenced.
4. The number of instalments by which the hire purchase price is to be paid, the amount of each of those instalments and the date *or* the mode of determining the date, upon which it is payable and the person to whom and the place where it is payable.
5. The goods to which the agreement relates, the manner sufficient to identify them.

3.0 TERMS USED IN HIRE PURCHASE AGREEMENT

Hirer	A 'Hirer' means a person who obtains *or* has obtained possession of the goods from an owner under a hire purchase agreement.
Hire Vendor	Hire Vendor means a person who delivers *or* has delivered the possession of goods to the hirer under a hire purchase agreement.
Cash Price	Cash Price means the price at which the goods may be purchased by the hirer for cash.
Down Payment	Down Payment means an initial payment payable by the hirer at the time of entering into a hire purchase agreement.
Hire Purchase Price	Hire Purchase Price means the total sum payable by the hirer under a hire purchase agreement in order to complete the purchase of *or* acquisition of property in the goods to which the agreement relates and includes any sum so payable by the hirer under the hire purchase agreement by way of deposit *or* other initial payment. In the form of an equation, hire purchase price may be shown as follows: Hire Purchase Price = Cash Price + Interest on Outstanding Balances
Hire Purchase Charges	Hire Purchase Charges means the difference between hire purchase price and the cash price as stated in the Hire Purchase Agreement. These hire purchase charges are popularly known as 'Interest'.

4.0 CALCULATION OF INTEREST WHEN BOTH THE CASH PRICE AND THE RATE OF INTEREST ARE GIVEN

The amount of interest may be calculated by preparing a table shown below:

TABLE SHOWING THE CALCULATION OF INTEREST FOR VARIOUS YEARS

A *Instalment No.*	*B* *Opening Balance*	*C = B x R/100* *Interest*	*D = B + C* *Opening Balance Plus Interest*	*E (Principal + Interest) Instalment Amount*	*F = D − E* *Closing Balance*
I	X_0	I_1	$X_0 + I_1$	Y_1	$X_1 = X_0 + I_1 - Y_1$
II	X_1	I_2	$X_1 + I_2$	Y_2	$1_2 = X_0 + I_2 - Y_2$
III	1_2	I_3	$1_2 + I_3$	Y_3	$X_3 = 1_2 + I_3 - Y_3$
IV	X_3	I_4	$X_3 + I_4$	Y_4	$X_4 = X_3 + I_4 - Y_4$

ILLUSTRATION 1

X purchased a machine. on hire purchase basis from Y on the following terms:

(a) Cash Price— ₹ 10,00,000 (b) Cash Down Payment—20% (c) Balance in Four annual equal instalments to be paid at the end of each year. The rate of interest charged by the vendor is 20% p.a. compounded annually. Calculate the amount of Interest and Instalments.

SOLUTION

STATEMENT SHOWING THE CALCULATION OF INTEREST AND INSTALMENT

A Instalment No.	*B Opening Balance*	*C = B × 20/100 Interest*	*D = B + C Opening Balance Plus Interest*	*E = 8/4 +C Instalment Amount*	*F = D – E Closing Balance*
1	8	1.6	9.6	3.6	6
2	6	1.2	7.2	3.2	4
3	4	0.8	4.8	2.8	2
4	2	0.4	2.4	2.4	0

ILLUSTRATION 2

C purchased a machine on hire purchase basis from D on the following terms:

(a) Cash Price— ₹ 10,00,000 (b) Cash Down Payment—20% (c) Balance in Four annual equal instalments to be paid at the end of each year. The rate of interest charged by the vendor is 20% p.a. compounded half yearly. Calculate the amount of Interest and Instalments.

SOLUTION

Principal	100
Add: Interest @ 20% p.a. for the 1st half year	10
Principal interest at the end of 1st half year	110
Add: Interest @ 20% p.a. for the 2nd half year	11
Principal for interest at the end of year	121

Thus, every payment of ₹ 121 includes an interest of ₹ 21.

STATEMENT SHOWING THE CALCULATION OF INTEREST AND INSTALMENT

A Instalment No.	*B Opening Balance*	*C = B × 21/100 Interest*	*D = B + C Opening Balance Plus Interest*	*E = 8/4 +C Instalment Amount*	*F = D – E Closing Balance*
1	8	1.68	9.68	3.68	6
2	6	1.26	7.26	3.26	4
3	4	0.84	4.84	2.84	2
4	2	0.42	2.42	2.42	0

ILLUSTRATION 3

E purchased a machine on hire purchase basis from F on the following terms:

(a) Cash Price— ₹10,00,000 (b) Cash Down Payment—40% (c) Balance in three Half yearly equal instalments to be paid at the end of each half year. The rate of interest charged by the vendor is 20% p.a. compounded half yearly. Calculate the amount of Interest and Instalments.

SOLUTION

STATEMENT SHOWING THE CALCULATION OF INTEREST AND INSTALMENT

A Instalment No.	B Opening Balance	C = B × 10/100 Interest	D = B + C Opening Balance Plus Interest	E = 6/3 +C Instalment Amount	F = D – E Closing Balance
1st half	6	0.6	6.6	2.6	4
2nd half	4	0.4	4.4	2.4	2
3rd half	2	0.2	2.2	2.2	0

5.0 CALCULATION OF INTEREST WHEN CASH PRICE IS GIVEN BUT RATE OF INTEREST IS NOT GIVEN

1 Mathematically speaking, the amount of interest should be allocated in ratio of benefit derived (i.e. outstanding cash price).

2 Since this would be too complicated to calculate the rate of interest mannualy, practically the amount of interest is allocated in the ratio of outstanding hire purchase price.

3 Unless otherwise stated, one may assume that (a) all the sales have been made at the beginning of the year *or* (b) sales have been made uniformly throughout the year. The latter assumption is considered to be *more* appropriate as compared to the former assumption since in practice, the sales will be taking place on different dates each year and not at the beginning of the year. Consider the following example:

"The hire purchase price of a machine is ₹ 25,000 payable by an initial deposit of ₹ 5,000 at the time of contract and the balance by 8 quarterly instalments of ₹ 2,500 each".

In such a case if all the sales are assumed to be in the beginning of the year, first 4 instalments will be recovered in the very first year and the last 4 instalments in the second year. If the sales are assumed to be uniform throughout the year, the first 2 instalments will be recovered in the first year, next 4 instalments in the second year and last 2 instalments in the third year.

4. **Practical Steps in Calculation of Interest**

Step 1: Hire Purchase Price = Down Payment + Instalments

Step 2: Total Interest = H.P. Price – Cash Price

Step 3: Calculate Ratio of Hire Purchase Price Outstanding in the Beginning of Each Year

A Year	B Outstanding H.P.P., in the Beginning of each year	C Instalment Paid	D = B – C Outstanding H.P.P. at the end of each year
I			
II			
III			
IV			

Ratio of outstanding H.P.P. at the beginning of each year =

Step 4: Calculate Interest for each year by dividing the Total Interest in the Ratio of outstanding H.P.P. at the beginning of each year.

ILLUSTRATION 4 [CALCULATION OF INTEREST WHEN RATE OF INTEREST IS NOT GIVEN AND INSTALMENTS ARE EQUAL]

X purchased a machine from Y on hire purchase basis on the following terms:

(a) Cash Price—₹ 10,00,000 (b) Cash Down Payment—20% (c) Four annual equal instalments of ₹ 2,50,000 each to be paid at the end of each year. Compute the payment of interest pertaining to each accounting year assuming that the sales were made at the beginning of the year.

SOLUTION

Step 1: Hire Purchase Price = Down Payment + Instalments

= ₹ 2,00,000 + ₹ 10,00,000 = ₹ 12,00,000

Step 2: Total Interest = H.P. Price – Cash Price = ₹ 12,00,000 – ₹ 10,00,000 = ₹ 2,00,000

Step 3:

CALCULATION OF RATIO OF HIRE PURCHASE PRICE OUTSTANDING IN THE BEGINNING OF EACH YEAR

A *Year*	*B* *Outstanding H.P.P., in the Beginning of each year*	*C* *Instalment Paid*	*D = B – C* *Outstanding H.P.P. at the end of each year*
I	10,00,000	2,50,000	7,50,000
II	7,50,000	2,50,000	5,00,000
III	5,00,000	2,50,000	2,50,000
IV	2,50,000	2,50,000	Nil

Ratio of outstanding H.P.P. at the beginning of each year = 100 : 75 : 50 : 25 *or* 4 : 3 : 2 : 1

Step 4: *Calculation of Interest for each year*

Interest for 1st year — ₹ 2,00,000 × 4/10 = ₹ 80,000

Interest for 2nd year — ₹ 2,00,000 × 3/10 = ₹ 60,000

Interest for 3rd year — ₹ 2,00,000 × 2/10 = ₹ 40,000

Interest for 4th year — ₹ 2,00,000 × 1/10 = ₹ 20,000

ILLUSTRATION 5 [CALCULATION OF INTEREST WHEN RATE OF INTEREST IS NOT GIVEN AND INSTALMENTS ARE EQUAL]

P purchased a machine from Q on hire purchase basis on the following terms:

(a) Cash Price—₹ 10,00,000 (b) Cash Down Payment—20% (c) Four annual equal instalments of ₹ 2,50,000 each to be paid at the end of each year. Compute the payment of interest pertaining to each accounting year assuming that the sales were made uniformly throughout the year.

SOLUTION

If the sales take place uniformly throughout the year, the average period over which the price will remain unpaid in the first year will be only six months.

STATEMENT SHOWING THE INTEREST PERTAINING TO EACH YEAR

A *Year ended on*	*B* *Amount used*	*C* *Period of use*	*D = B × C* *Product*	*E* *Ratio*	*F = ₹ 2,00,000 × E/300* *Amount of Interest for each accounting year*
31.12.2011	10,00,000	6	60,00,000	60	40,000

31.12.2012	10,00,000	6	60,00,000		
	7,50,000	6	45,00,000	105	70,000
31.12.2013	7,50,000	6	45,00,000		
	5,00,000	6	30,00,000	75	50,000
31.12.2014	5,00,000	6	30,00,000		
	2,50,000	6	15,00,000	45	30,000
31.12.2015	2,50,000	6	15,00,000	15	10,000
			Total	300	2,00,000

ILLUSTRATION 6 [CALCULATION OF INTEREST WHEN RATE OF INTEREST IS NOT GIVEN AND INSTALMENTS ARE UNEQUAL]

Tushar Tulsian purchased a machine on Hire Purchase System. The total cost price of the machine was ₹ 30,00,000 payable 20% down and four annual instalments of ₹ 8,40,000, ₹ 7,80,000, ₹ 7,20,000 and ₹ 6,60,000 at the end of the Ist year, 2nd year, 3rd year and 4th year respectively. Calculate the interest included in each year's instalment assuming that the sales were made at the beginning of the year.

SOLUTION

Step 1: Hire Purchase Price = Down Payment + Instalments

= ₹ 6,00,000 + (₹ 8,40,000 + ₹ 7,80,000 + ₹ 7,20,000 + ₹ 6,60,000)

= ₹ 36,00,000

Step 2: Total Interest = H.P. Price – Cash Price = 36,00,000 – ₹ 30,00,000 = ₹ 6,00,000

Step 3:

CALCULATION OF RATIO OF HIRE PURCHASE PRICE OUTSTANDING IN THE BEGINNING OF EACH YEAR

A *Year*	*B* *Outstanding H.P.P., in the Beginning of each year*	*C* *Instalment Paid*	*D = B – C* *Outstanding H.P.P. at the end of each year*
I	30,00,000	8,40,000	21,60,000
II	21,60,000	7,80,000	13,80,000
III	13,80,000	7,20,000	6,60,000
IV	6,60,000	6,60,000	Nil

Ratio of Outstanding H.P.P. at the beginning of year = 300 : 216 : 138 : 66

STEP 4: CALCULATION OF INTEREST FOR EACH YEAR

Interest for Ist year [₹ 6,00,000 × 300/720]	₹ 2,50,000
Interest for 2nd year [₹ 6,00,000 × 216/720]	₹ 1,80,000
Interest for 3rd year [₹ 6,00,000 × 138/720]	₹ 1,15,000
Interest for 4th year [₹ 6,00,000 × 66/720]	₹ 55,000
	₹ 6,00,000

6.0 CALCULATION OF INTEREST WHEN BOTH THE CASH PRICE AND THE RATE OF INTEREST ARE NOT GIVEN

1 The difference between any two successive instalments represents the least amount of interest charged in the last year assuming that the principal portion of each instalment is equal.

2 The amount of interest for each year is calculated as follows:

Interest for 1st year = Difference between two successive instalments × (N)

Interest for 2nd year = Difference between two successive instalments × (N – 1)

Interest for 3rd year = Difference between two successive instalments × (N – 2)

Interest for 4th year = Difference between two successive instalments × (N – 3)

Interest for 5th year onwards = Difference between two successive instalments × (N – 4)

Note: *'N'* denotes the number of instalments.

ILLUSTRATION 7 [CALCULATION OF INTEREST WHEN BOTH THE CASH PRICE AND THE RATE OF INTEREST ARE NOT GIVEN]

A purchased a machine on hire purchase basis from B on the following terms:

(a) Cash Down Payment—₹ 1,58,500 (b) Four Instalments of ₹ 2,21,900, ₹ 2,06,050, ₹ 1,90,200 & ₹ 1,74,350 at the end of the Ist year, 2nd year, 3rd year and 4th year respectively. (c) The Payment of cash price in each instalment—Uniform.

Required: Compute the amount of Interest.

SOLUTION

Difference between any two successive instalments represents the least amount of interest charged in the last year i.e. ₹ 2,21,900 – ₹ 2,06,050 = ₹ 15,850

Thus, Interest for 3rd year = Least amount of Interest × 2 = 31,700

Thus, Interest for 2nd year = ₹ 15,850 × 3 = 47,550

Thus, Interest for 1st year = ₹ 15,850 × 4 = 63,400

Thus, allocation of instalment between cash price and interest is as under:

Instalment (₹)	*Interest (₹)*	*Cash Price (₹)*
2,21,900	63,400	1,58,500
2,06,050	47,550	1,58,500
1,90,200	31,700	1,58,500
1,74,350	15,850	1,58,500
7,92,500	1,58,500	6,34,000

Total Cash Price = ₹ 6,34,000 + ₹ 1,58,500 = ₹ 7,92,500

7.0 CALCULATION OF CASH PRICE

Under Working Backward Method, the Cash Price may be calculated by taking the following steps:

Step 1: *Calculate the Closing Balance after the payment of instalment*

Step 2: *Calculate the Closing Balance before the payment of instalment as under:*

= Closing Balance after instalment + Instalment

Step 3: *Calculate the Interest included in the amount (as per step 2) as under:*

$$\text{Interest} = (\text{Amount as per Step 2}) \times \frac{\text{Rate}}{100 + \text{Rate}}$$

Step 4: *Calculate the Opening Balance due in the beginning as under:*

= Amount as per Step 2 – Amount as per Step 3

Step 5: *Go to Step 1 until Balance due in the beginning of first year is calculated.*

Step 6: *Calculate Cash Price as under:*

Cash Price = Balance due in the beginning of first year + Down Payment.

After taking the aforesaid steps the table showing the computation of cash price shall appear as follows:

TABLE SHOWING THE CALCULATION OF CASH PRICE AND INTEREST UNDER WORKING BACKWARD METHOD

A Instalment Number	*B Closing Balance after the payment of instalment*	*C Instalment Amount*	*D = B + C Closing Balance before the payment of instalment*	*E = D*R/(100 + R) Interest*	*F = D – E Opening Balance*
IV	*0*	Y_4	$0 + Y_4$	$I_4 = [(0 + Y_4)$ $r/(100 + R)]$	$X_3 = 0$ $+ Y_4 - I_4$
III	X_3	Y_3	$X_3 + Y_3$	$I_3 = [(X_3 + Y_3)$ $R/(100 + R)]$	$1_2 = X_3$ $+ Y_3 - I_3$
II	X_2	Y_2	$X_2 + Y_2$	$I_2 = [(X_2 + Y_2)$ $R/(100 + R)]$	$X_1 = X_2$ $+ Y_2 - I_2$
I	X_1	Y_1	$X_1 + Y_1$	$I_1 = [(X_1 + Y_1)$ $R/(100 + R)]$	$X_0 = X_1$ $+ Y_1 - I_1$

Note: *Cash Price =* X_0 *+ Cash Down payment.*

ILLUSTRATION 8 [CALCULATION OF CASH PRICE IN CASE OF ANNUAL INSTALMENTS]

X purchased a machine on hire purchase basis from Y on the following terms:

(a) Cash Down Payment—20% (b) Balance in In four annual instalments of ₹ 2,80,000, ₹ 2,60,000, ₹ 2,40,000 and ₹ 2,20,000 commencing from the end of a year from the date of down payment. The rate of interest charged by the vendor is 10% p.a. compounded annually. Calculate the Cash Price.

SOLUTION

COMPUTATION OF CASH PRICE AND PERIODIC INTEREST

A Instalment Number	*B Closing Balance after the payment of instalment*	*C Instalment Amount*	*D = B + C Closing Balance before the payment of instalment*	*E = D*R/(100 + R) Interest D*10/110*	*F = D – E Opening Balance*
IV	—	2,20,000	2,20,000	20,000	2,00,000
III	2,00,000	2,40,000	4,40,000	40,000	4,00,000

II	4,00,000	2,60,000	6,60,000	60,000	6,00,000
I	6,00,000	2,80,000	8,80,000	80,000	8,00,000

Let the Cash Price be 'X'

X = ₹ 8,00,000 + 20% of 'X'(i.e down payment)

0.8X = ₹ 8,00,000

X = ₹ 8,00,000/.8 = ₹ 10,00,000

ILLUSTRATION 9 [CALCULATION OF CASH PRICE IN CASE OF ANNUAL INSTALMENTS]

C purchased a machine from D on hire purchase basis on the following terms:

(a) Cash Down Payment—20% (b) Balance in Four annual instalments of ₹ 1,84,000, ₹ 1,63,000, ₹ 1,42,000 and ₹ 1,21,000 commencing from the end of a year from the date of down payment.

The rate of interest charged by the vendor is 20% p.a. compounded half yearly. Calculate the Cash Price

SOLUTION

Principal	₹ 100
Add: Interest @ 20% p.a. for 1st half year	₹ 10
Principal & Interest at the end of 1st half year	₹ 110
Add: Interest @ 20% p.a. for second half year	₹ 11
Principal & Interest at the end of second half year	₹ 121

Thus, every payment of ₹ 121 includes an interest of ₹ 21.

COMPUTATION OF CASH PRICE AND PERIODIC INTEREST

A Instalment Number	*B Closing Balance after the payment of instalment*	*C Instalment Amount*	*D = B + C Closing Balance before the payment of instalment*	*E = D*R/(100 + R) Interest D*21/121*	*F = D – E Opening Balance*
IV	—	1,21,000	1,21,000	21,000	1,00,000
III	1,00,000	1,42,000	2,42,000	42,000	2,00,000
II	2,00,000	1,63,000	3,63,000	63,000	3,00,000
I	3,00,000	1,84,000	4,84,000	84,000	4,00,000

Let the Cash Price be 'X'

X = ₹ 4,00,000 + 20% of X (i.e., down payment)

0.8X = ₹ 4,00,000

X = ₹ 4,00,000/0.8 = ₹ 5,00,000

ILLUSTRATION 10 [CALCULATION OF CASH PRICE WHEN 1ST INSTALMENT IS PAYABLE AFTER TWO YEARS]

On 1.1.2011 Tulsian purchased a machine on hire purchase basis. The terms of agreement provided for 40% as cash down payment and the balance in three instalments of ₹ 1,63,000 on 31.12.2012, ₹ 1,20,000 on 31.12.2013 and ₹ 1,10,000 on 31.12.2014. The rate of interest charged by the vendor is 10% p.a. compounded annually. Calculate the Cash Price.

SOLUTION

COMPUTATION OF CASH PRICE AND PERIODIC INTEREST

A *Instalment Number*	B *Closing Balance after the payment of instalment*	C *Instalment Amount*	*D = B + C* *Closing Balance before the payment of instalment*	*E = D*R/(100 + R)* *Interest D*10/110*	*F = D – E* *Opening Balance*
III	Nil	1,10,000	1,10,000	10,000	1,00,000
II	1,00,000	1,20,000	2,20,000	20,000	2,00,000
I	2,00,000	1,63,000	3,63,000	33,000	3,30,000
	3,30,000	—	3,30,000	30,000	3,00,000

Let Cash Price be X

X = ₹ 3,00,000 + 40% of X

0.6X = ₹ 3,00,000

X = ₹ 3,00,000/0.6 = ₹ 5,00,000

ILLUSTRATION 11 [CALCULATION OF CASH PRICE WHEN 2ND INSTALMENT IS PAYABLE AFTER TWO YEARS]

On 1.1.2011 Bharat purchased a machine from Gupta on hire purchase basis. The terms of agreement provided for 40% as cash down payment and the balance in three instalment of ₹ 1,30,000 on 31.12.2011, ₹ 1,42,000 on 31.12.2013 and ₹ 1,10,000 on 31.12.2014. The rate of interest charged by the vendor is 10% p.a. compounded annually. Calculate the cash price.

SOLUTION

COMPUTATION OF CASH PRICE AND PERIODIC INTEREST

A *Instalment Number*	B *Closing Balance after the payment of instalment*	C *Instalment Amount*	*D = B + C* *Closing Balance before the payment of instalment*	*E = D*R/(100 + R)* *Interest D*10/110*	*F = D – E* *Opening Balance*
III	Nil	1,10,000	1,10,000	10,000	1,00,000
II	1,00,000	1,42,000	2,42,000	22,000	2,20,000
	2,20,000	—	2,20,000	20,000	2,00,000
I	2,00,000	1,30,000	3,30,000	30,000	3,00,000

Let the Cash Price be X

X = ₹ 3,00,000 + 40% of X

0.6X = ₹ 3,00,000

X = ₹ 3,00,000/0.6 = ₹ 5,00,000

ILLUSTRATION 12 [CALCULATION OF CASH PRICE WHEN 3RD INSTALMENT IS PAYABLE AFTER 2 YEARS]

On 1.1.2011 Tushar purchased a machine from Bansal on hire purchase basis. The terms of agreement provided for 40% as cash down payment and the balance in three instalments of ₹ 1,30,000 on 31.12.2011, ₹ 1,20,000, on 31.12.2012 and ₹ 1,21,000, on 31.12.2014. The rate of interest charged by the vendor is 10% p.a. compounded annually. Calculate the Cash Price.

SOLUTION

COMPUTATION OF CASH PRICE AND PERIODIC INTEREST

A Instalment Number	*B Closing Balance after the payment of instalment*	*C Instalment Amount*	*D = B + C Closing Balance before the payment of instalment*	*E = D*R/(100 + R) Interest D*10/110*	*F = D – E Opening Balance*
III	Nil	1,21,000	1,21,000	11,000	1,10,000
	1,10,000	—	1,10,000	10,000	1,00,000
II	1,00,000	1,20,000	2,20,000	20,000	2,00,000
I	2,00,000	1,30,000	3,30,000	30,000	3,00,000

Let the Cash Price be X

X = ₹ 3,00,000 + 40% of X

0.6X = ₹ 3,00,000

X = ₹ 3,00,000/0.6 = ₹ 5,00,000

ILLUSTRATION 13 [CALCULATION OF CASH PRICE IN CASE OF HALF-YEARLY INSTALMENTS]

X, purchased a machinery on hire purchase basis from Y on the following terms:

(a) Cash Down Payment—33-1/3%, (b) Three half-yearly instalments of ₹ 16,400, ₹ 14,880 and ₹ 12,600, the first to commence at the end of 6 months from the date of cash down payment, (c) Interest to be charged by the vendor 10% p.a. calculated on half yearly rests. Compute the Cash Price of the Machine.

SOLUTION

COMPUTATION OF CASH PRICE AND PERIODIC INTEREST

A Instalment Number	*B Closing Balance after the payment of instalment*	*C Instalment Amount*	*D = B + C Closing Balance before the payment of instalment*	*E = D*R/(100 + R) Interest D*5/105*	*F = D – E Opening Balance*
3rd	Nil	12,600	12,600	600	12,000
2nd	12,000	14,880	26,880	1,280	25,600
1st	25,600	16,400	42,000	2,000	40,000

Let the Cash Price = X

X = ₹ 40,000 + 33–1/3% of X

66 – 2/3% of X = ₹ 40,000

X = ₹ 60,000

8.0 ACCOUNTING FOR HIRE PURCHASE TRANSACTIONS

The various methods of accounting for hire purchase transactions are shown below:

METHODS OF ACCOUNTING FOR HIRE PURCHASE TRANSACTIONS

1.0 Sales Method for goods of substantial sales values	2.0 Stock Methods for Goods of small sales values
	2.1 Debtors Method
	(a) Hire Purchase Trading Account (at cost)
	(b) Hire Purchase Trading Account (at hire purchase price)
	2.2 Stock and Debtors Method

9.0 SALES METHOD

MEANING OF SALES METHOD

Sales method follows a practical approach and practically (of course not technically) treats the hire purchaser as owner of the asset. Under this method, the asset is recorded at full cash price on the basis of **'substance over form'**. This method is *more* appropriate since the intention all along is to buy the asset.

JOURNAL ENTRIES UNDER SALES METHOD

The various accounting entries in the books of the hire purchaser and hire vendor are shown below:

JOURNAL ENTRIES UNDER SALES METHOD

Case	*In the Books of Hire Purchaser*	*In the Books of Hire Vendor*
1. On transfer of Possession	Asset A/c Dr. To Hire Vendor's A/c	Hire Purchaser's A/c Dr. To H.P. Sales A/c
2. On making Down Payment	Hire Vendor's A/c Dr. To Bank A/c	Bank A/c Dr. To Hire Purchaser's A/c
3. On making Interest due on unpaid balance	Interest A/c Dr. To Hire Vendor's A/c	Hire Purchaser's A/c Dr. To Interest A/c
4. On making payment of Instalment	Hire Vendor's A/c Dr. To Bank A/c	Bank A/c Dr. To Hire Purchaser's A/c
5. On providing Depreciation	Depreciation A/c Dr. To Asset A/c	No Entry
6. On closure of Depreciation A/c	Profit & Loss A/c Dr. To Depreciation A/c	No Entry
7. On closure of Interest A/c	Profit & Loss A/c Dr. To Interest A/c	Interest A/c Dr. To Profit & Loss A/c

DISCLOSURE IN BALANCE SHEET

At the end of each accounting period the balances of relevant accounts appear in the Balance Sheet as shown below:

DISCLOSURE IN BALANCE SHEET

Balance Sheet of Hire purchaser				Balance Sheet of Hire Vendor			
Liabilities	₹	*Assets*	₹	*Liabilities*	₹	*Assets*	₹
		Fixed Assets:				**Current Assets:**	
		Asset (at full cash price)	xxx			Hire Purchase Debtors	xxx
		Less: Dep. till date	xxx				
		Less: Balance in Hire Vendor's Account	xxx				
			xxx				xxx

ILLUSTRATION 14

On 1.1.2011 A purchased five Machines each costing ₹ 1,58,500 each from B Payment was to be made 20% down and the remainder in four equal annual instalments commencing from 31.12.2011 with interest at 10% p.a. A writes off depreciation @20% on the diminishing balance.

Required: Give the necessary journal entries and ledger accounts in the books of A and B under Sales Method. Also show how the relevant of items will appear in the Balance Sheet.

SOLUTION

JOURNAL

Journal of A		*Journal B*		*Dr. (₹)*	*Cr. (₹)*
01.01.2011					
(a) Machines A/c	Dr.	(a) A	Dr.	7,92,500	
To B		To HP Sales A/c			7,92,500
(b) B	Dr.	(b) Bank A/c	Dr.	1,58,500	
To Bank A/c		To A			1,58,500
31.12.2011					
(c) Interest A/c	Dr.	(c) A	Dr.	63,400	
To B		To Interest A/c			63,400
(d) B	Dr.	(d) Bank A/c	Dr.	2,21,900	
To Bank A/c		To A			2,21,900
(e) Depreciation A/c	Dr.	(e) No Entry		1,58,500	
To Machines A/c					1,58,500
(f) Profit & Loss A/c	Dr.	(f) No Entry		1,58,500	
To Depreciation A/c					1,58,500
(g) Profit & Loss A/c	Dr.	(g) Interest A/c	Dr.	63,400	
To Interest A/c		To Profit & Loss A/c			63,400

31.12.2012			
(a) Interest A/c Dr.	(a) A Dr.	47,550	
To B	To Interest A/c		47,550
(b) B Dr.	(b) Bank A/c Dr.	2,06,050	
To Bank A/c	To A		2,06,050
(c) Depreciation A/c	(c) No Entry	1,26,800	
To Machines A/c			1,26,800
(d) Profit & Loss A/c	(d) No Entry	1,26,800	
To Depreciation A/c			1,26,800
(e) Profit & Loss A/c	(e) Interest A/c Dr.	47,550	
To Interest A/c	To Profit & Loss A/c		47,550
31.12.2013			
(a) Interest A/c Dr.	(a) A Dr.	31,700	
To B	To Interest A/c		31,700
(b) B Dr.	(b) Bank A/c Dr.	1,90,200	
To Bank A/c	To A		1,90,200
(c) Depreciation A/c Dr.	(c) No Entry	1,01,440	
To Machines A/c			1,01,440
(d) Profit & Loss A/c Dr.	(d) No Entry	1,01,440	
To Depreciation A/c			1,01,440
(e) Profit & Loss A/c Dr.	(e) Interest A/c Dr.	31,700	
To Interest A/c	To Profit & Loss A/c		31,700
31.12.2014			
(a) Interest A/c Dr.	(a) A Dr.	15,850	
To B	To Interest A/c		15,850
(b) B Dr.	(b) Bank A/c Dr.	1,74,350	
To Bank A/c	To A		1,74,350
(c) Depreciation A/c Dr.	(c) No Entry	81,152	
To Machines A/c			81,152
(d) Profit & Loss A/c Dr.	(d) No Entry	81,152	
To Depreciation A/c			81,152
(e) Profit & Loss A/c Dr.	(e) Interest A/c Dr.	15,850	
To Interest A/c	To Profit & Loss A/c		15,850

LEDGER ACCOUNTS IN THE BOOK OF A

MACHINES ACCOUNT

Dr. *Cr.*

Date	*Particulars*	₹	*Date*	*Particulars*	₹
01.01.2011	To B	7,92,500	31.12.2011	By Depreciation A/c	1,58,500
				By Balance c/d	6,34,000
		7,92,500			7,92,500

01.01.2012	To Balance b/d	6,34,500	31.12.2012	By Depreciation A/c	1,26,800
				By Balance c/d	5,07,200
		6,34,000			6,34,000
01.01.2013	To Balance b/d	5,07,200	31.12.2013	By Depreciation A/c	1,01,440
				By Balance c/d	4,05,760
		5,07,200			5,07,200
01.01.2014	To Balance b/d	4,05,760	31.12.2014	By Depreciation A/c	81,152
				By Balance c/d	3,24,608
		4,05,760			4,05,760

Dr. **B 'S ACCOUNT** *Cr.*

Date	*Particulars*	₹	*Date*	*Particulars*	₹
01.01.2011	To Bank A/c		01.01.2011	By Machines A/c	7,92,500
	(Down Payment)	1,58,500	31.12.2011	By Interest A/c	63,400
31.12.2011	To Bank A/c	2,21,900		[(₹ 7,92,500 –	
	(₹ 1,58,500 + ₹ 63,400)			₹ 1,58,500) × 10/100]	
	To Balance c/d	4,75,500			
		8,55,900			8,55,900
31.12.2012	To Bank A/c	2,06,050	01.01.2012	By Balance b/d	4,75,500
	[1,58,500 + ₹ 47,550]		31.12.2012	By Interest A/c	47,550
	To Balance c/d	3,17,000		[₹ 4,75,500 × 10/100]	
		5,23,050			5,23,050
31.12.2013	To Bank A/c		01.01.2013	By Balance b/d	3,17,000
	[1,58,500 + 31,700]	1,90,200	31.12.2013	By Interest A/c	31,700
	To Balance c/d	1,58,500		[₹ 3,17,000 × 10/100]	
		3,48,700			3,48,700
31.12.2014	To Bank A/c		01.01.2014	By Balance b/d	1,58,500
	[1,58,500 + 15,850]	1,74,350	31.12.2014	By Interest A/c	15,850
				[₹ 1,58,500 × 10/100]	
		1,74,350			1,74,350

AN EXTRACT OF BALANCE SHEET OF A

Liabilities	*1st yr.*	*2nd yr.*	*3rd yr.*	*4th yr.*	*Assets*	*1st yr.* ₹	*2nd yr.* ₹	*3rd yr.* ₹	*4th yr.* ₹
					Fixed Assets:				
					Machines	7,92,500	7,92,500	7,92,500	7,92,500
					Less: Dep. till date	1,58,500	2,85,300	3,86,740	4,67,892
					Less: Bal. due to B	4,75,500	3,17,000	1,58,500	—
						1,58,500	1,90,200	2,47,260	3,24,608

LEDGER ACCOUNTS IN THE BOOKS OF B

A'S ACCOUNT

Dr. Cr.

Date	Particulars	₹	Date	Particulars	₹
01.01.2011	To Sales	7,92,500	01.01.2011	By Bank A/c (Down Payment)	1,58,500
31.12.2011	To Interest A/c	63,400	31.12.2011	By Bank A/c	2,21,900
				By Balance c/d	4,75,500
		8,55,900			8,55,900
01.01.2012	To Balance b/d	4,75,500	31.12.2012	By Bank A/c	2,06,050
31.12.2012	To Interest A/c	47,550	31.12.2012	By Balance c/d	3,17,000
		5,23,050			5,23,050
01.01.2013	To Balance b/d	3,17,000	31.12.2013	By Bank A/c	1,90,200
31.12.2013	To Interest A/c	31,700		By Balance c/d	1,58,500
		3,48,700			3,48,700
01.01.2014	To Balance b/d	1,58,500	31.12.2014	By Bank A/c	1,74,350
31.12.2014	To Interest A/c	15,850			
		1,74,350			1,74,350

AN EXTRACT OF BALANCE SHEET OF B

Liabilities	1st yr.	2nd yr.	3rd yr.	4th yr.	Assets	1st yr. ₹	2nd yr. ₹	3rd yr. ₹	4th yr. ₹
					Current Assets:				
					Hire Purchase Debtors—A	4,75,500	3,17,000	1,58,500	—

10.0 DEFAULT AND REPOSSESSION

If a hire purchaser fails to pay any instalment on the stipulated date, the hire purchaser is said to be at default. In case of default by the hire purchaser, the hire vendor may repossess the goods. Repossession means taking back the possession of goods by the hire vendor. Subject to agreement, the repossession may be either complete *or* partial.

MEANING OF COMPLETE OR FULL REPOSSESSION

In case of complete *or* full repossession the hire vendor takes back the possession of all the goods.

JOURNAL ENTRIES UNDER COMPLETE OR FULL REPOSSESSION

All Entries till the date of default are passed in the usual manner. The additional Entries are as follows:

Books of Hire Purchaser	***Books of Hire Vendor***
1. For Closing Hire Vendor's Account Hire Vendor's A/c Dr. To Asset A/c **Note:** *This entry is passed with the amount due to the hire-vendor.*	***1. On Repossession of goods*** Goods Repossessed A/c Dr. To Hire Purchaser's A/c **Note:** *This entry is passed with the revalued amount of goods repossessed.*

2. ***For Closing Asset Account*** *(i)* ***If the Book Value of the Asset exceeds the amount due to Hire-Vendor*** Profit & Loss A/c Dr. To Asset A/c *(ii)* ***If the amount due to Hire-Vendor exceeds the Book Value of the Asset*** Asset A/c Dr. To Profit & Loss A/c	2. ***For amount spent on reconditioning of Goods Repossessed*** Goods Repossessed A/c Dr. To Cash A/c/Bank A/c 3. ***For sale of Goods Repossessed*** Cash A/c/Bank A/c /Debtors A/c Dr. To Goods Repossessed A/c 4. ***For loss on sale of Goods Repossessed*** Profit & Loss A/c Dr. To Goods Repossessed A/c ***Note:*** *In case of profit, a reverse entry will be passed.*

ILLUSTRATION 15

On 1.1.2011, X purchased 5 Machines from Y. Payment was to be made—20% down and the balance in four annual instalments of ₹ 2,80,000, ₹ 2,60,000, ₹ 2,40,000 and ₹ 2,20,000 commencing from 31.12.2011. The vendor charged interest @ 10% p.a. X, writes off depreciation @ 20% p.a. on the original cost.

On X. 's failure to pay the instalment due on 31.12.2012, Y repossessed all the machines on 01.01.2013 and valued them on the basis of 40% p.a. depreciation on W.D.V. basis. Y after incurring ₹ 6,000 on repairs sold the machines for ₹ 2,66,000 on 30th June 2013. Prepare the relevant accounts in the books of X and Y.

SOLUTION

COMPUTATION OF CASH PRICE AND PERIODIC INTEREST

A *Instalment Number*	*B* *Closing Balance after the payment of instalment*	*C* *Instalment Amount*	*D = B + C* *Closing Balance before the payment of instalment*	*E = D*R/(100 + R)* *Interest D*10/110*	*F = D – E* *Opening Balance*
IV	—	2,20,000	2,20,000	20,000	2,00,000
III	2,00,000	2,40,000	4,40,000	40,000	4,00,000
II	4,00,000	2,60,000	6,60,000	60,000	6,00,000
I	6,00,000	2,80,000	8,80,000	80,000	8,00,000

Let the cash price by 'X'

X = ₹ 8,00,000 + 20% of X (i.e. down payment)

0.8X = ₹ 8,00,000

X = ₹ 8,00,000/0.8 = ₹ 10,00,000

LEDGER ACCOUNTS IN THE BOOK OF X
MACHINERY ACCOUNT

Dr. *Cr.*

Date	Particulars	₹	Date	Particulars	₹
01.01.11	To Y	10,00,000	31.12.11	By Depreciation A/c	2,00,000

				By Balance c/d	8,00,000
		10,00,000			10,00,000
01.01.12	To Balance b/d	8,00,000	31.12.12	By Depreciation A/c	2,00,000
				By Balance c/d	6,00,000
		8,00,000			8,00,000
01.01.13	To Balance b/d	6,00,000	01.01.13	By Y's A/c	6,60,000
	To P&L A/c (Profit)	60,000			
		6,60,000			6,60,000

Dr. **Y'S ACCOUNT** Cr.

Date	Particulars	₹	Date	Particulars	₹
01.01.11	To Bank A/c (Down Payment)	2,00,000	01.01.11	By Machinery A/c	10,00,000
31.12.11	To Bank A/c [₹2,00,000 + ₹80,000]	2,80,000	31.12.11	By Interest A/c [(₹10,00,000 – ₹2,00,000) × 10/100	80,000
	To Balance c/d	6,00,000			
		10,80,000			10,80,000
31.12.12	To Balance c/d	6,60,000	01.01.11	By Balance b/d	6,00,000
			31.12.12	By Interest a/c [(₹6,00,000 × 10/100)]	60,000
		6,60,000			6,60,000
01.01.13	To Machinery A/c	6,60,000	01.01.13	By Balance b/d	6,60,000

LEDGER ACCOUNTS IN THE BOOK OF Y

Dr. **X ACCOUNT** Cr.

Date	Particulars	₹	Date	Particulars	₹
01.01.11	To H.P. Sales A/c	10,00,000	01.01.11	By Bank A/c (Down Payment)	2,00,000
31.12.11	To Interest A/c [(₹10,00,00 – ₹2,00,000) × 10/100]	80,000	31.12.11	By Bank A/c [₹2,00,000 + ₹80,000]	2,80,000
				By Balance c/d	6,00,000
		10,80,000			10,80,000
01.01.12	To Balance b/d	6,00,000	31.12.12	By Balance c/d	6,60,000
31.12.12	To Interest A/c [₹ 6,00,000 × 10/100]	60,000			
		6,60,000			6,60,000
01.01.13	To Balance b/d	6,60,000	01.01.13	By H.P. Goods Repossessed A/c	3,60,000
				By Profit & Loss A/c	3,00,000
		6,60,000			6,60,000

Dr. **H.P. GOODS REPOSSESSED ACCOUNT** Cr.

Date	Particulars	₹	Date	Particulars	₹
01.01.13	To X's A/c	3,60,000	30.06.13	By Bank A/c	2,66,000
	To Bank A/c	6,000		By P & L A/c	1,00,000
		3,66,000			3,66,000

ILLUSTRATION 16

On 1st January, 2013, Ashok acquired furniture on the hire-purchase system from Real Aids, agreeing to pay four semi-annual instalments of ₹ 800 each, commencing on 30th June, 2013. The Cash price of the furniture was ₹ 3,010 and interest of 5% per annum at half yearly rest was chargeable. On 30th September, 2013, Ashok expresses his inability to continue and Real Aids seized the property. It was agreed that Ashok would pay the due proportion of the instalment upto the date of seizure and also a further sum of ₹ 200 towards depreciation. At the time of re-possession, Real Aids valued the furniture at ₹ 1,500. The company after incurring ₹ 200 towards repairs of the furniture, sold the items for ₹ 1,800 on 15th October, 2013.

Required: Prepare the Ledger accounts in the books of the Vendor and the Purchaser presuming that the purchaser charges depreciation @ 10% p.a.

SOLUTION

BOOKS OF ASHOK

Dr. **FURNITURE ACCOUNT** Cr.

Date	Particulars	₹	Date	Particulars	₹
01.01.13	To Real Aids	3,010.00	30.09.13	By Depreciation A/c (10% on ₹ 3,010 for 9 months)	225.75
				By Real Aids	1,713.82
				By P & L A/c (Loss)	1,070.43
		3,010.00			3,010.00

Dr. **REAL AIDS'S ACCOUNT** Cr.

Date	Particulars	₹	Date	Particulars	₹
30.06.13	To Cash A/c	800.00	01.01.13	By Furniture A/c	3,010.00
30.09.13	To Cash A/c (₹ 400 + ₹ 200)	600.00	30.06.13	By Interest A/c	75.25
30.09.13	To Furniture A/c	1713.82	30.09.13	By Interest (on ₹ 2,285.25 @ 5% p.a)	28.57
		3,113.82			3,113.82

Dr. **INTEREST ACCOUNT** Cr.

Date	Particulars	₹ P	Date	Particulars	₹ P
30.06.13	To Real Aids	75.25		By Profit & Loss A/c	103.82
30.09.13	To Real Aids	28.57			
		103.82			103.82

Dr. **AN EXTRACT OF PROFIT AND LOSS ACCOUNT OF ASHOK** Cr.

Date	Particulars	₹ P	Date	Particulars	₹ P
	To Interest	103.82			
	To Loss on Seizure of goods	1,070.43			
	To Dep. on Furniture	225.75			
		1,400.00			

BOOKS OF REAL AID

Dr. **ASHOK'S ACCOUNT** Cr.

Date	Particulars	₹ P	Date	Particulars	₹ P
01.01.13	To Hire Purchase Sales A/c	3,010.00	30.06.13	By Bank A/c	800.00
			30.06.13	By Bank A/c	600.00
30.06.13	To Interest A/c (on ₹ 3,010)	75.25	30.09.13	By Profit & Loss A/c (Loss on valuation of goods repossessed)	213.82
30.09.13	To Interest A/c (on ₹ 2,285.25)	28.57	30.09.13	By H.P. Goods Repossessed A/c	1,500.00
		3,113.82			3,113,82

Dr. **HIRE PURCHASE GOODS REPOSSESSED ACCOUNT** Cr.

Date	Particulars	₹ P	Date	Particulars	₹ P
30.09.13	To Ashok	1,500	15.10.13	By Cash A/c (Sales)	1,800
30.09.13	To Cash (Expenses)	200			
15.10.13	To Profit and Loss A/c (Profit on sale of repossessed goods)	100			
		1,800			1,800

Dr. **AN EXTRACT OF PROFIT AND LOSS ACCOUNT OF REAL AID** Cr.

Particulars	₹ P	Particulars	₹ P
To Loss on valuation of goods repossessed	213.82	By Interest on H.P. Sales	103.82
		By Hire Purchase Goods Repossessed A/c (Profit)	100.00

MEANING OF PARTIAL REPOSSESSION

In case of partial repossession, the hire vendor takes back the possession of a part of the goods.

PRACTICAL STEPS UNDER PARTIAL REPOSSESSION

Step 1: *Calculate Book value of Goods Repossessed*

A. Cost

B. Less: Depreciation upto date of repossession

C. Book value of Goods Repossessed

Step 2: *Calculate Agreed value of Goods Repossessed*

Step 3: *Loss on default = Book Value – Agreed Value*

JOURNAL ENTRIES UNDER PARTIAL REPOSSESSION

Entries till the date of default are passed in the usual manner. The additional Entries are as follows:

Books of Hire Purchaser	*Books of Hire Vendor*
1. **For transfer of the agreed value of Goods Repossessed** Hire Vendor's A/c Dr. To Asset A/c	1. **On Repossession of Goods at agreed value** H.P. Goods Repossessed A/c Dr. To Hire Purchaser's A/c
2. **For Transfer of Loss on default** Profit & Loss A/c Dr. To Asset A/c **Note:** *In case of profit on default, the reverse entry will be passed*	2, 3, 4—Same entries as in case of complete repossession

ILLUSTRATION 17

From the following particulars calculate:

(i) Value of plant taken back by the vendor.

(ii) Value of plant left with the purchaser.

(iii) Profit *or* loss on plant taken back.

(iv) Profit *or* loss on plant repossessed when sold by vendor.

Particulars:

(i) X purchased 3 plants from Y costing ₹ 1,00,000 each.

(ii) Purchaser charged depreciation @ 20% on diminishing balance method.

(iii) 2 plants were seized by the vendor when second instalment was not paid at the end of second year and vendor valued the plants at cost *less* 30% depreciation annually charged at diminishing balance method.

(iv) The vendor spent ₹ 40,000 on overhauling the plants and sold for ₹ 1,60,000.

SOLUTION

(I) VALUE OF PLANT TAKEN BACK BY THE VENDOR

Particulars	₹
A. Cost of 2 plants [₹ 1,00,000 × 2]	2,00,000
B. *Less:* Depreciation @ 30%	60,000
C. Agreed value [A – B]	1,40,000
D. *Less:* Depreciation @ 30%	42,000
E. Agreed value [C – D]	98,000

(II) BOOK VALUE OF PLANT LEFT WITH THE PURCHASER AND TAKEN BACK BY VENDOR

Particulars	1 left ₹	2 Repossessed ₹
A. Cost of Plants	1,00,000	2,00,000
B. *Less:* Depreciation @ 20%	20,000	40,000
C. Book value [A – B]	80,000	1,60,000
D. *Less:* Depreciation @ 20%	16,000	32,000
E. Book Value [C – D]	64,000	1,28,000

(iii) Loss = Agreed Value – Book Value = ₹ 98,000 – ₹ 1,28,000 = ₹ 30,000

(iv) Profit *or* Loss on Plant repressed when sold by vendor

Profit = Sale Proceeds – (Value of Plant taken back + Repairs)

= ₹ 1,60,000 – (₹ 98,000 + ₹ 40,000) = ₹ 22,000.

ILLUSTRATION 18

On 1.1.2011, X purchased 5 Machines from Y. Payment was to be made—20% down and the balance in four annual instalments of ₹ 2,80,000, ₹ 2,60,000, ₹ 2,40,000 and ₹ 2,20,000 commencing from 31.12.2011. The vendor charged interest @ 10% p.a. X, writes off depreciation @ 20% p.a. on the original cost. On X's failure to pay the instalment due on 31.12.2012, after negotiations on 1.1.2013 Y agreed to leave two machines with X adjusting the value of the other three machines against the amount due. The machines being valued at cost *less* 40% p.a. depreciation on W.D.V. basis, Y after spending ₹ 6,000 on repairs of each of such machines sold @ ₹ 70,000 on 30th June 2013. Prepare the relevant accounts in the books of X and Y

SOLUTION

COMPUTATION OF CASH PRICE AND PERIODIC INTEREST

A Instalment Number	*B Closing Balance after the payment of instalment*	*C Instalment Amount*	*D = B + C Closing Balance before the payment of instalment*	*E = D*R/(100 + R) Interest D*10/110*	*F = D – E Opening Balance*
IV	—	2,20,000	2,20,000	20,000	2,00,000
III	2,00,000	2,40,000	4,40,000	40,000	4,00,000
II	4,00,000	2,60,000	6,60,000	60,000	6,00,000
I	6,00,000	2,80,000	8,80,000	80,000	8,00,000

Let the cash price by 'X', X = ₹ 8,00,000 + 20% of X (i.e. down payment)

0.8X = ₹ 8,00,000, X = ₹ 8,00,000/0.8 = ₹ 10,00,000

LEDGER ACCOUNTS IN THE BOOK OF X
MACHINERY ACCOUNT

Dr. *Cr.*

Date	*Particulars*	₹	*Date*	*Particulars*	₹
01.01.11	To Y	10,00,000	31.12.11	By Depreciation A/c	2,00,000
				By Balance c/d	8,00,000
		10,00,000			10,00,000

01.01.12	To Balance b/d	8,00,000	31.12.12	By Depreciation A/c	2,00,000
				By Balance c/d	6,00,000
		8,00,000			8,00,000
01.01.13	To Balance b/d	6,00,000	01.01.13	By Y	2,16,000
				By P&L A/c	1,44,000
				(Loss on Default)	
			31.12.13	By Depreciation A/c	80,000
			31.12.13	By Balance c/d	1,60,000
		6,00,000			6,00,000

Dr. **Y 'S ACCOUNT** *Cr.*

Date	*Particulars*	₹	*Date*	*Particulars*	₹
01.01.11	To Bank A/c	2,00,000	01.01.11	By Machinery A/c	10,00,000
	(Down Payment)		31.12.11	By Interest A/c	80,000
31.12.11	To Bank A/c	2,80,000		[(₹ 10,00,000 –	
	[₹2,00,000 + ₹80,000]			₹ 2,00,000) × 10/100]	
	To Balance c/d	6,00,000			
		10,80,000			10,80,000
31.12.11	To Balance c/d	6,60,000	01.01.12	By Balance b/d	6,00,000
			31.12.12	By Interest A/c	60,000
				[₹ 6,00,000 × 10/100]	
		6,60,000			6,60,000
01.01.13	To Machinery A/c	2,16,000	01.01.13	By Balance b/d	6,60,000
	To Balance c/d	4,44,000			
		6,60,000			6,60,000

Working Notes:

1. CALCULATION OF BOOK VALUE OF GOODS REPOSSESSED

A. Cost [₹ 2,00,000 × 3]	₹ 6,00,000
B. *Less:* Depreciation for 2 years [₹ 6,00,000 × 20% × 2]	₹ 2,40,000
	₹ 3,60,000

2. CALCULATION OF AGREED VALUE OF GOODS REPOSSESSED

A. Cost [₹ 2,00,000 × 3]	₹ 6,00,000
B. *Less:* Depreciation for 1st year [40% of ₹ 6,00,000]	₹ 2,40,000
C. Book value in the beginning of 2nd year	₹ 3,60,000
D. *Less:* Depreciation for 2nd year [40% of ₹ 3,60,000]	₹ 1,44,000
E. Book Value at the end of 2nd year	₹ 2,16,000

3. **Loss on default** = Book value – Agreed value = ₹ 3,60,000 – ₹ 2,16,000 = ₹ 1,44,000

LEDGER ACCOUNTS IN THE BOOKS OF Y

X'S ACCOUNT

Dr. *Cr.*

Date	*Particulars*	₹	*Date*	*Particulars*	₹
01.01.11	To H.P. Sales A/c	10,00,000	01.01.11	By Bank A/c	2,00,000
31.12.11	To Interest A/c	80,000		(Down Payment)	
	[(₹ 10,00,00 – ₹ 2,00,000) × 10/100]		31.12.11	By Bank A/c [₹2,00,000 + ₹80,000]	2,80,000
				By Balance c/d	6,00,000
		10,80,000			10,80,000
01.01.12	To Balance b/d	6,00,000	31.12.12	By Balance c/d	6,60,000
31.12.12	To Interest A/c	60,000			
	[₹ 6,00,000 × 10/100]				
		6,60,000			6,60,000
01.01.13	To Balance b/d	6,60,000	01.01.13	By H.P. Goods Repossessed A/c	2,16,000
				By Balance c/d	4,44,000
		6,60,000			6,60,000

H.P. GOODS REPOSSESSED ACCOUNT

Dr. *Cr.*

Date	*Particulars*	₹	*Date*	*Particulars*	₹
01.01.13	To X's A/c	2,16,000	30.06.13	By Bank A/c	2,10,000
	To Bank A/c (Repairs)	18,000		By P&L A/c (Loss)	24,000
	(₹ 6,000 × 3)				
		2,34,000			2,34,000

ILLUSTRATION 19

On 1.1.2011, X purchased 5 Machines from Y. Payment was to be made—20% down and the balance in four annual instalments of ₹ 2,80,000, ₹ 2,60,000, ₹ 2,40,000 and ₹ 2,20,000 commencing from 31.12.2011. The vendor charged interest @ 10% p.a. X, writes off depreciation @ 20% p.a. on the original cost On X failure to pay the instalment due on 31.12.2012, Y repossessed 3 machines on 1.1.2013 and agreed to allow X a credit for the amount paid against 3 machines *less* 25%. Y spent ₹ 6,000 on repairs of these machines and sold one of such machines for ₹ 70,000 on 30th June 2013. Prepare the relevant accounts in the books of X and Y

SOLUTION

COMPUTATION OF CASH PRICE AND PERIODIC INTEREST

A *Instalment Number*	*B* *Closing Balance after the payment of instalment*	*C* *Instalment Amount*	*D = B + C* *Closing Balance before the payment of instalment*	*E = D*R/(100 + R)* *Interest D*10/110*	*F = D – E* *Opening Balance*
IV	—	2,20,000	2,20,000	20,000	2,00,000
III	2,00,000	2,40,000	4,40,000	40,000	4,00,000

II	4,00,000	2,60,000	6,60,000	60,000	6,00,000
I	6,00,000	2,80,000	8,80,000	80,000	8,00,000

Let the cash price by 'X'

X = ₹ 8,00,000 + 20% of X (i.e. down payment)

0.8X = ₹ 8,00,000

X = ₹ 8,00,000/0.8 = ₹ 10,00,000

LEDGER ACCOUNTS IN THE BOOK OF X

MACHINERY ACCOUNT

Dr. *Cr.*

Date	Particulars	₹	Date	Particulars	₹
01.01.11	To Y	10,00,000	31.12.11	By Depreciation A/c	2,00,000
				By Balance c/d	8,00,000
		10,00,000			10,00,000
01.01.12	To Balance b/d	8,00,000	31.12.12	By Depreciation A/c	2,00,000
				By Balance c/d	6,00,000
		8,00,000			8,00,000
01.01.13	To Balance b/d	6,00,000	01.01.13	By Y	1,80,000
				By P&L A/c (Loss on Default)	1,80,000
				By Depreciation A/c	80,000
				By Balance c/d	1,60,000
		6,00,000			6,00,000

Y 'S ACCOUNT

Dr. *Cr.*

Date	Particulars	₹	Date	Particulars	₹
01.01.11	To Bank A/c (Down Payment)	2,00,000	01.01.11	By Machinery A/c	10,00,000
31.12.11	To Bank A/c [₹2,00,000 + ₹80,000]	2,80,000	31.12.11	By Interest A/c [(₹ 10,00,000 – ₹ 2,00,000) × 10/100]	80,000
	To Balance c/d	6,00,000			
		10,80,000			10,80,000
31.12.12	To Balance c/d	6,60,000	01.01.12	By Balance b/d	6,00,000
			31.12.12	By Interest A/c [₹ 6,00,000 × 10/100]	60,000
		6,60,000			6,60,000
01.01.13	To Machinery A/c	1,80,000	01.01.13	By Balance b/d	6,60,000
	To Balance c/d	4,80,000			
		6,60,000			6,60,000

Working Notes

1. CALCULATION OF BOOK VALUE OF GOODS REPOSSESSED

A. Cost [₹ 2,00,000 × 3]	₹ 6,00,000
B. *Less:* Depreciation for 2 years [₹ 6,00,000 × 20% × 2]	₹ 2,40,000
	₹ 3,60,000

2. CALCULATION OF AGREED VALUE OF GOODS REPOSSESSED

A. Total amount of principal paid for 5 Machines	₹ 4,00,000
B. Total amount of principal paid for 3 machines [₹ 4,00,000 × 3/5]	₹ 2,40,000
C. Agreed value of 3 machines [₹ 2,40,000 – 25% of ₹ 2,40,000]	₹ 1,80,000

3. **Loss on Default** = Book Value – Agreed Value = ₹ 3,60,000 – ₹ 1,80,000 = ₹ 1,80,000

LEDGER ACCOUNTS IN THE BOOKS OF Y
X 'S ACCOUNT

Dr. Cr.

Date	Particulars	₹	Date	Particulars	₹
01.01.11	To H.P. Sales A/c	10,00,000	01.01.11	By Bank A/c (Down Payment)	2,00,000
31.12.11	To Interest A/c [(₹ 10,00,000 – ₹ 2,00,000) × 10/100]	80,000	31.12.11	By Bank A/c [₹2,00,000 + ₹80,000]	2,80,000
				By Balance c/d	6,00,000
		10,80,000			10,80,000
01.01.12	To Balance b/d	6,00,000	31.12.12	By Balance c/d	6,60,000
31.12.12	To Interest A/c [₹ 6,00,000 × 10/100]	60,000			
		6,60,000			6,60,000
01.01.13	To Balance b/d	6,60,000	01.01.13	By H.P. Goods Repossessed A/c	1,80,000
				By Balance c/d	4,80,000
		6,60,000			6,60,000

H.P. GOODS REPOSSESSED ACCOUNT

Dr. Cr.

Date	Particulars	₹	Date	Particulars	₹
01.01.13	To X's A/c	1,80,000	30.06.13	By Bank A/c	70,000
	To Bank A/c (Repairs)	6,000		By Balance c/d	1,24,000
	To P&L A/c (Profit) [₹ 70,000 – (₹ 1,86,000 × 1/3)	8,000			
		1,94,000			1,94,000

ILLUSTRATION 20

On April 1, 2011 Rahul purchased five machines on hire purchase system from Varun The cash price of each machine was ₹ 30,000 the terms of payment were:

(a) Down payment : ₹ 30,000.

(b) Six half yearly instalments of ₹ 23,500 each payable on September 30 and March 31 each year.

Rahul wrote off depreciation @ 10% p.a. on diminishing balance method.

Rahul paid instalments due upto March 31, 2013, but due to financial crisis he could not pay the instalment due on September 30, 2013. After negotiations, it was agreed that the vendor would repossess two machines for which Rahul would get credited for the amount paid towards the cost of the two machines *less* 25% thereof.

Varun sold both the machines for ₹ 23,800, after incurring ₹ 700 on repairs.

You are required to give:

(i) Varun A/c, Machines A/c in the books of Rahul.

(ii) Rahul A/c and Goods Repossessed A/c in the books of Varun

SOLUTION

BOOKS OF RAHUL
MACHINES ACCOUNT

Dr. *Cr.*

Date	*Particulars*	₹	*Date*	*Particulars*	₹
01.04.11	To Varun	1,50,000	31.03.12	By Depreciation A/c	15,000
				By Balance c/d	1,35,000
		1,50,000			1,50,000
01.04.12	To Balance b/d	1,35,000	31.03.13	By Depreciation A/c	13,500
				[1,35,000 × 10/100]	
				By Balance c/d	1,21,500
		1,35,000			1,35,000
01.04.13	To Balance b/d	1,21,500	30.09.13	By Varun	31,800
				By Depreciation A/c	2,430
				By P & L A/c (Loss)	14,370
				By Balance c/d	72,900
				[3/5 of 1,21,500]	
		1,21,500			1,21,500

VARUN

Dr. *Cr.*

Date	*Particulars*	₹	*Date*	*Particulars*	₹
01.04.11	To Cash A/c	30,000	01.04.11	By Machines A/c	1,50,000
	(Down Payment)		30.09.11	By Interest A/c	6,000
30.09.11	To Cash A/c	23,500	31.03.12	By Interest A/c	5,000
31.03.12	To Cash A/c	23,500			
	To Balance c/d	84,000			
		1,61,000			1,61,000

30.09.12	To Cash A/c	23,500	01.04.12	By Balance b/d	84,000
31.03.13	To Cash A/c	23,500	30.09.12	By Interest A/c	4,000
	To Balance c/d	44,000	31.03.13	By Interest A/c	3,000
		91,000			91,000
30.09.13	To Machines A/c	31,800	01.04.13	By Balance b/d	44,000
	To Balance c/d	14,200	30.09.13	By Interest A/c	2,000
		46,000			46,000

Working Notes:

(i) *Interest* = Total Hire Purchase Price – Total Cash Price

= [30,000 + (23,500 × 6)] – ₹ 1,50,000 = ₹ 21,000

Since the rate of interest has not been given, the amount of interest included each instalment will be ascertained by dividing the total interest in the ratio of hire purchase price outstanding in the beginning of each period. The ratio comes to 6 : 5 : 4 : 3 : 2 : 1.

Instalments	*Interest*
1	21,000 × 6/21 = ₹ 6,000
2	21,000 × 5/21 = ₹ 5,000
3	21,000 × 4/21 = ₹ 4,000
4	21,000 × 3/21 = ₹ 3,000
5	21,000 × 2/21 = ₹ 2,000
6	21,000 × 1/21 = ₹ 1,000

(II) CALCULATION OF LOSS ON MACHINES SEIZED BY VENDOR

		₹
A.	Book value of two Machines Repossessed Cost price of two machine (30,000 × 2)	60,000
	Less: Depreciation @ 10% on diminishing balance	6,000
	Book value of machines at year 1 end	54,000
	Less: Depreciation @ 10% on diminishing balance	(5,400)
	Book value of machines at year 2 end	48,600
	Less: Depreciation @ 10% on diminshing balance for half year	(2,430)
	Book value of machines at date of repossession	46,170
B.	Agreed value at which the machines were repossessed 2/5 [30,000 + (23,500 × 4) – 18,000 (Interest)	42,400
	Less: 25% of 42,400	10,600
		31,800
C.	Loss on Machines seized (A – B)	14,370

VARUN (HIRE VENDOR)
RAHUL'S ACCOUNT

Dr. Cr.

Date	*Particulars*	₹	*Date*	*Particulars*	₹
01.04.11	To H.P. Sales A/c	1,50,000	01.04.11	By Cash A/c	30,000

30.09.11	To Interest	6,000	30.09.11	By Cash A/c	23,500
31.03.12	To Interest	5,000	31.03.12	By Cash A/c	23,500
			31.03.12	By Balance c/d	84,000
		1,61,000			1,61,000
01.04.12	To Balance b/d	84,000	30.09.12	By Cash A/c	23,500
30.09.12	To Interest A/c	4,000		By Cash A/c	23,500
31.03.13	To Interest A/c	3,000	31.03.13	By Balance c/d	44,000
		91,000			91,000
01.04.13	To Balance b/d	44,000	30.09.13	By Goods Rep. A/c	31,800
30.09.13	To Interest A/c	2,000		By Balance c/d	14,200
		46,000			46,000

Dr. **GOODS REPOSSESSED ACCOUNT** *Cr.*

Particulars	₹	*Particulars*	₹
To Rahul's A/c	31,800	By Bank A/c	23,800
To Bank A/c (Repair)	700	By Profit & Loss A/c	8,700
	32,500		32,500

ILLUSTRATION 21

Deepak purchased four second-hand cars on hire-purchase system. Cash price being ₹ 52,500 each. The hire-purchase price for all the four cars was ₹ 2,40,000. The payment was to be made ₹ 60,000 on signing the agreement and three instalments of ₹ 60,000 each at the end of each of the three years. Deepak charges depreciation @ 10% per annum on Straight Line Method.

Deepak paid the down payment and first instalment but could not pay the second instalment. The vendor, after negotiations, took back three cars. These cars were taken back after depreciating them @ 20% per annum on written down value method. One car was left with the purchaser.

The Vendor spent ₹ 3,600 on repairs and sold two of these cars for ₹ 80,000.

Required: Show necessary ledger accounts in the books of both the parties.

SOLUTION

BOOKS OF DEEPAK

Dr. **CAR ON H.P. ACCOUNT** *Cr.*

Date	*Particulars*	₹	*Date*	*Particulars*	₹
1st Year	To Hire Vendor A/c	2,10,000	1st Year	By Depreciation A/c	21,000
				By Balance c/d	1,89,000
		2,10,000			2,10,000
IInd Year	To Balance b/d	1,89,000	IInd Year	By Depreciation A/c	21,000
				By Hire Vendor A/c	1,00,800
				By P & L A/c (Loss)	25,200
				By Balance c/d	42,000
		1,89,000			1,89,000

Dr. **HIRE VENDOR ACCOUNT** Cr.

Date	Particulars	₹	Date	Particulars	₹
1st Year	To Bank A/c		1st Year	By Car on H.P. system	2,10,000
	(Down Payment)	60,000		By Interest A/c	15,000
	To Bank A/c (Install.)	60,000			
	To Balance c/d	1,05,000			
		2,25,000			2,25,000
IInd Year	To Car A/c	1,00,800	IInd Year	By Balance b/d	1,05,000
	To Balance c/d	14,200		By Interest A/c	10,000
		1,15,000			1,15,000

BOOKS OF HIRE VENDOR

Dr. **DEEPAK ACCOUNT** Cr.

Date	Particulars	₹	Date	Particulars	₹
1st Year	To Sales on H.P.	2,10,000	1st Year	By Bank A/c	60,000
	To Interest A/c	15,000		By Bank A/c	60,000
				By Balance c/d	1,05,000
		2,25,000			2,25,000
IInd Year	To Balance b/d	1,05,000	IInd Year	By Goods Repossessed	1,00,800
	To Interest A/c	10,000		By Balance c/d	14,200
		1,15,000			1,15,000

GOODS REPOSSESSED ACCOUNT

Particulars	₹	Particulars	₹
To Deepak	1,00,800	By Bank A/c	80,000
To Bank Repair	3,600	By Balance c/d	34,800
To Profit & Loss A/c	10,400	[(1,00,800 + 3,600) × 1/3]	
	1,14,800		1,14,800

Working Notes:

1. **Calculation of Total Interest** = HPP – CP = ₹ 2,40,000 – ₹ 2,10,000 = 30,000

2. CALCULATION OF INTEREST INCLUDED IN CASH INSTALMENT

Year	Amount O/s in the beginning of each year	Ratio	Interest
1	1,80,000	3	30,000 × 3/6 = 15,000
2	1,20,000	2	30,000 × 2/6 = 10,000
3	60,000	1	30,000 × 1/6 = 5,000
		6	

3. **Value of Cars repossessed** = ₹ 1,57,500 × 80% × 80% = ₹ 1,00,800
4. **Value of car left** [₹ 52,500 – (₹ 52,500 × 10% × 2)] = ₹ 42,000

ILLUSTRAION 22

X Transport purchased from Delhi Motors 3 Tempos costing ₹ 50,000 each on the hire purchase system on 1.1.2011. Payment was to be made ₹ 30,000 down and the remainder in 3 equal annual instalments payable on 31.12.2011, 31.12.2012 and 31.12.2013 together with interest @ 9%. p.a. X Transport writes off depreciation at the rate of 20% p.a. on the diminishing balance. It paid the instalment due at the end of the first year i.e. 31.12.2011 but could not pay the next on 31.12.2012. Delhi Motors agreed to leave one Tempo with the purchaser on 31.12.2012 adjusting the value of the other 2 Tempos against the amount due on 31.12.2012. The Tempos were valued on the basis of 30% depreciation annually on W.D.V. basis.

Required: Show the necessary accounts in the books of X Transport for the year 2011, 2012, 2013.

SOLUTION

Dr. **TEMPOS ACCOUNT** *Cr.*

Date	Particulars	₹	Date	Particulars	₹
01.01.11	To Delhi Motors' A/c	1,50,000	31.12.11	By Depreciation A/c	
	(₹ 50,000 × 3)			(20% on ₹ 1,50,000)	30,000
				By Balance c/d	1,20,000
		1,50,000			1,50,000
01.01.12	To Balance b/d	1,20,000	31.12.12	By Depreciation A/c	24,000
			31.12.12	By Delhi Motors' A/c	
				(Value of 2 tempos taken away)	49,000
			31.12.12	By P & L A/c (Loss)	15,000
			31.12.12	By Balance c/d (Value	
				of one tempo left)	32,000
		1,20,000			1,20,000
01.01.13	To Balance b/d	32,000	31.12.13	By Depreciation A/c	6,400
			31.12.13	By Balance b/d	25,600
		32,000			32,000

Dr. **DELHI MOTOR'S ACCOUNT** *Cr.*

Date	Particulars	₹	Date	Particulars	₹
01.01.11	To Bank A/c		01.01.11	By Tempos A/c	
	(Down Payment)	30,000		(₹ 50,000 × 3)	1,50.000
			31.12.11	By Interest A/c (9% on	
31.12.11	To Bank A/c	50,800		₹ 1,20,000)	10,800
31.12.11	To Balance c/d	80,000			
		1,60,800			1,60,800
31.12.12	To Tempos A/c	49,000	01.01.12	By Balance b/d	80,000
31.12.12	To Balance c/d	38,200	31.12.12	By Interest A/c	
				(9% on ₹ 80,000)	7,200
		87,200			87,200

31.12.13	To Bank A/c	41,638	01.01.13	By Balance b/d	38,200
			31.12.13	By Interest A/c (9% on ₹ 38,200)	3,438
		41,638			41,638

Working Notes:

1. Value of a Tempo left with the buyer = ₹ 50,000 × 80/100 × 80/100 = ₹ 32,000
2. Value of Tempos taken away by the seller = ₹ 50,000 × 2 × 70/100 × 70/100 = ₹ 49,000
3. Loss on Tempos taken away = Book Value – Agreed Value
   = [2 × ₹ 50,000 × 80/100 × 80/100] – ₹ 49,000 = ₹ 15,000

ILLUSTRAION 23

On 1.1.2011 X, a television dealer, bought 5 television sets from Dolphin Television Co. on hire-purchase. The cash price of each set was ₹ 20,000. It was agreed that ₹ 25,000 should be paid immediately and the balance in three instalments of ₹ 30,000 each at the end of each year. The Television Co. charges interest @ 10% p.a. The buyer depreciates television sets at 20% p.a. on the diminishing balance method.

X paid cash down and two instalments but failed to pay the last instalment. Consequently, the Television Co. repossessed three sets, leaving two sets with the buyer and adjusting the value of 3 sets against the amount due. The sets repossessed were valued on the basis of 30% depreciation p.a. on the written down value. The sets repossessed were sold by the Television Co. for ₹ 30,000 after necessary repairs amounting to ₹ 5,000 on 30th June 2014.

Required: Open the necessary ledger account in the books of both the parties.

SOLUTION

IN THE BOOKS OF X

Dr. **TELEVISION ACCOUNT** *Cr.*

Date	Particulars	₹	Date	Particulars	₹
01.01.11	To Dolphin Television Co.	1,00,000	31.12.11	By Depreciation A/c	20,000
				By Balance c/d	80,000
		1,00,000			1,00,000
01.01.12	To Balance b/d	80,000	31.12.12	By Depreciation A/c	16,000
				By Balance c/d	64,000
		80,000			80,000
31.12.13	To Balance b/d	64,000	31.12.13	By Depreciation A/c	12,800
				By Dolphin Television Co-(Goods reposs.)	20,580
				By P & L A/c (Loss on default)	10,140
				By Balance c/d	20,480
		64,000			64,000

Dr. **DOLPHIN TELEVISION CO.** Cr.

Date	Particulars	₹	Date	Particulars	₹
01.01.11	To Cash A/c	25,000	01.01.11	By T.V. A/c	1,00,000
31.12.11	To Cash A/c	30,000	31.12.11	By Interest A/c	
	To Balance c/d	52,500		[(₹ 1,00,000 – ₹ 25,000) × 10/100]	7,500
		1,07,500			1,07,500
31.12.12	To Cash A/c	30,000	01.01.12	By Balance b/d	52,500
	To Balance c/d	27,750	31.12.12	By Interest A/c	5,250
				[52,500 × 10/100]	
		57,750			57,750
31.12.13	To T.V. A/c	20,580	01.01.13	By Balance b/d	27,750
	(Goods seized)		31.12.13	By Interest A/c	2,250
	To Balance c/d	9,420			
		30,000			30,000

Working Notes:

1. Total Interest = Hire Purchase Price – Cash Price
   = [₹ 25,000 + (₹ 30,000 × 3)] – (₹ 20,000 × 5)
   = ₹ 1,15,000 – ₹ 1,00,000 = ₹ 15,000
2. Interest for 3rd year = ₹ 15,000 – ₹ 7,500 – ₹ 5,250 = ₹ 2,250

3. Agreed Value of 3 TV Repossessed on the basis of depreciation @ 30% p.a.	₹
A. Cost (Cash Price) of 3 TV Sets	60,000
B. *Less:* Depreciation @ 30% p.a. for 3 years [₹ 18,000 + ₹ 12,600 + ₹ 8,820]	39,420
	20,580
4. Book Value of 3 TV Repossessed on the basis of depreciation @ 20% p.a.	
A. Cost (Cash Price) of 3 TV Sets	60,000
B. *Less:* Depreciation @ 20% WDV for 3 years [₹ 12,000 + ₹ 9,600 + ₹ 7,680]	29,280
	30,720

5. Loss on default = Book value—Agreed Value = ₹ 30,720 – ₹ 20,580 = ₹ 10,140

IN THE BOOKS OF DOLPHIN TELEVISION CO.

Dr. **X'S ACCOUNT** Cr.

Date	Particulars	₹	Date	Particulars	₹
01.01.11	To HP Sales A/c	1,00,000	01.01.11	By Cash A/c	25,000
31.12.11	To Interest A/c	7,500	31.12.11	By Cash A/c	30,000
				By Balance c/d	52,500
		1,07,500			1,07,500
01.01.12	To Balance b/d	52,500	31.12.12	By Cash A/c	30,000
31.12.12	To Interest A/c	5,250	31.12.12	By Balance c/d	27,750
		57,750			57,750

01.01.13	To Balance b/d	27,750	31.12.13	By Goods Repossessed	20,580
31.12.13	To Interest A/c	2,250		By Balance c/d	9,420
		30,000			30,000

Dr. **GOODS REPOSSESSED ACCOUNT** *Cr.*

Particulars	₹	*Particulars*	₹
To X	20,580	By Cash A/c	30,000
To Cash A/c (Repairs)	5,000		
To Profits & Loss A/c (Profit)	4,420		
	30,000		30,000

ILLUSTRAION 24

Bombay Roadways purchased three trucks costing ₹ 1,00,000 each from Hindustan Auto on 1st January, 2011 on the hire purchase system. The terms were: Payment on delivery ₹ 25,000 for each truck and balance of the principal amount by 3 equal instalments *plus* interest at 15% per annum to be paid at the end of each year. Bombay Roadways writes off 25% depreciation each year on the diminishing balance method. Bombay Roadways paid the instalments due on 31st December, 2011 and 31st December, 2012 but could not pay the final instalment. Hindustan Auto repossessed two trucks adjusting values against the amount due. The repossession was done on 1st January, 2014 on the basis of 40% depreciation on the diminishing balance method.

Required: (a) Write up the ledger accounts in the books of Bombay Roadways showing the above transactions upto 1.1.2014, and (b) Show the disclosure of the balance arising from the above in the Balance Sheet of Bombay Roadways as on 31st December 2013.

SOLUTION

Dr. **TRUCKS ACCOUNT** *Cr.*

Date	*Particulars*	₹	*Date*	*Particulars*	₹
01.01.11	To Hindustan Auto	3,00,000	31.12.11	By Depreciation A/c	75,000
				By Balance c/d	2,25,000
		3,00,000			3,00,000
01.01.12	To Balance b/d	2,25,000	31.12.12	By Depreciation A/c	56,250
				By Balance c/d	1,68,750
		2,25,000			2,25,000
01.01.13	To Balance b/d	1,68,750	31.12.13	By Depreciation A/c	42,188
				By Balance c/d	1,26,562
		1,68,750			1,68,750
01.01.14	To Balance b/d	1,26,562	01.01.14	By Hindustan Auto	43,200
				By Prov. for Loss on Repossession A/c	41,175
				By Balance c/d (1/3 of ₹ 1,26,562)	42,187
		1,26,562			1,26,562

Dr. **PROVISION FOR LOSS ON REPOSSESSION ACCOUNT** Cr.

Date	Particulars	₹	Date	Particulars	₹
31.12.13	To Balance c/d	41,175	31.12.13	By Profit & Loss A/c	41,175
01.01.14	To Trucks A/c	41,175	01.01.14	By Balance b/d	41,175

Dr. **HINDUSTAN AUTO ACCOUNT** Cr.

Date	Particulars	₹	Date	Particulars	₹
31.12.11	To Bank A/c	75,000	01.01.11	By Trucks A/c.	3,00,000
	To Bank		31.12.11	By Interest	
	(₹ 75,000 + ₹ 33,750)	1,08,750		(15% on ₹ 2,25,000)	33,750
	To Balance c/d	1,50,000			
		3,33,750			3,33,750
31.12.12	To Bank A/c	97,500	01.01.12	By Balance b/d	1,50,000
	To Balance c/d	75,000	31.12.12	By Interest	22,500
		1,72,500			1,72,500
31.12.13	To Balance c/d	86,250	01.01.13	By Balance b/d	75,000
			31.12.13	By Interest	
				(15% on ₹ 75,000)	11,250
		86,250			86,250
01.01.14	To Trucks A/c	43,200	01.01.14	By Balance b/d	86,250
	To Balance c/d	43,050			
		86,250			86,250

AN EXTRACT OF BALANCE SHEET OF THE BOMBAY ROADWAYS AS AT 31ST DEC., 2013

Previous year (₹)	Liabilities	₹	Previous year (₹)	Assets	₹
	Other Liabilities:			Fixed Assets:	
75,000	H.P. Instalments		3,00,000	Trucks Cost	3,00,000
	outstanding	75,000	1,31,250	*Less:* Depreciation	(1,73,438)
	Interest accrued on	11,250			
		86,250	1,68,750		1,26,562
	Provision for loss on repossession	41,175			

Working Notes:

1. AGREED VALUE OF TWO TRUCKS REPOSSESSED AT 40% DEPRECIATION

Particulars	2011 ₹	2012 ₹	2013 ₹
A. Cost/WDV in the beginning	2,00,000	1,20,000	72,000
B. *Less:* Depreciation for the year @ 40%	(80,000)	(48,000)	(28,800)
C. Book Value (A B)	1,20,000	72,000	43,200

2. LOSS ON RETURN OF TWO TRUCKS

	Particulars	₹
A.	Written down value of 3 trucks as on 01.01.2014	1,26,562
B.	*Less:* Value of one truck retained (₹ 1,26,562 × 1/3)	(42,187)
C.	Written down value of repossessed trucks (A – B)	84,375
D.	*Less:* Agreed value of repossessed trucks	(43,200)
E.	Loss on return of two trucks (C – D)	41,175

Tutorial Note: The company is aware of the default as the payment was due on 31st Dec., 2013. Hence the resulting loss must be provided for in the accounts for 2013.

ILLUSTRAION 25

Banerjee & Co. purchased seven trucks on hire purchase on 1st July. 2012. The cash purchase price of each truck was ₹ 50,000. The company has to pay 20% of the cash purchase price at the time of delivery and the balance in five half yearly instalment starting from 31st December, 2012 with interest at 5% per annum at half yearly rest. On the Company's failure to pay the instalment due on 30th June 2013, it was agreed that the Company would return 3 trucks to the vendor and the remaining four would be retained. The vendor agreed to allow him a credit for the amount paid against these 3 trucks *less* 25%. Vendor after spending ₹ 1,000 on repairs sold away all the three trucks for ₹ 40,000.

Required: Show the relevant Accounts in the books of the purchaser and vendor assuming the books are closed in June every year and depreciation @ 20% p.a. is charged on Trucks.

SOLUTION

IN BOOKS OF HIRE-PURCHASER (BANERJEE & CO.)

Dr. **TRUCKS ACCOUNT** *Cr.*

Date	Particulars	₹	Date	Particulars	₹
01.07.12	To Hire Vendor's A/c		30.06.13	By Depreciation A/c	70,000
	(Cost of 7 Trucks @ ₹ 50,000 each)	3,50,000		By Hire Vendor's A/c (Value of 3 Trucks returned to Vendor)	40,500
				By P & L A/c (Loss on default)	79,500
				By Balance c/d	1,60,000
		3,50,000			3,50,000

Dr. **HIRE VENDOR'S ACCOUNT** *Cr.*

Date	Particulars	₹	Date	Particulars	₹
01.07.12	To Bank A/c		01.07.12	By Trucks A/c	3,50,000
	(₹ 3,50,000 × 20/100)	70,000	31.12.12	By Interest A/c	7,000
				[₹ 2,80,000 × 5/100 × 6/12]	
31.12.12	To Bank A/c		30.06.13	By Interest A/c	5,600
	[(20% of ₹ 2,80,000) + ₹ 7,000]	63,000		[₹ 2,24,000 × 5/100 × 6/12]	

30.06.13	To Trucks A/c	40,500			
30.06.13	To Balance c/d	1,89,100			
		3,62,600			3,62,600

Working Notes:

1. CREDIT ALLOWED VENDOR AGAINST 3 TRUCKS

Particulars	₹
A. Total amount of principal paid against 7 trucks (₹ 70,000 + ₹ 56,000)	1,26,000
B. Total amount of principal paid against 3 trucks (₹ 1,26,000 × 3/7)	54,000
C. Credit allowed by Vendor (₹ 54,000 – 25% of ₹ 54,000)	40,500

2. LOSS ON RETURN OF 3 TRUCKS

Particulars	₹
A. Book value of 3 trucks returned [(₹ 50,000 × 3) *less* 20% of ₹ 1,50,000]	1,20,000
B. *Less:* Credit allowed by Vendor against these 3 Trucks	(40,500)
C. Loss on return of 3 Trucks (A – B)	79,500

IN THE BOOKS OF HIRE VENDOR
BANERJEE & CO'S ACCOUNT

Dr. *Cr.*

Date	*Particulars*	₹	*Date*	*Particulars*	₹
01.07.12	To Hire Sales A/c	3,50,000	01.07.12	By Bank A/c	70,000
31.12.12	To Interest A/c	7,000	31.12.12	By Bank A/c	63,000
30.06.13	To Interest A/c	5,600	30.06.13	By Goods Reposs. A/c	40,500
			30.06.13	By Balance c/d	1,89,100
		3,62,600			3,62,600

GOODS REPOSSESSED ACCOUNT

Dr. *Cr.*

Date	*Particulars*	₹	*Date*	*Particulars*	₹
30.6.13	To Banerjee & Co.	40,500	30.6.13	By Bank A/c (Sales)	40,000
30.6.13	To Cash A/c (exp.)	1,000	30.6.13	By Profit and Loss A/c (Loss on Sale)	1,500
		41,500			41,500

ILLUSTRAION 26

On 1 January 2012, X purchased from Y a plant valued at ₹ 7,45,000; payment to be made by four semi-annual instalments of ₹ 2,10,000 each; interest being charged at 5% per half year. X paid the first instalment on 1 July 2012 but failed to pay the next. Y repossessed the plant on 4 January 2013. On 5 January 2013, after negotiation, X was allowed to retain the plant of which the original cash price was ₹ 3,90,000 and he was to bear the loss on the remainder which was taken over by Y on that date for ₹ 3,75,000. Y waived the interest after 31 December 2012. Another agreement was signed for payment of the balance amount.

Required: Show by ledger accounts the necessary records in the books of X charging depreciation at 10% per annum half yearly on the written down value.

SOLUTION

Dr. **MACHINERY ACCOUNT** Cr.

Date	Particulars	₹	Date	Particulars	₹
1.1.2012	To Y 's A/c	7,45,000	30.6.2012	By Depreciation A/c	37,250
				By Balance c/d	7,07,750
		7,45,000			7,45,000
1.7.2012	To Balance b/d	7,07,750	31.12.2012	By Depreciation A/c	35,388
				By Balance c/d	6,72,362
		7,07,750			7,07,750
1.1.2013	To Balance b/d	6,72,362	5.1.2013	By Y 's A/c	3,75,000
	To P & L A/c (b.f.) [3,75,000–3,20,387]	54,613		By Balance c/d	3,51,975
		7,26,975			7,26,975

Dr. **Y 'S ACCOUNT** Cr.

Date	Particulars	₹	Date	Particulars	₹
30.6.2012	To Balance c/d	7,82,250	1.1.2012	By Plant on Hire Purch. A/c	7,45,000
			30.6.2012	By Interest A/c [₹ 7,45,000 × 5%]	37,250
		7,82,250			7,82,250
1.7.2012	To Bank A/c	2,10,000	1.7.2012	By Balance b/d	7,82,250
31.12.2012	To Balance c/d	6,00,863	31.12.2012	By Interest A/c [₹ 5,72,250 × 5%]	28,613
		8,10,863			8,10,863
5.1.2013	To Machinery A/c	3,75,000	1.1.2013	By Balance b/d	6,00,863
	To Balance c/d	2,25,863			
		6,00,863			6,00,863

Working Note:

CALCULATION OF BOOK VALUE OF PLANT REPOSSESSED AND RETAINED

Particulars	Repossessed (₹)	Retained (₹)
A. Cash Price of the Plant	3,55,000	3,90,000
B. *Less:* Depreciation @ 10% for 6 months	(17,750)	(19,500)
C. Book Value	3,37,250	3,70,500
D. *Less:* Depreciation @ 10% for 6 months	(16,863)	(18,525)
E. Book Value	3,20,387	3,51,975

ILLUSTRAION 27

Y sold 3 Machinery for a total cash sale price of ₹ 6,00,000 on hire purchase basis to X on 1.1.2011. The terms of agreement provided for 30% as cash down and the balance of the cash price in three equal instalments together with interest at 10% per annum compounded annually. The instalments were payable as per the following schedule:

1st instalment on 31.12.2012; 2nd instalment on 31.12.2013 and 3rd instalment on 31.12.2014. X paid the 1st instalment on time but failed to pay thereafter. On his failure to pay the second instalment, Y repossessed two machineries and valued them at 50% of the cash price. X charges 10% p.a. depreciation on straight line method.

Required: Prepare necessary ledger accounts in the books of X for 2011-2013.

SOLUTION

Dr. **MACHINERY ACCOUNT** *Cr.*

Date	*Particulars*	₹	*Date*	*Particulars*	₹
1.1.2011	To Y's Account	6,00,000	31.12.2011	By Depreciation A/c	60,000
				By Balance c/d	5,40,000
		6,00,000			6,00,000
1.1.2012	To Balance b/d	5,40,000	31.12.2012	By Depreciation A/c	60,000
				By Balance c/d	4,80,000
		5,40,000			5,40,000
1.1.2013	To Balance b/d	4,80,000	31.12.2013	By Depreciation A/c	60,000
				By Y's Account	2,00,000
				By Profit and Loss A/c *(Balancing figure)*	80,000
				By Balance c/d	1,40,000
		4,80,000			4,80,000

Dr. **Y'S ACCOUNT** *Cr.*

Date	*Particulars*	₹	*Date*	*Particulars*	₹
1.1.2011	To Bank A/c	1,80,000	31.12.2011	By Machinery A/c	6,00,000
31.12.2011	To Balance c/d	4,62,000		By Interest A/c [10% on (₹ 6,00,000 – ₹ 1,80,000)	42,000
		6,42,000			6,42,000
31.12.2012	To Bank A/c (1,40,000 + 42,000 + 46,200)	2,28,200	1.1.2012	By Balance c/d	4,62,000
	To Balance c/d	2,80,000	31.12.2012	By Interest A/c [10% on ₹ 4,62,000]	46,200
		5,08,200			5,08,200
31.12.2013	To Machinery A/c	2,00,000	1.1.2013	By Balance b/d	2,80,000
	To Balance c/d	1,08,000	31.12.2013	By Interest A/c	28,000
		3,08,000			3,08,000

Working Notes:

1. BOOK VALUE OF MACHINE LEFT AND REPOSSESSED

Particulars	*1 left*	*2 repossessed*
A. Costs	2,00,000	4,00,000
B. *Less:* Depreciation for 3 years @ 10%	(60,000)	(1,20,000)
	1,40,000	2,80,000

2. Agreed Value of 2 Machinery Repossessed = Cash Price – 50% of cash price
= ₹ 4,00,000 – 2,00,000 = ₹ 2,00,000

3. Loss on Default = Agreed Value – BookValue
= ₹ 2,00,000 – ₹ 2,80,000 = ₹ 80,000

11.0 ACCOUNTING FOR INSTALMENT PURCHASE

MEANING OF INSTALMENT PURCHASE AGREEMENT

Instalment Purchase Agreement means an agreement of sale under which:

1. The property in the goods (i.e. ownership of goods) is to pass to the buyer immediately on the signing of the contract of sale.
2. The buyer has no right to terminate the contract unless the seller defaults.
3. The seller has right only to sue for price if the buyer fails to pay any instalment (s). He can not take back the goods from the purchaser.
4. The buyer may dispose off the goods and give good title to the bona-fide purchaser.

DISTINCTION BETWEEN HIRE PURCHASE AGREEMENT AND INSTALMENT PURCHASE AGREEMENT

Hire Purchase Agreement differs from Instalment purchase Agreement in the following respects:

Basis of Distinction	***Hire Purchase Agreement***	***Instalment Purchase Agreement***
1. Act governing	It is governed by **Hire Purchase Act 1972.**	It is governed by the **Sale of Goods Act 1930.**
2. Nature of Contract	It is an **agreement of hiring.**	It is an **agreement of sale.**
3. Passing of Title (ownership)	The title to goods passes **on last payment.**	The title to goods passes **immediately** as in the case of usual sale.
4. Right to Return goods	The hirer **may return** goods without further payment, except for accrued instalment.	Unless seller defaults, goods are **not returnable.**
5. Seller's right to repossess	The seller **may take possession** of the goods if hirer is in default.	The seller can sue for price if the buyer is in default. He **cannot take** possession of the goods.
6. Right to Dispose off	Hirer **cannot** hire out, sell, pledge *or* assign entitling transferee to retain possession as against the hire vendor.	The buyer **may dispose off** the goods and give good title to the bonafide purchaser.

7. Responsibility for Risk of Loss	The **hirer is not responsible** for risk of loss of goods if he has taken reasonable precaution because the ownership has not yet transferred.	The **buyer is responsible** for risk of loss of goods because of the ownership has transferred.
8. Name of Parties involved	The parties involved are called **Hirer** and **Hire vendor.**	The parties involved are called **buyer** and **seller.**
9. Relationship between parties involved	The relationship between hirer and hire vendor is **that of Bailee and Bailor.**	The relationship between the buyer and seller is **that of a debtor and creditor** till last instalment is paid.
10. Component other than Cash Price	Component other than Cash Price included in Instalment is called **Hire charges.**	Component other than Cash price included in Instalment is called **Interest.**
11. Method of Accounting	1. Sales Method for goods of substantial sales values 2. Stock Methods for Goods of small sales values	Interest Suspense Method.

INTEREST SUSPENSE METHOD OF ACCOUNTING

Accounting for instalment purchase is done on the basis of Interest Suspense Method. Under this method, both the seller and buyer make the entries with full value and keep the unaccrued amount of interest in "Interest Suspense Account', from which a sum equivalent to the interest accrued is transferred to the Interest account periodically as and when accrued.

JOURNAL ENTRIES UNDER INTEREST SUSPENSE METHOD

Case	*In the Books of Purchaser*	*In the Books of Vendor*	*Amount with which debited or credited*
A. On transfer of possession	Asset A/c Dr. To Vendor's A/c Interest Suspense A/cDr. To Vendor' A/c	Purchaser's A/c Dr. To Sales A/c Purchaser'A/c Dr. To Interest Sus. A/c	(With the full cash price) (With the total unaccrued interest)
B. On making down payment	Vendor' A/c Dr. To Bank A/c	Bank A/c Dr. To Purchaser' A/c	(With the down payment
C. On making interest due on unpaid balance	Interest A/c Dr. To Interest Sus. A/c	Interest Sus. A/c Dr. To Interest A/c	(with the interest due on unpaid balance)
D. On making payment of instalment	Vendor's A/c Dr. To Bank A/c	Bank A/c Dr. To Purchaser' A/c	(With the amount of instalment)
E. On providing Depreciation	Depreciation A/c Dr. To Asset A/c Dr.	No Entry	With the amount of depreciation)
F. On closure of Depreciation A/c	Profit and Loss A/c Dr. To Depreciation A/c	No Entry	(With the amount of depreciation)
G. On closure of Interest A/c	Profit and Loss A/c Dr. To Interest A/c	Interest A/c Dr. To P & L A/c	(With the amount of interest)

DISCLOSURE IN BALANCE SHEET UNDER INTEREST SUSPENSE METHOD

Balance Sheet of Purchaser				Balance Sheet of Vendor			
Liabilities	₹	*Assets*	₹	*Liabilities*	₹	*Assets*	₹
Balance in Vendor's A/c	xxx	**Fixed Assets:**				Current Assets:	
		Asset (at full cash price)	xxx			Debtors	xxx
Less: Balance on Interest Sus. A/c	(xxx)	*Less:* Dep. till date	(xxx)			*Less:* Balance on Interest Sus. A/c	(xxx)
	xxx		xxx				xxx

ILLUSTRATION 28

On 1.1.2011, A purchased five Machines from B on instalment system. Payment was to be made 20% down and the balance in four annual instalments of ₹ 2,21,900, ₹ 2,06,050, ₹ 1,90,200 and ₹ 1,74,350 commencing from 31.12.2011. The vendor charged interest @ 10% p.a. A writes off depreciation @ 20% p.a. on the diminishing balance.

Required: Give the necessary journal entries in the books of A and B Show Machine Account, B's Account and Interest Suspense Account in the books of A and A's Account and Interest Suspense Account in the books of B Also show the relevant items in the Balance Sheet of A and B

SOLUTION

JOURNAL

Journal of A		*Journal B*		*Dr. (₹)*	*Cr. (₹)*
01.01.2011					
(a) Machines A/c	Dr.	(a) A	Dr.	7,92,500	
To B		To Sales A/c			7,92,500
(b) Interest Suspense A/c	Dr.	(b) A	Dr.	1,58,500	
To B		To Interest Suspense A/c			1,58,500
(c) B	Dr.	(c) Bank A/c	Dr.	1,58,500	
To Bank A/c		To A			1,58,500
31.12.2011					
(d) Interest A/c	Dr.	(d) Interest Suspense A/c	Dr.	63,400	
To Interest Suspense A/c		To Interest A/c			63,400
(e) B	Dr.	(e) Bank A/c	Dr.	2,21,900	
To Bank A/c		To A			2,21,900
(f) Depreciation A/c	Dr.	(f) No Entry			1,58,500
To Machinery A/c					1,58,500
(g) Profit & Loss A/c	Dr.	(g) No Entry			1,58,500
To Depreciation A/c					1,58,500
(h) Profit & Loss A/c	Dr.	(h) Interest A/c	Dr.	63,400	
To Interest A/c		To Profit & Loss A/c			63,400

31.12.2012					
(a) Interest A/c	Dr.	(a) Interest Suspense A/c	Dr.	47,550	
To Interest Suspense A/c		To Interest A/c			47,550
(b) B	Dr.	(b) Bank A/c	Dr.	2,06,050	
To Bank A/c		To A			2,06,050
(c) Depreciation A/c	Dr.	(c) No Entry			1,26,800
To Machinery A/c					1,26,800
(d) Profit & Loss A/c	Dr.	(d) No Entry			1,26,800
To Depreciation A/c					1,26,800
(e) Profit & Loss A/c	Dr.	(e) Interest A/c	Dr.	47,550	
To Interest A/c		To Profit & Loss A/c			47,550
31.12.2013					
(a) Interest A/c	Dr.	(f) Interest Suspense A/c	Dr.	31,700	
To Interest Suspense A/c		To Interest A/c			31,700
(b) B	Dr.	(a) Bank A/c	Dr.	1,90,200	
To Bank A/c		To A			1,90,200
(c) Depreciation A/c	Dr.	(b) No Entry			1,01,440
To Machinery A/c					1,01,440
(d) Profit & Loss A/c	Dr.	(c) No Entry			1,01,440
To Depreciation A/c					1,01,440
(e) Profit & Loss A/c	Dr.	(d) Interest A/c	Dr.	31,700	
To Interest A/c		To Profit & Loss A/c			31,700
31.12.2014					
(a) Interest A/c	Dr.	(a) Interest Suspense A/c	Dr.	15,850	
To Interest Suspense A/c		To Interest A/c			15,850
(b) B	Dr.	(b) Bank A/c	Dr.	1,74,350	
To Bank A/c		To A			1,74,350
(c) Depreciation A/c	Dr.	(c) No Entry			81,152
To Machinery A/c					81,152
(d) Profit & Loss A/c	Dr.	(d) No Entry			81,152
To Depreciation					81,152
(e) Profit & Loss A/c	Dr.	(e) Interest A/c	Dr.	15,850	
To Interest A/c		To Profit & Loss A/c			15,850

LEDGER ACCOUNTS IN THE BOOK OF A
MACHINES ACCOUNT

Dr. *Cr.*

Date	*Particulars*	₹	*Date*	*Particulars*	₹
01.01.11	To B	7,92,500	31.12.11	By Depreciation A/c	1,58,500
				By Balance c/d	6,34,000
		7,92,500			7,92,500

01.01.12	To Balance b/d	6,34,000	31.12.12	By Depreciation A/c	1,26,800
				By Balance c/d	5,07,200
		6,34,000			6,34,000
01.01.13	To Balance b/d	5,07,200	31.12.13	By Depreciation A/c	1,01,440
				By Balance c/d	4,05,760
		5,07,200			5,07,200
01.01.14	To Balance b/d	4,05,760	31.12.14	By Depreciation A/c	81,152
				By Balance c/d	3,24,608
		4,05,760			4,05,760

Dr. **B 'S ACCOUNT** *Cr.*

Date	*Particulars*	₹	*Date*	*Particulars*	₹
01.01.11	To Bank A/c (Down Payment)	1,58,500	01.01.11	By Machines A/c	7,92,500
31.12.11	To Bank A/c (₹1,58,500 + ₹63,400)	2,21,900	01.01.11	By Interest Suspense A/c	1,58,500
	To Balance c/d	5,70,600			
		9,51,000			9,51,000
31.12.12	To Bank A/c [1,58,500 + 47,550]	2,06,050	01.01.12	By Balance b/d	5,70,600
	To Balance c/d	3,64,550			
		5,70,600			5,70,600
31.12.13	To Bank A/c [1,58,500 + 31,700]	1,90,200	01.01.13	By Balance b/d	3,64,550
	To Balance c/d	1,74,350			
		3,64,550			3,64,550
31.12.14	To Bank A/c [1,58,500 + 15,850]	1,74,350	01.01.14	By Balance b/d	1,74,350
		1,74,350			1,74,350

Dr. **INTEREST SUSPENSE ACCOUNT** *Cr.*

Date	*Particulars*	₹	*Date*	*Particulars*	₹
01.01.11	To B	1,58,500	31.12.11	By Interest A/c	63,400
				By Balance c/d	95,100
		1,58,500			1,58,500
01.01.12	To Balance b/d	95,100	31.12.12	By Interest A/c	47,550
				By Balance c/d	47,550
		95,100			95,100
01.01.13	To Balance b/d	47,550	31.12.13	By Interest A/c	31,700
				By Balance c/d	15,850

		47,550			47,550
01.01.14	To Balance b/d	15,850	31.12.14	By Interest A/c	15,850

AN EXTRACT OF BALANCE SHEET OF A

Liabilities	*1st yr.*	*2nd yr.*	*3rd yr.*	*4th yr.*	*Assets*	*1st yr.* ₹	*2nd yr.* ₹	*3rd yr.* ₹	*4th yr.* ₹
Vendors B	5,70,600	3,64,550	1,74,350	—	**Fixed Assets:**				
Less: Balance in Interest Sus.	95,100	47,550	15,850	—	Machines	7,92,500	7,92,500	7,92,500	7,92,500
					Less: Dep. till date	1,58,500	2,85,300	3,86,740	4,67,892
	4,74,500	3,17,000	1,58,500	—		6,34,000	5,07,200	4,05,760	3,24,608

LEDGER ACCOUNT IN THE BOOKS OF B

Dr. **A'S ACCOUNT** *Cr.*

Date	*Particulars*	₹	*Date*	*Particulars*	₹
01.01.11	To Sales A/c	7,92,500	01.01.11	By Bank A/c	
01.01.11	To Interest Sus. A/c	1,58,500		(Down Payment)	1,58,500
			31.12.11	By Bank A/c	2,21,900
				By Balance c/d	5,70,600
		9,51,000			9,51,000
01.01.12	To Balance b/d	5,70,600	31.12.12	By Bank A/c	2,06,050
				By Balance c/d	3,64,550
		5,70,600			5,70,600
01.01.13	To Balance b/d	3,64,550	31.12.13	By Bank A/c	1,90,200
				By Balance c/d	1,74,350
		3,64,550			3,64,550
01.01.14	To Balance b/d	1,74,350	31.12.14	By Bank A/c	1,74,350

Dr. **INTEREST SUSPENSE ACCOUNT** *Cr.*

Date	*Particulars*	₹	*Date*	*Particulars*	₹
31.12.11	To Interest A/c	63,400	01.01.11	By A	1,58,500
	To Balance c/d	95,100			
		1,58,500			1,58,500
31.12.12	To Interest A/c	47,550	01.01.12	By Balance b/d	95,100
	To Balance c/d	47,550			
		95,100			95,100
31.12.13	To Interest A/c	31,700	01.01.13	By Balance b/d	47,550
	To Balance c/d	15,850			
		47,550			47,550
31.12.14	To Interest A/c	15,850	01.01.14	By Balance b/d	15,850

AN EXTRACT OF BALANCE SHEET OF B

Liabilities	*1st yr.*	*2nd yr.*	*3rd yr.*	*4th yr.*	*Assets*	*1st yr.* ₹	*2nd yr.* ₹	*3rd yr.* ₹	*4th yr.* ₹
					Current Assets:				
					Debtors—A	5,70,600	3,64,550	1,74,350	—
					Less: Balance in Interest Sus. A/c	95,100	47,550	15,850	
						4,75,500	3,17,000	1,58,500	

Working Note:

STATEMENT SHOWING THE CALCULATION OF CASH PRICE AND PERIODIC INTEREST

A *Instalment Number*	*B* *Closing Balance after the payment of instalment*	*C* *Instalment Amount*	*D = B + C* *Closing Balance before the payment of instalment*	*E = D*R/(100 + R)* *Interest D*10/110*	*F = D – E* *Opening Balance*
4th	Nil	1,74,350	1,74,350	15,850	1,58,500
3rd	1,58,500	1,90,200	3,48,700	31,700	3,17,000
2nd	3,17,000	2,06,050	5,23,050	47,550	4,75,500
1st	4,75,500	2,21,900	6,97,400	63,400	6,34,000

Cash Price = ₹ 6,34,000 + 25% of ₹ 6,34,000 (being Down Payment) = ₹ 7,92,500.

ILLUSTRATION 29

On January, 2011 A sells a truck to B, on instalment payment system, on the following conditions:

(a) The purchase price of the truck is ₹ 1,00,000.

(b) This amount is payable to A in four equal annual instalments alongwith 12% interest per annum on the outstanding balance, the first instalment being payable on the date of sale. B, in turn, hires out the truck to A for a monthly charge of ₹ 3,000 per month from 1st January, 2011. The hire charges are to be adjusted at the end of each year, against the amount due to A on account of principal and interest, any difference being settled in cash at the beginning of next year. B charges depreciation @20% p.a. (on the W.D.V. Method) on the truck. All payments are made as per agreement. On 1st January 2014, the truck, is sold by B to A for ₹ 15,000 in cash.

Required: Show in B's books the Truck Account, the Interest Suspense Account, the Hire Charges Account, Interest Account and A's Account.

SOLUTION

Dr. **TRUCK ACCOUNT** *Cr.*

Date	*Particulars*	₹	*Date*	*Particulars*	₹
01.01.11	To A	1,00,000	31.12.11	By Depreciation A/c	20,000
				By Balance c/d	80,000
		1,00,000			1,00,000
01.01.12	To Balance b/d	80,000	31.12.12	By Depreciation A/c	16,000
				By Balance c/d	64,000
		80,000			80,000

01.01.13	To Balance b/d	64,000	31.12.13	By Depreciation A/c	12,800
				By Balance c/d	51,200
		64,000			64,000
01.01.14	To Balance b/d	51,200	01.01.14	By A's A/c	15,000
				By Loss on sale of Truck	36,200
		51,200			51,200

Dr. **INTEREST SUSPENSE ACCOUNT** Cr.

Date	Particulars	₹	Date	Particulars	₹
01.01.11	To A's A/c	18,000	31.12.11	By Interest A/c	9,000
				By Balance c/d	9,000
		18,000			18,000
01.01.12	To Balance b/d	9,000	31.12.12	By Interest A/c	6,000
				By Balance c/d	3,000
		9,000			9,000
01.01.13	To Balance b/d	3,000	31.12.13	By Interest A/c	3,000

Dr. **HIRE CHARGES ACCOUNT** Cr.

Date	Particulars	₹	Date	Particulars	₹
31.12.11	To P & L A/c	36,000	01.01.11	By A's A/c	36,000
31.12.12	To P & L A/c	36,000	01.01.12	By A's A/c	36,000
31.12.13	To P & L A/c	36,000	01.01.13	By A's A/c	36,000

Dr. **INTEREST ACCOUNT** Cr.

Date	Particulars	₹	Date	Particulars	₹
31.12.11	To Interest Suspense A/c	9,000	31.12.11	By P & L A/c	9,000
31.12.12	To Interest Suspense A/c	6,000	31.12.12	By P & L A/c	6,000
31.12.13	To Interest Suspense A/c	3,000	31.12.13	By P & L A/c	3,000

Dr. **A'S ACCOUNT** Cr.

Date	Particulars	₹	Date	Particulars	₹
01.01.11	To Cash A/c	25,000	01.01.11	By Trucks A/c	1,00,000
31.12.11	To Hire Charges A/c	36,000		By Interest Sus. A/c	18,000
31.12.11	To Balance c/d	57,000			
		1,18,000			1,18,000
31.12.12	To Hire Charges A/c	36,000	01.01.12	By Balance b/d	57,000
	To Balance c/d	23,000		By Cash A/c	2,000
		59,000			59,000
31.12.13	To Hire Charges A/c	36,000	01.01.13	By Balance b/d	23,000
				By Cash A/c	5,000
				By Balance c/d	8,000

		36,000			36,000
01.01.14	To Balance b/d	8,000	01.01.14	By Cash A/c	23,000
	To Truck A/c	15,000			
		23,000			23,000

Working Notes:

1.CALCULATION OF INTEREST FOR

2011 on 75,000 @ 12%	₹ 9,000
2012 on 50,000 @ 12%	₹ 6,000
2013 on 25,000 @ 12%	₹ 3,000

2. CASH SETTLEMENT

Particulars	*Principal + Interest Due*	*Hire Charges + Sale Proceeds*	*Amount Received*
on 1.1.2012	25,000 + 9,000 = ₹ 34,000	36,000	₹ 2,000
on 1.1.2013	25,000 + 6,000 = ₹ 31,000	36,000	₹ 5,000
on 1.1.2014	25,000 + 3,000 = ₹ 28,000	36,000 + 15,000	₹ 23,000

13 ACCOUNTING FOR INVESTMENTS

LEARNING OBJECTIVES

After studying this chapter, you should be able to understand:

- ◇ Types of Scrips
- ◇ Fixed Income Bearing Scrips
- ◇ Format of Investment Account
- ◇ Variable Income Bearing Scrips

1.0 PROVISIONS OF AS – 13

WHAT ARE THE AREAS IN WHICH AS – 13 IS NOT APPLICABLE?

1. The bases for recognition of interest, dividends and rentals earned on investments which are covered by Accounting Standard 9 on Revenue Recognition;
2. Operating *or* Finance Leases;
3. Investments of Retirement Benefit Plans and Life Insurance Enterprises; and
4. Mutual Funds and/or the related asset management companies, banks and public financial institutions formed under a Central *or* State Government Act *or* so declared under the Companies Act, 1956.

WHAT IS MEANT BY TERM 'INVESTMENTS'?

Investments are assets held by an enterprise for earning income by way of dividends, interest, and rentals, for capital appreciation, *or* for other benefits to the investing enterprise.

Note: *Assets held as stocks - in - trade are not 'Investments'.*

WHAT IS MEANT THE TERM 'MARKET VALUE'?

Market value is the amount obtainable from the sale of an investment in an open market, net of expenses necessarily to be incurred on *or* before disposals.

WHAT IS MEANT BY THE TERM 'FAIR VALUE'?

Fair value is the amount for which an asset could be exchanged between a knowledgeable, willing buyer and a knowledgeable, wiling seller in an arm's length transaction. Under appropriate circumstances, market value net *or* net realizable value provides an evidence of fair value.

WHAT ARE THE COMPONENTS OF COST OF INVESTMENTS?

Cost of Investments includes:

1. Purchase Price;
2. Acquisition charges such as brokerage, fees and duties.

WHAT SHALL BE COST OF INVESTMENT IF IT IS ACQUIRED WHOLLY *or* PARTLY BY THE ISSUE OF SHARES *or* OTHER SECURITIES?

Cost of Investments = Fair Value of the securities issued (which in appropriate cases may be indicated by the issue price as determined by statutory authorities).

Note: *The fair value may not necessarily be equal to the nominal or par value of the securities issued.*

WHAT SHALL BE THE COST OF INVESTMENTS IF IT IS ACQUIRED IN EXCHANGE *or* PART EXCHANGE, FOR ANOTHER ASSET?

Cost of Investments = Either Fair Value of the asset given up *or* Fair Value of the investment acquired if it is more clearly evident.

WHAT IS THE ACCOUNTING TREATMENT OF INTEREST, DIVIDENDS AND RENTALS EARNED ON INVESTMENTS?

For Pre-acquisition period	• Should be credited to Investments Account
For Post-acquisition period	• Should be credited to Profit & Loss Account

WHAT IS THE COST OF INVESTMENTS WHEN RIGHTS ARE SUBSCRIBED?

Case	Treatment
1. When rights entitlement is received because of existing holding and right shares are subscribed.	The cost of the right shares is added to the carrying amount of the original holding.
2. When rights entitlement is purchased and right shares are subscribed.	Cost incurred in purchasing the rights entitlement *plus* the subscription price of the right shares shall constitute the cost of right share.
3. When rights entitlement is received because of cum-right purchase of investment & right shares are subscribed.	The cost of the right shares is added to the cum-right purchase price of investment.

WHAT SHOULD BE THE ACCOUNTING TREATMENT WHEN RIGHTS ARE SOLD IN THE MARKET?

Case	Treatment
1. When rights entitlement is received because of existing holding and rights entitlement is sold in the market.	The sale proceeds are taken to the Profit and Loss Statement.
2. When rights entitlement is purchased and sold in the market.	Difference between the Purchase Price and Sale Price of the rights sold should be sold in the market.
3. When rights entitlement is received because of cum-right purchase of investment and rights entitlement is sold in the market. (a) Where the market value of investments immediately after their becoming ex-right is lower than the cost for which they were acquired. (b) Where the market value of investments immediately after their becoming ex-right is equal to the cost for which they were acquired.	(a) Sale proceeds of rights up to the reduction in the value of investment should be credited to investment account and balance sale proceeds should be taken to Profit and Loss Statement. (b) Sale Proceeds should be taken to Profit and Loss Statement.

MEANING AND ACCOUNTING TREATMENT OF CURRENT INVESTMENTS

Meaning	A current investment is an investment that is by its nature readily realizable and is intended to be held for not more than one year from the date on which such investment is made.
Carrying	These should be carried **at the lower of cost and fair value** determined amount *either* on an individual investment basis *or* by category of investment, but not an overall (or global) basis.
Reduction & Reversal	Any reduction to fair value and any reversals of such reductions should be debited *or* credited to the Profit and Loss Statement.

MEANING AND ACCOUNTING TREATMENT OF LONG-TERM INVESTMENTS

Meaning	A long-term investment is an investment other than a current investment.
Carrying	These should be carried **at cost**. However, provision for diminution Amount shall be made to recognize a decline, other than temporary, in the value of the investments, such reduction being determined and made for each investment individually.
Reduction	Any reduction in the carrying amount and any reversals of & Reversal such reductions should be charged *or* credited to the Profit and Loss Statement.

MEANING AND ACCOUNTING TREATMENT OF INVESTMENT PROPERTIES

Meaning	An investment property is an investment in land *or* buildings that are not intended to be occupied substantially for use by, *or* in the operations of, the investing enterprise.
Accounting	As long term investments.
Cost of any Shares in a co-operative Society/a Company	The cost of any shares in a co-operative society *or* a company, the holding of which is directly related to the right to hold the estment property, is added to the carrying amount of the investment property.

ACCOUNTING TREATMENT OF OF DISPOSAL OF AN INVESTMENT

The difference between the carrying amount and net disposal proceeds should be **charged *or* credited to the Profit and Loss Statement.**

2.0 TYPES OF SCRIPS

The scrips purchased may be broadly classified into two categories viz. Fixed Income Bearing Scrips and Variable Income Bearing Scrips. A separate Investment Account is prepared for each scrip purchased.

3.0 FIXED INCOME BEARING SCRIPS

MEANING OF FIXED INCOME BEARING SCRIPS

Fixed Income Bearing Scrips include government securities/bonds, other debentures/bonds. Usually, the interest on such scrips is payable on fixed due dates (normally half yearly dates). In case of Registered scrips interest is payable to the registered holder of the scrips on the specified date. In case of Bearer scrips, the interest is payable to the holder of scrips on the specified date.

MEANING OF CUM-INTEREST AND EX-INTEREST

There are two ways of expressing the price quotations of such scrips viz Cum-Interest and Ex-Interest. Cum-Interest quotation includes the interest accrued from the last due date of interest to the date of transaction whereas Ex-Interest quotation does not include such accrued interest. Since the amount towards the cost of investment is to be entered in 'Cost Column' and the amount towards interest is to be entered in 'Interest column' of Investment account, it is always necessary to calculate the interest accrued from the last due date of interest to the date of transaction whether the price quotation is Cum-Interest *or* Ex-Interest. It may be noted that the interest is always calculated with reference to the face value (or nominal value) and the brokerage is always calculated with reference to quotation price (whether Cum-Interest *or* Ex-Interest).

The amount to be entered in 'Cost-Column' and 'Interest Column' may be calculated with the help of the following table:

Price Quotation	*Amount towards Cost ofInvestments to be entered in Cost Column*	*Amount towards Interest to be entered in interest column*
I. In case of Cum-Interest Quotation	C = Cum-Interest price ± Brokerage etc. – Interest	I = [Nominal Value × Rate/100 × *period/12]
II. In case of Ex-Interest Quotation	C = Ex-Interest Price ± Brokerage etc.	I = [Nominal Value × Rate/100 × *Period/12]

** months from the last due date of interest to the date of transaction.*

JOURNAL ENTRIES

The following journal entries are passed to account for various transactions relating to such scrips:

(a) On Purchase of Scrips

Investment A/c (Cost Column)	Dr.	[With the amount paid towards the cost of investments]
Investment A/c (Interest Column)	Dr.	[With the amount paid towards the interest accrued from the last due date of interest to the date of purchase]
To Cash A/c/Bank A/c		[With the total amount paid]

Note: *Cost of Investments = Ex-Interest Price + Brokerage, Securities Transaction Tax etc.*

(b) On Sale of Scrips

Cash A/c/Bank A/c	Dr.	[With the total amount received]
To Investment A/c (Cost Column)		[With the amount received towards the cost of Investments]
To Investment A/c (Interest Column)		[With the amount received towards the interest accrued from the last due date of interest to the date of sale]

Note: *Amount received towards the Cost of Investments = Ex-Interest Price —Brokerage, Securities Transaction Tax etc.*

(c) On receipt of Interest

Cash A/c/Bank A/c	Dr.	[With the interest received]
To Investment A/c (Interest Column)		

(d) On Transfer of the balance in the Interest column

Investment A/c (Interest column) Dr. [With the balance in Interest Column]

To Profit and Loss A/c

(e) On Transfer of the Profit on Sale of Scrip

Investment A/c (Cost Column) Dr. [With the amount of profit on sale]

To Profit and Loss A/c (if the investments are held as 'Current Assets') or,

To Capital Reserve A/c (if the investments are held as 'Fixed assets')

Notes:

(i) Profit on sale = Net Proceeds of Investments sold (towards the cost of investments) (i.e. Ex-interest Price) – Book Value of Investments sold.

(ii) In case of loss on sale, reverse of the above entry will be passed.

(f) On providing depreciation on Investments held as Current Investments where the fair value is lower than the cost

Profit and Loss A/c Dr. [With the excess of Cost over the fair value]

To Investment A/c (Cost Column)

Note: *Where the investments are held as 'Long-Inter Investments', the investments on hand should be valued at cost.*

TUTORIAL NOTES

(i) Unless otherwise stated, the price quotation will be treated as 'Ex-Interest' Quotation in case of government scrips and as 'Cum-interest' quotation in case of other scrips.

(ii) Interest is always calculated with reference to the face value (or nominal value) of the scrip.

(iii) Brokerage and Securities Transaction Tax (STT) are always calculated with reference to the quotation price (Whether Cum-interest or Ex-interest) of the transaction.

(iv) At the end of the accounting period, the investment on hand may be valued on First-in-First-out Method, Last-in First-out method or Average Cost Method.

(v) Generally scrips in India are quoted Cum-Interest/dividend. If the scrips are quoted ex-interest/dividend, the scrips sold/purchased are delivered after the expiry of the 'Record Date' (i.e., the last date fixed by the company for the purpose of payment of interest or dividend. The company makes the payment of interest or dividend only to those persons whose names appear in the Register as on the 'Record Date')

ILLUSTRATION 1

From the following information, calculate the profit *or* loss on sale of debentures and the value of closing balance of debentures if method of valuation is (a) FIFO (b) LIFO and (c) Weighted Average:

1.4.2016	Balance: 100, 12% Debentures of ₹ 100 each @ ₹ 95
5.4.2016	Purchased: 150, 12% Debentures of ₹ 100 each @ ₹ 90 Ex.
6.4.2016	Sold: 200, 12% Debentures of ₹ 100 each @ ₹ 93 Ex.

SOLUTION

Particulars	*FIFO* ₹	*LIFO* ₹	*Weighted Average* ₹
A. Sale Proceeds of 200 Debentures	18,600	18,600	18,600

B. *Less:* Cost of 200 Debentures			
FIFO [100 × ₹ 95) + (100 × ₹ 90)]	18,500	—	—
LIFO: [(150 × ₹ 90) + (50 × ₹ 95)]	—	18,250	—
Weighted Average: $\left[\frac{(100 \times ₹\ 95) + (150 \times ₹\ 90)}{250} \times 200\right]$	—	—	18,400
C. Profit [A – B]	100	350	200
D. Value of Closing Balance			
FIFO: 50 × ₹ 90	4,500	—	—
LIFO : 50 × ₹ 95	—	4,750	—
Weighted Average: $\left[\frac{(100 \times ₹\ 95) + (150 \times ₹\ 90)}{250} \times 50\right]$	—	—	4,600

3.0 FORMAT OF INVESTMENT ACCOUNT

A simple format of 'Investment Account' is given below:

INVESTMENT ACCOUNT...

For the year ending on...

[Here enter the Name of the scrip ....]

Dr. *[Here enter the Due Dates of Fixed Income Bearing Scrip]* *Cr.*

Date	*Particulars*	*Nominal value* ₹	**Interest **Dividend* ₹	*Cost* ₹	*Date*	*Particulars*	*Nominal value* ₹	**Interest **Dividend* ₹	*Cost* ₹
....	To Bal. b/d	....	....	....	....	By Bank A/c	....	....	....
....	To Bank A/c	....	....	....	....	(Sale)			
	(Pur.)					By P&L A/c			
....	To P&L A/c			....	....	(Loss)			....
	(Profit)					By Bank A/c	....	....	....
....	To P&L A/c		....		....	By P&L A/c		....	
	(T/F)					(T/F)			
					....	By Bal. c/d	....	....	....
		....	....	....			....	....	....

**If Investment Account relates to a Fixed income Bearing Scrip.*

***If Investment Account relates to a Variable Income Bearing Scrip.*

ILLUSTRATION 2

Mr. Investor furnishes the following details relating to his holding in 16% Debentures (₹ 100 each) of Y Ltd. held as current assets:

01.01.2013	Opening Balance—Face Value ₹ 60,000, Cost ₹ 59,000.

01.03.2013	100 Debentures purchased ex-interest at ₹ 98.
01.07.2013	Sold 200 Debentures ex-interest at ₹ 100.
01.10.2013	Purchased 50 Debentures at ₹ 98 cum-interest.
01.11.2013	Sold 200 Debentures ex-interest at ₹ 99.

Interest dates are 30th September and 31st March. Mr. Investor closes his books every 31st December. Brokerage @ 1% is to be paid for each transaction.

Required: Show the Investment Account as it would appear in his books. FIFO Method is to be assumed. Market Value of a 16% Debentures of Y Ltd on 31.12.2013 ₹ 99.

SOLUTION

INVESTMENT ACCOUNT FOR THE YEAR ENDING ON 31ST DECEMBER 2013
[SCRIP: 16% DEBENTURES OF Y LTD.]

Dr. *[Interest Payable on 31st March and 30th September]* *Cr.*

Date	*Particulars*	*Nominal value* ₹	*Interest* ₹	*Cost* ₹	*Date*	*Particulars*	*Nominal value* ₹	*Interest* ₹	*Cost* ₹
01.01.13	To Bal. b/d	60,000	2,400	59,000	31.03.13	By Bank A/c	—	5,600	—
01.03.13	To Bank A/c	10,000	667	9,898	01.07.13	By Bank A/c	20,000	800	19,800
01.07.13	To P & L A/c	—	—	133	30.09.13	By Bank A/c	—	4,000	—
01.10.13	To Bank A/c	5,000	—	4,949	01.11.13	By Bank A/c	20,000	267	19,602
31.12.13	To P & L A/c	—	—		01.11.13	By P&L A/c	—	—	64
	(Transfer)		9,000	—	31.12.13	By Bal. c/d	35,000	1,400	34,514
		75,000	12,067	73,980			75,000	12,067	73,980

Working Notes:

(i) *Cost of 100 Debentures purchased on 1st March*

= 100 × ₹ 98 + 1% of ₹ 9,800 = ₹ 9,898

(ii) *Sale Proceeds of 200 Debentures sold on 1st July*

= 200 × ₹ 100 – 1% of ₹ 20,000 = ₹ 19,800

(iii) *Cost of 50 Debentures purchased on 1st Oct.*

= 50 × ₹ 98 + 1% of ₹ 4,900 = ₹ 4,949

(iv) *Sale Proceeds of 200 Debentures on 1st Nov.*

= 200 × ₹ 99 – 1% of ₹ 19,800 = ₹ 19,602

(v) *Profit on sale of 200 Debentures on 1.7.20 X 1*

= Sale Proceeds – Book Value = (₹ 19,800) – (₹ 59,000 × 200/600) = ₹ 133.

(vi) *Loss on sale of 200 Debentures on 1.11.2013*

= Book Value – Sale Proceeds = (₹ 59,000 × 200/600) – ₹ 19,602 = ₹ 64.

ILLUSTRATION 3

Madhuri Dixit purchased on 1st March, 2013 ₹ 24,000 5% Bharat Debenture Stock @ 90 cum-interest, interest being payable on 31st March and 30th September each year. Stamp and expenses on purchase amounted to ₹ 20 and brokerage @ 2% was charged on cost; interest for the half-year was received on the due date. On 1st September ₹ 10,000 of the stock was sold @ 92 ex-interest *less* brokerage @ 2%. On 30th September, ₹ 8,000 stock was purchased @ 91 ex-interest *plus* brokerage @ 2% and charges ₹ 10. On 1st December, ₹ 6,000 stock was sold @ 94 cum interest *less* brokerage @ 2%. The market price of stock on 31st December was 88.5%. Show the Investment Account for the year ending on 31st December, 2013 assuming FIFO Method. Calculation should be made in the multiple of rupee. Madhuri Dixit holds the Bharat Debenture Stock as a current asset.

SOLUTION

INVESTMENT ACCOUNT FOR THE YEAR ENDING ON 31ST DECEMBER 2013
[SCRIP: 5% BHARAT DEBENTURE STOCK]

Dr. *[Interest Payable on 31st March and 30th September]* *Cr.*

Date	Particulars	Nominal value ₹	Interest ₹	Cost ₹	Date	Particulars	Nominal value ₹	Interest ₹	Cost ₹
01.03.13	To Bank A/c	24,000	500	21,552	31.03.13	By Bank A/c [₹ 24,000 × 5% × 6/12]	—	600	—
01.09.13	To P & L A/c	–	–	36					
30.09.13	To Bank A/c	8,000	200	7,436					
30.09.13	To P & L A/c	–	–	89	01.09.13	By Bank A/c	10,000	208	9,016
31.12.13	To P & L A/c	—	908	—	30.09.13	By Bank A/c [₹ 22,000 × 5% × 6/12]	—	550	—
					01.12.13	By Bank A/c	6,000	50	5,477
					31.12.13	By P & L A/c (Loss)	—	—	460
					31.12.13	By Bal.c/d	16,000	200	14,160
		32,000	1,608	29,113			32,000	1,608	29,113

Working Notes:

(i) *Cost of Debenture Stock purchased on 1st March*

= 90% of ₹ 24,000 + 2% of ₹ 21,600 + ₹ 20 – ₹ 500 (Interest) = ₹ 21,552

(ii) *Sale proceeds of Debentures Stock sold on 1st Sept.*

= 92% of ₹ 10,000 – 2% of ₹ 9,200 = ₹ 9,016

(iii) *Profit on Sale on 1st Sept.*

= ₹ 9,016 – (₹ 21,552 × 100/240) = ₹ 36

(iv) *Cost of Debentures Stock purchased on 30th Sept.*

= 91% of ₹ 8,000 + 2% of ₹ 7,280 + ₹ 10 = ₹ 7,436

(v) *Sale Proceeds of Debentures Stock sold*

= 94% of ₹ 6,000 – 2% of ₹ 5,640 – ₹ 50 (Interest) = ₹ 5,477

(vi) *Profit on Sale on 30th Sept.*

₹ 5,477 – (₹ 21552 × 60/240) = ₹ 89

(VII) VALUATION OF CLOSING BALANCE OF DEBENTURES STOCK ON FIFO BASIS:

Particulars	Nominal Value ₹	Actual Cost ₹	Market Value ₹
Balance out of March Purchase	8,000	7,184	7,080

Balance out of Sept. Purchase	8,000	7,436	7,080
	16,000	14,620	14,160

Closing Balance has been valued at ₹ 14,160 being lower than the actual cost.

(viii) Interest accrued on 31st Dec. = ₹ 16,000 × 5% × 3/12 = ₹ 200.

ILLUSTRATION 4

X Ltd. purchased on 1st May, 2013, 13.5% Convertible Debentures in Y Ltd. of face value of ₹ 5,00,000 @ 105 ex, Interest on the Debentures is payable each year on 31st March and 30th September. The accounting year is the calender year. The following other transactions were entered into during 2013.

Aug. 1	Purchased ₹, 2,50,000 Debentures @ 107 cum interest.
Oct. 1	Sale of ₹ 2,00,000 Debentures @ 103.
Dec. 31	Receipt of 10,000 Equity Shares in Y Ltd. of ₹ 10 each in conversion of 20% of the Debentures held, alongwith interest on Debentures converted.

The market price of a Debenture and an Equity shares in Y Ltd. at the end of 2013 was ₹ 106 and ₹ 15 respectively.

Required: Prepare the Debentures Investment Account in the books of X Ltd. on Average cost basis. (X Ltd. held the Debentures as current asset)

SOLUTION

INVESTMENT ACCOUNT FOR THE YEAR ENDING ON 31ST DECEMBER, 2013
[SCRIP: 13.5% CONVERTIBLE DEBENTURES IN X LTD.]

Dr. *[Interest Payable on 31st March and 30th September]* *Cr.*

Date	Particulars	Nominal value ₹	Interest ₹	Cost ₹	Date	Particulars	Nominal value ₹	Interest ₹	Cost ₹
01.05.13	To Bank A/c	5,00,000	5,625	5,25,000	30.09.13	By Bank A/c [₹ 7,50,000 × 13.5% × 6/12]	—	50,625	—
01.08.13	To Bank A/c	2,50,000	11,250	2,56,250	01.10.13	By Bank A/c	2,00,000	—	2,06,000
31.12.13	To P & L A/c (Interest)	—	52,313	—	01.10.13	By P & L A/c		2,333	
					31.12.13	By Equity's shares in Y L.	1,10,000		1,14,583
					31.12.13	By Bank A/c (Interest) (on Convertible Debentures)		3,713	
					31.12.13	By Bal. c/d	4,40,000	14,850	4,58,334
		7,50,000	69,188	7,81,250			7,50,000	69,188	7,81,250

Working Notes:

(i) *Cost of Debentures purchased on 1st Aug.*

= 107% of ₹ 2,50,000 – ₹ 11,250 (Interest) = ₹ 2,56,250

(ii) *Cost of Debentures sold on 1st Oct.*

= (₹ 5,25,000 + ₹ 2,56,250) × 2,00,000/7,50,000 = ₹ 2,08,333

(iii) *Loss on sale of Debentures* = ₹ 2,08,333 – ₹ 2,06,000 = ₹ 2,333

(iv) *Cost of Debentures converted.*

= (₹ 5,25,000 + ₹ 2,56,250) × 1,10,000/7,50,000 = ₹ 1,14,583

(v) *Cost of Debentures in hand on 31st Dec.*

= (₹ 5,25,000 + ₹ 2,56,250) × 4,40,000/7,50,000 = ₹ 4,58,334

(vi) *Interest on Debentures converted* = ₹ 1,10,000 × 13.5% × 3/12 = ₹ 3,713

(vii) Closing balance of Debentures has been valued at cost being lower than the market value (₹ 4,40,000 × 106%)

ILLUSTRATION 5

Bonanza Limited held on 1st April, 2013, ₹ 2,00,000 of 9% Government Loan (2009) at ₹ 1,90,000., (Face Value of Loan ₹ 100 each): Three month's interest had accrued on the above data. On 31st May, the company purchased the same Government Loan of the face value of ₹ 80,000 at ₹ 95 (net) cum-interest. On 1st June, ₹ 60,000 face value of the loan was sold at ₹ 94 (net) ex-interest. Interest on the loan was paid each year on 30th June and 31st December and was credited by the bank on the same date. On 30th November, ₹ 40,000 face value of the Loan was sold at ₹ 97 (net) cum-interest. On 1st December, the company purchased the same loan ₹ 10,000 at par ex-interest. On 1st March, the company sold ₹ 10,000 face value of the loan at ₹ 95 ex-interest. The market price of the loan on 31st March, 2014 was ₹ 96.

Required: Draw up the 9% Government Loan (20X5) Account in the books of Bonanza Limited. First in first out method shall be followed and the balance of the loan held by the company shall be valued at cost *or* market price whichever is lower. Calculation shall be made to the nearest rupee *or* multiple thereof.

SOLUTION

INVESTMENT ACCOUNT FOR THE YEAR ENDING ON 31ST MARCH, 2014
[SCRIP: 9% GOVERNMENT LOAN (2009)]

Dr. *[Interest payable on 30th June and 31st December]* *Cr.*

Date	*Particulars*	*Nominal value ₹*	*Interest ₹*	*Cost ₹*	*Date*	*Particulars*	*Nominal value ₹*	*Interest ₹*	*Cost ₹*
01.04.13	To Bal. b/d	2,00,000	4,500	1,90,000	01.06.13	By Bank A/c	60,000	2,250	56,400
31.05.13	To Bank A/c	80,000	3,000	73,000	30.06.13	By Bank A/c (2,20,000 × 9% × 6/12)	—	9,900	—
01.12.13	To Bank A/c	10,000	375	10,000					
31.03.14	To P & L A/c (Interest transferred)	—	18,525	—					
					30.11.13	By Bank A/c	40,000	1,500	37,300
					31.12.13	By Bank A/c	—	8,550	—
					01.03.14	By Bank A/c	10,000	150	9,500
					31.03.14	By P & L A/c (Loss on sale) [W.N. (iv)]	—	—	1,300
					31.03.14	By Bal. c/d [W.N. (v)&(vi)]	1,80,000	4,050	1,68,500
		2,90,000	26,400	2,73,000			2,90,000	26,400	2,73,000

Working Notes:

(i) Interest accrued on 1st April 2013 = ₹ 2,00,000 × 9% × 3/12 = ₹ 4,500

(ii) Cost of 9% Govt. Loan sold = ₹ 1,90,000 × 1,10,000/2,00,000 = ₹ 1,04,500

(iii) Sale Proceeds of 9% Govt. Loan sold = ₹ 56,400 + ₹ 37,300 + ₹ 9,500 = ₹ 1,03,200

(iv) Loss on sale of 9% Govt. Loan = ₹ 1,04,500 – ₹ 1,03,200 = ₹ 1,300

(V) VALUATION OF CLOSING BALANCE OF 9% GOVT. LOAN

Particulars	*Nominal Value* ₹	*Actual Cost* ₹	*Market Value* ₹
Balance out of opening stock	90,000	85,500	86,400
Balance out of May 2013 purchase	80,000	73,000	76,800
Balance out of Dec. 2013 purchase	10,000	10,000	9,600
	1,80,000	1,68,500	1,72,800

Closing Balance has been valued at cost being lower than the market value.

(vi) Interest accrued on 31.03.2014 = ₹ 1,80,000 × 9% × 3/12 = ₹ 4,050.

4.0 VARIABLE INCOME BEARING SCRIPS

MEANING OF VARIABLE INCOME BEARING SCRIPS

Variable Income Bearing Scrips refer to those scrips on which income is not fixed and include equity shares.

JOURNAL ENTRIES

The following journal entries are passed to account for various transactions relating to such scrips:

(a) On Purchase of Scrips

Investment A/c (Cost Column)	Dr.	[With the amount paid]
To Cash A/c/Bank A/c		

Notes:

(i) *Amount paid = Quotation Price + Brokerage etc.*

(ii) *The amount of dividend accruing between the date of last dividend payment and the date of purchase can not be immediately ascertained and hence not accounted for.*

(b) On Receipt of Dividend

Bank A/c	Dr.	[With total dividend received]
To Investment A/c (Cost Column)		[With the amount of dividend for the period for which the shares were not held by the investor, being a capital receipt]
To Investment A/c (Dividend column)		[With the amount of dividend for the post-acquisition period]

TUTORIAL NOTES

(i) *The Dividend received for a particular period is assumed to be evenly distributed over that period.*

(ii) *The dividend for the pre-acquisition period is treated as capital receipt and hence entered in 'Cost column' of Investment Account on the credit side.*

(iii) *The dividend for the post-acquisition period is treated as a revenue receipt and hence entered in 'Dividend Column' of Investment Account on the credit side.*

(c) On Sale of Scrips

Cash A/c /Bank A/c Dr. [With the amount received]

To Investment A/c (Cost column)

Notes:

(i) Amount received = Quotation Price – Brokerage etc.

(ii) The amount of dividend accruing between the date of last dividend payment and the date of sale can not be immediately ascertained and hence not accounted for.

(d) On Receipt of Bonus Shares.

The nominal value of 'Bonus Shares' is entered on the debit side in the 'Nominal column' of Investment Account. No amount is entered in the 'Cost Column' of Investment Account since the investor has not paid anything. It may be noted that bonus shares are entitled to prorata dividend from the date of their issue.

(e) On Subscription for Right Shares.

The nominal value and the cost of 'Right Shares' are entered on the debit side in the 'Nominal Column' and 'Cost column' of Investment Account respectively. It may be noted that right shares are entitled to prorata dividend from the date of their issue

(f)On Sale of Rights

The price realised by sale of rights is entered on the credit side in the 'Dividend/Income column' of the Investment Account. No amount is entered in the 'Nominal Column' of the Investment Account since the rights have been sold and not the shares.

ILLUSTRATION 6

On 1.1.2013, Sri Devi purchased 500 Equity Shares of ₹ 100 each in Reliance Ltd. @ ₹ 120 each Brokerage, Securities Transaction Tax etc. 2.5%. On 30.11.2013 bonus was declared in the ratio of 1:2. Before and after the record date of bonus shares, the shares were quoted at ₹ 175 per share and ₹ 90 per share. On 31.12.2013 Sri Devi sold bonus shares.Brokerage, Securities Transction Tax etc 2%. Shares are valued at average cost.

Required: Show the Investment Account in the books of Sri Devi who held the shares as current assets.

SOLUTION

INVESTMENT ACCOUNT FOR THE YEAR ENDING ON 31ST DECEMBER, 2013
[SCRIP: EQUITY SHARES OF RELIANCE LTD.]

Dr. *Cr.*

Date	*Particulars*	*Nominal value* ₹	*Cost* ₹	*Date*	*Particulars*	*Nominal value* ₹	*Cost* ₹
01.01.13	To Bank A/c	50,000	61,500	31.12.13	By Bank A/c	25,000	22,050
30.11.13	To Bonus Shares	25,000	—	31.12.13	By Balance c/d	50,000	41,000
31.12.13	To P & L A/c	—	1,550				
		75,000	63,050			75,000	63,050

Working notes:

(i) *Cost of Equity Shares purchased on 1st Jan*

= (500 × ₹ 120) + (2.5% of ₹ 60,000) = ₹ 61,500

(ii) *Sale proceeds of Equity shares sold on 31st Dec.*

= 250 × ₹ 90 – 2% of ₹ 22,500 = ₹ 22,050

(iii) *Profit on sale of Bonus shares on 31st Dec.*

= Sale Proceeds – Average cost = ₹ 22,050 – (₹ 61,500 × 25,000/75,000) = ₹ 1,550

(iv) *Valuation of Equity Shares on 31st Dec.*

Cost = (₹ 61,500 × 50,000/75,000) = ₹ 41,000,

Market Value = 500 × ₹ 90 = ₹ 45,000

Closing Balance has been valued at ₹ 41,000 being lower than the market value.

ILLUSTRATION 7

On 1st Jan. 2013, Singh had 20,000 equity shares in X Ltd. as current assets. Face value of the shares was ₹ 10 each but their book value was ₹ 16 per share. On 1st June 2013, Singh purchased 5,000 more equity shares in the company at a premium of ₹ 4 per share.

On 30th June, 2013, the Directors of X Ltd. announced a bonus and rights issue. Bonus was declared at the rate of one equity share for every five shares held and these shares were received on 2nd August, 2013. The terms of the rights issue were:

(a) Rights shares to be issued to the existing holders on 10th August, 2013. [Record Date 2.6.2013

(b) Rights issue would entitle the holders to subscribe for additional equity shares in the Company at the rate of one share per every three held at ₹ 15 per share-the whole sum being payable by 30th September, 2013.

(c) Existing shareholders may, to the extent of their entitlement, either wholly in *or* part, transfer their rights to outsiders.

(d) Singh exercised his option under the issue for 50% of his entitlements and the balance of rights he sold to Ananth for a consideration of ₹ 1.50 per share.

(e) Dividends for the year ending on 31st March, 2013, at the rate of 15% were declared by the Company and received by Singh on 20th October, 2013. [Record Date 2.6.2013]

(f) On 1st November, 2013, Singh sold 20,000 equity shares at a premium of ₹ 3 per share.

Required: Show the Investment Account as it would appear in Singh's books as on 31.12.2013 and the value of shares held on that date. (Market Price on 31.12. 2013 ₹ 13). Share are valued at average cost.

SOLUTION

INVESTMENT ACCOUNT FOR THE YEAR ENDING ON 31ST DECEMBER, 2013 [SCRIP: EQUITY SHARES IN X LTD.]

Dr. *Cr.*

Date	Particulars	Nominal value ₹	Divnd. ₹	Cost ₹	Date	Particulars	Nominal value ₹	Divnd. ₹	Cost ₹
01.01.13	To Bal. b/d	2,00,000	—	3,20,000	30.09.13	By Bank			
01.06.13	To Bank A/c	50,000	—	70,000		(Sale of rights)			
02.08.13	To Bonus Issue	50,000	—	—		(5,000 @			
30.09.13	To Bank					₹ 1.50)	—	7,500	–

	(Right)	50,000	—	75,000	20.10.13	By Bank A/c (Dividend)	—	30,000	7,500
01.11.13	To P & L A/c (transfer)		37,500	—	01.11.13	By Bank A/c	2,00,000		2,60,000
						By P & L A/c			1,429
					31.12.13	By Bal. c/d	1,50,000		1,95,000
						By P & L A/c			1,071
		3,50,000	37,500	4,65,000			3,50,000	37,500	4,65,000
01.01.13	To Bal. b/d	1,50,000		1,95,000					

Working Notes:

(i) Sale-proceeds of the rights being of revenue nature have been entered in the Dividend column of the Investment Account on the credit side as per AS 13.

(ii) Dividend received on 5,000 equity shares purchased on 1st June is for the period for which the shares were not held by the Investor and hence treated as of capital nature. Thus, such dividend being of capital nature has been entered in the Cost Column of the Investment Account on the credit side.

(iii) Net cost of 35,000 shares

= ₹ 3,20,000 + ₹ 70,000 + ₹ 75,000 – ₹ 7,500 = ₹ 4,57,500

(iv) Net cost of 20,000 shares sold = ₹ 4,57,500 × 20,000/35,000 = ₹ 2,61,429

(v) Loss on sale of 20,000 shares = ₹ 2,60,000 – ₹ 2,61,429 = ₹ 1,429

(vi) Valuation of 15,000 shares as on 31st Dec.

Cost (₹ 4,57,500 × 15,000/35,000) = ₹ 1,96,071,

Market Value = 15,000 × ₹ 13 = ₹ 1,95,000

Closing balance has been valued at ₹ 1,95,000 since the market value lower than the cost.

ILLUSTRATION 8

On 1.4.2013, Sundar has 25,000 equity shares of 'X' Ltd. at a book value of ₹ 15 per share (Face value ₹ 10). On 20th June, he purchased another 5,000 shares of the company @ ₹ 16 per share. The directors of 'X' Ltd. announced a bonus and rights issue. No dividend was payable on these issues. The terms of the issue are as follows:

Bonus basis 1:6 (Date 16th Aug.).

Rights basis 3:7 (Date 31st Aug.) Price ₹ 15 per share.

Due date for payment 30th Sept.

Shareholders can transfer their rights in full *or* in part. Accordingly, Sundar sold 33-1/3% of his entitlement of Sekhar for a consideration of ₹ 2 per share.

Dividends: Dividends for the year ended 31st March at the rate of 20% were declared by X Ltd. and received by Sundar on 31st Oct. Dividends for shares acquired by him on 20th June are to be adjusted against the cost of purchase.

On 15th Nov., Sundar sold 25,000 equity shares at a premium of ₹ 5 per share.

Required: Prepare in the books of Sundar: (a) Investment Account and (b) Profit & Loss Account For your exercise, assume that the books are closed on 31.12.2013 and shares are valued at average cost.

SOLUTION

INVESTMENT ACCOUNT FOR THE YEAR ENDING ON 31ST DEC. 2013 [EQUITY SHARES IN X LTD.]

Dr. *Cr.*

Date	Particulars	Nominal value ₹	Divnd. ₹	Amt. ₹	Date	Particulars	Nominal value ₹	Divnd. ₹	Amt. ₹
01.04.13	To Bal b/d	2,50,000		3,75,000	30.09.13	By Bank A/c			
20.06.13	To Bank A/c	50,000		80,000		(Sale of rights)		10,000	
16.08.13	To Bonus	50,000		—	31.10.13	By Bank A/c			10,000
30.09.13	To Bank A/c	1,00,000		1,50,000		(divnd. on			
	(Right shares)					share acquired			
						on 20th June)			
					31.10.13	By Bank A/c		50,000	
15.11.13	To P & L A/c			44,444	15.11.13	By Bank A/c			
						(Sale of share)	2,50,000		3,75,000
					31.12.13	By Bal. c/d	2,00,000		2,64,444
31.12.13	To P & L A/c		60,000						
		4,50,000	60,000	6,49,444			4,50,000	60,000	6,49,444

PROFIT & LOSS ACCOUNT

Dr. *Cr.*

Particulars	₹	Particulars	₹
To Balance c/d	1,00,000	By Investment A/c	50,000
		By Dividend	50,000
	1,00,000		1,00,000

Working Notes:

(i) Bonus Shares : $\frac{(25,000+5,000)}{6} = 5,000$ shares

(ii) Rights shares : $\frac{(25,000+5,000+5,000)}{7} \times 3 = 15,000$ shares

(iii) Rights shares renounced = [15,000 × 1/3] = 5,000 shares

(iv) Dividend received [25,000 × 10 × 20%] = ₹ 50,000

Dividend on share purchased on 20th June = 5,000 × 10 × 20% = ₹ 10,000 adjusted to Investment A/c

(v) Cost of shares on 31st Dec.

$$= \frac{(3,75,000+80,000+1,50,000+10,000)}{45,000} \times 20,000 = ₹2,64,444$$

ILLUSTRATION 9

The following transactions of COJIH Investment Ltd. took place during the year ended 31st March, 2014:

2013	
1st April	Purchased ₹ 12,00,000 8% bonds @ ₹ 80.5 cum-interest. Interest is payable on 1st November and 1st May.
12th April	Purchased 1,00,000 equity shares of ₹ 10 each in X Ltd. for ₹ 40,00,000.

1st May	Received half year's interest on 8% bonds.
15th May	X Ltd. made a bonus issue of three equity shares for every two held. Investor Ltd. sold 1,25,000 bonus shares @ ₹ 20 each.
1st July	Purchased 50,000 equity shares of ₹ 10 each in C Ltd. @ ₹ 7.75 each.
1st October	Sold ₹ 3,00,000 8% bonds @ ₹ 81 ex-interest.
1st November	Received half year's bond interest.
1st December	Received 18% dividend on equity shares in X Ltd.
2014	
1st January	C Ltd. made a rights issue of one equity share for every two held @ ₹ 5 per share. Rights sold in the market @ ₹ 2.25 per share.
1st March	Received 12.5% dividend on equity shares in C Ltd.

Required: Prepare the relevant investment accounts in the books of Investor Ltd. for the year ended 31st March, 2014. (Shares are valued at average cost)

SOLUTION

Dr. **8% BOND ACCOUNT** *Cr.*

Date	*Particulars*	*Nominal value* ₹	*Interest* ₹	*Cost* ₹	*Date*	*Particulars*	*Nominal value* ₹	*Interest* ₹	*Cost* ₹
2013					2013				
Apr.1	To Bank A/c	12,00,000	40,000	9,26,000	Mar 1	By Bank A/c	—	48,000	—
2014					Oct 1	By Bank A/c	3,00,000	10,000	2,43,000
Mar. 31	To P&L A/c (Interest)	—	84,000	—	Nov 1	By Bank A/c	—	36,000	—
					2014				
	To P&L A/c (Profit on Sale)	—	—	11,500	Mar. 31	By Bal. c/d	9,00,000	30,000	6,94,500
		12,00,000	1,24,000	9,37,500			12,00,000	1,24,000	9,37,500

Dr. **EQUITY SHARES IN X LTD.** *Cr.*

Date	*Particulars*	*Nominal value* ₹	*Dividend* ₹	*Cost* ₹	*Date*	*Particulars*	*Nominal value* ₹	*Dividend* ₹	*Cost* ₹
2013					2013				
April 12	To Bank A/c	10,00,000	—	40,00,000	May 15	By Bank A/c	12,50,000	—	25,00,000
May 15	To Bonus Issue A/c	15,00,000	—	—	Dec 1	By Bank A/c (Dividend)	—	2,25,000	—
2014					2014				
Mar 31	To P&L A/c (Divndend)	—	2,25,000	—	Mar 31	By Balance c/d	12,50,000	—	20,00,000
Mar 31	To P&L A/c (Profit on sale)	—	—	5,00,000					
		25,00,000	2,25,000	45,00,000			25,00,000	2,25,000	45,00,000

Dr. **EQUITY SHARES IN C LTD.** Cr.

Date	Particulars	Nominal value ₹	Dividend ₹	Cost ₹	Date	Particulars	Nominal value ₹	Dividend ₹	Cost ₹
2013					2014				
July 1	To Bank A/c	5,00,000	—	3,87,500	Jan 1	By Bank A/c (sale of right)		56,250	
2014									
Mar 31	To P & L A/c (Dividend)	—	1,18,750	—	Mar 1	By Bank A/c (Dividend)		62,500	
					Mar 31	By Bal. c/d.	5,00,000		3,87,500
		5,00,000	1,18,750	3,87,500			5,00,000	1,18,750	3,87,500

Working Note: *Calculation of Profit on Sale*

A. Cost per share after Bonus = ₹ 16

B. Profit = [(₹ 20 – ₹ 16) x 1,25,000] = ₹ 5,00,000

SOLVED PROBLEMS

PROBLEM 1

MY Ltd. had acquired 200 equity shares of YZ Ltd. at ₹105 per share on 1st Jan and paid ₹ 200 towards brokerage, stamp duty and STT. On 31st March, shares of YZ Ltd. were traded at ₹110 per share. At what value investment is to be shown in the Balance Sheet of MY Ltd. as at 31st March.

SOLUTION

Particulars	₹
Purchase Price of Equity shares of YZ Ltd. (200 shares x ₹105 per share)	21,000
Add: Brokerage, stamp duty and STT	200
Cost of investment	21,200

If the investment is a long term investment than it will be shown at cost. Therefore value of investment will be ₹ 21,200. However, if the investment is a current investment, then it will be shown at lower of cost (i.e. ₹ 21,200) *or* net realizable value (i.e. ₹ 200 x 110 = ₹ 22,000). Therefore value of investment will be ₹ 21,200.

PROBLEM 2

On 1st April, 2012, Mr. Neel purchased 5,000 equity shares of ₹100 each in X Ltd. @ ₹120 each from a Broker, who charged 2% brokerage. He incurred ½% as cost of shares transfer stamps. On 31st January, 2013, Bonus was declared in the ratio of 1:2. Before and after the record date of bonus shares, the shares were quoted at ₹175 per share and ₹90 per share respectively. On 31st March, 2013, Mr. Neel sold bonus shares to a broker, who charged 2% brokerage. Show the Investment Account in the books of Mr. Neel, who held the shares as current assets and closing value of investments shall be made at cost *or* Market value, whichever is lower.

SOLUTION

INVESTMENT ACCOUNT IN THE BOOKS OF MR. NEEL

for the year ended 31st March, 2013

Dr. **(SCRIP: EQUITY SHARES OF X LTD.)** Cr.

Date	Particulars	Nominal value ₹	Cost ₹	Date	Particulars	Nominal value ₹	Cost ₹
1.4.2012	To Bank A/c	5,00,000	6,15,000	31.3.2013	By Bank A/c	2,50,000	2,20,500
31.01.2013	To Bonus Shares	2,50,000	—	31.3.2013	By Balance c/d	5,00,000	4,10,000
31.03.2013	To P & LA/c	—	15,500				
		7,50,000	6,30,500			7,50,000	6,30,500

Working Notes:

(i) *Calculation of Cost of Equity Shares purchased*

= (5,000 × ₹120) + (2% of ₹6,00,000) + (½% of ₹6,00,000) = ₹6,15,000

(ii) *Calculation of Sale Proceeds of Equity Shares sold*

= (2,500 × ₹90) – (2% of ₹2,25,000) = ₹2,20,500

(iii) *Calculation of Profit on Sale of Bonus Shares*

= Sale proceeds – Average cost

$$= 2{,}20{,}500 - \left(6{,}15{,}000 \times \frac{2{,}50{,}000}{7{,}50{,}000}\right) = ₹15{,}500$$

(iv) *Valuation of equity shares at the end*

$$\text{Cost} = 6{,}15{,}000 \times \frac{5{,}00{,}000}{7{,}50{,}000} = ₹4{,}10{,}000$$

Market value = 5,000 shares × ₹90 = ₹4,50,000

Closing Balance has been valued at ₹4,10,000 i.e. at cost which is lower than the market value.

PROBLEM 3

On 01-04-2012, Mr. T. Shakharan purchased 5,000 equity shares of ₹ 100 each in V Ltd. @ ₹ 120 each from a broker, who charged 2% brokerage. he incurred 50 paisa per ₹ 100 as cost of shares transfer stamps. On 31-01-2013 bonus was declared in the ratio of 1 : 2. Before and after the record date of bonus shares, the shares were quoted at ₹ 175 per share and ₹ 90 per share respectively. On 31-02-02013, Mr. T. Shekharan sold bonus shares to a broker, who charged 2% brokerage.
Show the Investment Account in the books of T. Shekharan, who held the shares as Current Assets and closing value of investments shall be made at cost *or* market value whichever is lower.

SOLUTION

INVESTMENT ACCOUNT

for the year ended 31st March, 2013

Dr. **(SCRIP: EQUITY SHARES OF V LTD.)** Cr.

Date	Particulars	Nominal value ₹	Cost ₹	Date	Particulars	Nominal value ₹	Cost ₹
1.4.2012	To Bank A/c	5,00,000	6,15,000	31.3.2013	By Bank A/c	2,50,000	2,20,500

31.01.2013	To Bonus Shares	2,50,000	—	31.3.2013	By Balance c/d	5,00,000	4,10,000
31.03.2013	To P & LA/c	—	15,500				
		7,50,000	6,30,500			7,50,000	6,30,500

Working Notes:

(i) *Calculation of Cost of Equity Shares purchased*

$= (5{,}000 \times ₹120) + (2\% \text{ of } ₹6{,}00{,}000) + (\frac{1}{2}\% \text{ of } ₹6{,}00{,}000) = ₹6{,}15{,}000$

(ii) *Calculation of Sale Proceeds of Equity Shares sold*

$= (2{,}500 \times ₹90) - (2\% \text{ of } ₹2{,}25{,}000) = ₹2{,}20{,}500$

(iii) *Calculation of Profit on Sale of Bonus Shares*

= Sale proceeds – Average cost

$$= 2{,}20{,}500 - \left(6{,}15{,}000 \times \frac{2{,}50{,}000}{7{,}50{,}000}\right) = ₹15{,}500$$

(iv) *Valuation of equity shares at the end*

$$\text{Cost} = 6{,}15{,}000 \times \frac{5{,}00{,}000}{7{,}50{,}000} = ₹4{,}10{,}000$$

Market value = 5,000 shares × ₹90 = ₹4,50,000

Closing Balance has been valued at ₹4,10,000 i.e. at cost which is lower than the market value.

PROBLEM 4

H purchased 500 equity shares of ₹ 100 each in the ABC Company Limited for ₹ 62,500 inclusive of brokerage and stamp duty. Some years later the company decided to capitalise its profit and to issue to the holders of equity shares one equity shares one equity share as Bonus for every equity share held by them. Prior to capitalization, the shares of ABC Company Limited were quoted at ₹ 175 per share. After the capitalization, the shares were quoted at ₹ 92.50 per share. H sold the Bonus shares and received ₹ 90 per share. Show Investment A/c in H's books on average cost basis as per AS 13.

SOLUTION

Dr. **INVESTMENT ACCOUNT (EQUITY SHARES OF ABC CO. LTD.)** *Cr.*

Particulars	*Nominal value* ₹	*Cost* ₹	*Particulars*	*Nominal value* ₹	*Cost* ₹
To Balance b/d*	50,000	62,500	By Bank A/c	50,000	45,000
To Bonus Shares A/c	50,000	–	By Balance c/d	50,000	31,250
To Profit & Loss A/c		13,750			
(Profit on sale)					
	1,00,000	76,250		1,00,000	76,250

Working Notes:

(i) Profit on sale of bonus shares = (₹ 45,000 – (₹ 62,500 × 50,000/1,00,000) = ₹ 13,750

(ii) Value of investment will be least of market value ₹ 46,250 (i.e. 92.5% of ₹ 50,000) *or* average cost price (i.e. ₹ 31,250).

PROBLEM 5

On 1st April, 2012 XY Ltd. has 15,000 equity shares of ABC Ltd. at a book value of 15 per share (face value ₹ 10 per share). On 1st June, 2012, XY Ltd. acquired 5,000 equity shares of ABC Ltd. ₹ 1,00,000 on cum right basis. ABC Ltd. announced a bonus and right issue.

(1) Bonus was declared, at the rate of one equity share for every five shares held, on 1st July 2012.

(2) Right shares are to be issued to the existing shareholders on 1st September 2012. The company will issue one right share for every 6 shares at 20% premium. No dividend was payable on these shares.

(3) Dividend for the year ended 31.3.2012 were declared by ABC Ltd. @ 20%, which was received by XY Ltd. on 31st October 2012.

XY Ltd.

(i) Took up half the right issue.

(ii) Sold the remaining rights for ₹ 8 per share.

(iii) Sold half of its share holdings on 1st January 2013 at ₹ 16.50 per share. Brokerage being 1%

You are required to prepare Investment account of XY Ltd. for the year ended 31st March 2010 assuming the shares are being valued at average cost.

SOLUTION

INVESTMENT IN EQUITY SHARES OF ABC LTD.

Dr. *for the year ended 31st March, 2013* *Cr.*

Date	Particulars	No. ₹	Income ₹	Amount	Date	Particulars	No. ₹	Income ₹	Amount
2012	To Balance b/d	15,000	–	2,25,000	2012	By Bank A/c	–		16,000
April 1					Sept. 1				
June 1	To Bank A/c	5,000	–	1,00,000	2009	By Bank A/c	–	30,000	10,000
					Oct. 31	(W.N. 5)			
July 1	To Bonus Issue	4,000	–	–	2013	By Bank A/c	13,000	–	2,12,355
					Jan. 1				
Sept.1	To Bank A/c	2,000	–	24,000	March 31	By Balance c/d	13,000	–	1,61,500
2013	To P & L A/c	–	–	50,855					
March 31	To P & LA/c	–	–	30,000					
		26,000	**30,000**	**3,99,855**			**26,000**	**30,000**	**3,99,855**

Working Notes:

(i) **Bonus Shares** $= \frac{15{,}000 \text{ shares} + 5{,}000 \text{ shares}}{5} \times 1 = 4{,}000$ shares

(ii) **Right Shares** $= \frac{15{,}000 \text{ shares} + 5{,}000 \text{ shares} + 4{,}000 \text{ shares}}{6} = 4{,}000$ shares

Shares subscribed by XY Ltd. $= \frac{4{,}000}{2} = 2{,}000$ shares

Value of Right Shares subscribed = 2,000 shares @ 12 per share = 24,000

(iii) **Sale of Right Entitlement** = 2,000 shares × ₹ 8 per share = ₹ 16,000

(Since shares are purchased cum right basis, therefore, amount received from sale of rights will be credited to Investment Account)

(iv) **Profit on Sale of Shares**

Total holdings	=	15,000 shares	original
		5,000 shares	purchased
		4,000 shares	bonus
		2,000 shares	right shares
		26,000 shares	

50% of the holdings were sold i.e. 13,000 shares (26,000 x1/2) were sold.

Cost of total holdings of 26,000 shares (on average basis)

= ₹ 2,25,000 + ₹ 1,00,000 + 24,000 – ₹ 16,000 – ₹ 10,000 = ₹3,23,000

Average cost of 13,000 shares would be

= $\frac{3,23,000}{26,000} \times 13,000$ = ₹1,61,500

Particulars	₹
Sale Proceeds of 13,000 shares (13,000 × ₹ 16.50)	2,14,500
Less: 1% Brokerage	(2,145)
	2,12,355
Less: Cost of 13,000 shares	(1,61,500)
Profit on sale	50,855

(v) Dividend received on investment held as on 1st April

= 15,000 shares × ₹ 10 × 20% = 30,000 will be transferred to Profit and Loss A/c

Dividend received on shares purchased on 1st June

= 5,000 shares × ₹ 10 × 20% = ₹ 10,000 will be adjusted to Investment A/c

Note: *It is presumed that no dividend is received on bonus shares as bonus shares are declared on 1st July, 2009 and dividend pertains to the year ended 31st March*

(vi) Closing Value of shares (on average basis) = 13,000 × $\frac{3,23,000}{26,000}$ = ₹1,61,500.

PROBLEM 6

On 1st April, 2013, Rajat has 50,000 equity shares of P Lid. at a book value of ₹ 15 per share (face value ₹ 10 each). He provides you the further information:

(1) On 20th June, 2013, he purchased another 10,000 shares of P Ltd. at ₹ 16 per share.

(2) On 1st August 2013, P Ltd. issued one equity bonus share for every six shares held by the shareholders.

(3) On 31st October, 2013, the directors of P Ltd. announced a right sssue which entitle the holders to subscribe three shares for every seven shares at ₹ 15 per share. Shareholders can transfer their rights in full *or* in part.

Rajat sold 1/3rd of entitlement to Umang for a consideration of ₹ 2 per share and subscribe the rest on 5th November, 2013.

You are required to prepare Investment A/c in the books of Rajat for the year ending 31st March, 2014.

SOLUTION

INVESTMENT ACCOUNT IN THE BOOKS OF RAJAT (EQUITY SHARES IN P LTD.)

Dr. *Cr.*

Date	*Particulars*	*No. of Shares*	*₹*	*Date*	*Particulars*	*No. of Shares*	*₹*
1.4.13	To Balance b/d	50,000	7,50,000	5.11.13	By Bank A/c (sale of rights)	—	20,000
20.6.13	To Bank A/c	10,000	1,60,000	31.3.14	By Bal. c/d (b.f.)	90,000	11,90,000
1.8.13	To Bonus issue	10,000	—				
5.11.13	To Bank A/c (right shares)	20,000	3,00,000				
		90,000	12,10,000			90,000	12,10,000

Working Notes:

(i) Bonus Shares = (50,000 + 10,000)/6 = 10,000 shares

(ii) Right Shares = [(50,000 + 10,000 + 10,000)/7] × 3 = 30,000 shares

(iii) Sale of Rights = (30,000 shares × 1/3) × ₹ 2 = ₹ 20,000

(iv) Rights subscribed = (30,000 Shares × 2/3) × ₹ 15 = ₹ 3,00,000

INVESTMENT IN BONDS ACCOUNT

PROBLEM 7

On 1st April, 'X' purchased 12% debentures in 'M' Ltd. for ₹ 6,50,000. The face value of these debentures were ₹ 6,00,000. Interest on debentures falls due on 30th June and 31st December. Compute the cost of acquisition of debentures.

SOLUTION

COMPUTATION OF COST OF ACQUISITION OF DEBENTURES

Particulars	₹
Cum-interest purchase price of debentures	6,50,000
Less: Interest from the last date of payment of interest to the date of purchase [₹ 6,00,000 × 3/12 × 12%]	18,000
Cost of debentures at the time of acquisition	6,32,000

PROBLEM 8

The following information is presented by Mr. Z, relating to his holding in 9% Central Government Bonds.

Opening balance (face value) ₹1,20,000, Cost ₹1,18,000 (Face value of each unit is ₹100).

1.3.2012	Purchased 200 units, ex-interest at ₹98.
1.7.2012	Sold 500 units, ex-interest out of original holding at ₹100.
1.10.2012	Purchased 150 units at ₹ 98, cum interest.
1.11.2012	Sold 300 units, ex-interest at ₹ 99 out of original holdings.

Interest dates are 30th September and 31st March. Mr. Z closes his books every 31st December. Show the investment account as it would appear in his books.

SOLUTION

Dr. **9% CENTRAL GOVERNMENT BONDS (INVESTMENT) ACCOUNT** Cr.

Date 2012	Particulars	Face Value ₹	Interest ₹	Principal ₹	Date 2012	Particulars	Face Value ₹	Interest ₹	Principal ₹
Jan.1	To Balance b/d	1,20,000	2,700	1,18,000	March 31	By Bank A/c	-	6,300	-
March 1	To Bank A/c	20,000	750	19,600	July 1	By Bank A/c	50,000	1,125	50,000
July 1	To P&L A/c	-	-	833	Sept. 30	By Bank A/c	-	4,050	-
Oct. 1	To Bank A/c	15,000	-	14,700	Nov. 1	By Bank A/c	30,000	225	29,700
Nov. 1	To P&L A/c	-	-	200	Dec. 31	By Balance c/d	75,000	1,688	73,633
Dec. 31	To P&L A/c (Transfer)		9,938						
		1,55,000	13,388	1,53,333			1,55,000	13,388	1,53,333

Working Note:

CALCULATION OF CLOSING BALANCE

Particulars	Units	₹
From original holding (1,20,000 – 50,000 – 30,000) 40,000		
39,333 i.e., (1,18,000 / 1,20,000) × 40,000		
Purchased on 1st March	20,000	19,600
Purchased on 1st October	15,000	14,700
	75,000	73,633

INVESTMENT IN EQUITY SHARES ACCOUNT AND INVESTMENT IN BONDS ACCOUNT

PROBLEM 9

Mr.Brown has made following transactions during the financial year 2012-13:

Date	Particulars
01.05.2012	Purchased 24,000 12% Bonds of ₹ 100 each at ₹ 84 cum interest. Interest is payable on 30th September and 31st March every year.
15.06.2012	Purchased 1,50,000 Equity Shares of ₹ 10 each in Alpha Limited for ₹ 25 each through a Broker, who charged Brokerage at 2%.
10.07.2012	Purchased 60,000 Equity Shares of ₹ 10 each in Beeta Limited for ₹ 44 each through a Broker, who charged Brokerage at 2%.
14.10.2012	Alpha Limited made a Bonus Issue of two Shares for every three Shares held.
31.10.2012	Sold 80,000 Shares in Alpha Limited for ₹ 22 each.
01.01.2012	Received 15% Interim Dividend on Equity Shares of Alpha Limited.
15.01.2013	Beeta Limited made a Rights Issue of one Equity Share for every four Shares held at ₹ 5 per Share. Mr.Brown exercised his option for 40% of his entitlements and sold the balance rights in the market at ₹ 2.25 per Share.
01.03.2013	Sold 15,00012% Bonds at ₹ ex-interest.
15.03.2013	Received 18% Interim Dividend on Equity Shares of Beeta Limited. Interest on 12% Bonds was duly received on due dates.

Prepare separate Investment Account for 12% Bonds, Equity Shares of Alpha Limited and Equity Shares of Beeta Limited in the books of Mr.Brown for the year ended on 31st March 2013.

SOLUTION

Dr. **(I) INVESTMENT IN 8% BONDS ACCOUNT** *Cr.*

(₹ in '000)

Date	Item	FV	Int.	Cost	Date	Item	FV	Int.	Cost
1 May	To Bank A/c	2400	24	1992	30 Sept	By Bank A/c	–	144	–
1 Mar	To P&L A/c	–	–	105	1 Mar	By Bank A/c	1500	75	1350
31 Mar	To P&L A/c		249		31 Mar	By Bank A/c	–	54	
					31 Mar	By bal c/d	900		747
		2400	273	2,097			2400	273	2,097

Working Notes:

(i) Cost of Purchase = (24000 × ₹ 84) – (24,000 × ₹ 100 × 12% × 1/12) = 19,92,000

(ii) Profit / (Loss) on Sale of Investments = Sale Proceeds – Cost

= (15,000 × ₹ 90) – ₹ 19,92,000 × 15,00,000/24,00,000 = 1,05,000

Dr. **(II) INVESTMENT IN EQUITY SHARES OF ALPHA LTD.** *Cr.*

(₹ in '000)

Date	Item	Shares	Div.	Cost	Date	Item	Shares	Div.	Cost
15 June	To Bank A/c	15,0	–	38,25	31 Oct.	By Bank (Sale)	80	–	17,60
14 Oct.	To Bonus Shares	10,0	–	–	1 Jan	By Bank (Divnd.)	–	255	–
31 Mar	To P&L A/c (Divnd.)	–	255	–	1 Jan	To P&L A/c (Loss)			2,80
						By bal c/d	1,70	–	17,85
		2,50	255	3,825			250	255	3,825

Note: Cost of Investments Sold = ₹ 38,25,000 × $\frac{80,000 \text{ Shares}}{1,50,000 \text{ Shares}}$ = ₹ 20,40,000.

Hence, Loss on Sale = 20,40,000 – 17,60,000 = 2,80,000

Dr. **(III) INVESTMENT IN EQUITY SHARES OF BEETA LTD.** *Cr.*

Date	Item	Shares	Div.	Cost	Date	Item	Shares	Div.	Cost
10 Jul	To Bank A/c	60,000	–	26,92,800	31 Mar	By bal c/d	66,000	–	27,22,800
14 Oct	To Bank (Rights)	6,000	–	30,000*					
		66,000	–	27,22,800			66,000	–	27,22,800

*[(60,000 × 1/4 × 40% × ₹ 5)]

Note: The balance Right for 9,000 Shares are renounced at ₹ 2.25 per Share for ₹ 20,250. which will be credited to P&L A/c.

PROBLEM 10

Gaama Investment Company holds 1,000, 15% Debentures of ₹ 100 each in Beta industries Ltd, as on April 1, 2009 at a cost of ₹ 1,05,000. Interest is payable on June, 30 and December, 31 each year. On May 1, 2009, 500 debentures are purchased cum-interest at ₹ 53,500. On November 1, 2009, 600 debentures are sold ex-interest at ₹ 57,300. On November 30, 2009, 400 debentures are purchased ex-interest at ₹ 38,400. On December 31, 2009, 400 debentures are sold cum-interest for ₹ 55,000.

Require: Prepare the Investment Account showing value of holdings on March 31, 2010 at cost, using FIFO Method.

SOLUTION

Dr. **INVESTMENT ACCOUNT (15% DEBENTURES IN BETA INDUSTRIES LTD.)** *Cr.*

Date	*Particulars*	*Nominal value* ₹	*Interest* ₹	*Cost* ₹	*Date*	*Particulars*	*Nominal value* ₹	*Interest* ₹	*Cost* ₹
1.04.12	To Bal. b/d	1,00,000	3,750	1,05,000	30.06.12	By Bank A/c	—	11,250	—
1.05.12	To Bank A/c	50,000	2,500	51,000	1.11.12	By Bank A/c	60,000	3,000	57,300
30.11.12	To Bank A/c	40,000	2,500	38,400	1.11.12	By P&L A/c	—	—	5,700
31 12.12	To P&L A/c	—	—	10,000	31.12.12	By Bank A/c	40,000	3,000	52,000
31.03.13	To P&L A/c	—	18,625	—	31.12.12	By Bank A/c	—	6,750	—
					31.03.13	By Bank A/c	90,000	3,375	89,400
		1,90,000	27,375	2,04,400			1,90,000	27,375	2,04,400

Working Notes:

(i) Accrued Interest as on 1st April = ₹ 1,00,000 × $\frac{15}{100} \times \frac{3}{12}$ = ₹3,750

(ii) Accrued Interest = ₹50,000 × $\frac{15}{100} \times \frac{4}{12}$ = ₹ 2,500

(iii) Cost of Investment for purchase on 1st May = ₹ 53,500 – ₹2,500 = ₹51,000

(iv) Interest received = ₹1,50,000 × $\frac{15}{100} \times \frac{6}{12}$ = ₹11,250

(v) Accrued Interest = ₹60,000 × $\frac{15}{100} \times \frac{4}{12}$ = ₹3,000

(vi) Accrued Interest = ₹ 40,000 × $\frac{15}{100} \times \frac{5}{12}$ = ₹2,500

(vii) Accrued Interest = ₹40,000 × $\frac{15}{100} \times \frac{6}{12}$ = ₹3,000

(viii) Sale Price of Investment on 31st Dec. = ₹55,000 – ₹3,000 = ₹52,000

(ix) Accrued Interest = ₹90,000 × $\frac{15}{100} \times \frac{6}{12}$ = ₹6,750

(x) Accrued Interest = ₹90,000 × $\frac{15}{100} \times \frac{3}{12}$ = ₹3,375

(xi) Cost of investment as on 31st March = ₹ 51,000 + ₹ 38,400 = ₹ 89,400

(xii) Loss on debentures sold on 1st Nov. = ₹ 57,300 – (₹ 1,05,000 × 600/1000) = ₹ 5,200

(xiii) Profit on debentures sold on 31st Dec. = ₹ 52,000 – (₹ 1,05,00 × 400/1000) = ₹ 10,000

14 INSURANCE CLAIMS

LEARNING OBJECTIVES

After studying this chapter, you should be able to understand:

◇ Meaning of Insurance Contracts, Insuer, Insured, Premium

◇ When does the Liability Insurer Arise?

◇ What is the Extent of Liability of Insurer?

◇ Loss of Stock Policy

◇ Significance of Average Clause in Fire Insurance Policy

◇ Loss of Profit Policy

◇ Amount to be Insured under Loss of Profit Policy

1.0 MEANING OF INSURANCE CONTRACTS, INSUER, INSURED, PREMIUM

Insurance contracts are contracts of indemnity whereby one party, called the insurer, undertakes to indemnify the loss suffered by the other party, called the insured, on the happening of some unforeseen event in consideration of a fixed sum of money, called the Premium.

2.0 WHEN DOES THE LIABILITY INSURER ARISE?

The liability of the insurer to indemnify the loss suffered by the insured arises only on the happening of the event for which the policy is taken out.

3.0 WHAT IS THE EXTENT OF LIABILITY OF INSURER?

The liability of the insurer is limited to the amount of **loss actually suffered** by the insured ***or the policy amount (i.e. known as Sum Insured) whichever is less***. However, in case of under-insurance, (i.e. when the actual value of the property insured is greater than the insured value of the property) the liability of the insurer is limited to that proportion of the loss which the insured value bears to the actual value of the property insured if an Average Clause is included in the insurance policy.

4.0 LOSS OF STOCK POLICY

PRACTICAL STEPS INVOLVED IN THE DETERMINATION OF THE AMOUNT OF CLAIM UNDER LOSS OF STOCK POLICY

The various steps involved in the determination of the amount of claim under the loss of stock policy are shown below:

Step 1: *Calculate the Gross Profit Ratio*

$$\text{Gross Profit Ratio} = \frac{\text{Gross Profit}}{\text{Net Sales}} \times 100$$

While calculating the Gross Profit Ratio, the following factors should be taken into account:

(a) The opening and closing stocks should be adjusted at cost in case the stocks have been under/over valued.

(b) The effects of abnormal item (if any) should be excluded.

(c) Weighted average or geometric average may be taken if the percentages show a clear upward or downward trend.

Step 2: *Calculate the Estimated Value of Stock as at the date of fire*

While calculating the estimated value of stock as at date of fire, the following factors should be taken into account:

(a) Memorandum Trading Account should be prepared showing clearly the normal items and abnormal items. Its format may be as follows.

MEMORANDUM TRADING ACCOUNT FOR THE PERIOD FROM... TO...

Particulars	*Normal Items* ₹	*Abnormal Items* ₹	*Particulars*	*Normal Items* ₹	*Abnormal Items* ₹
To Opening Stock	xxx	xxx	By Sale	xxx	xxx
To Purchases	xxx	xxx	By Closing Stock (b/f.)	xxx	xxx
To Direct Expenses	xxx	xxx			
To Gross Profit	xxx	xxx			
	xxx	xxx		xxx	xxx

(b) Gross Profit Ratio (calculated as per Step No. 1) should be applied to Normal Sales only and not to Abnormal Sales.

(c) The effect of price-level changes(if any) should be excluded before applying the Gross Profit Ratio. Since the Gross Profit Ratio is based on previous year's price levels, the current year's figures of sales, purchases and direct expenses, should first be adjusted on previous year basis and then the Gross Profit Ratio should be applied.

(d) Unless otherwise stated, the estimated value of stock on date of fire consists of book value of normal Items and book value of abnormal items. Sometimes the specific valuation of abnormal items is given for the purposes of claim. Then instead of book value, such valuation should be taken.

Step 3: *Calculate the Value of Salvaged (Saved) Stock*

Step 4: *Calculate the Value of Stock lost by fire as under:*

(a) Value of Stock on the date of fire	xxx
(b) *Less:* Value of Salvaged Stock not handed over to Insurance Company	xxx
	xxx

Step 5: *Calculate the amount of claims*

(a) **In case of Over-Insurance** (i.e. where the sum insured exceeds the actual insurable value), the average clause does not apply at all and hence the amount of claim is equal to the value of stock lost by fire (as per Step No.4)

(b) **In case of Under-Insurance** (i.e. where the sum insured is *less* than the actual insurable value), the amount of claim according to the average clause (if inserted in the contract of insurance) will be calculated as follows:

$$\text{Amount of Claim} = \text{Loss suffered} \times \frac{\text{Sum Insured}}{\text{Actual Insurable Value}}$$

where, Actual Insurable Value = Estimated Value of Stock as at the date of fire.

Loss suffered = Estimated Value of Stock as at the date of loss *less* Value of Salvaged Stock.

5.0 SIGNIFICANCE OF AVERAGE CLAUSE IN FIRE INSURANCE POLICY

SIGNIFICANCE/OBJECTIVE

In order to discourage Under-Insurance (i.e. where the sum insured is *less* than the actual insurable value), fire insurance policies often include an average clause.

CALCULATION OF CLAIM

The amount of claim according to the average clause (if inserted in the contract of insurance) will be calculated as follows:

$$\text{Amount of Claim} = \text{Loss suffered} \times \frac{\text{Sum Insured}}{\text{Actual Insurable Value}}$$

where, Actual Insurable Value = Estimated Value of Stock as at the date of fire.

Loss suffered = Estimated Value of Stock as at the date of loss *less* Value of Salvaged Stock.

PRACTICAL EXAMPLE:

Actual value of stock as at date of fire ₹ 5,00,000

Value of salvaged stock ₹ 1,00,000

Sum Insured ₹ 2,50,000

Claim = (₹ 5,00,000 – ₹ 1,00,000) × ₹ 2,50,000/₹ 5,00,000

ACCOUNTING ENTRIES

The various accouting entries in the books of insured are given below:

(i) On recording the value of stock lost by fire	Stock Lost by Fire A/c To Trading A/c	Dr.	
(ii) On acceptance of the claim by the Insurance Co. *To Stock Lost by Fire A/c*	Insurance Co.'s A/c P & L A/cDr.	Dr.	(With claim admitted) (With claim not admitted) (with the Total)
(iii) On receipt of claim from Insurance Co.	Bank A/c To Insurance Co.'s A/c	Dr.	

ILLUSTRATION 1 [CALCULATION OF GROSS PROFIT RATIO]

Calculate the Gross Profit Ratio for the calender year 2013 in each of the following alternative cases:

Case (a) Opening Stock ₹ 6,40,000, Purchases ₹ 35,52,000, Wages ₹ 4,00,000, Sales ₹ 46,40,000, Closing Stock ₹ 8,80,000.

Case (b) Opening Stock ₹ 6,40,000 Purchases ₹ 37,52,000, Wages ₹ 4,00,000, Sales ₹ 46,40,000, Closing Stock ₹ 8,80,000 In June 2013 goods costing ₹ 2,00,000 were consigned but were lost in an accident against which insurance Co. paid only 40%.

Case (c) Opening Stock ₹ 5,76,000, Purchases ₹ 37,52,000, Wages ₹ 4,00,000, Sales ₹ 46,40,000, Closing Stock ₹ 9,68,000, Stock at the end of each year and till the end of calender year 2012 had been valued at cost *less* 10%. From 2013 however, there was a change in the valuation of Closing Stock which was ascertained by adding 10% to its cost. In June 2013, goods costing ₹ 2,00,000 were consigned but were lost in an accident against which the Insursnce Co. paid only 40%.

Case (d) Opening Stock ₹ 73,500, Purchases ₹ 3,98,000, Sales ₹ 4,87,000, Closing Stock ₹ 79,600. In valuing the Stock at 31-12-2013, ₹ 2,300 had been written off certain stock which was poor selling line, it having a cost of ₹ 6,900.

Case (e) Opening Stock ₹ 73,500, Purchases ₹ 3,98,000, Sales ₹ 4,90,200, Closing Stock ₹ 77,300. ₹ 2,300 had been written off certain Stock (out of current year's purchases) which was poor selling line, it having a cost of ₹ 6,900. A portion of these goods were sold in Dec., 2013 at a loss of ₹ 250 on original cost of ₹ 3,450.

SOLUTION

Case (a)

TRADING ACCOUNT FOR THE YEAR ENDING ON 31ST DEC 2013

Particulars	₹	*Particulars*	₹
To Opening Stock	6,40,000	By Sales	46,40,000
To Purchases	35,52,000	By Closing Stock	8,80,000
To Wages	4,00,000		
To Gross Profit (b.f.)	9,28,000		
	55,20,000		55,20,000

$$\text{G.P. Ratio} = \frac{\text{Gross Profit}}{\text{Net Sales}} \times 100 = \frac{₹9,28,000}{₹46,40,000} \times 100 = 20\%$$

Case (b)

TRADING ACCOUNT FOR THE YEAR ENDING ON 31ST DEC, 2013

Particulars	₹	*Particulars*	₹
To Opening Stock	6,40,000	By Sales	46,40,000
To Purchases	37,52,000	By Closing Stock	8,80,000
To Wages	4,00,000	By Bank A/c (claim)	80,000
To Gross Profit (b.f)	9,28,000	By Loss due to Accident A/c	1,20,000
	57,20,000		57,20,000

$$\text{G.P. Ratio} = \frac{\text{Gross Profit}}{\text{Net Sales}} \times 100 = \frac{₹9,28,000}{₹46,40,000} \times 100 = 20\%$$

Case (c)

TRADING ACCOUNT FOR THE YEAR ENDING ON 31ST DEC 2013

Particulars	₹	*Particulars*	₹
To Opening Stock	6,40,000	By Sales	46,40,000
(₹ 5,76,000 × 100/90)		By Closing Stock	
To Purchases	37,52,000	(₹ 9,68,000 × 100/110)	8,80,000

To Wages	4,00,000	By Bank A/c (claim)	80,000
To Gross Profit (b.f)	9,28,000	By Loss due to Accident A/c	1,20,000
	57,20,000		57,20,000

$$\text{G.P. Ratio} = \frac{\text{Gross Profit}}{\text{Net Sales}} \times 100 = \frac{₹9,28,000}{₹46,40,000} \times 100 = 20\%$$

Case (d)

TRADING ACCOUNT FOR THE YEAR ENDING ON 31ST DEC., 2013

Particulars	*Normal Items* ₹	*Abnormal Items* ₹	*Total Items* ₹	*Particulars*	*Normal Items* ₹	*Abnormal Items* ₹	*Total Items* ₹
To Opening Stock	66,600	6,900	73,500	By Sales	4,87,000	—	4,87,000
To Purchases	3,98,000	—	3,98,000	By Closing Stock	75,000	4,600	79,600
To Gross Profit (b.f)	97,400	—	97,400	By Gross Loss	—	2,300	2,300
	5,62,000	6,900	5,68,900		5,62,000	6,900	5,68,900

$$\text{G.P. Ratio} = \frac{\text{Gross Profit}}{\text{Net Sales}} \times 100 = \frac{₹97,400}{₹4,87,000} \times 100 = 20\%$$

Assumption: Stock written off was out of opening stock.

Case (e)

TRADING ACCOUNT FOR THE YEAR ENDING ON 31ST DEC. 2013

Particulars	*Normal Items* ₹	*Abnormal Items* ₹	*Total Items* ₹	*Particulars*	*Normal Items* ₹	*Abnormal Items* ₹	*Total Items* ₹
To Opening Stock	73,500	—	73,500	By Sales	4,87,000	3,200	4,90,200
To Purchases	3,91,100	6,900	3,98,000	By Closing Stock	75,000	2,300	77,300
To Gross Profit (b.f)	97,400	—	97,400	By Gross Loss	—	1,400	1,400
	5,62,000	6,900	5,68,900		5,62,000	6,900	5,68,900

$$\text{G.P. Ratio} = \frac{\text{Gross Profit}}{\text{Net Sales}} \times 100 = \frac{₹97,400}{₹4,87,000} \times 100 = 20\%$$

ILLUSTRATION 2 [CALCULATION OF CLOSING STOCK]

Calculate the Closing Stock as on 30.6.2013 in each of the following alternative cases:

Case (a) Stock as on 1.1.2013 ₹ 70,000, Purchases from 1.1.2013 to 30.6.2013 ₹ 6,00,000, Sales from 1.1.2013 to 30.6.2013 ₹ 8,80,000, G.P. Ratio for 2012 was 30%. In 2013, the cost of purchases and selling prices have increased by 20% and 10% respectively above the levels prevailing in 2012.

Case (b) Stock as on 1.1.2013 ₹ 1,20,000, Purchases from 1.1.2013 to 30.6.2013 ₹ 1,40,000, Sales from 1.1.2013 to 30.6.2013 ₹ 3,10,000, G.P.Rate for 2012 was 33-1/3%, Sales upto 30.6.2013 included ₹ 40,000 for which goods had not been despatched Purchases upto 30.6.2013 did not include ₹ 20,000 for which purchase invoice had not been received from suppliers, though the goods have been received at the godown.

Case (c) Stock as on 31.12.2012 ₹ 55,000, Trade Debtors (on 1.1.2013) ₹ 2,00,000, Trade Creditors (on 1.1.2013) ₹ 1,00,000. Trade Creditors (on 30.6.2013) ₹ 2,00,000, Collection from Trade Debtors from 1.1.2013 to 30.6.2013 ₹ 2,47,240, Payments made to Trade Creditors from 1.1.2013 to 30.6.2013 ₹ 8,750, Returns Inwards ₹ 760, Returns Outward ₹ 250, Cash

Sales 20% of Sales and Cash Purchases 25% of Purchases, G.P. Ratio for 2012 25%, Trade Debtors (on 30.6.2013) ₹ 1,00,000.

Case (d) Stock as on 31.12.2012 ₹ 79,600, Purchases from 1.1.2013 to 30.6.2013 ₹ 1,62,000, Sales from 1.1.2013 to 30.6.2013 ₹ 2,31,200. In valuing the Stock on 31.12.2012 ₹ 2,300 had been written off certain stock which was poor selling line, it having a cost of ₹ 6,900. A portion of these goods was sold in March, 2013 at a loss of ₹ 250 on the original cost of ₹ 3,450. The remainder of this stock was now estimated to be worth its original cost for the purposes of claim. Subject to above exception, gross profit remained at an uniform rate throught the year, G.P. Rate for 2012 was 20%.

SOLUTION

Case(a)

MEMORANDUM TRADING ACCOUNT FOR THE PERIOD FROM 01.01.2013 TO 30.06.2013

Particulars	*2012 basis* ₹	*2013* ₹	*Particulars*	*2012 basis* ₹	*2013* ₹
To Opening Stock	70,000	70,000	By Sales	8,00,000	8,80,000
To Purchases	5,00,000	6,00,000	By Closing Stock (b.f.)		
To Gross Profit @30%				10,000	12,000
on Normal Sales	2,40,000	2,22,000			
	8,10,000	8,92,000		8,10,000	8,92,000

Closing Stock: on FIFO Basis = ₹ 12,000, on LIFO Basis ₹ 10,000

Case (b)

MEMORANDUM TRADING ACCOUNT FOR THE PERIOD FROM 01.01.2013 TO 30.6.2013

Particulars	₹	*Particulars*	₹
To Opening Stock	1,20,000	By Sales (₹ 3,10,000 – ₹ 40,000)	2,70,000
To Purchases		By Closing Stock (b.f.)	1,00,000
(₹ 1,40,000 + ₹ 20,000)	1,60,000		
To Gross Profit @ 33-1/3%	90,000		
	3,70,000		3,70,000

Case (c)

(I) TOTAL CREDITORS ACCOUNT

Particulars	₹	*Particulars*	₹
To Bank A/c	8,750	By Opening Balance	1,00,000
To Returns Outward	250	By Credit Purchases (b.f.)	1,09,000
To Closing Balance	2,00,000		
	2,09,000		2,09,000

Net Purchases = Net Credit Purchases + Cash Purchases

= (₹ 1,09,000 – ₹ 250) + 33 – 1/3% of ₹ 1,08,750 = ₹ 1,45,000

(II) TOTAL DEBTORS ACCOUNT

Particulars	₹	Particulars	₹
To Opening Balance	2,00,000	By Bank A/c	2,47,240
To Credit Sales (Balancing figure)	1,48,000	By Returns Inward	760
		By Closing Balance	1,00,000
	3,48,000		3,48,000

Net Sales = Net Credit Sales + Cash Sales = (₹ 1,48,000 – ₹ 760) + 25% of ₹ 1,47,240 = ₹ 1,84,050

(III) MEMORANDUM TRADING ACCOUNT FOR THE PERIOD FROM 01.01.2013 TO 30.6.2013

Particulars	₹	Particulars	₹
To Opening Stock	55,000	By Sales	1,84,050
To Purchases	1,45,000	By Closing Stock	61,963
To Gross Profit	46,013	(Balancing figure)	
	2,46,013		2,46,013

Case (d)

MEMORANDUM TRADING ACCOUNT FOR THE PERIOD FROM 01.01.2013 TO 30.06.2013

Particulars	Normal Items ₹	Abnormal Items ₹	Total Items ₹	Particulars	Normal Items ₹	Abnormal Items ₹	Total Items ₹
To Opening Stock	75,000	4,600	79,600	By Sales	2,28,000	3,200	2,31,200
To Purchases	1,62,000	—	1,62,000	By Closing Stock	54,600	2,300	56,900
To Gross Profit	45,600	900	46,500				
	2,82,600	5,500	2,88,100		2,82,600	5,500	2,88,100

ILLUSTRATION 3 [CALCULATION OF THE AMOUNT OF INSURANCE CLAIM]

Stock as on the date of fire ₹ 58,050, Value of Salvaged Stock ₹ 5,800. Calculate the amount of claim if the sum insured to cover the loss of Stock by fire is (a) ₹ 60,000 (b) ₹ 50,000.

SOLUTION

Case (a) Since sum insured (₹ 60,000) exceeds the sum insurable (₹ 58,050), average clause will not apply at all and hence the amount of claim will be restricted to the value of Stock lost by fire ₹ 52,250 (i.e. ₹ 58,050 – ₹ 5,800).

Case (b) Since sum insured (₹ 50,000) is *less* than the Sum insurable (₹ 58,050), average clause will apply as under:

SOLUTION

$$\text{Loss suffered} \times \frac{\text{Sum Insured}}{\text{Actual Insurable Value}} = ₹52,250 \times \frac{₹50,000}{₹58,050} = ₹\ 45,004$$

ILLUSTRATION 4

On 12th June, 2013, a fire occurred in the premises of N.R. Patel, a paper merchant. Most of the stocks were destroyed, cost of stock salvaged being ₹ 11,200. In addition, some stock was salvaged in a damaged condition and its value in that condition was agreed at ₹ 10,400. From the books of account, the following particulars were available:

(i) His stock at the close of account on December 31,2012 was valued at ₹ 83,500.

(ii) His purchases from 1.1.2013 to 12.6.2013 amounted to ₹ 1,12,000 and his sales during that period amounted to ₹ 1,54,000.

On the basis of his accounts for the past three years, it appears that he earns on an average a gross profit of 25% on sales. Patel has insured his stock for ₹ 60,000. Compute the amount of the claim.

SOLUTION

STATEMENT OF CLAIM

	Particulars	₹
A.	Estimated Value of Stock as at date of fire	80,000
B.	Value of Salvaged Stock & damaged Stock (₹ 11,200 + ₹ 10,400)	21,600
C.	Estimated Value of Stock lost by fire (A – B)	58,400
D.	Amount of claim by applying Average clause:	
	$\text{Loss suffered} \times \frac{\text{Sum Insured}}{\text{Actual Insurable Value}} = ₹58,400 \times \frac{₹60,000}{₹80,000}$	43,800

Working Note: *Calculation of the value of Closing Stock as on the date of fire*

MEMORANDUM TRADING ACCOUNT FOR THE PERIOD FROM 01.01.2013 TO 12.06.2013

Particulars	₹	*Particulars*	₹
To Opening Stock	83,500	By Sales	1,54,000
To Purchases	1,12,000	By Closing Stock (Balancing figure)	80,000
To Gross Profit @ 25%	38,500		
	2,34,000		2,34,000

ILLUSTRATION 5

From the following, calculate the Closing Stock and claim as on date of fire:

(a) Opening Stock ₹ 29,700 was calculated at 10% *less* than the cost.

(b) Purchases ₹ 80,000 include the purchase of plant for ₹ 5,000.

(c) Wages ₹ 33,000 include wages of ₹ 500 for installation of plant.

(d) Goods costing ₹ 5,000 were taken by proprietor for his personal use.

(e) A sum of ₹ 2,200 was incurred by way of fire fighting expenses on the day of fire.

(f) Sales invoices raised upto date of fire ₹ 1,50,000. However, goods of the value of ₹ 10,000 had been returned by the customer before the date of fire.

(g) Stock to the value of ₹ 3,000 was salvaged out of which 10% was handed over to the Insurance Co., Rate of GP— on cost., Sum Insured—₹ 25,000

SOLUTION

STATEMENT OF CLAIM

	Particulars	₹
A.	Cost of stock as on date of fire	30,500

B. *Less:* Salvaged Stock not handed over to Insurance Co.	2,700
	27,800
C. *Add:* Fire Fighting Expenses	2,200
D. Total Loss	30,000
E. Claim = $\frac{\text{Sum Insured}}{\text{Actual Insurable Value}} \times$ Loss on date of fire = $\frac{₹25,000}{₹30,000} \times 30,000$	24,590

CALCULATION OF CLOSING STOCK
MEMORANDUM TRADING ACCOUNT

Particulars		₹	*Particulars*		₹
To Opening Stock		33,000	By Sales	1,50,000	
(₹ 29,700 × 100/90)			*Less:* Returns	10,000	1,40,000
To Purchases	80,000		By Closing Stock (b.f.)		30,500
Less: Cost of Plant	5,000				
Less: Drawings	5,000	70,000			
To Wages	33,000				
Less: Paid for Plant	500	32,500			
To GP @ 33-1/3% on					
Cost *or* 25% on sales		35,000			
		1,70,500			1,70,500

ILLUSTRATION 6

A fire occurred in the premises of Shri Ramesh on Ist April, 2013 and a considerable part of the stock was destroyed. The stock salvaged was ₹ 1,12,000. Shri Ramesh had taken a fire insurance policy for ₹ 6,84,000 to cover the loss of stock by fire. You are required to ascertain the insurance claim due from the insurance company for the loss of stock by fire. The following particulars are available;

Particulars	₹	*Particulars*	₹
Purchases for the year 2012	37,52,000	Stock on 1st January, 2012	5,76,000
Sales for the year 2012	46,40,000	Stock on 31st December, 2012	9,68,000
Purchases from 1st January, 2013 to 1st April, 2013	7,38,000	Wages paid during the year 2012	4,00,000
Sales from 1st January, 2013 to 1st April, 2013	9,60,000	Wages paid during 1st Jan, 2013 to 1st April, 2013	72,500

Shri Ramesh had in June, 2012 consigned good worth ₹ 2,00,000 which were lost in an accident. As there was no insurance the loss was borne by him in full. Stock at ends of each year prior to the year 2012 had been valued at cost *less* 10%. From 2012 however, there was a change in the valuation of closing stock which was ascertained by adding 10% to its cost.

Purchases for Jan 2013 include the purchase of plant for ₹ 5,000, Wages for 2013 include wages of ₹ 500 for installation of plant. Goods costing ₹ 5,000 were taken by proprietor for his personal use during the month of Jan 2013. A sum of ₹ 10,000 was incurred by way of fire fighting expenses on the day of fire.

SOLUTION

STATEMENT OF CLAIM

	Particulars	₹
A.	Estimated Value of Stock as at date of fire	9,12,000
B.	Value of Salvaged Stock & Damaged Stock	1,12,000
C.	Estimated Value of Stock Lost by fire (A – B)	8,00,000
D.	*Add:* Fire fighting expenses	10,000
E.	Total Loss	8,10,000
F.	Amount of claim by applying Average clause:	
	$\text{Loss suffered} \times \dfrac{\text{Sum Insured}}{\text{Actual Insurable Value}} = ₹8,10,000 \times \dfrac{₹6,84,000}{₹9,12,000}$	6,07,500

Working Notes:

(I) TRADING ACCOUNT FOR THE YEAR ENDING ON 31ST DEC, 2012

Particulars	₹	*Particulars*	₹
To Opening Stock		By Sales	46,40,000
(₹ 5,76,000 × 100/90)	6,40,000	By Closing Stock	
To Purchases	37,52,000	(₹ 9,68,000 × 100/110)	8,80,000
To Wages	4,00,000	By Loss due to Accident A/c	2,00,000
To Gross Profit (b.f)	9,28,000		
	57,20,000		57,20,000

$$\text{G. P. Ratio} = \frac{\text{Gross Profit}}{\text{Net Sales}} \times 100 = \frac{₹9,28,000}{₹46,40,000} \times 100 = 20\%$$

(II) MEMORANDUM TRADING ACCOUNT FOR THE PERIOD FROM 1.1.2013 TO 1.4.2013

Particulars		₹	*Particulars*	₹
To Opening Stock		8,80,000	By Sales	9,60,000
To Purchases7,38,000			By Closing Stock *(Balancing figure)*	9,12,000
Less: Cost of plant	(5,000)			
Less: Drawings	(5,000)	7,28,000		
To Wages (72,500 – 500)		72,000		
To Gross Profit @ 20%		1,92,000		
		18,72,000		18,72,000

ILLUSTRATION 7

From the following information, compute the amount of claim under loss of Stock Policy:

Sum Insured	₹ 6,000	Stock as on 1.1.2012	₹ 90,000
Accounting Year	Calender Year	Stock as on 31.12.2012	₹ 70,000
Reason for Damage on		Purchases during 2012	₹ 4,00,000

30-6-2013	Due to fire accident	Sales during 2012	₹ 6,00,000
Value of Salvaged Stock	₹ 5,000	Purchases from 1.1.2013 to	
G.P. Ratio	Uniform from year to year	30.6.2013	₹ 6,00,000
		Sales from on 1.1.2013 to	
		30.6.2013	₹ 8,80,000

You are informed that in 2013, the cost of purchases and selling prices have increased by 20% and 10% respectively above the levels prevailing in 2012.

SOLUTION

STATEMENT OF CLAIM

Particulars	₹
A. Estimated Value of Stock as at date of fire	12,000
B. Value of Salvaged Stock	5,000
C. Estimated Value of Stock lost by fire (A – B)	7,000
D. Amount of claim by applying Average clause	
$\text{Loss suffered} \times \frac{\text{Sum Insured}}{\text{Actual Insurable Value}} = ₹7,000 \times \frac{₹6,000}{₹12,000}$	3,500

Working Notes:

(I) TRADING ACCOUNT FOR THE YEAR ENDING ON 31ST DEC, 2012

Particulars	₹	*Particulars*	₹
To Opening Stock	90,000	By Sales	6,00,000
To Purchases	4,00,000	By Closing Stock	70,000
To Gross Profit (b.f)	1,80,000		
	6,70,000		6,70,000

$$\text{G. P. Ratio} = \frac{\text{Gross Profit}}{\text{Net Sales}} \times 100 = \frac{₹1,80,000}{₹6,00,000} \times 100 = 30\%$$

(II) MEMORANDUM TRADING ACCOUNT FOR THE PERIOD FROM 01.01.2013 TO 30.06.2013

Particulars	*2012 basis* ₹	*2013* ₹	*Particulars*	*2012 basis* ₹	*2013* ₹
To Opening Stock	70,000	70,000	By Sales	8,00,000	8,80,000
To Purchases	5,00,000	6,00,000	By Closing Stock (b.f.)	10,000	12,000
To Gross Profit @30%	2,40,000	2,22,000		10,000	12,000
	8,10,000	8,92,000		8,10,000	8,92,000

ILLUSTRATION 8

On 20th July, 2013, the godown and business premises of a merchant were affected by fire and from accounting records salvaged, the following information is made available to you:

Stock of goods at cost on 1st April, 2012	₹ 1,00,000

Stock of goods at 10% lower than cost as on 31.3.2013	₹ 1,08,000
Purchases of goods for the year from 1st April, 2012 to 31st March, 2013	₹ 4,20,000
Sales for the year 2012-2013	₹ 6,00,000
Purchases *less* returns for the period from 1st April, 2013 to 20th July, 2013	₹ 1,40,000
Sales *less* returns for the above period	₹ 3,10,000

Sales upto 20th July 2013 included ₹ 40,000 for which goods had not been despatched. Purchases upto 20th July, 2013 did not include ₹ 20,000 for which purchases invoices had not been received from suppliers, though goods have been recieved at the godown. Goods salvaged from the accident were worth ₹ 12,000 and these were handed over to the insured. Ascertain the value of the claim for loss of goods/stock which could be preferred on the insurer, and the amount of the claim if sum insured is ₹ 50,000.

SOLUTION

STATEMENT OF CLAIM

	Particulars	₹
A.	Estimated Value of Stock as at date of fire	1,00,000
B.	*Less:* Value of Salvaged Stock not handed over to Insurance Co.	—
C.	Estimated Value of Stock lost by fire (A – B)	1,00,000
D.	Amount of claim by applying Average clause	
	$\text{Loss suffered} \times \frac{\text{Sum Insured}}{\text{Actual Insurable Value}} = ₹1,00,000 \times \frac{₹50,000}{₹1,00,000}$	50,000

Working Notes:

(I) TRADING ACCOUNT FOR THE YEAR ENDING ON 31ST MAR, 2013

Particulars	₹	*Particulars*	₹
To Opening Stock	1,00,000	By Sales	6,00,000
To Purchases	4,20,000	By Closing Stock	
To Gross Profit (b.f.)	2,00,000	(₹ 1,08,000 × ₹ 100/90)	1,20,000
	7,20,000		7,20,000

$$\text{G. P. Ratio} = \frac{\text{Gross Profit}}{\text{Net Sales}} \times 100 = \frac{₹2,00,000}{₹6,00,000} \times 100 = 33\frac{1}{3}\%$$

(II) MEMORANDUM TRADING ACCOUNT FOR THE PERIOD FROM 01.04.2013 TO 20.07.2013

Particulars	₹	*Particulars*	₹
To Opening Stock	1,20,000	By Sales (₹ 3,10,000 – ₹ 40,000)	2,70,000
To Purchases (₹1,40,000 + ₹20,000)	1,60,000	By Closing Stock (Balancing figure)	1,00,000
To Gross Profit	90,000		
	3,70,000		3,70,000

ILLUSTRATION 9

On 1st April, 2013, the godown of Hindustan Limited was destroyed by fire. From the books of account, the following particulars are gathered:

Particulars	₹
Stock at Cost on 1st January, 2012	27,570
Sales during 2012	3,51,000
Stock as per Balance Sheet on 31st December, 2012	51,120
Sales from 1st January, 2013 to 31st March, 2013	91,500
Purchases during 2012	2,71,350
Value of goods salvaged	6,300
Purchases from 1st January, 2013 to 31st March, 2013	75,000

Goods of which original cost was ₹ 3,600 had been valued at ₹ 1,500 on 31st December, 2012. These were sold in March 2013 for ₹ 2,700. Except this transaction, the rate of gross profit has remained constant. On 31st March, 2013 goods worth ₹ 15,000 had been received by the godown-keeper, but had not been entered in the Purchase Account. Calculate the value of goods destroyed by fire and the amount of claim of loss by fire if sum insured is ₹ 39,000.

SOLUTION

STATEMENT OF CLAIM

Particulars	₹
A. Estimated Value of Stock As at date of fire	77,460
B. Value of Salvaged Stock	6,300
C. Estimated Value of Stock Lost by fire (A – B)	71,160
D. Amount of claim by applying Average clause:	
$\text{Loss suffered} \times \dfrac{\text{Sum Insured}}{\text{Actual Insurable Value}} = ₹71,160 \times \dfrac{₹39,000}{₹77,460}$	35,828

Working Notes:

(I) TRADING ACCOUNT FOR THE PERIOD FROM 1.1.2012 TO 31.12.2012

Particulars	Normal Items ₹	Abnormal Items ₹	Total Items ₹	Particulars	Normal Items ₹	Abnormal Items ₹	Total Items ₹
To Opening Stock	27,570	—	27,570	By Sales	3,51,000	—	3,51,000
To Purchases	2,67,750	3,600	2,71,350	By Closing Stock	49,620	1,500	51,120
To Gross Profit (b.f)	1,05,300	—	1,05,300	By Gross Loss	—	2,100	2,100
	4,00,620	3,600	4,04,220		4,00,620	3,600	4,04,220

$$\text{G. P. Ratio} = \frac{\text{Gross Profit}}{\text{Net Sales}} \times 100 = \frac{₹1,05,300}{₹3,51,000} \times 100 = 30\%$$

(II) MEMORANDUM TRADING ACCOUNT FOR THE PERIOD FROM 01.01.2013 TO 31.03.2013

Particulars	Normal Items ₹	Abnormal Items ₹	Total Items ₹	Particulars	Normal Items ₹	Abnormal Items ₹	Total Items ₹
To Opening Stock	49,620	1,500	51,120	By Sales	88,800	2,700	91,500
To Purchases (75,000 + 15,000)	90,000	—	90,000	By Closing Stock	77,460	—	77,460

To Gross Profit	26,640	1,200	27,840				
	1,66,260	2,700	1,68,960		1,66,260	2,700	1,68,960

ILLUSTRATION 10

From the following information, compute the amount of claim under loss of Stock Policy:

Sum Insured	₹ 50,000	Stock as on 1.1.2012	₹ 73,500
Accounting Year	Calender Year	Stock as on 31.12.2012	₹ 79,600
Value of Salvaged Stock	₹ 5,800	Purchases during 2012	₹ 3,98,000
G.P. Ratio	Uniform from year to year	Sales during 2012	₹ 4,87,000
Reason for Damage on 30-6-2013	Due to fire accident	Purchases from 1.1.2013 to 30.6.2013	₹ 1,62,000
		Sales from on 1.1.2013 to 30.6.2013	₹ 2,31,200

In valuing the stock at 31st December, 2012, ₹ 2,300 had been written off certain stock which was poor selling line, it having a cost of ₹ 6,900. A portion of these goods were sold in March, 2013 at a loss of ₹ 250 on original cost of ₹ 3,450. The remainder of this stock was now estimated to be worth its original cost for the purpose of claim. Subject to above exception, gross profit had remained at an uniform rate throughout the year.

SOLUTION

STATEMENT OF CLAIM

Particulars		₹
A. Estimated Value of Stock As at date of fire		
(a) Book-Value of Normal Items	₹ 54,600	
(b) Current Value of Abnormal Items [50% of ₹ 6,900]	₹ 3,450	58,050
B. Value of Salvaged Stock		5,800
C. Estimated Value of Stock Lost by fire (A – B)		52,250
D. Amount of claim by applying Average clause:		
$\text{Loss suffered} \times \frac{\text{Sum Insured}}{\text{Actual Insurable Value}} = ₹52,250 \times \frac{₹50,000}{₹58,050}$		45,004

Working Notes:

(I) TRADING ACCOUNT FOR THE YEAR ENDING ON 31ST DEC., 2012

Particulars	₹	*Particulars*		₹
To Opening Stock	73,500	By Sales		4,87,000
To Purchases	3,98,000	By Closing Stock Valued	₹ 79,600	
To Gross Profit (b.f)	97,400	*Add:* w/o	₹ 2,300	81,900
$GPR = \frac{₹97,400}{₹4,87,000} \times 100 = 20\%$				
	5,68,900			5,68,900

(II) MEMORANDUM TRADING ACCOUNT FOR THE PERIOD FROM 01.01.2013 TO 30.06.2013

Particulars	*Normal Items* ₹	*Abnormal Items* ₹	*Total Items* ₹	*Particulars*	*Normal Items* ₹	*Abnormal Items* ₹	*Total Items* ₹
To Opening Stock	75,000	4,600	79,600	By Sales	2,28,000	3,200	2,31,200
To Purchases	1,62,000	—	1,62,000	By Closing Stock	54,600	2,300	56,900
To Gross Profit@20%	45,600	900	46,500	By Gross Loss	—	—	—
	2,82,600	5,500	2,88,100		2,82,600	5,500	2,88,100

ILLUSTRATION 11

From the following information, compute the amount of claim under loss of Stock Policy:

Sum Insured	₹ 73,000	Stock as on 1.1.2012	₹ 1,80,000
Accounting Year	Calender Year	Stock as on 31.12.2012	₹ 2,70,000
Value of Salvaged Stock	₹ 6,000	Purchases during 2012	₹ 3,30,000
Reason for Damage on 30.6.2013	Due to fire accident	Purchases from 1.1.2013 to 30.6.2013	₹ 4,00,000
G.P. Ratio	Uniform from year to year	Sales during 2012	₹ 3,00,000
		Purchases from 1.1.2013 to 30.6.2013	₹ 4,00,000
		Sales from on 1.1.2013 to 30.6.2013	₹ 7,20,000

Stock as on 31st December, 2012 has been under valued by 10%. A stock taking conducted in March 2013 had revealed that stocks costing ₹ 80,000 were lying in a damaged condition.50 percent of these stock had ben sold in May, 2013 at 50% of the original cost and the balance was expected to be sold at 40% of the original cost.

SOLUTION

STATEMENT OF CLAIM

Particulars		₹
A. Estimated Value of Stock as at date of fire		
(a) Book-Value of Normal Items	₹ 1,30,000	
(b) Current Value of Abnormal Items	₹ 16,000	1,46,000
B. Value of Salvaged Stock		6,000
C. Estimated Value of Stock Lost by fire (A – B)		1,40,000
D. Amount of claim by applying Average clause		
$\text{Loss suffered} \times \frac{\text{Sum Insured}}{\text{Actual Insurable Value}} = ₹1,40,000 \times \frac{₹73,000}{₹1,46,000}$		70,000

Working Notes:

(I) TRADING ACCOUNT FOR THE YEAR ENDING ON 31ST DEC, 2012

Particulars	₹	*Particulars*	₹
To Opening Stock	1,80,000	By Sales	3,00,000

To Purchases	3,30,000	By Closing Stock Valued	₹ 2,70,000	
To Gross Profit (b.f)	90,000	*Add:* w/o	₹ 30,000	3,00,000
	6,00,000			6,00,000

(II) MEMORANDUM TRADING ACCOUNT FOR THE PERIOD FROM 01.01.2013 TO 30.06.2013

Particulars	*Normal Items* ₹	*Abnormal Items* ₹	*Total Items* ₹	*Particulars*	*Normal Items* ₹	*Abnormal Items* ₹	*Total Items* ₹
To Opening Stock	2,20,000	80,000	3,00,000	By Sales	7,00,000	20,000	7,20,000
To Purchases	4,00,000	—	4,00,000	By Closing Stock	1,30,000	40,000	1,70,000
To Gross Profit	2,10,000	—	2,10,000	By Gross Loss	—	20,000	20,000
	8,30,000	80,000	9,10,000		8,30,000	80,000	9,10,000

ILLUSTRATION 12

From the following information, compute the amount of claim under loss of Stock Policy:

Sum Insured	₹ 60,000	Stock as on 01.01.2012	₹ 37,500
Accounting Year	Calender Year	Stock as on 31.12.2012	₹ 52,000
Value of Salvaged Stock	₹ 7,200	Purchases during 2012	₹ 2,53,750
G.P. Ratio	Uniform from year to year	Sales during 2012	₹ 3,15,000
Collection from Trade Debtors during 2013	₹ 2,47,240	Trade Debtors as on 1.1.2013	₹ 2,00,000
Payments to Trade Creditors during 2013	₹ 8,750	Trade Creditors as on 30.6.2013	₹ 2,00,000
Reason for Damage on 30.6.2013	Due to fire accident	Trade Debtors as on 30.6.2013	₹ 1,00,000
		Trade Creditors as on 1.1.2013	₹ 1,00,000

In valuing the stock on 31st Dec, 2012, due to obsolescence 50% of the value of the stock of which original cost was ₹ 6,000 had been written off. In May, 2013, three-forth of this stock had been sold at 90% of the original cost and it is now expected that the balance of the obsolete stock would also realise the same price. Cash Sales - 20% of Total Sales (Net of Returns) and Cash Purchases 25% of Total Purchases (Net of Returns), Returns Inwards - ₹ 760 and Returns Outward ₹ 250.

SOLUTION

STATEMENT OF CLAIM

Particulars		₹
A. Estimated value of stock as at date of fire		
(a) Book-value of Normal Items	₹ 59,000	
(b) Current value of Abnormal Items	₹ 1,350	60,350
B. Value of Salvaged Stock		7,200
C. Estimated value of stock lost by fire (A–B)		53,150
D. Amount of claim by applying Average clause		

Loss suffered $\times \frac{\text{Sum Insured}}{\text{Actual Insurable Value}}$ = ₹53,150 $\times \frac{₹60,000}{₹60,350}$	52,842

Working Notes:

Dr. **(I) TRADING ACCOUNT FOR THE YEAR ENDING ON 31ST DEC, 2012** Cr.

Particulars	*Normal Items* ₹	*Abnormal Items* ₹	*Total Items* ₹	*Particulars*	*Normal Items* ₹	*Abnormal Items* ₹	*Total Items* ₹
To Opening Stock	31,500	6,000	37,500	By Sales	3,15,000	—	3,15,000
To Purchases	2,53,750	—	2,53,750	By Closing Stock	49,000	3,000	52,000
To Gross Profit	78,750		78,750	By Gross Loss (b.f.)	—	3,000	3,000
	3,64,000	6,000	3,70,000		3,64,000	6,000	3,70,000

(II) TOTAL CREDITORS ACCOUNT

Particulars	₹	*Particulars*	₹
To Bank A/c	8,750	By Balance b/d	1,00,000
To Returns Outward	250	By Credit Purchases (b.f.)	
To Balance c/d	2,00,000		1,09,000
	2,09,000		2,09,000

Net Purchases = Net Credit Purchases + Cash Purchases

= (₹ 1,09,000 – ₹ 250) + 33 – 1/3% of ₹ 1,08,750 = ₹ 1,45,000

(III) TOTAL DEBTORS ACCOUNT

Particulars	₹	*Particulars*	₹
To balance b/d	2,00,000	By Bank A/c	2,47,240
To Credit Sales (b.f.)	1,48,000	By Returns Inward	760
		By Balance c/d	1,00,000
	3,48,000		3,48,000

Net Sales = Net Credit Sales + Cash Sales

= (₹ 1,48,000 – ₹ 760) +25% of ₹ 1,47,240 = ₹ 1,84,050

(IV) MEMORANDUM TRADING ACCOUNT FOR THE PERIOD FROM 01.01.2013 TO 30.06.2013

Particulars	*Normal Items* ₹	*Abnormal Items* ₹	*Total Items* ₹	*Particulars*	*Normal Items* ₹	*Abnormal Items* ₹	*Total Items* ₹
To Opening Stock	49,000	3,000	52,000	By Sales	1,80,000	4,050	1,84,050
To Purchases	1,45,000	—	1,45,000	By Closing Stock	59,000	750	59,750
To Gross Profit	45,000	1,800	46,800				
	2,39,000	4,800	2,43,800		2,39,000	4,800	2,43,800

6.0 LOSS OF PROFIT POLICY

OBJECTIVE OF LOSS OF PROFIT POLICY

The purpose of any industrial business activity is to earn profit. The loss of profit insurance serves this basic need. A normal fire insurance policy covers the material damage to the property of a manufacturer, viz. his buildings, machinery and other plant against the risks of destruction by fire and/or other specified perils. Whilst this protection is afforded to the manufacturer, it is not possible for him to erect new buildings and/or instal new machinery and plant, put the factory into operation for production purpose immediately after the loss. It may take months and sometimes even years to replace/repair the loss/damage and reach pre-fire production/turnover level and resume to earn expected profits. During the period of interruption when there may be no profits *or* reduced profits, the manufacturer is saddled within certain fixed items of expenditure like rent, interest on capital etc., which he cannot avoid. Moreover, to fulfil the order schedule on hand he may have to incur extra cost for producing the goods elsewhere at much higher rates. The loss of profit insurance is designed to afford protection against such consequential loss following fire, viz

(i) Loss on account of standing charges,

(ii) Net profits before taxation, and

(iii) Increased cost of working.

The standing charges to be covered are as follows:

Interest on Debentures, Mortgages, Loans & Bank Overdrafts	Insurance Premium, Advertising Office expenses
Rent, Rates & Taxes (excluding Taxation chargable on Profit)	Postage, telegrams & telephone, Printing & Stationery
Salaries to permanent staff & wages to skilled employees	Electrical energy and/or power charges
Company's contribution to the Provident Fund	Maintenance of building, Plant & Machinery
Company's contribution to the Gratuity Fund	Depreciation (excluding stocks and stores)
Labour welfare charges	Miscellaneous Standing Charges not exceeding
Director's fees, Auditors fees, Legal expenses	5% of the amount of the Standing Charges specified.
Travelling expenses, Motor Car expenses	

PRACTICAL STEPS INVOLVED IN THE DETERMINATION OF THE AMOUNT OF CLAIM UNDER LOSS OF PROFIT POLICY

The various steps involved in the determination of the amount of claim under loss of profit policy are given below:

Step 1: ***Ascertain the period of claim by taking the 'Indemnity Period' or 'Dislocation Period whichever is less.***

Note: *Indemnity Period' refers to the period beginning with the occurence of the damage and ending not later than 12 months thereafter during which the results of the business shall be affected in consequence of the damage. 'Dislocation Period' refers to the period beginning with the occurence of the damage and ending with a date upto which the results of the business remain affected in consequence of the damages.*

Step 2: ***Calculate the Gross Profit Ratio based on the trading results of the last accounting year with due regard to the Special Circumstances Clause (if any, applicable) as under:***

In Case of Net Profit	*In Case of Net Loss*
G.P. Ratio = $\frac{\text{Net Profit} + \text{Insured Standing Charges}}{\text{Turnover of last accounting year}} \times 100$	G.P. Ratio = $\frac{\text{Insured Standing Charges} - \text{Net Loss}}{\text{Turnover of last accounting year}} \times 100$

Notes:

(i) *If all the standing charges are not insured, the amount of Net Loss must be reduced as under:*

(ii) *If the Special Circumstances Clause stipulates for the adjustment to be made in G.P Ratio to provide for the trend of the business, then the G.P. Ratio should be adjusted accordingly.*

Step 3: ***Calculate the Turnover lost in claim period with due regard to Special Circumstances Clause, (if any), as under:***

Particulars	₹
A. Turnover for the corresponding claim period in the preceding year	xxx
B. Add/Less Agreed increase/decrease (on account of upward/downward trend)	xxx
C. *Less:* Actual Turnover during the claim period	xxx
D. Turnover Lost during the claim period	xxx

Step 4: ***Calculate the Gross Profit lost during the claim period as under:***

Gross Profit lost = Turnover lost during the claim period x Agreed G.P. Ratio

Step 5: ***Calculate the Sum Insurable as under:***

Sum Insurable = Adjusted Turnover during 12 months immediately preceeding the date of fire × Agreed G.P. Ratio

Note: Adjusted Turnover = Turnover during 12 months immediately preceeding the date of fire + agreed increase/decrease

Step 6: ***Calculate the amount of Net claim for the Increased Cost of working as under:***

A.	Gross claim for Increased Cost of Working (*being the least of the following three amounts*)	xxx
1.	Actual Expenses	xxx
2.	Proportionate Increased Cost of Working	

$$\text{Increased Cost of Working} \times \frac{\text{Gross Profit on Adjusted Turnover}}{\text{Gross Profit as above} + \text{Uninsured Standing Charges}}$$

Note: Adjusted Turnover = Turnover during 12 months immediately preceding the date of fire ± agreed increase/decrease

3.	Maximum Saving of liability of the insurer = Reduction in Turnover avoided through Increased Cost of Working × Agreed G. P. Ratio	
B.	*Less:* Saving in Insured Standing Charges	xxx
C.	Net claim for Increased Cost of Working (A – B)	xxx

Step 7: ***Add the amount of Net Claim for the Increased Cost of Working to the Gross Profit lost during the claim period (i.e aggregate of amount as per Step No. 4&6).***

Step 8: ***Calculate the amount of claim to be considered by Insurance Co. as under:***

(a) **In case of over-insurance** (i.e. where the sum insured exceeds the sum insurable), the average clause (if any inserted in the 'Contract of Insurance) does not aply at all and hence the amount of claim is **equal to the sum calculated as per Step No. 7.**

(b) **In case of under-insurance** (i.e where the sum insured is *less* than the sum insurable), the amount of claim according to average clause (if inserted in the Contract of Insurance) **wiil be calculated as under:**

$$\left[\text{Gross P/L during claim period + the net claim for the increased cost of working} \times \frac{\text{Sum Insured}}{\text{Sum Insurable}}\right]$$

TUTORIAL NOTE

(i) *Unless otherwise stated, all standing charges should be treated as insured standing charges.*

(ii) *Unless otherwise stated, actual turnover in the claim period should be deemed to have been effected as a result of additional expenses.*

ILLUSTRATION 13 [CALCULATION OF PERIOD OF CLAIM]

Calculate the period of claim in each of following alternative cases:

Particulars	*Case I*	*Case II*
Indemnity Period	6 months	6 months
Dislocation Period	5 months	7 months

SOLUTION

The period of claim is the least of indeminity period and dislocation period. In Case I, the insurer would indeminify only for 5 months. In Case II, the insurer would indemnify only for 6 months.

ILLUSTRATION 14 [CALCULATION OF GROSS PROFIT RATIO]

Calculate the Gross Profit ratio in each of the following alternative cases:

Case (a) Net Profit ₹ 2,40,000, Turnover of last accounting year ₹ 40,00,000, Standing Charges (out of which ₹ 80,000 have not been insured) ₹ 5,60,000;

Case (b) Net Loss ₹ 2,40,000, Turnover of last accounting year ₹ 40,00,000, Standing Charges (out of which ₹ 80,000 have not been insured) ₹ 5,60,000;

Case (c) Net Profit ₹ 2,40,000, Turnover of last accounting year ₹ 40,00,000, Standing charges (out of which ₹ 80,000 have not been insured) ₹ 5,60,000, Special Circumstances Clause in the Policy allows for increase in the rate of Gross Profit by 2%

Case (d) Gross Profit Ratio for the last year 25%, Turnover for the last year ₹ 10,00,000, Total Standing Charges (out of which ₹ 50,000 have not been insured) ₹ 2,50,000

Case (e) Gross Profit Ratio for the last year 30%, Turnover for the last year ₹ 5,00,000, Uninsured Standing Charges ₹ 25,000, Net Profit ₹ 90,000

SOLUTION

Case (a) G. P. Ratio $= \frac{\text{Net Profit} + \text{Insured Standing Charges}}{\text{Turnover of last accounting year}} \times 100$

$= \frac{₹2,40,000 + ₹4,80,000}{₹40,00,000} \times 100 = 18\%$

Case (b) G. P. Ratio $= \frac{\text{Insured Standing Charges} - \text{Net Loss}}{\text{Turnover of last accounting year}} \times 100$

$= \frac{₹4,80,000 - ₹2,40,000}{₹40,00,000} \times 100 = 6\%$

Case (c) G. P. Ratio $= \frac{\text{Net Profit} + \text{Insured Standing Charges}}{\text{Turnover of last accounting year}} \times 100$

$$= \frac{₹2,40,000 + ₹4,80,000}{₹40,00,000} \times 100 = 18\%$$

Agreed Increase = 2%, Agreed G.P. Ratio = 18% + 2% = 20%

Case (d) Net Profit for last year = Gross Profit – Total Standing Charges

= 25% of ₹ 10,00,000 – ₹ 2,50,000 = 0

$$\text{G. P. Ratio} = \frac{\text{Net Profit} + \text{Insured Standing Charges}}{\text{Turnover of last accounting year}} \times 100$$

$$= \frac{0 + ₹2,00,000}{₹10,00,000} \times 100 = 20\%$$

Case (e) Total Standing Charges = Gross Profit – Net Profit

= 30% of ₹ 5,00,000 – ₹ 90,000 = ₹ 60,000

Insured Standing Charges = Total Standing Charges–Uninsured Standing Charges

= ₹ 60,000 – ₹ 25,000 = ₹ 35,000

$$\text{G. P. Ratio} = \frac{\text{Net Profit} + \text{Insured Standing Charges}}{\text{Turnover of last accounting year}} \times 100$$

$$= \frac{₹90,000 + ₹35,000}{₹5,00,000} \times 100 = 25\%$$

ILLUSTRATION 15 [CALCULATION OF TURNOVER LOST]

Calculate the Turnover lost during the Claim period from the following particulars:

Indeminity Period 6 Months	Turnover from 1.3.2013 to 31.7.2013 –₹ 8 lakhs
Disclocation Period from 1.3.2013 to 31.7.2013	Turnover from 1.3.2012 to 31.7.2012 –₹ 20 lakhs

Note: *Special Circumstances Clause in the policy provided for the increase of Turnover by 10%.*

SOLUTION

A.	Turnover for the corresponding claim period in the preceding year	₹ 20,00,000
B.	*Add:* Agreed Increase	₹ 2,00,000
C.	*Less:* Actual Turnover during the claim period	₹ 8,00,000
D.	Turnover lost in claim period (A + B – C)	₹ 14,00,000

ILLUSTRATION 16 [CALCULATION OF GROSS PROFIT LOST]

Calculate the Gross Profit lost during the Claim Period if the Turnover lost during the Claim Period is ₹ 14,00,000 and the agreed G.P.Ratio is 20%.

SOLUTION

Gross Profit lost = Turnover lost during the claim period × Agreed G.P. Ratio

= ₹ 14,00,000 × 20% = ₹ 2,80,000

ILLUSATRATION 17 [CALCULATION OF NET CLAIM FOR THE INCREASED COST OF WORKING]

Calculate the Net Claim for the increased Cost of working from the following information:

Agreed G.P. Ratio 20%, Net Profit for the last accounting year 2,40,000, Standing Charges (out of which ₹ 80,000 have not been insured) ₹ 5,60,000, actual turnover during claim period ₹ 8,00,000.

During the claim period, 50% of the total turnover of this period was maintained by incurring the additional expenses amounting to ₹ 1,50,000 and there was a saving in insured standing charges of 6.25% and in uninsured standing charges of ₹ 10,000. Turnover during 12 months preceding the date of fire ₹ 30,00,000. Agreed Increase 20%.

SOLUTION

1. Adjusted Turnover = ₹ 30,00,000 + 20% of ₹ 30,00,000 = ₹ 36,00,000
2. Net Claim for the increase cost of Working

A. Gross claim for Increased Cost of Working (being the least of the following three amounts) ₹ 80,000

1. Actual Expenses ₹ 1,50,000
2. Proportionate Increased Cost of Working

$$= \text{Increased Cost of Working} \times \frac{\text{Gross Profit on Adjusted Turnover}}{\text{Gross Profit as above} + \text{Uninsured Standing Charges}}$$

$$= 1,50,000 \times \frac{20\% \text{ of } ₹36,00,000}{₹7,20,000 + ₹80,000} = ₹\ 1,35,000$$

3. Maximum saving of liability of the insurer = Reduction in Turnover avoided through Increased Cost of Working × Agreed G.P. Ratio

= ₹ 4,00,000 × 20% = ₹ 80,000

B. *Less:* Saving In Insured Standing Charges (₹ 4,80,000 × 6.25%) = ₹ 30,000

C. Net claim for Increased Cost of Working (A – B) = ₹ 50,000

ILLUSTRATION 18 [CALCULATION OF THE AMOUNT OF SUM INSURABLE]

Calculate the amount of Sum Insurable from the following particulars: Date of fire 1.3.2013, Turnover from 1.3.2012 to 28.2.2013 ₹ 44,00,000, Agreed G.P. Ratio 20%, Special circumstances clause provided for the increase in turnover by 10%.

SOLUTION

Adjusted Turnover = Turnover during 12 Months preceding the date of fire + Agreed increase in Turnover

= ₹ 44,00,000 +10% of ₹ 44,00,000 = ₹ 48,40,000

Sum Insurable = Adjusted Turnover × Agreed G.P. Ratio

= ₹ 48,40,000 × 20/100 = ₹ 9,68,000

ILLUSTRATION 19 [CALCULATION OF THE AMOUNT OF INSURANCE CLAIM]

Calculate the amount of claim if sum insured is (a) ₹ 10,00,000 and (b) ₹ 7,50,000 from the following data:

Date of fire	1.3.2013	Turnover from 1.3.2012 to 28.2.2013	44,00,000
Gross profit lost during Claim period	2,80,000	Agreed G.P. Ratio	20%
Special Circumstances Clause provides for the increase in turnover by 10%		Net Claim for increased Cost of working	50,000

SOLUTION

(a) *If the Sum Insured is ₹ 10,00,000*

Sum Insurable = Adjusted Turnover during 12 months immediately preceding the date of fire x Agreed G.P. Ratio

= (₹ 44,00,000 + 10% of ₹ 44,00,000) × 20%

= ₹ 48,40,000 × 20% = ₹ 9,68,000

Since Sum Insured exceeds the Sum Insurable, Average Clause will not apply at all and hence the amount of claim will be calculated as under:

Total claim = Gross Profit on turn over lost during claim period + Net Claim for the increased cost of working

= ₹ 2,80,000 + ₹ 50,000 = ₹ 3,30,000

(b) *If the Sum Insured is ₹ 7,50,000*

Since Sum Insured is *less* than the Sum Insurable, the average clause will apply as under:

ILLUSTRATION 20

From the following information, compute the amount of claim under the loss of profit policy:

Sum Insured	₹ 1.95 Lakh
Indemnity Period	6 Months
Reason for Damage	Due to Fire Accident on1.3.2013
Period of Interruption	1.3.2013 to 31.7.2013
Accounting Year	Calender Year
Net Profit	₹ 0.60 Lakh
Increase in Cost of working	₹ 0.15 Lakh
Turnover For the year ended 31st December, 2012	₹ 5.250 Lakh
Turnover For the period from 1.3.2012 to 28.2.2013	₹ 5.850 Lakh
Turnover For the period from 1.3.2012 to 31.7.2012	₹ 1.275 Lakh
Turnover For the period from 1.3.2013 to 31.7.2013	₹ 0.600 Lakh
Sales were evenly throughout the period Standing Charges	₹ 1.50 Lakh
No clause for upward/downward trend	

SOLUTION

STATEMENT OF CLAIM

Particulars	₹
A. Gross Profit on Turnover lost in claim period	27,000
B. *Add:* Net claim for the Increased Cost of Working	15,000
C. Total Claim (A+B)	42,000
D. Net Claim = Total Claim $\times \frac{\text{Sum Insured}}{\text{Sum Insurable}} = \frac{₹42,000 \times ₹1,95,000}{₹2,34,000}$	35,000

Working Notes:

(i) Agreed G.P. Ratio = G.P. Ratio as per last accounting year + Agreed Increase/Decrease

$$\text{G. P. Ratio} = \frac{\text{Net Profit} + \text{Insured Standing Charges}}{\text{Turnover of last accounting year}} \times 100$$

$$= \frac{₹60,000 + ₹1,50,000}{₹5,25,000} \times 100 = 40\%$$

(ii) Claim Period being the least of the Indemnity Period (6 months) & Dislocation Period (5 months) is 5 months.

(III) CALCULATION OF TURNOVER LOST IN CLAIM PERIOD

A. Turnover for the corresponding claim period in the preceding year	1,27,500
B. *Add:* Agreed Increase	—
C. *Less:* Actual Turnover during the claim period	60,000
D. Turnover lost in claim period (A + B – C)	67,500

(iv) Gross Profit lost = Turnover lost during the claim period × Agreed G.P. Ratio
= ₹ 67,500 × 40% = ₹ 27,000

(v) Sum Insurable = Adjusted Turnover during 12 months immediately preceding the fire × Agreed G.P. Ratio
= ₹ 5,85,000 × 40% = ₹ 2,34,000

(VI) CALCULATION OF THE NET CLAIM FOR THE INCREASED COST OF WORKING

A. Gross claim for Increased Cost of Working *(being the least of the following three amounts)*	15,000
1. Actual Expenses	₹ 15,000
2. Proportionate Increased Cost of Working $\text{Increased Cost of Working} \times \frac{\text{Gross Profit on Adjusted Turnover}}{\text{Gross Profit as above} + \text{Uninsured Standing Charges}}$ $= 15,000 \times \frac{40\% \text{ of } 5,85,000}{2,34,000 \quad 0}$	₹ 15,000
3. Maximum saving of liability of the insurer = Reduction in Turnover avoided through Increased Cost of Working × Agreed G. P. Ratio = ₹ 60,000 × 40%	₹ 24,000
B. *Less:* Saving In Insured Standing Charges	—
C. Net claim for Increased Cost of Working (A – B)	₹ 15,000

(vii) In the absence of information, it has been assumed that the Actual Turnover during the claim period has been effected as a result of additional expenses.

(viii) In the absence of information, it has been assumed that all standing charges are insured.

ILLUSTRATION 21

From the following information, compute the amount of claim under the loss of profit policy:

Sum Insured	₹ 1.20 Lakh
Indemnity Period	6 Months
Reason for Damage	Due to Fire Accident on 1.3.2013
Period of Interruption	1.3.2013 to 31.7.2013

Accounting Year	Calender Year
Gross Profit Ratio	25%
Increase in Cost of working	₹ 0.30 Lakh
Saving in insured Standing Charges	₹ 0.09478 Lakh
Turnover For the year ended 31st Dec., 2012	₹ 10.00 Lakh
Turnover For the period from 1.3.2012 to 28.2.2013	₹ 9.00 Lakh
Turnover For the period from 1.3.2012 to 31.7.2012	₹ 5.00 Lakh
Turnover For the period from 1.3.2013 to 31.7.2013	₹ 3.00 Lakh
Sales were evenly throughout the period Standing Charges (out of which ₹ 50,000 have not been insured)	₹ 2.50 Lakh
No clause for upward/Downward Trend	

SOLUTION

STATEMENT OF CLAIM

	Particulars	₹
A.	Gross Profit on Turnover lost in claim period	40,000
B.	*Add:* Net claim for the Increased Cost of Working	14,000
C.	Total Claim (A + B)	54,000
D.	Net Claim Total Claim $\times \frac{\text{Sum Insured}}{\text{Sum Insurable}} = \frac{₹54,000 \times ₹1,20,000}{₹1,80,000}$	36,000

Working Notes:

(i) Agreed G.P. Ratio = G.P. Ratio as per last accounting year + Agreed Increase/Decrease

$$\text{G. P. Ratio} = \frac{\text{Net Profit} + \text{Insured Standing Charges}}{\text{Turnover of last accounting year}} \times 100$$

$$= \frac{0 + ₹2,00,000}{₹10,00,000} \times 100 = 20\%$$

Note: Net Profit for the year ended 31st Dec., 2012 = Gross profit – All Standing Charges

= 25% of ₹ 10,00,000 – ₹ 2,50,000 = 0

(ii) Claim Period being the least of the Indemnity Period (6 months) & Dislocation Period (5 months) is 5 months.

(III) CALCULATION OF TURNOVER LOST IN CLAIM PERIOD

A.	Turnover for the corresponding claim period in the preceding year	₹ 5,00,000
B.	*Add:* Agreed Increase	—
C.	*Less:* Actual Turnover during the claim period	₹ 3,00,000
D.	Turnover lost in claim period (A + B – C)	₹ 2,00,000

(iv) Gross Profit lost = Turnover lost during the claim period x Agreed G.P. Ratio

= ₹ 2,00,000 × 20% = ₹ 40,000

(v) Sum Insurable = Adjusted Turnover during 12 months immediately preceding the fire × Agreed G.P. Ratio

= ₹ 9,00,000 × 20% = ₹ 1,80,000

(VI) CALCULATION OF THE NET CLAIM FOR THE INCREASED COST OF WORKING

A.	Gross claim for Increased Cost of Working *(being the least of the following three amounts)*	₹ 23,478
1.	Actual Expenses	₹ 30,000
2.	Proportionate Increased Cost of Working $\text{Increased Cost of Working} \times \frac{\text{Gross Profit on Adjusted Turnover}}{\text{Gross Profit as above} + \text{Uninsured Standing Charges}}$ $= ₹30,000 \times \frac{20\% \text{ of } ₹9,00,000}{₹1,80,000 + ₹50,000}$	₹ 23,478
3.	Maximum saving of liability of the insurer = Reduction in Turnover avoided through Increased Cost of Working × Agreed G. P. Ratio = ₹ 3,00,000 × 20%	₹ 60,000
B.	*Less:* Saving In Insured Standing Charges	₹ 9,478
C.	Net claim for Increased Cost of Working (A – B)	₹ 14,000

(vii) In the absence of information, it has been assumed that the Actual Turnover in the claim period has been effected as a result of additional expenses.

ILLUSTRATION 22

From the following information, compute the amount of claim under the loss of profit policy:

Sum Insured	₹ 1,00,000
Indemnity Period	6 Months
Reason for Damage	Due to Fire Accident on 1.3.201
Period of Interruption	1.3.2013 to 31.7.2013
Accounting Year	Calender Year
Gross Profit Ratio	30%
Saving in insured Standing Charges	₹ 6,774
Increase in cost of working	₹ 20,000 for 80% of the turnover
No Clause for Upward/Downward Trend	during dislocation period
Turnover For the year ended 31st December, 2012	₹ 5,00,000
Turnover For the period from 1.3.2012 to 28.2.2013	₹ 5,20,000
Turnover For the period from 1.3.2012 to 31.7.2012	₹ 2,60,000
Turnover For the period from 1.3.2013 to 31.7.2013	₹ 1,00,000
Sales were evenly throughout the period Uninsurred Standing Charges	₹ 25,000
Net Profit	₹ 90,000

SOLUTION

STATEMENT OF CLAIM

	Particulars	₹
A.	Gross Profit on Turnover lost in claim period	40,000
B.	*Add:* Net claim for the Increased Cost of Working	10,000

C. Total Claim (A + B)	50,000
D. Net Claim = Total Claim $\times \frac{\text{Sum Insured}}{\text{Sum Insurable}} = \frac{₹50,000 \times ₹1,00,000}{₹1,30,000}$	38,462

Working Notes:

(i) Agreed G.P. Ratio = G.P. Ratio as per last accounting year + Agreed Increase/Decrease

$$\text{G. P. Ratio} = \frac{\text{Net Profit} + \text{Insured Standing Charges}}{\text{Turnover of last accounting year}} \times 100$$

$$= \frac{₹90,000 + ₹35,000}{₹5,00,000} \times 100 = 25\%$$

Notes: All Standing Charges = Gross Profit – Net profit

= 30% of ₹ 5,00,000 – ₹ 90,000 = ₹ 1,50,000–₹ 90,000 = ₹ 60,000

Insured Standing Charges = All Standing Charges *less* Uninsured Standing Charges

= ₹ 60,000 – ₹ 25,000 = ₹ 35,000

(ii) Claim Period being the least of the Indemnity Period (6 months) & Dislocation Period (5 months) is 5 months.

(III) CALCULATION OF TURNOVER LOST IN CLAIM PERIOD

A. Turnover for the corresponding claim period in the preceding year	₹ 2,60,000
B. *Add:* Agreed Increase	—
C. *Less:* Actual Turnover during the claim period	₹ 1,00,000
D. Turnover lost in claim period (A + B – C)	₹ 1,60,000

(iv) Gross Profit lost = Turnover lost during the claim period × Agreed G.P. Ratio

= ₹ 1,60,000 × 25% = ₹ 40,000

(v) Sum Insurable = Adjusted Turnover during 12 months immediately preceeding the fire × Agreed G.P. Ratio

= ₹ 5,20,000 × 25% = ₹ 1,30,000

(VI) CALCULATION OF THE NET CLAIM FOR THE INCREASED COST OF WORKING

A. Gross claim for Increased Cost of Working *(being the least of the following three amounts)*	₹ 16,774
1. Actual Expenses	₹ 20,000
2. Proportionate Increased Cost of Working $\text{Increased Cost of Working} \times \frac{\text{Gross Profit on Adjusted Turnover}}{\text{Gross Profit as above} + \text{Uninsured Standing Charges}}$ $= ₹20,000 \times \frac{25\% \text{ of } ₹5,20,000}{₹1,30,000 + ₹25,000}$	₹ 16,774
3. Maximum saving of liability of the insurer = Reduction in Turnover avoided through Increased Cost of Working × Agreed G. P. Ratio = ₹ 80,000 × 25%	₹ 20,000
B. *Less:* Saving In Insured Standing Charges	₹ 6,774
C. Net Claim for Increased Cost of Working (A – B)	₹ 10,000

ILLUSTRATION 23

From the following information, compute the amount of claim under the loss of profit policy:

Sum Insured	₹ 1,24,200
Indemnity Period	6 Months
Reason for Damage	Due to Fire Accident on 1.3.2013
Period of Interruption	1.3.2013 to 31.7.2013
Accounting Year	Calender Year
Net Profit for 2012	₹ 70,000
Increase in cost of working	₹ 6,700
Saving in insured Standing Charges	₹ 2,522
Turnover For the year ended 31st December, 2012	₹ 4,20,000
Turnover For the period from 1.3.2012 to 28.2.2013	₹ 4,50,000
Turnover For the period from 1.3.2012 to 31.7.2012	₹ 2,10,000
Turnover For the period from 1.3.2013 to 31.7.2013	₹ 75,000
Sales were evenly throughout the period Standing Charges (out of which ₹ 8,000 have not been insured)	₹ 64,000
Agreed Increase for upward trend in turnover	15%

SOLUTION

STATEMENT OF CLAIM

	Particulars	₹
A.	Gross Profit on Turnover lost in claim period	49,950
B.	*Add:* Net claim for the Increased Cost of Working	3,850
C.	Total Claim (A + B)	53,800
D.	Net Claim = Total Claim $\times \frac{\text{Sum Insured}}{\text{Sum Insurable}} = \frac{₹53,800 \times ₹1,24,200}{₹1,55,250}$	43,040

Working Notes:

(i) Agreed G.P. Ratio = G.P. Ratio as per last accounting year + Agreed Increase/Decrease

$$\text{G. P. Ratio} = \frac{\text{Net Profit} + \text{Insured Standing Charges}}{\text{Turnover of last accounting year}} \times 100 = \frac{₹70,000 + ₹56,000}{₹4,20,000} \times 100 = 30\%$$

(ii) Claim Period being the least of the Indemnity Period (6 months) & Dislocation Period (5 months) is 5 months.

(III) CALCULATION OF TURNOVER LOST IN CLAIM PERIOD

A.	Turnover for the corresponding claim period in the preceding year	₹ 2,10,000
B.	*Add:* Agreed Increase	₹ 31,500
C.	*Less:* Actual Turnover during the claim period	(₹ 75,000)
D.	Turnover lost in claim period (A + B – C)	₹ 1,66,500

(iv) Gross Profit lost = Turnover lost during the claim period × Agreed G.P. Ratio

= ₹ 1,66,500 × 30% = ₹ 49,950

(v) Sum Insurable = Adjusted Turnover during 12 months immediately preceeding the fire × Agreed G.P. Ratio
= ₹ 4,50,000 × 115% × 30% = ₹ 1,55,250

(VI) CALCULATION OF THE NET CLAIM FOR THE INCREASED COST OF WORKING

A. Gross claim for Increased Cost of Working *(being the least of the following three amounts)*	₹ 6,372
1. Actual Expenses	₹ 6,700
2. Proportionate Increased Cost of Working $\text{Increased Cost of Working} \times \frac{\text{Gross Profit on Adjusted Turnover}}{\text{Gross Profit as above} + \text{Uninsured Standing Charges}}$ $= ₹6,700 \times \frac{₹1,55,250}{₹1,55,250 + ₹8,000}$	₹ 6,372
3. Maximum saving of liability of the insurer = Reduction in Turnover avoided through increased Cost of Working x Agreed G. P. Ratio = ₹ 75,000 × 30%	₹ 22,500
B. *Less:* Saving In Insured Standing Charges	₹ 2,522
C. Net claim for Increased Cost of Working (A – B)	₹ 3,850

(vii) In the absence of information it has been assumed that the actual turnover during claim period has been effected as a result of additional expenses.

7.0 AMOUNT TO BE INSURED UNDER LOSS OF PROFIT POLICY

The amount to be insured should be the estimated specified standing charges *plus* the estimated net profit for selected period of indemnity based on the actual figures for the last financial year modified in accordance with the trend of business and market conditions. The various steps involved in the determination of the amount to be insured under a loss of profit policy are given below:

PRACTICAL STEPS INVOLVED IN THE DETERMINATION OF THE AMOUNT TO BE INSURED UNDER A LOSS OF PROFIT POLICY

Step 1: Calculate the estimated Turnover for the period for which policy is to be taken
Step 2: Calculate the estimated Gross Profit thereon
Step 3: Calculate the estimated increase in the amount of Insured standing charges.
Step 4: Calculate the amount of uninsured standing charges
Step 5: Calculate the amount of policy as follows:

A. Estimated Gross Profit (As per Step No. 2)	xxx
B. *Add:* Estimated Increase in Insured Standing Charges	xxx
C. *Less:* Uninsured Standing Charges (As per Step No.4)	xxx
D. Amount of Policy (A + B – C)	xxx

ILLUSTRATION 24

From the following calculation the sum insurable:

Variable Expenses	₹ 24.00 lakhs
Fixed Expenses	₹ 5.00 lakhs
Net Profit	₹ 4.20 lakhs

Misc. Income	₹ 0.70 lakhs
Expected Increase in Turnover	20%
Expected Increase in Standing Charges	9%

SOLUTION

Step 1: *Calculation of Gross Profit*

Dr. **TRADING & P&L ACCOUNT** *Cr.*

Particulars	₹	*Particulars*	₹
To Variable Expenses	24.00	By Sales	32.50
To Gross Profit	8.50		
	32.50		32.50
To Fixed Expenses	5.00	By Gross Profit b/d (b.f.)	8.50
To Net Profit	4.20	By Misc. Income	0.70
	9.20		9.20

Step 2: *Calculation of Sum Insurable*

Gross Profit on last year's Sales	8.50
Add: 20% Increase	1.70
Add: Increase in Standing Charges [9% of ₹ 5.00]	.45
Sum Insurable	10.65

ILLUSTRACTION 25

X Ltd. has decided to take out a loss of profits policy for the year 2013 and provides you the following figures for the last accounting year, 2012.

Variable Manufacturing Expenses ₹ 32,80,000, Standing Charges ₹ 4,80,000, Net Profits ₹ 2,45,000, Non-operating incomes ₹ 5,000, Turnover ₹ 40,00,000.

Compute the sum to be insured in each of the following alternative cases showing the anticipation for the year 2013:

(a) If Turnover will increase by 10%;

(b) If Turnover will increase by 10% and only 50% of the present standing charges are to be insured;

(c) If Turnover and standing charges will increase by 10%;

(d) If Turnover and variable expenses will increase by 10%;

(e) If Turnover will increase by 10% but variable expenses will decrease by 10%;

(f) If the turnover and standing charges will increase by 10% and variable expenses will decrease by 10% but only 50% of the present standing charges are to be insured:

SOLUTION

COMPUTATION OF SUM INSURED UNDER VARIOUS CASES *(₹ in lakhs)*

Particulars	*(a)* ₹	*(b)* ₹	*(c)* ₹	*(d)* ₹	*(e)* ₹	*(f)* ₹
A Turnover	44.00	44.00	44.00	44.00	44.00	44.00

B	*Less:* Variable Costs	36.08	36.08	36.08	39.688	32.472	32.472
C	Gross Profit (A – B)	7.92	7.92	7.92	4.312	11.528	11.528
D	*Add:* Increase in Insured Standing Charges	—	—	.48	—	—	.24
E	*Less:* Uninsured Standing Charges	—	(2.40)	—	—	—	(2.40)
F	Sum Insurable [C + D – E]	7.92	5.52	8.40	4.312	11.528	9.368

ILLUSTRATION 26

X Ltd. provides the following information:

(a) Claims made against and admitted by the Insurance Co.

Particulars	*Claimed* ₹	*Admitted* ₹	*Particulars*	*Claimed* ₹	*Admitted* ₹
Stock Damaged	40,000	30,000	Machinery	3,10,000	3,00,000
Stock Destroyed	50,000	35,000	Furniture	8,500	6,000
Loss of Profit	1,60,000	1,00,000	Fire Expenses	1,000	1,000
Building	3,25,000	3,15,000			

(b) Position of fixed assets on 1st day of accounting year, i.e., as on 1.4.2012

Particulars	*Accumulated Depreciation* ₹	*Original Cost* ₹
Building	60,000	3,00,000
Machinery	1,20,000	4,50,000
Furniture	5,000	15,000

(c) Annual Rates of Depreciation on W.D.V. Basis on Building (5%), Machinery (15%), Furniture (10%)

(d) The amount claimed and admitted for the loss of profit was half in respect of profits for 5 months and half in respect of heavy advertisement put to Advertising Suspense, now worthless.

(e) Repairs & Renovations to Building costs ₹ 19,000.

(f) Date of fire being 31st December, 2012.

Required: Give the necessary journal entries in the books of X Ltd.

SOLUTION

JOURNAL OF X LTD.

Particulars		*L.F.*	*Dr.* (₹)	*Cr.* (₹)
Insurance Company	Dr.		7,87,000	
To Buildings				3,15,000
To Machinery				3,00,000
To Furniture				6,000
To Stock damaged				30,000
To Stock destroyed				35,000

Particulars		Dr.	Cr.
To Profit & Loss A/c			30,000
To Profit & Loss Suspense A/c (Claim)			20,000
To Advertising Suspense A/c			50,000
To Fire Expenses			1,000
(Being the Claims admitted by the Insurance Co.)			
Bank A/c	Dr.	7,87,000	
To Insurance Company			7,87,000
(Being the payment received from the Insurance Company)			
Stock Damaged A/c	Dr.	40,000	
Stock Destroyed A/c	Dr.	50,000	
To Trading A/c			90,000
(Being the full value of stock credited to Trading Account)			
Profit and Loss A/c	Dr.	25,000	
To Stock Damaged A/c			10,000
To Stock Destroyed A/c			15,000
(Being the loss on account of difference between full value of stock and amount admitted transferred to Profit & Loss A/c)			
Depreciation A/c	Dr.	46,875	
To Building A/c			9,000
To Machinery A/c			37,125
To Furniture A/c			750
(Being the depreciation for 9 months on buildings @ 5% p.a and on Machinery at 15% p.a. and on furniture @ 10% p.a. on W.D.V. Basis)			
Building A/c	Dr.	84,000	
To Bank A/c			19,000
To Profit & Loss A/c			50,000
To Capital Reserve			15,000
(Being the amount recovered for building exceeds the book value *less* depreciation upto 31st Dec. 1995; the profit over the original cost credited to Capital Reserve & Payment for repairs etc. made)			
Profit & Loss A/c	Dr.	3,250	
To Furniture A/c			3,250
(Being the loss suffered on furniture since the amount recovered is *less* than the book value)			
Machinery A/c	Dr.	7,125	
To Profit & Loss A/c			7,125
(Being excess claim admitted)			

SOLVED PROBLEMS

PROBLEM 1 (A)

Calculate the Gross and Net claim for increased cost of working:

(a) Date of fire 15.6.2013

(b) Agreed Increase of Turnover in current year 25%

(c) Additional Expenditure during claim period ₹ 12,000

(d) Saving in Insured Standing Charges ₹ 2,000

(e) Total Standing charges ₹ 1,20,000

(f) Insured Standing charges ₹ 70,000

(g) Turnover from 16.6.2012 to 15.6.2013 ₹ 5,60,000

(h) Turnover for last accounting year ₹ 6,00,000

(i) Turnover from 15.6.2013 to 15.12.2013 ₹ 70,000

(j) Net Profit Ratio 15.6.2013 to 15.12.2013 — 13.1/3%

SOLUTION

(a) $\text{G. P. Ratio} = \dfrac{\text{Net Profit} + \text{Insured Standing Charges}}{\text{Turnover of last accounting year}} \times 100$

$$= \frac{13\frac{1}{3}\% \text{ of } ₹6,00,000 + ₹70,000}{₹6,00,000} \times 100 = 25\%$$

(b) Claim for increased cost of working least of the following:

(i) Actual Expenditure ₹ 12,000

(ii) $\text{Actual Expenditure} \times \dfrac{\text{GP on Adjusted Turnover}}{\text{GP as above} + \text{Uninsured Standing Charges}}$

$$= ₹12,000 \times \frac{25\% \text{ of } ₹7,00,000}{₹1,75,000 + ₹50,000} = ₹\ 9,333$$

Note: Adjusted Turnover = ₹ 5,60,000 + 25% of ₹ 5,60,000 = ₹ 7,00,000

(iii) GP on sales generated due to additional expenditure = 25% of ₹ 70,000 = ₹ 17,500

Hence, Gross Claim for increased cost of working = ₹ 9,333 (being least)

Net Claim = ₹ 9,333 – ₹ 2,000 (i.e. Savingin Insured Studing Charges) = ₹ 7,333

PROBLEM 1 (B)

Calculate the Gross and Net claim in Problem 1 above if additional expenditure was incurred to achieve 50% of the turnover during the disclocation period.

SOLUTION

GP on sales generated due to additional expenditure = 25% of (50% of ₹ 70,000) = ₹ 8,750

Thus, Gross claim is ₹ 8,750 (being least)

Net Claim = ₹ 8,750 – ₹ 2,000 = ₹ 6,750

PROBLEM 2

Compute the amount of claim from the following information:

Particulars	₹
Sum Insured against the loss of furniture	73,000
Value of Salvaged Furniture	6,000
Actual Value of furniture as on date of fire	1,70,000

SOLUTION

STATEMENT OF CLAIM

Particulars	₹
A. Estimated value of furniture as at date of fire	1,70,000
B. Value of Salvaged furniture	6,000
C. Estimated value of furniture lost by fire (A – B)	1,64,000
D. Amount of claim by applying Average clause:	
$\text{Loss suffered} \times \dfrac{\text{Sum Insured}}{\text{Actual Insurable Value}} = ₹1,64,000 \times \dfrac{₹73,000}{₹1,70,000}$	70,424

PROBLEM 3

The premises of Fire Proof Ltd. were destroyed by fire on 30.6.2014. The following figures were ascertained. You are required to prepare a statement of claim in respect of loss of stock to be submitted to the insurance company.

Particulars	*2011*	*2012*	*2013*	*1.1.2014 to 30.6.2014*
	₹	₹	₹	₹
Opening Stock	2,000	2,200	1,180	3,402
Purchases	16,000	14,500	17,000	3,500
Sales	20,000	19,850	18,750	2,600
Carriage Inwards	500	300	500	100
Freight Outwards	600	700	300	25

In 2011, while valuing closing stock, some defective goods costing ₹ 500 were valued at ₹ 400. These were sold for ₹ 450 in 2012. In 2012, an item costing ₹ 600 was wrongly valued at ₹ 700. This was sold for ₹ 550 in 2013. In 2013, item costing ₹ 1,200 were valued at ₹ 1,000,50% of these were sold in June, 2014 for ₹ 600. Subject to this, the gross profit rate is more *or less* uniform. The value of salvage was ₹ 800 and the sum insured was ₹ 4,500.

SOLUTION

STATEMENT OF CLAIM

Particulars		₹
A. Estimated value of stock as at date of fire		
(a) Book-value of Normal Items	4,402	

	(b) Current value of Abnormal Items	600	5,002
B.	Value of Salvaged Stock		800
C.	Estimated value of stock lost by fire (A – B)		4,202
D.	Amount of claim by applying Average clause		
	Loss suffered × $\frac{\text{Sum Insured}}{\text{Actual Insurable Value}}$ = ₹4,202 × $\frac{₹4,500}{₹5,002}$		3,780

Working Notes:

Dr. **(I) TRADING ACCOUNT FOR THE PERIOD FROM 01.01.2011 TO 31.12.2011** *Cr.*

Particulars	*Normal Items* ₹	*Abnormal Items* ₹	*Particulars*	*Normal Items* ₹	*Abnormal Items* ₹
To Opening Stock	1,500	500	By Sales	20,000	—
To Purchases	16,000	—	By Closing Stock	1,800	400
To Carriage Inwards	500	—	By Gross Loss		100
To Gross Profit	3,800				
	21,800	500		21,800	500

$$\text{G. P. Ratio} = \frac{\text{Gross Profit}}{\text{Net Sales}} \times 100 = \frac{₹3,800}{₹20,000} \times 100 = 19\%$$

Dr. **(II) TRADING ACCOUNT FOR THE PERIOD FROM 01.01.2012 TO 31.12.2012** *Cr.*

Particulars	*Normal Items* ₹	*Abnormal Items* ₹	*Particulars*	*Normal Items* ₹	*Abnormal Items* ₹
To Opening Stock	1,800	400	By Sales	19,400	450
To Purchases	13,900	600	By Closing Stock	480	700
To Carriage Inwords	300	—			
To Gross Profit	3,880	150			
	19,880	1,150		19,880	1,150

$$\text{G. P. Ratio} = \frac{\text{Gross Profit}}{\text{Net Sales}} \times 100 = \frac{₹3,800}{₹19,400} \times 100 = 20\%$$

Dr. **(III) TRADING ACCOUNT FOR THE PERIOD FROM 01.01.2013 TO 31.12.2013** *Cr.*

Particulars	*Normal Items* ₹	*Abnormal Items* ₹	*Particulars*	*Normal Items* ₹	*Abnormal Items* ₹
To Opening Stock	480	700	By Sales	18,200	550
To Purchases	15,800	1200	By Closing Stock	2,402	1,000
To Carriage Inwards	500	—	By Gross Loss	—	350
To Gross Profit	3,822	—			
	20,602	1,900		20,602	1,900

$$\text{G. P. Ratio} = \frac{\text{Gross Profit}}{\text{Net Sales}} \times 100 = \frac{₹3,822}{₹18,200} \times 100 = 21\%$$

(iv) Average of Gross Profit Ratio based on Profits of 3 years
= (19% + 20% + 21%)/3 = 20%

(V) MEMORANDUM TRADING ACCOUNT FOR THE PERIOD
from 01.01.2014 to 30.06.2014

Particulars	*Normal Items* ₹	*Abnormal Items* ₹	*Particulars*	*Normal Items* ₹	*Abnormal Items* ₹
To Opening Stock	2,402	1,000	By Sales	2,000	600
To Purchases	3,500	—	By Closing Stock	4,402	500
To Carriage Inwards	100	—			
To Gross Profit	400	100			
	6,402	1,100		6,402	1,100

PROBLEM 4

A fire occurred on 15th December, 2013 in the premises of CSDIG Co. Ltd. From the following figures, calculate the amount of claim to be lodged with the insurance company for loss of stock.

Particulars	₹
Stock at cost on 1st April, 2012	20,000
Stock at cost on 31st March, 2013	30,000
Purchases during the year ended 31st March, 2013	40,000
Purchases from 1st Aprll, 2013 to 15th Dec., 2013	88,000
Sales during the year ended 31st March, 2013	60,000
Sales from 1st April, 2013 to 15th December, 2013	1,05,000

During the current year cost of purchases have risen by 10% above last year's levels. Selling prices have gone up by 5%. Salvage value of stock after fire ₹ 2,000.

SOLUTION

Dr. **TRADING ACCOUNT FOR THE YEAR ENDING ON 31ST MARCH, 2013** *Cr.*

Particulars	₹	*Particulars*	₹
To Opening Stock	20,000	By Sales	60,000
To Purchases	40,000	By Closing Stock	30,000
To Gross Profit (50% on sales)	30,000		
	90,000		90,000

MEMORANDUM TRADING ACCOUNT
From 1st April, 2013 to 15th Dec., 2013

Particulars	*Normal Items* ₹	*Abnormal Items* ₹	*Particulars*	*Normal Items* ₹	*Abnormal Items* ₹
To Opening Stock	30,000	30,000	By Sales	1,05,000	1,00,000
To Purchases	88,000	80,000	By Closing Stock	66,000	60,000

To Gross Profit	53,000	50,000			
	1,71,000	1,60,000		1,71,000	1,60,000

Amount of Claim

The amount of claim shall be equal to the value of the closing stock—₹ 66,000 *less* salvage value of stock after fire—₹ 2,000 i.e. ₹ 64,000.

Notes:

(i) Gross profit from 1st April to 15th December, 2013 has been first calculated at last year's rates; i.e. 50% on sales ₹ 1,00,000.

(ii) Closing stock at last year's rates in the balancing figure, taking gross profit at ₹ 50,000.

(iii) Closing stock at current rates on FIFO basis shall be 10% higher than the one at previous year's rates and therefore, it comes to ₹ 66,000.

(iv) Last year's columns have been given only for information purposes.

15 ACCOUNTING FOR PARTNERSHIP FIRMS — FUNDAMENTALS

LEARNING OBJECTIVES

After studying this chapter, you should be able to understand:

- ◇ Meaning of Partnership
- ◇ Essential Elements of Partnership
- ◇ Nature of Partnership
- ◇ Meaning of Partners, Firm and Firm Name
- ◇ Maximum Limit of Partners
- ◇ Partnership Deed
- ◇ Provisions Affecting Accounting Treatment
- ◇ Some other Important Provisions of the Act
- ◇ Two Methods of Maintaining Capital Accounts of Partners
- ◇ Interest of Drawings
- ◇ Calculation of Interest on Capital
- ◇ Accounting Treatment of Interest on Capital
- ◇ Interest on Partner's Loan to the Firm
- ◇ Salary or Commission to a Partner
- ◇ Division of Profit Among Partners
- ◇ Past Adjustments
- ◇ Goodwill

1.0 MEANING OF PARTNERSHIP

According to Sec. 4 of the Indian Partnership Act, 1932, the term *'Partnership' is "the relation between two or more persons who have agreed to share the profits of a business carried on by all or any of them acting for all."*

2.0 ESSENTIAL ELEMENTS OF PARTNERSHIP

The essential elements of partnership are as follows:—

AT LEAST TWO PERSONS

There must be at least two persons to form a partnership and all such persons must be competent to contract. According to Section 11 of the Indian Contract Act, 1872, every person except the following, is competent to contract:

(i) Minor

(ii) Persons of unsound mind (e.g. lunatics, idiots), and

(iii) Persons disqualified by any law to which they are subject (e.g., alien enemies, insolvents).

EXAMPLE 1

Two brothers X (age 18 years), Y (age 17 years), decide to form a partnership with a provision that Y will share the profits only. Can they do so?

SOLUTION

Decision: They can not do so.

Reason: There must be at least two persons and such persons must be competent to contract. In the given case, Y is not competent to contract because he is a minor. Hence, there is only one person X who alone cannot form a partnership.

EXAMPLE 2

Three brothers, X (age 19 years), Y (age 18 years) and Z (age 17 years), decide to form a partnership with a provision that Z will share the profits only. Can they do so?

SOLUTION

Decision: They can not do so.

Reason: All the persons entering into partnership agreement must be competent to contract. Z is not competent to contract because he is a minor. It may be noted that no partnership can be formed with a minor partner. But after the formation of partnership, a minor can be admitted to the benefits of partnership with the consent of all other partners of the firm as per the provisions of Section 30 of the Act.

AGREEMENT

There must be an Agreement to form a Partnership. This agreement may be express (whether written *or* oral) *or* implied. This essential element is further clarified under Section 5. Section 5 provides that the relation of partnership arises from contract and not from status. ***For Example***, a Hindu undivided family carrying on a family business is not considered a partnership. The reason is that the coparceners (i.e. Members) of a Hindu undivided family acquire interest in the business because of their status (i.e., birth) in the family and not because of any agreement between them. Thus, partnership is voluntary and contractual in nature.

BUSINESS

There must exist a business. According to Section 2(b), the term 'Business' includes every trade, occupation and profession. ***For Example***, an association created for charitable, religious *or* social purpose cannot be regarded as partnership because there does not exist any business. It may also be noted that an agreement to carry on business at a future time does not result in partnership unless that time arrives and the business is started.

SHARING OF PROFITS

There must be sharing of profits. An agreement to share profits does not necessarily mean an agreement to share losses. ***For Example***, in case of Partner in profits only and minor there is only an agreement to share profits. Thus, sharing of losses is not an essential element of partnership. It may also be noted that sharing of profits is a *prima* facie evidence and not a conclusive evidence of partnership. That is why, everyone who shares the profits of business need not necessarily be a partner. ***For Example***, a manager who receives a particular share in the profits of a business as part of his remuneration, is simply an employee and not a partner.

MUTUAL AGENCY

There must exist a mutual agency relationship among the partners. 'Mutual Agency' relationship means that each partner is both an agent and a principal. Each partner is an agent in the sense that he has the capacity to bind other partners by his acts done. Each partner is a principal in the sense that he is bound by the acts of other partners. Such mutual agency relationship in case of a firm of X, Y and Z has been shown on below:

MUTUAL AGENCY RELATIONSHIP IN CASE OF A FIRM OF X, Y AND Z

	When X does an act	When Y does an act	When Z does an act
Who is an Agent	**X**	**Y**	**Z**
Who are Principals	**Y and Z**	**X and Z**	**X and Y**

The mutual relationship of agency is emphasised in Section 18 of the Indian Partnership Act, which reads as under:

"Subjec t to the provision of this Act, a partner is the agent of the firm for the business of the firm."

Moreover, the use of the words carried as all *or* by any of them acting for all, in Section 4 of the Act clearly emphasizes agency relationship.

Because of the existence of mutual agency relationship amongst the partners, the law of partnership is also regarded as an extension of the general law of agency. It may be noted that the mutual agency relationship is the true test of partnership and it distinguishes a partnership from simple agreement for sharing profits and co-ownership. ***For Example***, an Agreement between X and Y to share the Rental Income of a Joint Property owned by X and Y, can not be regarded as partnership because of absence of mutual agency between X and Y.

3.0 NATURE OF PARTNERSHIP

A partnership firm has no separate legal entity apart from the partners constituting it.

Thus, a firm itself cannot enter into a contract for partnership though its partners can. ***For Example***, two firms, namely, M/s A&B and M/s X & Y, themselves cannot form a new partnership though the partners of the individual firms can form a partnership.

4.0 MEANING OF 'PARTNERS', 'FIRM' AND 'FIRM NAME'

Partners	Persons who have entered into partnership with one another are individually called partners.
Firm	Persons who have entered into partnership with one another are collectively called a firm.
Firm Name	The name under which business is carried on is called firm name.
Maximum Limit of Partners	As per Rule 10 of The Companies (Miscellaneous) 201– **50 for any Business**

5.0 PARTNERSHIP DEED

Meaning	'Partnership Deed' is a written document which contains the terms and conditions of partnership agreed upon by all the partners.
Importance	1.It is important to have Partnership Deed in writing to settle any possible dispute with regard to the terms of partnership
	2.It serves as an evidence in the Courts of Law.
Signature	Partnership Deed must be signed by all the partners.
Stamping	Partnership Deed must be duly stamped as per Indian Stamp Act, 1889.
Is it essential to have a partnership deed?	No. It is not essential to have a partnership deed. In this case the relevant provisions of the Indian Partnership Act, 1932, would be applicable.
It is essential to have the partnership agreement in writing?	No since an agreement to form a partnership may be implied *or* express (oral *or* written).
Need for Partnership Deep	1. To Settle the dispute and misunderstanding with regard to the terms and conditions of partnership 2. To regulate the Rights, Duties and Liabilities of each Partner.
Contents	The Partnership Deed usually includes the following particulars— 1. Name of the firm; 2. Names and addresses of all partners; 3. Nature and place(s) of the business; 4. Duration of Partnership 5. Date of commencement of partnership; 6. Amount of capital contributed *or* to be contributed by each partner; 7. Ratio in which profits and losses are to be shared; 8. Interest on partners' capitals and drawings; 9. Interest on loan by a partner to the firm; 10. Salary, commission etc., if any, payable to a partner; 11. Method of computation and treatment of goodwill on the reconstitution of a firm; 12. Mode of settlement of accounts in case of retirement/death of a partner; 13. Mode of settlement of accounts in case of dissolution of a firm.
Terms of Partnership	Terms of Partnership may be changed by consent of all partners.

6.0 PROVISIONS AFFECTING ACCOUNTING TREATMENT

Where there is *neither* partnership deed *nor* express agreement *or* partnership deed is there but it is silent on any matter, then the relevant provisions of The Indian Partnership Act, 1932, would be applicable. Some of the provisions of the Act which have a direct bearing on the accounting treatment of the following items are as follows:

1. Salary/Commission to a partner	**No remuneration** for taking part in the conduct of business is to be allowed to any partner. [Sec 13 (a)]

2. Sharing of Profits & Losses	Profits & Losses are to be shared **equally.** [Sec 13(b)]
3. Interest on Capital	**No Interest** is to be allowed on Capital. [Sec 13(c)] If the agreement provides for interest on capital, such interest is payable only out of available profits.
4. Interest on Advances/ Loans by a partner	Interest @ **6% p.a.** is to be allowed on Advances/Loans. [Sec 13(d)]. Such interest is payable even if there are losses.
5. Interest on Drawings	**No Interest** is to be charged on Drawings.

7.0 SOME OTHER IMPORTANT PROVISIONS OF THE ACT

Registration	Registration of Firm is optional but not compulsory (Sec. 69)
Time of Registration	Registration of firm can be effected on *or* after the formation.
Suit by / against	No suit can be filed by unregistered firm *or* by its partners but third party can file suit against the unregistered firm *or* its partners.
Minor's Admission	A minor may be admitted to benefits of partnership with the consent of all partners (Sec. 30).
Admission of Partner	A person may be admitted as partner either with the consent of all partners *or* in accordance with express agreement among partners (Sec. 31)
Retirement of Partner	A partner may retire from firm either with the consent of all partners *or* in accordance with express agreement among partners (Sec. 32)
Dissolution of Firm	Unless otherwise agreed by partners, a firm may dissolve on the death of partner (Sec. 35)
Nature of Liability	Liability of partners is a joint and several (i.e. Unlimited Liability). Unlimited Liability of a partner means that Partners are liable for firm's debts jointly with other patners and also individually in their own capacity. Net Private Assets of a Partner (i.e. Private Assets – Private Debts) can be used to pay off Firm's Debts in case Firm's Assets are less than Firm's Debts.
Right to take part	Every partner has a right to take part in the conduct of the business. [Sec. 12]
Duty to Pay Personal Profit earned by a Partner	Every partner must pay to the firm the personal profits earned by him from any transaction of the firm *or* from the use of firm's property *or* from competing business. [Sec. 16]
Duty to bear Personal Loss	Every partner must bear the personal loss incurred by him from the use of firm's property.
Implied Authority	Every partner of a trading firm has an implied authority to purchase and sell the Goods but not an Immovable Property.

ILLUSTRATION 1

X and Y are partners They do not have any partnership agreement (partnership deed). What should be done in the following cases:

(a) X spends twice the time that Y devotes to business. X claims that he should get a salary of ₹ 6,000 per month for his extra time spent.

(b) Y has provided a capital of ₹ 50,000 whereas X has provided ₹ 5,000 only as capital. X however has provided ₹ 10,000 as loan to the firm. What interest (if any) will be given to X and Y?

(c) X wants to introduce his son Z into his business. Y objects to it.

(d) Y wants that profit should be distributed in the ratio of capitals but X wants that it should be distributed equally.

SOLUTION

(a) X is not entitled to any salary

(b) No interest on capital is allowed. X is entitled to claim an interest on his loan of ₹ 10,000 @ 6% p.a.

(c) X's son cannot be admitted as a partner if Y objects to it.

(d) Profits are to be distributed equally.

8.0 TWO METHODS OF MAINTAINING CAPITAL ACCOUNTS OF PARTNERS

The partners' Capital Accounts may be maintained according to Fluctuating Capital method *or* Fixed Capital method.

FLUCTUATING CAPITAL METHOD

1. Under Fluctuating Capital method, **only one account** (viz. Capital Account) for each partner is **maintained.**
2. All the transactions relating to a partner are recorded in his Capital Account.
3. As a result, the balance in the Capital Account keeps on fluctuating.
4. A Format of Capital Account under Fluctuating Capital Method is given below:

Dr. **PARTNER'S CAPITAL ACCOUNT UNDER FLUCTUATING CAPITAL METHOD** *Cr.*

Particulars	₹	*Particulars*	₹
*To Balance b/f	xxx	*By Balance b/f	xxx
To Cash/Bank A/c		By Cash/Bank A/c	xxx
[withdrawal of capital]	xxx	(Additional Capital)	
To Drawings	xxx	By Interest on Capital	xxx
To Interest on Drawings	xxx	By Salary	xxx
**To Profit & Loss A/c		By Commission	xxx
(Share of Loss)	xxx	**By P & L Appropriation A/c	xxx
***To Balance c/f	xxx	(Share of Profit)	
		***By Balance c/f	xxx
	xxx		xxx

*Only one figure will appear at a time.

**Only one figure will appear at a time.

***Only one figure will appear at a time.

FIXED CAPITAL METHOD

1. Under Fixed Capital method, **two accounts** (viz. Capital Account and Current Account) for each partner are **maintained.**

2. The transactions relating to introduction *or* withdrawal of Capital are recorded in Capital account.
3. Other transactions like Interest on Capital, Drawings, Salary, Commission, Share of Profit/loss are recorded in Current Account.
4. As a result of these, the Capital Account will continue to show the same balance from year to year unless some amount of Capital is introduced *or* withdrawn.
5. The balance of Current Account keeps on fluctuating.
6. Inspite of regular and consistent losses year after year, the Fixed Capital Account does not show a debit balance since all transactions relating to Interest on Capital, Drawings, Salary, Commission, Share of Profit/loss are recorded in Current Account and not in Capital Account.
7. The formats of Capital Account and Current Account under Fixed Capital Method are given on next page:

Dr. **PARTNER'S CAPITAL ACCOUNT UNDER FIXED CAPITAL METHOD** *Cr.*

Particulars	₹	*Particulars*	₹
To Cash/Bank A/c		By Balance b/f	xxx
(Withdrawal of Capital)	xxx	By Cash/Bank A/c	xxx
To Balance c/f	xxx	(Additional Capital)	
	xxx		xxx

Dr. **PARTNER'S CURRENT ACCOUNT UNDER FIXED CAPITAL METHOD** *Cr.*

Particulars	₹	*Particulars*	₹
*To Balance b/f	xxx	*By Balance b/f	xxx
To Bank A/c (Drawings)	xxx	By Interest on Capital	xxx
To Interest on Drawings	xxx	By Salary	xxx
**To P&L A/c (Share of Loss)	xxx	By Commission	xxx
***To Balance c/f	xxx	**By P & L Appropriation A/c (Share *or* Profit)	xxx
		***By Balance c/f	xxx
	xxx		xxx

*Only one figure will appear at a time.

**Only one figure will appear at a time.

*** Only one figure will appear at a time.

DISTINCTION BETWEEN FIXED CAPITAL METHOD AND FLUCTUATING CAPITAL METHOD

Fixed Capital method and Fluctuating Capital method in partnership accounts can be distinguished as follows:

Basis of Distinction	**Fixed Capital Method**	**Fluctuating Capital Method**
1. Change in Capital	The capital normally **remains unchanged** except under special circumstances.	The capital **fluctuates** quite frequently from period to period.
2. No. of Accounts maintained	**Two** accounts are maintained for each partner viz. (a) Fixed Capital Account, (b) Current Account.	Only **one** account (viz., Capital Account) is maintained for each year.

3. Adjustments for drawings etc.	All adjustments for drawings, interest on drawings, interest on capital, salary, share of profit/loss are made **in Current Account.**	All adjustments for drawings, interest on capital, salary, share of profit/loss are made **in Capital Account.**
4. Can Capital Account show a negative balance?	Fixed Capital Account can **never show** a negative balance.	Fluctuating Capital Account **can show** a negative balance.

ILLUSTRATION 2

State where the following items shall appear in case the capitals are fixed.

(a) Interest on Capital
(b) Withdrawal of Capital
(c) Interest on Drawings
(d) Drawings
(e) Share of loss
(f) Salary to Partners
(g) Fresh Capital introduced

SOLUTION

(a) On Credit side of Partner's Current A/c
(b) On Debit side of Partner's Capital A/c
(c) On Debit side of Partner's Current A/c
(d) On Debit side of Partner's Current A/c
(e) On Debit side of Partner's Current A/c
(f) On Credit side of Partner's Current A/c
(g) On Credit side of Partner's Capital A/c

9.0 INTEREST ON DRAWINGS

MEANING OF DRAWINGS

Drawings mean the amount withdrawn in cash *or* in kind for personal purposes. Drawings may be against profits *or* against capital.

DISTINCTION BETWEEN DRAWINGS AGAINST PROFITS AND DRAWINGS AGAINST CAPITAL

Drawings against Profits differ from drawings against Capital in the following respects:

Basis of Distinction	Drawings Against Profits	Drawings Against Capital
1. Part	It is part of **profits.**	It is part of **Capital.**
2. Whether considered for calculation of Interest on Capital	It is **not** considered to calculate interest on capital.	It is **considered** to calculate interest on capital.
3. Where debited?	It is debited in **Drawings Account.**	It is debited in **Capital Account.**
4. Whether reduces capital	It **does not** reduce capital.	It **reduces** Capital.
5. Popular Name	Drawings	Withdrawal of Capital

ACCOUNTING TREATMENT OF INTEREST ON DRAWINGS

When to charge	Interest on Drawings is to be charged from partners only when partnership agreement provides for the same.
Accounting Treatment	Interest on Drawings is a gain to the firm and hence is credited to Profit & Loss Appropriation Account. On the other hand, interest on drawings is a loss to the partner and hence is debited to his Capital Account *(in case of Fluctuating Capitals) or* Current Account *(in case of Fixed Capitals).* **JOURNAL ENTRIES** ***(a) Adjusting Entry to charge Interest on Drawings*** Partner's Capital A/c *(In case of Fluctuating Capitals)* Dr. or Partner's Current A/c *(In case of Fixed Capitals)* Dr. To Interest on Drawings A/c ***(b) Closing Entry to close the Interest on Drawings Account*** Interest on Drawings A/c Dr. To Profit & Loss Appropriation A/c

HOW CALCULATE INTEREST ON DRAWINGS

Interest on drawings is basically calculated with reference to the time period for which the money was withdrawn on the basis of Product Method. However, Short Cut Method may be used in case a Fixed Amount is withdrawn at uniform time-interval.

SHORT CUT METHOD

When a fixed amount is withdrawn at fixed dates, the interest on drawings may be calculated with the help of short cut formula as follows:

If Fixed Amount is Withdrawn...	*Interest on Drawings*
1. In the beginning of each month	$= \text{Total Drawings} \times \frac{\text{Rate of Interest}}{100} \times \frac{6\frac{1}{2}}{12}$ *
2. At the end of each month	$= \text{Total Drawings} \times \frac{\text{Rate of Interest}}{100} \times \frac{5\frac{1}{2}}{12}$ **
3. During the middle of each month	$= \text{Total Drawings} \times \frac{\text{Rate of Interest}}{100} \times \frac{6}{12}$
4. In the beginning of each quarter	$= \text{Total Drawings} \times \frac{\text{Rate of Interest}}{100} \times \frac{7\frac{1}{2}}{12}$ *
5. At the end of each quarter	$= \text{Total Drawings} \times \frac{\text{Rate of Interest}}{100} \times \frac{4\frac{1}{2}}{12}$ **
6. During the middle of each quarter	$= \text{Total Drawings} \times \frac{\text{Rate of Interest}}{100} \times \frac{6}{12}$

Note: *The above formulae have been given on the assumption that Total Period of Drawings is 12 months. In case the Period of Drawings is less than 12 months, the above formulae will change accordingly.*

* (Total Period + Time Interval)/2

**(Total Period – Time Interval)/2

PRODUCT METHOD

When an unequal amount is withdrawn at different dates, the interest on drawings is calculated with the help of Product Method as follows:

Step 1: *Calculate the Period for which amount withdrawn has been used.*

Step 2: *Calculate the Product as follows:*

$$\text{Product} = \text{Amount of Drawings} \times \text{Period of Use}$$

Step 3: *Calculate the Total Product*

Step 4: *Calculate the Interest on Drawings as follows:*

If Period is expressed in a month $= \text{Total Product} \times \dfrac{\text{Rate of Interest}}{100} \times \dfrac{1}{12}$

If Period is expressed in a day $= \text{Total Product} \times \dfrac{\text{Rate of Interest}}{100} \times \dfrac{1}{365}$

TUTORIAL NOTES

1. *If the date of drawing is not given the interest on Total Drawings is calculated for 6 months.*
2. *Interest @ 10% without word 'per annum' means interest is to be calculated without any reference to time period.*

ILLUSTRATION 3

Calculate the Interest on Drawings of Ram @ 10% p.a. for the year ended 31st Dec. 2012, if he withdrew ₹ 2,000 p.m. in the beginning of each month.

SOLUTION

$$\text{Interest on Drawings} = \text{Total Drawings} \times \frac{\text{Rate of Interest}}{100} \times \frac{6\frac{1}{2}}{12}$$

$$\text{Interest on Drawings} = ₹\ 24{,}000 \times \frac{10}{100} \times \frac{6\frac{1}{2}}{12} = ₹\ 1{,}300$$

ILLUSTRATION 4

Calculate the Interest on Drawings of Ram @ 10% p.a. for the year ended 31st Dec. 2012, if he withdrew ₹ 2,000 p.m. at the end of every month.

SOLUTION

$$\text{Interest on Drawings} = \text{Total Drawings} \times \frac{\text{Rate of Interest}}{100} \times \frac{5\frac{1}{2}}{12}$$

$$\text{Interest on Drawings} = ₹\ 24{,}000 \times \frac{10}{100} \times \frac{5\frac{1}{2}}{12} = ₹\ 1{,}100$$

ILLUSTRATION 5

Calculate the Interest on Drawings of Ram @ 10% p.a. for the year ended 31st Dec. 2012, if he withdrew ₹ 2,000 p.m. during the middle of each month.

SOLUTION

$$\text{Interest on Drawings} = \text{Total Drawings} \times \frac{\text{Rate of Interest}}{100} \times \frac{6}{12}$$

$$\text{Interest on Drawings} = ₹\ 24{,}000 \times \frac{10}{100} \times \frac{6}{12} = ₹\ 1{,}200$$

ILLUSTRATION 6

Calculate the Interest on Drawings of Ram @ 10% p.a. for the year ended 31st Dec. 2012, if he withdrew ₹ 6,000 in the beginning of each quarter.

SOLUTION

$$\text{Interest on Drawings} = \text{Total Drawings} \times \frac{\text{Rate of Interest}}{100} \times \frac{7.5}{12}$$

$$\text{Interest on Drawings} = ₹\ 24{,}000 \times \frac{10}{100} \times \frac{7.5}{12} = ₹\ 1{,}500$$

ILLUSTRATION 7

Calculate the Interest on Drawings of Ram @ 10% p.a. for the year ended 31st Dec. 2012, if he withdrew ₹ 6,000 at the end of each quarter.

SOLUTION

$$\text{Interest on Drawings} = \text{Total Drawings} \times \frac{\text{Rate of Interest}}{100} \times \frac{4.5}{12}$$

$$\text{Interest on Drawings} = ₹\ 24{,}000 \times \frac{10}{100} \times \frac{4.5}{12} = ₹\ 900$$

ILLUSTRATION 8

Calculate the Interest on Drawings of Ram @ 10% p.a. for the year ended 31st Dec. 2012, if he withdrew ₹ 6,000 per quarter.

SOLUTION

$$\text{Interest on Drawings} = \text{Total Drawings} \times \frac{\text{Rate of Interest}}{100} \times \frac{6}{12}$$

$$\text{Interest on Drawings} = ₹\ 24{,}000 \times \frac{10}{100} \times \frac{6}{12} = ₹\ 1{,}200$$

ILLUSTRATION 9

Calculate the Interest on Drawings of Ram @ 10% p.a. for the year ended 31st Dec. 2012, if his drawings during the year were ₹ 24,000.

SOLUTION

Assuming that the drawings were made evenly throughout the year, the interest on drawings has been calculated for an average period of 6 months.

$$\text{Interest on Drawings} = ₹\ 24{,}000 \times \frac{10}{100} \times \frac{6}{12} = ₹\ 1{,}200$$

ILLUSTRATION 10

Calculate the Interest on X's drawings @ 10% if he withdrew ₹ 24,000 during the year.

SOLUTION

Interest on Drawings = ₹ 24,000 × $\frac{10}{100}$ = ₹ 2,400

Note: *Interest has been calculated for 12 months since the given question specifies merely a rate of 10% and not 10% p.a.*

ILLUSTRATION 11

Calculate the Interest on Drawings of Ram @ 10% p.a. for the year ended 31st Dec. 2012. If he withdrew the following amounts as follows:

Jan. 31 ₹ 6,000, Mar. 31 ₹ 4,000, July 1 ₹ 8,000,

Sept. 30 ₹ 3,000, Nov. 1 ₹ 5,000,

SOLUTION

CALCULATION OF INTEREST ON DRAWINGS

A Date	*B* *Amount of Drawings*	*C* *Months for which amount has been withdrawn*	*D = B × C* *Product*
Jan. 31	6,000	11	66,000
Mar. 31	4,000	9	36,000
Jul. 1	8,000	6	48,000
Sept. 30	3,000	3	9,000
Nov. 1	5,000	2	10,000
		Sum of Products	1,69,000

Interest on Drawings = ₹ 1,69,000 × $\frac{10}{100} \times \frac{1}{12}$ = ₹ 1,408.33

10.0 CALCULATION OF INTEREST ON CAPITAL

RATIONALE BEHIND THE PROVISION FOR INTEREST ON CAPITAL

In case the profit sharing ratio differs from capital ratio, the provision for interest on capital compensates those partners who contribute capital more than the Proportionate Capital as per profit sharing ratio.

HOW TO CALCULATE INTEREST ON CAPITAL IN VARIOUS SITUATIONS

Interest is calculated at the given rate with reference to the time period for which the capital has been used as follows:

CALCULATION OF INTEREST

	Particulars	₹
A.	Interest on Opening Capital [Opening Capital × Rate/100 × 12/12]	xxx
B.	*Add:* Interest on Additional Capital [Additional Capital × Rate/100 × Period from the date of Introduction to the end of accounting period/12]	xxx

C. *Less:* Interest on Capital withdrawn = Capital withdrawn × Rate/100 × Period from the date of withdrawal to the end of accounting period/12]	(xxx)
D. Total Interest on Capital [A + B – C]	xxx

ILLUSTRATION 12

X and Y started business on 1st April, 2011 with capitals of ₹ 5,00,000 and ₹ 3,00,000 respectively.

On 1st May 2011, X introduced an additional capital of ₹ 1,00,000 and Y withdrew ₹ 50,000 from his capital. On 1st October 2011, X withdrew ₹ 2,00,000 from his capital and Y introduced ₹ 2,50,000. Interest on capital is allowed @ 6% p.a. calculate the interest on capital for the year ending 31st March, 2012.

SOLUTION

CALCULATION OF INTEREST

Particulars	*X* ₹	*Y* ₹
A. Interest on Opening Capital:		
X – ₹ 5,00,000 × $\frac{6}{100} \times \frac{12}{12}$	30,000	
Y – ₹ 3,00,000 × $\frac{6}{100} \times \frac{12}{12}$		18,000
B. *Add:* Interest on Additional Capital:		
X – ₹ 1,00,000 × $\frac{6}{100} \times \frac{11}{12}$	5,500	
Y – ₹ 2,50,000 × $\frac{6}{100} \times \frac{6}{12}$		7,500
C. *Less:* Interest on capital withdrawn:		
X – ₹ 2,00,000 × $\frac{6}{100} \times \frac{6}{12}$	–6,000	
Y – ₹ 50,000 × $\frac{6}{100} \times \frac{11}{12}$		–2,750
	29,500	22,750

ILLUSTRATION 13

X and Y started business on 1st April, 2011 with Capitals of ₹ 2,50,000 and ₹ 1,50,000 respectively. On 1st Oct. 2011, they decided that their capitals should be ₹ 2,00,000 each. The necessary adjustments in the capitals were made by introducing *or* withdrawing cash. Interest on capital is allowed at 8% p.a. Calculate the Interest on Capital on March 31, 2012.

SOLUTION

Interest on X's Capital:

On ₹ 2,50,000 for 6 months = ₹ 2,50,000 × 8/100 × 6/12 = ₹ 10,000

On ₹ 2,00,000 for 6 months = ₹ 2,00,000 × 8/100 × 6/12 = ₹ 8,000

Total Interest = ₹ 10,000 + ₹ 8,000 = ₹ 18,000

Interest on Y's Capital:

On ₹ 1,50,000 for 6 months = ₹ 1,50,000 × 8/100 × 6/12 = ₹ 6,000

On ₹ 2,00,000 for 6 months = ₹ 2,00,000 × 8/100 × 6/12 = ₹ 8,000

Total Interest = ₹ 6,000 + ₹ 8,000 = ₹ 14,000.

WHEN OPENING CAPITAL IS NOT GIVEN

Opening Capital is ascertained by adding those items which have already been subtracted (e.g. withdrawal of capital) and by subtracting those items which have already been added to the capital (e.g. Additional Capital).

CALCULATION OF OPENING CAPITAL

In case of Fixed Capitals	₹	*In case of Fluctuating Capitals*	₹
A. Closing Capital	xxx	A. Closing Capital	xxx
B. *Add:* Withdrawal of Capital	xxx	B. *Add:* Drawings	xxx
C. *Less:* Additional Capital	xxx	C. *Add:* Withdrawal of Capital	xxx
D. Opening Capital (A + B – C)	xxx	D. *Less:* Share of Profit	xxx
		E. *Less:* Additional Capital	xxx
		F. Opening Capital [A+B+C–D–E]	xxx

ILLUSTRATION 14

On 31st March, 2012 after the close of the accounts, the capital accounts of X and Y stood in the books of the firm at ₹ 4,00,000 and ₹ 5,00,000 respectively. On 1st May 2011, X introduced an additional capital of ₹ 1,00,000 and Y withdrew ₹ 50,000 from his capital. On 1st October 2011, X withdrew ₹ 2,00,000 from his capital and Y introduced ₹ 2,50,000. Interest on capital is allowed @ 6% p.a. Subsequently, it was discovered that interest on capital @ 6% p.a. had been omitted. The profits for the year ended 31st March, 2012 amounted to ₹ 2,00,000 and the partners' drawings had been: X ₹ 1,00,000 and Y ₹ 50,000. The profit sharing ratio of X and Y was 3 : 2.

Required: Calculate the interest on Capital if the Capitals are (a) fixed (b) fluctuating.

SOLUTION

(a) If the Capitals are Fixed

STEP 1: CALCULATION OF OPENING CAPITAL

Particulars	*X* (₹)	*Y* (₹)
A. Closing Capital	4,00,000	5,00,000
B. *Add:* Withdrawal of Capital	2,00,000	50,000
C. *Less:* Additional Capital	(1,00,000)	(2,50,000)
D. Opening Capital [A + B – C]	5,00,000	3,00,000

STEP 2: CALCULATION OF INTEREST ON CAPITAL

Particulars	*X*	*Y*
A. Interest on Opening Capital:		

X – ₹ 5,00,000 × $\frac{6}{100} \times \frac{12}{12}$	30,000	
Y – ₹ 3,00,000 × $\frac{6}{100} \times \frac{12}{12}$		18,000
B. *Add:* Interest on Additional Capital:		
X – ₹ 1,00,000 × $\frac{6}{100} \times \frac{11}{12}$	5,500	
Y – ₹ 2,50,000 × $\frac{6}{100} \times \frac{6}{12}$		7,500
C. *Less:* Interest on capital withdrawn:		
X – ₹ 2,00,000 × $\frac{6}{100} \times \frac{6}{12}$	(6,000)	
Y – ₹ 50,000 × $\frac{6}{100} \times \frac{11}{12}$		(2,750)
	29,500	22,750

(b) If the Capitals are Fluctuating

STEP 1: CALCULATION OF OPENING CAPITAL

Particulars	*X* (₹)	*Y* (₹)
A. Closing Capital	4,00,000	5,00,000
B. *Add:* Withdrawal of Capital	2,00,000	50,000
C. *Add:* Drawings	1,00,000	50,000
D. *Less:* Additional Capital	(1,00,000)	(2,50,000)
E. *Less:* Share of Profit	(1,20,000)	(80,000)
F. Opening Capital [A + B + C – D – E]	4,80,000	2,70,000

STEP 2: CALCULATION OF INTEREST ON CAPITAL

Particulars	*X*	*Y*
A. Interest on Opening Capital:		
X – ₹ 4,80,000 × $\frac{6}{100} \times \frac{12}{12}$	28,800	
Y – ₹ 2,70,000 × $\frac{6}{100} \times \frac{12}{12}$		16,200
B. *Add:* Interest on Additional Capital:		
X – ₹ 1,00,000 × $\frac{6}{100} \times \frac{11}{12}$	5,500	
Y – ₹ 2,50,000 × $\frac{6}{100} \times \frac{6}{12}$		7,500

C. *Less:* Interest on capital withdrawn:		
X – ₹ 2,00,000 × $\frac{6}{100} \times \frac{6}{12}$	(6,000)	
Y – ₹ 50,000 × $\frac{6}{100} \times \frac{11}{12}$		(2,750)
	28,300	20,950

11.0 ACCOUNTING TREATMENT OF INTEREST ON CAPITAL

PROVISIONS RELATING TO INTEREST ON CAPITAL

Case	Provision
I. If the Partnership Agreement is silent as to Interest on Capital.	I. **No Interest** on Capital will be allowed.
II. If the Partnership Agreement provides for Interest on Capital but is silent as to the treatment of interest as a charge *or* appropriation.	II. Interest on Capital will be **allowed** only if there are **profits.** [Sec 13(c)] (a) ***In case of Loss***— **No Interest** on Capital will be allowed. (b) ***In case Profit before interest is equal to or more than the interest.***— **Full Interest** on Capital will be **allowed.** (c) ***In case Profit before interest is less than the interest.***— **Profit** will be distributed **in the ratio of interest on Capital** of each partner.
III. If the Partnership Agreement provides for interest on capital as a charge (i.e. to be allowed whether there are profits *or* losses).	III. **Full Interest** on Capital will be allowed **whether** there are **profits** or **losses.**

JOURNAL ENTRIES

(a) Adjusting Entry to adjust Interest on Capital	
Interest on Capital A/c	Dr.
To Partner's Capital A/c *(In case of Fluctuating Capitals)*	
or	
To Partner's Current A/c *(In case of Fixed Capitals)*	
(b) Closing Entry to close the Interest on Capital Account	
Profit & Loss Appropriation A/c	Dr.
To Interest on Capital A/c	

ILLUSTRATION 15

X and Y are partners sharing the profits and losses in the ratio of 2 : 3 with capitals of ₹ 20,000 and ₹ 10,000 respectively. The partnership deed is silent as to the Interest on Capital and the trading profits for the year are ₹ 1,500. Show the distribution of profit/loss for the year 2011-12 by preparing the relevant account.

SOLUTION

PROFIT AND LOSS APPROPRIATION ACCOUNT

Dr. *for the year ending on 31st March, 2012* Cr.

Particulars	₹	Particulars	₹
To Profit transferred to:		By Profit & Loss A/c	1,500
X's Capital A/c	600	(Profit for the year)	
Y's Capital A/c	900		
	1,500		1,500

ILLUSTRATION 16

X and Y are partners sharing the profits and losses in the ratio of 2 : 3 with capitals of ₹ 20,000 and ₹ 10,000 respectively. Tthe partnership deed provides for Interest on Capital @ 6% p.a. and the trading loss for the year are ₹ 1,500. Show the distribution of profit/loss for the year 2011-12 by preparing the relevant account.

SOLUTION

***PROFIT AND LOSS ACCOUNT**

Dr. *for the year ending on 31st March, 2012* Cr.

Particulars	₹	Particulars		₹
To Loss for the year	1,500	By Loss transferred to:		
		X's Capital A/c	600	
		Y's Capital A/c	900	1,500
	1,500			1,500

*Profit & Loss Appropriation A/c should not be prepared because there is nothing to appropriate.

ILLUSTRATION 17

X and Y are partners sharing the profits and losses in the ratio of 2 : 3 with capitals of ₹ 20,000 and ₹ 10,000 respectively. The partnership deed provides for Interest on Capital @ 6% p.a and the trading profits for the year are ₹ 2,100. Show the distribution of profit/loss for the year 2011-12 by preparing the relevant account.

SOLUTION

PROFIT AND LOSS APPROPRIATION ACCOUNT

Dr. *for the year ending on 31st March, 2012* Cr.

Particulars		₹	Particulars	₹
To Interest on Capital:			By Profit & Loss A/c	2,100
X	1,200		(Profit for the year)	
Y	600	1,800		
To Profit transferred to:				
X's Capital A/c	120			
Y's Capital A/c	180	300		
		2,100		2,100

ILLUSTRATION 18

X and Y are partners sharing the profits and losses in the ratio of 2 : 3 with capitals of ₹ 20,000 and ₹ 10,000 respectively. The partnership deed provides for Interest on Capital @ 6% p.a. and the trading profits for the year are ₹ 1,500. Show the distribution of profit/loss for the year 2011-12 by preparing the relevant account.

SOLUTION

PROFIT AND LOSS APPROPRIATION ACCOUNT

Dr. *for the year ending on 31st March, 2012* *Cr.*

Particulars		₹	*Particulars*	₹
To Interest on Capital:			By Profit & Loss A/c	1,500
X	1,000		(Profit for the year)	
Y	500	1,500		
		1,500		1,500

Note: Since the amount of available profits is less than the total amount of interest on capital, the available profits have been distributed in the ratio of interest claims of X and Y i.e. ₹ 1,200 : ₹ 600.

ILLUSTRATION 19

X and Y are partners sharing the profits and losses in the ratio of 2 : 3 with capitals of ₹ 20,000 and ₹ 10,000 respectively. The partnership deed provides for Interest on Capital @ 6% p.a. even if it involves the firm in loss and the trading profits for the year are ₹ 1,500. Show the distribution of profit/loss for the year 2011-12 by preparing the relevant account.

SOLUTION

PROFIT AND LOSS ACCOUNT

Dr. *for the year ending on 31st March, 2012* *Cr.*

Particulars		₹	*Particulars*		₹
To Interest on Capital:			By Profits before Interest		1,500
X	1,200		By Loss transferred to:		
Y	600	1,800	X's Capital A/c	120	
			Y's Capital A/c	180	300
		1,800			1,800

*Profit & Loss Appropriation Account should not be prepared since all the charges against the profits are shown in Profit & Loss Account and all appropriations out of profits are shown in Profit & Loss Appropriation Account.

12.0 INTEREST ON PARTNER'S LOAN TO THE FIRM

	Case		Rate of Interest
Rate of Interest to be allowed	*I.*	***If there is an agreement as to the rate of interest on Loan.***	Partner is entitled to an interest on loan at an agreed rate of interest.
	II.	***If there is no agreement as to the rate of interest on Loan.***	Partner is entitled to interest on loan @ 6% p.a. [Sec. 13(d)]

Nature of Interest	Interest on Partner's loan is a **charge against the profits and not an appropriation out of profits.** In other words, interest on partner's loan is to be allowed whether there are profits *or* not.
If Profit is *less* than Interest	If the amount of available profits is less than the total amount of interest on loan, the total amount of interest on loan should be debited to P&L A/c & the resulting loss should be distributed in the profit sharing ratio.
Accounting Treatment	Interest on partner's loan is an expense for the firm and hence is debited to Profit & Loss Account. On the other hand, interest on partner's loan is a gain to partner in the capacity of a lender and hence is credited to his Loan Account and not his Capital Account. It may be noted that such interest on loan is a charge against the profits and hence must be **transferred to the debit of Profit & Loss Account and not to the debit of Profit & Loss Appropriation Account.** The following journal entries are passed to adjust Interest on Partners' Loan.Journal Entries ***(a) Adjusting Entry to provide for Interest on Partner's loan*** Interest on Partner's loan A/c Dr. To Partner's loan A/c ***(b) Closing Entry to close the Interest on Partner's loan Account*** Profit & Loss A/c Dr. To Interest on Partner's loan A/c

ILLUSTRATION 20

M and N are partners in a firm. M has given a loan of ₹ 8,000 to the firm on 1st July. The partnership deed is silent upon the question of provision of interest on partners' loan. Compute the amount of interest payable on the loan advanced by M to the firm assuming the books are closed on 31st March each year.

SOLUTION

When the partnership deed is silent as to the Interest on partner's loan, as per the Indian Partnership Act, 1932, interest @ 6% p.a. is to be allowed on loan by a partner. Hence M is entitled to an interest @ 6% on the loan of ₹ 8,000 for 9 months. (1st July to 31st March).

Interest payable by firm to M for loan = ₹ 8,000 × 6/100 × 9/12 = ₹ 360

ILLUSTRATION 21

X & Y are partners sharing the profits & losses in the ratio of 2 : 3 with Capitals of ₹ 20,000 & ₹ 10,000 respectively. On 1st Oct., 2011 X & Y granted loans of ₹ 40,000 and ₹ 20,000 respectively to the firm. The Partnership deed is silent as to the interest on Partner's Loan. The profits before any interest for the year amounted to ₹ 2,100. Show the distribution of profits/losses for the year 2011-2012.

SOLUTION

When the partnership deed is silent as to the Interest on partner's loan, as per the Indian Partnership Act, 1932, interest @ 6% p.a. is to be allowed on loan by a partner.

PROFIT AND LOSS ACCOUNT

Dr *for the year ending on 31st March, 2012* Cr.

Particulars	₹	*Particulars*	₹
To Interest on Loan:		By Profit before any interest	2,100

Particulars		₹	Particulars		₹
X	1,200				
Y	600	1,800			
To Net Profit transferred to:					
X's Capital A/c	120				
Y's Capital A/c	180	300			
		2,100			2,100

Working Notes:

1. Interest on X's Loan = ₹ 40,000 × 6/100 × 6/12 = ₹ 1,200
2. Interest on Y's Loan = ₹ 20,000 × 6/100 × 6/12 = ₹ 600

ILLUSTRATION 22

X and Y are partners sharing the profits and losses in the ratio of 2 : 3 with Capitals of ₹ 20,000 and ₹ 10,000 respectively. On 1st Oct., 2011 X and Y granted loans of ₹ 40,000 and ₹ 20,000 respectively to the firm. The Partnership deed is silent as to the interest on partner's loan. The profits before any interest for the year amounted to ₹ 1,500. Show the distribution of profits/losses for the year 2011-2012.

SOLUTION

When the partnership deed is silent as to the Interest on partner's loan, as per The Indian Partnership Act, 1932, interest @ 6% p.a. is to be allowed on loan by a partner.

PROFIT AND LOSS ACCOUNT

Dr *for the year ending on 31st March, 2012* *Cr.*

Particulars		₹	Particulars		₹
To Interest on Loan:			By Profit before any Interest		1,500
X	1,200		By Net Loss transferred to:		
Y	600	1,800	X's Capital A/c	120	
			Y's Capital A/c	180	300
		1,800			1,800

Working Notes:

1. Interest on X's Loan = ₹ 40,000 × 6/100 × 6/12 = ₹ 1,200
2. Interest on Y's Loan = ₹ 20,000 × 6/100 × 6/12 = ₹ 600

ILLUSTRATION 23

X and Y are partners sharing the profits and losses in the ratio of 2 : 3 with Capitals of ₹ 20,000 and ₹ 10,000 respectively. On 1st Oct., 2011 X and Y granted loans of ₹ 40,000 and ₹ 20,000 respectively to the firm. The loss before any interest for the year amounted to ₹ 1,500. The Partnership deed is silent as to the interest on partner's loan. Show the distribution of profits/losses for the year 2011-2012.

SOLUTION

When the partnership deed is silent as to the Interest on partner's loan, as per the Indian Partnership Act, 1932, interest @ 6% p.a. is to be allowed on loan by a partner.

PROFIT AND LOSS ACCOUNT

Dr *for the year ending on 31st March, 2012* Cr.

Particulars		₹	*Particulars*		₹
To Loss before any interest		1,500	By Net Loss transferred to:		
To Interest on Loan:			X's Capital A/c	1,320	
X	1,200		Y's Capital A/c	1,980	3,300
Y	600	1,800			
		3,300			3,300

Working Notes:

1. Interest on X's Loan = ₹ 40,000 × 6/100 × 6/12 = ₹ 1,200
2. Interest on Y's Loan = ₹ 20,000 × 6/100 × 6/12 = ₹ 600

ILLUSTRATION 24

A and B entered into partnership on 1st April, 2011 without any partnership deed. They introduced capitals of ₹ 5,00,000 and ₹ 3,00,000 respectively. On 31st October 2011,

A advanced ₹ 2,00,000 by way of loan to the firm without any agreement as to interest.

The Profit and Loss Account for the year ended 31.03.2012 showed a profit of ₹ 4,30,000, but the partners could not agree upon the amount of interest on loan to be charged and the basis of division of profits. Pass a journal entry for the distribution of the profit between the partners and prepare the Capital A/cs of both the partners and Loan A/c of A.

SOLUTION

JOURNAL

Date	*Particulars*	*L.F.*	*Dr. (₹)*	*Cr. (₹)*
31.03.12	Profit and Loss Appropriation A/c ...Dr.		4,25,000	
	To A's Capital A/c			2,12,500
	To B's Capital A/c			2,12,500
	(Being the Profits distributed equally)			

Dr. **PARTNER'S CAPITAL ACCOUNTS** Cr.

Date	*Particulars*	*A* ₹	*B* ₹	*Date*	*Particulars*	*A* ₹	*B* ₹
31.03.12	To Balance c/d	7,12,500	5,12,500	01.04.11	By Bank A/c	5,00,000	3,00,000
				31.03.12	By P&L App. A/c	2,12,500	2,12,500
		7,12,500	5,12,500			7,12,500	5,12,500

Dr. **A'S LOAN ACCOUNT** Cr.

Date	*Particulars*	₹	*Date*	*Particulars*	₹
31.03.12	To Balance c/d	2,05,000	31.10.11	By Bank A/c	2,00,000
			31.03.12	By Interest on Loan A/c	5,000
		2,05,000			2,05,000

Working Notes:

1. Interest on A's Loan = ₹ 2,00,000 × 6/12 × 5/12 = ₹ 5,000
2. Net Profit after interest on A's Loan = ₹ 4,30,000 – ₹ 5,000 = ₹ 4,25,000
3. Interest on Loan is credited to Loan A/c and not to Capital A/c.

RENT PAID TO A PARTNER

Rent paid to a partner is a charge against the profit and is not an appropriation out of profits. Hence it is debited to the Profit and Loss Account and not to the Profit and Loss Appropriation Account and credited to Partners' Current Accounts *(in case of Fixed Capitals) or* to Partners' Capital Accounts *(in case of Fluctuating Capitals).*

DISTINCTION BETWEEN CHARGE AGAINST PROFIT AND APPROPRIATION OF PROFIT

Basis	Charge Against Profit	Appropriation of Profit
1. Nature	It indicates deduction from Revenue to ascertain Net Profit/Loss.	It indicates distribution of Net Profit to different heads.
2. Recording	It is debited to Profit and Loss Account.	It is debited to Profit and Loss Appropriation Account.
3. When made	It is made even if there is loss.	It is made only when there is profit.
4. Priority over each other	It is done before appropriation of Profit.	It is done after creation of all charges.
5. Examples	Rent paid to a partner, Interest on Partner's Loan.	Interest on Capital, Salary to Partner, Transfer to General Reserve

13.0 SALARY OR COMMISSION TO A PARTNER

When to Allow	Salary *or* Commission to a partner is to be allowed if the partnership agreement provides for the same.
Nature	Salary *or* Commission to a partner is an **appropriation** out of profits and **not** a **charge** against the profits. In other words, it is to be allowed only if there are profits.
How to calculate	Commission may be allowed as percentage of Net Profit before charging such commission *or* after charging such commission. ***I—Commission as % of Net Profit before charging such Commission*** $= \text{Net Profit before Commission} \times \frac{\text{Rate of Commission}}{100}$ ***II—Commission as % of Net Profit after charging such Commission*** $= \text{Net Profit before Commission} \times \frac{\text{Rate of Commission}}{100 + \text{Rate of Commission}}$
If Profit is *less* than Salary/ Commission	If the amount of available profits is less than the amount of appropriations to be made, the available profits should be distributed in the ratio of appropriations to be made (i.e. no particular appropriation item like salary/ interest on capital has priority over another appropriation item).
Accounting Treatment	Salary *or* Commission to a partner is an **appropriation out of profits** and hence must be transferred to the **debit of Profit & Loss Appropriation Account and not** to the **debit of Profit & Loss Account.** The following journal entries are passed to adjust salary *or* commission:

	(a) Adjusting Entry to adjust salary or commission to a partner Salary *or* Commission A/c ... Dr. To Partner's Capital A/c *(In case of Fluctuating Capitals)*, or To Partner's Current A/c *(In case of Fixed Capitals)* ***(b) Closing Entry to close Salary or Commission Account*** Profit & Loss Appropriation A/c ... Dr. To Salary *or* Commission A/c

ILLUSTRATION 25

A and B are partners in a firm. A is to get a commission of 10% of Net Profit before charging any commission. B is to get a commission of 10% on Net Profit after charging all commissions. Net Profit before charging any commission was ₹ 55,000. Find out the commission of A and B.

SOLUTION

A's Commission = 10% of ₹ 55,000 = ₹ 5,500

B's Commission = (₹ 55,000 – ₹ 5,500) × 10/110 = ₹ 4,500.

ILLUSTRATION 26

X and Y are partners in a firm. X is entitled to a salary of ₹ 2,000 p.m. together with a commission of 10% of Net Profit before charging any commission. Y is entitled to a salary of ₹ 5,000 p.a. together with a commission of 10% of Net Profit after charging all commissions. Net profit before charging any commission for the year 2011-12 was ₹ 55,000. Show the distribution of Profit.

SOLUTION

PROFIT AND LOSS APPROPRIATION ACCOUNT

Dr. *for the year ending on 31st March, 2012* *Cr.*

Particulars		₹	*Particulars*	₹
To X's Salary		24,000	By Profit before Salary & Commission	
To Y's Salary		5,000	[₹ 55,000 + ₹ 24,000 (X's Salary)	
To X's Commission		5,500	+ ₹ 5,000 (Y's Salary)]	84,000
(₹ 55,000 × 10/100)				
To Y's Commission				
[(₹ 55,000 – ₹ 5,500) × 10/110]		4,500		
To Net Profit transferred to:				
X's Capital A/c	22,500			
Y's Capital A/c	22,500	45,000		
		84,000		84,000

ILLUSTRATION 27

X and Y are partners sharing the profits and losses in the ratio of 3 : 2. X being a non-working partner contributed ₹ 5,00,000 as his capital on 1st April, 2011. Y being a working partner agreed to work for the firm. The partnership deed provides for interest on capital @ 8% and salary to every working partner @ ₹ 2,000 p.m. On 31st October 2011, X advanced ₹ 2,00,000 by way of loan to the firm. Net

Profit before providing for any interest and partner's salary for the year 2011-12 was ₹ 25,000. Show the distribution of profit.

SOLUTION

PROFIT & LOSS APPROPRIATION ACCOUNT

Dr. *for the year ended 31st March 2012* *Cr.*

Particulars	₹	*Particulars*		₹
To Interest on X's Capital	12,500	By Net Profit as per P&L A/c		20,000
To Salary to Y	7,500	Given Profits	25,000	
		Less: Interest on Loan	5,000	
	20,000			20,000

Note: Interest on Loan = ₹ 2,00,000 × 5/12 × 6/100 = ₹ 5,000

Note: Since both interest on capital and salary to partner are appropriations and the available profits (₹ 25,000 – ₹ 5,000)are less than the amount of appropriations to be made, the available profits have been distributed in the ratio of appropriations to be made i.e. ₹ 40,000 (interest on capital ₹ 5,00,000 × 8/100) ₹ 24,000 (Salary (₹ 2,000 × 12).

14.0 DIVISION OF PROFIT AMONG PARTNERS

After ascertaining the Net Profit as per Profit & Loss Account, usually the Profit & Loss Appropriation Account is prepared.

Meaning	P&L Appropriation Account shows the distribution of Net Profits as per P&L A/c among the partners by way of Interest on Capital, Salary, Commission to partners, Transfer to Reserves.
Purpose	P & L Appropriation is prepared to show the distribution of Net Profit among the partners. The balance in Profit & Loss Appropriation Account may be used: 1. To provide for Interest on Capitals of Partners *(if Partnership Deed so provides).* 2. To provide for Salary *or* Commission to partners *(if Partnership Deed so provides).* 3. To transfer the profits to General Reserve *or* Specific Reserve. 4. To distribute the profits among the partners in their profit sharing ratio. 5. To retain the profits in the business by ploughing back of profits.
Debited with	It is debited with Interest on Capital, Salary, Commission to Partners, Transfer to Reserves, Share of Profit etc.
Credited with	It is credited with Opening Balance b/f, Interest on Drawings, etc.
Balance	Its balance is transferred to the partners' Capital (or Current) Accounts in their agreed profit sharing ratio (or equally if there is no agreed profit sharing ratio).

DIFFERENCE BETWEEN PROFIT & LOSS ACCOUNT AND PROFIL & LOSS APPROPRIATION ACCOUNT

Profit & Loss Account is prepared to ascertain the Net Profit whereas P & L Appropriation Account is prepared to the show the distribution of Net Profit among the partners.

DIFFERENCE BETWEEN PROFIT & LOSS APPROPRIATION ACCOUNT AND PROFIT & LOSS ADJUSTMENT ACCOUNT

P & L Appropriation Account is prepared to show the distribution of Net Profit among the partners whereas Profit & Loss Adjustment Account is prepared to show the effect of revaluation of assets and liabilities at the time of reconstitution of partnership. (i.e. Change in Profit sharing ratio, Admission, Retirement *or* Death of a Partner).

JOURNAL ENTRIES IN RELATION TO APPROPRIATION OF PROFITS

1. For Interest on Capital

(a) On allowing Interest on Capital

Interest on Capital A/c ... Dr.
  To Partner's Capital (or Current) A/c

(b) On Closure of Interest on Capital A/c

Profit & Loss Appropriation A/c ... Dr.
  To Interest on Capital A/c

2. For Interest on Drawings

(a) On Charging Interest on Drawings

Partner's Capital (or Current) A/c ... Dr.
  To Interest on Drawings A/c

(b) On Closure of Interest on Drawings A/c

Interest on Drawings A/c ... Dr.
  To Profit & Loss Appropriation A/c

3. For Partner's Salary/Commission

(a) On allowing Salary/Commission to Partner

Salary/Commission to Partner A/c ... Dr.
  To Partner's Capital (or Current) A/c

(b) On closure of Salary/Commission to Partner A/c

Profit & Loss Appropriation A/c ... Dr.
  To Salary/Commission to Partner A/c

4. For Transfer to Reserve

Profit & Loss Appropriation A/c ... Dr.
  To Reserve

5. For Transfer of Credit Balance (being Profit)

Profit & Loss Appropriation A/c ... Dr.
  To Partners' Capital (or Current) Accounts (Individually in profit sharing ratio)

FORMAT OF PROFIT AND LOSS APPROPRIATION ACCOUNT

PROFIT AND LOSS APPROPRIATION ACCOUNT

Dr. *for the year ending on ....* *Cr.*

Particulars	₹	*Particulars*	₹
To Interest on Capital:		By Profit & Loss A/c	xxx

A	xxx		(Net Profit subject to appropriations)		
B	xxx	xxx	By Interest on Drawings:		
To Salary to Partner		xxx	A	xxx	
To Commission to Partner		xxx	B	xxx	xxx
To Reserve		xxx			
To Profit transferred to:					
*A's Capital A/c	xxx				
**(or A's Current A/c)					
*B's Capital A/c	xxx				
**(or B's Current A/c)		xxx			
		xxx			xxx

**Under Fluctuating Capital Method*

***Under Fixed Capital Method*

ILLUSTRATION 28

Ram and Manohar are partners in a firm sharing profits and losses in the ratio of 7:3. According to the partnership deed, Ram was to be paid salary of ₹ 5,000 per month and Manohar was to get a bonus of ₹ 40,000 per annum. Interest on capital was to be allowed @ 10% per annum and interest on drawings was to be charged @ 8% per annum. Interest on Ram's drawings was ₹ 3,000 and on Manohar's drawings was ₹ 2,000. Their fixed capitals were ₹ 4,00,000 and ₹ 1,50,000 respectively. The firm earned a profit of ₹ 2,50,000 for the year ended 31.3.2012. Prepare Profit & Loss Appropriation A/c.

SOLUTION

Dr. **P & L APPROPRIATION ACCOUNT FOR THE YEAR ENDED 31ST MARCH, 2012** *Cr.*

Particulars		₹	*Particulars*		₹
To Ram's Salary (₹ 5,000 × 12)		60,000	By Net Profit as per P/L A/c		2,50,000
To Manohar's Bonus		40,000	By Interest on Drawings:		
To Interest on Capital:			Ram	3,000	
Ram	40,000		Manohar	2,000	5,000
Manohar	15,000	55,000			
To Profit t/f to Current A/c:					
Ram 7/10	70,000				
Manohar 3/10	30,000	1,00,000			
		2,55,000			2,55,000

ILLUSTRATION 29

A and B start business on April 1, 2011, each partner contributing ₹ 1,50,000 as his share of capital. On October 1, 2011, B makes an additional contribution of ₹ 1,00,000 which is treated as a loan. The profit for the period ending March 2012 was ₹ 85,000 before charging any interest. All the partners were entitled to a salary of ₹ 3,000 each, per quarter. The partners had drawn ₹ 24,000 each on 1 st January 2012. Prepare the P&L Appropriation Account for the period ended March 31, 2012.

SOLUTION

Dr. **PROFIT & LOSS APPROPRIATION ACCOUNT FOR THE PERIOD ENDED ON 31.3.2012** *Cr.*

Particulars		₹	*Particulars*		₹
To Salary:			By Net Profit as per P&L A/c	85,000	
A (3,000 × 4)	12,000		*Less:* Interest on B's Loan		
B (3,000 × 4)	12,000	24,000	(1,00,000 × 6/100 × 6/12)	3,000	82,000
To Profit t/f to Capital A/cs:					
A's 1/2	29,000				
B's 1/2	29,000	58,000			
		82,000			82,000

ILLUSTRATION 30

A and B are partners sharing profits in the ratio of 3 : 2 with capitals of ₹ 50,000 and ₹ 30,000 respectively. Interest on capital is agreed @ 6% p.a. B is to be allowed an annual salary of ₹ 2,500. During 2011-12 the profits of the year prior to calculation of interest on capital but after charging B's salary amounted to ₹ 12,500. A provision of 5% of the profits is to be made in respect of manager's commission. Prepare an account showing the allocation of profits and partners' capital accounts.

SOLUTION

Dr. **PROFIT & LOSS ACCOUNT** *Cr.*

for the year ended 31st March, 2012

Particulars	₹	*Particulars*	₹
To Manager's Commission		By Profit before B's salary	
(5% of ₹ 15,000)	750	(12,500 + 2,500)	15,000
To Net Profit t/f to P & L Appr. A/c	14,250		
	15,000		15,000

PROFIT AND LOSS APPROPRIATION ACCOUNT
Dr. **FOR THE YEAR ENDING ON 31ST MARCH 2012** *Cr.*

Particulars		₹	*Particulars*	₹
To Bs Salary		2,500	By Net Profit t/f from P & L A/c	14,250
To Interest on Capital:				
A	3,000			
B	1,800	4,800		
To Net Profit transferred to:				
A's Capital A/c	4,170			
B's Capital A/c	2,780	6,950		
		14,250		14,250

Dr. **PARTNERS' CAPITAL ACCOUNTS** *Cr.*

Particulars	*A* ₹	*B* ₹	*Particulars*	*A* ₹	*B* ₹
To Balance c/d	57,170	37,080	By Balance b/d	50,000	30,000
			By P & L Appropriation A/c		
			— Interest on Capital	3,000	1,800
			— Profit	4,170	2,780
			— Salary		2,500
	57,170	37,080		57,170	37,080

Note: Manager's Commission is a charge against the profits. Hence, it is required to be provided for before making any appropriation (such as partner's salary, interest on capital).

ILLUSTRATION 31

X and Y were partners in a firm sharing profits in the ratio of 3 : 2. On 1st April, 2011 their fixed capitals were ₹ 3,00,000 and ₹ 2,50,000 respectively. On 1st Oct, 2011, they decided that their total capital (fixed) should be ₹ 6,00,000 in their profit sharing ratio. Accordingly, they introduced extra capital *or* withdrew excess capital. The partnership deed provided for the following:

(i) Interest on capital @ 12% p.a.

(ii) Interest on drawing @ 18% p.a.

(iii) A monthly salary of ₹ 2,000 to X and a monthly salary of ₹ 1,500 to Y. The drawings of X and Y during the year were as follows:

Date	*X (₹)*	*Y (₹)*
on 30th Sept. 2011	20,000	15,000
on 31st Dec. 2011	20,000	25,000

During the year ended 31st March, 2012 the firm earned a net profit of ₹ 1,50,000. 10% of this profit was to be transferred to general reserve. You are required to prepare: (i) Profit and Loss Appropriation Account (ii) Partners' Capital Accounts, and (iii) Partners' Current Accounts.

SOLUTION

Dr. **PROFIT AND LOSS APPROPRIATION ACCOUNT** *Cr.*

Particulars	₹	*Particulars*	₹
To General Reserve	15,000	By P & L A/c (Net profit)	1,50,000
(₹ 1,50,000 × 10/100]		By Interest on Drawings:	
To Salary:		X	2,700
X [₹ 2,000 × 12]	24,000	Y	2,475
Y [₹ 1,500 × 12]	18,000		
To Interest on Capital:			
X	39,600		
Y	29,400		
To Profit t/f to:			
X's Current A/c	17,505		

Y's Current A/c	11,670		
	1,55,175		1,55,175

Dr. **PARTNERS' CAPITAL ACCOUNTS** Cr.

Particulars	X ₹	Y ₹	Particulars	X ₹	Y ₹
To Cash A/c	—	10,000	By Balance b/d	3,00,000	2,50,000
To Balance c/d	3,60,000	2,40,000	By Cash A/c	60,000	
	3,60,000	2,50,000		3,60,000	2,50,000

Dr. **PARTNERS' CURRENT ACCOUNTS** Cr.

Particulars	X ₹	Y ₹	Particulars	X ₹	Y ₹
To Drawings	40,000	40,000	By Salary	24,000	18,000
To Interest on Drawings	2,700	2,475	By Interest on Capital	39,600	29,400
To Balance c/d	38,405	16,595	By P&L App. A/c (Profit)	17,505	11,670
	81,105	59,070		81,105	59,070

Working Notes:

1. **Calculation of New capitals**

   ₹ 6,00,000 in the ratio of 3 : 2

   X's capital 3/5 of 6,00,000 = ₹ 3,60,000

   Y's capital 2/5 of 6,00,000 = ₹ 2,40,000

2. **Capital to be introduced by X** = ₹ 3,60,000 – ₹ 3,00,000 = ₹ 60,000

   Capital to be withdrawn by Y = ₹ 2,50,000 – ₹ 2,40,000 = ₹ 10,000

3. CALCULATION OF INTEREST ON CAPITAL

Particulars	X	Y
Upto 30th Sept	$3{,}00{,}000 \times \frac{12}{100} \times \frac{6}{12}$ = ₹ 18,000	$2{,}50{,}000 \times \frac{12}{100} \times \frac{6}{12}$ = ₹ 15,000
From 1st Oct. to 31st March	$3{,}60{,}000 \times \frac{12}{100} \times \frac{6}{12}$ = ₹ 21,600	$2{,}40{,}000 \times \frac{12}{100} \times \frac{6}{12}$ = ₹ 14,400
Total (₹)	39,600	29,400

4. CALCULATION OF INTEREST ON DRAWINGS

Particulars	X	Y
Upto 30th Sept	$20{,}000 \times \frac{18}{100} \times \frac{6}{12}$ = ₹ 1,800	$15{,}000 \times \frac{18}{100} \times \frac{6}{12}$ = ₹ 1,350
From 1st Oct. to 31st March	$20{,}000 \times \frac{18}{100} \times \frac{3}{12}$ = ₹ 900	$25{,}000 \times \frac{18}{100} \times \frac{3}{12}$ = ₹ 1,125
Total	₹ 2,700	₹ 2,475

ILLUSTRATION 32

X and Y started a partnership business on 1st April, 2011. They contributed ₹ 80,000 and ₹ 60,000 respectively as their capitals. On 1st Oct, 2011, X granted a loan of ₹ 20,000. The terms of the partnership agreement are as follows:

(a) 20% of Profits before charging Interest on Drawings but after making appropriations to be transferred to General Reserve.

(b) Interest on Capital @ 12% p.a. and Interest on Drawings @ 10% p.a.

(c) X to get a monthly salary of ₹ 2,000 and Y to get salary of ₹ 9,000 per quarter.

(d) X is entitled to a commission of 2% on Sales. Sales for the year were ₹ 3,50,000.

(e) Profits & Losses to be shared in the ratio of their Capital Contribution up to ₹ 70,000 and above ₹ 70,000 equally.

The profit for the year ended 31st March, 2012, before Interest on Partner's Loan was ₹ 1,84,400. The drawings of X and Y were ₹ 40,000 and ₹ 50,000 respectively.

Required: Pass the necessary journal entries relating to appropriations out of profits. Prepare Profit and Loss Appropriation Account and Partners' Capital Accounts.

SOLUTION

JOURNAL OF X AND Y

Date	*Particulars*		*L.F.*	*Dr. (₹)*	*Cr. (₹)*
2012 Mar. 31	Interest on X's Loan A/c [20,000 × 6% × 6/12] To X's Loan A/c (Being the adjustment made for Interest on Loan)	Dr.		600	 600
	Profit & Loss A/c To Interest on X's Loan A/c (Being the transfer of Interest on Loan to P&L A/c)	Dr.		600	 600
	Profit and Loss A/c To Profit and Loss Appropriation A/c (Being the transfer of Profit to P&L Appropriation A/c)	Dr.		1,83,800	 1,83,800
	Profit and Loss Appropriation A/c To General Reserve A/c (Being the transfer of 20% profits to General Reserve)	Dr.		20,000	 20,000
	Salary A/c To X's Capital A/c To Y's Capital A/c (Being the adjustment made for salary of X and Y)	Dr.		60,000	 24,000 36,000
	Profit and Loss Appropriation A/c To Salary A/c (Being the transfer of X & Y's Salary to P&L Appr. A/c)	Dr.		60,000	 60,000
	X's Commission A/c To X's Capital A/c (Being the adjustment made for X's Commission)	Dr.		7,000	 7,000

	Particulars		Dr.	Cr.
	Profit and Loss Appropriation A/c Dr. To X's Commission A/c (Being the transfer of X's Commission to P&L Appr. A/c)		7,000	7,000
	Interest on Capital A/c Dr. To X's Capital A/c To Y's Capital A/c (Being the adjustment made for interest on capital)		16,800	9,600 7,200
	Profit and Loss Appropriation A/c Dr. To Interest on Capital A/c (Being the transfer of Interest on Capital to P&L Appr. A/c)		16,800	16,800
	X's Capital A/c [₹ 40,000 × 10% × 6/12] Dr. Y's Capital A/c [₹ 50,000 × 10% × 6/12] Dr. To Interest on Drawings A/c (Being the adjustment made for interest on drawings)		2,000 2,500	4,500
	Interest on Drawings A/c Dr. To Profit and Loss Appropriation A/c (Being the t/f of Interest on drawings to P&L Appr. A/c)		4,500	4,500
	Profit and Loss Appropriation A/c Dr. To X's Capital A/c To Y's Capital A/c (Being the transfer of profit)		80,000	47,250 37,250

PROFIT & LOSS APPROPRIATION ACCOUNT
for the year ending on 31st Mar., 2012

Dr. Cr.

Particulars		₹	*Particulars*		₹
To Interest on Capital:			By P&L A/c [1,84,400 – 600]		1,83,800
X	9,600		By Interest on Drawings:		
Y	7,200	16,800	X	2,000	
To Salary:			Y	2,500	4,500
X	24,000				
Y	36,000	60,000			
To Commission to X					
[2% of ₹ 3,50,000]		7,000			
To General Reserve		20,000			
To Profit transferred to:					
70,000	*Balance*				
X's Capital A/c 40,000	+ 7,250	47,250			
Y's Capital A/c 30,000	+ 7,250	37,250			
		1,88,300			1,88,300

Dr. **PARTNERS' CAPITAL ACCOUNTS** *Cr.*

Particulars	*X* ₹	*Y* ₹	*Particulars*	*X* ₹	*Y* ₹
To Drawings	40,000	50,000	By Bank A/c	80,000	60,000
To Interest on Drawings	2,000	2,500	By Interest on Capital	9,600	7,200
To Balance c/d	1,25,850	87,950	By Salary	24,000	36,000
			By Commission	7,000	—
			By P&L App. A/c	47,250	37,250
	1,67,850	1,40,450		1,67,850	1,40,450

Notes:

1. As per The Indian Partnership Act, Interest on Loan is to be allowed @ 6% p.a.
2. Interest on Drawing has been calculated for an average period of 6 months as the date of drawing is not given.
3. T/f to Reserve = 20% of (1,83,800 – 16,800 – 60,000 – 7,000) = ₹ 20,000.

15.0 PAST ADJUSTMENTS

Meaning	Past Adjustments refer to those adjustments which affect the distribution of past profits like omission *or* commission in respect of Interest on Capital/ Drawings of a Partner, Salary/Commission to a Partner, Sharing of Profits.
How to carry out	Past Adjustments should be carried out directly through the Capital Accounts of the concerned partners.
How to Pass Single Adjusting Journal Entry	The passing of the necessary Adjusting Journal Entry involves the following steps: **Step 1:** ***Calculate the*** *amount already* ***recorded by way of Share of Profit, Interest on Capital, Salary, Commission etc.*** **Step 2:** *Calculate the* ***amount which should have been recorded*** *by way of Interest on Capital, Salary or Commission or Share of Profit etc.* **Step 3:** *Calculate the* ***difference*** *between the amounts calculated as per Step 1 and the amount calculated as per Step 2.* **Step 4:** *Find out the partner* ***who received excess*** *and the partner* ***who received short.*** **Step 5:** *Pass the Adjusting Journal Entry by* ***debiting*** *the Capital Account of Partner* ***who received excess*** *and by* ***crediting*** *the Capital Account of Partner* ***who received short.***
Format of Adjustment Table	A simplest format of Adjustment Table is given below:

ADJUSTMENT TABLE

Particulars	*X*	*Y*	*Total*
A. Amounts already recorded: (e.g.)			
Interest on Capital	....	....	....
Interest on Drawings	(....)	(....)	(....)
Salary/Commission to Partner	....	....	....
Share of Profit	....	....	....
	....	....	....

	B. Amounts which should have been recorded: (e.g.)			
	Interest on Capital	....	....	....
	Interest on Drawings	(....)	(....)	(....)
	Salary to Partner	....	....	....
	Commission to Partner	....	....	...
	Share of Revised Profit	....	....	....
		....	....	....
	C. Difference [A – B]	....	....	....
Single Adjusting Journal Entry	Gaining Partner's Capital A/c ***(who received excess)*** Dr. To Sacrificing Partner's Capital A/c ***(who received short)***			

ILLUSTRATION 33

X, Y, and Z are partners. Their Capitals as on 1st Jan., 2012 were: X ₹ 50,000, Y ₹ 1,00,000 and Z ₹ 1,50,000. Profits for the year 2012 amounting to ₹ 60,000 were distributed in the ratio of capitals without providing for the following:

(a) Interest on Capitals : X ₹ 5,000, Y ₹ 10,000, Z ₹ 15,000

(b) Interest on Drawings : X ₹ 3,000, Y ₹ 5,000, Z ₹ 8,000

(c) X 's Salary of ₹ 1,000 p.m. and Y's Commission of ₹ 4,000

The Partnership Deed was silent as to the sharing of Profits & Losses.

Required: Pass the necessary single Adjusting Entry.

SOLUTION

STEP 1: ADJUSTMENT TABLE

Particulars	*X*	*Y*	*Z*
I. Amounts already recorded:			
Share of Profit [₹ 60,000 in 1:2:3 ratio]	10,000	20,000	30,000
	10,000	20,000	30,000
II. Amounts which should have been recorded:			
Interest on Capital	5,000	10,000	15,000
Interest on Drawings	(3,000)	(5,000)	(8,000)
Salary [₹ 1,000 × 12]	12,000	—	—
Commission	—	4,000	—
Share of Profit [₹ 30,000* in 1:1:1 ratio]	10,000	10,000	10,000
	24,000	19,000	17,000
III. Difference [I – II]	**(14,000)**	**1,000**	**13,000**
	Sacrificing Partner	**Gaining Partner**	**Gaining Partner**

*Revised Profits = 60,000 – 5,000 – 10,000 – 15,000 + 3,000 + 5,000 + 8,000 – 12,000 – 4,000

= ₹ 30,000

STEP 2: ADJUSTING JOURNAL ENTRY

Date	*Particulars*	*L.F.*	*Dr. (₹)*	*Cr. (₹)*
	Y's Capital A/c		1,000	
	Z"s Capital A/c		13,000	
	To X's Capital A/c			14,000
	(Being the rectification for adjustment of profits as per Partnership Deed and The Indian Partnership Act, 1932)			

ILLUSTRATION 34

X, Y, and Z are partners. Their fixed capitals as on 1st Jan., 2012 were: X ₹ 50,000, Y ₹ 1,00,000 and Z ₹ 1,50,000. Profits for the year 2012 amounting to ₹ 30,000 were distributed in the ratio of capitals after providing for the following:

(a) Interest on Capitals : X ₹ 5,000, Y ₹ 10,000, Z ₹ 15,000

(b) Interest on Drawings : X ₹ 3,000, Y ₹ 5,000, Z ₹ 8,000

(c) X 's Salary of ₹ 1,000 p.m. and Y's Commission of ₹ 4,000

The Partnership Deed was silent as to the sharing of Profits & Losses, Interest on Capitals, Interest on Drawings and Partner's Salary and Commission.

Required: Pass the necessary single Adjusting Entry.

SOLUTION

STEP 1: ADJUSTMENT TABLE

Particulars	*X*	*Y*	*Z*
I. Amounts already recorded:			
Interest on Capital	5,000	10,000	15,000
Interest on Drawings	(3,000)	(5,000)	(8,000)
Salary[₹ 1,000 × 12]	12,000	—	—
Commission	—	4,000	—
Share of Profit [₹ 30,000 in 1:2:3 ratio]	5,000	10,000	15,000
	19,000	19,000	22,000
II. Amounts which should have been recorded:			
Share of Profit [₹ 60,000* in 1:1:1 ratio]	20,000	20,000	20,000
	20,000	20,000	20,000
III. Difference [I – II]	**(1,000)**	**(1,000)**	**2,000**
	Sacrificing Partner	**Sacrificing Partner**	**Gaining Partner**
			Partner

*Revised Profits = 30,000 + 5,000 + 10,000 + 15,000 – 3,000 – 5,000 – 8,000 + 12,000 + 4,000
= ₹ 60,000

STEP 2: ADJUSTING JOURNAL ENTRY

Date	Particulars	L.F.	Dr. (₹)	Cr. (₹)
	Z's Current A/c		2,000	
	To X's Current A/c			1,000
	To Y's Current A/c			1,000
	(Being the rectification for adjustment of profits as per The Indian Partnership Act)			

ILLUSTRATION 35

X and Y are partners in a firm. Their capital accounts as on March 31, 2012 showed balances of ₹ 70,000 and ₹ 60,000 respectively. The drawings of X and Y during the year 2011-2012 were ₹ 8,000 and ₹ 6,000 respectively. After distributing the profits of the year 2011-2012 which amounted to ₹ 40,000, it was subsequently found that the following items have been left out while preparing the final accounts of the year ended 31st March, 2012.

(i) The partners were entitled to Interest on capitals @ 6% p.a.

(ii) The interest on drawings was also to be charged @ 5% p.a.

(iii) X was entitled to salary of ₹ 10,000 and Y a commission of ₹ 4,000 for the whole year.

Required: Pass the necessary single Adjusting Entry.

SOLUTION

STEP 1: CALCULATION OF OPENING CAPITALS

Particulars	X (₹)	Y (₹)
A. Closing Capital	70,000	60,000
B. *Less:* Share of Profit [₹ 40,000 in 1:1 ratio]	(20,000)	(20,000)
C. *Add:* Drawings	8,000	6,000
D. Capital at the beginning [A – B + C]	58,000	46,000

Step 2: Calculation of Interest on Capital

For X: 58,000 × 6/100 = ₹ 3,480, For Y: 46,000 × 6/100 = ₹ 2,760

Step 3: Calculation of Interest on Drawings

For X: 8,000 × 5/100 × 6/12 = ₹ 200, For Y: 6,000 × 5/100 × 6/12 = ₹ 150

Step 4 Calculation of Revised Profits

= ₹ 40,000 – ₹ 3,480 – ₹ 2,760 + ₹ 200 + ₹ 150 – ₹ 10,000 – ₹ 4,000 = ₹ 20,110

Step 5: Calculation of Share of Profit

X's Share = ₹ 20,110 × 1/2 = 10,055, Y's Share = ₹ 20,110 × 1/2 = 10,055

STEP 6: ADJUSTMENT TABLE

Particulars	X	Y	Total
I. Amounts already recorded:			
Interest on Capital	—	—	—
Interest on Drawings	—	—	—

Salary	—	—	—
Share of Profit	20,000	20,000	40,000
	20,000	20,000	40,000
II. Amounts which should have been recorded:			
Interest on Capital	3,480	2,760	6,240
Interest on Drawings	(200)	(150)	(350)
Salary	10,000	—	10,000
Commission	—	4,000	4,000
Share of Profit (Refer to Step 5)	10,055	10,055	20,110
	23,335	16,665	40,000
III. Difference [I – II]	(3,335)	3,335	—

STEP 7: ADJUSTING JOURNAL ENTRY

Date	*Particulars*	*L.F.*	*Dr. (₹)*	*Cr. (₹)*
	Y's Capital A/c Dr.		3,335	
	To X's Capital A/c			3,335
	(Being the Omissions adjusted through Capital Accounts)			

ILLUSTRATION 36

A, B and C were partners in a firm. On 1.1.2012 their capitals stood at ₹ 50,000, ₹ 25,000 and ₹ 25,000 respectively. As per the provisions of the partnership deed:

(a) C was entitled for a salary of ₹ 1,500 p.m.

(b) Partners were entitled to interest on capital at 5% p.a.

(c) Profits were to be shared in the ratio of capitals.

The net profit for the year 2012 of ₹ 45,000 was divided equally without providing for the above terms.

Required: Pass an adjusting entry to rectify the above error.

SOLUTION

STEP 1: ADJUSTMENT TABLE

Particulars	*A* ₹	*B* ₹	*C* ₹
I. Amounts already credited:			
Share of Profit (in ratio of 1:1:1)	15,000	15,000	15,000
II. Amounts which should have been credited:			
C's Salary	–	–	18,000
Interest on Capital	2,500	1,250	1,250
Share of Profit (in ratio of 2:1:1)	11,000	5,500	5,500
	13,500	6,750	24,750
III. Difference (I – II)	1,500	8,250	(9,750)

STEP 2: ADJUSTING JOURNAL ENTRY

Date	Particulars	L.F.	Dr. (₹)	Cr. (₹)
	A's Capital A/c		1,500	
	Bs Capital A/c		8,250	
	To C's Capital A/c			9,750
	(Being the rectification for adjustment of profits as per partnership deed)			

ILLUSTRATION 37

X, Y, and Z are partners. Their fixed capitals as on 31st Dec., 2012 were: X ₹ 50,000, Y ₹ 1,00,000 and Z ₹ 1,50,000. Profits for the year 2012 amounting to ₹ 60,000 were distributed. Interest on Capital was credited @ 10% p.a. though there was no such provision in the partnership deed. Pass the necessary adjusting entry.

SOLUTION

STEP 1: ADJUSTMENT TABLE

Particulars	X ₹	Y ₹	Z ₹	Total ₹
I. Amount already credited by way of Interest on Capital	5,000	10,000	15,000	30,000
II. Amount which should have been credited by way of Share of Profit	10,000	10,000	10,000	30,000
III. Difference [I — II]	(5,000)	—	5,000	—

STEP 2: ADJUSTING JOURNAL ENTRY

Date	Particulars	L.F.	Dr. (₹)	Cr. (₹)
	Z's Current A/c Dr.		5,000	
	To X's Current A/c			5,000
	(Being the interest on wrongly provided, now adjusted)			

ILLUSTRATION 38

X, Y, and Z are partners. Their fixed capitals as on 31st Dec., 2012 were: X ₹ 50,000, Y ₹ 1,00,000 and Z ₹ 1,50,000. Profits for the year 2012 amounting to ₹ 60,000 were distributed. Interest on Capital was not credited @ 10% p.a. though there was such provision in the partnership deed. Pass the necessary adjusting entry.

SOLUTION

STEP 1: ADJUSTMENT TABLE

Particulars	X ₹	Y ₹	Z ₹	Total ₹
I. Amount already credited by way of share of profit	10,000	10,000	10,000	30,000

II. Amount which should have been credited by way of Interest on Capital	5,000	10,000	15,000	30,000
III. Difference [I — II]	5,000	—	(5,000)	—

STEP 2: ADJUSTING JOURNAL ENTRY

Date	*Particulars*	*L.F.*	*Dr. (₹)*	*Cr. (₹)*
	X's Current A/c Dr.		5,000	
	To Z's Current A/c			5,000
	(Being the interest omitted to be provided, now adjusted)			

ILLUSTRATION 39

X, Y, and Z are partners. Their fixed capitals as on 31st Dec., 2012 were: X ₹ 50,000, Y ₹ 1,00,000 and Z ₹ 1,50,000. Profits for the year 2012 amounting to ₹ 60,000 were distributed. Interest on Capital was credited @ 10% p.a. instead of 12% p.a. Pass the necessary adjusting entrys.

SOLUTION

STEP 1: ADJUSTMENT TABLE

Particulars	*X* ₹	*Y* ₹	*Z* ₹	*Total* ₹
A. Amount already credited by way of Interest on Capital @ 10%	5,000	10,000	15,000	30,000
Share of Profit [(₹ 36,000 – ₹ 30,000) in ratio of 1:1:1:]	2,000	2, 000	2,000	6,000
	7,000	12,000	17,000	3,6000
B. Amount that should have been credited by way of:				
Interest on Capital @ 12%	6,000	12,000	18,000	36,000
C. Difference [A — B]	1,000	—	(1,000)	—

STEP 2: ADJUSTING JOURNAL ENTRY

Date	*Particulars*	*L.F.*	*Dr. (₹)*	*Cr. (₹)*
	X's Current A/c Dr.		1,000	
	To Z's Current A/c			1,000
	(Being the interest on capital wrongly provided, now adjusted)			

ILLUSTRATION 40

X, Y, and Z are partners. Their fixed capitals as on 31st Dec., 2012 were: X ₹ 50,000, Y ₹ 1,00,000 and Z ₹ 1,50,000. Profits for the year 2012 amounting to ₹ 60,000 were distributed. Interest on Capital was credited @ 12% p.a. instead of 10% p.a. Pass the necessary adjusting entry.

SOLUTION

STEP 1: ADJUSTMENT TABLE

Particulars	X ₹	Y ₹	Z ₹	Total ₹
I. Interest on Capital already credited @ 12%	6,000	12,000	18,000	36,000
II. Amount that should have been credited by way of:				
Interest on capital @ 10%	5,000	10,000	15,000	30,000
Share of Profit [(₹ 36,000 – ₹ 30,000) in ratio of 1 : 1 : 1 :]	2,000	2,000	2,000	6,000
	7,000	12,000	17,000	36,000
III. Difference [I – II]	(1,000)	—	1,000	—

STEP 2: ADJUSTING JOURNAL ENTRY

Date	Particulars	L.F.	Dr. (₹)	Cr. (₹)
	Z's Current A/c Dr.		1,000	
	To X's Current A/c			1,000
	(Being the interest on capital wrongly provided, now adjusted)			

ILLUSTRATION 41

P, Q and R were partners in a firm sharing profits in the ratio of 1: 2 : 2.After division of the profits for the year ended 31.3.2012 their capitals were: P ₹ 1,50,000; Q ₹ 1,80,000 and R ₹ 2,10,000. During the year they withdrew ₹ 20,000 each. The profit of the year was ₹ 60,000. The partnership deed provided that interest on capital will be allowed @ 10% p.a. While preparing the final accounts, interest on partners' capital was not allowed.

Required: You are required to calculate the capital of P, Q and R as on 1.4.2011 and pass the necessary adjustment entry for providing interest on capital.

SOLUTION

STEP 1: CALCULATION OF OPENING CAPITALS

Particulars	P (₹)	Q (₹)	R (₹)	Total
A. Closing Capitals	1,50,000	1,80,000	2,10,000	5,40,000
B. *Add:* Drawings	20,000	20,000	20,000	20,000
C. *Less:* Share of Profit	12,000	24,000	24,000	60,000
D. Opening Capitals	1,58,000	1,76,000	2,06,000	5,00,000

STEP 2: ADJUSTMENT TABLE

Particulars	P (₹)	Q (₹)	R (₹)	Total
I. Share of Profit already credited	12,000	24,000	24,000	60,000
II. Amount which should have been Credited:				
(a) Interest on Capital @ 10%	15,800	17,600	20,600	54,000

(b) Share of Profit	1,200	2,400	2,400	6,000
	17,000	20,000	23,000	60,000
III. Difference [I – II]	–5,000	4,000	1,000	–

STEP 3: ADJUSTING JOURNAL ENTRY

Date	*Particulars*		*L.F.*	*Dr. (₹)*	*Cr. (₹)*
	Q's Capital A/c	Dr.		4,000	
	R's Capital A/c	Dr.		1,000	
	To P's Capital A/c				5,000
	(Being the omission of interest on capital rectified)				

ILLUSTRATION 42

A, B and C shared the profits of ₹ 75,000 in the ratio of 2:2:1 but the partnership deed was silent as to the profit sharing ratio. Pass the necessary adjusting entry.

SOLUTION

STEP 1: ADJUSTMENT TABLE

Particulars	*A (₹)*	*B (₹)*	*C(₹)*
I. Amount already credited by way of			
Share of Profit in the ratio of 2:2:1	30,000	30,000	15,000
II. Amount which should have been credited by way of Share of Profit in the ratio of 1:1:1]	25,000	25,000	25,000
III. Difference (I – II)	5,000 (Dr.)	5,000 (Dr)	–10,000 (Cr.)
	Excess	Excess	Short

STEP 2: ADJUSTING JOURNAL ENTRY

Date	*Particulars*		*L.F.*	*Dr. (₹)*	*Cr. (₹)*
	A's Capital A/c	Dr.		5,000	
	B's Capital A/c	Dr.		5,000	
	To C's Capital A/c				10,000
	(Being the profits distributed in wrong ratio, now rectified)				

ILLUSTRATION 43

Preeti, Mona and Nisha shared profits in the ratio of 3 : 2 : 1. The profits of the last three years were ₹ 1,40,000, ₹ 84,000 and ₹ 1,06,000 respectively. These profits were by mistake, shared equally for all the three years. It is now decided to correct the error. Pass necessary journal entry for the same.

SOLUTION

STEP 1: ADJUSTMENT TABLE

Particulars	*Preeti (₹)*	*Mona (₹)*	*Nisha (₹)*
Profits already received (3,30,000 in 1 : 1 : 1)	1,10,000	1,10,000	1,10,000
Profits to be received (3,30,000 in 3 : 2 : 1)	1,65,000	1,10,000	55,000
Difference	(55,000)	—	55,000
	Short		**Excess**

STEP 2: ADJUSTING JOURNAL ENTRY

Date	*Particulars*	*L.F.*	*Dr. (₹)*	*Cr. (₹)*
	Nisha's Capital A/c Dr.		55,000	
	To Preeti's Capital A/c			55,000
	(Being the adjustment made for profit divided in wrong ratio)			

ILLUSTRATION 44

X, Y and Z are partners sharing profits & losses in the ratio of 3:2:1. After the final accounts have been prepared, it was discovered that Interest on drawings had not been taken into consideration, the Interest on drawings of partners amounted to —X ₹ 250; Y ₹ 190 and Z ₹ 100. Pass the necessary adjusting journal entry.

SOLUTION

STEP 1: ADJUSTMENT TABLE

Particulars	*X* ₹	*Y* ₹	*Z* ₹
I. Amount which should have been debited by way of Interest on drawings	250	190	100
II. Amount which should have been credited by way of Share of Profit	270	180	90
III. Difference (I – II)	–20 (Cr.)	10 (Dr)	10 (Dr.)

STEP 2: ADJUSTING JOURNAL ENTRY

Date	*Particulars*	*L.F.*	*Dr. (₹)*	*Cr. (₹)*
	Y's Capital A/c Dr.		10	
	Z's Capital A/c Dr.		10	
	To X's Capital A/c			20
	(Being Interest on drawings omitted to be recorded, now adjusted)			

ILLUSTRATION 45

X, Y and Z are partners sharing profits and losses in the ratio of 3 : 2 : 1. After the final accounts have been prepared, it was discovered that interest on drawings @ 5% p.a. has not been taken into consideration. The drawings of the Partners were: X ₹ 15,000; Y ₹ 12,600; Z ₹ 12,000. Pass the necessary adjusting journal entry.

SOLUTION

Step 1: Calculation of Interest on Drawings:

Since date of drawings are not given, interest will be charged for 6 months.

Particulars	₹
X: ₹ 15,000 × 5/100 × 6/12	₹ 375
Y: ₹ 12,000 × 5/100 × 6/12	₹ 315
Z: ₹ 12,000 × 5/100 × 6/12	₹ 300
	₹ 990

STEP 2: ADJUSTMENT TABLE

Particulars		*X* ₹	*Y* ₹	*Z* ₹	*Total* ₹
I. Interest on Drawings	(Dr.)	375	315	300	990
II. Divisions of ₹ 990 in 3 : 2 : 1	(Cr.)	495	330	165	990
III. Difference [I – II]		Cr. 120	Cr. 15	Dr. 135	—

STEP 3: ADJUSTING JOURNAL ENTRY

Date	*Particulars*	*L.F.*	*Dr. (₹)*	*Cr. (₹)*
	Z's Capital A/c Dr.		135	
	To X's Capital A/c			120
	To Y's Capital A/c			15
	(Being the Adjustment of omission of Interest on drawings)			

ILLUSTRATION 46

R and S were partners in a firm sharing profits in 3 : 2 ratio. Their respective fixed capitals were ₹ 10,00,000 and ₹ 15,00,000. The partnership deed provided the following:

(i) Interest on capital @ 10% p.a., (ii) Interest on drawing @ 12% p.a.

During the year ended 31.3.2012, R's drawings were ₹ 1,000 per month drawn at the end of every month and S's drawings were ₹ 2,000 per month drawn in the beginning of the every month. After the preparation of final accounts for the year ended 31.3.2012 it was discovered that interest on R's drawings was not taken into consideration.

Required: Calculate Interest on R's drawings and Pass necessary Adjusting Entry for the same.

SOLUTION

Step 1: Interest on R's Drawings = 12,000 × 12/100 × 5.5/12 = ₹ 660

STEP 2: ADJUSTMENT TABLE

Particulars		R (₹)	S (₹)	Total (₹)
I. Amount which should have been debited (Interest on Drawings)	(Dr.)	660	660	
II. Amount which should have been credited (Share of Profit)	(Cr.)	396	264	660
III. Difference [I – II]		Dr. 264	Cr. 264	—

STEP 3: ADJUSTING ENTRY

Date	Particulars	L.F.	Dr. (₹)	Cr. (₹)
	R's Current A/c Dr.		264	
	To S's Current A/c			264
	(Being the Adjustment of omission of interest on drawings)			

ILLUSTRATION 47

Mohan, Vijay and Anil are equal partners, the balances in their capital accounts being ₹ 30,000, ₹ 25,000 and ₹ 20,000 respectively. In arriving at these figures, the profits for the year ended March 31st, 2012, ₹ 24,000 had already been credited to partners in the proportion in which they share profits. Their drawings were Mohan ₹ 5,000, Vijay ₹ 4,000 and Anil ₹ 3,000 during 2011-12. Subsequently, the following omissions were noticed and it was decided to bring them into account:

(i) Interest on Capital at 10% per annum.

(ii) Interest on Drawings was: Mohan ₹ 250, Vijay ₹ 200 and Anil ₹ 150.

Required: Make the necessary corrections through a journal entry.

SOLUTION

STEP 1: CALCULATION OF OPENING CAPITALS AND INTEREST ON CAPITALS

Particulars	Mohan ₹	Vijaj ₹	Anil ₹
A. Closing Capitals	30,000	25,000	20,000
B. *Add:* Drawings	5,000	4,000	3,000
C. *Less:* Shares of Profit Credited	(8,000)	(8,000)	(8,000)
D. Opening Capitals	27,000	21,000	15,000
E. Interest @ 10%	2,700	2,100	1,500

STEP 2: CALCULATION REVISED PROFITS

Revised Profits = Given Profits + Interest on Drawings – Interest on Capitals

= 24,000 + (250 + 200 + 150) – (2,700 + 2,100 + 1,500) = ₹ 18,300

STEP 3: ADJUSTMENT TABLE

Particulars	Mohan ₹	Vijaj ₹	Anil ₹
I. Amount already credited:	8,000	8,000	8,000

II.	**Amount which should have been credited:**			
	Interest on Capital	2,700	2,100	1,500
	Share of Profit (₹ 18,300 in 1 : 1 : 1)	6,100	6,100	6,100
	Interest on Drawings	(250)	(200)	(150)
		8,550	8,000	7,450
III.	**Amount to be adjusted [I – II]**	550	—	550

STEP 4: JOURNAL ENTRY

Date	*Particulars*	*L.F.*	*Dr. (₹)*	*Cr. (₹)*
	Anil's Capital A/c		550	
	To Mohan's Capital A/c			550
	(Being the adjusting entry to correct the amounts of profit transferred to Capital Accounts)			

ILLUSTRATION 48

A, B & C were partners. Their fixed capitals were A–₹ 30,000, B–₹ 20,000 and C–₹ 10,000 respectively. According to the Partnership Deed, they were entitled to an interest on capital at 5% p.a. In addition B was also entitled to draw a salary of ₹ 500 per month. C was entitled to a commission of 5% on the profits after charging the interest on capital, but before charging the salary payable to B. The net profits for the year were ₹ 30,000 distributed in the ratio of capitals without providing for any of the above adjustments. The profits were to be shared in the ratio of 5 : 2 : 3. Pass the necessary adjustment entry showing the working clearly.

SOLUTION

STEP 1: ADJUSTMENT TABLE

	Particulars	*A* ₹	*B* ₹	*C* ₹
I.	**Profit already wrongly credited [In 3 : 2 : 1]**	15,000	10,000	5,000
II.	**Amount which should have been credited:**			
	Interest on Capital	1,500	1,000	500
	Salary	—	6,000	—
	Commission	—	—	1,350
	Net Profit Distributed (5 : 2 : 3)	9,825	3,930	5,895
		11,325	10,930	7,745
III.	**Difference [I –II]**	3,675(Dr.)	930(Cr.)	2,745(Cr.)

STEP 2: ADJUSTING JOURNAL ENTRY

Date	*Particulars*	*L.F.*	*Dr. (₹)*	*Cr. (₹)*
	A's Current A/c ...Dr.		3,675	
	To B's Current A/c			930
	To C's Current A/c			2,745
	(Being the adjusting entry passed)			

ILLUSTRATION 49

The capitals of A, B and C as on 31st Dec, 2012 amounted to ₹ 30,000, ₹ 1,10,000 and ₹ 2,20,000 respectively. The profits amounting to ₹ 60,000 for the year 2012 were distributed in the ratio of 4:1:1 after allowing interest on Capitals @ 10% p.a. During 2012 each partner withdrew ₹ 1,20,000. The partnership deed was silent as to profit sharing ratio but provided for interest on capital @ 12%.

Required: Pass the necessary adjusting journal entry.

SOLUTION

STEP 1: ADJUSTMENT TABLE

Particulars	*X* ₹	*Y* ₹	*Z* ₹	*Total* ₹
I. Amount already credited				
Interest on Capital @ 10%	10,000	20,000	30,000	60,000
Share of Profit (in the ratio of 4:1:1)	40,000	10,000	10,000	60,000
	50,000	30,000	40,000	1,20,000
II. Amount which should have been credited:				
Interest on Capital @ 12%	12,000	24,000	36,000	72,000
Share of Profit (in the ratio of 1:1:1) (i.e. ₹ 1,20,000 – ₹ 72,000)	16,000	16,000	16,000	48,000
	28,000	40,000	52,000	1,20,000
III. Difference [I – II]	22,000	– 10,000	– 12,000	
	(Excess) Dr.	(Short) Cr.	(Short) Cr.	

STEP 2: ADJUSTING JOURNAL ENTRY

Date	*Particulars*	*L.F.*	*Dr. (₹)*	*Cr. (₹)*
	A's Capital A/c Dr.		22,000	
	To B's Capital A/c			10,000
	To C's Capital A/c			12,000
	(Being the short interest on capital provided and profits distributed in wrong ratio, now rectified)			

Working Note:

CALCULATION OF INTEREST ON CAPITAL ALREADY PROVIDED AND OPENING CAPITALS

	Particulars	*A* ₹	*B* ₹	*C* ₹
A	Closing Capitals	30,000	1,10,000	2,20,000
B	*Add:* Drawings already debited	1,20,000	1,20,000	1,20,000
C	*Less:* Profit already credited	40,000	10,000	10,000
D	Opening Capitals plus Interest on Capitals	1,10,000	2,20,000	3,30,000
E	*Less:* Interest on Capital (D × 10/110)	10,000	20,000	30,000
F	Opening Capitals (D – E)	1,00,000	2,00,000	3,00,000

ADJUSTING ENTRY WHEN MANAGER IS TREATED A PARTNER

Step 1: *Calculate the amount already credited to manager.*

Step 2: *Calculate the amount which should have been given as partner.*

Step 3: *Calculate the difference between these two amounts*

Step 4: Pass the following Adjusting Entry:

Old Partner's Capital A/cs	...Dr.	[In Old Ratio]
To Incoming Partner's Capital A/c		[With Credit still to be given]

Note: *Revised Profit for calculating Share of Profit = Given Profits + Amount already given as Manager – Amount to be given as Partner*

ILLUSTRATION 50 [MANAGER TREATED AS PARTNER]

A and B are partners sharing profits and losses in the ratio of 3:2. They employed C as their manager to whom they paid a salary of ₹ 750 p.m. C had deposited ₹ 20,000 on which interest was payable @ 9% per annum. At the end of 2012 (after division of the year's profits), it was decided that C should be treated as a partner with effect from 1st Jan. 2009 with 1/6th share of profits, his deposit being considered as capital carrying interest at 6% per annum like capitals of other partners. The firm's profits and losses after allowing interest on capitals were—2009 Profit ₹ 59,000; 2010 Profit ₹ 62,600; 2011 Loss ₹ 4,000; 2012 Profit ₹ 78,000. Record the necessary Journal Entries to give effect to the above. [Note: Interest on Capital is to be allowed as a charge]

SOLUTION

STEP 1: ADJUSTMENT TABLE

	Particulars	₹
I.	**Amount already credited to 'C':**	
	Interest on Loan (₹ 20,000 × 9/100 × 4)	7,200
	Salary (₹ 750 × 12 × 4)	36,000
		43,200
II.	**Amount which should have been credited to 'C':**	
	Interest on Capital (₹ 20,000 × 6/100 × 4)	4,800
	Share of Profit 1/6 of (₹ 1,95,600 + ₹ 43,200 – ₹ 4,800)	39,000
		43,800
III.	**Difference (credit still to be given) (I – II)**	– 600

STEP 2: ADJUSTING JOURNAL ENTRIES

Date	*Particulars*		*L.F.*	*Dr. (₹)*	*Cr. (₹)*
	C's Loan A/c	Dr.		20,000	
	To C's Capital A/c				20,000
	(Being C's Capital converted into Capital)				
	A's Capital A/c	Dr.		360	
	B's Capital A/c	Dr.		240	
	To C's Capital A/c				600

	(Being the adjustment made account of admission of C an existing manager, as a partner)		

16.0 GUARANTEE OF MINIMUM PROFIT TO A PARTNER

Guarantee to a Partner	It means assurance to give a minimum amount of Profit to a Partner.
Guaranteed Partner	A partner to whom guarantee of minimum profit has been provided is called **'Guaranteed Partner'**.
Guaranteeing Partners	The partner(s) who has (have) given guarantee of minimum profit is (are) called **'Guaranteeing Partners'**.
Guaranteed Amount	The minimum amount for which guarantee is given is called **'Guaranteed Amount'**.
Who can provide Guarantee and in what ratio?	The guarantee may be provided by one *or* some *or* all of the partners in an existing profit sharing ratio *or* in some other agreed ratio.
Personal Guarantee	When guarantee is given by one *or* some *or* all of the partners in a ratio different from existing profit sharing ratio, such guarantee is said to be personal guarantee.
Firm Guarantee	When guarantee is given by all the partners in an existing profit sharing ratio, such guarantee is said to be firm guarantee.
Effect of Guarantee	If in any year, the actual Share of Profit of a Guaranteed Partner is less than the Guaranteed Amount, then the deficiency (i.e., excess of Guaranteed Amount over actual Share of Profit) is borne by the Guaranteeing Partners in their agreed ratio.

PRACTICAL STEPS INVOLVED IN THE DISTRIBUTION OF PROFITS UNDER GUARANTEE ARRANGEMENT

Step 1: *Calculate the Actual Share of Profit/Loss of Guaranteed Partner for the given accounting period.*

Step 2: *Calculate the Amount of Deficiency as follows:*

Deficiency = Guaranteed Amount – Actual Share of Profit

or

= Guaranteed Amount + Actual Share of Loss

Step 3: *Distribute the Deficiency among the Guaranteeing Partners in their guaranteeing ratio*

Step 4: *Distribute the Actual Profits/Losses among all the partners in their profit sharing ratio as if there is no guarantee arrangement.*

Step 5: *Recover the Share of Deficiency (as per Step 3) from the Guaranteeing Partners and give credit for the same to Guaranteed Partner.*

ACCOUNTING TREATMENT

Case	*Accounting Entry to be passed*
I. In case the Actual Share is *less* than the Guaranteed Amount	**(a) On Distributing the Profits as if there is no Guarantee Arrangement** P & L Appropriation A/c Dr. To All Partners' Capital A/cs

	or **(a) On Distributing the Loss as if there is no Guarantee Arrangement** All Partners' Capital A/cs Dr. To P & L Appropriation A/c **(b) On Charging Deficiency to guaranteeing partner(s)** Guaranteeing Partners' Capital A/cs Dr. To Guaranteed Partner's Capital A/c
II. In case the Actual Share is more than the Guaranteed Amount	**On Distributing the Profits as if there is no guarantee arrangement** P&L Appropriation A/c Dr. To All Partners' Capital A/cs

TUTORIAL NOTE

Unless otherwise stated, it is presumed that all the existing partners (other than the Guaranteed Partner) have given such guarantee in their existing profit sharing ratio.

ILLUSTRATION 51 [GUARANTEE BY THE FIRM]

A and B are partners, sharing profits and losses in the ratio of 2: 1. On 1.4.2012, they admit C with 1/4th share in profits with Guaranteed Amount of ₹ 25,000. The profits for the year 2011-12 amounted to ₹ 76,000. Prepare Profit and Loss Appropriation Account.

SOLUTION

Step 1: *Calculation of New shares*

Let the Total Share be = 1, C's Share = 1/4

Remaining Share = 1 – 1/4 = 3/4, is to be divided among A and B in the ratio of 2:1 as under:

A's New Share = 2/3 × 3/4 = 2/4, B's new Share = 1/3 × 3/4 = 1/4

Step 2: C's Actual Share of Profit = 1/4 of ₹ 76,000 = ₹ 19,000

Step 3: Deficiency = Guaranteed amount – ₹ 19,000 = ₹ 25,000 – ₹ 19,000 = ₹ 6,000

Step 4: Deficiency is to be borne by A and B in the ratio of 2:1 as follows:

Deficiency to be borne by A = 2/3 × ₹ 6,000 = ₹ 4,000

Deficiency to be borne by B = 1/3 × ₹ 6,000 = ₹ 2,000

Step 5: Preparation of Profit & Loss Appropriation Account

PROFIT AND LOSS APPROPRIATION ACCOUNT

Dr. *for the year ending on 31st March, 2012* Cr.

Particulars		₹	*Particulars*	₹
To A's Capital A/c			By Profit & Loss A/c	76,000
(2/4 × ₹ 76,000)	38,000			
Less Deficiency borne				
(2/3 × ₹ 6,000)	(4,000)	34,000		
To B's Capital A/c				
(1/4 × ₹ 76,000)	19,000			

Less Deficiency borne				
(1/3 × ₹ 6,000)	(2,000)	17,000		
To C's Capital A/c				
(1/4 × ₹ 76,000)	19,000			
Add. Deficiency recovered from				
A	4,000			
B	2,000	25,000		
		76,000		76,000

ILLUSTRATION 52

A, B and C entered into partnership on 1st October 2011 to share profits & losses in the ratio of 4 : 3 : 3. A, however, personally guaranteed that C's share of profit after charging Interest on Capital @ 10% p.a. would not be less than ₹ 80,000 in any year. The Capital contributions were: A ₹ 3,00,000. B ₹ 2,00,000 and C ₹ 1,50,000.

The profit for the year ended on 31st March, 2012 amounted to ₹ 1,60,000.

Required: Prepare the Profit & Loss Appropriation Account.

SOLUTION

PROFIT & LOSS APPROPRIATION ACCOUNT
for the year ending on 31st March, 2012

Dr. *Cr.*

Particulars		₹	*Particulars*	₹
To Interest on Capital:			By Profit before appropriations	1,60,000
A	15,000			
B	10,000			
C	7,500	32,500		
To Net Profit transferred to:				
A (₹ 51,000 – ₹ 1,750)	49,250			
B (₹ 1,27,500 × 3/10)	38,250			
C (₹ 38,250 + ₹ 1,750)	40,000	1,27,500		
		1,60,000		1,60,000

Note: *Guaranteed Amount for half year = ₹ 80,000 × 1/2 = ₹ 40,000*

ILLUSTRATION 53 [GUARANTEE BY THE FIRM]

X, Y and Z entered into partnership on 1st April, 2010 to share profits and losses in the ratio of 12:8:5. It was provided that in no case Z's share in profits be less than ₹ 25,000 p.a. The profits and losses for the period ended 31st March were: 2010-11 Profit ₹ 1,00,000, 2011-12 Profit ₹ 1,50,000, 2012-13 Loss ₹ 1,00,000. Pass the necessary journal entries in the books of the firm.

SOLUTION

Particulars	*2010-11* ₹	*2011-12* ₹	*2012-13* ₹
I. Guaranteed Amount	25,000	25,000	25,000

II. Z's Actual Share as per profit sharing ratio	20,000 (1,00,000 × 5/25)	30,000 (1,50,000 × 5/25)	(20,000) (1,00,000 × 5/25)
III. Deficiency (I – II)	5,000	–	45,000

Since no specific ratio in which the deficiency is to be borne is given, it means the remaining partners (A & B) shall bear the deficiency in their agreed profit sharing ratio which is 12:8 *or* 3:2.

JOURNAL

Date	*Particulars*		*L.F.*	*Dr. (₹)*	*Cr. (₹)*
2010-11	P&L Appropriation A/c	Dr.		1,00,000	
	To X's Capital A/c				48,000
	To Y's Capital A/c				32,000
	To Z's Capital A/c				20,000
	(Being the distribution of profits as if there is no guarantee)				
	X's Capital A/c	Dr.		3,000	
	Y's Capital A/c	Dr.		2,000	
	To Z's Capital A/c				5,000
	(Being the deficiency met by guaranteeing partners)				
2011-12	P & L Appropriation A/c	Dr.		1,50,000	
	To X's Capital A/c				72,000
	To Y's Capital A/c				48,000
	To Z's Capital A/c				30,000
	(Being the distribution of profits)				
2012-13	X's Capital A/c	Dr.		48,000	
	Y's Capital A/c	Dr.		32,000	
	Z's Capital A/c	Dr.		20,000	
	To Profit & Loss A/c				1,00,000
	(Being the distribution of losses as if there is no guarantee)				
	X's Capital A/c	Dr.		27,000	
	Y's Capital A/c	Dr.		18,000	
	To Z's Capital A/c				45,000
	(Being the deficiency borne by guaranteeing partners)				

ILLUSTRATION 54

The Partners of a firm distributed the profits for the year ended 31st March, 2003, ₹ 90,000 in the ratio of 3 : 2 : 1 without providing for the following adjustments:

(i) A & B were entitled to a salary of ₹ 375 each per quarter.

(ii) B was entitled to a commission of ₹ 4,500.

(iii) B & C had guaranteed a minimum profit of ₹ 35,000 p.a. to A.

(iv) Profit were to be shared in the ratio of 3 : 3 : 2.

Required: Pass necessary journal entry for the above adjustments in the books of the firm.

SOLUTION

JOURNAL

Date	*Particulars*	*L.F.*	*Dr. (₹)*	*Cr. (₹)*
	A's Capital A/c Dr.		8,500	
	To B's Capital A/c			4,500
	To C's Capital A/c			4,000
	(Being adjustement entry passed for omission of salary, commission and change in profit sharing ratio of 3:3:2 arnong partners)			

Working Notes:

Dr. **ADJUSTED PROFIT AND LOSS ACCOUNT** *Cr.*

Particulars		₹	*Particulars*	₹
To Salary:			By P & L A/c	90,000
A's Capital	1,500			
B's Capital	1,500	3,000		
To Commission (B)		4,500		
To Profit transferred to:				
A	35,000			
B	28,500			
C	19,000	82,500		
		90,000		90,000

ADJUSTMENT TABLE

Particulars	*A*	*B*	*C*
Amount already recorded [₹ 90,000 in 3 : 2 : 1]	45,000	30,000	15,000
Amount to be recorded [Profit + Salary + Commission]	36,500	34,500	19,000
Adjustment	8,500	(4,500)	(4,000)

17.0 GOODWILL

Meaning of Goodwill	(a) Goodwill is the value of reputation of a firm in respect of the profits expected in future over and above the normal profits earned by other similar firms belonging to the same industry. Such excess of future profits over the normal profits is known as super profits. Thus, goodwill exists only when the firm earns super profits. (b) Any firm that earns only normal profits *or* is incurring losses has no goodwill. (c) If time value of money is considered, goodwill can be defined as the present value of anticipated super profits.
Nature of Goodwill	(a) Goodwill is regarded as an intangible asset and not a fictitious asset. (b) Goodwill is a valuable asset if the firms is earning profits and is a valueless asset if the firm is incurring losses.

	(c) However, in the periods of temporary recession, the goodwill of the firm which is incurring least losses as compared to other similar firms, may be a valuable asset.
Factors Affecting Goodwill	The factors giving rise to goodwill are as follows: 1. **Nature of Business** — A firm which produces high value added products *or* having a stable demand is able to earn more profits and therefore has more goodwill. 2. **Favourable Location** — When the business is centrally located *or* is at a place having heavy customer traffic, the goodwill tends to be high. 3. **Efficiency of Management** — A well-managed firm usually enjoys the advantages of high productivity and cost efficiency. This leads to higher profits and so the value of goodwill will also be high. 4. **Market situation** — The monopoly condition *or* limited competition enables the concern to earn high profits which leads to higher value of goodwill. 5. **Special Advantages** — The firm that enjoys special advantages like import licences, patents, trade marks, low rate and assured supply of electricity, long-term contracts for supply of materials, well-known collaborators etc. enjoy higher value of goodwill. 6. Technical know how 7. Quality of Products 8. After Sales Service 9. Producing/providing customers satisfying products 10. Management's attitude towards fulfillment of commitments (e.g. Timely delivery of goods to customers, timely payment to creditors, delivery of goods to customers at committed prices inspite of increase in market prices).
Need for Valuation of Goodwill	In case of a partnership firm, the need for valuation of goodwill may arise in the following circumstances: 1. When there is a change in profit-sharing ratio amongst the existing partners; 2. When a new partner is admitted; 3. When a partner retires; 4. When a partner dies; 5. When the firm is sold as a going concern; 6. When the firm is amalgamated with another firm.
Methods of Valuation of Goodwill	The various methods of valuing the goodwill are as follows:— 1. Average Profit Method, 2. Super Profits Method, and 3. Capitalisation Method.

AVERAGE PROFIT METHOD

(a) Goodwill under this method is ascertained by multiplying the Average Future Maintainable Profit by a certain number of years' purchases.

(b) It is based on the assumption that a new business will not be able to earn profits during the first few years of its operations.

(c) Hence the person who purchases an existing business has to pay in the form of Goodwill a sum equal to Average Future Maintainable Profits multiplied by the number of years during which he is likely to receive the profits for the first few years.

(d) While calculating past profits any abnormal gain is excluded by deducting from and any abnormal loss is excluded by adding to the past profits.

(e) The various steps involved under this method are given below:

PRACTICAL STEPS INVOLVED UNDER AVERAGE PROFITS METHOD

Step 1: Calculate Past profit for each of the relevant years (given) by adding abnormal losses and by deducting abnormal gains and Income from Non-trade Investments.

Step 2: Calculate Total Profits by adding each relevant year's past profit.

Step 3: Calculate Average Profits as under:

Average Profits = Total Profit/No. of relevant years

Step 4: Calculate Average Future Maintainable Profits after making future adjustments (if any)

Step 5: Calculate Goodwill as under:

Goodwill = Average Future Maintainable Profits × No. of years' Purchase.

ILLUSTRATION 55

Calculate the value of goodwill as on 1st Jan. 2013 on the basis of three years' purchases of the Average Profits of the last five years' profits. The profits & losses for the years were-2007 ₹ 30,000, 2008 Loss ₹ 40,000, 2009 ₹ 92,000, 2010 ₹ 55,000, 2011 ₹ 70,000, 2012 ₹ 90,000.

SOLUTION

Step 1: Total Profits = – 40,000 + 92,000 + 55,000 + 70,000 + 90,000 = ₹ 2,67,000

Step 2: Average Profits = ₹ 53,400

Step 3: Goodwill = Average profits × No. of years' Purchases = ₹ 53,400 × 3 = 1,60,200.

ILLUSTRATION 56

If in Previous Illustration. Profit on sale of a fixed asset during 2008 amounted to ₹ 2,000, during 2010 amounted to ₹ 5,000, Loss on sale of a fixed asset during 2012 amounted to ₹ 5,000. Calculate the Value of Goodwill.

SOLUTION

Step 1: *Calculation of Profits excluding abnormalities.*

Adjusted Loss for 2008 = ₹ 40,000 + ₹ 2,000 = ₹ 42,000

Adjusted Profit for 2010 = ₹ 55,000 – ₹ 5,000 = ₹ 50,000

Adjusted Profit for 2011 = ₹ 90,000 + ₹ 5,000 = ₹ 95,000

Step 2: Total Profits = ₹ – 42,000 + ₹ 92,000 + ₹ 50,000 + ₹ 70,000 + ₹ 95,000 = ₹ 2,65,000

Step 3: Average Profit = $\frac{\text{Total Profits}}{\text{No. of years}} \times \frac{₹\ 2,65,000}{5}$ = ₹ 53,000

Step 4: Goodwill = Average Profit × No. of years' Purchases = ₹ 53,000 × 3 = ₹ 1,59,000.

ILLUSTRATION 57

The following were the profits of a firm for the last three years.

Year ending March 31	Profit (₹)
2010	5,00,000 (including an abnormal gain of ₹ 1,50,000)
2011	4,00,000 (after charging an abnormal loss of ₹ 2,00,000)
2012	6,00,000 (excluding ₹ 2,00,000 payable on the insurance of plant and machinery)

Calculate the value of firm's goodwill on the basts of four years' purchase of the average profits for the last three years.

SOLUTION

STEP 1: CALCULATION OF AVERAGE MAINTAINABLE PROFITS

Year ended	*Profit*	
2010	(5,00,000 – 1,50,000)	3,50,000
2011	(4,00,000 + 2,00,000)	6,00,000
2012	(6,00,000 – 2,00,000)	4,00,000
Total		13,50,000

Step 2: Average Profit = 13,50,000/3 = ₹ 4,50,000

Step 3: Goodwill at 4 years' purchase of Average Profit = ₹ 4,50,000 × 4 = ₹ 18,00,000

WEIGHTED AVERAGE PROFIT METHOD

If there exists clear increasing trend of profits, it is better to give more weightage to the profits of the recent years than those of earlier years. In case the profits show increasing trend, weights like 1,2,3,4 etc. may be used. In case profits show decreasing trend, weights like 4, 3, 2, 1, etc. may be used. The various steps involved under this method are given as follows:

PRACTICAL STEPS INVOLVED UNDER WEIGHTED AVERAGE PROFITS METHOD

Step 1: ***Calculate profits for each of the given years.***

Step 2: ***Select the weights to be assigned***

Step 3: ***Calculate the weighted profit for each of the years by multiplying the simple profits by the respective weight.***

Step 4: ***Calculate the total of weights and total of weighted profits***

Step 5: ***Calculate Weighted Average Profits as follows:***

Weighted Average Profits = Total of Weighted Profits/Total of Weights

Step 6: ***Calculate the Value of Goodwill as under:***

Goodwill = Weighted Average Profit × Agreed Number of years' purchase.

ILLUSTRATION 58

The profits of a firm for the year ended 31st March for the last five years were as follows:

Year	*Profit (₹)*
2008	20,000

2009	30,000
2010	40,000
2011	50,000
2012	55,000

Calculate the value of goodwill on the basis of three years' purchase of weighted average profits after weights 1,2,3,4 and 5 respectively to the profits for 2008, 2009, 2010, 2011 and 2012.

SOLUTION

A *Year ended 31 March*	*B* *Profit (₹)*	*C* *Weight*	*D = B × C* *Product*
2008	20,000	1	20,000
2009	30,000	2	60,000
2010	40,000	3	1,20,000
2011	50,000	4	2,00,000
2012	55,000	5	2,75,000
Total		**15**	**6,75,000**

Weighted Average Profit = ₹ 6,67,000/15 = ₹ 45,000, Goodwill = ₹ 45,000 × 3 = ₹ 1,35,000

SUPER PROFIT METHOD

(a) Goodwill under this method is ascertained by multiplying the Super Profits by certain number of year's purchase.

(b) It is based on the assumption that a new business will not be able to earn excess profits (though it may earn normal profits) during the first few years of its operations.

(c) Hence the person who purchases an existing business has to pay in the form of Goodwill a sum equal to Super Profits multiplied by the number of years during which buyer is likely to receive excess profits for the first few years.

(d) The various steps involved under this method are given below:

PRACTICAL STEPS INVOLVED UNDER SUPER PROFIT METHOD

Step 1: Calculate Average Capital Employed as follows:

= (Opening Capital Employed + Closing Capital Employed)/2

or

= Closing Capital Employed – Half of current year's Profits + Half of Current year's Drawings

Note: Capital Employed = All assets (other than goodwill, fictitious assets and non-trade investments) less Outsiders' Liabilities.

Step 2: Calculate Normal Profits as follows:

Normal Profit = Average Capital Employed × Normal Rate of Return.

Note: Normal Rate of Return refers to the rate of return normally earned by an average firm belonging to the same industry.

Step 3: Calculate Average Future Maintainable Profits (according to steps given under Average Profits Method)

Step 4: Calculate Super Profits as follows:

Super Profits = Average Future Maintainable Profits – Normal Profits

Step 5: Calculate Goodwill as follows:
Goodwill = Super Profits × No. of years' Purchase.

ILLUSTRATION 59

The profits and losses for the previous years are: 2009 Profit ₹ 10,000, 2010 Loss ₹ 17,000, 2011 Profit ₹ 50,000, 2012 Profit ₹ 75,000. The Average Capital employed in the business is ₹ 2,00,000, the rate of interest expected from capital invested is 10%. The remuneration of partners is estimated to be ₹ 6,000 p.a. Calculate the value of goodwill on the basis of 2 years' purchases of Super Profits based on the average of 3 years.

SOLUTION

A. Total Profit for 3 years = – ₹ 17,000 + ₹ 50,000 + ₹ 75,000 = ₹ 1,08,000

B. Average Profits = $\frac{\text{Total Profits}}{\text{No. of years}} = \frac{₹\ 1{,}08{,}000}{3}$ = ₹ 36,000

Average Profits for Goodwill = ₹ 36,000 – Partners' Remuneration

= ₹ 36,000 – ₹ 6,000 = ₹ 30,000

C. Normal Profit = Interest on Capital employed

= ₹ 20,000 (i.e. ₹ 2,00,000 × 10/100) = ₹ 20,000

D. Super Profit = Average Profit – Normal Profit = ₹ 30,000 – ₹ 20,000 = ₹ 10,000

E. Goodwill = Super Profit × No. of years purchases = ₹ 10,000 × 2 = ₹ 20,000

ILLUSTRATION 60

On 1st April, 2012 an existing firm had assets of ₹ 75,000 including cash of ₹ 5,000. Its creditors amounted to ₹ 5,000 on that date. The firm had a Reserve Fund of ₹ 10,000 while partner's Capital accounts showed a balance of ₹ 60,000. If the Normal Rate of Return is 20% and the goodwill of the firm is valued at ₹ 24,000, at four year's purchase of super profit, find the average profits per year, of the existing firm.

SOLUTION

A. Capital employed = ₹ 75,000 – ₹ 5,000 = ₹ 70,000

B. Normal Profit = 20% of ₹ 70,000 = ₹ 14,000

C. Goodwill = ₹ 24,000

D. Super Profits = ₹ 24,000/4 = ₹ 6,000

E. Average Profits = Normal Profit + Super Profit = ₹ 14,000 + ₹ 6,000=₹ 20,000

DISTINCTION BETWEEN AVERAGE PROFITS & SUPER PROFITS

Basis of Distinction	Average Profit	Super Profit
1. Meaning	Average Profit is the **average of the profit of past few years.**	Super Profit is the **excess of Average Profits over Normal Profits.**
2. Whether Average Capital Employed considered for calculation	Average Capital Employed is **not considered** while calculating Average Profits.	Average Capital Employed is **considered** while calculating Super profits.

3. Whether Normal Rate of Return considered for calculation?	Normal Rate of Return is **not considered** while calculating Average Profits.	Normal Rate of Return is **Considered** while calculating Average Profits.
4. Relevance while Valuing Super Goodwill	Average Profit is relevant **for Average Profits Method, Super Profits Method and Capitalization Methods of** valuation of Goodwill.	Super profits is relevant **for Profits Method and Capitalization of Super Profits Method** of valuation of Goodwill.

CAPITALISATION OF SUPER PROFIT

The goodwill under this method is ascertained by capitalising the super profits on the basis of Normal Rate of Return. The various steps involved in valuing the goodwill according to this method are given below:

PRACTICAL STEPS INVOLVED UNDER CAPITALISATION OF SUPER PROFITS

Step 1: Calculate Super Profits (according to steps given under Super Profits Method)

Step 2: Calculate Goodwill as under:

$$\textit{Goodwill} = \textit{Super Profits} \times \frac{100}{\textit{Normal Rate of Return}}$$

ILLUSTRATION 61

A firm earns profits of ₹ 1,00,000. The Normal Rate of Return in a similar type of business is 10%. The value of total assets (excluding goodwill) and total outsiders' liabilities as on the date of valuation of goodwill are ₹ 11,00,000 and ₹ 2,80,000 respectively. Calculate the value of goodwill according to Capitalization of Super Profits Method.

SOLUTION

A. Average Profit (given) = ₹ 1,00,000

B. Normal Profit = (₹ 11,00,000 – ₹ 2,80,000) × 10/100
= ₹ 8,20,000 × 10/100 = ₹ 82,000

C. Super Profit = ₹ 1,00,000 – ₹ 82,000 = ₹ 18,000

D. Goodwill = ₹ 18,000 × 100/10 = ₹ 1,80,000

CAPITALIZATION OF AVERAGE PROFITS

The goodwill under this method is ascertained by deducting the actual capital employed (i.e. Net Assets as on the date of Valuation) in business from the Capitalised Value of the average profits on the basis of Normal Rate of Return. The various steps involved in valuing the goodwill according to this method are given below:

PRACTICAL STEPS INVOLVED UNDER CAPITALISATION OF AVERAGE PROFITS

Step 1: Calculate Average Future Maintainable Profits (according to steps given under Average Profits Method)

Step 2: Calculate the Capitalised Value of Average Profits as under:

$$\textit{Capitalised Value} = \frac{\text{Average Profit}}{\text{Normal Rate of Return}} \times 100$$

Step 3: Calculate the value of Net Assets as on the date of valuation of goodwill as under:

Net Assets = All Assets (other than goodwill, fictitious assets and non-trade investments) at their current values less Outsiders' Liabilities.

Step 4: Calculate Goodwill as under:

Goodwill = Capitalised Value – Net Assets

ILLUSTRATION 62

Calculate the value of Goodwill according to Capitalization of Average Profits Method in the previous Illustration.

SOLUTION

A. Average Profits = ₹ 1,00,000

B. Capitalised Value of Average Profits = ₹ 1,00,000 × 100/10 = ₹ 10,00,000.

C. Net Assets = Total Assets – Outsiders' Liabilities = ₹ 11,00,000 – ₹ 2,80,000 = ₹ 8,20,000

D. Goodwill = ₹ 10,00,000 – ₹ 8,20,000 = ₹ 1,80,000

COMPREHENSIVE REVISIONAL PROBLEMS

Objective: The following Problems have been given Only to Revise the Chapter. In Examination only some of the parts and not all the parts of such lengthy problems may be asked.

PROBLEM 1

X, Y and Z are in partnership with capital of ₹ 1,20,000 (Credit), ₹ 1,00,000 (Credit) and ₹ 8,000 (Debit) respectively on 1st April, 2011. Their partnership deed provides for the following:

(a) 7.5% of Net Profit to be transferred to General Reserve.

(b) Partners are to be only allowed interest on capital @ 5% p.a. and are to be charged interest on drawings @ 6% p.a.

(c) Z is entitled to a salary of ₹ 7,000.

(d) X is entitled to a remuneration of 10% of the net profit before making any appropriation.

(e) Y is also entitled to a commission of 8% of the net profit before charging Interest on Drawings but after making all appropriations.

During the year, X withdrew ₹ 1,000 at the beginning of every month, Y ₹ 1,000 during the month and Z ₹ 1,000 at the end of every month. On 1st Oct. 2011, Z granted a loan of ₹ 6,00,000.

The Manager is entitled to a salary of ₹ 1,000 p.m. and a commission of 10% of net profits after charging his salary & commission.

The net profit of the firm for the year ended on 31st March, 2012 before providing for any of the above adjustments was ₹ 1,62,000.

Required: Prepare Profit and Loss Appropriation Account for the year ended on 31st March, 2012.

SOLUTION

PROFIT & LOSS ACCOUNT

Dr. *for the year ended on 31st March, 2012* *Cr.*

Particulars	₹	*Particulars*	₹
To Interest on Z's Loan		By Net Profit before adjustments	1,62,000

[₹ 6,00,000 × 6/100 × 6/12]	18,000		
To Manager's Salary			
[₹ 1,000 × 12]	12,000		
To Manager's Commission			
[(₹ 1,62,000 – ₹ 18,000 – ₹ 12,000) × 10/110]	12,000		
To Net Profit t/f to P & L App.A/c	1,20,000		
	1,62,000		1,62,000

PROFIT & LOSS APPROPRIATION ACCOUNT

for the year ended on 31st March, 2012

Dr. *Cr.*

Particulars	₹	*Particulars*		₹
To General Reserve [7.5% of 1,20,000]	9,000	By Net Profit		1,20,000
		By Interest on Drawings:		
To Interest on Capital:		X	390	
X6,000		Y	360	
Y5,000	11,000	Z	330	1,080
To Z's Salary	7,000			
To X's Commission (10% of ₹ 1,20,000)	12,000			
To Y's Commission [(₹ 1,20,000 – 9,000 –11,000 – 7,000 – 12,000) × 8/108]	6,000			
To Profit transferred to:				
X's Capital A/c	25,360			
Y's Capital A/c	25,360			
Z's Capital A/c	25,360			
	1,21,080			1,21,080

Working Notes:

(i) Calculation of Interest on Drawings

Interest on X's Drawings: = ₹ 12,000 × $\frac{6.5}{12} \times \frac{6}{100}$ = ₹ 390

Interest on Y's Drawings: = ₹ 12,000 × $\frac{6}{12} \times \frac{6}{100}$ = ₹ 360

Interest on Z's Drawings: = ₹ 12,000 × $\frac{5.5}{12} \times \frac{6}{100}$ = ₹ 330

(ii) Interest on partner's loan and Manager's Salary & Commission are charges against the profits and not the appropriations out of profits. Hence these items have been debited to Profit & Loss Account and not Profit & Loss Appropriation Account.

PROBLEM 2

From the following information, calculate the value of goodwill of BHARAT and TUSHAR.

(i) At three years' purchase of Average Profit.

(ii) At three years' purchase of Super Profit.

(iii) On the basis of Capitalisation of Super Profit.

(iv) On the basis of Capitalisation of Average Profit.

Information:

(a) Average capital employed in the business–₹ 5,00,000.

(b) Net Trading results of the firm for the past years: Profit 2010 ₹ 1,50,000; Loss 2011–₹ 1,25,000; Profit 2012–₹ 4,25,000.

(c) Rate of interest expected from capital having regard to the risk involved–15%.

(d) Remuneration to each partner for his service–₹ 2,500 per month.

(e) Assets (excluding goodwill)–₹ 6,00,000; Liabilities–₹ 50,000.

SOLUTION

(i) Goodwill at 3 years' purchase of Average Profit:

Average Profit = [₹ 1,50,000 – ₹ 1,25,000 + ₹ 4,25,000/3] = ₹ 1,50,000

Average Profit for Goodwill = ₹ 1,50,000 – Remuneration of Partners

= ₹ 1,50,000 – (₹ 2,500 × 12 × 2)

= ₹ 1,50,000 – ₹ 60,000 = ₹ 90,000

Goodwill = Average Profit × 3 = ₹ 90,000 × 3 = ₹ 2,70,000

(ii) Goodwill at 3 years' purchase of Super Profit:

Normal Profit = Average Capital Employed × Normal Rate of Return

$= ₹\ 5,00,000 \times \frac{15}{100} = ₹\ 75,000$

Super Profit = Average Profit – Normal Profit = ₹ 90,000 – ₹ 75,000 = ₹ 15,000

Goodwill = Super Profit × 3 = ₹ 15,000 × 3 = ₹ 45,000

(iii) Goodwill under Capitalisation of Super Profit:

$\text{Goodwill} = \text{Super Profit} \times \frac{100}{\text{Normal Rate of Retum}} = ₹\ 15,000 \times 100/15 = ₹\ 1,00,000$

(iv) Goodwill under Capitalisation of Average Profit:

Step 1: Total Capitalised Value of the Firm $= \frac{\text{Average Profit}}{\text{Normal Rate of Return}} \times 100$

$= \frac{₹\ 90,000}{15} \times 100 = ₹\ 6,00,000$

Step 2: Net Assets = Total Assets (excluding goodwill) – Outsiders' Liabilities

= ₹ 6,00,000 – ₹ 50,000 = ₹ 5,50,000

Step 3: Goodwill = Total Capitalised Value of Business – Net Assets

= ₹ 6,00,000 – ₹ 5,50,000 = ₹ 50,000

PROBLEM 3

Shiv and Mohan are partners in a firm sharing profits and losses equally. On 31st March, 2013 the balances of their capital accounts were ₹ 3.00,000 and ₹ 2,00,000 respectively. The average profits of the firm are ₹ 1,36,000 and the rate of normal profit ts 20%.

On 1st April, 2013 they agreed to admit Hari as a partner for one fourth share. Hari will bring ₹ 1,00,000 as capital.

You are required to compute the value of the goodwill of the firm on admission of Hari, if goodwill is to be calculated on the basis of:

(1) 5 years' purchase of Super Profit (2) Capitalization Method

(3) 3 years' purchase of Average Profit.

SOLUTION

VALUATION OF GOODWILL

(1) 5 years' Purchase of Super Profit

Value of Goodwill = 5 × Super Profit = 5 × [₹ 1,36,000 – (20% of ₹ 5,00,000)] = ₹ 1,80,000

(2) Capitalisation Method

Value of Goodwill = Normal Value of business – Actual capital employed = 6,80,000

= [₹ 1,36,000/20%] – [₹ 3,00,000 + ₹ 2,00,000] = ₹ 1,80,000

(3) 3 years' Purchase of Average Profits

Goodwill = 3 × Average Profit = 3 × ₹ 1,36,000 = ₹ 4,08,000

SOLVED PROBLEMS

PROBLEM 1

Weak, Able and Lazy are in partnership sharing profits and losses in the ratio of 2 : 1 : 1. It is agreed that interest on capital will be allowed @ 10% per annum and interest on drawings will be charged @ 8 per cent per annum. (No interest will be charged/allowed on Current Accounts). The following are the particulars of the Capital and Drawings Accounts of the partners:

Particulars	*Weak* ₹	*Able* ₹	*Lazy* ₹
Capital (1.1.2013)	75,000	40,000	30,000
Current Account (1.1.2013)	10,000	5,000	(Dr.) 5,000
Drawings during 2013	15,000	10,000	10,000

The draft accounts for 2013 showed a net profit of ₹ 60,000 before taking into account interest on capitals and drawings and subject to following rectification of errors:

(a) Life Insurance premium of Weak amounting to ₹ 750 paid by the firm has been charged to Miscellaneous Expenditure Account.

(b) Repairs of Machinery amounting to ₹ 10,000 has been debited to Plant Account and depreciation there on charged @ 20%.

(c) Travelling expenses of ₹ 3,000 of Able for a pleasure trip to UK paid by the firm on 30th June, 2013 has been debited to Travelling Expenses Account.

Required: Prepare the Profit and Loss Appropriation Account for the year ending on 31st Dec. 2013 and partners' Current Accounts for the year.

SOLUTION

PROFIT AND LOSS APPROPRIATION ACCOUNT

Dr. *for the year ending on 31st Dec., 2013* *Cr.*

Particulars	₹	*Particulars*	₹
To Interest on Capital:		By Net Profit (Adjusted)	55,750

Weak	7,500		By Interest on Drawings:		
Able	4,000		Weak	630	
Lazy	3,000	14,500	Able	520	
To Partner's Current A/cs:			Lazy	400	1,550
Share of Profit Weak	21,400				
Able	10,700				
Lazy	10,700	42,800			
		57,300			57,300

Dr. **PARTNERS' CURRENT ACCOUNTS** Cr.

Particulars	*Weak* ₹	*Able* ₹	*Lazy* ₹	*Particulars*	*Weak* ₹	*Able* ₹	*Lazy* ₹
To Balance b/d	—	—	5,000	By Balance b/d	10,000	5,000	—
To Drawings	15,000	10,000	10,000	By P & L App. A/c			
To Life Insurance				(Int. on capital)	7,500	4,000	3,000
Premium	750	—	—	By P & L App. A/c	21,400	10,700	10,700
To Travelling Exps.	—	3,000	—	(Share of Profit)			
To P & L App. A/c				By Balance c/d	—	—	1,700
(Int. on Drawings)	630	520	400				
To Balance c/d	22,520	6,180	—				
	38,900	19,700	15,400		38,900	19,700	15,400

Working Notes:

(I) CALCULATION OF ADJUSTED PROFIT

			₹
A	Net Profit as per Profit & Loss A/c		60,000
B	*Add:* Drawings by Weak: (LIP charged to Misc. Exp)		750
C	*Add:* Drawings by Able (Travelling Expenses of Able charged to Travelling Expenses A/c of the firm)		3,000
D	*Less:* Repairs to Machinery wrongly capitalised	10,000	
	Less: Depreciation charged @ 20%	2,000	8,000
			55,750

(II) CALCULATION OF INTEREST ON DRAWINGS

	Particulars	*Weak* ₹	*Able* ₹	*Lazy* ₹
A	Drawings	15,000	10,000	10,000
B	*Add:* Rectificatory Adjustments	750	3,000	—
		15,750	13,000	10,000
D	Interest @ 8% p.a. for 6 months	630	520	400

PROBLEM 2

A, B and C were working in partnership, sharing profits and losses in the ratio of 2 : 1 : 1. It had been agreed that interest would be allowed at the rate of 10% per annum on partners' Capital Accounts. The balance in the Capital Accounts of A, B, C, on 1st Jan. 2012, were ₹ 15,000, ₹ 8,000 and ₹ 6,000 respectively. The account for the year ended 31st Dec., 2012 showed a net profit of ₹ 24,000 after taking into account interest on partners' capitals. The amounts and the shares in profit were credited to the currents accounts. During 2013, it was discovered that the following errors had occurred in the accounts for 2012.

(a) Rent of A's private house amounting to ₹ 300 and paid during 2012 had been included in Rent Account appearing in the P & L A/c. (b) Premium, amounting to ₹ 1,200 on B's life insurance and paid on 30th June, 2012 had been included in Insurance Expenses debited to the P & L. A/c. After the close of the year 2012, accounts, it was decided that, with effect from Jan. 1,2012, the rate of interest on capital should be increased to 12%.

Required: Pass the necessary adjusting entry.

SOLUTION

ADJUSTMENT TABLE

	Particulars	*A* ₹	*B* ₹	*C* ₹	*Total* ₹
A	**Amount already credited:**				
	(a) Interest on Capital	1,500	800	600	2,900
	(b) Share of Profit	12,000	6,000	6,000	24,000
		13,500	6,800	6,600	26,900
B	**Amounts which should have been credited (or debited):**				
	(a) Interest on Capital	1,800	960	720	3,480
	(b) Share of Profit	12,460	6,230	6,230	24,920
	(c) Private Expenses	(300)	(1,200)	—	(1,500)
		13,960	5,990	6,950	26,900
C	**Difference (A – B)**	(460)	810	(350)	—

ADJUSTMENT ENTRY

Date	*Particulars*	*L.F.*	*Dr. (₹)*	*Cr. (₹)*
	B's Current A/c Dr.		810	
	To A's Current A/c			460
	To C's Current A/c			350
	(Being the adjustments made through current accounts)			

Working Note:

COMPUTATION OF THE ACTUAL PROFIT FOR 2012

	Particulars	₹
A	Net Profit given	24,000
B	*Add:* Interest on Capital already debited	2,900

C	*Add:* Private Expenses wrongly debited (₹ 300 + ₹ 1,200)	1,500
D	Profit before Interest	28,400
E	*Less:* Interest on Capital @ 12%	3,480
F	Profit after Interest	24,920

PROBLEM 3

A and B have been carrying on business in partnership. They share profit equally. After the profit for 2013 had been divided, it was agreed that with effect from Jan. 1, 2013 they would share profits and losses as—A: 3/5 and B: 2/5. At that time, it was also discovered that while preparing accounts for 2012 and 2013, the following expenses which had occurred and those paid in advance have been erroneously ignored.

Particulars	2012 ₹	2013 ₹
Outstanding expenses	5,000	7,200
Expenses paid in advance	1,000	500
Accrued Income	200	300

The profit during 2013 was ₹ 30,000 according to the accounts already prepared.

Required: Give the necessary single adjusting journal entry to adjust the accounts of partners.

SOLUTION

JOURNAL

Date	Particulars		L.F.	Dr. (₹)	Cr. (₹)
	A's Capital A/c	Dr.		460	
	B 's Capital A/c	Dr.		5,940	
	Prepaid Expenses A/c	Dr.		500	
	Accrued Income A/c	Dr.		300	
	To Outstanding Expenses A/c				7,200
	(Being the expenses and income not taken into account adjusted)				

Working Note:

ADJUSTMENT TABLE

	Particulars	A ₹	B ₹
A	Amount already credited	15,000	15,000
	Share of Profit (in the ratio of 1 : 1)		
B	Amount which should have been credited		
	Share of Current Year's Profit (in the ratio of 3 : 2)		
	Profit = ₹30,000 + ₹5,000 – ₹1,000 – ₹200 – ₹7,200 + ₹500 + ₹300) = ₹27,400	16,440	10,960

C	Amount which should have been debited in respect of previous year's items (₹ 5,000 – ₹ 1,000 – ₹ 200) (in the ratio of 1 : 1)	(1,900)	(1,900)
D	Net Amount with which to be debited [A – B + C]	460	5,940

PROBLEM 4

The firm of A, B and C has existed for some years, profit being shared as 2/5, 2/5 and 1/5 respectively. C, however, feels that this arrangement has not been satisfactory to him and requires to be placed on some basis as regards profits as A and B. He further wants that this arrangement shall apply not only to future profits but also retrospectively to the profits of the past 3 years which were ₹ 10,000 ₹ 20,000 and ₹ 30,000. A and B have no objection to this. They further agree that in making such adjustment regard should be had to ₹ 5,000 value of goods which had been charged to profits but which actually were taken privately by B and ₹ 15,000 of office equipment no asset account had been opened in the books but charged to Profit and Loss Account. Plant and Machinery of the firm had not been depreciated over past years and it was estimated that the total of the amounts which should have been written off was ₹ 5,000. It was further agreed that after adjustments the capital accounts were to be equalized without, however, increasing *or* reducing the total capital of the firm.

Required: Show the Profit & Loss Adjustment Account and the Capital Accounts of the Partners after giving effect to the above agreement, assuming that immediately after the distribution of last year's profits, the capital accounts stood as: A—₹ 45,000; B—₹ 35,000 C—₹ 30,000.

SOLUTION

Dr. **PROFIT & LOSS ADJUSTMENT ACCOUNT** *Cr.*

Particulars	₹	*Particulars*	₹
To Dep. on Plant & Machinery	5,000	By A's Capital A/c	24,000
To Balance transferred to:		By B 's Capital A/c	24,000
A's Capital A/c	25,000	By C 's Capital A/c	12,000
B 's Capital A/c	25,000	By B 's Capital A/c (goods)	5,000
C 's Capital A/c	25,000	By Office Equipment A/c	15,000
	80,000		80,000

Dr. **CAPITAL ACCOUNTS OF PARTNERS** *Cr.*

Particulars	*A* ₹	*B* ₹	*C* ₹	*Particulars*	*A* ₹	*B* ₹	*C* ₹
To P&L Adjustment A/c	24,000	24,000	12,000	By Balance b/d	45,000	35,000	30,000
To Cash A/c	6,000	—	3,000	By P&L Adjustment A/c	25,000	25,000	25,000
To P&L Adjustment A/c	—	5,000	—	By Cash A/c	—	9,000	—
To Balance c/d	40,000	40,000	40,000				
	70,000	69,000	55,000		70,000	69,000	55,000

Notes:

(i) *In order to adjust the partners' capital accounts in accordance with the new arrangement, the past three years' profits, that were credited to partners in the ratio of 2 : 2 : 1 have been written back.*

(ii) *The total capital of the firm would be ₹ 1,20,000 (i.e. ₹ 1,10,000 plus ₹ 15,000 minus ₹ 5,000) and hence after equalising, each partner's capital would be ₹ 40,000 (i.e., one third of ₹ 1,20,000)*

PROBLEM 5

A and B were in partnership sharing profits and losses in the ratio of 2 : 3. On 1st April, 2012, they agreed to admit their sales manager 'C' as a partner with a one third share in the profits and a salary of ₹ 6,000 p.a. It is agreed that C's share shall not be less than his present salary of ₹ 9,000 p.a. together with a commission of 5% of the net profits after charging such salary & commission.

The profits for the year ended 31st March, 2013, before charging any commission and salary were ₹ 93,000. The excess of C's 1/3rd share in the profits over his remuneration is to be borne by A and B in the ratio of 3 : 2.

Required: Prepare a Statement showing the Distribution of Profits.

SOLUTION

STATEMENT SHOWING THE EXCESS OF C 'S SHARE AS PARTNER OVER HIS REMUNERATION AS MANAGER

	Particulars		₹
A	Remuneration of 'C' as manager		
	Salary		9,000
	Commission @ 5/105 of ₹ 84,000 being (₹ 93,000 – ₹ 9,000)		4,000
			13,000
B	Amount to be received by 'C's as Partner—	Salary	6,000
		Profit (₹ 87,000 × 1/3)	29,000
			35,000
C	Excess of C 's Share as Partner over his Remuneration as Manager, to be borne by A and B in the ratio of 3 : 2 (A – B)		22,000

DISTRIBUTION OF PROFITS

	Particulars	*A* ₹	*B* ₹	*C* ₹
A	Distribution of profits under old arrangement (₹ 93,000 – ₹ 13,000) divided in the ratio of 2 : 3	32,000	48,000	—
B	Share of 'C ' under old arrangement	—	—	13,000
C	Excess of Share of 'C ' as partner over his Remuneration as Manager divided in the ratio of 3 : 2	(13,200)	(8,800)	22,000
D	Share under new arrangement	18,800	39,200	35,000

PROBLEM 6

With effect from 1st January, 2013, 'M' the manager in the firm of R, S and T who were sharing profits and losses in the ratio of 1/2 and 1/3 and 1/6 respectively, was admitted as partner in the firm with a 1/10th share. It was agreed that should M's share of profits exceed his remuneration as Manager, R should bear the excess. As manager, M was entitled to a salary of ₹ 2,000 p.m. together with a commission of 2% on profit after charging the salary and commission when accounts were drawn up for 2013, by mistake the salary and commission as given above for M were debited to the Profit and Loss Account which then showed a credited balance of ₹ 3,00,000.

Required: Prepare a Statement showing the Distribution of Profits for 2013 together with necessary journal entries.

SOLUTION

JOURNAL

Date	Particulars	L.F.	Dr. (₹)	Cr. (₹)
	P & L Adjustment A/c Dr.		3,00,000	
	To R 's Capital A/c			1,50,000
	To S 's Capital A/c			1,00,000
	To T 's Capital A/c			50,000
	(Being the profits distributed as if 'M' is manager)			
	R 's Capital A/c Dr.		3,000	
	To M 's Capital A/c			3,000
	(Being the deficiency met out of share *or* R)			

DISTRIBUTION OF PROFITS

	Particulars	R ₹	S ₹	T ₹	M ₹
A	Distribution of profits under old arrangement (₹ 3,00,000 divided in the ratio of 3 : 2 : 1)	1,50,000	1,00,000	50,000	—
B	Share of M under old arrangement	—	—	—	30,000
C	Excess of Share of M as Partner over his remuneration as Manager to be borne by R	(3,000)	—	—	3,000
D	Profit under new arrangement	1,47,000	1,00,000	50,000	33,000

Working Notes:

	Particulars		₹
(i)	Calculation of Profit before charging salary and commission		
	I Profit after Salary & Commission	3,00,000	
	II Commission @ 2%	6,000	
	III Salary @ ₹ 2,000 p.m.	24,000	3,30,000
(ii)	Share of 'M' as partner (₹ 3,30,000 × 1/10)		33,000
(iii)	Remuneration of 'M' as Manager		30,000
(iv)	Excess of share as partner over remuneration as Manager to be borne by 'R'		3,000

PROBLEM 7

A, B and C are partners in a firm of which Partnership Deed includes the following provisions:

(a) B is entitled to a salary of ₹ 1,550 per month.

(b) C will get a salary of ₹ 950 per month to come out of B's share of Profit.

(c) In case C's share of profit, Interest on Capital and salary happens to be less than ₹ 50,000, the difference has to come out of A's share of profit.

(d) Partners are entitled to interest on capital @ 12% p.a.

On 31st March, 2012, the capital Accounts of A, B and C were ₹ 30,000, ₹ 60,000 and ₹ 80,000 respectively and they share the profits in the ratio of 3 : 2 : 1. Net profits of the firm for the year ending on March 31, 2013, were ₹ 1,59,000 before charging partners' salaries and interest on capital.

Required: Prepare Profit & Loss Appropriation Account.

SOLUTION

PROFIT AND LOSS APPROPRIATION ACCOUNT

Dr. *for the year ending on 31st March, 2013* *Cr.*

Particulars		₹	*Particulars*	₹
To Salary to Partners:			By Profit before Adjustments	1,59,000
B	18,600			
C	11,400	30,000		
To Interest on Capital:				
A	3,600			
B	7,200			
C	9,600	20,400		
To Profit transferred to Capital A/cs:				
A	51,000			
B	28,600			
C	29,000	1,08,600		
		1,59,000		1,59,000

Working Notes:

(i) Profits available for distribution (after Interest on Capital & B's salary) = ₹ 1,59,000 – ₹ 39,000 = ₹ 1,20,000.

(ii) Profits Shares of Partners: A ₹ 60,000; B ₹ 40,000; C ₹ 20,000.

(iii) C's deficiency in profit = ₹ 50,000 – ₹ 20,000 – ₹ 21,000 = ₹ 9,000.

(iv) Adjustments: A ₹ 60,000 – ₹ 9,000 = ₹ 51,000;
B ₹ 40,000 – ₹ 11,400 = ₹ 28,600.
C ₹ 20,000 + ₹ 9,000 = ₹ 29,000.

PROBLEM 8

Mehra and Ratnam are in partnership with capitals of ₹ 28,000, ₹ 14,000 respectively sharing profits and losses as 2 : 1. Interest on capital @ 5% per annum and salary of ₹ 2,800 per annum to Ratnam are allowable. Due to ill health Mehra ceased to take active part in the business with effect from 1st Jan. 2013, and the following terms were agreed upon:

(a) That the Manager, Jahar shall be taken as a partner with a capital of ₹ 5,000, he being entitled to a salary of ₹ 5,250 per annum, the excess over ₹ 2,800 (the salary received by him as Manager) to be borne by Mehra personally.

(b) That Ratnam shall get a salary of ₹ 3,500 per annum.

(c) That Jahar shall be entitled to one tenth of profits and losses after charging interest on capitals and partners' salaries.

(d) That interest on capital shall be allowed @ 5% per annum.

The net profit for the year ended 31st Dec., 2013, was ₹ 22,400 before charging interest on capital and partner's salaries.

Required: Show the division of the profit for the year 2013 between the partners.

SOLUTION

PROFIT AND LOSS APPROPRIATION ACCOUNT

Dr. *for the year ending on 31st Dec., 2013* *Cr.*

Particulars	₹	*Particulars*	₹
To Ratnam's Salary	3,500	By Net Profit b/d	22,400
To Jahar's Salary	5,250		
To Interest on Capital: Mehra 1,400			
Ratnam 700			
Jahar 250	2,350		
To Profit transferred to Capital Accounts:			
Mehra (Balance)	6,045		
Ratnam (3/10 of ₹ 13,750 profit after interest and salaries, taking Jahar's salary to be ₹ 2,800)	4,125		
Jahar (1/10 of ₹ 11,300 profit after interest and partners salaries)	1,130		
	22,400		22,400

Alternative Solution:

PROFIT AND LOSS APPROPRIATION ACCOUNT

Dr. *for the year ending on 31st Dec., 2013* *Cr.*

Particulars		₹	*Particulars*	₹
To Ratnam's Salary		3,500	By Net Profit	22,400
To Jahar's Salary		2,800		
To Interest on Capital:				
Mehra	1,400			
Ratnam	700			
Jahar	250	2,350		
To Balance c/d		13,750		
		22,400		22,400
To Profit transferred to:				
Mehra: (6/10)	8,250			
Less: Excess salary of Jahar	2,450	5,800	By Balance b/d	13,750
Ratnam (3/10)		4,125		
Jahar: (1/10)	1,375			
Add: From Mehra for Salary (Bal.)	2,450	3,825		
		13,750		13,750

Note: *The significant point seems to be that Ratnam should not suffer on account of increase in Jahar salary and that, for the purpose of ascertaining Ratnam's share, the salary of Jahar should be ₹ 2,800. From this point of view, the first solution is considered Proper. It cannot be that Jahar should derive a double benefit from increase in his salary and Mehra's agreeing to bear increased part of it.*

PROBLEM 9

M/s CANJA & CO.'s Balance Sheet as at 31st March, 2013:

Particulars		₹
Bank overdraft (State Bank)		54,000
Sundry Creditors		1,56,000
Capital Accounts:		
Mr A		
Balance as per last B/S	4,02,000	
Add: Profit for the year	95,400	
	4,97,400	
Less: Drawings	40,000	4,57,400
Mr B		
Balance as per last B/S	2,00,000	
Add: Profit for the year	95,400	
	2,95,400	
Less: Drawings	76,000	2,19,400
Cash at Bank of India		800
Sundry Debtors		2,80,000
Stock		1,00,000
Motor Cars cost as per last B/S	1,60,000	
Less: Depreciation till date	54,000	1,06,000
Machinery:		
Cost as per last B/S	3,00,000	
Less: Depreciation till date	1,40,000	1,60,000
Land and Buildings		2,40,000

You have examined the foregoing Draft of the Balance Sheet and have ascertained that the following adjustments are required to be carried out:

(i) Land and Buildings are shown at cost less ₹ 60,000 being the proceeds of the sale during the year of premises costing ₹ 70,000.

(ii) Machinery having a net book value of ₹ 4,300 had been scrapped during the year. The original cost was ₹ 12,300.

(iii) ₹ 2,000 paid for the Licence fees for the year ending 30th Sept., 2013 had been written off.

(iv) Debts amounting to ₹ 10,420 were considered to be bad and further debts amounting to ₹ 5,400 were considered doubtful and required 100% provision. Provision for doubtful debts had previously been made for ₹ 10,000.

(v) An item in the Inventory was valued at ₹ 37,400, but had a realisable value of ₹ 26,000 only. Scrap material having a value of ₹ 6,600 had been omitted from the stock valuation.

(vi) The cashier had misappropriated ₹ 700.

(vii) The cash-book for the year ending 31st March, 2013 included payments amounting to ₹ 6,924, the cheques having been made out, but not despatched by suppliers until April, 2013.

(viii) Interest is to be allowed on the Partners' opening Capital Account balances less drawings during the year at 9%.

You are required to prepare:

(a) Profit & Loss Adjustment Account for the year

(b) Capital Accounts of the Partners.

SOLUTION

Dr. **PROFIT AND LOSS ADJUSTMENT ACCOUNT** *Cr.*

Particulars		₹	*Particulars*		₹
To Land & Building Account (Loss on Sale)		10,000	By Partners' Capital Accounts:		
			Mr A	95,400	
To Machinery Account (Loss on Scraping)		4,300	Mr B	95,400	1,90,800
To Provision for Doubtful Debts (As per note below)		5,820	By Prepaid Expenses (Licence Fee)		1,000
To Stock Adjustment (Fall in Market Value)		11,400	By Stock Adjustment (Items omitted)		6,600
To Cash (Misappropriation)		700			
To Interest on Capitals:					
Mr A	32,580				
Mr B	11,160	43,740			
To Balance transfer to Capital Accounts:					
Mr A	61,220				
Mr B	61,220	1,22,440			
		1,98,400			1,98,400

Working Notes:

Dr. **(I) PROVISION FOR DOUBTFUL DEBTS ACCOUNT** *Cr.*

Particulars	₹	*Particulars*	₹
To Bad Debts	10,420	By Balance b/d	10,000
To Balance c/d (required)	5,400	By P & L Adjustment A/c (b.f.)	5,820
	15,820		15,820

Dr. **(II) CAPITAL ACCOUNT OF PARTNERS** *Cr.*

Particulars	*Mr. A* ₹	*Mr. B* ₹	*Particulars*	*Mr. A* ₹	*Mr. B* ₹
To Drawings	40,000	76,000	By Balance b/d	4,02,000	2,00,000
To P&L Adjustment A/c	95,400	95,400	By Profit for the year	95,400	95,400
To Balance c/d	4,55,800	1,96,380	By P&L Adjustment A/c:		
			Interest on Capital	32,580	11,160
			Profit for the year	61,220	61,220
	5,91,200	3,67,780		5,91,200	3,67,780

(iii) Misappropriation by cashier may be debited to cashier. In that case ₹ 700 will not be debited to P & L Adjustment Account and profit to partners will be ₹ 1,23,140 (Mr A ₹ 61,570 and Mr B ₹ 61,570). The capital accounts will accordingly be different.

(iv) The student may not reverse the distributed profit of last year. In that case Profit & Loss Adjustment A/c and Partners' Capital Accounts will differ from the solution. However, the balance of the Capital Accounts will remain the same.

PROBLEM 10

The partnership accounts of X and Y sharing in the ratio of 3 : 2 were maintained on cash basis right from its formation (in 2010). Now the partners decided to change into mercantile basis. Following details are given in this respect:

Particulars	*2010* ₹	*2011* ₹	*2012* ₹	*2013* ₹
Outstanding Salary	1,000	2,000	3,000	4,000
Prepaid Insurance Premium	1,500	3,000	4,500	6,000
Interest accrued but not received	2,000	4,000	6,000	8,000
Rent received in advance	3,000	6,000	9,000	12,000
Profits as per P & L A/c	10,500	20,500	30,500	40,500

Required: Pass the necessary single adjusting entry.

SOLUTION

CALCULATION OF PROFITS ON MERCANTILE BASIS

	Particulars	*2010* ₹	*2011* ₹	*2012* ₹	*2013* ₹
A	Cash Profits as given	10,500	20,500	30,500	40,500
B	*Add:* Outstanding Expenses in the beginning of current year	—	1,000	2,000	3,000
C	*Add:* Prepaid Expenses at the end of current year	1,500	3,000	4,500	6,000
D	*Add:* Accrued Income at the end of current year	2,000	4,000	6,000	8,000
E	*Add:* Unaccrued Income in the beginning of current year	—	3,000	6,000	9,000
F	*Less:* Outstanding Expenses at the end of current year	(1,000)	(2,000)	(3,000)	(4,000)
G	*Less:* Prepaid Expenses in the beginning of current year	—	(1,500)	(3,000)	(4,500)
H	*Less:* Accrued Income in the beginning of current year	—	(2,000)	(4,000)	(6,000)
I	*Less:* Unaccrued income at the end of current year	(3,000)	(6,000)	(9,000)	(12,000)
J	Profits on Mercantile Basis	10,000	20,000	30,000	40,000

ADJUSTING JOURNAL ENTRY

Date	*Particulars*		*L.F.*	*Dr. (₹)*	*Cr. (₹)*
	Prepaid Insurance Premium A/c	Dr.		6,000	
	Interest Accrued A/c	Dr.		8,000	
	X 's Capital A/c	Dr.		1,200	
	Y 's Capital A/c	Dr.		800	
	To Outstanding Salary A/c				4,000
	To Rent Received-in-advance A/c				12,000
	(Being the entry on Conversion of Cash Basis into Mercantile Basis)				

PROBLEM 11

Good, Better and Best are in Partnership sharing profits and losses in the ratio 3:2:4. Their Capital Account balances as on 31st March 2013 are as follows: Good ₹ 1,70,000 (Cr), Better ₹ 1,10,000 (Cr), Best ₹ 1,22,000 (Cr). Following further information provided:

1. ₹ 22,240 is to be transferred to General Reserve.
2. Good, Better and Best are paid monthly salary in cash amounting to ₹ 2,400, ₹ 1,600 and ₹ 1,800 rspectively.
3. Partners are allowed interest on their Closing Capital Balance at 6% p.a. and are charged interest on drawings at 8% p.a.
4. Good and Best are entitled to Commission at 8% and 10% respectively of the Net Profit before making any appropriation.
5. Better is entitled to Commission at 15% of the Net Profit before charging Interest on Drawings but after making all other appropriations.
6. During the year, Good withdrew ₹ 2,000 at the beginning of every month, Better ₹ 1,750 at the end of every month and Best ₹ 1,250 at the middle of every month.
7. The Firm's Accountant is entitled to a Salary of ₹ 2,000 per month and a Commission of 12% of Net Profit after charging such Commission.

The Net Profit of the Firm for the year ended 31st March 2013, before providing for any of the above adjustments was ₹ 2,76,000. You are required to prepare Profit and Loss Appropriation Account for the year ended on 31st March 2013.

SOLUTION

Dr. **PROFIT AND LOSS ACCOUNT** *Cr.*

Particulars	₹	*Particulars*	₹
To Accountant's Salary (2,000 × 12)	24,000	By Net Profit b/d	2,76,000
To Accountant's Commission [(2,76,000 – 24,000) × 12/112]	27,000		
To Net Profit c/d (bal. fig.)	2,25,000		
	2,76,000		2,76,000

Dr. **PROFIT AND LOSS APPROPRIATION ACCOUNT** Cr.

Particulars		₹	*Particulars*		₹
To General Reserve		22,240	By Net Profit b/d		2,25,000
To Salary:			By Interest on Drawings:		
Good (2,400 × 12)	28,800		Good (24,000 × 8% × 6.5 / 12)	1,040	
Better (1,600 × 12)	19,200		Better (21,000 × 8% × 5.5 / 12)	770	
Best (1,800 × 12)	21,600	69,600	Best (15,000 × 8% × 5.5 / 12)	600	2,410
To Interest on Capital:					
Good (1,70,000 × 6%)	10,200				
Better (1,10,000 × 6%)	6,600				
Best (1,22,000 × 6%)	7,320	24,120			
To Commission:					
Good (2,25,000 × 8%)	18,000				
Best (2,25,000 × 10%)	22,500				
Better (68,540 × 15%)	10,281	50,781			
To Net Profit tfrd to Capital A/c:					
Good (60,669 × 3/9)	20,223				
Better (60,669 × 2/9)	13,482				
Best (60,669 × 4/9)	26,964	60,669			
		2,27,410			2,27,410

Notes:

1. Salary and Commission to Firm's Accountant are in the nature of charges against Firm's Profits, and not an appropriation out of Profit to Partners. Hence, this amounts have been debited to Profit & Loss Account.
2. Better's Commission = [2,25,000 – 22,240 – 69,600 – 24,120 – 40,500] × 15% = ₹ 10,281

16 RECONSTITUTION OF PARTNERSHIP — CHANGE IN PROFIT SHARING RATIO

LEARNING OBJECTIVES

After studying this chapter, you should be able to understand:

- Meaning of Reconstitution of a Firm
- Occasions when Reconstitution of a Firm can take place
- Meaning of Change in Profit Sharing Ratio
- Need for Change in Profit Sharing Ratio
- Adjustments Required at the time of Change in Profit Sharing Ratio
- Meaning of Sacrificing Partners
- Meaning of Sacrificing Ratio
- Meaning of Gaining Partners
- Meaning of Gaining Ratio
- Meaning of New Profit Sharing Ratio
- Adjustment of Goodwill
- Adjustments of Profit/Loss on Revaluation of Assets & Liabilities
- Adjustment of Reserves and Accumulated Profits/Losses
- Adjustment of Capitals

1.0 RECONSTITUTION OF A FIRM

Meaning	Any change in existing agreement of partnership amounts to reconstitution of a firm. As a result, the existing agreement comes to an end and a new agreement comes into existence and the firm continues.
When Takes Place	Reconstitution of the firm can take place on the following occasions: 1. Change in the Profit Sharing Ratio of existing partners. 2. Admission of a new partner [e.g. Admission of Z as partner in the firm of X and Y] 3. Retirement of an existing partner [e.g. Continuity of business by X and Y after the retirement of a third partner Z]. 4. Death of a partner [e.g. Continuity of business by X and Y after the death of a third partner Z]. 5. Amalgamation of two partnership firms. [e.g. Merger of a firm of X and Y with the firm of P and Q.]

2.0 CHANGE IN PROFIT SHARING RATIO

Meaning	1. A change in profit sharing ratio is one of the modes of reconstituting the firm under which old partnership comes to an end and a new one comes nto existence. 2. A change in profit sharing ratio basically implies the purchase of share of profit by one partner from another partner. 3. Change in profit sharing ratio involves increase in share of profit of one *or* more partners and decrease in share of profit of one *or* more partners.
Need for Change in Profit Sharing Ratio	The need for change in profit sharing ratio arises in the following circumstances: 1. When the partners so decide. 2. When a new partner is admitted. 3. When a partner retires. 4. When a partner dies.
Adjustments Required	The various matters that need adjustment at the time of admission change in profit sharing ratio are given below: 1. Adjustment in Profit Sharing Ratio, 2. Adjustment of Goodwill, 3. Adjustment of Profit/Loss arising from the Revaluation of Assets and Liabilities, 4. Adjustment of Accumulated Profits, Reserves and Losses, 5. Adjustment of Capitals (if agreed).
Sacrificing Partners	The partners whose shares have decreased as a result of change are known as Sacrificing Partners.
Sacrificing Ratio	The ratio in which the partners have agreed to sacrifice their shares in profit in favour of other partner *or* partners, is known as sacrificing ratio. This ratio is calculated by taking out the difference between Old Profit Shares and New Profit Shares.
Gaining Partners	The partners whose shares have increased as a result of change are known as Gaining Partners.
Gaining Ratio	The ratio in which the partners have agreed to gain their shares in profit from the other partner *or* partners, is known as Gaining Partners. This ratio is calculated by taking out the difference between New Profit Shares and Old Profit Shares.
New Profit Sharing Ratio	The ratio in which all the partners share the future profits and losses is known as the New Profit Sharing Ratio.

ILLUSTRATION 1

X, Y and Z are sharing profits and losses in the ratio of 5 : 3 : 2. Calculate the new profit sharing ratio and the sacrificing ratio if Z acquires 1/10th share from Y.

SOLUTION

X's New Share = 5/10, Y's New Share = 3/10 – 1/10 = 2/10,

Z's New Share = 2/10 + 1/10 = 3/10

New Profit Sharing Ratio of X, Y and Z = 5/10 : 2/10 : 3/10 = 5 : 2 : 3

Share Sacrificed by Y = 1/10, Share Gained by Z = 1/10

ILLUSTRATION 2

X, Y and Z are sharing profits and losses in the ratio of 5 : 3 : 2. Calculate the new profit sharing ratio and the sacrificing ratio if Z acquires 1/10th share equally from X and Y.

SOLUTION

X's New Share = 5/10 – 1/20 = 9/20, Y's New Share = 3/10 – 1/20 = 5/20,

Z's New Share = 2/10 + 1/10 = 3/10

New Profit Sharing Ratio of X, Y and Z = 9/20 : 5/20 : 3/10 = 9 : 5 : 6

Share Gained by Z = 1/10

Sacrificing Ratio of X & Y = 1 : 1

ILLUSTRATION 3

X, Y and Z are sharing profits and losses in the ratio of 5 : 3 : 2. Calculate the new profit sharing ratio and the sacrificing ratio if X, Y and Z decide to share future profits & losses equally.

SOLUTION

New Profit Sharing Ratio of X, Y and Z = 1 : 1 : 1

X's Sacrifice = 5/10 – 1/3 = 5/30, Y's Gain = 3/10 – 1/3 = (1/30), Z's Gain = 2/10 – 1/3 = (4/30)

Y gains by 1/30th share, Z gains by 4/30th share and X sacrifices by 5/30th share.

3.0 ADJUSTMENT OF GOODWILL

Why Adjustment Required?	Whenever there is a change profit sharing ratio, the Gaining Partner (i.e., the partner whose share has increased as a result of change) must compensate the Sacrificing Partner (i.e., the partner whose share has decreased as a result of change).
Amount of Compensation	The amount of compensation must be equal to the proportionate value of firm's goodwill. Thus, Amount of Compensation Payable = Value of Firm's Goodwill × Share of Profit Gained
Recommendation of AS 26	(a) Internally generated goodwill should not be recognized as an asset because it is not an identifiable resource controlled by the enterprise that can be measured reliably at cost. (b) Hence, **when the goodwill is evaluated at the time of any change in the constitution of the firm** (by way of admission/retirement/death/ change in profit sharing ratio), the value of such goodwill should not be raised in the books of the firm. Rather the **value of such goodwill should be adjusted through concerned partners' capital accounts.**
Accounting Treatment	When there is a change in profit sharing ratio the following simplified approach is suggested to make adjustment for goodwill: **Step 1: Calculate the Share Gained and Share Sacrificed.** Share Gained = New Share – Old Share Share Sacrificed = Old Share – New Share

	Step 2: Calculate the Compensation payable by Gaining Partner (s) to Sacrifing Partner(s). Compensation = Firm's Goodwill × Share of Profit Gained **Step 3: Write off the Existing Book Value of goodwill (if any) appearing in the books of the firm** All Partners' Capital A/cs Dr. [In Old Ratio] To Goodwill A/c [With existing book value of Goodwill] (Being the existing goodwill written off in old ratio] **Step 4: Give Credit for Proportionate amount of Goodwill to Sacrificing Partners.** Gaining Partners' Capital A/cs Dr. [In Gaining Ratio] To Sacrificing Partners' Capital A/cs [In Sacrificing Ratio] (Being the adjustment made for goodwill on change in profit sharing ratio]

Tutorial Note: *Unless otherwise stated, the partners' capitals should be assumed to be fluctuating. Current Accounts are to be used in case of Fixed Capitals.*

ILLUSTRATION 4

X, Y and Z who are presently sharing profits & losses in the ratio of 5 : 3 : 2, decide to share future profits & losses equally with effect from 1st April, 2012. The goodwill of the firm has been valued at ₹ 1,80,000. Goodwill already appearing in the books is at ₹ 30,000. Show the necessary accounting treatment.

SOLUTION

STEP 1: CALCULATION OF GAIN/SECRIFICE OF PARTNERS

Particulars	*X*	*Y*	*Z*
New Shares	1/3	1/3	1/3
Old Shares	5/10	3/10	2/10
Difference	–5/30	1/30	4/30
	Sacrificing partner	Gaining partner	Gaining partner

Step 2: Compensation payable by Y to X = ₹ 1,80,000 × 1/30 = ₹ 6,000

Compensation payable by Z to X = ₹ 1,80,000 × 4/30 = ₹ 24,000

STEP 3 & 4: JOURNAL

Date	*Particulars*		*L.F.*	*Dr. (₹)*	*Cr. (₹)*
	X's Capital A/c [₹ 30,000 × 5/10]	Dr.		15,000	
	Y's Capital A/c [₹ 30,000 × 3/10]	Dr.		9,000	
	Z's Capital A/c [₹ 30,000 × 2/10]	Dr.		6,000	
	To Goodwill A/c				30,000
	(Being the existing goodwill w/o in old ratio on change in profit sharing ratio.)				

	Y's Capital A/c [₹ 1,80,000 × 1/30] Dr.		6,000	
	Z's Capital A/c [₹ 1,80,000 × 4/30] Dr.		24,000	
	To X's Capital A/c [₹ 1,80,000 × 5/30]			30,000
	(Being the adjustment made for goodwill on change in the profit sharing ratio)			

ILLUSTRATION 5

Anita, Asha and Amrit are partners sharing profits in the ratio of 3 : 2 : 1 respectively. From 1st January, 2012 they decided to share profits in the ratio of 2 : 3 : 1. The Partnership Deed provides that in the event of any change in profit-sharing ratio, the goodwill should be valued at three years' purchase of the average of five years' profits. The profits and losses of the preceding five years are:

Profit: 2007–₹ 1,20,000; 2008–₹ 3,00,000; 2009–₹ 3,40,000; 2010–₹ 3,80,000;

Loss: 2011–₹ 1,40,000.

Showing the working clearly, give the necessary Journal entry to record the above change.

SOLUTION

Step 1: Valuation of Goodwill:

Average Profits = (₹ 1,20,000 + ₹ 3,00,000 + ₹ 3,40,000 + ₹ 3,80,000 – ₹ 1,40,000)/5 = ₹ 2,00,000

Goodwill = ₹ 2,00,000 × 3 = ₹ 6,00,000

Step 2: Calculation of Gain *or* Sacrifice of Partners

Sacrifice Share = Old Share – New Share

Anita $= \frac{3}{6} - \frac{2}{6} = \frac{1}{6}$ (i.e., Sacrifice), Asha $= \frac{2}{6} - \frac{3}{6} = \left(\frac{1}{6}\right)$ (i.e. a Gain)

Amrit $= \frac{1}{6} - \frac{1}{6} = 0.$

Anita is a sacrificing partner and Asha is a gaining partner.

Step 3: Compensation payable by Asha to Anita = 6,00,000 × 1/6 = ₹ 1,00,000

STEP 4: JOURNAL

Date	*Particulars*	*L.F.*	*Dr. (₹)*	*Cr. (₹)*
01.01.12	Asha's Capital A/c Dr.		1,00,000	
	To Anita's Capital A/c			1,00,000
	(Being the adjustment for goodwill made on change in profit-sharing ratio)			

4.0 REVALUATION OF ASSETS AND LIABILITIES

WHY IS REVALUATION OF ASSETS AND LIABILITIES REQUIRED?

At the time of change in profit sharing ratio, the assets and liabilities are revalued so that the profit *or* loss arising on account of such revaluation upto the date of change in profit sharing ratio may be ascertained and adjusted in the partners' Capital Accounts in their old profit sharing ratio because such profit *or* loss relates to pre-change period and hence it is to be shared in Old Profit Sharing Ratio.

REVALUATION ACCOUNT

Meaning	Revaluation Account (or alternatively Profit & Loss Adjustment Account) is a Nominal Account.
Purpose	The purpose of Revaluation Account is to asertain the Profit/Loss arising on account of revaluation of assets and liabilities.
Contents	Revaluation Account is credited with increase in the value of assets and decrease in the amount of liabilities (it is a gain) and debited with any decrease in the value of assets and increase in the amount of liabilities (it is a loss). Unrecorded assets are recorded through the Revaluation Account as increase in assets. Unrecorded liabilities are recorded through the Revaluation Account as increase in liabilities.
Balance	The balance of Revaluation Account shows the net effect on account of revaluation which is transferred to the Partners' Capital accounts in their old profit sharing ratio.

ACCOUNTING ENTRIES TO RECORD THE REVALUATION OF ASSETS AND LIABILITIES

1. For Increase in the Value of an Asset	
Concerned Asset A/c	Dr.
To Revaluation A/c	
(Being the increase in the value of an asset recorded)	
2. For Decrease in the Value of an Asset	
Revaluation A/c	Dr.
To Concerned Asset A/c	
(Being the decrease in the value of an asset recorded)	
3. For increase in the Amount of a Liability	
Revaluation A/c	Dr.
To Concerned Liability A/c	
(Being the increase in the amount of a liability recorded)	
4. For Decrease in the Amount of a Liability	
Concerned Liability A/c	Dr.
To Revaluation A/c	
(Being the decrease in the amount of a liability recorded)	
5. For Recording an Unrecorded Asset	
Unrecorded Asset A/c	Dr.
To Revaluation A/c	
(Being an agreed value of an unrecorded asset brought into account)	
6. For Recording an Unrecorded Liability	
Revaluation A/c	Dr.
To Unrecorded Liability A/c	
(Being an agreed amount of an unrecorded liability brought into account)	
7. For Transfer of Balance in Revaluation Account	
(i) If credit side exceeds debit side (Net Gain)	

Revaluation A/c	Dr.
To Partners' Capital A/cs (Individually in Ratio)	
(Being the net gain on revaluation transferred to partners' capital accounts in old profit sharing ratio)	
(ii) If debit side exceeds credit side (Net Loss)	
Partners' Capital A/cs (Individually in Ratio)	Dr.
To Revaluation A/c	
(Being the net loss on revaluation transferred to partners' capital accounts in old profit sharing ratio)	

Tutorial Note: *When Revaluation Account is prepared, the assets and liabilities appear in the Balance Sheet of new firm at their* ***revised figures.***

FORMAT OF REVALUATION ACCOUNT

Dr. **REVALUATION ACCOUNT** *Cr.*

Particulars	₹	*Particulars*	₹
To Decrease in Value of Assets	....	By Increase in Value of assets	....
To Increase in Value of Liabilities	....	By Decrease in Value of Liabilities	....
To Unrecorded Liabilities	....	By Unrecorded Assets	....
To Profit* t/f to the Partners' Capital A/cs (in the Old Profit-Sharing Ratio)	....	By Loss* t/f to the Partners' Capital A/cs (in the Old Profit-Sharing Ratio)	....
	....		....

**Either Profit or Loss will appear.*

ILLUSTRATION 6

X, Y and Z who are presently sharing profits & losses in the ratio of 5 : 3 : 2, decide to share future profits & losses in the ratio of 2 : 3 : 5 with effect from 1st April, 2012. An extract of their Balance Sheet as at 31st March, 2012 is as follows:

Particulars		₹
Sundry Creditors		3,00,000
Outstanding Rent		10,000
Land & Building		2,50,000
Plant & Machinery		1,00,000
Stock		80,000
Debtors	3,00,000	
Less: Provision	10,000	2,90,000

It is decided that:

1. Land & Building be valued at ₹ 2,90,000.
2. Plant & Machinery be depreciated by 15%.
3. Stock is found overvalued by ₹ 38,000.
4. Provision for doubtful debts is to be made equal to 5% of the debtors.
5. An item of ₹ 30,000 included in sundry creditors is not likely to be claimed.

6. Rent of ₹ 4,000 still Outstanding
7. Out of the amount of insurance which was debited entirely to P & L A/c, ₹ 5,000 be carried forward as an unexpired insurance.
8. Out of total commission received ₹ 3,000 is to be treated as advance commission. This amount was earlier credited to Profit & Loss Account.

Required: Pass the necessary Journal Entries and prepare Revaluation Account.

SOLUTION

JOURNAL

Date	*Particulars*		*L.F.*	*Dr. (₹)*	*Cr. (₹)*
01.04.12	Land & Building A/c	Dr.		40,000	
	To Revaluation A/c				40,000
	(Being the increase in value of Land & Building recorded)				
	Revaluation A/c	Dr.		15,000	
	To Plant & Machinery A/c				15,000
	(Being the decrease in value of Plant & Machinery recorded)				
	Revaluation A/c	Dr.		38,000	
	To Stock A/c				38,000
	(Being the decrease in value of Stock recorded)				
	Revaluation A/c [₹15,000 – ₹10,000]	Dr.		5,000	
	To Provision for Doubtful Debts A/c				5,000
	(Being the short provision now created)				
	Creditors	Dr.		30,000	
	To Revaluation A/c				30,000
	(Being the decrease in the amount of creditors recorded)				
	Revaluation A/c	Dr.		4,000	
	To Outstanding Rent A/c				4,000
	(Being the Outstanding Rent recorded)				
	Prepaid Insurance	Dr.		5,000	
	To Revaluation A/c				5,000
	(Being the Prepaid Insurance Recorded)				
	Revaluation A/c	Dr.		3,000	
	To Commission received in advance A/c				3,000
	(Being the Commission received in advance recorded)				
	Revaluation A/c	Dr.		10,000	
	To X's Capital A/c				5,000
	To Y's Capital A/c				3,000
	To Z's Capital A/c				2,000

	(Being the transfer of Profit on Revaluation to Old Partners' Capital Accounts in their old profit sharing ratio)			

Dr. **REVALUATION ACCOUNT** Cr.

Particulars	₹	*Particulars*	₹
To Stock	38,000	By Land & Building	40,000
To Provision for Doubtful Debts	5,000	By Sundry Creditors	30,000
To Plant & Machinery A/c	15,000	By Prepaid Insurance	5,000
To Outstanding Rent A/c	4,000		
To Commission received in advance A/c	3,000		
To Profit on Revaluation t/f to:			
X 's Capital A/c	5,000		
Y 's Capital A/c	3,000		
Z 's Capital A/c	2,000		
	75,000		75,000

5.0 ADJUSTMENTS OF PROFIT/LOSS ON REVALUATION OF ASSETS AND LIABILITIES THROUGH CAPITAL ACCOUNTS ONLY

HOW TO ADJUST PROFIT/LOSS ON REVALUATION

When the partners decide to record the net effect of revaluation of assets and liabilities without affecting the old figures of assets liabilities, single adjusting entry involving the capital accounts of gaining partners and sacrificing partners is passed. The following steps may be taken in this regard:

PRACTICAL STEPS TO PASS SINGLE ADJUSTING ENTRY

				₹
Step 1:	***Calculate the Net Effect of Revaluation***			
	A. Increase in Value of Assets			xxx
	B. *Add:* Decrease in amount of Liabilities			xxx
	C. *Less:* Decrease in Value of Assets			xxx
	D. *Less:* Increase in Amount of Liabilities			xxx
	E. Net Effect of Revaluation			xxx
Step 2:	***Calculate Gain/Loss of Share***			
	Their New Shares	x	x	x
	Their Old Shares	x	x	x
	Difference	x	x	x
Step 3:	***Calculate the Share of Gaining Partner and Sacrificing Partner in the Net Effect of Revaluation***			
	For Gaining Partner = Share gained × Net Effect of Revaluation			
	For Sacrificing Partner = Share sacrificed × Net Effect of Revaluation			

Step 4: *Pass the following Single Adjusting Journal Entry:*	
In Case of Net Profit on Revaluation	**In Case of Net Loss on Revaluation**
Gaining Partner's Capital A/c Dr.	Sacrificing Partner's Capital A/c Dr.
To Sacrificing Partner's Capital A/c	To Gaining Partner's Capital A/c

Tutorial Note: *When the Profit/Loss on Revaluation of Assets and Liabilities is adjusted through Capital Accounts only, the Assets and Liabilities appear in the Balance Sheet of the New Firm at their* ***old figures.***

ILLUSTRATION 7

X, Y and Z are sharing profits & losses in the ratio of 5 : 3 : 2. They decide to share future profits & losses in the ratio of 2 : 3 : 5 with effect from 1st April 2012. They also decide to record the effect of following revaluations without affecting the book values of the assets & liabilities, by passing a single adjusting entry:

Particulars	*Book Figure*	*Revalued Figure*
Land & Building	₹ 1,00,000	₹ 1,50,000
Plant & Machinery	₹ 1,50,000	₹ 1,40,000
Trade Creditors	₹ 50,000	₹ 45,000
Outstanding Expenses	₹ 45,000	₹ 60,000

Required: Pass the necessary single adjusting entry.

SOLUTION

STEP 1: CALCULATION OF NET EFFECT OF REVALUATION

Particulars	₹
A. Increase in value of Land & Building	50,000
B. *Add:* Decrease in Amount of Creditors	5,000
C. *Less:* Decrease in Value of Plant & Machinery	10,000
D. *Less:* Increase in Amount of Outstanding Expenses	15,000
E. Net Profit on Revaluation	30,000

STEP 2: CALCULATION OF GAIN/LOSS OF SHARE

Particulars	*X*	*Y*	*Z*
Their New Shares	2/10	3/10	5/10
Their Old Shares	5/10	3/10	2/10
Difference	(3/10)	–	3/10

STEP 3: CALCULATION OF PROPORTIONATE AMOUNT OF NET PROFIT ON REVALUATION

For X = 3/10 × ₹ 30,000 = ₹ 9,000, For Z = 3/10 × ₹ 30,000 = ₹ 9,000

STEP 4: ADJUSTING JOURNAL ENTRY

Date	*Particulars*	*L.F.*	*Dr. (₹)*	*Cr. (₹)*
	Z's Capital A/c Dr.		9,000	

	To X's Capital A/c			9,000
	(Being the adjustment made for net profit on revaluation)			

6.0 ADJUSTMENT FOR RESERVES AND ACCUMULATED PROFITS/LOSSES

WHY IS ADJUSTMENT FOR RESERVES AND ACCUMULATED PROFITS/LOSSES REQUIRED?

If, at the time of change in Profit Sharing Ratio, any reserves *or* accumulated profits/losses exist in the books of the firm, these should be transferred to partners' Capital Accounts *(if capitals are fluctuating) or* Current Accounts *(if capital are fixed)* in their old profit sharing ratio since the reserves, accumulated profits/losses upto the date of change in profit sharing ratio belong to the partners in their old profit sharing ratio.

ACCOUNTING TREATMENT OF RESERVES, ACCUMULATED PROFITS/LOSSES

1. *For transfer of Reserves and Accumulated Profits*

Reserve A/c		Dr.
P & L A/c		Dr.
Workmen Compensation Reserve A/c	[Excess of Reserve over Actual Liability]	Dr.
Investment Fluctuation Reserve A/c	[Excess of Reserve over the difference between Book value and Market value]	Dr.
To Old Partners' Capital Accounts (individually)	(Old Ratio)	
(Being the Reserves & Profits transferred to old partners in their old ratio)		

2. *For transfer of Accumulated Losses*

Old Partners' Capital Accounts (individually)	Dr.	(Old Ratio)
To Profit & Loss A/c		
To Deferred Revenue Expenditure A/c		
(Being Accumulated Losses transferred to old partners in their old ratio)		

TUTORIAL NOTES

1. *Reserves, Accumulated Profits/Losses should always be distributed even if the question is silent.*
2. *Workmen Compensation Reserve is a reserve created out of profit to meet the Workment Compensation Liability, if any arise in future. Workmen Compensation Reserve (say ₹ 1,200) to the extent of liability (say ₹ 150) should be credited to Workmen Compensation Claim A/c and the balance of Workmen Compensation Reserve (₹ 1,050) should be credited to Partners' Capital Accounts.*
3. *Investment Fluctuation Reserve is a reserve created out of profit to adjust the difference between the Book Value and Market Value of Investments. Excess of Investment Fluctuation Reserve over difference between Book Value and Market Value is credited to partners in Profit Sharing Ratio.*
4. *Machinery Replacement Fund is in the nature of Accumulated Depreciation and not Accumulated Profits and hence it is not distributed among the partners.*
5. *Employees' Provident Fund represents statutory liability due to employees towards Provident Fund and is not an accumulated profit, hence it is not distributed among the partners.*

ILLUSTRATION 8

X, Y and Z are sharing profits & losses in the ratio of 5 : 3 : 2. They decide to share future profits & losses in the ratio of 2 : 3 : 5 with effect from 1st April, 2012. The following items appear in the Balance Sheet as at 31st March, 2012:

General Reserve	₹ 30,000
Contingencies Reserve	₹ 5,000
Advertisement Suspense A/c (Dr.)	₹ 20,000
Profit & Loss A/c (Cr.)	₹ 15,000

Required: Pass the necessary Journal Entries.

SOLUTION

JOURNAL

Date	*Particulars*		*L.F.*	*Dr. (₹)*	*Cr. (₹)*
2012	General Reserve	Dr.		30,000	
April 1	Contingencies Reserve	Dr.		5,000	
	Profit & Loss A/c (Cr.)	Dr.		15,000	
	To X's Capital A/c				25,000
	To Y's Capital A/c				15,000
	To Z's Capital A/c				10,000
	(Being the transfer of Reserves & Profits to old partners in their old ratio)				
	X's Capital A/c	Dr.		10,000	
	Y's Capital A/c	Dr.		6,000	
	Z's Capital A/c	Dr.		4,000	
	To Advertisement Suspense A/c				20,000
	(Being the transfer of balance of Advertisement Suspense A/c to old partners in their old ratio)				

ILLUSTRATION 9 [TREATMENT OF WORKMEN COMPENSATION RESERVE]

X, Y and Z who are presently sharing profits & losses in the ratio of 5 : 3 : 2, decide to share future profits & losses in the ratio of 2 : 3 : 5 with effect from 1st April, 2012. Workmen Compensation Reserve appears at ₹ 1,200 in the Balance Sheet as at 31st March, 2012.

Required: Show the accounting treatment in each of the following alternative cases:

Case I If there is no other information.

Case II If a claim on account of Workmen's Compensation is estimated at ₹ 150 only.

Case III If a claim on account of Workmen's Compensation is estimated at ₹ 2,250.

SOLUTION

JOURNAL

Date	Particulars		L.F.	Dr. (₹)	Cr. (₹)
2012	**Case I**				
April 1	Workmen Compensation Reserve A/c	Dr.		1,200	
	To X's Capital A/c				600
	To Y's Capital A/c				360
	To Z's Capital A/c				240
	(Being the transfer of Workmen Compensation Reserve to Partners' Capital Accounts in their old profit sharing ratio)				
	Case II				
	Workmen Compensation Reserve A/c	Dr.		150	
	To Provision for Workmen Compensation Claim A/c				150
	(Being the provision made for Workmen Compensation Claim)				
	Workmen Compensation Reserve A/c	Dr.		1,050	
	To X's Capital A/c				525
	To Y's Capital A/c				315
	To Z's Capital A/c				210
	(Being the transfer of surplus Workmen Compensation Reserve to Partners' Capital Account in their old profit sharing ratio)				
	Case III				
	Workmen Compensation Reserve A/c	Dr.		1,200	
	Revaluation A/c	Dr.		1,050	
	To Provision for Workmen Compensation Claim A/c				2,250
	(Being the provision created & short fall charged to Revaluation A/c)				
	X's Capital A/c	Dr.		525	
	Y's Capital A/c	Dr.		315	
	Z's Capital A/c	Dr.		210	
	To Revaluation A/c				1,050
	(Being the transfer of loss on revaluation to partners' capital accounts in their old profit sharing ratio)				

ILLUSTRATION 10 [TREATMENT OF INVESTMENT FLUCTUATION RESERVE]

X, Y and Z who are presently sharing profits & losses in the ratio of 5 : 3 : 2, decide to share future profits & losses in the ratio of 2 : 3 : 5 with effect from 1st April, 2012. An extract of their Balance Sheet as at 31st March, 2012 is as follows:

Particulars	₹
Investment Fluctuation Reserve	1,500
Investments (at cost)	20,000

Required: Show the accounting treatment in each of the following alternative cases:

Case I If there is no other information is given.

Case II If the market value of investments is ₹ 20,000.

Case III If the market value of investments is ₹ 19,000.

Case IV If the market value of investments is ₹ 18,000.

Case V If the market value of investments is ₹ 20,500.

SOLUTION

JOURNAL

Date	*Particulars*	*L.F.*	*Dr. (₹)*	*Cr. (₹)*
2012 April 1	**Case I** **1st Alternative** Assuming that the firm maintains Investment Fluctuation Reserve exactly equal to difference between the Cost & Market Price. No further entry is required. **2nd Alternative** Assuming that the market value of investment is ₹ 20,000.			
	Investment Fluctuation Reserve A/c Dr. To X's Capital A/c To Y's Capital A/c To Z's Capital A/c (Being the transfer of excess Investments Fluctuation Reserve to partners' capital accounts in their old profit sharing ratio)		1,500	 750 450 300
	Case II Same Solution as given in 2nd alternative of Case I			
	Case III Investment Fluctuation Reserve A/c Dr. To Investment A/c (Being the value of Investment brought upto market value)		 1,000	 1,000
	Investment Fluctuation Reserve A/c Dr. To X's Capital A/c To Y's Capital A/c To Z's Capital A/c		500	 250 150 100

	(Being the transfer of excess Investments Fluctuation Reserve to partners' capital accounts in their old profit sharing ratio)		
	Case IV		
	Investment Fluctuation Reserve A/c Dr.	1,500	
	Revaluation A/c Dr.	500	
	To Investment A/c		2,000
	(Being the value of investments brought down to market value)		
	X's Capital A/c Dr.	250	
	Y's Capital A/c Dr.	150	
	Z's Capital A/c Dr.	100	
	To Revaluation A/c		500
	(Being the transfer of loss on revaluation)		
	Case V		
	Investment Fluctuation Reserve A/c Dr.	1,500	
	To X's Capital A/c		750
	To Y's Capital A/c		450
	To Z's Capital A/c		300
	(Being the transfer of excess Investments Fluctuation Reserve to partners' capital accounts in their old profit sharing ratio)		
	Investment A/c Dr	500	
	To Revaluation A/c		500
	(Being the value of invsts. brought up to market value)		
	Revaluation A/c Dr.	500	
	To X's Capital A/c		250
	To Y's Capital A/c		150
	To Z's Capital A/c		100
	(Being the transfer of profit on revaluation)		

ILLUSTRATION 11

An Extract of Balance Sheet of X, Y and Z sharing profits and losses in the ratio of 5 : 3 : 2 respectively, on 31st March, 2012 is given below:

Particulars	₹
General Reserve	5,000
Contingencies Reserve	450
Profit and Loss Account	3,000
Investment Fluctuation Reserve	1,500
Machinery Replacement Fund	1,000
Workmen's Compensation Reserve	1,200

Employees' Provident Fund	2,000
Investment (Market Value ₹ 19,000)	20,000
Machinery Replacement Fund Investments	1,000
Advertisement Expenditure (Deferred Revenue)	1,000

With effect from April 1, 2012, they decided to share future profits & losses in the ratio of 2 : 3 : 5 respectively. A claim on account of workmen's compensation is estimated at ₹ 150 only.

Required: Give the necessary journal entries relating to the adjustment of accumulated profits and losses.

SOLUTION

JOURNAL

Date	*Particulars*		*L.F.*	*Dr. (₹)*	*Cr. (₹)*
2012	Workmen Compensation Reserve A/c	Dr.		150	
April, 1	To Provision for Workmen Compensation Claim A/c				150
	(Being the provision made for Workmen Compensation claim)				
	Workmen Compensation Reserve A/c	Dr.		1,050	
	To X's Capital A/c				525
	To Y's Capital A/c				315
	To Z's Capital A/c				210
	(Being the transfer of surplus Workmen Compensation Reserve to Partners' Capital Account in their old profit sharing ratio)				
	Investment Fluctuation Reserve A/c	Dr.		1,000	
	To Investment A/c				1,000
	(Being the value of Investment brought upto market value)				
	Investment Fluctuation Reserve A/c	Dr.		500	
	To X's Capital A/c				250
	To Y's Capital A/c				150
	To Z's Capital A/c				100
	(Being the transfer of excess Investments Fluctuation Reserve to partners' capital accounts in their old profit sharing ratio)				
	General Reserve	Dr.		5,000	
	Contigencies Reserve	Dr.		450	
	P & L A/c	Dr.		3,000	
	To A's Capital A/c				4,225
	To B's Capital A/c				2,535
	To C's Capital A/c				1,690
	(Being the transfer of accumulated profits to all the partners in their profit-sharing ratio)				

	A's Capital A/c	Dr.	500	
	B's Capital A/c	Dr.	300	
	C's Capital A/c	Dr.	200	
	To Advertisement Expenditure A/c			1,000
	(Being the transfer of accumulated loses to all the partners in their profit-sharing ratio)			

Working Notes:

1. Excess Investment Fluctuation Reserve Account has been transferred directly to partners' capital accounts. after providing for an anticipated loss of ₹ 1,000 (i.e. ₹ 20,000 – ₹ 19,000) according to Prudence (conservatism) concept.
2. Excess Workmen's Compensation Reserve Account has been transferred directly to partners' capital accounts.
3. Machinery Replacement Fund has not been transferred since it is in the nature of accumulated depreciation and not in nature of accumulated profits.
4. Employees' Provident Fund represents statutory liability due to employees towards Provident Fund and is not an Accumulated Profit and hence is not distributed among the partners.

7.0 ADJUSTMENTS OF ACCUMULATED PROFITS, LOSSES OR RESERVES THROUGH CAPITAL ACCOUNTS ONLY

HOW TO ADJUST ACCUMULATED PROFITS, LOSSES *or* RESERVES

When the partners decide to record the net effect of accumulated profits, losses *or* reserves without affecting the old figures of accumulated profits, losses *or* reserves, single adjusting entry involving the capital accounts of gaining partners and sacrificing partners is passed.

PRACTICAL STEPS TO PASS SINGLE ADJUSTING ENTRY

			₹
Step 1: ***Calculate the Net Effect of Accumulated Profits, Reserves & Losses***			
A. Accumulated Profits [e.g. P&L A/c (cr.)]			xxx
B. *Add:* Reserves [e.g. General Reserve, Contingency Reserve]			xxx
C. *Less:* Accumulated Losses			xxx
D. Net Effect			xxx
Step 2: ***Calculate Gain/Loss of Share***			
Their New Shares	x	x	x
Their Old Shares	x	x	x
Difference	x	x	x

Step 3: ***Calculate Share of Gaining Partner and Sacrificing Partner in the Net Accumulated Profits, Losses and Reserves.***

For Gaining Partner = Share gained × Net Effect.

For Sacrificing Partner = Share sacrificed × Net Effect.

Step 4: ***Pass the following Single Adjusting journal entry:***

In Case of Net Profit		In Case of Net Loss	
Gaining Partner's Capital A/c	Dr.	Sacrificing Partner's Capital A/c	Dr.
To Sacrificing Partner's Capital A/c		To Gaining Partner's Capital A/c	

Tutorial Note: *When Accumulated Profits, Reserves & Losses are adjusted through Capital Accounts only, then all Accumulated Profits, Reserves & Losses appear in the Balance Sheet of the new firm at their **old figures.***

ILLUSTRATION 12

X, Y and Z are sharing profits & losses in the ratio of 5 : 3 : 2. They decide to share future profits & losses in the ratio of 2 : 3 : 5 with effect from 1st April, 2012. They also decide to record the effect of the following accumulated profits, losses & reserves without affecting their book figures, by passing a single adjusting entry.

Particulars	*Book Figure*
General Reserve	₹ 30,000
Contigencies Reserve	₹ 5,000
Profit & Loss A/c (Cr.)	₹ 15,000
Advertisement Suspense A/c (Dr.)	₹ 20,000

Required: Pass the necessary single adjusting entry.

SOLUTION

STEP 1: CALCULATION OF NET EFFECT OF ACCUMULATED PROFITS/LOSSES *or* RESERVES

General reserve	₹ 30,000	
Contingencies Reserve	₹ 5,000	
Profit & Loss A/c	₹ 15,000	
Less: Advertisement Suspense A/c (Dr.)	(₹ 20,000)	₹ 30,000

STEP 2 ® CALCULATION OF GAIN/LOSS OF SHARE

Particulars	*X*	*Y*	*Z*
Their New Shares	2/10	3/10	5/10
Their Old Shares	5/10	3/10	2/10
Difference	(3/10)	–	3/10

STEP 3: CALCULATION OF SHARE OF SACRIFICING AND GAINING PARTNER IN THE NET ACCUMULATED PROFITS, LOSSES AND RESERVES

For X = 3/10 × ₹ 30,000 = ₹ 9,000, For Z = 3/10 × ₹ 30,000 = ₹ 9,000

STEP 4: ADJUSTING JOURNAL ENTRY

Date	*Particulars*	*L.F.*	*Dr. (₹)*	*Cr. (₹)*
	Z's Capital A/c Dr.		9,000	
	To X's Capital A/c			9,000
	(Being the adjustment made for net accumulated profits & reserves)			

8.0 ADJUSTMENT OF CAPITALS

The various steps involved in adjusting the capitals of partners according to new profit sharing ratio are given below:

PRACTICAL STEPS INVOLVED IN ADJUSTING THE CAPITALS OF PARTNERS

Step 1:* *Calculate the Adjusted Old Capitals of Partners (i.e., after all adjustments relating to goodwill, profit/loss on revaluation and accumulated profits/reserves/losses) by preparing their Capital Accounts.

Step 2:* *Calculate Total Capital of new firm (if not given in question) as under:

Total Capital = Aggregate of Adjusted Old Capitals of Partners.

Step 3:* *Calculate the New Capitals of partners as follows:

= Total Capital of New Firm × New Share

Step 4:* *Calculate the Shortage *or* ***(Surplus) in each of the Partner's Capital Account as follows:***

= New Capital – Adjusted Old Capital.

Step 5:* *Pass a Journal Entry to Adjust the Surplus by paying off *or* ***by transfer to the credit of his current account to and adjust the Shortage by asking the concerned partner to bring in the required amount*** *or* ***by transfer to the debit of his current account.***

Tutorial Note: *In the absence of any contract, Surplus or Shortage should be adjusted in Cash and not by transfer to Current Account.*

ILLUSTRATION 13

X, Y and Z are partners sharing profits and losses in the ratio of 5 : 3 : 2. they decide to share future profits & losses in the ratio of 2 : 3 : 5. Their capitals remaining after adjustments relating to goodwill, profit/loss on revaluation and accumulated profits, losses & reserves are ₹ 59,000, ₹ 30,000 and ₹ 11,000 respectively. They also decide that their capitals should also be in their new profit sharing ratio.

Required: Calculate the amount of actual cash to be paid off *or* brought in by the old partners for this adjustment and pass the necessary journal entries.

SOLUTION

Step 1: ***Calculation of Total Capital of the New Firm***

Total Capital = ₹ 59,000 + ₹ 30,000 + ₹ 11,000 = ₹ 1,00,000

Step 2 ® Calculation of New Capitals of all Partners

X	Y	Z
1,00,000 × 2/10 = 20,000,	1,00,000 × 3/10 = 30,000,	1,00,000 × 5/10 = 50,000

STEP 3: CALCULATION OF ACTUAL CASH TO BE PAID OFF OR BROUGHT IN BY OLD PARTNERS

Particulars	*X*	*Y*	*Z*
Their New Capitals	20,000	30,000	50,000
Their Adjusted New Capitals	59,000	30,000	11,000
	(39,000)	–	39,000

STEP 4: JOURNAL

Date	Particulars		L.F.	Dr. (₹)	Cr. (₹)
	Cash A/c	Dr.		39,000	
	To Z's Capital A/c				39,000
	(Being the shortage brought in by Z)				
	X's Capital A/c	Dr.		39,000	
	To Cash A/c				39,000
	(Being the excess amount withdrawn by X)				

COMPREHENSIVE ILLUSTRATION

ILLUSTRATION 14

X, Y and Z are partners in a firm sharing profits & losses in the ratio of 5 : 3 : 2. They decide to share future profits & losses in the ratio of 2 : 5 : 3 with effect from 1st April, 2012. Their Balance Sheet showed a debit balance of ₹ 4,000 in Profit & Loss Account and a balance of ₹ 24,000 in General Reserve. For this purpose, it was agreed that—

(a) the goodwill of the firm be valued at ₹ 30,000.

(b) the Land (having book value of ₹ 50,000) be valued at ₹ 80,000.

(c) the Stock (having book value of ₹ 50,000) be depreciated by 6%.

(d) Creditors amounting to ₹ 400 were not likely to be claimed.

(e) Unrecorded Investments to be valued at ₹ 22,600.

Required: Give the necessary single adjusting entry to record the above arrangement.

SOLUTION

STEP 1: CALCULATION OF GAIN/SACRIFICE OF SHARE

Particulars	X	Y	Z
Their Old Shares	5/10	3/10	2/10
Their New Shares	2/10	5/10	3/10
Difference	3/10	(2/10)	(1/10)
	Sacrificing Partner	*Gaining Partner*	*Gaining Partner*

STEP2 : CALCULATION OF NET EFFECT OF ADJUSTMENTS TO BE MADE

Particulars	₹
A. General Reserve	24,000
B. *Less:* Dr. Balance of P&L A/c	– 4,000
C. Value of Goodwill	30,000
D. Unrecorded Investments	22,600
E. Increase in Value of Land	30,000
F. Decrease in Value of Stock	– 3,000
G. Decrease in Creditors	400

H. Net Effect of Adjustment to be made	1,00,000

STEP 3: ADJUSTING JOURNAL ENTRY
JOURNAL

Date	*Particulars*		*L.F.*	*Dr. (₹)*	*Cr. (₹)*
	Y's Capital A/c [₹ 1,00,000 × 2/10]	Dr.		20,000	
	Z's Capital A/c [₹ 1,00,000 × 1/10]	Dr.		10,000	
	To X's Capital A/c [₹ 1,00,000 × 3/10]				30,000
	(Being the adjustment made on account of change in profit sharing ratio by debiting gaining partner and crediting sacrificing partners)				

COMPREHENSIVE REVISIONAL PROBLEMS

Objective: The following Illustrations have been given Only to Revise the Chapter. In Examination only some of the parts and not all the parts of such lengthy problems may be asked.

PROBLEM 1

X, Y and Z are partners in a firm sharing profit in the ratio of 2 : 2 : 1. Their Balance Sheet as at March 31, 2012 was as follows:

Particulars	₹
Creditors	30,000
Bills Payable	15,000
X's Capital	60,000
Y's Capital	30,000
Z's Capital	15,000
General Reserve	12,000
Land	30,000
Building	30,000
Plant	60,000
Stock	30,000
Debtors	9,000
Cash	3,000

X, Y and Z decided to share the profit equally, w.e.f. April 1, 2012. For this purpose it was agreed that:

(i) The goodwill of the firm should be valued at ₹ 18,000.

(ii) Land should be revalued at ₹ 48,000 and building should be depreciated by 6%.

(iii) Creditors amounting to ₹ 1,800 were not likely to be claimed and hence should be written off.

You are required to:—

(a) Record the necessary journal entries to give effect to the above agreement, without opening Revaluation Account;

(b) Prepare the Capital Accounts of the partners; and

(c) Prepare the Balance Sheet of the firm after reconstitution.

SOLUTION

JOURNAL

Date	Particulars		L.F.	Dr. (₹)	Cr. (₹)
01.04.2012	Z's Capital A/c	Dr.		2,400	
	To X's Capital A/c				1,200
	To Y's Capital A/c				1,200
	(Being the adjustment made for goodwill on change in profit sharing ratio)				
	Z's Capital A/c	Dr.		2,400	
	To X's Capital A/c				1,200
	To Y's Capital A/c				1,200
	(Being the adjustment made for profit on revaluation on change in the profit sharing ratio)				
	General Reserve A/c	Dr.		12,000	
	To X's Capital A/c				4,800
	To Y's Capital A/c				4,800
	To Z's Capital A/c				2,400
	(Being the transfer of General Reserve to partners' capital accounts on change in profit sharing ratio)				

Dr. **PARTNERS' CAPITAL ACCOUNTS** Cr.

Particulars	X ₹	Y ₹	Z ₹	Particulars	X ₹	Y ₹	Z ₹
To X's Capital A/c	–	–	1,200	By Balance b/d	60,000	30,000	15,000
To Y's Capital A/c	–	–	1,200	By Z's Capital A/c	1,200	1,200	–
To X's Capital A/c	–	–	1,200	By Z's Capital A/c	1,200	1,200	–
To Y's Capital A/c	–	–	1,200	By General Reserve	4,800	4,800	2,400
To Balance c/f	67,200	37,200	12,600				
	67,200	37,200	17,400		67,200	37,200	17,400

BALANCE SHEET OF X, Y AND Z AT 1.4. 2012

Liabilities	₹	Assets	₹
Creditors	30,000	Land	30,000
Bills Payable	15,000	Building	30,000
X's Capital	67,200	Plant	60,000
Y's Capital	37,200	Stock	30,000
Z's Capital	12,600	Debtors	9,000
		Cash	3,000
	1,62,000		1,62,000

PROBLEM 2

The Balance Sheet of A, B and C who are sharing profits in the ratio of 2:3:1, as at 31st March, 2012 is given below:

Particulars	₹
A's Capital	1,00,000
B's Capital	2,00,000
C's Capital	3,00,000
Workmen Compensation Reserve	20,000
Investment Fluctuation Reserve	10,000
Provision for Doubtful Debts	10,000
Sundry Creditors	3,00,000
Employees' Provident Fund	60,000
Goodwill	12,000
Land and Building	2,50,000
Investments [Market Value ₹ 46,000]	50,000
Stock	80,000
Debtors	3,00,000
Bank	2,96,000
Advertisement Suspense A/c	12,000
	10,00,000

A, B and C decide to alter their profits sharing ratio as 3 : 2 : 1 from 1st April, 2012.

1. Goodwill is to be valued at 2 years' purchase of average profits of last three completed years. The profits were - 2009-2010 ₹ 48,000, 2010-2011 ₹ 93,000, 2011-2012 ₹ 1,38,000.
2. Land & Building was found under valued by ₹ 20,000 and Stock was found overvalued by ₹ 38,000.
3. Provision for doubtful debts is to be made equal to 5% of the debtors.
4. Claim on account of workmen compensation is ₹ 8,000.
5. 10% of the sundry creditors be written back as no longer payable.
6. Out of the amount of insurance which was debited entirely to P&L A/c, ₹ 5,000 be carried forward as an unexpired insurance.

Required: Pass the necessary journal entries and prepare the necessary ledger accounts and the Balance Sheet.

SOLUTION

JOURNAL

Date	*Particulars*		*L.F.*	*Dr. (₹)*	*Cr. (₹)*
1	A's Capital A/c	Dr.		4,000	
	B's Capital A/c	Dr.		6,000	
	C's Capital A/c	Dr.		2,000	
	To Goodwill A/c				12,000
	(Being the existing goodwill w/o)				

2	A's Capital A/c	Dr.		31,000	
	To B's Capital A/c				31,000
	(Being the goodwill adjusted by debiting gaining partner and crediting sacrificing partner)				
3	Land & Building A/c	Dr.		20,000	
	Sundry Creditors	Dr.		30,000	
	Prepaid Insurance	Dr.		5,000	
	To Revaluation A/c				55,000
	(Being the increase in value of assets & decrease in Sundry Creditors recorded)				
4	Revaluation A/c	Dr.		43,000	
	To Stock A/c				38,000
	To Provision for Doubtful Debts A/c				5,000
	(Being the decrease in Value of assets & increase in provisions recorded)				
5	Revaluation A/c	Dr.		12,000	
	To A's Capital A/c				4,000
	To B's Capital A/c				6,000
	To C's Capital A/c				2,000
	(Being the transfer of profit on revaluation)				
6	Workmen Compensation Reserve A/c	Dr.		20,000	
	To Workmen Compensation Claim A/c				8,000
	To A's Capital A/c				4,000
	To B's Capital A/c				6,000
	To C's Capital A/c				2,000
	(Being the transfer of workmen compensation Reserve)				
7	Investment Fluctuation Fund A/c	Dr.		10,000	
	To Investment A/c				4,000
	To A's Capital A/c				2,000
	To B's Capital A/c				3,000
	To C's Capital A/c				1,000
	(Being the transfer of Investment Fluctuation Fund)				
8	A's Capital A/c	Dr.		4,000	
	B's Capital A/c	Dr.		6,000	
	C's Capital A/c	Dr.		2,000	
	To Advertisement Suspense A/c				12,000
	(Being the transfer of balance of Advertisement Suspense A/c)				

Ledger Accounts:

Dr. **1. REVALUATION ACCOUNT** Cr.

Particulars	₹	*Particulars*	₹
To Stock	38,000	By Land & Building	20,000
To Provision for Doubtful Debts	5,000	By Sundry Creditors	30,000
To Profit on Revaluation t/f to:		By Prepaid Insurance	5,000
A's Capital A/c	4,000		
B's Capital A/c	6,000		
C's Capital A/c	2,000		
	55,000		55,000

Dr. **2. PARTNERS' CAPITAL ACCOUNTS** Cr.

Particulars	*A* ₹	*B* ₹	*C* ₹	*Particulars*	*A* ₹	*B* ₹	*C* ₹
To Goodwill A/c	4,000	6,000	2,000	By Balance b/d	1,00,000	2,00,000	3,00,000
To B's Capital A/c	31,000	—	—	By A's Capital A/c	—	31,000	—
To Adv. Exp. Sus. A/c	4,000	6,000	2,000	By Revaluation A/c	4,000	6,000	2,000
To Balance c/d	71,000	2,34,000	3,01,000	By Work Com. Res.	4,000	6,000	2,000
				By Invest. Flus. Res.	2,000	3,000	1,000
	1,10,000	2,46,000	3,05,000		1,10,000	2,46,000	3,05,000

3. BALANCE SHEET AS AT 31ST MARCH, 2015

Liabilities	₹	*Assets*		₹
A's Capital	71,000	Land & Building		2,70,000
B's Capital	2,34,000	Investments		46,000
C's Capital	3,01,000	Stock		42,000
Sundry Creditors	2,70,000	Debtors	3,00,000	
Workmen Compensation Claim	8,000	*Less:* Provision	15,000	2,85,000
Employees' Provident Fund	60,000	Bank		2,96,000
		Prepaid Insurance		5,000
	9,44,000			9,44,000

Working Notes:

(I) CALCULATION OF GAIN/SACRIFICE OF SHARE

Particulars	*New Shares*	*Old Shares*	*Difference*
A.	3/6	2/6	3/6–2/6 = 1/6
B.	2/6	3/6	2/6–3/6 = –1/6
C.	1/6	1/6	—

(II) CALCULATION OF GOODWILL

A. Average Profits = $\frac{₹\ 48,000 + ₹\ 93,000 + ₹\ 1,38,000}{3}$ = ₹ 93,000

B. Firm's Goodwill = ₹ 93,000 × 2 = ₹ 1,86,000

A's Contribution = ₹ 1,86,000 × 1/6 = ₹ 31,000

B's Share = ₹ 1,86,000 × 1/6 = ₹ 31,000

17 RECONSTITUTION OF PARTNERSHIP — ADMISSION OF A PARTNER

LEARNING OBJECTIVES

After studying this chapter, you should be able to understand:

- ◇ Meaning of An Admission of a Partner
- ◇ How can a person be admitted as a Partner?
- ◇ Rights of a New Partner
- ◇ Adjustments required at the time of Admission of a New Partner
- ◇ Why is New Ratio determined even for Old Partners?
- ◇ Meaning of New Profit Sharing Ratio
- ◇ Meaning of Sacrificing Ratio
- ◇ Adjustment of Goodwill
- ◇ Adjustment of Profit/Loss on Revaluation of Assets and Liabilities
- ◇ Adjustment of Reserves and Accumulated Profits/Losses
- ◇ Adjustment of Capitals

1.0 AN ADMISSION OF A PARTNER

Meaning	Admission of a partner is one of the modes of reconstituting the firm under which old partnership comes to an end and a new one between all partners (including incoming partner) comes into existence.
How can be Admitted	According to the Sec 31(1) of Indian Partnership Act, 1932, a person can be admitted as a new partner only with the consent of all the existing partners unless otherwise agreed upon.
Two Main Rights of a New Partner	A new partner acquires two main rights in the firm — 1. Right to share the assets of the firm; 2. Right to share the future profits of the firm.
Why a New Partner brings in Capital	A New Partner brings in the agreed amount of Capital to acquire the right to share the Assets of the firm.
Why a New Partner brings in Goodwill	A New Partner brings in his share of Goodwill (also called Premium) to acquire the Right to share the future profits of the firm.
Adjustments Required	The various matters that need adjustment at the time of admission of a new partner are as follows: 1. Adjustment in Profit Sharing Ratio, 2. Adjustment of Goodwill, 3. Adjustment of Profit/Loss arising from the Revaluation of Assets & Liabilities, 4. Adjustment of Accumulated Profits, Reserves and Losses, 5. Adjustment of Capitals (if agreed).

2.0 NEW PROFIT SHARING RATIO AND SACRIFICING RATIO

Why to determine new ratio even for old partners?	When a new partner is admitted, he acquires his share in profits from the old partners. This reduces the old partners' shares in profits hence, profit sharing ratio for old partners have to be calculated.
New Profit Sharing Ratio	The ratio in which all partners (including incoming partner) share the future profits and losses is known as the new profit sharing ratio. The determination of new profit sharing ratio depends upon the ratio in which the incoming partner acquires his share from the old partners. An incoming partner may acquire his share: (a) from the old partners in their old profit sharing ratio; (b) from the old partners in some agreed ratio (other than old profit sharing ratio); (c) from one *or* more of old partners (but not from all partners). **Tutorial Note:** *Unless agreed otherwise, it is presumed that the new partner acquires his share in profits from the old partners in their old profit sharing ratio and the old partners continue to share the remaining profit in the old ratio and hence the New Profit Sharing Ratio of Old Partners will be the same as their Old Profit Sharing Ratio.*
Sacrificing Ratio	The ratio in which the old partners have agreed to sacrifice their shares in profit in favour of a new partner is called the sacrificing ratio. This ratio is calculated by taking out the difference between Old Profit Share and the New Profit Share. **Tutorial Note:** *Unless agreed otherwise it is presumed that the old partners sacrifice in their old profit sharing ratio and hence, Sacrificing Ratio of Old Partners will be the same as their Old Profit Sharing Ratio.*

DIFFERENCE BETWEEN '1/3RD OF SHARE' AND '1/3RD FROM SHARE

There exists difference between 'B surrenders 1/3rd of his share' and 'B surrenders 1/3rd from his share'. If B's share is 2/5th, it means in the former case he has surrendered 2/15th [i.e. (1/3) × (2/5)] share and B's New Share is 4/15 [i.e. (2/5) – (2/15)], in the latter case, he has surrendered 1/3rd share and B's New Share is 1/15 [i.e. (2/5) – (1/3)].

ILLUSTRATION 1

X and Y are partners in a firm sharing profits and losses in the ratio of 3 : 2. Z is admitted as partner with 1/5 share in the profits. Calculate the new profit sharing ratio and the sacrificing ratio.

SOLUTION

(a) Let the Total Share be = 1

(b) Share of Incoming Partner = 1/5

(c) Remaining Share [(a) – (b)] = 1 –1/5 = 4/5

(d) Existing Partners' shares are calculated by dividing the remaining share in their future profit sharing ratio (which in this case is old ratio since nothing is given as to how Z gets his share from X and Y) as under:

X's New Share = 3/5 of 4/5 = 12/25;

Y's New Share = 2/5 of 4/5 = 8/25.

(e) New Ratio of X, Y & Z = 12/25 : 8/25 : 5/25 = 12 : 8 : 5.

The sacrificing ratio is the same as the old ratio 3 : 2 on the presumption that the existing partners make sacrifice in their old profit sharing ratio.

ILLUSTRATION 2

X and Y are partners sharing profits and losses in the ratio of 7 : 5. They admit Z, a new partner, who acquires his share as 1/12th from X and 1/8th from Y. Calculate the new profit sharing ratio and the sacrificing ratio.

SOLUTION

New Share of Old Partner = Old Share – Share acquired by Incoming partner

X's New Share = 7/12 – 1/12 = 6/12

Y's New Share = 5/12 – 1/8 = 7/24

Share of Incoming Partner = 1/12 + 1/8 = 5/24

New Ratio of X, Y & Z = 12/24 : 7/24 : 5/24 = 12 : 7 : 5

Sacrificing Ratio = Share acquired from one existing partner: Share acquired from another existing partner

= 1/12 : 1/8 = 2 : 3

ILLUSTRATION 3

X and Y are partners in a firm sharing profits and losses in the ratio of 3 : 2. Z is admitted as partner with 1/4 share in profits. Z acquires his share from X and Y in the ratio of 2 : 1. Calculate the new profit sharing ratio.

SOLUTION

New Share of Old Partner = Old Share – Share acquired by Incoming Partner

Share acquired by Z from X = $\frac{2}{3} \times \frac{1}{4} = \frac{2}{12}$

Share acquired by Z from Y = $\frac{1}{3} \times \frac{1}{4} = \frac{1}{12}$ Z's Share = $\frac{2}{12} + \frac{1}{12} = \frac{3}{12}$

X's New Share = $\frac{3}{5} - \frac{2}{12} = \frac{26}{60}$ Y's New Share = $\frac{2}{5} - \frac{1}{12} = \frac{19}{60}$

New Ratio of X, Y & Z = 26/60 : 19/60 : 15/60 = 26 : 19 : 15

ILLUSTRATION 4

X and Y are partners sharing profits and losses in the ratio of 7 : 3. X surrenders 1/7th of his share and Y surrenders 1/3rd of his share in favour of Z, a new partner. Calculate the new profit sharing ratio and the sacrificing ratio.

SOLUTION

New Share of Old Partner = Old Share – Share surrendered by Old Partners

Share surrndered by X = $\frac{1}{7} \times \frac{7}{10} = \frac{1}{10}$

Share surrndered by Y = $\frac{1}{3} \times \frac{3}{10} = \frac{1}{10}$,

X's New Share = $\frac{7}{10} - \frac{1}{10} = \frac{6}{10}$,

Y's New Share $= \frac{3}{10} - \frac{1}{10} = \frac{2}{10}$

Z's Share $= \frac{1}{10} + \frac{1}{10} = \frac{2}{10}$

New Ratio of X, Y and Z $= \frac{6}{10} : \frac{2}{10} : \frac{2}{10} = 3 : 1 : 1$

Sacrificing Ratio of X & Y = Share surrendered by one existing partner: Share surrendered by another existing partner.

$= \frac{1}{10} : \frac{1}{10} = 1 : 1$

ILLUSTRATION 5

X and Y are partners sharing profits and losses in the ratio of 7 : 3. X surrenders 1/7th from his share and Y surrenders 1/3rd of his share in favour of Z, a new partner. Calculate the new profit sharing ratio and the sacrificing ratio.

SOLUTION

New Share of Old Partner = Old Share – Share surrendered by Old Partners

Share surrendered by X = 1/7,

Share surrendered by Y $= \frac{1}{3} \times \frac{3}{10} = \frac{1}{10}$

X's New Share $= \frac{7}{10} - \frac{1}{7} = \frac{39}{70}$

Y's New Share $= \frac{3}{10} - \frac{1}{10} = \frac{2}{10}$

Z's Share $= \frac{1}{7} + \frac{1}{10} = \frac{17}{70}$

New Ratio of X, Y & Z $= \frac{39}{70} : \frac{14}{70} : \frac{17}{70} = 39 : 14 : 17$

Sacrificing Ratio $= \frac{1}{7} : \frac{1}{10} = 10 : 7$

ILLUSTRATION 6

X and Y are partners sharing profits and losses in the ratio of 4 : 3. Z joins the firm as a new partner. The new profit sharing ratio of X, Y & Z is agreed at 7 : 4 : 3 respectively. Calculate the sacrificing ratio and the share of incoming partner.

SOLUTION

Share Sacrificed = Old Share – New Share

X's Sacrifice $= \frac{4}{7} - \frac{7}{14} = \frac{1}{14}$,

Y's Sacrifice $= \frac{3}{7} - \frac{4}{14} = \frac{2}{14}$

Sacrificing Ratio of X and Y $= \frac{1}{14} : \frac{2}{14} = 1 : 2$,

Share of Z $= \frac{1}{14} + \frac{2}{14} = \frac{3}{14}$

ILLUSTRATION 7

X and Y are partners in a firm sharing profits and losses in the ratio of 3 : 2. Z is admitted as partner with 1/8th share in profits. It is decided that X and Y will share profits and losses in future in the ratio of 4 : 3. Calculate the new profit sharing ratio and the sacrificing ratio.

SOLUTION

Let the Total Share be = 1, Share of Incoming Partner = 1/8

Remaining Share = $1-\frac{1}{8}=\frac{7}{8}$

Existing Partners' New shares are calculated by dividing the remaining share in their future profits sharing ratio (i.e. 4 : 3) as under:

X's New Share = $\frac{4}{7}\times\frac{7}{8}=\frac{28}{56}$;

Y's New Share = $\frac{3}{7}\times\frac{7}{8}=\frac{21}{56}$

New Ratio of X, Y & Z = $\frac{28}{56}:\frac{21}{56}:\frac{7}{56}$ = 28 : 21 : 7 = 4 : 3 : 1

Calculation of Sacrificing Ratio

Share Sacrificed = Old Share – New Share

X's Sacrifice = $\frac{3}{5}-\frac{4}{8}=\frac{4}{40}$;

Y's Sacrifice = $\frac{2}{5}-\frac{3}{8}=\frac{1}{40}$

Sacrificing Ratio of X and Y = $\frac{4}{40}:\frac{1}{40}$ = 4 : 1

ILLUSTRATION 8

X, Y and Z are partners in the ratio of 3 : 2 : 1. W is admitted with 1/6 share in profits. Z would retain his original share. Find out new profit sharing ratio.

SOLUTION

Let the total share be = 1

Share of Z and W = $\frac{1}{6}+\frac{1}{6}=\frac{1}{3}$

Remaining Share = $1-\frac{1}{3}=\frac{2}{3}$

New Shares of X and Y are calculated by dividing the remaining share in their future profit sharing ratio (which in this case is old ratio since nothing is given as to how W gets his share from X and Y) as under:

X's New Share = $\frac{3}{5}\times\frac{2}{3}=\frac{6}{15}$,

Y's New Share = $\frac{2}{5}\times\frac{2}{3}=\frac{4}{15}$

New Ratio of X, Y, Z and W = $\frac{6}{15}:\frac{4}{15}:\frac{1}{6}:\frac{1}{6}$ = 12 : 8 : 5 : 5

ILLUSTRATION 9

X and Y are partners sharing profits and losses in the ratio of 3 : 2. Z is admitted for 1/4th share. Thereafter W enters for 20 paise in the rupee. Compute the profit sharing ratio of X, Y, Z and W after W's admission.

SOLUTION

Calculation of New Ratio after Z's admission

Let the Total Share be = 1,

Share of Z = 1/4

Remaining Share = $1 - \frac{1}{4} = \frac{3}{4}$

X's New Share = $\frac{3}{5} \times \frac{3}{4} = \frac{9}{20}$

Y's New Share = $\frac{2}{5} \times \frac{3}{4} = \frac{6}{20}$

New Ratio of X, Y and Z = $\frac{9}{20} : \frac{6}{20} : \frac{5}{20}$ = 9 : 6 : 5.

Calculation of New Ratio after W's admission

Let the Total Share be = 1

W's Share = 1/5

Remaining Share = $1 - \frac{1}{5} = \frac{4}{5}$

X's New Share = $\frac{9}{20} \times \frac{4}{5} = \frac{36}{100}$

Y's New Share = $\frac{6}{20} \times \frac{4}{5} = \frac{24}{100}$

Z's New Share = $\frac{5}{20} \times \frac{4}{5} = \frac{20}{100}$

Share of W = 20/100

New ratio of X, Y, Z & W = 36 : 24 : 20 : 20 = 9 : 6 : 5 : 5.

ILLUSTRATION 10

A and B are partners sharing profits in the ratio of 2 : 1. They admit C into partnership and the profit sharing ratio of the three partners is agreed at 2 : 2 : 1 respectively. Calculate the gain *or* sacrifice of the partners.

SOLUTION

Particulars	*A*	*B*
(a)Their Old Shares	2/3	1/3
(b)Their New Shares	2/5	2/5
(c)Difference [(a) – (b)]	4/15	(1/15)

A has sacrificed 4/15 out of his share of which B gets 1/15 and C gets 1/5.

ILLUSTRATION 11

A and B are partners sharing profits in the ratio of 3:2. They admit C for 1/5th share in the profit. C acquires 1/5th of his share from A. Calculate the new profit sharing ratio and sacrificing ratio.

SOLUTION

Share acquired by C: from A $= \frac{1}{5} \times \frac{1}{5} = \frac{1}{25}$, **from B** $= \frac{4}{5} \times \frac{1}{5} = \frac{4}{25}$

A's New Share $= \frac{3}{5} - \frac{1}{25} = \frac{14}{25}$ B's New Share $= \frac{2}{5} - \frac{4}{25} = \frac{6}{25}$

New Profit Sharing Ratio of A, B and C = 14/25 : 6/25 : 5/25 = 14 : 6 : 5

Sacrificing Ratio of A and B = 1/25 : 4/25 = 1 : 4

ILLUSTRATION 12

A and B are partners sharing profits in the ratio of 3 : 2. They admit C, a new partner who acquires 1/5th of his share from A and 4/25th share from B. Calculate the new profit sharing ratio and sacrificing ratio.

SOLUTION

Step 1: Calculation of Share of Incoming Partner

Since C acquires 1/5th of his share from A, it means he acquires 4/5th (i.e. 1–1/5th) of his share from B.

If 4/5th shares = 4/25

1 share = $\frac{4}{25} \times \frac{5}{4} = \frac{1}{5}$

Step 2: Calculation of New Shares

Share acquired by C : from A $= \frac{1}{5} \times \frac{1}{5} = \frac{1}{25}$, **from B** = 4/25

A's New Share $= \frac{3}{5} - \frac{1}{25} = \frac{14}{25}$, B's New Share $= \frac{2}{5} - \frac{4}{25} = \frac{6}{25}$

Step 3: New Profit Sharing Ratio of A, B and C $= \frac{14}{25} : \frac{6}{25} : \frac{5}{25} = 14 : 6 : 5$

Step 4: Sacrificing Ratio of A and B $= \frac{1}{25} : \frac{4}{25} = 1 : 4$

ILLUSTRATION 13

X and Y share profits and losses in the ratio of 5 : 3. Z is admitted for 3/10th share of profits half of which was gifted by X and the remaining share was taken by Z equally from X and Y. Calculate the new profit sharing ratio.

SOLUTION

Share gifted by X $= \frac{1}{2} \times \frac{3}{10} = \frac{3}{20}$

Share acquired by Z : from X $= \frac{1}{2} \times \frac{3}{20} = \frac{3}{40}$, **from Y** =

X's New Share $= \frac{5}{8} - \frac{3}{20} - \frac{3}{40} = \frac{16}{40}$ Y's New Share $= \frac{3}{8} - \frac{3}{40} = \frac{12}{40}$

New Ratio of X, Y & Z = $\frac{16}{40} : \frac{12}{40} : \frac{12}{40}$ = 16 : 12 : 12 = 4 : 3 : 3

ILLUSTRATION 14

X and Y are sharing profits and losses in the ratio of 5 : 3. They admit Z and decide that the profit sharing ratio between Y and Z shall be the same as existing between X and Y. Calculate the new profit sharing ratio and the sacrificing ratio.

SOLUTION

As the Ratio of X and Y is 5 : 3, Ratio of Y and Z should be 5 : 3. Since Y's share is 60% of X's share, Z's share should also be 60% of Y's share. Thus, Z's share is 60% of 3 = 1.8 New Ratio of X, Y & Z = 5 : 3 : 1.8 *or* 25 : 15 : 9

Calculation of Sacrificing Ratio

Share Sacrificed = Old Share – New Share

X's Sacrifice $= \frac{5}{8} - \frac{25}{49} = \frac{45}{392}$, Y's Sacrifice $= \frac{3}{8} - \frac{15}{49} = \frac{27}{392}$

Sacrificing Ratio of X & Y $= \frac{45}{392} : \frac{27}{392} = 5 : 3$

3.0 ADJUSTMENT OF GOODWILL

Why is Adjustment of Goodwill required?	Whenever there is admission of a new partner the gaining partner (i.e., the partner whose share has increased as a result of change) must compensate the sacrificing partner (i.e., the partner whose share has decreased as a result of change). The new partner who gains by acquiring a right to share future profits must compensate the partner *or* partners who has *or* have made the sacrifice.
Amount of Compensation	The amount of compensation must be equal to the proportionate value of firm's goodwill. Thus, Amount of Compensation = Value of Firm's Goodwill × Share of Profit Sacrificed ***For Example***, Z, a new partner acquires his 1/5th share of profits from X, an existing partner and the present value of firm's goodwill is ₹ 50,000. In this case, Z is required to pay 1/5th of ₹ 50,000, i.e. ₹ 10,000 to X.
Recommendation of AS 26	1. Internally generated goodwill should not be recognized as an asset because it is not an identifiable resource controlled by the enterprise that can be measured reliably at cost. 2. Hence, **when the goodwill is evaluated at the time of any change in the constitution of the firm** (by way of admission/ retirement/death/change in profit sharing ratio), the value of such goodwill should not be raised in the books of the firm. Rather the **value of such goodwill should be adjusted through concerned partners' capital accounts.**

4.0 ACCOUNTING TREATMENT OF GOODWILL UNDER DIFFERENT SITUATIONS

SITUATION–I : WHEN THE INCOMING PARTNER PAYS HIS SHARE OF FIRM'S GOODWILL PRIVATELY

When the incoming partner pays his share of goodwill privately to the sacrificing partner(s) outside the business, no entry is passed in the books of the firm.

ILLUSTRATION 15

X and Y are partners in a firm sharing profits and losses in the ratio of 3 : 2. They admit Z as a partner for 1/5th share. Z paid ₹ 5,000 privately to X and Y as his share of goodwill. What should be the journal entry in the books of the firm?

SOLUTION

No journal entry will be passed in the books of the firm since Z has paid his share of goodwill to X and Y privately outside the firm.

SITUATION–II : WHEN THE INCOMING PARTNER BRINGS IN HIS SHARE OF FIRM'S GOODWILL IN CASH

When the incoming partner brings in his share of firm's goodwill in cash, the following simplified approach is suggested:

Step 1: Write off the Existing Book Value of Goodwill (if any) appearing in the books of the firm.		
Old Partners' Capital A/cs	Dr.	[In Old Ratio]
To Goodwill A/c		
(Being the existing goodwill written off in old ratio)		
Step 2: Record the Amount brought in by Incoming Partner		
Cash A/c/Bank A/c	Dr.	[With Capital & Share of Goodwill]
To Incoming Partner's Capital A/c		[With Capital]
To Premium for Goodwill A/c		[With Share of Goodwill brought in]
(Being the amount brought in by incoming partner)		
Step 3: Give Credit for Incoming Partner's Share of Goodwill to Sacrificing Partners.		
Premium for Goodwill A/c	Dr.	[With Share of Goodwill]
To Sacrificing Partners' Capital A/cs		[In Sacrificing Ratio]
(Being the share of incoming partner in firm's goodwill credited to sacrificing partners in their sacrificing ratio)		
Step 4: Record the Withdrawal (if any) of amount of goodwill by the Sacrificing Partner(s).		
Sacrificing Partners' Capital A/cs	Dr.	[To the extent of Withdrawal]
To Cash A/c/Bank A/c		
[Being the Goodwill amount withdrawn by Sacrificing Partner(s)]		

Tutorial Note: *Unless otherwise stated, the Partners' Capitals should be assumed to be fluctuating. Current Accounts are to be used in case of Fixed Capitals.*

ILLUSTRATION 16

A and B are partners sharing profits and losses in the ratio of 3 : 2. They admit C into partnership for 1/4th share. C brings in his requisite share of firm's goodwill in cash and ₹ 10,000 for capital. The goodwill of the firm is valued at ₹ 4,000. Goodwill already appears in the books at ₹ 500. Partners withdrew their share of goodwill. Give the necessary journal entries.

SOLUTION

JOURNAL

Date	Particulars		L.F.	Dr. (₹)	Cr. (₹)
	A's Capital A/c [₹ 500 × 3/5]	Dr.		300	
	B's Capital A/c [₹ 500 × 2/5]	Dr.		200	
	To Goodwill A/c				500
	(Being the existing value of goodwill w/o old ratio)				
	Cash A/c [10,000 + 1,000]	Dr.		11,000	
	To C's Capital A/c				10,000
	To Premium for Goodwill A/c				1,000
	(Being the amount brought in by C)				
	Premium for Goodwill A/c [₹ 4,000 × 1/4]	Dr.		1,000	
	To A's Capital A/c [₹ 1,000 × 3/5]				600
	To B's Capital A/c [₹ 1,000 × 2/5]				400
	(Being the goodwill credited to sacrificing partners in their sacrificing ratio)				
	A's Capital A/c	Dr.		600	
	B's Capital A/c	Dr.		400	
	To Cash A/c				1,000
	(Being the goodwill credited to sacrificing partners withdrawn by them)				

Note: Unless otherwise stated, Sacrificing Ratio is the same as Old Profit Sharing Ratio.

ILLUSTRATION 17

A and B are partners sharing profits in the ratio of 3 : 2. C is admitted paying a premium for 1/4th share of profit of which he acquires 1/6th from A and 1/12th from B. Goodwill of the firm is valued at ₹ 8,400. Goodwill already appears in the books at ₹ 5,000. Partners withdrew 50% of goodwill credited to them. Give the necessary journal entries.

SOLUTION

JOURNAL

Date	Particulars		L.F.	Dr. (₹)	Cr. (₹)
	A's Capital A/c [₹ 5,000 × 3/5]	Dr.		3,000	
	B's Capital A/c [₹ 5,000 × 2/5]	Dr.		2,000	
	To Goodwill A/c				5,000
	(Being the existing value of goodwill w/o in old ratio)				
	Cash A/c [₹ 8,400 × 1/4]	Dr.		2,100	
	To Premium for Goodwill A/c				2,100
	(Being the amount of goodwill brought in by C)				

	Premium for Goodwill A/c Dr.		2,100	
	To A's Capital A/c [₹ 2,100 × 2/3]			1,400
	To B's Capital A/c [₹ 2,100 × 1/3]			700
	(Being the goodwill credited to sacrificing partners in their sacrificing ratio of 2 : 1)			
	A's Capital A/c [₹ 1,400 × 1/2] Dr.		700	
	B's Capital A/c [₹ 700 × 1/2] Dr.		350	
	To Cash A/c [₹ 100 × 1/2]			1,050
	(Being 50% of goodwill credited to partners withdrawn by them)			

ILLUSTRATION 18

A and B are partners sharing profits and losses in the ratio of 3 : 2 respectively. They admit C paying premium for 1/4th share while A and B as between them sharing profits and losses equally. Goodwill already appears at ₹ 5,000. Partners withdrew half of the goodwill. Goodwill of the firm is valued at ₹ 4,000. Give the necessary journal entries.

SOLUTION

JOURNAL

Date	*Particulars*	*L.F.*	*Dr. (₹)*	*Cr. (₹)*
	A's Capital A/c [₹ 5,000 × 3/5] Dr.		3,000	
	B's Capital A/c [₹ 5,000 × 2/5] Dr.		2,000	
	To Goodwill A/c			5,000
	(Being the existing value of goodwill w/o in old ratio)			
	Cash A/c [₹ 4,000 × 1/4] Dr.		1,000	
	To Premium for Goodwill A/c			1,000
	(Being the amount of goodwill brought in by C)			
	Premimum for Goodwill A/c Dr.		1,000	
	To A's Capital A/c [₹ 1,000 × 9/10]			900
	To B's Capital A/c [₹ 1,000 × 1/10]			100
	(Being the goodwill credited to sacrificing partners in their sacrificing ratio of 9 : 1)			
	A's Capital A/c [₹ 900 × 1/2] Dr.		450	
	B's Capital A/c [₹ 100 × 1/2] Dr.		50	
	To Cash A/c [₹ 1,000 × 1/2]			500
	(Being 50% goodwill credited to sacrificing partners withdrawn by them)			

Working Note: *Calculation of Sacrificing Ratio*

Let Total Share = 1, Remaining Share for A & B = 1 – 1/4 = 3/4

A's New share = 3/4 × 1/2 = 3/8, B's New Share = 3/4 × 1/2 = 3/8

A's Sacrifice = 3/5 – 3/8 = 9/40, B's Sacrifies = 2/5 – 3/8 = 1/40

Hence, Sacrificing Ratio of A and B = 9 : 1

ILLUSTRATION 19

A and B are in partnership sharing profits and losses in the ratio of 5 : 3. C is admitted as a partner paying ₹ 40,000 as capital and the necessary amount of goodwill which is valued at ₹ 60,000 for the firm. Goodwill already appears in the books at ₹ 8,000. Partners withdrew half of goodwill. His share of profit is 1/5th of which he takes 1/10th from A and 1/10th from B. The profit for the first year of new partnership amounts to ₹ 24,000. Pass the necessary journal entries to adjust goodwill and to distribute profits.

SOLUTION

JOURNAL

Date	*Particulars*		*L.F.*	*Dr. (₹)*	*Cr. (₹)*
	A's Capital A/c [₹ 8,000 × 5/8]	Dr.		5,000	
	B's Capital A/c [₹ 8,000 × 3/8]	Dr.		3,000	
	To Goodwill A/c				8,000
	(Being the existing goodwill written off in old ratio)				
	Cash A/c [₹ 40,000 + (₹ 60,000 + 1/5)]	Dr.		52,000	
	To C's Capital A/c				40,000
	To Premium for Goodwill A/c				12,000
	(Being the amount of goodwill & capital brought in by C)				
	Premium for Goodwill A/c [₹ 60,000 × 1/5]	Dr.		12,000	
	To A's Capital A/c [₹ 12,000 × 1/2]				6,000
	To B's Capital A/c [₹ 12,000 × 1/2]				6,000
	(Being the goodwill credited to sacrificing partners in their sacrificing ratio of 1 : 1)				
	A's Capital A/c [₹ 6,000 × 1/2]	Dr.		3,000	
	B's Capital A/c [₹ 6,000 × 1/2]	Dr.		3,000	
	To Cash A/c [₹ 12,000 × 1/2]				6,000
	(Being 50% of goodwill credited to sacrificing partners withdrawn by them)				
	Profit & Loss A/c	Dr.		24,000	
	To A's Capital A/c [₹ 24,000 × 21/40]				12,600
	To B's Capital A/c [₹ 24,000 × 11/40]				6,600
	To C's Capital A/c [₹ 24,000 × 8/40]				4,800
	(Being the profit credited to all partners in their new profit sharing ratio of 21 : 11 : 8)				

Working Note: *Calculation of New Ratio*

A's New Share = 5/8 – 1/10 = 21/40, B's New Share = 3/8 – 1/10 = 11/40

Hence, New Ratio of A, B and C = 21/40 : 11/40 : 8/40 = 21 : 11 : 8

ILLUSTRATION 20

B and C are in partnership sharing profits and losses in the ratio of 3 : 1. They admit D for one third share of the profits. D brings ₹ 15,000 in cash for his share of goodwill. As between themselves, B and C agree to share future profits and losses equally. The amount of goodwill brought in cash is withdrawn by the concerned partners to the extent of 40% of what is credited to them. Draft Journal entries showing the appropriation of the premium money.

SOLUTION

JOURNAL

Date	*Particulars*	*L.F.*	*Dr. (₹)*	*Cr. (₹)*
	Cash A/c Dr. To Premium for Goodwill A/c (Being the amount brought in by D towards goodwill)		15,000	15,000
	Premium for Goodwill A/c Dr. To B's Capital A/c (Being the goodwill credited to sacrificing partner)		15,000	15,000
	C's Capital A/c [₹ 45,000 × 1/12] Dr. To B's Capital A/c (Being the adjustment made on account of change in profit sharing ratio. B loses 1/12th of profit and hence C compensates B for this loss in share of profit thus, 1/12th of ₹ 45,000, ₹ 3,750)		3,750	3,750
	B's Capital A/c [₹ 18,750 × 40/100] Dr. To Cash A/c (Being 40% of goodwill credited to sacrificing partner withdrawn by him)		7,500	7,500

Working Notes:

1. **Firm's Goodwill** = ₹ 15,000 × 3/1 = ₹ 45,000.
2. **Sacrificing Ratio**
   Let Total Share = 1, Remaining Share = 1 – 1/3 = 2/3
   B's New Share = 2/3 × 1/2 = 1/3, C's New Share = 2/3 × 1/2 = 1/3
   B's Sacrifice = 3/4 – 1/3 = 5/12, C's Gain = 1/4 – 1/3 = (1/12)

ILLUSTRATION 21

A, B and C are partners sharing profits and losses in the ratio of 3 : 2 : 1. D is admitted. The new profit sharing ratio between A, B, C and D will be 3 : 3 : 2 : 2. Goodwill of the firm is valued at ₹ 3,00,000. Goodwill already appears in the books at ₹ 6,000. D brings his share of firm's goodwill in cash. The amount of goodwill is withdrawn by the concerned partners to the extent of 30% of what is credited to them. Give the journal entries relating to adjustment of goodwill.

SOLUTION

JOURNAL

Date	*Particulars*	*L.F.*	*Dr. (₹)*	*Cr. (₹)*
	A's Capital A/c [₹ 6,000 × 3/6] Dr. B's Capital A/c [₹ 6,000 × 2/6] Dr.		3,000 2,000	

	C's Capital A/c [₹ 6,000 × 1/6] Dr.		1,000	
	To Goodwill A/c			6,000
	(Being the existing value of goodwill w/o in old ratio)			
	Cash A/c [₹ 3,00,000 × 2/10] Dr.		60,000	
	To Premium for Goodwill A/c			60,000
	(Being the amount of goodwill brought in by D)			
	C's Capital A/c [₹ 3,00,000 × 1/30] Dr.		10,000	
	Premium for Goodwill A/c [₹ 3,00,000 × 2/10] Dr.		60,000	
	To A's Capital A/c [₹ 3,00,000 × 2/10]			60,000
	To B's Capital A/c [₹ 3,00,000 × 1/30]			10,000
	(Being the adjustment for goodwill made on account of change in profit sharing ratio which resulted in loss of 6/30th to A and 1/30th to B and gain of 1/30th to C and 2/10th to D)			
	A's Capital A/c [₹ 60,000 × 30/100] Dr.		18,000	
	B's Capital A/c [₹ 10,000 × 30/100] Dr.		3,000	
	To Cash A/c [₹ 70,000 × 30/100]			21,000
	(Being the 30% of goodwill credited to sacrificing partner withdrawn by them)			

Working Note: *Calulation of Sacrificing Ratio*

A's Sacrifice = 3/10 – 3/6 = 6/30,

B's Sacrifice = 3/10 – 2/6 = 1/30

C's Gain = 1/6 – 2/10 = (1/30)

ILLUSTRATION 22

X and Y share profits & losses in the ratio of 5 : 3. Z is admitted for 3/10th share of profits half of which was gifted by X and the remaining share was taken by Z equally from X and Y. The goodwill of the firm is valued at ₹ 21,600. Z brings in his requisite share of firm's goodwill. The profit for the first year of new partnership amounts to ₹ 24,000. Pass the necessary journal entries to adjust goodwill and to distribute profits.

SOLUTION

JOURNAL

Date	Particulars	L.F.	Dr. (₹)	Cr. (₹)
	Cash A/c [₹ 21,600 × 3/20] Dr.		3,240	
	To Premium for Goodwill			3,240
	(Being the amount of goodwill brought in by Z for purchased share of profit i.e. 3/20)			
	Premium for Goodwill A/c Dr.		3,240	
	To X's Capital A/c [₹ 3,240 × 1/2]			1,620
	To Y's Capital A/c [₹ 3,240 × 1/2]			1,620
	(Being the goodwill credited to sacrificing partners in their sacrificing ratio of 1:1)			

	Profit and Loss A/c Dr.		24,000	
	To X's Capital A/c [₹ 24,000 × 4/10]			9,600
	To Y's Capital A/c [₹ 24,000 × 3/10]			7,200
	To Z's Capital A/c [₹ 24,000 × 3/10]			7,200
	(Being the profit credited to all partners in their new profit sharing ratio of 4 : 3 : 3)			

Working Note:

Calculation of New Profit Sharing Ratio-(Refer to Illustration 13).

SITUATION–III : WHEN THE INCOMING PARTNER BRINGS IN HIS SHARE OF GOODWILL IN KIND

(a) A new partner instead of bringing in cash may bring his share of goodwill in the form of assets.

(b) Usually, this happens in the case of a sole proprietorship. The incoming partner joins hands with others to carry on the business as a partnership firm.

(c) In such a situation, the assets brought in are debited and the incoming partner's capital account is credited with capital brought in and Premium Account is credited with amount of goodwill brought in.

(d) Afterwards, incoming partner's share of goodwill is transferred by debiting the Premium Account and crediting the capital accounts of the sacrificing partners in their sacrificing ratio.

(e) The two steps involved in this case are given below:

Step 1: Record Assets brought in by the Incoming partner		
Assets A/c	Dr.	[Individually]
To Incoming Partner's Capital A/c		[With amount of Capital]
To Premium for Goodwill A/c		[With share of Goodwill brought in]
Step 2: Give Credit for Incoming Partner's Share of Goodwill to Sacrificing Partner		
Premium for Goodwill A/c	Dr.	[With Share of Goodwill brought in]
To Sacrificing Partners' Capital A/cs		[In Sacrificing Ratio]

Tutorial Note: *Unless otherwise stated, the Partners' Capitals should be assumed to be fluctuating. Current Accounts are to be used in case of Fixed Capitals.*

ILLUSTRATION 23

X and Y are partners in a firm sharing profits in the ratio of 3 : 2. On April 1, 2012 they admit Z as a new partner. The new profit sharing ratio of X, Y and Z will be 5:5:3. Z contributed the following assets towards his capital and for his share of goodwill:

Stock ₹ 80,000, Debtors ₹ 70,000, Land ₹ 50,000. Plant and Machinery ₹ 90,000. On the date of admission of Z, the goodwill of the firm was valued at ₹ 6,50,000. Record the necessary journal entries in the books of the firm on Z admission.

SOLUTION

JOURNAL OF X, Y AND Z

Date	*Particulars*	*L.F.*	*Dr. (₹)*	*Cr. (₹)*
01.04.12	Stock Dr.		80,000	
	Debtors Dr.		70,000	

	Land Dr.		50,000	
	Plant and Machinery A/c Dr.		90,000	
	To Z's Capital A/c			1,40,000
	To Premium of Goodwill A/c			1,50,000
	(Being Stock, Debtors, Land and Plant and Machinery contributed by Z on his admission as his capital and his share of goodwill)			
01.04.12	Premium for Goodwill A/c [₹ 6,50,000 × 3/13] Dr.		1,50,000	
	To X's Capital A/c [₹ 1,50,000 × 14/15]			1,40,000
	To Y's Capital A/c [₹ 1,50,000 × 1/15]			10,000
	(Being the share of Z in goodwill credited to sacrificing partners in their sacrificing ratio)			

Working Note: *Calculation of Sacrificing Ratio*

Share Sacrificed = Old Share – New Share

X's Sacrifice = 3/5 – 5/13 = 14/65, Y's Sacrifice = 2/5 – 5/13 = 1/65,

Sacrificing Ratio = 14/65 : 1/65 = 14:1

ILLUSTRATION 24

A and B were sharing profits and losses in the ratio of 2 : 1 respectively. They admitted C for 2/7th share. The actual value of goodwill, however, on that date was ₹ 42,000. C contributed the following assets towards the payment of his capital and goodwill.

Cash ₹ 2,000, Sundry Debtors ₹ 10,000, Stock ₹ 12,000, Goodwill ₹ 10,000.

Required: Pass the journal entries to give effect to the above. Also give the new profit-sharing ratio.

SOLUTION

JOURNAL

Date	*Particulars*	*L.F.*	*Dr. (₹)*	*Cr. (₹)*
	Cash Dr.		2,000	
	Sundry Debtors Dr.		10,000	
	Stock Dr.		12,000	
	Goodwill Dr.		10,000	
	To C's Capital A/c [₹ 22,000 + (₹ 42,000 × 2/7)]			22,000
	To Premium for Goodwill A/c			12,000
	(Being the amount brought in by C)			
	Premium for Goodwill A/c [₹ 42,000 × 2/7] Dr.		12,000	
	To A's Capital A/c [₹ 12,000 × 2/3]			8,000
	To B's Capital A/c [₹ 12,000 × 1/3]			4,000
	(Being the goodwill credited to sacrificing partners in their sacrificing ratio i.e. 2 : 1)			

Calculation of New Profit Sharing Ratio

I. Let the total share be = 1

II. Share of incoming partner = 2/7

III. Remaining Share (A – B) = 1 – 2/7 = 5/7

IV. Existing Partners' New Shares are calculated by dividing the remaining share in the old Ratio as under:

A's New Share = 2/3 of 5/7 = 10/21, B's New Share = 1/3 of 5/7 = 5/21

V. New Ratio of A, B, C = 10/21 : 5 : 21 : 6/21 = 10 : 5 : 6

Working Notes:

(i) C's Share in Goodwill = ₹ 42,000 × 2/7 = ₹ 12,000

(ii) Calculation of Sacrificing Ratio

A's Sacrifice = 2/3 – 10/21 = 4/21

B's Sacrifice = 1/3 – 5/21 = 2/21.

Thus, Sacrificing Ratio between A & B = 4 : 2 = 2 : 1

ILLUSTRATION 25

A and B are partners in a firm sharing profits and losses equally. They admitted C as a partner for 1/5th share of profit. C brought into partnership "Book Debts" amounting to ₹ 20,000 (less provision for Doubtful Debts of 5%), the Goodwill of his connections valued at ₹ 40,000 and the balance amount in cash, borrowed from his friend D, so as to take his Capital of ₹ 1,20,000.

Required: Show the Journal Entry in the books of the firm.

SOLUTION

JOURNAL

Date	*Particulars*		*L.F.*	*Dr. (₹)*	*Cr. (₹)*
	Sundry Debtors A/c	Dr.		20,000	
	Goodwill A/c	Dr.		40,000	
	Cash A/c	Dr.		61,000	
	To Provision for Doubtful Debts A/c				1,000
	To C's Capital A/c				1,20,000
	(Being the amount brought in by C towards capital)				

SITUATION–IV : WHEN THE INCOMING PARTNER DOES NOT BRING HIS SHARE OF FIRM'S GOODWILL IN CASH

When the incoming partner does not bring in his share of firm's goodwill in cash, the following simplified approach is suggested:

Step 1: Write off the Existing Book Value of Goodwill (if any) appearing in the books

Old Partners' Capital A/cs Dr. [In Old Ratio]

To Goodwill A/c

(Being the existing goodwill written off in old ratio]

Step 2: Record the Amount brought in by Incoming Partner

Cash A/c/Bank A/c Dr. [With Capital brought in]

To Incoming Partner's Capital A/c

(Being the Capital brought in by Incoming Partner)

Step 3:	**Give Credit for Incoming Partner's Full Share of Goodwill to Sacrificing Partners.**		
	Incoming Partner's Capital A/c	Dr.	[With Unpaid Share of Goodwill in case of Fluctuating Capitals]
	To Sacrificing Partners' Capital A/cs		[In Sacrificing Ratio]
	(Being the share of incoming partner in firm's goodwill credited to sacrificing partners in their sacrificing ratio]		

Tutorial Note: *Unless otherwise stated, the Partners' Capitals should be assumed to be fluctuating. Current Accounts are to be used in case of Fixed Capitals.*

ILLUSTRATION 26

X and Y are partners in a firm sharing profits and losses in the ratio of 3 : 2. They admit Z as a partner for 1/5th share. Z acquires his share from X and Y in the ratio of 2 : 3. The goodwill of the firm has been valued at ₹ 25,000. Goodwill already appears in the books at ₹ 20,000. Z bring in ₹ 1,00,000 as his capital. Pass the necessary journal entries.

SOLUTION

JOURNAL

Date	Particulars	L.F.	Dr. (₹)	Cr. (₹)
(i)	X's Capital A/c [₹ 20,000 × 3/5] Dr.		12,000	
	Y's Capital A/c [₹ 20,000 × 2/5] Dr.		8,000	
	To Goodwill A/c			20,000
	(Being the existing goodwill written off in the old ratio, i.e. 3:2)			
(ii)	Cash A/c Dr.		1,00,000	
	To Z's Capital A/c			1,00,000
	(Being the amount brought in by Z as his capital)			
(iii)	Z's Capital A/c [₹ 25,000 × 1/5] Dr.		5,000	
	To X's Capital A/c [₹ 5,000 × 2/5]			2,000
	To Y's Capital A/c [₹ 5,000 × 3/5]			3,000
	(Being the share of Z in goodwill credited to X and Y in their sacrificing ratio, i.e. 2 : 3)			

SITUATION–V : WHEN INCOMING PARTNER BRINGS IN ONLY PART OF HIS SHARE OF FIRM'S GOODWILL IN CASH

When the incoming partner brings in only part of his share of firm's goodwill in cash, the following simplified approach is suggested:

Step 1:	**Write off the Existing Book Value of Goodwill (if any) appearing in the books**		
	Old Partners' Capital A/cs	Dr.	[In Old Ratio]
	To Goodwill A/c		
	(Being the existing goodwill written off in the old ratio]		
Step 2:	**Record the Amount brought in by Incoming partner**		
	Cash A/c/Bank A/c	Dr.	[With Capital & Share of goodwill]

	To Incoming Partner's Capital A/c [With Capital brought in]
	To Premium for Goodwill A/c [With Share of Goodwill brought in]
	(Being the amount brought in by Incoming Partner]
Step 3:	**Give Credit for Incoming Partner's Full Share of Firm's Goodwill to Sacrificing Partners as follows:**
	Premium for Goodwill A/c Dr. [With Share of Goodwill brought in]
	Incoming Partner's Capital A/c Dr. [With Unpaid Share of Goodwill in case of Fluctuating Capitals]
	To Sacrificing Partners' Capital A/cs [In Sacrificing Ratio]
	(Being the Share of Incoming Partner in firm's goodwill credited to Sacrificing Partners in their Sacrificing Ratio]
Step 4:	**Record the Withdrawal (if any) of amount of Goodwill by the Sacrificing Partner(s).**
	Sacrificing Partners' Capital Acs Dr. [To the extent of withdrawal]
	To Cash A/c/Bank A/c
	[Being the goodwill amount withdrawn by Sacrificing Partner(s)]

Tutorial Note: *Unless otherwise stated, the Partners' Capitals should be assumed to be fluctuating. Current Accounts are to be used in case of Fixed Capitals.*

ILLUSTRATION 27

X and Y are partners in a firm sharing profits and losses in the ratio of 3 : 2. They admit Z as a partner for 1/5th share. Z acquires his share from X and Y in the ratio of 2 : 3. The goodwill of the firm has been valued at ₹ 25,000. Goodwill already appears in the books at ₹ 20,000. Z brings in only 60% of his share of firm's goodwill and ₹ 1,00,000 as his capital in cash. The amount of goodwill is withdrawn by the concerned partners to the extent of 30% of what is credited to them. Pass the necessary journal entries.

SOLUTION

JOURNAL

Date	*Particulars*		*L.F.*	*Dr. (₹)*	*Cr. (₹)*
(i)	X's Capital A/c [₹ 20,000 × 3/5]	Dr.		12,000	
	Y's Capital A/c [₹ 20,000 × 2/5]	Dr.		8,000	
	To Goodwill A/c				20,000
	(Being the existing goodwill written off in the old ratio, i.e. 3:2)				
(ii)	Cash A/c [₹ 1,00,000 + 60% of ₹ 5,000]	Dr.		1,03,000	
	To Z's Capital A/c				1,00,000
	To Premium for Goodwill A/c				3,000
	(Being the amount brought in by Z for his share of goodwill and capital)				
(iii)	Premium for Goodwill A/c	Dr.		3,000	
	Z's Capital A/c	Dr.		2,000	
	To X's Capital A/c [₹ 5,000 × 2/5]				2,000

	To Y's Capital A/c [₹ 5,000 × 3/5]			3,000
	(Being share of Z in goodwill credited to X and Y in their sacrificing ratio i.e. 2 : 3)			
(iv)	X's Capital A/c [₹ 2,000 × 30/100] Dr.		600	
	Y's Capital A/c [₹ 3,000 × 30/100] Dr.		900	
	To Cash A/c [₹ 5,000 × 30/100]			1,500
	(Being 30% of the amount of goodwill credited to X & Y withdrawn by them)			

ILLUSTRATION 28

X and Y are partners in a firm sharing profits and losses in the ratio of 3:2. They admit Z as a new partner for 1/5th share. As between themselves, X and Y decide to share future profits & losses in the ratio of 13:7. The goodwill of the firm is valued at ₹ 25,000. Goodwill already appears in the books at ₹ 20,000. Z brings in 60% of his share of firm's goodwill and ₹ 1,00,000 as his capital in cash. The amount of goodwill is withdrawn by the concerned partners to the extent of 30% of what is credited to them. The profits for the first year of new partnership amount to ₹ 1,00,000.

Required: Give the necessary journal entries to adjust goodwill and to distribute profits.

SOLUTION

JOURNAL

Date	*Particulars*	*L.F.*	*Dr. (₹)*	*Cr. (₹)*
(i)	X's Capital A/c [₹ 20,000 × 3/5] Dr.		12,000	
	Y's Capital A/c [₹ 20,000 × 2/5] Dr.		8,000	
	To Goodwill A/c			20,000
	(Being the existing goodwill written off in the old ratio, i.e. 3:2)			
(ii)	Cash A/c [₹ 1,00,000 + 60% of ₹ 5,000] Dr.		1,03,000	
	To Z's Capital A/c			1,00,000
	To Premium for Goodwill A/c			3,000
	(Being the amount brought in by Z for his share of goodwill and capital)			
(iii)	Premium for Goodwill A/c Dr.		3,000	
	Z's Capital A/c Dr.		2,000	
	To X's Capital A/c [₹ 5,000 × 2/5]			2,000
	To Y's Capital A/c [₹ 5,000 × 3/5]			3,000
	(Being the share of Z in goodwill credited to sacrificing partners in their sacrificing ratio, i.e. 2 :3)			
(iv)	X's Capital A/c [₹ 2,000 × 30/100] Dr.		600	
	Y's Capital A/c [₹ 3,000 × 30/100] Dr.		900	
	To Cash A/c [₹ 5,000 × 30/100]			1,500
	(Being 30% of the amount of goodwill credited to X & Y withdrawn by them)			

(v)	Profit & Loss A/c Dr.		1,00,000	
	To X's Capital A/c [₹ 1,00,000 × 13/25]			52,000
	To Y's Capital A/c [₹ 1,00,000 × 7/25]			28,000
	To Z's Capital A/c [₹ 1,00,000 × 5/25]			20,000
	(Being the profit credited to all partners in their new profit sharing ratio]			

Working Note: *Calculate of New Profit Sharing Ratio and Sacrificing Ratio*

Let Total Share = 1. Z's Share = 1/5, Remaining Share = 1 – 1/5 = 4/5

X's New share = $\frac{13}{20} \times \frac{4}{5} = \frac{52}{100}$

Y's New Share = $\frac{7}{20} \times \frac{4}{5} = \frac{28}{100}$

New Ratio of X, Y and Z = $\frac{52}{100} : \frac{28}{100} : \frac{20}{100}$ = 52 : 28 : 20 = 13 : 7 : 5

X's Sacrifice = $\frac{3}{5} - \frac{52}{100} = \frac{8}{100}$

Y's Sacrifice = $\frac{2}{5} - \frac{28}{100} = \frac{12}{100}$

Sacrificing Ratio of X and Y = $\frac{8}{100} : \frac{12}{100}$ = 2 : 3

ILLUSTRATION 29

X and Y are partners in a firm sharing profits and losses in the ratio of 3 : 2. They admit Z as a partner for 1/4th share. Z acquires his share from X and Y in the ratio of 2 : 1. The goodwill of the firm has been valued at ₹ 24,000. Goodwill already appears at ₹ 15,000. Pass the necessary journal entries under each of the following alternative cases.

Case (a) If Z brings his requisite share of firm's goodwill in cash.

Case (b) If Z is unable to bring his requisite share of firm's goodwill in cash.

Case (c) If Z brings only 60% of his requisite share of firm's goodwill in cash.

SOLUTION

JOURNAL

Date	*Particulars*	*L.F.*	*Dr. (₹)*	*Cr. (₹)*
	Case (a)			
(i)	X's Capital A/c Dr.		9,000	
	Y's Capital A/c Dr.		6,000	
	To Goodwill A/c			15,000
	(Being the existing value of goodwill written off)			
(ii)	Cash A/c Dr.		6,000	
	To Premium of Goodwill A/c [₹ 24,000 × 1/4]			6,000
	(Being the amount of goodwill brought in by Z)			
(ii)	Premium of Goodwill A/c Dr.		6,000	
	To X's Capital A/c			4,000

	To Y's Capital A/c			2,000
	(Being the share of Z in goodwill credited to X and Y in their sacrificing ratio i.e. 2.1)			
	Case (b)			
(i)	X's Capital A/c	Dr.	9,000	
	Y's Capital A/c	Dr.	6,000	
	To Goodwill A/c			15,000
	(Being the existing value of goodwill written off)			
(ii)	Z 's Capital A/c	Dr.	6,000	
	To X's Capital A/c			4,000
	To Y's Capital A/c			2,000
	(Being the share of Z in goodwill credited to X and Y in their sacrificing ratio i.e. 2.1)			
	Case (c)			
(i)	X's Capital A/c	Dr.	9,000	
	Y's Capital A/c	Dr.	6,000	
	To Goodwill A/c			15,000
	(Being the existing value of goodwill written off)			
(ii)	Cash A/c	Dr.	3,600	
	To Premium of Goodwill A/c			3,600
	(Being 60% of the share of goodwill brought in by Z)			
(iii)	Premium of Goodwill A/c	Dr.	3,600	
	Z's Capital A/c	Dr.	2,400	
	To X's Capital A/c			4,000
	To Y's Capital A/c			2,000
	(Being the share of Z in goodwill credited to X and Y in their sacrificing ratio i.e. 2 : 1)			

ILLUSTRATION 30

A and B are in partnership sharing profits and losses in the ratio of 3 : 1. They admit C for one third share of the profits. As between themselves, A and B agree to share future profits and losses equally. Pass the necessary journal entries in each of the following alternative cases:

Case (a) If C brings in ₹ 15,000 in cash towards his share of firm's goodwill.

Case (b) If C brings in ₹ 5,000 in cash & machinery worth ₹ 10,000 towards his share of firm's goodwill.

Case (c) If C is unable to bring his share (₹ 15,000) of firm's goodwill in cash.

Case (d) If C brings in ₹ 9,000 out of his share of ₹ 15,000 for goodwill in Cash.

SOLUTION

(A) JOURNAL

Date	Particulars	L.F.	Dr. (₹)	Cr. (₹)
	Cash A/c Dr.		15,000	
	To Premium for Goodwill A/c			15,000
	(Being the amount brought in by C towards goodwill)			
	Premium for Goodwill A/c Dr.		15,000	
	To A's Capital A/c			15,000
	(Being the goodwill credited to sacrificing partner)			
	B's Capital A/c [₹ 45,000 × 1/12] Dr.		3,750	
	To A's Capital A/c			3,750
	(Being the adjustment made on account of change in profit sharing ratio. B loses 1/12th of profit and hence B compensates A for this loss in share of profit thus, 1/12th of ₹ 45,000, ₹ 3,750) (Firm's goodwill ₹ 15,000 × 3/1 = ₹ 45,000)			

Working Note: *Calculation of Sacrificing Ratio*

Let the Total Share be = 1, C's Share = 1/3

Remaining Share = 1 – 1/3 = 2/3

A's New Share = 1/2 × 2/3 = 2/6, B's Share = 1/2 × 2/3 = 2/6

Calculation of Sacrificing Ratio

Share Sacrificed (Gained) = Old Share – New Share

A's Sacrifice= 3/4 – 1/3 = 5/12, B's Gain = 1/4 – 1/3 = 1/12

(B) JOURNAL

Date	Particulars	L.F.	Dr. (₹)	Cr. (₹)
	Cash A/c Dr.		5,000	
	Machinery A/c Dr.		10,000	
	To Premium for Goodwill A/c			15,000
	(Being the amount brought in by C towards goodwill)			
	Premium for Goodwill A/c Dr.		15,000	
	To A's Capital A/c			15,000
	(Being the goodwill credited to sacrificing partner)			
	B's Capital A/c [₹ 45,000 × 1/12] Dr.		3,750	
	To A's Capital A/c			3,750
	(Being the adjustment made on account of change in profit sharing ratio. B loses 1/12th of profit and hence B compensates A for this loss in share of profit thus, 1/12th of ₹ 45,000, ₹ 3,750) (Firm's goodwill ₹ 15,000 × 3/1 = ₹ 45,000)			

Working Note: *Same as in Case (a)*

(C) JOURNAL

Date	Particulars		L.F.	Dr. (₹)	Cr. (₹)
	C's Capital A/c	Dr.		15,000	
	To A's Capital A/c				15,000
	(Being the goodwill credited to sacrificing partner)				
	B's Capital A/c [₹ 45,000 × 1/12]	Dr.		3,750	
	To A's Capital A/c				3,750
	(Being the adjustment made on account of change in profit sharing ratio. B loses 1/12th of profit and hence B compensates A for this loss in share of profit thus, 1/12th of ₹ 45,000, ₹ 3,750) (Firm's goodwill ₹ 15,000 × 3/1 = ₹ 45,000)				

Working Note: *Same as in Case (a)*

(D) JOURNAL

Date	Particulars		L.F.	Dr. (₹)	Cr. (₹)
	Cash A/c	Dr.		9,000	
	To Premium for Goodwill A/c				9,000
	(Being the amount brought in by C towards goodwill)				
	Premium for Goodwill A/c	Dr.		9,000	
	C's Capital A/c	Dr.		6,000	
	To A's Capital A/c				15,000
	(Being the goodwill credited to sacrificing partner)				
	B's Capital A/c [₹ 45,000 × 1/12]	Dr.		3,750	
	To A's Capital A/c				3,750
	(Being the adjustment made on account of change in profit sharing ratio. B loses 1/12th of profit and hence B compensates A for this loss in share of profit thus, 1/12th of ₹ 45,000, ₹ 3,750) (Firm's goodwill ₹ 15,000 × 3/1 = ₹ 45,000)				

Working Note: *Same as in Case (a)*

5.0 CALCULATION OF HIDDEN GOODWILL

When the value of the goodwill of the firm is not specifically given, the value of goodwill has to be inferred on the basis of the Net Worth of the firm as follows:

CALCULATION OF HIDDEN GOODWILL

	Particulars	₹
A.	Net Worth (including goodwill) on the basis of capital brought in by Incoming Partner (Incoming Partner's Capital × Reciprocal of Share of Incoming Partner)	xxx
B.	*Less:* Net Worth (excluding goodwill) of the reconstituted firm (including Incoming Partner's Capital)	xxx
C.	Value of Goodwill (A – B)	xxx

TUTORIAL NOTE

Net Worth = Sundry Assets – Outsiders' liabilities

or = Capitals of Partners + Net Accumulated Profits & Reserves (if any)

ILLUSTRATION 31

A and B are partners with capitals of ₹ 5,000 each. They admit C as a partner with 1/4th share in the profits of the firm. C brings ₹ 8,000. The Profit and Loss Account showed a credit balance of ₹ 4,000 as on date of admission of C. Give the necessary journal entries on C's admission with regard to Capital & Goodwill.

SOLUTION

JOURNAL

Date	*Particulars*		*L.F.*	*Dr. (₹)*	*Cr. (₹)*
	Bank A/c	Dr.		8,000	
	To C's Capital A/c				8,000
	(Being the amount brought in by C)				
	C's Capital A/c [₹ 10,000 × 1/4]	Dr.		2,500	
	To A's Capital A/c				1,250
	To B's Capital A/c				1,250
	(Being the share of C in the hidden goodwill adjusted through capital accounts by crediting sacrificing partners in their sacrificing ratio)				

Note: Hidden Goodwill $= \left(8{,}000 \times \frac{4}{1}\right)$ – (₹ 5,000 + ₹ 5,000 + ₹ 4,000 + ₹ 8,000) = ₹ 10,000

ILLUSTRATION 32

A and B who share the profits & losses in the ratio of 3 : 2 are partners with Capitals of ₹ 30,000 and ₹ 20,000. On date of C's admission, P&L A/c (Cr.) balance ₹ 6,000. Reserves ₹ 55,000, Advertisement Expenditure (Deferred Revenue) ₹ 1,000.

They admit C as a partner with 1/5th share in the profits of the firm. C brings ₹ 40,000. Give the necessary journal entries on C's admission with regard to capital and goodwill.

SOLUTION

JOURNAL

Date	*Particulars*		*L.F.*	*Dr. (₹)*	*Cr. (₹)*
	Bank A/c	Dr.		40,000	
	To C's Capital A/c				40,000
	(Being the amount brought in by C)				
	C's Capital A/c [₹ 50,000 × 1/5]	Dr.		10,000	
	To A's Capital A/c [₹ 10,000 × 3/5]				6,000
	To B's Capital A/c [₹ 10,000 × 2/5]				4,000

	(Being the share of C in the hidden goodwill adjusted through capital accounts by crediting sacrificing partners in their sacrificing ratio)			

Working Note:

CALCULATION OF HIDDEN GOODWILL

	Particulars	₹
A.	Net Worth (including goodwill) of new firm on the basis of Capital brought in by Incoming Partner (₹ 40,000 × 5/1)	2,00,000
B.	*Less:* Net Worth (excluding goodwill) of new firm (Adjusted old Capitals of old partners + Incoming Partner's Capital) [(₹ 30,000 + ₹ 20,000 + ₹ 55,000 + ₹ 6,000 – 1,000) + ₹ 40,000]	1,50,000
C.	Value of Goodwill [A – B]	50,000

ILLUSTRATION 33

Mr. A commenced business with a capital of ₹ 5,00,000 on 1st Jan. 2007. During the five years ending 31st Dec. 2011, the following profits and losses were made:

2007 Loss ₹ 10,000, 2008 Profit ₹ 26,000, 2009 Profit ₹ 34,000, 2010 Profit ₹ 40,000, 2011 Profit ₹ 50,000.

During this period, he had drawn ₹ 80,000 for his personal use. On 1st Jan. 2012, A admitted B into partnership on the following terms: B to bring capital equal to A's Capital for his half share in the business on 1st Jan. 2012 and to pay for one half share of goodwill of the business, on the basis of three times the average profits of the last five years. Prepare statement showing what amount B should invest to become a partner assuming that the goodwill is to be retained in the business and make entries to record the transactions pertaining to admission.

SOLUTION

(I) CALCULATION OF SHARE OF GOODWILL TO BE BROUGHT IN BY B

	Particulars	₹
A.	Total Profits for five years	1,40,000
B.	Average Profits (₹ 1,40,000/5)	28,000
C.	Amount of goodwill (₹ 28,000 × 3)	84,000
D.	Share of goodwill to be brought in by B (₹ 84,000/2)	42,000

(II) CALCULATION OF A'S CAPITAL AS ON 31-12-2011

	Particulars	₹
A.	Capital as on 1.1.2007	5,00,000
B.	*Add:* Net Profit for five years	1,40,000
C.	*Less:* Drawings	(80,000)
	Total	5,60,000

(iii) Calculation of amount to be invested by B

A's Capital after B's admission = ₹ 5,60,000 + Amount of goodwill to be brought in

= ₹ 5,60,000 + ₹ 42,000 .... Eq. I

Let B's Total investment be equal to X

X = Capital to be brought in by B + Goodwill to be brought in by B

or X = Capital + ₹ 42,000

or, Capital = X – ₹ 42,000 . . . . Eq. II

Since B has to bring capital equal to A's Capital, both the equations may be equated as under:

X – ₹ 42,000 = ₹ 5,60,000 + ₹ 42,000

X = ₹ 5,60,000 + ₹ 42,000 + ₹ 42,000 = ₹ 6,44,000.

JOURNAL

Date	*Particulars*		*L.F.*	*Dr. (₹)*	*Cr. (₹)*
01.01.12	Cash A/c (₹ 6,02, 000 + ₹ 42,000)	Dr.		6,44,000	
	To B's Capital A/c				6,02,000
	To Premium for Goodwill A/c				42,000
	(Being the amount brought in by B)				
	Premium for Goodwill A/c	Dr.		42,000	
	To A's Capital A/c				42,000
	(Being the amount of goodwill credited to A's Capital A/c)				

6.0 REVALUATION OF ASSETS AND LIABILITIES

Why is Revaluation Required?	At the time of admission of a partner, the assets and liabilities are revalued so that the profit *or* loss arising on account of such revaluation upto the date of admission of a new partner may be ascertained and adjusted in the old partners' Capital Accounts in their old profit sharing ratio since it belongs to old partners and not to new partner.
How to record the Effect of Revaluation	The effect of revaluation of assets and liabilities may be recorded either through **'Revaluation Account** *(if assets and liabilities are to appear* ***at revalued figures****)* ***or*** **through Capital Accounts** *(if assets and liabilities are to appear* ***at old figures).'***

REVALUATION ACCOUNT

Meaning	Revaluation Account (or *alternatively Profit & Loss Adjustment Account*) is a **Nominal Account.**
Purpose	The purpose of Revaluation Account is **to ascertain the profit/loss arising on account of Revaluation of Assets and Liabilities.**
Contents	Revaluation Account is **credited with increase in the value of assets and decrease in the amount of liabilities (it is a gain) and debited with decrease in the value of assets and increase in the amount of liabilities (it is a loss).** Unrecorded Assets are recorded through the Revaluation Account as increase in assets. Unrecorded Liabilities are recorded through the Revaluation Account as increase in liabilities.
Balance	The balance of Revaluation Account shows the net effect on account of revaluation which is **transferred to the Partners' Capital accounts in their Old Profit Sharing Ratio.**

ACCOUNTING ENTRIES TO RECORD THE REVALUATION OF ASSETS AND LIABILITIES

1. For Increase in the Value of an Asset	
Asset A/c	Dr.
To Revaluation A/c	
(Being the increase in the value of an asset recorded)	
2. For Decrease in the Value of an Asset	
Revaluation A/c	Dr.
To Asset A/c	
(Being the decrease in the value of an asset recorded)	
3. For Increase in the Amount of a Liability	
Revaluation A/c	Dr.
To Liability A/c	
(Being the increase in the amount of a liability recorded)	
4. For Decrease in the Amount of a liability	
Liability A/c	Dr.
To Revaluation A/c	
(Being the decrease in the amount of a liability recorded)	
5. For Recording an Unrecorded Asset	
Unrecorded Asset A/c	Dr.
To Revaluation A/c	
(Being an agreed value of an unrecorded asset brought into account)	
6. For Recording an Unrecorded Liability	
Revaluation A/c	Dr.
To Unrecorded Liability A/c	
(Being an agreed amount of an unrecorded liability brought into account)	
7. For Transfer of Balance in Revaluation Account	
(i) If credit side exceeds debit side (Net Gain)	
Revaluation A/c	Dr.
To Old Partners' Capital A/cs (Individually in Old Ratio)	
(Being the Net Gain on Revaluation transferred to Old Partners' Capital Accounts in Old Profit Sharing Ratio)	
(ii) If debit side exceeds credit side (Net Loss)	
Old Partners' Capital A/cs (Individually in Old Ratio)	Dr.
To Revaluation A/c	
(Being the Net Loss on Revaluation transferred to Old Partners' Capital Accounts in Old Profit Sharing Ratio)	

Tutorial Note: *When Revaluation Account is prepared, the Assets and Liabilities appear in the Balance Sheet of new firm at their revised figures.*

FORMAT OF REVALUATION ACCOUNT

Dr. **REVALUATION ACCOUNT** Cr.

Particulars	₹	*Particulars*	₹
To Decrease in Value of Assets	....	By Increase in Value of assets	....
To Increase in Value of Liabilities	....	By Decrease in Value of Liabilities	....
To Unrecorded Liabilities	....	By Unrecorded Assets	....
To Profit* t/f to the Partners' Capital A/cs (in the Old Profit-Sharing Ratio)	....	By Loss* t/f to the Partners' Capital A/cs (in the Old Profit-Sharing Ratio)	....
	....		....

**Either Profit or Loss will appear.*

ILLUSTRATION 34

X, Y and Z who are presently sharing profits & losses in the ratio of 5:3:2, decide to admit W for 1/6th share with effect from 1st April, 2012. An extract of their Balance Sheet as at 31st March, 2012 is as follows:

Laibilities	₹	*Assets*		
Sundry Creditors	3,00,000	Land & Building		2,50,000
Outstanding Rent	10,000	Plant & Machinery		1,00,000
		Stock		80,000
		Debtors	3,00,000	
		Less: Provision	10,000	2,90,000

It is decided that:

1. Land & Building be valued at ₹ 2,85,000.
2. Plant & Machinery be depreciated by 15%.
3. Stock is found overvalued by ₹ 38,000.
4. Provision for doubtful debts is to be made equal to 5% of the debtors.
5. An item of ₹ 30,000 included in Sundry Creditors is not likely to be claimed.
6. Rent of ₹ 4,000 still Outstanding.
7. Out of the amount of insurance which was debited entirely to P&L A/c, ₹ 5,000 be carried forward as an unexpired insurance.
8. Out of total commission received ₹ 3,000 is to be treated as advance commission. This amount was earlier credited to Profit & Loss Account.
9. An unaccounted accrued income of ₹ 1,000 be provided for.
10. A debtor whose dues of ₹ 5,000 were written off as bad debts paid ₹ 4,000 in full settlement.

Required: Pass the necessary Journal Entries and prepare Revaluation Account.

SOLUTION

JOURNAL

Date	*Particulars*		*L.F.*	*Dr. (₹)*	*Cr. (₹)*
1.	Land & Building A/c	Dr.		35,000	

	To Revaluation A/c (Being the increase in value of Land & Building recorded)			35,000
2.	Revaluation A/c To Plant & Machinery A/c (Being the decrease in value of Plant & Machinery recorded)	Dr.	15,000	15,000
3.	Revaluation A/c To Stock A/c (Being the decrease in value of Stock recorded)	Dr.	38,000	38,000
4.	Revaluation A/c [₹15,000 – ₹10,000] To Provision for Doubtful Debts A/c (Being the short provision now created)	Dr.	5,000	5,000
5.	Creditors To Revaluation A/c (Being the decrease in the amount of Creditors recorded)	Dr.	30,000	30,000
6.	Revaluation A/c To Outstanding Rent A/c (Being the Outstanding Rent recorded)	Dr.	4,000	4,000
7.	Prepaid Insurance To Revaluation A/c (Being the prepaid insurance recorded)	Dr.	5,000	5,000
8.	Revaluation A/c To Commission received in advance A/c (Being the commission received in advance recorded)	Dr.	3,000	3,000
9.	Accrued Income A/c To Revaluation A/c (Being the Accrued Income recorded)	Dr.	1,000	1,000
10.	Bad Debts Recovered A/c To Revaluation A/c (Being the Bad Debts recovered, recorded)	Dr.	4,000	4,000
11.	Revaluation A/c To X's Capital A/c To Y's Capital A/c To Z's Capital A/c (Being the transfer of profit on revaluation to old partners' capital accounts in their old profit sharing ratio)	Dr.	10,000	 5,000 3,000 2,000

Dr. **REVALUATION ACCOUNT** *Cr.*

Particulars	₹	*Particulars*	₹
To Stock	38,000	By Land & Building	35,000
To Provision for Doubtful Debts	5,000	By Sundry Creditors	30,000

To Plant & Machinery A/c	15,000	By Prepaid Insurance	5,000
To Outstanding Rent A/c	4,000	By Accured Income	1,000
To Commission received in adv. A/c	3,000	By Bad Debts Recovered	4,000
To Profit on Revaluation t/f to:			
X's Capital A/c	5,000		
Y's Capital A/c	3,000		
Z's Capital A/c	2,000		
	75,000		75,000

ILLUSTRATION 35

Pass Journal entries for the following on the admission of C, as a partner in the Journal of A and B.

(a) Unrecorded Investments worth ₹ 5,000.

(b) Unrecorded Liabilities towards suppliers for ₹ 1,500.

(c) An item of ₹ 650 included in Sundry Creditors is not likely to be claimed, hence should be written back.

SOLUTION

JOURNAL

Date	*Particulars*	*L.F.*	*Dr. (₹)*	*Cr. (₹)*
(a)	Investments A/c ...Dr.		5,000	
	To Revaluation A/c			5,000
	(Being the Investments recorded in books)			
(b)	Revaluation A/c ...Dr.		1,500	
	To Creditors A/c			1,500
	(Being the liability towards suppliers recorded)			
(c)	Sundry Creditors A/c ...Dr.		650	
	To Revaluation A/c			650
	(Being the item of creditors of ₹ 600 not likely to be claimed written back)			
(d)	Revaluation A/c (5,000 – 1,500 + 650) ...Dr.		4,150	
	To A's Capital A/c			2,075
	To B's Capital A/c			2,075
	(Being the t/f of Profit on Revaluation to Old Partners in Old Ratio)			

ILLUSTRATION 36

The Balance Sheet of A and B who share profits in the ratio of 3 : 1 as at 31st March, 2012 is as follows:

Liabilities	₹	*Assets*	₹
Sundry Creditors	41,500	Cash at Bank	26,500

A's Capital	33,000	Bills Receivable	3,000
B's Capital	17,000	Debtors	16,000
		Stock	20,000
		Furniture & Fixtures	1,000
		Land & Building	25,000
	91,500		91,500

On 31-03-2012, C was admitted into partnership for 1/5th share on the following terms:

(a) That C pays ₹ 10,000 as his capital for one fifth share.

(b) That C pays ₹ 5,000 for goodwill. Half of this sum is to be withdrawn by A and B.

(c) That Stock and Fixtures be reduced by 10% and a 5% Provision for Doubtful Debts be created on Sundry Debtors and Bills Receivable.

(d) That the value of Land and Buildings be appreciated by 20%.

(e) There being a claim against the firm for damages, liabilities to the extent of ₹ 1,000 should be created.

(f) An item of ₹ 650 included in sundry creditors is not likely to be claimed and hence should be written back.

Required: Pass the necessary journal entries & prepare the Balance Sheet of the reconstituted firm.

SOLUTION

JOURNAL

Date	*Particulars*		*L.F.*	*Dr. (₹)*	*Cr. (₹)*
	Bank A/c	Dr.		15,000	
	To C's Capital A/c				10,000
	To Premium for Goodwill A/c				5,000
	(Being the amount brought in by C)				
	Premium for Goodwill A/c	Dr.		5,000	
	To A's Capital A/c [₹ 5,000 × 3/4]				3,750
	To B's Capital A/c [₹ 5,000 × 1/4]				1,250
	(Being C's share of goodwill credited to sacrificing partners in their sacrificing ratio i.e. 3 : 1)				
	A's Capital A/c [₹ 3,750 × 50/100]	Dr.		1,875	
	B's Capital A/c [₹ 1,250 × 50/100]	Dr.		625	
	To Bank A/c [₹ 5,000 × 50/100]				2,500
	(Being 50% of goodwill withdrawn)				
	Revaluation A/c	Dr.		3,050	
	To Stock A/c [₹ 20,000 × 10/100]				2,000
	To Fixtures A/c [₹ 1,000 × 10/100]				100
	To Provision for Doubtful Debts A/c [₹ 16,000 × 5/100]				800
	To Provision for B/R A/c [₹ 3,000 × 5/100]				150
	(Being the fall in the value of assets recorded)				

	Land & Building A/c [₹ 25,000 × 20/100]	Dr.	5,000	
	Creditors A/c	Dr.	650	
	To Revaluation A/c			5,650
	(Being an increase in assets and decrease in liability recorded)			
	Revaluation A/c	Dr.	1,000	
	To Provision for damages A/c			1,000
	(Being the Provision for damages recorded)			
	Revaluation A/c	Dr.	1,600	
	To A's Capital A/c			1,200
	To B's Capital A/c			400
	(Being the transfer of profit on revaluation)			

BALANCE SHEET OF THE RECONSTITUTED FIRM

as at 31st March, 2012

Liabilities	₹	*Assets*		₹
Sundry Creditors	40,850	Cash at Bank		39,000
Provision for Damages	1,000	Bills Receivable	3,000	
A's Capital	36,075	*Less:* Provision	150	2,850
B's Capital	18,025	Debtors	16,000	
C's Capital	10,000	*Less:* Provision	800	15,200
		Stock		18,000
		Fixtures		900
		Land & Building		30,000
	1,05,950			1,05,950

ILLUSTRATION 37

The following was the Balance Sheet of A, B and C who were equal partners, on 31st March, 2012.

Liabilities	₹	*Assets*	₹
Bills Payable	3,300	Cash	600
Creditors	6,000	Debtors	10,800
Capital Accounts:		Stock	11,400
A	16,800	Furniture	2,400
B	12,600	Building	19,500
C	6,000		
	44,700		44,700

They agreed to take D into partnership and give him one-fourth share in the profits on the following terms:

(a) That D should bring in ₹ 9,000 for goodwill and ₹ 15,000 as capital.

(b) That one half of the goodwill shall be withdrawn by the old partners.

(c) That stock and furniture be depreciated by 10 per cent.

(d) That a provision of 5 per cent on debtors be created for doubtful debts.

(e) That a liability for ₹ 1,080 be created against bills discounted which was dishonoured.

(f) That the value of the building is undervalued by ₹ 8,500.

Required: Give the necessary entries to give effect to the above arrangement and prepare the Opening Balance Sheet of the firm as newly constituted.

SOLUTION

JOURNAL

Date	Particulars		L.F.	Dr. (₹)	Cr. (₹)
	Cash A/c [₹ 15,000 + ₹ 9,000]	Dr.		24,000	
	To D's Capital A/c				15,000
	To Premium for Goodwill A/c				9,000
	(Being the amount brought in by D)				
	Premium for Goodwill A/c	Dr.		9,000	
	To A's Capital A/c [₹ 9,000 × 1/3]				3,000
	To B's Capital A/c [₹ 9,000 × 1/3]				3,000
	To C's Capital A/c [₹ 9,000 × 1/3]				3,000
	(Being D's share of goodwill credited to sacrificing partners in their sacrificing ratio which is 1 : 1 : 1)				
	A's Capital A/c [₹ 3,000 × 50/100]	Dr.		1,500	
	B's Capital A/c [₹ 3,000 × 30/100]	Dr.		1,500	
	C's Capital A/c [₹ 3,000 × 50/100]	Dr.		1,500	
	To Cash A/c [₹ 9,000 × 50/100]				4,500
	(Being the amount withdrawn by sacrificing partners)				
	Revaluation A/c	Dr.		1,920	
	To Stock [₹ 11,400 × 10/100]				1,140
	To Furniture [₹ 2,400 × 10/100]				240
	To Provision for Doubtful Debts [₹ 10,800 × 5/100]				540
	(Being the record of decrease in value of assets)				
	Revaluation A/c	Dr.		1,080	
	To Liability against Bills Discounted A/c				1,080
	(Being the record of increase in liability)				
	Land & Buildings A/c	Dr.		8,500	
	To Revaluation A/c				8,500
	(Being the record of increase in value of asset)				
	Revaluation A/c	Dr.		5,500	
	To A's Capital A/c				1,833
	To B's Capital A/c				1,833
	To C's Capital A/c				1,834
	(Being the transfer of profit on revaluation)				

BALANCE SHEET OF RECONSTITUTED FIRM
as at 31st March, 2012

Liabilities	₹	*Assets*		₹
Bills Payable	3,300	Cash		20,100
Creditors	6,000	Debtors	10,800	
Liability for Bill Discounted	1,080	*Less:* Provision	540	10,260
Capital Accounts:		Stock		10,260
A	20,133	Furniture		2,160
B	15,933	Building		28,000
C	9,334			
D	15,000			
	70,780			70,780

7.0 ADJUSTMENT FOR RESERVES AND ACCUMULATED PROFITS/LOSSES

WHY IS ADJUSTMENT FOR RESERVES AND ACCUMULATED PROFITS/LOSSES REQUIRED?

If, at the time of admission of a partner, any reserves *or* accumulated profits/losses exist in the books of the firm, these should be transferred to Old Partners' Capital Accounts in their old profit sharing ratio since the reserves, accumulated profits/losses upto the date of admission of a new partner belong to the Old Partners only and not to the New Partner.

ACCOUNTING TREATMENT OF RESERVES, ACCUMULATED PROFITS/LOSSES

1. For transfer of Reserves and Accumulated Profits

Reserve A/c		Dr.
P & L A/c		Dr.
Workmen Compensation Reserve A/c	[Excess of Reserve over Actual Liability]	Dr.
Investment Fluctuation Reserve A/c	[Excess of Reserve over the difference between Book value and Market value]	Dr.
To Old Partners' Capital Accounts (individually)		(In Old Ratio)
(Being the Reserves & Profits transferred to old partners in their old ratio)		

2. For transfer of Accumulated Losses

Old Partners' Capital Accounts (individually)	Dr.(In Old Ratio)
To Profit & Loss A/c	
To Deferred Revenue Expenditure A/c	
(Being Accumulated Losses transferred to old partners in their old ratio)	

TUTORIAL NOTES

1. *Reserves, Accumulated Profits/Losses should always be distributed even if the question is silent.*
2. *Workmen Compensation Reserve* ***(say ₹ 1,200)*** *to the extent of liability* ***(say ₹ 150)*** *should be credited to Workmen Compensation Claim A/c and the balance of Workmen Compensation*

*Reserve (**₹ 1,050**) should be credited to Old Partners' Capital Accounts.*

3. *Excess of Investment Fluctuation Reserve over difference between Book Value and Market Value is credited to Old Partners' Capital Accounts.*
4. *Machinery Replacement Fund is in the nature of accumulated depreciation and not in nature of accumulated profits and hence is not distributed among the partners.*
5. *Employees' Provident Fund represents statutory liability due to employees towards Provident Fund and is not an accumulated profit, hence it is not distribted among the partners.*

ILLUSTRATION 38

X, Y and Z are sharing profits & losses in the ratio of 5:3:2. They decide to to admit W for 1/6th share with effect from 1st April, 2012. The following items appear in the Balance Sheet as at 31st March, 2012:

General Reserve	₹ 30,000
Contingencies Reserve	₹ 5,000
Profit & Loss A/c (Cr.)	₹ 15,000
Advertisement Suspense A/c (Dr.)	₹ 20,000

Required: Pass the necessary Journal Entries.

SOLUTION

JOURNAL

Date	*Particulars*		*L.F.*	*Dr. (₹)*	*Cr. (₹)*
2012	General Reserve	Dr.		30,000	
April 1	Contingencies Reserve	Dr.		5,000	
	Profit & Loss A/c (Cr.)	Dr.		15,000	
	To X's Capital A/c				25,000
	To Y's Capital A/c				15,000
	To Z's Capital A/c				10,000
	(Being the transfer of Reserves & Profits to Old Partners in their Old Ratio)				
	X's Capital A/c	Dr.		10,000	
	Y's Capital A/c	Dr.		6,000	
	Z's Capital A/c	Dr.		4,000	
	To Advertisement Suspense A/c				20,000
	(Being the transfer of balance of Advertisement Suspense A/c to Old Partners in their Old Ratio)				

ILLUSTRATION 39

A and B were partners in a firm sharing profits in 4 : 3 ratio. On 1st January they admitted C as a new partner. On the date of C's admission the Balance Sheet of A and B showed a General Reserve of ₹ 70,000 and a debit balance of ₹ 7,000 in the 'Profit and Loss Account'. Pass the necessary journal entries for the treatment of these items on C's admission.

SOLUTION

JOURNAL

Date	Particulars		L.F.	Dr. (₹)	Cr. (₹)
	General Reserve	Dr.		70,000	
	To A's Capital A/c				40,000
	To B's Capital A/c				30,000
	(Being General Reserve distributed between A & B)				
	A's Capital A/c	Dr.		4,000	
	B's Capital A/c	Dr.		3,000	
	To Profit & Loss A/c				7,000
	(Being debit balance of P & L A/c transferred to Capital A/cs)				

ILLUSTRATION 40

An extract of the Balance Sheet of A & B sharing profits & losses in the ratio of 3 : 2 as at 31st March, 2012 was as under:

Liabilities	₹	Assets	₹
General Reserve	5,000	Investments (Market Value ₹ 19,000)	20,000
Contingencies Reserve	450	Machinery Replacement Fund Invst.	1,000
P & L A/c	3,000	Advertisement Expenditure (Deferred Revenue)	1,000
Investment Fluctuation Reserve	1,500		
Workmen's Compensation Reserve	1,200		
Machinery Replacement Fund	1,000		
Employees' Provident Fund	2,000		

New partner C was admitted for 1/5th share of profits to be acquired from both 'A' and B. A claim on account of workmen's compensation is estimated at ₹ 150 only.

Required: Give the necessary journal entries to adjust accumulated profits and losses.

SOLUTION

JOURNAL

Date	Particulars		L.F.	Dr. (₹)	Cr. (₹)
	Investment Fluctuation Reserve A/c	Dr.		1,000	
	To Investments A/c				1,000
	(Being the value of investments brought down to market value)				
	Workmen Compensation Reserve A/c	Dr.		150	
	To Provision for Workmen Compensation Claim A/c				150
	(Being the workmen compensation claim provided for)				
	General Reserve	Dr.		5,000	
	Contingencies Reserve	Dr.		450	

	P & L A/c Dr.		3,000	
	Inves. Fluctuation Reserve A/c [1500 – (20,000 – 19,000)] Dr.		500	
	Workmen's Compensation Reserve A/c [₹ 1,200 – ₹ 150] Dr.		1,050	
	To A's Capital A/c			6,000
	To B's Capital A/c			4,000
	(Being the transfer of accumulated profits to Old Partners in their Old Profit Sharing Ratio)			
	A's Capital A/c Dr.		600	
	B's Capital A/c Dr.		400	
	To Advertisement Expenditure A/c			1,000
	(Being the transfer of accumulated losses to old partners in their old profit sharing ratio)			

Working Notes:

1. Investment Fluctuation Reserve Account has been transferred directly to Partners' Capital Accounts. after providing for an anticipated loss of ₹ 1,000 (i.e. ₹ 20,000 – ₹ 19,000) according to Prudence (conservatism) concept.
2. The balance of Workmen's Compensation Reserve Account after making Provision for Claim has been transferred directly to Partners' Capital Accounts.
3. Machinery Replacement Fund is in the nature of accumulated depreciation and not in nature of accumulated profits and hence is not distributed among the partners.
4. Employees' Provident Fund represents statutory liability due to employees towards Provident Fund and is not an accumulated profits, hence it is not distribted among the partners.

ILLUSTRATION 41

Following is the Balance Sheet of Shashi and Aashu sharing profits as 3 : 2:

Liabilities	₹	*Assets*		₹
Creditors	10,000	Goodwill		6,000
Employees' Provident Fund	8,000	Debtors	22,000	
Contingency Reserve	28,500	*Less:* Provision for D.D.	1,000	21,000
Workmen's Compensation Fund	15,000	Land & Building		18,000
Investment Fluctuation Fund	1,500	Plants & Machinery		7,000
Capitals:		Investment (Market Value ₹ 4,000)		5,000
Shashi	15,000	Stock		11,000
Aashu	10,000	Bank		15,000
		Advertisement Expenditure		5,000
	88,000			88,000

On admission of Tanya for 1/6th share in the profits it was decided that:

(a) Provision for doubtful debts to be increased by ₹ 1,500.

(b) Value of land and building to be increased to ₹ 21,000.

(c) Value of stock to be increased by ₹ 2,500.

(d) The liability of workmen's compensation fund was determined to be ₹ 12,000.

(e) Investments are to be brought down to market value.

(f) Tanya brought in as her share of goodwill ₹ 10,000 in cash.

(g) Tanya was to bring further cash of ₹ 15,000 for her capital.

(h) A unrecorded Furniture having a value of ₹ 6,000 is to be brought into the books.

Required: Prepare Revaluation A/c, Capital A/cs and Balance Sheet of the new firm.

SOLUTION

Dr. **REVALUATION ACCOUNT** *Cr.*

Particulars		₹	*Particulars*	₹
To Provision for Doubtful Debts		1,500	By Land & Building	3,000
To Profit on Revaluation t/f to:			By Stock	2,500
Shashi's Capital A/c	6,000		By Furniture	6,000
Aashu's Capital A/c	4,000	10,000		
		11,500		11,500

Dr. **PARTNERS' CAPITAL ACCOUNTS** *Cr.*

Particulars	*Shashi* ₹	*Aashu* ₹	*Tanya* ₹	*Particulars*	*Shashi* ₹	*Aashu* ₹	*Tanya* ₹
To Goodwill A/c	3,600	2,400	—	By Balance b/d	15,000	10,000	—
To Advertisement Exp.	3,000	2,000	—	By Contingency Res.	17,100	11,400	—
To Balance c/d	39,600	26,400	15,000	By Work Comp. Fund	1,800	1,200	—
				By Inves. Fluc. Fund	300	200	—
				By Revaluation A/c	6,000	4,000	—
				By Bank A/c	—	—	15,000
				By Premium for Goodwill	6,000	4,000	—
	46,200	30,800	15,000		46,200	30,800	15,000

BALANCE SHEET OF SHASHI, AASHU AND TANYA AS AT.....

Liabilities	₹	*Assets*		₹
Creditors	10,000	Debtors	22,000	
Employees' Provident Fund	8,000	*Less:* Provision	2,500	19,500
Liabilities for Workmen's Comp.	12,000	Land & Building		21,000
Capitals:		Plants & Machinery		7,000
Shashi	39,600	Investments		4,000
Aashu	26,400	Stock		13,500
Tanya	15,000	Bank		40,000
		Furniture		6,000
	1,11,000			1,11,000

ILLUSTRATION 42

A and B are partners sharing profits in the ratio of 3 : 1. Their Balance Sheet as on 31.03.2012 was as follows:

Liabilities	₹	*Assets*	₹
A's Capital	6,000	Bank	1,000
B's Capital	2,000	Debtors	6,000
Creditors	1,000	Stock	3,000
Workmen's Compensation Fund	2,000	Investments	5,000
Reserve	4,000	Goodwill	1,000
Employees' Provident Fund	1,000		
	16,000		16,000

C is admitted for 2/5th share in future profits. For this purpose following adjustments are agreed upon:

C will bring ₹ 8,000 for Capital and ₹ 2,000 for Goodwill.

Market value of Investment is ₹ 4,500; claim on account of Workmen's Compensation is ₹ 1,000. Goodwill is not to appear in the new firm at all.

Required: Prepare ledger accounts. i.e., Revaluation Account, Partners' Capital Accounts to record the above and show the Balance Sheet.

SOLUTION

Dr. **REVALUATION ACCOUNT** *Cr.*

Particulars	₹	*Particulars*	₹
To Investment A/c	500	By Loss on Revaluation t/f to:	
		A's Capital A/c	375
		B's Capital A/c	125
	500		500

Dr. **PARTNERS' CAPITAL ACCOUNTS** *Cr.*

Particulars	A ₹	B ₹	C ₹	*Particulars*	A ₹	B ₹	C ₹
To Revaluation A/c	375	125	—	By Balance b/d	6,000	2,000	—
To Goodwill A/c	750	250	—	By Workmen Com. Fund A/c	750	250	—
To Balance c/d	10,125	3,375	8,000	By Bank A/c	—	—	8,000
				By Premium for Goodwill	1,500	500	—
				By Reserve	3,000	1,000	—
	11,250	3,750	8,000		11,250	3,750	8,000

BALANCE SHEET OF THE RECONSTITUTED FIRM AS AT 31.03.2012

Liabilities	₹	*Assets*	₹
Workmen's Compensation Claim	1,000	Bank	11,000
Creditors	1,000	Debtors	6,000

Employees' Provident Fund	1,000	Stock		3,000
A's Capital	10,125	Investments	5,000	
B's Capital	3,375	*Less:* Reserve	500	4,500
C's Capital	8,000			
	24,500			24,500

ILLUSTRATION 43

Balance Sheet of A, B and C sharing profits in the ratio of 3 : 2 : 1 is given below:

Liabilities	₹	*Assets*		₹
A's Capital	4,00,000	Bank		40,000
B's Capital	4,00,000	Debtors	2,00,000	
C's Capital	2,00,000	*Less:* Provision	3,000	1,97,000
Contingency Reserve	60,000	Stock		2,03,000
Trade Creditors	1,60,000	Furniture		30,000
Employees' Provident Fund	20,000	Machinery		5,30,000
Workmen Compensation Fund	60,000	Building		3,00,000
	13,00,000			13,00,000

It was decided to admit D into partnership on the following terms and conditions :

(i) New Profit Sharing ratio between A, B, C and D will be 3 : 3 : 2 : 2.

(ii) Goodwill of the firm is valued at ₹ 3,00,000. D brings his share of goodwill in cash which is credited to the old partners.

(iii) D brings ₹ 1,50,000 as his share of capital.

(iv) Contingency Reserve is not required any more.

(v) Provision for Doubtful debt to be raised to 5% on debtors.

(vi) Machinery is overvalued by ₹ 30,000 and Building is undervalued by ₹ 67,000.

Required: Prepare Revaluation A/c. Capital A/cs. of A, B, C and D, and the Balance Sheet of the firm after D's admission. Also show the calculations regarding goodwill.

SOLUTION

Dr. **REVALUATION ACCOUNT** *Cr.*

Particulars		₹	*Particulars*	₹
To Provision for doubtful debts		7,000	By Building	67,000
To Machinery		30,000		
To Profit on Revaluation t/f to :				
A's Capital A/c	15,000			
B's Capital A/c	10,000			
C's Capital A/c	5,000	30,000		
		67,000		67,000

Dr. **A'S CAPITAL ACCOUNT** Cr.

Particulars	₹	*Particulars*	₹
To Balance c/d	5,35,000	By Balance b/d	4,00,000
		By Revaluation A/c	15,000
		By Contingency Reserve A/c	30,000
		By Workmen Compensation Fund	30,000
		By Premium for Goodwill A/c	51,429
		By C's Capital A/c	8,571
	5,35,000		5,35,000

Dr. **B'S CAPITAL ACCOUNT** Cr.

Particulars	₹	*Particulars*	₹
To Balance c/d	4,60,000	By Balance b/d	4,00,000
		By Revaluation A/c	10,000
		By Contingency Reserve A/c	20,000
		By Workmen Compensation Fund	20,000
		By Premium for Goodwill A/c	8,571
		By C's Capital A/c	1,429
	4,60,000		4,60,000

Dr. **C'S CAPITAL ACCOUNT** Cr.

Particulars	₹	*Particulars*	₹
To A's Capital A/c	8,571	By Balance b/d	2,00,000
To B's Capital A/c	1,429	By Revaluation A/c	5,000
To Balance c/d	2,15,000	By Contingency Reserve A/c	10,000
		By Workmen Compensation Fund	10,000
	2,25,000		2,25,000

Dr. **D'S CAPITAL ACCOUNT** Cr.

Particulars	₹	*Particulars*	₹
To Balance c/d	1,50,000	By Bank A/c	1,50,000
	2,10,000		1,50,000

BALANCE SHEET AS AT...

Liabilities	₹	*Assets*		₹
Trade Creditors	1,60,000	Bank		2,50,000
Employees' Provident Fund	20,000	Debtors	2,00,000	
A's Capital A/c	5,35,000	*Less:* Provision	10,000	1,90,000
B's Capital A/c	4,60,000	Stock		2,03,000
C's Capital A/c	2,15,000	Furniture		30,000

D's Capital A/c	1,50,000	Machinery	5,00,000
		Building	3,67,000
	15,40,000		15,40,000

Working Note: *Calculations regarding Goodwill.*

1. D's Share of Goodwill = ₹ 3,00,000 × 2/10 = ₹ 60,000
2. Change in profit sharing ratio will result in loss of 6/30th to A and 1/30 to B; gain of 1/30 to C and 2/10th to D. Hence the entry for adjustment of goodwill will be as under:

C's Capital A/c	Dr.	10,000 (i.e. 3,00,000 × 1/30)
Premium for Goodwill A/c	Dr.	60,000 (i.e. 3,00,000 × 2/10)
To A's Capital A/c		60,000 (i.e. 3,00,000 × 6/30)
To B 's Capital A/c		10,000 (i.e. 3,00,000 × 1/30)

ILLUSTRATION 44

P and S were partners in a firm sharing profits in the ratio of 3 : 2. Their Balance Sheet on 31.3.2012 was as follows:

Liabilities	₹	*Assets*	₹
Bank Overdraft	20,000	Cash	8,000
Creditors	30,000	Debtors	10,000
Provision for Doubtful debts	1,000	Bills Receivable	60,000
General Reserve	15,000	Stock	50,000
V's Loan	20,000	Building	90,000
Capitals:		Land	1,48,000
P	1,00,000		
S	1,80,000		
	3,66,000		3,66,000

On 1.4.2012 they admitted V as a new partner on the following conditions:

(i) V will get 1/8th share in the profits of the firm.

(ii) V's loan will be converted into his capital.

(iii) The goodwill of the firm was valued at ₹ 80,000 and V brought his share of goodwill premium in cash.

(iv) Provision for doubtful debts was to be made equal to 5% of the debtors.

(v) Stock to be depreciated by 7%, Land to be appreciated by 10%.

Required: Prepare Revaluation Account, Capital Accounts of P, S and V and the Balance Sheet of the New Firm.

SOLUTION

Dr. **REVALUATION ACCOUNT** *Cr.*

Particulars	₹	*Particulars*	₹
To Stock	3,500	By Land	14,800
To Profit on Revaluation t/f to:		By Provision for Doubtful Debts	500

P's Capital A/c	7,080	Existing	1,000	
S's Capital A/c	4,720	*Less:* Required	500	500
		[₹ 10,000 × 5/100]		
	15,300			15,300

Dr. **CAPITAL ACCOUNTS OF PARTNERS** *Cr.*

Particulars	*P*	*S*	*V*	*Particulars*	*P*	*S*	*V*
To Balance c/d	1,22,080	1,94,720	20,000	By Balance b/d	1,00,000	1,80,000	–
				By General Reserve	9,000	6,000	–
				By Revaluation A/c	7,080	4,720	–
				By V's Loan			
				for Goodwill A/c	–	–	20,000
				By Premium			
				for Goodwill A/c	6,000	4,000	–
	1,22,080	1,94,720	20,000		1,22,080	1,94,720	20,000

BALANCE SHEET AS AT 1.4.20X1

Liabilities	₹	*Assets*		₹
Bank Overdraft	20,000	Cash		18,000
Creditors	30,000	Debtors	10,000	
Capitals:		*Less:* Provision	500	9,500
P	1,22,080	Bills Receivable		60,000
S	1,94,720	Stock [₹ 50,000 – ₹ 3,500]		46,500
V	20,000	Building		90,000
		Land [₹ 1,48,000 + ₹ 14,800]		1,62,800
	3,86,800			3,86,800

ILLUSTRATION 45

X and Y were partners in a firm sharing profits in the ratio of 3:2. On 31.3.2012 their Balance Sheet was as follows:

Liabilities	₹	*Assets*	₹
Sundry Creditors	70,000	Land and Building	1,00,000
Outstanding Expenses	10,000	Machinery	80,000
Capital Accounts:		Stock	1,00,000
X	1,80,000	Debtors	40,000
Y	70,000	Cash	10,000
	3,30,000		3,30,000

On the above date Z was admitted as a new partner in the firm for 1/4 share in the profits on the following terms:

(i) Z was to bring ₹ 1,20,000 for his capital and ₹ 25,000 for his share as premium for goodwill but he actually contributed only ₹ 20,000 towards his share of Goodwill.

(ii) Machinery was to be depreciated by 10% and Land and Building was to be appreciated by ₹ 30,000.

(iii) Stock was overvalued by ₹ 20,000.

(iv) A provision of 5% was to be created for doubtful debts.

(v) Salary outstanding was ₹ 3,000. There was a claim against the firm for damages amounting to ₹ 2,000. The claim has now been accepted.

Required: Prepare Revaluation Account, Partners' Capital Accounts and the Balance Sheet of the new firm.

SOLUTION

Dr. **REVALUATION ACCOUNT** *Cr.*

Particulars	₹	*Particulars*		₹
To Machinery A/c	8,000	By Land and Building		30,000
To Stock A/c	20,000	By Loss of Revaluation t/f to:		
To Provision for Doubtful Debts	2,000	X's Capital A/c	3,000	
To Salary Outstanding	3,000	Y's Capital A/c	2,000	5,000
To Claim for Damages	2,000			
	1,35,000			35,000

Dr. **PARTNERS' CAPITAL ACCOUNTS** *Cr.*

Particulars	X ₹	Y ₹	Y ₹	*Particulars*	X ₹	Y ₹	Y ₹
To Revaluation A/c	3,000	2,000	–	By Balance b/d	1,80,000	70,000	–
To X's Capital A/c	—	—	3,000	By Cash A/c	–	–	1,20,000
To Y's Capital A/c	—	—	2,000	By Premium for Goodwill A/c	12,000	8,000	
To Balance c/d	1,92,000	78,000	1,15,000	By Z's Capital A/c	3,000	2,000	—
	1,95,000	80,000	1,20,000		1,95,000	80,000	1,20,000

BALANCE SHEET OF NEW FIRM AS AT 31.03.2012

Liabilities		₹	*Assets*		₹
Sundry Creditors		70,000	Land and Building		1,30,000
Outstanding Expenses		10,000	Machinery		72,000
Salary Outstanding		3,000	Stock		80,000
Claim for Damages		2,000	Debtors	40,000	
Capitals:			*Less:* Prov. for Doubtful Debts	2,000	38,000
X	1,92,000		Cash (10,000 + 1,20,000 + 20,000)		1,50,000
Y	78,000				
Z	1,15,000	3,85,000			
		4,70,000			4,70,000

ILLUSTRATION 46

Murari and Vohra were partners in a firm with capital of ₹ 1,20,000 and ₹ 1,60,000 respectively. On 1st April, 2012 they admitted Yadav as a partner for one-fourth share in profits on his payment of ₹ 2,00,000 as his capital and ₹ 90,000 for his one-fourth share of goodwill.

On that date the creditors of Murari and Vohra were ₹ 60,000 and Bank overdraft was ₹ 15,000. Their assets apart from Cash included Stock ₹ 10,000; Debtors ₹ 40,000; Plant and Machinery ₹ 80,000; Land and Building ₹ 2,00,000. It was agreed that Stock should be depreciated by ₹ 2,000; Plant and Machinery by 20%, ₹ 5,000 should be written off as bad debts and Land and Building should be appreciated by 25%.

Required: Prepare the Revaluation Account, Capital Accounts of Partners and the Balance Sheet of the new firm.

SOLUTION

Dr. **REVALUATION ACCOUNT** Cr.

Particulars		₹	*Particulars*	₹
To Stock A/c		2,000	By Land and Building A/c	50,000
To Plant and Machinery A/c		16,000		
To Bad Debts Written off		5,000		
To Profit on Revaluation transferred to:				
Murari's Capital A/c	13,500			
Vohra's Capital A/c	13,500	27,000		
		50,000		50,000

Dr. **PARTNERS' CAPITAL ACCOUNTS** Cr.

Particulars	*Murari (₹)*	*Vohra (₹)*	*Yadav (₹)*	*Particulars*	*Murari (₹)*	*Vohra (₹)*	*Yadav (₹)*
To Balance c/d	1,78,500	2,18,500	2,00,000	By Balance b/d	1,20,000	1,60,000	—
				By Cash/Bank A/c	—	—	2,00,000
				By Revaluation A/c (Profit)	13,500	13,500	—
				By Premium for Goodwill A/c	45,000	45,000	—
	1,78,500	2,18,500	2,00,000		1,78,500	2,18,500	2,00,000

BALANCE SHEET OF NEW FIRM
as at 1st April, 2012

Liabilities	₹	*Assets*		₹
Bank Overdraft	15,000	Cash in Hand		3,15,000
Creditors	60,000	Plant and Machinery	80,000	
Murari's Capital	1,78,500	*Less:* Depreciation	16,000	64,000
Vohra's Capital	2,18,500	Land and Building	2,00,000	
Yadav's Capital	2,00,000	*Add:* Appreciation	50,000	2,50,000
		Stock	10,000	
		Less: Depreciation	2,000	8,000

		Debtors	40,000	
		Less: Bad Debts	5,000	35,000
	6,72,000			6,72,000

Working Notes:

1. MEMORANDUM BALANCE SHEET (BEFORE YADAV'S ADMISSION)

Liabilities	₹	*Assets*	₹
Creditors	60,000	Land and Building	2,00,000
Bank Overdraft	15,000	Stock	10,000
Murari's Capital A/c	1,20,000	Debtors	40,000
Vohra's Capital A/c	1,60,000	Plant and Machinery	80,000
		Cash (Bal. Fig.)	25,000
	3,55,000		3,55,000

Dr. **2. CASH ACCOUNT** *Cr.*

Particulars	₹	*Particulars*	₹
To Balance b/d	25,000	By Balance c/d	3,15,000
To Premium for Goodwill	90,000		
To Yadav's Capital A/c	2,00,000		
	3,15,000		3,15,000

8.0 ADJUSTMENT OF CAPITAL

The capitals of the partners may be adjusted in any one of the following ways:

1. **Adjusting the Capitals of Old Partners on the Basis of the Capital of Incoming Partner when the Total Capital of New Firm is not given**

PRACTICAL STEPS INVOLVED IN ADJUSTING THE CAPITALS OF OLD PARTNERS

Step 1: ***Calculate New Profit Sharing Ratio***

Step 2: ***Calculate Total Capital of New Firm as follows:***

Total Capital = New Partner's Capital × Reciprocal of proportion of share of new partner.

Step 3: ***Calculate the New Capitals of Old Partners as follows:***

New Capital of Old Partner = Total Capital of New Firm × New Share of Old Partner

Step 4: ***Calculate the Adjusted Old Capitals of Old Partners as follows:***

	A	*B*
Old Capital before Adjustments	xxx	xxx
Share of Goodwill	xxx	xxx
Share of Profit (Loss) on Revaluation	xxx	xxx
Share of Reserve and Accumulated Profits (Loss)	xxx	xxx
	xxx	xxx

Step 5: ***Calculate the Shortage (Surplus) in each of the Old Partner's Capital A/c as follows:***

Shortage (Surplus) = New Capital – Adjusted Old Capital

Step 6: ***Pass a Journal Entry to Adjust Shortage in case the Adjusted Old Capital is** less **than the New Capital.***

Cash A/c or Concerned Partner's Current A/c — *Dr.*

To Concerned Partner's Capital A/c

or

Pass a Journal Entry to Adjust Surplus in case the Adjusted Old Capital Is more than the New Capital

Concerned Partner's Capital A/c — *Dr.*

To Cash A/c or Concerned Partner's Current A/c

TUTORIAL NOTES

1. *In the absence of any contract, Surplus or Deficiency should be adjusted in Cash and not by transfer to Current Account.*
2. *If the Capitals of Old Partners are to be adjusted on the basis of Capital of Incoming Partner and Incoming Partner is not bringing his full/part of his share of Goodwill in Cash, then Unpaid Share of Goodwill should be adjusted through his Current Account and not Capital Account. In this case Debit Balance of Current Account will appear on the Assets side of the Balance Sheet.*

ILLUSTRATION 47

A and B are in partnership sharing profits and losses in the ratio of 3 : 2. The capitals of A and B before adjustments are ₹ 69,000 and ₹ 51,000 respectively. Firm's Goodwill ₹ 50,000, Loss on Revaluation of Assets and Liabilities ₹ 5,000, General Reserve ₹ 15,000. They admit C as a partner who contributes ₹ 35,000 as capital for 1/5th share of profits to be acquired equally from both A and B. The capital accounts of old partners are to be adjusted on the basis of the proportion of C's capital to his share in the business. Calculate the amount of actual cash to be paid off *or* brought in by the old partners for the purpose and pass the necessary journal entries.

SOLUTION

Step 1: Calculation of New Profit Sharing Ratio

A's New Share = 3/5 – 1/10 = 5/10, B's New Share = 2/5 – 1/10 = 3/10

Hence, New Profit Sharing Ratio of A : B : C = 5/10 : 3/10 : 1/5 = 5 : 3 : 2

Step 2: Calculation of Total Capital of the reconstituted firm

Total Capital = ₹ 35,000 × 5/1 = ₹ 1,75,000

STEP 3: CALCULATION OF NEW CAPITALS OF ALL PARTNERS

Particulars	*A*	*B*	*C*
New Capitals (₹ 1,75,000 in ratio of 5 : 3 : 2)	₹ 87,500	₹ 52,500	₹ 35,000

STEP 4: ADJUSTED OLD CAPITALS OF OLD PARTNERS

Particulars	*A*	*B*
Old Capitals before Adjustments	69,000	51,000
Add: Share of Goodwill	5,000	5,000
Less: Share of Loss on Revaluation	(3,000)	(2,000)

Add: Share of General Reserve	9,000	6,000
	₹ 80,000	₹ 60,000

STEP 5: CALCULATION OF SHORTAGE/ SURPLUS

Particulars	*A*	*B*
(a) New Capitals (as per Step 3)	₹ 87,500	₹ 52,500
(b) Adjusted Old Capitals (as per Step 4)	₹ 80,000	₹ 60,000
(c) Surplus to be paid (Shortage to be brought in)	(₹ 7,500)	₹ 7,500

Step 6: Journal Entry

JOURNAL

Date	*Particulars*		*L.F.*	*Dr. (₹)*	*Cr. (₹)*
	Cash A/c	Dr.		7,500	
	To A's Capital A/c				7,500
	(Being the shortage brought in by A)				
	B's Capital A/c	Dr.		7,500	
	To Cash A/c				7,500
	(Being the excess amount withdrawn by B)				

ILLUSTRATION 48

A and B are in partnership sharing profits and losses in the proportion of two-third and one-third respectively. Their Balance Sheet on 31st March, 2012 was as follows:

Cash ₹ 1,000; Sundry Debtors ₹ 15,000; Stock ₹ 22,000; Plant and Machinery ₹ 4,000; Sundry Creditors ₹ 1,000; Employees' Provident Fund ₹ 1,000; Bank Overdraft ₹ 15,000; A's Capital ₹ 15,000 : B's Capital ₹ 10,000.

On 1st April, 2012, they admitted C into partnership on the following terms:

(a) C to purchase one quarter of the Goodwill for ₹ 3,000 and provide ₹ 10,000 as Capital. C brings necessary cash for goodwill and capital.

(b) Profits and Losses are to be shared in the proportion of one-half to A, one-quarter to B, and one quarter to C.

(c) Plant and Machinery is to be reduced by 10%, and ₹ 500 is to be provided for estimated bad debts. Stock is to be taken at a valuation of ₹ 24,940.

(d) By bringing in *or* withdrawing cash the capitals of A and B are to be made proportionate to that of C on their profit-sharing basis.

Required: Prepare the necessary ledger accounts and prepare the opening Balance Sheet of the new firm.

SOLUTION

Dr. **REVALUATION ACCOUNT** *Cr.*

Particulars	₹	*Particulars*	₹
To Plant and Machinery	400	By Stock	2,940
To Provision for doubtful debts	500		

To Profit on Revaluation t/f to:				
A's Capital A/c	1,360			
B's Capital A/c	680	2,040		
		2,940		2,940

Dr. **PARTNERS' CAPITAL ACCOUNTS** *Cr.*

Particulars	*A* ₹	*B* ₹	*C* ₹	*Particulars*	*A* ₹	*B* ₹	*C* ₹
To Cash A/c (b.f.)	—	**1,680**	—	By Balance b/d	15,000	10,000	—
To Balance c/d	20,000	10,000	10,000	By Revaluation A/c	1,360	680	—
				By Premium for Goodwill A/c	2,000	1,000	—
				By Cash A/c b.f.)	**1,640**	—	10,000
	20,000	11,680	10,000		20,000	11,680	10,000

Dr. **CASH ACCOUNT** *Cr.*

Particulars	₹	*Particulars*	₹
To Balance b/d	1,000	By B's Capital A/c	1,680
To A's Capital A/c	1,640	By Balance c/d	13,960
To C's Capital A/c	10,000		
To Premium for Goodwill A/c	3,000		
	15,640		15,640

BALANCE SHEET OF THE NEW FIRM AS AT 1ST APRIL., 2012

Liabilities	₹	*Assets*		₹
Sundry Creditors	1,000	Cash		13,960
Employees' Provident Fund	1,000	Debtors	15,000	
Bank Overdraft	15,000	*Less:* Provision	500	14,500
Capitals:		Stock		24,940
A	20,000	Plant and Machinery		3,600
B	10,000			
C	10,000			
	57,000			57,000

Note: Total Capital of Firm = ₹ 10,000 × 4/1 = ₹ 40,000

New Capital of A = ₹ 40,000 × 2/4 = ₹ 20,000, New Capital of B = ₹ 40,000 × 1/4 = ₹ 10,000

ILLUSTRATION 49

A, B and C are partners sharing profits and losses in the ratio of 2 : 3 : 5. On 31st March, 2012 their Balance Sheet was as follows :

Liabilities	₹	*Assets*	₹
A's Capital	36,000	Cash	18,000

B's Capital	44,000	Bills Receivable	24,000
C's Capital	52,000	Furniture	28,000
Creditors	64,000	Stock	44,000
Employees' Provident Fund	32,000	Debtors	42,000
Workmen Compensation Fund	14,000	Investment	32,000
		Machinery	34,000
		Goodwill	20,000
	2,42,000		2,42,000

They admit D into partnership on the following terms:

(a) Furniture, Investment and Machinery to be depreciated by 15%.

(b) Stock is revalued at ₹ 48,000.

(c) Goodwill to be valued at ₹ 24,000 and D brings his share in cash.

(d) Outstanding Rent amounted to ₹ 1,800.

(e) Prepaid Salaries ₹ 800.

(f) D to bring ₹ 32,000 towards capital for 1/6th share and partners to readjust their capital accounts on the basis of their profit sharing ratio.

(g) Adjustment of capitals to be made by cash.

Required: Prepare Revaluation account, Partners' capital accounts. Cash account and Balance Sheet of the new firm.

SOLUTION

Dr. **REVALUATION ACCOUNT** *Cr.*

Particulars	₹	*Particulars*	₹
To Furniture	4,200	By Stock	4,000
To Investments	4,800	By Prepaid Salaries	800
To Machinery	5,100	By Loss transferred to:	
To Outstanding Rent	1,800	A's Capital A/c	2,220
		B's Capital A/c	3,330
		C's Capital A/c	5,550
	15,900		15,900

Dr. **PARTNERS' CAPITAL ACCOUNTS** *Cr.*

Particulars	*A* ₹	*B* ₹	*C* ₹	*D* ₹	*Particulars*	*A* ₹	*B* ₹	*C* ₹	*D* ₹
To Goodwill A/c	4,000	6,000	10,000	—	By Balance b/d	36,000	44,000	52,000	—
To Revaluation A/c	2,220	3,330	5,550	—	By Workmen Comp. Fund	2,800	4,200	7,000	—
To Cash A/c (b.f.)	1,380	—	—	—	By Premium for Goodwill A/c	800	1,200	2,000	—
To Balance c/d	32,000	48,000	80,000	32,000	By Cash A/c (b.f.)	—	7,930	34,550	32,000
	39,600	57,330	95,550	32,000		39,600	57,330	95,550	32,000

Dr. **CASH ACCOUNT** Cr.

Particulars	₹	*Particulars*	₹
To Balance b/d	18,000	By A's Capital A/c	1,380
To B's Capital A/c	7,930	By Balance c/d	95,100
To C's Capital A/c	34,550		
To D's Capital A/c	32,000		
To Premium for Goodwill A/c	4,000		
	96,480		96,480

BALANCE SHEET OF A, B, C AS AT 31ST MARCH, 2012

Liabilities	₹	*Assets*	₹
Creditors	64,000	Cash	95,100
Employees' Provident Fund	32,000	Bills Receivable	24,000
Outstanding Rent	1,800	Debtors	42,000
Capitals:		Stock	48,000
A	32,000	Prepaid Salaries	800
B	48,000	Investments	27,200
C	80,000	Furniture	23,800
D	32,000	Machinery	28,900
	2,89,800		2,89,800

Working Note: *Calculation of Total Capital and New Capitals of Partners*

Total Capital of New Firm = ₹ 32,000 × 6/1 = ₹ 1,92,000

A's Capital = ₹ 1,92,000 × 2/12 = ₹ 32,000, B's Capital = ₹ 1,92,000 × 3/12 = ₹ 48,000

C's Capital = ₹ 1,92,000 × 5/12 = ₹ 80,000, D's Capital = ₹ 1,92,000 × 2/12 = ₹ 32,000

ILLUSTRATION 50

On 31st March, 2012 the Balance Sheet of W and R shared profits in 3 : 2 ratio was as follows:

Liabilities		₹	*Assets*		₹
Creditors		20,000	Cash		5,000
Profit & Loss A/c		15,000	Sundry Debtors	20,000	
Capital A/cs:			*Less:* Provision	700	19,300
W	40,000		Stock		25,000
R	30,000	70,000	Plant and Machinery		35,000
			Patents		20,700
		1,05,000			1,05,000

On this date B was admitted as a partner on the following conditions:

(i) B will get 4/15th share of profits.

(ii) B had to bring ₹ 30,000 as his capital to which amount other partners' capitals shall have to be adjusted.

(iii) He would pay cash for his share of goodwill which would be based on 2½ years' purchase of average profits of past 4 years.

(iv) The assets would be revalued as under:

Sundry debtors at book value *less* 5% provision for doubtful debts. Stock at ₹ 20,000, Plant and Machinery at ₹ 40,000.

(v) The profits of the firm for the years 2009, 2010 and 2011 were ₹ 20,000; ₹ 14,000 and ₹ 17,000 respectively.

Required: Prepare the Revaluation Account, Partners' Capital Accounts and the Balance Sheet of the new firm.

SOLUTION

Dr. **REVALUATION ACCOUNT** *Cr.*

Particulars	₹	*Particulars*		₹
To Provision for Doubtful Debts A/c	300	By Plant and Machinery A/c		5,000
To Stock A/c	5,000	By Loss transferred to:		
		W's Capital A/c	180	
		R's Capital A/c	120	300
	5,300			5,300

Dr. **PARTNERS' CAPITAL ACCOUNTS** *Cr.*

Particulars	*W (₹)*	*R (₹)*	*B (₹)*	*Particulars*	*W (₹)*	*R (₹)*	*B (₹)*
To Revaluation	180	120	—	By Balance b/d	40,000	30,000	—
To Cash A/c (b.f)	**5,920**	**7,280**	—	By P&L A/c	9,000	6,000	—
To Balance c/d	49,500	33,000	30,000	By Cash A/c	—	—	30,000
				By Premium for Goodwill A/c	6,600	4,400	—
	55,600	40,400	30,000		55,600	40,400	30,000

BALANCE SHEET OF THE NEW FIRM

as at 31st March, 2012

Liabilities	₹	*Assets*		₹
Creditors	20,000	Cash		32,800
Capital A/cs:		Sundry Debtors	20,000	
W	49,500	*Less:* Provision	1,000	19,000
R	33,000	Stock		20,000
B	30,000	Plant and Machinery		40,000
		Patents		20,700
	1,32,500			1,32,500

Working Notes:

1. **Average Profits** = (₹ 20,000 + ₹ 14,000) + ₹ 17,000 + ₹ 15,000)/4 = ₹ 16,500
2. **Value of Goodwill** = Average Profit × No. of years' Purchase = ₹ 16,500 × 5/2 = ₹ 41,250
3. **B's Share in Goodwill** = ₹ 41,250 × 4/15 = ₹ 11,000

4. **Calculation of New Profit Sharing Ratio**

Let Total Profit = 1

B's share = 4/15th share

Remaining Profit = 1 – 4/15 = 11/15

W's share = 11/15 × 3/5 = 33/75

R's share = 11/15 × 2/5 = 22/75

Ratio of W : R : B = 33/75 : 22/75 : 4/15 *or* 33 : 22 : 20

5. **Total Capital of New Firm and New Capitals of Partners**

Total Capital of New Firm = ₹ 30,000 × 15/4 = ₹ 1,12,500

W's Capital = ₹ 1,12,500 × 33/75 = ₹ 49,500

R's Capital = ₹ 1,12,500 × 22/75 = ₹ 33,000

B's Capital = ₹ 1,12,500 × 20/75 = ₹ 30,000

Dr. **6. CASH ACCOUNT** Cr.

Particulars	₹	*Particulars*	₹
To Balance b/d	5,000	By W's Capital A/c	5,920
To B's Capital A/c	30,000	By R's Capital A/c	7,280
To Premium for Goodwill	11,000	By Balance b/d	32,800
	46,000		46,000

ILLUSTRATION 51

Rao and Reddy were partners in a firm sharing profits in the ratio of 3 : 1. They admitted Kutty as a new partner for 3/8th share in the profits. The new profit-sharing ratio will be 3 : 2 : 3. Kutty brought ₹ 2,00,000 for his capital and ₹ 50,000 for his share of premium for goodwill. On 31st March, 2012, the date of Kutty's admission, the Balance Sheet of Rao and Reddy was:

Liabilities	₹	*Assets*	₹
Creditors	60,000	Cash	90,000
Bills Payable	20,000	Debtors	80,000
Capital A/cs:		Stock	1,50,000
Rao	4,00,000	Furniture	50,000
Reddy	1,00,000	Machinery	2,10,000
	5,80,000		5,80,000

It was agreed that

(i) Stock to be valued at ₹ 2,00,000.

(ii) Machinery will be depreciated by 12% and Furniture by ₹ 2,000.

(iii) A Provision of 5% for Doubtful Debts will be made on Debtors.

(iv) The Capital Accounts of all the partners were adjusted in the new profit-sharing ratio after admission. For surplus *or* deficiency, the Current Accounts were to be opened.

Required: Prepare the Revaluation Account, Partners' Capital Accounts and the Balance Sheet of the new firm.

SOLUTION

Dr. **REVALUATION ACCOUNT** Cr.

Particulars		₹	Particulars	₹
To Machinery A/c		25,200	By Stock A/c	50,000
To Furniture A/c		2,000		
To Provision for Doubtful Debts A/c		4,000		
To Profit on revaluation t/f to:				
Rao's Capital A/c (3/4)	14,100			
Reddy's Capital A/c (1/4)	4,700	18,800		
		50,000		50,000

Dr. **PARTNERS' CAPITAL ACCOUNTS** Cr.

Particulars	Rao (₹)	Reddy (₹)	Kutty (₹)	Particulars	Rao (₹)	Reddy (₹)	Kutty (₹)
To Rao's Current A/c (b.f.)	**2,64,100**	—	—	By Balance b/d	4,00,000	1,00,000	—
To Balance c/d	2,00,000	1,33,334	2,00,000	By Revaluation A/c	14,100	4,700	—
				By Bank A/c	—	—	2,00,000
				By Premium for Goddwill A/c	50,000	—	—
				By Reddy's Current A/c (b.f.)	—	**28,634**	—
	4,64,100	1,33,334	2,00,000		4,64,100	1,33,334	2,00,000

BALANCE SHEET OF THE NEW FIRM
as at 1st April, 2012

Liabilities	₹	Assets		₹
Creditors	60,000	Cash		3,40,000
Bills Payable	20,000	(₹ 90,000 + ₹ 2,00,000 + ₹ 50,000)		
Rao's Current A/c	2,64,100	Debtors	80,000	
Capital A/cs:		*Less:* Provision	4,000	76,000
Rao	2,00,000	Stock		2,00,000
Reddy	1,33,334	Furniture (₹ 50,000 – ₹ 2,000)		48,000
Kutty	2,00,000	Machinery (₹ 2,10,000 – ₹ 25,200)		1,84,800
		Reddy's Current A/c		28,634
	8,77,434			8,77,434

Working Notes:

1. **Calculation of Sacrificing Ratio**

   Sacrifice = Old Share – New Share

   Rao's sacrifice = $\frac{3}{4} - \frac{3}{8} = \frac{3}{8}$, Reddy's sacrifice = $\frac{1}{4} - \frac{2}{8}$ = Nil

   Only Rao sacrifices his share of profit.

2. Calculation of Partners' New Capitals

(a) Total Capital of the Firm = $\frac{\text{Capital of the New Partner (Kutty)}}{\text{Share of Profit of Kutty}}$

= ₹ 2,00,000 × 8/3 = ₹ 16,00,000/3

(b) New Capitals of Partners

Rao = $\frac{₹16,00,000}{3} \times \frac{3}{8}$ = ₹ 2,00,000; Reddy = $\frac{₹16,00,000}{3} \times \frac{2}{8}$ = ₹ 1,33,334

ILLUSTRATION 52

The following was the Balance Sheet of A, B and C sharing profits and losses in the ratio of 6 : 5 : 3 respectively:

Liabilities	₹	*Assets*	₹
Creditors	9,000	Goodwill	14,000
Employees' Provident Fund	3,000	Land & Building	24,000
Workmen Compensation Reserve	14,000	Furniture	3,500
Investment Fluctuation Reserve	7,000	Stock	14,000
A's Capital	19,000	Debtors	12,600
B's Capital	16,000	Cash	900
C's Capital	8,000	Advertisement Expenditure	7,000
	76,000		76,000

They agreed to take D into partnership and gave him a share of 1/8th in the rupee on the following terms:

(a) that D should bring in ₹ 4,200 as goodwill and ₹ 7,000 as his capital,

(b) that furniture be depreciated by 12%.

(c) that stock be depreciated by 10%.

(d) that a provision of 5% be created for doubtful debts.

(e) that the value of Land and Building be brought up to ₹ 31,000.

(f) that after making the above adjustments, the capital accounts of the old partners (who continue to share in the proportion as before) be adjusted on the basis of the proportion of D's capital to his share in the business, i.e., actual cash to be paid of *or* brought in by the old partners, as the case may be. Prepare the Revaluation Account, Cash Account and the opening Balance Sheet of the new firm.

SOLUTION

Dr. **REVALUATION ACCOUNT** *Cr.*

Particulars	₹	*Particulars*	₹
To Furniture	420	By Land & Building	7,000
To Stock	1,400		
To Provision for Doubtful Debts	630		
To Profit on Revaluation t/f to :			
A's Capital A/c	1,950		
B's Capital A/c	1,625		

C's Capital A/c	975		
	7,000		7,000

Dr. **CASH ACCOUNT** Cr.

Particulars	₹	*Particulars*	₹
To Balance b/d	900	By A's Capital A/c	1,750
To D's Capital A/c	7,000	By B's Capital A/c	1,625
To Premium for Goodwill A/c	4,200	By Balance c/d	9,350
To C's Capital A/c	625		
	12,725		12,725

BALANCE SHEET OF THE RECONSTITUTED FIRM AS AT...

Liabilities	₹	*Assets*		₹
Creditors	9,000	Cash		9,350
Employees' Provident Fund	3,000	Debtors	12,600	
A's Capital	21,000	*Less:* Provision	630	11,970
B's Capital	17,500	Stock		12,600
C's Capital	10,500	Furniture		3,080
D's Capital	7,000	Land & Building		31,000
	68,000			68,000

Working Notes:

1. Total Capital of New Firm = ₹ 7,000 × 16/2 = ₹ 56,000
2. New Capitals of Partners
   A's Capital = ₹ 56,000 × 6/16 = ₹ 21,000, B's Capital = ₹ 56,000 × 5/16 = ₹ 17,500
   C's Capital = ₹ 56,000 × 3/16 = ₹ 10,500 D's Capital = ₹ 56,000 × 2/16 = ₹ 7,000

3. CALCULATION OF ACTUAL CASH TO BE PAID OFF/BROUGHT IN BY THE OLD PARTNERS

Particulars	*A* ₹	*B* ₹	*C* ₹
(a) New Capital	21,000	17,500	10,500
(b) Adjusted Old Capital	22,750	19,125	9,875
(c) Cash to be paid off (to be brought in)	1,750	1,625	(625)

4. Adjusted Old Capitals have been ascertained after making adjustments for goodwill, accumulated profits & losses profit on revaluation of assets.

ILLUSTRATION 53

The following is the Balance Sheet of A and B who had been sharing profits in proportion of three-fourths and one-fourths, on 31st March, 2012.

Liabilities	₹	*Assets*	₹
Creditors	30,000	Goodwill	4,000

Employees' Provident Fund	7,500	Cash at Bank	22,500
Workmen Compensation Reserve	4,000	Bills Receivable	4,000
Investment Fluctuation Reserve	2,000	Debtors	16,000
A's Capital	33,000	Stock	20,000
B's Capital	17,000	Office Furniture	1,000
Provision for Doubtful Debts	1,000	Land & Building	25,000
		Advertisement Expenditure	2,000
	94,500		94,500

They agreed to take C into partnership on 1st April, 2012 on the following terms:

(a) That C pays ₹ 10,000 as his capital for one-fifth share in the future profits.

(b) That a Goodwill of the firm is valued at ₹ 20,000 but no goodwill is to appear in the books.

(c) That Stock and Furniture be reduced by 15% and 10% respectively and 5% provision for doubtful debts be created on debtors.

(d) That the Value of Land and Building be appreciated by 20%.

(e) That the Capital Accounts of the partners be re-adjusted on the basis of their profit sharing arrangement and any excess *or* deficiency be transferred to their Current Accounts. Prepare Revaluation Account, Partner's Capital Accounts and the Balance Sheet of the new firm.

SOLUTION

Dr. **REVALUATION ACCOUNT** *Cr.*

Particulars		₹	*Particulars*		₹
To Stock A/c		3,000	By Land & Building A/c		5,000
To Office Furniture A/c		100	By Provision for Doubtful Debts		
To Profit transferred to:			Existing	1,000	
A's Capital A/c	1,575		*Less:* Required		
B's Capital A/c	525	2,100	[₹ 16,000 × 5/100]	800	200
		5,200			5,200

Dr. **PARTNERS' CAPITAL ACCOUNTS** *Cr.*

Particulars	*A* ₹	*B* ₹	*C* ₹	*Particulars*	*A* ₹	*B* ₹	*C* ₹
To Goodwill A/c	3,000	1,000	—	By Balance b/d	33,000	17,000	—
To Current A/c (b.f.)	7,575	8,525	—	By Bank A/c	—	—	10,000
To Advertise Exp.	1,500	500	—	By C's Current A/c	3,000	1,000	—
To Balance c/d	30,000	10,000	10,000	By Revaluation A/c	1,575	525	—
				By Worr. Com. Res.	3,000	1,000	—
				By Invest. Fluc. Res.	1,500	500	—
	42,075	20,025	10,000		42,075	20,025	10,000

BALANCE SHEET AS AT 1ST APRIL, 2012

Liabilities	₹	*Assets*	₹
Creditors	30,000	Cash at Bank	32,500

Employees' Provident Fund		7,500	Bills Receivable		4,000
Capital Accounts:			Debtors	16,000	
A	30,000		*Less:* Provision	800	15,200
B	10,000		Stock		17,000
C	10,000	50,000	Office Furniture		900
Current Accounts:			Land & Building		30,000
A	7,575		C's Current A/c		4,000
B	8,525	16,100			
		1,03,600			1,03,600

Working Notes: *Calculation of Total Capital and New Capitals of Partners*

Total Capital = ₹ 10,000 × 5/1 = ₹ 50,000

A's Capital = ₹ 50,000 × 3/5 = ₹ 30,000, B's Capital = ₹ 50,000 × 1/5 = ₹ 10,000

2. Determining the New Partner's Capital on the Basis of Combined Capital of Old Partners

PRACTICAL STEPS INVOLVED IN THE DETERMINATION OF CAPITAL OF NEW PARTNER

Step 1: ***Calculate the New Profit Sharing Ratio***

Step 2: ***Calculate the Adjusted Old capitals of Old Partners:***

	A	B
Old Capital before Adjustments	xxx	xxx
Share of Goodwill	xxx	xxx
Profit (Loss) on Revaluation	xxx	xxx
Share of Reserve and Accumulated Profits (Loss)	xxx	xxx
	xxx	xxx

Step 3: ***Calculate the Total Capital of New Firm as follows:***

Total Capital = Total Adjusted Old Capitals of Old Partners × Reciprocal of proportion of Share of Old Partners

Step 4: ***Calculate the Proportionate Capital of New Partner as follows:***

New Partner's Capital = Total Capital × Proportion of Share of New Partner

Tutorial Note: *If Incoming Partner is bringing Proportionate Capital but is not bringing his full/part of his share of Goodwill in Cash, then Unpaid Share of Goodwill should be adjusted through his Current Account and not Capital Account. In this case Debit Balance of Current Account will appear on the Assets side of the Balance Sheet.*

ILLUSTRATION 54

A and B are in partnership sharing profits and losses in the ratio of 3 : 2. The capitals of A and B before adjustments are ₹ 69,000 and ₹ 51,000 respectively. Firm's Goodwill ₹ 50,000, Loss on Revaluation of Assets and Liabilities ₹ 5,000, General Reserve ₹ 15,000. They admit C as a partner who has to contribute sufficient capital to acquire 1/5th share of profits to be acquired equally from both A and B. Calculate the amount of capital to be brought in by C.

SOLUTION

Step 1: Calculation of New Profit Sharing ratio

New Profit Sharing Ratio = 5 : 3 : 2 (as calculated in Illustration 47)

STEP 2 CALCULATION OF TOTAL ADJUSTED OLD CAPITALS OF OLD PARTNERS

Particulars	A	B
Old Capitals before Adjustments	69,000	51,000
Add: Share of Goodwill	5,000	5,000
Less: Share of Loss on Revaluation	(3,000)	(2,000)
Add: Share of General Reserve	9,000	6,000
	₹ 80,000	₹ 60,000

Total Adjusted Capital of Old Partners = ₹ 80,000 + ₹ 60,000 = ₹ 1,40,000

Step 3: Calculation of Total Capital of New Firm

Total Share of Old Partners = 1 – Share of Incoming Partner = 1 – 1/5 = 4/5

Reciprocal of Proportion of Total Share of old partners = 5/4

Total Capital = ₹ 1,40,000 × 5/4 = ₹ 1,75,000

Alternative Method – Let us assume, the total capital of new firm be X

X = ₹ 80,000 + ₹ 60,000 + 1/5X or, X – 1/5X = ₹ 1,40,000

X = ₹ 1,40,000 × 5/4 = ₹ 1,75,000

Step 4: Calculation of Proportionate Capital of Incoming Partner

New Partner's Capital = Total Capital × Proportion of Share of New Partner

= ₹ 1,75,000 × 1/5 = ₹ 35,000

ILLUSTRATION 55

Assuming that in Previous Illustration, it is decided that the Capitals of old partners should also be in their new profit sharing ratio. Calculate the amount of actual cash to be paid off *or* brought in by the old partners for this adjustment.

SOLUTION

Step 1, 2, 3: Same as given in Previous Illustration.

Step 4: Calculation of New Capitals of Partners

A's New Capital = ₹ 1,75,000 × 5/10 = ₹ 87,500

B's New Capital = ₹ 1,75,000 × 3/10 = ₹ 52,500

STEP 5: CALCULATION OF ACTUAL CASH TO BE PAID OFF *or* BROUGHT IN BY OLD PARTNERS

(a) New Capitals	₹ 87,500	₹ 52,500
(b) Adjusted Old Capitals	₹ 80,000	₹ 60,000
(c) Cash to be paid (to be brought in) (a–b)	(₹ 7,500)	₹ 7,500

ILLUSTRATION 56

A and B are in partnership sharing profits and losses in the ratio of 3 : 2. The capitals of A and B after adjustments are ₹ 90,000 and ₹ 70,000 respectively. Calculate Incoming Partner's proportionate capital and surplus/shortage of existing capitals of old partners (if any) in each of the following alternative cases:

Case (a) If C is to contribute proportionate capital for his 1/5th share.

Case (b) If C is to contribute 1/5th of the total capital of the new firm.

Case (c) If C is to contribute 1/4th of the combined capitals of the existing partners.

Case (d) If C is to contribute proportionate capital for his 1/5th share and the capitals of all the partners are to be adjusted in new profit sharing ratio of 3 : 1 : 1.

SOLUTION

Case (a) Let the Total Capital be X

Thus, X = Adjusted Old Capitals of old partners + Incoming Partners' Capital

X = ₹ 90,000 + ₹ 70,000 + 1/5X, X–1/5X =₹ 1,60,000 = ₹ 1,60,000 × 5/4 = ₹ 2,00,000

Thus, Incoming Partner's proportionate capital = 1/5 of ₹ 2,00,000 = ₹ 40,000

Case (b) Same solution as in Case (a)

Case (c) Incoming Partner's Capital = 1/4 × (₹ 90,000 + ₹ 70,000) = ₹ 40,000

Case (d) Let the Total Capital be X

Thus, X = Adjusted Old Capitals of old partners + Incoming Partners' Capital

X = ₹ 90,000 + ₹ 70,000 + 1/5X

X–1/5X = ₹ 1,60,000 = ₹ 1,60,000 × 5/4 = ₹ 2,00,000

Thus, Incoming Partner's Proportionate Capital = 1/5 of ₹ 2,00,000 = ₹ 40,000.

Particulars	*A*	*B*
Their New Capitals	3/5 × ₹ 2,00,000 = ₹ 1,20,000	1/5 × 2,00,000 = 40,000
Their Adjusted Old Capitals	₹ 90,000	₹ 70,000
Shortage (Surplus)	₹ 30,000	(₹ 30,000)

ILLUSTRATION 57

On 31st March, 2012 the Balance Sheet of A and B, who are partners in a firm sharing profits in the ratio of 3:2 was as follows:

Liabilities	₹	*Assets*		₹
Capital Accounts:		Plant and Machinery		10,000
A	10,000	Land and Buildings		8,000
B	8,000	Debtors	12,000	
General Reserves	15,000	*Less:* Prov. for Doubt debts	1,000	11,000
Workmen's Compensation Fund	5,000	Stock		12,000
Creditors	12,000	Cash		9,000
	50,000			50,000

They agreed to admit C into partnership for 1/5th share of profits on the following terms:

(i) Provision for doubtful debts would be increased by ₹ 2,000.

(ii) The value of Land & Building would be increased to ₹ 18,000.

(iii) The value of Stock would be increased by ₹ 4,000

(iv) The liability against workmen's compensation fund is determined at ₹ 2,000.

(v) C brought in as his share of goodwill ₹ 10,000 in cash. C would bring further cash as would make his capital equal to 20% of the total capital of the new firm, after the above revaluation and adjustments are carried out.

Required: Pass Journal Entries relating to Goodwill, Reserves and Workmen Compensation Fund. Prepare Revaluation Account, Partners' Capital Accounts and the Balance Sheet of the firm after C's admission.

SOLUTION

JOURNAL

Date	*Particulars*		*L.F.*	*Dr. (₹)*	*Cr. (₹)*
1.	Cash A/c	Dr.		10,000	
	To Premium for Goodwill A/c				10,000
	(Being the Premium brought by C)				
2.	Premium for Goodwill A/c	Dr.		10,000	
	To A's Capital A/c				6,000
	To B's Capital A/c				4,000
	(Being the Premium divided among sacrificing partners)				
3.	General Reserve A/c	Dr.		15,000	
	To A's Capital A/c				9,000
	To B's Capital A/c				6,000
	(Being the General reserve distributed among partners)				
4.	Workmen's Compensation Fund	Dr.		5,000	
	To Liability for Workmen Compensation				2,000
	To A's Capital A/c				1,800
	To B's Capital A/c				1,200
	(Being the liability provided for and the balance amount of Workmen's Compensation Fund divided among Partners)				

Dr. **REVALUATION ACCOUNT** *Cr.*

Particulars		₹	*Particulars*	₹
To Provision for Doubtful Debts		2,000	By Land & Building A/c	10,000
To Profit transferred to			By Stock	4,000
A's Capital A/c	7,200			
B's Capital A/c	4,800	12,000		
		14,000		14,000

Dr. **PARTNERS' CAPITAL ACCOUNTS** *Cr.*

Particulars	*A (₹)*	*B (₹)*	*C (₹)*	*Particulars*	*A (₹)*	*B (₹)*	*C (₹)*
				By Balance b/d	10,000	8,000	
				By Revaluation A/c	7,200	4,800	
				By Work. Comp. Fund	1,800	1,200	
				By General Reserve	9,000	6,000	
To Balance c/d	34,000	24,000		By Premium for Goodwill A/c	6,000	4,000	
	34,000	24,000			34,000	24,000	

				By Balance b/d	34,000	24,000	
To Balance c/d	34,000	24,000	14,500	By Cash A/c	—	—	14,500
	34,000	24,000	14,500		34,000	24,000	14,500

BALANCE SHEET AS AT 31ST MARCH, 2012

Liabilities	₹	*Assets*		₹
Creditors	12,000	Plant		10,000
Liability for Workmen's Claim	2,000	Land & Building		18,000
A's Capital	34,000	Debtors	12,000	
B's Capital	24,000	*Less:* Pro. for Doubt. Debts	3,000	9,000
C's Capital	14,500	Stock		16,000
		Cash		33,500
	86,500			86,500

Working Notes:

1. Total Capital= (₹ 34,000 + ₹ 24,000) × 5/4 = 72,500.
2. C's Capital = ₹ 72,500 × 1/5 = ₹ 14,500

Dr. **3. CASH ACCOUNT** *Cr.*

Particulars	₹	*Particulars*	₹
To Balance b/d	9,000	By Balance c/d	33,500
To Premium for Goodwill A/c	10,000		
To C's Capital A/c	14,500		
	33,500		33,500

ILLUSTRATION 58

The Balance Sheet of Madan and Mohan who share profits and losses in the ratio of 3 : 2, as at 31st March, 2012 was as follows:

Liabilities	₹	*Assets*		₹
Creditors	28,000	Cash at Bank		10,000
Workmen's Compensation Fund	12,000	Debtors	65,000	
General Reserve	20,000	*Less:* Provision	5,000	60,000
Madan's Captial	60,000	Stock		30,000
Mohan's Captial	40,000	Investments		50,000
		Patents		10,000
	1,60,000			1,60,000

They decided to admit Gopal on 1st April, 2012 for 1/4th share on the following terms:

(a) Gopal shall bring ₹ 25,000 as his share of premium for goodwill.

(b) That unaccounted accrued income of ₹ 500 be provided for.

(c) The market value of investments was ₹ 45,000.

(d) A debtor whose dues of ₹ 1,000 were written off as bad debts paid ₹ 800 in full settlement.

(e) A claim of ₹ 2,000 on account of workmen's compensation to be provided for.

(f) Patents are undervalued by ₹ 5,000.

(g) Gopal to bring in capital equal to 1/4th of the total capital of the new firm after all adjustments.

Required: Prepare the Revaluation Account, Capital Accounts of the Partners and the Balance Sheet of the new firm.

SOLUTION

Dr. **REVALUATION ACCOUNT** *Cr.*

Particulars		₹	*Particulars*	₹
To Investments		5,000	By Accrued Income	500
To Profit transferred to:			By Bad Debts Recovered	800
Madan's Capital A/c	780		By Patents	5,000
Mohan's Capital A/c	520	1,300		
		6,300		6,300

Dr. **PARTNERS' CAPITAL ACCOUNTS** *Cr.*

Particulars	*Madan* (₹)	*Mohan* (₹)	*Gopal* (₹)	*Particulars*	*Madan* (₹)	*Mohan* (₹)	*Gopal* (₹)
To Balance c/d	93,780	62,520	52,100	By Balance b/d	60,000	40,000	—
				By General Reserve	12,000	8,000	—
				By Revaluation A/c	780	520	—
				By Workmen's Compensation Fund	6,000	4,000	—
				By Premium for Goodwill	15,000	10,000	—
				By Bank A/c	—	—	52,100
	93,780	62,520	52,100		93,780	62,520	52,100

BALANCE SHEET OF THE NEW FIRM

as at 1st April, 2012

Liabilities	₹	*Assets*		₹
Creditors	28,000	Cash at Bank		87,900
Workmen's Compensation Claim	2,000	Debtors	65,000	
Capital A/cs:		*Less:* Provision	5,000	60,000
Madan	93,780	Stock		30,000
Mohan	62,520	Investment		45,000
Gopal	52,100	Patents		15,000
		Accrued Income		500
	2,38,400			2,38,400

Working Notes:

1. **Total Capital of the Firm** = (₹ 93,780 + ₹ 62,520) × 4/3 = ₹ 2,08,400.
2. **Gopal's Capital in the New Firm** = ₹ 2,08,400 × 1/4 = ₹ 52,100.

Dr. **3. CASH ACCOUNT** Cr.

Particulars	₹	Particulars	₹
To Balance b/d	10,000	By Balance c/d	87,900
To Gopal's Capital A/c	52,100		
To Premium for Goodwill	25,000		
To Bad Debts Recovered	800		
	87,900		87,900

ILLUSTRATION 59

A and B are partners sharing profits and losses in the ratio of 3 : 2. Their Balance Sheet as at 31st March, 2012 was as follows:

Liabilities	₹	Assets		₹
Capital A/cs:		Fixed Assets		96,000
A	70,000	Investments		40,000
B	60,000	Stock		46,000
Workmen Compensation Fund	22,000	Debtors	38,000	
Bank Loan	18,000	*Less:* Provision	4,000	34,000
Creditors	70,000	Cash		24,000
	2,40,000			2,40,000

On 1st April, 2012, they admitted C for 25% share in profits on the following terms:

(a) C brings in capital proportionate to his share after all adjustments and ₹ 8,000 for goodwill out of his share of ₹ 14,000.

(b) Fixed Assets are overvalued by ₹ 3,000.

(c) Half of Investments was to be taken over by A and B in their profit-sharing ratio and remaining valued at ₹ 25,800.

(d) New Ratio will be 3 : 3 : 2.

(e) A claim of ₹ 2,000 on account of workmen compensation to be provided for

(f) A Provision for Doubtful Debts is to be maintained at 10% on Debtors.

Required: Prepare the Revaluation Account, Partners' Capital Accounts and the Balance Sheet and C's admission.

SOLUTION

Dr. **REVALUATION ACCOUNT** Cr.

Particulars		₹	Particulars		₹
To Fixed Assets		3,000	By Investments A/c		5,800
To Profit transferred to:			By Provision for Doubtful Debts		
A's Capital A/c	1,800		Existing	4,000	
B's Capital A/c	1,200	3,000	*Less:* Required	3,800	200
			[₹ 38,000 × 10/100]		
		6,000			6,000

Dr. **PARTNERS' CAPITAL ACCOUNTS** Cr.

Particulars	A (₹)	B (₹)	C (₹)	Particulars	A (₹)	B (₹)	C (₹)
To Investments A/c	12,000	8,000	—	By Balance b/d	70,000	60,000	—
To Balance c/d	84,400	62,600	49,000	By Cash A/c	—	—	49,000
				By C's Current A/c	5,400	600	—
				By Premium for Goodwill A/c	7,200	800	—
				By W. Comp. Fund	12,000	8,000	
				By Revaluation A/c	1,800	1,200	
	96,400	70,600	49,000		96,400	70,600	49,000

BALANCE SHEET OF A, B AND C

as at 1st April, 2012

Liabilities	₹	Assets		₹
Capital A/cs:		Fixed Assets [96,000 – 3,000]		93,000
A	84,400	Investments		25,800
B	62,600	Debtors	38,000	
C	49,000	*Less:* Provision for		
Bank Loan	18,000	Doubtful Debts	3,800	34,200
Creditors	70,000	C's Current A/c		6,000
Workmen Compensation Claim	2,000	Stock		46,000
		Cash ₹ (24,000 + 8,000 + 49,000)		81,000
	2,86,000			2,86,000

Working Notes:

1. **Sacrificing Ratio**

   A's sacrifice = 3/5 – 3/8 = 9/40,

   B's sacrifice = 2/5 – 3/8 = 1/40

   Hence SR = 9 : 1

2. **For Goodwill not brought in cash i.e., ₹ 6,000**

		Dr. (₹)	Cr. (₹)
C's Current A/c	...Dr.	6,000	
To A's Capital A/c			5,400
To B's Capital A/c			600

3. **Capital brought in by C**

   Total Capital of Firm = (₹ 84,400 + ₹ 62,600) × 4/3 = ₹ 1,96,000.

   C's Capital = ₹ 1,96,000 × 1/4 = ₹ 49,000.

9.0 ADMISSION OF A PARTNER DURING THE YEAR

Basis of Division of Profits	When a new partner is admitted during the year, the profits for the year should be divided between pre-admission period and post-admission period on some agreed basis (e.g., Time basis, Turnover basis). Unless otherwise agreed, the profits should be divided on time basis assuming that the profits are earned evenly throughout the year.

Profits for the Pre-admission period	Profits for the pre-admission period should be distributed among the Old Partners in Old Profit Sharing Ratio.
Profits for the post-admission period	Profits for the post-admission period should be distributed among All the Partners (including new one) in New Profit Sharing Ratio.

ILLUSTRATION 60

A and B are partners in a firm sharing profits and losses in the ratio of 3 : 2 with capital of ₹ 1,20,000 and ₹ 40,000 respectively. The amount of capital carries interest @ 10% p.a. They admit C into the partnership with effect from 1st Jan., 2012 on the following terms:

(a) That C is to bring in ₹ 10,000 for his share of goodwill in Cash.

(b) That C is to contribute ₹ 1,15,000 as his share of Capital;

(c) That the partners' capitals will carry interest @ 12% p.a.

(d) That the new profit sharing ratio of 'A', 'B' and 'C' will be 9 : 6 : 4.

(e) That A will be entitled to 5% commission on net profit.

(f) The profits for the year ending on 31st March, 2012 before providing for A's commission and interest on partners' capitals amounted to ₹ 76,000.

Required: Prepare Profit & Loss Appropriation Account for the year ending on 31st March, 2012.

SOLUTION

PROFIT AND LOSS APPROPRIATION ACCOUNT

Dr. *for the year ending on 31st March, 2012* *Cr.*

Particulars	*1.4.2011 to 31.12.2011* ₹	*1.1.2012 to 31.3.2012* ₹	*Particulars*	*1.4.2011 to 31.12.2011* ₹	*1.1.2012 to 31.3.2012* ₹
To Interest on Capital:			By Profit	57,000	19,000
A	9,000	4,860			
B	3,000	1,950			
C	—	3,450			
To Commission to A		950			
[5% of ₹ 19,000]	—				
To Net Profit t/f to:					
A	27,000	3,690			
B	18,000	2,460			
C	—	1,640			
	57,000	19,000		57,000	19,000

Working Notes:

1. CALCULATION OF SACRIFICING RATIO

Particulars	*A*	*B*
Existing Shares	3/5	2/5
New shares	9/19	6/19
Share Surrendered	12/95	8/95

Thus, Sacrificing Ratio of A and B = 12 : 8 *or* 3 : 2.

2. CALCULATION OF CAPITAL OF A AND B AS ON 1.1.2012

Particulars	*A*	*B*
Opening Capital	₹ 1,20,000	₹ 40,000
Share of Goodwill Credited	₹ 6,000	₹ 4,000
Interest on Capital	₹ 9,000	₹ 3,000
Share of Profit	₹ 27,000	₹ 18,000
Capital as on 1.1.2012	₹ 1,62,000	₹ 65,000

COMPREHENSIVE REVISIONAL PROBLEMS

Objective: The following Problems have been given Only to Revise the Chapter. In Examination only some of the parts and not all the parts of such lengthy problems may be asked.

PROBLEM 1

The Balance Sheet of A, B and C who are sharing profits in the ratio of 2:3:1, as at 31st March, 2012 is given below:

Liabilities	₹	*Assets*	₹
A's Capital	1,00,000	Goodwill	12,000
B's Capital	2,00,000	Land and Building	2,50,000
C's Capital	3,00,000	Investments [Market Value ₹ 46,000]	50,000
Workmen Compensation Reserve	20,000	Stock	80,000
Investment Fluctuation Reserve	10,000	Debtors	3,00,000
Provision for Doubtful Debts	10,000	Bank	2,96,000
Sundry Creditors	3,00,000	Advertisement Suspense A/c	12,000
Employees' Provident Fund	60,000		
	10,00,000		10,00,000

A, B and C decide to admit D as a new partner from 1st April, 2012 and fix their new profit sharing ratio as 1:2:3:4. D brings in ₹ 4,00,000 as his capital and brings in ₹ 5,000 in cash and machinery worth ₹ 25,000 towards his share of firm's goodwill.

1. Goodwill is to be valued at 2 years' purchase of average profits of last three completed years. The profits were — 2009-2010 ₹ 48,000, 2010-2011 ₹ 93,000, 2011-2012 ₹ 1,38,000.
2. Land & Building was found under valued by ₹ 20,000 and Stock was found overvalued by ₹ 38,000. Provision for doubtful debts is to be made equal to 5% of the debtors.
3. Claim on account of workmen compensation is ₹ 8,000. 10% of the sundry creditors be written back as no longer payable. Out of the amount of insurance which was debited entirely to P&L A/c, ₹ 5,000 be carried forward as an unexpired insurance.

Required: Pass the necessary journal entries and prepare the necessary ledger accounts and the Balance Sheet.

SOLUTION

JOURNAL

Date	Particulars	L.F.	Dr. (₹)	Cr. (₹)
1.	A's Capital A/c Dr.		4,000	
	B's Capital A/c Dr.		6,000	
	C's Capital A/c Dr.		2,000	
	To Goodwill A/c			12,000
	(Being the existing goodwill w/o)			
2.	Cash A/c Dr.		4,05,000	
	Machinery A/c Dr.		25,000	
	To D's Capital A/c			4,00,000
	To Premium for Goodwill A/c Dr.			30,000
	(Being D brought in ₹ 4,00,000 as capital and cash (₹ 5,000) & Machinery (₹ 25,000) out of his share of goodwill of ₹ 74,400 (i.e. ₹ 1,86,000 × 4/10)			
3.	D's Capital A/c Dr.		44,400	
	Premium for Goodwill A/c Dr.		30,000	
	To A's Capital A/c (₹ 74,400 × 14/32)			32,550
	To B's Capital A/c (₹ 74,400 × 18/32)			41,850
	(Being D's share of Goodwill (i.e. ₹ 74,400 credited to sacrificing partners)			
4.	C's Capital A/c (₹ 1,86,000 × 8/60) Dr.		24,800	
	To A's Capital A/c (₹ 24,800 × 14/32)			10,850
	To B's Capital A/c (₹ 24,800 × 18/32)			13,950
	(Being the adjustment made on account of change in profit sharing ratio-C's gain 8/60, A's sacrifice 14/60, B's sacrifice 18/60]			
5	Land & Building A/c Dr.		20,000	
	Sundry Creditors Dr.		30,000	
	Prepaid Insurance Dr.		5,000	
	To Revaluation A/c			55,000
	(Being the increase in value of assets & decrease in Sundry Creditors recorded)			
6	Revaluation A/c Dr.		43,000	
	To Stock A/c			38,000
	To Provision for Doubtful Debts A/c			5,000
	(Being the decrease in Value of assets & increase in provisions recorded)			
7.	Revaluation A/c Dr.		12,000	
	To A's Capital A/c			4,000
	To B's Capital A/c			6,000

	To C's Capital A/c			2,000
	(Being the transfer of profit on revaluation)			
8.	Workmen Compensation Reserve A/c	Dr.	20,000	
	To Workmen Compensation Claim A/c			8,000
	To A's Capital A/c			4,000
	To B's Capital A/c			6,000
	To C's Capital A/c			2,000
	(Being the transfer of workmen compensation Reserve)			
9.	Investment Fluctuation Fund A/c	Dr.	10,000	
	To Investment A/c			4,000
	To A's Capital A/c			2,000
	To B's Capital A/c			3,000
	To C's Capital A/c			1,000
	(Being the transfer of Investment Fluctuation Fund)			
10.	A's Capital A/c	Dr.	4,000	
	B's Capital A/c	Dr.	6,000	
	C's Capital A/c	Dr.	2,000	
	To Advertisement Suspense A/c			12,000
	(Being the t/f of bal. of Advertisement Suspense A/c)			

Ledger Accounts:

Dr. **1. REVALUATION ACCOUNT** *Cr.*

Particulars	₹	*Particulars*	₹
To Stock	38,000	By Land & Building	20,000
To Provision for Doubtful Debts	5,000	By Sundry Creditors	30,000
To Profit on Revaluation t/f to:		By Prepaid Insurance	5,000
A's Capital A/c	4,000		
B's Capital A/c	6,000		
C's Capital A/c	2,000		
	55,000		55,000

Dr. **2. PARTNERS' CAPITAL ACCOUNTS** *Cr.*

Particulars	*A (₹)*	*B (₹)*	*C (₹)*	*Particulars*	*A (₹)*	*B (₹)*	*C (₹)*
To Goodwill A/c	4,000	6,000	2,000	By Balance b/d	1,00,000	2,00,000	3,00,000
To A's Capital A/c	—	—	10,850	By Premium for Goodwill	13,125	16,875	—
To B's Capital A/c	—	—	13,950	By D's Capital A/c	19,425	24,975	—
To Adv. Exp. Sus. A/c	4,000	6,000	2,000	By C's Capital A/c	10,850	13,950	—
To Balance c/d	1,45,400	2,58,800	2,76,200	By Revaluation A/c	4,000	6,000	2,000
				By Work Com. Res.	4,000	6,000	2,000
				By Invest. Flus. Res.	2,000	3,000	1,000
	1,53,400	2,70,800	3,05,000		1,53,400	2,70,800	3,05,000

Dr. **3. D'S CAPITAL ACCOUNT** *Cr.*

Particulars	₹	*Particulars*	₹
To A's Capital A/c	19,425	By Cash A/c	4,00,000
To B's Capital A/c	24,975		
To Balance c/d	3,55,600		
	4,00,000		4,00,000

4. BALANCE SHEET AS AT 31ST MARCH, 2012

Liabilities	₹	*Assets*		₹
A's Capital	1,45,400	Machinery		25,000
B's Capital	2,58,800	Land & Building		2,70,000
C's Capital	2,76,200	Investments		46,000
D's Capital A/c	3,55,600	Stock		42,000
Sundary Creditors	2,70,000	Debtors	3,00,000	
Workmen Compensation Claim	8,000	*Less:* Provision	15,000	2,85,000
Employees' Provident Fund	60,000	Bank		2,96,000
		Cash		4,05,000
		Prepaid Insurance		5,000
	13,74,000			13,74,000

Working Notes:

1. CALCULATION OF GAIN/SACRIFICE OF SHARE

Particulars	*Old Share*	*New Share*	*Difference*
A.	2/6	1/10	2/6-1/10=14/60
B.	3/6	2/10	3/6-2/10 = 18/60
C.	1/6	3/10	1/6-3/10 = -8/60

2. CALCULATION OF GOODWILL

A. Average Profits = $\frac{₹48,000 + ₹93,000 + ₹1,38,000}{3}$ = ₹ 93,000

B. Firm's Goodwill = ₹ 93,000 × 2 = ₹ 1,86,000

C, D's Share of Goodwill = ₹ 1,86,000 × 4/10 = ₹ 74,400

D. D's Share of Goodwill not brought in = ₹ 74,400 – (₹ 5,000 + ₹ 25,000) = ₹ 44,400

PROBLEM 2

A and B are partners sharing profits in the ratio of 3:2. They admit C as a new partner from 1st April. A gives 1/3rd of his share while B gives 1/10th from his share. The Balance Sheet as at 31st March, 2012 is given below:

Liabilities	₹	*Assets*	₹
A's Capital	17,600	Goodwill	1,000
B's Capital	25,400	Land & Building	6,000

Workmen Compensation Fund	2,000	Investments [Market Value ₹ 4,500]	5,000
Investment Fluctuation Fund	1,000	Debtors	10,000
Employees' Provident Fund	1,000	Stock	30,000
Provision for Doubtful Debts	1,000	Bank Balance	25,000
C's Loan	30,000	Advertisement Suspense A/c	1,000
	78,000		78,000

Terms of C's admission are as follows:

1. C's loan will be converted into his capital. C brings in 60% of his share of goodwill in cash.
2. Goodwill is to be valued at 2 years' purchase of super profit of last three completed years. The profits were — 2009-2010 ₹ 48,000, 2010-2011 ₹ 93,000, 2011-2012 ₹ 1,38,000. The normal profits are ₹ 63,000. No Goodwill is to appear in the books of new firm.
3. Land & Building was found undervalued by ₹ 5,000, Stock was found overvalued by ₹ 7,000, Provision for doubtful debts is to be made equal to 5% of the debtors.
4. Claim on account of workmen compensation is ₹ 1,000. An Unaccounted Accrued Income of ₹ 1,000 be provided for. A Debtor whose dues of ₹ 5,000 were written off as bad debts paid ₹ 4,000 in full settlement.
5. Capital accounts of the partners be re-adjusted on the basis of their profit sharing ratio and any excess *or* deficiency be adjusted in cash.

Required: Prepare Revaluation Account, Partners' Capital Accounts and the Balance Sheet.

SOLUTION

Dr. **REVALUATION ACCOUNT** *Cr.*

Particulars	₹	*Particulars*		₹
To Stock	7,000	By Land & Building		5,000
To Profit on Revaluation t/f to:		By Provision for Doubtful Debts		
A's Capital A/c	2,100	By Accrued Income		1,000
B's Capital A/c	1,400	By Bad Debts Recovered		4,000
		Existing	1,000	
		Less: Required [₹10,000 × 5%]	500	5000
	10,500			10,500

Dr. **CAPITAL ACCOUNTS OF PARTNERS** *Cr.*

Particulars	*A (₹)*	*B (₹)*	*C (₹)*	*Particulars*	*A (₹)*	*B (₹)*	*C (₹)*
To Goodwill A/c	600	400	—	By Balance b/d	17,600	25,400	—
To Adv. Sus. A/c	600	400	—	By C's Loan A/c	—	—	30,000
To Balance c/d	31,400	32,600	30,000	By Premium for Goodwill A/c	7,200	3,600	—
				By C's Current A/c	4,800	2,400	—
				By Revaluation A/c	2,100	1,400	—
				By Work. Compt. F.	600	400	—
				By Invest. Flu. Fund	300	200	—
	32,600	33,400	30,000		32,600	33,400	30,000

To Bank A/c (b.f.)	—	2,600	—	By Balance b/d	31,400	32,600	30,000
To Balance c/d	40,000	30,000	30,000	By Bank A/c (b.f.)	8,600	—	—
	40,000	32,600	30,000		40,000	32,600	30,000

BALANCE SHEET AS AT APRIL 1, 2012

Liabilities	₹	*Assets*		₹
A's Capital	40,000	Land & Building		11,000
B's Capital	30,000	Investments		4,500
C's Capital	30,000	Debtors	10,000	
Employee Provident Fund	1,000	*Less:* Provision	500	9,500
Workmen Compensation Claim	1,000	Stock (30,000 – 7,000)		23,000
		Bank Balance		45,800
		Accured Income		1,000
		C's Current A/c		7,200
	1,02,000			1,02,000

Working Notes:

1. **Calculation of Incoming Partner's Share, Sacrificing Ratio and New Ratio.**

New Share = Old Share – Share surrendered

A's New Share = $\frac{3}{5} - \left(\frac{1}{3} \times \frac{3}{5}\right) = \frac{3}{5} - \frac{1}{5} = \frac{2}{5}$

B's New Share = $\frac{2}{5} - \frac{1}{10} = \frac{3}{10}$

C's Share = $\frac{1}{5} + \frac{1}{10} = \frac{3}{10}$

New Profit Sharing Ratio = $\frac{2}{5} : \frac{3}{10} : \frac{3}{10}$ = 4 : 3 : 3

Sacrificing Ratio of A and B = 1/5 : 1/10 = 2 : 1

2. **Calculation of Incoming Partner's Share of Goodwill.**

A. Average Profits = $\frac{₹48,000 + ₹93,000 + ₹1,38,000}{3}$ = ₹ 93,000

B. Normal Profits = ₹ 60,000

C. Super Profits = ₹ 93,000 – ₹ 63,000 = ₹ 30,000

D. Firm's Goodwill = ₹ 30,000 × 2 = ₹ 60,000

E. C's Share of Goodwill = ₹ 60,000 × 3/10 = ₹ 18,000

3. JOURNAL ENTRY WITH RESPECT TO GOODWILL

Bank A/c	Dr.	10,800	
To Premium For Goodwill A/c			10,800
Premium For Goodwill A/c	Dr.	10,800	
To A's Capital A/c			7,200
To B's Capital A/c			3,600

C's Current A/c Dr.	7,200	
To A's Capital A/c (₹ 7,200 × 2/3)		4,800
To B's Capital A/c (₹ 7,200 × 1/3)		2,400

4. **Total Capital** = ₹ 30,000 × 10/3 = ₹ 1,00,000

   A's New Capital = ₹ 1,00,000 × 4/10 = ₹ 40,000

   B's New Capital = ₹ 1,00,000 × 3/10 = ₹ 30,000

Dr. **5. BANK ACCOUNT** *Cr.*

Particulars	₹	*Particulars*	₹
To Balance b/d	25,000	By B's Capital A/c	2,600
To Premium for Goodwill A/c	10,800	By Balance c/d	45,800
To Bad Debts Recovered	4,000		
To A's Capital	8,600		
	48,400		48,400

PROBLEM 3

A, B and C were partners sharing profits and losses in the ratio of 3 : 2 : 1 On 1st April, 2011 they admitted D into partnership on the following terms:—

D to have one sixth share which he purchased entirely from A, paying A ₹ 40,000 for the share of goodwill through the books of the firm. Of this amount, A was to withdraw ₹ 30,000 and D to bring in proportionate capital. It was further agreed that investments should be reduced to their market value viz. ₹ 18,000 and that plant should be reduced to ₹ 39,000. A sum of ₹ 3,000 included in creditors was to be written back as there was no liability to pay the amount. The balance sheet of A, B and C as on 31st March, 2011 was as follows.

Liabilities	₹	*Assets*	₹
Creditors	1,05,000	Cash at Bank	40,000
Workmen Compensation Reserve	6,000	Debtors	60,000
A's Capital	57,000	Stock	50,000
B's Capital	38,000	Investments (at Cost)	30,000
C's Capital	19,000	Plant	45,000
	2,25,000		2,25,000

The profits for the year 2011-2012 were ₹ 60,000 and the drawings were ₹ 15,000 for A and B each and ₹ 7,500 for C and D each.

Required: Journalise the entries to be made on D's admission and give the Balance Sheet as at 31st March, 2012.

SOLUTION

JOURNAL

Date	*Particulars*	*L.F.*	*Dr. (₹)*	*Cr. (₹)*
	Bank A/c Dr.		40,000	
	To Premium for Goodwill A/c			40,000
	(Being the Share of Goodwill brought in by D)			

	Particulars		Dr. (₹)	Cr. (₹)
	Premium for Goodwill A/c	Dr.	40,000	
	To A's Capital A/c			40,000
	(Being the goodwill credited to A)			
	A's Capital A/c	Dr.	30,000	
	To Bank A/c			30,000
	(Being the part goodwill of ₹ 30,000 withdrawn by A)			
	Revaluation A/c	Dr.	18,000	
	To Investment A/c			12,000
	To Plant A/c			6,000
	(Being the fall in the value of assets recorded)			
	Sundry Creditors A/c	Dr.	3,000	
	To Revaluation A/c			3,000
	(Being the decrease in amount of creditors recorded)			
	A's Capital A/c	Dr.	7,500	
	B's Capital A/c	Dr.	5,000	
	C's Capital A/c	Dr.	2,500	
	To Revaluation A/c			15,000
	(Being the transfer of loss on revaluation)			
	Workmen Compensation Reserve A/c	Dr.	6,000	
	To A's Capital A/c			3,000
	To B's Capital A/c			2,000
	To C's Capital A/c			1,000
	(Being the transfer of Work. Comp. Res.)			
	Bank A/c	Dr.	23,000	
	To D's Capital A/c			23,000
	(Being the capital brought in by D)			

Dr. **CAPITAL ACCOUNTS OF OLD PARTNERS** *Cr.*

Particulars	*A (₹)*	*B (₹)*	*C (₹)*	*Particulars*	*A (₹)*	*B (₹)*	*C (₹)*
To Cash A/c	30,000	—	—	By Balance b/d	57,000	38,000	19,000
To Revaluation A/c	7,500	5,000	2,500	By Work. Com. Res.	3,000	2,000	1,000
To Balance c/d	62,500	35,000	17,500	By Premium			
					40,000	—	
	1,00,000	40,000	20,000		1,00,000	40,000	20,000
To Drawings A/c	15,000	15,000	7,500	By Balance b/d	62,500	35,500	17,500
To Balance c/d	67,500	40,000	20,000	By P & L A/c	20,000	20,000	10,000
	82,500	55,000	27,500		82,500	55,000	27,500

Dr. **D'S CAPITAL ACCOUNT** *Cr.*

Particulars	₹	*Particulars*	₹
To Drawings A/c	7,500	By Cash A/c	23,000

To Balance c/d	25,500	By P & L A/c	10,000
	33,000		33,000

BALANCE SHEET OF NEW FIRM AS AT 31ST MARCH, 2012

Liabilities	₹	*Assets*	₹
Creditors	1,02,000	Cash at Bank	88,000
A's Capital	67,500	Debtors	60,000
B's Capital	40,000	Stock	50,000
C's Capital	20,000	Investments	18,000
D's Capital	25,500	Plant	39,000
	2,55,000		2,55,000

Working Notes:

1. **Calculation of the amount to be brought in by D as capital**
   (a) Total Adjusted Capitals of Old Partners = ₹ 62,500 + ₹ 35,000 + ₹ 17,500 = ₹ 1,15,000
   (b) Total Capital of the New Firm = (₹ 1,15,000 × 6/5) = ₹ 1,38,000
   (c) Proportionate Capital of Incoming Partner = (₹ 1,38,000 × 1/6) = ₹ 23,000
2. **Calculation of Cash as on 31.3.2012**

Assuming that the profit earned during the year resulted in the change of cash balance only and no other assets, Cash balance is calculated as under.

Dr. **CASH AT BANK ACCOUNT** *Cr.*

Date	*Particulars*	₹	*Date*	*Particulars*	₹
01.04.11	To Balance b/f	40,000	2011-12	By A's Capital A/c	30,000
	To Premium			By Drawings	45,000
	for Goodwill A/c	40,000	31.03.12	By Balance c/f	88,000
	To D's Capital A/c	23,000			
2011-12	To Profit for the year	60,000			
		1,63,000			1,63,000

PROBLEM 4

Jain and Gupta were partners in a firm sharing profits and losses in the ratio of 4 : 3. The following is the balance Sheet of the firm as on 31st March, 2012.

Liabilities	₹	*Assets*		₹
Sundry Creditors	20,000	Cash		14,800
Bank Overdraft	17,000	Debtors	20,500	
Employees' Provident Fund	3,000	*Less:* Provision	300	20,200
Workmen Compensation Reserve	7,000	Stock	6,000	
Jain's Capital A/c	66,000	Investments		14,000
Gupta's Capital A/c	57,000	Plant		40,000
		Buildings		75,000
	1,70,000			1,70,000

They agreed to admit Mishra with effect from 1st April 2012 with 1/4th share in profit on the following terms:

(a) Mishra will bring in proportionate capital.

(b) Buildings are to be appreciated by ₹ 13,000 and plant to be depreciated to ₹ 33,000.

(c) The provision on debtors is to be raised to ₹ 1,000.

(d) The Goodwill of the firm has been valued at ₹ 21,000 but no goodwill is to appear in the books.

(e) Half of investments are to be taken over by Jain and Gupta in their profit sharing ratio and remaining valued at ₹ 8,000.

Required: Prepare the Revaluation account, Partners' Capital Accounts and the Balance Sheet of the firm after Mishra's admission.

SOLUTION

Dr. **REVALUATION ACCOUNT** *Cr.*

Particulars	₹	*Particulars*	₹
To Plant	7,000	By Building	13,000
To Provision on Debtors	700	By Investments	1,000
To Profit on Revaluation t/f to:			
Jain's Capital A/c	3,600		
Gupta's Capital A/c	2,700		
	14,000		14,000

Dr. **PARTNERS' CAPITAL ACCOUNTS** *Cr.*

Particulars	*Jain* ₹	*Gupta* ₹	*Mishra* ₹	*Particulars*	*Jain* ₹	*Gupta* ₹	*Mishra* ₹
To Investments	4,000	3,000	—	By Balance b/d	66,000	57,000	—
To Balance c/d	72,600	61,950	44,850	By Cash A/c	—	—	44,850
				By Workmen Com. Reserve	4,000	3,000	—
				By Revaluation A/c	3,600	2,700	—
				By Mishra's Curr. A/c	3,000	2,250	—
	76,600	64,950	44,850		76,600	64,950	44,850

BALANCE SHEET OF THE FIRM AS AT 01.04.2012

Liabilities	₹	*Assets*		₹
Sundry Creditors	20,000	Cash [₹ 14,800 + ₹ 44,850]		59,650
Bank Overdraft	17,000	Debtors	20,500	
Employees' Provident Fund	3,000	*Less:* Provision	1,000	19,500
Capitals:		Stock		6,000
Jain	72,600	Plant		33,000
Gupta	61,950	Building		88,000
Mishra	44,850	Investments		8,000
		Mishra's Current A/c		5,250
	2,19,400			2,19,400

Working Note: *Calculation of Mishra's Capital*

1. **Total Capital of New Firm**

   Let Total Capital of New Firm be X

   X = Jain's Capital + Gupta's Capital + Mishra's Capital

   X = ₹ 72,600 + ₹ 61,950 + 1/4X

   3/4X = ₹ 1,34,550 = ₹ 1,34,550 × 4/3 = ₹ 1,79,400

2. **Mishra's Capital** = ₹ 1,79,400 × 1/4 = ₹ 44,850

PROBLEM 5

A and B are partners sharing profits in the ratio of 3:2. They admit C as a new partner from 1st April. They decide to share future profits in the ratio of 4 : 3 : 3. The Balance Sheet as at 31st March, 2012 is given below:

Liabilities	₹	*Assets*	₹
A's Capital	17,600	Goodwill	1,000
B's Capital	25,400	Land & Building	6,000
Workmen Compensation Fund	2,000	Investments [Market Value ₹ 4,500]	5,000
Investment Fluctuation Fund	1,000	Debtors	10,000
Employees' Provident Fund	1,000	Stock	30,000
Provision for Doubtful Debts	1,000	Bank Balance	25,000
C's Loan	30,000	Advertisement Suspense A/c	1,000
	78,000		78,000

Terms of C's admission are as follows:

1. C contributes proportionate capital and 60% of his share of goodwill in cash.
2. Goodwill is to be valued at 2 years' purchase of super profit of last three completed years. The profits were — 2009-2010 ₹ 48,000, 2010-2011 ₹ 93,000, 2011-2012 ₹ 1,38,000. The normal profits are ₹ 53,000. No Goodwill is to appear in the books of new firm.
3. Land & Building was found undervalued by ₹ 10,000.
4. Stock was found overvalued by ₹ 7,000.
5. Provision for doubtful debts is to be made equal to 5% of the debtors.
6. Claim on account of workmen compensation is ₹ 1,000.

Required: Prepare Revaluation Account, Partners' Capital Accounts and the Balance Sheet.

SOLUTION

Dr. **REVALUATION ACCOUNT** *Cr.*

Particulars	₹	*Particulars*	₹
To Stock	7,000	By Land & Building	10,000
To Profit on Revaluation t/f to:		By Provision for Doubtful Debts	500
A's Capital A/c	2,100	Existing	1,000
B's Capital A/c	1,400	*Less:* Required [₹ 10,000 × 5/100]	500
	10,500		10,500

Dr. **CAPITAL ACCOUNTS OF PARTNERS** Cr.

Particulars	A (₹)	B (₹)	C (₹)	Particulars	A (₹)	B (₹)	C (₹)
To Goodwill A/c	600	400	—	By Balance b/d	17,600	25,400	—
To Adv. Sus. A/c	600	400	—	By C's Loan A/c	—	—	30,000
To Balance c/d	35,400	34,600	30,000	By Premium			
				for Goodwill A/c	9,600	4,800	—
				By C's Current A/c	6,400	3,200	—
				By Revaluation A/c	2,100	1,400	—
				By Work. Compt. F.	600	400	—
				By Invest. Flu. Fund	300	200	—
	36,600	35,400	30,000		36,600	35,400	30,000

BALANCE SHEET AS AT APRIL 1, 2012

Liabilities	₹	Assets		₹
A's Capital	35,400	Land & Building		16,000
B's Capital	34,600	Investments		4,500
C's Capital	30,000	Debtors	10,000	
Employee Provident Fund	1,000	*Less:* Provision	500	9,500
Workmen Compensation Claim	1,000	Stock (30,000 — 7,000)		23,000
C's Loan	30,000	Bank Balance		69,400
		C's Current A/c		9,600
	1,32,000			1,32,000

Working Notes:

1. CALCULATION OF INCOMING PARTNER'S SHARE, SACRIFICING RATIO

	Particulars	A	B
A	Their Old Shares	3/5	2/5
B	Their New Shares [A–B]	4/10	3/10
C	Share surrendered by old partners	3/5 – 4/10 = 2/10	2/5 – 3/10 = 1/10
D	C's Share = 3/10		
E	Sacrificing Ratio = 2/10 : 1/10 = 2 : 1		

2. CALCULATION OF INCOMING PARTNER'S SHARE OF GOODWILL

A. Average Profits = $\frac{₹48,000 + ₹93,000 + ₹1,38,000}{3}$ = ₹ 93,000

B. Normal Profits = ₹ 53,000, C. Super Profits = ₹ 93,000 – ₹ 53,000 = ₹ 40,000

D. Firm's Goodwill = ₹ 40,000 × 2 = ₹ 80,000

E. C's share of Goodwill = ₹ 80,000 × 3/10 = ₹ 24,000

3. JOURNAL ENTRY WITH RESPECT TO GOODWILL

Particulars		Dr.	Cr.
Bank A/c	Dr.	₹ 14,400	
To Premium for Goodwill A/c			₹ 14,400

Premium for Goodwill A/c	Dr.	₹ 14,400	
To A's Capital A/c			₹ 9,600
To B's Capital A/c			₹ 4,800
C's Current A/c	Dr.	₹ 9,600	
To A's Capital A/c (₹ 9,600 × 2/3)			₹ 6,400
To B's Capital A/c (₹ 9,600 × 1/3)			₹ 3,200

4. **Calculation of C's Capital**

Let Total Capital of New Firm be X

X = Adjusted Old Capitals of A & B + 3/10 X

X = ₹ 35,400 + ₹ 34,600 + 3/10 X

X − 3/10 X = ₹ 70,000, X = ₹ 70,000 × 10/7 = ₹ 1,00,000

C's Capital = ₹ 1,00,000 × 3/10 = ₹ 30,000

5. **Calculation of Closing Bank Balance**

Dr. **BANK ACCOUNT** *Cr.*

Particulars	₹	*Particulars*	₹
To Balance b/d	25,000	By Balance c/d	69,400
To Premium for Goodwill A/c	14,400		
To C's Capital A/c	30,000		
	69,400		69,400

PROBLEM 6

The Balance Sheet of Amit, Bhushan and Charan, who share profits and losses as 3 : 2 : 1 respectively, as on 01.04.2013 is as follows:

Liabilities	₹	*Assets*		₹
Capital Accounts: Amit	1,80,000	Machinery		1,50,000
Bhushan	1,60,000	Furniture		1,50,000
Charan	1,40,000	Debtors	80,000	
Current Accounts: Bhushan	16,000	*Less:* Provision	4,000	76,000
Creditors	1,20,000	Stock		2,10,000
		Cash		20,000
		Current Account: charan		10,000
	6,16,000			6,16,000

Dev is admitted as a partner on the above date for 1/5th share in the profit and loss. Following are agreed upon:

(1) The profit and loss sharing ratio among the old partners will be equal.

(2) Dev brings in ₹ 1,50,000 as capital but is unable to bring the required amount of premium for goodwill.

(3) The goodwill of the firm is valued at ₹ 60,000.

(4) Assets and liabilities are to be valued as follows:

Machinery ₹ 2,06,000 : Furniture ₹ 1,28,000 : Provision for doubtful debts @ 10% on debtors.

(5) Necessary adjustments regarding goodwill and Profit/loss on revaluation are to made through the Partner's Current Accounts.

(6) It is decided that the revalued figures of assets and liabilities will not appear in the Balance Sheet of the new firm.

(7) Capital Accounts of the oild partners in the new firm should be proportionate to the new profit and loss sharing ratio, taking Dev's Capital as base. The existing partners will not bring cash for further capital. The necessary adjustments are to be made through the partner's Current Account.

Prepare Partner's Capital & Current Account, and the Balance Sheet of the new firm after admission.

SOLUTION

Dr. **PARNTER'S CAPITAL ACCOUNTS** *Cr.*

Particular	*Amit*	*Bhushan*	*Charan*	*Dev*	*Particulars*	*Amit*	*Bhushan*	*Charan*	*Dev*
To Balance c/d	2,00,000	2,00,000	2,00,000	1,50,000	By Balance b/d	1,80,000	1,60,000	1,40,000	
					By Bank A/c	–	–	–	1,50,000
					By Partner'ps Current A/cs (bal. fig)	**20,000**	**40,000**	**60,000**	–
	2,00,000	2,00,000	2,00,000	1,50,000		2,00,000	2,00,000	2,00,000	1,50,000

Dr. **PARNTER'S CAPITAL ACCOUNTS** *Cr.*

Particular	*Amit*	*Bhushan*	*Charan*	*Dev*	*Particulars*	*Amit*	*Bhushan*	*Charan*	*Dev*
To Balance b/d	–	–	10,000	–	By Balance b/d		16,000	–	–
To Amit & Bhushan (Profit)			3,000	6,000	By Dev & Charan	7,000	2,000		–
To Amit and Bhushan (Goodwill adjustment)	–	–	6,000	12,000	By Dev and Charan (Goodwill adjustment)	14,000	4,000	–	
To Partners Capital A/cs	20,000	40,000	60,000	–	By Balance c/d	–	18,000	79,000	18,000
To Balance c/d	1,000	–	–						
	21,000	40,000	79,000	18,000		21,000	40,000	79,000	18,000

BALANCE SHEET OF NEW FIRM AFTER DEV'S ADMISSION

Liabilities	₹	*Assets*		₹
Amit	2,00,000	Machinery		1,50,000
Bhushan	2,00,000	Furniture		1,50,000
Charan	2,00,000	Stock		2,10,000
Dev	1,50,000	Debtors	80,000	
Current Account: Amit	1,000	*Less:* Provision	4,000	76,000
Creditors	1,20,000	Cash		1,70,000
		Current Accounts:		
		Bhushan	18,000	
		Charan	79,000	
		Dev	18,000	1,15,000
	8,71,000			8,71,000

Working Notes:

1. Dev. joins the business for 1/5th share and brings ₹ 1,50,000 as capital. Thus, total capital of new firm will be ₹ 7,50,000 (1,50,000 × 5). Total capital of Amit, Bhushan 7 Charan will be ₹ 6,00,000 (7,50,000 – 1,50,000) which will be shared by them equally i.e. 2,00,000 each.

2. NEW PROFIT SHARING RATIO

Amit	*Bhushan*	*Charan*	*Dev*
4/5 × 1/3 4/15	4/5 × 1/3 4/15	4/5 × 1/3 4/15	1/5 3/15
NR = 4:4:4:3			

3. ADJUSTMENT OF GOODWILL

Sacrifice/Gain of Partners

Amit	*Bhushan*	*Charan*	*Dev*
4/15 – 3/6 = 21/90 (Sacrifice)	4/15 – 2/6 = 6/90 (Sacrifice)	4/15 – 1/6 = 9/90 (gain)	1/5 (Gain)

JOURNAL ENTRY TO ADJUST GOODWILL

Charan [₹ 60,000 × 9/90]	Dr.	₹ 6,000	
Dev [₹ 60,000 × 1/5]	Dr.	₹ 12,000	
To Amit [₹ 60,000 × 21/90]			₹ 14,000
To Bhushan [₹ 60,000 × 6/90]			₹ 4,000

4. NET EFFECT OF REVALUATION OF ASSETS AND LIABILITIES

Increase in value of Machinery	₹ 56,000
Decrease in value of Furniture	(₹ 22,000)
Increase in Provision for Doubtful Debts	(₹ 4,000)
Journal Entry to Adjust Profit on Revolution	₹ 30,000

Charan [₹ 30,000 × 9/90]	Dr.	₹ 3,000	
Dev [₹ 30,000 × 1/5]	Dr.	₹ 6,000	
T Amit [30,000 × 21/90]			₹ 7,000
To Bhusan [30,000 × 6/90]			₹ 2,000

SOLVED PROBLEMS

PROBLEM 1

Gopal and Govind are partners sharing profits and losses in the ratio of 3 : 2. The firm's Balance Sheet as on 31.03.20X3 was as follows:

Liabilities	₹	*Assets*	₹
Capital Accounts:		Fixed Assets	3,00,000
Gopal	1,20,000	Investments	50,000
Govind	80,000	Current Assets	2,00,000
Long Term Loan	2,00,000	Loans and Advances	1,00,000
Current Liabilities	2,50,000		
	6,50,000		6,50,000

Due to financial difficulties, they have decided to admit Guru as a partner in the firm from 01.04.20X3 on the following terms:

(a) Guru will be paid 40% of the profits.

(b) Guru will bring in cash ₹ 1,00,000 as Capital. It is agreed that Goodwill of the firm will be valued at 2 years' purchase of 3 years' normal average profits of the firm and Guru will bring in his share of Goodwill. It was also decided that partners will not withdraw their share of goodwill *nor* will the goodwill appear in the books of account.

(c) The profits of the previous three years were as follows:

Foe the year ended 31.3.20X1 Profit ₹ 20,000 (includes insurance claim received of ₹ 40,000)

For the year ended 31.3.20X2 Loss ₹ 80,000 (includes voluntary retirement compensation paid ₹ 1,10,000)

For the year ended 31.3.20X3 Profit ₹ 1,05,000 (includes a profit of ₹ 25,000 on the sale of Assets)

(d) It was decided to revalue the assets on 31.3.20X3 as follows:

Fixed Assets (net) ₹ 4,00,000, Investment Nil, Current Assets ₹ 1,80,000, Loans and advances ₹ 1,00,000.

(e) The new profit sharing ratio after the admission of Guru was 35 : 25 : 40.

Required: Pass Journal Entries on admission, show goodwill calculation and prepare Revaluation Account, Partners' Capital Accounts and Balance-Sheet as on 01.04.20X3 after admission of Guru.

SOLUTION

Calculation of Sacrificing Ratio

Share sacrificed by Gopal = 60% – 35% = 25%

Share sacrificed by Govind = 40% – 25% = 15%

Sacrificing Ratio = 25% : 15% *or* 5 : 3

STATEMENT SHOWING THE CALCULATION OF GOODWILL

	Particulars	*For the year ending on*		
		31.3.20X1	*31.3.20X2*	*31.3.20X3*
A	Profit (loss)	20,000	(80,000)	1,05,000
B	*Add:* (less) : Abnormal Items	(40,000)	1,10,000	(25,000)
C	Net Profit (loss)	(20,000)	30,000	80,000

D Average Profits = [(₹ 20,000) + ₹ 30,000 + ₹ 80,000] /3 = ₹ 30,000

E Firm's Goodwill = ₹ 30,000 × 2 = ₹ 60,000

F Share of Goodwill of Guru = ₹ 60,000 × 40% = ₹ 24,000

G Gopal's Share in Goodwill brought in by Guru = ₹ 24,000 × 5/8 = ₹ 15,000

H Govind's Share in Goodwill brought in by Guru = ₹ 24,000 × 3/8 = ₹ 9,000

JOURNAL

Particulars		*L.F.*	*Dr. (₹)*	*Cr. (₹)*
Bank A/c	Dr.		1,24,000	
To Guru's Capital A/c				1,24,000
(Being the amount brought in by Guru in cash)				

Guru's A/c	Dr.	24,000	
To Gopal's Capital A/c			15,000
To Govind's Capital A/c			9,000
(Being the goodwill credited to sacrificing partners in their sacrificing ratio i.e. 5 : 3)			

Dr. **REVALUATION ACCOUNT** *Cr.*

Particulars	₹	*Particulars*	₹
To Investments	50,000	By Fixed Assets	1,00,000
To Current Assets	20,000		
To Profit on Revaluation transferred to:			
Gopal (60%)	18,000		
Govind (40%)	12,000		
	1,00,000		1,00,000

Dr. **PARTNERS' CAPITAL ACCOUNTS** *Cr.*

Particulars	*Gopal* ₹	*Govind* ₹	*Particulars*	*Gopal* ₹	*Govind* ₹
To Balance c/d	1,53,000	1,01,000	By Balance b/d	1,20,000	80,000
			By Guru's Capital A/c	15,000	9,000
			By Revaluation A/c	18,000	12,000
	1,53,000	1,01,000		1,53,000	1,01,000

BALANCE SHEET OF NEW FIRM AS AT 1ST APRIL, 20X3

Liabilities	₹	*Assets*	₹
Gopal's Capital	1,53,000	Fixed Assets	4,00,000
Govind's Capital	1,01,000	Current Assets	3,04,000
Guru's Capital	1,00,000	Loans & Advances	1,00,000
Long term Loan	2,00,000		
Current Liabilities	2,50,000		
	8,04,000		8,04,000

PROBLEM 2

A and B in partnership sharing profits and losses in the proportion of three-fourth and one fourth respectively. Their Balance Sheet on 31st March, 20X2 was as follows:

Cash ₹ 1,000; Sundry Debtors ₹ 25,000; Stock ₹ 22,000; Plant and Machinery ₹ 4,000; Sundry Creditors ₹ 12,000; Bank Overdraft ₹ 15,000; A's Capital ₹ 15,000; B's Capital ₹ 10,000

On 1st April, 20X2, they admitted C into partnership on the following terms:

(a) C to purchase one-third of the Goodwill for ₹ 2,000 and provide ₹ 10,000 as Capital. Goodwill not to appear in books.

(b) Future profits and losses are to be shared by A, B and C equally.

(c) Plant and Machinery is to be reduced by 10% and ₹ 5,000 is to be provided for estimated bad debts. Stock is to be taken at a valuation of ₹ 24,940.

(d) By bringing in *or* withdrawing cash the capitals of A and B are to be made proportionate to that of C on their profit sharing basis.

Required: Set out entries relating to the above arrangement in the firm's journal, give the partners' Capital Accounts in tabular form and submit the opening Balance Sheet of the new firm.

SOLUTION

JOURNAL

Particulars		*L.F.*	*Dr. (₹)*	*Cr. (₹)*
Cash A/c	Dr.		12,000	
To C 's Capital A/c				12,000
(Being the amount brought in by C as capital and share of goodwill)				
C 's Capital A/c	Dr.		2,000	
To A's Capital A/c				2,000
(Being the goodwill brought in by C credited to sacrificing partner, A)				
B 's Capital A/c	Dr.		500	
To A's Capital A/c				500
(Being an adjustment for goodwill made on account of purchase of 1/12th share by B from A)				
Revaluation A/c	Dr.		900	
To Plant and Machinery				400
To Provision for Doubtful Debts A/c				500
(Being Reduction in value of machinery and provision for doubtful debts adjusted)				
Stock A/c	Dr.		2,940	
To Revaluation A/c				2,940
(Being increase in value of Stock recorded)				
Revaluation A/c	Dr.		2,040	
To A's Capital A/c				1,530
To B 's Capital A/c				510
(Being the transfer of profit on Revaluation)				
A's Capital A/c	Dr.		9,030	
B 's Capital A/c	Dr.		10	
To Cash A/c				9,040
(Being the surplus amount withdrawn by the partners)				

Dr. **PARTNERS' CAPITAL ACCOUNTS** *Cr.*

Particulars	*A* ₹	*B* ₹	*C* ₹	*Particulars*	*A* ₹	*B* ₹	*C* ₹
To A's Capital A/c		500	2,000	By Balance b/d	15,000	10,000	
To Cash A/c	9,030	10		By Revaluation A/c	1,530	510	

To Balance c/d	10,000	10,000	10,000	By Cash A/c			12,000
				By B 's Capital A/c		500	
				By C 's Capital A/c		2,000	
	19,030	10,510	12,000		19,030	10,510	12,000

BALANCE SHEET OF A NEW FIRM AS AT 1 APRIL, 20X2

Liabilities	₹	*Assets*		₹
S. Creditors	12,000	Cash		3,960
Bank Overdraft	15,000	S. Debtors	25,000	
Capital Accounts:		*Less:* Provision	500	24,500
A	10,000	Stock		24,940
B	10,000	Plant & Machinery		3,600
C	10,000			
	57,000			57,000

Working Notes:

1. **Calculation of Sacrificing Ratio**

   A's Sacrifice = 3/4 – 1/3 = 5/12

   B's Gain = 1/4 – 1/3 = 1/12

2. **Value of Firm's Goodwill** = ₹ 2,000 × 3/1 = ₹ 6,000

   B has to be debited for = ₹ 6,000 × 1/12 = ₹ 500

   A has to be credited for = ₹ 6,000 × 5/12 = ₹ 2,500

Dr. **3. CASH ACCOUNT** *Cr.*

Particulars	₹	*Particulars*	₹
To Balance b/d	1,000	By A's Capital A/c	10
To C 's Capital A/c	12,000	By B 's Capital A/c	9,030
		By Balance c/d	3,960
	13,000		13,000

PROBLEM 3

A, B and C were in partnership, sharing profits and losses as to A one-half, B one-third and C one-sixth. As from 1st January, 20X2 they admitted D into partnership on the following terms:

D to have a one-sixth share which he purchased entirely from A paying A ₹ 8,000 for the share of Goodwill. Of this amount, A had withdrawn ₹ 6,000 and put the balance in the firm as additional capital. As a condition to admission of D as a partner D also brought ₹ 5,000 capital into the firm. It was further agreed that the investments should be valued at its market value of ₹ 3,600 and plant be valued at ₹ 5,800.

The Balance sheet of the old firm on 31.12.20X1 was as follows:

Cash at Bank ₹ 8,000; Debtors ₹ 12,000; Stock ₹ 10,000; Investments at Cost ₹ 6,000; Furniture ₹ 2,000; Plant ₹ 7,000; Creditors ₹ 21,000; Capital: A ₹ 12,000; B ₹ 8,000 and C ₹ 4,000.

The profits for the year 20X2 were ₹ 12,000 and the drawings were: A ₹ 6,000, B ₹ 6,000, C ₹ 3,000 and D ₹ 3,000.

Required: Journalise the opening adjustments, prepare the opening Balance Sheet of the new firm as on 1st January, 20X2 and give the capital account of each partner as on 31st December, 20X2.

SOLUTION

JOURNAL

Particulars		L.F.	Dr. (₹)	Cr. (₹)
Cash A/c	Dr.		13,000	
To D 's Capital A/c				13,000
(Being amount brought in by D)				
D 's Capital A/c	Dr.		8,000	
To A's Capital A/c				8,000
(Being goodwill credited to sacrificing partner 'A')				
A's Capital A/c	Dr.		6,000	
To Cash A/c				6,000
(Being Cash withdrawn by A)				
Revaluation A/c	Dr.		3,600	
To Investments A/c				2,400
To Plant A/c				1,200
(Being Revaluation of investments and plant recorded)				
A's Capital A/c	Dr.		1,800	
B 's Capital A/c	Dr.		1,200	
C 's Capital A/c	Dr.		600	
To Revaluation A/c				3,600
(Being Loss on Revaluation transferred to old partners in 3 : 2 : 1 ratio)				

OPENING BALANCE SHEET OF NEW FIRM AS ON 1 JAN., 20X2

Liabilities	₹	Assets	₹
Creditors	21,000	Cash at Bank	15,000
Capital Accounts:		Investments	3,600
A	12,200	Debtors	12,000
B	6,800	Stock	10,000
C	3,400	Furniture	2,000
D	5,000	Plant	5,800
	48,400		48,400

Dr. **CAPITAL ACCOUNTS OF PARTNERS AS ON 31ST DEC., 20X2** *Cr.*

Particulars	A ₹	B ₹	C ₹	D ₹	Particulars	A ₹	B ₹	C ₹	D ₹
To Drawings	6,000	6,000	3,000	3,000	By Balance b/d	12,200	6,800	3,400	—
To Balance c/d	10,200	4,800	2,400	4,000	By Cash A/c	—	—	—	5,000

					By P & L A/c	4,000	4,000	2,000	2,000
	16,200	10,800	5,400	7,000		16,200	10,800	5,400	7,000

PROBLEM 4

A, B and C who are sharing profits in the ratio of 2 : 3 : 1, decide to admit D as a new partner from 1st Jan. 20X7 and fix their new profit sharing ratio as 1 : 2 : 3 : 4. D brings in ₹ 4,00,000 as his capital and also brings in ₹ 5,000 in cash and machinery worth ₹ 5,000 towards part of his share of firm's goodwill.

The goodwill of the firm of the firm is to be determined on the basis of 2 years' purchase of the average profits from the business of the last 5 years. The particulars of the profits are 20X1 Profit ₹ 30,000, 20X2 Profit ₹ 20,000, 20X3 Loss ₹ 10,000, 20X4 Profit ₹ 20,000, 20X5 Profit ₹ 25,000, 20X6 Profit ₹ 30,000.

The above profits and losses are after charging the salary of A @ ₹ 500 per month. The profits for 20X2 included a profit of ₹ 30,000 on sale of a fixed asset and the loss for the year 20X3 was on account of loss by strike to the extent of ₹ 15,000 and loss on sale of another fixed asset to the extent of ₹ 5,000. The firm's assets also included 12% ₹ 10,000 Debentures purchased on 1.1.20X1 for ₹ 9,000. The following errors were also discovered:

(a) A Machinery costing ₹ 9,500 purchased in 20X4 was charged to purchases account, the installation charges of ₹ 500 being charged to Machinery Repairs Account. The firm charges depreciation on machinery @ 10% on W.D.V. basis.

(b) Goods of the invoice value of ₹ 51,150 sent on sale *or* return basis has been recorded in the Sales Day Book of 20X6. The firm's Gross Profit is 25% on Cost.

(c) ₹ 540 being the interest on trade investment due to the firm used by a partner for his personal expenses in 20X6.

(d) ₹ 1,200 received during 20X6 from a debtor towards rent of property sub-let was credited to his personal account instead of Rent Account so as to reduce his debit balance from ₹ 1,600 to ₹ 400 debit.

(e) Interest on 10% Mortgage loan of ₹ 12,000 was paid in advance upto 31st Dec., 20X7 and the whole amount was charged to Interest Account in 20X6.

Required: Calculate the value of goodwill as on 1.1.20X7 and pass the necessary journal entries on admission of new partner.

SOLUTION

STEP 1 CALCULATION OF CORRECT PROFITS FOR PREVIOUS YEARS

	Particulars	*20X2*	*20X3*	*20X4*	*20X5*	*20X6*
A	Profits as given	20,000	(10,000)	20,000	25,000	30,000
B	*Add:* X's salary	6,000	6,000	6,000	6,000	6,000
C	*Add:* Abnormal Losses	—	15,000	—	—	—
			5,000			
D	*Less:* Abnormal Profits	(30,000)				
E	*Less:* Income from Non-Trade Investments	(1,200)	(1,200)	(1,200)	(1,200)	(1,200)
F	*Add:* Machinery debited to Purchases A/c	—	—	9,500		

G	*Add:* Installation charges debited to Repairs			500		
H	*Less:* Depreciation @ 10% on W.D.V.	—	—	(1,000)	(900)	(810)
I	*Less:* Profits on Goods Sent on approval (20% of ₹ 51,150)	—	—	—	—	(10,230)
J	*Add:* Interest on Trade Investment	—	—	—	—	540
K	*Add:* Rent from sub-letting	—	—	—	—	1,200
L	*Add:* Interest on 10% Mortgage Loan	—	—	—	—	1,200
		(5,200)	14,800	33,800	28,900	26,700

Particulars	₹
Step 2 Total Profits for last 5 years	99,000
Step 3 Average Profits (₹ 99,000/5)	19,800
Step 4 Goodwill (₹ 19,800 × 2)	39,600

JOURNAL

Date	*Particulars*		*L.F.*	*Dr. (₹)*	*Cr. (₹)*
1	Cash A/c	Dr.		4,05,000	
	Machinery A/c	Dr.		5,000	
	To D's Capital A/c				4,10,000
	(Being D brought in ₹ 4,00,000 as capital and cash (₹ 5,000) & Machinery (₹ 5,000) out of his share of goodwill of ₹ 15,840 (i.e. ₹ 39,600 × 4/10)				
2	D's Capital A/c	Dr.		15,840	
	To A's Capital A/c (₹ 15,840 × 14/32)				6,930
	To B's Capital A/c (₹ 15,840 × 18/32)				8,910
	[Being D's share of Goodwill (i.e. ₹ 15,840) credited to sacrificing partners]				
3	C's Capital A/c (₹ 39,600 × 8/60)	Dr.		5,280	
	To A's Capital A/c (₹ 5,280 × 14/32)				2,310
	To B's Capital A/c (₹ 5,280 × 18/32)				2,970
	(Being the adjustment made on account of change in profit sharing ratio-C's gain 8/60, A's sacrifice 14/60, B's sacrifice 18/60]				

PROBLEM 5

Kapil, Chetan and minor Sachin are partners since 1.1.20X1. They decided to admit Sanjay as an equal partner from 1.1.20X4. Their Balance Sheet as at 31.12.20X3.

Liabilities	₹	*Assets*	₹
Capital Accounts:		Land and Building	56,000
Kapil	30,000	Plant and Machinery	32,875

Chetan	30,000	Stock in Trade	41,125
Minor Sachin	30,000	Sundry Debtors	36,500
Profit & Loss A/c	19,600	Cash & Bank Balance	3,500
Sundry Creditors	52,000		
Outstanding Expenses	8,400		
	1,70,000		1,70,000

(a) Profit and Loss Account consists of the followings: Profit of 20X1 ₹ 25,000 (including insurance claim of ₹ 10,000 received), Loss of 20X2 ₹ 15,400 (including voluntary Retirement compensation paid ₹ 5,000 and Profit on Sale of a Fixed Asset ₹ 1,000), Profit of 20X3 ₹ 10,000 (after adjusting a loss on sale of a Fixed Asset ₹ 6,000).

(b) The new partner is to bring the necessary amount towards goodwill in which the minor Sachin has no claim. Further, new partner to bring ₹ 30,000 towards his Capital.

(c) Goodwill of the firm is to be valued at 6 years' purchase of last 3 years' average corrected profits.

(d) Perusal of the books of accounts of the previous year disclosed the following errors.

(i) A Machinery cost ₹ 6,000, purchased on 1.1.20X2 was debited to Repairs Account. Firm provides 10% depreciation on its plant and machinery (on WDV basis).

(ii) Goods sent on sale *or* return basis costing ₹ 4,000 has been recorded as credit sale of 20X3. The firm's Gross Profit ratio is 25% on cost.

(iii) ₹ 540 being the fixed Deposit interest due to the firm used by Chetan for his personal expenses in 20X3.

Required: Prepare Balance Sheet of the reconstituted firm giving effect to the above adjustments.

SOLUTION

Step 1: *Old Ratio of Kapil, Chetan and Sachin 1:1:1 for profits and 1:1 for losses. Minor Sachin is not liable for losses. New Ratio of Kapil, Chetan Sachin and Sanjay 1:1:1:1 for Profit and 1:1:0:1 for losses.*

Step 2: *Computation of correct profit for various years*

	Particulars	*20X1* ₹	*20X2* ₹	*20X3* ₹	*Total*
A	Profit as per profit and Loss A/c	25,000	(15,400)	10,000	
B	*Add:* VRS compensation paid		5,000		
	Loss on Sale of a Fixed Asset			6,000	
	Machinery debited to Repairs		6,000		
	Fixed Deposit interest used by partner Chetan not recorded in the books			540	
C	*Less:* Insurance Claim	(10,000)			
	Profit on Sale of a Fixed Asset		(1000)		
	Depreciation on Machinery		(600)	(540)	
	Goods sent on sale *or* return Basis (₹ 4,000 × 25%)			(1,000)	
D	Correct Profit *or* (Loss) for the year	15,000	(6,000)	15,000	
	Share of Kapil	5,000	(3,000)	5,000	7,000

Share of Chetan	5,000	(3,000)	5,000	7,000
Share of Minor Sachin	5,000	—	5,000	10,000

Step 3: Goodwill = [(7,000 + 7,000 + 10,000)/3] × 6 = ₹ 48,000

Sanjay's Share of Goodwill = ₹ 48,000 × 1/4 = ₹ 12,000

Step 4:

Dr. **CAPITAL ACCOUNTS OF PARTNERS AS AT 31ST JAN., 20X4** *Cr.*

Particulars	*Kapil* ₹	*Chetan* ₹	*Minor Sachin* ₹	*Sanjay* ₹	*Particulars*	*Kapil* ₹	*Chetan* ₹	*Minor Sachin* ₹	*Sanjay* ₹
To Fixed Deposit	—	540	—	—	By Balance b/d	30,000	30,000	30,000	—
To Kapil's Capital A/c	—	—	—	6,000	By P & L A/c	7,000	7,000	10,000	—
					By Cash A/c	—	—	—	42,000
To Chetan's Capital A/c	—	—	—	6,000	By Sanjay's Capital A/c	6,000	6,000	—	—
To Balance c/d	43,000	42,460	40,000	30,000					
	43,000	43,000	40,000	42,000		43,000	43,000	40,000	42,000

BALANCE SHEET OF KAPIL, CHETAN, SANJAY AND MINOR SACHIN AS AT 1.1.20X4

Liabilities	₹	*Assets*	₹
Capital Accounts:		Land & Building	56,000
Kapil	43,000	Plant & Machinery	
Chetan	42,460	(32,875 + 6,000 – 1,140)	37,735
Sanjay	30,000	Stock in Trade (41,125 + 4,000)	45,125
Minor Sachin	40,000	Sundry Debtors (36,500 – 5,000)	31,500
Sundry Creditors	52,000	Cash on hand/Bank (3,500 + 42,000)	45,500
Outstanding Expenses	8,400		
	2,15,860		2,15,860

PROBLEM 6

X and Y are partners in a business started in 20X1, sharing profits and losses in the ratio of 5 : 4. After the accounts for the calendar year 20X4 were made up and their proportionate shares taken note of in their individual accounts, they decide to share profit and losses equally retrospectively for and from the year 20X4. It was also discovered that in ascertaining the results in prior years certain adjustments details of which are given, below had not been noticed.

Particulars	*20X1* ₹	*20X2* ₹	*20X3* ₹	*20X4* ₹
Profit as per accounts	72,000	78,000	90,000	1,08,000
Incomes not taken into account	5,400	4,500	3,600	6,300
Expenses not provided for	9,000	6,000	10,800	7,200

On 31st Dec., 20X3, Reserves stood at ₹ 54,000, Capitals of X and Y ₹ 1,26,000 and ₹ 96,000 respectively on 31st Dec. 20X4.

On 1st Jan. 20X5, Z was decided to be admitted as a partner and was allotted 1/5th share, Goodwill was decided to be ascertained by capitalising at 20% the average profit of the immediately two preceding years before admission. Z would bring in proportionate capital. Capitals of X and Y are to be equal, the differences to be adjusted in their current accounts.

Profits for 20X5, were ₹ 1,26,000, Drawings of X, Y and Z for the year were ₹ 54,000, ₹ 48,000 and ₹ 18,000 respectively. Incomes not taken into account are received in subsequent year. Expenses not provided for are paid in subsequent year. Prepare Capital and Current accounts of the partners for the year 20X5.

SOLUTION

Dr. **PARTNERS' CAPITAL ACCOUNTS** Cr.

Particulars	X ₹	Y ₹	Z ₹	Particulars	X ₹	Y ₹	Z ₹
31.12.20X4				31.12.20X4			
To P & L Adj. A/c	60,000	48,000	—	By Balance b/d	1,26,000	96,000	—
To P & L Adj. A/c	4,000	3,200	—	By P & L Adj. A/c	57,150	57,150	—
To X's Capital A/c				By Reserve	30,000	24,000	—
(Goodwill)	—	12,300	—	By Y's Capital A/c			
To Balance c/d	1,61,450	1,13,650	—	(Goodwill)	12,300	—	—
	2,25,450	1,77,150	—		2,25,450	1,77,150	—
01.01.20X5				01.01.20X5			
To Balance c/d	1,98,600	1,98,600	99,300	By Balance b/d	1,61,450	1,13,650	—
				By Z's Current A/c	22,140	22,140	—
				By Bank A/c	—	—	99,300
				By Current A/c	15,010	62,810	—
	1,98,600	1,98,600	99,300		1,98,600	1,98,600	99,300

Dr. **PARTNERS' CURRENT ACCOUNTS** Cr.

Particulars	X ₹	Y ₹	Z ₹	Particulars	X ₹	Y ₹	Z ₹
To X's Capital A/c	—	—	22,140	By P & L A/c	50,400	50,400	25,200
To Y's Capital A/c	—	—	22,140	By Balance c/d	18,610	60,410	37,080
To Drawings A/c	54,000	48,000	18,000				
To Capital A/c	15,010	62,810	—				
	69,010	1,10,810	62,280		69,010	1,10,810	62,280

Note: *Net outstanding expenses at the end of 20X3 (i.e. Outstanding Expenses 10,800 less accrued income ₹ 3,600) has been debited to capital accounts of X & y in the ratio of 5 : 4.*

Working Notes:

Dr. **1. PROFIT & LOSS ADJUSTMENT ACCOUNT FOR 20X4** Cr.

Particulars		₹	Particulars	₹
To Outstanding Expenses (20X4)		7,200	By Partners' Capital A/cs	7,200
To Net Profit t/f to Capital A/cs:			(net outstanding expenses for 20X3)	
X	57,150		By X 's Capital A/c	60,000
Y	57,150	1,14,300	By Y 's Capital A/c	48,000

		By Accrued Income (20X4)	6,300
	1,21,500		1,21,500

2. CALCULATION OF ADJUSTED PROFIT FOR 20X3 AND 20X4

	Particulars	*20X3* ₹	*20X4* ₹
A	Cash Profit	90,000	1,08,000
B	*Add:* Outstanding Expenses of previous year	6,000	10,800
C	*Add:* Accrued Income of current year	3,600	6,300
D	*Less:* Outstanding Expenses of current year	10,800	7,200
E	*Less:* Accrued Income of previous year	4,500	3,600
F	Adjusted Profit (A + B + C – D – E)	84,300	1,14,300

3. VALUATION OF GOODWILL ON CAPITALIZATION OF AVERAGE PROFIT BASIS

	Particulars	₹
A	Average Profit [(₹ 84,300 + ₹ 1,14,300)/2]	99,300
B	Capital of X & Y (including goodwill) (₹ 99,300 × ₹ 100/20)	4,96,500
C	Capital of X & Y (excluding goodwill) (₹ 1,61,450 + ₹ 1,13,650)	2,75,100
D	Value of Goodwill (B – C)	2,21,400

4. It has been assumed that total capital of the firm will not be increased on admission of Z otherwise Z will contribute 1/4 of the combined Capital of M/s X and Y i.e. 1/4 of ₹ 4,96,500.

5. X 's new Capital = ₹ 4,96,500 × 2/5 = ₹ 1,98,600,

   Y 's new Capital = ₹ 4,96,500 × 2/5 = ₹ 1,98,600,

   Z 's new Capital = ₹ 4,96,500 × 1/5 = ₹ 99,300

Note: *Though exact mode of valuation of goodwill on 1.1.20X4 is not given, On 31st Dec., 20X4 adjustment of goodwill may be recorded between X and Y—X has sacrificed 1/18 of his share of profit and Y has gained 1/18 share. Assuming value of goodwill on 1.1.20X4 to be identical to what it is on 31.12.20X4 i.e. ₹ 2,21,400, X has been credited by ₹ 12,300 and Y has been be debited by this amount.*

PROBLEM 7

Amit and Sumit are partners sharing profits and losses in the ratio of 3:2. Their Balance Sheet as on 31st March 2013 is given below:

Liabilities	₹	*Assets*		₹
Capital Accounts:		Land & building		3,20,000
Amit	1,76,000	Investments (Market value ₹ 55,000)		50,000
Sumit	2,54,000	Debtors	3,00,000	
Loan from Puneet	3,00,000	*Less:* Provision	10,000	2,90,000
General Resetve	30,000	Stock		1,10,000
Employer's provident fund	10,000	Cash at bank		50,000
Creditors	50,000			
	8,20,000			8,20,000

They decided to admit Puneet as a new partner from 1st April, 2013 on the following terms:

(1) Amit will give 1/3rd of his share and Sumit will give 1/4th of his share to Puneet.

(2) Puneet's loan account will be converted into his capital.

(3) The Goodwill of the firm is valued at ₹ 3,00,000. Puneet will bring his share of goodwill in cash and the same was immediately withdrawn by the partners.

(4) Land and building was found undervalued by ₹ 1,00,000.

(5) Stock was found overvalued by ₹ 60,000.

(6) Provision for doubtful debts will be made equal to 5% of debtors.

(7) Investments are to be valued at their market price.

It was decided that the total capital of the firm after admission of new partner would be ₹ 10,00,000. Capital accounts of partners will be readjusted on the basis of their profit sharing ratio and excess *or* deficiency will be adjusted in cash.

Required: Prepare (a) Revaluation A/c (b) Partners'capital A/cs (c) Balance Sheet of the firm after admission of a new partner

SOLUTION

Dr. **REVALUATION ACCOUNT** *Cr.*

Particulars	₹	*Particulars*	₹
To Stock	60,000	By Land & building	1,00,000
To Provision for doubtful debts	5,000	By Investments	5,000
To Profit transferred to:			
Amit's capital A/c	24,000		
Sumit's capital A/c	16,000		
	1,05,000		1,05,000

Dr. **PARTNERS' CAPITAL ACCOUNTS** *Cr.*

Particulars	*Amit* ₹	*Sumit* ₹	*Puneet* ₹	*Particulars*	*Amit* ₹	*Sumit* ₹	*Puneet* ₹
To Amit's				By Balance b/d	1,76,000	2,54,000	—
Capital A/c	—	—	60,000	By Puneets'			
To Puneet's	—	—	30,000	Loan A/'c	—	—	3,00,000
Capital A/c				By Puneet's			
To Bank A/c	60,000	30,000	—	capital A/c	60,000	30,000	—
To Balance c/d	4,00,000	3,00,000	3,00,000	By Bank A/c	—	—	90,000
				By Revaluation A/c	24,000	16,000	
				By General reserve	18,000	12,000	—
				By Bank	1,82,000	18,000	—
	4,60,000	3,30,000	3,90,000		4,60.000	3,30,000	3.90,000

BALANCE SHEET AS AT 1ST APRIL, 2013
(After admission of a new partner)

Liabilities	₹	*Assets*	₹
Capital accounts:		Land & Building	

Amit	4,00,000	(3,20,000 + 1,00,000)		4,20,000
Sumit	3,00,000	Investments		55,000
Puneet	3,00,000	Debtors	3,00,000	
Creditors	50,000	*Less:* Provision for		
Employers' Provident Fund	10,000	doubtful debts	(15,000)	2,85,000
		Stock (1,10,000 – 60,000)		50,000
		Cash at bank		2,50,000
	10,60,000			10,60,000

Working Notes:

(I) CALCULATION OF INCOMING PARTNER'S SHARE, NEW PROFIT SHARING RATIO AND SACRIFICING RATIO

Particulars	*Amit*	*Sumit*
Old profit sharing ratio	3/5	2/5
Surrendered by old partners	3/5 × 1 /3 = 1/5	2/5 × 1/4 = 1/10
Remaining share	3/5 – 1/5 = 2/5	2/5 – 1/10 = 3/10

Puneet's total share in profits = 1/5 + 1/10 = 3/10

New profit sharing ratio of Amit: Sumit: Puneet = 2/5 : 3/10 : 3/10 = 4:3:3

Sacrificing ratio of Amit: Sumit is 1/5 :1/10 : *or* 2:1

(ii) Share of Puneet in goodwill = ₹ 3,00,000 × 3/10 = ₹ 90,000

Goodwill will be distributed among the old partners in their sacrificing ratio of 2:1 i.e. ₹ 60,000 by Amit and ₹ 30,000 by Sumit.

Dr. **(III) BANK ACCOUNT** *Cr.*

Particulars	₹	*Particulars*	₹
To Balance b/d	50,000	By Amit's Capital A/c	60,000
To Puneefs Capital A/c	90,000	By Sumit's Capital A/c	30,000
To Sumit's Capital A/c	18,000	By Balance c/d	2,50,000
To Amit's Capita] A/c	1,82,000		
	3,40,000		3,40,000

PROBLEM 8

Laurel and Hardy are partners of the firm LH & Co., from 1.4.2009 Initially both of them contributed ₹ 1,00,000 each as capital. They did not contribute any capital thereafter. They maintain accounts of the firm on mercantile basis. They were sharing profits and losses in the ratio of 5:4. After the accounts for the year ended 31.3.2003 were finalized, the partners decided to share profits and losses equally with effect from 1. 4. 2009.

It was also discovered that in ascertaining the results in the earlier years certain adjustments, details of which are given below, had not been noted.

Year ended 31st March	*2010* ₹	*2011* ₹	*2012* ₹	*2013* ₹
Profit as per accounts prepaid and finalized	1,40,000	2,60,000	3,20,000	3,60,000

Expenses not provided for (as at 31st March)	30,000	20,000	36,000	24,000
Incomes not taken into account (as at 31st March)	18,000	15,000	12,000	21,000

The partners decided to admit Chaplin as a partner with effect from 1.4.2013. It was decided that Chaplin would be allotted 20% share in the firm and he must bring 20% of the combined capital of Laurel and Hordy.

Following is the Balance sheet of the firm as on 31.3.2013 before admission of Chaplin and before adjustment of revised profits between Laurel and Hardy.

BALANCE SHEET OF LH & CO. AS AT 31.3.2013

Liabilities	₹	*Assets*	₹
Capital Accounts:		Plant and Machinery	60,000
Laurel	2,11,500	Cash on hand	10,000
Hardy	1,51,500	Cash at bank	5,000
Sundry Creditors	2,27,000	Stock in trade	3,10,000
		Sundry Debtors	2,05,000
	5,90,000		**5,90,000**

You are required to prepare:

(i) Profit and Loss Adjustment account;

(ii) Capital accounts of the partners; and

(iii) Balance Sheet of the firm after the admission of Chaplin.

SOLUTION

Dr. **PROFIT & LOSS ADJUSTMENT ACCOUNT** Cr.

Particulars	₹	*Particulars*	₹
To Expenses not provided for (years 2004-2007)	1,10,000	By Income not considered (for years 2004-2007)	66,000
		By Partners' Capital A/c (loss)	
		Laurel	22,000
		Hardy	22,000
	1,10,000		1,10,000

Dr. **(II) PARTNER'S CAPITAL ACCOUNTS** Cr.

Particulars	*Laurel* ₹	*Hardy* ₹	*Dhaplin* ₹	*Particular*	*Laurel* ₹	*Hardy* ₹	*Dhaplin* ₹
To P & L Adjustment A/c	22,000	22,000	—	By Balance b/d	2,11,500	1,51,500	—
To Hardy	60,000			By Laurel	—	60,000	—
To Balance c/d	1,29,500	1,89,500	63,800	By Cash	—	—	63,800
	2,11,500	2,11,500	63,800		2,11,500	2,11,500	63,800

(III) BALANCE SHEET AS AT 1.4.2007 (AFTER ADMISSION OF CHAPLIN)

Liabilities	₹	*Assets*	₹
Capital Accounts:		Plant and machinery	60,000

Laurel	1,29,500	Sundry debtors	2,05,000
Hardy	1,89,500	Stock in trade	3,10,000
Chaplin	63,800	Accrued income	66,000
Sundry Creditors	2,27,000	Cash on hand (10,000 + 63,800)	73,800
Outstanding Expenses	1,10,000	Cash at bank	5,000
	7,19,800		7,19,800

Working Notes:

(i) Computation of Profit and Loss distributed among partners

Total Profit = ₹ 1,40,000 + ₹ 2,60,000, ₹ 3,20,000 + ₹ 3,60,000 = ₹ 10,80,000

Particulars	*Laurel* ₹	*Hardy* ₹	*Dhaplin* ₹
Profit shared in old ratio i.e. 5:4	6,00,000	4,80,000	10,80,000
Profit to be shared as per new ratio i.e. 1:1	5,40,000	5,40,000	10,80,000
Excess share	60,000		
Deficit share		(60,000)	

Laurel to be debited by ₹ 60,000 and Hardy to be credited by ₹ 60,000.

(ii) Capital brought in by Chaplin

Capital to be brought in by Chaplin must be equal to 20% of the combine capital of Laurel and Hardy

Particulars	₹
Capital of Laurel (2,11,500 – 22,000 – 60,000)	1,29,500
Capital of Hardy (1,1,500 – 22,000 + 60,000)	1,89,500
Combined Capital	3,19,000
20% of the combined capital brought in by Chaplin (20% of ₹ 3,19,000)	63,800

PROBLEM 16.2

P, Q, R are three doctors who are running a Polyclinic. Their capital on 31st March, 2012 was ₹ 1,00,000 each. They agreed to admit X, Y and Z as partners w.e.f. 1st April 2012. The terms for sharing profits & losses were as follows:

(a) 70% of the visiting fee is to go to the specialist concerned.

(b) 50% of the chamber fee will be payable to the individual specialist.

(c) 40% of operation fee and fee for pathological reports, X-rays and ECG will accrue in favour of the doctor concerned.

(d) Balance of profit *or* loss is shared equally.

(e) All the partners are entitled for 6% interest on capital employed.

They further agreed that:

(i) X, Y and I brought in ₹ 20,000 each as goodwill. Goodwill is shared by the existing partners equally.

(ii) X, Y and Z brought in ₹ 50,000 each as capital. Each of the original partners also contributed ₹ 50,000 by way of capital.

THE RECEIPTS FOR THE YEAR AFTER ADMISSION OF NEW PARTNERS WERE:

Name of doctors	*Particulars*	*Visiting Fees* ₹	*Chambers Fees* ₹	*Fees for reports, operation etc.* ₹
P	General Physician	1,50,000	2,00,000	—
Q	Gynecologist	25,000	1,75,000	1,00,000
R	Cardiologist		1,00,000	75,000
X	Child Specialist	1,00,000	1,50,000	—
Y	Pathologist			1,00,000
I	Radiologist		40,000	2,00,000
	Total	2,75,000	6,65,000	4,75,000

EXPENSES FOR THE YEAR WERE AS FOLLOWS

Particulars	₹
Medicines, injections and other consumables	1,00,000
Printing and stationery	5,000
Telephone expenses	5,000
Rent	42,000
Power and light	10,000
Nurses salary	20,000
Attendants wages	20,000
Total	**2,02,000**
Depreciation:	15,000
X-Ray machines	5,000
ECG equipments	5,000
Furniture	5,000
Surgical Equipments	5,000
Total	**30,000**

You are requested to:

(i) Pass necessary journal entries on admission of partners.

(ii) Prepare the Profit and Loss Account of the polyclinic for the year ended 31st March, 2013.

(iii) Prepare capital accounts of all the partners at the end of the financial year 2012-2013. Also show the distribution of profit among partners.

SOLUTION

(I) JOURNAL ENTRIES (ON ADMISSION OF PARTNERS)

Date	*Particulars*		*Dr. (₹)*	*Cr. (₹)*
01.04.12	X's Capital A/c	Dr.	20,000	
	Y's Capital A/c	Dr.	20,000	
	Z's Capital A/c	Dr.	20,000	

	To P's Capital A/c			20,000
	To Q's Capital A/c			20,000
	To R's Capital A/c			20,000
	(Being goodwill adjusted through capital accounts)			
	Bank A/c	Dr.	2,10,000	
	To X's capital A/c (20,000 + 50,000)			70,000
	To Y's capital A/c (20,000 + 50,000)			70,000
	To Z's capital A/c (20,000 + 50,000)			70,000
	(Being goodwill and capital brought in by new partners)			
	Bank A/c	Dr.	1,50,00	
	To P's capital A/c			50,000
	To Q's capital A/c			50,000
	To R's capital A/c			50,000
	(Being capital brought in by existing partners)			

(II) PROFIT & LOSS A/C FOR THE YEAR ENDED 31ST MARCH, 2013

Particulars		₹	*Particulars*	₹
To Medicines, injections and other consumables		1,00,000	By Visiting fee	2,75,000
			By Chamber fee	6,65,000
To Printing and stationery		5,000	By Fee for report, operation etc.	4,75,000
To Telephone expenses		5,000		
To Rent		42,000		
To Power and light		10,000		
To Nurses salary		20,000		
To Attendants wages		20,000		
To Depreciation				
X-ray machine	15,000			
ECG equipment	5,000			
Furniture	5,000			
Surgical equipment	5,000	30,000		
To Interest on capital		39,600		
To Net Profit		11,43,400		
		14,15,000		**14,15,000**

(II) PARTNERS' CAPITAL ACCOUNT FOR THE YEAR ENDED 31ST MARCH, 2013

Debit side

Particulars	*P* ₹	*Q* ₹	*R* ₹	*X* ₹	*Y* ₹	*Z* ₹
To P, Q, & R A/cs (Goodwill)	–	–	–	20,000	20,000	20,000
To Balance c/d	4,56,600	3,96,600	3,31,600	2,69,400	1,64,400	2,24.400
	4,56,600	**3,96,600**	**3,31,600**	**2,89,400**	**1,84,400**	**2,44,400**

Credit side

Particulars	*P* ₹	*Q* ₹	*R* ₹	*X* ₹	*Y* ₹	*Z* ₹
By Balance b/d	1,00,000	1,00,000	1,00,000	–	–	–
By X, Y & Z /cs (Goodwill)	20,000	20,000	20,000	–	–	–
By Bank A/c	50,000	50,000	50,000	70,000	70,000	70,000
By Interest on Capital	10,200	10,200	10,200	3,000	3,000	3,000
By Fee (share)	2,05,000	1,45,000	80,000	1,45,000	40,000	1,00,000
By Profit (share)	71,400	71,400	71,400	71,400	71,400	71,400
	4,56,600	**3,96,600**	**3,31,600**	**2,89,400**	**1,84,400**	**2,44,400**

Working Notes:

(I) STATEMENT SHOWING DISTRIBUTION OF FEE AMONG PARTNERS

Partner Name	*Visiting Fees (70%)* ₹	*Chambers Fees (50%)* ₹	*Operations Fees (40%)* ₹	*Total* ₹
P	1,05,000	1,00,000	—	2,05,000
Q	17,500	87,500	40,000	1,45,000
R	—	50,000	30,000	80,000
X	70,000	75,000	—	1,45,000
Y	—	—	40,000	40,000
Z	—	20,000	80,000	1,00,000
	1,92,500	3,32,500	1,90,000	7,15,000

(II) STATEMENT SHOWING DISTRIBUTION OF FEE AMONG PARTNERS

Particulars	₹
Profits as per profit and loss account	11,43,400
Less: Fee payable to partners	7,15,000
Profit to be divided equally among partners	**4,28,400**
Share of each partner in remaining profit = 4,28,400/6 = 71,400.	

(III) INTEREST ON CAPITAL EMPLOYED

Particulars	*P* ₹	*Q* ₹	*R* ₹	*X* ₹	*Y* ₹	*Z* ₹
Opening balance	1,00,000	1,00,000	1,00,000	—	—	—
Add: Goodwill	20,000	20,000	20,000	—	—	—
Add: Capital brought in cash	50,000	50,000	50,000	50,000	50,000	50,000
	1,70,000	1,70,000	1,70,000	50,000	50,000	50,000
Interest @ 6%	10,200	10,200	10,200	3,000	3,000	3,000

Total Interest = ₹ 39,600.

(iv) It is assumed that amount of premium for goodwill brought in by new partners X, Y and Z has not been withdrawn by old partners P, Q and R and it is still kept in the business.

18 RECONSTITUTION OF PARTNERSHIP-RETIREMENT/ DEATH OF A PARTNER

LEARNING OBJECTIVES

After studying this chapter, you should be able to understand:

- ◇ Meaning of Retirement of a Partner
- ◇ How can a Partner retire?
- ◇ Liability of a Retiring Partner
- ◇ Adjustments required at the time of Retirement of a Partner
- ◇ Meaning of New Profit Sharing Ratio
- ◇ Meaning of Gaining Ratio
- ◇ Distinction between Sacrificing Ratio and Gaining Ratio
- ◇ Adjustment of Goodwill
- ◇ Hidden Goodwill
- ◇ Adjustment of Profit/Loss on Revaluation of Assets and Liabilities
- ◇ Adjustment of Reserves and Accumulated Profits/Losses
- ◇ Adjustment of Capitals
- ◇ Disposal of the Amount Due to the Retiring Partner
- ◇ Retirement during the Accounting year
- ◇ Death of a Partner
- ◇ Accounting Treatment of Joint Life Policy and Individual Life Policy in Case of Death of a Partner
- ◇ Outgoing Partner's Share in the Profits of the year of Death/Retirement
- ◇ Deceased Partner's Share of Goodwill
- ◇ Calculation of Amount Payable to Executors of a Capital Account Deceased Partner
- ◇ Preparation of a Deceased Partner's Capital Account and His Excecutor's Account

1.0 RETIREMENT OF A PARTNER

Meaning	Retirement of a partner is one of the modes of reconstituting the firm under which an old partnership comes to an end and a new one between the continuing partners '(i.e., partners other than the outgoing partner) comes into existence. However, the firm continues its business.
How can a Partner retire?	A partner may retire — 1. with the consent of all other partners (whether implied *or* expressed); 2. in accordance with an express agreement by the partners*; or* 3. by giving notice in writing, to all other partners of his intention **to retire** in case of partnership at will [Sec. 32(1)].

Liability of a Retiring Partner	1. **Liability for the Firm's acts before his Retirement** Retiring Partner continues to be liable to the third party unless he discharges himself for the same by Notation (i.e., by tripartite agreement between him, third party and the continuing partners) [Sec. 32(2)]. 2. **Liability for the Firm's acts after his Retirement** Retiring Partner continues to be liable to third party until public notice of his retirement is given by himself *or* any of the other partners. But he will not be liable to any third party if the latter deals with the firm without knowing, that the former was a partner [Sec. 32(3) & (4)].
Adjustments Required	The various matters that need adjustment at the time of retirement of a partner are: 1. Adjustment in Profit Sharing Ratio 2. Adjustment for Goodwill 3. Adjustment of Profit/Loss arising on the Revaluation of Assets and Liabilities 4. Adjustment of Accumulated Profits, Reserves and Losses 5. Adjustment of Capitals (if agreed).

2.0 NEW PROFIT SHARING RATIO AND GAINING RATIO

New Profit Sharing Ratio	The ratio in which the continuing partners (i.e., partners other than an outgoing one) decide to share the future profits and losses, is known as new profit sharing ratio. **Tutorial Note:** *Unless agreed otherwise, it is presumed that the continuing partners acquire the outgoing partner's share in their old profit sharing ratio so that the continuing partners continue to share the future profits in the old ratio & hence their New Profit Sharing Ratio is same as their Old Profit Sharing Ratio.*
Gaining Ratio	The ratio in which the continuing partners acquire the outgoing (retired *or* deceased) partner's share is called as gaining ratio. This ratio is calculated by taking out the difference between New Profit Share and Old Profit Share. **Tutorial Note:** *Unless agreed otherwise it is presumed that, the Continuing Partners gain in their old profit sharing ratio and hence their Gaining Ratio is same as their Old Profit Sharing Ratio.*
Example	A, B and C are partners in a firm sharing profits in the ratio of 3 : 2 : 1. B died on 1st January 2012. C, the son of B, is of the opinion that he is the rightful owner of his father's share of profits, and the profits of the firm be shared between A and C equally. A does not agree. Settle the dispute between A and C according to Indian Partnership Act. **In the case C is not correct. Unless agreed otherwise, New Profit Sharing Ratio of Continuing Partners is same as their Old Profit Sharing Ratio i.e. 3 : 1.**

3.0 DISTINCTION BETWEEN SACRIFICING RATIO AND GAINING RATIO

Sacrificing Ratio and Gaining Ratio can be distinguished as follows:

Basis of Distinction	*Sacrificing Ratio*	*Gaining Ratio*
1. Meaning	It is the ratio in which the old partners have agreed to sacrifice their shares in profit in favour of new partner.	It is the ratio in which the continuing partners acquire the outgoing (retired *or* deceased) partners share.

2. Purpose	It is calculated to determine the amount of compensation to be paid by the incoming partner to the sacrificing partners.	It is calculated to determine the amount of compensation to be paid by each of the continuing partners to the outgoing partner.
3. How to calculate?	It is calculated by taking out the difference between Old Share and New Share.	It is calculated by taking out the difference between New Share and Old Share.
4. When to calculate?	It is calculated at the time of admission of a new partner and change in profit sharing ratio.	It is calculated at the time of retirement *or* death of a partner and change in profit sharing ratio.

ILLUSTRATION 1

X, Y and Z are partners sharing profits in the ratio of 1/2 : 3/10 : 1/5. Calculate the new profit sharing ratio and gaining ratio (a) If X retires (b) If Y retires (c) If Z retires.

SOLUTION

Let us convert the old ratio given in the form of fractions into one consisting of whole numbers, 1/2 : 3/10 : 1/5 = 5 : 3 : 2.

New Ratio In such case, new ratio will be the same as the old ratio which existed between the remaining partners since the remaining partners continue to share the future profits and losses in the old ratio as existed immediately before the going out of a partner unless agreed otherwise.

Thus, the new ratio will be as under:

(a) between Y & Z	3 : 2
(b) between X & Z	5 : 2
(c) between X & Y	5 : 3

Gaining Ratio In such a case, gaining ratio will be the same as the old ratio which existed between the remaining partners since the remaining partners gain in their old ratio unless agreed otherwise.

Thus, the gaining ratio will be as under: —

(a) between Y & Z	3 : 2
(b) between X & Z	5 : 2
(c) between X & Y	5 : 3

ILLUSTRATION 2

X, Y & Z are partners sharing profits and losses in the ratio of 1/5, 1/3 and 7/15 respectively. Z retires and his share is taken up by X and Y in the ratio of 3 : 2. Calculate the new profit sharing ratio and the gaining ratio.

SOLUTION

New Share of Remaining Partner = Old Share + Share acquired

Share acquired by X = $\frac{3}{5} \times \frac{7}{15} = \frac{21}{75}$

Share acquired by Y = $\frac{2}{5} \times \frac{7}{15} = \frac{14}{75}$

X's New Share = $\frac{1}{5} + \frac{21}{75} = \frac{36}{75}$

Y's New Share = $\frac{1}{3}+\frac{14}{75}=\frac{39}{75}$

Hence, New Ratio of X and Y = $\frac{36}{75}:\frac{39}{75}$ = 12 : 13

Gaining Ratio of X and Y = Share acquired by X : Share acquired by Y

= $\frac{21}{75}:\frac{14}{75}$ = 21 : 14 = 3 : 2

ILLUSTRATION 3

X, Y & Z are partners sharing, profits and losses in the ratio of 1/2, 3/10 and 1/5 respectively. Y retires from the firm and X and Z decide to share future profits and losses in the ratio of 3 : 2. Calculate the gaining ratio.

SOLUTION

Gain of a Partner = New Share – Old Share

X's Gain = $\frac{3}{5}-\frac{1}{2}=\frac{1}{10}$

Z's Gain = $\frac{2}{5}-\frac{1}{5}=\frac{2}{10}$

Hence, Gaining Ratio of X & Z = $\frac{1}{10}:\frac{2}{10}$ = 1 : 2

ILLUSTRATION 4

W, X, Y & Z are partners sharing profits and losses in the ratio of 1/3, 1/6, 1/3 and 1/6 respectively. Y retires and W, X & Z decide to share the profits and losses equally in future. Calculate the gaining ratio.

SOLUTION

Gain of a Partner = New Share – Old Share

W's Gain = $\frac{1}{3}-\frac{1}{3}=0$

X's Gain = $\frac{1}{3}-\frac{1}{6}=\frac{1}{6}$

Z's Gain = $\frac{1}{3}-\frac{1}{6}=\frac{1}{6}$

Hence, Gaining Ratio of X & Z = 1 : 1

ILLUSTRATION 5

X, Y & Z are partners sharing profits and losses in the ratio of 2/5, 2/5 & 1/5 respectively. Z retires and X & Y decide to share the future profits & losses in the ratio of 2 : 1 respectively. Calculate the gaining ratio.

SOLUTION

Gain (Sacrifice) of a Partner = New Share – Old Share

X's Gain = $\frac{2}{3}-\frac{2}{5}=\frac{4}{15}$

Y's Sacrifice = $\frac{1}{3}-\frac{2}{5}=\frac{1}{15}$

In this case, Only X is gaining partner. Z has sacrified his 1/5th share and Y has also sacrificed his share to the extent of 1/15 in favour of X who is required to compensate Z and Y for such sacrifice.

ILLUSTRATION 6

X, Y and Z are partners sharing the profits & losses in the ratio of 25 : 15 : 9. Y retires. It is decided that the profit sharing ratio between X and Z will be the same as existing between Y and Z. Calculate the new profit sharing ratio and gaining ratio.

SOLUTION

Ratio of Y and Z = 15 : 9 = 5 : 3

Therefore New Ratio of X & Z should be 5 : 3

Gain of a Partner = New Share – Old Share

X's Gain = $\frac{5}{8} - \frac{25}{49} = \frac{45}{392}$

Z's Gain = $\frac{3}{8} - \frac{9}{49} = \frac{75}{392}$

Hence, Gaining Ratio of X and Z = $\frac{45}{392} : \frac{75}{392}$ = 3 : 5

ILLUSTRATION 7

X, Y and Z are partners sharing profits & losses in the ratio of 4/9 : 1/3 : 2/9. Y retires and surrenders 1/9th of his share in favour of X and the remaining in favour of Z. Calculate the new profit sharing ratio and the gaining ratio.

SOLUTION

CALCULATION OF NEW RATIO

Particulars	*X*	*Z*
A. Their existing shares	4/9	2/9
B. Share surrendered by Y	1/9 × 1/3 = 1/27	8/9 × 1/3 = 8/27
C. New Share of remaining partner (A + B)	13/27	14/27
D. New Ratio of X and Z = 13 : 14		

Share surrendered in favour of X = $\frac{1}{9} \times \frac{1}{3} = \frac{1}{27}$

Shsare surrendered in favour of Z = $\frac{8}{9} \times \frac{1}{3} = \frac{8}{27}$

Hence, Gaining Ratio of X and Z = $\frac{1}{27} : \frac{8}{27}$ = 1 : 8

New Share = Old Share + Share acquired

X's New Share = $\frac{4}{9} + \frac{1}{27} = \frac{13}{27}$

Y's New Share = $\frac{2}{9} + \frac{8}{27} = \frac{14}{27}$

New Ratio of X and Z = $\frac{13}{27} : \frac{14}{27}$ = 13 : 14

ILLUSTRATION 8

X, Y and Z are partners sharing profits in the ratio of 4/9 : 1/3 : 2/9. Y retires and surrenders 1/9th from his share in favour of X and the remaining in favour of Z. Calculate the new profit sharing ratio and the gaining ratio.

SOLUTION

Share surrendered by Y in favour of X = 1/9

Share surrendered by Y in favour of Z = 3/9 – 1/9 = 2/9

Hence, Gaining Ratio of X and Z = 1/9 : 2/9 = 1 : 2

X's New share = $\frac{4}{9}+\frac{1}{9}=\frac{5}{9}$

Z's New share = $\frac{2}{9}+\frac{2}{9}=\frac{4}{9}$

New Ratio of X and Z = $\frac{5}{9}:\frac{4}{9}$ = 5 : 4

ILLUSTRATION 9

X, Y & Z share profits and losses in the ratio of 1/2, 3/10 & 1/5 respectively. Y retires and his share is taken up by X & Z in the ratio of 2 : 1. Then immediately, W is admitted for 1/4th share of profits, half of which was gifted by X and the remaining share was taken by W equally from X & Z. Calculate the new profit sharing ratio after W's admission.

SOLUTION

Particulars	*X*	*Z*
A. Their existing shares	1/2	1/5
B. Share acquired by remaining partners	2/3 x 3/10 = 2/10	1/3 x 3/10 = 1/10
C. New shares of remaining partners (A + B)	7/10	3/10
D. Share gifted by X	1/2 x 1/4 = 1/8	—
E. Share acquired by W (other than gift)	1/2 x 1/8 = 1/16	1/2 x 1/8 = 1/16
F. New Shares (C – D – E)	41/80	19/80
G. New Ratio, of X, Z & W = 41/80 : 19/80 : 20/80 = 41 : 19 : 20		

ILLUSTRATION 10

X, Y, & Z share profits and losses in the ratio of 4 : 3 : 2 respectively. Y retires and X & Z decide to share future profits & losses in the ratio of 5 : 3. Then W is admitted for 3/10th share of profits half of which was gifted by X and the remaining share was taken by W equally from X & Z. Calculate the gaining ratio of X & Z on Y's retirement and the new profit sharing ratio after W's admission.

SOLUTION

CALCULATION OF GAINING RATIO OF X & Z

X's Gain = $\frac{5}{8}-\frac{4}{9}=\frac{13}{72}$

Z's Gain = $\frac{3}{8}-\frac{2}{9}=\frac{11}{72}$

Hence, Gaining Ratio of X & Z = $\frac{13}{72}:\frac{11}{72}$ = 13 : 11

CALCULATION OF NEW RATIO OF X, Z & W

Particulars	*X*	*Z*
A. Their new shares after retirement	5/8	3/8
B. Gifted by X	1/2 of 3/10 = 3/20	—
C. Share acquired by W (other than gift)	1/2 of 3/20 = 3/40	1/2 of 3/20 = 3/40
D. New Shares after W's admission (A – B – C)	16/40	12/40
E. New Ratio of X, Z & W = 16/40 : 12/40 : 12/40 = 16 : 12 : 12 = 4: 3 : 3		

4.0 ADJUSTMENT OF GOODWILL

Why is Adjustment of Goodwill required?	When an existing partner of a firm decides to retire from the firm, the continuing partner(s) will gain in future profits. The continuing partner who gains by acquiring an additional right to share future profits must compensate the outgoing partner who sacrifices by foregoing his right to share future profits.
Amount of Compensation	The amount of compensation must be equal to the proportionate value of firm's goodwill. Thus, Outgoing Partner's Share of Goodwill = Value of Firm's Goodwill × Share of Profit Sacrificed
Accounting Treatment	The following simplified approach is suggested to make adjustment of goodwill:

PRACTICAL STEPS IN ADJUSTMENT OF GOODWILL

Step 1: Write off the Existing Book Value of Goodwill (if any) appearing in the books of the firm.

All Partners' Capital A/cs Dr. [In Old Ratio]

To Goodwill A/c [With Existing Book Value of Goodwill]

(Being the existing goodwill written off in Old Ratio)

Step 2: Give credit for Outgoing Partner's Share of Goodwill to Outgoing Partner

Gaining Partners' Capital A/cs Dr. [In Gaining Ratio]

To Outgoing Partner's Capital A/c [With his Share of Goodwill]

(Being the adjustment made for goodwill on retirement)

Step 3: If any Existing Partner (other than Outgoing Partner) is also sacrificing his share, a separate entry to adjust proportionate Goodwill should be passed as follows:

Gaining Partner's Capital A/cs Dr. [In Gaining Ratio]

To Sacrificing Partner's Capital A/c [Firm's Goodwill × Share Sacrificed]

ILLUSTRATION 11

X, Y & Z are partners sharing profits & losses in the ratio of 4 : 3 : 2. Y retires and the goodwill of the firm is valued at ₹ 21,600. Goodwill account already appears in the books at ₹ 9,000. Assuming that X and Z will share the future profits in the ratio of 5 : 3, pass the necessary journal entries.

SOLUTION

JOURNAL

Particulars		*L.F.*	*Dr. (₹)*	*Cr (₹)*
X's Capital A/c	Dr.		4,000	
Y's Capital A/c	Dr.		3,000	
Z's Capital A/c	Dr.		2,000	
To Goodwill A/c				9,000
(Being the existing goodwill written off in old ratio)				
X's Capital A/c [₹ 7,200 × 13/24]	Dr.		3,900	
Z's Capital A/c [₹ 7,200 × 11/24]	Dr.		3,300	
To Y's Capital A/c [₹ 21,600 × 3/9]				7,200
(Being Y's share of goodwill adjusted in the capital accounts of gaining partners in their gaining ratio of 13 : 11)				

Working Note: Calculation of Gaining Ratio

Gain of a Partner = New Share – Old Share

A gains = $\frac{5}{8}-\frac{4}{9}=\frac{13}{72}$; B gains = $\frac{3}{8}-\frac{2}{9}=\frac{11}{72}$. Gaining Ratio = $\frac{13}{72}:\frac{11}{72}$ *or* 13 : 11.

ILLUSTRATION 12

X, Y and Z are partners sharing profits & losses in the ratio of 14 : 5 : 6 respectively. Y retires and surrenders 5/25th of his share in favour of X. The goodwill of the firm is valued at 2 years' purchase of super profits based on average of last 3 years. The profits for the last 3 years are: ₹ 50,000, ₹ 55,000, ₹ 60,000. The normal profits for similar firm are ₹ 30,000. Goodwill already appears in the books of the firm at ₹ 75,000. The profit for the first year after Y's retirement was ₹ 1,00,000. Give the necessary journal entries to adjust goodwill and to distribute profits.

SOLUTION

JOURNAL

Particulars		*L.F.*	*Dr. (₹)*	*Cr (₹)*
X's, Capital A/c [₹ 75,000 × 14/25]	Dr.		42,000	
Y's Capital A/c [₹ 75,000 × 5/25	Dr.		15,000	
Z's Capital A/c [₹ 75,000 × 6/25]	Dr.		18,000	
To Goodwill A/c				75,000
(Being the existing goodwill written off in old ratio)				
X's Capital A/c [₹ 10,000 × 1/5]	Dr.		2,000	
Z's Capital A/c [₹ 10,000 × 4/5]	Dr.		8,000	
To Y's Capital A/c [₹ 50,000 × 1/5]				10,000
(Being Y's share of goodwill adjusted in the capital accounts of gaining partners in their gaining ratio of 1 : 4)				
Profit & Loss Appropriation A/c	Dr.		1,00,000	
To X's Capital A/c [₹ 1,00,000 × 3/5]				60,000

To Z's Capital A/c [₹ 1,00,000 × 2/5]			40,000
(Being the profits distributed among X & Z in their new profit sharing ratio)			

Working Notes:

1. CALCULATION OF NEW PROFIT SHARING RATIO

Particulars	*X*	*Z*
Their Old Shares	14/25	6/25
Share surrendered by Y	1/5 × 1/5 = 1/25	4/5 × 1/5 = 4/25
Their New Shares	14/25 × 1/25 = 1/25	6/25 × 4/25 = 10/25
Their Gaining Ratio 1/25 : 4/25 = 1:4		
Their New Ratio = 15/25 : 10/25 = 15:10 *or* 3:2		

2. CALCULATION OF GOODWILL

(i) Average Profits = (₹ 50,000 + ₹ 55,000 + ₹ 60,000)/3 = ₹ 55,000

(ii) Super Profits = ₹ 55,000 – ₹ 30,000 = ₹ 25,000

(iii) Goodwill = ₹ 25,000 × 2 = ₹ 50,000

(iv) Y's Share of Goodwill = ₹ 50,000 × 1/5 = ₹ 10,000

ILLUSTRATION 13

A, B, C & D are partners sharing profits and losses in the ratio of 3 : 3 : 2 : 2. D retires and A, B and C decide to share the future profits in the ratio of 3 : 2 : 1. Goodwill of the firm is valued at ₹ 3,00,000. Goodwill already appears in the books at ₹ 1,00,000. The profits for the first year after D's retirement amount to ₹ 6,00,000. Give the necessary journal entries to record Goodwill and to distribute the profits.

SOLUTION

JOURNAL

Particulars		L.F.	Dr. (₹)	Cr (₹)
A's Capital A/c [₹ 1,00,000 × 3/10]	Dr.		30,000	
B's Capital A/c [₹ 1,00,000 × 3/10]	Dr.		30,000	
C's Capital A/c [₹ 1,00,000 × 2/10]	Dr.		20,000	
D's Capital A/c [₹ 1,00,000 × 2/10]	Dr.		20,000	
To Goodwill A/c				1,00,000
(Being the existing goodwill w/o in old ratio)				
A's Capital A/c	Dr.		60,000	
B's Capital A/c	Dr.		10,000	
To C's Capital A/c				10,000
To D's Capital A/c				60,000
(Being the adjustment for goodwill made on account of change in profit sharing ratio which resulted in loss of 6/30th to D, 1/30th to C and gain of 1/30th to B and 2/10th to A)				

Profit & Loss Appropriation A/c	Dr.		6,00,000	
To A's Capital A/c [₹ 6,00,000 × 3/6]				3,00,000
To B's Capital A/c [₹ 6,00,000 × 2/6]				2,00,000
To C's Capital A/c [₹ 6,00,000 × 1/6]				1,00,000
(Being the amount of profit distributed among A & C in their new profit sharing ratio which is 3 : 2 : 1)				

ILLUSTRATION 14

A, B and C are partners sharing profits and losses in the ratio of 4 : 3 : 1. B retires selling his share of profit to A and C for ₹ 8,100—₹ 3,600 being paid by A and ₹ 4,500 by C. The profit for the year after B's retirement was ₹ 10,500. Give the necessary journal entries.

SOLUTION

JOURNAL

Particulars		*L.F.*	*Dr. (₹)*	*Cr (₹)*
Bank A/c	Dr.		8,100	
To A's Capital A/c				3,600
To C's Capital A/c				4,500
(Being the amount brought in by A and C to pay on his retirement)				
A's Capital A/c	Dr.		3,600	
C's Capital A/c	Dr.		4,500	
To B's Capital A/c				8,100
(Being B's share of goodwill adjusted in capital accounts of gaining partners in their gaining ratio of 12 : 15)				
B's Capital A/c	Dr.		8,100	
To Bank A/c				8,100
(Being the amount paid to B on his retirement for selling his share)				
Profit & Loss Appropriation A/c	Dr.		10,500	
To A's Capital A/c				7,000
To C's Capital A/c				3,500
(Being the amount of profit distributed among A & C in their new profit sharing ratio which is 2 : 1)				

Working Note: Calculation of New Profit Sharing Ratio

Gaining Ratio of A and C = 3,600 : 4,500 = 4 : 5

Share acquired by A = $\frac{4}{9} \times \frac{3}{8} = \frac{12}{72}$, Share acquired by C = $\frac{5}{9} \times \frac{3}{8} = \frac{15}{72}$

A's New Share = $\frac{4}{8} + \frac{12}{72} = \frac{48}{72}$, C's New Share = $\frac{1}{8} + \frac{15}{72} = \frac{24}{72}$

Hence, New Ratio of A & C = $\frac{48}{72} : \frac{24}{72}$ = 2 : 1

ILLUSTRATION 15

X, Y and Z share profits and losses in the ratio of 4 : 3 : 2 respectively. Y retires and X and Z decide to share future profits & losses in the ratio of 5 : 3. Then immediately W is admitted for 3/10th share of profits half of which was gifted by X and the remaining share was taken by W equally from X and Z. The Goodwill of the firm is valued at ₹ 21,600. W brings in the required amount of goodwill. The profit for the year after W's admission was ₹ 24,000. Give the necessary journal entries to adjust goodwill and to distribute profits.

SOLUTION

JOURNAL

Particulars		*L.F.*	*Dr. (₹)*	*Cr (₹)*
X's Capital A/c	Dr.		3,900	
Z's Capital A/c	Dr.		3,300	
To Y's Capital A/c				7,200
(Being Y's share of goodwill adjusted in the capital accounts of gaining partners in their gaining ratio of 13 : 11)				
Cash A/c	Dr.		3,240	
To Premium for Goodwill A/c				3,240
(Being the amount of goodwill brought in by W for purchased share of profit (i.e. 3/20)				
Premium for Goodwill A/c	Dr.		3,240	
To X's Capital A/c				1,620
To Z's Capital A/c				1,620
(Being the goodwill credited to sacrificing partners in their sacrificing ratio of 1 : 1)				
Profit & Loss Appropriation A/c	Dr.		24,000	
To X's capital A/c				9,600
To Z's Capital A/c				7,200
To W's Capital A/c				7,200
(Being the profit credited to all partners in their new profit sharing ratio of 4 : 3 : 3)				

Working Note: For calculation of gaining Ratio and New Ratio, Refer to Illustration 10.

.0 HIDDEN GOODWILL

f the firm has agreed to settle the account of retiring/deceased partner by paying him a lump-sum amount, then amount paid to him in excess of his capital and share in reserves/revaluation account etc. shall be treated as his share of goodwill. ***For Example***, X, Y and Z are partners. Z retires, his capital account, after making adjustments for reserves and profit on revaluation exists at ₹ 1,00,000. X and Y have agreed to pay him ₹ 1,50,000 in full settlement of his claim. It implies that ₹ 50,000 is Z's share in the goodwill of the firm. This will be treated by debiting ₹ 50,000 in the capital accounts of X and Y in their gaining ratio and crediting Z's capital account.

ILLUSTRATION 16

X, Y and Z are partners sharing profits in the ratio of 4 : 3 : 2. Y retires and his capital after making adjustments for reserves and profits on revaluation stands at ₹ 92,800. X and Z agreed to pay him ₹ 1,00,000 in full settlement of his claim. Record the necessary Journal entry for the treatment of goodwill if the new profit-sharing ratio is decided at 5 : 3.

SOLUTION

Particulars	₹
Amount agreed to be paid in full settlement	1,00,000
Less: C's Capital (after all adjustments)	92,800
Hidden Goodwill	7,200

JOURNAL

Particulars		*L.F.*	*Dr. (₹)*	*Cr (₹)*
X's Capital A/c	Dr.		3,900	
Z's Capital A/c	Dr.		3,300	
To Y's Capital A/c				7,200
(Being Y's share of goodwill adjusted in the capital accounts of gaining partners in their gaining ratio of 13 : 11)				

Working Note: Calculation of Gaining Ratio

Gain of a Partner = New Share – Old Share

A gains = $\frac{5}{8}-\frac{4}{9}=\frac{13}{72}$; B gains = $\frac{3}{8}-\frac{2}{9}=\frac{11}{72}$. Gaining Ratio = $\frac{13}{72}:\frac{11}{72}$ *or* 13 : 11.

6.0 REVALUATION OF ASSETS AND LIABILITIES

Why is Adjustment Required?	At the time of retirement of a partner, the assets and liabilities are revalued so that the due share of an outgoing partner in the profit/loss arising from such revaluation may be ascertained and adjusted in his Capital Account.
Accounting Treatment	For this purpose, a Revaluation Account *(or alternatively, Profit & Loss Adjustment Account)* is prepared exactly in the same manner as explained earlier in Chapter with regard to admission of a partner. Its **balance is transferred to the Capital Accounts of All the Partners (including the Outgoing Partner) in their Old Profit Sharing Ratio.**

ILLUSTRATION 17

The Balance sheet of A, B and C sharing profits & losses in the ratio of 5 : 3 : 2, on 31st March, 2012 was as under:

Liabilities	₹	*Assets*		₹
A's Capital	46,000	Land & Building		30,000
B's Capital	34,000	Plant & Machinery		35,000
C's Capital	25,000	Stock		12,800
Creditors	15,600	Debtors	₹ 16,000	

		Less: Provision	₹ 800	15,200
		Cash & Bank		27,600
	1,20,000			1,20,000

On the same date, B retires from the firm and A and C decide to share future profits and losses in the ratio of 3 : 2 respectively. The following adjustments were agreed upon:—

(a) that an amount of ₹ 1,100 included in Sundry Debtors be written off as no longer receivable;

(b) that a Provision for Doubtful Debts be maintained at an existing rate;

(c) that Stock be written down by ₹ 1,055;

(d) that Land and Building be written up by ₹ 11,500;

(e) that Plant & Machinery be reduced to ₹ 34,000;

(f) that an amount of ₹ 700 included in Sundry Creditors be written back as no longer payable;

(g) that provision of ₹ 600 be made for an outstanding repair bill;

(h) that B's Capital Account is to be transferred to his Loan Account.

Required: Pass the necessary journal entries and prepare the Revaluation Account.

SOLUTION

JOURNAL

Particulars		*L.F.*	*Dr. (₹)*	*Cr (₹)*
Bad Debts A/c	Dr.		1,100	
To Debtors A/c				1,100
(Being the bad debts written off)				
Provision for Doubtful Debts A/c	Dr.		800	
Revaluation A/c	Dr.		300	
To Bad debts A/c				1,100
(Being the balance in Bad Debts A/c transferred)				
Revaluation A/c	Dr.		1,055	
To Stock A/c				1,055
(Being the fall in value of stock recorded)				
Land & Building A/c	Dr.		11,500	
To Revaluation A/c				11,500
(Being an increase in value of building recorded)				
Revaluation A/c	Dr.		1,000	
To Plant & Machinery A/c				1,000
(Being the fall in value of plant recorded)				
Sundry Creditors A/c	Dr.		700	
To Revaluation A/c				700
(Being the fall in amount of creditors recorded)				
Revaluation A/c	Dr.		600	
To Outstanding Repairs A/c				600
(Being an unrecorded liability provided for)				

Revaluation A/c Dr.		745	
To Provision for Doubtful Debts A/c			745
(Being the provision created @ 5% on ₹ 14,900 i.e. ₹ 16,000 – ₹ 1,100)			
Revaluation A/c Dr.		8,500	
To A's Capital A/c			4,250
To B's Capital A/c			2,550
To C's Capital A/c			1,700
(Being the transfer of net profit on revaluation)			

Dr. **REVALUATION ACCOUNT** *Cr.*

Particulars	₹	*Particulars*	₹
To Bad Debts	300	By Land & Building	11,500
To Stock	1055	By Sundry Creditors	700
To Plant & Machinery	1,000		
To Provision for Doubtful Debt.	745		
To Outstanding Repairs	600		
To Profit on Revaluation t/f to:			
A's Capital A/c	4,250		
B's Capital A/c	2,550		
C's Capital A/c	1,700		
	12,200		12,200

7.0 ADJUSTMENT FOR RESERVES AND ACCUMULATED PROFITS/LOSSES

WHY IS ADJUSTMENT FOR RESERVES AND ACCUMULATED PROFITS/LOSSES REQUIRED?

If, at the time of retirement of a partner, any reserves, accumulated profits *or* losses exist in the books of the firm, these should be transferred to the **Capital Accounts of All the Partners (including Outgoing Partner) in their Old Profit Sharing Ratio** so that the due share of an outgoing partner in the reserves, accumulated profits/losses upto the date of retirement gets adjusted in his Capital Account.

ACCOUNTING TREATMENT OF RESERVES AND ACCUMULATED PROFITS/LOSSES

1. For transfer of Reserves and Accumulated Profits		
General Reserve		Dr.
P & L A/c		Dr.
Workmen Compensation Reserve	[Excess of Reserve over liability]	Dr.
Investment Fluctuation Reserve	[Excess of Reserve over difference between Book value and Market value]	Dr.
To All Partners' Capital A/cs	*(Individually in their Old Profit Sharing Ratio)*	

2.	***For transfer of Accumulated Losses [e.g. Profit & Loss Account (Dr Balance)]***		
	All Partners' Capital A/cs	Dr.	*[Individually in their Old Profit Sharing Ratio]*
	To Profit & Loss A/c		
	To Deferred Revenue Expenditure A/c		

TUTORIAL NOTES

1. *Reserves, Accumulated Profits/Losses should always be distributed even if the question is silent.*
2. *Workmen Compensation Reserve (say ₹ 1,200) to the extent of liability (say ₹ 150) should be credited to Workmen Compensation Claim A/c and the balance of Workmen Compensation Reserve (₹ 1,050) should be credited to Partners' Capital Accounts.*
3. *Excess of Investment Fluctuation Reserve over difference between Book Value and Market Value is credited to partners in Profit Sharing Ratio.*
4. *Machinery Replacement Fund is in the nature of accumulated depreciation and not in nature of accumulated profits and hence is not distributed among the partners.*
5. *Employees' Provident Fund represents statutory liability due to employees towards Provident Fund and is not an accumulated profit, hence it is not distribted among the partners.*

ILLUSTRATION 18

X, Y and Z are partners in a firm sharing profits and losses in the ratio of 5 : 3 : 2. Z retires from the firm on 31st March, 2012. On the date of Z's retirement, the following balances appeared in the books of the firm:

1. General Reserve ₹ 10,000; Profit and Loss Account (Dr.) ₹ 5,000.
2. Workmen's Compensation Reserve ₹ 20,000 out of which a liability of ₹ 8,000 is to be provided
3. Employees' Provident Fund ₹ 60,000.

Required: Pass the necessary Journal entries for the adjustment of these items on Z's retirement.

SOLUTION

JOURNAL

Date	*Particulars*		*L.F.*	*Dr. (₹)*	*Cr. (₹)*
31.03.12	General Reserve	...Dr.		10,000	
	To X's Capital A/c				5,000
	To Y's Capital A/c				3,000
	To Z's Capital A/c				2,000
	(Being the transfer of General Reserve to all partners)				
31.03.12	X's Capital A/c	...Dr.		2,500	
	Y's Capital A/c	...Dr.		1,500	
	Z's Capital A/c	...Dr.		1,000	
	To Profit and Loss A/c				5,000
	(Being the transfer of accumulated loss to all partners)				
31.03.12	Workmen's Compensation Reserve	...Dr.		20,000	
	To Liability for Workmen Compensation A/c				8,000

	To X's Capital A/c			6,000
	To Y's Capital A/c			3,600
	To Z's Capital A/c			2,400
	(Being the Workmen's Compensation Reserve transferred to Capital Accounts on Z's retirement)			

Note: *Employees Provident Fund is a statutory liability and is not an accumulated profit and hence is not distributed among the partners.*

ILLUSTRATION 19

P, Q and R were partners in a firm sharing profits in the ratio of 2:3:5. On 31.3.2012 their Balance Sheet was as follows:

Liabilities	₹	*Assets*		₹
Creditors	70,000	Bank		45,000
Capital Accounts:		Debtors	40,000	
P	80,000	*Less:* Provision for doubtful debts	5,000	35,000
Q	70,000	Stock		50,000
R	60,000	Building		1,40,000
		Profit & Loss A/c		10,000
	2,80,000			2,80,000

On the above date R retired from the firm due to his illness on the following terms:

(i) Building was to be depreciated by ₹ 40,000.

(ii) Provision for doubtful debts was to be maintained at 20% on debtors.

(iii) Salary outstanding ₹ 5,000 was to be recorded and creditors of ₹ 4,000 will not be claimed.

(iv) Goodwill of the firm was valued at ₹ 72,000.

(v) R was to be paid ₹ 15,000 in cash, through bank and the balance was to be transferred to his loan account.

Required: Prepare Revaluation Account, Partners' Capital Accounts and the Balance Sheet of P and Q after R's retirement.

SOLUTION

Dr. **REVALUATION ACCOUNT** *Cr.*

Particulars	₹	*Particulars*		₹
To Building	40,000	By Creditors		4,000
To Provision for Doubtful Debts	3,000	By Loss on Revaluation t/f to		
To Outstanding Salary	5,000	Capital A/cs:		
		P (2/10)	8,800	
		Q (3/10)	13,200	
		R (5/10)	22,000	44,000
	48,000			48,000

Dr. **PARTNERS' CAPITAL ACCOUNTS** Cr.

Particulars	*P* ₹	*Q* ₹	*R* ₹	*Particulars*	*P* ₹	*Q* ₹	*R* ₹
To Profit & Loss A/c	2,000	3,000	5,000	By Balance b/d	80,000	70,000	60,000
To Revaluation A/c	8,800	13,200	22,000	By P's Capital A/c	—	—	14,400
To R's Capital A/c	14,400	21,600	—	By Q's Capital A/c	—	—	21,600
To Bank A/c	—	—	15,000				
To R's Loan A/c			54,000				
To Balance c/d	54,800	32,200	—				
	80,000	70,000	96,000		80,000	70,000	96,000

BALANCE SHEET OF NEW FIRM AS AT 31.03.2012

Liabilities		₹	*Assets*		₹
Creditors		66,000	Bank (₹ 45,000 – ₹ 15,000)		30,000
Outstanding Salary		5,000	Debtors	40,000	
R's Loan		54,000	*Less:* Provision for		
Capital A/cs:			Doubtful Debts	8,000	32,000
P	54,800		Stock		50,000
Q	32,200	87,000	Building		1,00,000
		2,12,000			2,12,000

Note: *R's share of goodwill ₹ 36,000 (₹ 72,000 × 5/10) will be adjusted to gaining partners' capital a/cs in their gaining ratio 2 : 3.*

ILLUSTRATION 20

X, Y and Z were partners in a firm sharing profits in the ratio of 1/2: 1/3 : 1/6 respectively. The Balance Sheet of the firm on 31st March, 2012 stood as follows:

Liabilities	₹	*Assets*		₹
Creditors	9,500	Cash at Bank		1,250
Bills Payable	2,500	Debtors	8,000	
Reserve Fund	6,000	*Less:* Prov. for Doubt. Debts	250	7,750
Capitals:		Stock		12,500
X	20,000	Motor Vans		4,000
Y	15,000	Machinery		17,500
Z	12,500	Buildings		22,500
	65,500			65,500

Y retired from the firm on the above date subject to the following conditions:

(a) Goodwill of the firm be valued at ₹ 9,000 and is not to be shown in the books of the firm.

(b) Machinery would be depreciated by 10% and motor vans by 15%.

(c) Stock would be appreciated by 20% and Buildings by 10%.

(d) The provision for doubtful debts would be increased by ₹ 975.

(e) Liability for workmen's compensation to the extent of ₹ 825 would be created.

It was agreed that X and Z would share profits in future in the ratio of 3 : 1 : 2 respectively.

Required: Prepare the Revaluation Account, Capital Accounts of the partners and the Balance Sheet of the firm after the retirement of Y.

SOLUTION

Dr. **REVALUATION ACCOUNT** *Cr.*

Particulars	₹	*Particulars*	₹
To Machinery	1,750	By Stock	2,500
To Motor Van	600	By Building	2,250
To Provision for Doubtful Debts	975		
To Workmen's Claim	825		
To Profit transferred to Capital A/cs:			
X	300		
Y	200		
Z	100		
	4,750		4,750

Dr. **PARTNERS' CAPITAL ACCOUNTS** *Cr.*

Particulars	X	Y	Z	*Particulars*	X	Y	Z
To Y (Goodwill)	900		2,100	By Balance b/d	20,000	15,000	12,500
To Y's Loan		20,200		By Revaluation A/c	300	200	100
To Balance c/d	22,400		11,500	By General Reserve	3,000	2,000	1,000
				By X (Goodwill)		900	
				By Z (Goodwill)		2,100	
	23,300	20,200	13,600		23,300	20,200	13,600

BALANCE SHEET OF X AND Z AS AT 31ST MARCH, 2012

Liabilities	₹	*Assets*		₹
Creditors	9,500	Cash at Bank		1,250
Bills Payable	2,500	Debtors	8,000	
Workmen's Claim	825	*Less:* Prov. for Doubt. Debts	1,225	6,775
Y's Loan	20,200	Machinery	17,500	
Capitals:		*Less:* Depreciation	1,750	15,750
X	22,400	Motor Van	4,000	
Z	11,500	*Less:* Depreciation	600	3,400
		Stock	12,500	
		Add: Appreciation	2,500	15,000
		Building	22,500	
		Add: Appreciation	2,250	24,750
	66,925			66,925

Working Note:

X's Gaining Share = $\frac{3}{5} - \frac{3}{6} = \frac{18-15}{30} = \frac{3}{30}$

Z's Gaining Share = $\frac{2}{5} - \frac{1}{6} = \frac{12-5}{30} = \frac{7}{30}$

ILLUSTRATION 21

On 31st March, 2012, the Balance Sheet of M/s. A, B and C, sharing profits and losses in proportion to their capitals, stood as:

Liabilities	₹	*Assets*		₹
Creditors	1,08,000	Cash at Bank		80,000
Capital A/cs:		Debtors	1,00,000	
A	4,50,000	*Less:* Pro. for Doubtful Debts	2,000	98,000
B	3,00,000	Stock		90,000
C	1,50,000	Machinery		2,40,000
		Land and Building		5,00,000
	10,08,000			10,08,000

On that date, B retires from the firm and the remaining partners decide to carry on. The following readjustments of assets and liabilities have been agreed upon before the ascertainment of the amount payable to B:

(i) That out of the fire insurance premium paid during the year, ₹ 10,000 be carried forward as unexpired.

(ii) That the Land and Building be appreciated by 10%.

(iii) That the Provision for Doubtful Debts be brought up to 5% Debtors.

(iv) That Machinery be depreciated by 5%.

(v) That a provision of ₹ 15,000 be made in respect of an outstanding bill for repairs.

(vi) That the Goodwill of the entire firm be fixed at ₹ 1,80,000 and B's share of the same be adjusted in the accounts of A and C who share the future profits in the proportion of 3/4th and 1/4th respectively (no Goodwill Account being raised).

(vii) That B be paid ₹ 50,000 in cash and the balance be transferred to his Loan Account.

Required: Prepare the Revaluation Account, Capital Accounts of Partners and the Balance Sheet of the firm of A and C.

SOLUTION

Dr. **REVALUATION ACCOUNT** *Cr.*

Particulars	₹	*Particulars*	₹
To Provision for Doubtful Debts A/c (₹ 5,000 – ₹ 2,000)	3,000	By Unexpired Fire Insurance Premium A/c	10,000
To Depreciation on Machinery A/c [2,40,000 × 5/100]	12,000	By Land and Building A/c [5,00,000 × 10/100]	50,000
To Provision for Outstanding Repairs A/c	15,000		

To Profit transferred to:				
A's Capital A/c	15,000			
B's Capital A/c	10,000			
C's Capital A/c	5,000	30,000		
		60,000		60,000

Dr. **PARTNERS' CAPITAL ACCOUNTS** *Cr.*

Particulars	*A (₹)*	*B (₹)*	*C (₹)*	*Particulars*	*A (₹)*	*B (₹)*	*C (₹)*
To B's Capital A/c	45,000	—	15,000	By Balance b/d	4,50,000	3,00,000	1,50,000
To Bank A/c	—	50,000	—	By Revaluation A/c	15,000	10,000	5,000
To B's Loan A/c –Transfer	—	3,20,000	—	By A's Capital A/c	—	45,000	—
To Balance c/d	4,20,000	—	1,40,000	By C's Capital A/c	—	15,000	—
	4,65,000	3,70,000	1,55,000		4,65,000	3,70,000	1,55,000

BALANCE SHEET OF A AND C
as at 31st March, 2012

Liabilities	₹	*Assets*		₹
Creditors	1,08,000	Cash at Bank		30,000
Outstanding Bill for Repairs	15,000	Stock		90,000
B's Loan	3,20,000	Debtors	1,00,000	
Capital A/cs:		*Less:* Provision	5,000	95,000
A	4,20,000	Unexpired Fire Insurance		10,000
C	1,40,000	Machinery	2,40,000	
		Less: Depreciation	12,000	2,28,000
		Land and Building	5,00,000	
		Add: Appreciation	50,000	5,50,000
	10,03,000			10,03,000

Note: *B's Share of Goodwill has been debited to A and C in their gaining ratio i.e, 3 : 1.*

ILLUSTRATION 22

X, Y and Z were partners in a firm sharing profits in the proportions of 1/2, 1/3 and 1/6 respectively The Balance Sheet of the firm on 31st March, 2012 was as follows:

Liabilities	₹	*Assets*		₹
Trade Creditors	15,000	Goodwill		6,000
Employees' Provident Fund	6,000	Cash at Bank		5,750
Workmen Compensation Fund	12,000	Debtors	40,000	
Investment Fluctuation Fund	6,000	*Less:* Provision	2,000	38,000
X's Capital	68,000	Stock		30,000
Y's Capital	32,000	Investments [Market Value ₹ 17,600]		15,000
Z's Capital	21,000	Patents		10,000
		Plant and Machinery		50,000

		Advertisement Expenditure	5,250
	1,60,000		1,60,000

Z retired on the above date on the following terms.

(a) Goodwill of the firm was valued at ₹ 34,800 but it was not to remain in the books of the new firm.

(b) Value of Patents was to be reduced by 20% and that of Plant and Machinery to 90%.

(c) Provision for doubtful debts was to be raised to 6%.

(d) Z took over the investments at market value.

(e) Liability on account of Provident Fund was only ₹ 2,775.

(f) Liability for workmen compensation to the extent of ₹ 750 is to be created.

(g) Trade Creditors to the extent of 2½% are not likely to claim their dues.

(h) Amount due to Z is to be settled on the following basis:
50% on retirement, 50% of the balance within one year and the balance by a Bill of Exchange (without interest) at 3 months.

Required: Show the necessary journal entries for the treatment of Goodwill, prepare Revaluation account, Capital accounts of the partners and the Balance Sheet of X and Y after Z's retirement.

SOLUTION

JOURNAL

Particulars		*L.F.*	*Dr. (₹)*	*Cr (₹)*
X's Capital A/c	Dr.		3,000	
Y's Capital A/c	Dr.		2,000	
Z's Capital A/c	Dr.		1,000	
To Goodwill A/c				6,000
(Being the existing book value of goodwill w/o)				
X's Capital A/c	Dr.		3,480	
Y's Capital A/c	Dr.		2,320	
To Z's Capital A/c				5,800
(Being the Z's share of goodwill credited to him by debiting gaining partners in their gaining ratio of 3 : 2)				

Dr. **REVALUATION ACCOUNT** *Cr.*

Particulars	₹	*Particulars*	₹
To Patents	2,000	By Investments	2,600
To Plant & Machinery	5,000	By Provident fund	3,225
To Provision for Doubtful debts	400	By Creditors	375
		By Loss on Revaluation t/f to:	
		X's Capital A/c	600
		Y's Capital A/c	400
		Z's Capital A/c	200
	7,400		7,400

Dr. **PARTNERS' CAPITAL ACCOUNTS** Cr.

Particulars	X ₹	Y ₹	Z ₹	*Particulars*	X ₹	Y ₹	Z ₹
To Goodwill A/c	3,000	2,000	1,000	By Balance b/d	68,000	32,000	21,000
To Z's Capital A/c	3,480	2,320	—	By Work Com. F.	5,625	3,750	1,875
To Revaluation A/c	600	400	200	By Invest. Fluc. Fund	3,000	2,000	1,000
To Advertisement Exp.	2,625	1,750	875	By X's Capital A/c	—	—	3,480
To Investment A/c	—	—	17,600	By Y's Capital A/c	—	—	2,320
To Bank A/c	—	—	5,000				
To Loan from Z A/c	—	—	2,500				
To Bills Payable A/c	—	—	2,500				
To Balance c/d	66,920	31,280	—				
	76,625	37,750	29,675		76,625	37,750	29,675

BALANCE SHEET AS AT 31ST MARCH, 2012

Liabilities	₹	*Assets*		₹
Trade Creditors	14,625	Cash at Bank [₹ 5,750 – ₹ 5,000]		750
Liability for Workmen Compensation	750	Debtors	40,000	
Provident Fund	2,775	*Less:* Provision	2,400	37,600
Bill Payable	2,500	Stock		30,000
Loan from Z	2,500	Patents		8,000
X's Capital	66,920	Plant & Machinery		45,000
Y's Capital	31,280			
	1,21,350			1,21,350

8.0 ADJUSTMENT OF CAPITALS

The capitals of the continuing partners may be required to be adjusted in any one of the following three ways:

1. WHEN THE TOTAL CAPITAL OF THE NEW FIRM IS GIVEN

The various steps involved in adjusting the capitals of the partners are given below:

PRACTICAL STEPS INVOLVED IN ADJUSTING THE CAPITALS [WHEN THE TOTAL CAPITAL OF THE NEW FIRM IS GIVEN]

Step 1: ***Calculate New Profit Sharing Ratio & Gaining Ratio of Continum®ing Partners (if not given)***

Step 2: ***Calculate the Adjusted Old Capitals of Continuing Partners as follows:***

Particulars	*A*	*B*	*C*
Old Capital before Adjustments	xxx	xxx	xxx
Share of Goodwill Credited (Debited)	xxx	xxx	xxx
Share of Profit (Loss) on Revaluation	xxx	xxx	xxx
Share of Reserve and Accumulated Profit (Loss)	xxx	xxx	xxx
	xxx	xxx	xxx

Step 3: *Calculate the New Capitals of Continuing Partners as follows:*

= Total Capital of New Firm × New Share of Continuing Partner

Step 4: *Calculate the Shortage to be brought in* *or* ***Surplus to be paid off as follows:***

= New Capital – Adjusted Old Capital

Step 5: *Pass a Journal Entry in Case the Adjusted Old Capital is* *less* ***than the New Capital (i.e. Shortage to be brought in)***

Cash A/c or Concerned Partner's Current A/c *Dr.*

To Concerned Partner's Capital A/c

or

Step 6: *Pass a Journal Entry in Case the Adjusted Old Capital is more than the New Capital (i.e. Surplus to be paid off)*

Concerned Partner's Capital A/c *Dr.*

To Cash A/c or Concerned Partner's Current A/c

Tutorial Note: *In the absence of any contract Surplus or Deficiency should be adjusted in Cash and not by transferring it to Current Account.*

ILLUSTRATION 23

A, B & C were partners sharing profits and losses in the ratio of 4 : 3 : 2 respectively. B retired on 31st March, 2012 when the capitals of A, B & C before the necessary adjustments stood at ₹ 21,950, ₹ 11,400 & ₹ 11,650 respectively. Firm's Goodwill ₹ 21,600, Loss on Revalutation of Assets & Liabilities ₹ 2,700. General Reserve ₹ 6,300. The entire capital of the newly constituted firm is fixed at ₹ 28,000 between A and C in the proportion of five-eighths and three-eighths after passing entries in their accounts for adjustments. Calculate the actual cash to be paid off *or* to be brought in by the continuing partners and pass the necessary journal entries.

SOLUTION

Step 1: Calculation of Gaining Ratio: Gain of a Partner = New Share – Old Share

A gains = $\frac{5}{8}-\frac{4}{9}=\frac{13}{72}$; C gains = $\frac{3}{8}-\frac{2}{9}=\frac{11}{72}$. Gaining Ratio = $\frac{13}{72}:\frac{11}{72}$ *or* 13 : 11.

STEP 2: ADJUSTED OLD CAPITALS

Old Capital before Adjustments	21,950	7,200	(3,300)
Share of Goodwill	(3,900)	7,200	(3,300)
Share Loss on Revalutation	(1,200)	(9,00)	(6,00)
Share of General Reserve	2,800	2,100	1,400
	19,650	19,800	9,150

Particulars	*A*	*C*
Step 3: New Capital (₹ 28,000 in the ratio of 5 : 3)	₹ 17,500	₹ 10,500

STEP 4: CALCULATION OF SHORTAGE TO BE BROUGHT IN *or* SURPLUS TO BE PAID OFF

Particulars	*A*	*C*
I. New Capital (₹ 28,000 in the ratio of 5 : 3)	₹ 17,500	₹ 10,500
II. Adjusted Old Capital	19,650	9,150
III. Cash to be brought in (paid off) (I – II)	(2,150)	1,350

STEP 5: JOURNAL

Particulars		L.F.	Dr. (₹)	Cr (₹)
A's Capital A/c	Dr.		2,150	
To Cash A/c				2,150
(Being the excess withdrawn by A)				
Cash A/c	Dr.		1,350	
To C's Capital A/c				1,350
(Being the shortage brought in by C)				

ILLUSTRATION 24

The Balance Sheet of A, B & C who are partners in a firm sharing profits according to their capitals as on 31st March, 2012 was as under:

Liabilities	₹	*Assets*		₹
Creditors	21,000	Buildings		1,00,000
A's Capital	80,000	Machinery		50,000
B's Capital	40,000	Stock		18,000
C's Capital	40,000	Debtors	20,000	
General Reserve	20,000	*Less:* Provision	1,000	19,000
		Cash at Bank		14,000
	2,01,000			2,01,000

On that date B decided to retire from the firm and was paid for his share in the firm subject to the following:

(a) Building to be appreciated by 20%.

(b) Provision for Doubtful Debts to be increased to 15% on Debtors.

(c) Machinery to be depreciated by 20%.

(d) Goodwill of the firm is valued at ₹ 72,000 and the retiring partner's share is adjusted through the Capital Accounts of remaining partners.

(e) The Capital of the new firm be fixed at ₹ 1,20,000. Prepare Revaluation Account, Capital Accounts of the partners and the Balance Sheet after retirement of B.

SOLUTION

Dr. **REVALUATION ACCOUNT** *Cr.*

Particulars		₹	*Particulars*	₹
To Provision for Doubtful Debts		2,000	By Building	20,000
To Machinery		10,000		
To Revaluation Profit transferred to:				
A	4,000			
B	2,000			
C	2,000	8,000		
		20,000		20,000

Dr. **PARTNERS' CAPITAL ACCOUNTS** Cr.

Particulars	*A* ₹	*B* ₹	*C* ₹	*Particulars*	*A* ₹	*B* ₹	*C* ₹
To Bank A/c	—	65,000	—	By Balance b/d	80,000	40,000	40,000
To B's Capital	12,000		6,000	By General Res.	10,000	5,000	5,000
To Bank A/c	2,000		1,000	By A's Capital A/c (G)		12,000	
To Balance c/d	80,000		40,000	By C's Capital A/c (G)		6,000	
				By Reval. A/c (Profit)	4,000	2,000	2000
	94,000	65,000	47,000		94,000	65,000	47,000

Dr. **BANK ACCOUNT** Cr.

Particulars	₹	*Particulars*	₹
To Balance b/d	14,000	By A's Capital A/c	2,000
To Balance c/d	54,000	By B's Capital A/c	65,000
		By C's Capital A/c	1,000
	68,000		68,000

BALANCE SHEETS AS AT 31ST MARCH, 2012

Liabilities	₹	*Assets*		₹
Creditors	21,000	Building		1,20,000
Bank Overdraft	54,000	Machinery		40,000
A's Capital	80,000	Stock		18,000
C's Capital	40,000	Debtors	20,000	
		Less: Provision	3,000	17,000
	1,95,000			1,95,000

ILLUSTRATION 25

Jyoti, Ruchi and Yogesh were sharing profits and losses in proportion to their capitals. Their Balance Sheet on 31st March, 2012 was as under:

Liabilities	₹	*Assets*		₹
Sundry Creditors	20,000	Buildings		1,00,000
Employees' Provident Fund	1,600	Machinery		48,000
Contingency Reserve	4,500	Stock		18,000
Employees' Compensation Reserve	4,500	Debtors	20,000	
Jyoti	76,000	*Less:* Provision	400	19,600
Ruchi	57,000	Bank		8,000
Yogesh	38,000	Cash		8,000
	2,01,600			2,01,600

Ruchi decided to retire due to old age. They agreed to the following adjustments in the books of accounts to decide Ruchi's share:

(a) Buildings to be appreciated by 20%.

(b) Provision for doubtful debts is to be increased to 5% on debtors.

(c) Out of total insurance premium paid ₹ 3,000 is to be treated as prepaid insurance. This amount was earlier debited to Profit and Loss Account.

(d) Machinery is to be depreciated by 20%.

(e) Goodwill of the entire firm is to be valued at ₹ 72,000. Ruchi's share is to be adjusted in the accounts of Jyoti and Yogesh.

(f) Jyoti and Yogesh also decide that the total capital of the firm after Ruchi's retirement will be ₹ 1,80,000 in their profit-sharing ratio i.e. actual cash to be brought in *or* paid to a partner as the case may be.

Required: Prepare Revaluation Account, the Capital Accounts of all the partners and the Balance Sheet of Jyoti and Yogesh.

SOLUTION

Dr. **REVALUATION ACCOUNT** *Cr.*

Particulars	₹	*Particulars*	₹
To Prov. for Doubtful Debts	600	By Unexpired Insurance	3,000
To Machinery	9,600	By Land & Building	20,000
To Profit on Revaluation t/f to:			
Jyoti's Capital A/c	5,689		
Ruchi's Capital A/c	4,267		
Yogesh's Capital A/c	2,844		
	23,000		23,000

Dr. **CAPITAL ACCOUNTS OF PARTNERS** *Cr.*

Particulars	*Jyoti*	*Ruchi*	*Yogesh*	*Particulars*	*Jyoti*	*Ruchi*	*Yogesh*
To Ruchi's Capital A/c	16,000	—	8,000	By Balance b/d	76,000	57,000	38,000
(for Goodwill)				By Jyoti's Capital A/c	—	16,000	—
To Bank A/c	—	88,267	—	By Yogesh Capital A/c			
To Balance c/d	1,20,000	—	60,000	(for goodwill)	—	8,000	—
				By Revaluation A/c	5,689	4,267	2,844
				By Contingency Reserve	2,000	1,500	1,000
				By Employees' Compensation Reserve	2,000	1,500	1,000
				By Bank A/c	50,311	—	25,156
	1,36,000	88,267	68,000		1,36,000	88,267	68,000

BALANCE SHEET OF JYOTI AND YOGESH AS AT 31ST MARCH, 2012

Liabilities	₹	*Assets*		₹
Creditors	20,000	Cash at Bank		3,200
Employees' Provident Fund	1,600	Debtors	20,000	
Jyoti's Capital A/c	1,20,000	*Less:* Provision	1,000	19,000
Yogesh's Capital A/c	60,000	Stock		18,000
		Machinery		38,400

		Land & Building	1,20,000
		Unexpired Insurance	3,000
	2,01,600		2,01,600

ILLUSTRATION 26

The Balance Sheet of A, B and C who were sharing profits in proportion to their capitals, stood as follows on 31st March 2012:

Liabilities	₹	*Assets*		₹
Sundry Creditors	6,000	Goodwill		9,000
Employees' Provident Fund	900	Cash at Bank		5,500
A's Capital A/c	20,000	Sundry Debtors	5,000	
B's Capital A/c	15,000	*Less:* Provision	100	4,900
C's Capital A/c	10,000	Stock		8,000
Workmen Compensation Reserve	9,900	Plant & Machinery		8,500
		Factory Land & Building		25,000
		Advertisement Expenditure A/c		900
	61,800			61,800

B retires and the following re-adjustments of the assets and liabilities have been agreed upon before the ascertainment of the amount payable by the firm to B:

(a) That the Stock be depreciated by 6 per cent.

(b) That the Provision for doubtful debts be brought up to 5% on Debtors.

(c) That the Factory Land and Building be appreciated by 20%.

(d) That a provision of ₹ 770 be made in respect of outstanding legal charges.

(e) That the Goodwill of the entire firm be fixed at ₹ 10,800 and B's share of the same be adjusted into the accounts of A and C who are going to share in future in the proportion of five-eighths and three-eighths respectively (No goodwill account is to be raised).

(f) That the entire capital of the firm as newly constituted be fixed at ₹ 28,000 between A and C in the proportion of five-eighths and three-eighths after passing entries in their accounts for adjustments (i.e., actual cash to be paid off *or* to be brought in by the continuing partners as the case may be).

Required: Pass the necessary journal entries to give effect to the above arrangement and prepare the Balance Sheet of A & C transferring the amount due to B to a separate Loan Account in his name.

SOLUTION

JOURNAL

Particulars		*L.F.*	*Dr. (₹)*	*Cr (₹)*
Revaluation A/c	Dr.		1,400	
To Stock Reserve A/c				480
To Provision for Doubtful Debts A/c				150
To Provision for Legal Charges A/c				770
(Being the fall in value of assets and increase in amount of Provision recorded)				

Particulars		L.F.	Dr. ₹	Cr. ₹
Land and Building A/c	Dr.		5,000	
To Revaluation A/c				5,000
(Being the increase in value of assets recorded)				
Revaluation A/c	Dr.		3,600	
To A's Capital A/c				1,600
To B's Capital A/c				1,200
To C's Capital A/c				800
(Being the transfer of profit on revaluation)				
A's Capital A/c	Dr.		4,000	
B's Capital A/c	Dr.		3,000	
C's Capital A/c	Dr.		2,000	
To Goodwill A/c				9,000
(Being the existing book value of Goodwill A/c)				
A's Capital A/c	Dr.		1,950	
C's Capital A/c	Dr.		1,650	
To B's Capital A/c				3,600
(Being B's share of goodwill credited to B and debited to the remaining partners in their gaining ratio which is 13 : 11)				
Workmen Compensation Reserve A/c	Dr.		9,900	
To A's Capital A/c				4,400
To B's Capital A/c				3,300
To C's Capital A/c				2,200
(Being the transfer of Workmen Comp. Reserve)				
A's Capital A/c	Dr.		400	
B's Capital A/c	Dr.		300	
C's Capital A/c	Dr.		200	
To Advertisement Expenditure A/c				900
(Being the transfer of Advertisement Expenditure)				
B's Capital A/c	Dr.		19,800	
To B's Loan A/c				19,800
(Being the transfer of amount due to B to his Loan A/c)				
Bank A/c	Dr.		1,350	
To C's Capital A/c				1,350
(Being the short amount brought in by C)				
A's Capital A/c	Dr.		2,150	
To Bank A/c				2,150
(Being the excess amount withdrawn by A)				

BALANCE SHEET OF A AND C AS AT 31ST MARCH, 2012

Liabilities	₹	*Assets*	₹
Sundry Creditors	6,000	Cash at bank	4,700

Employees' Provident Fund	900	Debtors	5,000	
Provision for legal charges	770	*Less:* Provision	250	4,750
B's Loan A/c	19,800	Stock	8,000	
A's Capital A/c	17,500	*Less:* Reserve	480	7,520
C's Capital A/c	10,500	Plant		8,500
		Land & Building		30,000
	55,470			55,470

Working Note:

1. **Calculation of Gaining Ratio**

Gain of a Partner = New Share – Old Share

A gains = $\frac{5}{8} - \frac{4}{9} = \frac{13}{72}$;

B gains = $\frac{3}{8} - \frac{2}{9} = \frac{11}{72}$.

Gaining Ratio $\frac{13}{72} : \frac{11}{72}$ = *or* 13 : 11.

2. **Calculation of New Capitals of A & C**

(a) Total Capital of the reconstituted firm = ₹ 28,000

(b) A's New Capital = ₹ 28,000 × 5/8 = ₹ 17,500

(c) C's New Capital = ₹ 28,000 × 3/8 = ₹ 10,500

3. **Calculation of Cash to be paid off/brought in by remaining partners.**

Dr. **CAPITAL ACCOUNTS OF PARTNERS** *Cr.*

Particulars	*A* ₹	*B* ₹	*C* ₹	*Particulars*	*A* ₹	*B* ₹	*C* ₹
To Goodwill A/c	4,000	3,000	2,000	By Balance b/d	20,000	15,000	10,000
To B's Capital A/c	1,950	—	1,650	By Revaluation A/c	1,600	1,200	800
To Advertisement Exp.	400	300	200	By Contingency Res.	4,400	3,300	2,200
To Bank A/c (b.f.)	2,150	—	—	By A's Capital A/c	—	1,950	—
To B's Loan A/c	—	19,800	—	By C's Capital A/c	—	1,650	—
To Balance c/d	17,500	—	10,500	By Bank A/c (b.f.)	—	—	1,350
	26,000	23,100	14,350		26,000	23,100	14,350

ILLUSTRATION 27

On 31st March 2012 the Balance Sheet of A, B and C who were sharing profits and losses in proportion to their capitals stood as follows:

Liabilities	₹	*Assets*		₹
Creditors	20,000	Goodwill		6,000
Employees' Provident Fund	1,600	Cash at Bank		16,000
A's Capital A/c	78,000	Debtors	20,000	
B's Capital A/c	52,000	*Less:* Provision	400	19,600
C's Capital A/c	26,000	Stock		18,000

Contingency Reserve	30,000	Machinery	48,000
Workmen Compensation Reserve	6,000	Land & Building	1,00,000
	2,13,600		2,13,600

B retires and the following re-adjustments of the assets and liabilities have been agreed upon before the ascertainment of the amount payable to B:

(a) That out of the amount of insurance which was debited entirely to Profit and Loss Account, ₹ 2,000 be carried forward as an unexpired insurance.

(b) That the Land and Building be appreciated by 10%.

(c) That the Provision for Doubtful Debts be brought up to 5% on Debtors.

(d) That Machinery be depreciated by 5%.

(e) That a provision of ₹ 3,000 be made in respect of an outstanding bill for repairs.

(f) That the Goodwill of the entire firm be fixed at ₹ 36,000.

(g) That the entire capital of the firm as newly constituted be fixed at ₹ 1,20,000 between A and C in the proportion of 3/4 and 1/4 after passing entries in their accounts for adjustments i.e. actual cash to be paid off *or* to be brought in by the continuing partners as the case may be.

(h) That B be paid ₹ 6,000 in Cash and the balance be transferred to his loan account.

Required: Prepare the Revaluation Account, the Capital Accounts of the Partners and the Balance Sheet of the firm of A and C.

SOLUTION

Dr. **REVALUATION ACCOUNT** *Cr.*

Particulars	₹	*Particulars*	₹
To Provision for Doubtful Debts	600	By Unexpired Insurance	2,000
To Machinery	2,400	By Land & Building	10,000
To Outstanding Repairs	3,000		
To Profit on Revaluation t/f to:			
A's Capital A/c	3,000		
B's Capital A/c	2,000		
C's Capital A/c	1,000		
	12,000		12,000

Dr **CAPITAL ACCOUNTS OF PARTNERS** *Cr.*

Particulars	*A* ₹	*B* ₹	*C* ₹	*Particulars*	*A* ₹	*B* ₹	*C* ₹
To Goodwill A/c	3,000	2,000	1,000	By Balance b/d	78,000	52,000	26,000
To B's Capital A/c	9,000	—	3,000	By Revaluation A/c	3,000	2,000	1,000
(for goodwill)				By A's Capital A/c			
To Advertisement Exp.	3,000	2,000	1,000	(for goodwill)	—	9,000	—
To Bank A/c	—	6,000	—	By C's Capital A/c			
To B's Loan A/c	—	68,000	—	(for goodwill)	—	3,000	—
To Balance c/d	90,000	—	30,000	By Cont. Reserve	15,000	10,000	5,000
				By Work. Com. Reserve	3,000	2,000	1,000

				By Bank A/c	6,000	—	2,000
	1,05,000	78,000	35,000		1,05,000	78,000	35,000

BALANCE SHEET OF A AND C AS AT 31ST MARCH, 2012

Liabilities	₹	*Assets*		₹
Creditors	20,000	Cash at Bank		18,000
Employees' Provident Fund	1,600	Debtors	20,000	
Liability for repairs	3,000	*Less:* Provision	1,000	19,000
B 's Loan A/c	68,000	Stock		18,000
A's Capital A/c	90,000	Machinery		45,600
C's Capital A/c	30,000	Land & Building		1,10,000
		Unexpired Insurance		2,000
	2,12,600			2,12,600

Working Note:

Dr. **1. CASH AT BANK ACCOUNT** *Cr.*

Particulars	₹	*Particulars*	₹
To Balance b/d	16,000	By B's Capital A/c	6,000
To A's Capital A/c	6,000	By Balance c/d	18,000
To C's Capital A/c	2,000		
	24,000		24,000

ILLUSTRATION 28

Dowell & Co. is a partnership firm with partners Mr. A, Mr. B and Mr. C, sharing profits and losses in the ratio of 10: 6: 4. The Balance Sheet of the firm as at 31st March, 2012 is as under:

Liabilities	₹	*Assets*	₹
A's Capital	90,000	Goodwill	20,000
B's Capital	26,000	Land	10,000
Cs Capital	34,000	Buildings	2,00,000
Contingency Reserves	5,000	Plant and Machinery	1,30,000
Workmen Compensation Reserve	15,000	Furniture	43,000
Investment Fluctuation Reserve	5,000	Investments [Market value ₹ 15,000]	12,000
Employees' Provident Fund	10,000	Stock	1,30,000
Long Term Debt	3,00,000	Debtors	1,39,000
Bank Overdraft	44,000	Advertisement Expenditure	5,000
Trade Creditors	1,60,000		
	6,89,000		6,89,000

It was mutually agreed that Mr. B will retire from partnership and in his place Mr. D will be admitted as a partner with effect from 1st April, 2012. For this purpose, the following adjustments are to be made:

(i) Goodwill is valued at ₹ 1 lakh and D brings in his share of goodwill in cash.

(ii) Buildings and Plant and Machinery are to be depreciated by 5 percent and 20 percent respectively. Investments are to be taken over by the retiring partner at market value. Provision of 20 percent is to be made on debtors to cover doubtful debts.

(iii) In the reconstituted firm, the total capital will be ₹ 2 lakhs which will be contributed by Mr. A, Mr. C and Mr. D in their new profit sharing ratio, which is 2 : 2 : 1.

(iv) The surplus funds, if any, will be used for repaying the Bank Overdraft.

(v) The amount due to his retiring partner shall be transferred to his loan account.

Required: Prepare (a) Revaluation A/c; (b) Partner's Capital Accounts; (c) Bank Account; and (d) Balance Sheet of the reconstituted firm as at 1st April, 2012.

SOLUTION

Dr. **REVALUATION ACCOUNT** *Cr.*

Particulars	₹	*Particulars*	₹
To Building A/c	10,000	By Investments A/c	3,000
To Plant and Machinery A/c	26,000	By Loss on Revaluation T/f to:	
To Provision for doubtful debts A/c	27,800	A's Capital A/c	30,400
		B's Capital A/c	18,240
		C's Capital A/c	12,160
	63,800		63,800

Dr. **CAPITAL ACCOUNTS OF PARTNERS** *Cr.*

Particulars	A ₹	B ₹	C ₹	D ₹	*Particulars*	A ₹	B ₹	C ₹	D ₹
To Goodwill A/c	10,000	6,000	4,000		By Balance b/d	90,000	26,000	34,000	—
To Revaluation A/c	30,400	18,240	12,160	—	By Cont. Res. A/c	2,500	1,500	1,000	—
To A's Capital A/c	—	—	10,000	—	By Inves. Fluc. Res.	2,500	1,500	1,000	—
To B's Capital A/c	—	—	10,000	—	By Inves. Fluc. Res.	2,500	1,500	1,000	—
To Investments A/c		15,000	—	—	By Workmen C. R.	7,500	4,500	3,000	—
To Advert. Exp. A/c	2,500	1,500	1,000	—	By C Cap. A/c	10,000	10,000	—	—
To B's Loan A/c	—	22,760	—	—	By Premium for Goodwill	—	20,000	—	—
To Balance c/d	80,000	—	80,000	40,000	By Bank A/c (b.f.)	10,400	—	78,160	40,000
	1,22,900	63,500	1,17,160	40,000		1,22,900	63,500	1,17,160	40,000

Dr. **BANK ACCOUNT** *Cr.*

Particulars	₹	*Particulars*	₹
To A's Capital A/c	10,400	By Balance b/d (Bank Overdraft)	44,000
To Cs Capital A/c	78,160	By Balance c/d	1,04,560
To Premium for Goodwill A/c	20,000		
To D's Capital A/c	40,000		
	1,48,560		1,48,560

BALANCE SHEET OF DOWELL & CO. AS AT 1ST APRIL, 2012

Liabilities	₹	*Assets*	₹
Capital Accounts:		Land	10,000

A	80,000	Buildings		1,90,000
C	80,000	Plant and Machinery		1,04,000
D	40,000	Furniture		43,000
Long Term Debt	3,00,000	Stock		1,30,000
Trade Creditors	1,60,000	Debtors	1,39,000	
Employees' P.F.	10,000	*Less:* Provision	27,800	1,11,200
B's Loan Account	22,760	Balance at Bank		1,04,560
	6,92,760			6,92,760

ILLUSTRATION 29

On 31st March, 2012 the Balance Sheet of M/s Ram, Hari & Mohan sharing profits and losses in the ratio of 2 : 3 : 2, stood as follows:

Liabilities	₹	*Assets*	₹
Capital Accounts:		Goodwill	7,00,000
Ram	10,00,000	Land and Buildings	10,00,000
Hari	15,00,000	Machinery	17,00,000
Mohan	10,00,000	Closing Stock	5,00,000
Workmen Compensation Reserve	10,50,000	Sundry Debtors	6,00,000
Sundry Creditors	5,00,000	Cash and Bank Balances	5,50,000
	55,50,000		55,50,000

On same date Hari desired to retire from the firm and the remaining partners decided to carry on. It was agreed to revalue the Assets and Liabilities on that date on the following basis:

(a) Land & Buildings be appreciated by 30%.

(b) Machinery be depreciated by 20%.

(c) Closing Stock to be valued at ₹ 4,50,000.

(d) Provision for doubtful debts be made at 5%.

(e) Old credit balances of Sundry Creditors ₹ 50,000 be written back.

(f) Goodwill of the entire firm be valued at ₹ 6,30,000. Ram and Mohan decided to share the future profits & losses in the ratio of 3 : 2.

(g) The total capital of the firm is to be the same as before retirement. Individual capitals be in their profit sharing ratio.

(h) Amount due to Hari is to be settled on the following basis: 50% on retirement and the balance 50% within one year.

Required: Prepare Revaluation Account, Capital Accounts of Partners, Cash Account and Balance Sheet of New Firm.

SOLUTION

Dr. **REVALUATION ACCOUNT** *Cr.*

Particulars	₹	*Particulars*	₹
To Machinery	3,40,000	By Land & Building	3,00,000
To Closing Stock	50,000	By Creditors written back	50,000

To Provision for doubtful debts	30,000	By Loss on Revaluation t/f to:	
		Ram's Capital A/c	20,000
		Hari's Capital A/c	30,000
		Mohan's Capital A/c	20,000
	4,20,000		4,20,000

Dr. **PARTNERS' CAPITAL ACCOUNTS** Cr

Particulars	Ram ₹	Hari ₹	Mohan ₹	Particulars	Ram ₹	Hari ₹	Mohan ₹
To Goodwill A/c	2,00,000	3,00,000	2,00,000				
To Revaluation A/c	20,000	30,000	20,000	By Balance b/d	10,00,000	15,00,000	10,00,000
To Hari (Goodwill)	1,98,000	—	72,000	By Work.Comp. Res.	3,00,000	4,50,000	3,00,000
To Cash A/c	—	9,45,000	—	By Ram(Goodwill)	—	1,98,000	—
To Hari's Loan A/c	—	9,45,000	—	By Mohan(Goodwill)	—	72,000	—
To Balance c/d	21,00,000		14,00,000	By Cash A/c	12,18,000		3,92,000
	25,18,000	22,20,000	16,92,000		25,18,000	22,20,000	16,92,000

Dr. **CASH AND BANK ACCOUNT** Cr

Particulars	₹	Particulars	₹
To Balance b/d	5,50,000	By Hari's Capital A/c	9,45,000
To Ram's Capital A/c	12,18,000	By Balance c/d	12,15,000
To Mohan's Capital A/c	3,92,000		
	21,60,000		21,60,000

BALANCE SHEET OF M/S RAM & MOHAN AS AT 1ST APRIL, 2012

Liabilities	₹	Assets		₹
Capital Accounts:		Land & Building		13,00,000
Ram	21,00,000	Machinery		13,60,000
Mohan	14,00,000	Closing Stock		4,50,000
Sundry Creditors	4,50,000	Sundry Debtors:		
Hari's Loan A/c	9,45,000	Balance	6,00,000	
		Less: Provision	30,000	5,70,000
		Cash and Bank Balances		12,15,000
	48,95,000			48,95,000

Working Notes:

1. **Calculation of Gaining Ratio:** Ram's Gain = 3/5 – 2/7 = 11/35,
   Mohan's Gain = 2/5 – 2/7 = 4/35 Thus, Gaining Ratio of Ram and Mohan = 11 : 4
2. **Hari's Share of Goodwill** = ₹ 6,30,000 × 3/7 = ₹ 2,70,000 which is to be contributed by Ra[m] and Mohan in their Gaining Ratio of 11 : 4 as under:
   Ram: ₹ 2,70,000 × 11/15 = ₹ 1,98,000, Mohan ₹ 2,70,000 × 4/15 = ₹ 72,000

2. WHEN THE TOTAL CAPITAL OF THE NEW FIRM IS NOT GIVEN

The various steps involved in adjusting the Capitals of the partners are given below:

PRACTICAL STEPS INVOLVED IN ADJUSTING THE CAPITALS [WHEN THE TOTAL CAPITAL OF THE NEW FIRM IS NOT GIVEN]

Step 1: ***Calculate the Adjusted Old Capitals of Continuing Partners after all other adjustments (as explained under Para 8.1)***

Step 2: ***Calculate Total Capital of the New Firm as follows:***

Total Capital of the New Firm = Total of Adjusted Old Capitals of Continuing Partners

Step 3: ***Then, Steps 3 to 5 as given in Para 8.1 should be taken.***

ILLUSTRATION 30

A, B & C were partners sharing profits and losses in the ratio of 4 : 3 : 2 respectively. B retired on 31st March 2012 when the capitals of A, B and C after all necessary adjustments stood at ₹ 19,650, ₹ 19,800 and ₹ 9,150 respectively. The entire capital of the reconstituted firm will be readjusted by bring in *or* paying off cash so that the future capital of A & C be in their future profit-sharing ratio. Calculate the amount of cash to be paid off *or* to be brought in the continuing partners.

SOLUTION

Total Capital of New Firm = ₹ 19,650 + ₹ 9,150 = ₹ 28,800

CALCULATION OF ACTUAL CASH TO BE PAID OFF *or* BROUGHT IN

Particulars	*A*	*C*
I. New Capital (₹ 28,800 in the ratio of 2 : 1)	₹ 19,200	₹ 9,600
II. Adjusted Old Capital	₹ 19,650	₹ 9,150
III. Cash to be brought in (paid off) (I – II)	(₹ 450)	(₹ 450)

3. WHEN THE OUTGOING PARTNER IS TO BE PAID THROUGH CASH BROUGHT BY THE CONTINUING PARTNERS IN SUCH A WAY AS TO MAKE THEIR CAPITALS PROPORTIONATE TO THEIR NEW PROFIT SHARING RATIO

The various steps involved in adjusting the capitals of partners are given below:

PRACTICAL STEPS INVOLVED IN ADJUSTING THE CAPITALS OF PARTNERS

Step 1: ***Calculate the Adjusted Old Capitals of Continuing Partners after all other adjustments (as explained under Para 8.1)***

Step 2: ***Calculate Total Capital of the New Firm as follows:***

= Total Adjusted Old Capitals of Continuing Partners + Shortage of Cash to be brought in by Continuing Partners in order to make payment to Outgoing Partner

Step 3: ***Then, the Steps 3 to 5 given in Para 8.1 should be taken.***

ILLUSTRATION 31

A, B & C were partners sharing profits and losses in the ratio of 5 : 3 : 2 respectively. B retired on 31st March 2012 when the Capitals of A, B and C after all necessary adjustments stood at ₹ 43,200, 36,600 and ₹ 11,200 respectively. The cash and bank balance on 31st March, 2012 amounted to 4,000. B was to be paid through cash brought in by A and C in such a way as to make their capitals proportionate to their new profit sharing ratio of 3 : 2. Calculate the amount of cash to be paid off *or* to be brought in by the continuing partners assuming that a minimum Cash & Bank Balance of ₹ 3,000 was to be maintained.

SOLUTION

(I) CALCULATION OF TOTAL CAPITAL OF THE FIRM AFTER B'S RETIREMENT

Balance of Capital A/cs of A & C after adjustment of Goodwill & effect of revaluation	
(a) Adjusted Old Capital of A	₹ 43,200
(b) Adjusted Old Capital of C	₹ 11,200
(c) Shortage of Cash to be brought in by A & C in order to make payment to 'B' (₹ 36,600 – ₹ 1,000)	₹ 35,600
	₹ 90,000

(II) CALCULATION OF ACTUAL CASH TO BE PAID OFF *or* BROUGHT IN

Particulars	*A*	*C*
(a) New Capital (₹ 90,000 in the ratio of 3 : 2)	₹ 54,000	₹ 36,000
(b) Adjusted Old Capital	₹ 43,200	₹ 11,200
(c) Cash to be brought in (a – b)	₹ 10,800	₹ 24,800

ILLUSTRATION 32

A, B and C were partners sharing profits and losses in the ratio of 5 : 3 : 2. On 31st March, 2012 the Balance Sheet of the firm stood as under:

Particulars	₹
Sundry Creditors	26,500
Employees' Provident Fund	3,500
Workmen Compensation Reserve	15,000
A's Capital	1,10,000
B's Capital	56,000
C's Capital	44,000
Bank (Minimum Balance)	10,000
Debtors	65,000
Stock	55,000
Fixed Assets	1,25,000

B retires on 31st March 2012. For the purpose the following adjustments were agreed upon:—

(a) That Goodwill be valued at ₹ 75,000 but no goodwill is to appear in the books of new firm.

(b) That Fixed Assets be appreciated by 20%;

(c) That Stock be reduced to ₹ 50,000

(d) That B be paid through cash brought in by A and C in such a way as to make their capitals proportionate to their new profit sharing ratio which is to be A-3/5 & C - 2/5;

Required: Give the Partners' Capital A/cs & the Balance Sheet of A and C.

OLUTION

Dr. **CAPITAL ACCOUNTS OF PARTNERS** Cr.

Particulars	A ₹	B ₹	C ₹	Particulars	A ₹	B ₹	C ₹
To B's Capital A/c	7,500	—	15,000	By Balance b/d	1,10,000	56,000	44,000
To Cash A/c	—	89,000	—	By Revaluation A/c	10,000	6,000	4,000
To Balance c/d	1,47,000	—	98,000	By Workmen Com. Reserve A/c	7,500	4,500	3,000
				By A's Capital A/c	—	7,500	—
				By C's Capital A/c	—	15,000	—
				By Cash A/c	27,000	—	62,000
	1,54,500	89,000	1,13,000		1,54,500	89,000	1,13,000

BALANCE SHEET OF A & C AS AT 31ST MARCH, 2012

Liabilities	₹	Assets	₹
A's Capital	1,47,000	Fixed Assets	1,50,000
C's Capital	98,000	Stock	50,000
Sundry Creditors	26,500	Debtors	65,000
Employees' Provident Fund	3,500	Bank	10,000
	2,75,000		2,75,000

Working Notes:

1. **Calculation of Gaining Ratio**

   Gain of a Partner = New Share – Old Share

   A's Gain = $\frac{3}{5} - \frac{1}{2} = \frac{1}{10}$

   C's Gain = $\frac{2}{5} - \frac{1}{5} = \frac{2}{10}$

   Hence, Gaining Ratio of A & C = $\frac{1}{10} = \frac{2}{10} = 1:2$

2. **Profit on Revaluation** = (20% of ₹ 1,25,000) – (₹ 55,000 – ₹ 50,000) = ₹ 20,000

3. **Total Capital of New Firm** = Adjusted Old Capitals of A & C + Shortage of Cash

   = (₹ 1,20,000 + ₹ 36,000) + ₹ 89,000 = ₹ 2,45,000

4. **A's New Capital** = ₹ 2,45,000 × 3/5 = ₹ 1,47,000

   C is New Capital = ₹ 3,20,000 × 2/5 = ₹ 1,28,000

5. CALCULATION OF ACTUAL CASH TO BE PAID OFF *or* BROUGHT IN BY A AND C

Particulars	A	C
a) New Capital (₹ 2,45,000 in the ratio of 3 : 2)	₹ 1,47,000	₹ 98,000
b) Adjusted Old Capital	₹ 1,20,000	₹ 36,000
c) Cash to be brought in (a – b)	₹ 27,000	₹ 62,000

9.0 DISPOSAL OF THE AMOUNT DUE TO THE RETIRING PARTNER

HOW TO DISCHARGE THE AMOUNT DUE TO A RETIRING PARTNER

The amount due to the retiring partner is settled in the manner prescribed in the partnership deed. The amount due is either paid off immediately *or* is paid in instalments with *or* without interest as per agreement. In the absence of an agreement in this regard, the outgoing partner at his option is entitled to receive either interest @ 6% p.a. till the amount is paid off *or* a share of the profit which has been earned by using the amount due to him. [Section 37]

ACCOUNTING ENTRIES RELATING TO DISPOSAL OF THE AMOUNT DUE TO AN OUTGOING PARTNER

Entry for raising Loan from Bank	Bank A/c ...Dr. To Loan from Bank A/c **Note:** *Loan from bank will appear on the liabilities side of Balance Sheet.*
Entry for discharging Outgoing Partner's Claim	Outgoing Partner's Capital A/c ...Dr. To Investment/ Asset A/c [with agreed value of asset *(if any)*] To Bills Payable A/c *(if B/E is accepted)* To Cash/ Bank A/c *(if some immediate payment is made)* To Outgoing Partner's Loan A/c *(if amount is transferred to Loan A/c)* **Note:** *If all Investments have been taken over by an outgoing partner, Investments will not appear in the Balance Sheet.*
Entries for Interest on Partner's Loan	Interest on Loan A/c ...Dr. To Outgoing Partner's Loan A/c
Entries for Payment of Partner's Loan	Outgoing Partner's Loan A/c ...Dr. To Bank / Cash A/c

ILLUSTRATION 33 (A)

A, B and C are in partnership sharing profits and of 5 : 3 : 2 respectively. 'A' retires from the firm as on 1st January, 2011 when his Capital Account shows a net credit balance of ₹ 82,100 after the necessary adjustments. 'A' is to be paid ₹ 82,100 in cash immediately on retirement. Show the necessary ledger accounts.

SOLUTION

Dr. **A'S CAPITAL ACCOUNT** *Cr.*

Particulars	₹	*Particulars*	₹
To Bank A/c	82,100	By Balance b/d (Net amount due)	82,100

ILLUSTRATION 33 (B)

A, B and C are in partnership sharing profits and of 5 : 3 : 2 respectively. 'A' retires from the firm as on 1st January, 2011 when his Capital Account shows a net credit balance of ₹ 82,100 after the necessary adjustments. 'A' is to be paid ₹ 22,100 in cash immediately on retirement and the balance in three equal annual instalments together with interest @ 5% p.a. on diminishing balance. Show the necessary ledger accounts.

SOLUTION

Dr. **A'S CAPITAL ACCOUNT** Cr.

Particulars	₹	*Particulars*	₹
To Bank A/c	22,100	By Balance b/d (Net amount due)	82,100
To A's Loan A/c	60,000		
	82,100		82,100

Dr. **A'S LOAN ACCOUNT** Cr.

Date	*Particulars*	₹	*Date*	*Particulars*	₹
31.12.11	To Bank A/c	23,000	01.01.11	By A's Capital A/c	60,000
	To Balance c/d	40,000	31.12.11	By Interest A/c	3,000
		63,000			63,000
31.12.12	To Bank A/c	22,000	01.01.12	By Balance b/d	40,000
	To Balance c/d	20,000	31.12.12	By Interest A/c	2,000
		42,000			42,000
31.12.13	To Bank A/c	21,000	01.01.13	By Balance b/d	20,000
			31.12.13	By Interest A/c	1,000
		21,000			21,000

Working Note:

Amount of each instalment (towards principal only) = (₹ 82,100 – ₹ 22,100)/3 = ₹ 20,000

ILLUSTRATION 33 (C)

A, B and C are in partnership sharing profits and of 5 : 3 : 2 respectively. 'A' retires from the firm as on 1st January, 2011 when his Capital Account shows a net credit balance of ₹ 82,100 after the necessary adjustments. 'A' is to be paid ₹ 22,100 in cash immediately on retirement and the balance in three equal annual instalments of ₹ 22,034 each (including interest @ 5% p.a.). Show the necessary ledger accounts.

SOLUTION

Dr. **A'S CAPITAL ACCOUNT** Cr.

Particulars	₹	*Particulars*	₹
To Bank A/c	22,100	By Balance b/d (Net amount due)	82,100
To A's Loan A/c	60,000		
	82,100		82,100

Dr. **A'S LOAN ACCOUNT** Cr.

Date	*Particulars*	₹	*Date*	*Particulars*	₹
31.12.11	To Bank A/c	22,034	01.01.11	By A's Capital A/c	60,000
	To Balance c/d	40,966	31.12.11	By Interest A/c	3,000
		63,000			63,000

31.12.12	To Bank A/c	22,034	01.01.12	By Balance b/d	40,966
	To Balance c/d	20,980	31.12.12	By Interest A/c	2,048
		43,014			43,014
31.12.13	To Bank A/c	22,034	01.01.13	By Balance b/d	20,980
			31.12.13	By Interest A/c	1,054
		22,034			22,034

Note: *During the last year (2013) the amount of interest @ 5% p.a. comes to ₹ 1,049 but due to approximation used while computing the installment of ₹ 22,034, the difference has been adjusted in the final figure of interest.*

ILLUSTRATION 34

A, B and C are partners in a firm. B retires and his claim including his capital and his share of goodwill is ₹ 60,000. He is paid in kind a vehicle valued at ₹ 30,000 unrecorded in the books of the firm till the date of retirement and the balance in cash. Give the journal entries for recording the payment to B in the books of the firm.

SOLUTION

JOURNAL

Particulars		*L.F.*	*Dr. (₹)*	*Cr. (₹)*
Vehicle A/c	Dr.		30,000	
To Revaluation A/c				30,000
(Being the unrecorded vehicle recorded)				
Revaluation A/c	Dr.		30,000	
To A's Capital A/c				10,000
To B's Capital A/c				10,000
To C's Capital A/c				10,000
(Being the transfer of profit on revaluation)				
B's Capital A/c	Dr.		70,000	
To Vehicle A/c				30,000
To Cash A/c				40,000
(Being B's claim discharged)				

ILLUSTRATION 35

A, B and C are partners in a firm, B retires and his claim including his capital and his share of goodwill is ₹ 60,000. There was some unrecorded furniture estimated at ₹ 3,000, half of which was handed over to an unrecorded liability of ₹ 6,000 in settlement of claim of ₹ 3,000 and remaining half was handed over to B at a discount of 10% in part satisfaction of his claim. Balance of B's claim was discharged in cash. Give the journal entries to record this arrangement.

SOLUTION

JOURNAL

Particulars		*L.F.*	*Dr. (₹)*	*Cr. (₹)*
Furniture A/c	Dr.		1,350	

To Revaluation A/c (Being the unrecorded furniture recorded)			1,350
Revaluation A/c Dr. To Unrecorded Liability A/c (Being the unrecorded liability recorded)		3,000	3,000
A's Capital A/c Dr. B's Capital A/c Dr. C's Capital A/c Dr. To Revaluation A/c (Being the transfer of Loss on Revaluation)		550 550 550	1,650
B's Capital A/c Dr. To Furniture A/c To Cash A/c (Being B's claim discharged)		59,450	1,350 58,100

ILLUSTRATION 36

A, B, and C were partners in a firm sharing profits in 3 : 2 : 1 ratio. On 31st March 2012 B retired. On the date of his retirement the balance in his capital account was ₹ 35,000. The other assets and liabilities of the firm on that date were as follows:

Cash ₹ 10,000, Building ₹ 1,00,000, Plant & Machinery ₹ 40,000, Stock ₹ 20,000, Debtors ₹ 20,000 and Investments ₹ 30,000.

The following was agreed between the partners on B's retirement:

(a) Building to be appreciated by 20%.

(b) Plant and Machinery to be depreciated by 10%.

(c) A provision of 5% on debtors to be created for doubtful debts.

(d) Stock was to be valued at ₹ 18,000 and Investments at ₹ 35,000.

(e) An old photocopier previously written off was sold for ₹ 2,000.

(f) Partners had to pay ₹ 5,000 to the family of an employee who died in an accident. B was paid ₹ 10,000 in cash and the balance in three equal yearly instalments with interest @ 10% p.a. starting from 31.03.2013.

Required: Pass the necessary journal entries to record the above adjustments, prepare Revaluation Account and B's loan account till it is finally paid. The firm closes its book on 31st March every year.

SOLUTION

JOURNAL

Particulars	*L.F.*	*Dr. (₹)*	*Cr. (₹)*
Building A/c Dr. Investment A/c Dr. Photocopier A/c Dr. To Revaluation A/c (Being increase in Assets recorded)		20,000 5,000 2,000	27,000

Revaluation A/c Dr. To Plant and Machinery A/c To Provision for Doubtful Debts To Stock A/c To Employees' claim A/c (Being decrease in asset recorded)		12,000	 4,000 1,000 2,000 5,000
Revaluation A/c Dr. To A's Capital A/c To B's Capital A/c To C's Capital A/c (Being Profit on Revaluation t/f to all partners in their profit sharing ratio)		15,000	 7,500 5,000 2,500
Cash A/c Dr. To Photocopier A/c (Being Photocopier sold)		2,000	 2,000
Employees' Claim A/c Dr. To Cash A/c (Being Cash paid for the Employees' claim)		5,000	 5,000
B's Capital A/c Dr. To Cash A/c To B's Loan A/c (Being Cash paid to B and rest transferred to his loan A/c)		40,000	 10,000 30,000

Dr. **REVALUATION ACCOUNT** Cr.

Particulars	₹	*Particulars*	₹
To Plant & Machinery	4,000	By Building A/c	20,000
To Provision for doubtful debts	1,000	By Investment A/c	5,000
To Stock A/c	2,000	By Photocopier A/c	2,000
To Employees' Claim A/c	5,000		
To Revaluation Profit t/f to:			
A's Capital A/c	7,500		
B's Capital A/c	5,000		
C's Capital A/c	2,500		
	27,000		27,000

Dr. **B'S CAPITAL ACCOUNT** Cr.

Date	*Particulars*	₹	*Date*	*Particulars*	₹
31.3.2012	To Cash A/c	10,000	31.3.2012	By Balance b/d	35,000
31.3.2012	To B's Loan A/c	30,000	31.3.2012	By Revaluation A/c (Profit)	5,000
		40,000			40,000

Dr. **B'S LOAN ACCOUNT** Cr.

Date	Particulars	₹	Date	Particulars	₹
31.3.2012	To Balance c/d	30,000	31.3.2012	By B's Capital A/c	30,000
31.3.2013	To Bank A/c		01.4.2012	By Balance b/d	30,000
	(10,000 + 3,000)	13,000	31.3.2013	By Interest A/c	
	To Balance c/d	20,000		[30,000 × 10/100 × 12/12]	3,000
		33,000			33,000
31.3.2014	To Cash A/c		01.4.2013	By Balance b/d	20,000
	[₹ 10,000 + 2,000]	12,000	31.3.2014	By Interest A/c	
	To Balance c/d	10,000		[20,000 × 10/100 × 12/12]	2,000
		22,000			22,000
31.3.2015	To Cash A/c		01.4.2014	By Balance b/d	10,000
	[₹ 10,000 + 1,000]	11,000	31.3.2015	By Interest A/c	
				[10,000 × 10/100 × 12/12]	1,000
		11,000			11,000

RETIREMENT DURING THE ACCOUNTING YEAR

When a partner retires from the firm during the accounting year, the retiring partner is entitled to the share of profits of the current year up to the date of retirement, in addition to reserve, his share of goodwill and profits on revaluation of assets and reassessment of liabilities. His share of interim profits is calculated as per the provisions of the Partnership Deed. If the Partnership Deed is silent, the amount of profits should be calculated in the manner as agreed among the partners. When it calculated on the basis of last year's profit, the last year's profit is calculated for the period up to the date of retirement and then share of profits of retiring partner is calculated.

The share of retiring partner on the basis of the average profits of the past few years is calculated and adjusted as follows:

PRACTICAL STEPS IN ADJUSTMENT OF SHARE OF RETIRING PARTNER IN CURRENT YEAR'S PROFITS

Step 1: *Take the Total Profits of the given number of years.*

Step 2: *Calculate the Average Annual Profits = Total Profits/No. of years*

Step 3: *Calculate Profits for the period up to the date of his retirement = Average Annual profits × Period up to date of Retirement/12 months.*

Step 4: *Calculate the Share of Profits of the Retiring Partner = Profit for the period (as per Step 3) × Share of Retiring Partner*

Step 5: *Pass the following Journal Entry:*

Profit and Loss Suspense A/c Dr. [Retiring Partner's Share of Profit]

To Retiring Partner's Capital A/c

***Note:** Reverse Entry in Case of Loss.*

TUTORIAL NOTES

1. The balance of the Profit and Loss Suspense Account is transferred to the Profit and Loss Appropriation Account at the end of accounting period.

2. The balance of Profit and Loss Suspense Account is shown in the interim Balance Sheet, i.e Balance Sheet after retirement.
3. Retiring Partner's share of the profits will be credited to his Capital Account and debited to th continuing partners' Capital Accounts in the ***Gaining Ratio*** when the profit-share ratio of th continuing partners, in between them, does not remain the same.

Continuing Partners' Capital A/cs Dr. [In Gaining Ratio]

To Retiring Partner's Capital A/c

ILLUSTRATION 37

The Partnership deed of C and D contains a clause that any partner may retire from the firm on th following terms by giving six months' notice in writing:

The retiring partner shall be paid—

(a) The amount standing to the credit of his Capital Account and Current Account.

(b) His share of profit to the date of retirement, calculated on the basis of the average profits the three preceding completed years.

(c) His share of the goodwill of the firm calculated on the basis of 1½ times the average profits the three preceding completed years.

C gave notice to retire with effect from 30th September 2012, on 31st March 2012, when the balan of his Capital was ₹ 16,000 and his Current Account (in debit) ₹ 500. The profit for the three precedi completed years were: year ended 31st March 2010, ₹ 3,000, year ended 31st March 2011, ₹ 2,0 and year ended 31st March, 2012, ₹ 1,600.

Required: What amount is due to C in accordance with the partnership agreement?

SOLUTION

Dr. **C'S CURRENT ACCOUNT** C

Particulars	₹	*Particulars*	₹
To Balance b/d	500	By P & L Suspense A/c	55
To C's Capital A/c	1,700	By D's Current A/c	1,65
		(Share of Goodwill)	
	2,200		2,20

Dr. **C'S CAPITAL ACCOUNT**

Particulars	₹	*Particulars*	₹
To Balance c/d	17,700	By Balance b/d	16,00
		By C's Current A/c	1,70
	17,700		17,70

Working Note: Calculation of C's Share of Goodwill

A. Average Profits = (₹ 3,000 + ₹ 2,000 + ₹ 1,600)/3 = ₹ 2,200.

B. Estimated Profit to the date of retirement = ₹ 2,200 × 6/12 = ₹ 1,100.

C. C's Share of profit to the date of retirement = ₹ 1,100 × 1/2 = ₹ 550.

D. Value of firm's goodwill = ₹ 2,200 × 3/2 = ₹ 3,300.

E. C's Share of goodwill = ₹ 3,300 × 1/2 = ₹ 1,650.

ILLUSTRATION 38

X, Y and Z are partners' sharing profits and losses in the ratio of 5 : 3 : 2. Z retires on 31st March, 2012. The Balance Sheet of the firm as at 31st December, 2011 stood as follows:

Liabilities	₹	*Assets*	₹
X's Capital	5,50,000	Land and Building	9,00,000
Y's Capital	5,70,000	Investments	2,00,000
Z's Capital	3,80,000	Stock	3,00,000
Workmen Compensation Reserve	5,00,000	Sundry Debtors	5,00,000
Sundry Creditors	1,00,000	Cash & Bank	3,00,000
Employees Provident Fund	1,00,000		
	22,00,000		22,00,000

In order to arrive at the balance due to Z, it was mutually agreed that:

(a) Land and Building be valued at ₹ 11,00,000.

(b) Investments to be valued at ₹ 1,50,000.

(c) Stock be taken at ₹ 4,00,000.

(d) Goodwill be valued at two years' purchase of the average profit of the past five years. Goodwill will not appear in the books of reconstituted firm.

(e) Z's share of profits up to the date of retirement be calculated on the basis of average profit of the preceding three years.

The profits of the preceding five years were as under:

Year	2007	2008	2009	2010	2011
Profits (₹)	2,00,000	2,50,000	3,00,000	4,00,000	3,50,000

(f) Amount payable to Z to be transferred to his Loan Account carrying interest @ 10% p.a.

Required: Prepare the Revaluation Account, Partners' Capital Accounts, and the Balance Sheet as at 31st March, 2012.

SOLUTION

Dr. **REVALUATION ACCOUNT** *Cr.*

Particulars		₹	*Particulars*	₹
To Investments A/c		50,000	By Land and Building A/c	
[2,00,000 – 1,50,000]			[11,00,000 – 9,00,000]	2,00,000
To Profit on Reval. t/f to Capital A/cs:			By Stock A/c [4,00,000 – 3,00,000]	1,00,000
X	1,25,000			
Y	75,000			
Z	50,000	2,50,000		
		3,00,000		3,00,000

Dr. **PARTNERS' CAPITAL ACCOUNTS** *Cr.*

Particulars	*X* ₹	*Y* ₹	*Z* ₹	*Particulars*	*X* ₹	*Y* ₹	*Z* ₹
To Z's Capital A/c	75,000	45,000	—	By Balance b/d	5,50,000	5,70,000	3,80,000

To Z's Loan A/c	—	—	6,67,500	By X's Capital A/c	—	—	75,000
To Balance A/c	8,50,000	7,50,000	—	By Y's Capital A/c	—	—	45,000
				By W.C. Reserve	2,50,000	1,50,000	1,00,000
				By Revaluation A/c	1,25,000	75,000	50,000
				By P&L Susp. A/c (WN 2)	—	—	17,500
	9,25,000	7,95,000	6,67,500		9,25,000	7,95,000	6,67,500

BALANCE SHEET OF A AND B
as at 31st March, 2012

Liabilities	₹	*Assets*	₹
Capital A/cs:		Land and Building	11,00,000
X	8,50,000	Investments	1,50,000
Y	7,50,000	Stock	4,00,000
10% Z's Loan	6,67,500	Sundry Debtors	5,00,000
Sundry Creditors	1,00,000	Cash & Bank	3,00,000
Employees' Provident Fund	1,00,000	Profit & Loss Suspense A/c	17,500
	24,67,500		24,67,500

Working Notes:

1. **Calculation of Goodwill**

   Average Profit = (₹ 2,00,000 + ₹ 2,50,000 + ₹ 3,00,000 + ₹ 4,00,000 + ₹ 3,50,000)/5
   = ₹ 3,00,000

   Goodwill = 2 years' purchase of average profit = 2 × ₹ 3,00,000 = ₹ 6,00,000

   Z's Share of Goodwill = 6,00,000 × 2/10 = 1,20,000.

2. **Calculation of Z's Share of Profit:**

   (a) Average Profit = (₹ 3,00,000 + ₹ 4,00,000 + ₹ 3,50,000)/3 = ₹ 3,50,000

   (b) Profit (upto 3 months) = ₹ 3,50,000 × 3/12 = 87,500.

   (c) Z's Share of Profits = ₹ 87,500 × 2/10 = ₹ 17,500.

11.0 DEATH OF A PARTNER

BASIC DIFFERENCES BETWEEN THE RETIREMENT OF A PARTNER AND DEATH OF A PARTNER

The basic differences between the two situations are: (a) that the retirement of a partner may be planned to be effective from a particular date whereas the death of a partner may occur any time during the year; (b) that the payment of the amount due is made to the retiring partner in case of retirement of a partner whereas the payment of the amount due is made to the legal representatives of a deceased partner in case of death of a partner.

HOW TO ASCERTAIN THE SHARE OF A DECEASED PARTNER

When a partner dies, the deceased partner's share in the firm is calculated in the same manner as in case of a retiring partner.

Dr. **FORMAT OF A DECEASED PARTNER'S CAPITAL ACCOUNT** Cr.

Particulars	₹	Particulars	₹
To Goodwill A/c [Existing Goodwill w/o]	xxx	By Balance b/d	xxx
To Drawings	xxx	By Gaining Partner's Capital A/c	
To Interest on Drawings	xxx	(Share of Goodwill)	xxx
To Undistributed Losses	xxx	By P & L Suspense A/c	
To Revaluation A/c	xxx	(Share of Profits)	xxx
(Share of Loss on Revaluation)		By Reserves (Share of Reserves)	xxx
To Deceased Partner's Executors' A/c	xxx	By Interest on Capital A/c	xxx
[Balancing Figure]		By Revaluation A/c	xxx
		[Share of Profit on Revaluation]	
	xxx		xxx

2.0 OUTGOING PARTNER'S SHARE IN THE PROFITS OF THE YEAR OF DEATH/RETIREMENT

HOW TO CALCULATE OUTGOING PARTNER'S SHARE IN THE PROFITS

The calculation of outgoing partner share in profits earned from the date of last Balance Sheet to date of death/retirement, involves the following two steps:

Step 1: Calculate the Profits of the firm from the date of last Balance Sheet to the date of death/retirement — Subject to agreement, such profit may be determined either on time basis *or* on sales basis using previous year's profits *or* average profits of the past years.

(i) **On Time Basis:** In such a case, the previous year's profits *or* average profits of past years are divided between pre-death (or retirement) period and post-death (or retirement) period on the basis of time assuming that the profits are earned evenly throughout the year as under:

$$\text{Profit from the date of last Balance Sheet to the date of death/retirement} = \frac{\text{No. of days } or \text{ months from the date of last Balance Sheet to the date of death/retirement}}{\text{365 days or 12 months}} \times \text{Previous year's profits or Average profits of a given number of past years}$$

(ii) **On Sales Basis:** In such a case, the previous year's profits *or* average profits of past years are apportioned between the pre-death (or retirement) period and post-death (or retirement) period on the basis of turnover as under:

$$\text{Profit from the date of last Balance Sheet to the date of death/retirement} = \frac{\text{Sales from the date of the last Balance Sheet to the date of death/retirement}}{\text{Previous year's Sales or Average Sales of a given number of past years}} \times \text{Previous year©s profits or Average profits of a given number of past years}$$

Step 2: Calculate Outgoing Partner's Share in Profits

Outgoing Partner's Share in Profits = (Profits of the firm from the date of last Balance Sheet to the date of death/retirement) × (Proportion of Share of Outgoing Partner)

ILLUSTRATION 39

X, Y and Z were partners sharing profits & losses in the ratio of 3 : 2 : 1 respectively. X died on 31st March, 2012. The partnership deed provided that the share of profit till the date of death be estimated at the sum calculated on the average of the last three completed years' profits. The book showed the profits for the calendar years as under: 2007–₹ 5,000; 2008–₹ 5,000; 2009 ₹ 8,000; 2010–₹ 7,600 & 2011–₹ 9,000.

Calculate his share of profit during the accounting year 2012.

SOLUTION

Particulars	₹
A. Total Profits for last three years (₹ 8,000 + ₹ 7,600 + ₹ 9,000)	24,600
B. Average Profits (₹ 24,600/3)	8,200
C. Estimated Profits for the period from 1.1.20X6 to 31.3.20X6 (₹ 8,200 × 3/12)	2,050
D. Share of X (₹ 2,050 × 3/6)	1,025

ILLUSTRATION 40

X, Y and Z were partners sharing profits & losses in the ratio of 3 : 2 : 1 respectively. X died on 31st March, 2012. The partnership deed provided that the share of profit till the date of death be estimated at the sum calculated on the sales till the date of death by applying the ratio of Net Profit to Sales for the last accounting year. Sales from 1.1.2012 to 31.3.2012 amounted to ₹ 30,000. Sales and Net Profit for the year 2011 amounted to ₹ 3,60,000 and ₹ 54,000 respectively. Calculate his share of profit during the accounting year 2012.

SOLUTION

Particulars	₹
A. Estimated Profits for the period from 1.1.20X6 to 31.3.20X6 = ₹ 30,000/3,60,000 × 54,000	4,500
B. Share of X (₹ 4,500 × 3/6)	2,250

ACCOUNTING TREATMENT OF OUTGOING PARTNER'S SHARE IN THE PROFITS

The outgoing partner's share in the profits may be adjusted in either of the following ways:

I. **Through Profit and Loss Suspense Account** — The Outgoing Partner's share in the profits between the date of last balance sheet and the date of death/retirement, should be credited to Outgoing Partner's Capital Account through Profit & Loss Suspense Account by passing the following Journal Entry:

Case	Accounting Entry to be passed
I. **In Case of Profit**	Profit & Loss Suspense A/c Dr. To Outgoing Partner's Capital A/c
II. **In Case of Loss**	Reverse of the above entry is passed.

TUTORIAL NOTES

1. The Profit & Loss Suspense Account should be closed by transferring its balance to the Profit & Loss Account at the end of accounting period.
2. This treatment is appropriate only when the new profit sharing ratio of continuing partners does not differ from their old profit sharing ratio.

II Through Capital Accounts of the Gaining Partners — Instead of using Profit & Loss Suspense Account, only the Outgoing Partner's share in the profits/losses may be adjusted through the Capital Accounts of the Gaining Partners in their gaining ratio. The following journal entry is passed to record such an adjustment:

Case	Accounting Entry to be passed
I. In Case of Profit	Gaining Partner's Capital A/cs Dr. [Gaining Ratio] To Outgoing Partner's Capital A/c
II. In Case of Loss	Reverse of the above entry is passed.

Tutorial Note: *In case the new profit sharing ratio of continuing partners differ from their old profit sharing ratio, outgoing partner's share of profits must be adjusted through the Capital Accounts of Gaining Partners only.*

ILLUSTRATION 41

A, B & C were partners sharing profits & losses in the ratio of 3 : 2 : 1 respectively. B died on 31st March, 2012. The profits from 1.1.2012 to 31.3.2012 amounted to ₹ 4,500. A and C decided to share the future profits in the ratio of 3 : 2 respectively with effect from 1.4.2012. Pass the necessary journal entry to record the B's share of profit to the date of death.

SOLUTION

JOURNAL

Date	*Particulars*		*L.F.*	*Dr. (₹)*	*Cr. (₹)*
31.3.12	Profit & Loss Suspense A/c	Dr.		1,500	
	To B's Capital A/c				1,500
	(Being B's Share of profits to the date of death adjusted)				
	Alternative Treatment:				
	A's Capital A/c	Dr.		450	
	C's Capital A/c	Dr.		1,050	
	To B's Capital A/c				1,500
	(Being B's share of profit to the date of death adjusted in the capital accounts of A & C in their gaining ratio of 3 : 7)				

14.0 DECEASED PARTNER'S SHARE OF GOODWILL

A deceased partner's share of goodwill is calculated and adjusted in the same manner as in case of a retiring partner.

ILLUSTRATION 42

A, B and C are in partnership sharing profits in the ratio of 4 : 3 : 1. B died on 30th June 2012. The firm's profits for various years were-2007 (Profits ₹ 6,48,888), 2008 (Profits ₹ 1,60,000), 2009 (Profits ₹ 20,000), 2010 (Losses ₹ 20,000), 2011 (Profits ₹ 80,000), 2012 (Profits ₹ 1,00,000). A and C decided to share future profits in the ratio of 3 : 2. Goodwill is to be valued on the basis of 2 years' purchase of average profits of 4 completed years immediately preceding the year of death of a partner. Pass a Journal Entry to record B's Share of Goodwill.

SOLUTION

A's Gain = $\frac{3}{5} - \frac{4}{8} = \frac{4}{40}$, C's Gain = $\frac{2}{5} - \frac{1}{8} = \frac{11}{40}$

Gainin Ratio of A and C = $\frac{4}{40} : \frac{11}{40}$ = 4 : 11

A. Average Profits of 4 years = (₹ 1,60,000 + ₹ 20,000 – ₹ 20,000 + ₹ 80,000)/4 = ₹ 60,000

B. Firm's Goodwill = ₹ 60,000 × 2 = ₹ 1,20,000

C. B's Share of Goodwill = ₹ 1,20,000 × 3/8 = ₹ 45,000

JOURNAL ENTRY

Particulars		*L.F.*	*Dr. (₹)*	*Cr. (₹)*
A's Capital A/c	Dr.		12,000	
C's Capital A/c	Dr.		33,000	
To B's Capital A/c				45,000
(Being the B's share of goodwill credited to B and debited to A and C in their gaining ratio of 4 : 11)				

ILLUSTRATION 43

A, B and C are in partnership sharing profits in the ratio of 4 : 3 : 1. B died on 30th June 2012. The firm's profits for various years were-2007 (Profits ₹ 6,48,888), 2008 (Profits ₹ 1,60,000), 2009 (Profits ₹ 20,000), 2010 (Losses ₹ 20,000), 2011 (Profits ₹ 80,000), 2012 (Profits ₹ 1,00,000). A and C decided to share future profits in the ratio of 3 : 2. Goodwill is to be valued on the basis of such partner's share of 2 years' profits calculated on the average of 5 completed years' profits immediately preceding the year of death *less* 10%. Pass a Journal Entry to record B's Share of Goodwill.

SOLUTION

A. Average Profits = (₹ 6,48,888 + ₹ 1,60,000 + ₹ 20,000 – ₹ 20,000 + ₹ 80,000)/5 = ₹ 1,77,777.6

B. 2 years' Average profits = ₹ 1,77,777.6 × 2 = 3,55,555.2

C. B's Share of 2 years' Average Profits = ₹ 3,55,555 × 3/8 = ₹ 1,33,333.2

D. Firm's Goodwill = ₹ 1,33,333 – 10% of ₹ 1,33,333 = ₹ 1,20,000

E. B's Share of Goodwill = ₹ 1,20,000 × 3/8 = ₹ 45,000

Gaining Ratio and Journal Entry - Same as in Illustration 44 (A).

ILLUSTRATION 44

A, B and C are in partnership sharing profits in the ratio of 4 : 3 : 1. B died on 30th June 2012. The firm's profits for various years were-2007 (Profits ₹ 6,48,888), 2008 (Profits ₹ 1,60,000), 2009 (Profits ₹ 20,000), 2010 (Losses ₹ 20,000), 2011 (Profits ₹ 80,000) 2012 (Profits ₹ 1,00,000). A and C decided to share future profits in the ratio of 3 : 2. Deceased partner's share of goodwill is to be valued at one half of the net profit credited to his account during the last four completed years immediately preceding the year of death. Pass a Journal Entry to record B's Share of Goodwill.

SOLUTION

A. Total Profits of 4 years = (₹ 1,60,000 + ₹ 20,000 – ₹ 20,000 + ₹ 80,000 = ₹ 2,40,000

B. B's Share of profit credited during 4 years = ₹ 2,40,000 × 3/8 = ₹ 90,000

C. B's Share of Goodwill = ₹ 90,000 × 1/2 = ₹ 45,000

Gaining Ratio & Journal Entry - Same as in Illustration 44 (A).

ILLUSTRATION 45

A, B and C are in partnership sharing profits in the ratio of 4 : 3 : 1. B died on 30th June 2012.The firm's profits for various years were-2007 (Profits ₹ 6,48,888), 2008 (Profits ₹ 1,60,000), 2009 (Profits ₹ 20,000), 2010 (Losses ₹ 20,000), 2011 (Profits ₹ 80,000), 2012 (Profits ₹ 1,00,000). A and C decided to share future profits in the ratio of 3 : 2. Goodwill is to be valued at three years' purchase of average profits of three years upto the date of death. Pass a Journal Entry to record B's Share of Goodwill.

SOLUTION

A. Average Profits, of three years upto date of death comprise the profits earned from 1st July 20X3 to 30th June 20X6

= (50% of ₹ 20,000 – ₹ 20,000 + ₹ 80,000 + 50% of ₹ 1,00,000)/3 = ₹ 40,000

B. Firm's Goodwill = ₹ 40,000 × 3 = ₹ 1,20,000

C. B's share of Goodwill = ₹ 1,20,000 × 3/8 = ₹ 45,000

Gaining Ratio & Journal Entry - Same as in Illustration 44(A)

ILLUSTRATION 46

P, R and S are partners sharing profits in the ratio of 4 : 3 : 1 respectively. It is provided under the 'partnership deed that on the death of any partner his share of goodwill is to be valued at one half of the net profits credited to his account during the last 4 completed years and share of profit to the date of death is to be based on the average profits of the last three completed years, *plus* 10% (books of accounts are closed on 31st December). R died on 14th March 2013. The firm's profits for the last 4 years were as follows: 2009 (Profits ₹ 1,20,000); 2010 (Profits ₹ 60,000), 2011 (Losses ₹ 20,000) and 2012 (Profits ₹ 80,000)

Pass a journal entries to adjust R's Share of Goodwill and Profit assuming that profit sharing ratio between P and S in future will be 3 : 2.

SOLUTION

1. Calculation of R's Share of goodwill

A. Total Profits = 1,20,000 + 60,000 – 20,000 + 80,000 = ₹ 2,40,000

B. R's Share of Profits credited during 4 years = ₹ 2,40,000 × 3/8 = ₹ 90,000

C. R's Share of Goodwill ₹ 90,000 × 1/2 = ₹ 45,000

2. Calculation of R's Share of Profits

Average Profits = [(₹ 60,000 – ₹ 20,000 + ₹ 80,000)/3] + 10%

= ₹ 40,000 + 10% of ₹ 40,000 = ₹ 44,000

R's Share of Profits = ₹ 44,000 × 73/365 × 3/8 = ₹ 3,300

(B) JOURNAL ENTRIES

Date	*Particulars*	*L.F.*	*Dr. (₹)*	*Cr. (₹)*
	P's Capital A/c Dr.		12,000	
	S's Capital A/c Dr.		33,000	
	To R's Capital A/c			45,000
	(Being R's Share of goodwill credited to R and debited to P and S in their Gaining Ratio of 4 : 11)			

	Profit & Loss Suspense A/c Dr.		3,300	
	To R's Capital A/c			3,300
	(Being R's Share of Profits to the date of death adjusted)			

Working Note: *Calculation of Gaining Ratio*

P's Gain = $\frac{3}{5} - \frac{4}{8} = \frac{4}{40}$, S's Gain = $\frac{2}{5} - \frac{1}{8} = \frac{11}{40}$

Gaining Ratio of P & S = $\frac{4}{40} : \frac{11}{40}$ = 4: 11

CALCULATION OF AMOUNT PAYABLE TO EXECUTORS OF A DECEASED PARTNER

ILLUSTRATION 47

The Balance Sheet of Jassal, Jaipaul and Jyoti who are partners sharing profit in the ratio of 2 : 2 : 1, as on 31st March, 2012 is as follows:

Liabilities	₹	*Assets*	₹
Creditors	30,000	Goodwill	30,000
Employees' Provident Fund	10,000	Fixed Assets	60,000
Contingency Reserve	30,000	Stock	10,000
Jassal's Capital	30,000	Sundry Debtors	20,000
Jaipaul's Capital	25,000	Cash at Bank	15,000
Jyoti's Capital	15,000	Advertisement Expenditure	5,000
	1,40,000		1,40,000

Jaipaul died on 15th June. 2012. According to the Deed, his legal representatives were entitled to:

(a) Balance in Capital Account.

(b) Share of goodwill valued on the basis of thrice the average of the past four years' profits.

(c) Share in profits upto the date of death on the basis of average profits for the past four years.

Profits for the years ending on March 31st, of 2009, 2010, 2011 and 2012 respectively were ₹ 15,000; ₹ 17,000; ₹ 19,000 and ₹ 13,000.

(d) Interest on Capital @ 12% p.a.

Jaipaul's legal representatives were to be paid the amount due. Jassal and Jyoti continued as partners by taking over Jaipaul's share equally.

Required: Work out the amount payable to Jaipaul's legal representatives

SOLUTION

1. **Calculation of Share of Goodwill**

   A. Value of Goodwill = [(15,000 + 17,000 + 19,000 + 13,000)/4] × 3 = ₹ 48,000

   B. Jaipaul's Share of Goodwill = ₹ 48,000 × 2/5 = ₹ 19,200

2. **Calculation of Share of Profits**

   A. Average Profit = ₹ 16,000

   B. Estimated Profit upto date of death = (₹ 16,000/12) × 2½ = ₹ 3,333.33

   C. Jaipaul's Share of Profits = ₹ 3,333.33 × 2/5 = ₹ 1,333.33

3. **Interest on Capital** = ₹ 25,000 × 2.5/12 × 12/100 = ₹ 625

4. **Jaipaul's Share of Reserve** = ₹ 30,000 × 2/5 = ₹ 12,000

5. **Jaipaul's Share of Advertisement Expenditure** = ₹ 5,000 × 2/5 = ₹ 2,000.

6. TOTAL AMOUNT PAYABLE TO JAIPAUL'S LEGAL REPRESENTATIVE.

Opening balance	25,000
Goodwill	19,200
Less: Goodwill w/o (₹ 30,000 × 2/5)	(12,000)
Profits	1,333
Interest on Capital	625
Reserve Fund	12,000
Less: Advertisement Expenditure	(2,000)
	44,158

PREPARATION OF A DECEASED PARTNER'S CAPITAL ACCOUNT AND HIS EXECUTOR'S ACCOUNT

ILLUSTRATION 48

A and B are in partnership sharing profits and losses in the ratio of 3 : 2. B dies three months after the date of the last Balance Sheet. According to the partnership deed, the executors of B are entitled to the following:—

(a) His capital as per the last Balance Sheet.

(b) Interest on capital at 3% p.a. to date of death.

(c) His share of goodwill on the basis of 2 years' purchase of average profit of 3 Completed years preceding the death of a partner.

(d) His share of profit to date of death calculated on the basis of 1st year's profits

His drawings are to bear interest at an average rate of 2% on the amount. The net profits for the 3rd, 2nd, and 1st year, were ₹ 34,000, ₹ 56,000 and ₹ 60,000 respectively. B's capital as per Balance Sheet was ₹ 80,000 and his drawings to date of death were ₹ 10,000. Draw B's Capital Account to be tendered to his representatives.

SOLUTION

Dr. **B'S CAPITAL ACCOUNT** *Cr.*

Particulars	₹	*Particulars*	₹
To Drawings	10,000	By Balance b/d	80,000
To Interest on Drawings	200	By Interest on Capital	600
(₹ 10,000 × 2/100)		(₹ 80,000 × 3/100 × 3/12)	
To B's Executors' A/c	1,16,400	By P & L Suspense A/c	6,000
		(Share of profit)	
		By A's Capital A/c (Share of goodwill)	40,000
	1,26,600		1,26,600

Working Note:

1. **Average Profits** = (₹ 34,000 + ₹ 56,000 + ₹ 60,000)/3 = ₹ 50,000
2. **Firm's Goodwill** = ₹ 50,000 × 2 = ₹ 1,00,000.

3. **B's Share of Goodwill** = ₹ 1,00,000 × 2/5 = ₹ 40,000.
4. **B's Share of Profit** = ₹ 60,000 × 2/5 × 3/12 = ₹ 6,000

ILLUSTRATION 49

A, B & C are equal partners of a trading firm. The capital of the firm is ₹ 60,000 held equally by the partners.

Under the partnership deed:

(a) A and B were entitled to be credited at the close, of each year with partnership salaries of 1,800 and ₹ 1,600 respectively.

(b) In the event of death of a partner, Goodwill was to be valued at one year's the average profits of the three years preceding the year of death.

(c) Partners were to be charged 5% interest on their drawings and were to be allowed 5% interest on their capital irrespective of the period.

B died on 31st Dec. 2012. His drawings during 2012 amounted to ₹ 2,000. The profits of the three years preceding the death were: 2009 profit ₹ 8,000, 2010 profit ₹ 24,400, 2011 loss ₹ 5,400, 2012 profit ₹ 9,000.

Required: Prepare B's Current A/c and Capital A/c and Executors' A/c.

SOLUTION

Dr. **B'S CURRENT ACCOUNT** *Cr.*

Particulars	₹	*Particulars*	₹
To Drawings	2,000	By Salary	1,600
To Interest on Drawings (2,000 × 5/100)	100	By P & L Suspense A/c (Share of Profit) (9,000 × 1/3)	3,000
To B's Capital A/c	6,500	By A's Current A/c (Share of goodwill)	1,500
		By C's Current A/c (Share of goodwill)	1,500
		By Interest on Capital(20,000 × 5/100)	1,000
	8,600		8,600

Dr. **B'S CAPITAL ACCOUNT** *Cr.*

Particulars	₹	*Particulars*	₹
To B's Executors' A/c	26,500	By Balance b/d (₹ 60,000/3)	20,000
		By B's Current A/c	6,500
	26,500		26,500

Dr. **B'S EXECUTORS' ACCOUNT** *Cr.*

Particulars	₹	*Particulars*	₹
To Balance c/d	26,500	By B's Capital A/c	26,500

Working Notes:

1. **Average Profits** = (₹ 8,000 + ₹ 24,400 – ₹ 5,400)/3 = ₹ 9,000
2. **Firm's Goodwill** = ₹ 9,000 × 1 = ₹ 9,000.
3. **B's Share of Goodwill** = ₹ 9,000 × 1/3 = ₹ 3,000.

ILLUSTRATION 50

In the partnership agreement between A, B and C who were sharing profits & losses in the ratio of 4 : 2 : 2, the goodwill was to be valued on the death of any partner on the basis of such partner's share of 4 years' profits calculated on the average of 5 years profits immediately preceding the year of death *less* 10%. The firm's profits were ₹ 20,000 in 2007, ₹ 60,000 in 2008, ₹ 80,000 in 2009 and, losses of ₹ 10,000 in 2010 and ₹ 4,000 in 2011. The deceased partner's share of profits for the period of his life-time in the year of death was to be based on the average of profits of the previous 3 years *plus* 10%.

A died on 31st May, 2012. His Capital Account showed a credit of ₹ 20,000 on 1st Jan, 2012 and he had drawn ₹ 3,000 since that date. Interest on Capital is to be allowed and interest on drawings is to be charged @ 5% irrespective of the period.

Required: Prepare A's Capital Account and A's Executor's A/c.

SOLUTION

Dr. **A'S CAPITAL ACCOUNT** *Cr.*

Particulars	₹	*Particulars*	₹
To Drawings	3,000	By Balance b/d	20,000
To Interest on Drawings (3,000 × 5/100)	150	By Interest on Capital (₹ 20,000 × 5/100)	1,000
To A's Executors' A/c	49,172	By P & L Suspense A/c (Share of profit)	5,042
		By B's Capital A/c (Share of goodwill)	13,140
		By C's Capital A/c (Share of goodwill)	13,140
	52,322		52,322

Dr. **A'S EXECUTORS' ACCOUNT** *Cr.*

Particulars	₹	*Particulars*	₹
To Balance c/d	49,172	By A's Capital A/c	49,172

Working Notes:

1. **Calculation of A's Share of Goodwill**

A. Average Profit of 5 years = (₹ 20,000 + ₹ 60,000 + ₹ 80,000 – ₹ 10,000 – ₹ 4,000)/5 = ₹ 29,200.

B. 4 years' average profits = ₹ 29,200 × 4 = ₹ 1,16,800

C. A's share of aforesaid profits = ₹ 1,16,800 × 4/8 = ₹ 58,400.

D. Value of firm's goodwill = ₹ 58,400 – 10% of ₹ 58,400 = ₹ 52,560.

E. A's share of Goodwill = ₹ 52,560 × 4/8 = ₹ 26,280

2. **Calculation of A's Share of Profits**

A. Average profits of 3 years = (₹ 80,000 – ₹ 10,000 – ₹ 4,000)/3 = ₹ 22,000

B. Estimated Profits for 2012 = ₹ 22,000 + 10% of ₹ 22,000 = ₹ 24,200.

C. Estimated Profits for 5 months = ₹ 24,200 × 5/12 = ₹ 10,083

D. A's Share of Profits = ₹ 10,083 × 1/2 = ₹ 5,042

ILLUSTRATION 51

X and Y are partners. The Partnership deed provides inter alia:—

(a) That the accounts be balanced on 31st December in each year.

(b) That the profits be divided as follows: X one-half, Y one-third and carried to a Reserve Account one-sixth.

(c) That in the event of the death of a partner, his executors be entitled to be paid out:

   (i) The Capital to his credit at date of death.

   (ii) His proportion of profits to date of death based on the average profits of the last three completed years.

   (iii) By way of Goodwill, his proportion of the total profits for the three preceding years.

(d) The Balance Sheet as at 31st Dec., 2011

Particulars	₹
X's Capital	9,000
Y's Capital	6,000
Contingency Reserve	3,000
Creditors	2,000
Employees' Provident Fund	1,000
Sundry Assets	21,000

The Profits for three years were: 2009-₹ 4,200; 2010-₹ 3,900; 2011-₹ 4,500. Y died on 1st May, 2012.

Required: Prepare Y's Capital Account and Y's Executors Account.

SOLUTION

Dr. **Y'S CAPITAL ACCOUNT** *Cr.*

Particulars	₹	*Particulars*	₹
To Y's Executors A/c	12,800	By Balance b/d	6,000
		By Conting. Reserve (₹ 3,000 × 2/5)	1,200
		By P & L Suspense A/c	
		(Share of Profit)	560
		By X's Capital A/c (Share of Goodwill)	5,040
	12,800		12,800

Dr. **Y'S EXECUTORS' ACCOUNT** *Cr.*

Particulars	₹	*Particulars*	₹
To Balance c/d	12,800	By Y's Capital A/c	12,800

Working Notes:

1. Ratio between X and Y = 1/2 : 1/3 = 3 : 2

2. CALCULATION OF Y'S SHARE OF GOODWILL

A. Total Profits for previous three years	₹ 12,600
B. Y's Share of Goodwill (₹ 12,600 × 2/5)	₹ 5,040

3. CALCULATION OF Y'S SHARE OF PROFITS

A. Total Profit for previous three years	₹ 12,600
B. Average Profits (₹ 12,600/3)	₹ 4,200
C. Profit from 1.1.2012 to 30.4.2012 (₹ 4,200 × 4/12)	₹ 1,400
D. Y's Share of Profits (₹ 1,400 × 2/5)	₹ 560

ILLUSTRATION 52

R, S and T were partners sharing profits and losses in the ratio of 5 : 3 : 2 respectively. On 31st December 2011. Their Balance Sheet stood as under:

Liabilities	₹	*Assets*	₹
Sundry Creditors	50,000	Goodwill	25,000
Employees' Provident Fund	5,000	Leasehold	1,00,000
Contingency Reserve	20,000	Patents	30,000
Employees' Compensation Reserve	10,000	Machinery	1,50,000
Capital Accounts:		Stock	50,000
R	1,50,000	Debtors	40,000
S	1,25,000	Cash at Bank	40,000
T	75,000		
	4,35,000		4,35,000

T died on 1st May, 2012. It was agreed that:

(a) Goodwill to be valued at 2½ years' purchase of last four years' average profits which were: 2008-₹ 65,000. 2009-₹ 60,000, 2010-₹ 80,000 and 2011-₹ 75,000.

(b) Machinery be valued at ₹ 1,40,000; Patents be valued at ₹ 40,000; Leasehold be valued at ₹ 1,25,000.

(c) For the purpose of calculating T's share in the profits to 2012, the profits in 2012 should be taken to have accrued on the same scale as in 2011.

(d) A sum of ₹ 21,000 to be paid immediately to the executors of T and the balance to be paid in four equal half-yearly instalments together with interest @ 10% per annum.

Required: Pass the necessary journal entries to record the above transactions and T's Executors' Account for 2012.

SOLUTION

JOURNAL

Particulars		*L.F.*	*Dr. (₹)*	*Cr. (₹)*
Revaluation A/c	Dr.		10,000	
To Machinery A/c				10,000
(Being the decrease in value of asset recorded)				
Patents A/c	Dr.		10,000	
Leasehold A/c	Dr.		25,000	
To Revaluation A/c				35,000
(Being the increase in value of assets recorded)				

Particulars		Dr. (₹)	Cr. (₹)
Revaluation A/c	Dr.	25,000	
To R's Capital A/c			12,500
To S's Capital A/c			7,500
To T's Capital A/c			5,000
(Being the transfer of profit on revaluation)			
R's Capital A/c	Dr.	12,500	
S's Capital A/c	Dr.	7,500	
T's Capital A/c	Dr.	5,000	
To Goodwill A/c			25,000
(Being the existing goodwill w/o)			
R's Capital A/c [₹ 35,000 × 5/8]	Dr.	21,875	
S's Capital A/c [₹ 35,000 × 3/8]	Dr.	13,125	
To T's Capital A/c [₹ 1,75,000 × 2/10]			35,000
(Being T's share of goodwill adjusted through capital accounts)			
Profit & Loss Suspense A/c	Dr.	5,000	
To T's Capital A/c			5,000
(Being T's share of profit to date of death credited)			
Contingency Reserve A/c	Dr.	20,000	
To R's Capital A/c			10,000
To S's Capital A/c			6,000
To T's Capital A/c			4,000
(Being the transfer of Contingency Reserve)			
Employees' Compensation Reserve	Dr.	10,000	
To R's Capital A/c			5,000
To S's Capital A/c			3,000
To T's Capital A/c			2,000
(Being the transfer of Workmen Compensation Reserve)			
T's Capital A/c	Dr.	1,21,000	
To T's Executor's A/c			1,21,000
(Being the transfer of T's capital A/c to his executor's A/c)			
T's Executor's A/c	Dr.	21,000	
To Bank A/c			21,000
(Being partial payment made to R's Executors)			

Dr. **T'S CAPITAL ACCOUNT** *Cr.*

Particulars	₹	*Particulars*	₹
To Goodwill A/c	5,000	By Balance b/d	75,000
To T's Executor's A/c	1,21,000	By Revaluation A/c	5,000
		By R's Capital A/c (Goodwill)	21,875
		By S's Capital A/c (Goodwill)	13,125

		By Profit and Loss A/c	5,000
		By Contingency Reserve	4,000
		By Employees' Comp. Reserve	2,000
	1,26,000		1,26,000

Dr. **T'S EXECUTORS' ACCOUNT** *Cr.*

Date	*Particulars*	₹	*Date*	*Particulars*	₹
01.05.12	To Bank A/c	21,000	01.05.12	By T's Capital A/c	1,21,000
31.10.12	To Bank A/c	30,000	31.10.12	By Interest A/c	
31.10.12	To Balance c/d	75,000		(1,00,000 × 10/100 × 6/12)	5,000
		1,26,000			1,26,000
31.12.12	To Balance c/d	76,250	01.11.12	By Balance b/d	75,000
			31.12.12	By Interest A/c (accrued)	
				(75,000 × 10/100 × 6/12)	1,250
		76,250			76,250

Working Notes:

1. CALCULATION OF GOODWILL

Particulars	₹
A. Total profits for first 4 years	2,80,000
B. Average Profit (₹ 2,80,000/4)	70,000
C. Goodwill (₹ 70,000 × 2½)	1,75,000
D. T's share [₹ 1,75,000 × 2/10]	35,000

2. **T's Share of Profit to the date of death** = ₹ 75,000 × 4/12 × 2/10 = ₹ 5,000
3. It may be noted that R's Executor's A/c has been required for 2012.

ILLUSTRATION 53

A, B and C were partners in a firm sharing profits and losses in the ratio of 5 : 3 : 2 respectively. A died on 28th February, 2012. The Balance Sheet on that date was as follows:

Liabilities	₹	*Assets*	₹
A's Capital	12,000	Goodwill	6,000
B's Capital	16,000	Machinery	35,000
C's Capital	12,000	Furniture	6,000
Contingency Reserve	12,000	Stock	9,000
Creditors	20,000	Debtors	15,000
Employees' Provident Fund	2,000	Cash	3,000
	74,000		74,000

The Partnership Deed provided that on the death of a partner the assets and liabilities are to be revalued.

The assets and liabilities were revalued as follows on A's death:

(a) Machinery ₹ 45,000 and furniture ₹ 7,000.

(b) A provision of 10% was created for doubtful debts.

(c) A provision of ₹ 15,000 was made for taxation.

(d) The Goodwill of the firm was valued at ₹ 21,000 on A's death.

(e) The amount payable to A was transferred to his executor's account.

You are required to prepare:

(i) Revaluation Account

(ii) Capital Accounts of the partners, and

(iii) Balance Sheet of B and C.

SOLUTION

Dr. **REVALUATION ACCOUNT** *Cr.*

Particulars	₹	*Particulars*	₹
To Provision for Doubtful Debts	1,500	By Machinery	10,000
To Provision for Taxation	15,000	By Furniture	1,000
		By Loss on Revaluation t/f to:	
		A's Capital A/c	2,750
		B's Capital A/c	1,650
		C's Capital A/c	1,100
	16,500		16,500

Dr. **PARTNERS' CAPITAL ACCOUNTS** *Cr.*

Particulars	*A* ₹	*B* ₹	*C* ₹	*Particulars*	*A* ₹	*B* ₹	*C* ₹
To Goodwill A/c	3,000	1,800	1,200	By Balance b/d	12,000	16,000	12,000
To A's Capital A/c	—	6,300	4,200	By Cont. Reserve	6,000	3,600	2,400
To Revaluation A/c	2,750	1,650	1,100	By B's Capital A/c	6,300	—	—
To A's Executor's A/c	22,750	—	—	By C's Capital A/c	4,200	—	—
To Balance c/d	—	9,850	7,900				
	28,500	19,600	14,400		28,500	19,600	14,400

BALANCE SHEET OF B AND C (AFTER A'S DEATH) AS AT 28.02.2012

Liabilities	₹	*Assets*		₹
B's Capital	9,850	Machinery		45,000
C's Capital	7,900	Furniture		7,000
A's Executors	22,750	Stock		9,000
Creditors	20,000	Debtors	15,000	
Provision for Taxation	15,000	*Less:* Provision	1,500	13,500
Employees' Provident Fund	2,000	Cash		3,000
	77,500			77,500

ILLUSTRATION 54

The following is the balance Sheet of Ram, Mohan and Sohan as on 31st December, 2011.

Liabilities	₹	*Assets*	₹
Sundry Creditors	10,000	Goodwill	5,000
Workmen Compensation Reserve	7,500	Tools	3,000
Ram's Capital	20,000	Furniture	13,000
Mohan's Capital	10,000	Stock	16,000
Sohan's Capital	10,000	Debtors	12,000
		Cash at bank	8,000
		Cash in hand	500
	57,500		57,500

Ram, Mohan and Sohan shared profits and losses in the ratio of 2 : 2 : 1. Sohan died on 31st March 2012. Under the Partnership agreement the executor of Sohan was entitled to:

(a) Amount standing to the credit of his Capital Account.

(b) Interest on Capital @ 6% p.a.

(c) Share of Goodwill on the basis of twice the average of past three years' profits.

(d) Share of profit from the closing of last financial year to the date of death on the basis of average profits of past three years.

Profits for 2009, 2010 and 2011 were ₹ 10,000, ₹ 15,000 and ₹ 20,000 respectively. Sohan's executor was paid ₹ 1,400 on 1st April, 2012 and the balance in four equal yearly instalments from 31.3.2013 with interest @ 6% p.a.

Required: Pass necessary Journal entries and draw up Sohan's Account to be rendered to his executor and Sohan's Executor's Account till it is finally paid.

SOLUTION

JOURNAL

Particulars		*L.F.*	*Dr. (₹)*	*Cr. (₹)*
Interest on Capital	Dr.		150	
To Sohan's Capital A/c				150
(Being the interest on Capital provided)				
Ram's Capital A/c [₹ 5,000 × 2/5]	Dr.		2,000	
Mohan's Capital A/c [₹ 5,000 × 2/5]	Dr.		2,000	
Sohan's Capital A/c [₹ 5,000 × 1/5]	Dr.		1,000	
To Goodwill A/c				5,000
(Being the existing goodwill w/o)				
Ram's Capital A/c	Dr.		3,000	
Mohan's Capital A/c	Dr.		3,000	
To Sohan's Capital A/c				6,000
(Being the Share of goodwill credited)				
Profit & Loss Suspense A/c	Dr.		750	
To Sohan's Capital A/c				750

(Being the Share of profit credited)			
Workmen Compensation Reserve	Dr.	1,500	
To Sohan's Capital A/c			1,500
(Being the Share of reserve credited)			
Sohan's Capital A/c	Dr.	17,400	
To Sohan's Executors' A/c			17,400
(Being the transfer of Balance in Sohan's Capital A/c to Sohan's Executor's A/c)			
Sohan's Executor's A/c	Dr.	1,400	
To Cash A/c			1,400
(Being the cash Paid to Sohan's Executors)			

Dr. **SOHAN'S CAPITAL ACCOUNT** Cr.

Particulars	₹	*Particulars*	₹
To Goodwill A/c	1,000	By Balance b/d	10,000
To Sohan's Executor's A/c	17,400	By Interest on Capital	150
		By Ram's Capital A/c	3,000
		By Mohan's Capital A/c	3,000
		By P & L Suspense A/c	750
		By Workmen Comp. Reserve A/c	1,500
	18,400		18,400

Dr. **SOHAN'S EXECUTOR'S ACCOUNT** Cr.

Date	*Particulars*	₹	*Date*	*Particulars*	₹
2012			2012		
April 1	To Bank A/c	1,400	Mar. 31	By Sohan's Capital A/c	17,400
Dec. 31	To Balance c/d	16,720	Dec. 31	By Interest A/c [(17,400 – 1,400) × 6/100 × 9/12]	720
		18,120			18,120
2013			2013		
Mar 31	To Cash A/c [₹ 4,000 + ₹ 960]	4,960	Jan 1	By Balance b/d	16,720
			March 31	By Interest A/c [16,000 × 6/100 × 3/12]	240
Dec. 31	To Balance c/d	12,540	Dec. 31	By Interest A/c [12,000 × 6/100 × 9/12]	540
		17,500			17,500
2014	To Cash A/c		2014		
Mar 31	[₹ 4,000 + ₹ 720]	4,720	Jan 1	By Balance b/d	12,540
Dec 31	To Balance c/d	8,360	Mar 31	By Interest A/c	180

				[12,000 × 6/100 × 3/12]	
			Dec. 31	By Interest A/c	360
				[8,000 × 6/100 × 9/12]	
		13,080			13,080
2015	To Cash A/c		2015		
Mar. 31	[₹ 4,000 + ₹ 480]	4,480	Jan. 1	By Balance b/d	8,360
Dec. 31	To Balance c/d	4,180	Mar. 31	By Interest A/c	120
				[8,000 × 6/100 × 3/12]	
			Dec 31	By Interest A/c	180
				[4,000 × 6/100 × 9/12]	
		8,660			8,660
2016			2016		
Mar 31	To Cash A/c		Jan 1	By Balance b/d	4,180
	[₹ 4,000 + ₹ 240]	4,240	Mar 31	By Interest A/c	
				[4,000 × 6/100 × 3/12]	60
		4,240			4,240

Note: The date of closing the accounts is 31st Dec. and date of payment of instalment is 31st March.

Working Notes:

1. **Calculation of Share of Goodwill**
   A. Present Value of Goodwill = [(₹ 10,000 + ₹ 15,000 + ₹ 20,000)/3] × 2 = ₹ 30,000
   B. Deceased Partner's share of Goodwill = ₹ 30,000 × 1/5 = ₹ 6,000
2. **Calculation of Share of Profits**
   A. Average Profits = (₹ 10,000 + ₹ 15,000 + ₹ 20,000)/3 = ₹ 15,000
   B. Estimated Profits upto date of death = ₹ 15,000 × 3/12 = ₹ 3,750
   C. Deceased Partner's Share of Profits = ₹ 3,750 × 1/5 = ₹ 750

ILLUSTRATION 55

On 31st December 2011, the Balance Sheet of P, Q and R who were partners in a firm, was as under:

Liabilities	₹	*Assets*	₹
Sundry Creditors	25,000	Building	26,000
Reserves Fund	20,000	Investments	11,000
P's Capital A/c	13,000	Debtors	15,000
Q's Capital A/c	9,000	Bills Receivable	6,000
R's Capital A/c	9,000	Stock	12,000
		Cash	6,000
	76,000		76,000

The partnership deed provides that the profits be shared in the ratio of 2 : 1 : 1 and that in the event of death of the partner, his executors will be entitled to be paid out:

(a) The capital to his credit at the date of last Balance Sheet;

(b) His proportion of Reserve at the date of last Balance Sheet;

(c) His proportion of profits to the date of death based on the average profits of the last three completed years, *plus* 10%.

(d) By way of goodwill, his proportion of the total profits for the three preceding years

(e) The Net Profits for the last three years were:

2009 ₹ 16,000, 2010 ₹ 16,000, 2011 ₹ 15,400

R died on 1st April, 2012. He had withdrawn ₹ 5,000 to the date of his death. The Investments were sold for ₹ 15,000 and R's executors were paid off.

Required: Prepare Partners' Capital Accounts, R's Executor's Account and Balance Sheet of the surviving partners P and Q.

SOLUTION

Dr. **PARTNERS' CAPITAL ACCOUNTS** *Cr.*

Particulars	*P* ₹	*Q* ₹	*R* ₹	*Particulars*	*P* ₹	*Q* ₹	*R* ₹
To R's Capital	7,900	3,950		By Balance b/d	13,000	9,000	9,000
To Cash A/c			5,000	By Reserve Fund	10,000	5,000	5,000
To R's Executors' A/c			22,936	By P & L Susp. A/c			1,086
To Balance c/d	17,100	11,050		By P's Capital A/c			7,900
				By Q's Capital A/c			3,950
				By Revaluation A/c	2,000	1,000	1,000
	25,000	15,000	27,936		25,000	15,000	27,936

Dr. **CASH ACCOUNT** *Cr.*

Particulars	₹	*Particulars*	₹
To Balance b/d	6,000	By R's Capital A/c (Drawings)	5,000
To Investments	15,000	By R's Executors' A/c (Amount Due)	22,936
To Balance c/d (b.f.) (Overdraft Bal)	6,936		
	27,936		27,936

Dr. **R'S EXECUTOR ACCOUNT** *Cr.*

Particulars	₹	*Particulars*	₹
To Cash A/c	22,936	By R's Capital A/c	22,936
	22,936		22,936

BALANCE SHEET OF P AND Q AS AT 1ST APRIL, 2012

Liabilities	₹	*Assets*	₹
Sundry Creditors	25,000	Building	26,000
P's Capital A/c	17,100	Debtors	15,000
Q's Capital A/c	11,050	Bills Receivable	6,000
Overdraft	6,936	Stock	12,000
		P & L Suspense A/c	1,086
	60,086		60,086

Working Notes:

1. **R's Share of Profits**

Average Profits $= \frac{16,000 + 16,000 + 15,400}{3} + 10\%$

$= 15,800 + 10\%$ of ₹ 15,800 = ₹ 17,380

R's Share of Profits = 17,380 × 3/12 × 1/4 = ₹ 1,086

2. **R's Share in Goodwill** = 47,400 × 1/4 = ₹ 11,850

ILLUSTRATION 56

Arti, Bharati and Seema are partners in a firm sharing profits in the proportion of 3:2:1. Their Balance Sheet as at 31st March, 2012 stood as follows:

Liabilities	₹	*Assets*	₹
Bills Payable	12,000	Buildings	21,000
Creditors	14,000	Cash in hand	4,250
General Reserve	12,000	Cash at Bank	21,450
Capital Accounts:		Debtors	12,000
Arti	20,000	Bills Receivable	4,300
Bharati	12,000	Stock	1,750
Seema	8,000	Investments	13,250
	78,000		78,000

Bharati died on 30th June, 2012 and according to the deed of the said partnership her executors are entitled to be paid as under:

(i) The capital to her credit at the time of her death and interest thereon @ 10% per annum.

(ii) Her proportionate share of general reserve.

(iii) Her share of profits for the intervening period will be based on the sales during that period. Sales were calculated as ₹ 1,20,000. The rate of profit during past three years had been 10% on sales.

(iv) Goodwill according to her share of profit to be calculated by taking twice the amount of profits of the last three years *less* 20%. The profits of the previous three years were:

2009-10	₹ 8,200
2010-11	₹ 9,000
2011-12	₹ 9,800

The investments were sold at par and her executors were paid out in full.

Required: Prepare Bharati's Capital Account and her Executor's Account.

SOLUTION

Dr. **BHARTI'S CAPITAL ACCOUNT** *Cr.*

Date	*Particulars*	₹	*Date*	*Particulars*	₹
30.06.12	To Bharti's Executor A/c	34,700	01.04.12	By Balance b/d	12,000
	(Balancing Figure)		30.06.12	By General Reserve	4,000
			30.06.12	By Interest on Capital	300

			30.06.12	By P&L Suspense A/c	4,000
			30.06.12	By Aarti's Capital A/c	10,800
			30.06.12	By Seema's Capital A/c (Goodwill)	3,600
		34,700			34,700

Dr. **BHARTI'S EXECUTOR'S ACCOUNT** Cr.

Date	*Particulars*	₹	*Date*	*Particulars*	₹
30.06.12	To Bank A/c (Bal. fig.)	34,700	30.06.12	By Bharti's Capital A/c	34,700
		34,700			34,700

Working Notes:

1. **Interest on Capital** = 12,000 × 10/100 × 3/12 = ₹ 300
2. **Share in General Reserve** = 12,000 × 2/6 = ₹ 4,000
3. **Share of Profit** = 1,20,000 × 10/100 = ₹ 12,000, Bharti's Share = 2/3 × 12,000 = ₹ 4,000
4. **Share of Goodwill**

   Total Profit of Last 3 Years = 8,200 + 9,00 + 9,800 = ₹ 27,000

   Firm's Goodwill = (27,000 × 2) – (20% of ₹ 54,000) = 43,200

   Share of Goodwill = 43,200 × 2/6 = 14,400

Date	*Particulars*		*L.F.*	*Dr. (₹)*	*Cr. (₹)*
	Arti's Capital	Dr.		10,800	
	Seema's Capital A/c	Dr.		3,600	
	To Bharti's Capital A/c				14,400
	(For Bharti's share of goodwill given to her by Arti and Seema in gaining ratio)				

ILLUSTRATION 57

Ramesh, Naresh and Sudesh were partners in a firm sharing profits in the ratio of 2 : 2 : 1. On 31st December, 2011, their Balance Sheet was as follows:

Liabilities		₹	*Assets*	₹
Creditors		60,000	Bank	90,000
Bills Payable		40,000	Stock	70,000
General Reserve		30,000	Debtors	40,000
Capital A/cs:			Land and Building	5,00,000
Ramesh	3,00,000		Profit and Loss A/c	1,60,000
Naresh	3,00,000			
Sudesh	1,30,000	7,30,000		
		8,60,000		8,60,000

Naresh died on 31st March, 2012. The Partnership Deed provided for the following on the death of a partner.

(i) Goodwill of the firm was to be valued at 2 years' purchase of the average profit of last 5 years. The profits for the years ended 31st December, 2010, 31st December, 2009, 31st December,

2008 and 31st December, 2007 were ₹ 50,000; ₹ 80,000; ₹ 1,10,000 and ₹ 2,20,000 respectively.

(ii) Naresh's share of profit *or* loss till the date of his death was to be calculated on the basis of the profit *or* loss for the year ended 31st December, 2011.

You are required to calculate the following:

(i) Goodwill of the firm and Naresh's share of goodwill at the time of his death.

(ii) Naresh's share in the profit *or* loss of the firm till the date of his death.

(iii) Prepare Naresh's Capital Account at the time of his death to be presented to his executors.

SOLUTION

(i) Firm's Goodwill = [(50,000 + 80,000 + 1,10,000 + 2,20,000 – 1,60,000)/5] × 2 = ₹ 1,20,000.

Naresh's Share of goodwill = ₹ 1,20,000 × 2/5 = ₹ 48,000, which is contributed by Ramesh and Sudesh in their Gaining Ratio of 2 : 1.

Ramesh's Contribution = ₹ 48,000 × 2/3 = ₹ 32,000 and

Sudesh's Contribution = ₹ 48,000 × 1/3 = ₹ 16,000.

(ii) Naresh's Share in Loss = ₹ 1,60,000 × 3/12 × 2/5 = ₹ 16,000.

Dr. **(III) NARESH'S CAPITAL ACCOUNT** *Cr.*

Particulars	₹	*Particulars*	₹
To P & L A/c (₹ 1,60,000 × 2/5)	64,000	By Balanced b/d	3,00,000
To P & L Suspense A/c	16,000	By General Reserve (₹ 30,000 × 2/5)	12,000
To Naresh's Executor's A/c	2,80,000	By Ramesh's Capital A/c (Goodwill)	32,000
		By Sudesh's Capital A/c (Goodwill)	16,000
	3,60,000		3,60,000

ILLUSTRATION 58

Khanna, Seth and Mehta were partners in a firm sharing profits in the ratio of 3 : 2 : 5. On 31-12-2011 the Balance Sheet of Khanna, Seth and Mehta was as follows:

Liabilities	₹	*Assets*	₹
Khanna's Capital	5,00,000	Goodwill	3,00,000
Seth's Capital	2,05,000	Fixed Assets	6,60,000
Mehta's Capital A/c	3,00,000	Investments	10,000
Workmen Compensation Reserve	1,00,000	Stock	30,000
Employees' Provident Fund	20,000	Debtors	1,20,000
Loan from Seth	50,000	Cash	50,000
Creditors	51,000	P&L Account (for the year 2011)	60,000
Provision for Doubiful Debts	4,000		
	12,30,000		12,30,000

On 14th March 2012, Seth died. He had withdrawn ₹ 5,000 during 2012.

The partnership deed provided that on the death of a partner the executor of the deceaused partner is entitled to:

(i) Balance in Capital Account:

(ii) Share in Profits upto the date of death on the basis of Last year's profit;

(iii) His Share in Profit/Loss on Revaluation of Assets and re-assessment of liabilities which were as follows:

  (a) Fixed Assets were to be valued at ₹ 7,35,000.

  (b) Stock was overvalued by ₹ 11,000

  (c) A provision of 2½% for doubtful debts was to maintained on Debtors;

  (d) Creditors of ₹ 2,000 are not to be paid.

  (e) Investments were sold for ₹ 20,000

(iv) Half of the net amount payable to Seth's executors was paid immediately and the balance was transferred to his loan account which was to be paid later.

Required: Prepare Revaluation Account, Partners' Capital Accounts, Seth's Executors A/c and the Balance Sheet of Khanna and Mehta who decided to continue the business keeping their capital balances in their new profit sharing ratio. Any surplus *or* deficit to be transferred to Current Accounts of the partners.

Note: Firm enjoys Bank Overdraft facility.

SOLUTION

Dr. **1. REVALUATION ACCOUNT** *Cr.*

Particulars	₹	*Particulars*		₹
To Stock A/c	11,000	By Fixed Assets		
To Profit on Revaluation t/f to:		[₹ 7,35,000 – ₹ 6,60,000]		75,000
Khanna's Capital A/c	23,100	By Provision for Doubtful		
Seth's Capital A/c	15,400	Existing	4,000	
Mehta's Capital A/c	38,500	*Less:* Required	3,000	1,000
		[₹ 1,20,000 × 2.5/100]		
		By Creditors		2,000
		By Investments		10,000
	88,000			**88,000**

Dr. **2. PARTNER'S CAPITAL ACCOUNTS** *Cr.*

Particulars	*Khanna* ₹	*Seth* ₹	*Mehta* ₹	*Particulars*	*Khanna* ₹	*Seth* ₹	*Mehta* ₹
To Cash A/c (Drawings)	—	5,000	—	By Balance b/d	5,00,000	2,05,000	3,00,000
To Goodwill A/c (w/o)	90,000	60,000	1,50,000	By W. Comp Reserve	30,000	20,000	50,000
To Profit & Loss A/c	18,000	12,000	30,000	By Revaluation A/c (Profit)	23,100	15,400	38,500
To P&L Susp. A/c (Loss)	—	2,400	—				
To Seth's Executor's A/c	—	1,61,000	—				
To Balance c/d	4,45,100	—	2,08,500				
	5,53,100	**2,40,400**	**3,88,500**		**5,53,100**	**2,40,400**	**3,88,500**

Dr. **3. SETH'S EXECUTOR'S ACCOUNT** *Cr.*

Particulars	₹	*Particulars*	₹
To Cash A/c	1,05,500	By Seth's Capital A/c	1,61,000

To Seth's Excecutor's Loan A/c	1,05,500	By Seth's Loan A/c	50,000
	2,11,000		**2,11,000**

4. BALANCE SHEET OF KHANNA & MEHTA

as at 14th March, 2012

Liabilities	₹	*Assets*		₹
Khanna's Capital	2,45,100	Fixed Assets		7,35,000
Mehta's Capital	4,08,500	Stock		19,000
Creditors [51,000 – 2,000]	49,000	Debtors	1,20,000	
Seth's Executors' Loan A/c	1,05,500	*Less:* Provision	3,000	1,17,000
Profit & Loss Suspense A/c	2,400	Mehta's Current A/c		2,00,000
Khanna's Current A/c	2,00,000			
Bank Overdraft	40,500			
Employees' Provident Fund	20,000			
	10,71,000			10,71,000

Working Notes:

1. **Calculation of Seth's Share in Loss** = ₹ 60,000 ×73/365 × 2/10 = ₹ 2,400
2. **Calculation of Khanna's New Capital and Mehta's New Capital**

   Total Capital on New Firm = Total Adjusted Old Capitals = ₹ 4,45,100 + ₹ 2,08,500 = ₹ 6,53,600

   Khanna's New Capital = ₹ 6,53,600 × 3/8 = ₹ 2,45,100

   Mehta's New Capital = ₹ 6,53,600 × 5/8 = ₹ 4,08,500

   T/f to Khanna's Current A/c (Cr.) = ₹ 4,45,100 – ₹ 2,45,100 = ₹ 2,00,000

   T/f to Mehta's Current A/c (Dr.) = ₹ 2,08,500 – ₹ 4,08,500 = ₹ 2,00,000

Dr. **CASH ACCOUNT** *Cr.*

Particulars	₹	*Particulars*	₹
To Balance b/d	50,000	By Seth's Capital A/c (Drawings)	5,000
To Investments	20,000	By Seth's Executors's A/c	1,05,500
To Bank Overdraft (Bal. Figure)	40,500		
	1,10,500		1,10,500

Note: Due to Shortage of Cash, Bank Overdraft has been taken.

COMPREHENSIVE REVISIONAL PROBLEMS

Objective: The following Problems have been given Only to Revise the Chapter. In Examination only some of the parts and not all the parts of such lengthy problems may be asked.

PROBLEM 1

The Balance Sheet of A, B and C sharing profits and losses in the ratio of 5 : 3 : 2 respectively, on 31st March, 2012:

Liabilities	₹	*Assets*	₹
A's Capital	40,000	Land and Building	30,000

B's Capital	30,000	Plant and Machinery	35,000
C's Capital	25,000	Investment (Market Value ₹ 19,000)	20,000
General Reserve	5,000	Machinery Replacement Fund Invsts.	1,000
Profit and Loss Account	3,450	Current Assets	28,000
Investment Fluctuation Reserve	1,500	Advt. Expnd. (Deferred Revenue)	1,000
Machinery Replacement Fund	1,000		
Workmen's Compensation Reserve	1,200		
Employees' Provident Fund	2,000		
Creditors	5,850		
	1,15,000		1,15,000

On this date, B retires from the firm and A and C continue to share future profits & losses in the ratio of 3 : 2 respectively. A claim on account of workmen's compensation is estimated at ₹ 150 only.

Required: Pass the necessary journal entries relating to the adjustment of accumulated profits and losses.

SOLUTION

JOURNAL

Particulars		*L.F.*	*Dr. (₹)*	*Cr. (₹)*
Investment Fluctuation Reserve A/c	Dr.		1,000	
To Investment A/c				1,000
(Being the value of investments brought down to market value)				
Workmen Compensation Reserve A/c	Dr.		150	
To Provision for Workmen Compensation Claim A/c				150
(Being the workmen's compensation claim provided to the extent of ₹ 150)				
General Reserve	Dr.		5,000	
P & L A/c	Dr.		3,450	
Investment Fluctuation Reserve A/c [1,500– (20,000–19,000)]	Dr.		500	
Workmen's Compensation Reserve A/c	Dr.		1,050	
To A's Capital A/c				5,000
To B's Capital A/c				3,000
To C's Capital A/c				2,000
(Being the transfer of accumulated profits to all the partners in their profit-sharing ratio)				
A's Capital A/c	Dr.		500	
B's Capital A/c	Dr.		300	
C's Capital A/c	Dr.		200	
To Advertisement Expenditure A/c				1,000
(Being the transfer of accumulated loses to all the partners in their profit-sharing ratio)				

Working Notes:

1. Investment Fluctuation Reserve Account has been transferred directly to partners' capital accounts. after providing for an anticipated loss of ₹ 1,000 (i.e. ₹ 20,000 – ₹ 19,000) according to Prudence (conservatism) concept.
2. The balance of Workmen's Compensation Reserve Account after making Provision for Claim has been transferred directly to partners' capital accounts.
3. Machinery Replacement Fund is in the nature of accumulated depreciation and not in nature of accumulated profits and hence is not distributed among the partners.
4. Employees' Provident Fund represents statutory liability due to employees towards Provident Fund and is not an accumulated profits, hences it is not distribted among the partners.

PROBLEM 2

The Balance Sheet of A, B and C who are sharing profits in the ratio of 2:3:1, as at 31st March, 2012 is given below:

Liabilities	₹	*Assets*	₹
A's Capital	1,00,000	Goodwill	12,000
B's Capital	2,00,000	Land and Building	2,50,000
C's Capital	3,00,000	Investments [Market Value ₹ 46,000]	50,000
Workmen Compensation Reserve	20,000	Stock	80,000
Investment Fluctuation Reserve	10,000	Debtors	3,00,000
Provision for Doubtful Debts	10,000	Bank	2,96,000
Sundry Creditors	3,00,000	Advertisement Suspense A/c	12,000
Employees' Provident Fund	60,000		
	10,00,000		10,00,000

C retires from 1st April, 2012 and A and B decide to share future profits losses in the ratio of 3:2 and 50% is to be paid immediately and the balance in two equal annual instalments together with interest @ 10% p.a.

1. Goodwill is to be valued at 2 years' purchase of average profits of last three completed years. The profits were - 2009-2010 ₹ 48,000, 2010-2011 ₹ 93,000, 2011-2012 ₹ 1,38,000.
2. Land & Building was found under valued by ₹ 20,000 and Stock was found overvalued by ₹ 38,000.
3. Provision for doubtful debts is to be made equal to 5% of the debtors.
4. Claim on account of workmen compensation is ₹ 8,000.
5. 10% of the sundry creditors be written back as no longer payable.
6. Out of the amount of insurance which was debited entirely to P&L A/c, ₹ 5,000 be carried forward as an unexpired insurance.

Required: Pass the necessary journal entries and prepare the necessary ledger accounts and the Balance Sheet.

SOLUTION

JOURNAL

Date	*Particulars*		*L.F.*	*Dr. (₹)*	*Cr. (₹)*
(1)	A's Capital A/c	Dr.		4,000	

	B's Capital A/c	Dr.	6,000	
	C's Capital A/c	Dr.	2,000	
	To Goodwill A/c			12,000
	(Being the existing goodwill w/o)			
(2)	A's Capital A/c (₹ 1,86,000 × 8/30)	Dr.	49,600	
	To B's Capital (₹ 1,86,000 × 3/30)			18,600
	To C's Capital A/c (₹ 1,86,000 × 5/30)			31,000
	(Being the goodwill adjusted by debiting gaining partner (A for 8/30) and crediting Sacrificing partners (B for 3/30) and (C for 1/6)]			
(3)	Land & Building A/c	Dr.	20,000	
	Sundry Creditors	Dr.	30,000	
	Prepaid Insurance	Dr.	5,000	
	To Revaluation A/c			55,000
	(Being the increase in value of assets & decrease in SundryCreditors recorded)			
(4)	Revaluation A/c	Dr.	43,000	
	To Stock A/c			38,000
	To Provision for Doubtful Debts A/c			5,000
	(Being the decrease in Value of assets & increase in provisions recorded)			
(5)	Revaluation A/c	Dr.	12,000	
	To A's Capital A/c			4,000
	To B's Capital A/c			6,000
	To C's Capital A/c			2,000
	(Being the transfer of profit on revaluation)			
(6)	Workmen Compensation Reserve A/c	Dr.	20,000	
	To Workmen Compensation Claim A/c			8,000
	To A's Capital A/c			4,000
	To B's Capital A/c			6,000
	To C's Capital A/c			2,000
	(Being the transfer of workmen compensation Reserve)			
(7)	Investment Fluctuation Fund A/c	Dr.	10,000	
	To Investment A/c			4,000
	To A's Capital A/c			2,000
	To B's Capital A/c			3,000
	To C's Capital A/c			1,000
	(Being the transfer of Investment Fluctuation Fund)			
(8)	A's Capital A/c	Dr.	4,000	
	B's Capital A/c	Dr.	6,000	
	C's Capital A/c	Dr.	2,000	

	To Advertisement Suspense A/c			12,000
	(Being the transfer of balance of Advertisement Suspense A/c)			
(9)	C's Capital A/c	Dr.	3,32,000	
	To Bank A/c			1,66,000
	To C's Loan A/c			1,66,000
	(Being 50% paid and the balance t/f to Loan A/c)			

Ledger Accounts:

Dr. **1. REVALUATION ACCOUNT** *Cr.*

Particulars	₹	*Particulars*	₹
To Stock	38,000	By Land & Building	20,000
To Provision for Doubtful Debts	5,000	By Sundry Creditors	30,000
To Profit on Revaluation t/f to:		By Prepaid Insurance	5,000
A	4,000		
B	6,000		
C	2,000		
	55,000		55,000

Dr. **2. PARTNERS' CAPITAL ACCOUNTS** *Cr.*

Particulars	A ₹	B ₹	C ₹	*Particulars*	A ₹	B ₹	C ₹
To Goodwill A/c	4,000	6,000	2,000	By Balance b/d	1,00,000	2,00,000	3,00,000
To B's Capital A/c	18,600	—		By A's Capital A/c	—	18,600	31,000
To C's Capital A/c	31,000	—	—	By Revaluation A/c	4,000	6,000	2,000
To Adv. Exp. Sus. A/c	4,000	6,000	2,000	By Work Com. Res.	4,000	6,000	2,000
To Bank A/c	—	—	1,66,000	By Invest. Flus. Res.	2,000	3,000	1,000
To C's Loan A/c	—	—	1,66,000				
To Balance c/d	52,400	2,21,600	—				
	1,10,000	2,33,600	3,36,000		1,10,000	2,33,600	3,36,000

3. BALANCE SHEET AS AT 31ST MARCH, 2012

Liabilities	₹	*Assets*		₹
A's Capital	52,400	Land & Building		2,70,000
B's Capital	2,21,600	Investments		46,000
C's Loan	1,66,000	Stock		42,000
Sundary Creditors	2,70,000	Debtors	3,00,000	
Workmen Compensation Claim	8,000	*Less:* Provision	15,000	2,85,000
Employees' Provident Fund	60,000	Bank		1,30,000
		Prepaid Insurance		5,000
	7,78,000			7,78,000

Working Notes:

1. **Gain/Sacrifice** = New Share – Old Share

   A's Gain = 3/5 – 2/6 = 8/30, B's Gain = 2/5 – 3/6 = –3/30

2. **Calculation of Goodwill**

   A. Average Profits = $\frac{₹\ 48,000 + ₹\ 93,000 + ₹\ 1,38,000}{3}$ = ₹ 93,000

   B. Firm's Goodwill = ₹ 93,000 × 2 = ₹ 1,86,000

PROBLEM 3

The Balance Sheet to A, B and C who were sharing profits in proportion in their capitals stood as follows as on 31st Dec., 2011.

Liabilities	₹	*Assets*		₹
Expenses Owing	900	Goodwill		9,000
Trade Creditors	5,000	Cash at Bank		15,500
Employees' Provident Fund	1,000	Sundry Debtors	5,000	
Reserve Fund	5,400	*Less:* Provision	100	4,900
Workmen Compensation Reserve	1,200	Stock		9,000
Investment Fluctuation Fund	1,900	Investments [Market value ₹ 8,700]		9,700
A's Capital	21,600	Land and Building		15,000
B's Capital	16,200	Advertisement Expenditure		900
C's Capital	10,800			
	64,000			64,000

B retires on 31.12.2011, and the following readjustments of the assets and liabilities have been agreed upon before the ascertainment of the amount payable to B:

(a) That the Stock be written down to ₹ 8,520.

(b) That the provision for doubtful debts be brought upto 5% on debtors.

(c) That the Land and Building be written up by ₹ 5,000.

(d) That a provision of ₹ 4,420 be made in respect of outstanding legal charges.

(e) That out of the amount of insurance which was debited entirely to P & L A/c, ₹ 2,000 be carried forward as an unexpired insurance.

(f) That Expenses owing to be brought down to ₹ 625.

(g) That Trade Creditors agree to allow a discount of 2½%.

(h) That 'X' an old customer whose account was written off as bad had promised in writing to pay ₹ 350 in settlement of his full debt of ₹ 500.

(i) That claim on account of workmen's compensation is estimated at ₹ 300.

(j) That A and C are going to share in future in the proportion of five eighths and three eighths respectively.

(k) That the goodwill is to be valued at 2 years' purchase of the average profits of 3 completed years preceding the date of retirement. The profits for 2007 ₹ 3,000, for 2008 ₹ 3,520, for 2009 ₹ 6,600, for 2010, ₹ 7,700, 2011 ₹ 8,000. No goodwill account is to be raised.

(l) That the investments are taken over by B at market value.

(m) B is to be paid the amount due to him by raising a loan of ₹ 7,000 on the security of land and building and ₹ 460 by a Bill of Exchange (without interest) payable at the expiry of 3 months and carrying the remainder to be paid in four equal half yearly instalments together with interest @ 6% p.a. on half yearly rests.

Required: Pass the necessary journal entries, Prepare Partners' Capital Accounts and the Balance Sheet after B's retirement:

SOLUTION

JOURNAL

Particulars		*L.F.*	*Dr. (₹)*	*Cr. (₹)*
Revaluation A/c	Dr.		5,050	
To Stock Reserve A/c				480
To Provision for Doubtful Debts A/c				150
To Provision for Outstanding Legal Charges A/c				4,420
(Being the fall in value of assets and increase in amount of provision recorded)				
Land & Building	Dr.		5,000	
Prepaid Insurance	Dr.		2,000	
Expenses Owing	Dr.		275	
Reserve for Discount on Trade Creditors	Dr.		125	
Mr. X	Dr.		350	
To Revaluation A/c				7,750
(Being the increase in value of assets, decrease in liabilities and Reserve for discount on creditors recorded)				
Revaluation A/c	Dr.		2,700	
To A's Capital A/c				1,200
To B's Capital A/c				900
To C's Capital A/c				600
(Being the transfer of profit on revaluation to all partners in their profit sharing ratio of 4 : 3 : 2)				
Workmen Compensation Reserve	Dr.		1,200	
To Provision for Workmen Compensation Claim A/c				300
To A's Capital A/c				400
To B's Capital A/c				300
To C's Capital A/c				200
(Being provision made for workmen compensation and surplus Workmen Compensation reserve transferred)				
Investment Fluctuation Reserve A/c	Dr.		1,900	
To Investments A/c				1,000
To A's Capital A/c				400
To B's Capital A/c				300
To C's Capital A/c				200
(Being investments brought down to its market value and surplus t/f to capital a/cs)				

Reserve Fund	Dr.	5,400	
To A's Capital A/c			2,400
To B's Capital A/c			1,800
To C's Capital A/c			1,200
(Being the transfer of reserve to all partners in their profit sharing ratio of 4 : 3 : 2)			
A's Capital A/c	Dr.	400	
B's Capital A/c	Dr.	300	
C's Capital A/c	Dr.	200	
To Advertisement Expenditure A/c			900
(Being the transfer of Advertisement Expenditure to all partners in their profit sharing ratio of 4 : 3 : 2)			
A's Capital A/c	Dr.	4,000	
B's Capital A/c	Dr.	3,000	
C's Capital A/c	Dr.	2,000	
To Goodwill A/c			9,000
(Being the existing book value of Goodwill w/o)			
A's Capital A/c	Dr.	2,145	
C's Capital A/c	Dr.	1,815	
To B's Capital A/c			3,960
(Being share of goodwill credited to B and debited to the remaining partners in their gaining ratio which is 13 : 11)			
Bank A/c	Dr.	7,000	
To Loan from Bank A/c			7,000
(Being the loan from Bank raised on the security of Land & Building)			
B's Capital A/c	Dr.	20,160	
To Investments A/c			8,700
To Bank A/c			7,000
To Bills Payable A/c			460
To 6% B's Loan A/c			4,000
(Being B's claim discharged-Investments ₹ 8,700, Cheque ₹ 7,000, B/P ₹ 460 and the balance transferred to his LoanA/c)			

Dr. **CAPITAL ACCOUNTS OF PARTNERS** *Cr.*

Particulars	*A* ₹	*B* ₹	*C* ₹	*Particulars*	*A* ₹	*B* ₹	*C* ₹
To Goodwill A/c	4,000	3,000	2,000	By Balance b/d	21,600	16,200	10,800
To B's Capital A/c	2,145	—	1,815	By Revaluation A/c	1,200	900	600
To Adv. Exp. A/c	400	300	200	By Work. Comp. Res.	400	300	200
To Investments A/c	—	8,700	—	By Invest. Flu. Res.	400	300	200
To Bills Payable A/c	—	460	—	By Reserve A/c	2,400	1,800	1,200

To Bank A/c	—	7,000		By A's Capital A/c	—	2,145	—
To B's Loan A/c	—	4,000		By C's Capital A/c	—	1,815	—
To Balance c/d	19,455	—	8,985				
	26,000	23,460	13,000		26,000	23,460	13,000

BALANCE SHEET OF A AND C AS AT 31ST DEC., 2011

Liabilities		₹	*Assets*		₹
Expenses Owing		625	Cash at Bank		15,500
Trade Creditors	5,000		Sundry Debtors	5,000	
Less: Reserve	125	4,875	*Less:* Provision	250	4,750
Employees' Provident Fund		1,000	Mr X		350
Provision for Workmen's			Prepaid Insurance		2,000
Compensation claim		300	Stock	9,000	
Provision for Outstanding Legal			*Less:* Reserve	480	8,520
Charges		4,420	Land & Building		20,000
Bills Payable		460			
Loan from Bank		7,000			
6% B's Loan		4,000			
A's Capital		19,455			
C's Capital		8,985			
		51,120			51,120

Working Notes:

1. **Average Profits** = (₹ 3,520 + ₹ 6,600 + ₹ 7,700)/3 = ₹ 5,940
2. **Firm's Goodwill** = ₹ 5,940 × 2 = ₹ 11,880
3. **B's Share of Goodwill** = ₹ 11,880 × 3/9 = ₹ 3,960
4. *Alternatively:* Excess Workmen Compensation Reserve (i.e., ₹ 1,050) may directly be transferred to the Capital accounts of partners in their profit sharing ratio and accordingly the profit on revaluation will be reduced by ₹ 1,050.

PROBLEM 4

A, B and C were partners sharing profits and losses in the ratio of 5 : 3 : 2. On 31.12.2011, the Balance Sheet was as under:

Liabilities	₹	*Assets*	₹
Trade Creditors	26,500	Bank	20,000
Employees' Provident Fund	3,500	Debtors	30,000
Reserve	20,000	Stock	55,000
A's Capital	1,00,000	Fixed Assets	1,15,000
B's Capital	50,000	Goodwill	15,000
C's Capital	40,000	Advertisement Expenditure	5,000
	2,40,000		2,40,000

B retires on 1.1.2012. For the purpose, the following adjustments were agreed upon:

(a) That the goodwill be valued at 2 years' purchase of the average profits of 3 completed years preceding the date of retirement. The profits for previous years were: 2008 ₹ 45,000, 2009 ₹ 50,000, 2010 ₹ 55,000, 2011 ₹ 60,000.

(b) That Fixed Assets were found undervalued by ₹ 25,000.

(c) That Stock was found overvalued by ₹ 5,000.

(d) That the new profit sharing ratio of A and C will be 3 : 2

(e) That B be paid through cash brought in by A and C in such a way as to make their capitals proportionate. Minimum Bank Balance is to be maintained at ₹ 10,000.

(f) The partners decide that Goodwill is not to appear in the Balance Sheet of New Firm.

Required: Prepare Revaluation Account, Capital Account of Partners & the Balance Sheet of A & C.

SOLUTION

Dr. **REVALUATION ACCOUNT** *Cr.*

Particulars	₹	*Particulars*	₹
To Stock	5,000	By Fixed Assets	25,000
To Profit on Revaluation t/f to:			
A's Capital A/c (5/10)	10,000		
B's Capital A/c (3/10)	6,000		
C's Capital A/c (2/10)	4,000		
	25,000		25,000

Dr. **CAPITAL ACCOUNTS OF PARTNERS** *Cr.*

Particulars	*A (₹)*	*B (₹)*	*C (₹)*	*Particulars*	*A (₹)*	*B (₹)*	*C (₹)*
To B's Capital A/c	2,000	—	4,000	By Balance b/d	1,00,000	50,000	40,000
To Goodwill A/c	7,500	4,500	3,000	By Revaluation	10,000	6,000	4,000
To B's Capital A/c	9,000	—	18,000	By Reserve	10,000	6,000	4,000
To Adv. Exp. A/c	2,500	1,500	1,000	By A's Capital A/c	—	11,000	—
To Balance c/d	99,000	89,000	22,000	By C's Capital A/c	—	22,000	—
	1,20,000	95,000	48,000		1,20,000	95,000	48,000
To Bank A/c	—	89,000	—	By Balance b/d	99,000	89,000	22,000
To Balance b/d	1,20,000	—	80,000	By Bank A/c	21,000	—	58,000
	1,20,000	89,000	80,000		1,20,000	89,000	80,000

BALANCE SHEET OF A AND C AS AT 1ST JAN., 2012

Liabilities	₹	*Assets*		₹
A's Capital	1,20,000	Fixed Assets		1,40,000
C's Capital	80,000	Stock	55,000	
Sundry Creditors	26,500	*Less:* Reserve	5,000	50,000
Employees' Provident Fund	3,500	Debtors		30,000
		Bank		10,000
	2,30,000			2,30,000

Working Notes:

1. **Average Profits** = (₹ 50,000 + ₹ 55,000 + ₹ 60,000)/3 = ₹ 55,000
2. **Firm's Goodwill** = ₹ 55,000 × 2 = ₹ 1,10,000
3. **B's Share of Goodwill** = ₹ 1,10,000 × 3/10 = ₹ 33,000
4. **Shortage of Cash** = ₹ 89,000 – ₹ 10,000 (i.e. ₹ 20,000 — ₹ 10,000) = ₹ 79,000
5. **Total Capital of New Firm** = ₹ 99,000 + ₹ 22,000 + ₹ 79,000 = ₹ 2,00,000
6. **A's New Capital** = ₹ 2,00,000 × 3/5 = ₹ 1,20,000,

   C's New Capital ₹ 2,00,000 × 2/5 = ₹ 80,000.

PROBLEM 5

The Balance Sheet to A, B and C who were sharing profits in proportion in their capitals stood as follows as on 31st Dec., 2011.

Liabilities	₹	*Assets*		₹
Expenses Owing	900	Goodwill		9,000
Trade Creditors	5,000	Cash at Bank		15,500
Employees' Provident Fund	1,000	Sundry Debtors	5,000	
Reserve Fund	5,400	*Less:* Provision	100	4,900
Workmen Compensation Reserve	1,200	Stock		9,000
Investment Fluctuation Fund	1,900	Investments [Market value ₹ 8,700]		9,700
A's Capital	21,600	Land and Building		15,000
B's Capital	16,200	Advertisement Expenditure		900
C's Capital	10,800			
	64,000			64,000

B retires on 31.12.2011, and the following readjustments of the assets and liabilities have been agreed upon before the ascertainment of the amount payable to B:

(a) That the Stock be written down to ₹ 8,520.

(b) That the provision for doubtful debts be brought upto 5% on debtors.

(c) That the Land and Building be written up by ₹ 5,000.

(d) That a provision of ₹ 4,420 be made in respect of outstanding legal charges.

(e) That out of the amount of insurance which was debited entirely to P & L A/c, ₹ 2,000 be carried forward as an unexpired insurance.

(f) That Expenses owing to be brought down to ₹ 625.

(g) That Trade Creditors agree to allow a discount of 2½%.

(h) That 'X' an old customer whose account was written off as bad had promised in writing to pay ₹ 350 in settlement of his full debt of ₹ 500.

(i) That claim on account of workmen's compensation is estimated at ₹ 300.

(j) That A and C are going to share in future in the proportion of five eighths and three eighths respectively.

(k) That the goodwill is to be valued at 2 years' purchase of the average profits of 3 completed years preceding the date of retirement. The profits for 2007 ₹ 3,000, for 2008 ₹ 3,520, for 2009 ₹ 6,600, for 2010, ₹ 7,700, 2011 ₹ 8,000. No goodwill account is to be raised.

(l) That the investments are taken over by B at market value.

(m) B is to be paid through Cash brought in by A and C in such a way as to make their capitals proportionate to their new profit sharing ratio subject to the condition that a bank balance of ₹ 10,000 is to be maintained.

Required: Pass the necessary journal entries, Prepare Partners' Capital Accounts and the Balance Sheet after B's retirement:

SOLUTION

JOURNAL

Particulars		*L.F.*	*Dr. (₹)*	*Cr. (₹)*
Revaluation A/c	Dr.		5,050	
To Stock Reserve A/c				480
To Provision for Doubtful Debts A/c				150
To Provision for Outstanding Legal Charges A/c				4,420
(Being the fall in value of assets and increase in amt. of pro. recorded)				
Land & Building	Dr.		5,000	
Prepaid Insurance	Dr.		2,000	
Expenses Owing	Dr.		275	
Reserve for Discount on Trade Creditors	Dr.		125	
Mr. X	Dr.		350	
To Revaluation A/c				7,750
(Being the increase in value of assets, decrease in liabilities and Reserve for discount on creditors recorded)				
Revaluation A/c	Dr.		2,700	
To A's Capital A/c				1,200
To B's Capital A/c				900
To C's Capital A/c				600
(Being the transfer of profit on revaluation to all partners in their profit sharing ratio of 4 : 3 : 2)				
Workmen Compensation Reserve	Dr.		1,200	
To Provision for Workmen Compensation Claim A/c				300
To A's Capital A/c				400
To B's Capital A/c				300
To C's Capital A/c				200
(Being provision made for workmen compensation and surplus Workmen Compensation reserve transferred)				
Investment Fluctuation Reserve A/c	Dr.		1,900	
To Investments A/c				1,000
To A's Capital A/c				400
To B's Capital A/c				300
To C's Capital A/c				200
(Being investments brought down to its market value and surplus t/f to capital a/cs)				

Reserve Fund Dr.		5,400	
To A's Capital A/c			2,400
To B's Capital A/c			1.800
To C's Capital A/c			1,200
(Being the transfer of reserve to all partners in their profit sharing ratio of 4 : 3 : 2)			
A's Capital A/c Dr.		400	
B's Capital A/c Dr.		300	
C's Capital A/c Dr.		200	
To Advertisement Expenditure A/c			900
(Being the transfer of Advertisement Expenditure to all partners in their profit sharing ratio of 4 : 3 : 2)			
A's Capital A/c Dr.		4,000	
B's Capital A/c Dr.		3,000	
C's Capital A/c Dr.		2,000	
To Goodwill A/c			9,000
(Being the existing book value of Goodwill w/o)			
A's Capital A/c Dr.		2,145	
C's Capital A/c Dr.		1,815	
To B's Capital A/c			3,960
(Being share of goodwill credited to B and debited to the remaining partners in their gaining ratio which is 13 : 11)			
B's Capital A/c Dr.		20,160	
To Investments A/c			8,700
To Bank A/c			11,460
(Being B's Claim discharged)			
Bank A/c Dr.		5,960	
To A's Capital A/c			2,045
To C's Capital A/c			3,915
(Being the additional cash brought In by remaining partners)			

Dr. **CAPITAL ACCOUNTS OF PARTNERS** *Cr.*

Particulars	*A (₹)*	*B (₹)*	*C (₹)*	*Particulars*	*A (₹)*	*B (₹)*	*C (₹)*
To Goodwill A/c	4,000	3,000	2,000	By Balance b/d	21,600	16,200	10,800
To B's Capital A/c	2,145	—	1,815	By Revaluation A/c	1,200	900	600
To Adv. Exp. A/c	400	300	200	By Work. Com. Res.	400	300	200
To Investments A/c	—	8,700	—	By Invest. Fluc. Res.	400	300	200
To Balance c/d	19,455	11,460	8,985	By Reserve A/c	2,400	1,800	1,200
				By A's Capital A/c	—	2,145	—
				By C's Capital A/c	—	1,815	—
	26,000	23,460	13,000		26,000	23,460	13,000

To Bank A/c	—	11,460	—	By Balance b/d	19,455	11,460	8,985
To Balance c/d	21,500	—	12,900	By Bank A/c (b.f.)	2,045	—	3,915
	21,500	11,460	12,900		21,500	11,460	12,900

BALANCE SHEET OF A AND C AS AT 31ST DEC., 2011

Liabilities		₹	*Assets*		₹
Expenses Owing		625	Cash at Bank		10,000
Trade Creditors	5,000		Sundry Debtors	5,000	
Less: Reserve	125	4,875	*Less:* Provision	250	4,750
Employees Provident Fund		1,000	Mr X		350
Provision for Workmen Compensation Claim		300	Prepaid Insurance		2,000
			Stock	9,000	
Provision for Outstanding Legal Charges			*Less:* Reserve	480	8,520
			Land & Building		20,000
Legal Charges		4,420			
A's Capital		21,500			
C's Capital		12,900			
		45,620			45,620

Working Notes:

1. **Shortage of Cash** = ₹ 11,460 – ₹ 5,500 (i.e. ₹ 15,500 — ₹ 10,000) = ₹ 5,960
2. **Total Capital of New Firm** = ₹ 19,455 + ₹ 8,985 + ₹ 5,960 = ₹ 34,400
3. **A's New Capital** = ₹ 34,400 × 5/8 = ₹ 21,500,

   C's New Capital = ₹ 34,400 × 3/8 = ₹ 12,900

PROBLEM 6

X and Y are partners. The partnership deed provides as under:

(a) That the account be balanced on 31st Dec. each year.

(b) That the profit be divided as follows: X one half, Y one third and carried to a Reserve Account one sixth.

(c) That in the event of the death of a partner, his executors be entitled to be paid out:

(i) The capital to his credit.

(ii) His proportion of profit to the date of death based on the average of profits of the last 3 completed years immediately preceding the year of death.

(iii) By way of goodwill, his proportion of total profits for 3 preceding years.

(iv) Interest on Capital @ 3% p.a.

His drawings are to bear interest at an average rate of 2% on the amount. Their Balance Sheet as on 31.12.2011 were as under:

Liabilities	₹	*Assets*	₹
X's Capital	9,000	Fixed Assets	15,000
Y's Capital	6,000	Investments	5,000

Reserve	4,000	Current Assets	1,000
Creditors	3,000	Advertisement Expenditure	1,000
	22,000		22,000

The profit for 2008 ₹ 1,000, 2009 ₹ 4,200, 2010 ₹ 3,900, 2011 ₹ 4,500. Y died on 1st May 2012. His drawings in 2012 amounted to ₹ 1,000.

On 1st May, 2012, the Investments of the firm were sold for ₹ 10,000 and proceeds were given to executors. Prepare Y's Capital Account and Y's Executors' Account.

SOLUTION

Dr. **Y'S CAPITAL ACCOUNT** *Cr.*

Particulars	₹	*Particulars*	₹
To Drawings	1,000	By Balance b/d	6,000
To Interest on Drawings		By Reserve (₹ 4,000 × 2/5)	1,600
(2% of ₹ 1,000)	20	By P & L Suspense A/c	560
To Adv. Exp. [₹ 1,000 × 2/5]	400	(share of profits)	
To Y's Executors' A/c	13,840	By X's Capital A/c (share of goodwill)	5,040
		By Interest on Capital	
		[6,000 × 3/100 × 4/12]	60
		By Revaluation A/c (₹ 5,000 × 2/5)	2,000
	15,260		15,260

Dr. **Y'S EXECUTORS' ACCOUNT** *Cr.*

Particulars	₹	*Particulars*	₹
To Bank A/c	10,000	By Y's Capital A/c	13,840
To Balance c/d	3,840		
	13,840		13,840

Working Notes:

1. **Ratio between X and Y** = 1/2 : 1/3 = 3 : 2

2. CALCULATION OF Y'S SHARE OF GOODWILL

	Particulars	₹
A.	Total Profits for previous three years	12,600
B.	Y's Share of Goodwill (₹ 12,600 × 2/5)	5,040

3. CALCULATION OF Y'S SHARE OF PROFITS

	Particulars	₹
A.	Total Profits for previous three years	12,600
B.	Average Profits (₹ 12,600/3)	4,200
C.	Profit from 1.1.20X5 to 30.4.20X5 (₹ 4,200 × 4/12)	1,400
D.	Y's Share of Profits (₹ 1,400 × 2/5)	560

4. CALCULATION OF Y'S SHARE OF MATURED POLICIES

Particulars	₹
A. Sum Assured of Joint Life Policy	75,000
B. Sum Assured of Individual Life Policy	7,500
C. Total Sum Assured of Matured Policies (A + B)	82,500
D. Y's Share of Matured policies (₹ 82,500 × 2/5)	33,000

5. CALCULATION OF Y'S SHARE IN SURRENDER VALUE OF UNMATURED POLICY

Particulars	₹
A. Surrender value of X's individual life policy (50% of ₹ 15,000)	7,500
B. Y's share (₹ 7,500 × 2/5)	3,000

PROBLEM 7

The Balance Sheet of A, B and C who are sharing profits in the ratio of 2:3:1, as at 31st March, 2012 is given below:

Liabilities	₹	Assets	₹
A's Capital	1,00,000	Goodwill	12,000
B's Capital	2,00,000	Land and Building	2,50,000
C's Capital	3,00,000	Investments [Market Value ₹ 46,000]	50,000
Workmen Compensation Reserve	20,000	Stock	80,000
Investment Fluctuation Reserve	10,000	Debtors	3,00,000
Provision for Doubtful Debts	10,000	Bank	2,96,000
Creditors	3,60,000	Advertisement Suspense A/c	12,000
	10,00,000		10,00,000

C dies on 1st April, 2012 and A and B decide to share future profits & losses in the ratio of 3:2 and 50% is to be paid immediately and the balance in two equal annual instalments together with interest @ 10% p.a.

1. Goodwill is to be valued at 2 years' purchase of average profits of last three completed years. The profits were - 2009-2010 ₹ 45,000, 2010-2011 ₹ 90,000, 2011-2012 ₹ 1;35,000.
2. Land & Building was found under valued by ₹ 25,000 and Stock was found overvalued by ₹ 8,000.
3. Provision for doubtful debts is to be made equal to 5% of the debtors.
4. Claim on account of workmen compensation is ₹ 8,000. Pass the necessary journal entries and prepare the necessary ledger accounts and the Balance Sheet.

SOLUTION

JOURNAL

Date	Particulars		L.F.	Dr. (₹)	Cr. (₹)
(1)	A's Capital A/c	Dr.		4,000	
	B's Capital A/c	Dr.		6,000	
	C's Capital A/c	Dr.		2,000	

	To Goodwill A/c (Being the existing goodwill w/o)			12,000
(2)	A's Capital A/c (₹ 1,80,000 × 8/30) To B's Capital (₹ 1,80,000 × 3/30) To C's Capital A/c (₹ 1,80,000 × 5/30) (Being the goodwill adjusted by debiting gaining partner (A for 8/30) and crediting Sacrificing partners (B for 3/30) and (C for 1/6)]	Dr.	48,000	 18,000 30,000
(3)	Land & Building A/c To Revaluation A/c (Being the increase in value of assets recorded)	Dr.	25,000	 25,000
(4)	Revaluation A/c To Stock A/c To Provision for Doubtful Debts A/c (Being the decrease in Value of assets & increase in provisions recorded)	Dr.	13,000	 8,000 5,000
(5)	Revaluation A/c To A's Capital A/c To B's Capital A/c To C's Capital A/c (Being the transfer of profit on revaluation)	Dr.	12,000	 4,000 6,000 2,000
(6)	Workmen Compensation Reserve A/c To Workmen Compensation Claim A/c To A's Capital A/c To B's Capital A/c To C's Capital A/c (Being the transfer of workmen compensation Reserve)	Dr.	20,000	 8,000 4,000 6,000 2,000
(7)	Investment Fluctuation Fund A/c To Investment A/c To A's Capital A/c To B's Capital A/c To C's Capital A/c (Being the transfer of Investment Fluctuation Fund)	Dr.	10,000	 4,000 2,000 3,000 1,000
(8)	A's Capital A/c B's Capital A/c C's Capital A/c To Advertisement Suspense A/c (Being the t/f of balance of Advertisement Suspense A/c)	Dr. Dr. Dr.	4,000 6,000 2,000	 12,000
(9)	C's Capital A/c To C's Executors' A/c (Being the balance in C's Capital t/f to Executor's A/c)	Dr.	3,31,000	 3,31,000

(10)	C's Executors A/c	Dr.	1,65,500	
	To Bank A/c			1,65,500
	(Being 50% paid to C's Executors)			

Ledger Accounts:

Dr. **1. REVALUATION ACCOUNT** *Cr.*

Particulars	₹	*Particulars*	₹
To Stock	8,000	By Land & Building	25,000
To Provision for Doubtful Debts	5,000		
To Profit on Revaluation t/f to:			
A	4,000		
B	6,000		
C	2,000		
	25,000		25,000

Dr. **2. PARTNERS' CAPITAL ACCOUNTS** *Cr.*

Particulars	*A (₹)*	*B (₹)*	*C (₹)*	*Particulars*	*A (₹)*	*B (₹)*	*C (₹)*
To Goodwill A/c	4,000	6,000	2,000	By Balance b/d	1,00,000	2,00,000	3,00,000
To B's Capital A/c	18,000	—	—	By A's Capital A/c	—	18,000	30,000
To C's Capital A/c	30,000	—	—	By Revaluation A/c	4,000	6,000	2,000
To Adv. Exp. Sus. A/c	4,000	6,000	2,000	By Work Com. Res.	4,000	6,000	2,000
To C's Executors' A/c	—	—	3,31,000	By Invest. Flus. Res.	2,000	3,000	1,000
To Balance c/d	54,000	2,21,000	—				
	1,10,000	2,33,000	3,35,000		1,10,000	2,33,000	3,35,000

3. BALANCE SHEET AS AT 31ST MARCH, 2012

Liabilities	₹	*Assets*		₹
A's Capital	54,000	Land & Building		2,75,000
B's Capital	2,21,000	Investments		46,000
C's Executors'	1,65,500	Stock		72,000
Creditors	3,60,000	Debtors	3,00,000	
Workmen Compensation Claim	8,000	*Less:* Provision	15,000	2,85,000
		Bank		1,30,500
	8,08,500			8,08,500

Working Notes:

1. CALCULATION OF GAIN/SACRIFICE OF SHARE

Particulars	*New Share*	*Old Share*	*Difference*
A.	3/5	2/6	3/5 – 2/6 = 8/30
B.	2/5	3/6	2/5 – 3/6 = – 3/30

2 Calculation of Goodwill

A. Average Profits = $\frac{₹\,45,000 + ₹\,90,000 + ₹\,1,35,000}{3}$ = ₹ 90,000

B. Firm's Goodwill = ₹ 90,000 × 2 = ₹ 1,80,000

PROBLEM 8

A, B and C were partners sharing profits and losses in the ratio of 5 : 3 : 2. On 31st December, 2011 their Balance Sheet was as follows:

Liabilities	₹	*Assets*	₹
Sundry Creditors	11,000	Goodwill	5,000
Investment Fluctuation Reserve	3,500	Patents	26,000
Workmen Compensation Reserve	3,500	Machinery	31,200
A's Capital	67,500	Investments	3,000
B's Capital	47,500	Stock	10,000
C's Capital	37,000	Sundry Debtors	12,000
		Loan to C	1,000
		Cash at Bank	5,800
		Advertisement Expenditure	1,000
		Profit & Loss A/c (2011)	75,000
	1,70,000		1,70,000

C died on 1st May, 2012. C has withdrawn ₹ 5,000 during 2012. It was agreed between his executors and the remaining partners that:—

(a) Goodwill be valued at 2-1/2 years' purchase of average of four completed years' profits which were: 2008 ₹ 1,01,000; 2009 ₹ 14,000; 2010 ₹ 16,000.

(b) C's Share of profit from the closure of last accounting year till date of death be calculated on the basis of the average of three completed years' profits before death.

(c) Patents undervalued by ₹ 17,000; Machinery overvalued by ₹ 3,200.

(d) Investments be sold for ₹ 4,200 and a sum of ₹ 5,200 be paid to C's Executors immediately. The remainder to be paid in four equal half-yearly instalments together with interest @ 10% p.a. at half-yearly rest.

You are required:

(a) to give the necessary journal entries to be passed on C's death;

(b) to prepare the Capital Accounts of all the partners;

(c) to prepare the Balance Sheet of A and B immediately after C's death;

(d) to prepare C's Executor's Account till it is finally settled.

SOLUTION

JOURNAL

Date	*Particulars*		*L.F.*	*Dr. (₹)*	*Cr. (₹)*
1.	A's Capital A/c	Dr.		2,500	
	B's Capital A/c	Dr.		1,500	
	C's Capital A/c	Dr.		1,000	

	To Goodwill A/c (Being the existing goodwill written off)			5,000
2.	A's Capital A/c [₹ 7,000 × 5/8] B's Capital A/c [₹ 7,000 × 3/8] To C's Capital A/c [₹ 35,000 × 2/10] (Being C's share of goodwill adjusted)	Dr. Dr.	4,375 2,625	 7,000
3.	C's Capital A/c To Profit & Loss Suspense A/c (Being C's share of loss to date of death recorded)	Dr.	1,000	 1,000
4.	Investment Fluctuation Reserve Workmen Compensation Reserve To A's Capital A/c To B's Capital A/c To C's Capital A/c (Being the transfer of reserves)	Dr. Dr.	3,500 3,500	 3,500 2,100 1,400
5.	A's Capital A/c B's Capital A/c C's Capital A/c To Advertisement Expenditure A/c (Being the transfer of Advertisement Expenditure)	Dr. Dr. Dr.	500 300 200	 1,000
6.	A's Capital A/c B's Capital A/c C's Capital A/c To Profit & Loss A/c (Being the transfer of Accumulated Loss)	Dr. Dr. Dr.	37,500 22,500 15,000	 75,000
7.	Revaluation A/c To Machinery A/c (Being the decrease in value of asset recorded)	Dr.	3,200	 3,200
8.	Patents A/c To Revaluation A/c (Being the increase in value of assets recorded)	Dr.	17,000	 17,000
9.	Revaluation A/c To A's Capital A/c To B's Capital A/c To C's Capital A/c (Being the transfer of profit on revaluation)	Dr.	13,800	 6,900 4,140 2,760
10.	Bank A/c To Investments A/c (Being the investments sold)	Dr.	4,200	 4,200

			Dr.	Cr.
11.	Investments A/c	Dr.	1,200	
	To A's Capital A/c			600
	To B's Capital A/c			360
	To C's Capital A/c			240
	(Being the profit on sale of investments transferred)			
12.	C's Capital A/c	Dr.	1,000	
	To Loan to C A/c			1,000
	(Being the transfer of Loan to C A/c to his capital A/c)			
13.	C's Capital A/c	Dr.	25,200	
	To C's Executors' A/c			25,200
	(Being the transfer of C's Capital A/c to his executors' A/c)			
14.	C's Executors' A/c	Dr.	5,200	
	To Bank A/c			5,200
	(Being partial payment made to C's Executors)			

Dr. **CAPITAL ACCOUNTS OF PARTNERS** Cr.

Particulars	A (₹)	B (₹)	C (₹)	Particulars	A (₹)	B (₹)	C (₹)
To Bank A/c	—	—	5,000	By Balance b/d	67,500	47,500	37,000
To Goodwill A/c	2,500	1,500	1,000	By Revaluation A/c	6,900	4,140	2,760
To P & L A/c	37,500	22,500	15,000	By A's Capital A/c	—	—	4,375
To C's Capital A/c	4,375	2,625	—	By B's Capital A/c	—	—	2,625
To P & L Suspense A/c	—	—	1,000	By Invest. F. Res.	1,750	1,050	700
To Loan to C A/c	—	—	1,000	By Work. Comp. Res.	1,750	1,050	700
To Adv. Exp.	500	300	200	By Investments A/c	600	360	240
To C's Executors' A/c	—	—	25,200				
To Balance c/d	33,625	27,175	—				
	78,500	54,100	48,400		78,500	54,100	48,400

BALANCE SHEET OF A AND B AS AT 1ST MAY 2012

Liabilities	₹	Assets	₹
Sundry Creditors	11,000	Patents	43,000
C's Executors' Account	20,000	Machinery	28,000
A's Capital	33,625	Stock	10,000
B's Capital	27,175	Sundry Debtors	12,000
P & L Suspense A/c	1,000		
Bank Overdraft	200		
	93,000		93,000

Dr. **C'S EXECUTORS' ACCOUNT** Cr.

Date	Particulars	₹	Date	Particulars	₹
01.05.12	To Bank A/c	5,200	01.05.12	By C's Capital A/c	25,200

31.10.12	To Bank A/c (5,000 + 1,000)	6,000	31.10.12	By Interest A/c [20,000 × 10/100 × 6/12]	1,000
31.10.12	To Balance c/d	15,000			
		26,200			26,200
31.12.12	To Balance c/d	15,250	01.11.12	By Balance b/d	15,000
			31.12.12	By Interest A/c (Accrued) [15,000 × 10/100 × 2/12]	250
		15,250			15,250
30.04.13	To Bank A/c (5000 + 250 + 500)	5,750	01.01.13	By Balance b/d	15,250
30.04.13	To Balance c/d	10,000	30.04.13	By Interest A/c [15,000 × 10/100 × 4/12]	500
		15,750			15,750
31.10.13	To Bank A/c (5,000 + 500)	5,500	01.05.13	By Balance b/d	10,000
31.10.13	To Balance c/d	5,000	31.10.13	By Interest A/c [10,000 × 10/100 × 6/12]	500
		10,500			10,500
31.12.13	To Balance c/d	5,083	01.11.13	By Balance b/d	5,000
			31.12.13	By Interest A/c (Accured) [5,000 × 10/100 × 2/12]	83
		5,083			5,083
30.4.14	To Bank A/c [5,000 + 83 + 167]	5,250	01.01.14	By Balance b/d	5,083
			30.04.14	By Interest A/c [5,000 × 10/100 × 4/12]	167
		5,250			5,250

Working Notes:

1. **C's Share of Goodwill**

   Firm's Goodwill = [(1,01,000 + 14,000 + 16,000 – 75,000)/4] × 2.5 = ₹ 35,000

   C's Share of Goodwill = ₹ 35,000 × 2/10 = ₹ 7,000

2. **C's Share of Profit (Loss) till date of death**

   Average Profit (Loss) of Last 3 years = (14,000 + 16,000 – 75,000)/3 = (₹ 15,000)

   C's Share of Loss = (₹ 15,000) × 4/12 × 2/10 = (₹ 1,000)

Dr. **3. BANK ACCOUNT** *Cr.*

Particulars	₹	*Particulars*	₹
To Balance b/d	5,800	By C's Capital A/c (Drawings)	5,000
To Investments	4,200	By C's Executors' A/c	5,200
To Balance c/d (b.f.)	**200**		
	10,200		10,200

SOLVED PROBLEMS

PROBLEM 1

Wise, Clever and Dull were trading in partnership sharing profits and losses in the ratio of 4 : 3 : 3 respectively. The accounts of the firm made up to 31st December every year. The partnership provided, inter alia, that :

On the death of a partner, the goodwill was to be valued at three years' purchase of average profits of three years upto the date of death after deducting interest @ 8per cent on capital employed and a fair remuneration of each partner. The profits are assumed to be earned evenly throughout the year.

On 30th June, 20X4, Wise died and it was agreed on his death to adjust goodwill in the capital accounts without showing any amount of goodwill in the Balance Sheet. For the purpose of valuation of goodwill, the fair remuneration for work by each partner would be ₹ 15,000 per annum and that the capital employed would be ₹ 1,56,000. Clever and Dull were to continue the partnership, sharing profits and losses equally after death of wise. The following were the amount of profits of earlier years before charging interest on capital employed.

20X1 ₹ 67,200, 20X2 ₹ 75,600, 20X3 ₹ 72,000, 20X4 ₹ 62,400

Required: Compute the value of goodwill and show the adjustment thereof in the books of the firm.

SOLUTION

(i) Average Profit for three years, ending 30th June before death:

Profit for the Year ending 30th June, 20X2 = 1/2 of 20X1 + 1/2 of 20X2
= ₹ 33,600 + ₹ 37,800 = ₹ 71,400

Profit for the Year ending 30th June, 20X3 = 1/2 of 20X2 + 1/2 of 20X3
= ₹ 37,800 + ₹ 36,000 = ₹ 73,800

Profit for the Year ending 30th June, 20X4 = 1/2 of 20X3 + 1/2 of 20X4
= ₹ 36,000 + ₹ 31,200 = ₹ 67,200

(a) Total Profits for 3 years = ₹ 2,12,400

(b) Average Profits (₹ 2,12,400/3) = ₹ 70,800

(ii) Super Profit = Average Profit – Partner's remuneration – 8% on Capital employed
= ₹ 70,800 – ₹ 45,000 – ₹ 12,480 = ₹ 13,320

(iii) Goodwill @ three years' Purchase (13,320 × 3) = ₹ 39,960

Adjusting Entry for Goodwill:

JOURNAL

Particulars		*L.F.*	*Dr. (₹)*	*Cr. (₹)*
Clever's Capital A/c	Dr.		7,992	
Dull's Capital A/c	Dr.		7,992	
To Wise's Capital A/c				15,984
(Being Wise's share of goodwill adjusted in the capital accounts of gain partners in their gaining ratio of 1 : 1)				

PROBLEM 2

On 31st March, 20X2, the Balance Sheet of M/s A, B & C sharing profits and losses in proportionate to their capitals stood as follows:

Liabilities	₹	*Assets*	₹
Capital Accounts:		Land and Buildings	2,00,000
A	2,00,000	Machinery	3,00,000
B	3,00,000	Closing Stock	1,00,000
C	2,00,000	Sundry Debtors	1,00,000
Sundry Creditors	1,00,000	Cash and Bank Balances	1,00,000
	8,00,000		8,00,000

On 31st March, 20X2, A desired to retire from the firm and the remaining partners decided to carry on. It was agreed to revalue the Assets and Liabilities on the date on the following basis:

(a) Land & Buildings be appreciated by 30% (b) Machinery the depreciated by 20%. (c) Closing stock to be valued at ₹ 75,000. (d) Provision for doubtful debts be made at 5%. (e) Old credit balances of Sundry Creditors ₹ 20,000 be written back. (f) Joint Life Policy of the partners surrendered and cash obtained ₹ 80,000. (g) Goodwill of the entire firm be valued at ₹ 1,40,000 and A's share of the Goodwill be adjusted in the accounts of B and C who share the future profits equally. No Goodwill Account being raised. (h) The total capital of the firm is to be the same as before retirement. Individual capitals be in their profit sharing ratio. (i) Amount due to A is to be settled on the following basis: 50% on retirement and the balance 50% within one year.

Required: Prepare Revaluation Account, Capital Accounts of Partners, Cash Account and Balance Sheet as at 31st March, 20X2 of M/s B & C.

SOLUTION

Dr. **REVALUATION ACCOUNT** *Cr.*

Particulars	₹	*Particulars*	₹
To Machinery	60,000	By Land and Building	60,000
To Stock	25,000	By Creditors	20,000
To Provision for doubtful debts	5,000	By Loss on Revaluation t/f to:	
		A's Capital A/c	2,857
		B 's Capital A/c	4,286
		C 's Capital A/c	2,857
	90,000		90,000

Dr. **PARTNERS' CAPITAL ACCOUNTS** *Cr.*

Particulars	*A (₹)*	*B (₹)*	*C (₹)*	*Particulars*	*A (₹)*	*B (₹)*	*C (₹)*
To Revaluation A/c	2,857	4,286	2,857	By Balance c/d	2,00,000	3,00,000	2,00,000
To A (Goodwill)	—	10,000	30,000	By Insurance Co. A/c	22,857	34,286	22,857
To Cash A/c	1,30,000	—	—	By B (Goodwill)	10,000	—	—
To A's Loan A/c	1,30,000	—	—	By C (Goodwill)	30,000	—	—
To Balance c/d	—	3,50,000	3,50,000	By Cash A/c	—	30,000	1,60,000
	2,62,857	3,64,286	3,82,857		2,62,857	3,64,286	3,82,857

Dr. **CASH AND BANK ACCOUNT** *Cr.*

Particulars	₹	*Particulars*	₹
To Balance b/d	1,00,000	By A's Capital A/c	1,30,000

To Insurance Co (Joint Life Policy)	80,000	By Balance c/d	2,40,000
To B 's Capital A/c	30,000		
To C 's Capital A/c	1,60,000		
	3,70,000		3,70,000

BALANCE SHEET OF B AND C AS ON 31ST MARCH, 20X2

Liabilities	₹	*Assets*		₹
B 's Capital	3,50,000	Land & Buildings		2,60,000
C 's Capital	3,50,000	Machinery		2,40,000
A's Loan	1,30,000	Stock		75,000
Creditors	80,000	Debtors	1,00,000	
		Less: Provision	5,000	95,000
		Cash & Bank Balance		2,40,000
	9,10,000			9,10,000

PROBLEM 3

Peter, Paul and Prince were partners sharing profits and losses in the ratio of 2 : 1 : 1. It was provided in the partnership deed that in the event of retirement/death of a partner, he/his legal representatives would be paid:

(a) The balance in the Capital Account.

(b) His share of Goodwill of the firm valued at two years' purchase of normal average profits (after charging interest on fixed capital) for the last three years up to 31st of December preceding his retirement *or* death.

(c) His share of profits from the beginning of the accounting year to the date of retirement *or* death, which shall be taken on proportionate basis of profits of the previous years as increased by 25%.

(d) Interest on Fixed Capital @ 10% p.a. though payable to the partners will not be payable in the year of death *or* retirement.

(e) All the assets are to be revalued on the date of retirement *or* death and the profit *or* loss to be debited/credited to Partners in the profit sharing ratio.

Peter died on 30th Sep., 20X4. The books of Account are closed on calendar year basis from 1st January to 31st December. The balance in the Fixed Capital Accounts as on 1st January, 20X4 were: Peter ₹ 10,000, Paul ₹ 5,000 and Prince ₹ 5,000. The balance in the Current Accounts as on 1st January, 20X4 were: Peter ₹ 20,000, Paul ₹ 10,000 and Prince ₹ 7,000. Drawings of Peter till 30th Sep. 20X4 ₹ 10,000. The Profits of the firm before charging interest on capital for the calendar years 20X1, 20X2 and 20X3 were ₹ 1,00,000, ₹ 1,20,000 and ₹ 1,50,000 respectively. The profits include the following abnormal items of credit:—

Particulars	*20X1*	*20X2*	*20X3*
Profit on sale of Assets	5,000	7,000	10,000
Insurance claim received	3,000		12,000

The firm has taken out a Joint Life Policy for ₹ 1,00,000. Besides, the partners had severally insured their lives for ₹ 50,000 each, the premium, in respect thereof being charged to the Profit and Loss Account. The surrender value of the Policies were 30% of the face value. On 30th June, 20X4, the firm received notice from the insurance company that the insurance premium in respect of a fire policy had been undercharged to the extent of ₹ 6,000 in the year 20X3 and the firm has to pay immediately. The revaluation of the assets indicate an upward revision in value of assets to the extent of ₹ 20,000. Prepare an account showing the amount due to Peter's legal representatives as on 30th September, 20X4 alongwith necessary workings.

SOLUTION

Dr. **PETER'S CURRENT ACCOUNT** *Cr.*

Particulars	₹	*Particulars*	₹
To Drawings	10,000.00	By Balance b/d	20,000.00
To Profit & Loss Adjustment A/c	3,000.00	By Paul A/c (Goodwill)	53,500
(Share in Pre. undercharged)		By Prince A/c (Goodwill)	53,500
To Peter's Executor's A/c	2,81,031.25	By Insurance Co.	
		(Share of Matured Policies)	75,000.00
		By Paul's Current A/c	7,500.00
		By Prince's Current A/c	7,500.00
		(Share of Unmatured Policies)	
		By Revaluation A/c	10,000.00
		By P & L Suspense A/c	67,031.25
		(Share of Profit)	
	2,94,031.25		2,94,031.25

Dr. **PETER'S EXECUTOR'S ACCOUNT** *Cr.*

Particulars	₹	*Particulars*	₹
To Balance c/d	2,91,031.25	By Peter's Capital A/c	10,000.00
		By Peter's Current A/c	2,81,031.25
	2,91,031.25		2,91,031.25

Working Notes:

1. CALCULATION OF PETER'S SHARE OF GOODWILL

	Particulars	*20X1* ₹	*20X2* ₹	*20X3* ₹
A	Profit as per Profit & Loss A/c	1,00,000	1,20,000	1,50,000
B	*Less:* Interest on Capital	2,000	2,000	2,000
C	*Less:* Insurance Premium	—	—	6,000
D	*Less:* Abnormal Items:			
	Profit on Sale of Assets	5,000	7,000	10,000
	Insurance Claim received	3,000	—	12,000
E	Adjusted Past Profits	90,000	1,11,000	1,20,000
F	Average Profits (₹ 90,000 + ₹ 1,11,000 + ₹ 1,20,000)/3 = ₹ 1,07,000			
G	Goodwill at 2 years' Purchases = (1,07,000 × 2) = ₹ 2,14,000			
H	Peter's Share (₹ 2,14,000 × 2/4) = ₹ 1,07,000			

2. CALCULATION OF PETER'S SHARE OF INSURANCE POLICIES

Sum Assured of Joint Life Policy of all Partners	₹ 1,00,000
Sum Assured of Individual Life Policy of Peter	₹ 50,000
Total Sum Assured of Matured Policies	₹ 1,50,000
Peter's Share (₹ 1,50,000 × 2/4)	₹ 75,000
Surrender Value of Policies of Paul & Prince: 30% of (₹ 50,000 + ₹ 50,000)	₹ 30,000
Peter's Share (₹ 30,000 × 2/4)	₹ 15,000

3. Calculation of Peter's Share of Profits

(a) Correct Profit for the year 20X3 = ₹ 1,50,000 – ₹ 6,000 – ₹ 1,000 (being Interest payable to other partners)

= ₹ 1,43,000

(b) Estimated Profit for 20X4 = 125% of ₹ 1,43,000 = ₹ 1,78,750

(c) Proportionate till 30.9.20X4 (₹ 1,78,750 × 9/12) = ₹ 1,34,062.50

(d) Peter's Share (₹ 1,34,062.50 × 2/4) = ₹ 67,031.25

4. Peter's Share of Profit on Revaluation of Assets = ₹ 20,000 × 2/4 = ₹ 10,000

5. Peter's share of Insurance Premium undercharged for the year 2013

= ₹ 6,000 × 2/4 = ₹ 3,000

PROBLEM 4

X, Y and Z were in partnership sharing profits and losses as one-half, one fourth and one-fourth respectively. It was agreed that interest should be allowed at the rate of 10% per annum on partners' capital accounts and charged at the rate of 8 per cent per annum on their drawings. No interest was to allowed *or* charged on current accounts.

The following are the particulars of their capital accounts, current accounts and drawings (as shown by the draft accounts):

Particulars	*Capital Account balance on 1.1.20X1* ₹	*Current Account balance on 1.1.20X1* ₹	*Drawings for year ended 31st Dec. 20X1* ₹	*Interest on Drawings* ₹
X	1,50,000 Cr.	20,000 Cr.	30,000	2,000
Y	80,000 Cr.	10,000 Cr.	20,000	760
Z	60,000 Cr.	10,000 Dr.	20,000	1,400

The draft accounts for the year up to 31st December, 20X1 showed a net profit of ₹ 1,20,000 before taking into account interest on partners' capital account balances and drawings. The audit of the draft accounts revealed the following errors:

(a) The rent of X's private house, amounting to ₹ 1,500 and paid on 31st December, 20X1 had been included in rents charged in profit and loss account.

(b) Repairs amounting to ₹ 20,000 had been treated as additions to machinery, depreciation on which had been charged at the rate of 20 per cent.

(c) The premium, amounting to ₹ 6,000, on Y's Life Insurance Policy, and paid on 30th June, 20X1 had been included as insurance charges in the profit and loss account.

Z retired from the partnership on 31st December, 20X1 and agreed to leave the amount due to him from the firm as a loan repayable by agreed instalments. X and Y agreed to continue in partnership, sharing profits and losses as two-third and one-third. In ascertaining the amount due to Z from the firm and for the purposes of the new partnership, it was agreed to make the following adjustments: (a) Goodwill to be valued at ₹ 1,44,000, but no account for goodwill to be raised in the books. (b) The value of freehold premises to be increased by ₹ 40,000. (c) The provision for doubtful debts to be increased by ₹ 12,000.

You are required to prepare (a). The Profit and Loss Appropriation account for the year ended 31st December 20X1, making all the necessary adjustments for the errors revealed, and (b) Partners' Capital and Current Accounts (in columnar form) for the year ended 31st December, 20X1 incorporating the adjustment on Z's retirement;

SOLUTION

STATEMENT SHOWING THE CALCULATION OF NET PROFIT FOR THE YEAR

	Particulars	₹
A	Amount as per draft accounts	1,20,000
B	*Add:* Rent of X wrongly charged	1,500
	Depreciation wrongly debited	4,000
	Premium on Y 's Life policy wrongly charged	6,000
		1,31,500
C	*Less:* Repairs previously capitalised	20,000
D	Net Profit (A + B – C)	1,11,500

PROFIT AND LOSS APPROPRIATION ACCOUNT

Dr. *for the year ending on 31st December, 20X1* *Cr.*

Particulars		₹	*Particulars*		₹
To Interest on Capital:			By Net Profit (as calculated above)		1,11,500
X		15,000	By Interest on Drawings:		
Y		8,000	X	2,000	
Z		6,000	Y (₹ 760 + ₹ 240)	1,000	
			Z	1,400	4,400
To Net Profit t/f to Current A/cs:					
X	43,450				
Y	21,725				
Z	21,725	86,900			
		1,15,900			1,15,900

Dr. **PARTNERS' CURRENT ACCOUNTS** *Cr.*

Particulars	*X* ₹	*Y* ₹	*Z* ₹	*Particulars*	*X* ₹	*Y* ₹	*Z* ₹
To Balance b/d	—	—	10,000	By Balance b/d	20,000	10,000	—
To Drawings	30,000	20,000	20,000	By Interest on Capital	15,000	8,000	6,000
To Rent of House	1,500	—	—	By Z 's Capital A/c	—	—	6,675
To Life Policy Premium	—	6,000	—	By P & L Appropriation A/c	43,450	21,725	21,725
To Interest on Drawings	2,000	1,000	1,400				

To Provision for Doubtful Debts	6,000	3,000	3,000				
To Balance c/d	38,950	9,725	—				
	78,450	39,725	34,400		78,450	39,725	34,400

Dr. **PARTNERS' CAPITAL ACCOUNTS** Cr.

Particulars	*X* ₹	*Y* ₹	*Z* ₹	*Particulars*	*X* ₹	*Y* ₹	*Z* ₹
To Z (Goodwill)	24,000	12,000	—	By Balance b/d	1,50,000	80,000	60,000
To Z 's Currrent A/c	—	—	6,675	By X (Goodwill)	—	—	24,000
To Z 's Loan Account	—	—	99,325	By Y (Goodwill)	—	—	12,000
To Balance c/d	1,46,000	78,000	—	By Freehold Premises	20,000	10,000	10,000
	1,70,000	90,000	1,06,000		1,70,000	90,000	1,06,000

PROBLEM 5

The Balance Sheet X & Y as at 31st March, 20X2 was as follows:

Liabilities	₹	*Assets*	₹
X 's Capital	32,000	Stock	56,000
Y 's Capital	29,000	Debtors	3,000
Creditors	6,000	Bank	8,000
	67,000		67,000

On the same date, X by agreement, retires and his son Z joins the firm for one-third share of profit. Sufficient money is to be introduced so as to enable X to be paid off and leave ₹ 4,000 in Bank. Y and Z are to provide such as to make their capitals proportionate to their shares of profit. X agrees to contribute from his capital half of the amount Z has to provide.

Required: Assuming that the agreement was carried out, show the necessary journal entries and prepare the Balance Sheet.

SOLUTION

JOURNAL

Particulars		*L.F.*	*Dr. (₹)*	*Cr. (₹)*
Bank A/c	Dr.		9,500	
X 's Capital A/c	Dr.		9,500	
To Z 's Capital A/c				19,000
(Being ₹ 9,500 transferred to Z 's A/c from X 's A/c and balance brought in by Z)				
Bank A/c	Dr.		9,000	
To Y 's Capital A/c				9,000
(Being the amount brought in by Y)				
X 's Capital A/c	Dr.		22,500	
To Bank A/c				22,500
(Being the amount paid to X)				

BALANCE SHEET OF Y AND Z AS AT 31ST MARCH, 20X2

Liabilities	₹	*Assets*	₹
Y 's Capital	38,000	Stock	56,000
Z 's Capital	19,000	Debtors	3,000
Sundry Creditors	6,000	Cash at Bank	4,000
	63,000		63,000

Working Notes:

1. **Total Capital of reconstituted firm** = Stock + Debtors + Bank – Creditors
   = ₹ 56,000 + ₹ 3,000 + ₹ 4,000 – ₹ 6,000 = ₹ 57,000
2. **Y's New Capital** = ₹ 57,000 × 2/3 = ₹ 38,000,
   Z's New Capital = ₹ 57,000 × 1/3 = ₹ 19,000

3. CALCULATION OF CASH TO BE BROUGHT IN BY Y AND Z

Particulars	*Y*	*Z*
(a) Their New Capitals	₹ 38,000	₹ 19,000
(b) Their Adjusted Old Capitals	₹ 29,000	
(c) Capital transferred from X's Capital A/c		₹ 9,500
(d) Amount to be brought in	₹ 9,000	₹ 9,500

PROBLEM 6

A, B and C are in partnership sharing profits and losses in the ratio of 2 : 3 : 5. A retires on 31st March 20X5 and D is admitted to partnership on the same date, the new profit sharing ratio between B, C and D being 2 : 3 : 1. Following is the Balance Sheet of A, B and C on 31st March, 20X5.

Liabilities	₹	*Assets*	₹
A's Capital	10,000	Land & Building	10,000
B 's Capital	15,000	Machinery	30,000
C 's Capital	20,000	Stock	20,000
General Reserve	40,000	Debtors	30,000
Loan from D	50,000	Cash in hand	2,000
Sundry Creditors	50,000	Cash at Bank	93,000
	1,85,000		1,85,000

D is admitted on the following terms:

(a) Machinery is to be depreciated by 10%, (b) Land and building is revalued at 300%, (c) Stock is to be written off to the extent of ₹ 5,000 (d) Provision @ 5% for Doubtful Debts is to be made. (e) General Reserve is to be apportioned among the partners. (f) The firm's goodwill is to be valued at two years' purchase profits for the last three financial years. The figures are: For 20X1-20X2 Profit ₹ 20,000, for 20X2-20X3 Loss ₹ 15,000, 20X3-20X4 Profit ₹ 40,000. (g) The amount due to A is to be retained in the business as loan. (h) D's Capital contribution should be 1/5th of the combined capital of B and C after making the above adjustments. D's share of capital will be transferred from his Loan A/c.

Required: Pass the necessary journal entries to give effect to the above.

SOLUTION

JOURNAL

Particulars		L.F.	Dr. (₹)	Cr. (₹)
Revaluation A/c	Dr.		9,500	
To Machinery A/c				3,000
To Stock A/c				5,000
To Provision for Doubtful Debts A/c				1,500
(Being the fall in value of assets recorded)				
Land & Building A/c	Dr.		20,000	
To Revaluation A/c				20,000
(Being an increase in value of assets recorded)				
Revaluation A/c	Dr.		10,500	
To A's Capital A/c				2,100
To B 's Capital A/c				3,150
To C 's Capital A/c				5,250
(Being the transfer of profit on revaluation)				
General Reserve A/c	Dr.		40,000	
To A's Capital A/c				8,000
To B 's Capital A/c				12,000
To C 's Capital A/c				20,000
(Being the transfer of general reserve)				
B 's Capital A/c	Dr.		1,000	
D 's Capital A/c	Dr.		5,000	
To A's Capital A/c				6,000
(Being the Goodwill Credited to A & debited to sacrificing partners)				
A's Capital A/c	Dr.		26,100	
To A's Loan A/c				26,100
(Being the transfer of A's capital A/c to his loan A/c)				
D's Loan A/c	Dr.		14,880	
To D 's Capital A/c				14,880
(Being the transfer of D 's Capital contribution on his admission, from his Loan Account)				

Working Notes:

1. CALCULATION OF VALUE OF GOODWILL

(a) Total Profit for previous three years	₹ 45,000
(b) Average Profit (₹ 45,000/3)	₹ 15,000
(c) Goodwill (₹ 15,000 × 2)	₹ 30,000

2. CALCULATION OF CAPITAL OF D

(a) Aggregate capital (after all other adjustments) of B and C	₹ 74,400
(b) D 's Capital (₹ 74,400 × 1/5)	₹ 14,880

PROBLEM 7

Jeet, Meet, and Reet were partners sharing profits and losses in the ratio of 2/5, 2/5 and 1/5. On 1st Jan. 20X1 their Balance Sheet stood as follows:

Liabilities	₹	*Assets*	₹
Creditors	40,000	Fixed Assets	1,00,000
Reserve	10,000	Stock	25,000
Capital Accounts:		Debtors	35,000
Jeet	50,000	Cash	10,000
Meet	40,000		
Reet	30,000		
	1,70,000		1,70,000

The firm had taken out a Joint Life Policy for ₹ 1,00,000 the premiums on which were charged to the Profit and Loss Accounts. On 1st July, 20X2 Reet died. His representatives agree that:

(a) Goodwill of the firm be valued at ₹ 50,000; (b) Fixed assets be written down by ₹ 10,000; and (c) In lieu of profits, upto his death, Reet should be paid interest at the rate of 25% p.a. on his capital as on 1st Jan. 20X1. The policy money was received on December 31, 20X1 and Reet's heirs were paid the total amount due to them. The accounts reveal that the firm had made a profit of ₹ 40,500 during the year after writing off ₹ 9,500 as depreciation on fixed assets (of which ₹ 5,000 was up to 1st July. 20X1). At the end of the year. the creditors had been reduced by ₹ 5,000 and debtors by ₹ 6,000 and stock had increased by ₹ 8,000 (as compared to the figures on 1st Jan, 20X1. The drawings of the partners were;

Particulars	*Up to 1st July 20X1* ₹	*After 1st July 20X1* ₹
Jeet	4,125	5,000
Meet	4,125	5,000
Reet	1,750	—

Required: Prepare the Balance Sheet of the firm as on 31st Dec, 20X1, assuming that remaining partners did not retain goodwill in their books.

SOLUTION

BALANCE SHEET OF JEET AND MEET AS ON 31ST DEC., 20X1

Liabilities	₹	*Assets*		₹
Sundry Creditors	35,000	Fixed Assets:	90,000	
Capital Accounts:		*Less:* Depreciation	9,500	80,500
Jeet	90,938	Current Assets:		
Meet	80,939	Stock		33,000
		Debtors		29,000

		Cash in hand	64,377
	2,06,877		2,06,877

Working Notes:

Dr. **(I) PROFIT & LOSS ACCOUNT FROM 1ST JAN, 20X2 TO 30TH JUNE, 20X1** Cr.

Particulars	₹	*Particulars*	₹
To Reet's Capital A/c		By Profit	20,000
(interest in lieu of profit)	3,750	[(₹ 40,500 + ₹ 9,500)/2 – ₹ 5,000]	
To Profit transferred to Capital A/cs:			
Jeet	8,125		
Meet	8,125		
	20,000		20,000

(II) PROFIT AND LOSS ACCOUNT OF JEET AND MEET

Dr. *from 1st july, 20X1 to 31st Dec, 20x1* Cr.

Particulars	₹	*Particulars*	₹
To Reet's Executors' A/c	6,623	By Profit	20,500
To Profit transferred to capital A/cs:		[(₹ 40,500 + ₹ 9,500)/2 – ₹ 4,500]	
Jeet	6,938		
Meet	6,939		
	20,500		20,500

Dr. **(III) CAPITAL ACCOUNTS (FROM 1.1.20X1 TO 30.6.20X1)** Cr.

Particulars	*Jeet* ₹	*Meet* ₹	*Reet* ₹	*Particulars*	*Jeet* ₹	*Meet* ₹	*Reet* ₹
To Reet	5,000	5,000	—	By Balance b/d	50,000	40,000	30,000
To Fixed Assets A/c	4,000	4,000	2,000	By Reserve	4,000	4,000	2,000
To Drawings A/c	4,125	4,125	1,750	By Jeet A/c	—	—	5,000
To Reet's Executor's A/c	—	—	42,000	By Meet A/c	—	—	5,000
To Balance c/d	49,000	39,000	—	By Profit & Loss A/c	8,125	8,125	3,750
	62,125	52,125	45,750		62,125	52,125	45,750

Dr. **(IV) CAPITAL ACCOUNTS (FROM 1.7.20X1 TO 31.12.20X1)** Cr.

Particulars	*Jeet* ₹	*Meet* ₹	*Reet's Ex* ₹	*Particulars*	*Jeet* ₹	*Meet* ₹	*Reet's Ex* ₹
To Drawings A/c	5,000	5,000	—	By Balance b/d	49,000	39,000	42,000
To Cash A/c	—	—	68,623	By Joint Life Policy	40,000	40,000	20,000
To Balance c/d	90,938	80,939	—	By Profit & Loss A/c	6,938	6,939	6,623
	95,938	85,993	68,623		95,938	85,993	68,623

Dr. **(V) CASH ACCOUNT** Cr.

Particulars	₹	*Particulars*	₹
To Balance b/d	10,000	By Reet's Executor's A/c	68,623

To Joint Life Policy	1,00,000	By Decrease in Sundry Creditors		5,000
To Profit *plus* Depreciation	50,000	By Increase in Stock		8,000
To Decrease in Debtors	6,000	By Drawings:		
		Jeet	9,125	
		Meet	9,125	
		Reet	1,750	20,000
		By Balance c/d		64,377
	1,66,000			1,66,000

Working Notes:

1. Capitals on 1st July, 20X1 have been ascertained without taking into account the Joint Life Policy (since the amount has not yet received) but after crediting the goodwill to all partners.
2. Profit for the year 20X1 has been segregated into two parts—profits before Reet's death and after Reet's death. Total profit for the year, before depreciation, is ₹ 40,500 + ₹ 9,500 *or* ₹ 50,000. It has also been assumed that profit is earned evenly throughout the year. Hence profit before depreciation upto 30th June, 20X1 is ₹ 25,000 and profit after depreciation for the same period is ₹ 20,000.
3. According to Sec. 37 of Indian Partnership Act 1932, Reet's executors have an option to claim either of the following two amounts:

   (a) Share of Profits $= \frac{\text{Reet's Capital on 1.7.20X1}}{\text{Total Capital of the firm on 1.7.20X1}} \times \text{Profit}$

   $= \frac{42,000}{1,30,000} \times 20,500 = ₹\ 6,623$

   (b) Interest = ₹ 42,000 × 6/100 × 6/12 = ₹ 1,260

   The remaining profit shall be shared by Jeet and Meet in their profit sharing ratio.
4. Cash Account is prepared on the assumption that:

   (a) Profit for the year is realised in cash; and

   (b) Increase in the value of assets and decrease in the value of liabilities mean reduction in cash and vice versa.

PROBLEM 8

Avinash, Basuda Ltd. and Chinmoy Ltd. were in partnership sharing profits and losses in the ratio of 9 : 4 : 2. Basuda Ltd. retired from the partnership on 31st March, 20X5, when the firm's balance sheet was as under:

₹ in thousands

Liabilities	₹	*Assets*	₹
Sundry Creditors	600	Cash and Bank	284
Capital accounts:		Sundry Debtors	400
Avinash	2,700	Stock	800
Basuda Ltd.	1,200	Furniture	266
Chinmoy Ltd.	600	Plant	850
		Land and Building	2,500
	5,100		5,100

Basuda Ltd.'s share in goodwill and capital was acquired by Avinash and Chinmoy Ltd. in the ratio of 1 : 3, the continuing partners bringing in the necessary finance to pay off Basuda Ltd. The partnership deed provides that on retirement *or* admission of a partner, the goodwill of the firm is to be valued at three times the average annual profits of the firm for the four years ended on the date of retirement *or* admission. The profits of the firm during the four years ended 31st March, 20X5 in thousands of rupees were:

20X1-20X2 ₹ 450, 20X2-20X3 ₹ 250, 20X3-20X4 ₹ 600, 20X4-20X5 ₹ 700.

The deed further provided that goodwill account is not to appear in the books of accounts at all.

The continuing partners agreed that with effect from 1st April, 20X5, Ghanashyam, son of Avinash is to be admitted as a partner with 25% share of profits and Capital of all partners are to b e in Profit sharing ratio.

Avinash gifts to Ghanashyam, by transfer from his capital account, an amount sufficient to cover up 12.5% of capital and goodwill requirement. The balance 12.5% of capital and goodwill requirement is purchased by Ghanashyam from Avinash and Chnimoy Ltd. in the ratio of 2 : 1.

The firm asks you to:

(i) Prepare a statement showing the continuing partners' shares;

(ii) Pass journal entries including for bank transactions; and

(iii) Prepare the balance sheet of the firm after Ghanshyam's admission.

SOLUTION

(I) STATEMENT SHOWING THE PARTNERS' SHARES

	Particulars	*Avinash Ltd.*	*Basuda Ltd.*	*Chinmoy*	*Ghanashyam*
I	Their existing shares	9/15	4/15	2/15	
II	Share acquired from retiring partner	(+)1/15	—	(+)3/15	
III	New ratio before admission of Ghanashyam [I + III]	10/15		5/15	
IV	Gift by Avinash (12.5/100)	(–)1/8			1/8
V	Purchase from Avinash & Chinmoy Ltd.	(–)2/24		(–)1/24	(+)3/24
VI	New Ratio [IV + V]	11/24		7/24	6/24

(II) JOURNAL

Date	*Particulars*		*L.F.*	*Dr. (₹)*	*Cr. (₹)*
31.03.2015	Avinash's Capital A/c	Dr.		1,00,000	
	Chinmoy Ltd.'s Capital A/c	Dr.		3,00,000	
	To Basuda Ltd.'s Capital A/c				1,00,000
	(Being purchase by Avinash and Chinmoy Ltd. of share from Basuda Ltd.)				
04.04.2015	Avinash's Capital A/c	Dr.		7,50,000	
	Bank A/c	Dr.		9,37,500	
	To Ghanashyam's Capital A/c				16,87,500
	(Being gift made by Avinash to G and remaining capital brought in by Ghanshyam)				

	Bank A/c	Dr.	16,00,000	
	To Avinash's Capital A/c			4,00,000
	To Chinmay Ltd.'s Capital A/c			12,00,000
	(Being continuing partners brought in the necessary finance to pay off Barmuda Ltd.)			
	Basuda Ltd.'s Capital A/c	Dr.	16,00,000	
	To Bank A/c			16,00,000
	(Being final payment made to Basuda Ltd. on retirement)			
	Ghanashyam's Capital A/c	Dr.	1,87,500	
	To Avinash's Capital A/c			1,25,000
	To Chinmoy Ltd.'s Capital A/c			62,500
	(Being goodwill credited to sacrificing partners for share purchaed in the ratio of 2 : 1)			
	Bank A/c	Dr.	15,00,000	
	To Avinash's Capital A/c			3,75,000
	To Chinmoy Ltd.'s Capital A/c			1,87,500
	To Ghanashyam's Capital A/c			9,37,500
	(Being capital brought in by the partners)			

(III) BALANCE SHEET AS AT 1ST APRIL, 20X5

Liabilities	₹	*Assets.*	₹
Sundry Creditors	6,00,000	Cash and Bank	17,84,000
Capital accounts:		Sundry Debtors	4,00,000
Avinash	27,50,000	Stock	8,00,000
Chinmoy Ltd.	17,50,000	Furniture	2,66,000
Ghanashyam	15,00,000	Plant	8,50,000
		Land and Building	25,00,000
	66,00,000		66,00,000

Working Notes:

(₹ in thousands)

1. **Adjustment of Goodwill on Retirement**

   Value of Goodwill = (450 + 250 + 600 + 700) × 3/4 = 1,500

   Share of Basuda Ltd. = 1,500 × 4/15 = 400

   Adjustment through partners' capital accounts

   Avinash: 1/4 × 400 = 100 (Dr.)

   Basuda Ltd.: 4/15 × 1500 = 400 (Cr.)

   Chinmoy Ltd.: 3/4 × 400 = 300 (Dr.)

2. **Closing Balances of Capital Accounts**

   A Adjusted old Capital of Continuing Partners 4,500

   B Total Capital of New firm = Adjujsted Old Capital + Incoming Partner's Capital

$X = 4,500 + 25\% \text{ of } X$

$(3/4)X = 4,500$

$X = 4,500 \times 4/3 = 6,000$

C New Capital of Partners: Avinash = ₹ 6,000 × 11/24 = ₹ 2,750,

Chinmay = ₹ 6,000 × 7/24 = ₹ 1,750

Ghanshyam = ₹ 6,000 × 6/24 = ₹ 1,500

3. Adjustment of Goodwill on Admission

Goodwill of the firm = 1,500

Total Share of Ghanshyam = 1500 × 1/4 = 375

Goodwill to be brought in share Purchased by Avinash = 375 × 1/2 = 187.5

Amount to be brought in by Ghanashyam = 750 + 187.50 = 937.50

(a) Gift by Avinash = 1/2 × 375 = 187.5
(included in the gift of 750 – see W.N. (ii)

(b) Purchase from Avinash and Chinmoy Ltd. = 187.5
(in 2 : 1 ratio)

Thus, adjustment of goodwill purchased through capital accounts

Avinash: 187.5 = 125 (Cr.)

Chinmoy Ltd.: 187.5 = 62.5 (Cr.)

Ghanashyam: 375 = 187.5 (Dr.)

4. Amount brought in by Partners

Dr. **PARTNERS' CAPITAL ACCOUNTS** *Cr.*

Particulars	*Avinash*	*Basuda*	*Chinmoy*	*Ghana-shyam*	*Particulars*	*Avinash*	*Basuda*	*Chinmoy*	*Ghana-shyam*
To Basuda Ltd.	100	—	300	—	By Balance b/d	2,700	1,200	600	—
To Ghanashyam	750	—	—		By Avinash and Chinmoy Ltd.	—	400	—	—
To Avinash and Chinmoy Ltd.	—	—	—	187.5	By Bank A/c	400	—	1,200	—
To Cash & Bank	—	1,600	—	—	By Cash&Bank (b.f)	375	—	187.5	937.5
To Balance c/d	2,750	—	1,750	1,500	By Avinash			—	750
					By Ghanashyam	125	—	62.5	—
	3,600	1,600	2,050	1,687.5		3,600	1,600	2,050	1,687.5

5. CASH AND BANK

Particulars	₹
Amount given	284
Amount brought in by partners	3,100
	3,384
Less: Payment to Basuda Ltd.	1,600
	1,748
Net Increase = 1,500 (Equivalent to the value of goodwill)	

PROBLEM 9

Manish, Jatin and Paresh were partners sharing Profits/Losses in the ratio of Manish 40 per cent, Jatin 35 per cent, and Paresh 25 per cent. The draft Balance Sheet of the partnership as on 31st December, 20X3 was as follows:

Liabilities		₹	*Assets*		₹
Sundry Creditors		30,000	Cash on hand and at Bank		67,000
Bills payable		8,000	Stock		42,000
Loan from Jatin		30,000	Sundry Debtors	34,000	
Current Accounts:			*Less:* Pro. for Doubtful Debts	6,000	28,000
Manish	12,000		Plant and Machinery (at cost)	80,000	
Jatin	8,000		*Less:* Depreciation	28,000	52,000
Paresh	6,000	26,000	Premises (at cost)		75,000
Capital Accounts:					
Manish	90,000				
Jatin	50,000				
Paresh	30,000	1,70,000			
		2,64,000			2,64,000

Jastin retired on 31st December, 20X3. Manish and Paresh continued in partnership sharing Profits/ Losses in the ratio of Manish 60 per cent and Paresh 40 per cent. 50 per cent of Jatin's loan was repaid on 1-1-20X4 and it was agreed that of the amount then remaining due to him a sum of ₹ 80,000 should remain as loan to partnership and the balance to be carried forward as ordinary trading liability. The following adjustments were agreed to be made to the above mentioned Balance Sheet:

(i) ₹ 10,000 should be written off from the premises.

(ii) Plant and Machinery was revalued at ₹ 58,000.

(iii) Provision for doubtful debts to be increased by ₹ 1,200.

(iv) ₹ 5,000 due to creditors for expenses had been omitted from the books of account.

(v) ₹ 4,000 to be written off stocks.

(vi) Provide ₹ 1,200 for professional charges in connection with revaluation.

As per the deed of partnership, in the event of the retirement of a partner, goodwill was to be valued at an amount equal to one year's purchase of the average profits of the preceding three years on the date of retirement. Before determining the said average profits a notional amount of ₹ 80,000 should be charged for remuneration to partners. The necessary profits before charging such remuneration were:

Year ending 31.12.20X1	₹ 1,44,000
Year ending 31.12.20X2	₹ 1,68,000
Year ending 31.12.20X3	₹ 1,88,200 (as per draft accounts)

It was agreed that, for the purpose of valuing goodwill, the amount of profit for the year 20X3 be recomputed after charging the loss on revaluation in respect of premises and stock, the unprovided expenses (except professional expenses) and increase in the provision for doutful debts. The continuing partners decided to eliminate goodwill account from their books.

You are required to prepare:

(i) Revaluation Account;

(ii) Capital Accounts (merging current accounts therein);

(iii) Jatin's Accounts showing balance due to him; and

(iv) Balance Sheet of Manish and Paresh as at 1st January, 20X4.

SOLUTION

Dr. **(I) REVALUATION ACCOUNT** *Cr.*

Particulars	₹	*Particulars*		₹
To Premises	10,000	By Plant & Machinery		6,000
To Provision for Doubtful Debts	1,200	By Loss transferred to Capital A/c's:		
To Outstanding Expenses	5,000	Manish (40%)	6,160	
To Stock	4,000	Jatin (35%)	5,390	
To Provision for Profess. Charges	1,200	Paresh (25%)	3,850	15,400
	21,400			21,400

Dr. **(II) CAPITAL ACCOUNTS OF PARTNERS** *Cr.*

Particulars	*Manish* ₹	*Jain* ₹	*Paresh* ₹	*Particulars*	*Manish* ₹	*Jain* ₹	*Paresh* ₹
To Revaluation A/c (Loss)	6,160	5,390	3,850	By Balance b/f	90,000	50,000	30,000
To Jatin's Capital A/c	16,000	—	12,000	By Current A/c	12,000	8,000	6,000
To Personal A/c (b.t.)	—	80,610	—	By Manish Capital A/c	—	16,000	—
To Balance c/f	79,840	—	20,150	By Paresh's Capital A/c	—	12,000	—
	1,02,000	86,000	36,000		1,02,000	86,000	36,000

Dr. **(III) JATIN'S PERSONAL ACCOUNT** *Cr.*

Particulars	₹	*Particulars*	₹
To Bank (50% of old loan)	15,000	By Capital Account	
To Loan Account (new transferred)	80,000	(Balance transferred)	80,160
To Balance c/d	15,610*	By Loan Account (old)	30,000
	1,10,610		1,10,610

* For the balance amount due to Jatin, candidates may show Jatin's loan account at ₹ 95,000 (consisting of old loan ₹ 15,000 and new loan ₹ 80,000) and the balance i.e. ₹ 610 can be carried as an ordinary trading liability.

(IV) BALANCE SHEET OF M/S MANISH AND PARESH

as on 1st January 20X4

Liabilities	₹	*Assets*		₹
Bills Payable	8,000	Current Assets:		
Sundry Creditors	30,000	Cash in hand & at Bank		52,000
Jatin's Personal A/c	15,610	Sundry Debtors	34,000	
Creditors For Expenses	6,200	*Less:* Provision	7,200	26,800
Loan A/c—Jatin	80,000	Stock in Trade		38,000
Mr. Manish's Capital	79,840	Fixed Assets:		

Mr. Paresh's Capital	20,150	Plant & Machinery		
		As Ravalued	86,000	
		Less: Deprecation	28,000	58,000
		Premises (at cost)	75,000	
		Less: Written off	10,000	65,000
	2,39,800			2,39,800

Working Notes:

1. PROFIT FOR THE YEAR ENDING 31ST DECEMBER 20X3

Particulars		₹
As per Draft A/c		1,88,200
Less: Premises Written off	10,000	
Provision for Doubtful Debts	1,200	
Outstanding Expenses	5,000	
Stock	4,000	20,200
		1,68,800

2. VALUATION OF GOODWILL

Particulars		₹
Profit for the year ended 31st December 20X3 (adjusted)	1,68,000	
Profit for the year ended 31st December 20X2	1,68,000	
Profit for the year ended 31st December 20X1	1,44,000	4,80,000
Average Profits, before Partners' Salaries		1,60,000
Less: Partners' Salaries (notional)		80,000
Super profit and Goodwill (one year's Purchase)		80,000

PROBLEM 10

A, B and C were partners, sharing profits and losses in the ratio of 5 : 3 : 2 respectively. On 31st March, 20X4 their Balance Sheet stood as follows:

Liabilities	₹	*Assets*	₹
A's Capital	7,79,000	Plant and Machinery	13,62,000
B's Capital	7,07,800	Furniture and Fittings	2,36,000
C's Capital	6,86,200	Stock	7,02,000
Creditors	4,91,000	Debtors	1,91,000
		Cash at Bank	1,73,000
	26,64,000		26,64,000

On 31st July 20X4 A died. According to partnership deed, on the death of a partner, the capital account of the deceased partner was to be credited with:

(i) his share of profit for the relevant part of the year of death calculated on the basis of profit earned during the immediately preceding accounting year, and

(ii) his share of goodwill.

Goodwill was to be valued at two years' purchase of the average profits of immediately preceding three accounting years. The profits, as per books of account, were as follows:

Particulars	₹
For accounting year ended 31st March, 20X2	3,29,000
For accounting year ended 31st March, 20X3	3,46,000
For accounting year ended 31st March, 20X4	3,78,000

However, while going through the books of account on A's death, it came to light that ₹ 30,000 worth of wages were spent on installation of a new machinery, but the sum was not capitalised; the machinery was put into operation on 1st October, 20X3. Depreciation was provided on the machinery @ 20% per annum.

On 1st October, 20X4 A's son D was admitted into partnership with immediate effect on the following terms:

(a) D would get one-fourth share in the profit of the firm, while the relative profit sharing ratio between B and C would remain unchanged.

(b) The final balance of A's capital account would be credited to D's Capital Account.

(c) An adjustment would be made in the Capital Accounts for D's share of goodwill. The basis of valuation of firm's goodwill would be the same as was adopted of the time of the death of his father.

On 31st March, 20X5 the Profit and Loss Account of the firm showed that the firm had earned a profit of ₹ 4,16,000 for the year. The respective drawings accounts showed that while B and C had withdrawn ₹ 60,000 each during the year, D's drawing totalled ₹ 30,000. The Drawings Accounts are closed at the end of the year by transfer to respective capital accounts.

You are required to:

(i) Prepare a statement showing distribution of profits for the accounting year ended 31st March, 20X5; and

(ii) Pass journal entries for all the transactions relating to death of the partner, D's admission into partnership, and at the end of the year relating to transfer of Drawings Accounts and distribution of profit for the year.

SOLUTION

(I) STATEMENT SHOWING DISTRIBUTION OF PROFITS FOR THE ACCOUNTING YEAR ENDED 31ST MARCH 20X5

Particulars	₹	₹
Net Profit for the year ended 31.03.20X5		4,16,000
A's Share		
(Profit distributed to deceased partner A & his executor)		
(a) Profit for 4 months (1.4.20X4 – 31.7.20X4) (W.N.1)	67,500	
(b) Application of Sec. 37 (1.8.20X4 – 30.9.20X4) (W.N.5)	28,021	95,521
B's Share		
(a) Profit for 4 months (1.4.20X4 – 31.7.20X4) (W.N.3)	42,700	
(b) Profit for 2 months (1.8.20X4 – 30.9.20X4) (W.N.6)	24,787	
(c) Profit for 3 months (1.10.20X4) – 31.3.20X5) (W.N.10)	93,600	1,61,087
C's share		

(a) Profit for 4 months (1.4.20X4 – 31.7.20X4) (W.N.3)	28,467	
(b) Profit for 2 months (1.8.20X4 – 30.9.20X4) (W.N.6)	16,525	
(c) Profit for 6 months (1.10.20X4 – 31.3.20X5) (W.N.10)	62,400	1,07,392
D's Share		
(a) Profit for 6 months (1.10.20X4 – 31.3.20X5) (W.N.10)	52,000	52,000
		4,16,000

(II) JOURNAL

Date	*Particulars*		*L.F.*	*Dr. (₹)*	*Cr. (₹)*
20X4	Machinery A/c	Dr.		27,000	
July 31	To A's Capital A/c				13,500
	To B's Capital A/c				8,100
	To C's Capital A/c				5,400
	(Wages spent on installation of new machinery captialised and credited to partners' capital accounts after providing depreciation for six months ended 31st March, 2000)				
	Profit and Loss Suspense A/c	Dr.		67,500	
	To A's Capital A/c				67,500
	(A's share of profit for four months as calculated in W.N. 1 credited to his capital to his capital account)				
	B's Capital A/c	Dr.		2,16,000	
	C's Capital A/c	Dr.		1,44,000	
	To A's Capital A/c				3,60,000
	(Goodwill credited to A)				
	A's Capital A/c	Dr.		12,20,000	
	To A's Executor's A/s				12,20,000
	(Balance due to A transferred to his executor's account)				
	Profit & Loss Suspense A/c	Dr.		28,021	
	To A's Executor's A/c				28,021
	(Profit earned out of the unsettled capital credited to A's executor's account as per W.N. 5)				
Oct. 1	A's Executor's A/c	Dr.		12,48,021	
	To D's Capital A/c				1248,021
	(Final balance of A's executor's account transferred to D's capital account)				
	D's Capital A/c	Dr.		1,80,000	
	To B's Capital A/c				1,08,000
	To C's Capital A/c				72,000
	(Goodwill Credited to sacrificing partners in the ratio of 3 : 2)				

Mar. 31	B's Capital A/c	Dr.	60,000	
	C's Capital A/c	Dr.	60,000	
	D's Capital A/c	Dr.	30,000	
	To B's Drawings A/c			60,000
	To C's Drawings A/c			60,000
	To D's Drawing A/c			30,000
	(Drawings debited to partners' capital accounts)			
Mar. 31	Profit and Loss Appropriation A/c	Dr.	4,16,000	
	To Profit and Loss Suspense A/c (₹ 67,500 + 28,021)			95,521
	To B's Capital A/c			1,61,087
	To C's Capital A/c			1,07,392
	To D's Capital A/c			52,000
	(Division of profits as shown in statement of distribution of profits and balance of profit & loss suspense account transferred to profit and loss appropriation account)			

Working Notes:

1. **Computation of A's Share in profit for the period 1.4.20X4 – 31.7.20X4**

   A's share in profits for the period of 1st April, 20X4 to 31st July, 20X4 is to be calculated on the basis of profit earned during the immediately previous accounting year i.e., year ended on 31st March, 20X4

	Particulars	₹
A.	Profit for the year ended 31st March, 20X4	3,78,000
B.	*Add:* Capital expenditure of wages spent on installation of new machinery, treated, treated as revenue expenditure	30,000
		4,08,000
C.	*Less:* Dep. on ₹ 30,000 (being the value of machinery @ 20% p.a. for 6 months)	3,000
D.	Correct profit for the year ended 31st March, 20X4	4,05,000
E.	Profit for 4 months on the basis of last year's profit [₹ 4,05,000 × 4/12]	1,35,000
F.	A's share in profit [1,35,000 × 5/10	67,500

2. VALUATION OF GOODWILL

Profit for the year ended 31st March, 20X2	3,29,000
Profit for the year ended 31st March, 20X3	3,46,000
Profit for the year ended 31st March, 20X4	4,05,000
Total Profit	10,80,000
Average profit = ₹ 10,80,000/3 = ₹ 3,60,000	
Goodwill (at two years' purchase) = ₹ 3,60,000 × 2 = ₹ 7,20,000	

3. DISTRIBUTION OF PROFITS FOR 4 MONTHS ENDED 31ST JULY, 20X4

Particulars	₹
Net Profit [₹ 4,16,000 × 4/12]	1,38,667

A's share [as per Working Note (i)]	67,500
B's share [₹ 71,167 × 3/5]	42,700
C's share [₹ 71,167 × 2/5]	28,467

Dr. **4. PARTNERS' CAPITAL ACCOUNTS AS ON 31ST JULY, 20X4** *Cr.*

Particulars	*A* ₹	*B* ₹	*C* ₹	*Particulars*	*A* ₹	*B* ₹	*C* ₹
To A's Capital A/c	—	2,16,000	1,44,000	By Balance b/d	7,79,000	7,07,800	6,86,200
To Drawings	—	20,000	20,000	By Plant & Machinery	13,500	8,100	5,400
To A's Executor's A/c	12,20,000	—	—	By B's Capital A/c	2,16,000	—	—
To Balance c/d	—	5,22,600	5,56,067	By C's Capital A/c	1,44,000	—	—
				By Share in profit (W.N. 3)	67,500	42,700	28,467
	12,20,000	7,58,600	7,20,067		12,20,000	7,58,600	7,20,067

5. **Application of Section 37 of the Indian Partnership Act, 1932 Either**

(i) Interest of ₹ 12,20,000 × 6/100 × 2/12 = ₹ 12,200

or

(ii) Profit earned out of unsettled capital

$$₹\ 4,16,000 \times \frac{2}{12} \times \frac{₹\ 12,20,000}{₹\ (12,20,000 + 9,54,600 + 8,44,067)} = ₹\ 28,021 \text{ (approx.)}$$

In the absence of specific agreement amongst partners on the above subject matter, the representatives of the deceased partner can receive at their option, interest at the rate of 6% p.a. *or* share of profit earned for the amount due to the deceased partner.

In the above case, it would be rational to assume that A's representatives would opt for ₹ 28,021.

6. DISTRIBUTION OF PROFIT FOR 2 MONTHS ENDED 31ST OCT., 20X4

Particulars	₹
Net profit (₹ 4,16,000 × 2/12)	69,333
A's executor's share [as per Working Note (v)]	28,021
B's share (₹ 41,312 × 3/5)	24,787
C's share (₹ 41,312 × 2/5)	16,525

Dr. **7. A'S EXECUTOR'S ACCOUNT** *Cr.*

Particulars	₹	*Particulars*	₹
To D's Capital A/c	12,48,021	By A's Capital A/c	12,20,000
		By Share in profit (W.N. 6)	28,021
	12,48,021		12,48,021

8. PARTNERS' CAPITAL ACCOUNTS

Dr. *(1st August, 20X4 to 30th Sept., 20X4)* *Cr.*

Particulars	*B* ₹	*C* ₹	*Particulars*	*B* ₹	*C* ₹
To Drawings	10,000	10,000	By Balance b/d	5,22,600	5,56,067

To Balance c/d	5,37,387	5,62,592	By P & L A/c	24,787	16,525
	5,47,387	5,72,592		5,47,387	5,72,592

9. **Computation of new profit sharing ratio between B, C & D**

D is admitted for 1/4 share

B's new ratio = 3/4 × 3/5 = 9/20

C's new ratio = 3/4 × 2/5 = 6/20

D's new ratio = 1/4 = 5/20

New profit sharing ratio = 9 : 6 : 5

10. DISTRIBUTION OF PROFIT FOR 6 MONTHS ENDED 31ST MARCH, 20X5

Particulars	₹
Net profit (₹ 4,16,000 × 6/12)	2,08,000
B's share (₹ 2,08,000 × 9/20)	93,600
C's share (₹ 2,08,000 × 6/20)	62,400
D's share (₹ 2,08,000 × 5/20)	52,000

Dr. **11. PARTNERS' CAPITAL ACCOUNTS AS ON 31ST MARCH, 20X5** *Cr.*

Particulars	*B* ₹	*C* ₹	*D* ₹	*Particulars*	*B* ₹	*C* ₹	*D* ₹
To B's Capital A/c	—	—	1,08,000	By Balance b/d	5,37,387	5,62,592	—
To C's Capital A/c	—	—	72,000	By A's Executor's A/c	—	—	12,48,021
To Drawings	30,000	30,000	30,000	By D's Capital A/c	1,08,000	72,000	—
To Balance c/d	7,08,987	6,66,992	10,90,021	By Share of profit (W.N. 10)	93,600	62,400	52,000
	7,38,987	6,96,992	13,00,021		7,38,987	6,96,992	13,00,021

12. It is assumed that profit was earned uniformly throughout the year. Although notional profit was calculated for the first four months, it is to be transferred from the current year's profit (as calculated in working note 3). The question requires that A's share of profit for this period is to be calculated on the basis of profit earned during year ended 31st March, 20X4. The balance amount after calculating his share has been credited to B and C in ratio 3 : 2.

13. It is assumed that drawings were made evenly throughout the year. However, single entry has been given at the year end in the main solution relating to transfer of drawings and distribution of profit but the Partners' capital accounts shown in the working notes include entries of drawings and distribution of profit of respective dates within the year.

PROBLEM 6 RETIREMENT OF A PARTNER

Atul, Balbir and Chatur were carrying on a business in partnership sharing profits in the ratio of 5 : 3: 2 respectively. On 31st March, 2013 their Balance Sheet stood as follows:

Liabilities	₹	*Assets*	₹
Atul's Capital	6,25,000	Goodwill	80,000
Balbir's Capital	3,75,000	Land & Buildings	7,00,000
Chatur's Capital	2,50,000	Furniture	1,65,000
General Reserve	1,00,000	Stock	2,86,000

Trade Creditors	2,10,000	Trade Debtors	1,80,000	
		Less: Provision	3,600	1,76,400
		Cash at Bank		1,52,600
	15,60,000			15,60,000

Atul retired on the above mentioned date and partners agreed that:

(i) The current value of goodwill be taken to be equal to the book value of the asset.

(ii) Land and Buildings be considered worth ₹ 9,00,000.

(iii) The provision for bad debts on trade debtors be raised to 5%.

(iv) Provision be made for compensation of ₹ 5,000 to an ex-employee.

(v) Half of the amount due to Atul be paid immediately in cash and tghe balance be treated as 10% loan, repayable within 3 years.

In order to facilitate cash payment to Atul, Balbir and Chatur brought in ₹ 3,00,000 in the ratio of 3 : 2 respectively.

Prepare Revaluation Account, the Capital of all tghe partners and Bank Account. Also draw the initial Balance Sheet of Balbir and Chatur, immediately after Atul's retirement.
(16 Marks)

SOLUTION 6:

Dr. **REVALUATION ACCOUNT** *Cr.*

Particulars	₹	*Particulars*	₹
To Provision for Doubtful Debts	5,400	By Building	2,00,000
To Provision for compensation	5,000		
To Profit on Revaluation t/f to:			
Atul	94,800		
Balbir	56,880		
Chatur	37,920		
	2,00,000		2,00,000

Dr. **PARTNERS' CAPITAL ACCOUNTS** *Cr.*

Particulars	*Atul* ₹	*Balbir* ₹	*Chatur* ₹	*Particulars*	*Atul* ₹	*Balbir* ₹	*Chatur* ₹
To Goodwill A/c	40,000	24,000	16,000	By Balance b/d	6,25,000	3,75,000	2,50,000
To Cash A/c	3,84,900			By General Reserve	50,000	30,000	20,000
To 10% Loan	3,84,900			By Revaluation A/c	94,800	56,880	37,920
To Atul Capital A/c	—	24,000	16,000	By Balbir & Chatur's A/c	40,000		
To Balance c/d		5,93,880	3,95,920	By Cash A/c		1,80,000	1,20,000
	8,09,800	6,41,880	4,27,920		8,09,800	6,41,880	4,27,920

BANK ACCOUNT

Particulars	₹	*Particulars*	₹
To Balance b/s	1,52,600	By Atul's Capital A/c	3,84,900
To Balbir's capital A/c	1,80,000	By Balance c/d	67,700

To Chatur's capital A/c	1,20,000		
	4,52,000		4,52,600

BALANCE SHEET OF AS AT 31.03.2013 (ATUL'S RETIREMENT)

Liabilities	₹	*Assets*		₹
Balbir's Capital	5,93,880	Land and Building		9,00,000
Chatur's Capital	3,95,920	Furniture		1,65,000
10% Loan from Atul	3,84,900	Stock		2,86,000
Trade Creditors	2,10,000	Trade Debtors	1,80,000	
Provision for Compensation	5,000	*Less:* Provision	9,000	1,71,000
		Cash at Bank		67,700
	15,89,700			15,89,700

PROBLEM 12 DEATH OF A PARTNER

The Balance Sheet of Amitabh, Abhishek and Amrish as at 31.12.2008 stood as follows: X

Liabilities	₹	*Assets*		₹
Capitals:		Land & Buildings		74,000
Amitabh	60,000	Investments		10,000
Abhishek	40,000	Goodwill		37,800
Amrish	40,000	Life Policy (at surrender value):		
Creditors	25,800	Amitabh		2,500
General Reserve	8,000	Abhishek		2,500
Investment Fluctuation Reserve	2,400	Amrish		1,000
		Stock		20,000
		Debtors	20,000	
		Less: Provision	1,600	18,400
		Cash & bank balance		10,000
	1,76,200			1,76,200

Amrish died on 31 March, 2009, due to this reason the following adjustments were agreed upon:

(i) Land and Buildings be appreciated by 50%.

(ii) Investment be valued at 6% *less* than the cost.

(iii) All debtors (except 20% which are considered as doubtful) were good.

(iv) Stock to be reduced to 94%.

(v) Goodwill to be valued at 1 year's purchase of the average profits of the past five years.

(vi) Amrish's share of profit to the date of death be calculated on the basis of average profits of the three completed years immediately preceeding the year of death.

The profits of the last five years are as follows:

Year	₹
2004	23,000
2005	28,000

2006	18,000
2007	16,000
2008	20,000

The life policies have been shown at their surrender values representing 10% of the sum assured in each case. The annual premium of ₹ 1,000 is payable every year on 1st August.

Give the necessary Journal Entries in the books of account and prepare the Balance Sheet of the reconstituted firm.

SOLUTION

JOURNAL

Date	*Particulars*		*Dr. (₹)*	*Cr. (₹)*
1.	Insurance Company's A/c	Dr.	10,000	
	To Life Policy A/c			10,000
	(Being the policy on the life of Amrish matured on his death)			
2.	Life Policy A/c	Dr.	9,000	
	To Amitabh's Capital A/c			3,000
	To Abhishek's Capital A/c			3,000
	To Amrish's Capital A/c			3,000
	(Being the transfer of balance in life policy account to all partners' capital accounts)			
3.	Amitabh's Capital A/c	Dr.	12,600	
	Abhishek's Capital A/c	Dr.	12,600	
	Amrish's Capital A/c	Dr.	12,600	
	To Goodwill A/c			37,800
	(Being goodwill standing in the books written off fully)			
4.	Land & Buildings A/c	Dr.	37,000	
	To Revaluation A/c			37,000
	(Being an increase in the value of assets recorded)			
5.	Investment Fluctuation Reserve A/c	Dr.	600	
	To Investment A/c			600
	(Being reduction in the cost of investment adjusted through Investment Fluctuation Reserve)			
6.	Revaluation A/c	Dr.	3,600	
	To Stock A/c			1,200
	To Provision for Doubtful Debts A/c			2,400
	(Being the fall in value of assets recorded)			
7.	Amitabh's Capital A/c	Dr.	3,500	
	Abhishek's Capital A/c	Dr.	3,500	
	To Amrish's Capital A/c			7,000
	(Being the share of Amrish's revalued goodwill adjusted through capital accounts of the remaining partners)			

8.	Profit & Loss Suspense Account	Dr.	1,500	
	To Amrish's Capital A/c			1,500
	(Being Amrish's Share of profit to date of death credited to his account)			
9.	Revaluation A/c	Dr.	33,400	
	To Amitabh's Capital A/c			11,133
	To Abhishek's Capital A/c			11,133
	To Amrish's Capital A/c			11,134
	(Being the transfer of profit on revaluation)			
10.	General Reserve A/c	Dr.	8,000	
	Investment Fluctuation Reserve A/c (₹ 2,400 – ₹ 600)	Dr.	1,800	
	To Amitabh's Capital A/c			3,267
	To Abhishek's Capital A/c			3,267
	To Amrish's Capital A/c			3,266
	(Being the transfer of accumulated profits to capital accounts)			
11.	Amrish's Capital A/c	Dr.	53,300	
	To Amrish's Executor's A/c			53,300
	(Being the transfer of Amrish's Capital A/c to his Executor's A/c)			

BALANCE SHEET AS AT 31ST MARCH, 2009

Liabilities	₹	*Assets*		₹
Amithabh's Capital Account	61,300	Land & Building		1,11,000
Abhishek's Capital Account	41,300	Life Policy: Amitabh	2,500	
Amrish's Executor's Account	53,300	Abhishek	2,500	5,000
Sundry Creditors	25,800	Investments		9,400
		Stock		18,800
		Debtors	20,000	
		Less: Provisions	4,000	16,000
		Insurance Company		10,000
		Cash & Bank Balance		10,000
		Profit and loss Suspense A/c		1,500
	1,81,700			1,81,700

Working Notes:

(i) Calculation of Amrish's Share of Profit

Average Profit (₹ 18,000 + 16,000 + 20,000) = ₹ 18,000

Profit for 3 months = 18,000 × 3/12 = 4,500, Amrish's share of Profit = 4,500 × 1/3 = 1,500

(ii) Calculation of Goodwill

Total profits for last five years = ₹ 1,05,000

Average Profit = 1,05,000/5 = ₹ 21,000

Goodwill at one year's purchase = ₹ 21,000 × 1 = ₹ 21,000

PROBLEM 17.6

Ramu, Shamu and Raju were partners sharing profits and tosses in the ratio of 3 : 2 : 2. Their Balance Sheet as on 01-01-2009 was as follows:

Liabilities	₹	*Assets*	₹
Capital Accounts:		Fixed assets	80,000
Ramu	30,000	Stock	15,000
Shamu	20,000	Debtors	12,000
Raju	20,000	Cash & bank	1,951
Reserves	14,000		
Creditors	24,951		
	1,08,951		1,08,951

On 1st October, 2009, Ramu died. His heirs agreed that:

(i) Goodwill of the firm be valued at 2 years' purchase of average profit of past three years. Profits for the year 2006, 2007 and 2008 were ₹ 30,000, ₹ 40,000 and ₹ 47,600 respectively.

(ii) Fixed assets be revalued at ₹ 1,01,000

(iii) Profit to be shared, earned in subsequent period after death of Ramu till settlement of his executors' claim.

Ramu's heirs account was settled on 31-12-2009 by bringing in required cash by remaining partners in equal proportion leaving cash balance of ₹ 1,234. Each partner had drawn @ ₹ 1,000 per month for personal use.

Profit for the current year after charging depreciation of ₹ 9,000 (₹ 6,000 for first three quarters and ₹ 3,000 for last quarter) was ₹ 46,600 earned evenly through-out the year. You are requested to prepare Profit & Loss Appropriation A/c, Cash & Bank A/c, Ramu's's Executor's A/c and Partners' Capital Accounts for the year ended on 31-12-2009 assuming remaining partners' decided not to retain goodwill in the books.

SOLUTION

Dr. **(I) PROFIT & LOSS ACCOUNT** *Cr.*

Particulars	₹ (for 9 months)	₹ (for 3 months)	*Particulars*	₹ (for 9 months)	₹ (for 3 months)
To Dep. A/c	6,000	3,000	By Profit	041,700	13,900
To Net Profit	35,700	10,900			
	41,700	**13,900**		**41,700**	**13,900**

Dr. **PROFIT & LOSS APPROPRIATION ACCOUNT** *Cr.*

Particulars	₹ (for 9 months)	₹ (for 3 months)	*Particulars*	₹ (for 9 months)	₹ (for 3 months)
To Partners' capital A/cs			By Net Profit	35,700	10,900
Ramu	15,300				
Shamu	10,200	3,043			
Raju	10,200	3,044			
To Ramu's Elxecutor A/c		4,813			
	35,700	**10,900**		**35,700**	**10,900**

Dr. **(II) PARTNER'S CAPITAL ACCOUNTS AS ON 1ST OCTOBER, 2009** Cr.

Particulars	Ramu ₹	Shamu ₹	Raju ₹	Particulars	Ramu ₹	Shamu ₹	Raju ₹
To Drawings	9,000	9,000	9,000	By Balance b/d	30,000	20,000	20,000
To Ramu's Executors A/c	87,414	–	–	By Reserves	6,000	4,000	4,000
To Balance c/d	–	55,276	55,276	By Goodwill*	36,114	24,076	24,076
				By Fixed Assets**	9,000	6,000	6,000
				By P & L Appropriation A/c	15,300	10,200	10,200
	96,414	**64,276**	**64,276**		**96,414**	**64,276**	**64,276**

Dr. **(III) PARTNERS' CAPITAL ACCOUNTS AS ON 31.12.2009** Cr.

Particulars	Shamu ₹	Raju ₹	Particulars	Shamu ₹	Raju ₹
To Drawings	3,000	3,000	By Balance b/d	55,276	55,276
To Goodwill	42,133	42,133	By Cash A/c	62,255	62,255
To Balance c/d	5,441	75.442	By P&L Appropriation A/c	3,043	3,044
	1,20,574	**1,20,575**		**1,20,574**	**1,20.575**

Dr. **RAMU'S EXECUTORS' A/C AQS ON 31.12.2009** Cr.

Particulars	₹	Particulars	₹
To BankA/c	92,227	By Balance b/d	87,414
		By P & L Appropriation A/c	4,813
	92,227		92,227

Dr. **CASH & BANK ACCOUNT** Cr.

Particulars	₹	Particulars	₹
To Balance b/d	1,951	By Ramu's executors A/c	92,227
To Shamu's capital A/c	62,255	By Partners' Capital A/cs (Drawings):	
To Raju's capital A/c	62,255	Ramu	9,000
		Shamu	12,000
		Raju	12,000
		By Balance c/d	1,234
	1,26,461		1,26,461

(iv) As per para 36 of AS 10, 'Accounting for fixed Assets, 'goodwill should be recorded in the books only when some consideration in money *or* money's worth has been paid for it. However, in the above solution, goodwill has been raised in the books at the time of death of a partner and written off by the remaining partners, as per the information given in the question.

(v) Appreciation of fixed assets may also be recorded through "Revaluation Account".

Working Notes:

(i) Profit for the year before depreciation = ₹ 46,600 + ₹ 9,000 = ₹ 55,600

(ii) As per section 37 of Partnership Act, in case of settlement of deceased partner's account on the date other then the date of death, the executor of deceased partner has a choice to take

Either-

(A) Profit earned on un-settled capital= Profix × $\frac{\text{Unsettled capital as on1.10.09}}{\text{Total capital as on 1.10.09}}$

$$= 10,900 \times \frac{87,414}{(87,414 + 55,276 + 55,276)}$$

$$= 10,900 \times \frac{87,414}{1,97,966} = ₹\,4,813$$

Or

(B) Interest on capital @ 6% i.e. 87,414 × 6% × 3/12 = 1,311

Option A is beneficial, therefore heirs of Ramu will opt for proportionate share of profit i.e. 4,813.

(III) VALUATION OF GOODWILL:

Particulars	₹	*Weight*	*Product*
Profit for 2006	30,000	1	30,000
2007	40,000	2	80,000
2008	47,600	3	1,42,800
	1,17,600	6	2.52.800

Weighted Average Profit = 2,52,000/6 = ₹ 42,133

Goodwill = 2 year's purchase of average profit = ₹ 42,133 × 2 = ₹ 84,266.

PROBLEM 13

A, B and C were partners of a firm sharing profits and losses in the ratio of 3 : 4 : 3. The Balance sheet of the firm, as at 31st March, 1998 was as under:

Liabilities	₹	*Assets*	₹
Capital Accounts:		Fixed Assets	1,00,000
A	48,000	Current Assets	
B	64,000	Stock	30,000
C	48,000	Debtors	60,000
Reserve	20,000	Cash and Bank	30,000
Creditors	40,000		
	2,20,000		2,20,000

The firm had taken a Joint Life Policy for ₹ 1,00,000; the premium periodically paid was charged to Profit and Loss Account. Partner C died on 30th September, 1998. It was agreed between the surviving partners and the legal representatives of C that:

(i) Goodwill of the firm will be taken at ₹ 60,000.

(ii) Fixed Assets will be written down by ₹ 20,000.

(iii) In lieu of profits, C should be paid at the rate of 25% per annum on his capital as on 31st March, 1998.

Policy money was received and the legal hairs were paid off. The profits for the year ended 31st March, 1999, after charging depreciation of ₹ 10,000 (Depreciation upto 30th September was agreed to be ₹ 6,000) were ₹ 48,000. Partner's Drawings Accounts showed balances as under:

A ₹ 18,000 (drawn evenly over the year)

B ₹ 24,000 (drawn evenly over the year)

C (up-to-date of death) ₹ 20,000

On the basis of the above figures, please indicate the entitlement of the legal heirs of C, assuming that they had not been paid anything other then the share in the Joint Life Policy.

SOLUTION

COMPUTATION OF ENTITLEMENT OF LEGAL HEIRS OF C
(I) PROFITS FOR THE HALF YEAR ENDED 31ST MARCH, 1999

Particulars	₹
Profits for the year ended 31st March, 1999 (after depreciation)	48,000
Add: Depreciation	10,000
Profit before depreciation	58,000
Profits for the first half (assumed: evenly spread)	29,000
Less: Depreciation for the first half	6,000
Profit for the first half year (after depreciation)	23,000
Profits for the second half (i.e., 1st October, 1998 to 31st March, 1999)	29,000
Less: Depreciation for the second half	4,000
Profits for the second half year (after depreciation)	25,000

Dr. **(II) CAPITAL ACCOUNTS OF PARTNERS AS ON 30TH SEPTEMBER, 1998** *Cr.*

Particulars	*A* ₹	*B* ₹	*C* ₹	*Particulars*	*A* ₹	*B* ₹	*C* ₹
To Fixed Assets				By Balance b/d	48,000	64,000	48,000
(loss on revaluation)	6,000	8,000	6,000	By Reserve	6,000	8,000	6,000
To Drawings	9,000	12,000	20,000	By Goodwill	18,000	24,000	18,000
To C Executor's A/c	—	—	52,000	By P&L Appro priation A/c			
To Balance c/d	57,000	76,000	—	(Interest on ₹ 48,000			
				@ 25% for 6 months)	—	—	6,000
	72,000	96,000	78,000		72,000	96,000	78,000

(iii) Application of Section 37 of the Partnership Act

Legal heirs of C have not been paid anything other than the share in joint life policy. The amount due to the deceased partner carries interest at the mutually agreed upon rate. In the absence of any agreement, the representatives of the deceased partner can receive at their option interest at the rate of 6% per annum *or* the share of profit earned for the amount due to the deceased partner.

Thus, the representatives of C can opt for

Either,

(i) Interest on ₹ 52,000 for 6 months @ 6% p.a. = ₹ 1,560 or

(ii) Profit earned out of unsettled capital (in the second half year ended 31st March, 1999)

$$₹\ 25{,}000 \times \frac{52{,}000}{57{,}000 + 76{,}000 + 52{,}000} = ₹\ 7{,}027 \text{ (approx.)}$$

In the above case, it would be rational to assume that the legal heirs would opt for ₹ 7,027.

(IV) AMOUNT DUE TO LEGAL HEIRS OF C

Particulars	₹
Balance in C's Executor's account	52,000
Amount of profit earned out of unsettled capital [calculated in (3)]	7,027
Amount due	59,027

PROBLEM 14 RETIREMENT CUM ADDMISSION

A, B and C are partners of the firm ABC & Co., sharing profits and losses in the ratio of 5:3:2. Following is the Balance Sheet of the firm as at 31.3.2013:

Liabilities	₹	*Assets*	₹
Partners' capital accounts:		Goodwill	1,00,000
A	4,50,000	Building	10,50,000
B	1,30,000	Machinery	6,50,000
C	1,70,000	Furniture	2,15,000
Investment fluctuation reserve	1,00,000		
Contingency reserve	75,000	Investments (market) value ₹ 75,000	60,000
Long-term loan	15,00,000	Stock	6,50,000
Bank overdraft	2,20,000	Sundry debtors	6,95,000
Sundry creditors	8,00,000	Advertisement suspense	25,000
	34,45,000		34,45,000

It was decided that B would retire from the partnership on 1.4.2008 & D would be admitted as a partner on the same date. Following adjustments are agreed amongst the partners for the retirement/admission:

(i) Goodwill is to be valued at ₹ 5,00,000, but the same will not appear as an asset in the books of the firm.

(ii) Building and machinery are to be revalued at ₹ 10,00,000 and ₹ 5,20,000 respectively.

(iii) Investments are to be taken over by B at the market value.

(iv) Provision for doubtful debts is to be maintained at 20% on sundry debtors.

(v) The capital of the reconstituted firm will be ₹ 10,00,000 to be contributed by the partners A, C and D in their new profit sharing ratio of 2 :2 : 1.

(vi) Surplus funds, if any will be used to pay the bank overdraft.

(vii) Amount due to retiring partner B will be transferred to his loan account.

Prepare:

(i) Revaluation Account;

(ii) Capital Accounts of the partners; and

(iii) Balance Sheet of the firm after reconstitution.

SOLUTION

Dr. **(I) REVALUATION ACCOUNT** *Cr.*

Particulars	₹	*Particulars*	₹
To Building	50,000	By Investments	15,000

To Machinery (Loss on revaluation)	1,30,000	By Partners' capital A/cs		
To Provision for doubtful debts	1,39,000	A	1,52,000	
		B	91,200	
		C	60,800	3,04,000
	3,19,000			3,19,000

Dr. **(II) PARTNERS' CAPITAL ACCOUNTS** Cr.

Particulars	*A* ₹	*B* ₹	*C* ₹	*D* ₹	*Particulars*	*A* ₹	*B* ₹	*C* ₹	*D* ₹
To Revaluation A/c	1,52,000	91,200	60,800	–	By Balance b/d	4,50,000	1,30,000	1,70,000	–
To Goodwill	50,000	30,000	20,000	–	By Contingency Reserve	37,500	22,500	15,000	–
To A and B	–	–	1,00,000	1,00,000	By Investment Fluctuation Reserve	50,000	30,000	20,000	–
To Investments	–	75,000	–	–	By C and D	50,000	1,50,000	–	–
To Advertisement suspense	12,500	7,500	5,000	–	By Bank (b.f.)	27,000	–	3,80,800	3,00,000
To B's Loan A/c(b.f.)	–	1,28,800	–	–					
To Balance c/d	4,00,000	–	4,00,000	2,00,000					
	6,14,500	3,32,500	5,85,800	3,00,000		6,14,500	3,32,500	5,85,800	3,00,000

(III) BALANCE SHEET AS AT 01.04.2008
(AFTER RETIREMENT OF B AND ADMISSION OF D)

Liabilities	₹	*Assets*		₹
Partners' Capital Accounts :		Building		10,00,000
A	4,00,000	Machinery		5,20,000
C	4,00,000	Furniture		2,15,000
D	2,00,000	Stock		6,50,000
Long term loan	15,00,000	Debtors	6,95,000	
B's loan	1,28,800	*Less:* Provision for doubtful debts	1,39,000	5,56,000
Sundry creditors	8,00,000	Cash at bank		4,87,800
	34,28,800			34,28,800

Working Notes:

Dr. **(I) BANK ACCOUNT** Cr.

Particulars	₹	*Particulars*	₹
To A's capital A/c	27,000	By Balance b/d (Overdraft)	2,20,000
To C's capital A/c	3,80,800	By Balance c/d (Bal. fig.)	4,87,800
To D's capital A/c	3,00,000		
	7,07,800		7,07,800

(ii) Goodwill, already shown in the Balance Sheet of ₹ 1,00,000, is firstly written off and then an adjusting entry is passed for revalued goodwill of ₹ 5,00,000 in sacrificing and gaining ratio of partners. This treatment is given based on the para 36 of AS 10, which states that goodwill should be recorded in the books only when some consideration in money *or* money's worth has been paid for it.

(iii) Calculation of sacrificing and gaining ratio

Partners	*New share*	*Old share*	*Share Sacrificed*	*Share Gained*
A	2/5	5/10	2/5 – 5/10 = 1/10	
B		3/10		3/10
C	2/5	2/10	2/5 – 2/10 = 1/5	
D	1/5			1/5

ADJUSTING ENTRY TO ADJUST GOODWILL

Particulars		*Dr. (₹)*	*Cr. (₹)*
C's Capital A/c (₹ 5,00,000 × 1/5)	Dr.	1,00,000	
D's Capital A/c (₹ 5,00,000 × 1/5)	Dr.	1,00,000	
To A's Capital A/c (₹ 5,00,000 × 1/10)			50,000
To B's Capital A/c (₹ 5,00,000 × 3/10)			1,50,000

(IV) CAPITALS OF A, C AND D AS PER NEW RATIO

Particulars	₹
Total Capital of the firm after admission	10,00,000
A's share [10,00,000 × 2/5]	4,00,000
C's share [10,00,000 × 2/5]	4,00,000
D's share [10,00,000 × 1/5]	2,00,000

PROBLEM 17.3

Ram, Rahim and Robert are partners, sharing Profits and Losses in the ratio of 5 : 3 : 2. It was decided that Robert would retire on 31.3.2005 and in his place Richard would be admitted as a partner with new profit sharing between Ram, Rahim and Richard at 3 : 2 : 1.

BALANCE SHEET OF RAM, RAHIM AND ROBERT AS AT 31.3.2005

Liabilities	₹	*Assets*	₹
Capital Accounts:		Cash in Hand	20,000
Ram	1,00,000	Cash at Bank	1,00,000
Rahim	1,50,000	Sundry Debtors	5,00,000
Robert	2,00,000	Stock in Trade	2,00,000
General Reserve	2,00,000	Plant & Machinery	3,00,000
Sundry Creditors	8,00,000	Land & Building	5,30,000
Loan from Richard	2,00,000		
	16,50,000		16,50,000

Retirement of Robert and admission of Richard is on the following terms:

(a) Plant & Machinery to be depreciated by ₹ 30,000.

(b) Land and Building to be valued at ₹ 6,00,000.

(c) Stock to be valued at 95% of book value.

(d) Provision for doubtful debts @ 10% to be provided on debtors.

(e) General Reserve to be apportioned amongst Ram, Rahim and Robert.

(f) The firm's goodwill to be valued at 2 years' purchase of the average profits of the last 3 years. The relevant figures are:
Year ended 31.3.2002 – Profit ₹ 50,000
Year ended 31.3.2003 – Profit ₹ 60,000
Year ended 31.3.2004 – Profit ₹ 55,000

(g) Out of the amount due to Robert ₹ 2,00,000 would be retained as loan by the firm and the balance will be settled immediately.

(h) Richard's capital should be equal to 50% of the combined capital of Ram and Rahim.

Required: **Prepare**

(i) Capital accounts of the partners; and

(ii) Balance Sheet of the reconstituted firm.

SOLUTION

Dr. **PARTNERS' CAPITAL ACCOUNTS** *Cr.*

Particulars	*Ram* ₹	*Rahim* ₹	*Robert* ₹	*Richard* ₹	*Particulars*	*Ram* ₹	*Rahim* ₹	*Robert* ₹	*Richard* ₹
To Revaluation A/c	10,000	6,000	4,000	—	By Balanceb/d	1,00,000	1,50,000	2,00,000	—
To Loan from Robert A/c	—	—	2,00,000	—	By General Reserve	1,00,000	60,000	40,000	—
					By Goodwill	55,000	33,000	22,000	—
To Bank	—	—	58,000	—		—	—	—	—
To Balance c/d	2,45,000	2,37,000	—	—					
	2,55,000	2,43,000	2,62,000	—		2,55,000	2,43,000	2,62,000	
To Goodwill*	55,000	36,667	—	18,333	By Balance b/d	2,45,000	2,37,000	—	—
To Balance c/d	1,90,000	2,00,333	—	1,95,167	By Loan A/c-transfer	—	—	—	2,00,000
					By Bank	—	—	—	13,500
	2,45,000	2,37,000	—	2,13,500		2,45,000	2,37,000	—	2,13,500

BALANCE SHEET OF THE RECONSTITUTED FIRM (AFTER ADMISSION OF RICHARD)

Liabilities	₹	*Assets*	₹
Capital Accounts:		Land and Building	6,00,000
Ram	1,90,000	Plant and machinery	2,70,000
Rahim	2,00,333	Stock	1,90,000
Richard	1,95,167	Debtors	4,50,000
Sundry Creditors	8,00,000	Cash at bank	55,500
Loan from Robert	2,00,000	Cash in hand	20,000
	15,85,500		15,85,500

Working Notes:

(i) Calculation of Goodwill:

Average Profit = (₹ 50,000 + ₹ 60,000 + ₹ 55,000)/3 = ₹ 55,000

Goodwill = ₹ 55,000 × 2 years = ₹ 1,10,000.

As per para 36 of AS-10, 'Accounting for Fixed Assets', goodwill should be recorded in the books only when some consideration in money *or* money's worth has been paid for it. Therefore, the goodwill raised at the time of retirement of Robert is to be written off in new raio among remaining partners including new partner—Richard.

Dr. **(II) BANK ACCOUNT** Cr.

Particulars	₹	Particulars	₹
To Balance b/d	1,00,000	By Robert's Capital A/c	58,000
To Richard's Capital A/c	13,500	By Balance c/d	55,500
	1,13,500		1,13,500

(III) REVALUATION ACCOUNT

Particulars	₹	Particulars	₹
To Plant and Machinery	30,000	By Land and building	70,000
To Stock	10,000	By Partners' Capital Accounts.	
To Debtors	50,000	Ram	10,000
		Rahim	6,000
		Robert	4,000
	90,000		90,000

PROBLEM 17.4

E, F and G were partners sharing Profits and Losses in the ratio of 5:3:2 respectively. On 31st March, 2009 Balance Sheet of the firm stood as follows:

Liabilities	₹	Assets	₹
Capital A/cs:		Buildings	55,000
E	50,000	Furniture	25,000
F	40,000	Stock	42,000
G	28,000	Debtors	20,000
Creditors	33,500	Cash at Bank	11,200
Outstanding Expenses	1,700		
	1,53,200		1,53,200

On 31st March, 2009, E decided to retire and F and G decided to continue as equal partners. Other terms of retirement were as follows:

(i) Building be appreciated by 20%.

(ii) Furniture be depreciated by 10%.

(iii) A provision of 5% be created for bad debts on debtors.

(iv) Goodwill be valued at two years' purchase of profit for the latest accounting year. The firm's profit for the year ended 31st March, 2009 was ₹ 25,000. No goodwill account is to be raised in the books of accounts.

(v) Fresh capital be introduced by F and G to the extent of ₹ 10,000 and ₹ 35,000 respectively.

(vi) Out of sum payable to retiring partner E, a sum of ₹ 45,000 be paid immediately and the balance be transferred to his loan account bearing interest @ 12% per annum. The loan is to be paid off by 31st March, 2011.

One month after E's retirement, F and G agreed to admit E's son H as a partner with one-forth share in Profits/Losses. E agreed that the balance in his loan account be converted into H's Capital. E also agreed to forgo one month's interest on his loan.

It was also agreed that H will bring in, his share of goodwill through book adjustment, valued at the price on the date of E's retirement. No goodwill account is to be raised in the books.

You are requested to pass necessary Journal Entries to give effect to the above transactions and prepare Partner's Capital Accounts.

SOLUTION

JOURNAL

Date.	*Particulars*		*Dr. (₹)*	*Cr. (₹)*
1.	Building A/c	Dr.	11,000	
	To Revaluation A/c			11,000
	(Being building appreciated)			
2.	Revaluation A/c	Dr.	3,500	
	To Furniture A/c			2,500
	To Provision for Doubtful Debts A/c			1,000
	(Being furniture depreciated by 10% and Provision for doubtful debts created @ 5% on Debtors)			
3.	Revaluation A/c	Dr.	7,500	
	To E's Capital A/c			3,750
	To F's Capital A/c			2,250
	To G's Capital A/c			1,500
	(Being profit on revaluation transferred to capital accounts of partners)			
4.	F's Capital A/c	Dr.	10,000	
	G's Capital A/c	Dr.	15,000	
	To E's Capital A/c			25,000
	(Being adjustment for E's share of goodwill)			
5.	Bank A/c	Dr.	45,000	
	To F's Capital A/c			10,000
	To G's Capital A/c			35,000
	(Being fresh capital introduced by F and G)			
6.	E's Capital A/c	Dr.	78,750	
	To Bank A/c			45,000
	To E's Loan A/c			33,750
	(Being settlement of E's capital on his retirement)			
7.	E's Loan A/c	Dr.	33,750	
	To H's Capital A/c			33,750
	(Transfer of E's Loan Account to H's Capital Account)			
8.	H's Capital A/c	Dr.	12,500	
	To F's Capital A/c			6,250
	To G's Capital A/c			6,250
	(Being adjustment entry passed for H's share of goodwill)			

Dr. **PARTNER'S CAPITAL ACCOUNTS** Cr.

Particulars	E ₹	F ₹	G ₹	H ₹	Particulars	E ₹	F ₹	G ₹	H ₹
To E (Goodwill)	—	10,000	15,000	—	By Balance b/d	50,000	40,000	28,000	—
To Bank	45,000	—	—	—	By Revaluation A/c	3,750	2,250	1,500	—
To E's Loan A/c	33,750	—	—	—	By F (Goodwill)	10,000	—	—	—
To Balance c/d	—	42,250	49,500	—	By G (Goodwill)	15,000	—	—	
					By Bank(fresh capital)	—	10,000	35,000	—
	78,750	52,250	64,500	—		78,750	52,250	65,500	—
To F (Goodwill)	—	—	—	6,250	By Balance b/d		42,250	49,500	—
To G (Goodwill)	—	—	—	6,250	By E's Loan A/c	—	—	—	33.750
To Balance c/d	—	48,500	55,750	21,250	By H (goodwill)		6,250	6,250	—
	—	48,500	55,750	33,750		—	48,500	55,750	33,750

Working Notes:

(I) CALCULATION OF GAINING RATIO

Partners	New ratio	Old ratio	Gain	Sacrifice
E		5/10		5/10
F	1/2	3/10	1/2 – 3/10 = 2/10	
G	1/2	2/10	1/2 – 2/10 = 3/10	

Hence, ratio of gain between F and G = 2:3

(ii) Value of Total Goodwill of the firm = ₹ 25,000 × 2 = ₹ 50,000

E's Share = ₹ 50,000 × 5/10 = ₹ 25,000

F will bear = ₹ 25,000 × 2/5 = ₹10,000

G will bear = ₹ 25,000 × 3/5 = ₹ 15,000

(iii) H's share of goodwill = ₹ 50,000 × 1/4 = ₹ 12,500

F and G share equal profits. Therefore, their sacrificing ratio will also be equal

Hence, each of them will be credited with ₹ 6,250.

PROBLEM 15

P, Q and R were partners sharing profits and losses in the ratio of 2 : 2 : 1. R wants to retire from partnership on 31-3-2011 and S wants to join the partnership on the same date, to which both P & Q agreed. The Balance Sheet of the partnership firm as on 31-03-2011 and other information were as detailed below:

BALANCE SHEET AS AT 31-03-2011

Liabilities	₹	Assets	₹
Partners' Capital A/cs:		Fixed assets	6,00,000
P	4,80,000	Stockinhand	2,00,000
Q	3,20,000	Sundry debtors	2,80,000
R	2,40,000	Cash at bank	1,60,000
General reserve	40,000	Cash in hand	40,000

Sundry creditors	2,00,000		
	12,80,000		12,80,000

P, Q and S agree to share profits and losses in equal ratio in future. Value of goodwill is taken to be ₹ 1,80,000. Fixed assets are revalued upwards by ₹ 1,20,000 and stock by ₹ 40,000. A debtor from whom ₹ 20,000 was due, become insolvent. No amount will be received from him in future and same is not recorded in the books and balance sheet as above. Claim of R will be settled in full. P, Q and S agree to make their capital proportionate to their new profits sharing ratio. Balance amount receivable from/payable to partners will be brought in by partners/paid to partners immediately. All these transactions viz., claim of R and amount receivable/payable to partners will be routed through bank only. New partners also want to maintain ₹ 3,20,000 bank balance for working capital requirement. However, they don't want to show goodwill in the books of accounts.

(i) Revaluation account

(ii) Capital accounts of partners and

(iii) Balance Sheet of the firm as newly constituted.

SOLUTION

Dr. **REVALUATION ACCOUNT** *Cr.*

Particulars	₹	*Particulars*	₹
To Sundry Debtors	20,000	By Fixed assets	1,20,000
To Profit on Revaluation t/f to:		By Stock in hand	40,000
P's Capital A/c	56,000		
Q's Capital A/c	56,000		
R's Capital A/c	28,000		
	1,60,000		1,60,000

Dr. **PARTNERS' CAPITAL ACCOUNTS** *Cr.*

Particulars	P ₹	Q ₹	R ₹	S ₹	*Particulars*	P ₹	Q ₹	R ₹	S ₹
To P, Q, and R	—	—	—	60,000	By Balance b/d	4,80,000	3,20,000	2,40,000	—
To Bank (b.f.)	1,04,000	—	3,12,000	—	By General reserve	16,000	16,000	8,000	—
To Balance c/d	4,60,000	4,60,000	—	4,60,000	By Reva. profit	56,000	56,000	28,000	—
					By S	12,000	12,000	36,000	—
					By Bank (Bal. fig)	—	56,000	—	5,20,000
	5,64,000	4,60,000	3,12,000	5,20,000		5,64,000	4,60,000	3,12,000	5,20,000

BALANCE SHEET AS AT 31.03.2011 (AFTER RETIREMENT OF R AND ADMISSION OF S)

Liabilities		₹	*Assets*	₹
Partners' capital A/cs (Bal. fig.)			Fixed assets	7,20,000
P	4,60,000		Stock in hand	2,40,000
Q	4,60,000		Sundry debtors	2,60,000
S	4,60,000	13,80,000	Cash at bank	3,20,000
Sundry Creditors		2,00,000	Cash in hand	40,000
		15,80,000		15,80,000

Working Notes:

(I) ADJUSTMENT OF GOODWILL

Particulars	*P* ₹	*Q* ₹	*R* ₹	*S* ₹	*Total* ₹
Credited to old partners in 2:2:1	72,000	72,000	36,000	—	1,80,000
Written off among remaining partners including Sin 1:1:1	60,000	60,000	—	60,000	1,80,000
Cr.	12,000	12,000	36,000		
Dr.				60,000	

(ii) As per balance sheet as on 31.03.2011 (after retirement of R and admission of S), balancing figure of total partners' capital is ₹ 13,80,000 (i.e. Total assets ₹ 15,80,000 – Sundry creditors ₹ 2,00,000). Since partners agree to make their capital proportionate to their new profit sharing ratio i.e. 1:1:1, capital of each partnerwill be ₹ 4,60,000 (i.e. ₹ 13,80,000/3).

(III) BANK ACCOUNT

Dr. *Cr.*

Particulars	₹	*Particulars*	₹
To Balance b/d	1,60,000	By P's Capital A/c	1,04,000
To Q's Capital A/c	56,000	By R's Capital A/c	3,12,000
To S's Capital A/c	5,20,000	By Balance c/d	3,20,000
	7,36,000		7,36,000

PROBLEM 17.5

Anuj, Ayush and Piyush are in partnership sharing profits and losses in the ratio 2 : 2 : 1. Their Balance Sheet as on 31.3.2014 is as follows:

Liabilities	₹	*Assets*	₹
Anuj's Capital	3,75,000	Fixed Assets: Plant	7,87,000
Ayush's Capital	2,80,000	Stock	1,03,000
Piyush's Capital	2,25,000	Debtors	1,56,000
General Reserve	1,88,000	Bank FD	2,25,000
Creditors	2,16,000	Bank balance	13,000
	12,84,000		12,84,000

Anuj decided to retire with effect from 1.4.2014.

The remaining partners agreed to share profits and losses equally in future.

The following adjustments were agreed to be made upon retirement of Anuj:

(i) Goodwill was to be valued at 1 year purchase of the average profits of the preceding 3 years on the date of retirement.

The average profits of the past 3 years were as follows:

Year ended	₹
31.3.2014	3,30,000 (as per draft accounts)
31.3.2013	2,32,000
31.3.2012	2,20,000

The partners decided not to raise goodwill account in the books.

(ii) Plant to be depreciated by 10%; Creditors amounting to ₹ 10,000 were omitted to be recorded; ₹ 6,000 is to be written off from stock; Provision for doubtful debts to be created @ 5% of the debtors; Interest accrued on FD amounting to ₹ 9,000 was omitted to be recorded.

The above adjustments were to be made from the profit for the year ended 31.3.2014 before calculation of goodwill.

(iii) Anuj agreed to make over the bank FD including interest accrued thereon in part payment of his dues and the balance would remain as a loand carrying interest of 8% p.a.

(iv) Ayush and Piyush agree to bring in sufficient cash to make their capital proportiionate and maintain a bank balance of ₹ 1,50,000.

You are required to prepare

(1) Capital accounts of parnters as on 1.4.2014 giving effect to the above adjustments.

(2) Balance Sheet as on 1.4.2014 after Anuj's retirement.

SOLUTION

Dr. **CAPITAL ACCOUNTS OF PARTNERS** *Cr.*

Particulars	*Anuj* ₹	*Ayush* ₹	*Piyush* ₹	*Particulars*	*Anuj* ₹	*Ayush* ₹	*Piyush* ₹
To Anuj's Capital A/c		22,950	68,850	By Balance b/d	3,75,000	2,80,000	2,25,000
To Bank FD A/c	2,25,000			By General Reserve A/c	75,200	75,200	37,600
To Accrued interest on FD	9,000			By Ayush's			
To Revaluation A/c	37,400	37,400	18,700	Capital A/c	22,950		–
To Anuj's Loan A/c	2,70,600			Capital A/c	68,850		
To Balance C/f	–	3,03,450	3,03,450	By Bank A/c	–	8,600	1,28,400
	5,42,000	3,63,800	3,91,000		5,42,000	3,63,800	3,91,000

BALANCE SHEET AS ON 31.3.2014 (AFTER ANUJ'S RETIREMENT)

Liabilities		₹	*Assets*		₹
Capital A/cs:			Plant	7,87,000	
Ayush (8,77,500/2)	3,03,450		*Less:* Depreciation	(78,700)	7,08,300
Pyish (8,77,500/2)	3,03,450	6,06,900	Stock	1,03,000	
Creditrors [2,16,000 – 10,000]		2,26,000	*Less:* Written off	(6,000)	97,000
Anuj's Loan		2,70,600	Debtors	1,56,000	
			Less: Provisions	(7,800)	1,48,200
			Interest Accrued on FD	9,000	—
			Less: Taken over by Anuj	(9,000)	—
			Bank FD	2,25,000	
			Less: Taken over by Anuj	(2,25,000)	—
			Bank Balance		1,50,000
			(13,000 + 8,600 + 1,28,400)		
		11,03,500			11,03,500

Working Notes:

Dr. **REVALUATION ACCOUNT** Cr.

Particulars	₹	*Particulars*		₹
To Plant A/c	78,700	By interest accrued on FD		9,000
To Creditors A/c	10,000	By Capital A/c:		
To Stock A/c	6,000	Anuj	37,400	
To RDD A/c	7,800	Ayush	37,400	
		Piyush	18,700	93,500
	1,02,500			1,02,500

(2) Goodwill adjustment:

(a) Goodwill valuation:

Profit for the year ended 31.3.2012		₹ 2,20,000
Profit for the year ended 31.3.2013		₹ 2,32,000
Profit for the year ended 31.3.2014:		
Profit as per draft accounts	3,30,000	
Less: Depreciation on plant	(78,700)	
Less: Unrecorded creditors/purchases	(10,000)	
Less: Amount written off from stock	(6,000)	
Less: Provision	(7,800)	
Add: Interest accrued on FD	9,000	₹ 2,36,500
Total Profit for 3 years		₹ 6,88,500
Average Profit = 6,88,500/3 year = 2,29,500		
Goodwill = 2,29,500 × 1 years' purchase = ₹ 2,29,500		

(B) GOODWILL ADJUSTMENT:

Particulars	*Anuj* ₹	*Ayush* ₹	*Piyush* ₹
Goodwill raised (2:2:1)	91,800 Cr	91,800 Cr	45,900 Cr
Goodwill written off (1:1)	—	1,14,750 Dr	1,14,750 Dr
Net effect	91,800 Cr	22,950 Dr	68,850 Dr

19 ACCOUNTING IN COMPUTERISED ENVIRONMENT

LEARNING OBJECTIVES

After studying this chapter, you should be able to understand:

- ◇ Meaning of a Computer
- ◇ Capabilities of a Computer
- ◇ Role of Computers in Accounting
- ◇ Manual Accounting System and Computerised Accounting System
- ◇ When can a Computerised Accounting System be used?
- ◇ How can Computerised Accounting System be used?
- ◇ Salient Features of Computerised Accounting System
- ◇ Significance of Computerised Accounting System
- ◇ Classification and Codification of Accounts
- ◇ Pre-Packaged Accounting Software
- ◇ Advantages of Pre-Packaged Accounting Software
- ◇ Disadvantage of Pre-Packaged Accounting Software
- ◇ Considerations for Selection of Pre-Packaged Accounting Software
- ◇ Customised Accounting Software
- ◇ Advantages of a Customised Accounting Package
- ◇ Disadvantages of a Customised Accounting Package
- ◇ Accounting Software as part of Enterprise Resource Planning (ERP)
- ◇ Outsourcing of Accounting Function
- ◇ Generating Reports from Software

1.0 MEANING OF A COMPUTER

A computer is an electronic machine which operates on given instructions and PROCESSES the INPUT DATA, to convert it into some OUTPUT (i.e., INFORMATION). Let us consider a simple real life example to make 'Rice Pulao' in the kitchen to understand the meaning of Data, Information and Processing.

In Kitchen	In Computer
Raw 'Rice', Water, Salt, pepper and other ingredients	DATA *or* INPUT
Act of steaming the above ingredients in a pressure cooker by putting them on fire	Processing
Cooked Rice Pulao	Information *or* output

Thus,

1. **Data** is collection of facts and figures which has no meaning when collected. ***For Example***, somebody asks names of the students of your class and enters these in the computer without any sequence.
2. **Processing** is the sequence of actions taken on data to convert it into information which is meaningful to the user. It can be calculations, comparisons *or* decisions taken by the computer.
3. **INFORMATION** is the final result *or* output which we get after processing of the data.

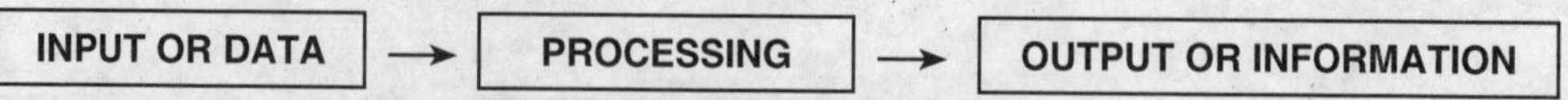

The computer is also called a faithful, never tiring but a foolish servant.

It is **faithful** in the sense that it follows the given set of instructions without fail. It does not deviate a bit from the instructions and follows them in the prescribed order.

It **never tires** because it is a machine and has phenomenal stamina. It can process any volume of data and can make any number of complex calculations on a variety of variables effortlessly.

It is a **foolish servant** in the sense that it has no thinking ability. It only does what it is asked to do that too only in the language it understands. It cannot by itself discern any error in the data *or* information fed to it. Also it is not capable of taking any initiative in a contingency.

2.0 CAPABILITIES OF A COMPUTER

The capabilities of a computer are as follows:

1. **Accuracy** — Computer is a 100% accurate machine. The accuracy of the computer depends upon the quality of the input and instructions. Thus, computer is as accurate as the input and instructions are.
2. **Speed** — Computer can process the data at very high speed. It makes calculations at a very high speed. A powerful computer is capable of adding together 10 digits numbers in 300 to 400 nano seconds (i.e., about 3 million calculations per second). It can process and retrieve huge volume of data very quickly.
3. **Storage** — Computer can store huge data, information and softwares (i.e., programme files) in its storage space depending upon the capacity of hard disk installed.

   The unit which is used to store the programs and data is known as storage unit (main memory). The main memory of a computer is divided into various cells. Each cell holds certain amount of information depending on the word length which may be 8 bits, *or* 16 bits *or* 32 bits depending on the technical structure of the computer. The memory is usually a multiple of 4,096 which represents 64* 64 core array. Commercially thousands words are designated by K and the capacity of 4,096 is taken roughly as 4K.

   Units of Storage Capability

   8 Bits = 1 Byte
   1024 Bytes = 1 Kilo bytes (KB)
   1024 Kilo bytes = 1 Mega bytes (MB)
   1024 Mega bytes = 1 Giga bytes (GB)

   Now-a-days, hard disks of the capacities of 10 GB, 20 GB, 40 GB and 80 GB are available.
4. **Consistency** — Computer given the same results without any variations on consistent basis irrespective of the number of times the programme is run. This property of repeating the same results without variation is known as consistency.

3.0 ROLE OF COMPUTERS IN ACCOUNTING

Nowadays, computers are used in almost all aspects of accounting. The most common applications of a computer in accounting covers the following:

1. **Transaction Recording** — Computers can be used for maintaining the records of day-to-day transactions upto date. As the number of transactions increases, it becomes difficult to keep the records of all the transactions up-to-date manually. The required information is readily available which can be used by the management for planning, decision-making *or* control purposes.
2. **Debtors Accounting** — Computers can be used for maintaining the records of debtors up-to-date. Debtors Ledger, Statement of Account, Collection List, Analysis of Debtors Outstandings by age and credit limit can be prepared and maintained up-to-date.
3. **Inventory Accounting** — Computers can be used for maintaining the store records up-to-date. Stores Ledger, Material Cost Analysis by cost centres and cost units, Stores Inventory, Slow Moving Inventory, etc., can be prepared and maintained up-to-date.
4. **Payroll Accounting** — Computers can be used for maintaining the payroll records up-to-date. Payroll and Pay slips, Income-tax, ESI and Provident Fund Deduction Statements. Annual Provident Fund Statements, Employee's Loan Accounts, Wages Analysis by cost centres, cost units can be prepared and maintained up-to-date.
5. **Financial Accounting** — Computer facilitates the preparation of —
   - (i) Vouchers — Cash, Non-Cash, Transfer
   - (ii) Cash Memos and Credit Invoices
   - (iii) Books of Accounts — Cash Book, Purchases Book, Sales Book, Sales Returns Book, Purchase Returns Book, Bills Receivable Book, Bills Payable Book, Journal Proper.
   - (iv) Ledger Accounts
   - (v) Trial Balance
   - (vi) Trading & Profit & Loss Account
   - (vii) Balance Sheet
   - (ix) Chart showing various ratios
   - (x) Loan Repayment Schedules
6. **Cost Accounting** — Computer facilitates the preparation of — (a) Cost Reports, (b) Cost Sheet
7. **Budgetary Control** — Computerised accounting system facilitates to exercise budgetary control efficiently. It facilitates the quick preparation of several budgets (for example, Sales Budget, Production Budget, Purchase Budget, Expenses Budget, Cash Budget) and several Budget Reports showing control ratios etc.
8. **Standard Costing** — Computerised accounting system facilitates the use of standard costing in efficient manner. It can calculate the various variances (i.e. difference between Standard Data and Actual Data) and can give analysis of variances.
9. **Sensitivity Analysis** — Computerised Accounting facilitates sensitivity analysis (i.e., analyzing the effects under various situations of changed conditions) with a view to ascertain the most sensitive factor(s).
10. Break Even Analysis
11. Evaluation of Capital Budgeting Decisions
12. Evaluation of Capital Structure Decisions
13. Evaluation of Dividend Policy Decisions
14. Evaluation of Working Capital Management Policies

4.0 DISTINCTION BETWEEN MANUAL ACCOUNTING SYSTEM AND COMPUTERISED ACCOUNTING SYSTEM

Computerised Accounting System differs from Manual Accounting System in the following respects:

Basis of Distinction	Manual Accounting System	Computerised Accounting System
1. **Speed**	The speed of performing tasks manually is very **slow** as compared to computers.	Computers are able to perform all the tasks at **high** speed. It can process a millions of instructions (MIS) per second.
2. **Accuracy**	Humans are prone to errors. Managing accounts manually involves **great chances of errors.**	Computer results are accurate. Once the right instructions have bene given to it, the **chances of the committing errors** are almost **zero.**
3. **Consistency**	A man gets **tired** after some time and needs break in between to work again.	The computer **never tires.** It can give a consistently good performance hour after hour.
4. **Storage**	**Lots of ledger books and files** have to be **maintained** in a manual system.	It **can store a large amount of data** in its memory. Storage of data and information on the computer allows reduction of paper filing and other mundane tasks.
5. **Duplicacy**	There **can be** duplicacy of records.	Due to some advanced features, duplication of records is **not possible.**
6. **Modification**	Updation & deletion of records is a tough and **complicated task** if done manually. It is also time consuming.	Modification can be **easily done.** Data can be easily updated, added *or* deleted in a computer system.
7. **Data Sharing**	In a manual system, same data **cannot be shared** by different persons at the same time.	Sharing of data is **possible** through networking.
8. **Deligence**	A man gets **bored** doing same type of task again and again.	It performs the same task again and again **without getting bored.**
9. **Efficiency**	Human efficiency **decreases** with age.	A computer's efficiency **does not decrease** by age.

For a very long period of time organisations are maintaining their accounts manually. Still prevalent, manual accounting system, now and by large has been replaced by computerised accounting system which provides more accuracy, efficiency and speed with seldom errors and consistency. A manual system where one gets tired and bored after some time because of performing the same task again and again, computer proves to be delegant and efficient.

The basic differences between a manual accounting system and a computerised accounting system are as follows:

5.0 WHEN CAN A COMPUTERISED ACCOUNTING SYSTEM BE USED?

A Computerised Accounting System can be used under the following conditions:

1. **High Speed Required** — When accounts are to be processed at high speed. ***For Example***, in case of accounting for Credit Card, Debit Card, ATM Card.

2. **Large Volume of Transactions** — When the volume of transactions is very large.
3. **Accuracy Required** — When accounts are to be maintained error free.
4. **Storage Required** — When a large amount of accounting data is required to be stored.
5. **Modification Required** — When accounting data are to be updated, added *or* deleted on consistent basis.
6. **Data Sharing Required** — When accounting data are to be shared by several persons for several functions at the same time.

6.0 HOW CAN COMPUTERISED ACCOUNTING SYSTEM BE USED?

A Computerised Accounting System can be used by using own developed accounting software *or* market accounting softwares such as TALLY, BUSY, MUNIMJI etc.

The advantages of a computer accounting system over a manual accounting system has enabled the computer to be used in various fields of life. Some of the areas where a computerised accounting system can be used are:

1. **Financial Statements** — Computerised accounting system facilitates the quick preparation of accurate financial statements (i.e. Income Statement, Balance Sheet and Cash Flow Statement).
2. **Inventory** — It facilitates the recording of details of purchases and sales of goods and the ascertainment of closing stocks of various goods in hand after each & every transaction of purchase and sale.
3. **Billing** — Computers can be used to prepare Cash Memos and Credit Invoices in respect of sale of goods.
4. **Banking** — Banks use computers to make their job of keeping accounts much easier. It also helps them to give better customer service. ATM *or* Automatic Teller Machine is a very good example of computerised machine. Everytime a customer deposits *or* withdraws money, his account gets updated automatically.
5. **Tickets Reservation** — Railways and airline tickets for various places can be booked from different places.
6. **Automatic Vending Machines** — Computerised system facilitates the installation and maintaining the automatic vending machines such as Playwin Lottery, Weighing Machines, Pure Drink Machines.
7. **Budgetary Control** — Computerised accounting system facilitates to exercise budgetary control efficiently. It facilitates the quick preparation of several budgets (for example, Sales Budget, Production Budget, Purchase Budget, Expenses Budget, Cash Budget) and several Budget Reports showing control ratios etc.
8. **Standard Costing** — Computerised accounting system facilitates the use of standard costing in efficient manner. It can calculate the various variances (i.e. difference between Standard Data and Actual Data) and can give analysis of variances.
9. **Sensitivity Analysis** — Computerised Accounting facilitates sensitivity analysis (i.e., analysing the effects under various situations of changed conditions) with a view to ascertain the most sensitive factor(s).

   For example, a company is selling 1,000 units of a product at ₹ 10 each.

   The variable cost per unit is ₹ 4 and fixed cost per unit is ₹ 2.

   Computerised Accounting System can be used to answer the following questions:

(a) What will the impact on profits if sales volume increases by 20%.

(b) What will the impact on profits if sales volume decreases by 20%.

(c) What will the impact on profits if selling price increases by 20%.

(d) What will the impact on profits if selling price decreases by 20%.

(e) What will the impact on profits if variable cost increases by 20%.

(f) What will the impact on profits if variable cost decreases by 20%.

(g) What will the impact on profits if fixed cost increases by 20%.

(h) What will the impact on profits if fixed cost decreases by 20%.

(i) What will the impact on profits if total cost increases by 20%.

(j) What will the impact on profits if selling price increases by 20% but sales volume decreases by 20%.

(k) What will the impact on profits if selling price decrease by 20% but sales volume increases by 20%.

10. Apart from all these areas, there are offices and organisations that use the computes to increase their productivity and profits.

7.0 SALIENT FEATURES OF COMPUTERISED ACCOUNTING SYSTEM

Computer information system environment exists when one *or* more computer(s) of any type *or* size is (are) involved in the processing of any information, whether those computers are operated by the entity *or* by a third party. A computerised accounting environment will therefore have the following salient features:

1. The processing of information will be by one *or* more computers.
2. The computer *or* computers may be operated by the entity *or* by a third party.
3. The processing of financial information by the computer is done with the help of one *or* more computer softwares.
4. A computer software includes any program *or* routine that performs a desired function *or* set of functions and the documentation required to describe and maintain that program *or* routine.
5. The computer software used for the accounting system may be an acquired software *or* may be developed specifically for the business.
6. Acquired software may consist of a spread sheet package *or* may be prepackaged accounting software.

8.0 SIGNIFICANCE OF COMPUTERISED ACCOUNTING SYSTEM

1. The speed with which accounts can be maintained is several fold higher.
2. Automatic Correct Balancing of Ledger Accounts
3. Automatic Tailied Trial balance unless some mistake is made while recording the opening balance.
4. Automatic Income Statement
5. Automatic Balance Sheet

Threat to Computerised Accounting System

The only concerns that has increased today are concerns for controls, security and integrity of the computer system as more and more information is stored not in the hard print but as soft copies inside the computer. Issue like unauthorised access to the data either through the local area network *or* through the internet by hacking into the company server are becoming potential threat to the computer usage.

9.0 CLASSIFICATION AND CODIFICATION OF ACCOUNTS

Some computerised accounting softwares support a coded accounting system and some support even a non-coded accounting system. A coded accounting system is more convenient where there are numerous account heads and the complexity is high. It also to some extent reduces the possibility of the same account existing in several names due to spelling mistakes *or* abbreviations used.

A proper codification requires a systematic grouping of accounts. The major groups *or* heads could be Assets, Liabilities, Revenue Receipts, Capital Receipts, Revenue Expenditure, Capital Expenditure. The sub-groups *or* minor heads could be "Cash" *or* "Receivables" *or* "Payables" and so on. The grouping and codification is dependant upon the type of organisation and the extent of sub-division required for reporting on the basis of profit centres *or* product lines. There could a classification based on geographical location as well.

The main unit of classification in accounts should be the **major head** which should be divided into **minor heads**, each of which should have a number of subordinate heads, generally shown as **sub-heads**. The sub-heads are further divided into **detailed heads**. Sometimes major heads may be divided into 'sub-major heads' before their further division into minor heads.

The Major heads, Minor heads, Sub-heads and Detailed heads together may constitute a four tier arrangement of the classification structure of Accounts.

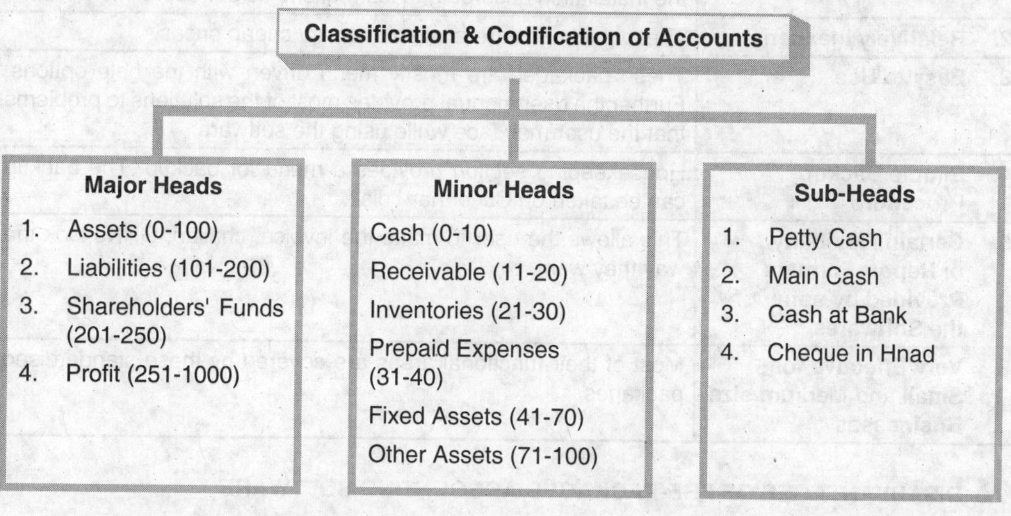

10.0 PRE-PACKAGED ACCOUNTING SOFTWARE

1. There are several prepackaged accounting software which are available in the market and are used extensively for small and medium sized organisations.
2. These softwares are easy to use, relatively inexpensive and readily available.
3. The installation of these softwares are very simple. An installation diskette *or* CD is provided with the software which can be used to install the software on a personal computer. A network version of this software is also generally available which needs to be installed on the server and work can be performed from the various workstations *or* nodes connected to the server.
4. Along with the software an user's manual is provided which guides the user on how to use the software.
5. After installation of the software, the user should check the version of the software to ensure that they have been provided with the latest.
6. The vendor normally provides regular updates to take care of the changes of law as well as add features to the existing software.

7. These softwares normally have a section which provides for the creation of a company. The name, address, phone numbers and other details of the company like VAT registration number, PAN and TAN numbers are feeded into the system. The accounting period has to be set by inserting the first and the last day of the financial year.

The next step in the use of this software could be the creation of accounts. This is done by adding the accounts along with their codes into the master file files. Each account has to be classified into whether it is an asset *or* liability *or* an income *or* expenditure to the system. The opening balances are to be entered into the master file files. The company parameters need to be set at this point of time so that the accounts which are the cash, bank, sundry debtors, sundry creditors, etc. are known to the system. The customers' names, addresses and other basic details are also entered in the customer master file. Similarly, the creditors details are entered into the creditor master file files. Product details are entered through the product master file files. Here the unit of measurement and the opening stock quantities including the values are provided. The system of valuation of stock like the FIFO, LIFO, Weighted average, etc. are defined in the product master file files.

11.0 ADVANTAGES OF PRE-PACKAGED ACCOUNTING SOFTWARE

1. Easy to Install	The CD containing set up file is to be inserted and run to complete the installation according to instructions as per user's manuals.
2. Relatively Inexpensive	These packages are available at very cheap prices.
3. Easy to Use	These packages are mostly menu driven with the help options. Further the user manual provides most of the solutions to problems that the user may face while using the software.
4. Simple Backup Procedure	Housekeeping section provides a menu for backup. The backup can be taken on CD *or* hard disk.
5. Certain Flexibility of Report Formats Provided by some of the Softwares	This allows the user to make the invoice, challan, GRNs look the way they want.
6. Very Effective for Small and Medium size Businesses	Most of their functional areas are covered by these standardised packages.

12.0 DISADVANTAGES OF PRE-PACKAGED ACCOUNTING SOFTWARE

1. Does not cover Peculiarities of Specific Business	A standard package may not be able to take care of the complexities of a specific business.
2. Does not cover all Functional Areas	These packages may not cover all functional areas such as production process.
3. Customisation may not be Possible: is not Sufficient or Serve the Purpose:	These packages may not be customised as per needs of customers.
4. Reports Generated	All reports required for exercising management control may not be available in a standard package.
5. Lack of Security	Security is generally missing in a pre-packaged accounting package since any person can view data of all companies with common access password.

6. **Bugs in the software**	Certain bugs may remain in the software which takes long to be rectified by the vendor and is common in the initial years of the software.

13.0 CONSIDERATIONS FOR SELECTION OF PRE-PACKAGED ACCOUNTING SOFTWARE

The following factors should be considered while selecting pre-packaged accounting software:

1. **Fulfillment of Business Requirements**	The purchaser should ensure whether the available software meets all the business requirements.
2. **Completeness of Reports:**	The purchaser should ensure whether the available software can provide all the reports required by business.
3. **Ease of Use**	The purchaser should ensure whether the available software is easy to operate.
4. **Cost**	The software should not involve very high installation and running cost.
5. **Reputation of the vendor**	It should be ensured whether the vendor has good reputation and good track records *or* not.
6. **Regular updates**	It should be ensured whether the vendor is prepared to give updates.

14.0 CUSTOMISED ACCOUNTING SOFTWARE

Meaning — A customised accounting software is one which is developed on the basis of specific requirements of the organisation.

A feasibility study is first made before the decision to develop a software is made. The life cycle of a customised accounting software begins with the organisation providing the user requirements. Based on the these user requirement the system analyst prepares a requirement specification which is given for approval by the user management. Once the requirement specification is approved, the designing process begins. Development, testing and implementation are the other components of the system development life cycle.

15.0 ADVANTAGES OF A CUSTOMISED ACCOUNTING PACKAGE

1. The functional areas which are not covered in pre-packaged software gets computerised.
2. The input screens can be tailor made to match the input documents for ease of data entry.
3. It provides many MIS reports as per the specification of the organisation.
4. It facilitates the use of Bar-code scanners as input devices suitable for the specific needs of an individual organisation.
5. It can suitably match with the organisational structure of the company.

16.0 DISADVANTAGES OF A CUSTOMISED ACCOUNTING PACKAGE

1. Requirement specifications are incomplete *or* ambiguous resulting in a defective *or* incomplete system.
2. Bugs may remain in the software because of Inadequate testing.
3. Documentation may not complete.
4. Frequent changes made to the system with inadequate change management procedure may result in in system compromise.

5. Vendor may not be unwilling to give support of the software due to other commitments.
6. Vendor may not be willing to part with the source code *or* enter into an escrow agreement.
7. Control measures may be inadequate.
8. There may be delay in completion of the software due to problems with the vendor *or* inadequate project management.

The choice of customised accounting packages is made on the basis of evaluation of vendor proposals. The proposals are evaluated as to the suitability, completeness, cost and vendor proposals. Generally preference is given to a vendor won has a very good track record of deliverables.

17.0 ACCOUNTING SOFTWARE AS PART OF ENTERPRISE RESOURCE PLANNING (ERP)

MEANING OF ERP

An ERP is an integrated software package that manages the business process across the entire enterprise.

ADVANTAGES OF USING AN ERP

The advantages of using an ERP for maintaining accounts are as follows:

(a) Standardised Processes and Procedures	An ERP is a generalised package which covers most of the common functionalities of any specific module.
(b) Standardised Reporting	Majority of the desired reports are available in an ERP package. These reports are standardised across industry and are generally acceptable to the users.
(c) Avoid Duplication	Duplication of data entry is avoided as it is an integrated package.
(d) Availability of more Information	Greater information is available through the package.

DISADVANTAGES OF AN ERP

The disadvantages of an ERP are the following:

(a) Lesser Flexibility	The user may have to modify their business procedure at times to be able to effectively use the ERP.
(b) Implementation Hurdles	Many of the consultants doing the implementation of the ERP may not be able to fully appreciate the business procedure to be able to do a good implementation of an ERP.
(c) Very Expensive	ERP are normally priced at an amount which is often beyond the reach of small and medium sized organisation. However, there are some ERP coming into the market which are moderately priced and may be useful to the small businesses.
(d) Complexity of the Software	Generally an ERP package has large number of options to choose from. Further the parameter settings and configuration makes it a little complex for the common users.

CONSIDERATIONS FOR CHOICE OF AN ERP

Choice of an ERP depends upon the following factors:

(a) Functional Requirements of the Organisation	The ERP that matches most of the requirements of an organisation is preferred over the others.

(b) Reports available in the ERP	The organisation ascertains the reporting requirements and chooses a vendor which fulfils its reporting requirements.
(c) Background of the Vendors	The service and deliverable record of a vendor is extremely important in choosing the vendor.
(d) Cost Comparisons	The budget constraints and fund position of an enterprise often becomes the deciding factor for choosing a particular package.

18.0 OUTSOURCING OF ACCOUNTING FUNCTION

MEANING OF OUTSOURCING OF ACCOUNTING FUNCTION

Outsourcing of Accounting Function means assigning accounting function to a third who records, processes the accounting data and provides information in the form of reports as per requirement of organisation.

ADVANTAGES OF OUTSOURCING THE ACCOUNTING FUNCTIONS

The advantages of outsourcing the accounting functions are the following:

1. Saving Time	The organisation that outsources is able to save time to concentrate on the core area of business activity.
2. Utilisation of Expertise of Third Party	The organisation is able to utilise the expertise of the third party in undertaking the accounting work.
3. Data Management by Professional	Storage and maintenance of the data is in the hand of professional people.
4. Less Dependence on Key Accounting Positions	The organisation is not bothered about people leaving the organisation in key accounting positions.
5. Economical	The proposition often proves to be economically more sensible.

DISADVANTAGES OF OUTSOURCING THE ACCOUNTING FUNCTIONS

The disadvantages of outsourcing the accounting functions are the following:

1. Lack of Security & Confidentiality	The data of the organisation is handed over to a third party: This raises two issues, one of security and second of confidentiality. There have been instances of information leaking out of the third party data centres.
2. Inadequate Services Provided	The third party is unable to meet the standards desirable.
3. High Cost	The cost may ultimately be higher than initially envisaged.
4. Delay in Obtaining Services	The third party service providers are catering to number of clients thereby processing as per priority basis.

CONSIDERATIONS FOR CHOICE OF OUTSOURCING VENDOR

The choice of outsourcing vendor is made on the basis of evaluation of the proposals received from these vendors. The proposals should be evaluated on the basis of following factors:

1. The amount of services provided and whether the same matches with the requirements.
2. The reputation and background of the vendor.
3. The comparative costs of the various propositions.
4. The assurance of quality.

CONSIDERATIONS FOR CHOICE OF SPREAD SHEET PACKAGES, PRE-PACKAGED ACCOUNTING SOFTWARE, CUSTOMISED ACCOUNTING PACKAGE, ERP PACKAGE AND OUTSOURCING THE ACCOUNTING FUNCTION TO A THIRD PARTY. SUCH CHOICE DEPENDS UPON THE FOLLOWING

1. Size of Business Operation	If the size of the operation is small *or* medium the organisation can opt for a prepackaged accounting package. However, if the size is big, the organisation may decide upon a customised software *or* an ERP package.
2. Complexity of Operation	If the operation is complex with several functional areas which needs to be computerised the choice is usually a customised software *or* an ERP package.
3. Business Requirement	If the organisation has several non-standard requirements then customised software could be the solution.
4. Budgetary Constraints	Cost consideration could also be a deciding factor for the choice of a particular alternative. Normally the spread sheet and the prepackaged accounting software works out to be the cheapest. The customized software and the ERP are of higher cost considerations.

19.0 GENERATING REPORTS FROM SOFTWARE

Spreadsheet softwares can be utilised to generate accounting reports. Formats have to be defined by the user and can be used to view *or* print the reports. In a pre-packaged accounting software reports are generated from the package. The user is allowed to define the period of the report which should fall within the accounting period for which the report is required. Reports from the pre-packaged software is mostly in a pre-determined format. However, some of the softwares allow certain customisation of the formats of the report. ***For Example*** the format of the invoice *or* challan can be printed according to the style normally used by the organisation.

THEORETICAL QUESTIONS

Short Answer Type Questions

1. What is a computer?
2. State the main features of a Computer.
3. Identify the major applications of a computer in an accounting.
4. What is the significance of a computerised accounting system?
5. How is computerised accounting system is different from a manual system? Explain in brief.
6. How do we chose a pre-packaged accounting software?
7. How will you select a customised accounting software vendor?

Long Answer Type Questions

8. What are the advantages and disadvantages of a pre-packaged accounting software?
9. What are the advantages and disadvantages of a customised accounting software? How is it different from a pre-packaged accounting software?
10. What are the advantages and disadvantages of using ERP for maintaining accounts?
11. List the factors affecting the choice of ERP.
12. What are the advantages and disadvantages of outsourcing of accounting function?
13. List the factors for choice of outsourcing vendor for accounting function.
14. List the factors for choice of Spread Sheet Package,Pre-packaged Software, Customised Software, ERP Package, Outsourcing Accounting Function.

PAPER–1: ACCOUNTING (GROUP I)

SECTION–B

ACCOUNTING STANDARDS

[PREFACE TO AS, APPLICABILITY OF AS, AS 1, AS 2, AS 3, AS 6, AS 7, AS 9, AS 10, AS 13, AS 14]

1 PREFACE TO ACCOUNTING STANDARDS

THEORETICAL BASE

1.0 MEANING OF ACCOUNTING STANDARD

1. **An accounting standard is a selected set of accounting policies or broad guidelines regarding the principles and methods to be chosen out of several alternatives.** Standards conform to applicable laws, customs, usage and business environment. So there is no universally acceptable set of standards.
2. Accounting Standards (ASs) are written policy documents issued by expert accounting body or by government or other regulatory body covering the aspects of recognition, measurement, presentation and disclosure of accounting transactions in the financial statements.
3. Accounting Standards deal with the issues of:
   (i) **recognition** of events and transactions in the financial statements,
   (ii) **measurement** of these transactions and events,
   (iii) **presentation** of these transactions and events in the financial statements in a manner that is meaningful and understandable to the reader, and
   (iv) **the disclosure requirements** which should be there to enable the public at large and the stakeholders and the potential investors in particular, to get an insight into what these financial statements are trying to reflect and thereby facilitating them to take prudent and informed business decisions.

2.0 OBJECTIVE OF ACCOUNTING STANDARD

1. The main objective of accounting standards is **to harmonise the diverse accounting policies and practices** at present in use in India. However, harmonisation does not mean that accounting standards should become very rigid. In fact, harmonisation of accounting standards do permit flexibility to make the necessary adjustments to suit their purpose.

3.0 SIGNIFICANCE OF ACCOUNTING STANDARDS

1. The adoption and application of accounting standards ensures uniformity, comparability and qualitative improvement in the preparation and presentation of financial statements.
2. The accounting standards seek to describe the accounting principles, the valuation techniques and the methods of applying the accounting principles in the preparation and presentation of financial statements so that they may give a true and fair view.
3. The ostensible purpose of the standard setting bodies is to promote the dissemination of timely and useful financial information to investors and certain other parties having an interest in companies' economic performance.
4. Accounting Standards standardize diverse accounting policies with a view to eliminate, to the maximum possible extent, (i) the non-comparability of financial statements and thereby improving the reliability of financial statements, and (ii) to provide a set of standard accounting policies, valuation norms and disclosure requirements.

5. In brief, the accounting standards aim at improving the quality of financial reporting by promoting comparability, consistency and transparency, in the interests of users of financial statements. Good financial reporting not only promotes healthy financial markets, it also helps to reduce the cost of capital because investors can have faith in financial reports and consequently perceive lesser risks.

4.0 ADVANTAGES OF SETTING ACCOUNTING STANDARDS

1. Reduction in Variations	Standards reduce to a reasonable extent or eliminate altogether confusing variations in the accounting treatments used to prepare financial statements.
2. Disclosure Beyond that Required by Law	There are certain areas where important information is not statutorily required to be disclosed. Standards may call for disclosure beyond that required by law.
3. Facilitates Comparison	The application of accounting standards would, to a limited extent, facilitate comparison of financial statements of companies situated in different parts of the world and also of different companies situated in the same country. However, it should be noted in this respect that differences in the institutions, traditions and legal systems from one country to another give rise to differences in accounting standards practised in different countries.

5.0 ARGUMENTS AGAINST SETTING ACCOUNTING STANDARDS

However there are some arguments against setting accounting standards:

1. Restriction on Choice of Alternative Treatments	Alternative solutions to certain accounting problems may each have arguments to recommend them. A standard which insists on one particular solution may be unduly restrictive. This can sometimes be avoided either by allowing a permitted choice between different accounting treatments, or by defining closely the circumstances where different treatments may be appropriate.
2. Rigidity	There may be a trend towards rigidity in applying the accounting standards. Michael Alexander, Director of Research and Technical Activities at the Financial Accounting Standards Board (FASB) said, 'the demand for standards comes largely from an insatiable appetite for rules. The reliance on judgment in technical accounting matters seems to have gone'.
3. Cannot Override the Statute	Accounting standards cannot override the statute. The standards are required to be framed within the ambit of prevailing statutes.

6.0 EVOLUTION OF ACCOUNTING STANDARDS

1. As early as in 1932-34, the American Institute of Accountants (now known as American Institute of Certified Public Accountants), collaborated with the New York Stock Exchange in the formulation of five 'rules or principles' of accounting to narrow down the variations in accounting policies, recommend disclosures for significant items, and suggest improvement in disclosures required by accounting standards keeping in view the company law and other regulatory requirements.
2. In 1959, the American Institute of Certified Public Accountants (AICPA) established the Accounting Principles Board (APB) with the objective of carrying on research so as to provide a solid conceptual base for its opinions.

3. In 1973APB was replaced by Financial Accounting Standards Board (FASB). Accounting Standards Committee (ASC) was set up in United Kingdom to lay down 'standards' which could produce greater uniformity in financial accounting practices.
4. Prior to 1970s, very few academicians paid much attention to the standard setting process in accounting. However, it became clear that standard setting was a fascinating process that had intertwined with the economic self-interests of the affected parties. Currently, standard setting boards or committees are active in number of countries including the United States, United Kingdom, Australia, Canada, India etc. In the same direction, the International Accounting Standards Committee (now known as IASB), the London based group responsible for developing International Accounting Standards, was set up in June 1973. The IASC comprises the professional accountancy bodies of over 75 countries (including the Institute of Chartered Accountants of India).
5. In 1978, another professional body, the International Federation of Accountants (IFAC) was established.

7.0 ACCOUNTING STANDARDS BOARD OF INDIA [ASB]

1. **Formation of the Accounting Standards Board** The Institute of Chartered Accountants of India, recognising the need to harmonise the diverse accounting policies and practices at present in use in India, constituted an Accounting Standards Board (ASB) on April 21, 1977.
2. **Scope and Function of Accounting Standards Board**
   (a) The main function of ASB is to formulate accounting standards so that such standards may be established by the Council of the Institute in India.
   (b) While formulating the accounting standards, ASB will take into consideration the applicable law, customs, usages and business environment.
   (c) The Institute is one of the members of the International Accounting Standards Committee (IASC) and has agreed to support the objectives of IASC.
   (d) While formulating the accounting standards, ASB will give due consideration to International Accounting Standards issued by IASC and try to integrate them, to the extent possible, in the light of the conditions and practices prevailing in India.
   (e) The accounting standards will be issued under the authority of the Council. ASB has also been entrusted with the responsibility of propagating the accounting standards and of persuading the concerned parties to adopt them in the preparation and presentation of financial statements.
   (f) ASB will issue guidance notes on the accounting standards and give clarifications on issues arising therefrom.
   (g) ASB will also review the accounting standards at periodical intervals.
3. **Procedure for Issuing Accounting Standards** Broadly, the following procedure will be adopted for formulating Accounting Standards:

Step 1: To determine the broad areas in which accounting standards need to be formulated and the priority in regard to the selection thereof.

Step 2: To hold a dialogue with the representatives of the government, public sector undertakings, industry and other organizations for ascertaining their views.

Step 3: On the basis of the work of the study groups and the dialogue with the representatives, to prepare and issue the exposure of draft of the proposed standard for comments by members of the Institute and the public at large.

Step 4: To finalise the draft of the proposed standard after taking into consideration the comments received.

Step 5: To submit the final draft of the proposed standard to the Council of the Institute.

The Council of the Institute will consider the final draft of the proposed standard, and if found necessary, modify the same in consultation with ASB. The accounting standard on the relevant subject will then be issued under the authority of the Council.

8.0 ACCOUNTING STANDARDS ISSUED SO FAR

1. In India, The Council of the Institute of Chartered Accountants of India has so far issued 32 Accounting Standards but effectively there are 31 as at present since AS-8 has been withdrawn consequent to the issuance of AS 26 on 'Intangible Assets'.
2. These accounting standards are mandatory in the sense that these are binding on the members of the Institute.
3. These accounting standards are as follows:

AS No.	AS Title	Date	Scope
1	Disclosure of Accounting Policies	01/04/1993	All Level
2	Valuation of Inventories (Revised)	01/04/1999	All Level
3	Cash Flow Statement (Revised)	01/04/2001	Level I
4	Contingencies and Events Occurring after the Balance Sheet Date	01/04/1998	All Level
5	Net Profit or Loss for the Period, Prior Period Items and Changes in Accounting Policies (Revised)	01/04/1996	All Level
6	Depreciation Accounting (Revised)	01/04/1995	All Level
7	Construction Contracts (Revised)	01/04/2002	All Level
8	Research & Development	Now included	in AS – 26
9	Revenue Recognition	01/04/1993	All Level
10	Accounting for Fixed Assets	01/04/1993	All Level
11	The Effects of Changes in Foreign Exchange Rates (Revised)	01/04/2004	All Level
12	Accounting for Government Grants	01/04/1994	All Level
13	Accounting for Investments	01/04/1995	All Level
14	Accounting for Amalgamations	01/04/1995	All Level
15	Employee Benefits	01/04/2006	All Level
16	Borrowing Costs	01/04/2000	All Level
17	Segment Reporting	01/04/2001	Level I
18	Related Party Disclosures	01/04/2001	Level I
19	Leases	01/04/2001	All Level
20	Earning Per Share	01/04/2001	Level I
21	Consolidated Financial Statement	01/04/2001	Enterprises preparing CFS*
22	Accounting for Taxes on Income	01/04/2001 01/04/2002 01/04/2006	Listed Companies Other Companies All Enterprises
23	Accounting for Investment in Associates in Consolidated Financial Statement	01/04/2002	Enterprises preparing CFS

24	Discontinuing Operations	01/04/2004	Level I
25	Interim Financial Statement	01/04/2002	Level I
26	Intangible Assets	01/04/2003	All Level
27	Financial Reporting of Interests in Joint Ventures	01/04/2002	Enterprises preparing CFS
28	Impairment of Assets	01/04/2004 01/04/2006 01/04/2008	Level I Level II Level III
29	Provisions, Contingent Liabilities and Contingent Assets	01/04/2004	All Level
30	Financial Instruments - Recognition and Measurement		
31	Financial Instruments - Presentation		
32	Financial Instruments - Disclosure		

9.0 APPLICABILITY OF ACCOUNTING STANDARDS

In assessing whether an Accounting Standard is applicable, one must find correct answer to the following three questions:

(a) Does it apply to the enterprise concerned? If yes, the next question is:

(b) Does it apply to the financial statement concerned? If yes, the next question is:

(c) Does it apply to the financial item concerned?

The preface to the statements of accounting standards answers the above questions.

1. Enterprises to which the Accounting Standards apply

Accounting Standards apply in respect of any enterprise (whether organised in corporate, co-operative or other forms) **engaged in commercial, industrial or business activities,** whether or not profit oriented and even if established for charitable or religious purposes. Exclusion of an enterprise from the applicability of the Accounting Standards would be permissible only if no part of the activity of such enterprise is commercial, industrial or business in nature. Even if a very small proportion of the activities of an enterprise were considered to be commercial, industrial or business in nature, the Accounting Standards would apply to all its activities including those, which are not commercial, industrial or business in nature.

2. Implication of Mandatory Status

Where the statute governing the enterprise does not require compliance with AS (e.g. a Partnership Firm)	In discharging their attest functions, the members of the Institute are required to examine whether the financial statements are prepared in compliance with the applicable accounting standards. In the event of any deviation from the accounting standards, they have the duty to make adequate disclosures in their reports so that the users of financial statements may be aware of such deviations.
Where the statute governing the enterprise requires compliance with AS (e.g. Companies)	The duty of compliance is primarily on the enterprise presenting the financial statements. The auditor is required by section 227(3)(d) to report whether, in his opinion, the Profit and Loss Account and Balance Sheet of the company audited, comply with the accounting standards referred to in Section 211(3C).

Notes:

(i) As per section 211(3C), the expression 'accounting standards', for the purpose of section 211(3A), means standards of accounting recommended by the ICAI, as may be prescribed by the Central Government in consultation with the National Advisory Committee on Accounting Standards established u/s 210A (1). It is also provided that, till the time the Central Government prescribes accounting standards, the accounting standards specified by the ICAI shall be deemed to be accounting standards for the purpose of section 211(3A). Till date, the Central Government has not prescribed any accounting standards. For the purpose of section 211(3A) and Section 227(3)(d), the institute has specified all mandatory accounting standards. In other words, companies are required to comply with all applicable mandatory standards issued by the ICAI.

(ii) Enterprises in insurance business are required to comply with the accounting standards by the Insurance Regulatory and Development Authority (Preparation of Financial Statements and Auditor's Report of Insurance Companies) Regulations, 2000. The standards to be complied by these enterprises are those, made applicable to them.

3. **Financial Items to which the Accounting Standards Apply**

   The Accounting Standards are intended to apply **only to material items.** An item is considered material, if its omission or misstatement is likely to affect economic decision of the user. Materiality is not necessarily a function of size; it is the information content if the financial item which is important. A penalty of ₹ 50,000 paid for breach of law by a company can seem to be a relatively small amount for a company incurring crores of rupees in a year, yet is a material item because of the information it conveys. The materiality should therefore be judged on case-to-case basis. If an item is material, it should be shown separately instead of clubbing it with other items. For example it is not appropriate to club the penalties paid with legal charges.

10.0 CONFLICT BETWEEN REQUIREMENTS OF ACCOUNTING STANDARD AND COURT/TRIBUNAL ORDER

On 17 November 2004, the Council of the ICAI has announced that if an item in the financial statement of an enterprise is treated differently pursuant to an Order made by the Court/Tribunal, as compared to the treatment required by an Accounting Standard, following disclosures should be made in the financial statements of the year in which different treatment has been given:

A description of the accounting treatment made along with the reason that the same has been adopted because of the Court/Tribunal Order.

(a) Description of the difference between the accounting treatment prescribed in the Accounting Standard and that followed by the enterprise.

(b) The financial impact, if any, arising due to such a difference.

11.0 ACCOUNTING STANDARD AND INCOME TAX ACT

1. The Guidance Note on Audit u/s 44AB of Income Tax Act, requires all financial statements prepared under mercantile system of accounting to comply with all applicable mandatory accounting standards issued by the Institute. The financial statements prepared under cash basis of accounting however, need not adhere to the accounting standards issued by the Institute.
2. It follows from above, that a member of the Institute reporting for tax audit purposes, is under an obligation to see whether the audited financial statements, if prepared under mercantile system of accounting, comply with all applicable mandatory standards issued by the Institute. In case of any deviation, the member should consider making qualification/appropriate disclosure in his reports.

3. It should be noted that the Central Government has notified two accounting standards, viz. AS (IT) 1, Disclosure of Accounting Policies and AS (IT) 2, Disclosure of Prior Period and Extra Ordinary Items and Disclosure of Accounting Policies for the purpose of taxation. Section 145 of Income Tax Act requires all assesses keeping their books by the mercantile system of accounting to comply with these two standards. Also, requirements of AS (IT) 1 and AS (IT) 2 are practically same as the corresponding AS 1 and AS 5 issued by the institute. The mandatory compliance of AS (IT) 1 and AS (IT) 2 are nevertheless required for the limited purpose of income tax.

4. Mandatory accounting standards issued by the ICAI apply to all financial statements prepared under mercantile system irrespective of the requirements of Income Tax Act. The differences between requirements of Income Tax Act and those of accounting standards cause taxable profit to differ from the accounting profit before tax.

12.0 ACCOUNTING STANDARD INTERPRETATIONS (ASI)

1. The Accounting Standard Interpretations address questions that arise in course of application of a standard. These are therefore issued after issue of the relevant standard. Authority of an interpretation is same as that of the Accounting Standard to which it relates. So far, 30 interpretations have been issued.

   A brief summary of these interpretations is given below.

ASI No.	Related AS	Topic
1	16	Interpretation of the term 'substantial period'
2	2, 10	Treatment of machinery spares
3	22	Computation of deferred tax during tax holiday u/s 80-IA and 80-IB (Revised)
4	22	Computation of deferred tax in respect of losses under the head Capital Gains
5	22	Computation of deferred tax during tax holiday u/s 10A and 10B
6	22	Computation of current and deferred tax subject to MAT u/s 115JB
7	22	Disclosure of deferred tax assets/liabilities in balance sheet
8	21, 23, 27	Interpretation of the term 'near future'
9	22	Interpretation of the term 'virtual certainty'
10	16	Computation of exchange difference to be treated as borrowing cost
11	22	Computation of deferred tax in case of Amalgamations
12	20	Applicability of AS 20 to unlisted companies
13	18	Aggregation of related party disclosures
14	9	Manner of disclosure of excise duty
15	21	Notes to the Consolidated Financial Statements (CFS)
16	23	Treatment in CFS: Dividend proposed by an associate
17	23	Treatment in CFS: Changes in equity not included in P & L A/c
18	23	Consideration of potential equity to ascertain whether the investee is an associate
19	18	Interpretation of the term 'intermediary'
20	17	Disclosure of segment information in certain cases (Revised)
21	18	Non-executive directors; whether related parties
22	17	Interest expenses; whether to treat as segment expenses

23	18	Remuneration paid to key management personnel; whether related party transaction
24	21	Subsidiaries having two parents
25	21	Shares held as stock-in-trade
26	21	Consolidation of current and deferred tax
27	25	Applicability of AS 25
28	21, 27	Disclosure of post-acquisition reserves in Consolidated Financial Statements
29	7	Turnover in case of contractors
30	29	Applicability of AS 29 to onerous contracts

13.0 COMPLIANCE OF ACCOUNTING STANDARDS

1. During the period an accounting standard is recommendatory in nature, the members of the Institute should, while discharging their attest function, examine whether the standard has been followed or not. If the same has not been followed, the members should consider whether, keeping in view the circumstances of the case, a disclosure in their audit reports is necessary.
2. Once the standard becomes mandatory, it will be the duty of the members of the Institute to examine, while discharging their attest function, whether this accounting standard is complied with in the presentation of financial statements covered by their audit. In the event of any deviation from the accounting standard, it will be their duty to make adequate disclosures in their audit reports so that the users of financial statements may be aware of such deviations.
3. For the purpose of compliance of the Accounting Standards, all enterprises in India are classified into three broad categories:

Level I Enterprise	• Enterprises, whose equity or debt securities are either listed or is in the process to be listed in India or outside India. • Banks, Insurance Companies and Financial Institutions. • All commercial, industrial and other reporting business enterprises, whose **total turnover** during the previous year **exceeds ₹ 50 crores** (as per the audited financial statement). • All commercial, industrial and other reporting business enterprises, whose **total borrowings including public deposits** during the previous year **exceeds ₹ 10 crores** (as per the audited financial statement). • Holding or subsidiary company of any of the above enterprises any time during the year.
Level II Enterprise	• All commercial, industrial and other reporting business enterprises, whose **total turnover** during the previous year **exceeds ₹ 1 crore but does not exceed ₹ 50 crores** (as per the audited financial statement). • All commercial, industrial and other reporting business enterprises, whose **total borrowings including public deposits** during the previous year **exceeds ₹ 1 crore but does not exceed ₹ 10 crores** (as per the audited financial statement). • Holding or subsidiary company of any of the above enterprises any time during the year.
Level III Enterprise	All the enterprises not covered in above two levels come under this level.

2 APPLICABILITY OF ACCOUNTING STANDARDS

THEORETICAL BASE

QUESTION 1: What is the meaning of "small and medium sized company" as per the companies Accounting Standards) Rules, 2006?

ANSWER: As per the companies (Accounting Standards) Rules, 2006 "Small and Medium Sized Company" (SMC) means, a company which satisfies all the following 5 conditions at the end of relevant accounting period.

1. Non-Listed	Whose equity or debt securities are not listed or are not in the process of listing on any stock exchange, whether in India or outside India.
2. Non-Banking etc.	Which is not a bank, financial institution or an insurance company;
3. Turnover up to 50 Crores	Whose turnover (excluding other income) does not exceed ₹ 50
4. Borrowings up to 10 crore	crores crore in the immediately preceding accounting year; Whose total borrowings (including public deposits) does not exceed₹ 10 crore at any time during the immediately preceding accounting year; and
5. Neither Holding nor Subsidiary	Which is not a holding or subsidiary company of a company which is not small and medium-sized company.

QUESTION 2: XYZ, with a turnover of ₹ 35 lakhs and borrowing of ₹ 10 lakhs during any time in the previous year, wants to avail the exemptions available in adoption of Accounting Standard applicable to companies for the year ended 31.3.2015. Advise the management the exemptions that are available as per Companies (AS) Rules, 2006.

ANSWER:

(a) XYZ, is a small and medium sized enterprise (SME) company as per Companies (AS) Rules, 2006. Since its turnover does not exceed ₹ 50 crores and its borrowings do not exceed ₹ 10 crores. It is assumed that its shares are not listed and it is neither Banking Co. nor a financial institution nor an insurance Co. nor a holding Co. nor a subsidiary Co. of a company which is not SMC.

(b) The following relaxations and exemptions are available.

1. As 3 "Cash Flow Statements" is not mandatory.
2. As 17 "Segment Reporting" is not mandatory.
3. SMEs are exempt for some paragraphs of AS 19 "Leases".
4. SMEs are exempt for disclosures of diluted EPS (both including and excluding extraordinary items).
5. SMEs are allowed to measure the 'value in use' on the basis of reasonable estimate thereof instead of computing the value in use by present value technique under AS 28 "impairment of Assets".
6. SMEs are exempt from disclosure requirements of paragraphs 66 and 67of AS 29 "Provisions , Contingent Liabilities and Contingent Assets".
7. SMEs are exempt from certain requirements of AS 15 "Employee Benefits".
8. Accounting Standards 21, 23, 27 are not applicable to SMEs.

If XYZ is not a company, it will be treated as a level III enterprise instead of level II enterprise; XYZ Ltd. will be exempt from requirements of AS 18 "Related Party Disclosures" and AS 24 "Discontinuing Operations".

QUESTION 3: Is XYZ Ltd, on Indian company (having Turnover & Borrowing each of ₹ 60 crores listed on NASDAQ only and having 51% Equity in S Ltd., an Indian Unlisted company with negligible Turnover and Borrowings required to prepare consolidated financial statements?

ANSWER: XYZ Ltd. is not required to prepare Consolidated Financial Statements even though it is non-SMC enterprise becouse SEBI requires only those Indian companies whose shares are listed on Indian Stock exchange, to prepare CFS.

QUESTION 4: X Ltd. an US company (having Turnover of 51 crores and Borrowings of ₹ 1 crore) is listed on NASDAQ only, has acquired 51% equity in S Ltd. an Indian unlisted company (having Turnover & Borrowings of ₹ 40 lakhs each). Is X Ltd. required to prepare Consolidated Financial Statement (CFS)? Is S Ltd. required to prepare Cash Flow Statement?

ANSWER:

(a) X Ltd is not required to prepare. CFS even though it is non SMC since its equity is not listed in India.

(b) S Ltd is not required to prepare Cash Flow Statement since it is a subsidiary of non-Indian holding company.

QUESTION 5: Y Ltd avail Sales Tax deferral benefit under which it is required to pay the Tax collected after 5 years to the Govt. Such Tax collected of ₹ 11 crores is shown as Unsecured Loan. Is Y Ltd a SMC or Non-SMC enterprise?

ANSWER: Y Ltd is a SMC since Tax deferral would not be considered as 'Borrowing' for the purposes of determine SMC or Non-SMC enterprise since the amount has not been actually borrowed.

QUESTION 6: Is Z Ltd. engaged only in insurance broking business a SMC on Non-SMC enterprise?

ANSWER: Z Ltd. is a SMC enterprise since Insurance broking business would not be considered as "Insurance Business' for the purpose of determining SMC or Non-SMC enterprise.

QUESTION 7: W Ltd., an unlisted and a Not-for-profit company registered u/s 25 of The Companies Act. provides micro finance to backward classes and its interest income is ₹ 40 crores. Is W Ltd. a SMC or non-SMC enterprise?

ANSWER: W Ltd. is a Non-SMC enterprise since it is engaged in commercial activities (i.e. providing loans & earning Interest therefrom). The objective of formation of enterprise is not relevant for the purpose of determining SMC or Non-SMC enterprises.

QUESTION 8: An organization whose objects are charitable or religious, holds that the Accounting Standards are not applicable to it since only a very small proportion of its activities are business in nature. Comment.

ANSWER: Accounting Standards apply in respect of any enterprise (whether organised in corporate, co-operative or other forms) engaged in commercial, industrial or business activities, whether or not profit oriented and even if established for charitable or religious purposes. Exclusion of an enterprise from the applicability of the Accounting Standards would be permissible only if no part of the activity of such enterprise is commercial, industrial or business in nature. Even if a very small proportion of the activities of an enterprise were considered to be commercial, industrial or business in nature, the Accounting Standards would apply to all its activities including those, which are not commercial, industrial or business in nature.

QUESTION 9: Comment whether the following Companies can be classified as a Small and Medium Sized Company (SMC) as per the Companies (Accounting standards) Rules, 2006:

(i) A Pvt. Ltd., a subsidiary of a multinational company listed on London Stock Exchange. It has a turnover of ₹.12 crores and borrowings of ₹ 5 crores.

(ii) B Pvt. Ltd. has a turnover of ₹ 45 crores, other income of ₹ 7 crores and bank borrowings of ₹ 9 crores.

(iii) C Ltd. Has appointed Merchant bankers to prepare a Red-herring prospectus for the purpose of filing the same with Securities and Exchange Board of India.

ANSWER:

(a) As per the Companies (Accounting Standards) Rules 2006, "Small and Medium Sized Company" (SMC) means, a company:

(i) Whose equity or debt securities are not listed or are not in the process of listing on any stock exchange, whether in India or outside India;

(ii) Which is not a bank, financial institution or an insurance company;

(iii) Whose turnover (excluding other income) does not exceed rupee; fifty crore in the immediately preceding accounting year,

(iv) Which does not have borrowings (including public deposits) in excess of rupees ten crore at any time during the immediately preceding accounting year; and

(v) which is not a holding or subsidiary company of a company which is not a small and medium-sized company.

Explanation: For the purposes of clause (f) , a company shall qualify as a Small and Medium Sized Company, if the conditions mentioned. therein are satisfied as at the end of the relevant accounting period.

(a) As per the definition of SMC, point (v), a company will be a SMC if it is not a holding or subsidiary company of another company which is not a SMC. Since A Pvt. Ltd. is a subsidiary of another Company which is listed, on London Stock Exchange (and is therefore not a SMC), A Pvt. Ltd. cannot be a SMC. The turnover and borrowings are not relevant in this case.

(b) As per the definition of SMC, point (iii), a company will be a SMC if its turnover does not exceed ₹ 50 corers or borrowings do not exceed ₹ 10 crore. For calculating this turnover, other income is not to be included. Since B Pvt. Ltd. has a turnover of ₹ 45 corers and borrowing; of ₹ 9 corers, it will satisfy the definition and can be classified as SMC.

(c) As per the definition of SMC, point (i) a company will be a SMC if it is not listed or in the process of listing. Since C Pvt. Ltd. has appointed merchant bankers to prepare a Red Herring Prospectus for the purpose of filling the same with SEBI, it is in the process of listing on a Stock Exchange. Hence C Ltd. cannot be classified as a SMC.

(i) A Ltd. is a subsidiary of a multinational company listed on London Stock Exchange. It has a turnover of ₹ [illegible] crores and borrowings of ₹ [illegible] crores.

(ii) P Pvt. Ltd. has a turnover of ₹ [illegible] crores, other income of ₹ [illegible] crores and borrowings of ₹ [illegible] crores.

(iii) C Ltd. has appointed merchant bankers to prepare Red Herring Prospectus [illegible] for listing its [illegible] with [illegible] Stock Exchange [illegible].

ANSWER

(a) As per the Companies (Accounting Standards) Rules, 2006, Small and Medium Sized Company (SMC) means, a company:

(i) Whose equity or debt securities are not listed or are not in the process of listing on any stock exchange, whether in India or outside India;

(ii) Which is not a bank, financial institution or an insurance company;

(iii) Whose turnover (excluding other income) does not exceed rupees fifty crore in the immediately preceding accounting year;

(iv) Which does not have borrowings (including public deposits) in excess of rupees ten crore at any time during the immediately preceding accounting year; and

(v) Which is not a holding or subsidiary company of a company which is not a small and medium-sized company.

Explanation: For the purpose of clause [illegible], a company shall qualify as a small and medium sized company, if the conditions mentioned therein are satisfied as at the end of the relevant accounting period.

(i) As per the definition of SMC, point (v), a company will be a SMC if it is not a holding or subsidiary company of another non-SMC company. Since A Ltd. is a subsidiary of another Company which is listed on London Stock Exchange [illegible], A Ltd. cannot be a SMC [illegible] turnover and borrowings [illegible] in this case.

(ii) As per the definition of SMC, point [illegible], a company will be a SMC if its turnover does not exceed [illegible] crores [illegible] other income is not [illegible] P Pvt. Ltd. [illegible] turnover [illegible] and borrowings [illegible] definition and can be classified as SMC.

(iii) As per the definition of SMC, point (i), a company will be a SMC if it is not listed or in the process of listing. Since C Ltd. has appointed merchant bankers to prepare Red Herring Prospectus for the purpose of listing, the same will be in the process of listing on a stock exchange. Hence C Ltd. cannot be classified as a SMC.

3 AS 1 – DISCLOSURE OF ACCOUNTING POLICIES

THEORETICAL BASE

QUESTION 1: What is meant by Accounting Policies?

ANSWER: Accounting Policies refer to-

(i) Specific Accounting Principles. For example, valuations of inventories at lower of Cost or Net Realizable Value or Systematic allocation of cost of fixed assets in different accounting years.

(ii) Methods of applying those Principles. For example, using First In First Out Method (FIFO) or Weighted Average Method for valuation of inventories or using Straight Line or Written Down Value method for providing depreciation.

QUESTION 2: Mention six areas in which different accounting policies are followed by companies.

ANSWER:

1. Valuation of Fixed Assets
2. Valuation of Investments
3. Valuation of Inventories
4. Methods of Depreciation, Depletion and Amortization.
5. Treatment of Goodwill.
6. Treatment of Expenditure during construction

QUESTION 3: State the Three Considerations in Selection of Accounting Policies.

ANSWER:

1. Prudence [Ignore Anticipated Profits but Make Provision for Known Liabilities]
2. Substance Over Form
3. Materiality

QUESTION 4: State the Disclosures Requirements as to Accounting Policies.

ANSWER: All significant Accounting Policies should be disclosed normally at one place & should form part of Financial Statements.

QUESTION 5: When is the Change in Accounting Policy recommended?

A change in the Accounting Policy should be made only if adoption of different Accounting Policy is required

- by Statute, or
- For compliance with an Accounting Standard, or
- If it is considered that the change would result in more appropriate presentation of financial statements.

QUESTION 6: State the Disclosures Requirements as to Change in Accounting Policies.

ANSWER:

Case	What is to be disclosed ?
(a) ***When the change has material effect in current Period*** the	(i) The nature of change. (ii) Financial effect of change on items to period extent ascertainable. (iii) Where the amount is not ascertainable in wholly or part then indicate this fact.
(b) ***When the change hasmaterial effect in later period(s).***	(i) The nature of change. (ii) The fact that change in accounting policies has an effect in later period.

For example, if depreciation method is changed from straight-line method to written-down value method, or if cost formula used for inventory valuation is changed from weighted average to FIFO, or if interest is capitalized which was earlier not in practice, or if proportionate amount of interest is changed to inventory which was earlier not the practice, all these may increase or decrease the net profit. Unless the effect of such change in accounting policy is quantified, the financial statements may not help the users of accounts. Therefore, it is necessary to quantify the effect of change on financial statement items like assets, liabilities, profit/loss.

QUESTION 7: State the Three Fundamental Accounting Assumptions. Also State the Disclosures Requirements as to Fundamental Accounting Assumptions.

ANSWER: Accounting Standard (AS) 1 recognizes three fundamental accounting assumptions. These are as follows:

1. **Going Concern:** The financial statements are normally prepared on the assumption that an enterprise will continue its operations in the foreseeable future and neither there is intention, nor there is need to materially curtail the scale of operations.
2. **Consistency:** The principle of consistency refers to the practice of using same accounting policies for similar transactions in all accounting periods unless the change is required (i) by a statute, (ii) by an accounting standard or (iii) for more appropriate presentation of financial statements.
3. **Accrual basis of accounting:** Under this basis of accounting, transactions are recognised as soon as they occur, whether or not cash or cash equivalent is actually received or paid.

Disclosure Requirements

Case	What is to be disclosed ?
(a) **If All FAA are followed.**	No specific disclosure is required.
(b) **If any of FAA is not followed.**	The fact that accounting assumption is notfollowed must be disclosed.

QUESTION 8: What are Financial indicators to be considered for evaluating the assumption of Going Concern.

ANSWER:

1. Negative Net Worth or Negative Working without realistic prospects.
2. Fixed-term borrowings approaching maturity without realistic prospects.
3. Adverse key financial ratios.
4. Substantial Operating Losses.
5. Substantial Negative Cash Flows from Operations.
6. Arrears of Discontinuance of Dividends.
7. Inability to pay Creditors on due dates.

8. Difficulty in complying with the terms of Loan Agreements.
9. Change from credit to Cash-on-delivery transactions with suppliers.
10. Inability to obtain financing for essential new product development or other essential investments.
11. Entering into a scheme of arrangement with creditors for reduction of liability.

QUESTION 9: X Ltd. sold its building to Mini Ltd. for Rs 60 lakhs on 30.09-2014 and gave possession of the property to Mini Ltd. However, documentation and legal formalities are pending. Due to this,the company has not recorded the sale and has shown the amount received as an advance.The book value of the building is Rs 25 lakhs as on 31st March, 2015. Do you agree with this treatment? If you do not agree, explain the reasons with reference to the accounting standard.

ANSWER:

PROVISION OF AS 1

Principles of prudence, substance over form and materiality should be looked into, to ensure true and fair consideration in a transaction.

ADVICE

The economic reality and substance of the transaction is that the rights and beneficial interest in the property has been transferred although legal title has not been transferred. Hence, X Ltd. should record the sale and recognize the profit of Rs 35 lakhs in its financial statements for the year ended 31st March, 2015; value of building should be removed balance sheet. Therefore the treatment given by the company is not correct.

QUESTION 10: XYZ Company is engaged in the business of financial services and is undergoing tight liquidity position, since most of the assets of the company are blocked in various claims/ petitions in a Special Court. XYZ has accepted Inter-Corporate Deposits (ICDs) and, it making its best efforts of settle the dues. There were claims at varied rates of interest, from lenders, from the due date of ICDs to the date of repayment. The company has provided interest, as per the terms of the contract till the due date and a note for non-provision of interest on the due date to date of repayment was effected in the financial statements. On account of uncertainties existing regarding the determination of the amount and in the absence of any specific legal obligation at present as per the terms of contracts, the company considers that these claims are in the nature of "claims against the company not acknowledged as debt", and the same has been disclosed by way of a note in the accounts instead of making a provision in the Profit & Loss Account. State whether the treatment done by the company is correct or not.

ANSWER:

PROVISION OF AS 1

Pare 17 of AS-1 'Disclosure of Accounting Policies' recognises 'prudence' as one of the major consideration governing the selection and application of accounting policies. In view of the uncertainty attached to future events, profits are not anticipated but recognised only when realised through not necessarily in cash. Provision is made for all known liabilities and losses even through the amount cannot be determined with certainty and represents only a best estimated in the light of available information.

Also as per para 10 of the AS 1, 'accrual' is one of the fundamental accounting assumptions. Irrespective of the terms of the contract, so long as the principal amount of a loan is not repaid, the lender cannot be replaced in a disadvantageous position of non-payment of interest in respect of overdue amount.

ADVICE

It is apparent that the company has an obligation on account of the overdue interest. In this situation, the company should provide for the liability (since it is not waived by the lenders) at an amount estimated or on reasonable basis based on facts and circumstances of each case. However, in respect of the overdue interest amounts, which are settled, the liability should be accrued to the extend of amounts settled. Non-provision of the overdue interest liability amounts to violation of accrual basis of accounting. Therefore, the treatment, done by the company, of not providing the interest amount from due date to the date of repayment is not correct.

4 AS 2 – VALUATION OF INVENTORIES

THEORETICAL BASE

QUESTION 1: State the areas to which AS 2 is not applicable.

ANSWER:

1. Work - in - progress arising under construction contracts, including directly related service contracts (see AS-7: Accounting for Construction Contracts);
2. Work - in - progress arising in ordinarily course of business of service providers;
3. Shares, debentures and other financial instruments held as stock - in - trade; and
4. Producers' inventories of live stock, agriculture and forest product and mineral oils, ores and gases to the extent that they are measured at Net Realizable Value in accordance with well-established practices in those industries.

QUESTION 2: State the Meaning of Inventory.

ANSWER: Inventories are assets that are -

(a) held for sale in ordinary business;e.g.Finished Goods

(b) in the process of production for such sale; e.g. WIP or

(c) in the form of materials or supplies to be consumed in the production process or in the rendering of services. e.g.Raw Materials

INVENTORY = FINISHED GOODS+ WIP+ RAW MATERIALS

Note: Machinery spares which are specific to a particular item of fixed asset should be capitalized in accordance with AS - 10 and should not be treated as inventories for the purpose of AS - 2.

QUESTION 3: What are the items that are to be included in determination of the cost of inventories as per AS-2?

ANSWER:

1. **Cost of Purchase.**

   [**INCLUDES** Purchase Price+ Duties & Taxes (which are NOT subsequently recoverable) + other expenditure directly attributable to acquisition (Like Freight Inward) **BUT EXCLUDES** Trade Discount, Rebates, Duty Drawbacks Subsidies and Taxes (which are subsequently recoverable)]

2. **Cost of Conversion.**

   [**INCLUDES** Direct Labour, Direct Expenses, Sub Contracted Work and Production Overheads absorbed on the basis of Normal Capacity]

3. **Other Costs** incurred in bringing the inventories to their present location and condition. e.g. costs incurred in designing products for specific customers

QUESTION 4: What are the items that are to be excluded in determination of the cost of inventories as per AS-2?

ANSWER: Items that are to be excluded in determination of the cost of inventories as per para 13 of AS 2 on 'Valuation of Inventories' are:

(1) Abnormal Amounts of wasted materials, labour or other production costs.

(2) Storage Costs unless those costs are necessary in the production process prior to a further production stage.

(3) Administrative Overheads that do not contribute to bringing the inventories to their present location and condition; and

(4) Selling and Distribution Costs.

Question 5: State the Techniques for Allocating Production Cost.

ANSWER:

1. Standard Costing
2. Retail Cost Method

Question 6: State the Cost Formulae to be used As per AS 2.

Item of Inventory	Cost Formulae to be used
1. For items that are not ordinarily interchangeable and goods or services produced and segregated for specific projects	Specific Identification of Cost Method
2. For Other Items	First-In-First-Out Method (FIFO) or Weighted Average Method

Question 7: State the Rule of Lower of Cost or Net Realizable Value.

ANSWER: The inventories should be valued at the lower of cost and net realizable value at each Balance Sheet date.

Note: *Net Realizable Value = Estimated Selling Price – Estimated Costs of Completion – Estimated Costs necessary to make the sale.*

Question 8: State the Two Methods of Comparision of Cost with NRV

ANSWER:

1. Item by item Method
2. Group Method

Note: *The Comparison of Cost with NRV ON Aggregate basis is not permissible.*

Question 9: How are Materials and Other Supplies valued as per AS 2?

ANSWER:

Case	Valuation of Materials
1. If Finished Product are expected to be sold at or above the cost	Materials and other supplies should be valued at cost even if there is decline in the price of materials.
2. If Finished Product are expected to be sold below cost	Materials and other supplies should be valued at NRV if there is decline in the price of materials. In such circumstances, the replacement cost of the materials may be the best available measure of their net realizable value.

Question 10: State the Disclosure Requirements as per AS 2.

ANSWER:

1. Accounting Policies

2. Cost Formula Used
3. Total Carrying Amount of Inventories

PRACTICAL QUESTIONS FOR PRACTICE

APPLICABILITY OF AS 2

QUESTION 1: Following persons valued the year end inventory on Net Realizable Value on the ground that AS-2 dose not apply to their inventory:

(a) A whole seller in agriculture and forest product

(b) A Dealer in Shares, Debentures and other Financial Instruments

(c) A whole seller in live stock

(d) A whole seller in mineral oils, ores and gases

Comment on the practice adopted.

ANSWER

Case	Practice	Reason
(a)	**Incorrect**	AS-2 does not apply to producers of agriculture and forest product but applies to traders in agriculture and forest product. Hence the inventory should be valued at lower of cost or Net Realizable Value.
(b)	**Correct**	AS-2 does not apply to Shares, Debentures and other Financial Instruments held as stock - in – trade. Hence the inventory can be valued at Net Realizable Value.
(c)	**Incorrect**	AS-2 does not apply to producers of live stock but applies to traders in live stock. Hence the inventory should be valued at lower of cost or Net Realizable Value.
(d)	**Incorrect**	AS-2 does not apply to producers of mineral oils, ores and gases but applies to traders in mineral oils, ores and gases. Hence the inventory should be valued at lower of cost or Net Realizable Value.

QUESTION 2: BHARAT LTD. manufacturing cars has installed several machines, valued the year end inventory of all Machinery spares(of which some are specific to a particular Machine and some are common to all Machines) on Net Realizable Value on the ground that AS-2 dose not apply to their inventory. Comment on the practice adopted.

ANSWER

1. Machinery spares which are specific to a particular item of fixed asset should be capitalized in accordance with AS - 10 and should not be treated as inventories for the purpose of AS - 2.Hence the practice adopted is incorrect.
2. Machinery spares which are not specific to a particular item of fixed asset should be treated as inventories for the purpose of AS – 2 and the inventory should be valued at lower of cost or Net Realizable Value Hence the practice adopted is incorrect.

QUESTION 3: Night Ltd. sells beer to customers; some of the customers consume the beer in the bars run by Night Limited. While leaving the bars, the consumers leave the empty bottles in the bars and the company takes possession of these empty bottles. The company has laid down a detailed internal record procedure for accounting for these empty bottles which are sold by the company by calling for tenders. Keeping this in view.

(i) Decide whether the stock of empty bottles is an asset of the company;

(ii) If so, whether the stock of empty bottles existing as on the date of Balance Sheet is to be considered as inventories of the company and valued as per AS-2 or to be treated as scrap and show at realizable value with corresponding credit to 'Other Income"?

ANSWER:

(i) Tangible objects or intangible right carrying probable future benefits, owned by an enterprise are called assets. Night Ltd. sells these empty bottles by calling tenders. It means further benefits are accrued on its sale. Therefore, empty bottles are assets for the company.

(ii) As per AS 2 "Valuation of Inventories", inventories are assets held for sale in the ordinary course of business. Stock of empty bottles existing on the Balance Sheet date is the inventory and Night Ltd. has detailed controlled recording and accounting procedure which duly signify its materiality. Hence stock of empty bottles cannot be considered as scrap and should be valued as inventory in accordance with AS 2.

CALCULATION OF COST OF CLOSING STOCK WHEN THERE IS NO NORMAL/ABNORMAL LOSS

QUESTION 4:

Particulars		*Kg.*	*₹*
Opening Stock	**Finished goods**	**1,000**	**25,000**
	Raw materials	**1,100**	**11,000**
Purchases		**10,000**	**1,00,000**
Labour			**76,500**
Overheads (Fixed)			**75,000**
Sales		**10,000**	**2,80,000**
Closing Stock	**Raw Materials**	**900**	
	Finished goods	**1,200**	

The expected production for the year was15,000 kg. of the finished good product. Due to fall in market demand the sales price for the finished goods was ₹ 20 per kg. and the replacement cost for the raw material was ₹ 9.50 Kg. on the closing day.

Required: Calculate the Value of the Closing Stock

ANSWER:

CALCULATION OF COST PER UNIT

Particulars	*Amount (₹)*	*Quantity (units)*	*Per unit cost*
Purchases	1,00,000	10,000	10.00
Add: Opening Stock	11,000	1,100	10.00
Less: Closing stock of materials	9000	900	10.00
Cost of Purchases	1,02,000	10,200	10.00
Add: Direct labour	76,500		7.50
Add: Production Overhead (Fixed)	75,000		5.00
			(75,000/15,000)
Total Cost per unit			22.50

Hence closing stock should be valued at NRV (i.e. ₹ 20 per unit), since it is less than cost (i.e ₹. 22.50 per unit).

CALCULATION OF COST OF STOCK WHEN THERE IS NORMAL AND ABNORMAL LOSS

QUESTION 5: In a production process, normal waste is 5% of input. 5,000 MT of input were put in process resulting in a wastage of 300 MT. Cost per MT of input is ₹ 1,900. The entire quantity of waste is on stock at the year end. State with reference to Accounting standard the treatment of normal loss and abnormal loss and also find out the amount of abnormal loss, if any and the value of closing inventories.

ANSWER:

1. Normal Loss Qty = 5% of 5,000 MT = 250 MT

   Treatment: No entry is passed for normal loss. However, normal loss increases the cost per good unit
2. Cost of Good units = Total Cost/(Total Qty – Normal Loss Qty) = (5000 × ₹1,900)/(5000 – 250) = ₹ 2,000
3. Abnormal Loss Qty = Total Loss – Normal Loss = 300 MT – 5% of 5,000 MT = 50 MT

   Cost of Abnormal Loss = 50MT × ₹ 2,000= ₹ 1,00,000

   Treatment: As per AS 2, abnormal amounts of waste materials, labour and other production costs are excluded from cost of inventories and such costs are recognized as expenses in the period in which they are incurred.. Hence, the Cost of Abnormal Loss of ₹ 1,00,000 should be charged to Profit & Loss A/c.
4. Closing Inventory Qty = 5,000 MT – 250 MT – 50 MT = 4,700 MT

   Cost of Closing Inventory =4,700 MT × ₹ 2,000= ₹ 94,00,000

QUESTION 6: Tulsian Limited took Bank Overdraft at an interest rate of 15% p.a. specifically for the purpose of purchasing 10,000 kg. of certain material at ₹ 100 per kg. The purchase price includes excise duty ₹ 10 per kg., in respect of which full CENVAT credit is admissible. Freight, loading and unloading charges incurred amounted to ₹ 40,800. Interest on such Bank Overdraft amounted to ₹ 25,000. Normal Transit Loss is 2%. The enterprise actually received 9,760 kg. and consumed 9,500 kg. Determine cost of inventory and allocation of material cost as per AS 2 "Valuation of Inventory".

ANSWER:

DETERMINATION OF NORMAL COST PER KG

Particulars	*Amount (₹)*
Purchase price (10,000 kg. × ₹ 100)	10,00,000
Less: CENVAT credit (10,000 kg. × 10)	(1,00,000)
Add: Freight, loading and unloading charges	40,800
Total Material Cost	9,40,800
Number of units after normal loss (i.e. 98% of 10,000 kg.)	9,800
Norma Cost per kg.	₹ 96

Note: Interest and other borrowing costs are usually considered as overheads that don't contribute to bringing the inventories to their present location and condition.Hence, Interest on bank overdraft will not form part of cost of production.

ALLOCATION OF MATERIAL COST

	Kg.	*₹/Kg.*	*Amount (₹)*
Material consumed	9,500	63	9,12,000
Closing inventory (9,760 – 9,500)	260	96	24,960
Abnormal Loss (9,800 – 9,760)	40	96	3,840
Total material cost	9,800	96	9,40,800

VALUATION OF CLOSING STOCK AS PER RETAIL METHOD

QUESTION 7: The retailer has large numbers of rapidly changing inventory items that have similar margins and for which it is impracticable to use other costing methods. He furnishes the following details:

Particulars	*Items*	*Cost*	*Retail Price*
Opening stock	10,000 units	50 per unit	80 per unit
Purchases	1,00,000 units	60 per unit	100 per unit
Sales ₹ 86,40,000			

Calculate the value of closing stock as per retail method.

ANSWER:

VALUATION OF CLOSING STOCK AS PER RETAIL METHOD

Particulars	*Cost*	*Retail Price*
A Opening stock	5,00,000	8,00,000
B Purchases	60,00,000	1,00,00,000
C Total [A + B]	65,00,000	1,08,00,000
D Sales		86,40,000
E Closing Stock at Retail Price		21,60,000
F Closing Stock at Cost [E × 65 / 108]	13,00,000	

COST FORMULAE: FIFO AND WEIGHTED AVERAGE METHOD

QUESTION 8: From the following data, find out value of inventory as on 30th April using (a) LIFO method, and (b) Weighted Average Method:

1. 1st April Purchased	10 units @₹.70 per unit
2. 6th April Sold	5 units @ ₹.90 per unit
3. 9th April Purchased	20 units @ ₹.75 per unit
4. 18th April Sold	14 units @₹.100 per unit

ANSWER:

(A) VALUATION OF CLOSING INVENTORY BY LIFO METHOD

Date	*Receipts*			*Issue*			*Balance*		
	Unit	*Cost/unit*	*Amount*	*Unit*	*Cost/unit*	*Amount*	*Unit*	*Cost/unit*	*Amount*
Apr. 1	10	70	700				10	70	700
Apr. 6				5	70	350	5	70	350
Apr. 9	20	75	1500				5	70	350
							20	75	1500
Apr. 18				14	75	1,050	5	70	350
							6	75	450

Value of Closing Inventory as per LIFO Method =(4 units × ₹ 70)+(6 units × ₹ 75)= ₹ 730

(B) VALUATION OF CLOSING INVENTORY BY WEIGHTED AVERAGE METHOD

Date	*Receipts*			*Issue*			*Balance*		
	Unit	*Cost/unit*	*Amount*	*Unit*	*Cost/unit*	*Amount*	*Unit*	*Cost/unit*	*Amount*
Apr. 1	10	70	700				10	70	700
Apr. 6				5	70	350	5	70	350
Apr. 9	20	75	1500				25	74	1850
Apr. 18				14	74	1,036	11	74	814

Value of Closing Inventory as per WEIGHTED AVERAGE Method: = ₹ 814

QUESTION 9: HP is a leading distributor of petrol. A detail inventory of petrol in hand is taken when the books are closed at the end of each month. At the end of month following information is available:

Sales:	₹ 47,25,000
General overheads cost	₹ 1,25,000
Inventory at beginning	1,00,000 litres @ ₹ 15 per litre

Purchases:

June 1 two lakh litres @ ₹ 14.25

June 30 one lakh litres @ ₹ 15.15

Closing inventory 1.30 lakh litres

Compute the following by the FIFO as per AS 2:

(i) Value of Inventory on June, 30.

(ii) Amount of cost of goods sold for June.

(iii) Profit/Loss for the month of June.

ANSWER:

		₹
(i)	**Cost of closing inventory for 1,30,000 litres as on 30th June**	
	1,00,000 litres @ ₹ 15.15	15,15,000
	30,000 litres @ ₹ 14.25	4,27,500
	Total	19,42,500
(ii)	**Calculation of Cost of Goods Sold**	₹
	Opening inventories (1,00,000 litres @ ₹ 15)	15,00,000
	Purchases: June-1 (2,00,000 litres @ ₹ 14.25)	28,50,000

	June-30 (1,00,000 litres @ ₹ 15.15)	15,15,000
		58,65,000
Less:	Closing inventories	19,42,500
Cost of goods sold		39,22,000

(iii) Profit = ₹ 47,25,000 – (₹ 39,22,500 + ₹ 1,25,000) = ₹ 6,77,500

LOWER OF COST OR NRV RULE

QUESTION 10:

Unsold units with Agent	**1,000**
Cost per unit	**₹ 10**
Estimated Selling Price per unit as at Balance Sheet Date	**₹ 8**
Agent's Commission on Sales	**5 %**

What should be the Value of Closing Stock?

ANSWER:

I. Cost of Closing Stock (1,000 × ₹ 10)	₹ 10,000
II. Net Realizable Value	
A. Total Realizable Value (1,000 × ₹ 8)	₹ 8,000
B. *Less:* Realizable Expenses (here agent's commission is realizable expense) (₹ 8,000 × 5/100)	₹ 400
C. Net Realizable Value (A – B)	₹ 7,600
III. Valuation since out of cost (which is ₹ 10,000 as calculated above) and NRV (which is ₹ 7,600), NRV is lower, the said unsold stock should be valued at ₹ 7,600.	

QUESTION 11: On 31st March 2015 a business firm finds that cost of a partly finished unit on that date is ₹ 530. The unit can be finished in 2015-2016 by an additional expenditure of ₹ 310. The finished unit can be sold for ₹ 750 subject to payment of 4% brokerage on selling price. The firm seeks your advice regarding:

(i) the amount at which the unfinished unit should be valued as at 31st Mach, 2015 for preparation of final accounts and

(ii) the desirabilty or otherwise of producing the finished unit.

ANSWER:

VALUATION OF UNFINISHED UNIT

Particulars	₹
Net selling price	750
Less: Estimated cost of completion	(310)
	440
Less: Brokerage (4% of 750)	30
Net Realisable Value	410
Cost of inventory	530
Value of inventory (Lower of cost and net realisable value)	410

Incremental cost ₹ 310 (cost to complete) is less than incremental revenue ₹ 720 (₹ 750 – ₹ 30). The enterprise will therefore decide to finish the unit for sale at ₹ 750.

Note: The above answer is given on the assumption that partly finished unit cannot be sold in semi finished form and its NRV is zero without processing it further.

QUESTION 12: X Ltd. has 5,000 AC in stock on 31st March, 2010. The cost of each AC amount to ₹ 10,000. There is firm commitment of sale of 1,000 AC by the company in April, 2010 @ ₹ 15,000 per AC. However, the general price of this AC at year end amounts to ₹ 9,500 per AC. Calculate the Value of Stock.

ANSWER:

CALCULATION OF VALUE OF STOCK

	Particulars	₹
A	Value of 1,000 AC covered under firm commitment at Cost	1,00,00,000
B	Value of 4,000 AC not covered under firm commitment at NRV since it is less than cost	3,80,00,000
C	Total Value of Stock [A + B]	4,80,00,000

QUESTION 13: As a Company Auditor how would you react of the following situations? Inventories of a Car manufacturing company include the value of items, required for the manufacture of a model which was removed from the production line five years back, at cost price.

ANSWER:

PROVISION OF AS-2

As per AS-2 on "Valuation of Inventories" the cost of inventories may not be recoverable if those inventories are damaged, or have become wholly or partially obsolete, or if their selling prices have declined. Accordingly, the auditor should examine whether appropriate allowance has been made for the defective, damaged, obsolete and slow-moving inventories in determining the Net Realizable Value.

ADVICE

Items required for the manufacture of a model which has been withdrawn from the production line five years ago are included in the stock at cost price resulting in overstatement of inventory and profit. It becomes necessary to write down the obsolete. Inventory to 'Net Realizable Value' if the cost is not recoverable. Under the circumstance, the auditor should qualify the Audit Report appropriately.

TWO METHODS OF COMPARISION OF COST WITH NRV

QUESTION 14: From the following data, calculate the value of stock, to be shown

(i) by the item-by-item method

(ii) by the group method.

Article	Group	No. of units	Cost (₹) per unit	Realizable value (₹) per unit.	Realization Expenses
1	A	100	100	120	8-1/3 %
2	B	200	200	200	10 %
3	C	300	150	156	8-1/3 %
4	D	400	250	290	10 %

ANSWER:

VALUATION OF STOCK ACCORDING TO ITEM BY ITEM METHOD

Article	*Cost (₹)*	*NRV (₹)*	*Lower of cost/ NRV ₹*
1	10,000	11,000	10,000
2	40,000	36,000	36,000
3	45,000	42,900	42,900
4	1,00,000	1,04,400	1,00,000
			1,88,900

VALUATION OF STOCK ACCORDING TO GROUP METHOD

GROUP 'A'

Article	*Cost (₹)*	*NRV (₹)*	*Lower of cost/ NRV ₹*
1	10,000	11,000	
3	45,000	42,900	
	55,000	53,900	53,900

GROUP 'B'

Article	*Cost (₹)*	*NRV (₹)*	*Lower of cost/ NRV ₹*
2	40,000	36,000	
4	1,00,000	1,04,400	
	1,40,000	1,40,400	1, 40,000

Value of Closing Stock = ₹ 53,900 + ₹ 1, 40, 000 = ₹ 1,93,900

QUESTION 15: Best Ltd. deals in five products, P, Q, R, S, and T which are neither similar nor interchangeable. At the time of closing of its accounts for the year ending 31st March 2013, the historical cost and net realizable value of the items of the dosing stock are determined as follows:

Items	*Historical Cost ₹*	*Net Realizable Value ₹*
P	5,70,000	4,75,000
Q	9,80,000	10,32,000
R	3,16,000	2,89,000
S	4,25,000	4,25,000
T	1,60,000	2,15,000

What will be the value of closing stock as at 31st March 2013 as per AS 2 "Valuation of Inventories"?

ANSWER: As per para 5 of AS 2 "Valuation of Inventories, inventories should be valued at the lower of cost and net relizable value. Inventories should be written down to net realizable value on an item-by-item basis.

VALUATION OF INVENTORY (ITEM WISE) AS AT 31ST MARCH 2013

Item	*Historical Cost ₹*	*Net realizable value ₹*	*Valuation of closing stock ₹*
P	5,70,000	4,75,000	4,75,000

Q	9,80,000	10,32,000	9,80,000
R	3,16,000	2,89,000	2,89,000
S	4,25,000	4,25,000	4,25,000
T	1,60,000	2,15,000	1,60,000
			23,29,000

The value of inventory as at 31st March 2013 = ₹ 23,29,000.

VALUATION OF MATERIALS AND OTHER SUPPLIES

QUESTION 16: Tulsian Ltd. which manufactures three products namely 'OM', 'NAMO' and 'SHIVAY' using raw materials M1. M2 and M3 respectively provides you the following information about the Closing Stock:

Items	*Historical Cost (₹ in Lakhs)*	*Net Realizable Value (₹ in Lakhs)*	*Replacement Value (₹ in Lakhs)*
OM	10	11	12
NAMO	20	18	19
SHIVAY	30	27	28
M1	5		3
M2	6		5
M3	7		8

Required: Calculate the value of Closing Stock.

ANSWER:

Items	*Historical Cost (₹ in Lakhs)*	*Net Realizable Value (₹ in Lakhs)*	*Valuation of Stock (₹ in Lakhs)*
OM	10	11	10
NAMO	20	18	18
SHIVAY	30	27	27
M1	5	3 (Replacement Cost)	5 (Since Finished Product is expected to be sold at above cost)
M2	6	5 (Replacement Cost)	5 (Since Finished Product is expected to be sold below cost)
M3	7	8 (Replacement Cost)	7
		Total	72

QUESTION 17: U.S.A Ltd. purchased raw material @ ₹ 400 per kg. Company does not sell raw material but uses in production of finished goods. The finished goods in which raw material is used are expected to sold at below cost. At the end of the accounting year, company is having 10,000 kg of raw material in stock. As the company never sells the raw material, it does not know the selling price of raw material and hence can not calculate the realizable value of the raw material for valuation of inventories at the end of the year. However replacement cost of raw material is ₹ 300 per kg. How will you value as inventory of raw material?

ANSWER:

PROVISION OF AS 2

As per Para 24 of **AS** 2 (Revised) " Valuation of Inventories", materials and other supplies held for use in the production of inventories are not written down below cost if the finished products in which they will be incorporated are expected to be sold at or above cost. However, when there has been a decline in the price of materials and it is estimated that the cost of the finished products will exceed net realizable value, the materials are written down to net realizable value. In such circumstances, the replacement cost of the materials may be the best available measure of their net realizable value.

ADVICE

USA Ltd. should value the stock of raw material at ₹ 30,00,000 (i.e. 10,000 Kg @₹ 300 per kg.).

QUESTION 18: Raw materials inventory of a company includes certain material purchased at ₹100 per kg The price of the material is on decline and replacement cost of the inventory at the year end is ₹ 75 per kg. It is possible to convert the material into finished product at conversion cost of ₹ 125.

Decide whether to make the product or not to make the product if selling price is (i) ₹ 175 and (ii) ₹ 225. Also find out the value of inventory in each case.

ANSWER: As per para 24 of AS 2 'Valuation of Inventories', materials and other supplies held for use in the production of inventories are not written down below cost if the finished products in which they will be incorporated are expected to be sold at or above cost. However, when there has been a decline in the price of materials and it is estimated that the cost of the finished products will exceed net realizable value, the materials are written down to net realisable value. In such circumstances, the replacement cost of the materials may be the best available measure of their net realisable value.

(i) When selling price is ₹ 175

Incremental Profit = ₹ 175 – ₹ 125 = ₹ 50

Current price of the material = ₹ 75

Therefore, it is better not to make the product. Raw material inventory would be valued at net realisable value i.e. ₹ 75 because the selling price of the finished product is less than ₹225 (100 + 125) per kg.

(ii) When selling price is ₹ 225

Incremental Profit = ₹ 225 – ₹ 125 = ₹ 100

Current price of the raw material = ₹ 75.

Therefore, it is better to make the product.

Raw material inventory would be valued at ₹ 100 per kg because the selling price of the finished product is not less than ₹ 225.

QUESTION 19: Calculate the value of raw materials and closing stock based on the following information:

Row material X	
Closing Balance	500 units
	₹ per unit
Cost price including excise duty	200
Exercise duty (Cenvat credit is receivalbe on the excise duty paid)	10
Freight inward	20
Unloading charges	10
Replacement cost	150

Finished good Y	
Closing Balance	1200 units
	₹ per unit
Material consumed	220
Direct labour	60
Direct overhead	40

Total Fixed overhead for the year was ₹ 2,00,000 on normal capacity of 20,000 units.

Calculate the value of the closing stock, when

(i) Net Realizable Value of the Finished Goods Y is ₹ 400.

(ii) Net Realizable Value of the Finished Goods Y is ₹ 300.

ANSWER:

Situation (i)

When Net Realisable Value of the Finished Goods Y is ₹ 300

NRV is greater than the cost of Finished Goods Y i.e. ₹ 330

Hence, Raw Material and Finished Goods are to be valued at cost

VALUE OF CLOSING STOCK

	Qty	*Rate*	*Amount (₹)*
Raw Material X	500	220	1,10,000
Finished Goods Y	1,200	330	3,96,000
Total Cost of Closing Stock			5,06,000

Situation (ii)

When Net Realisable Value of the Finsihed Goods Y is ₹ 300

NRV is less than the cost of Finished Goods Y i.e. ₹ 330

Hence, Raw Material is to be valued at replacement cost and

Finished Goods are to be valued at NRV since NRV is less than the cost

VALUE OF CLOSING STOCK

	Qty	Rate	₹
Raw Material X	500	150	75,000
Finished Goods Y	1,200	330	3,60,000
Total Cost of Closing Stock			4,35,000

Note: It has been considered that Raw Material X is used for the production of Finished Goods Y.

WORKING NOTES:

Raw Materials X	₹
Cost Price	200
Less: Cenvat Credit	(10)
Add: Freight Inward	20
Unloading charges	10
Cost	220
Finished goods Y	1

Materials consumed	220
Direct Labour	60
Direct overhead	40
Fixed overhead (₹ 2,00,000/20,000 units)	10
Cost	330

MISCELLANEOUS

QUESTION 20: A private limited company manufacturing fancy terry towels had valued its closing stock of inventories of finished goods at the realizable value, inclusive of profit and the export cash incentives. Firm contracts had been received and goods were packed for export, but the ownership in these goods had not been transferred to the foreign buyers.

Comment on the valuation of the stocks by the company.

ANSWER:

PROVISION OF AS-2 AND AS 9

Revenue cannot be recognized on the goods since sale is not complete m accordance with AS-9. Such goods should be valued at Cost or Net Realizable Value which ever is lower as per AS 2.

ADVICE

The closing stock of the finished goods (fancy terry towel) should be valued at lower of cost, and Net Realizable Value and not at Net Realizable value, Further, export incentives are recorded only in the year the export sale takes place. Therefore, the policy adopted by the company for valuing its closing stock of inventory of finished goods is not correct as per AS 9 since the ownership has not been transferred.

QUESTION 21: Vintage Ltd. has been in the business of sale of Vintage Wines for the last 12 years and is an extremely cash rich company. In FY 2014-2015 the Board of the company decided to venture into new areas of business and identified the activity of acquiring Vintage Properties such as old Bungalows, Heritage buildings and the like at prime locations and after carrying out renovation and refurbishment of the same to let out these properties on lease to willing parties. The new business was commenced as a separate division of the company in FY 2014-2015 during which the company managed to identify 19 such properties of which 17 were acquired and 9 given on lease. Being the initial year of operations and also since some of the lease arrangements were entered into at the fag end of the year the income from leasing was only a paltry amount. After the acquisition of the properties as aforesaid very attractive offers for sale of 14 of the properties were received. Vintage Ltd. after negotiation accepted 12 of the offers and sold these 12 properties making large profits in the bargain. The accountant of Vintage Ltd. hasc accounted the acquisition and disposals of properties as ₹Purchases' and ₹Sales' in the Profit & Loss account of the Property Division and treated the lease incomes as part of the other income of the company. The contention of the accountant of Vintage Ltd., was that since a majority of the properties were disposed off within a short span of time, the properties are to be considered as stock in trade only. Further since the lease income was insignificant it does not become the main source of income and hence considered as part of other income. You are required to examine the correctness of the contentions of the accountant of Vintage Ltd. considering the relevant Accounting Standards and provisions of Schedule III of Companies Act, 2013.

ANSWER:

PROVISION OF AS 2

As per para 3 of AS 2 "Valuation of Inventories", inventories are assets that are (a) held for sale in the ordinary course of business; (b) in the process of production for such sale; or (c) in the form of materials or supplies to be consumed in the production process or in the rendering of services. The properties acquired by Vintage Ltd. Should not be construed as stock in trade in spite of the fact that they are being sold within a short span of time.

ADVICE

As per AS 10, a fixed asset is one which is held with the intention of being used for the purpose of producing goods or services and is not held for sale in the normal course of business. The acquisition of the heritage properties is done by the company with the intention to provide the service of leasing of such properties. Hence the intention of the company was to use such property for generating revenue for the company by leasing out such properties. The sale of 12 properties can't be considered as part of normal business operations of the company. Hence the treatment of the properties as 'Stock-in-Trade' is incorrect as the properties are to be considered only as Fixed Assets of the company. The purchase and sale in short span of time to make huge profit will require disclosure as per AS 5 'Net Profit or Loss for the Period, Prior Period Items and Changes in Accounting Policies'. The lease income from these properties will be considered as main business income and cannot be considered as part of other income. Such income will be disclosed under the head Revenue from operations.

Thus the contentions of the accountant regarding accounting the acquisition and sale of these properties as sale and purchase, treating them as stock in trade, considering lease income as other income are incorrect in line with provisions of relevant accounting standards.

QUESTION 22: T. Ltd. Commenced its manufacturing activities from 1st April, 2014. In the course of production the company generated certain by-products. As at 31st March 2015 the company did not value the by-products considering the value as insignificant. The auditor of the company is of the opinion that the by-products are inventory of the company and it should be valued and brought into books of account. Comment.

ANSWER:

PROVISION OF AS 2

As per AS-2 on "Valuation of Inventories", a production process may result in more than one product being produced simultaneously. This is the case when joint products are produced or when there is a main product & by-products. If the costs of conversion of each product are not separable, they are allocated on a rational & consistent basis.Most of the by-products as well as scrap or waste materials, by their nature, are immaterial. They are often measured at net realizable value & this value is deducted from the cost of the main product. In the given case, as the value of the by-products is insignificant, the realizable value of by products should be ascertained and it should be deducted from the cost of the main product. An asset is a resource controlled by an enterprise as a result of past events from which the future economic benefits are expected. As per AS 2- Inventories are assets (a) held for sale in the ordinary course of business (b) in the process of production for such sale (c) in the form of materials or supplies to be consumed in the production process or in the rendering of services.

ADVICE

As the stock of by-product is a resource controlled by T Ltd., it is an asset and it is inventory because it is held for sale in the ordinary course of business. T Ltd. should deduct the realizable value of its by products from the cost of production of main product.

ANSWER:

5 AS 3 – CASH FLOW STATEMENT

THEORETICAL BASE

QUESTION 1: What is meant by Cash Flow Statement?

ANSWER: The Cash Flow Statement means the Statement of Changes in Cash and Cash equivalents during a particular accounting period. It shows—

1. **Net Cash flows from Operating Activities;**
2. **Net Cash flows from Investing Activities;**
3. **Net Cash flows from Financing Activities;**
4. **Net Change in Cash and Cash Equivalents.**

QUESTION 2: What is meant by Cash Flows as per AS-3?

ANSWER: Cash Flows are inflows and outflows of Cash and Cash equivalents.

QUESTION 3: What is meant by Cash as per AS-3?

ANSWER: Cash comprises Cash on hand and Demand Deposits with banks.

QUESTION 4: What is meant by Cash Equivailents as per AS-3? Give two examples.

ANSWER: Cash Equivalents are short term, highly liquid investments that are readily convertible into known amounts of cash and which are subject to an insignificant risk of changes in value.

Examples: Treasury Bills, Commercial Papers, Commercial Bills, Call Money, Certificate of Deposit

QUESTION 5: What is the purpose of the term 'Cash Equivalents' as per AS-3?

ANSWER: Cash Equivalents are held for the purpose of meeting short-term cash commitments rather than for Investment *or* other purposes.

QUESTION 6: What are the Two Conditions for an investment to qualify as 'Cash Equivalents as per AS-3?

ANSWER:

1. It must be readily convertible to a known amount of cash.
2. It must be subject to an insignificant risk of changes in value. Therefore, an investment normally qualifies as a cash equivalent only when it has a short maturity of, say, 3 months *or* less from the date of acquisition.

QUESTION 7: What is meant by Operating Activities as per AS-3? Give two examples.

ANSWER: Operating Activities are the principal revenue-producing activities of the enterprise and other activities that are not investing *or* financing activities.

Examples: Purchase/Sale of Goods, Payments received from Trade Debtors, Payments made to Trade Creditors, Payments of Operating Expenses.

QUESTION 8: What is meant by Investing Activities as per AS-3? Give two examples.

ANSWER: Investing Activities are the acquisition and disposal of Long-term Assets and other Investments not included in Cash Equivalents.

Examples: Purchase/Sale of Non-Current Assets, Income received from Investments.

QUESTION 9: What is meant by Financing Activities as per AS-3? Give two examples.

ANSWER: Financing Activities are activities that result in changes in the size and composition of the Owners' Capital (including Preference Share Capital in the case of a company) and Borrowings (whether Short term *or* Long term) of the enterprise.

Examples: Issue/Buy Back of Equity Shares, Issue/Redmption of Pref. Shares/Debentures/Loans, Payment of Interest on Borrowings, Payment of Interim Dividend/Final Dividend

QUESTION 10: Garden Lid. acquired fixed assets viz. plant and machinery for ₹ 20 lakhs. During the same year it sold its furniture and fixtures for ₹ 5 lakhs. Can the company disclose, net cash outflow towards purchase of fixed assets in the cash flow statement as per AS-3?

ANSWER:

PROVISION OF AS 3

As per Para 21 of AS 3 (Revised) 'Cash Flow Statements', an enterprise should report separately major classes of gross cash receipts and gross cash payments arising from investing and financing activities, except to the extent that cash flows described in paragraphs 22 and 24 are reported en a net basis. Acquisition and disposal of fixed assets is not prescribed in para 22 and 24 of the standard.

ADVICE

Hence, the company cannot disclose net cash flow in respect of acquisition of plant and machinery and disposal of furnitures and fixtures.

QUESTION 11: Intelligent Ltd., a non financial company has the following entries in its Bank Account. It has sought your advice on the treatment of the same for preparing Cash Flow Statement.

1. **Loans and Advances given to the following and interest earned on them:**
   (a) **to suppliers**
   (b) **to employees**
   (c) **to its subsidiaries companies**
2. **Investment made in subsidiary Smart Ltd. and dividend received**
3. **Dividend paid for the year**
4. **TDS on interest income earned on investments made**
5. **TDS on interest earned on advance given to suppliers**
6. **Insurance claim received against loss of fixed asset by fire**

Discuss in the context of AS 3 Cash Flow Statement.

ANSWER:

1. Loans and advances given and interest earned	
(a) to supliers	Operating Cash flow
(b) to employees	Operating Cash flow
(c) to its subsidiary companies	Investing Cash flow
2. Investment made in subsidiary company and dividend received	Investing Cash flow
3. Dividend paid for the year	Financing Cash Outflow
4. TDS on interest income earned on investments made	Investment Cash Outflow
5. TDS on interest earned on advance given to suppliers	Operating Cash Outflow
6. Insurance claim received against loss of fixed asset by fire	Extraordinary item to be shown under a separate heading as 'Cash inflow from Operating activities'.

6 AS 6 – DEPRECIATION ACCOUNTING

THEORETICAL BASE

QUESTION 1: What are the areas in which AS – 6 is not applicable? Does AS – 6 apply to land?

ANSWER:

1. Forests, Plantations and Similar Regenerative Natural Resources;
2. Wasting Assets including expenditure on the exploration for and extraction of Minerals, Oils, Natural Gas and similar Non-Regenerative Resources;
3. Expenditure on Research and Development;
4. Goodwill;
5. Livestock.

AS - 6 does not apply to land unless it has a limited useful life for the enterprise.

QUESTION 2: What is the meaning of term 'Depreciation'?

ANSWER:

1. Depreciation is a measure of the wearing out, consumption or other loss of value of a depreciable asset arising from use, effluxion of time or obsolescence through technology and market changes.
2. Depreciation is allocated so as to charge a fair proportion of the depreciable amount in each accounting period during the expected useful life of the asset.
3. Depreciation includes amortization of assets whose useful life is predetermined.

QUESTION 3: What are Depreciable Assets?

ANSWER:

Depreciable assets are assets which-

(i) are expected to used during more than one accounting period; and

(ii) have a limited useful life; and

(iii) are held by an enterprise for use in the production or supply of goods and services, for rental to others, or for administrative purposes and not for the purpose of sale in the ordinary course of business.

QUESTION 4: What are the factors which determine the amount of depreciation?

ANSWER:

1. **Historical Cost:** It represents its money outlay or its equivalent in connection with its acquisition, installation and commissioning as well as for additions to or improvement to thereof. The historical cost of a depreciable asset may undergo subsequent changes arising as a result of price adjustments, changes in duties or similar factors.
2. **Expected Useful Life:** It is the period over which a depreciable asset is expected to be used by the enterprise; or the number of production or similar units expected to be obtained from the use of the asset by the enterprise.

3. **Estimated Residual Value:** It is value expected to be realized on its sale or exchange on the expiry of its useful life.

QUESTION 5: What is the meaning of term 'Depreciable Amount'? How should depreciable amount be allocated?

ANSWER:

1. Depreciable amount of a depreciable asset is its historical cost, or other amount substituted for historical cost in the financial statements, *less* the estimated residual value.
2. The depreciable amount of a depreciable asset should be allocated on a systematic basis to each accounting period during the useful life of the asset.

QUESTION 6: At which rate depreciation should be provided Management's Rate *or* Statute Rate?

ANSWER: The statute governing an enterprise may provide the basis for computation of the depreciation. *For example*, the Companies Act, 2013 lays down the rates of depreciation in respect of various assets.

Case	Rate
(i) ***Where the management's estimate of the useful life of an asset is shorter than that envisaged under the statute.***	The depreciation provision should appropriately be computed by applying a higher rate of management.
(ii) ***Where the management's estimate of the useful life of an asset is longer than that envisaged under the statute.***	The depreciation provision should appropriately be computed by applying a higher rate of statute.

QUESTION 7: When should the change in the method of depreciation be made? How should the change in the method of depreciation be accounted for? What are the disclosure requirements regarding change in accounting method?

ANSWER:

When	A change in the method of depreciation should be made only if - - Adoption of different accounting policy is required by statute or - For compliance with an accounting standard or - If it is considered that the change would result in more appropriate presentation.
How	**Step 1:** *Recalculate depreciation as per new method from the date of the asset coming into use.* **Step 2:** *Calculate Deficiency or Surplus* **Step 3:** *Charge Deficiency OR Credit Surplus in the Statement of Profit and Loss for the year in which the method of depreciation is changed.*
Disclosure Requirements	Such a change should be treated as a change in accounting policy and its effect should be quantified and disclosed.

QUESTION 8: How should Depreciation be provided in the following cases?

(a) after review of useful life

(b) after the change in historical cost due to change in long-term liability

(c) after revaluation of assets

(d) after addition or extension

ANSWER:

Case	How to provide Depreciation
After Review of Useful Life	The unamortized depreciable amount should be charged over the revised remaining useful life.
After the Change in Historical Cost due to Change in Long-term Liability	The depreciation on the revised unamortized depreciable amount should be provided prospectively over the residual useful life of the asset.
After Revaluation of Assets	1. The Provision for depreciation should be based on the revalued amount and on the estimate of the remaining useful lives of such assets. 2. In case the revaluation has a material effect on the amount of depreciation, the same should be disclosed separately in the year in which revaluation is carried out.
After addition or extension ***(i) Where any addition or extension becomes an integral part of the existing asset.***	1. Such addition or extension should be depreciated over the remaining useful life of that existing asset of which any addition or extension becomes an integral part of existing asset, or 2. The depreciation on such addition or extension may also be provided at the rate applied to the existing asset.
(ii) Where an addition or extension retains a separate identity and is capable of being used after the existing asset is disposed of	Depreciation should be provided independently on the basis of an estimate of its own useful life.

QUESTION 9: What are the disclosure requirements as to (a) each class of depreciable assets (b) depreciation policy?

ANSWER:

For each class of Depreciable Assets	1. the Historical Cost or other amount substituted for historical cost of each class of depreciable assets; 2. Total Depreciation for the period for each class of assets; and 3. the related Accumulated Depreciation.
For Depreciation Policy	1. Depreciation Methods used; and 2. Depreciation Rates or the Useful Lives of the assets, if they are different from the principal rates specified in the statute governing the enterprise.

PRACTICAL QUESTIONS FOR PRACTICE

CALCULATION OF DEPRECIABLE AMOUNT

QUESTION 1: X Ltd. set up a new factory in the backward area and purchased plant for ₹ 500 Lakhs for the purpose. Purchases were entitled for the Cenvat credit of 2% and along with this Government agreed to extend 30% subsidy for backward area development. Estimated residual value at the end of Useful life ₹ 43 Lakhs Compute depreciable amount for the Asset.

ANSWER:

CALCULATION OF DEPRECIABLE AMOUNT

Particulars	₹ In Lakhs
A. Purchase price of the plant	500
B. *Less:* Cenvat Credit @ 2%	10
C. Balance (A – B)	490
D. *Less:* Government Subsidy @ 30%	147
E. *Less:* Estimated Residual Value	43
F. Depreciable Amount	300

CALCULATION OF DEPRECIATION AFTER REVIEW OF USEFUL LIFE

QUESTION 2: A computer costing ₹ 60,000 is depreciated on straight line basis, assuming 10 years working life and Nil residual value, for three years. The estimate of remaining useful life after third year was reassessed at 5 years. Calculate Depreciation as per the provisions of AS - 6 "Depreciation Accounting".

ANSWER: Present Book Value (i.e. after three years) [₹ 60,000 – (₹ 6,000 × 3 yrs) = ₹ 42,000
Depreciation for the current year and onwords [₹ 42,000/5 years] = ₹ 8,400 p.a.

QUESTION 3:

Machinery purchased	**₹ 1,00,000**
Estimated residual value at the end of the 10th year	**₹ 10,000**
Method of providing depreciation in use	**Straight line method.**

At the end of the 4th year due to change in technology the total useful life of an asset is reduced to 8 years and residual value at the end of 8th year is ₹3000.

ANSWER:

CALCULATION OF UNAMORTIZED AMOUNT TO BE DEPRECIATED

Particulars	₹
Cost	1,00,000
Less: Depreciation for Year 1	9,000
Balance	91,000
Less: Depreciation for Year 2	9,000
Balance	82,000
Less: Depreciation for Year 3	9,000
Balance	73,000
Depreciation for the Year 4 and onwards = (₹ 73,000 – ₹ 3,000) / 5 = ₹14,000	

CALCULATION OF DEPRECIATION AFTER THE CHANGE IN HISTORICAL COST DUE TO CHANGE IN LONG-TERM LIABILITY

QUESTION 4: A machinery was purchased on 1st April, 2011 for ₹ 1,50,000 and the useful life of the machine is estimated to be 10 years. The net book value of the machinery on 1st April, 2014 was ₹ 1,05,000. The liability for acquiring this machine was increased by ₹ 14,000 due to

price adjustments on 31st March, 2015. What will be the depreciation for the year 2014-2015 and onwards? (Assume depreciation has been provided on SLM)

ANSWER:

COMPUTATION OF DEPRECIATION

Net Book Value on 1st April, 2014	₹ 1,05,000
Add: Increase in liability on 31st March, 2015	14,000
Total unamortized amount	1,19,000

Depreciation for year 2014 - 2015 and onwards (₹ 1,19,000/7) = ₹ 17,000

CALCULATION OF DEPRECIATION AFTER REVALUATION OF ASSETS

QUESTION 5:

Cost of machine	**₹ 1, 30, 000**
Residual value	**NIL**
Useful life	**10 years**
Method of Depreciation in use	**Straight line method**

After 8 years, the machine was revalued to ₹ 80,000

ANSWER:

COMPUTATION OF DEPRECIATION

	Particulars	₹
A	Original cost	1,30,000
B	*Less:* Aggregate Depreciation up to 8 years [(₹1,30,000 – NIL) × 8/10]	1,04,000
C	Existing Unamortized Depreciable Amount (A – B)	26,000
D	*Add:* Profit on revaluation (80,000 – 26,000)	54,000
E	Revised unamortized depreciable amount (C + D)	80,000
F	Depreciation for 9th year (₹ 80,000 / 2)	40,000

Note: Remaining useful life is 2 years.

QUESTION 6: A building costing ₹ 12,00,000 is depreciated for three years on straight line basis, assuming 10 years working life and ₹ 2,00,000 residual value. At the beginning of fourth year, the building was revalued upwards by ₹ 3,00,000. Residual value also revalued upwards by ₹ 1,00,000. The remaining useful life was reassessed as 10 years. Find depreciation to be charged for the fourth year onwards.

ANSWER:

A.	Original Cost	12,00,000
B.	*Less:* Depreciation till Revaluation [₹ (12,000,000 – ₹ 2,00,000) × 3 years]	(3,00,000)
C.	Book value [A – B]	9,00,000
D.	*Add:* Upward Revaluation	3,00,000
E.	Revised Value	12,00,000
F.	Depreciation from the fourth year onwards = (₹ 12,00,000 – ₹ 3,00,000)/10 years = ₹ 90,000 per year.	

QUESTION 7: On 01.04.2012 a machine was acquired at ₹ 4,00,000. The machine was expected to have a useful life of 10 years. The residual value was estimated at 10% of the original cost. At the end of the 3rd year, an attachment was made to the machine at a cost of ₹ 1,80,000 to enhance its capacity. The attachment was expected to have a useful life of 10 years and zero terminal value. During the same time the original machine was revalued upwards by ₹ 90,000 and remaining useful life was reassessed at 9 years and residual value was reassessed at NIL.

Calculate depreciation for the year, if

(i) attachment retains its separate identity.

(ii) attachment becomes integral part of the machine

ANSWER:

1. DEPRECIATION ON ORIGINAL MACHINE

Particulars	₹
A. Depreciation for 3 Years [(₹ 4,00,000 – ₹ 40,000) × 10 × 3]	1,08,000
B. Written down value at the end of 3rd year (4,00,000 – 1,08,000)	2,92,000
C. *Add:* Revaluation	90,000
D. Total Book Value after revaluation	3,82,000
E. Ressessed remaining useful life	9 Years
F. Depreciation per year from 2015-2016 [D/E]	42,444

2. Depreciation on Attachment = ₹ 1,80,000/10 = ₹ 18,000

(i) Total Depreciation for the year if Arttachment retains its separate identity
= ₹ 42,444 + ₹ 18,000 = ₹ 60,444

(ii) Total Depreciation for the year if Attachment becomes integral part of the Machine
= (₹ 3,82,000 + ₹ 1,80,000)/9 = ₹ 62,444

Note: Since, upward revaluation of the machine and ressesment of remaining useful life had been made at the end of the 3rd year, it is implied that depreciation for the 3rd year has been charged on the basis of old calculation & remaining useful life of 9 years is to be calculated from the beginning of the 4th year onwards.

QUESTION 8: Tulsian Ltd. provides you the following information:

Machinery purchased on 1st April, 2011	**₹ 1,00,000**
Estimated residual value at the end of 5th year	**₹ 5,000**
Method of Depreciation	**Written down value method**
Rate of Depreciation	**55 %**
Addition to machinery on 1st April, 2012	**₹ 50,000**
Estimated Residual Value at the end of 4th year	**₹ 2,000**

This addition becomes an integral part of the existing asset.

Calculate depreciation for the year, if

1. **Addition retains its separate identity.**
2. **Addition becomes integral part of the machine**

ANSWER:

Particulars	Case 1			Case 2
	Existing	New Asset	Total	
Cost as on 1.4.2011	1,00,000	0	1,00,000	1,00,000
Less: Depreciation for 2011-2012	55,000	0	1,00,000	55,000

Balance/Addition as on 1.4.2012	45,000	50,000	95,000	95,000
Less: Depreciation for 2012-2013	24,750	25,000	49,750	52,250
Balance as on 1.4.2013	20,250	25,000	45,250	42,750
Less: Depreciation for 2013-2014	11,138	12,500	23,638	23,513
Balance as on 1.04.2014	9,112	12,500	21,612	19,237
Less: Depreciation for 2014-2015	5,012	6,250	11,262	10,580
Balance as on 1.4.2015	4,100	6,250	10,350	8,657

*Rate of depreciation is calculated by the formula $=1-\sqrt[n]{s/c}=1-\sqrt[4]{5,000/50,000}=50\%$

CHANGE IN THE METHOD OF DEPRECIATION

QUESTION 9: M/s. Son Ltd. charged depreciation on its assets on SLM basis. In the year ended 31st March, 2015 it changed to WDV basis. The impact of the change when computed from the date of the assets putting into use amounts to ₹ 18 lakhs being additional depreciation. Discuss, when should an enterprise change method of charging depreciation and how it should be dealt with in Profit and Loss A/c.

ANSWER:

PROVISION OF AS 6

As per AS 6 'Depreciation Accounting', an enterprise can change one method of charging depreciation to another method only if the adoption of the new method is required by statute or for compliance with an accounting standard or if it is considered that the change would result in a more appropriate preparation or presentation of the financial statements of the enterprise.

When such a change in the method of depreciation is made, depreciation should be recalculated in accordance with the new method from the date of the asset coming into use. The deficiency or surplus arising from retrospective recomputation of depreciation in accordance with the new method should be adjusted in the accounts through statement of profit and loss in the year in which the method of depreciation is changed. In case the change in the method results in deficiency in depreciation in respect of past years, the deficiency should be charged in the statement of profit and loss.

ADVICE

Additional Depreciation of ₹ 18 lakhs should be provided for as under:

Date	Particulars		Dr. (₹)	Cr.(₹)
	Profit & Loss A/c	Dr.	₹ 18 lakhs	
	To Assets A/c			₹ 18 lakhs
	(Being the additional depreciation due to change in the method of depreciation w/o to Profit & Loss A/c)			

QUESTION 10:

Machinery purchased ₹ 1,00,000

Estimated residual value at the end of the 10th year ₹ 10,000

Method of providing depreciation in use Straight line method.

From 5th year, company decided to change the method of depreciation from Straight Line Method to Written Down Value Method @ 20%.

ANSWER:

COMPUTATION OF DEFICIENCY / SURPLUS

Particulars	Straight Line Method	Written Down Value Method
Cost	1,00,000	1,00,000
Less: Dep. for Year 1	9,000	20,000
Balance	91,000	80,000
Less: Dep. for Year 2	9,000	16,000
Balance	82,000	64,000
Less: Dep. for Year 3	9,000	12,800
Balance	73,000	51,200
Less: Dep. for Year 4	9,000	10,240
Balance	64,000	40,960
Total Depreciation provided	36,000	59,040
Deficiency = ₹ 59,040 – ₹ 36,000 = ₹ 23, 040		

JOURNAL ENTRY TO ADJUST DEFICIENCY

Date	Particulars		Dr. (₹)	Cr.(₹)
	Profit & Loss A/c	Dr.	₹ 23,040	
	To Machinery A/c			₹ 23,040
	(Being the backlog depreciation relating to past years now adjusted)			

QUESTION 11: A company acquired a machine on 1.4.2011 for ₹ 5,00,000. The company charged depreciation upto 2013-2014 on straight line basis with estimated working life of 10 years and scrap value of ₹ 50,000. From 2014-2015, the company decided to change depreciation method at 20% on reducing balance method. Compute the amount of depreciation to be debited to Profit and Loss Account for the year 2014-2015.

ANSWER:

Annual depreciation charged by the company up to 2013-2014

= (Cost – Scrap Value)/Useful Life

= (5,00,000 – 50,0000)/10 = 45,000

WDV of machine at the end of 2013-2014 by Straight Line Method (SLM)

= ₹ 5,00,000 – {₹ 45,000 × 3} = ₹ 3,65,000

DEPRECIATION BY REDUCING BALANCE METHOD (RBM)

Year	Cost / WDV at the beginning of the year ₹	Depreciation ₹	WDV at the end of the year ₹	
2011-2012	5,00,000	5,00,000 × 20%	1,00,000	4,00,000
2012-2013	4,00,000	4,00,000 × 20%	80,000	3,20,000
2013-2014	3,20,000	3,20,000 × 20%	64,000	2,56,000
				2,44,000
2014-2015	2,56,000	2,56,000 × 20%	51,200	2,04,800

DEPRECIATION TO BE CHARGED IN 2014-2015

Particulars	₹
Book value of the machine as per SLM as on 1.4.2014	3,65,000
Less: Book value of the machine as per RBM as on 1.4.2014	(2,56,000)
Add: Depreciation for the year 2014-2015 as per RBM	51,200
Total Depreciation to be debited to Profit and Loss Account in the year 2014-2015	1,60,200

Such a change should be treated as a change in accounting policy and its effect should be quantified and disclosed as per AS 5. "Net Profit loss for the period, prior period items and changes in Accounting Policies).

QUESTION 12: An item of machinery was purchased on 1-04-2013 for ₹ 2,00,000. The WDV depreciation rate applicable to the machinery was 15%. The written down value of the machinery as on 31-03-2015 was ₹ 1,44,500. On 1-04-2015, the enterprise decided to change the method from written down value (WDV) to straight line method (SLM). The enterprise decided to write off the book value of ₹ 1,44,500, over the remaining useful life or machinery i.e., 5 years. Out of the total useful life 7 years, 2 years have already elapsed.

Required: Comment whether the accounting treatment is correct. If not, given the correct accounting treatment with reasons.

ANSWER:

PROVISION OF AS 6

As per para 15 of Accounting Standard 6, 'Depreciation Accounting', when the method of depreciation is changed, depreciation is recalculated in accordance with the new method form the date of the assets coming into use. The deficiency or surplus arising from retrospective re-computation of depreciation in accordance with the new method is adjusted in the statement of profit & loss in the year in which the method of depreciation is changed.

ADVICE

CALCULATION OF SURPLUS/DEFICIENCY DUE TO CHANGE IN METHOD OF DEPRECIATION

Particulars	₹
Purchase Price of Plant as on 01-04-2013	2,00,000
Less: Depreciation as per SLM, for the years 2013-2014 & 2014-2015 (Rs 2,00,000 × 2/7)	57,143
Balance as on 31-3-2015	1,42,857
Book Value as per WDV method [Given]	1,44,500
Book Value as per SLM	1,42,857
Excess Depreciation already provided	1,643

1. Such Excess Depreciation should be written back in the year of change by passing the following Journal Entry:

   Machinery A/c Dr. ₹1,643

   To Profit and Loss A/c ₹1,643

2. As a result of above entry, the balance of Machinery Account will be Rs 1,44,500 as on 1.4.2015
3. Depreciation should be charged @ 15% on WDV basis from the year 2015-16 onwards.

QUESTION 13: In the Trial Balance of M/s Sun Ltd. as on 31-3-2015, balance of machinery appears at ₹ 5,60,000. The company follows rate of depreciation on machinery @ 10% p.a. on WDV basis. On scrutiny it was found that a machine appearing in the books on 1-4-2014 at ₹ 1,60,000 was disposed of on 30-9-2014 at ₹ 1,35,000 in part exchange of a new machine costing ₹ 1,50,000.

You are required to calculate:

(i) Total depreciation to be charged in the Profit and Loss Account.

(ii) Loss on exchange of machine.

(iii) Book value of machinery in the Balance Sheet as on 31-3-2015.

ANSWER:

(I) TOTAL DEPRECIATION TO BE CHARGED IN THE PROFIT AND LOSS ACCOUNT

Particulars	₹
Depreciation on old machinery in use [10% of (5,60,000 – 1,60,000)]	40,000
Add: Depreciation on new machine [(1,50,000 × 10%) × 6/12]	7,500
Add: Depreciation on machine disposed of [(1,60,000 × 10%)6/12]	8,000
Total Depreciation to be charged in Profit and Loss A/c	55,500

(II) LOSS ON EXCHANGE OF MACHINE

Particulars	₹
Book value of machine as on 1.4.2012	1,60,000
Less: Depreciation for 6 months @ 10%	(8,000)
Written Down Value as on 30.9.2012	1,52,000
Less: Exchange value	(1,35,000)
Loss on exchange of machine	17,000

(III) BOOK VALUE OF MACHINERY IN THE BALANCE SHEET AS ON 31.03.2015

Particulars	₹
Balance as per trial balance	5,60,000
Less: Book value of machine sold	(1,60,000)
Add: Purchase of new machine	1,50,000
Less: Depreciation on machinery in use [40,000 + 7,500]	(47,500)

QUESTION 14: In the books of Optic Fiber Ltd., plant and machinery stood at ₹ 6,32,000 on 1.4.2014. However on scrutiny it was found that machinery worth ₹ 1,20,000 was included in the purchases on 1.6.2013. On 30.6.2014 the company disposed a machine having book value of ₹ 1,89,000 on 1.4.2014 at ₹ 1,75,000 in part exchange of a new machine costing ₹ 2,56,000. The company charges depreciation @ 20% WDV on plant and machinery.

You are required to calculate:

(i) Depreciation to be charged to P/L

(ii) Book value of Plant and Machinery A/c as on 31.3. 2015

(iii) Loss on exchange of machinery.

ANSWER:

RECTIFYING ENTRY

Machinery A/c	Dr.	₹ 1,20,000	
To Purchases A/c			₹ 1,20,000

1. DEPRECIATION TO BE CHARGED TO P/L ACCOUNT

(6,32,000 – 189,000) × 20%	₹ 88,600
1,89,000 × 20% × 3/12	₹ 9,450
2,56,000 × 20% × 9/12	₹ 38,400
1,20,000 × 20% × 10/12	₹ 20,000
	₹ 1,56,450

2. BOOK VALUE OF PLANT AND MACHINERY AS ON 31.3.2015

Book value of Plant and machinery before depreciation	₹ 8,19,000
(4,43,000 + 1,20,000 + 2,56,000)	
Less: Depreciation on existing assets (88,600 + 38,400 + 20,000)	₹ 1,47,000
	₹ 6,72,000

3. LOSS ON EXCHANGE OF MACHINERY

WDV of machinery disposed in part exchange	₹ 1,89,000
Less: Depreciation for 3 months	₹ 9,450
Book value of machinery on date of Exchange	₹ 1,79,550
Exchange Value	₹ 1,75,000
Loss on Exchange	₹ 4,550

MANAGEMENT'S RATE VS. STATUTE RATE

QUESTION 15: Narmada Ltd. purchased an existing bottling unit from Kaveri Ltd. Kaveri Ltd. followed straight line method of charging depreciation on machinery of the sold unit whereas Narmada Ltd. followed written down value method in its other units. The directors of Narmada Ltd. want to continue to charge depreciation for the acquired unit in Straight Line Method which is not consistent with the WDV method followed in other units.

Discuss the contention of the directors with reference to the Accounting Standard. Further during the year, Narmada Ltd. set up a new plant on coastal land. In view of the corrosive climate, the Company felt that its machine life is reducing faster. Can the Company charge a higher rate of depreciation?

ANSWER:

PROVISION OF AS 6

According to para 12 of AS 6 'Depreciation Accounting', there are several methods of allocating depreciation over the useful life of the assets. The management of a business selects the most appropriate method(s) based on various important factors e.g., (i) type of asset, (ii) the nature of the use of such asset and (iii) circumstances prevailing in the business. A combination of more than one method is sometimes used. A company may adopt different methods of depreciation for different types of assets, provided the same methods are followed consistently.

The statute governing an enterprise may provide the basis for computation of the depreciation. For example, the Companies Act lays down the rates of depreciation in respect of various assets. Where the management's estimate of the useful life of an asset of the enterprise is shorter than that envisaged under the provisions of the relevant statute, the depreciation provision is appropriately computed by applying a higher rate.

ADVICE

The Company can charge higher rates of depreciation based on its estimate of the useful life of machinery, provided that such estimate is not less than the rate prescribed by the Companies Act, for that class of assets. However, such higher depreciation rates and/or the reduced useful lives of the assets should be disclosed by way of notes to the accounts in the Financial Statements. Thus Narmada Ltd. can continue to charge depreciation for the acquired unit as per straight line method.

QUESTION 16: Progressive Company Limited has not charged depreciation for the year ended on 31st March 2015, in respect of a Spare Bus purchased during the Financial Year 2014-2015 and kept ready by the Company for use as a stand-by, on the ground that, it was not actually used during the year. State your views with reference to AS - 6 "Depreciation Accounting".

ANSWER:

PROVISION OF AS 6

Depreciation is to be charged if asset is "ready for use", whether put to use or not.

7 AS 7 – CONSTRUCTION CONTRACTS

THEORETICAL BASE

QUESTION 1: What Is Construction Contract?

ANSWER: A construction contract is a contract specifically negotiated for the construction of an asset or a combination of assets that are closely interrelated or interdependent in terms of their design, technology and function or their ultimate purpose or use.

It may also include:

(a) Contracts for the rendering of services which are directly related to the construction of the asset, ***For example***, those for the services of project managers and architects; and

(b) Contracts for destruction or restoration of assets, and the restoration of the environment following the demolition of assets. *For example* contract for demolition of unauthorized storey of a building.

QUESTION 2: What are the types of construction contracts?

ANSWER: Construction contracts may be formulated in a number of ways. Some general types of contracts are given below:–

(i) Fixed Price Contracts	The contractor agrees to fixed contract price, or a fixed rate per unit of output, which in some cases is subject to cost escalation clauses;
(ii) Cost Plus Contracts	The contractor is reimbursed for allowable or otherwise defined costs, and is also allowed a percentage of these costs or a fixed fee.
(iii) Mixed Types of Contracts	These types of construction contracts may contain characteristics of both of fixed price contracts and cost plus contracts.
(iv) Real Estate Project	Some real estate projects indicate significant characteristics of construction contracts. These real estate projects then are subject to this standard.

QUESTION 3: State the items which constitute Contract Revenue.

ANSWER:

1. Initial amount of revenue agreed in the contract;
2. Variations in contract work;
3. Claims;
4. Incentive payments.

QUESTION 4: How should Contract Revenue be measured?

ANSWER: Contract Revenue should be measured at the consideration received or receivable.

QUESTION 5: Can original estimated contract revenue be revised?

ANSWER: Contract revenue is affected by number of uncertainties that depend on outcome of future events. Estimates are often reconsidered when events occur in future and / or uncertainties are resolved. Hence contract revenue as determined originally may change from one reporting period to the next reporting period. **When contract revenue is revised it is treated as changed in estimates.**

QUESTION 6: State the items which constitute Contract Costs.

ANSWER:

1. **Costs that are directly related to the specific contract**; *For Example*:
   (a) Site Labour Costs, including site supervision;
   (b) Costs of materials used in construction;
   (c) Depreciation of plant and equipment used on the contract;
   (d) Costs of moving plant, equipment and materials to and from the contract site;
   (e) Costs of hiring plant and equipment;
   (f) Costs of design and technical assistance that is directly related to the contract;
   (g) the estimated costs of rectification and guarantee work, including expected warranty costs; and
   (h) Claims from third parties.
2. **Costs which are generally related to the contract activity and are allocable to the specific contract;** *For Example:*
   (a) insurance;
   (b) costs of design and technical assistance that is not directly related to a specific contract; and
   (c) construction overheads which may include cost such as the preparation and processing of construction personnel payroll.
3. **Borrowing Costs;**
4. **Costs which are specifically chargeable to the customer under contract terms;**(i.e. those costs for which reimbursement is specific provided as per contract terms and may include some general administration cost and development cost.)
5. **Pre-contract Costs** (i.e. those costs which are incurred in securing the contract.)

QUESTION 7: State the costs which are not included in contract cost?

ANSWER:

1. general administration costs for which reimbursement is not specified in the contract;
2. selling costs;
3. research and development costs for which reimbursement is not specified in the contract; and
4. depreciation of idle plant and equipment that is not used on a particular contract.

QUESTION 8: State the accounting treatment of miscellaneous incomes .

ANSWER: Any miscellaneous income i.e. Rental Income, Sale of Surplus material, disposal of plant and equipment shall be **reduced from contract cost.**

QUESTION 9: When should contract revenue and contract cost should be recognized as revenue and expenses respectively?

ANSWER:

1. Contract revenue and contract cost should be recognized as revenue and expenses respectively by reference to the **stage of completion of the contract activity at the reporting period.**
2. However, recognization should only be done when the outcome of a construction contract can be **estimated reliably.**

QUESTION 10: When can the outcome of a construction contract be estimated reliably?

ANSWER: This degree of reliability would be provided if the following conditions are satisfied:

In case of Fixed Price Contracts	In case of Cost Plus Contracts
1. It is probable that the economic benefits associated with the contract will flow to the enterprise;	1. It is probable that the economic benefits associated with the contract will flow to the enterprise; and
2. total Contract Revenue can be measured reliably;	2. the contract costs attributable to the contract, whether or not specifically reimbursable, can be clearly identified and measured reliably.
3. both the contract costs to complete the contract and the stage of contract completion at the reporting date can be measured reliably; and	
4. the contract costs attributable to the contract can be clearly identified and measured reliably so that actual contract costs incurred can be compared with prior estimates.	

QUESTION 11: What is meant by term 'Stage of Completion Method' (Percentage Completion Method)?

ANSWER:

1. The stage of completion of contract is determined at the reporting date.
2. Contract Revenue is recognized as a certain percentage of Total Contract Revenue.
3. This revenue is matched with the contract cost incurred in reaching the stage of completion.
4. It is applied on a specific contract from year to year on a cumulative basis

QUESTION 12: What should be the treatment of an amount already recognized as contract revenue when an uncertainty arises about its collectability?

ANSWER:

Such amount should be recognized as an expense in the period in which uncertainty arises about the amount collectability.

QUESTION 13: What should be the treatment of contract cost the recovery of which is not probable?

ANSWER: Contract cost, the recovery of which is not probable should be recognized as expense.

QUESTION 14: What should be the treatment when the outcome of a construction contract cannot be estimated reliably?

ANSWER:

Revenue:– It should be recognized to the extent of contract cost incurred of which recovery is probable.

Expense:– Contract cost should be recognized as an expense in the period in which they are incurred.

QUESTION 15: What is Expected Loss? What should be the treatment of Expected Loss?

ANSWER:

MEANING OF EXPECTED LOSS

Expected loss is the excess of total contract cost over total contract revenue.

TREATMENT OF EXPECTED LOSS

When it is probable that expected loss shall occur, it should be recognized as an expense immediately irrespective of

(i) Whether or not work has commenced on the contract;

(ii) Whether or not the outcome of contract can be estimated reliably;

(iii) The stage of completion of contract activity;

(iv) The amount of profit expected on other contracts not treated as single contracts (i.e. segmented from single contract).

QUESTION 16: What is Contract Work – in – progress?

ANSWER: Contract costs incurred up to reporting date may include certain costs which relates to future activity on the contract. Such costs should not be matched with contract revenue recognized. Instead such contract costs should be recognized as an asset if it is probable that it shall be recovered and are classified as contract work – in – progress.

QUESTION 17: How should Contract Work in progress be determined?

ANSWER: Contract work in progress should be determined in the following manner:

Dr. **CONTRACT WORK IN PROGRESS ACCOUNT** **Cr.**

Particulars	₹	Particulars	₹
To balance b/d*	xxx	By balance b/d*	xxx
To Contract Cost incurred during current accounting period	xxx	By contract expense to be recognized during current accounting period	xxx
To Contract Revenue to be recognized during current accounting period	xxx	By costs, the recovery of which is not possible recognized as an expense during current accounting period	xxx
To balance c/d**	xxx	By Expected loss recognized during current accounting period	xxx
		By Miscellaneous income not recognized as contract revenue during current accounting period	xxx
		By Progress Billings during current accounting period	xxx
		By balance c/d**	xxx

*Only one of the figures shall appear at a time.

**Only one of the figures shall appear at a time.

Disclosure of Debit Balance: If there is debit balance in an account, then it shall be shown as an asset under the head **Gross amount due from customer for contract work.**

Disclosure of Credit Balance: If there is credit balance in an account, then it shall be shown as liability under the head **Gross amount due to customer for contract work**

QUESTION 18: What are the Disclosure Requirements AS TO construction contracts AND contracts in progress?

ANSWER:

For Construction Contract	1. the amount of contract revenue recognized as revenue in the period; 2. the methods used to determine the contract revenue recognized in the period; and 3. the methods used to determine the stage of completion of contracts in progress.
For Contracts in progress	1. the aggregate amount of costs incurred and recognized profits (less recognized losses) up to the reporting date; 2. the amount of advances received; 3. the amount of retentions.

STATEMENT SHOWING THE COMPUTATION OF VARIOUS AMOUNTS AS PER REQUIREMENTS OF AS – 7 FOR VARIOUS ACCOUNTING PERIODS.

Particulars	Years			
	1	2	3	4
A Opening Balance				
B Additions during the year Cost Incurred during the year Cost Incurred during the year				
Total [B]				
C Deductions during the year Expenses recognized during the year Costs not recoverable Expected loss Miscellaneous income				
Total [C]				
D Balance [A + B – C] **[As per disclosure requirement of AS – 7]**				
E Progress Billings				
F Cumulative Progress billings				
G Amount due from customers for contract work /(Amount due to customers for contract work) [D – F]				

A. Work Certified	500
B. Work Not Certified	105
C. Cost incurred till date/ Contract Expense[A + B]	605
D. Estimated Additional Cost	495
E. Estimated Total Cost [C + D]	1100
F. Contract Price	1000

G. Total Estimated Profit [F – E] OR Total Expected Loss [E – F]	
H. % of Completion [(C/E) × 100]	55%
I. Contract Revenue to be recognised as Turnover [Contract Price × % of Completion]	550
J. Loss for the current year [I – C]	55
K. Expected Loss to be recognized immediately as per para 35 of AS 7 [G – J]	45
L. Progress Billings [Progress Payment Received + To be Received]	540
M. Retentions (billed but not received from contractee)	140
N. Gross amount due to customers [C – G – L]	35

PRACTICAL QUESTIONS FOR PRACTICE

QUESTION 1: On 31st October, 2014 , Bharat Construction Co. Ltd. undertook a contract to construct a Flyover for ₹ 215 crores. On 31st March, 2015, company found that its work certified is for ₹ 100 crores and work to be certified is for ₹ 35 crores. Prudent estimate of additional cost for completion was ₹ 90 crores. What amount should be charged to Revenue in the final accounts for the year ended 31st March, 2015 as per provisions of Accounting Standard 7 (revised).

ANSWER:

PROVISION OF AS 7

1. As per AS-7 when the outcome of a construction contract can be estimated reliably, contract revenue and contract costs associated with the construction contract should be recognised as revenue and expenses respectively by reference to stage of completion of the contract activity at the reporting date.
2. As per AS-7 an expected loss on the Construction contract should be recognized as an expense immediately irrespective of (i) whether or not the work has commenced on the contract; or (ii) the stage of completion of the contract: or (iii) the amount of profits expected to arise in other contracts.

ADVICE

Particulars	₹ (crores)
A.Work Certified	100
B. Work Not Certified	35
C. Cost incurred till date/ Contract Expense [A + B]	135
D. Estimated Additional Cost	90
E. Estimated Total Cost [C + D]	225
F. Contract Price	215
G. Total Expected Loss [E – F]	10
H. % of Completion [(C/E) × 100]	60%
I. Contract Revenue to be recognised as Turnover [Contract Price × % of Completion]	129
J. Loss for the current year [I – C]	6
K. Expected Loss to be recognized immediately as per para 35 of AS 7 [G – J]	4

DISCLOSURES AS PER AS – 7

Particulars	₹ (crores)
Contract Revenue	129
Contract Expenses Charged	(135)
Provision for Expected Loss	(4)

QUESTION 2: X Limited undertook a contract to construct a building for ₹ 3 Crores on 1st September, 2014. On 31st March 2015, the Company found that it had already spent ₹ 1 Crore 80 Lakhs on the construction of which 60% has been certified. Prudent estimate of additional cost of completion was ₹ 1 Crore 40 Lakhs. What amount should be charged, to revenue in the final accounts for the year ended on 31st March 2015, as per the provisions of AS -7?

ANSWER:

PROVISION OF AS 7

1. As per AS-7 when the outcome of a construction contract can be estimated reliably, contract revenue and contract costs associated with the construction contract should be recognised as revenue and expenses respectively by reference to stage of completion of the contract activity at the reporting date.
2. As per AS-7 an expected loss on the Construction contract should be recognized as an expense immediately irrespective of (i) whether or not the work has commenced on the contract; or (ii) the stage of completion of the contract: or (iii) the amount of profits expected to arise in other contracts.

ADVICE

Particulars	₹ (lakhs)
A.Work Certified	108
B. Work Not Certified	72
C. Cost incurred till date/ Contract Expense [A + B]	180
D. Estimated Additional Cost	140
E. Estimated Total Cost [C + D]	320
F. Contract Price	300
G. Total Expected Loss [E – F]	20
H. % of Completion [(C/E) × 100]	56.25%
I. Contract Revenue to be recognised as Turnover [Contract Price × % of Completion]	168.75
J. Loss for the current year [I – C]	11.25
K. Expected Loss to be recognized immediately as per para 35 of AS 7 [G – J]	8.75

DISCLOSURES AS PER AS – 7

Particulars	₹ Lakhs
Contract Revenue	168.75
Contract Expenses	(180.00)
Provision for Expected Loss	(8.75)

QUESTION 3: An amount of ₹ 9,90,000 was incurred on a contract work upto 31.03.2013. Certificates have been received to date to the value of ₹ 12,00,000 against which ₹ 10,80,000 has been received in cash. The cost of work done but not certified amounted to ₹ 22,500. It is estimated that by spending an additional amount of ₹ 60,000 (including provision for contingencies) the work can be completed in all respects in another two months. The agreed contract price of work is ₹ 12,50,000. Compute a conservative estimate of the profit to be taken to the Profit and Loss Account as per AS 7.

ANSWER:

PROVISION OF AS 7

As per AS-7 when the outcome of a construction contract can be estimated reliably, contract revenue and contract costs associated with the construction contract should be recognised as revenue and expenses respectively by reference to stage of completion of the contract activity at the reporting date.

ADVICE

A.Work Certified	9,67,500
B. Work Not Certified	30,000
C. Cost incurred till date/ Contract Expense [A + B]	9,97,500
D. Estimated Additional Cost	52,500
E. Estimated Total Cost [C + D]	10,50,000
F. Contract Price	12,50,000
G. Total Estimated Profit [F – E]	2,00,000
H. % of Completion [(C/E) × 100]	95%
I. Contract Revenue to be recognised as Turnover [Contract Price × % of Completion]	11,87,500
J. Profit for the current year [I – C]	1,90,000

QUESTION 4: PRARTHANA LTD, a firm of contractors provides the following details for the year ended 31st March, 2013:

Particulars	(₹ in lakhs)
Total Contract Price	₹ 1,000 lacs
Work Certified	500
Work not Certified	105
Estimated further Cost to Completion	495
Progress Payment Received	400
To be Received	140

Required: Show the relevant disclosures under AS 7.

ANSWER:

PROVISION OF AS 7

1. As per AS-7 when the outcome of a construction contract can be estimated reliably, contract revenue and contract costs associated with the construction contract should be recognised as revenue and expenses respectively by reference to stage of completion of the contract activity at the reporting date.

2. As per AS-7 an expected loss on the Construction contract should be recognized as an expense immediately irrespective of (i) whether or not the work has commenced on the contract; or (ii) the stage of completion of the contract: or (iii) the amount of profits expected to arise in other contracts.

ADVICE

A. Work Certified	500
B. Work Not Certified	105
C. Cost incurred till date/ Contract Expense [A + B]	605
D. Estimated Additional Cost	495
E. Estimated Total Cost [C + D]	1100
F. Contract Price	1000
G. Total Expected Loss [E – F]	100
H. % of Completion [(C/E) × 100]	55%
I. Contract Revenue to be recognised as Turnover [Contract Price × % of Completion]	550
J. Loss for the current year [I – C]	55
K. Expected Loss to be recognized immediately as per para 35 of AS 7 [G – J]	45

DISCLOSURES AS PER AS – 7

Particulars	₹ Lakhs
Contract Revenue	550
Contract Expenses	(605)
Provision for Expected Loss	(45)
Progress Billings [Progress Payment Received + To be Received]	540
Retentions (billed but not received from Contractee)	140
Gross amount due to customers [605 – 100 – 540]	35

QUESTION 5: A firm of contractors obtain a contract for construction of a bridge across river Hindan. The following details are available in the records kept for the year ended 31st March, 2015:

Particulars	₹ in lakhs
Total Contract Price	**2,000**
Work Certified	**1,400**
Work Not Certified	**400**
Estimated Further Cost to Completion	**700**
Progress Payment: Received	**1,000**
To be Received	**200**

The firm seeks your advice and assistance in the presentation of accounts keeping in view the requirements of AS – 7.

ANSWER:

AMOUNT TO BE DISCLOSED AS PER DISCLOSURE REQUIREMENTS OF AS – 7

	Particulars	₹ In Lakhs
A	Additions during the year	
	Cost Incurred during the year (1,400 + 400)	1,800
	Revenue recognized during the year (2,000 × 1,400)/2,500	1,120
	Total [A]	2,920
B	Deductions during the year	
	Expenses recognized during the year (Work certified)	1,400
	Expected loss [(₹ 1,400 lakhs + ₹ 400 lakhs + ₹ 700 lakhs)	
	₹ 2,000 lakhs] – [₹ 1,400 lakhs – ₹ 1,120]	220
	Total [B]	1,620
C	Balance [A – B] As per disclosure requirement of AS – 7]	1,300
D	Progress Billings	1,200
E	Amount due from customers for contract work [D – E]	100
F	Progress payment received	1,000
G	Retentions [D – F]	200

QUESTION 6: The following information is extracted from the books of X Ltd. for the year ending 31st March, 2015.

Particulars	Contract			
	A	B	C	D
Contract revenue recognized during the year	50,000	1,25,000	1,00,000	2,00,000
Contract expense recognized during the year	50,000	1,00,000	1,20,000	1,50,000
Contract cost incurred during period	70,000	1,00,000	150,000	1,40,000
Expected loss		20,000		30,000
Progress billings	50,000	12,00,000	1,00,000	2,10,000
Advance received during year	20,000			10,000
Opening balance of contract work in progress			10,000	10,000
(Progress billing was not taken into consideration while determining this account)				

Required: How should this information should be disclosed as per AS – 7?

ANSWER:

AMOUNT TO BE DISCLOSED AS PER DISCLOSURE REQUIREMENTS OF AS – 7

Particulars	₹
Contract revenue recognized as revenue in the period	4,75,000
Aggregate amount of costs incurred and recognized profits	4,85,000
(less recognized losses) upto the reporting date	
Amount of advances received	30,000

Gross amount due from customers for contract work as an asset	15,000
Gross amount due to customers for contract work as a liability	10,000

Working Note:

	Particulars	Contracts				
		A	B	C	D	Total
A	Opening Balance			10,000	10,000	20,000
B	Additions during the year					
	Cost Incurred during the year	70,000	1,00,000	1,50,000	1,40,000	4,60,000
	Revenue recognized during the year	50,000	1,25,000	1,00,000	2,00,000	4,75,000
	Total B	1,20,000	2,25,000	2,50,000	3,40,000	9,35,000
C	Deductions during the year					
	Expenses recognized during the year	50,000	1,00,000	1,20,000	1,50,000	4,20,000
	Expected loss	20,000		30,000		50,000
	Total C	70,000	1,00,000	1,50,000	1,50,000	4,70,000
D	Balance [A + B – C]	50,000	1,25,000	1,10,000	2,00,000	4,85,000
E	Progress billings	50,000	1,20,000	1,00,000	2,10,000	4,80,000
F	Amount due from customers	0	5,000	10,000	0	15,000
G	Amount due to customers	0	0	0	10,000	10,000

8 AS 9 – REVENUE RECOGNITION

THEORETICAL BASE

QUESTION 1: State the Revenues with which AS – 9 deals.

ANSWER:

AS 9 deals with the basis for recognition of revenue arising in the course of the ordinary activities of the enterprise from:

1. the sale of goods,
2. the rendering of services, and
3. the use by others of enterprise resources yielding interest, royalties and dividends

QUESTION 2: State the Revenues with which AS – 9 does not deal.

ANSWER:

1. Revenue arising from construction contracts;
2. Revenue arising from hire-purchase, lease agreements;
3. Revenue arising from government grants and other similar subsidies;
4. Revenue of insurance companies arising from insurance contracts.

QUESTION 3: Define the term ' Revenue'as per AS – 9.

ANSWER:

Revenue is the gross inflow of cash, receivables or other consideration arising in the course of the ordinary activities of an enterprise from:

1. the sale of goods,
2. the rendering of services, and
3. the use by others of enterprise resources yielding interest, royalties and dividends

Note: *In an agency relationship, the revenue is the amount of commission and the not the gross inflow of cash, receivables or other consideration.*

QUESTION 4: State the Items not included in the term 'Revenue'.

ANSWER:

1. Realized gains resulting from the disposal of, and unrealized gains resulting from the holding of, non-current assets e.g. appreciation in the value of fixed assets;
2. Unrealized holding gains resulting from the change in value of current assets, and the natural increases in herds and agricultural and forest products;
3. Realized or unrealized gains resulting from changes in foreign exchange rates and adjustments arising on the translation of foreign currency financial statements;
4. Realized gains resulting from the discharge of an obligation at less than its carrying amount;
5. Unrealized gains resulting from the restatement of the carrying amount of an obligation.

QUESTION 5: State the Meaning of Revenue Recognition.

ANSWER:

Revenue recognition means identifying the revenues for a particular accounting period. Revenue recognition is mainly concerned with the timing of recognition of revenue in the Statement of Profit and Loss of an enterprise.

QUESTION 6: When should revenue from sale of goods be recognized?

ANSWER:

Revenue from sale of goods should be recognized when:

1. The seller of goods has transferred to the buyer the property in the goods for a price or all significant risks and rewards of ownership have been transferred to the buyer and the seller retains no effective control of the goods transferred to a degree usually associated with ownership;
2. No significant uncertainty exists regarding the amount of the consideration that will be derived from the sale of goods.
3. At the time of performance it is reasonable to expect ultimate collection (i.e. there is a reasonable certainty of ultimate collection).

QUESTION 7: When should revenue from service transactions be recognized?

ANSWER:

Revenue from service transactions should be recognized when

1. No significant uncertainty exists regarding the amount of the consideration that will be derived from the rendering the service.
2. At the time of performance it is reasonable to expect ultimate collection.

QUESTION 8: When and on what basis should revenue from from Interest, Royalties and Dividends be recognized?

ANSWER:

WHEN SHOULD REVENUE BE RECOGNIZED?

Revenue arising from the use by others of enterprise resources yielding interest, royalties and dividends should only be recognized **when no significant uncertainty as to measurability or collectability exists.**

BASIS OF REVENUE RECOGNISION

Case	Basis of Revenue Recognision
(i) Interest	**On a time proportion basis** taking into account the amount outstanding and the rate applicable.
(ii) Royalties	**On an accrual basis** in accordance with the terms of the relevant agreement.
(iii) Dividends from	When the owner's **right to receive** investment in payment is **established** (i.e. the Date of declaration of Final Dividend & ate of Payment of Interim Dividend)

Notes:

(i) Revenue arising from the use by others of enterprise resources yielding interest, royalties and dividends should only be recognized when no significant uncertainty as to measurability or collectability exists.

(ii) When interest, royalties and dividends from foreign countries require exchange permission and uncertainty in remittance is anticipated, revenue recognition may need to be postponed.

QUESTION 9: How should uncertainties about revenue recognition be treated?

ANSWER:

(i) Where the ability to assess the ultimate collection with reasonable certainty is lacking at the time of raising any claim, e.g., for escalation of price, export incentives, interest etc.	Revenue recognition is **postponed** to the extent of uncertainty involved. In such cases, it may be appropriate to recognize revenue only when it is reasonably certain that the ultimate collection will be made. However, where there is no uncertainty as to ultimate collection, revenue is recognized at the time of sale or rendering of service even though payments are made by installments.
(ii) When the uncertainty relating to collectability arises subsequent to the time of sale or the rendering of the service	A separate provision to reflect the uncertainty rather than to adjust the amount of revenue originally recorded.
(iii) Where consideration receivable for the sale of goods, the rendering of services or from the use by others of enterprise resources is not reasonably determinable.	Recognition of revenue is postponed till it is reasonably determinable.

QUESTION 10: State the Disclosure Requirements AS PER AS 9.

ANSWER: In addition to the disclosures required by Accounting Standard 1 on 'Disclosure Of Accounting Policies' (AS 1), an enterprise should also disclose the circumstances in which revenue recognition has been postponed pending the reANSWERof significant uncertainties.

QUESTION 11: How is excise duty disclosed in presentation of revenue from sales transaction?

ANSWER: As per ASI 14, the amount of turnover should be disclosed in the following manner on the face of the statement of profit and loss:

Turnover (Gross)	XXX
Less: Excise Duty	XXX
Turnover (Net)	XXX

PRACTICAL QUESTIONS FOR PRACTICE

QUESTION 1: M/s. SEA Ltd. recognized ₹ 5.00 lakhs on accrual basis income from dividend during the year 2014-2015, on shares of the face value of ₹ 25.00 lakhs held by it in Rock Ltd. as at 31st March, 2015. Rock Ltd. proposed dividend @ 20% on 10th April, 2015. However, dividend was declared on 30th June, 2015. Please state with reference to relevant Accounting Standard, whether the treatment accorded by SEA Ltd. is in order.

ANSWER:

PROVISION OF AS 9

As per AS 9 "Revenue Recognition" states that dividend from investments in shares are not recognized in the statement of Profit and Loss until the right to receive dividend is established.

ADVICE

The dividend is proposed on 10th April, 2015, while it was declared on 30th June, 2015. Hence, the right to receive dividend is established on 30th June, 2015 only. Therefore, on applying the provisions stated in the standard, income from dividend on shares should be recognized by Sea Ltd. in the financial year 2015-2016 only.

Therefore, the recognition of income from dividend of ₹ 5 iakhs, on accrual basis, in the financial year 2014-2015 is not in accordance with AS 9.

QUESTION 2: Y Co. Ltd., used certain resources of X Co. Ltd. In return X Co. Ltd. received ₹ 10 lakhs and ₹ 15 lakhs as interest and royalties respectively from Y Co. Ltd. during the year 2014-2015. You are required to state whether and on what basis these revenue can be recognised by X Co. Ltd.

ANSWER: As per AS-9 on Revenue Recognition, revenue arising from the use by other of enterprise resources yielding interest and royalties should only be recognised when no significant uncertainty as to measurability or collectability exists. These revenues are recognised on the following bases:

(i) **Interest:** on a time proportion basis taking into amount outstanding and the rate applicable.

(ii) **Royalties:** on an accrual basis in accordance with the terms of the relevant agreement.

QUESTION 3: AQ Ltd., an investment company is finalizing its account for the Financial Year ending 2015 in the month of August 2015.

How will the following incomes be accounted for in the books of AQ Ltd.?

(1) X Ltd., has declared interim dividend which has not been received till 31-3-2015 but received on 25-4-2015.

(2) Y Ltd., has declared dividend on 8th May 2015 for the year ending 31-3-2015 which has been approved by the shareholders of the company on 30th June 2015.

(3) Z Ltd., a subsidiary of AQ Ltd., has declared dividend for the year ended 31-3-2015 on 25th May 2015 the AGM for which is to be held on September 2015.

ANSWER:

PROVISION OF AS-9

As per AS 9 "Revenue Recognition", dividends from investment in shares is recognized in the statement of Profit and Loss only when the owner's right to receive the payment is established.

ADVICE

(i) Since interim dividend was declared by X Ltd. before 31st March 2015 it means that the dividend had been vested (acrrued) to the shareholders of AQ Ltd. in the year 2014-2015. Therefore, though it is received on 25.4.2015 (before finalization of accounts) yet it should be recognized in the financial statements for the year ended 31st March, 2015.

(ii) Dividend declared by Y Ltd and approved by the shareholders of AQ Ltd. after balance sheet date but before finalization of accounts will be accounted for 2015-2016 as the right to receive dividend will arise when the AGM will approve the dividend i.e. on 30th June 2015. Since right to receive the dividend was not established on or before 31st March, 2015, it will not be accounted for in the books for the year ended 31st March, 2015.

(iii) Dividend declared by Z Ltd. will be approved in the AGM to be held on 30th September, 2015. Before that right to receive dividend cannot be established. Hence it will not be accounted for in the financial year ended on 31st March, 2015.

QUESTION 4: In the course of audit of T Ltd. you observed that export incentives are not accounted on accrual basis. The company's management contended that these would be accounted on cash basis citing the uncertainty about its receipts as they are not admitted as due by the customs authorities. Comment.

ANSWER:

PROVISION OF AS-9

As per AS 9 'Revenue Recognition", if at the time of raising the claim for incentive, it is unreasonable to expect ultimate collection, revenue recognition should be postponed. Therefore, as per accounting standard, if there is uncertainty is the receipt of the amounts, then the revenue in respect of such incentives ought not to be recognized in the books of accounts.

ADVICE

The exporters receive certain incentives (monetary or non-monetary) from the Government of India on export of goods. However due to various procedural delay sand laws involved which keep changing frequently, there is generally a delay in actual receipt of the export incentives. Further the receipt of the export incentives may not be assured in certain situations due to frequent changes in the policies of the Government. In such cases, ti may be reasonable to presume that the receipt of the incentives in uncertain till the time they are actually received.

The contention of management of T Ltd. to record the export incentive on cash basis is correct. There revenue is to be recognized only when there is reasonable certainty in the receipt of the same.

An Alternative view: Since the export incentives are due as and when the exports have been made from India, though customs authorities does not acknowledge them as due. This does not mean that an uncertainty arises about its receipt. If at all customs authorities have an objection it should be at the time of clearance of the goods for export. The only uncertainty is the timing of the receipt of such incentives, but not the incentive itself. Hence T Ltd. has to account the export incentives on Accrual basis.

QUESTION 5: X Ltd. entered into an agreement with Y Ltd. for sale of goods costing ₹ 2,00,000 at a profit of 20 % on sale. The sale transaction took place on 1st February, 2015. On the same day X Ltd. entered into another agreement with Y Ltd. for repurchasing the same goods at ₹ 2,80,000 on 1st August, 2015. State the treatment of above transaction in the financial statements of X Ltd. for the year 2014–2015. The predetermined repurchasing price covers, inter alia, the holding cost of Y Ltd.

ANSWER:

In this case X Ltd. concurrently agrees to repurchase the same goods from Y Ltd. at a later date. Also, the repurchase price is predetermined and covers Y Ltd. purchasing and holding costs. Hence, the transaction between X Ltd. and Y Ltd. on 1st February, 2015 should be accounted for as a financing transaction rather as a sale. The resulting cash inflow of ₹ 2,50,000 [i.e. ₹ 2,00,000 / (1.00 – 0.20)] is not revenue as per AS - 9.

Therefore the pattern of journal entries, required to be made in the books of X Ltd. during the year 2014-2015, are as follows:

JOURNAL

Date	Particulars	Dr. (₹)	Cr. (₹)
1.2.2015	Bank A/c ... Dr.	2,50,000	
	To Advance from Y Ltd. A/c		2,50,000
	(Being amount received from Y Ltd. as per sale and repurchase agreement)		
31.3.2015	Financing charges A/c ... Dr.	10,000	
	To Advance from Y Ltd. A/c		10,000
	[Being financing charges on ₹ 2,50,000 for 2 months (i.e. (₹.2,80,000 – ₹ 2,50,000) x (2 months / 6months)]		

31.3.2015	Profit and Loss A/c ...Dr.	10,000	
	To Financing charges		10,000
	(Financing charges transferred)		

Disclosures:

(I) AT EXTRACT OF BALANCE SHEET OF X LTD. AS AT 31ST MARCH 2015

Particulars	₹	₹
Current Liabilities:		
Advance money from Y Ltd.	2,50,000	
Add: Accrued finance charges	10,000	2,60,000
Current Assets:		
Goods lying with Y Ltd.		2,00,000

(ii) By way of notes:

(a) Goods lying with Y Ltd. costing ₹ 2,00,000 to be purchased after 6 months at ₹ 2,80,000

(b) Goods sold to Y Ltd. for ₹ 2,50,000 (cost ₹ 2,00,000) on repurchase agreement. The difference between sales price and repurchase price is treated as financing charge and located proportionately in the current accounting period.

QUESTION 6: B Ltd. entered into an agreement on 1st March, 2015 to buy computer spares from S Ltd. at prevailing market price for ₹ 1200 lakhs on which S Ltd. made a profit of 20% and received full advance payment. The transaction was concluded on 15th March, 2015. On the same day S Ltd. agrees to buy on 15th Sept., 2015 the same goods from B Ltd. at 20% over cost. The 20% mark up compensates B Ltd. for its inventory holding costs till sale date. You are required to show how both the buyer and seller account for the above transaction in the year 2015-2016 explaining in brief the justification for your treatment and also draft the Notes on Account on disclosure if any required in the annual accounts of year ended 31st March, 2015.

ANSWER: The transaction between S Limited and B Limited should be accounted for as financing transaction rather than as sale since S Ltd. concurrently agrees to repurchase the same goods from B Ltd. at a later date. Also, the repurchase price is predetermined and covers B Limited's purchasing and holding costs. Hence, the resulting cash inflow of ₹ 1,200 lakhs is not revenue as per AS-9 'Revenue Recognition'.

JOURNAL OF S LIMITED

Date	Particulars	Dr. (₹)	Cr. (₹)
15.3.2015	Bank A/c Dr.	1,200	
	To Advance from B Limited A/c		1,200
	(Being amount received from B Ltd. as per sale and repurchasing agreement)		
31.3.2015	Financing Charges A/c Dr.	20	
	To Advance from B Ltd. A/c		20
	(Being the Financing charges 20% of ₹ 1200 lakhs for 1/2 month i.e. 240 x 0.5/6)		
31.3.2015	Profit and Loss A/c Dr.	20	
	To Financing charges		20
	(Being amount transferred to profit and loss account)		

Disclosure in the Balance Sheet

1. **An Extract of Balance Sheet of S Ltd. as at 31.3.2015**

Particulars	(₹) in lakhs
Assets (Under the head "Current Assets")	
Short-term loans and advances	
Goods lying with B Limited (under sale and repurchase agreement)	1,000*
Liabilities (under the head "Secured Loans')	
Advance from B Limited	1,200
Add: Accrued finance charges	20
	1,220

2. **Notes to accounts:**
   (a) Goods lying with B Limited costing ₹ 1,000 lakhs to be repurchased after 6 months at ₹ 1,440 lakhs.
   (b) Goods sold to B Limited for ₹ 1,200 lakhs (cost ₹ 1,000 lakhs) on repurchase agreement. The difference between sale price and repurchase price is treated as financing charges and allocated proportionately in the current accounting period.

JOURNAL OF B LTD. **₹ in lakhs**

Date	Particulars		Dr. (₹)	Cr. (₹)
15.3.2015	Advance from B Limited A/c	Dr.	1,200	
	To Bank A/c		1,200	
	(Being amount paid to S Ltd. as per sale and repurchase agreement)			
31.3.2015	Accrued Finance Income A/c	Dr.	20	
	To Finance income			20
	(Financing charges 20% of ₹ 1200 lakhs for 1/2 month i.e. 240 × 0 .5/6)			
31.3.2015	Financing Income A/c	Dr.	20	
	To Profit and Loss A/c			20
	(Being financing charges received transferred to profit and loss account)			

Disclosure in the Balance Sheet

1. **An extract of Balance sheet of B Ltd. as on 31.3.2015**
   Assets (Under the head 'Current Assets)'
   Short-term loans and advances
   Advance to S Ltd. (Under sale and repurchase agreement) ₹ 1,200 lakhs
   Accrued Finance income ₹ 20 lakhs
   (This advance is fully secured by goods of S Ltd. Market value of ₹ 1,200 lakhs lying with company as security)
2. **Notes to Account**
   ₹ 1,200 lakhs paid to S Limited against the sale and repurchase agreement against the security of goods of S Limited whose market value is ₹ 1,200 Lakhs.
   The transaction is in the nature of a financing arrangement and hence is not recognized as a sale and hence the excess of repurchase price over sale price amounting to ₹ 240 lakhs have been treated as Finance charges allocated proportionately between accounting periods

2015-2016 and 2015-2016. The value of the computer spares lying with B Ltd. on Balance Sheet date is considered as part of the company's inventory held as security for the Financing obligation.

QUESTION 7: On 25th September, 2015, Planet Advertising Limited obtained advertisement rights to World Cup Hockey Tournament to be held in Nov./Dec., 2015 for ₹ 520 lakhs.

They furnish the following information:

1. **The company obtained the advertisements for 70% of available time for ₹ 700 lakhs by 30th September, 2015.**
2. **For the balance time they got bookings in October, 2015 for ₹ 240 lakhs.**
3. **All the advertisers paid the full amount at the time of booking the advertisements.**
4. **40% of the advertisements appeared before the public in Nov. 2015 and balance 60% appeared in the month of December, 2015.**

You are required to calculate the amount of profit/loss to be recognized for the month November and December, 2015 as per Accounting Standard-9.

ANSWER:

PROVISION OF AS 9

As per AS 9 in a transaction involving the rendering of services, performance should be measured either under the completed service contract method or under the proportionate completion method, whichever relates the revenue to the work accomplished. Further, appendix to AS 9 states that revenue from advertising should be recognized when the service is completed. The service as regards advertisement is deemed to be completed when the related advertisement appears before the public.

ADVICE

In the given QUESTION, 40% of the advertisement appeared before the public in November, and balance 60% in December.

CALCULATION OF TOTAL PROFIT

Particulars	₹ in lakhs
Advertisement for 70% of available time obtained by 30th September, 2013	700
Advertisement for 30% of available time obtained in by October, 2013	240
Total	940
Less: Cost of advertisement rights	(520)
Profit	420

The profit amounting ₹ 420 lakhs should be apportioned in the ratio of 40:60 for the months of November and December, 2015. Thus, the company should recognise ₹ 168 lakhs (i.e. ₹ 420 lakhs × 40%) in November, 2015 and rest ₹ 252 lakhs (i.e. ₹ 420 lakhs × 60%) in December, 2015.

QUESTION 8: ABC Advertisers obtained advertisement rights for one day world cup cricket tournament to be held in May 2015 for ₹ 800 lakhs in February 2015.

By 31/3/2014, they had paid ₹ 500 lakhs to secure these advertisements rights. The balance ₹ 300 lakhs was paid in April 2015. By March 2015, they procured advertisement for 75% of the available time for ₹ 1000 lakhs. The advertisers paid 60 % of the amount by that date. The balance 40 % was received in April 2015. Advertisements for balance 25 % time were procured in April 2015 for ₹ 200 lakhs. The advertisers paid the full amount while booking the advertisement. 25 % of the advertisement time is expected to be available in May 2015 and balance in June 2015. Journalise.

ANSWER:

JOURNAL ₹ in Lakhs

Date	Particulars		Dr. (₹)	Cr. (₹)
2014 Feb.	Advertisement rights	...Dr.	800	
	To Creditors for advertisement rights			800
	(Being advertisement rights obtained in February)			
March	Creditors for advertisement rights	...Dr.	500	
	To Bank A/c			500
	(Being payment made by 31st March)			
March	Debtors for advertisement rights	...Dr.	1,000	
	To Advertisement rights			1,000
	(Being 75 % of advertisement rights are booked)			
March	Bank A/c	...Dr.	600	
	To Debtors for advertisement rights			600
	(Being 60 % of the amount paid by the debtors)			
April	Creditors for advertisement rights	...Dr.	300	
	To Bank A/c			300
	(Being balance payment made in April)			
April	Bank A/c	...Dr.	400	
	To Debtors for advertisement rights			400
	(Being 40 % of the amount paid by the debtors who booked the time for advertisement in March)			
April	Bank A/c	...Dr.	200	
	To Advertisement rights			200
	(Being 25 % of advertisement rights are booked and paid)			
May	Advertisement rights	...Dr.	100	
	To Revenue from advertisement rights			100
	(Being 25 % of the advertisement rights (i.e. 25 % of ₹ 400 lakhs) availed in May)			
June	Advertisement rights	...Dr.	300	
	To Revenue from advertisement rights			300
	(Being balance of the advertisement rights (i.e. 75 % of ₹ 400 lakhs) availed in June)			

Note: *As per AS - 9, in a transaction involving the rendering of services, performance should be measured either under the completed service contract method or under the proportionate completion method, whichever relates the revenue to the work accomplished. Such performance should be regarded as being achieved when no significant uncertainty exists regarding the amount of consideration that will be delivered from rendering the service. Further, the revenue from advertising should be recognized when the service is completed. In this case the service as regards advertisement is deemed to be completed when the related advertisement appears before the public.*

As the 25 % of the advertisement appeared in May, 2015 and 75 % in June, 2015, therefore the net revenue of ₹ 400 lakhs [i.e. (₹ 1000 lakhs + ₹ 200 lakhs) - (₹ 800 lakhs)], should be apportioned in the ratio of 25 % and 75 % in May, 2013 and in June, 2015 respectively.

QUESTION 9: XYZ Ltd. purchased goods on credit from ABC Ltd. for ₹ 250 crores for export. The export order was cancelled. XYZ Ltd. decided to sell the same goods in the local market with a price discount. ABC Ltd. was requested to offer a price discount of 15 %. The directors of ABC Ltd. want to adjust the sales figure to the extent of the discount requested by XYZ Ltd. Comment.

ANSWER:

PROVISION OF AS 9

As per AS 9 trade discounts and volume rebates are not encompassed within the definition of revenue. Trade discounts and volume rebates given should be deducted in determining the revenue.

ADVICE

However, the price discount of 15 % in the instant case, is not the discount given during the ordinary course of the trade. Hence, it cannot be treated in the nature of discount eligible for deduction from sales price, the better alternate is to treat the amount as bad debt, therefore the contentions of directors of XYZ Ltd. are not correct.

QUESTION 10: M Ltd. manufactures machinery used in steel plants. It quotes prices in various tenders issued by steel plants. As per terms of contract, full price of machinery is not released by the steel plants, but 10% thereof is retained and paid after one year if there is satisfactory performance of the machinery supplied. The company accounts for only 90% of the invoice value as sales income and the balance amount in the year of receipt to the extent of actual receipts only. Comment.

ANSWER:

PROVISION OF AS 9

As per AS 9 Revenue from sale of goods should be recognized if the seller has transferred to the buyer the property in the goods for a price or all significant risks and rewards of ownership have been transferred to the buyer and the seller retains no effective control of the goods transferred to a degree usually associated with ownership and no significant uncertainty exists regarding the amount of consideration.

ADVICE

In this case, the goods as well as risks and rewards of ownership have been transferred. The invoice raised is for the full price but 10 % of the invoice amount is withheld from recognition of revenue. This is incorrect treatment since revenue in this case shall be recognized at full invoice amount. However, depending on the past experience of recovering the balance of 10 %, the **company may make a provision for receivables whose collectability is not certain.**

QUESTION 11: M/s Prima Co. Ltd. sold goods worth ₹ 50,000 to M/s Y and Company. M/s Y and Co. asked for discount of ₹ 8,000 which was agreed by M/s Prima Co. Ltd. The sale was effected and goods were despatched. After receiving, goods worth ₹ 7,000 was found defected, which they returned immediately. They made the payment of ₹ 35,000 to M/s Prima Co. Ltd. Accountant booked the sales for ₹ 35,000. Please discuss.

ANSWER:

PROVISION OF AS 9

As per AS 9, revenue is the gross inflow of cash, receivable or other consideration arising in the course of the ordinary activities of an enterprise from the sale of goods, from the rendering of services, and from the use by others of enterprise resources yielding interest, royalties and dividends.

ADVICE

M/s Prima. Co. Ltd. should record the sales at gross value of ₹ 50,000. Discount of ₹ 8,000 in price and goods returned worth ₹ 7,000 are to be adjusted by suitable provisions. M/s Prime Co. Ltd. might have sent the credit note of ₹ 15,000 to M/s Y and Co. to account for these adjustments. The contention of the accountant to book the sales for ₹ 35,000 is not correct.

QUESTION 12: Golden Eagle Ltd., has been successful jewellers for the past 100 years and sales are against cash only. The company diversified into apparels. A young senior executive was put in charge of Apparels business and sales increased 5 times. One of the conditions for sales that dealers can return the unsold stocks within one month of the end of season. Sales return for the year was 25% of sales. Suggest a suitable Revenue Recognitions Policy with references to AS 9.

ANSWER:

PROVISION OF AS 9

As per AS 9, "Revenue Recognition", revenue recognition is mainly concerned with the timing of recognition of revenue in Statement of Profit and Loss of an enterprise. The amount of revenue arising on a transaction is usually determined by the agreement between the parties involved in the transaction. When uncertainties exist regarding the determination of the amount, or its associated costs, these uncertainties may influence the timing of revenue recognition.

ADVICE

In the case of the Jewellery Business the company is selling for cash and returns are negligible. Hence, revenue can be recognized on sales. One the other hand, in Apparels industry, the dealers have a right to return the unsold goods within one month of the end of the season. In this case, the company is bearing the risk of sales return and therefore, the company should not recognize the revenue to the extent of 25% of its sales. The company may disclose suitable revenue recognition policy in its financial statements separately for both Jewellery and Apparels business. Thus, in a present case revenue recognition should be postponed until the ultimate collection becomes certain.

QUESTION 13: When do you recognize revenue in the following cases?

1. **'Bill and hold' scales i.e., delivery is delayed at buyer's request but buyer takes title and accepts billing.**
2. **Shipped subject to cash on delivery.**
3. **Installation fee.**
4. **Advertising commission.**

ANSWER:

1. Although physical delivery has been delayed, revenue should be recognized so long as there is every expectation that delivery will be made. But goods sold must be in hand, identified and ready for delivery. This should not be simply the items to be manufactured or procured at the time of delivery.
2. Revenue should be recognized on receipt of the cash by seller or his agent.
3. If installation are other than incidental to the sale of products, they should be recognized as revenue after installation of the equipment and acceptance by the customer.
4. For advertising agencies media commission will be recognized normally when the related advertisement or commercial appears before the public.

QUESTION 14: The Board of Directors decided on 31.3.2015 to increase the sale price of certain items retrospectively from 1st January, 2015.

In view of this price revision with effect from 1st January, 2015, the company has to receive ₹ 15 lakhs from its customers in respect to sales made from 1st January, 2012 to 31st March,

2015 and Accountant cannot make up his mind whether to include ₹ 15 lakhs in the Sales for 2014-2015.

ANSWER: If the company is able to assess the ultimate collection with reasonable certainty, then additional revenue arising out of the said price revision may be recognised in 2014-2015.

QUESTION 15: Some of the Transport claims lodged in 2014-2015 has been settled by the carrier in February, 2015 by paying ₹ 1,15,000. These claims were not recorded in the books of the company so far Comment.

ANSWER:

PROVISION OF AS 9

As per AS 9 where the ability to assess the ultimate collection with reasonable certainty is lacking at the time of raising any claim, revenue recognition is postponed to the extent of uncertainty involved. It is also that when recognition of revenue is postponed due to the effect of uncertainties, it is considered as revenue of the period in which it is reasonable certain that ultimate collection will be made

ADVICE

In this case, it may be assumed that collectability of claim was not certain in the earlier years. So this transaction cannot be taken as 'Prior-period item'.

It will not be treated as extra ordinary item as per AS-5. However, AS-5 states that when item of income and expense within profit and loss for ordinary activities are of such size, nature or incidence that their disclosure is relevant to explain the performance of enterprise for the period, the nature and amount of such items should be disclosed separately. Accordingly, the nature and amount of this item should be disclosed separately as per AS-5.

QUESTION 16: XYZ Company has taken a Transit Insurance Policy. Suddenly in the year 2014-2015 the percentage of accident has gone upto 10 % and company wants to recognize insurance claim as revenue in year 2014-2015 in accordance with relevant Accounting Standards. Comment.

ANSWER:

PROVISION OF AS 9

As per AS 9 the revenue should be recognized if it can be measured reliably and there is not any significant uncertainty in its ultimate collection.

ADVICE

In the instant case it appears that these are uncertainties in measuring the claim and the settlement of the insurance claim. Hence, insurance claim can be recognized only if the amount can be measured reliably and ultimate collection is reasonably certain.

QUESTION 17: ABC Ltd. sells agriculture products to dealers. One of the condition of sale is that interest is payable at the rate of 2 % per month, for delayed payments. Percentage of intent recovery is only 10 % on such overdue outstanding due to various reasons. During the year 2014-2015 the company wants to recognize the entire interest receivable. Do you agree?

ANSWER:

PROVISION OF AS 9

As per AS 9 to recognize the revenue there should not be significant uncertainty in ultimate collection of the amount.

ADVICE

In the instant case it appears that there are uncertainties in the collection of interest. Therefore income can be recognized only if the amount can be measured reliably and ultimate collection is reasonably certain.

QUESTION 18: Sale of goods costing ₹ 60,000 with a profit margin of 25 % on selling price is included in the inventory as delivery of goods was postponed at buyer's request. Comment.

ANSWER:

PROVISION OF AS 9

As per AS 9 Revenue from sale of goods should be recognized if the seller has transferred to the buyer the property in the goods for a price or all significant risks and rewards of ownership have been transferred to the buyer and the seller retains no effective control of the goods transferred to a degree usually associated with ownership. The transfer of property in goods, in most cases, results in or coincides with the transfer of significant risks and rewards of ownership.

ADVICE

In this case, all significant risks and rewards of ownership have been transferred to the buyer and the seller retains no effective control of the goods transferred to a degree usually associated with ownership but delivery is postponed at the buyer's request. Hence this transaction should be recognized as revenue. Thus, ₹ 60,000 should be deducted from inventory, and the amount of ₹ 80,000 [i.e. ₹ 60,000 / (1.00 – 0.25)] should be included in sales with correspondence increase in Debtor's balances.

QUESTION 19: A suit for damages of ₹ 1 lakhs for breach of contract of sale (breach occurred in 2009) was decreed in favour of May Ltd. in March 2015. The Company has included the amount in its turnover for the financial year 2014-2015.

ANSWER: The expression "turnover" normally implies the amount for which the sales are affected or services rendered by an enterprise. Thus, apparently as per this definition, the amount received on account of breach of contract of sales would not form part of the turnover.

QUESTION 20: A company is engaged in the business of ship building and ship repair. On completion of the repair work, a work completion certificate is prepared and countersigned by ship owner (customer). Subsequently invoice is prepared based on the work completion certificate describing the nature of work done together with the rate and the amount.

Customer scrutinizes the invoice and any variation is informed to the company. Negotiations take place between the company and the customer. Negotiations may result in a deduction being allowed from the invoiced amount either as a lumpsum or as a percentage of the invoiced amount The accounting treatment followed by the company is as follows:

(i) When the invoice is raised, the customer's account is debited and Ship Repair Income Account is credited with the invoiced amount.

(ii) Deduction, if any arrived after negotiation is treated as trade discount by debiting the Ship Repair Income Account.

(iii) At the close of the year, negotiation in respect of certain invoices had not been completed. In such cases, based on past experience, a provision for anticipated loss is created by debiting the Profit and Loss account. The provision is disclosed in Balance Sheet.

Following two aspects are settled in the negotiations:

(i) Errors in billing arising on account of variation between the quantities as per work completion certificate and invoice and other clerical errors in preparing the invoice.

(ii) Disagreement between the company and customer about the rate/cost on which prior agreement has not been reached between them.

Comment:

(i) Whether the accounting treatment of deduction as trade discount is correct? If not state the correct accounting treatment.

(ii) Whether the disclosure of the provision for anticipated loss in Balance Sheet is correct, if not state the correct accounting treatment.

ANSWER:

(i) As per AS 9 "Revenue Recognition", revenue is recognized at the time when the invoice is raised to the customers; however the treatment of deduction as trade discount is not in accordance with AS 9. Considering the treatment prescribed by adjustment of the difference between the invoice amount and the amount finally settled against 'Ship Repair Income' Account is in order. Events occurring up to the date of approval of the accounts by the Board of Directors should be taken into consideration in determining the amount of adjustment to be made in the regard. The description of the difference as 'trade discount' is not appropriate,

(ii) In respect to ship repair jobs for which negotiations between the ship owners and the company are not over, the accounting treatment is not appropriate. Instead, the amount of difference between the invoiced amount and the amount likely to the finally settled (as estimated on the basis of past experience) should be adjusted in the "Ship Repair Income" by a corresponding credit to the accounts of the respective ship owners. Consequently, the figure of sundry debtors included in the balance sheet would be net of adjustment for such difference. In other words, the amount of the difference would be neither shown under the head Provision nor shown as a deduction from the sundry debtors in the Balance Sheet.

QUESTION 21: Excel Ltd. is a Manufacturing Company in durable consumer goods with an annual turnover of ₹ 1,000 lakhs. The Company receives orders from its commission agents all over the country, but goods are despatched directly to the customers. The documents including Transport bills are sent through the bank for collection.

At the end of 6th year, it is found that documents covering the despatch of goods worth ₹ 100 lakhs were still lying with the banks not cleared by the customers even though the normal collection period of 20 days from the date of despatch has expired. Should Revenue be recognised in the above case?

ANSWER:

PROVISION OF AS 9

As per AS 9 Revenue can be recognised if the seller of goods has transferred to the buyer the property in the goods for a price or all significant risks and rewards of ownership have been transferred to the buyer and the seller retains no effective control of the goods transferred to a degree usually associated with the ownership. It is subject to the fact that there should not be any significant uncertainty about the realisation of price. Both these conditions are required to be evaluated with reference to various others relevant factors pertaining to specific circumstances e.g., intention of the parties for retaining the shipping documents, any explicit term in the contract, etc.

ADVICE

Applying these tests to the facts of case, since the transport bills were sent through the bank for collection, it may be said that the seller has retained effective control over his ownership. Further since the documents were not cleared by the customer even after the expiry of the normal period of collection, there is an uncertainty in the realisation of sale proceeds. Apparently, the amount also appears to be quite material being 10% of total turnover. Hence, revenue should not be recognised in this case.

9 AS 10 – ACCOUNTING FOR FIXED ASSETS

THEORETICAL BASE

QUESTION 1: What are the areas to which AS – 10 is not applicable?

ANSWER:

1. Accounting for Fixed Assets under Inflation Accounting
2. Accounting for Forests, Plantations and similar Regenerative Natural Resources;
3. Accounting for Wasting Assets including Mineral Rights, expenditure on the exploration for and extraction of Minerals, Oil and Natural Gas and similar Non - Regenerative Resources;
4. Accounting for Expenditure on Real Estate Development;
5. Accounting for Live stock.
6. Allocation of the Depreciable Amount of Fixed Assets to future periods which is dealt with AS 6
7. Treatment of Government Grants and subsidies which is dealt with AS 12
8. Assets under Leasing Rights.
9. Borrowing Cost which is dealt with AS 16
10. Assets acquired in an Amalgamation or Merger which is dealt with AS 14

QUESTION 2: What is meant by the term 'Fixed Asset'?

ANSWER: Fixed asset is an asset held with the intention of being used for the purpose of producing or providing goods or services and is not held for sale in the normal course of business

QUESTION 3: What is meant by the term 'Gross Book Value of a Fixed Asset'?

ANSWER:

Gross Book Value = Historical Cost or other amount substituted 'for historical cost in the books of account of financial statements.

Net Book Value = Gross Book Value – Accumulated Depreciation

QUESTION 4: What is meant by term 'Fair Market Value of a Fixed Asset?

ANSWER: FMV is the price that would be agreed to in an open and unrestricted market between knowledgeable and willing parties dealing at arm's length who are fully informed and are not under any compulsion to transact.

QUESTION 5: What are the various components of cost of Fixed Asset?

ANSWER:

1. Purchase Price (Less any Trade Discounts and Rebates)
2. Import Duties and other non Refundable Taxes or Levies;
3. Directly attributable cost of bringing the asset to its working condition for its intended use. (e.g. site preparation, initial delivery and handling costs installation cost, such as special foundations for plant, professional fees of architects and engineers)

4. Finance Cost as dealt in AS-16.
5. Expenditure incurred on start-up and commissioning of the project,(including the expenditure incurred on test runs and experimental production)

Note: Administration and other general overhead expenses not relating to a specific fixed asset are usually excluded from the cost of fixed assets.

QUESTION 6: What is the treatment of expenses incurred ?

(a) upto the date of commencement of commercial production

(b) between the date at which a project is ready to commence commercial production and the date at which commercial production actually begins

(c) after the date of commencement of commercial production

ANSWER:

TREATMENT OF EXPENDITURE

1. Expenditure incurred upto the date of commencement of commercial production	Should be capitalized
2. Expenditure incurred between the date at which the project becomes ready to commence commercial production and the date at which commercial production actually begins	Should be treated as Revenue/Deferred Revenue Expenditure.
3. Subsequent Expenditures	Should be capitalized only if they increase the future benefits from the existing asset beyond its previously assessed standard of performance

QUESTION 7: How is the Gross Book Value of Self Constructed Fixed Asset computed?

ANSWER: It should comprise those costs that—

(a) relate directly to the specific asset, and

(b) that are attributable to the construction activity in general and can be allocated to the specific asset.

Note: Any internal profits are eliminated in arriving at such costs.

QUESTION 8: How is the fixed asset acquired in exchange of another asset recorded?

ANSWER: The cost of such asset acquired should be recorded either—

(a) at FMV of the asset given up or the asset acquired, whichever is more clearly evident. or

(b) at the Net Book Value of the asset given up, (*plus/minus* other consideration, if any)

QUESTION 9: How is the fixed asset acquired in exchange of Securities recorded?

ANSWER: The cost of such asset acquired should be recorded either at FMV of Asset acquired or Securities issued whichever is more clearly evident.

QUESTION 10: How should first revaluation of asset be accounted for?

ANSWER:

1. Surplus should be credited to Revaluation Reserve.
2. Deficiency should be charged to Profit & Loss A/c.

QUESTION 11: How should the subsequent revaluation be accounted for?

ANSWER:

1. Surplus to the extent of decrease arising on revaluation previously charged to Profit & Loss A/c should be credited to Profit & Loss A/c and remaining surplus should be credited to Revaluation Reserve.
2. Deficiency to the extent of increase arising on revaluation previously credited to Revaluation Reserve should be reversed or utilized and remaining deficiency should be charged to Profit & Loss A/c

QUESTION 12: Should Accumulated Depreciation existing at the date of upward revaluation be credited to P&L A/c?

ANSWER: No

QUESTION 13: How should the Balance of Revaluation Reserve after Disposal be treated?

ANSWER: T/F to General Reserve. It is not mandatory.

QUESTION 14: Can Business losses be adjusted against Revaluation Reserve?

ANSWER: No

QUESTION 15: State the Accounting Treatment of Profit/Loss on Disposal of Fixed Asset.

ANSWER:

Case	Treatment
1. Profit on Retirement/Disposal	Credit to Profit & Loss A/c
2. Loss on Retirement/Disposal	
(i) Related to increase already credited to Revaluation Reserve	Credit to Revaluation Reserve
(ii) Other Loss	Debit to Profit & Loss A/c

QUESTION 16: How should the Fixed Assets retired from active use and held for disposal be stated in the financial statements?

ANSWER: These should be stated at the **lower** of their Net Book Value *or* Net Realizable Value and shown appropriately in the financial statements.

QUESTION 17: How are the Fixed Assets owned by the enterprise jointly with others disclosed?

ANSWER:

1. In the case of fixed assets owned by the enterprise jointly with others, the extent of the enterprise's share in such assets, and the proportion of the original cost, accumulated depreciation and written down value should be stated in the balance sheet.
2. Alternatively, the pro-rata cost of such jointly owned assets may be grouped together with similar fully owned assets with an appropriate disclosure thereof

QUESTION 18: How is the value apportioned to fixed assets when various fixed assets are purchased for a consolidated price?

ANSWER: Where several assets are purchased for a consolidated price, the consideration should be apportioned to the various assets on a fair basis as determined by competent valuers.

QUESTION 19: When should Goodwill be recorded ? How should Goodwill be amortized?

ANSWER:

1. Goodwill should be recorded in the books only when some consideration in money or money's worth has been paid for it.
2. It should be amortized as per AS 26.

QUESTION 20: State the Disclosure Requirements as per AS 10.

ANSWER:

1. Gross and net book values of fixed assets at the beginning and at the end of an accounting period showing additions, disposals, acquisitions and other movements;
2. Expenditure incurred on account of fixed assets in the course of construction or acquisition; and
3. Revalued amounts substituted for historical costs of fixed assets, the method adopted to compute the revalued amounts, the nature of indices used, the year of any appraisal made, and whether an external valuer was involved, in case where fixed assets are stated at revalued amounts.

PRACTICAL QUESTIONS FOR PRACTICE

COST OF NEW ASSET ACQUIRED AS PER AS 10

QUESTION 1: S Ltd. acquired a land for their factory site for ₹ 100 Lakhs. It demolished an old building constructed on land and sold the scrap for ₹ 1 lakhs. From the data given below compute the amount to be capitalized in Land A/c.

Particulars	₹ in Lakhs
Legal fees for registration of Sale deed.	**2**
Title Gurantee Insurance	**1**
Cost of demolition of old building	**3**

ANSWER:

CALCULATION OF COST OF LAND TO BE CAPITALIZED AS PER AS 10

Particulars	₹ in Lakhs	
A. Purchase Cost		100
B. Legal fees for registration of Sale deed.		2
C. Title Gurantee Insurance		1
D. Cost of demolition of old building	₹ 3 Lakhs	
Less: Sale proceeds from sale of the scrap	₹ 1 Lakhs	2
E. Cost of land to be capitalized		105

QUESTION 2: X Ltd. purchased machinery from Y Ltd. on 30th Sept. 2014. The price was 522.50 lakhs after charging 10 % Vat and giving a trade discount of 5% on the quoted price. Transport charges were 0.25 % on the quoted price and installation charges come to 1% on the quoted price.

A loan of ₹ 500 lakhs was taken from bank on which interest at 15 % per annum was to be paid.

Expenditure incurred on the trial run was: Material ₹ 50,000, wages ₹ 40,000 and overheads ₹ 30,000.

Machinery was ready for use on 1st Dec. 2014. However it was actually put to use only on 1st May, 2015. Find out the cost of the machine and suggest the accounting treatment for the expenses incurred in the interval between the dates 1st Dec. 2014 to 1st May 2015. The entire loan amount remained unpaid on 1st May 2015. X Ltd. does not intend to utilize the input tax paid on capital good.

ANSWER:

CALCULATION OF COST OF MACHINE TO BE CAPITALIZED AS PER AS 10

Particulars		₹ in lakhs
A. Quoted Price of machine		500.00
B. Trade discount @ 5 % on ₹ 500		25.00
C. Price after discount [A – B]		475.00
D. VAT @ 10 % on ₹ 475		47.50
E. Selling Price [C + D]		522.50
F. Transportation charges [0.25 % of ₹ 500]		1.25
G. Installation charges [1 % of ₹ 500]		5.00
H. Borrowing cost [₹ 500 lakhs × 15% × 2/12]		12.50
I. Expenditure on Trial Run		
Material:	0.50	
Wages:	0.40	
Overheads:	0.30	1.20
J. Total Cost of the machinery to be capitalized [E + F + G + H + I]		542.45

As per AS - 16, the capitalization of interest should cease when substantially all the activities necessary for intended use are completed. Therefore, interest for the period 01.12.2014 to 01.05.2015 should be expensed.

Working notes:

1. Selling Price before VAT = ₹ 522.50 lakh × 100/110 = ₹475 lakhs
2. Quoted Price before Trade Discount = ₹475 lakh × 100/95 = ₹500 lakhs
3. As per As 16 interest should be capitalized only for the period when substantially all the activities necessary for intended use are completed. In present case machinery was ready for use on 1st Dec. 2012. Hence in this case capitalization of interest should be done for only two months (i.e. from 30th Sept. 2014 to 1st Dec., 2014)

   Interest for the two months = 500 lakhs × 15 % × (2 months/12 months) = 12.50 lakhs.

QUESTION 3: Amna Ltd. contracted with a supplier to purchase a specific machinery to be installed in Department A in two months time. Special foundations were required for the plant, which were to be prepared within this supply lead time. The cost of site preparation and laying foundations were ₹ 47,290. These activities were supervised by a technician during the entire period, who is employed for this purpose of ₹ 15,000 per month. The technician's services were given to Department A by Department B, which billed the services at ₹ 16,500 per month after adding 10% profit margin.

The machine was purchased at ₹ 52,78,000. Sales Tax was changed at 4% on the invoice ₹ 18,590 transportation charges were incurred to bring the machine to the factory. An Architect

was engaged at a fee of ₹ 10,000 to supervise machinery installation at the factory premises. Also, payment under the invoice was due in 3 months. However, the Company made the payment in 2nd month. The company operates on Bank Overdraft@ 11%.

Ascertain the amount at which the asset should be capitalized under AS 10.

ANSWER:

CALCULATION OF COST OF FIXED ASSET (I.E. MACHINE)

Particulars	₹
Purchase Price (Given)	52,78,000
Add: Sales Tax at 4% (₹ 52,78,000 × 4%)	2,11,120
Site Preparation Cost (Given)	47,290
Technician's Salary (Specific/Attributable overheads for 2 months)	30,000
Initial Delivery Cost (Transportation)	18,590
Professional Fees for Installation (Architect's Fees)	10,000
Total Cost of Asset	55,95,000

Notes:

1. Interest on Bank Overdraft for earlier payment of invoice is not relevant under AS 10. It may be noted that overdraft facility is generally used for working capital purpose.
2. Internally booked profits should be eliminated in arriving at the cost of Fixed Assets.
3. In the absence of information about excise, CENVAT credit has been ignored.
4. It has been assumed that the purchase price of ₹ 52,78,000 excludes amount of sales tax.

QUESTION 4: W Ltd. purchased machinery for ₹ 80 lakhs from X Ltd. during 2014-2015 and installed the same immediately. Price includes excise duty of ₹ 8 lakhs. During the year 2014-2015, the company produced exciseable goods on which excise duty of ₹ 7.20 lakhs was charged.

Give necessary entries explaining the treatment of Cenvat Credit.

ANSWER:

JOURNAL **₹ in lakhs**

Particulars		Dr.	Cr.
(a) Machinery A/c	Dr.	72	
Cenvat credit receivable on capital goods A/c	Dr.	8	
To Bank A/c or Creditors A/c			80
(Being capitalization of machinery)			
(b) Excise duty A/c	Dr.	7.2	
To Cenvat credit receivable on capital goods A/c			4.0
To Bank A/c			3.2
(Being excise duty set off to the extent of 50% of excise duty paid in the first year of acquisition of capital asset)			

QUESTION 5: Comptech Ltd. having office at Chennai, acquired a sophisticated three dimensional (3D) computer printer having all inclusive MRP (Maximum Retail Price) of ₹ 50 lakhs from a supplier located at New Delhi. The terms of the purchase were as under:

- **(i) The supplier would buy back the existing unit with Comptech that has carrying amount of ₹ 10.20 lakhs. Prevailing CST rate is 2%.**
- **(ii) The supplier would give a special discount of 10% on MRP to Comptech considering their long standing relationship.**
- **(iii) A cash payment of ₹ 38.25 lakhs would be made by Comptech Ltd. to the supplier.**
- **(iv) Accessories required to operate the machine costing ₹ 7.60 lakhs (inclusive of all taxes) will be purchased by Comptech.**
- **(v) The supplier will deliver free of cost certain heavy duty cables etc. having MRP of ₹ 5.75 lakhs, that are required to run the machine.**
- **(vi) Transit insurance cost will be borne by Comptech @ 2% of MRP.**
- **(vii) Freight and other incidentals amounting to ₹ 2.30 lakhs is borne by Comptech.**

You are required to arrive at the cost of the new asset and show the profit/(loss) incurred by Comptech on the buy back arrangement and also draft the Journal Entries to record the above transaction.

ANSWER:

PROVISION OF AS 10

As per para 22 of AS 10 ₹ Accounting for Fixed Assets', when a fixed asset is acquired in part exchange for another asset, the cost of the asset acquired should be recorded either at fair market value or at the net book value of the asset given up, adjusted for any balancing payment. In the given question the FMV of the new machine is its MRP net of special concession given to the buyer.

CALCULATION OF COST OF NEW ASSET

Particulars	₹ in lakhs
MRP of Printer	50
Less: Special Discount 10% of MRP	5
Add: Accessories	7.6
Add: Transit Insurance Cost (2% of 50 lakh)	1
Add: Freight and other incidental amount	2.30
	55.9

PROFIT /LOSS INCURRED ON BUY-BACK ARRANGEMENT

Particulars	₹ in lakhs
Discounted price of new machine	45.00
Less: Cash portion thereof	38.25
FMV of old machine	6.75*
Less: Book Value thereof	10.20
Loss on Buy back	3.45
*This includes CST of 2%. Thus the CST will be 6.75 × 2/102 = 0.13 lakh	

JOURNAL

Particulars		Dr. (₹ in lakhs)	Cr. (₹ in lakhs)
1. 3D Computer Printer A/c	Dr.	49.15	
To Cash A/c			49.15
(Being the expenses incurred for purchase of 3D computer – cash payment 38.25 + accessory 7.6 + insurance 1 and freight 2.3)			
2. 3D Computer Printer A/c	Dr.	6.75	
Loss on buy back of old machine A/c	Dr.	3.45	
To Old Machine A/c			10.20
(Being the transfer of FMV of ₹ 6.75 lakhs of old machine to new printer under buy-back scheme and recognition of loss on buy back)			

Note: It is assumed that the cash payment of ₹ 38,25 lakhs is the full and final payment to the supplier for the printer.

TREATMENT OF SUBSEQUENT EXPENDITURES

QUESTION 6: List 4 Examples of Subsequent Expenditures which are treated as (a) Capital Expenditure (b) Revenue Expenditure.

ANSWER:

Examples of Subsequent Expenditures to be treated as Capital Expenditure	Examples of Subsequent Expenditures to be treated as Revenue Expenditure
1. Cost of Improvements which will increase earning capacity.	1. Routine Repairs & overhauling of Machinery to maintain it in good condition
2. Cost of Improvements which will decrease cost.	2. Cost of Dismantling and re-erection.
3. Cost of Replacements which doubled the output.	3. Expenses on shifting existing machine on new site.
4. Compensation to existing tenants so as to lease the property at higher rates.	4. Cost of Building of a new foundation to shift an existing machine.
5. Cost of Trial Run sub-standard Production.	

QUESTION 7: From the following information state the amount to be capitalized as per AS 10 with reason. ₹ 5 lakhs as routine repairs and ₹ 1 lakh on partial replacement of a part of a machine. ₹ 10 lakhs on replacement of part of a machinery which will improve the efficiency of a machine.

ANSWER:

PROVISION OF AS 10

1. As per AS 10 "Accounting for Fixed Assets", expenditure on repairs and improvements to the asset should be capitalised if it increases the efficiency of the asset or the expected useful life of the asset or if it reduces the operating cost of the asset.
2. Expenditure in the nature of routine repairs which is incurred to maintain the asset is required to be expensed in the year in which it is incurred.

DECISION

1. ₹ 5 Lakhs incurred as routine repairs and ₹ 1 Lakhs on partial replacement of a part a machine should be expensed as these do not increase pre-assessed benefits from the assets.
2. ₹ 10 Lakhs spent on improvement of machinery will be capitalized as it improves the efficiency of the asset.

QUESTION 8: X Ltd. purchases a building that already has non moving tenants. Subsequently X Ltd. pays significant compensation to these tenants, so that the property could be leased to a third party at much higher rates. Advise X Ltd. on the treatment of the compensation.

ANSWER:

PROVISION OF AS 10

As per AS 10 Subsequent expenditures that increases the future benefits from the existing asset beyond its previously assessed standard of performance is capitalized.

ADVICE

In a present situation, compensation paid to the tenants increases the future benefits of the building beyond its previously assessed standard of performance. Hence, the compensation paid to the tenants should be capitalized as cost of the building.

QUESTION 9: A company undertook a repair and overhauling of its machinery at cost of ₹ 3 crores to maintain them in good condition and capitalized the amount as it is more than 30% of the original cost of the machinery. What should be your comment as a company auditor.

ANSWER:

PROVISION OF AS 10

As per AS 10 expenditure that increases the future benefits from the existing asset beyond its previously assessed standard of performance should be capitalized.

ADVICE

In present case *neither* the earning capacity has increased *nor* there is any reduction in the cost of production, hence there is no increase in future benefits beyond its originally assessed standard of performance. In the absence of these criteria, it is to be treated as revenue expenditure. The mere fact that expenditure on maintenance is more than 30 % of the original cost of the machinery would not change its nature. Consequently, the auditor would be required to qualify his report.

QUESTION 10: During the year, P Limited incurred the following expenses on machinery: ₹ 2.50 lacs as routine repairs and ₹75,000 on partial replacement of a part. ₹ 7 lacs on replacement of part of a machinery which will improve the efficiency of the machine. Which amount should be capitalized as per AS 10?

ANSWER:

PROVISION OF AS 10

As per only those expenditures that increase the future benefits from the existing assets, is to be included in the gross book value. Example: Increase in capacity.

ADVICE

₹3.25 lacs spent on repairs and partial replacement of a part of the machinery should be charged to Profit and Loss Account as they will help in maintaining the capacity but will not improve the efficiency of the machine. However, ₹ 7 lacs incurred on replacement of a part of the machinery, which will increase the efficiency, should be capitalized by inclusion in the gross book value of assets,

QUESTION 11: A company is in the process of setting up a production line for manufacturing a new product. Based on trial runs conducted by the company, it was noticed that the production lines output was not of the desired quality. However, company has taken a decision to manufacture and sell the sub-standard product over the next one year due to the huge investment involved. In the background of the relevant accounting standard, advice the company on the cut - off date for capitalization of the project cost.

ANSWER:

PROVISION OF AS 10

As per AS 10 the expenditure incurred after the plant has begun commercial production i.e., production intended for sale or captive consumption is not capitalized and is treated as revenue expenditure

ADVICE

In the present case, the company decided to sell the sub - standard production, and therefore, the expenditure incurred to this date will be capitalized as it will be deemed that commercial production intended for sale has begun and the cut - off date would be the date when the trial run of sub - standard product was completed.

QUESTION 12: A company has scrapped a semi - automatic part of a machine (not written off) and replaced with a more expensive fully automatic part, which has doubled the output of the machine. At the time to the machine was moved to a more suitable place in the factory, which involved the building of a new foundation in addition to the cost of dismantling and re-erection. The company wants to charge the whole expenditure to revenue. As an auditor give your comments for this situation.

ANSWER:

Subsequent Expenditure on fully automatic part	It should be capitalized as it has doubled the output of the machine, hence it has increased future benefits beyond the machines' pre - assessed standard of performance
Expenses for shifting the machine and building of a new foundation & the cost of dismantling	These costs should be charged to profit and loss statement. Since these do not contribute to any new future benefit from the existing asset. They only serve to maintain performance of the machine.

CALCULATION OF GROSS BOOK VALUE OF SELF CONSTRUCTED FIXED ASSET

QUESTION 13: PQR Ltd. constructed a fixed asset and incurred the following expenses on its construction:

Particulars	₹
Materials	**16,00,000**
Direct Expenses	**3,00,000**
Total Direct Labour	**6,00,000**
(1/15th of the total labour time was chargeable to the construction)	
Total Office & Administrative Expenses	**9,00,000**
(4% is chargeable to the construction)	
Depreciation on assets used for the construction of this asset	**15,000**

Calculate the Cost of the fixed asset.

ANSWER:

CALCULATION OF COST OF FIXED ASSETS

Particulars	₹
Materials	16,00,000
Direct expenses	3,00,000
Direct labour 1/15th of ₹ 6,00,000)	40,000
Office and administrative expenses (4% ₹ 9,00,000)	36,000
Depreciation on assets	15,000
Cost of fixed asset	19,91,000

Note: It is assumed that 4% of office and administrative expenses are specifically attributable to construction of a fixed asset. Alternatively, it may be assumed that 4% of office and administraive expenses are only allocated to construction project and is not specifically attributable to it. In such a case, the cost of fixed assets will be ₹19,55,000.

QUESTION 14: A company has made additions to its factory buildings by its own workmen, at cost of ₹8,00,000 for wages and materials. The lowest estimate from an outsider contractor to carry out the same work was for ₹10,00,000. The directors contend that as they were fully entitled to employ an outside contractor, it is reasonable to debit the factory building account with ₹10,00,000. As an auditor of the company, what shall be your advice in the above case.

ANSWER:

PROVISION OF AS 10

As per AS 10 cost of a self-constructed fixed asset should comprise those costs that relate directly to the specific asset and those that are attributable to the construction activity in general and can be allocated to the specific asset. Any internal profits are eliminated in arriving at such costs.

ADVICE

Hence the factory building should be capitalized with ₹8,00,000 and not ₹10,00,000 as contended by the Board.

RECORDING OF FIXED ASSET ACQUIRED IN EXCHANGE OF ANOTHER ASSET

QUESTION 15:

Book value of old assets exchanged **₹ 8,000**

Additional cash given for exchange of asset **₹ 5,000**

Determine the cost of new asset acquired and show the accounting treatment in this regard in the following cases:

(a) If no other information is given

(b) Fair market value of old asset exchanged is ₹18,000

(c) Fair market value of new asset acquired in exchange of old asset is ₹25,000

ANSWER:

Case (a) When the market value of asset given up/ acquired is not clearly evident

JOURNAL

New Asset A/c	...Dr.	₹ 13,000	
To Bank A/c			₹ 5,000
To Old Asset A/c			₹ 8,000
(Being the cost of asset acquired is recorded at the book value of asset given up and adjusted for payment.)			

Case (b) When the market value of asset given up is more clearly evident

JOURNAL

New Asset A/c	...Dr.	₹ 23,000	
To Bank A/c			₹ 5,000
To Old Asset			₹18,000
(Being the cost of asset acquire d is recorded at the fair market value of asset given up and adjusted for payment)			
Old Asset A/c	...Dr.	₹10,000	
To Profit & loss A/c			₹10,000
(Being the excess of fair market value over book value is transferred to P&L A/c)			

Case (c) When the market value of asset acquired is more clearly evident

JOURNAL

New Asset A/c	...Dr.	₹ 25,000	
To Bank A/c			₹ 5,000
To Old Asset A/c			₹ 20,000
(Being the cost of asset acquired is recorded at its fair market value)			
Old Asset A/c	...Dr.	₹ 12,000	
To Profit & Loss A/c			₹ 12,000
(Being credit balance in Old Asset A/c is transferred to P&L A/c)			

QUESTION 16: One customer from whom ₹5 lakhs are recoverable for credit sales gives a motorcar in full settlement of the dues. The directors estimate that the market value of the motorcar transferred is ₹5.25 lakhs. As on the date of balance sheet the car has not been registered in the name of the auditee.Comment.

ANSWER:

PROVISION OF AS 10

As per AS 10 the asset acquired in an exchange of assets should be valued at the fair market value of assets acquired or the asset given up, whichever is more clearly evident.

ADVICE

Here fair market value of the assets given up obviously more clearly evident. Hence, the motorcar should be valued at ₹5 lakhs. Also the motorcar should be recognized as an asset even though it is not yet registered in auditee's name. This is because legal title is not necessary for an asset to exist. What is necessary is control as per the framework for preparation and presentation of financial statements. Applying substance over form it is concluded that since price has been settled, the auditee has control, hence it should be reflected as an asset along with a note to the effect that the registration in auditee name is pending.

RECORDING OF FIXED ASSET ACQUIRED IN EXCHANGE OF SECURITIES

QUESTION 17: XYZ Ltd. issue 1,00,000 equity shares of ₹10 each (fully paid up) in consideration for supply of a machinery by PQR Ltd. The shares exchanged for machinery are quoted on National Stock Exchange (NSE) at ₹25 per share, at the time of transaction. In the absence of fair market value of the machinery acquired, how the value of machinery would be recorded in the books of company.

ANSWER:

PROVISION OF AS 10

As per AS 10, fixed asset acquired in exchange for shares or other securities in the enterprise should be recorded at the fair market value of the asset acquired or the fair market value of the securities issued, whichever is more clearly evident.

ADVICE

Since, the market value of the shares exchanged for the asset is more clearly evident, the company should record the value of machinery at ₹ 25,00,000 (i.e. 1,00,000 shares × ₹ 25 per share being the market price). Journal entry in respect of this transaction is as follows:

JOURNAL

Machinery A/c ...Dr.	25,00,000	
To Share Capital A/c		10,00,000
To Securities Premium A/c		15,00,000
(Being machinery recorded at the fair market value of the securities issued in consideration for machinery acquired)		

ACCOUNTING FOR FIRST AND SUBSEQUENT REVALUATION OF ASSET AND TREATMENT OF PROFIT/LOSS ON DISPOSAL OF FIXED ASSET

QUESTION 18: Tulsian Ltd. provides you the following information:

Particulars	Plot of Land 1	Plot of Land 2	Plot of Land 3	Plot of Land 4	Plot of Land 5
Book Value on 1st April, 2013	1,00,000	1,00,000	1,00,000	1,00,000	1,00,000
Revalued on 31st March, 2014	1,20,000	1,20,000	80,000	80,000	1,20,000
Revalued on 31st March, 2015	1,15,000	95,000	1,00,000	1,05,000	1,15,000
Sold on 1st April, 2015	1,20,000	90,000	90,000	90,000	1,10,000

Pass the Journal Entries on 31st March, 2014, on 31st March, 2015 and 1st April, 2015.

ANSWER:

JOURNAL

Date	Particulars	Dr. (₹)	Cr. (₹)
31.03.2014	Asset 1 A/c ...Dr.	20,000	
	To Revaluation Reserve A/c		20,000
	(Being whole of the surplus arising on revaluation transferred to Revaluation Reserve A/c.)		
31.03.2014	Asset 2 A/c ...Dr.	20,000	
	To Revaluation Reserve A/c		20,000
	(Being whole of the surplus arising on revaluation transferred to Revaluation Reserve A/c.)		
31.03.2014	Profit & Loss A/c ...Dr.	20,000	
	To Asset 3 A/c		20,000
	(Being whole of the deficiency arising on revaluation transferred to P & LA/c.)		
31.03.2014	Profit & Loss A/c ...Dr.	20,000	
	To Asset 4 A/c		20,000
	(Being whole of the deficiency arising on revaluation transferred to P & LA/c.)		
31.03.2014	Asset 5 A/c ...Dr.	20,000	
	To Revaluation Reserve A/c		20,000
	(Being whole of the surplus arising on revaluation transferred to Revaluation Reserve A/c.)		
31.03.2015	Revaluation Reserve A/c ...Dr.	5,000	
	To Asset 1 A/c		20,000
	(Being deficiency to the extent of increase arising on revaluation previously credited to Revaluation Reserve utilized)		
31.03.2015	Revaluation Reserve A/c ...Dr.	20,000	
	Profit & Loss A/c ...Dr.	5,000	
	To Asset 2 A/c		25,000
	(Being deficiency to the extent of increase arising on revaluation previously credited to Revaluation Reserve utilized and remaining deficiency charged to Profit & Loss A/c)		
31.03.2015	Asset 3 A/c ...Dr.	20,000	
	To Profit & Loss A/c		20,000
	(Being Surplus to the extent of decrease arising on revaluation previously charged to Profit & Loss A/c credited to P & L A/c)		

31.03.2015	Asset 4 A/c ...Dr. To Profit & Loss A/c To Revaluation Reserve A/c (Being Surplus to the extent of decrease arising on revaluation previously charged to Profit & Loss A/c credited to P & L A/c and remaining surplus credited to Revaluation Reserve A/c)	25,000	 20,000 5,000
31.03.2015	Revaluation Reserve A/c ...Dr. To Asset 5 A/c (Being deficiency to the extent of increase arising on revaluation previously credited to Revaluation Reserve utilized)	5,000	 20,000
01.04.2015	Bank A/c ...Dr. To Asset 1 A/c (Being the Asset sold)	1,20,000	 1,20,000
01.04.2015	Asset 1 A/c ...Dr. To Profit & Loss A/c (Being profit on sale of land transferred to P & L A/c)	5,000	 5,000
01.04.2015	Revaluation Reserve A/c ...Dr. To General Reserve A/c (Being balance of Revaluation Reserve A/c transferred to General Reserve A/c.)	15,000	 15,000
01.04.2015	Bank A/c ...Dr. To Asset 2 A/c (Being the Asset sold)	90,000	 90,000
01.04.2015	Profit & Loss A/c ...Dr. To Asset 2 A/c (Being Loss on sale of land transferred to P & L A/c)	5,000	 5,000
01.04.2015	Bank A/c ...Dr. To Asset 3 A/c (Being the Asset sold)	90,000	 90,000
01.04.2015	Profit & Loss A/c ...Dr. To Asset 3 A/c (Being Loss on sale of land transferred to P & L A/c)	10,000	 10,000
01.04.2015	Bank A/c ...Dr. To Asset 4 A/c (Being the Asset sold)	90,000	 90,000
01.04.2015	Revaluation Reserve A/c ...Dr. Profit & Loss A/c ...Dr. To Asset 4 A/c (Being loss to the extent it is related to an increase previously credited to Revaluation Reserve A/c utilized.)	5,000 10,000	 15,000

01.04.2015	Bank A/c ...Dr. To Asset 5 A/c (Being the Asset sold)	1,10,000	1,10,000
01.04.2015	Revaluation Reserve A/c ...Dr. To Asset 5 A/c (Being loss to the extent it is related to an increase previously credited to Revaluation Reserve A/c utilized.)	5,000	5,000
01.04.2015	Revaluation Reserve A/c ...Dr. To General Reserve A/c (Being balance of Revaluation Reserve A/c transferred to General Reserve A/c.)	10,000	10,000

QUESTION 19: The company has written up its fixed assets by ₹ 100 lakhs and transferred the accumulated depreciation of ₹25 lakhs to Profit & Loss A/c. Advice the company on changes to be affected in the draft financial statements. Give reasons in support of advice.

ANSWER:

PROVISION OF AS 10

As per AS 10 when fixed assets are revalued upwards, the accumulated depreciation existing on the date of revaluation should not be credited to profit and loss account. The increase on account of revaluation should be credited to Revaluation Reserve Account.

ADVICE

Hence, the transfer of accumulated depreciation of ₹25 lakhs to profit and loss account is contrary to principles laid down in AS 10.

QUESTION 20: At the beginning of the year, the company has a capital of ₹10 crores, free reserves of ₹2 crores and Revaluation Reserve of ₹8 crores. In the relevant year under audit, the company has incurred a loss of ₹7 crores. The company proposes to adjust the loss with the Revaluation Reserve. As a statutory auditor of a Public Limited Company, how would you deal with such situation?

ANSWER:

PROVISION OF AS 10

As per AS 10 Losses and accumulated losses cannot be adjusted against the revaluation reserves which were created on the revaluation of assets.

ADVICE

Hence, in a present case, the contentions of the company are not correct.

QUESTION 21: The Directors of ABC Ltd. are of the opinion that before declaration of dividends, it would be necessary to set off the carried forward amount of debit balance in the profit and loss account against current revenue profits but the same could be set off against existing revaluation reserve. As an auditor of the company do you agree with the contentions of directors?

ANSWER:

PROVISION OF AS 10

If the debit balance in the Profit and Loss Account is set off against revaluation reserve, and then dividend is declared from out of revenue profits, it should amount to payment of dividend out of capital without making good the lower of loss or depreciation.

ADVICE

Such a declaration shall be violation of the provisions of Section 123 of the Companies Act, 2013. Hence, the opinion of the directors of ABC Ltd. is not correct.

TREATMENT OF FIXED ASSETS RETIRED FROM ACTIVE USE AND HELD FOR DISPOSAL

QUESTION 22: Tulsian Ltd. provides you the following information:

Particulars	Plot of Land 1	Plot of Land 2	Plot of Land 3	Plot of Land 4	Plot of Land 5
Book Value on 1st April, 2013	1,00,000	1,00,000	1,00,000	1,00,000	1,00,000
Revalued on 31st March, 2014	1,20,000	1,20,000	80,000	80,000	1,20,000
Revalued on 31st March, 2015	1,15,000	95,000	1,00,000	1,05,000	1,15,000
Estimated Net Realizable Value on 1st April, 2015	1,20,000	90,000	90,000	90,000	1,10,000

How shall the retirement of land from active use on 1st April, 2015 be accounted for?

ANSWER:

JOURNAL

Date	Particulars		Dr. (₹)	Cr. (₹)
01.04.2015	Revaluation Reserve A/c (Asset 1)	...Dr.	15,000	
	To General Reserve A/c			15,000
	(Being balance of Revaluation Reserve A/c transferred to General Reserve A/c.)			
01.04.2015	Profit & Loss A/c	...Dr.	5,000	
	To Asset 2 A/c			5,000
	(Being Loss on sale of land transferred to P & L A/c)			
01.04.2015	Profit & Loss A/c	...Dr.	10,000	
	To Asset 3 A/c			10,000
	(Being Loss on sale of land transferred to P & L A/c)			
01.04.2015	Revaluation Reserve A/c	...Dr.	5,000	
	Profit & Loss A/c	...Dr.	10,000	
	To Asset 4 A/c			15,000
	(Being loss to the extent it is related to an increase previously credited to Revaluation Reserve A/c utilized.)			

01.04.2015	Revaluation Reserve A/c ...Dr. To Asset 5 A/c (Being loss to the extent it is related to an increase previously credited to Revaluation Reserve A/c utilized.)	5,000	 5,000
01.04.2015	Revaluation Reserve A/c ...Dr. To General Reserve A/c (Being balance of Revaluation Reserve A/c transferred to General Reserve A/c.)	10,000	 10,000

QUESTION 23: F Limited includes those items of Fixed assets which have not been in active use and held for disposal, as inventory item in the Schedule of Inventory.

ANSWER:

PROVISION OF AS 10

AS-10 "Accounting for Fixed Assets", requires that the item of fixed assets that have been retired form active used and are held for disposal be stated at the lower of their net book value and net realizable value and are shown separately in the financial statements. As per AS-2 "Valuation of Inventories", "inventories" are assets' held for sale in the ordinary course of business in the process of production for such sale; or in the form of materials or supplies to be consumed in the production process or in the rendering of services.", whereas, the sale of fixed assets cannot be treated as sale arising from the ordinary course of business.

ADVICE

Thus, F Ltd's inclusion of fixed assets not in active use and held for disposal, as inventory item in the schedule of inventory is not in line with the requirements of AS-10 and AS-2. Such fixed assets should be stated at lower of net book value and net realizable value and are shown separately in financial statements.

TREATMENT OF FIXED ASSETS OWNED BY THE ENTERPRISE JOINTLY WITH OTHERS

QUESTION 24: A computerized machinery was purchased by two companies jointly. The price shared equally. It was also agreed that they would use the machinery equally and show in their Balance Sheets, 50% of the value of machinery and charge 50% of the depreciation in their respective books of account.

ANSWER:

PROVISION OF AS 10

As per AS 10 in case of fixed assets owned jointly by enterprises, the extent of the entity's share in such assets, and the proportion in the original cost, accumulated depreciation and written down value should be stated in the Balance Sheet *Alternatively*, AS-10 also recommends that the pro-rata cost of such jointly owned assets may be grouped together with similar fully owned assets and appropriate disclosure of the same should be made.

ADVICE

Accordingly, the treatment followed by the companies reflecting 50% of the value of the machinery and charging 50% in their respective books of accounts is proper. However such jointly owned assets should be indicated, separately in the Fixed Asset Register maintained by the company.

MISCELLENEOUS QUESTIONS

QUESTION 25: On 1st April, 2011. BHARAT TUSHAR Ltd. purchased a Fixed Asset worth ₹ 125 lakhs. The Salvage Value at the end of useful life of 4 years was estimated at ₹ 51.20 lakhs. The Asset was revalued upward by 60% on 1.4.2012. The Asset was revalued downward by 25% on 1.4.2013. The asset was sold on 1.4.2014 at a Loss @5%. The company charged straight line depreciation. The company also charged the excess depreciation to Revaluation Reserve.

Required: Show Fixed Assets A/c, Depreciation A/c, Revaluation Reserve A/c.

ANSWER:

Dr. **FIXED ASSETS ACCOUNT** **Cr.**

Date	Particulars	₹ lakhs	Date	Particulars	₹ lakhs
1.4.2011	To Bank A/c	125.00	31.3.2012	By Depreciation A/c [(125 – 51.2)/4]	18.45
				By Balance c/d	106.55
		125.00			125.00
1.4.2012	To Balance b/d	106.55	31.3.2013	By Depreciation A/c [(106.55 + 63.93 – 51.2)/3]	39.76
1.4.2012	To Revaluation Reserve [106.55 × 60%]	63.93		By Balance c/d	130.72
		170.48			170.48
1.4.2013	To Balance b/d	130.72	1.4.2013	By Revaluation Reserve [(130.72 × 25%)]	32.68
			31.3.2014	By Depreciation A/c [(130.72 – 32.68 – 51.2)/2]	23.42
				By Balance c/d	74.62
		130.72			130.72
1.4.2014	To Balance b/d	74.62	1.4.2014	By Revaluation Reserve A/c [74.62 × 5%]	3.371
				By Bank A/c [74.62 × 95%]	70.889
		74.62			74.62

Dr. **DEPRECIATION ACCOUNT** **Cr.**

Date	Particulars	₹ lakhs	Date	Particulars	₹ lakhs
31.3.2012	To Fixed Assets A/c	18.45	31.3.2012	By P & L A/c	18.45
31.3.2013	To Fixed Assets A/c	39.76	31.3.2013	By P & L A/c	18.45
				By Revaluation Reserve	21.31
		39.76			39.76
31.3.2014	To Fixed Assets A/c	23.42	31.3.2014	By P & L A/c	18.45
				By Revaluation Reserve	4.97
		23.42			23.42

Dr. **REVALUATION RESERVE ACCOUNT** Cr.

Date	Particulars	₹ lakhs	Date	Particulars	₹ lakhs
31.3.2013	To Depreciation A/c [63.93/3]	21.31	1.4.2012	By Fixed Assets A/c	63.93
	To Balance c/d	42.62			
		63.93			63.93
31.3.2014	To Fixed Assets A/c	32.68	1.4.2013	By Balance b/d	42.62
	To Depreciation A/c [(42.62 – 32.68)/2]	4.97			
	To Balance c/d	4.97			
		42.62			42.62
1.4.2014	To Fixed Assets A/c	3.731	1.4.2014	By Balance b/d	4.97
	To General Reserve	1.239			
		4.97			4.97

QUESTION 26: ABC Ltd. purchased fixed assets worth ₹ 200 lakhs on 1st April, 2011. The life of the assets is 10 years and they are to be depreciated on straight - line basis. The assets were revalued on 1st April, 2013 when 50 % of the assets were assessed at 15 % less than the book value, and the remaining assets were at 20 % higher than book value. The assets were ultimately sold on 01.04.2015 for ₹ 120 lakhs. Excess depreciation on revaluation, if any should be charged to Revaluation Reserve.

Required: **Prepare Fixed Assets Account, Depreciation Account and Revaluation Reserve Account, supported by workings wherever necessary.**

ANSWER:

Dr. **FIXED ASSETS ACCOUNT** Cr.

Date	Particulars	₹ lakhs	Date	Particulars	₹ lakhs
1.4.2011	To Bank A/c	200	31.3.2012	By Depreciation A/c [200/10]	20
				By Balance c/d	180
		200			200
1.4.2012	To Balance b/d	180	31.3.2013	By Depreciation A/c	20
				By Balance c/d	160
		180			180
1.4.2013	To Balance b/d	160	31.3.2014	By Profit & Loss A/c (80 × 15%)	12.00
	To Revaluation Reserve A/c (80 × 20%)	16	31.3.2014	By Depreciation A/c (8.50 + 12)	20.50
				By Balance c/d	143.50
		176			176
1.4.2014	To Balance b/d	143.50	31.3.2015	By Depreciation A/c [74.62 × 5%]	20.50
				By Balance c/d	123.00
		143.50			143.50

1.4.2015	To Balance b/d	123	1.4.2015	By Revaluation Reserve A/c	3
				By Bank A/c	120
		123			123

Dr. **DEPRECIATION ACCOUNT** **Cr.**

Date	Particulars	₹ lakhs	Date	Particulars	₹ lakhs
31.3.2012	To Fixed Assets A/c	20	31.3.2012	By P & L A/c	20
31.3.2013	To Fixed Assets A/c	20	31.3.2013	By P & L A/c	20
31.3.2014	To Fixed Assets A/c	20.50	31.3.2014	By P & L A/c	18.50
				By Revaluation Reserve	2.00
		20.50			20.50
31.3.2015	To Fixed Assets A/c	20.50	31.3.2015	By P & L A/c	18.50
				By Revaluation Reserve	2.00
		20.50			20.50

Dr. **REVALUATION RESERVE ACCOUNT** **Cr.**

Date	Particulars	₹ lakhs	Date	Particulars	₹ lakhs
31.3.2014	To Depreciation A/c [16/8]	2	1.4.2013	By Fixed Assets A/c	16
	To Balance c/d	14			
		16			16
31.3.2015	To Depreciation A/c	2	1.4.2014	By Fixed Assets A/c	14
	To Balance c/d	12			
		14			14
1.4.2015	To Fixed Assets A/c	3	1.4.2015	By Balance b/d	12
	To General Reserve	9			
		12			12

QUESTION 27: BHARAT TUSHAR Ltd. purchased machinery from Y Ltd. on 30.09.2008. The price was 480.70 lakhs after charging 10 % Vat and giving a trade discount of 5 % on the quoted price. Transport charges were 0.25 % on the quoted price and installation charges come to 1% on the quoted price. A loan of ₹460 lakhs was taken from bank on which interest at 15 % per annum was to be paid. The entire loan amount remained unpaid on 01.04.2009.

Expenditure incurred on the trial run was: Material ₹ 1,00,000, Wages ₹ 60,000 and Overheads ₹ 45,000.Machinery was ready for use on 01.12.2008. However it was actually put to use only on 01.04.2009. X Ltd. does not intend to utilize the input tax paid on capital good.

On 1st April, 2009. it got Government grant of ₹ 250 lakhs. The Salvage Value at the end of useful life of 4 years was estimated at ₹ 102.40 lakhs. The company charged depreciation on Written Down Value basis. From 3rd year, company decided to change the method of depreciation from Written Down Value Method to Straight Line Method . On 1.4.2012, the Asset 's useful life was reassessed at 6 years instead of 4 years and it was revalued upward by 60%. On 1.4.2013 the Asset was revalued downward by 25%. On 31.3.2015 the asset was retired from active use but not disposed off. Estimated Realizable Value and Realizable Expenses were ₹ 52 lakhs and ₹ 80,000 respectively. The company also charged the excess depreciation to Revaluation Reserve.

Required: (a)Find out the cost of the machine (b) suggest the Accounting Treatment for the expenses incurred in the interval between the dates 01.12.2008 to 01.04.2009.(c)Prepare Fixed Assets A/c, Depreciation A/c, Revaluation Reserve A/c.

ANSWER:

(A) CALCULATION OF COST OF MACHINE AS PER AS 10

Particulars		₹ in lakhs
A. Quoted Price of machine		460.00
B. *Less:* Trade discount @ 5 % on ₹460		23.00
C. Price after discount [A – B]		437.00
D. *Add:* VAT @ 10 % on ₹437		43.70
E. Selling Price [C + D]		480.70
F. *Add:* Transportation charges [0.25 % of ₹460]		1.15
G. *Add:* Installation charges [1 % of ₹460]		4.60
H. *Add:* Borrowing cost upto 01.12.2008 [₹460 lakhs × 15% × 2/12]		11.50
I. *Add:* Expenditure on Trial Run:		
Material:	1.00	
Wages:	0.60	
Overheads:	0.45	2.05
J. Total Cost of the machinery to be capitalized [E + F + G + H + I]		500.00

Working Notes:

1. Selling Price before VAT = ₹ 480.7 lakh=100/110 = ₹ 437 lakhs
2. Quoted Price before Trade Discount = ₹ 437 lakh = 100/95 = ₹ 460 lakhs
3. As per As 16 interest should be capitalized only for the period when substantially all the activities necessary for intended use are completed. In present case machinery was ready for use on 01.12.2008. Hence in this case capitalization of interest should be done for only two months (i.e. from 30.09.2008 to 30.11.2008)

   Interest for the two months = 460 lakhs × 15 % × (2 months / 12 months) = 11.50 lakhs.

(b) Accounting Treatment for Interest for the period 01.12.2008 to 01.04.2009: It should be expensed since As per AS – 16, the capitalization of interest should cease when substantially all the activities necessary for intended use are completed

Dr. FIXED ASSETS ACCOUNT Cr.

Date	Particulars	₹ lakhs	Date	Particulars	₹ lakhs
1.4.2009	To Bank A/c	500.00	1.4.2009	By Govt. Grant A/c	250.00
			31.3.2010	By Depreciation A/c	50.00
				By Balance c/d	200.00
		500.00			500.00
1.4.2010	To Balance b/d	200.00	31.3.2011	By Depreciation A/c	40.00
				By Balance c/d	160.00
		200.00			200.00

1.4.2011	To Balance b/d	160.00	31.3.2012	By Depreciation A/c	36.90
	To Profit & Loss A/c	16.20		By Balance c/d	139.30
		176.20			176.20
1.4.2012	To Balance b/d	139.30	31.3.2013	By Depreciation A/c [(139.30 + 83.58 – 102.4)/3]	40.16
1.4.2012	To Revaluation Reserve [139.3 × 60%]	83.58			182.72
				By Balance c/d	182.72
		222.88			222.88
1.4.2013	To Balance b/d	180.72	1.4.2013	By Revaluation Reserve [180.72 × 25%]	45.18
			31.3.2014	By Depreciation A/c [(180.72 – 45.18 – 102.4)/2]	16.57
				By Balance c/d	118.97
		180.72			180.72
1.4.2014	To Balance b/d	118.97	31.3.2015	By Depreciation A/c	16.57
				By Profit & Loss A/c	51.20
				By Balance c/d	51.20
		118.97			118.97

Dr. **DEPRECIATION ACCOUNT** Cr.

Date	Particulars	₹ lakhs	Date	Particulars	₹ lakhs
31.3.2010	To Fixed Assets A/c	50.00	31.3.2010	By P & L A/c	50.00
31.3.2011	To Fixed Assets A/c	40.00	31.3.2011	By P & L A/c	40.00
31.3.2012	To Fixed Assets A/c	36.90	31.3.2012	By P & L A/c	36.90
31.3.2013	To Fixed Assets A/c	40.16	31.3.2013	By P & L A/c	12.30
				By Revaluation Reserve	27.86
		40.16			40.16
31.3.2014	To Fixed Assets A/c	16.57	31.3.2014	By P & L A/c	11.30
				By Revaluation Reserve	5.27
		16.57			16.57
31.3.2015	To Fixed Assets A/c	16.57	31.3.2015	By P & L A/c	11.30
				By Revaluation Reserve	5.27
		16.57			16.57

Dr. **REVALUATION RESERVE ACCOUNT** Cr.

Date	Particulars	₹ lakhs	Date	Particulars	₹ lakhs
31.3.2013	To Depreciation A/c [83.58/3]	27.86	1.4.2012	By Fixed Assets A/c	83.58
	To Balance c/d	55.72			
		83.58			83.58

31.3.2014	To Fixed Assets A/c	45.18	1.4.2013	By Balance b/d	55.72
	To Depreciation A/c [(55.72 – 45.18)/2]	5.27			
	To Balance c/d	5.27			
		55.72			55.72
31.3.2015	To Depreciation A/c	5.27	1.4.2014	By Balance b/d	5.27
		5.27			5.27

Working Notes:

1. WDV Depreciation Rate (on 1.4.2009) = $1 - \sqrt[4]{102.40/250}$
   $= 1 - 0.8 = 0.2$ or 20%
2. WDV Depreciation for 2 years = [250 – (250 × 80% × 80%)] = ₹ 90 lakhs
3. SLM Depreciation p.a. = [(250 – 102.4)/4] = ₹ 36.90 lakhs
4. SLM Depreciation for 2 years = ₹ 36.90 lakhs × 2 = ₹ 73.80 lakhs
5. Excess Depreciation provided = ₹ 90 lakhs – ₹ 73.80 lakhs = ₹ 16.20 lakhs

QUESTION 28: A company transferred land from 'fixed assets' to 'current assets' at market price and adjusted the excess value under capital reserve instead of Revaluation Reserve. In subsequent years, the value was written down gradually as 'decline in market value' - whether this would constitute unusual accounting?

ANSWER:

The treatments in different situations are as follows:

(1) In case where enterprise wants to deal in the assets

(a) Fixed assets reclassified as current assets should be valued at their carrying amount appearing in the balance sheet or at the net realizable value, whichever is lower. In this case, no appreciation would be recognized either in the capital reserve or in the revaluation reserve or

(b) It would be appropriate to value assets which were until now classified as fixed assets at their market price in order to determine the correct profit on sale of such assets in the ordinary course of business. The excess of market value over the carrying amount at the date of reclassification can be transferred to the revaluation reserve. It is noted that revaluation reserve arising in a situation where a fixed asset is revalued and continues to be a fixed asset then balance in such a revaluation reserve cannot be utilized. However in case of an asset which was previously classified as fixed asset and currently classified as current asset, the profit on revaluation can be transferred to capital reserve instead of revaluation reserve. It may be noted that under Companies Act, 1956 the capital reserve is not free for distribution.

(2) In case the intention of the enterprise is not to deal in the assets which were until now treated as fixed assets, but assets retired from active use and held for disposal, these should continue to be classified as fixed assets and treated as per AS 10 which requires that such items should be stated at the lower of their net book value and net realizable value and shown separately in the financial statements.

QUESTION 29: A Ltd. entered into a binding contract with C Ltd. to buy a machine for ₹ 1,00,000. The machine is to be delivered on 15th February, 2015. On 1st January, 2015, A Ltd. changed its process of production. The new process will not require the machine ordered and it shall have to be scrapped after delivery. The expected scrap value of the machine is nil. Explain how A Ltd. should recognise the entire transaction in the books of account for the year ended 31st March, 2015.

ANSWER: A Ltd. entered into a binding contract with C Ltd. and therefore, it should recognise a liability of ₹1,00,000. The entire amount of purchase price of the machine should be recognised in the year ended 31st March, 2013 as loss because future economic benefit from the machine to the enterprise is improbable.

JOURNAL ENTRY

Particulars		Dr. (₹)	Cr. (₹)
Profit & Loss A/c	...Dr.	1,00,000	
To C Ltd.			1,00,000
(Being value of machinery fully depreciated because of change in the process of production i.e. obsolescence)			

QUESTION 30: A company is engaged in the manufacture of electronic products and systems. As per Chief Accountant a prototype system was installed at one of the customer's locations in June 2014 for getting acceptance on the performance of the system. The Chief Accountant has stated that as the ownership of the system installed for field trials was vested with the company for accounting and control purposes, the prototype system installed at customer's location in 2014 was capitalized in the accounts for the year 2014-2015 at its bought-out cost. State whether the accounting treatment adopted by the company is correct or not?

ANSWER:

PROVISION OF AS 10

As per para 3 of AS-2 'Valuation of invemtories', inventories mean assets held for sale in the ordinary course of business, or in the process of production for which sale, or for consumption in the production of goods or services for sale, including maintenance supplies and consumables other than machinery spares.

And as per para 6.1 of 10 'Accounting for fixed assets', fixed asset is an asset held with the intention of being used for the purpose of producing of providing goods or services and is not held for sale in the normal course of business.

ADVICE

Accordingly, the system installed by the company at customer's site for the acceptance, based on the field trials of the system, is an item of inventory, and is not a fixed asset. Installation of such prototype system at customers' sites for their acceptance is akin to sale of goods on approval basis. Therefore, the capitalisation of such prototype system is at its bought-out-cost is not correct.

At the time of installation of such systems at the customers' site, value of the same should be transferred to a separate account such as 'Goods sent for approval account'.

As it does not qualify the definition of fixed assets, therefore, no depreciation can be charged on it.

QUESTION 31: In the notes to accounts of C Co. Ltd. as on 31-03-2015 Note No. 11 states that 'Certain machinery items are lying at customer warehouses and company has paid ₹1000 lakhs up to 30-0-6-2014 as detention changes, out of which a sum of ₹ 600 lakhs is written back during the year 2014-2015 based on settlement with the concemed authorities in respect of a major spares of machinery. For the remaining machinery items negotiations are pending and a provision of ₹ 50 lakhs is made. As such total amount of ₹ 450 lakhs paid/provided on account of detention charges have been capitalized and included in the Fixed Assets/Capital work in progress. The management is of the view that these expenses are directly attributable to the acquisition of the related Fixed Asset. Comment.

ANSWER:

PROVISION OF AS 10

As per AS 10 "Accounting for Fixed Assets", the cost of an item of fixed asset comprise its purchase price, including import duties and other non-refundable taxes or levies and any directly attributable cost of bringing the asset to its working condition for its intended use.

ADVICE

Generally, detention charges represent an abnormal expenditure, as these expenditures are not directly attributable to the cost of asset.

The auditor will quality the report appropriately in the paragraph before stating that the balance sheet gives that and fair view and the Profit and Loss Account show true and fair profit to the year ending on 31-03-2015. The qualification will be as follows:

"Attention is invited to Note No. 11 regarding Capitalization of detention charges to ₹450 lakhs during the year and on account of delays in respect of clearing from custom werehouses for certain machinery items". In our opinion the detention charge are not directly attributable to the acquisition of related fixed assets. The said amount of ₹450 lakhs should have been written off in the Profit & Loss Account. Had these expenses been so written off the profit for the year would have been lower by ₹ 450 lakhs and Reserves & Surplus as well as Fixed Assets/Capital WIP would have been lower by ₹450 lakhs.

QUESTION 32: Tulsian Ltd. provides in the following information:

1. On 01.04.2014 Book Value of Plant and Machinery ₹ 10,00,000
2. On 01.04.2014, out of the above a Machine having book value ₹2,00,000 has been retired from use and held for disposal. The net realizable value of the same is ₹ 20,000.
3. On 01.04.2014 Book value of old Machine No. 1 exchanged for ₹ 1,00,000. Additional cash given for exchange of asset ₹ 10,000, Fair market value of new Machine No. 100 acquired in exchange of old Machine is ₹ 40,000
4. On 01.04.2014 Issued 1,00,000 equity shares of ₹ 10 each (fully paid up) in consideration for supply of a machinery by PQR Ltd. The shares exchanged for machinery are quoted on National Stock Exchange (NSE) at ₹ 25 per share, at the time of transaction
5. Rate of depreciation is 10% p.a. on WDV basis
6. Goodwill was valued at ₹1,20,000 by independent valuers and no consideration was paid. The Company has not yet recorded the same.

Required: Prepare the Journal for the year 2014-2015. How will you dislose the relevent items in the Financial Statements of the company.

ANSWER:

JOURNAL

Date	Particulars		Dr. (₹)	Cr. (₹)
01.04.2014	Profit & Loss A/c	...Dr.	1,80,000	
	To Plant and Machinery A/c			1,80,000
	(Being the Loss on retirement charged to P & L A/c)			

01.04.2014	New Asset A/c ...Dr. To Bank A/c To Old Asset A/c (Being the cost of asset acquired is recorded at its fair market value)	40,000	 10,000 30,000
01.04.2014	Old Asset A/c ...Dr. To Profit & Loss A/c (Being credit balance in Old Asset A/c is transferred to P&L A/c)	70,000	 70,000
01.04.2014	Machinery A/c ...Dr. To Share Capital A/c To Securities Premium A/c (Being machinery recorded at the fair market value of the securities issued in consideration for machinery acquired)	25,00,000	 10,00,000 15,00,000
31.03.2015	Depreciation A/c ...Dr. To Plant and Machinery A/c [Being the Depreciation provided @10% on ₹ 32,40,000(i.e. 10,00,000 – 2,00,000 – 1,00,000 + 40,000 + 25,00,000)]	3,24,000	 3,24,000
31.03.2015	Profit & Loss A/c ...Dr. To Depreciation A/c (Being the T/F of Depreciation A/c to P & L A/c)	3,24,000	 3,24,000

AN EXTRACT OF STATEMENT OF PROFIT & LOSS FOR THE YEAR ENDED 31.03.2015

Loss on retirement	₹ 1,80,000
Loss on Exchange of an Old Machine	₹ 70,000
Depreciation on Plant and Machinery	₹ 3,24,000

AN EXTRACT OF BALANCE SHEET AS AT 31.03.2015

Share Capital (Issued for Consideration other than Cash)	₹ 10,00,000
Reserves & Surplus (Securities Premium)	₹ 25,00,000
Plant and Machinery	₹ 32,40,000
Machine retired from use and held for disposal(at NRV)	₹ 20,000

Treatment of Goodwill: As per para 16 of AS 10 'Accounting for Fixed Assets' goodwill is to be recorded only when some consideration in money or money's worth has been paid for it.; Since the goodwill is self generated and no money or money's worth has been paid for the same, therefore, it is not to be recorded in the books.

Note: As per para 11 of the AS 10, the new machine has been recorded at the Fair Market Value of the securities issued as it is more clearly evident.

QUESTION 33: Ascertain the value at which various items of Fixed Assets are to be shown in the Financial Statements of Velvet Ltd. and amount to be debited to the Profit and Loss Account in the context of the relevant Acounting Standard.

Narrations for the adjustments made should form part of the answer:

(i) **Goodwill was valued at ₹1,20,000 by independent valuers and no consideration was paid. The Company has not yet recorded the same.**

(ii) **Balance of Office Equipment as on 01.04.2013 is ₹ 1,20,000. On 01.04.2013, out of the above office equipment having book value ₹20,000 has been retired from use and held for disposal. The net realizable value of the same is ₹ 2,000. Rate of depreciation is 15% p.a. on WDV basis.**

(iii) **Book Value of Plant and Machinery as on 01.04.2013 was ₹ 7,20,000. On 01.08.2013 an item of machinery was purchased in exchange for 500 equity shares of face value ₹10. The Fair Market value of the equity shares on 01.08.2013 was ₹120. Rate of depreciation is 10% p.a. on WDV basis.**

ANSWER:

TREATMENT AND VALUE OF VARIOUS ITEMS OF FIXED ASSETS

Item of Fixed Assets (₹)		Amount Debited to P & L in current year	Amount	Narration	Closing Balance to be shown in the Financial Statements
(i) Goodwill		0			
Opening Balance					
Closing Balance					0
(ii) Office Equipment	1,20,000				
Opening Balance	20,000				
Less: Retired from use	1,00,000				
Less: Depreciation @ 15%	15,000		15,000	Depreciation	
Closing Balance	85,000				
Office Equipment (Retired from use)					85,000
Opening balance		20,000			
Less: Closing Balance (At NRV)		2,000			2,000
Loss on retirement charged to P&L		18,000	18,000	Loss on retirement of asset	
(iii) Plant and Machinery	7,20,000				7,04,000
Opening Balance	60,000				
Add: Machine purchased					
	7,80,000				
Less: Depreciation					
on old machine	72,000				
On New machine	4,000	76,000	76,000	Depreciation	
Closing Balance		7,04,000			
		1,09,000			7,91,000

Notes:

1. As per para 16 of AS 10 'Accounting for Fixed Assets' goodwill is to be recorded only when some consideration in money or money's worth has been paid for it.; Since the goodwill is self generated and no money or money's worth has been paid for the same, therefore, it is not to be recorded in the books.
2. Office equipment having book value of ₹ 20,000 has been retired from use. As per Para II of AS 10 It has been recorded at Net Realisable Value (NRV) as the NRV is lower than the book value and shown separatley in the financial statements.
3. As per para 11 of the AS 10, the new machine has been recorded at the Fair Market Value of the securities issued as it is more clearly evident.

10 AS 13 – ACCOUNTING FOR INVESTMENTS

THEORETICAL BASE

QUESTION 1: What are the areas in which AS – 13 is not applicable?

ANSWER:

1. The bases for recognition of interest, dividends and rentals earned on investments which are covered by Accounting Standard 9 on Revenue Recognition;
2. Operating or Finance Leases;
3. Investments of Retirement Benefit Plans and Life Insurance Enterprises; and
4. Mutual Funds and/or the related asset management companies, banks and public financial institutions formed under a Central or State Government Act or so declared under the Companies Act, 1956.

QUESTION 2: What is meant by term 'Investments'?

ANSWER: Investments are assets held by an enterprise for earning income by way of dividends, interest, and rentals, for capital appreciation, or for other benefits to the investing enterprise.

Note: *Assets held as stocks - in - trade are not 'Investments'.*

QUESTION 3: What is meant the term 'Market Value'?

ANSWER: Market value is the amount obtainable from the sale of an investment in an open market, net of expenses necessarily to be incurred on or before disposals.

QUESTION 4: What is meant by the term 'Fair value'?

ANSWER: Fair value is the amount for which an asset could be exchanged between a knowledgeable, willing buyer and a knowledgeable, wiling seller in an arm's length transaction. Under appropriate circumstances, market value net or net realizable value provides an evidence of fair value.

QUESTION 5: What are the components of Cost of Investments?

ANSWER: Cost of Investments includes:

1. Purchase Price;
2. Acquisition charges such as brokerage, fees and duties.

QUESTION 6: What shall be Cost of Investment if it is acquired wholly or partly by the issue of shares or other securities?

ANSWER:

Cost of Investments = Fair Value of the securities issued (which in appropriate cases may be indicated by the issue price as determined by statutory authorities).

Note: *The fair value may not necessarily be equal to the nominal or par value of the securities issued.*

QUESTION 7: What shall be the cost of investments if it is acquired in exchange or part exchange, for another asset?

ANSWER:

Cost of Investments = Either Fair Value of the asset given up or Fair Value of the investment acquired if it is more clearly evident.

QUESTION 8: What is the Accounting Treatment of Interest, Dividends and Rentals earned on Investments?

ANSWER:

For Pre-acquisition period	• Should be credited to Investments Account
For Post-acquisition period	• Should be credited to Profit & Loss Account

QUESTION 9: What is the Cost of Investments when rights are subscribed?

ANSWER:

Case	Treatment
1. When rights entitlement is received because of existing holding and right shares are subscribed.	The cost of the right shares is added to the carrying amount of the original holding.
2. When rights entitlement is purchased and right shares are subscribed.	Cost incurred in purchasing the rights entitlement plus the subscription price of the right shares shall constitute the cost of right share.
3. When rights entitlement is received because of cum-right purchase of investment and right shares are subscribed.	The cost of the right shares is added to the cum-right purchase price of investment.

QUESTION 10: What should be the Accounting Treatment when rights are sold in the market?

ANSWER:

Case	Treatment
1. When rights entitlement is received because of existing holding and rights entitlement is sold in the market.	The sale proceeds are taken to the Profit and Loss Statement.
2. When rights entitlement is purchased and sold in the market.	Difference between the Purchase Price and Sale Price of the rights sold should be sold in the market.
3. When rights entitlement is received because of cum-right purchase of investment and rights entitlement is sold in the market. (a) Where the market value of investments immediately after their becoming ex-right is lower than the cost for which they were acquired. (b) Where the market value of investments immediately after their becoming ex-right is equal to the cost for which they were acquired.	(a) Sale proceeds of rights up to the reduction in the value of investment should be credited to investment account and balance sale proceeds should be taken to Profit and Loss Statement. (b) Sale Proceeds should be taken to Profit and Loss Statement.

QUESTION 11: State the meaning and accounting treatment of Current Investments.

ANSWER:

Meaning	A current investment is an investment that is by its nature readily realizable and is intended to be held for not more than one year from the date on which such investment is made.
Carrying	These should be carried **at the lower of cost and fair value** determined amount *either* on an individual investment basis *or* by category of investment, but not an overall (or global) basis.
Reduction & Reversal	Any reduction to fair value and any reversals of such reductions should be debited or credited to the Profit and Loss Statement.

QUESTION 12: State the meaning and accounting treatment of Long-term Investments.

ANSWER:

Meaning	A long-term investment is an investment other than a current investment.
Carrying	These should be carried **at cost**. However, provision for diminution Amount shall be made to recognize a decline, other than temporary, in the value of the investments, such reduction being determined and made for each investment individually.
Reduction	Any reduction in the carrying amount and any reversals of & Reversal such reductions should be charged or credited to the Profit and Loss Statement.

QUESTION 13: State the meaning and accounting treatment of Investment Properties.

ANSWER:

Meaning	An investment property is an investment in land or buildings that are not intended to be occupied substantially for use by, or in the operations of, the investing enterprise.
Accounting	As long term investments.
Cost of any Shares in a co-operative Society/a Company	The cost of any shares in a co-operative society or a company, the holding of which is directly related to the right to hold the estment property, is added to the carrying amount of the investment property.

QUESTION 14: State the accounting treatment of of Disposal of An Investment.

ANSWER: The difference between the carrying amount and net disposal proceeds should be **charged or credited to the Profit and Loss Statement.**

QUESTION 15: State the Disclosure Requirements as to Investments as per AS 13.

ANSWER:

1. The accounting policies for determination of carrying amount of investments;
2. Classification of investments
3. The amounts included in Profit and Loss Statement for:
   (i) Interest, Dividends (showing separately dividends from subsidiary companies), and rentals on Investments showing separately such income from long-term and current investments. Gross income should be stated, the amount of income tax deducted at a source being included under Advance Tax Paid;
   (ii) Profits and Losses on disposal of Current Investments and changes in the carrying amount of such investments; and

(iii) Profits and Losses on disposal of long-term investments and changes in the carrying amount of such investments.

4. Significant restrictions on the right of ownership, realisability of investments or the remittance of income and proceeds of disposals;
5. The aggregate amount of quoted and unquoted investments, giving the aggregate market value of quoted investments;
6. Other disclosures as specifically required by the relevant statute governing the enterprise.

PRACTICAL QUESTIONS FOR PRACTICE

QUESTION 1:

Par Value of Shares	**₹ 18,000**
Fair Market Value of Shares	**₹ 20,000**
Fair Market value of an Investment acquired	**₹ 25,000**
Additional Cash Given for acquisition of an Investment	**₹ 4,000**

Determine the Cost of Investment acquired and show the accounting treatment in this regard.

ANSWER:

JOURNAL

Date	Particulars	Dr. (₹)	Cr. (₹)
	Investment A/c ...Dr.	₹ 24,000	
	To Bank A/c		₹ 4,000
	To Equity Share Capital A/c		₹18,000
	To Securities Premium A/c		₹ 2,000
	(Being the Cost of Investment acquired recorded at the Fair Value of Shares issued)		

QUESTION 2:

Book Value of Old Asset given up	**₹ 18,000**
Fair Market Value of old asset exchanged	**₹ 20,000**
Fair Market Value of an investment acquired in exchange of old asset	**₹ 25,000**
Additional Cash given for acquisition of an investment	**₹ 4,000**

Determine the cost of investment acquired and show the accounting treatment in this regard.

ANSWER:

1st Alternative

JOURNAL

Date	Particulars	Dr. (₹)	Cr. (₹)
	Investment A/c ...Dr.	₹ 24,000	
	To Bank A/c		₹ 4,000
	To Old Asset A/c		₹ 20,000
	(Being the Cost of Investment acquired recorded at the Fair Market Value of Asset given up and adjusted for payment)		

	Old Asset A/c ...Dr. To Profit & Loss A/c. (Being the Excess of Fair Market Value over Book Value transferred to P & L A/c)	₹ 2,000	₹ 2,000

2nd Alternative

JOURNAL

Date	Particulars	Dr. (₹)	Cr. (₹)
	Investment A/c ...Dr. To Bank A/c To Old Asset A/c (Being the Cost of Investment acquired recorded at its Fair Market Value)	₹ 25,000	₹ 4,000 ₹ 21,000
	Old Asset A/c ...Dr. To Profit & Loss A/c. (Being the credit balance in Old Asset A/c transferred to P&L A/c)	₹ 3,000	₹ 3,000

QUESTION 3:

Cum - right purchase price of 100 shares on 1st Feb. 2015 **₹ 15,000**

Rights sold on 1st March 2015 **₹ 4,000**

Show the treatment of sale proceeds of rights if:

Ex - right purchase price of 100 shares on 31st Mar. 2015.

(a) **₹ 11,000**

(b) **₹ 12,000**

(c) **₹ 15,000**

(d) **₹ 16,000**

ANSWER:

Case	Amount to be transferred to the credit of Investment Account	Amount to be transferred to the credit of Profit & Loss Account
(a)	₹ 4,000	NIL
(b)	₹ 3,000	₹ 1,000
(c)	NIL	₹ 4,000
(d)	NIL	₹ 4,000

QUESTION 4: Mention two categories of investments defined by AS 13 and also state their valuation principles.

ANSWER: As per para 7 and 8 of AS 13 'Accounting for Investments', there are two categories of investments, viz., Current Investments and Long Term Investments. According to para 14 of the standard, the carrying amount for current investments is the lower of cost and fair value whereas para 17 states that Long Term Investments are valued at cost less permanent diminutions in value of investment. For current investments, para 16 of the standard states that, any reduction to fair value and any reversals of such reductions are included in the profit and loss statement.

QUESTION 5: Rose Ltd. had made an investment ot ₹ 500 lakhs in the equity shares of Nose Ltd. on 10.01. 2015. The realisable value of such investment, on 31.03.2015 became ₹.200 lakhs as Nose Ltd. lost a case of patent rights. Rose Ltd. follows financial year as accounting year. How will you recognize this reduction in Financial statements for the year 2014-2015.

ANSWER: Recognition of reduction in value of investment would depend upon the nature of investment and nature of decline as per Accounting Standard 13 "Accounting for Investments". As per provisions of the standard, if the investments were acquired for long term and decline is temporary in nature, reduction in value will not be recognized and investments would be carried at cost. If the decline is of permanent nature, it will be charged to Profit and Loss Account. If the investments are current investments, then the reduction should be recognized and charged to Profit and Loss Account as the current investments are carried at cost or fair value, *whichever is less.*

QUESTION 6: Innovative Garments Manufacturing Company Limited invested in the Shares of another Company on 1st October 2014, at a cost of ₹ 2,50,000. It also earlier purchased Gold of ₹ 4,00,000 and Silver of ₹ 2,00,000 on 1st March 2012. Market Value as on 31st March 2015 of above Investments are: Shares ₹ 2,25,000, Gold ₹ 6,00,000 and Silver ₹ 3,50,000.

How will the above Investments be shown in the books of accounts of Innovative Garments Manufacturing Limited for the year ending 31st March 2015, as per the provisions of AS-13?

ANSWER:

TREATMENT AS PER AS 13

Type of Investment	Valuation Principle	Carrying Amount
Equity Shares	Lower of Cost *or* Market Value	₹ 2,25,000
Gold	Cost (Long Term Investment, since the asset is held for more than 3 years)	₹ 4,00,000
Silver	Cost (Long Term Investment, since the asset is held for more than 3 years)	₹ 2,00,000
	Total	₹ 15,50,000

QUESTION 7: A unquoted long term investment is carried in the books at its cost of ₹ 5 lakhs. The Published Accounts of the unlisted company received in May, 2015 showed that the company was incurring cash losses with declining market share and the long term investment may not fetch more than ₹ 80,000.

ANSWER:

PROVISION OF AS 13

Investments classified as long term investments should be carried in the financial statements at cost. However, provision for diminution shall be made to recognise a decline, other than temporary, in the value of the investments, such reduction being determined and made of each investment individually. Para 17 to AS 13 'Accounting for Investments' states that indicators of the value of an investment are obtained by reference to its market value, the investee's assets and results and the expected cash flows from the investments.

ADVICE

The facts of the given case clearly suggest that the provision for diminution should be made to reduce the carrying amount of long term investment to ₹ 80,000 in the financial statements for the year ended 31st March, 2015.

PROVISION OF AS 30

As per AS 30, An Impairment Loss should be recognised in the Statement of Profit and Loss if there is an objective evidence that an impairment loss has been incurred on an unquoted equity instrument that is not carried at fair value.

ADVICE

Hence, An Impairment Loss of ₹ 4,20,000 (i.e.₹ 5,00,000 –₹ 80,000) should be recognised in the Statement of Profit and Loss for the year ended 31st March, 2015.

QUESTION 8: Anischit Finance Ltd. is a non-banking finance company. It makes available to you the costs and market price of various investments held by it for Trading as on 31.3.2015.

Particulars		(Figures in ₹ Lakhs)
	Cost	Market Price
Scripts:		
A. Equity Shares		
A	60.00	61.20
B	31.50	24.00
C	60.00	36.00
D	60.00	120.00
E	90.00	105.00
F	75.00	90.00
G	30.00	6.00
B. Mutual funds		
MF-1	39.00	24.00
MF-2	30.00	21.00
MF-3	6.00	9.00
C. Government Securities-		
GV-1	60.00	66.00
GV-2	75.00	72.00

(i) Can the company adjust depreciation of a particular item of investments within a category?

(ii) What should be the value of investments as on 31.3.2015?

(iii) Is it possible of off-set depreciation investment in mutual funds against appreciation of the value of investment in equity shares and government securities?

ANSWER:

(i) Quoted current investments for each category shall be valued at cost of market value, whichever is lower. For this purpose, the investments in each category shall be considered scrip-wise and the cost and market value aggregated for all investments in each category. If the aggregate market value for the category is less than the aggregate cost for that category, the net depreciation shall be provided for or charged to the profit and loss account. If the aggregate market value for the category exceeds the aggregate cost for the category, the net appreciation shall be ignored. Therefore, depreciation of a particular item of investments can be adjusted within the same category in investments.

(ii) Value of investments as on 31.3.2015

Type of investment	Valuation Principle	Value ₹ in lakhs
Equity Shares (Aggregated)	Lower of cost or market Value	406.50
Mutual Funds	NAV (market value, assumed)	54.00
Government securities	Cost	135.00
		595.50

As per par 14 of AS 13 "Accounting for investments", the carrying amount for current investments is the lower of cost and market price. Sometimes, the concern of an enterprise may be with the value of a category of related current investments and not with each individual investments, and accordingly, the investments may be computed at the lower of cost and market value computed category wise.

(iii) Inter category adjustments of appreciation and depreciation in values of investments cannot be done. It is possible to offset depreciation in investment in mutual funds against appreciation of the value of investments in equity shares and Government securities.

PROVISION OF AS 30

As per AS 30 Financial Instrument should be measured at Fair Value on the Date of Acquisition and on Subsequent Measurement. Any Gain or Loss on Subsequent Measurement is to be recognised in the Statement of Profit and Loss.

ADVICE

A. Total Maket Value of Investments = 61.2 + 24 + 36 + 120 + 105 + 90 + 6 + 24 + 21 + 9 + 66 + 72 = ₹ 634.2 lakhs

B. Total Cost of Investments = 60 + 31.5 + 60 + 60 + 90 + 75 + 30 + 39 + 30 + 6 + 60 + 75 = ₹ 616.5 lakhs

C. Total Gain [A – B] = ₹ 17.7 lakhs

Total Gain of ₹ 17.7 lakhs) should be recognised in the Statement of Profit and Loss for the year ended 31st March, 2015.

QUESTION 9: Suram Ltd. wants to re-classify its investment in accordance with AS 13. Decide on the treatment to be given in each of the following cases.

(i) A portion of Current Investments purchased for ₹ 20 lakhs to be reclassified as long-term investments, as the company has decided to retain them. The market value as on the date of Balance Sheet was ₹ 25 lakhs.

(ii) Another portion of Current Investments purchased for ₹ 15 lakhs has to be reclassified as Long-term Investments. The market value of these Investments as on the date of Balance Sheet was ₹ 6.5 Lakhs.

(iii) Certain Long-term Investments no longer considered for holding purposes have to be re-classified as Current Investments. The original cost of these was ₹ 18 lakhs but they had been written down to ₹ 12 lakhs to recognize permanent decline as per AS 13.

ANSWER: As per Para 24 of AS 13 'Accounting for Investments', where investments are reclassified from current to long-term, transfers are made at the lower of cost and fair value at the date to transfer.

(i) The market value of the investments is ₹ 25 Lakhs, which is higher than its cost i.e., ₹ 20 lakhs. Therefore, the transfer to long term investments should be carried at cost i.e., ₹ 20 lakhs.

(ii) The market value of the investment is ₹ 6.5 lakhs, which is lower than its cost i.e., ₹ 15 lakhs. Therefore, the transfer to long term investments should be carried in the books at the market value i.e., ₹ 6.5 lakhs. The loss of ₹ 8.5 lakhs should be charged to Profit and Loss account.

(iii) As per para 23 of AS 13, where long-term investments are reclassified as current investments, transfer are made at the lower of cost and carrying amount at the date of transfer.

The book value for the investment is ₹ 12 lakhs, which is lower than its cost i.e., ₹ 18 lakhs. Here, the transfer should be at carrying amount and hence this reclassified current investments should be carried at ₹ 12 lakhs.

PROVISION OF AS 30

As per AS 30 Financial Instrument should be measured at Fair Value on the Date of Acquisition and on Subsequent Measurement. Any Gain or Loss on Subsequent Measurement is to be recognised in the Statement of Profit and Loss.

ADVICE

(i) Gain of ₹ 5 lakhs should be recognised in the Statement of Profit and Loss.

(ii) Loss of ₹ 8.5 lakhs should be recognised in the Statement of Profit and Loss.

(ii) Loss of ₹ 6 lakhs should be recognised in the Statement of Profit and Loss.

QUESTION 10: Albert Finance Ltd, has made the following investments.

(i) Purchased the following equity shares from stock exchange on 1st June, 2014.

Particulars	Cost
Scrip X	1,80,000
Scrip Y	50,000
Scrip Z	1,70,000
	4,00,000

(i) Purchased gold of ₹ 3,00,000 on 1st April, 2011.

(iii) Invested in mutual funds at a cost of ₹ 6,00,000 on 31st March, 2014.

(iv) Purchased government securities at a cost of ₹ 5,00,000 on 1st April, 2014.

How will you treat these investments as per applicable AS in the books of the company for the year ended on 31st March, 2015, if the values of these investments are as follows:

Shares		
Scrip X	1,90,000	
Scrip Y	40,000	
Scrip Z	70,000	3,00,000
Gold		5,00,000
Mutual Funds		4,50,000
Government securities		7,00,000

Also explain is it possible to off-set depreciation in investment in mutual funds against appreciation of the value of investment in government securities?

ANSWER:

PROVISION OF AS 13

As per As 13 'Accounting for Investment' current investments should be carried in the financial statements at lower of cost and fair value determined either on an individual investment basis or by category of investment but not on an overall (or global) basis and long-term investments are carried at cost except when there is a decline, other than temporary, in the value of a long term investment, the carrying amount is reduced to recognize the decline.

ADVICE

(i) If the investment in shares is intended to he held for not more than one year from the date on which such investment is made: Scrip X should be valued at cost, i.e., ₹ 1,80,000 (lower of cost and fair value); Scrip Y should be valued at fair value, i.e., ₹ 40,000 (lower of cost and fair value) and Scrip Z should be valued at fair value i.e., ₹ 70,000 (lower of cost and fair value). The total loss of ₹ 1,00,000 (₹ 4,00,000 – ₹ 3,00,000) on scrip purchased on 1st June, 2014, is to be charged to Profit and Loss Account for the year ended 31st March, 2015.

If investment is intended to be held for long term period: Investment will continue to be shown at cost in the Balance sheet of the company. However, provision for diminution shall be made to recognize a decline, other than temporary, in the value of investments, such reduction being determined and made for each investment individually.

(ii) Investment in gold (purchased in April, 2011) shall continue to be shown at cost of ₹ 3,00,000 in the balance sheet as on 31.3.2015.

(iii) If mutual funds are intended to be held for short term period it will be valued at ₹ 4,50,000 as on 31st March, 2015 and if its is intended to be held for long term, then it should be valued at its cost i.e., ₹ 6,00,000.

(iv) Value of government securities (Purchased on 1st April, 2014) is to shown at cost of ₹ 5,00,000 in the balance sheet as on 31.3.2015.

Inter category adjustments of appreciation and depreciation in value of investments cannot be done. It is not possible to offset depreciation in investment in mutual funds against appreciation in value of investment in government securities.

PROVISION OF AS 30

As per AS 30 Financial Instrument should be measured at Fair Value on the Date of Acquisition and on Subsequent Measurement. Any Gain or Loss on Subsequent Measurement is to be recognised in the Statement of Profit and Loss.

ADVICE

A. Total Maket Value of Investments(except Gold)=1.9+0.4+0.7+4.5+7=₹ 14.5 lakhs

B. Total Cost of Investments(except Gold)=15 lakhs

Total Loss of ₹ 0.5 lakh should be recognised in the Statement of Profit and Loss.

Gold (not being a Financial Instrument) shall continue to appear at cost of ₹ 3 lakhs.

QUESTION 11: ABC Ltd. has acquired 100% of the equity shares of Company 'X' during 2012. Company 'X' is a defunct company. The net worth of the Company 'X' is represented by land and building it owns. ABC Ltd acquired the shares of Company 'X' only for the land and building owned by it. ABC Ltd. had proposed to start a software development facility at this site at the time of share purchase. The software development facility has not yet been set up, as Company's existing facility itself is under utilized.

In the financials of the year 2013, the above investment was classified fixed assets under the head 'land and building' to reflect the substance of the transaction, as the intention to acquire the shares was to use the land and building owned by Company 'X'.

During the year 2015, the Company has decided to sell these shares and has passed a reANSWER authorizing the chairman to negotiate and settle the price. As of March 2015, this investment is reflected as fixed assets in the books. The property is prime one and is an ideal one for setting up new software units, ware houses etc.

(a) Should the above shares be classified under investments or is the current treatment of grouping it under fixed assets correct?

(b) If the current treatment of disclosing the shares as land and building is correct, should we disclose the same as assets held for disposal, with appropriate classification and disclosures?

ANSWER:

PROVISION OF AS 13

AS per AS 1 'Disclosure of Accounting, Policies 'The substance of the transaction is an investment in fixed assets, through the "form" is acquisition of shares.

ADVICE

(a) In the given case, the acquisition of shares in Company X was with the sole motive of using the land and buildings, and not for earning income by way of dividends.

In view of this, the accounting treatment so far accorded by the Company, in classifying the shares as fixed assets is correct.

(b) Since the original intention has undergone a change, therefore, on account of the changed intention, i.e., "to dispose of the shares", the accountant should reclassify the holding in the Company X as investments as available for sale and bring the same in the books at Fair Value if it is reliably determinable otherwise at carrying amount.

QUESTION 12: JVR Limited has made investment of ₹ 97.84 Crores in Equity Shares of QSR Limited in pursuance of Joint Venture agreement in 2015-2016. The investment has been made at par. QSR Limited has been in continuous losses for the last 2 years. JVR Limited is willing to re–assess the carrying amount of its investment in QSR Limited and wish to provide for diminution in value of investment. However, QSR Limited has futuristic and profitable business plans and projection for the coming years. Discuss whether the connection of JVR Limited to bring down the Carrying Amount of Investment in QSR Limited is in accordance with Accounting Standards

ANSWER:

PROVISION OF AS 13

(i) **Carrying Amount:** Long–Term Investments are usually carried at Cost.

(ii) **Basis:** Long–Term Investments are of individual importance to an enterprise. So, the Carrying Amount is determined on an individual basis.

(iii) **Decline in Value:**

(a) When there is a permanent decline in the value of a long–term investment, the Carrying Amount is reduced in order to recognise the decline. The reduction in value shall be determined and made for each investment individually.

(b) Temporary Fall in the value of long–term investments need not be provided for.

ADVICE

If QSR Ltd has demonstrative future maintainable profits, then the present losses can be considered as "Temporary" in nature. Hence as there is no permanent decline in the value, there is no need for creating any provision for loss on value of investments.

QUESTION 13: K Ltd. had 5 subsidiaries as at 31st March 2015 and the investments in-subsidiaries are considered as long term and valued at cost. Two of the subsidiaries net worth eroded as at 31st March 13 and the prospects of their recovery are very bleak and the other three subsidiaries are doing exceptionally well. The company did not provide for the decline in the value of investments in two subsidiaries because the overall investment portfolio in subsidiaries did not suffer any decline' as the other three subsidiaries are doing exceptionally well. Comment.

ANSWER:

PROVISION OF AS 13

As per AS 13, "Accounting for Investments" long-term investments are usually of individual importance to the investing enterprise. The carrying amount of long-term investments is therefore determined on an individual investment basis. Investments classified as long term investments should be carried in the financial statements at cost. However, provision for diminution shall be made to recognize a decline, other than temporary, in the value of the investments, such reduction being determined and made for each investment individually.

ADVISE

K Ltd should provide for the decline in the value of investments in two subsidiaries despite the fact that the overall investment portfolio in subsidiaries did not suffer any decline.

QUESTION 14: Blue-chip Equity Investments Ltd., wants to re-classify its investments in accordance with AS 13.

(i) Long term investments in Company A, costing ₹ 8.5 lakhs are to be re-classified as current. The comp0any had reduced the value of these investments to ₹ 6.5 lakhs to recognize a permanent decline in value. The fair value on date of transfer is ₹ 6.8 lakhs.

(ii) Long term investments in Company B, costing ₹ 7 lakhs are to be re-classified as current. The fair value on date of transfer is ₹ 8 lakhs and book value is ₹ 7 lakhs.

(iii) Current investment in Company C, costing ₹ 10 lakhs are to be re-classified as long term as the company wants to retain them. The market value on date of transfer is ₹ 12 lakhs.

(iv) Current investment in Company D, costing ₹ 15 lakhs are to be re-classified as long term. The market value on date of transfer is ₹ 14 lakhs.

ANSWER:

As per AS 13 "Accounting for Investments", in case of reclassification of investment from long-term to current, transfer is to be made at lower of cost or carrying amount at the date of transfer. If investment is reclassified from current to long term, transfer is to be made at lower of cost and fair value. Keeping in view this provision, the answer is given below:

(i) Reclassification from Long term to Current: Cost is ₹ 8.5 Lakhs and carrying amount is ₹ 6.5 Lakhs. Hence transfer will be made at ₹ 6.5 Lakhs.

(ii) Reclassification from Long term to current: Cost is ₹ 7 Lakhs and carrying amount is ₹ 7 Lakhs. Hence transfer will be made at ₹ 7 Lakhs.

(iii) Reclassification from current to Long term: Cost is ₹ 10 Lakhs and Fair Value is ₹ 12 Lakhs. Hence transfer will be made at ₹ 10 Lakhs.

11 AS 14 – AMALGAMATION

THEORETICAL BASE

QUESTION 1. What are the two main methods of accounting for amalgamations?
ANSWER:

1. The Pooling of Interests Method	Under this Method, the Assets, Liabilities and Reserves of the transferor company are recorded by the transferee company at their existing carrying amounts after making the adjustments required in para 11 of AS-14 to ensure uniformity of accounting policies.
2. The Purchase Method	Under this Method, tthe Assets, Liabilities and Reserves of the transferor company are recorded by the transferee company at their existing carrying amounts **or** on the basis of their individual fair values on the date of amalgamation.

QUESTION 2. As per Accounting Standard-14, what are the conditions which must be satisfied for an amalgamation in the nature of merger?

ANSWER: According to AS-14 "Accounting for Amalgamations", Amalgamation in the nature of merger is an amalgamation which satisfies all the followings conditions:

1. Transfer of All Assets & Liabilities	All the assets and liabilities of the transferor company (i.e., the company which is amalgamated into another company) become, after amalgamation, the assets and liabilities of the transferee company (i.e., the company into which a transferor company is amalgamated).
2. Same Equity Shareholders Holding 90%	Shareholders holding at least 90% of the face value of the equity shares of the transferor company (other than the equity shares already held therein, immediately before the amalgamation, by the transferee company or its subsidiaries or their nominees) become equity shareholders of the transferee company by virtue of the amalgamation.
3. Purchase Consideration in Equity Shares	The consideration for the amalgamation receivable by those equity shareholders of the transferor company who agree to become equity shareholders of the transferee company is discharged by the transferee company wholly by the issue of equity shares in the transferee company, except that cash may be paid in respect of any fractional shares.
4. Same Business	The business of the transferor company is intended to be carried on, after the amalgamation, by the transferee company.
5.Recording of Assets & Liabilities at Book Values	No adjustment is intended to be made to the book values of the assets and liabilities of the transferor company when they are incorporated in the financial statements of the transferee company except to ensure uniformity of accounting policies.

QUESTION 3. State the Meaning of Purchase Consideration as per AS 13.

ANSWER: Consideration for the amalgamation means the aggregate of the shares and other securities issued and the payment made in the form of cash or other assets by the transferee company to the shareholders of the transferor company.

The analysis of the aforesaid definition of 'Purchase Consideration' makes it clear that the payments made by the transferee company to discharge the debentureholders and other outside liabilities and the reimbursement of cost of winding up of transferor company shall not be considered as part of purchase consideration.

QUESTION 4. What disclosures should be made in the first financial statements following the amalgamation?

ANSWER: As per Para 24 of AS 14 'Accounting for Amalgamations' states that for all amalgamations (whether for amalgamations accounted for under the pooling of interests method or amalgamations accounted for under the purchase method), the following disclosures are considered appropriate in the first financial statements following the amalgamation:

(a) Names and general nature of business of the amalgamating companies;
(b) Effective date of amalgamation for accounting purposes;
(c) The method of accounting used to reflect the amalgamation; and
(d) Particulars of the scheme sanctioned under a statute.

QUESTION 5. A Ltd. is amalgamating with B Ltd. They are undecided on the method of accounting to be followed. You are required to advice the management of B Ltd. on the method of accounting that can be adopted under AS-14.

ANSWER: An amalgamation may be either – an amalgamation in the nature of merger, or an amalgamation in the nature of purchase. The selection of method of accounting for amalgamation (pooling of interests or purchase method) is to be judged after considering the intentions of the both the companies.

If genuine pooling of all assets, liabilities, shareholders' interest is intended; separate businesses of both the companies are continued and their amalgamation scheme satisfies all the conditions necessary for merger as specified in AS 14 Accounting for Amalgamations, pooling of interests method is adopted. However, if B Ltd. or A Ltd. wants to acquire the other company, then purchase method needs to be adopted. In that case, the shareholders of the acquired company don't continue to have proportional share in equity of the combined company and the business of the acquired company is not intended to be continued. The object of the purchase method is to account for the amalgamation by applying the same principles as are applied in the normal purchase of assets.

Thus choice of accounting method depends on the fact whether B Ltd. wants to continue its business or not.

QUESTION 6. How shall Investment Allowance Reserve A/c of a transferor company be recorded in the books of transferee company if the amalgamation is in the nature of (a) Purchase (b) Merger?

ANSWER:

Date	Particulars	Dr. (₹)	Cr. (₹)
(a)	Amalgamation Adjustment A/c Dr.		
	To Investment Allowance Reserve A/c		
(b)	Assets (taken over)		
	To Liabilities (taken over)		
	To Investment Allowance Reserve A/c		
	To Business Purchase A/c		

QUESTION 7. How shall the Amalgamation Expenses incurred by transferee company be recorded in clase of amalgamation is the nature of (a) Purchase (b) Merger?

ANSWER:

Date	Particulars		Dr. (₹)	Cr. (₹)
(a)	Goodwill A/c	Dr.		
	To Bank A/c			
(b)	P&L A/c	Dr.		
	To Bank A/c			

QUESTION 8. How shall the profit included in unsold stock (sold by transferor Co.) of Transferee Co. be dealt with in case Amalgamation is in the nature of (a) Purchase (b) Merger?

ANSWER:

Date	Particulars		Dr. (₹)	Cr. (₹)
(a)	Goodwill A/c	Dr.		
	To Stock A/c			
(b)	P&L A/c	Dr.		
	To Stock A/c			

SECTION – C

QUESTIONS BASED ON REVISED SCHEDULE III TO THE COMPANIES ACT, 2013

QUESTIONS BASED ON SCHEDULE III TO THE COMPANIES ACT, 2013

THEORETICAL BASE

SPECIMEN OF STATEMENT OF PROFIT & LOSS

NAME OF THE COMPANY.........................
STATEMENT OF PROFIT AND LOSS FOR THE YEAR ENDED ....

	Particulars	*Note No.*	*Figures for the Current Reporting Period*	*Figures for the Previous Reporting Period*
			₹	₹
I.	Revenue from Operations	1	xxx	xxx
II.	Other Income	2	xxx	xxx
III.	**Total Revenue [I + II]**		xxx	xxx
IV.	**Expenses:**			
	Cost of Materials consumed	3	xxx	xxx
	Purchases of Stock-in-Trade		xxx	xxx
	Changes in Inventories	4	xxx	xxx
	Employee Benefits Expense	5	xxx	xxx
	Finance Costs	6	xxx	xxx
	Depreciation and Amortization Expense	7	xxx	xxx
	Other Expenses	8	xxx	xxx
	Total Expenses		xxx	xxx
V.	**Profit before Tax(III–IV)**		xxx	xxx
VI.	**Exceptional Items**		xxx	xxx
VII.	**Profit Before Extraordinary**		xxx	xxx
	Items and Tax (V – VI)			
VIII.	**Extraordinary Items**		xxx	xxx
IX.	**Profit before tax (VII – VIII)**		xxx	xxx
X.	**Tax Expense:**			
	(1) Current Tax		xxx	xxx
	(2) Deferred Tax		xxx	xxx
			xxx	xxx
XI.	**Profit (Loss) for the period**		xxx	xxx
XII.	**Earnings per Equity Share:**			

(1) Basic		xxx	xxx
(2) Diluted		xxx	xxx

Notes to Accounts:

NOTE 1: REVENUE FROM OPERATIONS

(a) From Sale of Products	xxx	xxx
(b) From Sale of Services	xxx	xxx
(c) From Other Operating Revenues [Trading Commission]	xxx	xxx
(d) *Less:* Excise Duty	(xxx)	(xxx)
	xxx	xxx

NOTE 2: OTHER INCOME

(a) Interest Income (in case of a company other than a finance company)	xxx	xxx
(b) Dividends From Subsidiary Companies	xxx	xxx
(c) Dividend Income From Companies other than Subsidiary Companies	xxx	xxx
(d) Net Gain/Loss on Sale of Investments [Gain – Loss)]	xxx	xxx
(e) Other Non-Operating Income (Net of Expenses directly attributable to such income) [Income – Expenses)]	xxx	xxx
(f) Net Gain on Foreign Currency Transaction of Translation (other than considered as Finance Cost)	xxx	xxx
	xxx	xxx

NOTE 3: COST OF MATERIALS CONSUMED

(a) Opening Stock of Materials	xxx	xxx
(b) *Add:* Purchases of Materials	xxx	xxx
(c) *Less:* Closing Stock of Materials	(xxx)	(xxx)
Cost of Materials consumed	xxx	xxx

NOTE 4: CHANGES IN INVENTORIES

Particulars	*Work-in-Progress* (₹)	*Finished Goods* (₹)	*Total*
Closing Stock	xxx	xxx	xxx
Less: Opening Stock	(xxx)	(xxx)	(xxx)
	xxx	xxx	xxx

NOTE 5: EMPLOYEE BENEFITS EXPENSE

Salaries and Wages	xxx	xxx
Contribution To Provident and Other Funds	xxx	xxx
Expense On Employee Stock Option Scheme (ESOP) and Employee Stock Purchase Plan (ESPP)	xxx	xxx

Staff Welfare Expenses	xxx	xxx
	xxx	xxx

NOTE 6: FINANCE COSTS

(a) Interest Expense	xxx	xxx
(b) Other Borrowing Costs	xxx	xxx
(c) Applicable Net Gain/Loss on Foreign Currency Transactions and Translation	xxx	xxx
	xxx	xxx

NOTE 7: DEPRECIATION AND AMORTIZATION EXPENSE

Buildings	xxx	xxx
Plant and Equipment	xxx	xxx
Vehicles	xxx	xxx
Office Equipment	xxx	xxx
Brands	xxx	xxx
Computer Software	xxx	xxx
	xxx	xxx

NOTE 8: OTHER EXPENSES

(a) Consumption of Stores and Spare Parts	xxx	xxx
(b) Power and Fuel	xxx	xxx
(c) Rent.	xxx	xxx
(d) Repairs to Buildings	xxx	xxx
(e) Repairs to Machinery	xxx	xxx
(f) Insurance	xxx	xxx
(g) Rates and Taxes [Excluding Taxes on Income]	xxx	xxx
(h) Miscellaneous Expenses	xxx	xxx
(i) Provisions for Losses of Subsidiary Companies	xxx	xxx
(j) Net Gain on Foreign Currency Transaction of Translation (other than considered as Finance Cost)	xxx	xxx
(k) Provisions, if material	xxx	xxx
(l) Withdrawl from Provisions, if material	xxx	xxx
(m) Expenditure on Corporate Social Responsibility (CSR)	xxx	xxx
(j) Payments to the Auditor as:		
(a) Auditor	xxx	xxx
(b) For Taxation Matters	xxx	xxx
(c) For Company Law Matters	xxx	xxx
(d) For Management Services	xxx	xxx
(e) For Other Services	xxx	xxx

(f) For Reimbursement of Expenses	xxx	xxx
	xxx	xxx

NOTE: SURPLUS I.E. BALANCE IN THE STATEMENT OF PROFIT AND LOSS TO BE TAKEN TO BALANCE SHEET

Opening Balance	xxx	xxx
Add: Profit for the period	xxx	xxx
Less: Transfer to Reserve	(xxx)	(xxx)
Less: Interim Dividend	(xxx)	(xxx)
Less: Proposed Preference Dividend	(xxx)	(xxx)
Less: Proposed Equity Dividend	(xxx)	(xxx)
Less: Dividend Distribution Tax	(xxx)	(xxx)
Closing Balance	xxx	xxx

Notes:

1. Any item of Income *or* Expenditure which exceeds **1% of the Revenue from Operations *or* ₹ 1,00,000, *whichever is higher*** is to be disclosed separately.
2. The Statement of Profit and Loss shall also contain by way of a note the following information, namely:

(a) **Value of imports calculated on C.I.F. basis** by the company during the financial year in respect of—

I. Raw Materials; II. Components and spare parts; III. Capital Goods;

(b) **Expenditure in Foreign Currency** during the financial year on account of royalty, know-how, professional and consultation fees, interest, and other matters;

(c) **Total Value of all imported raw materials, spare parts and components** consumed during the financial year and the total value of all indigenous raw materials, spare parts and components similarly consumed and the percentage of each to the total consumption;

(d) **The amount remitted during the year in Foreign Currencies** on account of dividends with a specific mention of the total number of Non-Resident Shareholders, the total number of shares held by them on which the dividends were due and the year to which the dividends related.

(e) **Earnings in Foreign Exchange** classified under the following heads, namely:—

I. Export of Goods calculated on F.O.B. basis;
II. Royalty, know-how, professional and consultation fees;
III. Interest and Dividend;
IV. Other Income, indicating the nature thereof.

FORM OF PREPARING A BALANCE SHEET OF A COMPANY

VERTICAL FORM OF BALANCE SHEET

Part I of Schedule III to The Companies Act, 2013 prescribes only vertical form of Balance Sheet.

GENERAL INSTRUCTIONS FOR PREPARATION OF BALANCE SHEET

1. Current Assets	An asset shall be classified as current when it satisfies any of the following **criteria**: (a) it is expected to be realized in, *or* is intended for sale *or* consumption in, the company's normal operating cycle; (b) it is held primarily for the purpose of being traded; *or*

	(c) it is expected to be realized within 12 months after the reporting date; or (d) it is cash *or* cash equivalent unless it is restricted from being exchanged *or* used to settle a liability for at least 12 months after the reporting date.
2. Non-Current Assets	All other assets shall be classified as non-current.
3. An Operating Cycle	An operating cycle is the time between the acquisition of assets for processing and their realization in cash *or* cash equivalents. Where the normal operating cycle cannot be identified, it is assumed to have a duration of 12 months.
3. Current Liabilities	A liability shall be classified as current when it satisfies **any of the following criteria:** (a) it is expected to be settled in the company's normal operating cycle; (b) it is held primarily for the purpose of being traded; (c) it is due to be settled within 12 months after the reporting date; *or* (d) the company does not have an unconditional right to defer settlement of the liability for at least twelve months after the reporting date. Terms of a liability that could, at the option of the counterparty, result in its settlement by the issue of equity instruments do not affect its classification.
4. Non-Current Liabilities	All other liabilities shall be classified as non-current.
5. Trade Receivable	A receivable shall be classified as a 'Trade Receivable' if it is in respect of the amount due on account of goods sold *or* services rendered in the normal course of business.
6. Trade Payable	A payable shall be classified as a 'Trade Payable' if it is in respect of the amount due on account of goods purchased *or* services received in the normal course of business.
7. Use of Prefix 'At' instead of 'On'	It may be noted that the prescribed form of Balance Sheet prefixes 'At' instead of 'On'. For example, if a Balance Sheet of X Ltd. is prepared on 31st march, then the date of the balance-sheet will be stated as 'At 31st March, 2015' and not as 'On 31st March, 2015. The word 'On' refers to the entire duration (which consists of 24 hours) of the day whereas the word 'At' refers to a specific point of time. Since the balance-sheet is prepared to represent the financial position of the concern at a particular point of time (viz. at the end of the day's business hours), it is **appropriate to use the word 'At' instead of 'On'.**

VERTICAL FORM OF SUMMARISED BALANCE SHEET [WITH MAJOR HEADINGS ONLY]

...NAME OF THE COMPANY...
BALANCE SHEET AS AT...

(Rupees in. ..)

Particulars	*Note No.*	*Figures for the Current Reporting Period*	*Figures for the Previous Reporting Period*
I. EQUITY AND LIABILITIES			
(1) Shareholders' Funds		xxx	xxx
(2) Share Application Money pending Allotment		xxx	xxx
(3) Non-Current Liabilities		xxx	xxx
(4) Current Liabilities		xxx	xxx
Total		xxx	xxx
II. ASSETS			
(1) Non-Current Assets		xxx	xxx
(2) Current Assets		xxx	xxx
Total		xxx	xxx

VERTICAL FORM OF DETAILED BALANCE SHEET

...NAME OF THE COMPANY...
BALANCE SHEET AS AT. ..

(Rupees in. ..)

Particulars	*Note No.*	*Figures for the Current Reporting Period*	*Figures for the Previous Reporting Period*
I. EQUITY AND LIABILITIES			
(1) Shareholders' Funds			
(a) Share Capital	1	....	....
(b) Reserves and Surplus [e.g. Debit Balance of Profit & Loss A/c as negative figure]	2	....	....
(c) Money received against Share Warrants		....	....
(2) Share Application Money pending Allotment		....	....
(3) Non-Current Liabilities			
(a) Long-term Borrowings [e.g. Bonds/ Debentures/Loans repayableafter 12 months]	3	....	....
(b) Deferred Tax Liabilities (Net)		....	....
(c) Other Long term Liabilities [e.g. Trade Payables to be settled after 12 months]		....	....

(d) Long-term Provisions [e.g. Provision for Employee Benefits to be settled after 12 months]		....	....
(4) Current Liabilities			
(a) Short-Term Borrowings [e.g. Loans repayable on demand *or* within 12 months]	4	....	....
(b) Trade Payables [e.g. Trade Creditors,Bills Payables to be settled within 12 months]	5	....	....
(c) Other Current Liabilities [e.g. Bank Overdraft,Unpaid Dividend/ matured Deposits/ matured Debentures, That portion of Long-term Borrowings repayable within 12 months, Interest accrued(whether due *or* not) on borrowings,Calls-in-Advance,Outstanding Expenses, Tax Payable]	6		
(d) Short-Term Provisions [e.g. Provision for Tax, Proposed Dividend, Provision for Employee Benefits to be settled within 12 months]	7	....	....
Total		....	....
II. ASSETS			
(1) Non-Current Assets			
(a) Fixed Assets			
(i) Tangible Assets [e.g. Land, Buildings, Plant & Equipment]	8	....	....
(ii) Intangible Assets [e.g.Goodwill Purchased, Goodwill on Consolidation,Brands/Trademarks]	9	....	....
(iii) Capital Work-in-Progress [e.g. Building under construction]		....	....
(iv) Intangible Assets under Development [e.g. Computer Software under Development]		....	....
(b) Non-Current Investments [e.g. Investment in Property/Partnership Firms]	10	....	....
(c) Deferred Tax Assets (Net)		....	....
(d) Long-Term Loans and Advances [e.g. Capital Advances, Security Deposits, Loans & Advances receivable after 12 months]	11	....	....

(e) Other Non-Current Assets [e.g.Unamortised Expenses like Discount/Loss on issue of Debentures to be amortised after 12 months, Amalgamation Adjustment A/c]	12	....	....
(2) Current Assets			
(a) Current Investments	13	....	....
(b) Inventories [e.g. Raw- Materials, Work-in-Progress, Finished Goods,Loose Tools,Stores & Spares]	14	....	....
(c) Trade Receivables [e.g. Trade Debtors,Bills Receivables to be realized within 12 months, Provision for Doubtful Debts by way of deduction]	15	....	....
(d) Cash and Cash Equivalents [e.g. Cheques/Drafts on hand, Bank Deposits with more than 12 months maturity]	16	....	....
(e) Short-term Loans and Advances [e.g. Loans & Advances receivable within 12 months]	17	....	....
(f) Other Current Assets [e.g.Prepaid Expenses]	18	....	....
Total		....	....

Notes To Accounts:

NOTE 1: SHARE CAPITAL

Particulars	₹	₹
Authorised Capital		
..... Shares of ₹. .. each	xxx	xxx
Issued Capital		
..... Shares of ₹. .. each	xxx	xxx
Subscribed Capital and fully paid		
..... Shares of ₹. .. each ₹. .. per share paid up	xxx	xxx
*Subscribed Capital but not fully paid		
..... Shares of ₹. .. each ₹. .. per share paid up	xxx	xxx
Less: Calls unpaid:		
(a) by Directors & Officers	(xxx)	(xxx)
(b) by Others	(xxx)	(xxx)
Add: Forfeited Shares	xxx	xxx
	xxx	xxx

Notes:

For the period of 5 years immediately preceding the date as at which the Balance Sheet is prepared

(a) Aggregate Number and Class of **Shares** allotted as fully paid up pursuant to a contract **without payments being received in cash**

(b) Aggregate Number and Class of **Shares** allotted as fully paid up by way of **Bonus Shares**

(c) Aggregate Number and Class of Shares bought back

2. Shares in the company held by each shareholder holding more than 5% shares specifying the number of shares
3. Shares Reserved for issue under options and contracts/commitments for the sale of shares/disinvestment, including the terms and amounts
4. Shares held by Holding Company/Ultimate Holding Company/Subsidiaries/Associates of Holding Company/Ultimate Holding Company.
5. **Reconciliation** of the No of shares outstanding at the beginning and at the end of the reporting period

	Particulars	*Figures for the Current Reporting Period*	*Figures for the Previous Reporting Period*
A.	Shares at the beginning of the year		
B.	*Add:* Shares allotted as fully paid up pursuant to a contract without payments being received in cash		
C.	*Add:* Shares issued on RIght/Preferential/Private Placement basis		
D.	*Add:* Shares allotted as fully paid up by way of Bonus Shares		
E.	*Add:* Shares Issued on exercise of Employee Stock Options		
F.	*Add:* Shares Issued on conversion/surrender of Debentures/Bonds/Term Loan.		
G.	*Less:* Shares cancelled on buy back of Shares		
H.	*Less:* Shares Foreited but not ressued during the current year		
I.	Shares at the end of the year		

***Note:** *Subscribed and Paid up Share Capital will include Unpaid Amount on Shares subscribed by Subscribers to Memorandum of Association and such Unpaid Amount will be disclosed under the head* **'Current Assets' and sub-head 'Other Current Assets'.**

NOTE 2: RESERVES AND SURPLUS

Particulars	₹	₹
Capital Reserve		
Capital Redemption Reserve		
Securities Premium Reserve		
Debenture Redemption Reserve		
Revaluation Reserve		
Share Options Outstanding Account		
Other Reserves – (specify the nature and purpose of each reserve and the amount in respect thereof)		
General Reserve, Dividend Equalisation Reserve, Reserve for Contingent Liabilities, Reserve for bad debts, Tonnage Tax Reserve created under the Income-tax Act, 1961.		

Surplus i.e. Balance in Statement of Profit & Loss		
Opening Balance		
Add: Profit for the period		
Less: Transfer to Reserve		
Less: Used for Bonus Shares		
Less: Interim Dividend		
Less: Proposed Preference Dividend		
Less: Proposed Equity Dividend		
Less: Dividend Distribution Tax		
Closing Balance		

Notes:

1. Debit Balance of Profit & Loss A/c is to be shown as negative figure.
2. Similarly Debit Balance of Reserve & Surplus is shown as negative figure.
3. 'Fund' is to be used if Reserve is earmarked for specific purpose.

NOTE 3: LONG-TERM BORROWINGS

Particulars	₹	₹
Bonds/Debentures		
Term Loans from Banks		
Term Loans from Other Parties		
Deferred Payment Liabilities		
Deposits		
Loans and Advances from Related Parties		
Long term Maturities of Finance Lease Obligations		
Other Loans and Advances (specify nature)		

Notes:

1. Aggregate Amount of Secured Borrowings along with Nature of security.
2. Aggregate Amount of Unsecured Borrowings
3. Aggregate Amount of Loans guaranteed by Directors *or* Others under each head
4. Bonds/debentures (along with the Rate of Interest and particulars of redemption *or* conversion, as the case may be) in descending order of maturity *or* conversion, starting from farthest redemption *or* conversion date, as the case may be. Where bonds/debentures are redeemable by installments, the date of maturity for this purpose must be reckoned as the date on which the first installment becomes due.
5. Particulars of any Redeemed Bonds/Debentures which the company has power to reissue shall be disclosed.
6. Terms of Repayment of Term Loans and Other Loans
7. Period and amount of continuing default as on the Balance Sheet Date in repayment of Loans and Interest

NOTE 4: SHORT-TERM BORROWINGS

Particulars	₹	₹
Loans repayable on demand from Banks		
Loans repayable on demand from Other Parties		

Loans and Advances from Related Parties		
Deposits		
Other Loans and Advances (specify nature)		

Notes:

1. Aggregate Amount of Secured Borrowings along with Nature of security and Unsecured Borrowings.
2. Aggregate Amount of Unsecured Borrowings
3. Aggregate Amount of Loans guaranteed by Directors *or* Others under each head
4. Period and amount of continuing default as on the Balance Sheet Date in repayment of Loans and Interest

NOTE 5: TRADE PAYABLES

Particulars	₹	₹
Sundry Creditors		
Bills Payables		

NOTE 6: OTHER CURRENT LIABILITIES

Particulars	₹	₹
Current maturities of Long-term Debt		
Current maturities of Finance Lease Obligations		
Interest accrued but not due on Borrowings		
Interest accrued and due on Borrowings		
Income received in advance		
Unpaid Dividends		
Application Money received for allotment of securities and due for refund and interest accrued thereon.		
Unpaid matured Deposits and Interest accrued thereon		
Unpaid matured Debentures and Interest accrued thereon		
Other Payables (specify nature e.g.)		
Bank Overdraft		
Outstanding Expenses		
Calls-in-Advance		

NOTE 7: SHORT-TERM PROVISIONS

Particulars	₹	₹
Provision for Employees' Benefit		
Provision for Income Tax		
Provision for Dividend Distribution Tax		
Proposed Equity Dividend		
Proposed Preference Dividend		

NOTE 8: TANGIBLE ASSETS

Asset	*Original Cost in the beg*	*Additions*	*Disposal*	*Original Cost at the end*	*Total Depreciation in the beg*	*Depreciation for Current year*	*Depreciation on Asset Disposed off*	*Total Depreciation at the end*	*W.D.V at the end*
A	*B*	*C*	*D*	*E = B + C − D*	*F*	*G*	*H*	*I = F + G − H*	*J = E − I*
Land									
Building									
Plant & Equipment									
Furniture and Fixtures									
Vehicles									
Office Equipment									
Others (specify nature)									
Assets under Lease									

Notes:

1. Impairment Losses/Reversals
2. Every Balance Sheet subsequent to date of Capital Reduction/Revaluation must show the reduced *or* increased figures and must by way of a note also show the amount of the reduction *or* increase together with the date thereof for the first 5 years subsequent to the date of such reduction *or* increase.

NOTE 9: INTANGIBLE ASSETS

Asset	*Original Cost in the beg*	*Additions*	*Disposal*	*Original Cost at the end*	*Total Depreciation in the beg*	*Depreciation for Current year*	*Depreciation on Asset Disposed off*	*Total Depreciation at the end*	*W.D.V at the end*
A	*B*	*C*	*D*	*E = B + C − D*	*F*	*G*	*H*	*I = F + G − H*	*J = E − I*
Goodwill									
Brands									
Trademarks									
Computer Software									
Mastheads and Publishing Titles.									
Mining Rights.									
Copyrights, and Patents and Other Intellectual Property Rights, Services & Operating Rights.									

Recipes, Formulae, Models, Designs and Prototypes.									
Licenses and Franchise.									
Others (Specify Nature).									

Notes: Same as for Tangible Assets

NOTE 10: NON-CURRENT INVESTMENTS

Particulars	₹	₹
Trade Investments		
Investment in Property		
Investments In Equity Instruments		
Investments In Preference Shares		
Investments In Government *or* Trust Securities		
Investments In Debentures *or* Bonds		
Investments In Mutual Funds		
Investments In Partnership Firms		
Other Non-Current Investments (Specify Nature)		

Notes:

1. Basis for Valuation in case of Investments carried at other than at cost
2. Aggregate amount of Quoted Investments and Market Value thereof;
3. Aggregate amount of Unquoted Investments;
4. Aggregate Provision for Diminution in Value of Investments

NOTE 11: LONG-TERM LOANS AND ADVANCES

Particulars	₹	₹
Capital Advances		
Security Deposits		
Loans and Advances to Related Parties		
Other Loans and Advances (specify nature)		

Notes:

1. Amount of Secured Loans & Advances considered good
2. Amount of Unsecured Loans & Advances considered good
3. Amount of Loans & Advances considered Doubtful
4. Allowance for Bad and Doubtful on Loans and Advances
5. Loans and advances due by directors *or* other officers of the the company *or* any of them either severally *or* jointly with any other persons *or* amounts due by firms *or* private companies respectively in which any director is a partner *or* a director *or* a member

NOTE 12: OTHER NON-CURRENT ASSETS

Particulars	₹	₹
Long Term Trade Receivables (including trade receivables on deferred credit terms)		
Others (specify nature e.g.)		
Discount/Loss on Issue of Debentures		
Amalgamation Adjustment A/c		

Notes: Same as for Long-term Loans and Advances

NOTE 13: CURRENT INVESTMENTS

Particulars	₹	₹
Investments In Equity Instruments		
Investments In Preference Shares		
Investments In Government *or* Trust Securities		
Investments In Debentures *or* Bonds		
Investments In Mutual Funds		
Investments In Partnership Firms		
Other Current Investments (Specify Nature)		

Notes: Same as for Non-Current Investments

NOTE 14: INVENTORIES

Particulars	₹	₹
Raw- Materials		
Work-in-Progress		
Finished Goods		
Stock-in-Trade		
Stores & Spares		
Loose Tools		
Others (specify nature)		

Notes:

1. Goods-in-transit
2. Mode of Valuation

NOTE 15: TRADE RECEIVABLES

Particulars	₹	₹
Sundry Debtors		
Less: Provision for Doubtful Debts		
Bills Receivables		

Notes:

1. Aggregate amount of Trade Receivables outstanding for a period exceeding six months from the date they are due for payment
2. Other Notes Same as for Long-term Loans and Advances

NOTE 16: CASH AND CASH EQUIVALENTS

Particulars	₹	₹
Bank Balance		
Cheques/Drafts on hand		
Cash Balance		
Others (specify nature)		

Notes:

1. Earmarked balances with banks(for example for unpaid dividend)
2. Balances with banks to the extent held as margin money *or* security against the borrowings, guarantees, other commitments
3. Repatriation restrictions, if any, in respect of cash and bank balances
4. Bank deposits with more than 12 months maturity

NOTE 17: SHORT-TERM LOANS AND ADVANCES

Particulars	₹	₹
Loans and Advances to Related Parties		
Other Loans and Advances (specify nature)		

Notes: Same as for Long-term Loans and Advances

NOTE 18: OTHER CURRENT ASSETS (SPECIFY NATURE E.G.)

Particulars	₹	₹
Prepaid Expenses		
Unpaid Amount on Shares subscribed by Subscribers to Memorandum of Association		

NOTE 19: CONTINGENT LIABILITIES AND COMMITMENTS (TO THE EXTENT NOT PROVIDED FOR)

Particulars	₹	₹
(i) CONTINGENT LIABILITIES		
(a) Claims against the company not acknowledged as debt (e.g., Towards Excise, Customs, VAT, Service Tax, Income Tax, Suppliers, Customers)		
(b) Guarantees (e.g. to Banks on behalf of others)		
(c) Other money for which the company is contingently liable (e.g.Bills Discounted but not yet matured)		
(ii) COMMITMENTS		
(a) Estimated amount of contracts remaining to be executed on Capital Account and not provided for;		
(b) Uncalled Liability on Shares and Other Investments(e.g. Debentures) partly paid		
(c) Other Commitments (e.g. Arrears of Fixed Cumulative Dividends on Preference Shares)		

PRACTICAL QUESTIONS FOR PRACTICE

QUESTION 1: How will you disclose the following items while preparing the Balance Sheet of a company?

ANSWER:

Item	Major Head	Sub- Head	Sub- Sub- Head
Preference Shares whose redemption overdue	Shareholders' Funds *[As per ICAI's Guidance Note]*	Share Capital	
Share Application Money pending Allotment-Not exceeding Issued Capital and to the extent not refundable	Shareholders' Funds	Share Capital	
Share Application Money pending Allotment- to the extent refundable	Current Liabilities	Other Current Liabilities	
Debit Balance of Profit & Loss A/c	Shareholders' Funds	Reserves and Surplus *[As a Negative Figure]*	
Loans repayable after Operating Cycle	Non-Current Liabilities	Long-term Borrowings	
Loans repayable within Operating Cycle/12 months	Current Liabilities	Short-Term Borrowings	
Loans repayable on demand	Current Liabilities	Short-Term Borrowings	
Trade Payables to be settled after Operating Cycle	Non-Current Liabilities	Other Long term Liabilities	
Trade Payables to be settled within Operating Cycle/12 months	Current Liabilities	Trade Payables	
Interest accrued on Share Application Money	Current Liabilities	Other Current Liabilities	
Interest accrued and due on Long-term Borrowings	Current Liabilities	Other Current Liabilities	
Interest accrued but not due on Long-term Borrowings	Current Liabilities	Other Current Liabilities	
Outstanding Expenses	Current Liabilities	Other Current Liabilities	
Tax Payable	Current Liabilities	Other Current Liabilities	
Bank Overdraft	Current Liabilities	Other Current Liabilities	

Unpaid/Unclaimed Dividend	Current Liabilities	Other Current Liabilities	
Matured Deposits	Current Liabilities	Other Current Liabilities	
Matured Debentures	Current Liabilities	Other Current Liabilities	Current Maturities of Long-term Debt
That portion of Long-term Borrowings repayable within 12 months	Current Liabilities	Other Current Liabilities	
Provision for Tax	Current Liabilities	Short-Term Provisions	
Proposed Dividend	Current Liabilities *[**Note:** This treatment is as per ICAI's Guidance Note and AS 4]*	Short-Term Provisions	It may be noted that Revised Schedule VI requires merely the disclosure in **Notes to Accounts.**
Provision for Employee Benefits to be settled within 12 months	Current Liabilities	Short-Term Provisions	
Provision for Employee Benefits to be settled after 12 months	Non-Current Liabilities	Long-term Provisions	
Provision for Employee Provident Fund to be settled after 12 months	Non-Current Liabilities	Long-term Provisions	
Live Stock	Non-Current Assets	Fixed Assets	Tangible Assets
Brands	Non-Current Assets	Fixed Assets	Intangible Assets
Intellectual Property Rights	Non-Current Assets	Fixed Assets	Intangible Assets
Licenses and Franchise	Non-Current Assets	Fixed Assets	Intangible Assets
Building under construction	Non-Current Assets	Fixed Assets	Capital Work-in-Progress
Computer Software under Development	Non-Current Assets	Fixed Assets	Intangible Assets under Development
Investment in Property	Non-Current Assets	Non-Current Investments	
Capital Advances	Non-Current Assets	Long-Term Loans and Advances	
Security Deposits	Non-Current Assets	Long-Term Loans and Advances	
Deposits with Custom Authorities	Non-Current Assets	Long-Term Loans and Advances	
Loans & Advances receivable after 12 months	Non-Current Assets	Long-Term Loans and Advances	

Discount/Loss on issue of Debentures/Share Issue Exp. to be w/o after 12 months		Non-Current Assets	Other Non-Current Assets
Preliminary Expenses	As per Para 56 of AS 26, 'Intangible Assets', Preliminary Expenses are to be recognized as expenses as and when they are incurred. Hence, Preliminary Expenses are not to appear in the Balance Sheet.		
Work-in-Progress	Current Assets	Inventories	
Loose Tools	Current Assets	Inventories	
Stores & Spares	Current Assets	Inventories	
Trade Receivables to be realized within 12 months/ Operating Cycle	Current Assets	Trade Receivables	
Provision for Doubtful Debts	Current Assets	Trade Receivables [Shown by way of deduction]	
Cheques/Drafts on hand	Current Assets	Cash and Cash Equivalents	
Bank Deposits with more than 12 months maturity	Current Assets	Cash and Cash Equivalents	
Loans & Advances receivable within 12 months	Current Assets	Short-term Loans and Advances	
Prepaid Expenses	Current Assets	Other Current Assets	
Interest accrued on Investments	Current Assets	Other Current Assets	
Unpaid Amount on Shares subscribed by Subscribers to Memorandum of Association	Current Assets *[**Note:** Subscribed and Paid up Share Capital will include such Unpaid Amount]*	Other Current Assets	
Calls Unpaid on Shares (othe than those subscribed by Subscribers to Memorandum of Association)	**Notes to Accounts** *[**Note:** Subscribed and Paid up Share Capital will be net of Calls Unpaid]*		
Guarantees	Notes to Accounts	Contingent Liabilities and Commitments	Contingent Liabilities

Bills Discounted but not yet matured	Notes to Accounts	Contingent Liabilities and Commitments	Contingent Liabilities
Uncalled Liability on partly paid Shares held as Investments	Notes to Accounts	Contingent Liabilities and Commitments	Commitments
Uncalled Liability on partly paid Debentures held as Investments	Notes to Accounts	Contingent Liabilities and Commitments	Commitments
Arrears of Fixed Cumulative Dividends on Preference Shares	Notes to Accounts	Contingent Liabilities and Commitments	Commitments
Allocations and Appropriations such as Dividend, Bonus Shares and Transfer to/ from Reserves	Notes to Accounts	Reserves and Surplus	Surplus

QUESTION 2: State under which head these accounts should be classified in Balance Sheet, as per Schedule III to The Companies Act 2013:

(i) Share application money received in excess of issued share capital.
(ii) Share option outstanding account.
(iii) Unpaid matured debenture and interest accrued thereon.
(iv) Uncalled liability on shares and other partly paid investments.
(v) Calls unpaid.
(vi) Intangible Assets under development.
(vii) Money received against share warrant.
(viii) Long term maturity of finance lease obligation.

ANSWER:

CLASSIFICATION OF FOLLOWING ACCOUNTS FOR THE PRESENTATION IN SCHEDULE III TO THE COMPANIES ACT, 2013

Sl. No.	*Accounts*	*Head*
(i)	Share application money received in excess of issue share capital	Other Current Liabilities
(ii)	Share option outstanding account	Reserve & Surplus
(iii)	Unpaid matured debenture and interest accrued thereon	Other Current Liabilities
(iv)	Uncalled liability on shares and other partly paid investments	Contingent Liabilities and commitments-commitments to the extent not provided for
(v)	Calls unpaid	Share Capital
(vi)	Intangible Assets under development	Fixed Assets
(vii)	Money received against share warrant	Shareholder's Funds
(viii)	Long term maturity of finance lease obligation	Long Term Borrowings

QUESTION 3: State the disclose requirement of Proposed Dividend while preparing Financial Statements on company.

ANSWER:

Revised Schedule VI	The Revised Schedule VI, classifies 'Proposed Dividend' as commitments'.
AS 4	Paragraph 14 of AS 4 requires that "Dividends stated to be in respect of the period covered by the financial statements, which are proposed or declared by the enterprise after the Balance Sheet date but before approval of the financial statements, should be adjusted." Accounting Standards now have overriding impact over Revised Schedule VI. Therefore, unless Para 14 of AS 4 is changed, Proposed Dividend shall be adjusted.
ICAI Guidance Note	The ICAI Guidance Note on the Revised Schedule VI has clarified that the 'Proposed Dividend' is a provision.

QUESTION 4: How will you disclose the following items while preparing the Balance Sheet of a company?

1. **Trade Receivables**
2. **Trade Payables**
3. **Current Maturities of Long-term Debt**

ANSWER:

1. Trade Receivables are to be classified as Current Assets if Expected Realisation Period is either within the Operating Cycle Period or within the 12 Months Period.
2. Trade Payables are to be classified as Current Liabilities if Expected Payment Period is either within the Operating Cycle Period or within the 12 Months Period.
3. Current Maturities of Long-term Debt represents that portion of Long-term Borrowings which is due within 12 Months from the date of Balance Sheet or with in Operating Cycle Period. It appears under the head 'Current Liabilities' and sub-head 'Other Current Liabilities'. For Example, 12% Debentures of Reliance Ltd. ₹ 100 lacs [20% Redeemable within 1 year]. ₹ 20 lacs will appear as Current Maturities of Long-term Debt under the head 'Current Liabilities' and sub-head 'Other Current Liabilities' and ₹ 80 lacs will appear under the head 'Non-Current Liabilities' and sub head 'Long-term Borrowings'.

QUESTION 5: X Ltd. provides you the following information:

1. **Raw material stock holding period: 3 months**
2. **Work-in-progress holding period: 1 month**
3. **Finished goods holding period: 4 months**
4. **Debtors collection period: 6 months**

You are required to compute the operating cycle

ANSWER:

As per Schedule III "An operating cycle is the time between the acquisition of assets for processing and their realization in cash or cash equivalents".

Operating Cycle = Raw material stock holding period + Work-in-progress holding period + Finished goods holding period + Debtors collection period = 3 + 1 + 4 + 6 = 14 months.

QUESTION 6: State giving reason whether the Trade Receivables are Current Assets or Non-Current Assets as per Schedule III in the following cases:

Case	Operating Cycle Period	Expected Realisation Period
1.	11 Months	10 Months
2.	11 Months	12 Months
3.	11 Months	13 Months
4.	14 Months	13 Months
5.	14 Months	15 Months

ANSWER:

Case	*Current Assets or Non-Current Assets*	*Reason*
1.	Current Assets	Expected Realisation Period — is less than the Operating Cycle Period and — is within 12 Months.
2.	Current Assets	Expected Realisation Period is within 12 Months although it is more than the Operating Cycle Period.
3.	Non-Current Assets	Expected Realisation Period is more than the Operating Cycle Period and 12 Months Period.
4.	Current Assets	Expected Realisation Period is less than the Operating Cycle Period although it is more than the 12 Months Period .
5.	Non-Current Assets	Expected Realisation Period is more than the Operating Cycle Period and the 12 Months Period .

QUESTION 7: State giving reason whether the Trade Payables are Current Liabilities or Non-Current Liabilities as per Schedule III in the following cases:

Case	Operating Cycle Period	Expected Payment Period
1.	11 Months	10 Months
2.	11 Months	12 Months
3.	11 Months	13 Months
4.	14 Months	13 Months
5.	14 Months	15 Months

ANSWER:

Case	*Current Assets or Non-Current Assets*	*Reason*
1.	Current Assets	Expected Payment Period — is less than the Operating Cycle Period and — is within 12 Months.
2.	Current Assets	Expected Payment Period is within 12 Months although it is more than the Operating Cycle Period.
3.	Non-Current Assets	Expected Payment Period is more than the Operating Cycle Period and 12 Months Period.
4.	Current Assets	Expected Payment Period is less than the Operating Cycle Period although it is more than the 12 Months Period .

5.	Non-Current Assets	Expected Payment Period is more than the Operating Cycle Period and the 12 Months Period .

QUESTION 8: PCT Ltd. is in the process of finalizing its accounts for year ended 31st March, 2015 and furnishes the following information:

- **(i) Finished goods normally are held for 1 month before sale.**
- **(ii) Sales realization from Debtors usually takes 2 months from date of credit invoice.**
- **(iii) Raw materials are held in stock to cover 1 month's production requirements.**
- **(iv) Packing materials, being specifically made for the company and having lead time of 3 months is held in stock for 3 months.**
- **(v) The holding period in respect of unfinished goods is 1 month.**
- **(vi) Being a monopoly KAY Ltd. enjoys a credit period of 12.5 months from its suppliers who sometimes at the end of their credit period opt for conversion of their dues into long term debt of KAY Ltd.**

You are required to compute the operating cycle of PCT Ltd. as per Schedule III of The Companies Act, 2013. As the suppliers of the company are paid off after a credit period of 12.5 months should this be part of Current Liability? Would your answer be the same if the creditors are settled in 330 days?

ANSWER:

Operating Cycle = 1 + 1 + 3 + 1 + 2 = 8 months

Classification of liability to suppliers: Schedule III provides that:

"A liability shall be classified as current when it satisfies any of the following criteria:

- (i) it is expected to be settled in the company's normal operating cycle;
- (ii) it is held primarily for the purpose of being traded;
- (iii) it is due to be settled within 12 months after the reporting date; or
- (iv) the company does not have an unconditional right to defer settlement of the liability for at least 12 months after the reporting date. Terms of a liability that could, at the option of the counterparty, result in its settlement by the issue of equity instruments and do not affect its classification."

  - (a) **When credit period is 12.5 months:** It will be treated as non-current liability since it is not due to be settled within 12 months after the reporting date.
  - (b) **When credit period is 330 days (i.e. 11 months approx.):** It will be treated as current liability since it is due to be settled within 12 months after the reporting date.

QUESTION 9: The management of X Ltd. contends that the work in process is not valued since it is difficult to ascertain the same in view of the multiple processes involved. They opined that the value of opening and closing work in process would be more or less the same. Accordingly, the management had not separately disclosed work in process in its financial statements. Comment in line with Schedule III.

ANSWER: Schedule III to the Companies Act, 2013 requires the disclosure of opening and closing WIP under broad heads by way of additional information [General Instructions 5 (iii)]. In addition, AS-2 also requires the valuation of WIP. Therefore, the non-disclosure in the financial statements by the company amounts to violation of Schedule III.

QUESTION 10: TULSIAN Ltd is having the following Fixed Deposit Receipts:

Bank	Date of FDR	Maturity Date	Amount
Yes Bank Limited	**01–Jan–2015**	**2–Jan–2016**	**30,00,000**
Bank of Baroda	**01–Jan–2015**	**31–Mar–2016**	**20,00,000**

State Bank of India	**28–Feb–2015**	**30–May–2015**	**10,00,000**
ICICI Bank	**1–Jan–2014**	**1–Apr–2016**	**40,00,000**

Prepare Notes to Accounts showing the above Deposits in accordance with the requirements of Schedule III as at the Balance Sheet date i.e. 31st March, 2015.

ANSWER:

NOTE 'X': CASH & BANK BALANCES AS AT 31.03.2015 (BALANCE SHEET DATE)

Particulars	₹
A. Cash in Hand	xxx
B. Balances with Bank	
(i) Less than or equal to 12 Months Maturity.	
– Cash Equivalent as per AS–3 (less than 3 Months Maturity) [SBI]	10,00,000
– Other Bank Balances [30,00,000 + 20,00,000]	50,00,000
(ii) More than 12 Months Maturity [ICICI]	40,00,000
	100,00,000

QUESTION 11: Z Ltd. has flexi deposit linked current account with various banks. Cheques are issued from the current amount and as per the requirements of funds, the flexi deposits are encashed and transferred to current accounts. As of 31st March 2015 certain cheques issued to vendors are not presented for payment resulting in the credit balance in the books of the company. The management wants to present the books overdraft under current liabilities and flexi deposits under cash and bank balances. Comment.

ANSWER:

Schedule III	Presentation of Bank Overdraft as per Schedule III: The instructions in accordance with which "Cash and Cash Equivalents" should be presented as per Schedule III to the Companies Act, 2013 are as follows: (i) Cash and Cash Equivalents shall be classified as: (a) Balances with banks; (b) Cheques, drafts on hand; (c) Cash on hand; (d) Others (specify nature). (ii) Earmarked balances with banks (for example, for unpaid dividend) shall be separately stated. (iii) Balances with banks to the extent held as margin money or security against the borrowings, guarantees, other commitments shall be disclosed separately (iv) Repatriation restrictions, if any, in respect of cash and bank balances shall be separately stated. (v) Bank deposits with more than 12 months maturity shall be disclosed separately.
Advice	It is evident that is substance the position is that the composite bank balance including the balance in flexi deposit accounts are positive, even though physical set-off has not been made as on the balance sheet date. Further the bank has got the right to set off of flexi deposits against the cheques issued and hence it would be more information and useful to the readers of the financial statements to disclosed the book credit balance as a set-off from the flexi deposit accounts. The disclosure of the said book credit balance as book overdraft under the head current liabilities as proposed by the management is not correct.

QUESTION 12: Is non-disclosure of source from which Bonus shares have been issued, a violation of Schedule III to the Companies Act, 2013?

ANSWER: No since Schedule III does not require such disclosure. Schedule III merely requires the disclosure of aggregate number and class of shares allotted as fully paid up bonus shares for a period of 5 years immediately preceding the Balance Sheet date in the Notes to Accounts.

QUESTION 13: X Ltd. paid ₹ 25 lakhs as advance to Y Ltd. towards the purchase of printing machinery on 15-01-2015 with delivery instruction to deliver the same in the last week of June, 2015. Further on 15-02-2015 X Ltd. purchased two diesel generator sets from Y Ltd. for ₹ 30 lakhs on 90 days Credit term. In the accounts for 2014-15, X Ltd. intends to adjust the advance paid against Credit purchase and show the net amount of ₹ 5 lakhs as due from them. As the statutory auditor, how would you deal with this?

ANSWER: Since X Ltd. has paid advance amount to the supplier of machinery to be used in the project, such advance amount should be grouped under the main heading 'Non-Current Assets' with the sub-head as Fixed Assets with a sub-classification as 'Capital Work-in-Progress.' This is as per requirement of Schedule III to The Companies Act, 2013 and the existing accounting practice.

If the advance is for purchase of other machinery, it should be grouped under a separate head – 'Long Term Loan and Advance' with a sub-classification as 'Capital advance' under the main heading 'Non-current Assets'. In view of the above, the proposal of X Ltd., to show the net balance in the personal account of Y Ltd. is not correct. Such proposal will conceal the two material items in the balance sheet – one, expenditure towards capital asset and the other current liability for purchase of the generator set.

Hence, the auditor should advice X Ltd., to show these tow items separately. If X Ltd. does not accept the advice, the auditor should qualify his report with suitable quantification of amount involved.

asset and the other current liability for purchase of the generator set.

Hence, the auditor should advice X Ltd., to show these tow items separately. If X Ltd. does not accept the advice, the auditor should qualify his report with suitable quantification of amount involved.

QUESTION 14: Y Ltd. purchased an existing bottling unit. The method of charging depreciation on machinery of the acquired unit was different from that followed by the company in its other units. The company wants to continue to charge depreciation for the acquired unit, in the method followed earlier by them and which was too consistent with their own method. Comment

ANSWER:

Guidance Note	Guidance Note on Accounting for Depreciation in companies issued by the Institute recommends that a company may adopt more than one method of depreciation. Therefore, it is permissible to adopt or follow different method of depreciation, for different types of assets, provided the same methods are consistently adopted every year in term of section 205(2) of the Companies Act, 1956. Also units in different geographical locations can follow different methods of depreciation on machinery provided the same are consistently followed.
Advice	Y Ltd. could continue to follow the previous method of charging depreciation for the acquired company, even if it is not in agreement with the method followed by Y Ltd. for their other units.

QUESTION 15: S Ltd. issued Bonds to the tune of ₹ 100 lacs and provided security to the tune of ₹ 80 lacs for the same. It insists that it will disclose the Bonds as "Secured" in the Balance Sheet of the Company. Comment.

ANSWER: Prima facie, the Bonds issued to the tune of ₹ 100 lacs are provided with security to the tune of ₹ 80 lacs i.e. neither fully secured nor unsecured. Guidance Note on the 'Terms used in Financial Statements" issue by ICAI, states "Secured Loans" as loan secured wholly or partly against tan asset. Hence the Bond should be classified under 'Secured Loans' for the purpose of disclosure in the balance Sheet. However the nature of security should be clearly specified.

QUESTION 16: The Balance Sheet of G Ltd is as under: Comment on the presentation in terms of Schedule III and Accounting Standards issued by NACAS.

BALANCE SHEET AS AT ... *(Rupees in ...)*

Particulars	Note No.	31.03.2015	31.03.2014
I. EQUITY AND LIABILITIES			
Share Capital	1	xxx	xxx
Reserves & Surplus	2	0	0
Employee stock option outstanding	3	xxx	xxx
Share application money	4	xxx	xxx
Non-Current Liabilities			
Deferred tax liability (Arising from Indian Income Tax)	5	xxx	xxx
Current Liabilities			
Trade Payables	6	xxx	xxx
Total		xxx	xxx
II. ASSETS			
Non-Current Assets			
Fixed Assets-Tangible	7	xxx	xxx
CWIP (including capital advances)	8	xxx	xxx
Current Assets			
Trade Receivables	9	xxx	xxx
Deferred Tax Asset (Arising from Indian Income Tax)	10	xxx	xxx
P & L Debit balance			
Total		xxx	xxx

ANSWER: Following Errors are noticed in presentation as per Schedule III:

(i) Share Capital & Reserve & Surplus are to be reflected under the heading "Shareholders' funds", which is not shown while preparing the balance sheet. Although it is a part of Equity and Liabilities yet it must be shown under head "shareholders' funds". The heading "Shareholders' funds" is missing in the balance sheet given in the question.

(ii) Reserve & Surplus is showing zero balance, which is not correct in the given case. Debit balance of statement of profit & Loss should be shown as a negative figure under the head 'Surplus'. The balance of 'Reserves and Surplus', after adjusting negative balance of surplus shall be shown under the head 'Reserves and Surplus' even if the resulting figure is in the negative.

(iii) Schedule III requires that Employee Stock Option outstanding should be disclosed under the heading "Reserves and Surplus"

(iv) Share application money refundable shall be shown under the sub-heading "Other Current Liabilities". As this is refundable and not pending for allotment, hence it is not a part of equity.

(v) Deferred Tax Liability has been correctly shown under Non-Current Liabilities. But Deferred tax assets and deferred tax liabilities, both, cannot be shown in balance sheet because only the net balance of Deferred Tax Liability or Asset is to be shown

(vi) Under the main heading of Non-Current Assets, Fixed Assets are further classified as under:
  (i) Tangible assets
  (ii) Intangible assets
  (iii) Capital work in Progress
  (iv) Intangible assets under development.

Keeping in view the above, the CWIP shall be shown under Fixed Assets as Capital Work in Progress. The amount of Capital advances included in CWIP shall be disclosed under the sub-heading "Long term loans and advances" under the heading Non-Current Assets.

(vii) Deferred Tax Asset shall be shown under Non-Current Asset. It should be the net balance of Deferred Tax Asset after adjusting the balance of deferred tax

QUESTION 17: On 30th September, 2012 BHARAT Ltd. was incorporated with a Authorised Capital of ₹ 50 lakhs. It first accounts were closed on 31st March, 2013 by which time it had become a listed company with an issued, subscribed and paid up capital of ₹ 40 lakhs in 4,00,000 Equity Shares of ₹ 10 each.

The company started off with two lines of business namely 'Engineering Division' and 'Chemicals Division', with equal asset base with effect from 1st April, 2013. The 'Ceramic Division' was added by the company on 1st April, 2014. The following data is gathered form the books of account of BHARAT Ltd:

TRIAL BALANCE AS ON 31ST MARCH 2015 *(₹ in 000's)*

Particulars	*Dr.*	*Cr.*
Engineering Division sales	—	**6,000**
Cost of engineering Division sales	**2,600**	—
Chemicals Division sales	—	**8,000**
Cost of sales of Chemicals Division	**4,300**	—
Ceramic Division Sales	—	**1,500**
Cost of sales of Ceramic Division	**900**	—
Administration cost	**2,000**	—
Distribution cost	**1,500**	—
Dividend-Interim	**1,200**	—
Fixed Asset at cost	**9,000**	—
Depreciation on Fixed Assets	—	**1,500**
Closing Stock	**400**	—
Trade Debtors	**440**	—
Cash at Bank	**160**	—
Trade Creditors	—	**500**
Equity Shares Capital is shares of ₹ 10 each	—	**4,000**
Retained Profits	—	**1,000**
	22,500	**22,500**

Additional Information:

(a) Administration costs should be split between the Divisions in the ratio 5 : 3 : 2.

(b) Distribution costs should be spread over the Divisions in the ratio 3 : 1 : 1.

(c) Directors have proposed Final Dividend of ₹ 800 thousands and transfer to reserve @10%.

(d) Some of the users of ceramics Division are unhappy with the product and have lodged claims against the company for damages of ₹ 750 thousands. The claim is hotly contested by the company on legal advice.

(e) Fixed Assets worth ₹ 3000 thousand were added in the Ceramic Division of 1.4.2014.

(f) Fixed Assets are written off over a period of 10 years on straight line basis in the books. However for Income tax purposes depreciation at 20% on written down value of the assets is allowed by Tax Authorities.

(g) Income tax rate may be assumed at 35% and Dividend Distribution Tax @ 16.2225%.

(h) During the year Engineering Division has sold to Alpha Ltd. goods having a sales value of ₹ 2500 thousands. Mr. BHARAT, the Managing Director of BHARAT Ltd. owns 100% of the issued Equity Shares of Alpha Ltd. The sales made of Alpha Ltd. were at normal selling price of BHARAT Ltd.

Required: Prepare Statement of Profit and Loss for the year ended 31st March, 2015 and the Balance Sheet as at the date as per Schedule III to The Companies Act, 2013. Your answer should include notes and disclosures as per Accounting Standards.

ANSWER:

BHARAT LTD.
PROFIT AND LOSS ACCOUNT FOR THE YEAR ENDING 31ST MARCH 2015

Particulars		Note No.	(₹ '000)
I. Revenue from Operations (6,000 + 8,000 + 1,500)			15,500
II. Total Revenue			15,500
III. Expenses:			
Cost of Sales			7,800
Distribution costs			1,500
Administration costs			2,000
Total Expenses			11,300
IV. Profit before tax			4,200
V. Tax Expenses			
Current tax	1,239		
Deferred tax	231		1,470
VI. Profit or Loss for the period			2,730

BHARAT LTD.
BALANCE SHEET AS AT 31ST MARCH, 2015

Particulars	Note No.	(₹ '000)
I. Equity and Liabilities		
(1) Shareholder's Funds		
(a) Share Capital	1	4,000.0
(b) Reserves and Surplus	2	1,187.8
(2) Current Liabilities		
Trade payable		500.0
Other Current Liabilities	3	1,573.2
Short term Provisions	4	1,239.0

Total		8,500
II. Assets		
(1) Non-Current Assets		
Fixed assets		
Tangible assets	5	7,500
(2) Current Assets		
(a) Inventories		400
(b) Trade Receivables		440
(c) Cash and Cash Equivalents		160
Total		8,500

Notes to Accounts:

(₹ '000)

Particulars	₹	₹
1. Share Capital		
Authorised Shares Capital		
5,00,000 Equity Shares of ₹ 10 each		5,000
Issued and subscribed		
4,00,000 Shares of ₹ 10 each, fully paid up		4,000
2. Reserves and Surplus		
Retained Profit brought forward (₹ 1,000 – ₹ 210)		790.00
Profit after tax of the current year	2,730	
Amount transferred to General Reserve (10% of ₹ 2,730)	(273)	
Amount transferred to CDT* (16.2225% of ₹ 2,000)	(324.45)	
Dividends (₹ 1,200 + ₹ 800)	(2,000)	
Profit for the years		132.55
Total Profit		922.55
Reserves		273.00
		1,195.55
3. Other Current Liabilities		
Proposed dividend	800.00	
Dividend Distribution Tax	324.45	
Deferred Tax Liability (₹ 210 + ₹ 231)	441.00	1,565.45
4. Short term Provisions		
Provision for tax		
5. Tangible Assets		1,239
Fixed Assets		
Gross Block	9,000	
Less: Depreciation	(1,500)	7,500

*The dividend distributed by an Indian Company is exempt from income tax in the hands of shareholders. However, the Indian company is liable to pay Dividend Distribution Tax (DDT) @ 16.2225% (i.e., inclusive of surcharge and eduction cess on such dividend).

Disclosures

1. SEGMENTS DISCLOSURE (BUSINESS SEGMENTS) *(₹ in '000)*

Particulars	*Engineering Division*	*Chemical Division*	*Ceramics Division*	*Total*
Sales	6,000	8,000	1,500	15,500
Cost of Sales	2,600	4,300	900	7,800
Administration Cost (5 : 3 : 2)	1,000	600	400	2,000
Distribution Cost (3 : 1 : 1)	9000	300	300	1,500
Profit/Loss	1,500	2,800	(100)	4,200
	6,000	8,000	1,500	15,500
Original cost of Assets (Equal Capital Base)	3,000	3,000	3,000	9,000
Depreciation @ 10% p.a.				
For the year ended 31.3.2014	300	300	NIL	600
For the year ended 31.3.2015	300	300	300	300

Note: Ceramic division is a reportable segment as per assets criteria.

2. SEGMENTS DISCLOSURE (BUSINESS SEGMENTS) *(₹ in '000)*

Particulars	*₹ in '000*
Opening Timing Difference on 1.4.2014	
WDV of fixed assets as per books	5,400
WDV of fixed assets as per Income Tax Act	4,800
Difference	600
Deferred Tax Liability @ 35% on ₹ 600	210
This has been adjusted against opening balance of retained profits.	
Current year (ended 31st March, 2015)	
Depreciation as per books	900
Depreciation as per Income Tax Act (₹ 480 + ₹ 480 + ₹ 600)	1,560
Difference	660
Deferred Tax Liability @ 35% on ₹ 660 (to be carried forward)	231

3. **Contingent Liabilities no provided:** Company is contesting claim for damages for ₹ 7,50,000 and as such the same is not acknowledged as debts.

4. **Related Party Disclosure:** Para 3 AS 18 lists out related party relationships. The includes individuals owning, directly or indirectly, an interest in voting power of reporting enterprise which given them control or significant influence over the enterprises, and relatives of any such individual. In the instant case, Mr. BHARAT as a managing director controls operating and financial actions of BHARAT Ltd. He is also owing 100% share capital of Alpha Ltd. thereby exercising control over it. Hence, Alpha Ltd. is related party as per para 3 of AS 18.

   Disclosure to be made:

   Name of the related party — Alpha Ltd.
   Nature of relationship — common director
   Nature of the transaction — Sale of goods at normal commercial terms
   Volume of the transaction — Sales to Alpha Ltd. worth ₹ 2500 thousands

Working Note:

TAX COMPUTATION

Particulars	₹
Profit before tax for the year ended 31.3.2015	4,200
Add: Depreciation provided in the books (₹ 300 + ₹ 300 + ₹ 300)	900
	5,100
Less: Depreciation as per Income Tax Act (₹ 480 + ₹ 480 + rs 600)	(1,560)
Taxable Income	3,540
Tax at 35% on ₹ 3,540	1,239